PRINCIPLES OF AUSTRALIAN EQUITY AND TRUSTS
Cases and Materials

PRINCIPLES OF AUSTRALIAN EQUITY AND TRUSTS
Cases and Materials

Peter Radan

BA, LLB, PhD (Syd), Dip Ed (SCAE)
Solicitor of the Supreme Court of New South Wales
and High Court of Australia
Professor of Law, Macquarie Law School, Macquarie University

Cameron Stewart

BEc LLB (Hons) (Macq), Grad Dip Juris (Syd), Grad Dip Leg Prac
(NSW College of Law), PhD (Syd), FACLM (Hon)
Associate Professor and Director of the Centre for Health Governance,
Law and Ethics, Sydney Law School
Associate Professor, Centre for Values, Ethics and the Law in Medicine,
Faculty of Medicine, University of Sydney

Ilija Vickovich

BA (Hons), LLB (Syd), LLM (Macq)
Roll of Legal Practitioners, New South Wales
Lecturer, Macquarie Law School, Macquarie University

LexisNexis Butterworths
Australia 2010

LexisNexis

AUSTRALIA	LexisNexis Butterworths 475–495 Victoria Avenue, Chatswood NSW 2067 On the internet at: www.lexisnexis.com.au
ARGENTINA	LexisNexis Argentina, BUENOS AIRES
AUSTRIA	LexisNexis Verlag ARD Orac GmbH & Co KG, VIENNA
BRAZIL	LexisNexis Latin America, SAO PAULO
CANADA	LexisNexis Canada, Markham, ONTARIO
CHILE	LexisNexis Chile, SANTIAGO
CHINA	LexisNexis China, BEIJING, SHANGHAI
CZECH REPUBLIC	Nakladatelství Orac sro, PRAGUE
FRANCE	LexisNexis SA, PARIS
GERMANY	LexisNexis Germany, FRANKFURT
HONG KONG	LexisNexis Hong Kong, HONG KONG
HUNGARY	HVG-Orac, BUDAPEST
INDIA	LexisNexis, NEW DELHI
ITALY	Dott A Giuffrè Editore SpA, MILAN
JAPAN	LexisNexis Japan KK, TOKYO
KOREA	LexisNexis, SEOUL
MALAYSIA	Malayan Law Journal Sdn Bhd, SELANGOR DURAL EHSAN
NEW ZEALAND	LexisNexis, WELLINGTON
POLAND	Wydawnictwo Prawnicze LexisNexis, WARSAW
SINGAPORE	LexisNexis, SINGAPORE
SOUTH AFRICA	LexisNexis Butterworths, DURBAN
SWITZERLAND	Staempfli Verlag AG, BERNE
TAIWAN	LexisNexis, TAIWAN
UNITED KINGDOM	LexisNexis UK, London, EDINBURGH
USA	LexisNexis Group, New York, NEW YORK LexisNexis, Miamisburg, OHIO

National Library of Australia Cataloguing-in-Publication entry

Author:	Radan, Peter.
Title:	Principles of Australian Equity and Trusts—Cases and Materials.
Edition:	1st edition.
ISBN:	9780409324518 (pbk).
Notes:	Includes index.
Subjects:	Equity–Australia. Trusts and trustees—Australia.
Other Authors/Contributors:	Stewart, Cameron; Vickovich, Ilija.
Dewey Number:	346.94004

Typeset in Stone Serif and Frutiger.

Printed in Australia by Ligare Pty Ltd (NSW).

Visit LexisNexis Butterworths at www.lexisnexis.com.au

CONTENTS

DETAILED CONTENTS

PREFACE

Lawyers will often argue about important cases and which of them best represent this or that principle. Issues of judicial style and substance are much debated, with some, for example, preferring the incisive exactness of the judgments of Gleeson CJ, the careful and exhaustive inclusiveness of Kirby J or the brutal honesty and razor wit of Meagher JA. Academics often prepare their own volumes of favourites and will dedicate hours to their selection, sometimes to the delight, and sometimes to the horror, of students.

Debates about cases resemble arguments between music lovers over which contemporary songs deserve to be placed in a list of the 'top 10' songs for this or that genre. Our own musical preferences are diverse. For the record, Peter's tastes are eclectic. His musical immortals include Elvis, Frank Zappa, The Band, Doc Watson, Louis Jordan, Hank Williams, Bill Monroe, Nina Simone, and the incomparable Milija Spasojević. For Cameron the industrial rock of Hunters & Collectors, and the dizzy pop-rock of the Hoodoo Gurus, was all he could ask for while growing up, although now he devotes much time to the sounds of Stevie Ray Vaughan, John Mayer and David Gray. Ilija can't understand why Claude Debussy, Aaron Copland, Oscar Peterson and Leon Redbone are not household names. All three authors are old enough to remember creating 'mixed tapes' of their favourite songs. They would also like to think themselves young enough to understand how to create playlists on their digital music devices. We shall leave questions regarding the effect of copyright on these practices for others more able.

This casebook represents our own mixed tape of Equity's greatest hits. Like all compilations, it is based on some agreed rules of selection, but, to be honest, these have been honoured more in the breach. Our basic guiding principle was to select cases which best communicated a rule or principle of Equity. We preferred to select cases from courts of high authority and we also had a preference for cases from Australian courts. But we were not beyond breaking any of these principles if we thought readers would gain more from reading one case rather than another.

This casebook has been designed for use in conjunction with Radan & Stewart, *Principles of Australian Equity and Trusts*, 2010. We avoided adding to the extracts any significant substantive background and commentary as it would involve unnecessary repetition of content to be found in the companion textbook. We have, on occasion, highlighted some of the historical background to the case and personal information about the litigants, when this might add to the reader's understanding of the dispute (or enhance the reader's enjoyment).

In this casebook we have used a standard template which was designed for another text co-authored by Peter and Ilija with John Gooley, *Principles of Australian Contract Law - Cases and Materials*. For each case we have aimed to clearly set out: (i) a summary of the relevant facts (ii) the issue(s) before the court (iii) the decision of the court and (iv) the matter(s) addressed by the extracts. At the end of each extracted case we have referred readers to the relevant parts of the Radan & Stewart textbook where the case and relevant content are discussed. Where we thought appropriate we also have made comments and references to other literature where the case is discussed in more detail.

In following the path of the said contract law casebook we have referred to the parties by name rather than by their procedural appellation such as plaintiff and defendant, appellant and respondent and so on. This will hopefully make it easier for the reader to understand the extracts. We also deleted some references and edited the extracts to place cited cases into footnotes, even though that may not have occurred in the report of the case.

Furthermore, in preparing this casebook we resolved not to extract relevant statutory materials. In so deciding we were, of course, not denying the importance of statute in particular areas of equity and trusts. Our decision was principally driven by the fact that, in an age when internet access is so widespread, accessing statutory material is relatively quick and simple.

We would like to thank a number of people for their help in preparing this volume. We must acknowledge the love, support, encouragement and, most of all, the understanding of our families: Sybil, Rade, Andrija and Aleksandra Radan; Nerida, Maxwell, Hannah, Beth, Angus and Eadie Stewart; and Aleksandar, Daniel and Damien Vickovich. They all had to make sacrifices so that we could complete this task.

We also express our heartfelt thanks to Zoe Hutchison, Andrija Radan, Rowan Platt and Emily Christie, who provided invaluable research assistance.

Peter would like to dedicate his work on this casebook to his wife Sybil and his children, Rade, Andrija and Aleksandra.

Cameron would like to thank his colleagues Gillian Triggs, Lee Burns, Fiona Burns, Shae McCrystal, Jamie Glister, Rosalind Croucher, Patrick Parkinson, Pat Lane, Joellen Riley and Roger Magnusson. His chapters were completed as part of sabbatical leave and he thanks his faculty for that support. He also wishes to thank Gareth Jones, Grant Gillet, Lynley Anderson, Neil Pickering, Peter Skegg and Nicola Peart from the medical and law Faculties of the University of Otago, and Ron Paterson and Jo Manning from the Faculty of Law, University of Auckland, who were his most gracious hosts while on that leave.

Ilija would like to dedicate his work on this casebook to the memory of his father Danilo and the health of his mother Neda.

At LexisNexis we wish to thank Kate Hickey, Elise Carney, Annabel Adair, Jocelyn Holmes, and Banita Dimitrioska for their support, understanding and patience, as well as their efficiency in turning a manuscript into a book.

We hope that the reader enjoys our mixed tape of Equity and Trusts. We look forward to the inevitable debates about our selections.

Peter Radan
Cameron Stewart
Ilija Vickovich
29 April 2010

TABLE OF CASES

References are to paragraphs: bold case names indicate a case extract;
bold paragraph numbers indicate where the case is extracted

TABLE OF STATUTES

References are to paragraphs

1

HISTORY OF EQUITY

Introduction

1.1   This chapter deals with the historical development of equitable principles in England and their reception in the Australian colonies. The historical development of equity is crucial for an understanding of its principles and their place within Australian law.

The extracts in this chapter discuss the following:

- the emergence, in medieval England, of equity as a body of principles based upon the notion of conscience: Christopher St Germain, 'What is Equytie';
- the possible influence of the Islamic *waqf* on the emergence of the institution of the trust: Avisheh Avini, 'The *Waqf* and the Trust';
- the social importance of trusts in Victorian England: Chantal Stubbings, 'The Trust in Victorian England';
- the significance of family settlements: Malcolm Voyce, 'The Significance of the Capital Income Distinction in Trusts';
- the extent to which equity historically impacted on the rights of women: Rosemary Auchmuty, 'Equity "Looking After" Women';
- the Court of Chancery and equitable procedures in the early nineteenth century: Charles Dickens, 'In Chancery';
- the impact of the introduction of the judicature system: Keith Mason, 'Variety and Stages of Fusion'; and
- the reception of equity's principles in the British Empire: B H McPherson, 'Judicial Reception of Equity'.

Equity in medieval times

1.2   St Germain, 'What is Equytie'

Source: J A Guy, *Christopher St Germain on Chancery and Statute*, Seldon Society, London, 1985.

Extracts: The extracts from Christopher St Germain (1460–1541) set out his influential views on the meaning of equity and the principle of conscience that underpinned the manner in which Chancery's cases were decided by medieval chancellors. The first extract, which describes equity, as understood by St Germain, comes from Chapter 16 of the first dialogue in *Dialogue Between a Doctor and Student*, first published in Latin in 1528 and then in English in 1531. The second extract comes from *A Little Treatise concerning Writs of Subpoena* which was written, it is believed, in 1532, but not published until 1787. It discusses St Germain's understanding of the notion of conscience as underpinning the principles of equity.

What is equytie

[72] Equyte is a ryghtwysenes that consideryth all the pertyculer cyrcumstaunces of the dede, the whiche also is temperyd with the swetnes of mercye. And such an equytye must alway be obseruyd in euery lawe of man, and in euery generall rewle therof, & that knewe he wel that sayd thus. Laws couet to be rewlyd by equytye ... And for the playner declaracyon what equytie is thou shalt vnderstande that syth the dedes and actes of men, for whiche lawes ben ordayned happen in dyuers maners infynytlye. It is not possyble to make any generall rewle of the lawe, but that it shall fayle in some case. And therefore makers of lawes take hede to such thynges as may often come and not to euery particular case, for they coulde not though they wolde And therefore to folowe the wordes of the lawe, were in some case both agaynst Iustyce & the common welthe: wherefore in some cases it is *good and even* necessary to leue the wordis of the lawe, & to folowe that reason and Justyce requyreth, & to that intent equytie is ordeyned, that is to say to temper and myttygate the rygoure of the lawe. And it is called also by some men epicaia. The whiche is no other thynge but an excepcyon of the lawe of god, or of the lawe of reason, from the generall rewles of the lawe of man: when they by reason of theyr generalytye wolde in any particular case Iuge agaynste the lawe of god, or the lawe of reason, the whiche excepcion is secretely vnderstande in euery generall rewle of euery posytyue lawe.

A little treatise concerning writs of subpoena

[123] Another objection ... is this: in what uncertayntie (seyth he) shall the kinges subgiettes stande when they shalbe out from the lawe of the reame, and bee compellede to be ordrede by the discrecion and conscience of oon man; and namelie, for asmoche as conscience is a thinge of great uncertayntie, for summe men (he saieth) thinke that if they treade upon two straws that lye acrosse, that they offende yn conscience, and that summe man thinkith that if he lak mony, and another hathe too moche, that he may take parte of his with conscience; and so divers men, divers consciences, for every man knoweth not what conscience is *aswell* (saieth *he*) as you, Masiter Doctour doo. And to that it may be aunswered, that the said two consciences by hym before remembrede, wherof thone is a scrupilous conscience and the other an erroniouse conscience, are not suche a conscience as the Chauncellor or any other is bounde to followe. But they ar [deleted: defaultes] errours yn conscience; *and* errours *in conscyence* cumme vij manner of waies as is expressede yn the saide firste dialogue yn the xvth chapitre, which he that will kepe hym self yn a cleane conscience mustse clearlie abjecte and caste away. But the conscience that the Chauncellor is bounde to followe is that conscience which is groundede upon the lawe God, and the lawe of *reason, and upon the lawe of* the realme not contrary to the saide lawes of God nor *to ye* lawe of reason. And therfore to be rulede by such a conscience semethe neyther to be against the law of God, the lawe of reason, nor

the common welthe of the realme, as it is supposede yn the saide treatise *it shuld be.* And that the chauncellor is bounde to ordre his conscience after the lawe of God and the lawe of reason, it is evidente of it self and nedeth no further prove. And that he is also bounde sumtyme to ordre his conscience after the lawe of the realme, and afer non other lawe of man, it may appere thus. Yf a man seasede of landes yn fee makethe his will that another shall have it to hym and to his heyres, and after dieth seasede; yf it cumme afterwards yn question yn the chauncerye whether this will be goode, the chauncellor ys bounde yn conscience to juge yt to be voyde yn conscience, bicause it is voide by the law.

Comments

1. See Radan & Stewart at **1.9–1.16, 1.20**.
2. In William Holdsworth, *Some Makers of English Law, The Tagore Lectures 1937-38*, Cambridge University Press, Cambridge, 1938, pp 96–7, the author assesses the significance of St Germain's *Dialogue Between a Doctor and Student*, as follows:

   That it was a very important book can be seen from the fact that it is cited by every writer on equity down to Blackstone's day. The reasons why it is so important are as follows: First, the English version of the first dialogue put into a popular and intelligible form the canonist learning as to the reason for the existence of a system of equity … St Germain's exposition of … [conscience] theory made it the basis and starting-point of the English system of equity. Secondly, the time when the book appeared was very opportune. It came at the close of the period during which the court of Chancery had been presided over by ecclesiastical Chancellors, and at the beginning of the period when its development was to be guided by common lawyers. Thus it helped to promote a larger amount of continuity in the development of equity than would otherwise have been possible. Thirdly, the popular form in which these canonist principles were expressed, and the manner in which they were applied in detail to many different rules of English law, facilitated the development of these principles on native lines. St Germain did for the principles of the canon law what Bracton did for the principles of Roman civil law. Both adapted foreign principles to an English environment. Both by this adaptation forwarded a native development of the law. In neither case was there any reception in detail of foreign law.

   Holdsworth's third point asserting that equity did not involve the 'reception in detail of any foreign law' is by no means universally accepted, as is seen in the debate over the foreign influences on the development of the institution of the trust, an issue addressed in the following extract.

The origins of the trust

1.3   Avini, 'The *waqf* and the trust'

Source: Avisheh Avini, 'The Origins of the Modern English Trust Revisited' (1995–96) 70 *Tulane Law Review* 1139.

> **Extracts:** The extracts from Avini's article argue that if the development of the English law of trusts was influenced by comparable institutions in other legal systems, the most likely source of such influence is the Islamic notion of *waqf* which had developed some five centuries earlier within the framework of Islamic law.

[1140] The origin of the English trust, known as the *use* before the passage of the Statute of Uses in 1535, has been the subject of debate among some of the greatest legal minds of historical jurisprudence ... Until the nineteenth century, the Roman *fideicommissum* was believed to have inspired the trust. This Roman legal institution permitted a testator to devise property to a legally incompetent beneficiary by transmitting the property to a capable legatee. The legatee would then fulfill his promise of delivering the property to the otherwise ineligible [1141] beneficiary. ...

A more recent theory has been offered which suggests that the trust was modeled on the Islamic law of *waqf* (pl. *awqaf*). In general, *awqaf* were of two types: family endowments (*waqf ahli* or *dhurri*) and charitable endowments (*waqf khairi*). A *waqf* was created by a donor (the *waqif*) for use by designated beneficiaries (*mustahiqq*, pl. *mustahiqqun*). It was administered by a trustee (the *mutawalli*) who, in turn, was under the supervision of a local judge (the *qadi*).

The Roman *fideicommissum*, ... the Islamic *waqf*, and the English trust all emerged as a result of positive-law deficiencies and restrictions concerning the ownership and devolution of property. ...

[1153] The *waqf* is created upon the declaration of the owner (the *waqif*) that the income of the subject property is to be permanently reserved for a specific purpose, at which point his ownership is 'arrested' or 'detained.' There is no requirement that the *waqf* be in a written form, although it is usually expressed in such manner. When declaring a property as *waqf*, the *waqif* must clearly express his intentions, appending to his declaration the phrase, 'it must neither be sold nor given away nor bequeathed.' In addition, the *waqif* must accurately describe the property, the purpose of the endowment, and the beneficiaries.

Three conditions must be satisfied before a *waqf* may be considered valid. First, the endowment must be made in perpetuity. This, essentially, renders the property inalienable. Second, the *waqf* must become immediately effective; no provision can exist for postponing it, except in cases in which the *waqf* arises by testament. [1154] Finally, the dedication of property to a *waqf* must be irrevocable. The only way in which a *waqf* may be extinguished is if the *waqif* secedes from Islam. Because the ultimate purpose of a *waqf* is always charitable, the *waqf* property is even immune from confiscation by temporal authorities.

In addition to the above requirements, the *waqif* must be legally competent and have unrestricted ownership of the property. The property to be dedicated as *waqf* must be of a permanent nature and yield a usufruct. Most importantly, the purpose of the endowment must be a work pleasing to God (*qurba*) and not violate any of the laws of Islam.

Although the ostensible purpose of the *waqf* was always charitable, the *waqifs* of *awqaf* also had many undeclared motives in creating a *waqf*. Because the *waqf* is the only form of perpetuity in Islamic law, it was bound to fulfill many other functions. Some of these secular uses included evasion of taxation, control over the [1155] excesses of heirs, accession of power over the masses by paying their religious leaders, and most prominently, immunity from government confiscation. There is also evidence that conquered peoples forced to convert to Islam used the *waqf* to circumvent the constraints of the Islamic law of inheritance. ...

[1157] In dedicating property as *waqf*, the *waqif* was free to determine the terms and conditions of the *waqf*'s operation. For example, the *waqif* could make provisions for the selection of beneficiaries (or *mustahiqqun*), appointment of the trustee (*mutawalli*), and distribution of *waqf* income. He may also reserve to himself the right to appoint and dismiss the trustee, or even act as trustee himself. [1158] In no event, however, was the *waqif* allowed to appoint himself as a beneficiary because this would invalidate the *waqf*.

The trustee of a *waqf* was obligated to implement the wishes of the *waqif* as expressed in the *waqf* instrument. The trustee himself was required to be 'a Muslim, legally responsible, [and] able to carry out his functions with knowledge and experience.' The duties of the trustee varied according to the wishes of the *waqif* as expressed in the *waqf* document. In general, however, these duties included the preservation and maintenance of the *waqf* property, collection and distribution of *waqf* income, payment to beneficiaries, and resolution of disputes involving the *waqf* property.

The trustee was to perform his duties under the supervision of the judge (*qadi*) within whose jurisdiction the *waqf* property was located. In the event that the *waqif* neither designated a trustee nor set the criteria for a trustee, the *qadi* was to appoint a trustee and, in certain cases, act as trustee himself. Although the *qadi* could dismiss the trustee for cause, he could only dismiss the trustee without cause if the trustee was the *qadi*'s own appointee.

The designated beneficiaries of a *waqf* were entitled to share in the usufruct of the *waqf* property according to the provisions of the *waqf* document. The beneficiaries, however, would not receive their shares if they failed to comply with the conditions set forth in the *waqf* instrument. If a beneficiary failed to perform his duties, the trustee was free to replace that beneficiary with another. This, however, occurred only in cases in which the beneficiary violated an express and unambiguous condition of the *waqf*. ...

[1159] The Islamic theory on the origin of the English trust proposes that the concept behind the *waqf* was imported to England by Franciscan Friars returning from the Crusades in the thirteenth century. By the twelfth century, the *waqf* had developed into a fully refined and widespread legal device throughout the Middle East. During this period, Islamic culture was more advanced than that of the West. Because the direction of influence proceeds naturally from the more advanced culture to one of less advancement, it is reasonable to expect that Islam could have influenced the West in certain respects. ...

[1160] The *waqf* and the *use* share many similarities in purpose, theory, and structure. Both of these devices were used to circumvent proscriptions on land ownership as well as to avoid the financial burdens of land ownership. Both involved the separation of ownership and usufruct, the vesting in beneficiaries of a right of enjoyment of the [1161] usufruct only, and the right of the settlor to vest the usufruct in a succession of beneficiaries, both present and future. Furthermore, both institutions shared the same structure — the *waqif* is analogous to the person making the *enfeoffment* (settlor); the *mutawalli* is the same as the *feoffee to uses* (trustee); and the beneficiaries (both present and future) exist in both institutions. Even the differences between the *waqf* and the trust highlight the similarity between the two. The trust, originally in the form of the *use*, was made in perpetuity and was, like the *waqf*, devoid of juristic personality. Therefore, the *waqf* and the *use*, as the trust was originally known, are almost identical institutions. ...

[1163] [I]f an outside paradigm for the English *use* is to be located, the Islamic *waqf's* parallel structure and historical proximity indicate that it was the *waqf* which most prominently influenced the development of the *use*. It can hardly be doubted that the stifling legal environment of thirteenth-century feudal England was the motivating force behind the *use*. And it was precisely at this time that the *waqf* was at its apogee, having become fully established throughout the Middle East. One need not venture far to conceive of a means of transmission of this commonplace instrument to a receptive climate.

Comments

1. See Radan & Stewart at **1.17–1.19**.
2. For a detailed analysis of the *waqf* and its connection to the development of the trust see Gilbert Paul Verbit, *The Origins of the Trust*, Xlibris Corporation, 2002.

The social importance of trusts in Victorian England

1.4   Stebbings, 'The trust in Victorian England'

Source: Chantal Stebbings, *The Private Trustee in Victorian England*, Cambridge University Press, Cambridge, 2002.

Extracts: The extracts from Stebbings' book detail the importance of the private trust in the social structures of Victorian England.

---

[4] In 1740 Lord Hardwicke LC expressed the original and traditional conception of the trust when he observed that, in general, his court looked upon it 'as honorary, and a burden upon the honour and conscience of the person intrusted, and not undertaken upon mercenary views'.[1] Trustees were to embrace the sacred duty of trusteeship with no receipt, or indeed thought, of financial reward. They were, furthermore, expected to undertake the burden personally, and were to devote themselves wholeheartedly to the well being and security of their beneficiaries. The beneficiaries were pre-eminent in Chancery's concern. Early Equity adopted a view of somewhat extreme paternalism, and perceived the beneficiary as a victim ripe for exploitation. The courts had to be supremely vigilant, for if trustees were given an inch, they would take a mile. Accordingly errant trustees had to be dealt with swiftly and severely to serve as an example to others. The voluntary nature of the trust was additional justification. The law neither encouraged nor permitted deviation from this ideal. Throughout the eighteenth and the early years of the nineteenth century the fundamental principles of Equity were settled and subsequently

---

1.   *Ayliffe v Murray* (1740) 26 ER 433 at 434.

elaborated by Lord Hardwicke and then by Lord Eldon. They laid the foundations of trusts jurisprudence in the Victorian period.

The dawn of the Victorian age saw the trust fully established in law and in English society and culture. It was familiar to and understood by the landed classes, who had employed it in the preservation [5] of family estates and the provision for their families for over a hundred years. Its fundamental doctrines were largely settled and a considerable body of law had grown up around it. It was, furthermore, supported by an infrastructure, though still general in nature, of legal and other professional expertise. The Victorians embraced the trust with the same enthusiasm which they showed in all aspects of their lives. An intense curiosity about art, literature, history, science, medicine and the natural world was continued into the more prosaic sphere of government and social and legal institutions. Legal concepts and devices were addressed, examined, reformed, refined, developed and adopted, and, thus adapted, played their full part in the vibrant and dynamic society of Victorian England.

Since the trust was a purely private arrangement, with no requirements of registration and with significant fluctuations in the value of trust funds, it is impossible to state with accuracy how much property was held in trust in the nineteenth century. It was widely believed by contemporaries to be considerable, and to be increasing as the country became wealthier with more money available to be settled. In 1895 it was said that 'an enormous amount of personal property, as well as a great deal of land', was held in trust, and some believed it was as much as one-tenth of the property in Great Britain. One estimate was £1,000 million. As a result Lord St Leonards could say that there were 'few social questions of more importance' than the trust relationship in Victorian England,[2] and as early as 1857 the trust could accurately be described as 'one of the most ordinary relations of life', and the positions of trustee and beneficiary as 'among the most common and the most necessary'.[3] Writing in the early years of the next century, Frederic Maitland observed that the trust 'seems to us almost essential to civilization'.[4] Where such numbers were concerned, trusteeship was a concept which formed an integral part of Victorian society and the issue of [6] trustees' powers, duties and liabilities was one of considerable legal and popular importance.

Being a relationship based on property, the trust was not one employed or enjoyed by the abject poor, but whereas in the eighteenth century it had been the province principally, though not exclusively, of the aristocracy and the landed classes, Victorian England saw its widespread adoption by the emerging middle class. This was a class with unprecedented power and influence in national life. These businessmen, bankers, lawyers, doctors, clergymen, civil servants and shopkeepers were, as a class, self-reliant, educated and commercially astute. An income of £1,000 a year put a man towards the top of the middle class, and many men were worth considerably more. They also had confidence, both in themselves and in the future of their country's political and economic standing. The complex family settlements of the landed estates of the aristocracy continued in their pattern of creation and renewal, but the principal innovation of the nineteenth century was the growth of the small — and not so small — family trust of personalty.

---

2. Lord St Leonards, *A Handy Book on Property Law*, 2nd ed, Edinburgh & London, 1858, p 159.
3. *Parliamentary Debates*, vol 145, ser 3, col 673, 21 May 1857 (HC).
4. F W Maitland, *Equity*, 2nd ed, Cambridge, 1949, p 23.

Not only did this reflect the decline in the political, economic and social value of land and the increased tendency to express wealth in terms of money, it also reflected the congenial nature of the trust in its fulfilment of the social, moral, religious and financial expectations of Victorian society. All sections of the middle classes, and some of the skilled working classes, employed the trust. Gentlemen, clerks in holy orders, butchers, printers, merchants and yeomen were typical of the range of middle-class settlors. In practice their creation reflected the most significant human rite of passage — marriage — and the most final — death — the former, moreover, implicitly embracing birth. Some individuals settled considerable amounts of property, others more modest fortunes, but it was clearly perceived as an accessible and flexible legal device which met — or at least had the potential to meet — the diverse needs of the new Victorian order.

Social structures in nineteenth-century England were unambiguously hierarchical and fixed, though movement could and did occur between the classes. Inherent in the psyche of the middle classes was the desire to rise through this hierarchy, and this was often expressed through the imitation and adoption of the habits and institutions [7] of the social classes above them. In this context the adoption of the trust was unsurprising. The trust, however, was much more than a mark of social aspirations, for it provided a home for the new wealth which the middle classes produced. But central to its use was its traditional nature as a vehicle to support their wives and often numerous children, the family being the centre of Victorian life. There was no welfare state to speak of. Illness and epidemic made life itself uncertain, and the possibility of a parent left alone to raise infant children, or indeed infant children left as orphans, was very real. Children had to be supported and educated, since survival to adulthood brought exposure to a harsh world in which a living had to be sought and made. The liberal education essential to entry into the learned professions of medicine, the church and the law, and the support of young men while they were establishing themselves, was a considerable and long-term expense. Towards the end of the century entry into the new professions, and the introduction of competitive entry to the traditional ones, increased the importance of a sound and relevant — and preferably public-school — education. Married women were entirely dependent on their husbands because they were, until the latter part of the century, incapable of holding property at Common Law. Widows, as indeed all single women of the middle class, had few opportunities to earn their own living for most of the nineteenth century. The trust addressed these issues and allowed the settlor to arrange his fortune in order to ensure that on his death his wife and children would not be left unprovided for, indeed that they would have a measure of that independence which was so highly valued as a measure of respectability in Victorian England. While the settlor desired their security above all else, he also wished his trustees to take financial decisions in unexpected circumstances to ensure his infant children were appropriately provided for in the social and economic context in which he himself had lived. Once a family had arrived in the middle class, it tended to want to stay there. As long as men in contemplation of their death wanted to consign their property to a trusted friend or relation to look after it for the benefit of their wives and children, and to regulate their enjoyment of it, there would be a need for the trust. In this sense trusts were regarded as a powerful and essential tool in family provision.

[8] Even if the motive were the support of the family, the trust also satisfied the natural human desire to preserve and transmit family wealth to the next generation. The aims

of Victorian settlors, and accordingly the powers they purported to give to their trustees, were, however, noticeably short-term in nature. The desire was not the preservation of a specific landed estate for future generations, but rather the preservation and growth of a fund for the support of the next immediate generation or the support of dependants in the event of an early death. The danger in the nineteenth century was not that of taxation, for the rates were too low to make that a significant factor, but rather the natural decline in the value of property if it were not carefully attended to and placed, as well as the possibilities of dissipation by the current owners or appropriation by subsequent marriage. Accordingly, most trusts in Victorian England were trusts of a mixed fund, or of personalty, established for the benefit of persons in succession, generally the wife for life, remainder to the children of the marriage …

[9] As well as achieving its purpose in providing long-term financial support within a quasi-familial context for the middle classes, the trust strengthened the position of the class itself. It perpetuated that class through provision for subsequent generations, and furthermore the infrastructure of the trust in the Victorian period was itself middle class. It was to a large extent dependent on the lower branches of the legal profession and on the new professions of surveyor and accountant for its efficient administration. This supported and strengthened those same professions and, in turn, the class from which both sprang. The social and commercial interaction between settlors, trustees, beneficiaries and the supporting professions, with their shared values and outlook, reinforced the importance of the Victorian trust and facilitated its development.

Comment

1. See Radan & Stewart at **1.27**.

Family settlements

1.5 Voyce, 'The significance of the capital income distinction in trusts'

Source: Malcom Voyce, 'Governing from a Distance: The Significance of the Capital Income Distinction in Trusts' in S Scott-Hunt & H Lim (eds), *Feminist Perspectives on Equity and Trusts*, Cavendish Publishing Ltd, London, 2001, p 153.

Extracts: The extracts from Voyce's article discuss why family settlements were prevalent and important in England, but not so in Australia.

---

[158] It has been said of strict settlements that:

There is nothing, perhaps, in the institutions of modern Europe which comes so near to an *imperium in imperio* [an empire within an empire] as the settlement of a great English estate. The settlor is a kind of absolute lawgiver for two generations; his will suspends for that time the operation of the common law of the land and substitutes for it an elaborate constitution of his own making. The trustees of a family settlement are something like the constitutional safeguards of a complex political system; their presence is, in ordinary circumstances, hardly perceived, but they hold great powers in reserve, which may be used with effect on an emergency.[5]

Wealthy families in England developed over the centuries a particular form of the trust device, called the strict settlement, to keep family property intact in [159] the hands of successive oldest sons. Its principal aim was to inhibit any disposal of family estates by the heirs out of the family. The strict settlement has been simply described as a complicated series of life estates which could be set up at any one time, but the most common event leading to its creation was the coming of age of the eldest son. Generally, there had to be a resettlement in every generation if the constraints on disposal were to be maintained. Every substantial landowner in the 18th and 19th century in England was subject to strong pressure from the landowning class to adopt strict settlement, as a means of controlling land estates and guaranteeing the political position of the 'landed estate' class in the country. By the end of the 17th century, a fairly standard form of strict settlement had evolved at the hands of eminent conveyancers and was endorsed by the courts. This form of conveyance survived until the beginning of the 20th century, when death duties led to its demise and lack of effectiveness.

Strict settlements made a significant contribution to the consolidation and preservation of wealth and power of the landowning classes of England. By the mid-18th century, such devices had been imposed on up to half, or perhaps even three-quarters of English land. New families could obtain access to this class through the purchase of land, which was difficult given the limited number of hereditary titles available. The only means to buy new land were to mortgage existing properties or to arrange for an advantageous marriage to a wealthy heir. As a buttress against the possibility of family ownership of land the strict settlement was a line of defence against short-sighted sales by an heir or heiress ...

Australia, for a variety of reasons, never used strict settlements. Historians have indicated the reasons for this: there existed vestiges of moral economy imported by the convicts; resentment over the treatment of labour in [160] the era of industrial capitalism; the suspicion of efforts to reproduce English social relations; and the scorn that was heaped on efforts to establish a 'bunyip aristocracy'. English dynastic notions of property were foreign to Australian soil. While the colonial gentry had prospered and retained substantial political power, it did not successfully transplant, on the whole, the British 'customs of patronage and deference in such an uncongenial soil'.[6] In short, colonial aristocracy was on the defensive, and governors of States had to take into account popular sentiment, such as the needs of squatters' access to land. While ownership of rural land in Britain was consolidated in a few hands and continued to be the social and political base of the dominant classes, the opposite was generally true in Australia, in that land was freely available. In essence, property was a commodity.

The above may be a partial explanation of why the strict settlement was not employed in Australia. To date, at least, historians have not suggested other reasons. Since the founding of Australia, the formal device of strict settlement has been extremely rare. Greater use was made of life estates set up with a trust in a will and trusts under the Settled Land Acts.

---

5. F Pollock, *The Land Laws*, Rothman, Littleton CO, 1896, p 117.
6. S McIntyre, *Winners and Losers: The Pursuit of Social Justice in Australian History*, Allen & Unwin, Sydney, 1985.

Such arrangements are usually called trusts rather than settlements, and are governed by the various State Trustee Acts. In effect, the universal form of trust and the power politics behind it were remodelled in a different form through life estate trusts and family trusts. In effect, then, we may recast Pollock's observation, cited above, that while trusts did not act as constitutional safeguards in the English sense, they did allow trustees to hold great powers in reserve, not only to be used in emergency, but as vehicles for the enforcement of trustee autocratic power.

Comment
1. See Radan & Stewart at **1.27**.

Equity and the rights of women

1.6   Auchmuty, 'Equity "Looking After" Women'

Source: Rosemary Auchmuty, 'The Fiction of Equity' in S Scott-Hunt & H Lim (eds), *Feminist Perspectives on Equity and Trusts*, Cavendish Publishing Ltd, London, 2001, p 1.

Extracts: The extracts from Auchmuty's article analyse the extent to which equitable principles shielded women compared with rules of common law that restricted the rights of women as compared to the rights of men.

[13] Accounts of the development of property law have represented the courts of equity as particularly sympathetic to women's sufferings under the common law. Scholars have argued that women's legal position improved across the 16th, 17th and 18th centuries, largely because of the increasingly sophisticated use of trusts in marriage settlements. Until recently, the strict settlement has been explained as a property device which owed its origins in part to the desire of loving fathers to provide for their daughters and younger sons instead of simply following the rules of primogeniture. The restraint on anticipation, invented by Lord Thurlow in 1791 to prevent a married woman from alienating her separate property, was justified throughout the century and a half of its existence as a safeguard for women's rights. The object of the restraint was to make it impossible for a husband to force his wife to transfer her property to him or to offer it as security for his debts — to 'kick or kiss' her out of her entitlement. The woman thus shielded was (in Dicey's words), 'absolutely guarded against the possible exactions or persuasions of her husband, and received a kind of protection which the law of England does not provide for any other person except a married woman'.[7] More recently, Lord Denning made chivalrous use of equitable principles to try to produce justice for women in the context of disputes over the family home ...

---

7.   A V Dicey, *Lectures on the Relation Between Law and Public Opinion in England During the Nineteenth Century*, 2nd ed, Macmillan, London, 1962, p 379.

[14] More recent research by legal feminists has all but dismantled equity's claim to offer women special protection. Tim Stretton's exhaustive study of *Women Waging Law* in the (equitable) Court of Requests in Tudor times has demonstrated that 'it is misleading to represent equity as women's legal saviour'.[8] Eileen Spring has challenged the traditional view of strict settlements as providing for women who would have lost out under common law rules. She has shown that, on the contrary, the common law rules were perceived as allowing property to fall into women's hands much too frequently, and the strict settlement was developed to restrict or actually deny their access to it.[9] ...

As for the restraint on anticipation ... it can equally plausibly be seen as protection for the assets of the woman's family of origin against an interloping husband, and it operated as a severe check on married women's ability to make use of their capital or anticipate their income. This meant that the 19th century wife, unlike her 18th century predecessor, could not conduct her own business or even provide for her family in the event of her husband's inability to do so. In *Re Wood* (1885), for example, a solicitor's clerk in his 50s lost his job through illness and was unable to find another. His wife applied to release some of the funds in her marriage settlement to pay for the children's education. The Court of Appeal refused: '[T]hey did not consider it would be for the benefit of the family that the small property should be eaten up. On the contrary, it might be for their benefit that the husband, who had hitherto been unable to get work and on whom there was not the slightest imputation, should not have the stimulus to induce him to procure work in any way removed'.[10] Yet the debates over the restraint on anticipation, which was not abolished until well into the 20th century, raises many of the same issues as Belinda [16] Fehlberg's work on women sureties. The reality of patriarchal power within 19th century marriage meant that many husbands did put pressure on their wives to give up their separate property or use it to secure their husbands' business debts. Indeed, the restraint had been created in direct response to the sad case of Mrs Vernon who, not realising the consequences of her action, conveyed her separate estate as security for her husband's debts; thus, 'while the wax was yet warm upon the deed,' as the report most graphically puts it, 'the creditors got a claim on it'.[11] A century later, successive Vice Chancellors were still commenting on the stream of applications coming to court where 'it has been evident that the object of removing the restraint was in reality to benefit the husband'.[12] ...

[17] What does emerge clearly, however, is that women under settlements were obliged to rely on the skill and honesty of male trustees and solicitors (some of whom lacked both), instead of being able to control their own finances and develop the competence that comes with experience. Tim Stretton makes this point about women in the 16th and 17th centuries: 'Parents made arrangements with parents and future sons-in-law or with trustees, and while

---

8. T Stretton, *Women Waging War in Elizabethan England*, Cambridge University Press, Cambridge, 1998, p 28.
9. E Spring, *Studies in Legal History, Law, Land and Family: Aristocratic Inheritance in England 1300-1800*, Carolina University Press, Chapel Hill, 1993.
10. *Re Wood* (1885) 1 TLR 192 at 193.
11. *Pybus v Smith* (1791) 29 ER 570.
12. *Tamplin v Miller* [1882] WN 44.

daughters were consulted, their involvement was often circumscribed'.[13] It was always men who prepared and signed the documents, and women tended to accept any financial arrangements their husbands proposed.[14] ...

The lessons to be learnt from this account of some of equity's claims to protect women are that, across the centuries, women have indeed required protection from the abuse of patriarchal power and that equity has from time to time operated to 'mitigate the harshness of the common law' (as the textbooks put it), as it impacts on women ... and at other times not. What is most striking is that equitable interventions which have the potential to assist women are, nevertheless, susceptible of co-option and use by men against women ...

[18] The fact that women prioritise loyalty and trust and looking after the family over safeguarding their own legal position and standing up for their own rights and wishes means that their version of events will continue to conflict with the way the law sees it — and this will almost always act to women's detriment. Equity has come to the aid of women many a time, but it has never spoken for women, nor represented women's viewpoint. It is but another of patriarchy's discourses and, despite its heroic reputation, it does not embody [an] ethic of care, and it still lets women down.

Comment
1. See Radan & Stewart at **1.28**.

Dickens' Chancery in 'Bleak House'

1.7   Dickens, 'In Chancery'

Source: Charles Dickens, *Bleak House*, first published in instalments from March 1852 to September 1853. Extracts are from the edition published by Oxford University Press (Oxford World's Classics paperback edition), Oxford, 1998.

Extracts: The extracts from the opening pages of Dickens' ninth novel are a devastating critique on the Court of Chancery as it operated in the first half of the nineteenth century. Dickens' views of Chancery were very much informed by his own experiences as a plaintiff in Chancery during the 1840s in relation to an injunction application against the unauthorised exploitation of his novella, A *Christmas Carol*, that had been published in 1843. Even though Dickens' claim was upheld, Blount notes that 'the whole affair became for him a source of expense and worry' which ended with him having 'to pay more or less all the costs and what had been intended as a mortal blow to the pirates eventually cost him about £700', leaving him to complain that he had been 'treated as if I were the robber instead of the robbed'.[15]

---

13. Stretton, *Women Waging War*, note 8 above, p 120.
14. See, for example, *Mara v Browne* [1895] 2 Ch 69 at 89.
15. Trevor, Blount, 'The Documentary Symbolism of Chancery in *Bleak House*' (1966) *The Dickension*, Vol 62, No 350, 47–52, pp 48–9.

[11] London. Michaelmas Term lately over, and the Lord Chancellor sitting in Lincoln's Inn Hall. Implacable November weather ...

Fog everywhere. Fog up the river, where it flows among green aits and meadows; fog down the river, where it rolls defiled among the tiers of shipping, and the waterside pollutions of a great (and dirty) city. Fog on the Essex marshes, fog on the Kentish heights. Fog creeping into the cabooses of collier–brigs; fog lying out on the yards and hovering in the rigging of great ships; fog drooping on the gunwales of barges and small boats. Fog in the eyes and throats of ancient Greenwich pensioners, wheezing by the firesides of their wards; fog in the stem and bowl of the afternoon pipe of the wrathful skipper, down in his close cabin; fog cruelly pinching the toes and fingers of his shivering little 'prentice boy on deck. Chance people on the bridges peeping over the parapets into a nether sky of fog, with fog all round them, as if they were up in a balloon and hanging in the misty clouds ...

[12] The raw afternoon is rawest, and the dense fog is densest, and the muddy streets are muddiest, near that leaden–headed old obstruction, appropriate ornament for the threshold of a leaden–headed old corporation, Temple Bar. And hard by Temple Bar, in Lincoln's Inn Hall, at the very heart of the fog, sits the Lord High Chancellor in his High Court of Chancery.

Never can there come fog too thick, never can there come mud and mire too deep, to assort with the groping and floundering condition which this High Court of Chancery, most pestilent of hoary sinners, holds, this day, in the sight of heaven and earth.

On such an afternoon, if ever, the Lord High Chancellor ought to be sitting here— as here he is—with a foggy glory round his head, softly fenced in with crimson cloth and curtains, addressed by a large advocate with great whiskers, a little voice, and an interminable brief, and outwardly directing his contemplation to the lantern in the roof, where he can see nothing but fog. On such an afternoon, some score of members of the High Court of Chancery bar ought to be—as here they are—mistily engaged in one of the ten thousand stages of an endless cause, tripping one another up on slippery precedents, groping knee–deep in technicalities, running their goat–hair and horsehair warded heads against walls of words and making a pretence of equity with serious faces, as players might. On such an afternoon, the various solicitors in the cause, some two or three of whom have inherited it from their fathers, who made a fortune by it, ought to be—as are they not?—ranged in a line, in a long matted well (but you might look in vain for Truth at the bottom of it) between the registrar's red table and the silk gowns, with bills, cross–bills, answers, rejoinders, injunctions, affidavits, issues, references to masters, masters' reports, mountains of costly nonsense, piled before them. Well may the court be dim, with wasting candles here and there; well may the fog hang heavy in it, as if it would never get out; well may the stained–glass windows lose their colour, and admit no light of day into the place; well may the uninitiated from the streets, who peep in through the glass panes in the door, be deterred from entrance by its owlish aspect, and by the drawl languidly echoing to the roof from the padded dais where the Lord High Chancellor looks into the lantern that has no light in it, [13] and where the attendant wigs are all stuck in a fog–bank! This is the Court of Chancery; which has its decaying houses and its blighted lands in every shire; which has its worn–out lunatic in every madhouse, and its dead in every churchyard; which has its ruined suitor, with his slipshod heels and threadbare dress borrowing and begging through the round of every man's acquaintance; which gives to monied might the means abundantly of wearing out the right; which so exhausts finances, patience, courage, hope; so overthrows the brain and breaks the heart; that there is not an honorable man among its practitioners who would not give—who does not often give—the warning, 'Suffer any wrong that can be done you rather than come here!'

Who happen to be in the Lord Chancellor's court this murky afternoon besides the Lord Chancellor, the counsel in the cause, two or three counsel who are never in any cause, and the well of solicitors before mentioned? There is the registrar below the Judge, in wig and gown; and there are two or three maces, or petty–bags, or privy purses, or whatever they may be, in legal court suits. These are all yawning, for no crumb of amusement ever falls from JARNDYCE AND JARNDYCE (the cause in hand), which was squeezed dry years upon years ago. The short–hand writers, the reporters of the court, and the reporters of the newspapers, invariably decamp with the rest of the regulars when Jarndyce and Jarndyce comes on. Their places are a blank. Standing on a seat at the side of the hall, the better to peer into the curtained sanctuary, is a little mad old woman in a squeezed bonnet, who is always in court, from its sitting to its rising, and always expecting some incomprehensible judgment to be given in her favour. Some say she really is, or was, a party to a suit; but no one knows for certain, because no one cares. She carries some small litter in a reticule which she calls her documents; principally consisting of paper matches and dry lavender. A sallow prisoner has come up, in custody, for the half–dozenth time, to make a personal application 'to purge himself of his contempt'; which, being a solitary surviving executor who has fallen into a state of conglomeration about accounts of which it is not pretended that he had ever any knowledge, he is not at all likely ever to do. In the meantime his prospects in life are ended. Another ruined suitor, who periodically appears from Shropshire, and breaks out into efforts to address the Chancellor at the close of the day's business, and who can by no means be made to understand that the Chancellor is [14] legally ignorant of his existence after making it desolate for a quarter of a century, plants himself in a good place and keeps an eye on the Judge, ready to call out 'My Lord!' in a voice of sonorous complaint, on the instant of his rising. A few lawyers' clerks and others who know this suitor by sight, linger, on the chance of his furnishing some fun, and enlivening the dismal weather a little.

Jarndyce and Jarndyce drones on. This scarecrow of a suit has, in course of time, become so complicated, that no man alive knows what it means. The parties to it understand it least; but it has been observed that no two Chancery lawyers can talk about it for five minutes, without coming to a total disagreement as to all the premises. Innumerable children have been born into the cause; innumerable young people have married into it; innumerable old people have died out of it. Scores of persons have deliriously found themselves made parties in Jarndyce and Jarndyce, without knowing how or why; whole families have inherited legendary hatreds with the suit. The little plaintiff or defendant, who was promised a new rocking–horse when Jarndyce and Jarndyce should be settled, has grown up, possessed himself of a real horse, and trotted away into the other world. Fair wards of court have faded into mothers and grandmothers; a long procession of Chancellors has come in and gone out; the legion of bills in the suit have been transformed into mere bills of mortality; there are not three Jarndyces left upon the earth perhaps, since old Tom Jarndyce in despair blew his brains out at a coffee–house in Chancery Lane; but Jarndyce and Jarndyce still drags its dreary length before the court, perennially hopeless.

Jarndyce and Jarndyce has passed into a joke. That is the only good that has ever come of it. It has been death to many, but it is a joke in the profession. Every master in Chancery has had a reference out of it. Every Chancellor was 'in it', for somebody or other, when he was counsel at the bar. Good things have been said about it by blue–nosed, bulbous–shoed old benchers, in select port–wine committee after dinner in hall. Articled clerks have been in the habit of fleshing their legal wit upon it. The last Lord Chancellor handled it neatly, when, correcting Mr Blowers the eminent silk gown who said that such a thing might happen when the sky rained potatoes, he observed, 'or when we get through Jarndyce and Jarndyce, Mr Blowers;'—a pleasantry that particularly tickled the maces, bags, and purses.

How many people out of the suit, Jarndyce and Jarndyce has [15] stretched forth its unwholesome hand to spoil and corrupt, would be a very wide question. From the master, upon whose impaling files reams of dusty warrants in Jarndyce and Jarndyce have grimly writhed into many shapes; down to the copying–clerk in the Six Clerks' Office, who has copied his tens of thousands of Chancery-folio-pages under that eternal heading; no man's nature has been made better by it. In trickery, evasion, procrastination, spoliation, botheration, under false pretences of all sorts, there are influences that can never come to good. The very solicitors' boys who have kept the wretched suitors at bay, by protesting time out of mind that Mr Chizzle, Mizzle, or otherwise, was particularly engaged and had appointments until dinner, may have got an extra moral twist and shuffle into themselves out of Jarndyce and Jarndyce. The receiver in the cause has acquired a goodly sum of money by it, but has acquired too a distrust of his own mother, and a contempt for his own kind. Chizzle, Mizzle, and otherwise have lapsed into a habit of vaguely promising themselves that they will look into that outstanding little matter, and see what can be done for Drizzle—who was not well used—when Jarndyce and Jarndyce shall be got out of the office. Shirking and sharking, in all their many varieties, have been sown broadcast by the ill–fated cause; and even those who have contemplated its history from the outermost circle of such evil, have been insensibly tempted into a loose way of letting bad things alone to take their own bad course, and a loose belief that if the world go wrong, it was, in some off–hand manner, never meant to go right.

Thus, in the midst of the mud and at the heart of the fog, sits the Lord High Chancellor in his High Court of Chancery.

Comments
1. See Radan & Stewart at **1.40**.
2. The story of the case of *Jarndyce v Jarndyce* that is told in *Bleak House* is set in Chancery during the time when Lord Eldon was Lord Chancellor. For a description of Chancery during Lord Eldon's tenure as Lord Chancellor see R A Melikan, *John Scott, Lord Eldon, 1751–1838: The Duty of Loyalty*, Cambridge University Press, Cambridge, 1999, pp 295–325. In a chapter entitled 'Lord Endless', Melikan, at 414–5, notes that 'Eldon was generally averse to altering either the office of Chancellor or the practice of Chancery ... because he genuinely believed in the strength, if not the perfection, of the existing structure'.

3. For a discussion and assessment of Dickens' *Bleak House* as a work of legal history see William S Holdsworth, *Charles Dickens as a Legal Historian*, Haskell House Publishers Ltd, New York, 1972 (originally published in 1928), pp 79–115.

4. For an analysis of the impact of *Bleak House* to the reform of Chancery in the nineteenth century see K Dolin, *Fiction and the Law, Legal Discourse in Victorian and Modernist Literature*, Cambridge University Press, Cambridge, 1999, pp 71–96.

The effect of the Judicature Acts' reforms

1.8   Mason, 'Variety and Stages of Fusion'

Source: Keith Mason, 'Fusion: Fallacy, Future or Finished?' in S Degeling & J Edelman, *Equity in Commercial Law*, Lawbook Co, Sydney, 2005, p 41.

Extracts: The extracts from Mason's article discuss the introduction of the judicature system and the way it presently operates in practice.

[45] When we speak about the fusion of law and equity we need to distinguish between four types of fusion: fusion of administration, procedure, remedies and doctrines. We must examine caselaw and legal theory as much as statutory developments. And we need to be on guard against distraction by sometimes fictional passwords like trustee, trust property and fiduciary.[16] Care is also needed in the use of different words to describe similar legal concepts and the use of the same word to serve different purposes.[17]

As fast as we distinguish the varieties of fusion, we must acknowledge that developments in one field have impacted on others. We inhabit a legal system that regards jurisdictional questions as primary, thinks of doctrines in terms of causes of action, views rights through remedies, and approaches remedies through procedure.

It is often stated that fusion of law and equity in England occurred in 1875, but this is quite misleading. Fusion of whatever nature represents an ongoing and interactive process, not an event that occurred in its definitive form at a particular moment of time. The processes and levels of integration (or non-integration) may differ from one law area to another. In any event, Judicature Acts are only constitutional in nature if you choose

---

16. Equity's counterparts of 'agent': *Pinkstone v The Queen* (2004) 219 CLR 444 at 465–7. 'Trust property' is often used fictionally to explain a company's right to trace and follow misdirected funds. Millett LJ described the use of 'trust' as a precursor to a personal remedy as 'nothing more than a formula for equitable relief': *Paragon Finance plc v DB Thakerar & Co* [1999] 1 All ER 400 at 409. Labels touching the status of company directors ('trustee' or 'agent') led to unseemly and expensive conflicts between Chancery and the common law courts in the mid nineteenth century.

17. Cf the variety of words used to describe an award of compensation (damages, compensation, indemnity, *Lord Cairns' Act* damages) and the use of 'injunction' to describe orders that were never part of classical equity or which were or now are statutory: *Cardile v LED Builders Pty Ltd* (1999) 198 CLR 380 at 394, 412.

to treat them that way; and all Constitutions would surprise their founders more than a century after promulgation.

To my knowledge, debates about fusion have arisen in every legal system deriving from English law. Different attitudes about the relationship between law and equity are however, more than a product of when English law was received and when and how 'law' and 'equity' were statutorily fused. Academic cultures have also played their part.[18]

I shall hereafter use 'general law' when referring to the inheritance of judge-made common law, equity, ecclesiastical and maritime law derived from English law. 'Common law' in its stricter sense refers to the systems of law practised at trial level in England before 1875 in the Queens Bench, Exchequer and Common Pleas Courts. I suppose that is an accurate definition, although it is something of a mystery why no one treats 'common law' in the same way as equity (usually spelt with a capital 'E') in the present universe of discourse.

[44] Can it be that common law scholars (if they exist in the same sense that we talk of equity scholars) have simply moved on? To my knowledge, no law school teaches 'common law' as a subject.

In referring to a modern judicature System, we envisage trial courts of general jurisdiction (subject to monetary limits in some cases) whose judges hear and determine disputes, whether arising under statute law or general law in all of its manifestations. These courts may have specialist lists, but litigants can advance claims and defences however arising. Proceedings will be moved sideways to appropriate judges or courts if commenced in an inappropriate forum or list. The choice of initiating process, pleading system, method of adducing evidence, interlocutory procedures, method of trial and right of appeal are generally unaffected by concerns as to whether asserted rights or defences are statutory, legal, equitable, ecclesiastical or maritime in derivation. There may be pockets of resistance in matters of practice (for example, the order of addresses), or culture (for example, the style or volume of counsel), but these are diminishing. Trial of 'common law' matters by jury is now very exceptional.

Modern pleadings concentrate first on facts giving rise to substantive causes of action based, for example, on contract, tort, trust, statutory obligation etc. They then claim a variety of remedies in the alternative. Very few causes of action or remedies will be exclusively equitable in historical derivation and even these are now statutory in most cases.

Some court statutes, like the *Supreme Court Act 1970* (NSW), contain provisions re-enacting nineteenth century steps towards procedural fusion, but in a form that usually confers the power to award any variety of injunctions, declarations etc. This is not to imply that the reader does not need to know the circumstances in which the particular remedies are available. He or she is, however, more likely to go to the applicable specialist text on substantive law (torts, defamation, contract, trusts) or to practice books or books on remedies generally, rather than to equity texts to find the remedial and procedural rules referable to a field of law.

---

18. The role of Sydney University Law School cannot be ignored. It has produced generations of well-informed defenders of equity. When I was an undergraduate, Sydney Law School prided itself on historically based, black letter law. My teachers in equity were proud to be practitioners in the world's last pre-judicature system.

Other statutes, like the *Trade Practices Act 1974* (Cth) offer a smorgasbord of remedies in terms that indicate the need for real caution lest judges wrongly assume that traditional 'equitable' principles apply to the minority of available remedies that would have been available only in Chancery before 1875. It can be misleading to approach statutes like the *Trade Practices Act* with preconceptions about the continuing role of equity doctrine, even when what formerly were purely equitable remedies like rescission and injunction are mentioned.

[47] In the twenty-first century it is hard to think of a non-Judicature system. Priestley JA once quipped that 'even in New South Wales all common law judges are chancellors now'.[19] Advocacy is becoming increasingly specialised, but the lines of division have nothing to do with any doctrinal common law/equity division. There may be different levels of complexity between different types of case, but this is presently irrelevant. I estimate that less than 10 per cent of the work done in the Equity Division of the Supreme Court of New South Wales involves equity in the sense explained to Socrates. Some is probate, much is contract, most is statutory (for example, *Family Provision Act*, *Corporations Act*, revenue law).

Occasionally we are reminded of the problems inherent in a pre-judicature system. This is when Parliament creates specialist courts with exclusive jurisdiction. Then it really can matter that the plaintiff has filed in the wrong court or that part of the matter in dispute lies outside that court's jurisdiction.

All four types of fusion of law and equity identified above were addressed in the *Judicature Act 1873* (UK), although it was not itself the original model for fusion.

The *Judicature Act 1873* created a single Supreme Court of Judicature divided into the Court of Appeal and the High Court of Justice (with five Divisions, merged into three in 1881). Section 24 addressed the relationship between legal and equitable procedures, with the general object of securing a complete and final determination of all matters in controversy between the parties and avoiding multiplicity of proceedings. The section gave all branches of the Court power to administer equitable remedies, enabled equitable defences to be invoked, required all branches of the Court to recognise equitable titles, prohibited the issue of common injunctions within the Court and gave general power of determination of legal titles.

The predominant feature of the common law system of pleading had been the requirement that the plaintiff choose a cause of action in which to bring the claim. The parties thereafter exchanged pleadings that were designed to produce either an issue of law by way of demurrer or an issue of fact for decision by the jury. There were many technicalities and fictions, although some were abolished by pleading reforms in the mid-nineteenth century.

In Chancery, the plaintiff pleaded by Bill in equity, a complex, prolix and repetitive document. Once again mid-nineteenth century reforms removed a number of technical excrescences, requiring the Bill to state the material facts, matters and circumstances relied on.

The Rules of Court made under the Judicature Acts prescribed the modern system of pleading which sought to combine the best features of the two former systems, the brevity and the simplified forms of the common law with the [48] equity principle of stating

---

19. *Renard Constructions (ME) Pty Ltd v Minister for Public Works* (1992) 26 NSWLR 234 at 269.

facts and not the legal conclusion which the pleader put upon the facts. This system enabled parties to allege in one process facts giving rise to causes of action, defences or replies recognised at law, in equity or by statute. The origin of a right did not need to be stated unless silence might take the opponent by surprise.

The *Judicature Act 1873* was mainly procedural in motivation. Lord Selborne LC said as much during the debate on the Bill. So too did Sir George Jessel MR in *Salt v Cooper* in 1880 when he said that the Act 'simply transferred the old jurisdictions of the Courts of Law and Equity to the new tribunal, and then gave directions to the new tribunal as to the mode in which it should administer the combined jurisdictions'.[20] Section 25 addressed areas of substantive clash, but initially it was thought that most bases had been covered and that the catch-all provision (subs 11) would have little work to do.

Contrary to what one sometimes reads, the reformers perceived that a system of fused administration might provide the means of ironing out inconsistencies and discordances in the practical administration of the law. Thus, the Judicature Commission responsible for the *Judicature Act* reported in 1869 that:

The litigation arising out of joint Stock Companies has constituted a very large proportion of the business which has engaged the attention of Court of Law and Equity for some years. Directors of Joint Stock Companies fill the double character of agents and trustees for the companies and shareholders; and the effect of their acts and representations has frequently been brought into question in both jurisdictions, and sometimes with opposite results. The expense thus needlessly incurred has been so great, and the perplexity thereby occasioned in the conduct of business so considerable, as to convince most persons, who have followed the development of this branch of the law, of the necessity that exists for a tribunal invested with full power of dealing with all the complicated rights and obligations springing out of such transactions, and of administering complete and appropriate relief, no matter whether the rights and obligations involved are what are called legal or equitable.[21]

The merging of administration, procedure and remedies (with rule-making power that would enable further developments in that direction over the years to come) was the cornerstone of a system of fused administration of law and equity. But it was not the first or last legislative step on the topic in England. Earlier in the nineteenth century, statute provided the Common Law Courts with a limited power to grant injunctions;[22] and Chancery the power to decide legal titles,[23] together with a power to award damages[24] ...

As the years progressed after 1875, statute law and court rules further integrated common law and equity procedure. As early as 1879 the English **[49]** Court of Appeal held that, in cases where no rule of practice was laid down by the Rules made under the *Judicature Act*, and there was a variance in the old practice of the Chancery and Common

---

20. *Salt v Cooper* (1880) 16 Ch D 544 at 549. Lord Jessel expressed a different view in *Walsh v Lonsdale* (1882) 21 Ch D at 14 when, in the context of estates in land, he said 'there is only one Court, and equity rules prevail in it'.
21. First Report at 7.
22. *Common Law Procedure Act 1854*.
23. 15 & 16 Vict c 86, s 62, a later version being 25 and 26 Vict c 42, s 1 (*Sir John Rolt's Act*).
24. *Chancery Amendment Act 1858* (known as *Lord Cairns' Act*).

Law Courts, that practice was to prevail which was considered most convenient.[25] Procedural coalescence continued in the twentieth century with the gradual abolition of jury trial, greater use of the summons as an initiating process, increasing resort to evidence by affidavit or statement and other developments.

Other legal systems proceeded towards administrative, procedural, remedial and substantive fusion in different ways and at different times.[26]

Thus, administration within a single Supreme Court came to New South Wales from the founding of the colony, whereas full procedural and substantive fusion only arrived in 1972. But long before then, several of England's pre-1873, 1873 and post-1873 reforms were introduced piecemeal.

The English legislation of 1854 that had conferred on the common law Courts limited powers to grant injunctions and to recognise equitable defences was adopted in New South Wales by the *Common Law Procedure Act 1857*. But the latter provision was held to be only available in circumstances entitling the claiming of an absolute, perpetual unconditional injunction, otherwise it was still necessary to seek a common injunction in separate proceedings in the equity side of the Supreme Court. An attempt to plug this gap on condition that the proceedings were transferred into the jurisdiction of the Court in Equity was enacted in 1957.[27] Continuing difficulties with this provision were a fillip for the complete fusion enacted in New South Wales by the *Supreme Court Act 1970*.

> **Comment**
> 1. See Radan & Stewart at **1.42–1.44**.

The reception of equity in the British Empire

> ### 1.9 McPherson, 'Judicial Reception of Equity'
>
> **Source:** B H McPherson, *The Reception of English Law Abroad*, Supreme Court of Queensland Library, Brisbane, 2007.
>
> **Extracts:** The extracts from McPherson's book outline the reception of equity principles in the British Empire.

[439] The High Court of Chancery was another court in England which like King's Bench ranked as a superior court. Its English side evolved from the function of the Lord Chancellor of doing what conscience demanded in individual cases to ameliorate the rigidity of

---

25. *Newbiggin-By-The-Sea Gas Co v Armstrong* (1879) 13 Ch D 310.
26. As to Canada, see P M Perrell, 'A Legal History of the Fusion of Law and Equity in the Supreme Court of Ontario' (1988) *Advocates Quarterly* 472. As to the United States, see C T McCormick, 'The Fusion of Law and Equity in United States Courts' (1928) 6 *NCL Rev* 283; D B Dobbs, *Law of Remedies*, 2nd ed, West, St Paul, Minneapolis, 1993, pp 148ff.
27. *Supreme Court Procedure Act 1957*, replacing s 98 of the *Common Law Procedure Act 1899*.

the common law and supplement its deficiencies. Over time, this jurisdiction in equity was extended to a wide range of matters including charities, trusts, administration of estates, fraud, misrepresentation and undue influence, mistake, forfeitures and penalties, partnerships, specific performance injunctions, and so on. There was also a common law or 'Latin' side covering the repeal of letters patent including crown grants of land, traverses of office, petitions of right and guardianship of the persons and property of those suffering from mental disabilities; with a [440] comparable power over infants delegated to the Lord Chancellor by the king as *parens patriae* or guardian of the nation.

Equity and chancery jurisdiction were slow to make their way to some parts of the empire, especially New England, Pennsylvania and India. For this there were several reasons. It was not until some time after the first colonial settlements in the 17th century that in England equity evolved into a system of identifiable principles capable of being transmitted abroad. When it did, there were not enough practitioners with the specialist skills in Chancery procedure available in the colonies to support a system of equity courts in the colonies. In addition, many settlers in the early American colonies were hostile to courts which sat without juries, and, in places where equitable powers were conferred locally, they were often limited in scope and entrusted to courts of law. Furthermore, on a narrow view of the colonial birthright, it was restricted to the common law, and only much later was it clearly recognised as including equity and equitable principles. Added to all this was the fact that the Court of Chancery to some extent met the prevailing need by exercising its jurisdiction *in personam* in England in matters and transactions taking place in the colonies, which it did with some frequency.

Imperial policy in the 18th century insisted on the creation of colonial courts by executive action on the part of the crown rather [441] than by local legislation sourced in the assembly. As keepers of the colonial seal, governors of colonies were, by a somewhat strained analogy, credited with all the equitable jurisdiction of the Lord Chancellor in England, which they exercised either alone or with members of their executive councils. In this regard, opposition from the legislative assemblies of New York and Pennsylvania accounts for the inclusion in the Declaration of Independence of complaints against the British government of obstructing the administration of justice. It may have helped to influence later professional and judicial opinion in England to accept the view that legislation was essential for the creation of courts exercising jurisdiction otherwise than at common law. The experiment of invoking the equity jurisdiction of the Exchequer Court in England attempted by Governor Cosby in New York in 1732 seems not to have been repeated elsewhere. In later British settlements, newly created colonial Supreme Courts, which from early in the 19th century were being invested with equity jurisdiction, invariably derived their authority from legislation, imperial or local, which specifically declared them to be courts of equity with all the powers of the Lord Chancellor or of the Chancery Court in England.[28]

Introduction of the Judicature Act or 'reformed' procedure, once it was adopted throughout the colonial empire and the United States in places where English law prevailed, had the effect of finally removing the jurisdictional barriers that had [442] existed against combining the administration of law and equity. After 1875 orders in council made

---

28. See, for example, *New South Wales Act 1923*; 4 Geo 4, c 96, s 9. Third Charter of Justice for New South Wales, 13 October 1823, art 18 (guardianship of infants and lunatics).

under the Foreign Jurisdiction Acts establishing superior courts in protectorates in Africa, the Pacific and elsewhere invariably provided for the concurrent administration of law and equity. It was not, however, until as recently as the 1970s that New South Wales, Massachusetts and Prince Edward Island fully unified and combined the procedures and administration of the two branches in a single court. Only the Delaware Chancery Court now retains a completely separate, but flourishing, existence as a court of equity.

Comment
1. See Radan & Stewart at **1.48–1.49**.

2

THE NATURE OF EQUITY

Introduction

2.1 This chapter deals with the nature of equity and its place within the Australian legal system and highlights the idea that the notion of conscience underpins equitable doctrine and its manifestation in the maxims of equity.

The extracts in this chapter discuss the following:

- the notion of conscience as the organising idea behind equitable doctrines: Patrick Parkinson, 'The Conscience of Equity';
- the function of the maxims of equity: Paul Jackson, 'The Maxims of Equity Revisited'; and
- the origins and history of the 'clean hands' maxim: *FAI Insurances Ltd v Pioneer Concrete Services Ltd* (1987) 15 NSWLR 552.

Conscience and equity

2.2   Parkinson, 'The Conscience of Equity'

Source: Patrick Parkinson, 'The Conscience of Equity' in P Parkinson (ed), *The Principles of Equity*, 2nd ed, Lawbook Co, Sydney, 2003, p 29.

Extracts: The extracts from Parkinson's article discuss the idea that equity's central organising theme is the requirement of conscientious conduct on the part of persons when exercising their legal rights.

[29] Equitable intervention on behalf of a plaintiff is frequently based upon the fact that there is something in the conduct of the defendant which makes it unconscionable for her or him to insist on the preservation or enforcement of the strict legal rights arising under the law of contract or the law of property. Unconscionability is thus the basis of a range of doctrines. It is also a theme of equity jurisprudence which has seen a considerable revitalisation in recent years. It has been said that unconscionability is an emerging preoccupation of the judiciary in the common law world, not only in Australia, but also in Canada, New Zealand and especially the United States. It has been described as a 'universal talisman in many fields of equity'.[1]

---

1. A Mason, 'Themes and Prospects' in P D Finn (ed), *Essays in Equity*, Law Book Co Sydney, 1985, p 244.

The historic basis of equity's concern with unconscionability is the prevention of 'fraud'. In this context, however, 'fraud' does not have its ordinary meaning, in the English language, of an act of wilful deceit to gain an advantage, nor, at common law, of an intentional or reckless disregard for truth.[2] This common meaning of 'fraud' is narrower than fraud in equity; indeed, a distinction is made between [30] 'actual fraud', and 'constructive fraud' or 'equitable fraud' ...

[30] Relief from fraud, in the equitable sense, may be said to be the leitmotif of equitable intervention to modify strict legal rights generally ... [31] Equitable fraud is a deliberately fluid concept. The great 18th-century judge, Lord Hardwicke, wrote that:

> As to relief against frauds, no invariable rules can be established. Fraud is infinite, and were a Court of Equity once to lay down rules, how far they would go, and no farther, in extending their relief against it, or to define strictly the species or evidence of it, the jurisdiction would be cramped, and perpetually eluded by new schemes, which the fertility of man's invention would contrive.[3]

However, a clear understanding of the way in which the conscience of equity is expressed through its doctrines and remedies is necessary, for, without such an understanding of 'unconscionability', the notion can decline all too readily into a generalised justification for the courts doing whatever they deem to be fair. In Australian law, such an approach has clearly been rejected.[4]

[32] The current emphasis on unconscionability in Australian law is important, because beneath the detail of individual cases lies an ideological shift. Increasingly, courts are curtailing the pursuance of self-interest, where, in times past, it would have been encouraged as a virtue. For example, no longer is it likely that judges will say, as did Wills J in *Allen v Flood*, that 'any right given by contract may be exercised as against the giver by the person to whom it is granted, no matter how wicked, cruel or mean the motive may be which determines the enforcement of the right'.[5] One may now observe the growth of obligations to have concern for others' interests in areas of the law where hitherto such obligations would not have been countenanced. In the commercial world, in Australia at least, this translates into more stringent obligations of good faith and fair dealing in pre-contractual negotiations and in the performance of contracts, careful scrutiny of the steps taken to ensure that the consent of guarantors is not procured by unfair pressure, influence or exploitation, and a refusal by the courts to allow the harsh or oppressive use of forfeiture provisions ...

[34] A distinction is sometimes drawn between procedural and substantive unconscionability.[6] The terms refer, respectively to situations where the unconscionability lies in the process by which one party gained the benefit which is under challenge, and cases in which the rationale for judicial intervention is founded upon the unconscionability of the outcome which would otherwise prevail. Clearly, of course, the two are interrelated. Much of the concern with unfairness in the process of gaining a contract is because of the

---

2. *Derry v Peek* (1889) 14 App Cas 337.
3. Letter to Lord Kames cited in L Sheridan, *Fraud in Equity: A Study in English and Irish Law*, Pittman, London, 1957, p 2.
4. See Deane J in *Muschinski v Dodds* (1985) 160 CLR 583 at 516.
5. *Allen v Flood* [1898] AC 1 at 46.
6. *West v AGC (Advances) Ltd* (1986) 5 NSWLR 610 at 620.

unconscionability outcomes which arise from one-sided bargains. Furthermore, grossly unfair outcomes inevitably lead to an inquiry about the negotiating process ...

Thus the ideas about what is, or is not, an unfair outcome may have a strong influence upon decisions about whether aspects of the process should be deemed 'unconscionable'. Nonetheless, procedural unconscionability has been the traditional focus of legal doctrine, both at common law and in equity. The doctrines of undue influence, unconscionable dealing, unilateral mistake, relief from fraud, misrepresentation and duress, may all be explained on this basis.[7] What attracts the exceptional intervention of the court to set aside transactions [35] which would otherwise stand, or to interfere with legal rights which would otherwise be enforced, is that those against whom claims are raised have so acted that it would be inequitable and against conscience for them to set up those legal rights. It is the words or conduct of the party with the claimed right which justify the court in refusing to enforce that right, or enforcing it subject to a trust, or other qualification upon legal title.

Increasingly, however, there are signs that courts are justifying intervention on the basis of unconscionable outcomes, with requiring proof that the defendant has engaged in some form of unfair dealing.[8] Here, the unconscionability lies in the insistence on one's strict legal rights, in circumstances where to do so is considered to be contrary to equity and good conscience, because of the hardship which would thereby be caused to the other party. Courts have usually proceeded cautiously in this area, however, since without a focus upon specific acts of wrongful conduct, the notion of unconscionability can become all too subjective. A principle which was meant to be used to restrain people like the Sheriff of Nottingham should not be used to empower a judge to act like Robin Hood.

Comments

1. See Radan & Stewart at **2.4–2.7**.
2. Parkinson's use of the term 'unconscionability' should be read in light of the High Court's comment in *Tanwar Enterprises Pty Ltd v Cauchi* (2003) 217 CLR 315 at 324, that the term 'unconscientious' is a more accurate term than 'unconscionable' to describe the basis for equitable intervention.

The maxims of equity

2.3 Jackson, 'The Maxims of Equity Revisited'

Source: Paul Jackson, The Maxims of Equity Revisited' in S Goldstein (ed), *Equity and Contemporary Legal Developments*, Harry and Michael Sacher Institute for Legislative Research and Comparative Law, the Hebrew University of Jerusalem, Jerusalem, 1992, p 72.

Extracts: The extracts from Jackson's article discuss the relevance and place of the maxims of equity in terms of equitable principles and doctrines and cautions against an over-estimation of their worth in resolving cases and the development of principles.

---

7. *Commercial Bank of Australia Ltd v Amadio* (1983) 151 CLR 447 at 461.
8. See especially *Bridgewater v Leahy* (1998) 194 CLR 457, in which the High Court indicated that the passive acceptance of a benefit may be unconscionable.

[73] Textbooks on Equity ... usually include[e] a chapter on 'The Maxims of Equity'. The significance of these maxims in modern equity has, however, been doubted; they have been described as being 'of uncertain application ... not of real importance in the modern law' or dismissed as 'a collection of mottoes in which aspects of conscience become pickled and to a degree trivialised'.[9] Spry suggests that the use of well known equitable maxims can be 'commonly misleading' and that 'Often, indeed, when they are used or referred to it is found, on a careful analysis, that their purpose has been merely to justify or explain or confirm a decision which has already been reached on other grounds through a more close application of equitable principles'.[10] Few teachers would be likely nowadays to agree with Holdsworth that a 'satisfactory course of lectures on the general principles of equity can be grouped round some of the most important of these maxim's'.[11] Hanbury had foreseen the risk of the traditional maxims degenerating into 'useless and deceptive catchwords' while hoping on the other hand that they might continue to 'fill the place that they have hitherto held, the worthy place of coadjutors to the study [74] of equity jurisprudence'.[12] ...

[75] Textbooks devote little attention to what distinguishes maxims from rules, to their relationship to common law concepts such as public policy or *ex turpi causa non oritur actio* or whether there may be other forms of principles or concepts which should properly be taken into account in deciding cases on a basis of equity.

Certainly no one could confuse the maxims of equity with an attempt to state rationally a series of juristic deductions from a philosophical concept of equity ... Some maxims are so widely expressed that, if taken literally, they [76] would dissolve all legal rules and concepts; for example, Equity does not suffer a wrong to be without a remedy — which may have meaning as a description of the original of equity's auxiliary jurisdiction ...

[80] Whatever the importance historically or today of particular maxims ... the maxim equity acts *in personam* is unique as a description of the foundation of equitable jurisdiction and more controversially as defining the nature of equitable rights. No doubt it is in the words of Snell 'of less significance now than formerly'[13] but the development of *Anton Piller* orders and *Mareva* injunctions have seen it frequently cited to justify these new jurisdictions ...

[81] Concentration on the traditional equitable maxims in contrast to equitable rules can, however, obscure resort by courts to other manifestations [82] of general standards when they wish to avoid applying rules. The most general and abstract such standard is 'general equitable principles'. These were invoked by Phillimore L J in *Greenwood v Bennett*[14] to allow a claim for money expended on repairing a stolen car by a bona fide purchaser after the true owner had established his title ... In *The Alaska Trader*[15] Lloyd J, in considering the right of the innocent party to insist on the performance of a contract

9. J Hackney, *Understanding Equity and Trusts*, 1987, p 29.
10. I C F Spry, *The Principles of Equitable Remedies*, 3rd ed, Law Book Co, Sydney, 1984, p 6.
11. Holdsworth, *History of English Law*, vol xii, p 191.
12. Hanbury, *Essays in Equity*, 1934, p 54. This essay, 'The Field of Modern Equity', originally appeared in (1929) 45 *Law Quarterly Review* 196.
13. R P Meagher, W M C Gummow and J F R Lehane, *Equity, Doctrines and Remedies* (2nd ed, 1984) p 42.
14. [1973] QB 195.
15. *Clea Shipping Corporation v Bulk Oil International (No 2)* [1984] 1 All ER 129.

... , concluded that a point would come at which the court would cease to allow such insistence 'on general equitable principles'.

Other cases have invoked in varying terms, principles apparently common to law and equity. Thus, *qui sentit commodum sentire debet et onus* has been invoked in recent decisions as

> the simple principle of ordinary fairness and consistency that from the earliest days most of us have heard in the form 'you can't have it both ways' or 'you can't eat your cake and have it too' or 'you can't blow hot and cold'.[16]

and described by Lord Fraser in *Newbury D C v Secretary of State for the Environment*[17] as a maxim of law and equity ...

[84] The common law too recognises and applies general principles and moral standards. Indeed, well known maxims of equity such as where the equities are equal the first in time prevails are just as properly regarded as maxims of the common law, which in this instance, as others, was indebted to Roman law. In the Latin form *Qui prior est in tempore* it is treated ... as a legal maxim and cited as the basis for primogeniture, acquisition of title by occupancy and the right of property in wreck, derelicts, waifs and strays ...

[87] [Furthermore, t]hree maxims particularly focus on the unmeritorious conduct of the plaintiff: He who comes into equity must come with clean hands and equity will not allow a statute to be used as an instrument of fraud both refer to conduct before an action is brought. He who seeks equity must do equity (sometimes in the form, he that seeks equity should do equity) is normally said to look to the future although this distinction is not always drawn ... With these equitable maxims may be compared common law reliance on *ex turpi non oritur action* and public policy.

Comment

1. See Radan & Stewart at **2.13–2.14**.

Origins and history of the 'clean hands' maxim

2.4   FAI Insurances Ltd v Pioneer Concrete Services Ltd (1987) 15 NSWLR 552

Court: Supreme Court of New South Wales

Facts: In relation to proceedings concerning certain share transactions, notices of motion were filed seeking to amend the statements of claim and defences and to strike out interrogatories.

Issue: One of the issues before the Supreme Court was whether the defence of unclean hands was available in this case.

---

16. *Tito v Waddell (No 2)* [1977] Ch 106 at 289.
17. [1981] AC 578 at 606.

Decision: Young J held that the defence of unclean hands is only available where the right is one which, if protected, would mean that the plaintiff was taking advantage of its own wrong.

Extracts: The extracts from the judgment of Young J outline the origins and history of the maxim that 'one who comes to equity must come with clean hands'.

Young J

[557] I now turn to the matters of the equitable defences of clean hands or clean hands mingled with illegality.

There has been quite a debate before me as to how far the doctrine goes ... I have thought it necessary to go back in history and to look closely at the content of the clean hands doctrine in order to answer this question. Equity textbooks often refer to ... the [view] that the rule ... is of relatively recent origin ...

However, it does not seem to me that such a position is historically justified. Spence points out that the maxim 'He who comes to equity must come with clean hands' is closely related to the maxim 'He who seeks equity must do equity' and that both derive from [558] the ecclesiastical law which in turn derived from the Roman law.[18] Without going into the matter too deeply, it would seem that the basis is the Roman law exceptio doli which came into Roman law shortly after 66 BC.[19] The central idea behind this exceptio was to provide a defence which would prevent the plaintiff's action succeeding when the plaintiff had acted dishonestly in bringing the action.

The ecclesiastical law developed the conception in matrimonial cases by allowing defences of recrimination. Although it is sometimes broadly put that only a person who had by him or herself preserved the sanctity of marriage could petition for divorce, the principle was in fact narrower ... If there was a petition for divorce on the ground of adultery, then the petitioner's own adultery would normally bar relief, but if the petitioner had merely been cruel, it would not bar relief. This is because the bar only arose 'where both parties are in eodem delicto, and that in cases of cruelty and adultery the delictum is not of the same kind ... No cruelty can, ... justify the violation of the marriage-bed'.[20] I think this is significant when considering the equitable doctrine of 'clean hands' ...

[R]esearch shows that the equitable maxim was first used in Francis' *Maxims of Equity* (1728), where he summed up some of the seventeenth century cases by saying: 'He that hath committed iniquity shall not have equity'. This is acknowledged to be the author's own deduction from study of cases.[21]

Francis based his maxim on cases such as *Rich v Sydenham*.[22] In that case, the plaintiff held a bond for 1,600 pounds to secure a debt of 800 pounds based upon a loan transaction of 90 pounds. The plaintiff sought to attach equitable property of the defendant. The

---

18. Spence, *Equitable Jurisdiction* (1846).
19. See Lee's *Elements of Roman Law*, 4th ed (1956) p 450.
20. *Otway v Otway* (1888) 13 PD 141 at 149.
21. See Pound, 'On Certain Maxims of Equity', *Cambridge Legal Essays* (1926) at 263 and Holdsworth's *History of English Law*, vol 12, p 188.
22. *Rich v Sydenham* (1671) 22 ER 762.

defendant objected that the security was got from him when he was drunk and the report says: 'the Lord Keeper would not give the Plaintiff any Relief in Equity, not so much as for the Principal he had really lent; and so the Bill was dismist'. Other examples are *Bodly's* case,[23] and the other ancient cases about to be discussed.

The report of *Jones v Lenthal*[24] is instructive. That case involved a bill to be relieved from a debt owing by bond. In an earlier suit, the plaintiff had sworn that the debt had been fully satisfied, but this was to avoid a sequestration. Because this iniquity was not done against the defendant, the court ignored it. The editor of the reports adds this note:

> For though the Rule be, That he who has committed Iniquity (as here, in the false Answer) shall not have Equity; yet it seems, that is to be understood, when the Iniquity is done to the Defendant himself: As where a Lessee is sued at Law on a Forfeiture of his Lease for Non-payment of Rent or the like; if such Lease was obtained by Fraud or false Suggestion, Equity will not relieve ...

Next in point of time comes the famous case of *Dering v Earl of Winchelsea*. That was a case before the Court of Exchequer on its equity side. A guarantor was suing his co-sureties for contribution and the allegation of the defendants was that the plaintiff was the brother of the [559] defaulter and he encouraged his brother in gaming knowing that his brother had insufficient income of his own so would probably be resorting to moneys that did not belong to him. The court did not consider this a valid defence. Eyre CB said:

> ... It is not laying down any principle to say that his ill-conduct disables him from having any relief in this court. If this can be founded on any principle, it must be that a man must come into a court of equity with clean hands, but when this is said it does not refer to a general depravity; it must have an immediate and necessary relation to the equity sued for; it must be a depravity in a legal as well as in a moral sense. In a moral sense, the companion, and perhaps the conductor, of Thomas Dering, may be said to be the author of the loss, but to legal purposes Thomas Dering himself is the author of it; and if the evil example of the plaintiff led him on, this is not what the court can take cognisance of. Cases indeed might be put in which the proposition would be true. If a contribution were demanded from a ship and cargo for goods thrown overboard to save the ship, if the plaintiff had actually bored a hole in the ship, he would in that case be certainly the author of the loss, and would not be entitled to any contribution.[25] ...

It should be noted that it would appear that the first reported judicial use of the expression 'clean hands' was by Lord Mansfield in proceedings at law to be relieved from a usurious contract in *Fitzroy v Gwillim* on 5 May 1786, where his Lordship used the current maxim as equivalent to 'He who seeks equity must do equity'.[26] The descent of the clean hands principle from that other maxim is attested by strong authority.[27] It is useful to observe that in Viner's *Abridgement on the Maxims of Equity*, the maxim 'He who seeks equity must do equity' is also limited to doing equity in the same transaction.

---

23. (1679) 22 ER 824.
24. (1669) 22 ER 739.
25. *Dering v Earl of Winchelsea* (1787) 29 ER 1184 at 1185.
26. *Fitzroy v Gwillim* (1786) ER 1025 at 1026.
27. Spence, *Equitable Jurisdiction* (1846) p 423.

There were then a series of cases dealing with unconscionable conduct in conveyancing cases. It was clearly held that misrepresentations or the like would destroy a contract and operate as a personal bar to the person who had practised it,[28] but that one could not, as a plaintiff in a specific performance suit, get something more than one could get under the contract at law because of the defendant's misrepresentation, a distinction which is referred to in the cases summed up by the Privy Council in *Fisher v Tully*.[29]

In *Attwood v Small* Lord Brougham said:

> ... that general fraudulent conduct signifies nothing; that general dishonesty of purpose signifies nothing; that attempts to overreach go for nothing; that an intention and design to deceive may go for nothing unless all this dishonesty of purpose, all this fraud, all this intention and design, can be connected with the particular transaction, and not only connected with the particular transaction, but must be made to be the very ground upon which this transaction took place, and must have [560] given rise to this contract. If a mere general intention to overreach were enough, I hardly know a contract, even between persons of very strict morality, that could stand.[30]

Coming to the twentieth century, we again find some cases where what is really a defence of public policy or illegality is sometimes given the tag of clean hands. One such illustration is *Glyn v Weston Feature Film Co*, where Younger J said of a book which was 'calculated ... to mislead into the belief that she may without danger choose the easy life of sin many a poor romantic girl striving amidst manifold hardships and discouragements to keep her honour untarnished' was a book of 'such a cruelly destructive tendency no protection will be extended by a Court of Equity'.[31] Apart from these cases, there were others which clearly dealt with the scope of the unclean hands rule.

In the High Court in *Meyers v Casey*, Isaacs J said of the case before him:

> It is altogether different from the cases where the right relied on, and which the Court of equity is asked to protect or assist, is itself to some extent brought into existence or induced by some illegal or unconscionable conduct of the plaintiff, so that protection for what he claims involves protection for his own wrong. No Court of equity will aid a man to derive advantage from his own wrong, and this is really the meaning of the maxim.[32]

In *Moody v Cox*, the English Court of Appeal reaffirmed that:

> ... Equity will not apply the principle about clean hands unless the depravity, the dirt in question on the hand, has an immediate and necessary relation to the equity sued for. In this case the bribe has no immediate relation to rectification.[33]

The next case that should be considered is *Kettles and Gas Appliances Ltd v Anthony Hordern & Sons Ltd*. In essence, the facts of that case were that the plaintiff sought an injunction to restrain passing-off in respect of kettles which closely resembled its 'Captain Kettle'. The plaintiff would have obtained relief but for its improper branding of its own kettles with the words 'patented, copyrighted' in a prominent place which did not represent

---

28. *Clermont (Viscount) v Tasburgh* (1819) 37 ER 318.
29. (1878) 3 App Cas 627 at 639.
30. *Attwood v Small* (1838) 7 ER 684 at 765.
31. *Glyn v Weston Feature Film Co* [1916] 1 Ch 261 at 270.
32. *Meyers v Casey* (1913) 17 CLR 90 at 124. See also Barton ACJ at 101–02.
33. *Moody v Cox* [1917] 2 Ch 71 especially at 85–8.

the correct position. Long Innes J said that he was satisfied that this was done by the plaintiff with the deliberate intention of deceiving the public and of deterring others from manufacturing or vending a similar kettle.[34] This matter was sufficient to induce the court not to give the plaintiff any relief.

In *Gill v Lewis*,[35] Hodson LJ said that the court would not give relief against forfeiture where the conduct of the applicant was such as to make it inequitable that relief should be given to him such as the case where he had been conducting the premises as a disorderly house. This case is listed by *Snell Principles of Equity*,[36] as an instance of the unclean hands defence. I was disturbed by this because it did seem to me that this extended the net of clean hands wider than the plaintiff's naughtiness with respect to the lessor and the transaction. On more reflection, however, it either fits into the class of cases which are really based **[561]** on public policy or alternatively, comes within the footnote to *Jones v Lenthal* set out above. I do not believe that *Gill v Lewis* modifies the rule.

Although *Snell* says that American authorities have not always appreciated the limitations of the clean hands doctrine ... modern American authority appears to say exactly the same as the authorities in England and Australia[37] ...

Finally, I should refer to two recent decisions in this Division. In *Dow Securities Pty Ltd v Manufacturing Investments Ltd*,[38] Wootten J considered the situation where to endeavour to obtain protection against winding up for a debt a company wished to rely on an illegal loan agreement with a director who was connected with the creditor company. The judge held that the debt involved in the winding up proceedings was not brought into existence or induced by the conduct relating to the alleged illegal director's loan, so that clean hands was not a defence. His Honour rejected the submission ... that the decision ... in *Hewson v Sydney Stock Exchange Ltd*,[39] had relaxed this requirement. I also reject it. In *Dewhirst v Edwards*,[40] Powell J sets out the cases dealing with the limitations of the clean hands rule including *Hewson's* case, with no suggestion that the exceptions to the rule have been watered down.

I have gone through such a lengthy history and examination of the rule because, it seems to me ... that ... the more one examines the rule in its application in the cases, the more one can see that it is only if the right being sought to be vindicated by the plaintiff in a court of equity, is one which if protected, would mean the plaintiff was taking advantage of his own wrong, that the court will either debar him from relief or perhaps say he is not a proper plaintiff in a representative suit.

Comments
1. See Radan & Stewart at **2.31**.
2. For a discussion of a case applying the defence of unclean hands see *Black Uhlans Inc v New South Wales Crime Commission* [2002] NSWSC 1060. This case is extracted in Chapter 31.

---

34. *Kettles and Gas Appliances Ltd v Anthony Hordern & Sons Ltd* (1934) 35 SR (NSW) 108 at 128.
35. [1956] 2 QB 1 at 17.
36. Snell, *Principles of Equity*, 28th ed (1982), p 33.
37. See *Republic Molding Corporation v BW Photo Utilities* 319 F (2d) 347, 349 (1963).
38. (1981) 5 ACLR 501.
39. (1967) 87 WN (Pt 1) (NSW) 422.
40. [1983] 1 NSWLR 34 at 51.

3

THE RELATIONSHIP OF LAW AND EQUITY

Introduction

3.1 This chapter deals with the relationship between the principles of the common law and equity following the introduction of the judicature system which ended the system of separate courts of common law and equity and created a single court that administered both sets of principles. A crucial aspect of the judicature system has been its impact on the development of legal doctrine, particularly the extent to which there has been, or can be, a fusion of the principles of the common law and equity.

The extracts in this chapter discuss the following:

- the development of legal principles in the context of the single court created by the judicature system: Keith Mason, 'Substantive Fusion and the Judicature Act'; and
- the doctrine of *Walsh v Lonsdale*: *Walsh v Lonsdale* (1882) 2 Ch D 9; *Chan v Cresdon Pty Ltd* (1989) 168 CLR 242.

Fusion under the judicature system

3.2   Mason, 'Substantive Fusion and the Judicature Act'

Source: Keith Mason, 'Fusion: Fallacy, Future or Finished?' in S Degeling & J Edelman, *Equity in Commercial Law*, Lawbook Co, Sydney, 2005, p 41.

Extracts: The extracts from Mason's article, written at a time when he was President of the New South Wales Court of Appeal, argue that the introduction of the judicature system did not preclude the unified court that it created from thereafter fusing the principles of the common law and equity.

[54] Section 25 of the *Judicature Act 1873* (UK) also directly fused substantive law and equity. On the orthodox view, it did so, only to a limited degree. It is, however, possible to see s 25(11) as the statutory capping of a process that had started in 1615. Parliament confirmed equity's precedence as a matter of last resort (if Judges of a single Court could not sort out remedial and doctrinal differences between Law and Equity by their own devices).

The side-note to s 25 was 'rules of law upon certain points'. Subsections (1) to (10) dealt with particular conflicts between law and equity in respect of the same subject matter.

The 'conflicts or variances' thereby resolved related to assignments of choses in action, stipulations as to time in contract, the custody [55] of infants, equitable waste, merger of estates, administration of insolvent estates and actions for trespass by mortgagors in possession. Resolution was generally in favour of Chancery's rule, but a statutory amalgam of law and equity was devised as regards assignments. The miscellany of topics is itself testimony to the extent to which the two systems were treading on each other's toes when administered separately.

Section 25(11) was the catch-all, providing:

> Generally in all matters not herein-before particularly mentioned, in which there is any conflict or variance between the rules of equity and the rules of the common law with reference to the same matter, the rules of equity shall prevail.

By the time that New South Wales took its great leap forward to the nineteenth century by enacting the *Supreme Court Act 1970*[1] most of the matters covered by s 25(1)–(10) of the *Judicature Act 1873* (UK) had already been addressed by the New South Wales Parliament. It was only thought necessary to enact a modern variant of subs (11).[2]

The framers of the English statute thought that s 25(11) would have little work to do. It turned out that they underestimated the situations in which later courts would discover direct 'conflict or variance' between law and equity 'with reference to the same matter'. Later caselaw disclosed several topics where equity and law were seen to produce different outcomes on the same issue, areas where the pre-1875 Chancery rule prevailed in accordance with the subsection.

Section 25 was never intended to do away with the distinction between law and equity. Maitland in his *Equity Lectures*[3] was, however, at pains to stress the general absence of conflict between law and equity, thereby explaining the minimal scope of s 25(11). He expounded equity as a gloss on the common law, albeit a collection of appendices between which there was no very close connexion. Using a Biblical metaphor, he stated that:

> Equity had come not to destroy the law, but to fulfil it. Every jot and every tittle of the law was to be obeyed, but when all this has been done something might yet be needed, something that equity would require ...

There was a flaw in Maitland's gloss metaphor, with its message of continuing confluence between law and equity, like Ashburner's reference to 'two streams of jurisdiction [which], though they run in the same channel, run side by side and do not mingle their waters'.[4] Congruence, stemming from [56] Equity's supremacy before and after 1875, was a more accurate picture than confluence. Hohfeld answered Maitland in a famous article on 'The Relations between Equity and Law' when he pointed out that:

---

1. It commenced on 1 July 1972.
2. Section 64, later re-enacted so as to apply in the *Law Reform (Law and Equity) Act 1972*. The New South Wales Law Reform Report on *Law and Equity* (LRC 13, 1971) at 9–10, documents the earlier adoption in New South Wales of subs (1) to (10) of s 25 of the *Judicature Act 1873* (UK). For example, subs (3)–(7) were addressed in the *Conveyancing Act 1919* (NSW).
3. J Brunyate (ed), *Equity A Course of Lectures by F W Maitland*, Rev ed, Cambridge University Press, Cambridge, 1947.
4. D Brown, *Ashburner's Principles of Equity*, 2nd ed, Butterworths, London, 1933, p 18.

As against the proposition that there is no appreciable conflict between law and equity, the thesis of the present writer is this: while a large part of the rules of equity harmonise with the various rules of law, another large part of the rules of equity — more especially those relating to the so-called exclusive and auxiliary jurisdictions of equity — conflict with legal rules and, as a matter of substance, annul or negative the latter pro Canto. As just indicated, there is, it is believed, a very marked and constantly recurring conflict between equitable and legal rules relating to various jural relations; and whenever such conflict occurs, the equitable rule is, in the last analysis, paramount and determinative. Or, putting the matter in another way, the so-called legal rule in every such case has, to that extent, only an apparent validity and operation as a matter of genuine law. Though it may represent an important stage of thought in the solution of a given problem, and may also connote very important possibilities as to certain other, closely associated (and valid) jural relations, yet as regards the very relation in which it suffers direct competition with a rule of equity, such a conflicting rule of law is, pro tanto, of no greater force than an unconstitutional statute.[5]

On this basis, Hohfeld wrote, s 25(11) had been added only out of an abundance of caution. Its fundamental idea was 'anything but a novelty'.[6] Arguments that the *Judicature Act* directly changed substantive rules (outside the working out of s 25) have been rebuffed on the few occasions that they surfaced. One of the earliest examples is *Britain v Rossiter*[7] where the English Court of Appeal rejected a submission that the *Judicature Act* permitted damages to be awarded with respect to an unwritten contract where the conduct of the parties did not attract the doctrine of part performance that triggered resort to *Lord Cairns' Act* as a source of the power to award damages. The substantive doctrine of part performance as a key to equitable remedies was in truth too firmly fixed to justify further expansion of an already bold doctrine without clear legislative endorsement.

But it was or should have been equally clear that the *Judicature Act* did not forbid the continuing development of law and equity, including development in the direction of integration of principles, if the single Court otherwise considered this an appropriate application of earlier precedents. *Walsh v Lonsdale* was decided in 1883. Unloved for its boldness by *Meagher, Gummow and Lehane's Equity*, and others, it nevertheless became undoubted authority for the proposition that a specifically enforceable agreement for lease would, in a *Judicature Act* court, be regarded as between the original parties as the equivalent of a lease at law.[8]

There is a more specific corollary to the proposition that s 25(11) and its counterparts have limited direct effect. Outside cases falling within its scope, [57] courts are free to develop the law in a principled manner by preferring legal rather than equitable analogies or precedents. This was the stance affirmed by the English Court of Appeal as early as 1879 in procedural matters.[9] A much more recent example is *AMEV-UDC Finance Ltd v Austin* where, in the area of penalties, modern equity chose to follow the common law

---

5. W Hohfeld, 'The Relations Between Equity and Law' (1913) 11 *Michigan Law Review* 537 at 543–4.
6. Hohfeld, 'The Relations Between Equity and Law', note 5 above at 543–4.
7. (1883) 11 QBD 123.
8. *Chan v Cresdon Pty Ltd* (1989) 168 CLR 242 at 252.
9. *Newbiggin-By-The-Sea Gas Co v Armstrong* (1879) 13 Ch D 310.

and, with the advent of the Judicature System, allow a discordant stream of equitable doctrine to 'wither ... on the vine'[10] in the interests of coherence in the law generally. As I pointed out in *Harris*,[11] many of the instances when this borrowing has occurred (before and after 1875) are parked in equity texts under the rubrics of the maxim 'equity follows the law' or equity's 'concurrent jurisdiction' ...

Section 25(11) did not purport to stop or even affect the development of legal and equitable doctrine. Nothing in the *Judicature* reforms precluded the continuing trend towards a more integrated, internally-consistent and principled system of general law, a task assisted by progressive steps (before and after the *Judicature Act*) taken towards a single system of court administration, procedure and remedies.

Despite his attitude to s 25(11), Maitland in his lectures nevertheless forecast that:

> The bond which kept [these doctrines] under the head of Equity was the jurisdictional and procedural bond. All these matters were within the cognizance of courts of equity, and they were not within the cognizance of the courts of the common law. That bond is now broken by the judicature acts. Instead of it we find but a mere historical bond — 'these rules used to be dealt with by the Court of Chancery' — and the strength of that bond is being diminished year by year. The day will come when lawyers will cease to inquire whether a given rule be a rule of equity or a rule of the common law: suffice that it is a well-established rule administered by the High Court of Justice.[12]

Maitland's prediction is yet to be fulfilled, although matters have hastened in the last couple of decades ... For the moment, I draw attention to his observation that the procedural coalescence of the separate courts would be as much a trigger for fusion as s 25(11).

Comments
1. See Radan & Stewart at **3.4–3.22**.
2. For a similar understanding of the *Judicature Acts* see Hon Justice Michael Kirby, 'Equity's Australian Isolationism' (2008) 8 *Queensland University of Technology Law & Justice Journal* 444 and P Jaffey, *Private Law and Property Claims*, Hart Publishing, Oxford, 2007, Ch 4. Jaffey, at pp 120 and 125, states:

> Since the Judicature Acts, equity and the common law have been applied together in the same courts and it has been practicable for analogical reasoning to operate across the two bodies of law. It should operate to eliminate false differentiation and assimilate rules concerning the same issue into a single body of law. This is what is meant by substantive fusion. Substantive fusion is the natural consequence of the ordinary judicial function of analogical reasoning ... [T]he Judicature Acts themselves do not require or authorise substantive fusion: their purpose and effect was procedural fusion ... [However,] the argument for substantive fusion does not rely on the Judicature Acts. The justification for substantive fusion is the value of coherence that lies behind analogical reasoning. Procedural fusion merely made explicit the need for substantive fusion and facilitated it by bringing the two bodies of law in front of the same judges. This point also shows why substantive fusion is necessarily a gradual process.

10. *AMEV-UDC Finance Ltd v Austin* (1986) 162 CLR 170 at 191.
11. *Harris v Digital Pulse Pty Ltd* (2003) 56 NSWLR 298 at 326.
12. Brunyate, *Equity A Course of Lectures by F W Maitland*, note 3 above.

The doctrine of *Walsh v Lonsdale*

3.3   Walsh v Lonsdale (1882) 2 Ch D 9

Court: Court of Appeal of England and Wales

Facts: Lonsdale (the landlord) agreed to grant Walsh (the tenant) a lease of a mill for seven years at a rent payable quarterly in arrears, with a provision entitling the landlord to demand a year's rent in advance. Walsh entered into possession and paid rent in accordance with the agreement for 18 months. However, it transpired that the lease was void at common law because it was never executed under seal as required by statute. Lonsdale then demanded a year's rent in advance in accordance with the agreement, which Walsh failed to pay. Lonsdale levied for distress at common law, seeking to seize Walsh's chattels in lieu of payment. Walsh sought an injunction against the distress, as well as damages for illegal distress, arguing that the agreement was not a valid common law lease and that it amounted to no more than a tenancy from year to year under which rent was payable quarterly, with the consequence that there was no basis for Lonsdale's distress action. Walsh also argued that Lonsdale should have first sought specific performance of the agreement to lease.

Issue: The issue before the Court of Appeal was whether Lonsdale's common law remedy of distress was permitted despite the absence of a lease at common law.

Decision: The Court of Appeal (Jessel MR, Cotton and Lindley LJJ) unanimously found in favour of the landlord Lonsdale. It was held that a written lease not in proper form will give rise to an equitable relationship of landlord and tenant, but it will not be treated as a legal lease unless it can support an order for specific performance. Because the equitable lease in this case could be equated to a lease at law, breach of the tenant's liability to pay rent was capable of supporting the common law remedy of distress.

Extracts: The extracts from the judgment of Jessel MR highlight the Court of Appeal's view that, because there was an agreement to lease which the parties conceded was specifically enforceable, the rights of the parties could be determined as if the lease had been entered into in accordance with the requirements of statute.

Jessel MR

[14] It is not necessary on the present occasion to decide finally what the rights of the parties are. If the Court sees that there is a fair question to be decided it will take security so that the party who ultimately succeeds may be in the right position. The question is one of some nicety. There is an agreement for a lease under which possession has been given. Now since the *Judicature Act* the possession is held under the agreement. There are not two estates as there were formerly, one estate at common law by reason of the payment of the rent from year to year, and an estate in equity under the agreement. There is only one Court, and the equity rules prevail in it. The tenant holds under an agreement for a lease. He holds, therefore, under the same terms in equity as if a lease had been granted, it being a case in which both parties admit that relief is capable of being given by [15] specific performance.

That being so, he cannot complain of the exercise by the landlord of the same rights as the landlord would have had if a lease had been granted. On the other hand, he is protected in the same way as if a lease had been granted; he cannot be turned out by six months' notice as a tenant from year to year. He has a right to say, 'I have a lease in equity, and you can only re-enter if I have committed such a breach of covenant as would if a lease had been granted have entitled you to re-enter according to the terms of a proper proviso for re-entry'. That being so, it appears to me that being a lessee in equity he cannot complain of the exercise of the right of distress merely because the actual parchment has not been signed and sealed.

Comments

1. See Radan & Stewart at **3.28–3.38**.
2. For a discussion of this case, in the context of Sir George Jessel's other decisions following the introduction of the judicature system, see D O'Keefe, 'Sir George Jessel and the Union of Judicature' (1982) 26 *American Journal of Legal History* 227, esp 243–6.
3. In P Sparkes, '*Walsh v Lonsdale*: The Non-Fusion Fallacy' (1988) 8 *Oxford Journal of Legal Studies* 350, the author argues that *Walsh v Lonsdale* can only be supported on the basis that the *Judicature Acts* did bring about a substantive fusion of the principles of common law and equity and that the decision resulted in the recognition of equitable rent as a new equity that could be enforced by a legal remedy. A more radical approach to the case is evident in S Gardner, 'Equity, Estate Contracts and the Judicature Acts: *Walsh v Lonsdale* Revisited' (1987) 7 *Oxford Journal of Legal Studies* 60, where the author argues that the *Judicature Acts* did bring about a substantive fusion of principles and that the agreement for lease of the kind that occurred in *Walsh v Lonsdale* does not need to be specifically enforceable for rights to arise thereunder. However, Gardner's analysis is inconsistent with subsequent authority which insists upon the agreement for lease being specifically enforceable.

3.4   Chan v Cresdon Pty Ltd (1989) 168 CLR 242

Court: High Court of Australia

Facts: Cresdon (the landlord) agreed in writing to lease Torrens title land in Queensland to Sarcourt Pty Ltd (the tenant) for a term exceeding three years. The agreement contained the terms of the lease as an annexure, but the lease was never registered despite being duly executed. Robert and Grace Chan (the guarantors) were also parties to the agreement because, pursuant to clause 23.01 of the annexure, they guaranteed the tenant's obligations. Sarcourt defaulted under the lease and Cresdon took action against the guarantors. Cresdon's action against the guarantors was stated as being one taken on the guarantee 'under this lease'. The guarantors argued that the lease's registration was a condition precedent to their liability and that, until registration, there were no obligations to be performed under the lease. They also contended that third parties were not subject to the rule in *Walsh v Lonsdale*, and that the rule did not mean that a term recognised in equity would necessarily be sufficient to satisfy the condition of a legal term. Cresdon argued that a lease that remained unregistered, although ineffectual at law, was not void or ineffective for all purposes.

Issue: The issue before the High Court was whether the guarantee was enforceable notwithstanding that the lease had not been registered as required by statute. It also had to consider the application of the rule in *Walsh v Lonsdale* to the facts in this case.

Decision: The majority of the High Court (Mason CJ, Brennan, Deane and McHugh JJ; Toohey J dissenting) decided against the landlord and ruled that, because there was no registered lease, there was no enforceable guarantee. It also held that, although the rule in *Walsh v Lonsdale* meant that an agreement to lease gave rise to an equitable lease, it did not create a legal interest. Further, the operation of the rule depended upon the availability of specific performance of the agreement to lease. The facts in this case did not support such a finding. The guarantee of obligations 'under this lease' referred to obligations in a legal lease. Because no legal lease existed, there was no enforceable guarantee.

Extracts: The extracts from the joint majority judgment focus on the High Court's interpretation of the rule in *Walsh v Lonsdale* and the relationship between legal and equitable principles.

Mason CJ, Brennan, Deane and McHugh JJ

[250] The [landlord's] next contention is that the unregistered lease amounts to an equitable lease to which the relevant covenants may be related. The argument, which invokes the doctrine in *Walsh v Lonsdale*, is that the lease, though ineffective to create a 'legal' lease until registration, was effective to bring into existence an equitable lease for a term of five years on the footing that equity regards as done what ought to be done. The most favourable statement of the position, from the [landlord's] viewpoint, was that made by Sir George Jessel MR in *Walsh v Lonsdale*:

> There is an agreement for a lease under which possession has been given. Now since the *Judicature Act* the possession is held under the agreement. There are not two estates as there were formerly, one estate at common law by reason of the payment of the rent from year to year, and an estate in equity under the agreement. There is only one Court, and the equity rules prevail in it. The tenant holds under an agreement for a lease. He holds, therefore, under the same terms in equity as if a lease had been granted, it being a case in which both parties admit that relief is capable of being given by specific performance.[13]

These remarks were made in an appeal from an order granting interlocutory relief to a landlord who had been sued by a tenant after purporting to levy a distress for unpaid rent under an agreement to grant a lease for a term of seven years, the right to specific performance of that agreement being conceded. Jessel MR appears to have regarded the agreement as amounting to an equitable lease which was the equivalent of a lease at law so as to give rise to a liability for rent for which the common law remedy of distress could be levied ...

[251] The weight of English authority is against Sir George Jessel ...

---

13. *Walsh v Lonsdale* (1882) 21 Ch D 9 at 14–15.

[252] For present purposes [the] authorities establish two propositions. First, the court's willingness to treat the agreement as a lease in equity, on the footing that equity regards as done what ought to be done and equity looks to the intent rather than the form, rests upon the specific enforceability of the agreement. Secondly, an agreement for a lease will be treated by a court administering equity as an equitable lease for the term agreed upon and, as between the parties, as the equivalent of a lease at law, though the lessee does not have a lease at law in the sense of having a legal interest in the term.

The first proposition requires some elaboration or qualification in order to accommodate what has been said in later cases. Although it has been stated sometimes that the equitable interest is commensurate with what a court of equity would decree to enforce the contract, whether by way of specific performance,[14] [253] injunction or otherwise,[15] the references in the earlier cases to specific performance should be understood in the sense of Sir Frederick Jordan's explanation adopted by Deane and Dawson JJ in *Stern v McArthur*:[16]

> Specific performance in this sense means not merely specific performance in the primary sense of the enforcing of an executory contract by compelling the execution of an assurance to complete it, but also the protection by injunction or otherwise of rights acquired under a contract which defines the rights of the parties.[17]

In relation to the second proposition stated above Maitland ... commented:

> An equitable right is not equivalent to a legal right; between the contracting parties an agreement for a lease may be as good as a lease ... But introduce the third party and then you will see the difference.[18]

So, in *Lowther v Heaver*[19] Cotton LJ said that the rights of a tenant holding under an agreement for lease of which specific performance would be decreed ought to be dealt with in the same way as if a lease had been granted to him. Subsequently, in *Foster v Reeves*,[20] where the landlord brought an action for rent in the County Court on an agreement for lease for a term of three years, relying on the doctrine of *Walsh v Lonsdale*, he failed but only on the ground that the County Court lacked a concurrent jurisdiction in equity as well as law. In conformity with this approach, in *Manchester Brewery Co v Coombs*, Farwell J observed that the application of the doctrine in *Walsh v Lonsdale*:

> involves two questions: (1) Is there a contract of which specific performance can be obtained? (2) If Yes, will the title acquired by such specific performance justify at law the act complained of, or support at law the action in question? It is to [254] be treated

---

14. *Connolly v Ryan* (1922) 30 CLR 498 at 506–7; *Brown v Heffer* (1967) 116 CLR 344 at 349; *Chang v Registrar of Titles* (1976) 137 CLR 177 at 184–5, 189–90.
15. *Tailby v Official Receiver* (1888) 13 App Cas 523 at 546–9; *Redman v Permanent Trustee Co* (1916) 22 CLR 84 at 96; *Legione v Hateley* (1983) 152 CLR 406 at 446, 456.
16. (1988) 165 CLR 489 at 522.
17. Sir Frederick Jordan, 'Chapters in Equity in New South Wales', *Select Legal Papers*, 6th ed, 1947, p 52.
18. F W Maitland, *Lectures on Equity*, 2nd ed, 1936, p 158.
19. (1889) 41 Ch D 248 at 264.
20. [1892] 2 QB 255.

as though before the Judicature Acts there had been, first, a suit in equity for specific performance, and then an action at law between the same parties; and the doctrine is applicable only in those cases where specific performance can be obtained between the same parties in the same court, and at the same time as the subsequent legal question falls to be determined.[21]

His Lordship plainly considered that, if specific performance could be so obtained, then the agreement for lease was enforceable between the parties as a lease at law, as though the lease had been granted pursuant to the agreement before the decree for specific performance.[22]

The operation thus attributed to the Judicature Acts had the effect of enabling a party to an agreement to enforce, against another party to the agreement, legal remedies in respect of equitable rights and interests. In this respect the English cases referred to in the preceding paragraph proceed on the footing that the Judicature Acts have a procedural operation. This can be demonstrated by reference to the fact that, although there is no recorded instance of a court of equity exercising a jurisdiction to make an order for the payment of rent under an equitable lease, there was a jurisdiction to backdate specific performance to enable an action to be brought at law on the covenants in the lease. As Mr Sparkes observes, '… before the Judicature Acts, equity did not recognise rent due under an agreement for a lease. Rent was recoverable by action only in the common law courts.'[23] In *Cox v Bishop* Turner LJ observed:

> Courts of equity do not, as I think, in ordinary cases, decree the payment of rent or the performance of covenants upon a mere agreement for a lease. In such cases the Court does not treat the relation of landlord and tenant as completed by the agreement, and decree the rent to be paid and the covenants to be performed accordingly, but it decrees the execution of the lease, and leaves the parties to their remedies at law consequent upon the relation created by the execution of it.[24]

Again, in *Vincent v Godson*,[25] Stuart V-C held that an actual demise was required in order to provide priority in the form of a distress for unpaid rent as a specialty debt. He said:

> The contract itself is a mere agreement for a lease, on which if [255] the land were in England there could be no right of distress, or equivalent right, this being a matter remaining entirely in contract.[26]

Precisely the same approach was taken by Lord Cranworth LC in *Walters v Northern Coal Mining Co* where the question of awarding specific performance retrospectively, after the expiration of the term, arose. His Lordship said:

---

21. *Manchester Brewery Company v Coombs* [1901] 2 Ch 608 at 617.
22. *Manchester Brewery Company v Coombs* [1901] 2 Ch 608 at 618.
23. Peter Sparkes, 'Walsh v Lonsdale: The Non-Fusion Fallacy' (1988) 8 *Oxford Journal of Legal Studies* 350 at 356.
24. *Cox v Bishop* (1857) 44 ER 604 at 608.
25. (1853) 65 ER 168; affd (1854) 43 ER 620.
26. *Vincent v Godson* (1853) 65 ER 168 at 173.

Perhaps Sir Thomas Plumer was right in declining to say that there might not be a case in which it might be fitting for the Court to decree the specific performance of a contract for a lease after the term had expired. But certainly the circumstances of the case must be very special indeed to warrant such an interposition of this Court. What the Court really would be decreeing in such case would not be the specific performance of an agreement for a lease, but merely that the lessee should make himself a specialty debtor in respect of past benefits received. No lease properly so called could be made after the expiration of the time.

The demise, which was the very object of the contract, could not be made, or if made in words would in substance be a mere fiction.[27]

Before the Judicature Acts, the jurisdiction to backdate specific performance of an agreement for a lease in order to enable an action at law to be brought on covenants in the lease seems to have been exercised in one case only, *Mundy v Joliffe*,[28] and then only as between the lessor and the lessee.[29]

The pre-Judicature Acts cases have a dual importance. They indicate that there was a jurisdiction to backdate specific performance and that it was a jurisdiction to be exercised sparingly. The existence of that jurisdiction supports the view that, notwithstanding the broad language of Jessel MR, the decision in *Walsh v Lonsdale* involved no more than giving the Judicature Acts a procedural operation. But the fact that the jurisdiction was exercised so sparingly demonstrates that in the present case it would be imprudent to assume that specific performance would be awarded as a matter of course. As Evatt J observed in *Dimond v Moore*, with reference to suits for specific performance:

[256] Many circumstances may prevent a plaintiff from succeeding in such a suit, although there was originally a binding agreement for a lease and the plaintiff entered into possession under such agreement. Great difficulties will arise if, in Courts where the judicature system is adopted, a person in possession of land under an agreement is to be treated for all purposes as though specific performance has been decreed from the moment of entry, and the agreement has already been converted into an actual lease on the terms of the agreement.[30]

The [landlord's] failure to register, or procure registration, of the lease, which may have been due to the [landlord] granting a mortgage to Citibank Ltd which was registered in 1987, was a factor which would require to be taken into consideration in deciding whether to award or refuse specific performance. So would the question whether the lease came to an end before the expiration of the term by reason of [the tenant's] default.

But even if it be assumed that specific performance would be awarded in favour of the [landlord], that is not enough, in our opinion, to establish liability on the part of [the Chans] as guarantors. What they guaranteed was the 'obligations [of the tenant] under this lease', that is, the instrument of lease in its character as a lease. In our view, only

27. *Walters v Northern Coal Mining Co* (1855) 43 ER 1015 at 1019.
28. (1839) 9 LJ Ch 95 at 97–8.
29. See Peter Sparkes, 'Back-Dating Specific Performance' (1989) 10 *Journal of Legal History* 29 at 33.
30. *Dimond v Moore* (1931) 45 CLR 159 at 186.

a lease at law would meet this description for the purposes of the guarantee. In *Ankar Pty Ltd v National Westminster Finance (Australia) Ltd*, Mason ACJ, Wilson, Brennan and Dawson JJ observed:

> At law, as in equity, the traditional view is that the liability of the surety is strictissimi juris and that ambiguous contractual provisions should be construed in favour of the surety.[31]

In the light of this settled principle governing the interpretation of contracts of guarantee, there is no justification for reading cl 23.01 as extending to obligations which, at best, as between the landlord and the lessee, arise, not under the lease at law but under an equitable lease which is the equivalent of the lease at law.

In any event, s 43 of the [*Property Law*] Act [1974 (Qld)] presents an insuperable obstacle to the [landlord's] success. The section provides, in relation to land under the Act, that, until registration, no instrument of transfer shall be effectual to pass an estate or interest in the land. Notwithstanding this provision, it has been said from time to time that unregistered instruments may confer equitable estates and interests.[32] These statements need to be read in conjunction with **[257]** the remarks of Isaacs J in *Barry v Heider*. His Honour, in the context of s 41 of the *Real Property Act* 1900 (NSW), the counterpart of s 43 of the Act, said:

> [S]ec 41, in denying effect to an instrument until registration, does not touch whatever rights are behind it. Parties may have a right to have such an instrument executed and registered; and that right, according to accepted rules of equity, is an estate or interest in the land. Until that instrument is executed, sec 41 cannot affect the matter, and if the instrument is executed it is plain its inefficacy until registered — that is, until statutory completion as an instrument of title — cannot cut down or merge the pre-existing right which led to its execution.[33]

The point made in this passage is that, though the unregistered instrument is itself ineffective to create a legal or equitable estate or interest in the land, before registration, the section does not avoid contracts or render them inoperative. So an antecedent agreement will be effective, in accordance with the principles of equity, to bring into existence an equitable estate or interest in the land. But it is that antecedent agreement, evidenced by the unregistered instrument, not the instrument itself, which creates the equitable estate or interest. In this way no violence is done to the statutory command in s 43.

In *Brunker v Perpetual Trustee Co (Ltd)*, Latham CJ, in dissent, though not on this point, speaking with reference to s 41 of the *Real Property Act* (NSW), said:

> Thus the instrument of transfer in itself cannot be effectual to vest in the defendant either a legal or an equitable interest in the land. But where there is a transaction for value which is recorded in a contract followed by an instrument of transfer, or where

---

31. *Ankar Pty Ltd v National Westminster Finance (Australia) Ltd* (1987) 162 CLR 549 at 561.
32. See *National Trustees, Executors and Agency Co of Australasia Ltd v Boyd* (1926) 39 CLR 72 at 81–2; *York House Pty Ltd v Federal Commissioner of Taxation* (1930) 43 CLR 427 at 435–6; *Progressive Mailing House Pty Ltd v Tabali Pty Ltd* (1985) 157 CLR 17 at 26–7.
33. *Barry v Heider* (1914) 19 CLR 197 at 216.

there is a transaction for value which itself is recorded in a transfer, then 'the transaction behind the instrument' and upon which it rests may create an equitable interest in the land which will be recognised in the courts.[34] ...

If we assume that the agreement for lease would have been specifically enforced in equity and that, as a result, an equitable lease for a term of five years came into existence between the [258] [parties as landlord and tenant], that equitable lease is a thing different from the unregistered form of lease executed by the parties. Although such an equitable lease would incorporate the terms of the unregistered lease, by virtue of s 43 it necessarily arises not from the instrument but from the agreement which lies behind it. On this score alone, it would be impossible to conclude that a liability to pay rent under the equitable lease was an obligation 'under this lease' within the meaning of cl 23.01.

Comments

1. See Radan & Stewart at **3.34** and **3.37–3.38**.
2. In B Fitzgerald, 'Walsh v Lonsdale: Eighties Style?' (1990) 6 *Queensland University of Technology Law Journal* 119 at 124, the author makes the following comment on the High Court's reasoning:

   Their Honours explain that Jessel MR [in *Walsh v Lonsdale*] merely used the jurisdiction of Chancery to back-date specific performance and thereupon facilitated recovery of rent (due under the agreement) pursuant to a remedy at law. With respect, this writer fails to see the magical powers of retrospective specific performance, because even with this new found device an interim fiction is still required. On the court's current explanation there is a period of time wherein between lessor and lessee a relationship is defined in terms of remedies at law but no interest at law exists ... [The High Court's] judgment [at 256] does intimate that an interim fiction regarding the legal interest exists by saying: 'obligations which, at best, as between the landlord and the lessee, arise, not under the lease at law but under an equitable lease which is the equivalent of the lease at law' ... [T]he coherence of this ... approach to *Walsh v Lonsdale* is reduced if one accepts ... that retrospective specific performance when it was invoked created an anomalous occurrence ... *Chan v Cresdon Pty Ltd* offers an interesting interpretation but one that is premised on a fiction, ie that the lessor and lessee hold legal interests. Without that fiction *Walsh v Lonsdale* cannot be labelled a 'procedural fusion' case. But the fiction is too fatal a one to accept, as to do so would give an equitable right a legal remedy ... To let *Walsh v Lonsdale* stand perpetuates fusion fallacy and denies the correct view of the unison of law and equity.

---

34. *Brunker v Perpetual Trustee Co (Ltd)* (1937) 57 CLR 555 at 581.

4

NATURE OF EQUITABLE ESTATES AND INTERESTS

Introduction

4.1 This chapter deals with the recognition and nature of equitable proprietary interests and highlights the fact that such interests are varied in terms of the characteristics they possess and that an equitable right may be classified as proprietary in some contexts, but as non-proprietary in other contexts.

The extracts in this chapter discuss the following:

- when equitable proprietary interests arise: *Commissioner of Stamp Duties (Qld) v Livingston* [1965] AC 694; *Horton v Jones* (1935) 53 CLR 475; and
- the multiple classification of equitable interests: *Latec Investments Ltd v Hotel Terrigal Limited* (1965) 113 CLR 265; Samantha Hepburn, 'The Benefits of Equitable Classification'.

The recognition of equitable interests

4.2   Commissioner of Stamp Duties (Qld) v Livingston [1965] AC 694

Court: Judicial Committee of the Privy Council

Facts: In July 1950 Mrs Coulson died intestate. At the time of her death she was entitled to a one-third share in the residue of the deceased estate of Livingston, her first husband. However, at this time Livingston's estate had not been administered and her share had not been exactly ascertained. The executors of Livingston's estate were domiciled in New South Wales. Livingston's estate included personal and real property in both Queensland and New South Wales. The Stamp Duties Commissioner in Queensland claimed that, at her death, Mrs Coulson owned an equitable interest in real and personal property in Queensland in relation to the share of Livingston's deceased estate that she was to have inherited, and, in applying that state's succession legislation, levied succession duty.

Issue: The issue before the Privy Council was whether Mrs Coulson, at the date of her death, had an equitable interest in relation to her share of Livingston's unadministered estate. If she did, the Stamp Duties Commissioner was entitled to levy succession duty.

Decision: The Privy Council (Viscount Radcliffe, Lords Reid, Evershed, Pearce and Upjohn) held that, at the date of her death, Mrs Coulson did not have any proprietary interest in Livingston's unadministered estate. Accordingly, no succession duty was payable.

Extracts: The extracts from the speech of Viscount Radcliffe, who delivered the judgment of the Privy Council, discuss the nature of Mrs Coulson's interest in Livingston's unadministered estate and explain why it was not an equitable proprietary interest.

Viscount Radcliffe

[704] It is essential to the decision of this case that Mrs Coulson's rights at her death were the rights of a person interested in a dead man's unadministered estate ... [706] [I]f there is to be a taxable succession, it must be because she died owning a beneficial interest in real property in Queensland or had beneficial personal property interests locally situate in Queensland ...

[707] When Mrs Coulson died she had the interest of a residuary legatee in the testator's unadministered estate. The nature of that interest has been conclusively defined by decisions of long established authority, and its definition no doubt depends upon the peculiar status which the law accorded to an executor for the purposes of carrying out his duties of administration. There were special rules which long prevailed about the devolution of freehold land and its liability for the debts of a deceased, but subject to the working of these rules whatever property came to the executor virtute officii came to him in full ownership, without distinction between legal and equitable interests. The whole property was his. He held it for the purpose of carrying out the functions and duties of administration, not for his own benefit; and these duties would be enforced upon him by the Court of Chancery, if application had to be made for that purpose by a creditor or beneficiary interested in the estate. Certainly, therefore, he was in a fiduciary position with regard to the assets that came to him in the right of his office, and for certain purposes and in some aspects he was treated by the Court as a trustee. 'An executor', said Kay J *In Re Marsden*, 'is personally liable in equity for all breaches of the ordinary trusts which in Courts of Equity are considered to arise from his office'.[1] He is a trustee 'in this sense'.

It may not be possible to state exhaustively what those trusts are at any one moment. Essentially, they are trusts to preserve the assets, to deal properly with them, and to apply them in a due course of administration for the benefit of those interested according to that course, creditors, the death duty authorities, legatees of various sorts, and the residuary beneficiaries. They might just as well have been termed 'duties in respect of the assets' as trusts. What equity did not do was to recognise or create for residuary legatees a beneficial interest in the assets in the executor's hands during the course of administration. Conceivably, this could have been done, in the sense that the assets, whatever they might be from time to time, could have been treated as a present, though fluctuating, trust fund held for the benefit of all those interested in the estate according to the measure of their respective interests. But it never was done. It would have been

---

1. *In Re Marsden* (1884) 26 Ch D 783 at 789.

a clumsy and unsatisfactory device from a [708] practical point of view; and, indeed, it would have been in plain conflict with the basic conception of equity that to impose the fetters of a trust upon property, with the resulting creation of equitable interests in that property, there had to be specific subjects identifiable as the trust fund. An unadministered estate was incapable of satisfying this requirement. The assets as a whole were in the hands of the executor, his property; and until administration was complete no one was in a position to say what items of property would need to be realised for the purposes of that administration or of what the residue, when ascertained, would consist or what its value would be. Even in modern economies, when the ready marketability of many forms of property can almost be assumed, valuation and realisation are very far from being interchangeable terms.

At the date of Mrs Coulson's death, therefore, there was no trust fund consisting of Mr Livingston's residuary estate in which she could be said to have any beneficial interest, because no trust had as yet come into existence to affect the assets of his estate ... Mr Livingston's property in Queensland, real or personal, was vested in his executors in full right, and no beneficial property interest in any item of it belonged to Mrs Coulson at the date of her death ...

[712] A ... criticism has occasionally been expressed to the effect that it is incredible ... to deny to a residuary legatee all beneficial interest in the assets of an unadministered estate. Where, it is asked, is the beneficial interest in those assets during the period of administration? It is not, ex hypothesi, in the executor: where else can it be but in the residuary legatee? This dilemma is founded on a fallacy, for it assumes mistakenly that for all purposes and at every moment of time the law requires the separate existence of two different kinds of estate or interest in property, the legal and the equitable. There is no need to make this assumption. When the whole right of property is in a person, as it is in an executor, there is no need to distinguish between the legal and equitable interest in that property, any more than there is for the property of a full beneficial owner. What matters is that the court will control the executor in the use of his rights over assets that come to him in that capacity; but it will do it by the enforcement of remedies which do not involve the admission or recognition of equitable rights of property in those assets. Equity in fact calls into existence and protects equitable rights and interests in property only where their recognition has been found to be required in order to give effect to its doctrines ...

[T]he terminology of our legal system has not produced a sufficient variety of words to represent the various meanings which can be conveyed by the words 'interest' and 'property'. Thus propositions are advanced or rebutted by the employment of terms that have not in themselves a common basis of definition. For instance, there ... is the remark of Jordan CJ in *McCaughey's* case, 'The idea that beneficiaries in an unadministered or partially administered estate have no beneficial interest in the items which go to make up the estate is repugnant to elementary and fundamental [713] principles of equity.'[2] If 'by beneficial interest in the items' it is intended to suggest that such beneficiaries have any property right at all in any of those items, the proposition cannot be accepted as either elementary or fundamental. It is, as has been shown, contrary to the principles of equity. But, on the other hand, if the meaning is only that such beneficiaries are not without

---

2. *McCaughey v Commissioner of Stamp Duties* (1945) 46 SR (NSW) 192 at 204.

legal remedy during the course of administration to secure that the assets are properly dealt with and the rights that they hope will accrue to them in the future are safeguarded, the proposition is no doubt correct. They can be said, therefore, to have an interest in respect of the assets, or even a beneficial interest in the assets, so long as it is understood in what sense the word 'interest' is used in such a context.

Similarly with the passage from the High Court's judgment in *Smith v Layh*:

> ... it is not the consequence that the residuary legatee or next-of-kin has no right of property in the totality of assets forming the residue of the intestate estate. The beneficial interest is not vested in the legal personal representative, subject to the rights of creditors. The right of the next-of-kin or residuary legatee to have the estate properly administered and to receive payment of the net balance gives them an equitable interest in the totality and therefore in the assets of which it is composed.[3]

With all respect, that cannot be taken as an exact statement of the law without some further definition of terms. For its expressions would have to be reconciled with the authorities that deny to the residuary legatee any property at all in any specific asset while administration proceeds and with the fact that 'residue' cannot come into existence in the eyes of the law until administration is completed. Therefore, while it may well be said in a general way that a residuary legatee has an interest in the totality of the assets, (though that proposition in itself raises the question what is the local situation of the 'totality'), it is in their Lordships' opinion inadmissible to proceed from that to the statement that such a person has an equitable interest in any particular one of those assets ...

[717] [T]heir Lordships regard it as clearly established that Mrs Coulson was not entitled to any beneficial interest in any property in Queensland at the date of her death. What she was entitled to in respect of her rights under her deceased husband's will was a chose in action, capable of being invoked for any purpose connected with the proper administration of his estate; and the local situation of this asset, as much under Queensland law as any other law, was in New South Wales, where the testator had been domiciled and his executors resided and which constituted the proper forum of administration of his estate.

Comments

1. See Radan & Stewart at **4.24–4.28**.

2. In *Raymond Saul & Co v Holden* [2008] EWHC 2731 (Ch), at [49]–[52] and [61], in a case concerning the right of a residuary beneficiary in an unadministered estate, Richard Snowden QC, after a thorough review of relevant authorities, including *Livingston*, said:

   > The authorities to which I have referred establish that upon death of a testator, a residuary legatee has an immediate entitlement, arising from the terms of the will, to have transferred to him, at the completion of the administration of the estate, such assets (if any) as then form the residue of the estate. This entitlement does not give the residuary legatee any present property interest in any of the individual assets forming the estate whilst it is being administered. Nor can it give the legatee any immediate

---

3. *Smith v Layh* (1953) 90 CLR 102 at 108–109.

interest of a proprietary nature in what is called 'the residue of the estate', because that is simply a concept which has no existence independent of the assets which are eventually found to comprise it, as and when the estate has been fully administered.

The residuary legatee's immediate entitlement to future payment (if there are any assets left to form the residue) is, however, recognised and protected whilst the estate is in the course of administration by a right of action to compel the due administration of the estate. As Viscount Radcliffe explained in *Livingston*, the due administration of the estate, by its very nature, involves the application of the assets for the benefit of the creditors, the taxation authorities, legatees of various sorts, and (finally) the residuary beneficiaries. Because the entitlement to receive such assets as may comprise the residue in the future is the very foundation for the legatee's right to compel due administration of the estate, it seems to me that there is no sensible basis upon which the two can be separated. The right of action would not be given to a stranger to the estate who had no possibility of receiving such assets in the future.

It is therefore correct to describe the right of the residuary legatee as a composite right to have the estate properly administered and to have the residue (if any) paid to him as and when the administration is complete. That composite right is a chose in action, which is transmissible, and accordingly falls within the first limb of the definition of 'property' in section 436 [of the relevant bankruptcy legislation].

On that basis, it must follow that when a residuary legatee becomes bankrupt, the chose in action which vests in his trustee in bankruptcy is the composite right that includes the right to have the assets comprised in the residuary estate paid over to him at the end of the administration of the estate. Once that right vests in the trustee, the right will not revest in the bankrupt unless and until his bankruptcy debts and costs have been paid; and the right will be capable of being asserted by the trustee in bankruptcy against the executors, so as to preclude them from giving priority to any rival claims to the assets comprising the residue at the end of the administration ...

In summary, ... the law has long recognised that a residuary legatee has an immediate 'interest' of some kind in the assets that will in the future form the residuary estate of a testator. The precise nature of the interest is unclear, but at [the] very least it must give the holder of the interest the right to receive the residue (if any) as and when ascertained.

4.3   Horton v Jones (1935) 53 CLR 475

Court: High Court of Australia

Facts: Horton looked after Jones who was old and sick. In return Jones made an oral promise to leave 'his fortune' to Horton. The agreement was never reduced to writing. When Jones died, he had rights as next-of-kin in the unadministered estates of his four children who in turn had interests in the unadministered estate of Jones' father. These unadministered estates included land. After Jones' death Horton sued his estate on the oral contract.

Issue: The issue before the High Court was whether Horton's oral agreement with Jones was enforceable.

Decision: The High Court of Australia (Rich, Starke, Dixon, Evatt and McTiernan JJ) unanimously held that there was no enforceable agreement entered into between Horton and Jones. Evatt and McTiernan JJ dismissed the claim on the ground that the agreement was void for uncertainty. Dixon and Rich JJ ruled that, as the property that Jones stood to inherit from the unadministered estates of his children included land, Horton's oral agreement with Jones was unenforceable because of non-compliance with the statutory requirement of writing in relation to contracts involving land or any interest in land set out in s 54A(1) of the *Conveyancing Act 1919* (NSW).[4] Starke J held that the agreement failed on grounds of uncertainty as well as for non-compliance with s 54A(1).

Extracts: The extracts from the joint judgment of Rich and Dixon JJ explain what is meant by an interest in land for the purposes of s 54A and why Jones had such an interest in relation to the unadministered estates of his children.

Rich and Dixon JJ

[484] We are prepared to assume that ... it was open to a jury to find that [Horton's] promise was to act as [Jones'] housekeeper and attendant under his reasonable and lawful directions. If this was its meaning, it was not too vague or uncertain to afford a consideration for his promise to leave what he called his 'fortune' to her. Even so, we think his promise would not be actionable without a writing ...

[485] The question whether the alleged contract, so far as it related to the deceased's interest in his father's estate, fell within s 54A of the *Conveyancing Act* 1919–1930, depends upon an ascertainment of the nature of his rights in that estate and upon its condition or possible condition of investment ...

[486] Upon [the] facts [of this case] the first question is whether, although the estate of [Jones'] father be regarded as including interests in land, the interest in that estate taken by [Jones] himself as sole next-of-kin of his sons can be so regarded. It was suggested that, because [Jones] had no more than a right to have the estates of his deceased children administered in due course and to receive the net surplus, and that these estates in turn comprised no more than an analogous right in the residue of [Jones'] father's estate, no right in any specific asset in the estate of the [Jones'] father subsisted in [Jones]. This may at once be conceded.[5] But it is not the consequence that no right of property subsisted in [Jones], nor that no right of property subsisted involving an interest in land. [Jones] possessed equitable rights enforceable in respect of the assets considered as a whole. It is

---

4. The equivalent provisons to s 54A(1) in other Australian jurisidictions are: *Civil Law (Property) Act 2006* (ACT) s 204(1); *Law of Property Act 2000* (NT) s 62; *Property Law Act 1974* (Qld) s 59; *Law of Property Act 1936* (SA) s 26; *Conveyancing and Law of Property Act 1884* (Tas) s 36(1); *Instruments Act 1958* (Vic) s 126; *Property Law Act 1969* (WA) s 34(1).

5. See *Sudeley v Attorney-General* [1897] AC 11; *Vanneck v Benham* [1917] 1 Ch 60; *Barnardo's Homes v Special Income Tax Commissioner* [1921] 2 AC 1; *Baker v Archer-Shee* [1927] AC 844; *In re Rowe* [1926] VLR 452.

true that he had no immediate right to possession or enjoyment, and that his precise rights involved, at any rate prima facie, administration, and possibly necessitated conversion and calling in of investments. But, none the less, he had more than a mere equity. He had an equitable interest, and it related to assets which included interests in lands.[6] **[487]** But this does not completely dispose of the question whether the alleged contract falls within s 54A and amounts to a contract for the sale or other disposition of land. For, although [Jones'] interest in his father's estate might or did at the time of the making of the alleged agreement amount to or include an interest in land, this arose only from its state of investment, which, from the point of view of the contracting parties was a mere accident. When [Jones] came to fulfil his promise it might no longer be so invested. The contract was to leave that interest whatever form it might take or happen to be in. Indeed, it may be said that the substance of the contract was to leave to [Horton] whatever [Jones] might have at his death, representing that interest, and his life insurance policies. We think that these considerations do not take the contract set up out of the *Statute of Frauds*. The contract is to leave property by will whatever form it may be in. At the time of contracting, it involved an interest in land. It is therefore a contract to leave that interest or the proceeds thereof if thereafter called in and invested in some other form of security or distributed. It appears to us that this is a contract which relates to an identifiable asset or assets which have the character of an interest in land, although consistently with the contract and before its performance is complete, they may have lost that character. Such a contract at its inception relates to an interest in land and promises a disposition of that interest or its proceeds. The alternative expressed in the words 'or its proceeds' does not make the contract fail to answer the description of s 54A. That provision has, we think, substantially the same effect as the *Statute of Frauds* so far as it related to interests in land. We cannot agree in the construction of the curiously drawn definition of 'disposition' in s 7 of the *Conveyancing Act* 1919–1930 which excludes disposition by will.

Starke J

[489] [T]he contract alleged is, in my opinion, a contract within the provisions of the … *Conveyancing Act* 1919–30 of New South Wales, s 54A. A contract to leave by will 'all my real and personal property' would, I think, be clearly within the statute, for it expressly stipulates for the disposition of any land belonging to or coming to the contracting party, or an interest therein. And the cases are not distinguishable, to my mind, where the contract is for 'all my property' or for 'all my fortune,' for they too extend to and cover the disposition of any land belonging or coming to the contracting party, or any interest therein. The *Statute of Frauds* is directed to agreements concerning, covering, or extending to lands or interests therein, whether the contracting party has title to them or not. The present case is even stronger. The agreement of the parties stipulated … for so much of the estate of Jones' father, namely, four-sevenths thereof, as was within Jones' power of disposition, and it was proved that part of the father's **[490]** estate was at the time of the agreement invested upon mortgages of land … [A] mortgage of land constitutes an interest in land. It was contended, however, that Jones had no interest in

---

6. See *Cooper v Cooper* (1874) LR 7 HL 53; *Blake v Bayne* [1908] AC 371 at 383–4; *Brook v Badley* (1868) LR 3 Ch 672 at 674–5; *Ashworth v Munn* (1878) 15 Ch D 363 at 368, 370; *Re Dawson; Pattisson v Bathurst* [1915] 1 Ch 626 at 639.

these mortgages, but only a right to the administration of his father's estate. The learned Chief Justice [of the Supreme Court of New South Wales] satisfactorily disposed of the argument in the following passage of his judgment:

> But the fact that the interest is not identifiably attached to any specific asset does not ... prevent it from being in fact and in law a beneficial interest in all the assets for the time being existing in their actual condition, for the purposes of the *Statute of Frauds*.[7]

The form in which these assets were invested might, indeed, as was contended, change from time to time, but nevertheless the assets about which the parties stipulated, and to which they attached their agreement, was the interest as it then existed, and was an interest in land, whatever form it afterwards assumed, or was converted into.

Comment
1. See Radan & Stewart at **4.29–4.32**.

The multiple classification of equitable interests

4.4   Latec Investments Ltd v Hotel Terrigal Pty Limited (1965) 113 CLR 265

Court: High Court of Australia

Facts: Hotel Terrigal was the owner of a hotel which was mortgaged to Latec Investments. Hotel Terrigal defaulted on its mortgage obligations. Latec Investments exercised its power of sale under the mortgage and sold the property to Southern Hotels, which was a totally owned subsidiary of Latec Investments. The mortgagee sale was thus fraudulent. A year later Southern Hotels gave MLC Nominees, as trustees for debenture holders, a security by way of a floating charge over the hotel property. Following the default of Southern Hotels the floating charge crystallised. Hotel Terrigal subsequently sought to have the fraudulent mortgagee sale to Southern Hotels set aside. In effect Hotel Terrigal was asserting the priority of its right to set aside the fraudulent mortgagee sale of the hotel over MLC Nominee's equitable proprietary interest in the hotel pursuant to the floating charge.

Issue: The issue before the High Court was a priority dispute over which of Hotel Terrigal and MLC Nominees had the better claim to first exercise their rights over the hotel.

Decision: The High Court (Kitto, Taylor and Menzies JJ) unanimously ruled in favour of MLC. Kitto and Menzies JJ ruled that Hotel Terrigal's right was a mere equity only and as such gave way to MLC Nominee's equitable proprietary interest. Taylor J ruled Hotel Terrigal's right was an equitable interest, although one with an impediment that meant it had to give way to Hotel Terrigal's equitable interest. Arguably, his Honour's view is in substance the same as that of Kitto and Menzies JJ.

---

7.   *Horton v Jones* (1934) SR (NSW) 359 at 366.

> **Extracts:** The extracts from the judgment of Kitto J discuss the nature of Hotel Terrigal's right as a mere equity and why the right of MLC Nominees prevailed over it. The extracts from the judgment of Menzies J discuss the point that Hotel Terrigal's right can be differently classified depending upon the context in which the right is asserted.

Kitto J

[274] If [Hotel Terrigal] had sought the intervention of the court without delay, the findings of fact ... [in this case] would necessarily have led to a decree setting aside the sale as against [Latec Investments] and [Southern Hotels] and granting consequential relief. But nearly five years went by before proceedings were commenced, and it is necessary to consider whether [Hotel Terrigal's] right to relief is affected by what occurred in that time. First let me be clear about the nature of the right which [Hotel Terrigal] might have asserted ... [275] The right which [Hotel Terrigal] had immediately before the sale was a right to have [Latec Investments] ordered (notwithstanding that the contractual date for payment had passed) to receive what should be found on a taking of accounts to be owing under the mortgage and thereupon to execute a discharge of the mortgage ...

But ... [Hotel Terrigal] took no step to establish its equity of redemption for nearly five years ... [I]f there were nothing more to consider than the bare fact of the delay it may be that [Hotel Terrigal] would not be precluded from asserting its rights even after so long a time. But an important change in the situation occurred a little more than a year after the sale. On 18th March 1960, [there was] executed a trust deed in respect of debentures to be issued, and it put out to the public a series of prospectuses which led many [276] persons to take up debentures. The prospectuses showed, as the fact was, that ... [Southern Hotels], had joined in the trust deed as a guarantor and had given [MLC Nominees] ... a floating charge over all its assets as security for the debentures. Each prospectus, moreover, contained an explicit statement that the Hotel Terrigal was owned by [Southern Hotels]. The statement, of course, would have been true if [Southern Hotel's] title had been unimpeachable by [Hotel Terrigal], and neither [MLC Nominees] nor the persons who took up debentures were given any cause to doubt it ... After another two and a half years the floating charge crystallized.

In these circumstances [MLC Nominees] ... contends that [Hotel Terrigal] ought not to be given the relief to which, according to the views I have expressed, it would otherwise be entitled. As between [MLC Nominees] and [Hotel Terrigal] I am of opinion the contention should succeed. In all cases where a claim to enforce an equitable interest in property is opposed on the ground that after the interest is said to have arisen a third party innocently acquired an equitable interest in the same property, the problem, if the facts relied upon as having given rise to the interests be established, is to determine where the better equity lies. If the merits are equal, priority in time of creation is considered to give the better equity. This is the true meaning of the maxim *qui prior est tempore potior est jure*.[8] But where the merits are unequal, as for instance where conduct on the part of the owner of the earlier interest has led the other to acquire his interest on the supposition that the earlier did not exist, the maxim may be displaced and priority accorded to the

---

8. *Rice v Rice* (1853) 61 ER 646 at 648.

later interest. In the present case it seems to me that there is much to be said for holding that, since during the long period of [Hotel Terrigal's] delay in setting up the invalidity of [Southern Hotel's] title persons were induced to lend money on debentures in the belief that an unencumbered fee simple in the subject property formed part of the security under [MLC Nominee's] floating charge, [Hotel Terrigal] ought not to be allowed to insist upon its equity of redemption as against the equitable interest of [MLC Nominees] ...

[277] [I]n my opinion the equitable charge of [MLC Nominees] for the debenture holders stands in the way of [Hotel Terrigal's] success because it was acquired for value and without any notice either of the existence of [Hotel Terrigal's] right to set aside the sale or of any facts from which such a right might be inferred. [MLC Nominees], of course, has not the legal estate; its rights are purely equitable; but the case falls within one of the categories described in the judgment of Lord *Westbury* in *Phillips v Phillips* in which the legal estate is not required in order that a defence of purchase for value without notice may succeed. It is the case of a suit 'where there are circumstances that give rise to an equity as distinguished from an equitable estate — as, for example, an equity to set aside a deed for fraud, or to correct it for mistake'.[9] In such a case, his Lordship said, if the purchaser under the instrument maintains the plea of purchase for value without notice 'the Court will not interfere'.[10] It is true that if [Hotel Terrigal] ... was entitled to have [Latec Investments'] sale set aside it had more than a mere equity: it had, as I have pointed out, an equity of redemption, and such an interest, being in respect of an estate in fee simple, has been considered an equitable estate ever since Lord *Hardwicke* decided *Casborne v Scarfe*.[11] But each of the illustrations Lord *Westbury* chose was also a case where the equity was accompanied by an equitable interest which might constitute an equitable estate. So much had been shown by decisions of most eminent judges, at least twice in the ten years before his Lordship spoke,[12] and Lord *Westbury's* judgment gives every indication of an intention to state systematically the effect of previous decisions, and not to depart from them in any degree. The illustrations therefore make it clear, it seems to me, that the cases to which his Lordship was referring were not only those in which there is an assertion of an equity unaccompanied by an equitable interest ... — indeed he may not have had them in mind at all — but those in which an equity is asserted which must be made good before an equitable interest can be held to exist. In the latter class of cases the equity is distinct from, because logically antecedent to, the equitable [278] interest, and it is against the equity and not the consequential equitable interest that the defence must be set up. That the defence of purchase for value without notice (in the absence of the legal estate) is a good defence against the assertion of the equity in such a case had been established long before Lord *Westbury's* time. In *Malden v Menill*, for example, Lord Hardwicke had refused rectification of an instrument for mistake, as against a purchaser of an equitable interest without notice, on the ground that the mistake should not 'turn to the prejudice of a fair purchaser'.[13] ... The reason of the matter ... is that the purchaser who has relied upon the instrument as taking effect according to its terms and the party

---

9. *Phillips v Phillips* (1861) 45 ER 1164 at 1167.
10. *Phillips v Phillips* (1861) 45 ER 1164 at 1167.
11. (1737) 26 ER 377. See also (1738) 37 ER 600.
12. See *Stump v Gaby* (1852) 42 ER 1015; *Gresley v Mousley* (1859) 45 ER 31.
13. *Malden v Menill* (1737) 26 ER 402 at 405.

whose rights depend upon the instrument being denied that effect have equal merits, and the court, finding no reason for binding the conscience of either in favour of the other, declines to interfere between them. Consequently the party complaining of the fraud or mistake finds himself unable to set up as against the other the equitable interest he asserts; but the fact remains that it is against the preliminary equity, and not against the equitable interest itself, that the defence of purchase for value without notice has succeeded. The maxim *qui prior est tempore* is not applicable, for it applies only as between equitable interests, the logical basis of it being that in a competition between equitable interests the conveyance in virtue of which the later interest is claimed is considered, as Lord *Westbury* pointed out, to be innocent, in the sense of being intended to pass that which the conveyor is justly entitled to and no more.[14] Where a claim to an earlier equitable interest is dependent for its success upon the setting aside or rectification of an instrument, and the court, notwithstanding that the fraud or mistake (or other cause) is established, leaves the instrument to take effect according to its terms in favour of a third party whose rights have intervened, the alleged earlier equitable interest is unprovable against the third party, and consequently, so far as the case against him discloses, there is no prior equitable interest to which his conveyance can be held to be subject.

On the principle to which Lord *Westbury* referred it seems to me inevitable that [Hotel Terrigal's] claim in the present case to have [Latec Investments'] sale and the transfer to [Southern Hotels] 'set aside,' **[279]** … should fail as against [MLC Nominees as] trustee for the debenture holders, though it should succeed as against [Latec Investments] and [Southern Hotels].

Menzies J

[288] If the maxim *'Qui prior est tempore potior est jure'* applies, [Hotel] Terrigal's right to have the conveyance set aside and to be restored to the register, without regard to MLC Nominees' equitable interest, prevails, but [MLC Nominees'] is that this right is a mere equity and the maxim has no application when the contest is between such an equity and an equitable interest of the character held by MLC Nominees. This contention rests upon the line of authority based upon *Phillips v Phillips*.[15] …

[289] There is, however … another line of cases, [such as *Stump v Gaby*[16]], the authority of which is beyond question, establishing that where there is an equity to have the voidable conveyance of an estate set aside, there remains in the conveyor, notwithstanding the conveyance, an equitable estate which may be devised or transferred …

[290] If there is a difference between the two lines of authority, that difference seems to me to arise from concentration upon different aspects of what follows from a voidable conveyance. Thus, *Phillips v Phillips*, in so far as it says that a person with the right to have a voidable conveyance set aside has but a mere equity, directs attention to the right to have the conveyance set aside as a right to sue which must be successfully exercised as a necessary condition of there being any relation back of the equitable interest established by the suit. *Stump v Gaby* directs attention to the result of **[291]** the eventual avoidance of the conveyance upon the position *ab initio* and throughout of the persons by whom

---

14. *Phillips v Phillips* (1861) 45 ER 1164 at 1166.
15. (1861) 45 ER 1164.
16. (1852) 42 ER 1015.

and to whom the conveyance of property was made and says that, in the event of a successful suit (which may be maintained by a devisee), the conveyor had an equitable estate capable of devise and that the conveyee holds, and has always held, as trustee.

There is no doubt that the two lines of authority are well established. Furthermore, there is room for the application of each in appropriate circumstances. Thus, if [Hotel] Terrigal were a person instead of a company and the question were whether, in the circumstances here, that person had a devisable interest in the hotel property by virtue of his equity to have the conveyance to Southern [Hotels] set aside, *Stump v Gaby* would require an affirmative answer on the footing that, in the circumstances, [Hotel] Terrigal had an equitable interest in the hotel property. Where, however, the question arises in a contest between [Hotel] Terrigal and MLC Nominees, the holders of an equitable interest in the hotel property acquired without notice of [Hotel] Terrigal's rights, the authority of *Phillips v Phillips* is (i) that the contest is between [Hotel] Terrigal's equity to have the conveyance set aside and the equitable interest of MLC Nominees and (ii) that in that contest, [Hotel] Terrigal's equity is not entitled to priority merely because it came into existence at an earlier time than the equitable interest of MLC Nominees. In the circumstances here, therefore, the maxim '*Qui prior est tempore potior est jure*' has no application.

Comments

1. See Radan & Stewart at **4.38–4.42**.
2. For discussions of the mere equities see M Neave & M Weinberg, 'The Nature and Function of Equities' (1979) 6 *University of Tasmania Law Review* 24 (Part I), 115 (Part II) and D Skapinker, 'Equitable Interests, Mere Equities, "Personal" Equities and "Personal Equities" — Distinctions With a Difference' (1994) 68 *Australian Law Journal* 593.

4.5   Hepburn, 'The Benefits of Equitable Classification'

Source: Samantha Hepburn, 'Reconsidering the Benefits of Equitable Classification' (2005) 12 *Australian Property Law Journal* 157.

Extracts: The extracts from Hepburn's article discuss the utility of the hierarchical classification of equitable rights and argue that such a classification provides important structural guidance for assessing unconscionable or unconscientious conduct and the appropriate form of equitable relief to be provided for such conduct.

---

[161] It has been suggested that there is no actual *need* to categorise equitable rights. The division between personal, mere and full equitable interests have resulted in 'different authors stating different conclusions regarding the same equitable interests'.[17] ... There is no doubt that indistinct equitable categories have encouraged a diverse range of

---

17. D Wright, 'The Continued Relevance of Divisions in Equitable Interests in Real Property' (1995) 3 *Australian Property Law Journal* 163 at 177.

judicial and academic opinion. Nevertheless, this fact in itself is one of the reasons why classification has become so important. Classification provides a basic methodology for the independent examination and assessment of rights ...

The clarity that the classification of equitable interests can provide is outlined in this article in three significant ways. First, the division of equitable interests into primary and secondary rights highlights the continuum of equitable relief. The personal right to seek equitable relief against land is a right which crystallises at the point when the unconscionable behaviour occurs even though equitable in rem ownership may be dependent upon judicial discretion. The requirement of court assistance for full equitable ownership should not deny the existence of a lesser right at an earlier stage. The existence of preliminary proprietary and non-proprietary rights is imperative. They illustrate the restorative scope of the equitable jurisdiction. For example, a defrauded mortgagor can seek equitable rescission of a fraudulent mortgagee sale and subsequently demand compliance with the security objectives of the mortgage upon being reinstated as the holder of the equity of redemption. The personal remedy complements the proprietary remedy but the right upon which it is founded is fundamentally different. To ignore the distinction between the right to set an improper mortgagee sale aside and the right [162] acquired when such a mortgage is set aside is to disregard the shifting functions of the equitable jurisdiction.

Secondly, the classification of equitable interests justifies the application of different priority rules to different categories of equitable rights. Full equitable interests are traditionally prioritised in accordance with the rule that the prior equity will defeat the subsequent equity if both are equal in status. By contrast, a mere, preliminary equity will be defeated by a bona fide purchaser of the full equity. The ancillary status of the mere equity as a quasi proprietary interest justifies its defeat at the hands of a bona fide purchaser for value without notice. If the mere equity was not classified in this way, the application of a priority principle so fundamentally different from the merit analysis, may appear unjustified ...

[164] A third and significant benefit flowing from the classification of equitable interests is the structure and scope such a framework provides for the application of equitable principles to the Torrens system. An indefeasible title acquired by a registered proprietor will not be amenable to general law priority rules and will only be regarded as defeasible if established exceptions can be proven. The two exceptions that intersect with the equitable jurisdiction are statutory fraud and the in personam principle. Statutory fraud must be brought home to the registered proprietor or his or her agent and amounts to something more than mere notice. Whilst statutory fraud is not positively defined, the orthodox view is that it requires some active dishonesty, committed by the registered proprietor in the process of seeking registration ... The in personam exception on the other hand upholds the 'right of a plaintiff to bring against a registered proprietor a claim in personam, founded in law or in equity, for such relief as a court acting in personam may grant'.[18]

The scope of these two exceptions is particularly broad. Where a registered proprietor is involved in 'personal dishonesty' or 'moral turpitude' it may amount to statutory fraud and confer equitable rights upon the defrauded party. Statutory fraud

---

18. *Frazer v Walker* [1967] AC 569 at 585.

is merely a qualification to registered title and is not, in itself 'directly generative of legal rights and obligations, its role being to qualify the operation of the doctrine of indefeasibility upon what would have been the rights and remedies of the complainant if the land in question were held under unregistered title'.[19] Dishonest and unconscionable behaviour is a source of equitable relief and registration cannot alter this jurisdictional nucleus. Indeed, the Torrens system of title by registration 'does not interfere with the ordinary operation of contractual or other personal relations, or the effect of instruments at law or in equity'.[20] The registration system [165] never intended to abolish equitable rights and interests ...

It is important to ensure that the application of equitable principles to the Torrens system is properly and effectively structured. Classification of equitable interests will clarify the personal responsibilities of the registered proprietor thereby promoting greater certainty and assurance. This is consistent with the objectives of a system promoting indefeasibility. As noted by Owen J in *Conlan v Registrar of Titles*:

> It is clear from the authorities that the in personam claim must be based on more than an innate sense of fairness. It must be a recognised legal or equitable cause of action. A court needs to proceed with caution. It must not, through sympathy for the plight of unregistered investors, develop a rule of equitable principle that is so broad as to make inroads into the principle of indefeasibility.[21]

Effective classification may also encourage a more structured approach to the enforceability of equitable rights against registered interest holders. Currently, while it is well established under the in personam principle that a full equitable beneficial interest will be enforceable against a trustee/registered proprietor, the enforceability of a mere equitable interest is less clear and has been the subject of some academic debate. Professor Butt has concluded that the personal equities principle should not be used to 'cut back on the benefits of indefeasibility'.[22] However, there is some authority to suggest that it is legitimate to enforce mere equitable interests against registered proprietors ...

[166] Known equitable actions ... should be enforceable against a registered title holder. There is no reason why the in personam defence should be limited to full equitable interests arising under express, constructive or resulting trusts. Nevertheless, Bradbrook et al have stated that the in personam exception:

> ... acknowledges that the concept of indefeasibility of title enshrined in the Torrens legislation does not affect the personal obligations of the registered proprietor. At its [167] simplest level, the exception means that a registered proprietor is subject to contracts he or she has entered into and also to trusts, whether express or implied, over the property.[23]

---

19. *Bank of South Australia Ltd v Ferguson* (1998) 192 CLR 248 at 256.
20. *Groongal Pastoral Co Ltd v Falkiner* (1924) 35 CLR 157 at 163.
21. *Conlan v Registrar of Titles* (2001) 24 WAR 299 at 289.
22. P Butt, 'Indefeasibility and Sleights of Hand' (1992) 66 *Australian Law Journal* 596 at 597.
23. A J Bradbrook, S V McCallum & A P Moore, *Australian Real Property Law*, 3rd ed, Law Book Co, 2002, pp 150–1.

This is a narrow view. It assumes that the equitable responsibilities of registered proprietors do not extend beyond the trust relationship. Such a limitation is difficult to justify within a vigilant and expansive equitable jurisdiction ...

[168] Registration cannot and did not intend to eradicate personal equitable responsibility. As noted by Brennan J in *Bahr v Nicolay*, the enforcement of equitable obligations:

> ... do not infringe the indefeasibility provisions of the Act. Those provisions are designed to protect a transferee from defects in the title of a transferor, not to free him from interests with which he has burdened his own title.[24]

The clear endorsement of a well structured equitable classification may encourage a more logical and consistent relationship between equitable principles and statutory indefeasibility. The tortured limitations and exceptions that have evolved under the guise of reconciling the 'certainty' of indefeasibility with the 'ambiguity' of a jurisdiction directed at individualised justice may be removed, or at least diminished, with the promotion of a distinct classification of equitable rights.

The classification or 'labelling' of different forms of equitable interest is a methodology that judges have never abandoned. It provides structural guidance for the assessment of distinctive forms of unconscionable conduct and the application of appropriate equitable relief. It configures a jurisdiction comprised of established normative principles and evolving ethical potential. There is no danger in dissecting established equitable rights on the basis of their personal and proprietary content. It will not impede or frustrate the future capacity of an evolving equitable jurisdiction because its aims are administrative rather than instructive. The overriding utility of equitable classification is not simply its capacity to rationalise, clarify and explain different perspectives of equitable rights, but its explicit articulation of a diverse equitable landscape. This exposition, in the words of Professor Newman, 'eliminates the no man's land between honesty and dishonesty'.[25]

Comments

1. See Radan & Stewart at **4.38–4.42**.
2. Hepburn's views can be contrasted to those of Wright who has argued against the classification of equitable rights. He suggests, in relation to the categorisation of such rights as equitable interests and mere equities, that '[l]egal history stands against their continuance' and that '[a]uthority exists against their continued use and other means, such as the priorities rule, are available to take into account all the issues which might cause an equitable interest to be considered an equitable estate, a mere equity or a personal equity': D Wright, 'The Continued Relevance of Divisions in Equitable Interests to Real Property' (1995) 3 *Australian Property Law Journal* 163 at 164.

---

24. *Bahr v Nicolay (No 2)* (1988) 164 CLR 604 at 654.
25. R A Newman, 'Equity in the World's Legal Systems' in *An Introduction to Equity in the World's Legal Systems*, 1973, Ch 1, p 25.

5

THE LAW OF ASSIGNMENT

Introduction

5.1 This chapter deals with the assignment or transfer of interests in property. Property can be assigned either at law or in equity. The importance of this topic is illustrated by the example of the creation of a trust. A trust can be created by the transfer of property from one person (the settlor) to another (the trustee) for the trustee to hold on behalf of certain beneficiaries. Such a trust requires the assignment of the property to the trustee before the trust can be constituted. The assignment of the property can be a legal or an equitable assignment.

If property is capable of being assigned, whether it has been effectively assigned depends on a variety of matters such as: any relevant statutory requirements; whether the property is presently existing or future property; whether it is a legal or equitable interest in property; and whether the assignment is for consideration or not.

The extracts in this chapter discuss the following:

- the extent to which the right to litigate is assignable: Andrew Tettenborn, 'Champerty and Assignments'; *Trendtex Trading Corporation v Credit Suisse* [1982] AC 679;
- equitable assignments and the requirement of an intention to assign: *Comptroller of Stamps (Victoria) v Howard-Smith* (1936) 54 CLR 614;
- the assignment of future property: *Norman v Federal Commissioner of Taxation* (1962) 109 CLR 9; *Shepherd v Commissioner of Taxation of the Commonwealth of Australia* (1965) 113 CLR 385;
- the assignment of future property and the nature of the assignee's interest: *In re Lind, Industrials Finance Syndicate Ltd v Lind* [1915] 2 Ch 345; and
- the voluntary assignment of property in equity: *Corin v Patton* (1990) 169 CLR 540.

Champerty and assignments of the right to litigate

5.2   Tettenborn, 'Champerty and Assignments'

Source: Andrew Tettenborn, 'Assignment of rights to compensation' [2007] *Lloyd's Maritime and Commercial Law Quarterly* 392.

Extracts: The extracts from Tettenborn's article reject the view that the restrictions against assignments of the bare right to litigate can be justified on the principle of avoiding champerty. Later in his article he suggests that such rights should be assignable, although he recognises that there are specific situations where substantive or policy-based arguments justify prohibiting or restricting the right to assign.

[401] In particular, it is suggested that, however venerable and however liberally applied, the 'avoidance of champerty' rationale cannot be made to work. This is admittedly a drastic claim, but there are at least three reasons to make it.

To begin with, it is suggested that the tie between assignment and champerty is actually an arbitrary one, due to history and nothing else. It is linked inextricably with the pre-Judicature Act process of equitable assignment. Under this the so-called assignor did not [402] transfer his rights as such, because he could not. Instead the job was done indirectly by subjecting the 'assignor' to an equitable obligation to enforce his right against the debtor in his own name for the benefit of the 'assignee', the latter in turn indemnifying him for costs. Structured thus, the transaction could not but be champertous in principle. The assignee was, after all, agreeing to bankroll the assignor's suit in exchange for a proportion of the spoils (in this case 100%). Conversely, the only way out of this bind (short of the unthinkable one of disallowing all assignments, even in equity) was to limit legal recognition to those transfers that were covered by the existing exceptions to champerty, such as the right of a person to interfere in litigation where he had sufficient interest to justify his doing so. Indeed, the irony goes further. It might have been thought that, after the introduction in 1873 of statutory assignment, under which an assignment did indeed 'pass and transfer the legal right to such debt or thing in action' to the assignee, the champerty problem would go away, since now an assignee enforced his own right directly and not the assignor's indirectly. But it was quickly established — though, if one may say so, without much thought — that matters that would have invalidated an equitable assignment equally nullified a statutory one, and hence this escape route was closed off. In short, it is difficult to avoid the conclusion that, had English common law followed the logical route of Scots law and other civil law systems and developed a theory of assignment as an alienation of an intangible, rather than the ramshackle scheme of A enforcing his rights for the benefit of B, things would have been different. In such a case it is hard to see how anyone could have thought champerty had anything to do with the issue. On the contrary: either the right would have been validly transferred to the 'assignee' so as to allow the latter to enforce it, or it would not, in which case the assignee would have no rights anyway.

Secondly, even if we leave aside history, champerty mismatches assignment because the two concepts deal with different things. The proper limits on assignability are a substantive matter: how far should the policy of the law allow an intangible right originally vested in A to be consensually transferred to, and thereafter enforced by, B? [403] Champerty, by contrast, concerns procedural sin: the law disapproves of it because it thinks it a misuse of the legal process when people muscle in on lawsuits that are none of their business. Of course it is true that there may be some fortuitous connection between the two. If the assignee B cannot get his money without buying A's promise to testify in a particular way in a suit against the defendant, then allowing B to sue at all may indeed put the legal system under some strain; and this in turn might be a reason for invalidating the transfer of rights in the first place. But the difference in subject matter remains: and, apart from special cases like the one just mentioned, it is not apparent why possible abuse of the litigation process should have anything to do with the question of assignability as such.

Thirdly, saying that a purported assignment from A to B is bad if it savours of champerty actually begs the question. Champerty, it is worth remembering, is about interfering without good reason in the enforcement of *other people's* claims. *Ex hypothesi*, it has nothing to say about steps taken to enforce one's own rights. But, once we accept that a claimant's own rights include those rights validly assigned to him, then we reach an impasse. Faced with a purported assignment from A to B, we cannot know whether the rights B is trying to enforce are his own (which is legitimate) or someone else's (potentially champertous) until we know if the assignment from A to him is valid. We thus end up in a circle. When is an assignment ineffective? When the assignee's action savours of champerty. When is this so? When the assignment is bad. And so on.

It is therefore submitted that champerty is an irrelevance that cannot make sense of restrictions on assignability. If this is right, moreover, a further consequence must follow: once abandon the link to champerty, and the *Trendtex* 'legitimate commercial interest' must go with it. If champerty is not a rationally defensible obstacle to assignment, then there is no more reason to think that the lack of it, in the form of the presence of some 'legitimate commercial interest', should be able to validate it. It certainly seems hard to see any independent justification for such a requirement. After all, no such rule applies to tangibles: there, a person either is or is not an owner; and, if he is, the question whether he had any genuine or legitimate interest in acquiring the thing is beside the point.

Comment

1. See Radan & Stewart at **5.9–5.10**.

5.3   Trendtex Trading Corporation v Credit Suisse [1982] AC 679

Court: House of Lords

Facts: Trendtex sued the Central Bank of Nigeria (CBN) in relation to a letter of credit issued by CBN which the bank failed to honour. Trendtex then assigned its cause of action against CBN to Credit Suisse for a price of US$800,000. At that time Trendtex owed Credit Suisse a substantial sum of money which Credit Suisse had no hope of recovering unless Trendtex's claim against CBN succeeded. Five days later Credit Suisse assigned the cause of action to an unidentified third party for a price of US$1.1m. In the following month the case against CBN was settled for US$8m. Trendtex then sued Credit Suisse claiming that the assignment of its contractual claim against CBN was void because it was an assignment of a bare right to litigate. Credit Suisse sought a stay of the proceedings on the ground that the matter was properly one to be heard by the courts of Switzerland because the proper law of the agreement between Trendtex and Credit Suisse was Swiss law.

Issues: The main issue before the House of Lords was whether the proceedings should be heard by the Swiss courts, although the issue of the validity of Trendtex's assignment to Credit Suisse was also raised.

Decision: The House of Lords (Lords Wilberforce, Edmund-Davies, Fraser of Tullybelton, Keith of Kinkel and Roskill) unanimously held that the English proceedings should be stayed because the validity of Trendtex's assignment to Credit Suisse was a matter to be determined by the courts in Switzerland. Nevertheless, their Lordships observed that, had Credit Suisse not assigned Trendtex's claim against CBN to the unidentified third party, the assignment by Trendtex to Credit Suisse would have been valid under English law. However, the further assignment to the third party rendered the earlier assignment invalid.

Extracts: The extracts from the speech of Lord Roskill discuss the law relating to the assignment of the bare right to litigate and explain why, in the circumstances of this case, the assignment by Trendtex to Credit Suisse violated that law.

Lord Roskill

[702] My Lords, it is clear, when one looks at the cases upon maintenance in this century and indeed towards the end of the last, that the courts have adopted an infinitely more liberal attitude towards the supporting of litigation by a third party than had previously been the case …

My Lords, one of the reasons why equity would not permit the assignment of what became known as a bare cause of action, whether legal or equitable, was because it savoured of maintenance. If one reads the well known judgment of Parker J in *Glegg v Bromley*,[1] one can see how the relevant law has developed. Though in general choses in action were assignable, yet causes of action which were essentially personal in their character, such as claims for defamation or personal injury, were incapable of assignment for the reason already given. But even so, no objection was raised to assignments of the proceeds of an action for defamation as in *Glegg v Bromley*, for such an assignment would in no way give the assignee the right to intervene in the action and so be contrary to public policy.[2]

My Lords, just as the law became more liberal in its approach to what was *lawful* maintenance, so it became more liberal in its approach to the [703] circumstances in which it would recognise the validity of an assignment of a cause of action and not strike down such an assignment as one only of a bare cause of action. Where the assignee has by the assignment acquired a property right and the cause of action was incidental to that right, the assignment was held effective. *Ellis v Torrington* is an example of such a case. Scrutton LJ stated that the assignee was not guilty of maintenance or champerty by reason of the assignment he took because he was buying not in order to obtain a cause of action but in order to protect the property which he had bought.[3] But, my Lords, as I read the cases it was not necessary for the assignee always to show a property right to support his assignment. He could take an assignment to support and enlarge that which he had already acquired as, for example, an underwriter by subrogation.[4] My Lords, I am afraid that, with respect, I cannot agree with the learned Master of the Rolls [Lord Denning] when he said in the instant case that 'The old saying that you cannot assign a "bare right to litigate" is gone'.[5] I venture to think that that still remains a fundamental principle

---

1. [1912] 3 KB 474 at 490.
2. See *Glegg v Bromley* [1912] 3 KB 474 at 488–9.
3. *Ellis v Torrington* [1920] 1 KB 399 at 412–3.
4. See *Compania Colombiana de Seguros v Pacific Steam Navigation Co* [1965] 1 QB 101.
5. *Trendtex Trading Corporation v Credit Suisse* [1980] QB 629 at 657.

of our law. But it is today true to say that in English law an assignee who can show that he has a genuine commercial interest in the enforcement of the claim of another and to that extent takes an assignment of that claim to himself is entitled to enforce that assignment unless by the terms of that assignment he falls foul of our law of champerty, which, as has often been said, is a branch of our law of maintenance. For my part I can see no reason in English law why Credit Suisse should not have taken an assignment to themselves of Trendtex's claim against CBN for the purpose of recouping themselves for their own substantial losses arising out of CBN's repudiation of the letter of credit upon which Credit Suisse were relying to refinance their financing of the purchases by Trendtex of this cement from their German suppliers ...

If the assignment is of a property right or interest and the cause of action is ancillary to that right or interest, or if the assignee had a genuine commercial interest in taking the assignment and in enforcing it for his own benefit, I see no reason why the assignment should be struck down as an assignment of a bare cause of action or as savouring of maintenance.

But, my Lords ... [that] does not mean that ... [the assignment by Trendtex to Credit Suisse] is not objectionable as being champertous, for it is not an assignment designed to enable Credit Suisse to recoup their own losses by enforcing Trendtex's claim against CBN to the maximum amount recoverable. Though your Lordships do not have the agreement between Credit Suisse and the anonymous third party, it seems to me obvious, as **[704]** already stated, that the purpose of [the assignment by Trendtex to Credit Suisse] was to enable the claim against CBN to be sold on to the anonymous third party for that anonymous third party to obtain what profit he could from it, apart from paying to Credit Suisse the purchase price of US $1,100,000. In other words, the 'spoils', whatever they might be, to be got from CBN were in effect being divided, the first US $1,100,000 going to Credit Suisse and the balance, whatever it might ultimately prove to be, to the anonymous third party. Such an agreement, in my opinion, offends for it was a step towards the sale of a bare cause of action to a third party who had no genuine commercial interest in the claim in return for a division of the spoils, Credit Suisse taking the fixed amount which I have already mentioned.

Comment

1. See Radan & Stewart at **5.14–5.20**.

The intention to assign in equity

5.4   Comptroller of Stamps (Victoria) v Howard-Smith (1936) 54 CLR 614

Court: High Court of Australia

Facts: Howard-Smith was the residuary beneficiary under his deceased wife's estate. He wrote a letter to the executor and trustee of the will, who held a power of attorney from him, requesting that certain payments be made to named individuals from his interest as residuary beneficiary. These payments were made as requested. The Comptroller of Stamps in Victoria assessed the letter to be dutiable, claiming that stamp duty was payable under the *Stamps Act 1928* (Vic). The Supreme Court of Victoria found the gift was not liable for stamp duty. The Comptroller of Stamps appealed to the High Court.

Issue: The issue before the High Court was whether Howard-Smith's letter was an assignment of property and therefore liable for stamp duty or merely an authorisation having no dispositive effect with no liability for stamp duty.

Decision: The High Court (Starke, Dixon and McTiernan JJ) unanimously dismissed the Comptroller of Stamps' appeal and affirmed the lower court decision that Howard-Smith's letter did not operate as an equitable assignment. It was merely an authorisation with no dispositive effect.

Extracts: The extracts from the judgments of Starke J and Dixon J discuss the relevant principles as to the presence or absence of an intention to assign property.

Starke J

[619] The question is whether the document operates as a gift of any property to the persons and institutions mentioned therein, or declares any trust in their favour. A man may voluntarily dispose of his equitable estates or interests if he choose to do so. No [620] particular form of words is required for the purpose, but he must make clear his intention that he divests himself of the property and gives it over to another, or that he creates a trust in the property in favour of another. A mere mandate from a principal to his agent gives no right or interest in the subject of the mandate. Now, all we have to go on in this case is the letter from H B Howard-Smith to the executor of the will of his wife and his own attorney. It simply 'requests' the executor and attorney to pay certain amounts out of his residuary interest. It is left to the discretion of the executor and attorney whether the payment shall be in shares or in money. And, so far as appears from the facts stated in the case, the document, when executed, was not communicated to the persons or institutions named as the recipients of Howard-Smith's bounty. The absence of communication suggests that the appropriation was not irrevocable. The document, it appears to me, operates as an authority to the executor and attorney to make the payments mentioned, and is not a transfer or assignment of any interest to the persons or institutions named, nor the creation of any trust in their favour. The fact that the authority contained in the document has been acted upon is irrelevant to the question whether the document itself operated as a gift or constituted a trust in favour of the persons or institutions therein named.

Dixon J

[620] The question which this appeal raises for decision is whether a certain document under hand amounts to an equitable assignment. The [Comptroller of Stamps] claims ... that it is an instrument liable to stamp duty ... His claim cannot succeed unless by the instrument itself equitable interests were made over to the various persons and bodies intended to benefit ...

[621] As a residuary legatee, the husband was not entitled to specific items of property, but to equitable interest in the entire mass. There is thus no question of an assignment of

a legal chose in action. The property dealt with was simply an equitable interest. Further, there is no question of consideration. The distribution directed by the letter was by way of gift.

A voluntary disposition of an equitable interest may take one of at least three forms. It may consist of an expression or indication of intention on the part of the donor that he shall hold the equitable interest vested in him upon trust for the persons intended to benefit. In that case he retains the title to the equitable interest, but [622] constitutes himself trustee thereof, and, by his declaration, imposes upon himself an obligation to hold it for the benefit of others, namely, the donees.

In the second place, the disposition may consist of a sufficient expression of an immediate intention to make over to the persons intended to benefit the equitable interest vested in the donor, or some less interest carved out of it. In that case communication to the trustee or person in whom the legal title to the property is vested is not required in order effectually to assign the equitable property. Notice to the trustee may be important to bind him to respect the assignment and in order to preserve priorities. But it is not a condition precedent to the operation of the expression of intention as an assignment. Nor does it appear necessary that the intention to pass equitable property shall be communicated to the assignee. What is necessary is that there shall be an expression of intention then and there to set over the equitable interest, and, perhaps, it should be communicated to someone who does not receive the communication under confidence or in the capacity only of an agent for the donor.

In the third place, the intending donor for whom property is held upon trust may give to his trustee a direction requiring him thenceforth to hold the property upon trust for the intended donee.

A beneficiary who is *sui juris* and entitled to an equitable interest corresponding to the full legal interest in property vested in his trustee may require the transfer to him of the legal estate or interest. He may then transfer the legal interest upon trust for others. Without going through these steps he may simply direct the existing trustee to hold the trust property upon trust for the new beneficiaries. He cannot without the trustee's consent impose upon him new active duties. But he may substitute a new object, at any rate in the case of any passive trust. Accordingly, a voluntary disposition of an equitable interest may be effected by the communication to the trustee of a direction, intended to be binding on him, thenceforward to hold the trust property upon trust for the donee. But it must be a direction, and not a mere authority revocable until acted upon. Such an authority is not in itself an assignment. It may, it is true, result in a transfer of an equitable interest. For the trustee acting [623] upon it may make an effectual appropriation of the trust property to the new beneficiary, or may acknowledge to him that he holds the trust property thenceforward on his behalf. If the authority contemplates or allows such a method of imparting an equitable interest to the donee, the action of the trustee may be effectual to bring about the result. But, in such a case, it is not the donor's expression of intention which *per se* constitutes the assignment. It is the dealing with the trust property under his authorization. The distinction is, of course, of great importance in considering whether a document is itself an assignment, and, as such, liable to stamp duty ...

In the present case, the question is whether the document is no more than an authorization having no dispositive effect until the trustee acts upon it by distributing the shares and money. It is evident upon its face that it cannot operate as a declaration of trust by the husband constituting himself trustee for the persons and bodies intended to benefit. But the document comes very near to expressing an immediate intention to make over an interest to each of the named persons and bodies, and very near to conveying **[624]** to the trustee a direction thenceforward to hold the residue upon new trusts. Upon consideration, however, I have come to the conclusion that it fails to do either of these things. The reasons for this conclusion consist in indications appearing in the text of the document, which, while none of them is in itself decisive, combine to show that it was not the intention of the proposing donor then and there to impart an interest to any of the intended donees. His intention, in my opinion, was that they should take on distribution by the trustee company and not before. In the first place, it is to be noticed that each is to receive a definite sum of money or an equivalent in shares. It is to be received out of an undefined mass, the administration of which is only about to begin. The trustee company is to determine the precise form in which each intended donee is to take the gift, and, in case of a deficiency, is to make a proportionate abatement. Then it is not unimportant that the language is that of request. Finally, the trustee is addressed in its character of attorney under power of the signatory of the document, as well as in that of executor of his wife's estate.

The nature of the gifts intended, the very different character of the interest of the intending donor, the language of the request and the reference to his power of attorney, all support the view that the letter means to convey an authorization and no more.

Comment

1. See Radan & Stewart at **5.58**.

The assignment of future property

5.5   Norman v Federal Commissioner of Taxation (1962) 109 CLR 9

Court: High Court of Australia

Facts: In 1956 Norman purported to assign two items of property to his wife. First, there was 'all his right title and interest in and to the income being payable' on a loan of £3000 owed to Norman, which the borrower was entitled to repay to Norman at any time and without notice. Second, there was his interest in and dividends on certain shares in which Norman had an equitable interest as the beneficiary of a deceased estate. The assignments were by means of a voluntary deed. After the deed was executed the shares were registered in Norman's name. The Commissioner of Taxation argued that, because the assignments were voluntary, they were ineffective on the basis that they involved future property, not presently existing property. (Future property can only be validly assigned if the assignee gives valuable consideration for the assignment.) If the Commissioner's argument was correct, the interest on the loan (£450) and the dividends (£460) earned in the 1958 financial year constituted part of Norman's taxable income, and not that of his wife.

Issue: The issue before the High Court in relation to both assignments was whether present or future property had been assigned.

Decision: In relation to the dividends, the High Court (Dixon CJ, McTiernan, Windeyer, Menzies and Owen JJ) unanimously held that the assignment was not effective because it involved future property for which the assignee did not provide valuable consideration. A bare majority (Dixon CJ, Menzies and Owen JJ; McTiernan and Windeyer JJ dissenting) came to the same conclusion in relation to the interest on the loan.

Extracts: The extracts from the judgment of Menzies J illustrate the approach of the majority on the question of the interest on the loan. The extracts from the judgment of Windeyer J illustrate the view of the court on the dividends as well as the minority view on the issue of the interest on the loan. Windeyer J also discusses, in detail, the principles relating to the assignment of property in equity.

Menzies J

[20] The debt was for no fixed term and the [borrower] was at liberty to repay it or any part of it at any time without notice. The lender was required to give eighteen months' notice if he should require payment of the debt or any part of it and in that event interest was from the date of the notice reduced to 1½ per cent per annum. No notice in writing of the assignment was given to the [borrower]. It is common ground that the assignment did not operate as a legal assignment of interest or the taxpayer's right to it, and the real question is whether there was an effectual equitable assignment of a right to interest. I do not think there was because what was assigned was not an existing right but was no more than a right which might thereafter come into existence and so could not be effectually assigned in equity without consideration.

In general future property was not assignable at common law[6] but in equity after-acquired property was assignable for value according to the principles stated by Lord [21] Macnaghten in *Tailby v Official Receiver*[7] but only for value notwithstanding the assignment was by deed. If then interest that may arise under a contract has the character of a future rather than an existing right, the deed, lacking consideration, was not effective to entitle the assignee to the interest in question as and when it became due and payable. I regard interest which may accrue in the future upon an existing loan repayable without notice as having the character of a right to come into existence rather than of a right already in existence ... What was said in *Horwood v Millar's Timber and Trading Co Ltd* has application here. There, the question [22] of the assignability of wages to be earned arose and *Warrington* LJ, speaking, I think, without any reference to the *Judicature Act*, s. 25 (6), said:

> The assignment with which we have to deal is not the assignment of an actual debt, not the assignment of a chose in action which is in existence, but the assignment of a chose in action, wages which a man is going to earn, which may hereafter come into existence. Now the effect of that is nothing more than to create a contractual obligation between the two parties. That was stated by Lord *Macnaghten* in his speech to the House of Lords in *Tailby v Official Receiver* in these terms: 'It has long been settled that future property,

---

6. *Lunn v Thornton* (1845) 135 ER 587.
7. (1888) 13 App Cas 523.

possibilities and expectancies are assignable in equity for value. The mode or form of assignment is absolutely immaterial provided the intention of the parties is clear. To effectuate the intention an assignment for value, in terms present and immediate, has always been regarded in equity as a contract binding on the conscience of the assignor and so binding the subject-matter of the contract when it comes into existence, if it is of such a nature and so described as to be capable of being ascertained and identified'.[8] In other words, the real effect of such an assignment where property is not in existence is that it is carried into effect not because it passes the property, but because it is a contractual obligation binding upon the assignor, and one which can be specifically enforced if the contract and the subject-matter of it are sufficiently definite.[9]

Under the contract of loan now under consideration, there was no liability for or right to interest until it began to accrue in an annual period and in 1956 the borrowers were under no liability for and the lender had no right to interest for 1958. It is not that interest for 1958 was not payable in 1956; it is that in 1956 interest for 1958 was nothing but an expectancy. It appears to me that the entries which were made in the books of the firm, clearly enough with the approval of both the assignor and the assignee, accorded with the true legal position in that the taxpayer was credited with all interest falling due upon his loan and his account was then debited and his wife's account was then credited with so much of the interest as was interest upon £3,000 of the debt. To put it shortly, there were gifts of interest paid but not a gift of interest to be paid.

Windeyer J

[23] The ultimate question in this case is whether before 1st July 1957 the taxpayer had effectually assigned his right to receive certain moneys that would otherwise have been receivable by him and been part of his income for the year ending on 30th June 1958 ...

[24] (i) As to attempted assignments of things not yet in existence:

As it is impossible for anyone to own something that does not exist, it is impossible for anyone to make a present gift of such a thing to another person, however sure he may be that it will come into existence and will then be his to give. He can, of course, promise that when the thing is his he will make it over to the intended donee. But in the meantime he may change his mind and when the time comes refuse to carry out his promise, even though it were by deed. A court of law could not compel him to perform it. A court of equity would not. Courts of equity never had the objections to all agreements about future interests that, until the seventeenth century, were deeply rooted in the common law. Equity did not share the view that such agreements were void on the ground of maintenance. But things not yet in existence could only be the subject of agreement, not of present disposition. And, in relation to promises and agreements, equity has been faithful to its maxim that it does not come to the aid of volunteers. For equity a deed does not make good a want of consideration.

If we turn from attempted gifts of future property to purported dispositions of it for value, the picture changes completely. The common law objection remains. But in equity

8. *Tailby v Official Receiver* (1888) 13 App Cas 523 at 543.
9. *Horwood v Millar's Timber and Trading Co Ltd* [1917] 1 KB 305 at 315.

a would-be present assignment of something to be acquired in the future is, when made for value, construed as an agreement to assign the thing when it is acquired. A court of equity will ensure that the would-be assignor performs this agreement, his conscience being bound by the consideration. The purported assignee thus gets an equitable interest in the property immediately the legal ownership of it is acquired by the assignor, assuming it to have been sufficiently described to be then identifiable. The prospective interest of the assignee is in the meantime protected by equity ...

[25] [A] purported assignment of a thing before the thing exists can have no effect at law, except as a covenant or contract to assign. The earliest moment at which the property in the thing can actually pass is when it first becomes extant ...

[26] (ii) As to assignments of choses in action:

In *Lampet's Case*, *Coke* spoke of 'the great wisdom and policy of the sages and founders of our law, who have provided that no possibility, right, title, nor thing in action, shall be granted or assigned to strangers, for that would be the occasion of multiplying of contentions and suits'.[10] It was a somewhat unsophisticated view of legal rights that led the common lawyers to classify choses in action and debts with mere possibilities, and to condemn all assignments of them as leading to maintenance.

Assignment means the immediate transfer of an existing proprietary right, vested or contingent, from the assignor to the assignee. Anything that in the eye of the law can be regarded as an existing subject of ownership, whether it be a chose in possession or a chose in action, can to-day be assigned, unless it be excepted from the general rule on some ground of public policy or by statute. But a mere expectancy or possibility of becoming entitled in the future to a proprietary right is not an existing chose in action. It is not assignable, except in the inexact sense into which ... lawyers slipped when it is said to be assignable in equity for value.

The distinction between a chose in action, which is an existing legal right, and a mere expectancy or possibility of a future right is of cardinal importance in this case, as will appear. It does not, in my view, depend on whether or not there is a debt presently recoverable by action because presently due and payable. A legal right to be paid money at a future date is, I consider, a present chose in action, at all events when it depends upon an existing contract on the repudiation of which an action could be brought for anticipatory breach.

The common law doctrine that debts and other choses in action were not assignable never applied to Crown debts; and, by the influence of the law merchant, bills of exchange and promissory notes were outside it. And it was never accepted in equity ... [27] What had happened was that the common law rule came to be circumvented in various ways. One was by novation. Another was by the assignor giving a power of attorney to the assignee to sue the debtor at law in the assignor's name, without having to render an account ... And courts of equity would come to the assistance of the assignee if the assignor refused to do whatever was necessary to enable the assignee to get the benefit of the assignment. Thus a recalcitrant assignor would be required, on having an indemnity for his costs, to permit his name to be used in an action to recover the debt; or an assignor would be restrained from receiving the debt for himself ... Because the

---

10. *Lampet's Case* (1612) 77 ER 994 at 997.

assistance of equity was available, it was generally not needed. The common law courts recognized that an assignee might sue in the assignor's name. So that in 1849 it could be said that 'the courts of law have adopted the doctrines of the court of chancery in regard to assignments of choses in action'; so much so that 'In ordinary cases, where the plaintiff has an easy remedy by suing in the name of the assignor, the court (scil. the Court of Chancery) will not entertain jurisdiction, but leave the party to his remedy at law'.[11] Therefore, ... it is somewhat misleading to say, as is often said, that before the *Judicature Act* the common law would not allow assignments of legal choses in action. Long before 1873 the development of common law processes and the impact of equity had pushed the common law prohibition of the assignment of choses in action back into history. Nevertheless the original doctrine survived, to this extent that, until the *Judicature Act*, 1873, s 25(6), and the corresponding statutory provisions in Australia and elsewhere came into operation, an assignee of a legal debt could not in his own name bring an action against the debtor to recover the debt. The original creditor must be the plaintiff on the record. He remained in law the owner of the chose in action. What the provision of the *Judicature Act*, 1873, did was to render unnecessary the previous circumlocutions. Debts and other legal choses in action were made directly assignable by the statutory method. But this, while it simplified [28] assignments, has not simplified the law surrounding them ...

It is settled that any assignment that satisfies the requirements of the statute is valid and fully effectual although it be voluntary. That is to say the law now provides a means whereby the legal owner of a chose in action may make a complete and perfect gift of it. That being so, and as equity does not perfect an imperfect gift, can there ever now be an effectual voluntary assignment unless all the statutory requirements are met? The question is not an easy one if a purely logical answer be sought. Equity intervened to assist the assignments of choses in action because they were not assignable at law. Now that they are, why, it may be asked, should equity aid imperfect attempts at voluntary assignments of them. On the other hand, it can be urged that the statute provides a method or machinery whereby assignment may be effected, but that it does not detract from the validity of any transaction that would have been effective in equity if it had occurred before the statute came into operation ... [T]he weight of authority is, I think in favour of the view that in equity there is a valid gift of property transferable at law if the donor, intending to make, then and there, a complete disposition and transfer to the donee, does all that *on his part* is necessary to give effect to his intention and arms the donee with the means of completing the gift according to the [29] requirements of the law. I think therefore that, if a man, meaning to make an immediate gift of a chose in action that is his, executes an instrument that meets the requirements of the statute and delivers it to the donee, actually or constructively, he has put it out of his power to recall his gift. It is true that until notice is given to the debtor or person against whom the chose is enforceable at law, all the requirements of the statute have not been complied with. But the notice can be given by the donee; and, if the donee has express or implied authority to give it, I think that equity would not allow the donor to deny the right of the donee to do so and so intercept his gift. I reach this conclusion with some hesitation ... But it

---

11. Spence, *Equitable Jurisdiction of the Court of Chancery*, vol 2 at 853, 854; and see *Roxburghe v Cox* (1881) 17 Ch D 520 at 526.

accords, it seems to me with general principle. For these reasons I consider that, if the debt that the deed in this case purported to assign had been an existing chose in action assignable by the statutory procedure, the only question would be whether the assignor had purported to make an absolute assignment of it, and whether he did all that on his part had to be done to that end ...

(iii) As to assignments of part of a debt:

It has been held that the statutory method of assignment is not available for the assignment of parts of debts or choses in action.[12] There were some earlier decisions to the contrary; but they must be taken to be overruled. The later decisions should, I consider, be followed by this Court. They are in accordance with general principle. The conclusion does not depend simply on a literal interpretation of the statutory language and of the phrase 'absolute assignment'. Before the statute an assignee was permitted to bring his action at law in the name of the assignor when he was seeking to recover a whole debt assigned to him. If a debt had been broken into parts this procedure was not appropriate. A creditor cannot recover a debt piecemeal in a court of law. Therefore, when part of a debt was assigned, proceedings to enforce the assignment had to be brought in a court of equity. And the assignee, not the assignor, would be the plaintiff in the suit. The assignor (the creditor) as legal owner, the debtor and any assignee of other **[30]** parts of the debt were all necessary parties, so that all the obligations of the debtor and the rights of all persons interested in the fund might be established by the decree. This was the rule of the Chancery Court. It is still the law.[13] As an assignment of part of a debt is still necessarily an equitable assignment, the question arises can it be made by way of gift; and, if so, how?

(iv) As to whether consideration is required for the equitable assignment of a chose in action not assignable at law:

One might have expected that this would long ago have been authoritatively settled. But ... Lord Evershed said in *In re McArdle (dec'd)* that the problem is 'vexed and difficult'.[14] ... I do not think it necessary to discuss all the cases that were cited to us in argument, nor all those on this topic that I have read since then. I shall state the conclusions that I have reached on matters that are significant for the determination of the case before us.

There are several senses in which the phrase 'equitable assignment' may be used; and the question, Is consideration necessary for an equitable assignment?, does not admit of a single short answer covering all of them.

If the interest to be assigned is a creature of equity, such as the beneficial interest of a cestui que trust, then, apart from any statutory provisions, an assignment of it can, of course, only be effected in equity; for the common law does not know it. Any present assignment of such an interest, that is to say of a chose in equity, is therefore necessarily an equitable assignment. Such an assignment can be by way of gift; and, except that writing is required by s 9 of the *Statute of Frauds*, no formality is necessary beyond a clear expression of an intention to make an immediate disposition. In short, there is no reason at all why a person should not give away any beneficial interest that is his ...

---

12. *Williams v Atlantic Assurance Co* [1933] 1 KB 81; *Re Steel Wing Co Ltd* [1921] 1 Ch 349.
13. See *Performing Right Society Ltd v London Theatre of Varieties Ltd* [1924] AC 1 at 14, 20, 30, 31.
14. *In re McArdle (dec'd)* [1951] 1 Ch 669 at 673.

It is, of course, necessary that the transaction should take the form of, and be intended as, an immediate [31] transfer of the beneficial interest of the assignor, as distinct from an agreement to assign it. The distinction is critical, for consideration is always necessary to attract the support of equity to a transaction that is a contract rather than a conveyance ...

Turning, from assignments that are equitable because the property assigned is a chose in equity, to assignments that are equitable because the property assigned is a legal chose in action not assignable except by the aid of equity: It has been said that historically there could be no equitable assignment of a debt except for value. Whether this be correct or not as a general proposition, it never meant that there must be consideration as now understood in the law of contract. An assignment in satisfaction, or part satisfaction, of an antecedent debt was taken in equity as made for value. And this was what had happened in case after case appearing in the reports in which assignments were upheld in equity before the *Judicature Act*. Whether equity would then give any aid to an assignment of a chose in action made for no value at all, but as a pure gift, is less clear ...

[32] It seems to me that, in principle, so far as a deed has any efficacy in connexion with equitable assignments, it is not that a deed takes the place of valuable consideration where that is needed to attract the aid of equity. Rather it is that, in cases where value is not so required but a clear expression of intention is, the delivery of a deed couched in terms of present gift manifests, in the best possible way, the intention of the assignor to make an immediate and irrevocable transfer.

[33] The intervention of equity in support of assignments of choses in action has been ascribed historically, in the main, to one or other of two grounds. One is to hold men to agreements and promises which they have made for value; the other is the analogy of a trust. *Story* put the two somewhat together when ... he said: 'Every such assignment is considered in equity as in its nature amounting to a declaration of trust, and to an agreement to permit the assignee to make use of the name of the assignor to recover the debt, or to reduce the property into possession'.[15] An assignment, of course, differs from a declaration of trust. And it is trite to say that an ineffectual attempt to assign property will not be rescued by equity by being construed as a valid declaration of trust.[16] Nevertheless, the analogy between the creation of a trust and an equitable assignment of a chose in action, which creates an equitable interest in the assignee, is significant.

An agreement to assign will be effective as an equitable assignment if it be for value; for then equity looks on that as done which ought to be done. But this does not mean that there cannot be in equity an actual assignment of a chose in action as distinct from an agreement to assign. I think there can, and that it can be by way of gift. In such a case equity enforces the assignment, not by compelling the assignor to do something, but by refusing to allow him to act in a way inconsistent with what he has done, that is by restraining him from derogating from his gift. His conscience becomes bound, not by value received, but because, as between him and the assignee, his gift was complete ...

[34] Why should consideration be said to be necessary to bind the conscience in the one case when it is not necessary in the other? Before 1873 a chose in equity and

---

15. Story, *Equity Jurisprudence* 7th ed (1857), para 1040.
16. *Milroy v Lord* (1862) 45 ER 1185.

a chose in action were both transferable in equity and only in equity. The assignments were alike made effective because of the remedies that a court of equity could provide. To speak of equity not perfecting an imperfect gift seems beside the point where no gift could be made except in equity. To say that the donor must do everything that according to the nature of the property is necessary to transfer it means little when it is in law not transferable; for equity looks to the intent not the form. These considerations have added weight in the case of part of a debt; for a part of a debt never was assignable so as to be recoverable at law even in an indirect way. It being necessary for the decision of this case to come to a conclusion on a vexed question, my conclusion is that the deed that [Norman] executed did not fail because it was voluntary. The whole of a debt being now voluntarily assignable under the statute, it would be a strange anomaly if a part could not be the subject of voluntary equitable assignment. To say, 'you can give away the whole, but you cannot give away a part, for a part you must get a price' would seem to contradict common sense. And I do not think it necessary to do so.

(v) As to the facts: ...

[37] It is true too that the interest, to the extent of £450, that the deed assigned was not due and payable at the date of the deed. But a contract to pay a sum of money on a future day, call it interest or what you will, calculable in amount according to conditions presently agreed, is in my view a presently existing chose in action. [38] As between the parties to a contract of money lent at interest the borrower is simply a debtor who must pay a sum or sums (called interest) that he has, for good consideration (the forbearance of the creditor) contracted to pay to his creditor at the time or times stipulated. Why should not the creditor before the date when this debt becomes due and payable, assign his right to receive payment on the due date? He could assign the whole under the statute.[17] Why not part in equity? What he assigns is not, it seems to me, a right to arise in the future but a present contractual right to be paid at a future date a sum of money, to be calculated in the agreed manner. In *Brice v Bannister*, Lord Coleridge CJ said 'that a debt to become due is a chose in action, is clear'.[18] Interest on money lent is recoverable by action at law as a debt separate from the principal, as the common indebitatus count for interest shows.

But it was urged this case is not like a case of a loan for a fixed term. What was owing might, it is pointed out, have been repaid by the partnership, or reduced below £3,000, after the date of the deed of assignment and before 1st July 1957. As a matter of law, no doubt that is so. But it does not, I think, follow that [Norman] had for that reason no assignable right. He had a present right to be paid interest at a future date on the money he had lent, unless in the meantime the loan was repaid. [Norman] assigned the benefit of this contract, to the extent of £450 to become due conditionally in 1958, to his wife by the deed of 1956. I consider that the deed was an effectual equitable assignment. It operated, I think, upon its delivery as a deed. The assignee had notice of it and assented. It was valid and binding as between assignor and assignee ...

[40] Is a dividend that may become payable in the future upon shares presently held something that can be assigned in equity? Is it a present chose in action or a mere possibility? Is it property in existence, or something not in existence and therefore

---

17. *Walker v Bradford Old Bank Ltd* (1884) 12 QBD 511.
18. *Brice v Bannister* (1878) 3 QBD 569 at 573.

not capable of being assigned in the absence of consideration? I think it is the latter. The court will not compel directors to declare a dividend.[19] A dividend is not a debt until it is declared. Until then it is in the eye of the law a possibility only. When it is declared it becomes a debt for which a shareholder who is on the register at the date of the declaration may sue. The companies paid the dividends to the registered holder of the shares, [Norman]. They knew nothing of the purported assignment. Depending perhaps in some cases on their articles of association, they might have paid the dividends directly to [Norman's] wife had they been directed by him to do so. But, in the absence of consideration, such a direction would have been merely a revocable mandate, not an assignment. Dividends that may be declared are to my mind quite unlike the interest that will become due according to an existing contract of loan if the loan be not repaid.

Comment

1. See Radan & Stewart at **5.62–5.72**.

5.6 Shepherd v Commissioner of Taxation of the Commonwealth of Australia (1965) 113 CLR 385

Court: High Court of Australia

Facts: In the early 1950s Shepherd granted Cowen a licence to manufacture castors in return for royalty payments based upon the gross sales of castors manufactured pursuant to the licence. In 1957 Shepherd assigned 'absolutely and unconditionally' by way of gift to a number of persons 'all my right title and interest in and to an amount equal to ninety per centum of the income which may accrue during a period of three years from the date this assignment from royalties' payable by Cowen pursuant to the licence agreement with Shepherd. Shepherd then directed Cowen to pay royalties to the named persons set out in the deed of assignment.

The Commissioner of Taxation argued that, because the assignments were voluntary, they were ineffective on the basis that they involved future property, not presently existing property. (Future property can only be validly assigned if the assignee gives valuable consideration for the assignment.) If the Commissioner's argument was correct, the royalties paid to the named persons constituted part of Shepherd's taxable income, and not part of the taxable incomes of the persons named in the deed of assignment.

Issue: The issue before the High Court was whether what Shepherd had assigned was present or future property.

Decision: The majority of the High Court (Barwick CJ and Kitto J; Owen J dissenting) held in favour of Shepherd on the basis that the voluntary deed of assignment was an effective assignment of presently existing property.

---

19. *Bond v Barrow Haematite Steel Co* (1902) 1 Ch 353.

> **Extracts:** The extracts from the judgment of Barwick CJ discuss the basis upon which the assignment was held to be an assignment in equity of presently existing property. They also stress the importance of a proper construction of the wording of an assignment in determining whether it involves future or presently existing property.

Barwick CJ

[390] [Cowen] was under promise to pay royalties to [Shepherd]. That promise in its entirety would have been assignable at law pursuant to the provisions of s 134 of the *Property Law Act* 1958 (Vict). But part of it could not be so assigned, nor could the royalties as after acquired property be assigned at law. Thus, whether the deed poll be construed as an attempted assignment of part of the promise to pay royalties or an attempted assignment of part of the royalties themselves when received, it will in either case be ineffective at law. In my opinion, the deed poll is not capable of being regarded as or as containing a covenant by [Shepherd] to pay money in the future to the named persons, the amount to be paid being quantified in relation to the amount of royalties received by [Shepherd]. The function of the expression 'an amount equal to' in the operative words of the deed poll is not, in my opinion, to make the purported assignment a covenant to pay money but … its purpose, in my opinion, is to work out the fraction of the right to royalties which in total is being assigned to the donees. Indeed, I see in the employment of the words 'an amount equal to' an indication that it is the right to the royalties rather than the royalties as after acquired property which is the subject matter of the assignment …

In my opinion, the situation of the deed poll is that it is ineffective at law to confer on any of the named persons any legal right whether to any part of the promise to pay royalties or of the royalties themselves when received.

However, a part or parts of a chose in action can be assigned in equity. In my opinion, if the assignment of a part of the chose in action consisting of the promise to pay royalties is complete, [391] it is effective to vest the appropriate part of the right equitably in the assignee, whether or not the assignment is for consideration or by way of gift. It is only if the donee needs the assistance of equity to complete the gift, as distinct from enforcing the right given, that he can be met with the defence that equity will not assist a volunteer. Here, if there was an immediate gift of a proportion of the right to the royalties, the donees need seek no assistance. If the deed upon its true construction evidences an intention presently to assign part of the right, the assignment would be complete within the doctrines of equity. If, on the other hand, the deed purports to assign the stated proportion of the royalties as after-acquired property the assignment would be ineffective in equity for want of consideration. The question therefore, in my opinion, is a narrow one, namely, whether upon its true construction the deed purports to assign part of the right to the royalties or of the royalties themselves as after-acquired property …

The task in construing the deed is to find the meaning intended by [Shepherd] as expressed. No form of words is required for an equitable assignment but it is necessary to find the expression of an intention to assign. The deed does purport in terms presently to assign its subject matter and to do so absolutely and unconditionally. In describing what he considered he had done by the operative words of the deed, [Shepherd] in the second paragraph of the deed, speaks of the persons 'to whom my right title and interest … is assigned'. The difficulty in the case arises in the description of the subject matter of the gift. That description begins with the words 'all my right title and interest in and to' which words are appropriate to the assignment of a chose in action as distinct from its ultimate produce. But the words that follow create the problem, 'an amount equal to ninety per centum of the income which may arise during a period of three years from the date of this assignment'.

Had [Shepherd] been dealing with his entire right to royalties, probably the description of the subject matter of the intended gift would not have been difficult. But because the deed was to deal with only part of that right and that only for a limited period of years, the draftsman, it seems to me, has been led into the use [392] of the awkward words which I have quoted. I think it not inappropriate when seeking the intended meaning of the words to notice the consequences of not finding in the language of the deed, as a whole, an intention to make a present gift of part of the right to royalties arising under the licence to manufacture. For if the deed poll is not an equitable assignment of part of that right it must be, in my opinion, an attempted equitable assignment of the royalties as after-acquired property. Equity would treat such an assignment as or as evidencing a promise to hand over the royalties when received: but the promise being voluntary would not be enforced by it. The directions given by [Shepherd] to [Cowen] subsequent to the execution of the deed poll would then be no more than revocable mandates ...

No doubt to speak of the subject matter of the gift as an amount of income to accrue from royalties would seem to support the conclusion that what is to be given is the property in the form of money produced by the promise to pay royalties. But the full description of the subject matter of the assignment is of 'the right' to such amounts — an unlikely expression to describe the money itself. In my opinion, it indicates that [Shepherd] was not intending to promise that he would pay money measured by the amount of royalties accrued or that he was intending to assign the royalties themselves. Its use rather suggests, to my mind, that he was intending to place the persons he wished to benefit in the position of being able themselves to assert a right to receive the appropriate amounts from [Cowen].

As I have mentioned, the dominant consideration is the intention of [Shepherd] as expressed in the deed. The expressed indications of an intent presently to assign portions of his right to royalties are strong enough, in my view, to overbear any contrary indication which might possibly be derived from the words which I have just discussed. These clumsy expressions are used, in my opinion, as I have said, in an endeavour to attain the two desiderata of a gift of part only of the right and only for a limited period of years. They are not in any case really so inappropriate to a present gift of a part of the right to royalties that they should be allowed to dominate the construction and to displace the evident intention expressed in the earlier part of the deed.

I have come to the conclusion that upon the true construction of the deed poll [Shepherd] did thereby equitably assign to the named donees the stated proportions of his right during [393] the ensuing three years to royalties from [Cowen] under the licence to manufacture the patented article.

It was also submitted by the Commissioner that the subject matter of the intended assignment was a mere *spes* or possibility which could not be voluntarily assigned. This argument concedes the intention to assign, but attacks its subject matter as insusceptible of assignment by way of gift. If there is no such intention to assign evidenced, the Commissioner would succeed on other grounds, as I have mentioned.

The basis of this submission is that in the event there may not be any amount payable for royalties because no sales of castors may be made. But this misconceives the matter. That a promise may not be fruitful does not make it incapable of assignment. Reference was made on behalf of the Commissioner in this connexion to *Norman v Federal Commissioner of Taxation*.[20] But that case did not decide anything to the contrary of what I have just said ... The case, in my opinion, has no relevance to the problem raised by the language of this deed poll as applied to the facts of this case.

Comment

1. See Radan & Stewart at **5.73–5.74**.

The assignment of future property and the nature of the assignee's interest

---

5.7   Re Lind, Industrials Finance Syndicate Ltd v Lind [1915] 2 Ch 345

Court: Court of Appeal of England and Wales

Facts: Lind had an expectancy under his mother's will. Prior to her death he borrowed from two separate sources (Norwich Union and Arnold), in each case assigning the expectancy as security for the loan. Lind was then declared bankrupt, from which he was subsequently discharged. He then borrowed money from a third source (Industrials Finance Syndicate) and again assigned his expectancy as security for the loan. His mother then died.

Issue: The issue before the Court of Appeal was whether the third assignee's interest in the property inherited by Lind pursuant to his mother's will had priority over the interests of the first two assignees. This in turn depended upon whether the first two assignments survived Lind's bankruptcy. If they had not, then the first two assignees had no claim to the property inherited by Lind. If the first two assignments had survived bankruptcy, then on the rules relating to priority between competing equitable interests, they, being first in time, prevailed over the interest of the third assignee.

Decision: The Court of Appeal (Swinfen Eady, Phillimore and Bankes LJJ) unanimously ruled in favour of the first two assignees. The court found that the first two assignments survived Lind's bankruptcy. All three judges rejected the notion that the rights of an assignee of future property rested purely in contract. Rather, there was a higher right. The crucial factor establishing this higher right was the fact that an assignee of future property obtains an equitable interest in the property immediately and automatically upon the property coming into existence or into the possession of the assignor. This attribute of the assignment of future property meant that the rights of the assignee were sufficiently proprietary in nature to attract the rules relating to priorities between

---

20. (1963) 109 CLR 9.

competing interests in the property that was the subject of the assignment. If the rights of the first two assignees had been merely contractual they would have been completely discharged by Lind's bankruptcy and no priorities issue would have arisen with the third assignee.

Extracts: The extracts from the three judgments in the Court of Appeal discuss the principles relating to the assignment in equity of future property as well as the nature of the rights of the assignee in relation to that property, especially in the period between the date of the assignment and the date when it subsequently comes into existence and becomes presently existing property.

Swinfen Eady LJ

[357] [Industrials Finance] contend that the securities of the [first two assignees] are of no value, and that [Industrials Finance] are now absolutely entitled to the share under their deeds of 1911 and 1914, free from any incumbrance. They base this claim upon the bankruptcy of … Lind and his discharge while Florence Lind was still living. They say that the rights of the [first two assignees] rested only in contract, and amounted only to contracts to assure in the future, and by way of security for their mortgage debts; that by reason of the bankruptcy [Lind] has been released from the mortgage debts; that the contracts to assure his expectant interest gave rise only to a right of proof which was not exercised; that any covenant for further assurance was only ancillary to and for the purpose of securing the mortgage debts, and that as the debts are discharged by the bankruptcy and discharge of the debtor, the covenant for further assurance is no longer in force …

Is the contention well founded that the rights of mortgagees of an expectancy rest only in contract, giving rise to a right of proof if the assignor shall become bankrupt before the expectancy vests in interest, but otherwise barred by the bankruptcy, and discharge of the bankrupt? In my opinion the answer must be in the negative; the security of the mortgagee remains in force, and becomes effective whenever the expectancy vests in interest …

[358] In *Holroyd v Marshall* it was held by the House of Lords that an assignment by way of mortgage of machinery to be acquired in the future gave a good title to such machinery from the moment when it was acquired, and without any novus actus interveniens. Lord Westbury LC there said:

> If a vendor or mortgagor agrees to sell or mortgage property, real or personal, of which he is not possessed at the time, and he receives the consideration for the contract, and afterwards becomes possessed of property answering the description in the contract, there is no doubt that a Court of Equity would compel [359] him to perform the contract, and that the contract would, in equity, transfer the beneficial interest to the mortgagee or purchaser immediately on the property being acquired. This, of course, assumes that the supposed contract is one of that class of which a Court of Equity would decree the specific performance. If it be so, then immediately on the acquisition of the property described the vendor or mortgagor would hold it in trust for the purchaser or mortgagee, according to the terms of the contract. For if a contract be in other respects

good and fit to be performed, and the consideration has been received, incapacity to perform it at the time of its execution will be no answer when the means of doing so are afterwards obtained.[21]

In the same case Lord Chelmsford considered the nature of the equity created by agreements to transfer or to charge future acquired property, whether it is a personal equity to be enforced by suit, or to be made available by some act to be done between the parties, or is in the nature of a trust attaching upon and binding the property at the instant of its coming into existence, and decided in favour of the latter view. He added:

> At law property non-existing, but to be acquired at a future time, is not assignable; in equity it is so. At law (as we have seen), although a power is given in the deed of assignment to take possession of after-acquired property, no interest is transferred, even as between the parties themselves, unless possession is actually taken; in equity it is not disputed that the moment the property comes into existence the agreement operates upon it.[22]

In *Tailby v Official Receiver* Lord Macnaghten stated that *Holroyd v Marshall* laid down no new law, nor did it extend the principles of equity in the slightest degree. Long before *Holroyd v Marshall* was determined it was well settled that an assignment of future property for value operates in equity by way of agreement, binding the conscience of the assignor, and so binding the property from the moment when the contract becomes capable of being performed, on the principle that equity considers as done that which ought to be done. Lord Macnaghten then dealt with Lord Westbury LC's reference **[360]** in *Holroyd v Marshall* to the subject of specific performance, and proceeded to point out that considerations applicable to suits for specific performance ought not to be transferred to cases of equitable assignment where nothing remained to be done in order to define the rights of the parties. He added:

> The truth is that cases of equitable assignment or specific lien, when the consideration has passed, depend on the real meaning of the agreement between the parties ... When that is ascertained you have only to apply the principle that equity considers that done which ought to be done if that principle is applicable under the circumstances of the case. The doctrines relating to specific performance do not, I think, afford a test or a measure of the rights created.[23] ...

It is clear from these authorities that an assignment for value of future property actually binds the property itself directly it is acquired — automatically on the happening of the event, and without any further act on the part of the assignor — and does not merely rest in, and amount to, a right in contract, giving rise to an action. The assignor, having received the consideration, becomes in equity, on the happening of the event, trustee for the assignee of the property devolving upon or acquired by him, and which he had previously sold and been paid for.

---

21. *Holroyd v Marshall* (1862) 11 ER 999 at 1007.
22. *Holroyd v Marshall* (1862) 11 ER 999 at 1010.
23. *Tailby v Official Receiver* (1888) 13 App Cas 523 at 547.

Phillimore LJ

[364] In order that the assignment [of future property] may survive [the assignor's bankruptcy] and have its effect it must give to the assignee something more than a mere right in contract, something in the nature of an estate or interest.

The real question in this case is whether the assurances by ... Lind remained in contract, or whether upon the property coming into existence they automatically, and without any novus actus interveniens, passed his estate or interest in his share of his mother's personal estate to the assignees.

That the assurances remain in contract might be inferred from some language of Lord Westbury LC in *Holroyd v Marshall* which I venture to quote:

> But if a vendor or mortgagor agrees to sell or mortgage [365] property, real or personal, of which he is not possessed at the time, and he receives the consideration for the contract, and afterwards becomes possessed of property answering the description in the contract, there is no doubt that a Court of Equity would compel him to perform the contract, and that the contract would, in equity, transfer the beneficial interest to the mortgagee or purchaser, immediately on the property being acquired. This, of course, assumes that the supposed contract is one of that class of which a Court of Equity would decree the specific performance. If it be so, then immediately on the acquisition of the property described the vendor or mortgagor would hold it in trust for the purchaser or mortgagee, according to the terms of the contract. For if a contract be in other respects good and fit to be performed, and the consideration has been received, incapacity to perform it at the time of its execution will be no answer when the means of doing so are afterwards obtained.[24] ...

If the right of [the mortgagee or purchaser] has to be enforced by a suit for specific performance of a contract, involving as it does 'some of the nicest distinctions and most difficult questions that come before the Court,'[25] then the right is in contract only and the statutory discharge in bankruptcy should operate ...

But notwithstanding these allusions to the doctrine of specific performance of contracts, it is I think well and long settled that the right of the assignee is a higher right than the right to have specific performance of a contract, that the assignment creates [366] an equitable charge which arises immediately upon the property coming into existence. Either then no further act of assurance from the assignor is required, or if there be something necessary to be done by him to pass the legal estate or complete the title, he has to do it not by reason of a covenant for further assurance the persistence of which through bankruptcy it is unnecessary to discuss, but because it is due from him as trustee for his assignee.

Bankes LJ

[369] The assignments [in this case] were assignments of a mere expectancy, and I do not think it is material to discuss the nature of the expectancy ... In speaking of assignments of a similar kind to the present, Lord Herschell, in *Tailby v Official Receiver*, said:

---

24. *Holroyd v Marshall* (1862) 10 HLC 191 at 211.
25. *Tailby v Official Receiver* (1888) 13 App Cas 523 at 544.

I confess I am unable to see any sound distinction between an instrument assigning future book debts which may become due to the assignor in any business carried on by him and one assigning future bequests and devises to which he may under any will become entitled. The subjects of both assignments are equally wide, equally incapable of ascertainment at the time of the assignment, but equally capable of identification [370] when the subject has come into existence and it is sought to enforce the security.[26]

For the purpose of this judgment I propose to treat the assignments as if they were assignments of after-acquired property merely. It has long been settled that a Court of Equity will give effect to an assignment for good consideration of a mere expectancy though such an interest was not assignable at law ... One way in which equity supports such an assignment is by treating the transaction, though in form an assignment, as containing or importing a covenant to do that which is necessary to effect the validity of the assignment.[27] And one method by which a Court of Equity would compel the performance of such a covenant would, in a proper case, be by granting a decree for specific performance ...

[371] The real question [in this case] is as to the exact effect which equity gives to the assignments in question and as to the operation of the Bankruptcy Acts upon the covenant which equity imports into them. I will deal with this last point first. There is no decision precisely in point, but there is a body of judicial opinion upon the question. The covenant which has to be considered is a covenant to assign after-acquired property. The question which has to be determined is whether the existence of that covenant at the date of the bankruptcy created without more a mere liability within the meaning of s 37(8) of the *Bankruptcy Act*, 1883, which must be deemed to be a debt provable in the bankruptcy. If it did, then the discharge in bankruptcy operated as a discharge from all liability under the covenant. If it did not, then the matter is [372] one outside the Bankruptcy Acts altogether, and the covenant is unaffected by the bankrupt's discharge ... [On the basis of the relevant authorities[28]] I ... have ... no hesitation in ... saying that the covenants to assign the after-acquired interests in [Lind's] mother's property were not affected by [his] discharge in bankruptcy.

There remains the other question, as to whether these assignments do not in equity give the [first two assignees] an interest in the property itself. Upon this question there is again no decision precisely in point, if the question is regarded from the point of view of the effect of a discharge in bankruptcy, but there is in my opinion abundant authority which settles the question in principle. If the view of a Court of Equity on this point had been [373] that the only way in which to do equity in the case of an assignment of after-acquired property was to construe the assignment as a covenant to assign it, then in cases where the property came into existence something would have had to be done by the covenantor to give effect to his covenant; but I find that time after time it has been laid down, perhaps not always in the same words, that directly the property comes into existence the assignment fastens on it and without any actus interveniens the property is regarded in equity as the property of the assignee ... [In this respect,] [t]he language

---

26. *Tailby v Official Receiver* (1888) 13 App Cas 523 at 530.
27. See *In re Mudge* [1914] 1 Ch 115 at 122.
28. See *Robinson v Ommanney* (1882) 21 Ch D 780; (1883) 23 Ch D 285; *Hardy v Fothergill* (1888) 13 App Cas 351; *In re Reis* [1904] 2 KB 769.

of Lords Watson and Macnaghten in [*Tailby v Official Receiver*] is very emphatic. Lord Watson says:

> There is but one condition which must be fulfilled in order to make the assignee's right attach to a future chose in action, which is, that, on its coming into existence, it shall answer the description in the assignment, or, in other words, that it shall be capable of being identified as the thing, or as one of the very things assigned. When there is no uncertainty as to its identification, the beneficial interest will immediately vest in the assignee.[29]

[A]nd Lord Macnaghten says:

> Long before *Holroyd v Marshall* was determined it was well settled that an assignment of future property for value operates in equity by way of agreement, binding the conscience of the assignor, and so binding the property from the moment when the contract becomes capable of being performed, on the principle that equity considers as done that which ought to be done, and in accordance with the maxim which Lord Thurlow[30] said he took to be universal, 'that whenever persons agree concerning any particular subject, that, in a Court of Equity, as against the party himself, and any claiming under him, voluntarily or with notice, raises a trust'.[31]

It appears to me to be manifest from these statements of the law that equity regarded an assignment for value [374] of future acquired property as containing an enforceable security as against the property assigned quite independent of the personal obligation of the assignor arising out of his imported covenant to assign. It is true that the security was not enforceable until the property came into existence, but nevertheless the security was there, the assignor was the bare trustee of the assignee to receive and hold the property for him when it came into existence.

Comment

1. See Radan & Stewart at **5.84–5.93**.

The voluntary assignment of property in equity

5.8 Corin v Patton (1990) 169 CLR 540

Court: High Court of Australia

Facts: Mr and Mrs Patton owned Torrens title land as joint tenants in the Sydney suburb of Belrose. Mrs Patton was terminally ill and, on the assumption that she would die before her husband, the land was to pass to him automatically upon her death in

---

29. *Tailby v Official Receiver* (1888) 13 App Cas 523 at 533.
30. *Legard v Hodges* (1792) 30 ER 447 at 447.
31. *Tailby v Official Receiver* (1888) 13 App Cas 523 at 546.

accordance with the principle of survivorship that applies to land held in joint tenancy. Mrs Patton did not want this to happen upon her death. She wanted her share of the property to go to her children. To achieve this result she wanted to sever the joint tenancy and thereby exclude the operation of the principle of survivorship upon her death. One way in which a joint tenancy can be severed is if a joint tenant assigns his or her interest in the property to another person. With this in mind Mrs Patton executed three documents. The first was a memorandum of transfer of her interest in the property to her brother, Mr Corin. The transfer was stated as being subject to a mortgage to the State Bank of New South Wales, which held the relevant certificate of title. The second document was a trust deed by which Mr Corin declared that he held the interest transferred to himself by Mrs Patton on trust for her. The third document was a will by which Mrs Patton left her estate to her children in equal shares. At the time of her death the transfer to Mr Corin had not been registered, nor had any steps been taken to have the State Bank produce the certificate of title to enable the transfer to be registered.

Issue: The issue before the High Court was whether Mrs Patton had assigned, either at law or in equity, her interest in the property to Mr Corin before she died. If she had, the joint tenancy with Mr Patton would have been severed with the consequence that Mrs Patton's interest in the property would have passed to her children in accordance with the terms of her will. If Mrs Patton had not assigned her interest in the property before her death, the joint tenancy would not have been severed and Mr Patton would become the sole owner of the property in accordance with the principle of survivorship.

Decision: The High Court (Mason CJ, Brennan, Deane, Toohey and McHugh JJ) unanimously ruled that there had been no assignment, that the joint tenancy had not been severed, and that Mr Patton became the sole owner of the property upon the death of his wife.

In coming to that conclusion it was clear that there had not been a legal assignment of the property to Mr Corin because the transfer had not been registered in accordance with the requirements of s 41 of the *Real Property Act 1900* (NSW). Furthermore, the court held that there had been no assignment in equity. Because no effort had been made to produce the certificate of title to enable registration of the transfer, there had been no equitable assignment on any of the three views set out in *Anning v Anning* as to the meaning of the principle in *Milroy v Lord* in relation to what was required to be done by an assignor to effect an equitable assignment of property in circumstances similar to this case. The most liberal view, that of Griffith CJ, would have required production of the title documents, because that was an act that only Mrs Patton, as assignor, could have compelled the State Bank to perform. Although it was not necessary, strictly speaking, for the court to express a considered position about which of the three views in *Anning v Anning* was correct, a majority of the court (Mason CJ, McHugh and Deane JJ) endorsed the stance of Griffith CJ.

Extracts: The extracts from the joint judgment of Mason CJ and McHugh J and the judgment of Deane J outline the basis upon which the views of Griffith CJ in *Anning v Anning* were to be preferred and why there was no assignment in equity on the facts of this case.

Mason CJ and McHugh J

[549] [In *Milroy v Lord*] Turner LJ stated:

> I take the law of this Court to be well settled, that, in order to render a voluntary settlement valid and effectual, the settler [sic] must have done everything which, according to the nature of the property comprised in the settlement, was necessary to be done in order to transfer the property and render the settlement binding upon him. He may of course do this by actually transferring the property to the person for whom he intends to provide, and the provision will then be effectual, and it will be equally effectual if he transfers the property to a trustee for the purposes of the settlement, or declares that he himself holds it in trust for those purposes; ... but, in order to render the settlement binding, one or other of these modes must, as I understand the law of this Court, be resorted to, for there is no equity in this Court to perfect an imperfect gift. The cases I think go further to this extent, that if the settlement is intended to be effectuated by one of the modes to which I have referred, the Court will not give effect to it by applying another of those modes. If it is intended to take effect by transfer, the Court will not hold the intended transfer to operate as a [550] declaration of trust, for then every imperfect instrument would be made effectual by being converted into a perfect trust.[32] ...

Two propositions emerged from the observations of Turner LJ. First, the donor must have done everything necessary to be done, according to the nature of the property, in order to transfer the property and render the gift binding. Secondly, if the gift was intended to have been effectuated by one means, the court will not give effect to it by another means. However, as the later cases were to reveal, there was an element of uncertainty in the first proposition. Did it require that the donor must have done himself all that was necessary to be done in order to transfer the property or did he only have to do all that was necessary to be done by *him* in order to achieve that result?

This question clearly emerged for the first time in *Anning v Anning* ... [In that case] each member of the Court had a different understanding of the principle to be applied.

Griffith CJ said:

> I think that the words 'necessary to be done', as used by Turner LJ in *Milroy v Lord*, mean necessary to be done by the donor ... If, however, anything remains to be done by the donor, in the absence of which the donee cannot establish his title to the property as against a third person, the gift is imperfect, and in the absence of consideration the Court will not aid the donee as against the donor. But, if all that remains to be done can be done by the donee himself, so that he does [551] not need the assistance of the Court, the gift is, I think, complete.[33]

Isaacs J took a stricter view of the matter. His Honour said:

> If the legal title is assignable at law it must be so assigned or equity will not enforce the gift. If for any reason, whether want of a deed by the assignor, or a specifically prescribed method of transfer, or registration, or statutory notice, the transfer of the

---

32. *Milroy v Lord* (1862) 45 ER 1185 at 1189–90.
33. *Anning v Anning* (1907) 4 CLR 1049 at 1057.

legal title is incomplete when the law permits it to be complete, equity regards the gift as still imperfect and will not enforce it. In such a case, the fact that the assignor has done all that he can be required to do is not applicable.[34]

Higgins J appeared to adopt an intermediate position. His Honour stated that the word 'necessary' refers to the nature of the property, not to any obligation upon the donor, and went on to say:

What the Courts look at is what the donor *might* have done. This point has been put so fully in the judgment of Mr Justice Isaacs that I need not deal with it further.[35]

Despite the reference to the judgment of Isaacs J, it seems that Higgins J would have been prepared to recognize in equity a gift which the donor could have done no more to perfect, for example, a gift incomplete simply because the transfer, lodged for registration, remained unregistered, the donor having done all that he could do. Isaacs J would not have recognized such a gift because the transfer of the legal title was incomplete ...

[556] The view of Higgins J, to the extent that it differs from that of Isaacs J, has not found support in the later cases. Moreover, the difficulties which would be presented by an inquiry into what was within the power of the donor to achieve in a particular case constitute a sufficient reason for discarding his Honour's view.

The stricter approach of Isaacs J is consistent with the historic attitude of equity in developing rules applicable to intended gifts where no means of effecting a transfer at law were available.[36] There is also perhaps a conceptual difficulty in accepting, in accordance with the broader view, that a donor has done everything necessary to be done by him to complete a legal transfer in a case where the donor could in fact have procured a legal transfer, for example by seeing to registration personally. And, as we have already noted, Isaacs J's view conforms to the notion, underpinned by the two equitable maxims, that equity will not assist a volunteer to perfect a title which is incomplete. Equity's refusal may be justified on the footing that the donor should be at liberty to recall his gift at any time before it is complete.

Although Griffith CJ did not expressly advert in *Anning v Anning* to the maxim that equity will not assist a volunteer, the divergent approaches adopted by Griffith CJ and Isaacs J in that case may be taken to imply different understandings of the maxim. Isaacs J considered that equity [557] would pay no regard at all to voluntary transactions which were insufficient to create proprietary or contractual rights at law. Thus, equity would not heed the volunteer's plea for recognition of his interest. On the other hand, Griffith CJ must be taken to have regarded the maxim as an injunction against equity making its remedies available to perfect an imperfect gift. On this footing the recognition of the volunteer's interest did not amount to the provision of assistance in violation of the maxim.

Of course it would be a mistake to set too much store by the maxim. Like other maxims of equity, it is not a specific rule or principle of law. It is a summary statement of a broad theme which underlies equitable concepts and principles. Its precise scope is necessarily

---

34. *Anning v Anning* (1907) 4 CLR 1049 at 1069.
35. *Anning v Anning* (1907) 4 CLR 1049 at 1082.
36. See *William Brandt's Sons & Co v Dunlop Rubber Co* [1905] AC 454 at 461–2.

ill-defined and somewhat uncertain. It is subject to certain clearly established exceptions such as the rule in *Strong v Bird*[37] and the doctrine of equitable estoppel, where an equity arises in favour of an intended donee from the conduct of the donor after the making of the voluntary promise by the donor. These exceptions have no bearing on the present case except in so far as they demonstrate that the maxim does not enunciate an inflexible or universal rule. What is of importance is that this and the related maxim that equity will not perfect an imperfect gift are primarily associated with the rule that a voluntary covenant is not enforceable in equity, a rule which itself has become the subject of critical scrutiny in some of its applications.[38] Thus, a volunteer who is the object of an intended trust will only succeed if the trust has been completely constituted. This means, so it is said, that the trust must be constituted by a present declaration of trust or by a transfer by the settlor of the legal title to the intended trustee. And that brings us back to the statement of principle by Turner LJ in *Milroy v Lord*.

But there is a distinction between the enforcement of a voluntary covenant to create a trust and the enforcement of a transfer by way of intended gift when the donor has done all that was within his power to vest title to the property in trustees for the donee or in the donee. In the first case, equity will not compel specific performance of the voluntary covenants, there being no completely constituted trust; in the second case, as the transaction is complete as far as the donor is concerned, no question of withholding specific performance can arise and equity will hold the donor to the completed [558] transaction on the footing that title has been divested.[39] The point is, as Page Wood V-C noted in *Donaldson v Donaldson*, that where there is an imperfect gift 'which requires some other act to complete it on the part of the assignor or donor, the Court will not interfere *to require anything else to be done by him*' (our emphasis).[40]

These specific statements, which necessarily circumscribe the area of operation of the equitable maxims, were apt to apply to those situations in which legal title passed not on the delivery of an executed conveyance or transfer of property but subsequently on registration of a transfer, as is the case with stocks and shares in companies. The statements are equally apt to apply to the transfer of estates in land under the Torrens system.

The rationale for refusing to complete an incomplete gift is that a donor should not be compelled to make a gift, the decision to give being a personal one for the donor to make. However, that rationale cannot justify continued refusal to recognize any interest in the donee after the point when the donor has done all that is necessary to be done on his part to complete the gift, especially when the instrument of transfer has been delivered to the donee. Just as a manifestation of intention plus sufficient acts of delivery are enough to complete a gift of chattels at common law, so should the doing of all necessary acts by the donor be sufficient to complete a gift in equity. The need for compliance with subsequent procedures such as registration, procedures which the donee is able to satisfy,

---

37. *Strong v Bird* (1874) LR 18 Eq 315.
38. See M R T Macnair, 'Equity and Volunteers' (1988) 8 *Legal Studies* 172.
39. See *Ellison v Ellison* (1802) 31 ER 1243 at 1246; *Ex parte Pye* (1811) 34 ER 271 at 274, where Lord Eldon LC observed 'if the act is completed, though voluntary, the Court will act upon it'; *Fletcher v Fletcher* (1844) 67 ER 564 at 567, where, in the words of Wigram V-C, the covenant being 'complete', the court was 'not called upon to do any act to perfect it'.
40. *Donaldson v Donaldson* (1854) 69 ER 303 at 306.

should not permit the donor to resile from the gift. Once the transaction is complete so far as the donor is concerned, he has no locus poenitentiae. Viewed in this light, Griffith CJ's approach has the advantage that it gives effect to the clear intention and actions of the donor rather than insisting upon strict compliance with legal forms. It is a reflection of the maxim 'equity looks to the intent rather than the form'. By avoiding unnecessarily rigid adherence to the general rule and endeavouring to give effect to the donor's intention, the law avoids unjust and arbitrary results.

[559] In any event there is stronger support in the later cases for the view of Griffith CJ than that of Isaacs J ... Accordingly, we conclude it is desirable to state that the principle is that, if an intending donor of property has done everything which it is necessary for him to have done to effect a transfer of legal title, then equity will recognize the gift. So long as the donee has been equipped to achieve the transfer of legal ownership, the gift is complete in equity. 'Necessary' used in this sense means necessary to effect a transfer. From the viewpoint of the intending donor, the question is whether what he has done is sufficient to enable the legal transfer to be effected without further action on his part.

Although Griffith CJ did not explicitly say so, his proposition implicitly recognizes that the donee acquires an equitable estate or interest in the subject matter of the gift once the transaction is complete so far as the donor is concerned. So much was acknowledged by the English Court of Appeal in *In re Rose*. There the Court concluded that the donor had executed and delivered transfers and share certificates to the donee with the intention of transferring title to the shares to him and had placed him in a position to secure the legal title to the shares by registration subject to an exercise by the directors of their discretion to register the transfers. In this situation the donor could not recall the gift or invoke the aid of the court to prevent registration. The Court held that the donor had parted with his beneficial interest and had become a constructive trustee for the donee. This conclusion did not affect the second proposition in Turner LJ's judgment in *Milroy v Lord*. As Evershed MR stated:

> ... if a document is apt and proper to transfer the property — is in truth the appropriate way in which the property must be transferred — then it does not seem to me to follow from the statement of Turner LJ that, as a result, either during some limited period or otherwise, a trust may not arise, for the purpose of giving effect to the transfer.[41] ...

[560] [I]f we accept that *In re Rose* correctly states the consequences of the approach taken by Griffith CJ in *Anning v Anning*, there remains the problem of accommodating that approach to the injunction contained in s 41 of the *Real Property Act* [NSW] to the effect that, until registration, an instrument of transfer shall be ineffectual to pass an estate or interest in the land. Although that injunction applies to equitable as well as legal estates, it 'does not touch whatever rights are behind' the instrument.[42] ... Where a donor, with the intention of making a gift, delivers to the donee an instrument of transfer in registrable form with the certificate of title so as to enable him to obtain registration, an equity arises, not from the transfer itself, but from the execution and delivery of the transfer and the delivery of the certificate of title in such circumstances as will enable

---

41. *In re Rose* [1952] Ch 499 at 510.
42. *Barry v Heider* (1914) 19 CLR 197 at 216; *Chan v Cresdon Pty Ltd* (1989) 168 CLR 242 at 256–8.

the donee to procure the vesting of the legal title in himself. Accordingly, s 41 does not prevent the passing of an equitable estate to the donee under a completed transaction.

The question is then whether Mrs Patton did all that it was necessary for her to do in order to effect a transfer. Two obstacles are suggested to completion of the gift. First, the certificate of title remained throughout with the mortgagee and Mrs Patton took no steps to arrange for its production for the purposes of registration. Secondly, it is not clear whether or not [the solicitor] held the executed transfer on Mrs Patton's instructions or those of Mr Corin.

Whether or not it is correct to say that the production of a certificate of title is 'necessary' to achieve registration of a transfer of Torrens system land, it is apparent that a gift of such land cannot be regarded as complete in equity while the donor retains possession or control of the certificate of title.[43] That is because it can scarcely be said that the donor has done everything necessary to be done by him if he has retained the certificate of title, by virtue of the possession of which the gift might well be thwarted.

In the present case Mrs Patton gave no authority for the [561] mortgagee bank to hand the certificate of title to Mr Corin for the purposes of registration. At least, if she authorized [the solicitor] to obtain the certificate, there is no clear evidence to that effect ...

Accordingly, the transactions failed to pass the equitable property in the land to Mr Corin ... Further, because the gift was incomplete, Mrs Patton could have recalled the transfer at any time. But it is not strictly relevant to ask whether or not Mrs Patton could have recalled the gift; that is not a criterion but rather a result of the efficacy or otherwise of the gift ...

[I]t should be observed that the instrument of transfer cannot take effect in equity as a declaration of trust. Mrs Patton clearly did not intend to constitute herself trustee for Mr Corin and the terms of the instrument provide no support for such an interpretation.

Deane J

[582] In my view ... the test for determining whether the stage has been reached when a gift of *Real Property Act* land under an unregistered memorandum of transfer is complete and effective in equity ... is a twofold one. It is whether the donor has done all that is necessary to place the vesting of the legal title within the control of the donee and beyond the recall or intervention of the donor. Once that stage is reached and the gift is complete and effective in equity, the equitable interest in the land vests in the donee and, that being so, the donor is bound in conscience to hold the property as trustee for the donee pending the vesting of the legal title. In that regard, it is not a matter of equity ignoring the provisions of s 41 of the Act and treating the unregistered transfer as effective of itself to assign the beneficial interest in the land. It is simply that equity, acting upon the 'fact or circumstance' that the donor has placed the vesting of the legal title within the control of the donee and beyond the donor's recall or intervention, looks at the substantial effect of [583] what has been done and regards the gift as complete.[44]

---

43. Dixon J in *Brunker v Perpetual Trustee Co Ltd* (1937) 57 CLR 555 at 600–5; *Scoones v Galvin and the Public Trustee* [1934] NZLR 1004.
44. *Olsen v Dyson* (1969) 120 CLR 365 at 375–6.

In the present case, the fact that Mrs Patton had taken no step to enable Mr Corin to procure the production of the duplicate certificate of title which was held by the bank meant that she had not done all that was necessary to place the vesting of the common law title within Mr Corin's control ... It is true that there was a theoretical possibility that the Registrar-General would register the transfer without production of the certificate of title. The plain fact remains, however, that registration of the transfer and vesting of the legal title could not be said to be within Mr Corin's control for so long as he was not entitled to procure production of the document of title. In any event, it is apparent that it remained in Mrs Patton's power to intervene to prevent the vesting of any legal interest in him. In circumstances where Mr Corin's only involvement was as a bare trustee for Mrs Patton, she was entitled to terminate the trust at any time and demand the return of the unregistered transfer. It was submitted on behalf of the appellants that Mrs Patton's position as beneficiary under the deed of trust should be disregarded. Her role as donor should not, it was said, be confused with any other role. The answer to that submission is that, in so far as equity is concerned, Mrs Patton's role as prospective transferor and prospective beneficiary were inextricably connected. All that Mrs Patton intended to confer and conferred upon Mr Corin was the limited entitlement of a bare trustee. It was the limited content of that entitlement that resulted in the situation where, for so long as the memorandum of transfer remained unregistered, Mrs Patton could recall the document and prevent the vesting of any legal title to the land in him.[45]

Comments

1. See Radan & Stewart at **5.99–5.110**.
2. For a discussion of this case see K Bell, 'Corin v Patton: Solving the Riddle of the Perfect Gift' (1990) 6 *Queensland University of Technology Law Journal* 126.

---

45. See *Brunker v Perpetual Trustee Co Ltd* (1937) 57 CLR 555 at 602–3, and cf *Cope v Keene* (1968) 118 CLR 1 at 12–13; *McNab v Earle* [1981] 2 NSWLR 673 at 677.

6

DISPOSITIONS OF EQUITABLE INTERESTS AND THE REQUIREMENT OF WRITING

Introduction

6.1   This chapter primarily deals with the disposition of equitable interests in personal property and the extent to which such dispositions need to be evidenced in writing. All Australian jurisdictions have legislation imposing a writing requirement on the disposition of subsisting equitable interests in property.[1]

The extracts in this chapter discuss the following:

- dispositions of equitable interests in personal property by means of a direction to a trustee: *Grey v Inland Revenue Commissioners* [1960] AC 1; *Vandervell v Inland Revenue Commissioners* [1967] 2 AC 291; and
- dispositions of equitable interests in personal property by oral agreement: *Oughtred v Inland Revenue Commissioners* [1960] AC 206.

Dispositions of equitable interests in personal property by direction to a trustee

6.2   Grey v Inland Revenue Commissioners [1960] AC 1

Court: House of Lords

Facts: Hunter was the beneficiary under a bare trust of 18,000 shares. Grey and Randolph were the trustees (the Trustees). On 18 February 1955 Hunter orally and irrevocably directed the Trustees to hold those shares on various trusts for Hunter's grandchildren with the intention that such direction should result in Hunter ceasing to have any equitable interest in the shares. One week later, Hunter executed various declarations of trust confirming the effect of the oral direction given to the Trustees. Stamp duty was payable on these documents.

---

1.   *Civil Law (Property) Act 2006* (ACT) s 201(3); *Conveyancing Act 1919* (NSW) s 23C(1)(c); *Law of Property Act 2000* (NT) s 10(1)(c); *Property Law Act 1974* (Qld) s 11(1)(c); *Law of Property Act 1936* (SA) s 29(1)(c); *Conveyancing and Law of Property Act 1884* (Tas) s 60(2)(c); *Property Law Act 1958* (Vic) s 53(1)(c); *Property Law Act 1969* (WA) s 34(1)(c).

The IRC assessed the documents as being liable to stamp duty based upon the value of the shares (*ad valorem* duty). They argued that the executed declarations of trust, and not Hunter's earlier oral direction, effected the disposition of the equitable interest in the shares. The Trustees contested this assessment on the basis that the earlier oral direction was effective to dispose of the equitable interest in the shares and that the later written declarations merely confirmed what had taken place earlier. On this basis, the Trustees argued that the later written declarations did not effect the disposition of the equitable interest in the shares and were thus only liable to nominal stamp duty. The Trustees' argument could only succeed if the oral direction to them was *not* a disposition within the meaning of s 53C(1)(c) of the *Law of Property Act 1925* (UK), which stipulated that 'a disposition of an equitable interest or trust subsisting at the time of the disposition, must be in writing signed by the person disposing of the same, or by his agent thereunto lawfully authorised in writing or by will'.

Issue: The issue before the House of Lords was whether Hunter's oral direction to the Trustees was a disposition within 53C(1)(c) of the *Law of Property Act 1925* (UK). If it was, it was ineffective with the consequence that the later written declarations of trust were liable to be assessed for stamp duty on an *ad valorem* basis.

Decision: The House of Lords (Viscount Simonds, Lords Radcliffe, Cohen and Keith of Avonholm) upheld the IRC's claim that the written declarations of trust were assessable for stamp duty on an *ad valorem* basis because s 53C(1)(c) rendered ineffective Hunter's oral direction to the Trustees. The oral direction did not constitute an effective disposition of the equitable interest to Hunter's grandchildren.

Extracts: The extracts from the speeches of Viscount Simonds and Lord Radcliffe discuss the meaning of disposition in s 53C(1)(c).[2]

Viscount Simonds

[12] If the word 'disposition' is given its natural meaning, it cannot, I think, be denied that a direction given by Mr Hunter, whereby the beneficial interest in the shares theretofore vested [13] in him became vested in another or others, is a disposition. But it is contended by the [Trustees] that the word 'disposition' is to be given a narrower meaning and (so far as relates to inter vivos transactions) be read as if it were synonymous with 'grants and assignments' and that, given this meaning, it does not cover such a direction as was given in this case. As I am clearly of the opinion, which I understand to be shared by your Lordships, that there is no justification for giving the word 'disposition' a narrower meaning than it ordinarily bears, it will be unnecessary to discuss the interesting problem that would otherwise arise. It was for this reason that your Lordships did not think it necessary to hear learned counsel for the [Trustees] in reply on this part of the case.

---

2. The Australian equivalents of s 53(1)(c) are: *Civil Law (Property) Act 2006* (ACT) s 201(3); *Conveyancing Act 1919* (NSW) s 23C(1)(c); *Law of Property Act 2000* (NT) s 10(1)(c); *Property Law Act 1974* (Qld) s 11(1)(c); *Law of Property Act 1936* (SA) s 29(1)(c); *Conveyancing and Law of Property Act 1884* (Tas) s 60(2)(c); *Property Law Act 1958* (Vic) s 53(1)(c); *Property Law Act 1969* (WA) s 34(1)(c).

Lord Radcliffe

[15] My Lords, if there is nothing more in this appeal than the short question whether the oral direction that Mr Hunter gave to his trustees on February 18, 1955, amounted in any ordinary sense of the words to a 'disposition of an equitable interest or trust subsisting at the time of the disposition', I do not feel any doubt as to my answer. I think that it did. Whether we describe what happened in technical or in more general terms the full equitable interest in the 18,000 shares concerned, which at that time was his, was (subject to any statutory invalidity) diverted by his direction from his ownership into the beneficial ownership of the various equitable owners, present and future, entitled under his six existing settlements.

But that is not the question which has led to difference of opinion in the courts below. Where opinions have differed is on the point whether his direction was a 'disposition' within the [16] meaning of section 53(1)(c) of the Law of Property Act, 1925, the argument for giving it a more restricted meaning in that context being that section 53 is to be construed as no more than a consolidation of three sections of the Statute of Frauds, sections 3, 7 and 9. So treated, 'disposition', it is said, is merely the equivalent of the former words of section 9, 'grants and assignments', except that testamentary disposition has to be covered as well, and a direction to a trustee by the equitable owner of the property prescribing new trusts upon which it is to be held is a declaration of trust but not a grant or assignment. The argument, concludes, therefore, that neither before January 1, 1926, nor since did such a direction require to be in writing signed by the disponor or his agent in order to be effective.

In my opinion, it is a very nice question whether a parol declaration of trust of this kind was or was not within the mischief of section 9 of the Statute of Frauds. The point has never, I believe, been decided and perhaps it never will be. Certainly it was long established as law that while a declaration of trust respecting land or any interest therein required writing to be effective, a declaration of trust respecting personalty did not. Moreover, there is warrant for saying that a direction to his trustee by the equitable owner of trust property prescribing new trusts of that property was a declaration of trust. But it does not necessarily follow from that that such a direction, if the effect of it was to determine completely or pro tanto the subsisting equitable interest of the maker of the direction, was not also a grant or assignment for the purposes of section 9 and therefore required writing for its validity. Something had to happen to that equitable interest in order to displace it in favour of the new interests created by the direction: and it would be at any rate logical to treat the direction as being an assignment of the subsisting interest to the new beneficiary or beneficiaries or, in other cases, a release or surrender of it to the trustee.

I do not think, however, that that question has to be answered for the purposes of this appeal. It can only be relevant if section 53(1)(c) of the Law of Property Act, 1925, is treated as a true consolidation of the three sections of the Statute of Frauds concerned ...

[17] I think that there is no direct link between section 53(1)(c) of the Act of 1925 and section 9 of the Statute of Frauds. The link was broken by the changes introduced by the amending Act of 1924, and it was those changes, not the original statute, that section 53 must be taken as consolidating. If so, it is inadmissible to allow the construction of

the word 'disposition' in the new Act to be limited or controlled by any meaning [18] attributed to the words 'grant' or 'assignment' in section 9 of the old Act.

Comments

1. See Radan & Stewart at **6.16–6.20**.

2. For a contextual analysis of this case see B Green, 'Grey, Oughtred and Vandervell – A Contextual Reappraisal' (1984) 47 *Modern Law Review* 385, at 388–395.

6.3   Vandervell v Inland Revenue Commissioners [1967] 2 AC 291

Court: House of Lords

Facts: The National Provincial Bank was a bare trustee of shares for Vandervell. Vandervell orally directed the bank to transfer the shares to the Royal College of Surgeons. His intention was that the college acquire both the legal and equitable interest in the shares. Pursuant to relevant income tax legislation, the IRC assessed Vandervell as being liable for a surtax on the dividends earned by the shares. A provision of the income tax legislation stipulated that if Vandervell had 'divested himself absolutely' of his interest in the shares, the surtax was not payable. Vandervell argued that his oral direction to the Bank meant that he had so divested himself of his shares. The IRC also argued that Vandervell had not disposed of his equitable interest in the shares in accordance with the requirements of s 53C(1)(c) of the *Law of Property Act 1925* (UK), which stipulated that 'a disposition of an equitable interest or trust subsisting at the time of the disposition, must be in writing signed by the person disposing of the same, or by his agent thereunto lawfully authorised in writing or by will'.

Issues: The issues before the House of Lords were whether Vandervell's oral direction fell within the provision in the income tax legislation that meant that no surtax was payable, and whether the oral declaration was a disposition within the scope of s 53C(1)(c).

Decision: The House of Lords (Lords Reid, Pearce, Upjohn, Donovan and Wilberforce) unanimously held that Vandervell's oral direction was not a disposition caught by s 53C(1)(c). However, a majority of their Lordships (Lords Pearce, Upjohn and Wilberforce; Lords Reid and Donovan dissenting) held that Vandervell's oral direction did not mean that Vandervell had 'divested himself absolutely' of his interest in the shares in accordance with the requirements of the income tax legislation. As a result, Vandervell was held liable to pay the surtax.

Extracts: The extracts from the speeches of Lords Upjohn, Donovan and Wilberforce discuss the reasons why an oral direction to a trustee to transfer the legal and equitable interest in personalty is not a disposition within s 53C(1)(c).[3]

---

3.   The Australian equivalents of s 53(1)(c) are set out in note 1 above.

Lord Upjohn

[310] The question is whether notwithstanding the plainly expressed intention of the [Vandervell] ... the absence of writing prevented any equitable or beneficial interest in the shares passing to the college so that contrary to his wishes and understanding they remained bare trustees for him. This depends entirely upon the true construction of section 53(1)(c) of the Law of Property Act, 1925, which the Crown maintain makes writing necessary to pass the beneficial interest. This section was generally thought to re-enact section 9 of the Statute of Frauds and that section had never been applied to a trust of an equitable interest of pure personalty. Before the cases of *Grey v Inland Revenue Commissioners*[4] *and Oughtred v Inland Revenue Commissioners*,[5] both in your Lordships' House, this argument would have been quite untenable.

[311] It was shown in those cases that the Law of Property Act, 1925, was not re-enacting section 9 but that it had been amended by the Law of Property Act, 1924. The relevant words of section 53 are:

' ... a disposition of an equitable interest or trust subsisting at the time of the disposition, must be in writing signed by the person disposing of the same ...'

Those words were applied in *Grey* and *Oughtred* to cases where the legal estate remained outstanding in a trustee and the beneficial owner was dealing and dealing only with the equitable estate. That is understandable; the object of the section, as was the object of the old Statute of Frauds, is to prevent hidden oral transactions in equitable interests in fraud of those truly entitled, and making it difficult, if not impossible, for the trustees to ascertain who are in truth his beneficiaries. But when the beneficial owner owns the whole beneficial estate and is in a position to give directions to his bare trustee with regard to the legal as well as the equitable estate there can be no possible ground for invoking the section where the beneficial owner wants to deal with the legal estate as well as the equitable estate ...

[I]f the intention of the beneficial owner in directing the trustee to transfer the legal estate to X is that X should be the beneficial owner I can see no reason for any further document or further words in the document assigning the legal estate also expressly transferring the beneficial interest; the greater includes the less. X may be wise to secure some evidence that the beneficial owner intended him to take the beneficial interest in case his beneficial title is challenged at a later date but it certainly cannot, in my opinion, be a statutory requirement that to effect its passing there must be some writing under section 53(1)(c).

Counsel for the Crown admitted that where the legal and beneficial estate was vested in the legal owner and he desired to transfer the whole legal and beneficial estate to another he did not have to do more than transfer the legal estate and he did not have to comply with section 53(1)(c); and I can see no relevant difference between that case and this.

[312] As I have said, that section is ... directed to cases where dealings with the equitable estate are divorced from the legal estate and I do not think any of their Lordships in *Grey*

---

4. [1960] AC 1.
5. [1960] AC 206.

and *Oughtred* had in mind the case before your Lordships. To hold the contrary would make assignments unnecessarily complicated; if there had to be assignments in express terms of both legal and equitable interests that would make the section more productive of injustice than the supposed evils it was intended to prevent.

Lord Donovan

[317] My Lords, section 53(1)(*c*) of the Law of Property Act, 1925, ... clearly refers to the disposition of an equitable interest as such. If, owning the entire estate, legal and beneficial, in a piece of property, and desiring to transfer that entire estate to another, I do so by means of a disposition which ex facie deals only with the legal estate, it would be ridiculous to argue that section 53(1)(*c*) has not been complied with, and that therefore the legal estate alone has passed.

The present case, it is true, is different in its facts in that the legal and equitable estates in the shares were in separate ownership; but when Mr Vandervell, being competent to do so, instructed the bank to transfer the shares to the college, and made it abundantly clear that he wanted to pass, by means of that transfer, his own beneficial, or equitable, interest, plus the bank's legal interest, he achieved the same result as if there had been no separation of the interests. The transfer thus made pursuant to his intentions and instructions was a disposition not of the equitable [318] interest alone, but of the entire estate in the shares. In such a case I see no room for the operation of section 53(1)(*c*).

Lord Wilberforce

[329] There remains the alternative point taken by the Crown that in any event, by virtue of section 53(1)(*c*) of the Law of Property Act, 1925, [Vendervell] never effectively disposed of the beneficial interest in the shares to the Royal College of Surgeons. This argument I cannot accept. Section 53(1)(*c*) ... has recently received a new lease of life as an instrument in the hands of the Revenue. The subsection ... is certainly not easy to apply to the varied transactions in equitable interests which now occur. However, in this case no problem arises. The shares in question ... were, prior to November 14, 1958, registered in the name of the National Provincial Bank Ltd upon trust for [Vandervell] absolutely. On November 14, 1958, [Vandervell's] solicitor received from the bank a blank transfer of the shares, executed by the bank, and the share certificate. So at this stage [Vandervell] was the absolute master of the shares and only needed to insert his name as transferee in the transfer and to register it to become the full legal owner. He was also the owner in equity. On November 19, 1958, the solicitor ... on behalf [330] of Mr Vandervell, who intended to make a gift, handed the transfer to the college which, in due course, sealed it and obtained registration of the shares in the college's name. The case should then be regarded as one in which [Vandervell] himself has, with the intention to make a gift, put the college in a position to become the legal owner of the shares, which the college in fact became. If [Vandervell] had died before the college had obtained registration, it is clear on the principle of *In re Rose*[6] that the gift would have been complete, on the basis that he had done everything in his power to transfer the legal interest, with an intention to give, to the college. No separate transfer, therefore, of the equitable interest ever came to

---

6.   [1949] Ch 78.

or needed to be made and there is no room for the operation of the subsection. What the position would have been had there simply been an oral direction to the legal owner (viz the bank) to transfer the shares to the college, followed by such a transfer, but without any document in writing signed by Mr Vandervell as equitable owner, is not a matter which calls for consideration here. The Crown's argument on this point fails.

Comments

1. See Radan & Stewart at **6.21–6.26**.
2. Lord Wilberforce's comment, at 330, that, if Vandervell had died before his direction to the trustee had been carried out, the gift would nevertheless have been valid, was rejected in *Parker & Parker v Ledsham* [1988] WAR 32 at 37, where Rowland J held that in such circumstances the direction to the trustee would be revoked by the death of the person making the direction.
3. For a contextual analysis of this case see B Green, 'Grey, Oughtred and Vandervell – A Contextual Reappraisal' (1984) 47 *Modern Law Review* 385, at 404–13.

Dispositions of equitable interests in personal property by oral agreement

---

6.4   Oughtred v Inland Revenue Commissioners [1960] AC 206

Court: House of Lords

Facts: Mrs Oughtred held a beneficial life estate in certain shares. Her son Peter held the equitable reversionary interest in those shares. Mrs Oughtred was also the absolute owner of a number of other shares in the same company. By an oral agreement of 18 June 1956 Mrs Oughtred and her son agreed that on 26 June 1956 she would transfer to him the shares in the company that she owned absolutely and in return Peter would surrender to her his equitable reversionary interest in the shares in which Mrs Oughtred had an equitable life estate, thereby making her the absolute beneficial owner of those shares.

On 26 June 1956 three documents were executed to effectuate the earlier oral agreement. The first document was a deed of release which noted that the shares formerly held by trustees on trust for Mrs Oughtred for life with an equitable reversionary interest to Peter, were now held on trust for Mrs Oughtred absolutely and that it was intended to transfer legal title to her whereupon the trustees would be released from their trusteeship. The second document transferred to Peter, for nominal consideration, the shares that Mrs Oughtred formerly owned absolutely. The third document was a transfer, for nominal consideration, of the legal title to the shares referred to in the first document from the trustees to Mrs Oughtred. The third document was assessed by the IRC as liable for the payment of *ad valorem* stamp duty on the basis that the earlier oral contract was ineffectual in transferring Peter's equitable reversionary interest to Mrs Oughtred because such a transaction had to be in writing as a disposition within the meaning of s 53(1)(c) of the *Law of Property Act 1925* (UK). The IRC argued that it was the third document which effected the disposition in favour of Mrs Oughtred and was therefore liable to *ad valorem* stamp duty. Mrs Oughtred claimed that only nominal duty was payable because the oral agreement created a constructive trust for which writing was not required pursuant to s 53(2) of the Act. This stipulated that the writing requirement set out in s 53(1)(c) does not affect the creation and operation of resulting, implied or constructive trusts. If this argument was correct, the later written instrument did not effect a disposition and was therefore liable only for nominal stamp duty.

Issue: The issue before the House of Lords was whether the oral agreement of 18 June 1956 was ineffective as a disposition because it was not in writing as required by s 53(1)(c) of the *Law of Property Act 1925* (UK), or whether the oral agreement gave rise to a constructive trust, in which case the later documentation attracted only nominal stamp duty.

Decision: The majority of the House of Lords (Lords Keith of Avonholm, Denning and Jenkins; Lords Radcliffe and Cohen dissenting) found in favour of the IRC, with the result that *ad valorem* stamp duty was payable on the relevant written documentation executed on 26 June 1956. For the majority, Lords Keith of Avonholm and Jenkins took the view that *ad valorem* stamp duty was payable because the transfer from the trustees to Mrs Oughtred related to a dealing in property and as such attracted *ad valorem* stamp duty under the relevant stamp duty legislation. This approach made it unnecessary for their Lordships to determine whether or not s 53(1)(c) or s 53(2) applied. However, they suggested that, even if the earlier oral agreement had created a constructive trust, the later transfer to Mrs Oughtred from the trustees would have conferred upon her rights superior to those gained on the creation of the constructive trust. In such circumstances, the transfer would be dutiable at *ad valorem* rates under the stamp duty legislation. Lord Denning took the view that even if the oral agreement of 18 June 1956 had effectively disposed of Peter's equitable reversionary interest to his mother, the subsequent transfer from the trustees to Mrs Oughtred attracted *ad valorem* stamp duty. However, Lord Denning was also of the view that the oral agreement was ineffective to dispose of Peter's equitable reversionary interest because of the requirement of writing in s 53(1)(c). In his Lordship's view s 53(2) did not dispense with that requirement.

For the minority, Lord Radcliffe accepted the view that the oral agreement of 18 June 1956 gave rise to a constructive trust and that the disposition was effected by the oral agreement. In such a situation s 53(2) dispensed with the need for writing. The transfer from the trustees to Mrs Oughtred of 26 June 1956 did not dispose of Peter's reversionary interest and accordingly was only liable to nominal stamp duty. Lord Cohen accepted the view that Peter became constructive trustee of his equitable reversionary interest as a result of the oral agreement of 18 June 1956. He also conceded that if the transfer from the trustees to Mrs Oughtred of 26 June 1956 had transferred an equitable interest in the shares to Mrs Oughtred it would have been liable to *ad valorem* stamp duty. However, he took the view that the documentation did not do this. Mrs Oughtred was absolutely entitled to the shares as at 26 June 1956, not because the documentation of 26 June 1956 had transferred an equitable interest to her, but because Peter, having become constructive trustee of his equitable reversionary interest by virtue of the earlier oral agreement, could not have disputed Mrs Oughtred's title to the shares. Accordingly, no *ad valorem* stamp duty was payable.

Extracts: The extracts from the speech of Lord Radcliffe explain why s 53(2)[7] and not s 53(1)(c)[8] applied to the facts of this case. Although his Lordship dissented in this case, as is detailed in the Comments below, his views were adopted and followed in later cases.

Lord Radcliffe

[227] [T]he law with regard to liability to stamp duty is clear enough. The duty is charged on instruments, if they exist and come within any of the categories prescribed by the Act. It is not charged on transactions. Thus property such as chattels, which by law pass on delivery, can be transferred from one owner to another without attracting duty. Again, though an agreement for sale may be chargeable ad valorem, since the Act has so required, an oral agreement for the sale of property involves no charge to duty because no instrument is brought into existence to effect or to record it. The whole point of the present appeal seems to me to turn on the question whether it is open to a court of law to deduce from the documents of this case that Mrs Oughtred's title to her son's equitable reversionary interest rested upon anything more than the oral agreement which admittedly took place.

My Lords, on this short point my opinion is that such a deduction is not open to a court of law. The materials that would support it are simply not there ...

The reasoning of the whole matter, as I see it, is as follows: On June 18, 1956, the son owned an equitable reversionary interest in the settled shares: by his oral agreement of that date he created in his mother an equitable interest in his reversion, since the subject-matter of the agreement was property of which specific performance would normally be decreed by the court. He thus became a trustee for her of that interest sub modo: having regard to subsection (2) of section 53 of the Law of Property Act, 1925, subsection (1) of that section did not operate to prevent that trusteeship arising by operation of law. On June 26 Mrs Oughtred transferred to her son the shares which were the consideration for her acquisition of his equitable interest: upon this transfer he became in a full sense and without more the trustee [228] of his interest for her. She was the effective owner of all outstanding equitable interests. It was thus correct to recite in the deed of release to the trustees of the settlement, which was to wind up their trust, that the trust fund was by then held on trust for her absolutely. There was, in fact, no equity to the shares that could be asserted against her, and it was open to her, if she so wished, to let the matter rest without calling for a written assignment from her son. Given that the trustees were apprised of the making of the oral agreement and of Mrs Oughtred's satisfaction of the consideration to be given by her, the trustees had no more to do than to transfer their legal title to her or as she might direct. This and no more is what they did.

---

7. The Australian equivalents of s 53(2) are: *Civil Law (Property) Act 2006* (ACT) s 201(4)(a); *Conveyancing Act 1919* (NSW) s 23C(2); *Law of Property Act 2000* (NT) s 10(2); *Property Law Act 1974* (Qld) s 11(2); *Law of Property Act 1936* (SA) s 29(2); *Conveyancing and Law of Property Act 1884* (Tas) s 60(2); *Property Law Act 1958* (Vic) s 53(2); *Property Law Act 1969* (WA) s 34(2).
8. The Australian equivalents of s 53(1)(c) are set out in note 1 above.

It follows that, in my view, this transfer cannot be treated as a conveyance of the son's equitable reversion at all. The trustees had not got it: he never transferred or released it to them: how then could they convey it? With all respect to those who think otherwise, it is incorrect to say that the trustees' transfer was made either with his authority or at his direction. If the recital as to Mrs Oughtred's rights was correct, as I think that it was, he had no remaining authority to give or direction to issue. A release is, after all, the normal instrument for winding up a trust when all the equitable rights are vested and the legal estate is called for from the trustees who hold it. What the release gave the trustees from him was acquittance for the trust administration and accounts to date, and the fact that he gave it in consideration of the legal interest in the shares being vested in his mother adds nothing on this point. Nor does it, with respect, advance the matter to say, correctly, that at the end of the day Mrs Oughtred was the absolute owner of the shares, legal and equitable. I think that she was: but that is description, not analysis. The question that is relevant for the purpose of this appeal is how she came to occupy that position; a position which, under English law, could be reached by more than one road.

Lastly, I ought perhaps to say that I do not myself see any analogy between the operations embraced by the oral agreement and documents and the common case of a sale of shares by an owner for whom they are held by a nominee or bare trustee. What is sold there is the shares themselves, not the owner's equitable interest. What is passed by the transfer executed by his nominee is the shares, according to the contract, without any incumbrance on the title, equitable or legal. It is, I think, a misunderstanding of the law to speak of the nominee as transferring his beneficiary's previous equitable interest to the purchaser.

Comments

1. See Radan & Stewart at **6.27–6.39**.

2. Lord Radcliffe's views were adopted and followed by a unanimous Court of Appeal in England in *Neville v Wilson* [1997] Ch 144 at 158. *Neville v Wilson* has been accepted in Australia by Priestley JA (Mason P concurring) in the Court of Appeal in New South Wales in *Baloglow v Konstanidis* [2001] NSWCA 451 at [120]–[125], the Queensland Court of Appeal in *Reef & Rainforest Travel Pty Ltd v Commissioner of Stamp Duties* [2002] 1 Qd R 683 at 688, and by Heydon J in the High Court in *Halloran v Minister Administering National Parks and Wildlife Act 1974* (2006) 229 CLR 545 at 573–4.

3. For a contextual analysis of this case see B Green, 'Grey, Oughtred and Vandervell – A Contextual Reappraisal' (1984) 47 *Modern Law Review* 385, at 399–404. For a technical analysis of this case see D S K Ong, *Trusts Law in Australia*, 3rd ed, Federation Press, Sydney, 2007, pp 141–8.

7

PRIORITIES

Introduction

7.1 This chapter deals with the resolution of competing claims to the same property. These priority disputes are resolved by applying the relevant rules depending upon whether the interests are legal or equitable in nature, with the exception of Torrens title land, in which case the interests are either registered or unregistered.

The extracts in this chapter discuss the following:

- priority between competing equitable interests: *Moffett v Dillon* [1999] 2 VR 480;
- postponing conduct and priority between competing equitable interests: *Heid v Reliance Finance Corporation Pty Ltd* (1983) 154 CLR 326; *Walker v Linom* [1907] 2 Ch 104;
- the rule in *Dearle v Hall*: *In re Dallas* [1904] 2 Ch 385;
- priority between registered and unregistered interests in relation to Torrens title land: *Bahr v Nicolay (No 2)* (1988) 164 CLR 604;
- priority and *in personam* rights in relation to Torrens title land: *Vassos v State Bank of South Australia* [1993] 2 VR 316; and
- priority and the failure to lodge a caveat in relation to Torrens title land: *Person-to-Person Financial Services Pty Ltd v Sharari* [1984] 1 NSWLR 745; *Jacobs v Platt Nominees Pty Ltd* [1990] VR 147.

Competing equitable interests

7.2 Moffett v Dillon [1999] 2 VR 480

Court: Court of Appeal of Victoria

Facts: Dillon executed a charge over her Torrens title property in the Melbourne suburb of Essendon to secure a sum of money that she owed to Moffett. Moffett lodged a caveat on the title in relation to this charge. Subsequently, Dillon borrowed money from Westpac Bank and executed a mortgage over the Essendon property in favour of the bank as security for the loan. The bank wrote to Moffett's solicitors seeking his consent to the registration of the mortgage. The consent was not given. By mistake, the mortgage was registered. However, the dispute between the parties was litigated on the basis that the bank's mortgage had not been registered.

Issue: The issue before the Court of Appeal was whether Moffett's unregistered interest (the charge) had priority over the bank's unregistered mortgage.

Decision: The Court of Appeal (Brooking, Ormiston and Buchanan JJA) unanimously ruled in favour of Moffett because his interest was the first in time and there was no basis upon which that priority could be displaced in favour of the bank.

Extracts: The extracts from the judgments of Brooking JA (Buchanan JA agreeing) and Ormiston JA discuss the relevance of notice in the context of the rules as to priorities between competing equitable (unregistered in the case of Torrens title land) interests. The difference between the two judgments relates to whether notice of an earlier equitable interest forms a separate rule to the 'better equity' principle or whether notice is but one of the factors that goes to determining which interest holder has the 'better equity'.

Brooking JA

[485] It is conceded that at the time the bank took its mortgage it had full actual knowledge, not casually acquired, of the creation and continued existence of the charge. At least in the circumstances of the present case, this is fatal to the contention that the later equitable interest should prevail over the earlier. I know of no decision in which a later equity has been held to prevail where its holder acquired it with knowledge of the creation and continued existence of the earlier equity. I defer consideration of whether circumstances are conceivable in which that result [486] could be arrived at. One might ask rhetorically how it can be equitable to postpone the prior interest to one which was acquired by a person who knew that an interest already existed and chose to proceed with the transaction and acquire a competing interest which he would then contend defeated the pre-existing interest. Knowing that someone was already the holder of an equitable interest, he has chosen to acquire a rival one from a person who in the eye of equity is not entitled to create that interest.[1] He then comes before a court of equity claiming that the very conflict he has chosen to create should be resolved in his favour. What do the cases, and what does the principle, suggest the response of the court should be?

The authorities use language suggesting that a later equitable interest can never prevail over an earlier one where the holder of the later interest had at the time of its acquisition notice of the earlier interest. (I exclude the case where although there was notice of the coming into existence of the earlier interest the holder of the later interest had by the time of its acquisition a belief that the earlier interest no longer existed.) The rule is correctly stated in terms of 'notice' of the earlier interest. The present case is one of admitted actual and full knowledge. This is either to be regarded as actual notice or, according to the analysis of Pomeroy,[2] to be treated as having the same consequences as notice ...

[489] The best known doctrine of equity regarding the effect of notice on priorities concerns the bona fide purchaser for value of the legal estate. ... The rule applies whether the estate or interest taken by the purchaser is legal or equitable and whether the equity

---

1. *Phillips v Phillips* (1861) 45 ER 1164.
2. Pomeroy, *Equity Jurisprudence*, 5th ed, (1941), paras 591 et seq.

held by a third person in relation to the same subject matter does or does not amount to an equitable interest according to the distinction that has been drawn between 'mere equities' and equitable interests. The rule is illustrated, as regards the taking of an equitable interest with notice of a pre-existing one, by the early case of *Willoughby v Willoughby*.[3] There Lord Hardwicke LC said that it was against conscience that an equitable mortgagee who had taken with notice of a prior equitable interest should assert that his mortgage was entitled to priority ...

[492] I have said that there are two rules or principles at work in cases like the present, the rule that a person taking with notice an equity takes subject to it and the rule where the equities are equal the first in time prevails. As regards the second rule, I have referred to the wide view taken by Mason and Deane JJ in *Heid v Reliance Finance Corp Pty Ltd* that broad principles of right and justice will guide the court in determining whether the equities are equal.[4] As what I have already written should make plain, I do not regard the question whether a person who acquired an equity did so with notice of a prior equity as no more than a consideration to which regard is to be had in determining whether one of the equities is better than the other. I regard the rule about notice as a distinct and fundamental one and I do not consider that Mason and Deane JJ intended to question its existence or to subsume this particular matter of notice under a broad question so as to make it no more than a consideration bearing upon which was the better equity ...

[493] The [trial] judge was right in this case to hold that [Moffett's] charge had not lost its priority over the subsequent mortgage [to the bank].

Ormiston JA

[499] I have had the benefit of reading the judgment of Brooking JA in draft form and, subject to what appears below, I agree both in the reasoning and in the conclusion which he has reached ...

The issue is not which document is easier to enforce or which creates the better or more effective security, but which party has the better *equity*. In other words, which of the [500] parties should be entitled first to enforce their securities or other interests, which in the ordinary course of events will be the security or interest first created unless there be some act or default which, having regard to 'broad principles of right and justice' would make it inequitable as between the parties that the holder of the first interest should retain its initial priority. Expressions such as 'the merits' and 'the better equity' unfortunately connote, even though they have not been intended to express, some inquiry as to which security is objectively the more effective and they also connote, which perhaps is more objectionable, that in some way ordinarily one can ascertain the 'better' equity as a matter of determining comparative strength or enforceability, an inquiry which, apart from asking which is first in point of time, is one to be avoided. Merits, in equity, are those matters which impinge, broadly speaking, on the conscience of those who seek its aid or are otherwise subject to its jurisdiction. So priority is to be resolved against the holder of the prior equity only if the other party can establish the first holder's want of 'merits' or comparative lack of 'merit'. That is essentially a negative inquiry into behaviour on the part of the holders of each of the equitable interests as to whether they

---

3. (1787) 99 ER 1366.

4. *Heid v Reliance Finance Corp Pty Ltd* (1983) 154 CLR 326 at 341.

can be shown to have been obtained or enforced in a manner which is so unconscionable or otherwise inequitable so as to deprive the holder of the earlier interest of the priority to which it is otherwise entitled, whether that behaviour be evidenced by fraud, unfairness, negligence, the wrongful creation of particular assumptions by representations or the like or in a number of other ways which reflect on the behaviour of the holders of each of the interests ...

[501] As to the other basis upon which Brooking JA would ... give priority to [Moffett's] charge, I have greater difficulty and, for the present, I feel obliged, regrettably, to withhold my concurrence with it ...

[504] What Brooking JA says as to notice and its importance in the law of equity is ... most persuasive and there seems ... to be much force in the contention that notice is critical to the ascertainment of priorities, even in relation to equitable interests. However, I am not entirely [convinced] that ... knowledge or notice [should be given] any greater significance that any of the other matters which may be taken into account to determine whether an interest is postponed 'in fairness and in justice'. In the absence of detailed argument on that subject I would prefer to reserve my opinion on that. I must emphasise, nevertheless, that it still seems to me that one ought to take the interest first created and then inquire whether any even has occurred which would result in that interest being postponed to a later interest. If that still be the correct approach, as I believe it to be, then the existence of notice or knowledge of the kind here admitted is strictly speaking irrelevant, for that is not a factor which would permit a court exercising its equitable jurisdiction to conclude that the later interest should be preferred. It would only become relevant if there were some other factor which might point to the later equitable interest as being the 'better equity', were it not for the existence of relevant notice or knowledge which would deny that characterisation of the later interest and would deny its being preferred ...

It seems to me the present issue can be resolved in the same way whichever approach one takes. I have preferred to conclude ... that Moffett as holder of equitable interest first in time should be preferred unless and until the bank established that it had the better equity in the sense of a better equitable interest, and that is what the bank failed to do.

There are, however, real questions of the principle at issue as to whether the doctrine of notice is relevant to priority between two equitable interests. It may be seen that upon the test I have preferred there was no question of [Moffett's] establishing the existence of notice in the bank. What the bank would have had to do is to show that it took its interest for value without notice or had the better equity for some other reason, or that is what I believe is the essence of the present difference of opinion.

The better view, although I would not wish to resolve it finally in present circumstances, seems to be that the principle favouring the bona fide purchaser without notice has been one not ordinarily applied (except in circumstances which have been criticised) as between competing equitable interests. [505] The reason for this broad proposition may be traced, at least in part, to the observation of Lord Westbury in *Phillips v Phillips*:

> I take it to be a clear proposition that every conveyance of an equitable interest is an innocent conveyance, that is to say, the grant of a person entitled merely in equity passes only that which he is justly entitled to and no more. If, therefore, a person seised of an equitable estate (the legal estate being outstanding), makes an assurance by way of mortgage or grants an annuity, and afterwards conveys the whole estate to a purchaser,

he can grant to the purchaser that which he has, viz, the estate subject to the mortgage or annuity, and no more. The subsequent grantee takes only that which is left in the grantor. Hence grantees and incumbrancers claiming an equity take and are ranked according to the dates of their securities; and the maxim applies, 'qui prior est tempore potior est jure'. The first grantee is potior — that is, potentior. He has a better and superior — because a prior — equity. The first grantee has a right to be paid first, and it is quite immaterial whether the subsequent incumbrancers at the time when they took their securities and paid their money had notice of the first incumbrance or not.[5]

This passage has been cited on numerous occasions subsequently … Nevertheless, … there are statements by judges both in England and the United States which would appear to expand the doctrine to give the purchaser without notice rights where the later interest acquired is only an equitable interest …

Perhaps the solution lies in Lord Westbury's analysis which would allow of the second interest holder to take an interest but only subject to the earlier equity. If that be so, that later holder of an equitable interest would have to show why he or she should be preferred over the earlier equitable interest holder. This might involve some nice balancing of competing equities … but, as a generalisation only, such an inquiry may be cut short by it being demonstrated that the later holder knew of the earlier interest when he or she took. So, subject to the possible existence of rights under a prioritisation or subordination deed or other contract or by reason of a common assumption created by the holder of the prior interest at the time the later holder acquired his or her interest (or the like), there would [506] be little reason for further examination as to which party held the 'better equity', the later holder facing an effectively insuperable hurdle at that stage. However, without resolving all these difficulties, I would prefer to reiterate that Mr Moffett's interest was created first in time and nothing had been demonstrated in this case to show that the bank's later interest should be preferred in equity.

Comments
1. See Radan & Stewart at **7.6–7.7**.
2. For a discussion of this case and the role of notice in resolving priority disputes between holders of competing equitable interests see S Rodrick, 'Resolving Priority Disputes Between Competing Equitable Interests in Torrens System Land – Which Test?' (2001) 9 *Australian Property Law Journal* 172, where the author argues that the approach of Ormiston JA should be preferred to that of Brooking JA.

Postponing conduct and priority between competing equitable interests

---

7.3 Heid v Reliance Finance Corporation Pty Ltd (1983) 154 CLR 326

Court: High Court of Australia

---

5.   *Phillips v Phillips* (1861) 45 ER 1164 at 1166.

Facts: Heid sold Torrens title land to Connell Investments. Gibby, an employee of Connell Investments did the paperwork for this transaction. Part of the proceeds of sale to be received by Heid was to be applied to a particular investment by Connell Investments on behalf of Heid. The balance of the proceeds of sale was to be secured by a mortgage over the land from Connell Investments in favour of Heid. To facilitate these arrangements Heid executed a contract for the sale of the land to Connell Investments, a memorandum of transfer and a mortgage. These documents were handed to Connell Investments. Connell Investments never invested part of the sale proceeds as it had agreed to do, nor was the transfer and mortgage in favour of Heid registered. In these circumstances Heid had two equitable interests in the land, namely, a vendor's lien in relation to the money that was not invested as instructed, and an equitable mortgage.

Connell Investments borrowed money from Reliance Finance Corporation, executing a mortgage in its favour and handing it to Reliance Finance together with the certificate of title and the memorandum of transfer from Heid to Connell Investments. Reliance had the transfer registered and it lodged a caveat in relation to its mortgage. Thus, Reliance gained an equitable interest in the land. Connell Investments then executed a mortgage in favour of Alexander in respect of a loan from Alexander, who in turn lodged a caveat in relation to the mortgage. Subsequently Heid lodged a caveat in relation to his equitable mortgage. Reliance Finance and Alexander had no notice of Heid's equitable interests in the land at the time they made their loans to Connell Investments.

Issue: The issue before the High Court was whether Heid's earlier equitable interests had priority over the subsequent equitable interests of Reliance Finance and Alexander.

Decision: The High Court (Gibbs CJ, Mason, Murphy, Wilson and Deane JJ) unanimously ruled in favour of Reliance Finance and Alexander. Heid's conduct in handing over title documents to Connell Investments had postponed the priority that he would otherwise have had based upon the fact that his equitable interests were first in point of time.

Extracts: The extracts from the judgment of Gibbs CJ and the joint judgment of Mason and Deane JJ discuss the theoretical basis of the principles governing priorities between competing equitable interests and explain why, when applied in this case, they resulted in the equitable interests of Reliance Finance and Alexander having priority over those of Heid.

Gibbs CJ

[333] [I]t is convenient first to discuss the question which arises between [Heid] and Reliance Finance. Each of those parties had an equitable interest in the land — [Heid] because of his vendor's lien, and Reliance Finance as an equitable mortgagee. 'In all cases where a claim to enforce an equitable interest in property is opposed on the ground that after the interest is said to have arisen a third party innocently acquired an equitable interest in the same property, the problem, if the facts relied upon as having given rise to the interests be established, is to determine where the better equity lies. If the merits

are equal, priority in time of creation is considered to give the better equity. This is the true meaning of the maxim qui prior est tempore potior est jure.[6] But where the merits are unequal, as for instance where conduct on the part of the owner of the earlier interest has led the other to acquire his interest on the supposition that the earlier did not exist, the maxim may be displaced and priority accorded to the later interest'.[7] In the present case the interest of [Heid] was first in time. The question therefore is whether his conduct in handing to Gibby a completed memorandum of transfer, containing an acknowledgement of payment and accompanied by the certificate of title, thus enabling Connell Investments to represent itself to Reliance Finance as having a title free from outstanding equitable interests, has the consequence that Reliance Finance has the better equity, and that [Heid's] interest should be postponed to that of Reliance Finance.

In *Rimmer v Webster*, Farwell J stated the following proposition which appears to govern cases such as the present:

> If the owner of property clothes a third person with the apparent ownership and right of disposition thereof, not merely by transferring it to him, but also by acknowledging that the transferee has paid him the consideration for it, he is estopped from asserting his title as against a person to whom such third party has disposed of the property, and who took it in good faith and for value.[8]

There is no doubt as to the general correctness of that proposition. [334] It is illustrated by the decision in *Rice v Rice*. In that case the vendors, who had not in fact received the purchase money, delivered to the purchaser the title deeds indorsed with a receipt acknowledging payment. The purchaser made a mortgage by deposit of the deeds. It was held that possession of the deeds and the fact of the indorsement of the receipt gave the mortgagee a better equity, so that his equitable interest prevailed over that of the unpaid vendor. Kindersley VC said:

> ... they [the vendors] voluntarily armed the purchaser with the means of dealing with the estate as the absolute legal and equitable owner, free from every shadow of incumbrance or adverse equity. In truth it cannot be said that the purchaser, in mortgaging the estate by the deposit of the deeds, has done the vendors any wrong, for he has only done that which the vendors authorized and enabled him to do.[9]

This passage was cited with approval in the judgment of the Judicial Committee [of the Privy Council] in *Abigail v Lapin*.[10] In that case the respondents (Mr and Mrs Lapin), one of whom was indebted to one Heavener, transferred certain land to Mrs Heavener as her husband's nominee. The transfers were absolute in form but were in fact given as security for the debt. After the transfer was registered, Mrs Heavener executed a registrable mortgage in favour of the appellant (Abigail) as security for advances made by him. It was held that the equitable mortgage of Abigail took priority over the Lapins' equitable right to redeem. Lord Wright, who delivered the judgment of the Judicial

---

6. *Rice v Rice* (1854) 61 ER 646 at 648.
7. *Latec Investments Ltd v Hotel Terrigal Pty Ltd (in liq)* (1965) 113 CLR 265 at 276.
8. *Rimmer v Webster* [1902] 2 Ch 163 at 173.
9. *Rice v Rice* (1893) 61 ER 646 at 650.
10. (1934) 51 CLR 58 at 68.

Committee, approved[11] the reasons of Gavan Duffy and Starke JJ in this court which concluded as follows:

> In our opinion, the Lapins are bound by the natural consequences of their acts in arming Olivia Sophia Heavener with the power to go into the world as the absolute owner of the lands and thus execute transfers or mortgages of the lands to other persons, and they ought to be postponed to the equitable rights of Abigail to the extent allowed by the Supreme Court.[12]

Lord Wright went on to say:

> Apart from priority in time, the test for ascertaining which encumbrancer has the better equity must be whether either has been guilty of some act or default which prejudices his claim; in the present case the respondents on the one hand enabled the [335] Heaveners to represent themselves as legal owners in fee simple, while on the other hand it cannot be said that Abigail did or omitted to do anything which he should have done in lending the money on the security, though he might, by registering the mortgage, have secured the legal title.[13]

Lord Wright pointed out that it was only in an artificial sense that it could be said that the Lapins had made any representations to Abigail[14] and continued:

> It is true that in cases of conflicting equities the decision is often expressed to turn on representations made by the party postponed, as, for instance, in *King v King*.[15] But it is seldom that the conduct of the person whose equity is postponed takes or can take the form of a direct representation to the person whose equity is preferred: the actual representation is, in general, as in the present case, by the third party, who has been placed by the conduct of the party postponed in a position to make the representation, most often as here because that party has vested in him a legal estate or has given him the *indicia* of a legal estate in excess of the interest which he was entitled in fact to have, so that he has in consequence been enabled to enter into the transaction with the third party on the faith of his possessing the larger estate.[16]

The decisions in such cases as *Rimmer v Webster* and *Abigail v Lapin* may be based, alternatively, on the principle that a person who hands over title deeds to an agent with authority to deal with the property in a restricted manner cannot rely on the restrictions as against the third party who had no notice of them, and on the doctrine of estoppel. The former principle is said to have its origins in equity, and has been distinguished from estoppel, but it seems to me that it may be regarded as a particular form of estoppel. However, either principle will determine the present case, and it is sufficient to deal with the question whether the ordinary rules of estoppel prevent [Heid] from asserting his equitable interest against [Reliance Finance and Alexander]. The essential elements

---

11. *Abigail v Lapin* (1934) 51 CLR 58 at 64.
12. *Lapin v Abigail* (1930) 44 CLR 166 at 198.
13. *Abigail v Lapin* (1934) 51 CLR 58 at 68–9.
14. *Abigail v Lapin* (1934) 51 CLR 58 at 70.
15. [1931] 2 Ch 294.
16. *Abigail v Lapin* (1934) 51 CLR 58 at 71.

of an estoppel by representation, summarily stated, are that there must have been a representation (by words or conduct or, if there was a duty to speak or act, by silence or inaction) upon the faith of which the representee has acted to his detriment. No direct representation in the present case was made by [Heid] to Reliance Finance but, as Lord Wright explained in *Abigail v Lapin*, that is immaterial. The act of [Heid] in allowing Gibby to have the certificate of title and the memorandum of transfer which acknowledged receipt of the purchase price armed Gibby's employer **[336]** with the means of dealing with the land as absolute legal and equitable owner; in other words it armed Connell Investments 'with the power of going into the world under false colours'.[17] When in these circumstances Reliance Finance acted to its detriment on the assumption, to which [Heid's] conduct had contributed, that no adverse equitable interest existed, [Heid] is estopped from setting up his equitable interest. The result may be explained in point of principle by saying ... that [Heid] is bound by the natural consequences of his acts, although I would prefer to say, in the words of Griffith CJ in *Barry v Heider*, that 'the transfer operated as a representation, addressed to any person into whose hands it might lawfully come without notice,'[18] that Connell Investments had an absolute interest ...

[338] For these reasons ... the equitable interest of Reliance Finance as mortgagee prevailed over that of [Heid]. By the same reasoning, the interest of Mr Alexander also takes priority over the interest of [Heid]. By the time that Mr Alexander made the advance to Connell Investments, that company had become registered as proprietor of the land, and although Mr Alexander did not see the memorandum of transfer ... the registration allowed Connell Investments to hold out to Mr Alexander that, subject to the interest of Reliance Finance, it had a good title, and ... Mr Alexander acted on the faith of this representation. ... In the case of Mr Alexander also, all the elements necessary to ground an estoppel are present.

Mason and Deane JJ

[339] The theoretical basis for granting priority, in such circumstances, to the later interest has been the subject of debate. Some have found the basis in the doctrine of estoppel; others have identified a more general principle that a preference should be given to what is the better equity on an examination of the circumstances, especially the [340] conduct of the owner of the first equity ...

It is difficult, if not impossible, to accommodate all the cases of postponement of an equity under the umbrella of estoppel. In *Dixon v Muckleston*, Lord Selborne LC pointed out that the holder of the first equity might arm the third party with the indicia of title by means of express representation, positive act or omission, or negligence, though he unnecessarily confined it to 'wilful and unjustifiable neglect'.[19] As the Judicial Committee noted in *Abigail v Lapin*,[20] it is seldom that the conduct of a person whose equity is postponed takes the form of a direct representation to the person whose equity is preferred or is otherwise such as to found a conventional estoppel in pais. The actual representation is usually made by the third party who has been enabled to make it by the holder of the first equity, who has, for example, armed the third party with the indicia

---

17. *Dixon v Muckleston* (1872) LR 8 Ch App 155 at 160.
18. *Barry v Heider* (1914) 19 CLR 197 at 208.
19. *Dixon v Muckleston* (1892) LR 8 Ch App 155 at 160.
20. (1934) 51 CLR 58 at 71.

of title. In this situation, it is the adoption of the fiction that what the third party does is within the actual authority given by the holder of the first equity that fits the case to [341] the doctrine of estoppel. But the true position is that in the situation contemplated, where there is fraud on the part of the third party, the first holder gives no authority, express or implied, to him to make the representation to the second holder.[21] While the conduct of the holder of the first equity may, in such a case, be blameworthy, the operative representation was neither made nor authorized by him.

For our part we consider it preferable to avoid the contortions and convolutions associated with basing the postponement of the first to the second equity exclusively on the doctrine of estoppel and to accept a more general and flexible principle that preference should be given to what is the better equity in an examination of the relevant circumstances. It will always be necessary to characterize the conduct of the holder of the earlier interest in order to determine whether, in all the circumstances, that conduct is such that, in fairness and in justice, the earlier interest should be postponed to the later interest. Thus in *Latec Investments* Kitto J said that the case where the conduct of the prior owner leads the later owner to acquire his interest on the supposition that the earlier interest does not exist ... was just one 'instance' of a case when the merits are unequal.[22] To say that the question involves general considerations of fairness and justice acknowledges that, in whatever form the relevant test be stated, the overriding question is: 'whose is the better equity, bearing in mind the conduct of both parties, the question of any negligence on the part of the prior claimant, the effect of any representation as possibly raising an estoppel and whether it can be said that the conduct of the first or prior owner has enabled such a representation to be made'.[23] Thus elements of both negligence and [342] estoppel will often be found in the statements of general principle.

It may be that an equitable interest will not be postponed to an equitable interest created later in time merely because there is a causal nexus between an act or omission on the part of the prior equitable owner and an assumption on the part of the later equitable owner as to the non-existence of the prior equity. Fairness and justice demand that we be primarily concerned with acts of a certain kind — those acts during the carrying out of which it is reasonably foreseeable that a later equitable interest will be created and that the holder of that later interest will assume the non-existence of the earlier interest ...

In deciding whose is the better equity in this case it is necessary to ask whether there has been an act, neglect or default of the kind mentioned on the part of [Heid]. We need to consider what are the reasonably foreseeable consequences of his act in entrusting Gibby with the instrument of transfer and the authority to collect the certificate of title ...

[343] There are two elements of special significance in [Heid's] conduct. The first is that the instrument of transfer signed by [Heid] contained an acknowledgement of the receipt by him of the purchase money which was in fact unpaid and which lay at the heart of his equitable lien. The second is that [Heid] left the signed instrument of transfer together with the authority to collect the certificate of title with Gibby, who, as far as [Heid] was led to believe, was a solicitor acting for [Connell Investments] as well as for [Heid] ...

---

21. See the discussion by Starke J in *Thompson v Palmer* (1933) 49 CLR 507 at 526–7.
22. *Latec Investments Ltd v Hotel Terrigal Pty Ltd (in liq)* (1965) 113 CLR 265 at 276.
23. Edward Sykes, *The Law of Securities*, 3rd ed, 1978, p 336.

[345] [W]e ... look at [this] case as one in which [Heid] handed the documents to an employee of [Connell Investments]. The delivery of the documents to the employee armed [Connell Investments] with the capacity to represent itself to be the true owner of the property and to engage in fraudulent and deceptive conduct of the kind which took place. The risk of [Connell Investments] engaging in that conduct was reasonably foreseeable. Indeed, that conduct, though not intended by [Heid], was the natural consequence of his positive act in handing over the documents to Gibby — in effect to [Connell Investments] — without taking any steps, as for instance, by lodging a caveat, to protect himself and others who might otherwise be deceived by misuse of the documents.

The inevitable conclusion therefore is that there was negligence on the part of [Heid]. It led ... to an assumption by Reliance Finance and by Mr Alexander that [Heid's] interest no longer existed. It follows that, in all the circumstances, Reliance Finance and Mr Alexander have the better equities.

Comments

1. See Radan & Stewart at **7.15–7.16, 7.27–7.31**.
2. The approach of Mason and Deane JJ in relation to the theoretical basis upon which priority between competing equitable interests is determined has been subsequently supported in *Jacobs v Platt Nominees Pty Ltd* [1990] VR 146 at 151–4; *Elderly Citizens Homes of SA Inc v Balnaves* (1998) 72 SASR 210 at 225; and *Mercury Geotherm Ltd (In Receivership) v McLachlan* [2006] 1 NZLR 258 at 272.

7.4   Walker v Linom [1907] 2 Ch 104

Court: Chancery Division of the High Court of England and Wales

Facts: Walker created an equitable interest in certain property he owned in favour of his wife pursuant to a marriage settlement. The trustees of the marriage settlement failed to get title documents to that property from Walker who was therefore able to hold himself out as being the absolute owner of the property. Walker subsequently mortgaged the property and defaulted under the mortgage. The mortgagee, in exercise of its power of sale under the mortgage, sold the property to Linom. Neither the mortgagee nor Linom had any notice of Mrs Walker's equitable interest.

Issue: The issue before the Chancery Division was whether Mrs Walker's earlier equitable interest as beneficiary under a trust had priority over Linom's later equitable interest as purchaser of the property from the mortgagee.

Decision: Parker J ruled that although all the parties except Walker had acted honestly, the negligence of the trustees meant that their legal estate had to be postponed to Linom's subsequent equitable interest as purchaser from the mortgagee. His Honour also held that Mrs Walker's interest was in no better position than that of the trustees. Accordingly, Linom's equitable interest in the property had priority over Mrs Walker's beneficial interest under the marriage settlement.

Extracts: The extracts from the judgment of Parker J examine the principles and authorities that resulted in Mrs Walker's earlier equitable interest being postponed to Linom's later equitable interest.

Parker J

[110] Now it cannot be disputed that the settlement constituted a conveyance for value, and that the trustees have the legal estate. The circumstances under which a mortgagee or purchaser with the legal estate is, by reason of some conduct on his part in relation to the title deeds, postponed to some person having only an equitable interest is discussed fully in the case of *Northern* [111] *Counties of England Fire Insurance Co v Whipp*,[24] in which Fry LJ delivered the considered judgment of the Court of Appeal. The Lord Justice states the question for decision by referring to the rival contentions of the parties. 'It has been contended,' he says, 'on the part of the plaintiffs that nothing short of fraud will justify the Court in postponing the legal estate. It has been contended by the defendant that gross negligence is enough.' He then divides the cases which may assist in answering the question for decision into two categories, namely, (1) those which relate to the conduct of the holder of the legal estate in not getting possession of the deeds, and (2) those which relate to the conduct of such holder in dealing with the deeds after he has got them. In the former category the question may be between the holders of the legal estate and either a prior or a subsequent incumbrancer or purchaser. In the latter case it can only be between the holder of the legal estate and a subsequent incumbrancer or purchaser. The two classes, he says, will not be found to differ in the principles by which they are to be governed, but they do differ much in the kind of fraud which is to be most naturally looked for. In the former case you would naturally look for some such 'dolus malus' as indicated by Lord Hardwicke in *Le Neve v Le Neve*.[25] In the latter case you look for some actual concurrence in the fraudulent design of another. The learned Lord Justice next discusses at length the judgment of Lord Eldon in *Evans v Bicknell*,[26] and comes to the conclusion that the language of Lord Eldon in that case, though loose and difficult to construe, points to fraud as the necessary conclusion before the Court can deprive the holder of the legal estate of the rights derived therefrom. 'This fraud,' he continues, 'no doubt, may be arrived at either by direct evidence or by evidence circumstantial and indirect, and it does not cease to be fraud, because the particular object in contemplation of the parties may have been a fraud in some respects different from the fraud actually accomplished; or because the person intended to have been defrauded may be different from the person actually defrauded; [112] or because the original fraudulent intention had no particular person in view'.[27] That fraud, and fraud alone, is the ground for postponing the legal estate is, he says, confirmed by the judgments of Lord Hardwicke in *Le Neve v Le Neve*, Sir William Grant in *Barnett v Weston*,[28] and James LJ in *Ratcliffe v Barnard*.[29]

---

24. (1884) 26 Ch D 482 at 486.
25. (1747) 27 ER 291 at 294–5.
26. (1801) 31 ER 998.
27. *Northern Counties of England Fire Insurance Co v Whipp* (1884) 26 Ch D 482 at 490.
28. (1806) 33 ER 50.
29. (1871) LR 6 Ch 652.

He then subdivides the cases relating to the conduct of the holder of the legal estate in not getting possession of the deeds into various classes, the first class being where no inquiry has been made for the deeds and the holder of the legal estate has therefore been postponed either to a prior equitable estate, as in *Worthington v Morgan*,[30] or, as in *Clarke v Palmer*,[31] to a subsequent equitable owner who has obtained the deeds. In these cases he says the Courts have considered the conduct of the holder of the legal estate in making no inquiry to be evidence of the fraudulent intent to escape notice of a prior equity, and, in the latter case, that a subsequent mortgagee who has in fact been misled by the mortgagor taking advantage of the conduct of the legal mortgagee could, as against him, take advantage of the fraudulent intent. I need not consider the other classes.

The Lord Justice next subdivides and considers the cases relating to the conduct of the holder of the legal estate in dealing with the deeds after he has got them. The case with which he was actually dealing was a case under this category.

The conclusion he ultimately arrives at is that in order to postpone a prior legal to a subsequent equitable estate there must be fraud as apart from negligence, and this conclusion is stated in language wide enough to cover cases of postponement based upon the conduct of the holder of the legal estate in not getting possession of the title deeds as well as cases of postponement based upon the conduct of such holder in dealing with the title deeds after he has got them. It would seem at first sight that the Lord Justice uses the word 'fraud' throughout this judgment as connoting a dishonest intent, notwithstanding that in the case of fraud to be gathered from conduct in relation to [113] not getting in the title deeds he refers to such cases as *Le Neve v Le Neve* and *Ratcliffe v Barnard*.

Now, ... I cannot under the circumstances of this case find that anyone concerned in the 1896 settlement, with the exception of George Church Walker, acted otherwise than honestly, and, if I treat Fry LJ's judgment as meaning that in no case can a prior legal estate be postponed to a subsequent equitable estate without the existence of fraud in its ordinary common law sense as necessarily connoting a dishonest intention, I must hold that the trustees are not postponed. There are, however, subsequent cases which suggest that at any rate in cases of postponement, based on no inquiry having been made for the deeds, fraud is not necessary. It is, for example, clear from the case of *Oliver v Hinton*[32] that a purchaser obtaining the legal estate, but making no inquiry for the title deeds, or making inquiry and failing to take reasonable means to verify the truth of the excuse made for not producing them or handing them over, is, although perfectly honest, guilty of such negligence as to make it inequitable for him to rely on his legal estate so as to deprive a prior incumbrancer of his priority. In this case Lindley MR disapproves of the passage in the judgment of James LJ in *Ratcliffe v Barnard*, quoted by Fry LJ in *Northern Counties of England Fire Insurance Co v Whipp*, and distinctly says that to deprive a purchaser for value without notice of a prior equitable incumbrance of the benefit of the legal estate it is not essential that he should have been guilty of fraud. And Sir F H Jeune, referring also to the judgment of James LJ in *Ratcliffe v Barnard*, comes to the conclusion that the word 'fraud,' as there used, did not mean such conduct as would justify a jury or judge in finding that there

---

30. (1849) 60 ER 987.
31. (1882) 21 Ch D 124.
32. [1899] 2 Ch 264.

had been actual fraud, but such conduct as would justify the Court of Chancery in concluding that there had been fraud in some artificial sense. Similarly in *Berwick & Co v Price* Joyce J says: 'The omission by a purchaser to investigate the title or to require [114] delivery or production of the title-deeds is not to my mind either fraudulent or culpable, nor does it, since the judgment of Lindley MR in *Oliver v Hinton*, seem necessary to characterize it by any such epithet; but the consequence of such omission or wilful ignorance is that it is held to be unjust to prefer the purchaser to the previous mortgagee who has the deeds although such mortgage be equitable and the purchaser have the legal estate'.[33]

In both the cases last referred to the question was between a prior equitable and a subsequent legal estate, and I think the later case was actually decided on constructive or imputed notice. But the Master of the Rolls expressly refused to decide *Oliver v Hinton* on any such ground. The question, however, arises whether the principle laid down in *Oliver v Hinton* is equally applicable between the holder of the legal estate who has omitted to make inquiry for the title deeds and a subsequent equitable estate the creation of which has been rendered possible by such omission. In my opinion any conduct on the part of the holder of the legal estate in relation to the deeds which would make it inequitable for him to rely on his legal estate against a prior equitable estate of which he had no notice ought also to be sufficient to postpone him to a subsequent equitable estate the creation of which has only been rendered possible by the possession of deeds which but for such conduct would have passed into the possession of the owner of the legal estate. This must, I think, have been the opinion of Fry LJ in *Northern Counties of England Fire Insurance Co v Whipp*; for he explains both *Worthington v Morgan* and *Clarke v Palmer* as based upon the same sort of fraud. I do not think, therefore, that there is anything in the authorities to preclude me from holding, and I accordingly hold, that the trustees, although they have the legal estate, are postponed to [Linom].

Passing now to the position of [Mrs Walker] herself, her interest is prior in time to [Linom's], and both are equitable. The usual rule is, the equities in other respects being equal, that which is prior in point of time prevails. The question, therefore, [115] is whether the equities are in other respects equal. It is argued that [Mrs Walker's] equity is affected by the conduct of the trustees, and that her position cannot be better than the position of her trustees. The case of *Lloyd's Banking Co v Jones* is cited as an authority for this proposition ... The facts in *Lloyd's Banking Co v Jones* were very like the facts in the present case. A lady who under a will became entitled to leaseholds subject to an equitable mortgage to certain bankers settled them upon her marriage, the trusts being for herself for life, with remainder to the infant defendant. The trustees who took the legal estate made no inquiry for the deeds, which were with the bankers. The lady subsequently paid off the equitable mortgage, but left the deeds in the bankers' hands as security for her husband's overdraft. Under these circumstances the trustees were held to be postponed to the bankers. It was argued that the defendant had a better equity than the trustees. 'I demur,' said Pearson J, 'to that proposition entirely. I think I should be introducing a most fatal doctrine if I were to say that, when the legal estate in property is vested in a trustee under a marriage settlement, the simple fact that his cestuis que trustent are ignorant what he is doing gives them a prior equity over any person who has

---

33. *Berwick & Co v Price* [1905] 1 Ch 632 at 640.

dealings with him, and who is equally ignorant of the existence of the settlement and of the rights of the cestuis que trustent'.[34] ...

On the other hand, my attention was called to a series of authorities which do not appear to be entirely consistent with the principle enunciated by Pearson J. in the passage I have quoted. For example, there is the case of *Cory v Eyre*. In this case the trustee of an equitable mortgage transferred it to a purchaser for value who had no notice of the trust: it was held that the interest of the cestui que trust had priority over the interest of the transferee. It was argued that the cestui que trust was in no better position than his trustee, [116] because he was bound to make inquiries into the conduct of the trustee. It was held that there was no such obligation. Turner LJ says: 'The very first principle of trusts is, that the cestui que trust places confidence in his trustee, and if it is to be held that a cestui que trust is to be postponed upon the mere ground that he did not inquire into the acts or conduct of his trustee, that principle would, as it seems to me, be in a great measure, if not wholly, destroyed'.[35] Again, Turner LJ in effect says that the possession of the title deeds gave the transferee of the mortgage no priority.[36] It was not, he conceived, the doctrine of the Court that in the case of mere equitable interests priority could be gained through the medium of a breach of trust or duty. The decision in *Taylor v London and County Banking Co*[37] is to the same effect ...

[118] It was urged in argument that *Cory v Eyre* and *Taylor v London and County Banking Co* ... are inconsistent with the principle enunciated by Pearson J in *Lloyd's Banking Co v Jones*, and that I ought to treat that case as overruled. It is to be observed, however, that all these cases had reference to the conduct of trustees or persons in some other fiduciary relationship with reference to title deeds which they held in trust for or otherwise on account of the persons who were their cestuis que trust, or towards whom the fiduciary relationship subsisted, and the effect of such conduct on the rights of such persons respectively, whereas the case of *Lloyd's Banking Co v Jones* related to the conduct of trustees in not getting possession of the title deeds. It may well be, therefore, that Pearson J's decision is right even if the principle he lays down is not one of general application to all cases ...

I have to ask myself, therefore, whether, so far as it affects the rights of their cestuis que trust, there is any real ground for drawing a distinction between the wrongful conduct of trustees in relation to title deeds in their possession as trustees and the wrongful conduct in relation to title deeds which as a fact never came into their possession, and are therefore never held by them upon trust at all. In my opinion there is such a real ground of distinction. In the former case the trustees hold the deeds for their cestuis que trust, and are bound to deal with them in [119] accordance with the trusts upon which they are held. In the latter case the trustees never held the deeds for their cestuis que trust, and their breach of duty lies in not obtaining them. In the former case the trusteeship, so far as the deeds are concerned, is complete, and the deeds cannot be dealt with improperly if the trustees do their duty, and the cestuis que trust may fairly assume that they will do their duty. In the latter case the trusteeship, so far as the deeds are concerned, is incomplete, and the person who retains them is in a position to deal with them without

---

34. *Lloyd's Banking Co v Jones* (1885) 29 Ch D 221 at 227–8.
35. *Cory v Eyre* (1863) 46 ER 58 at 66.
36. *Cory v Eyre* (1863) 46 ER 58 at 66.
37. [1901] 2 Ch 231 at 260.

reference to the trustees, so that the cestuis que trust have no one on whose possession of the deeds they are entitled to rely as standing between them and the perpetration of a fraud.

I hold, therefore, in the present case, on the authority of *Lloyd's Banking Co v Jones*, that [Mrs Walker] is in no better position than her trustees, and is postponed to [Linom].

Comment

1. See Radan & Stewart at **7.32–7.36**.

The rule in *Dearle v Hall*

7.5   Re Dallas [1904] 2 Ch 385

Court: Court of Appeal of England and Wales

Facts: Dallas was the appointed executor and beneficiary of a legacy under his father's will. Prior to his father's death Dallas assigned his expectancy by way of security for certain loans, firstly from Stuart and then from Brooks-Jenkins. Following his father's death Dallas renounced probate and his sister, Beedell, successfully applied for letters of administration in relation to her deceased father's estate. The day after the grant of letters of administration to Beedell, Brooks-Jenkins gave her notice of its assignment. Six days later Stuart became aware for the first time that Beedell had been granted letters of administration. Stuart gave notice of his assignment to her the following day.

Issue: The issue before the Court of Appeal was who, of Brooks-Jenkins and Stuart, had priority pursuant to the rule in *Dearle v Hall* in relation to the legacy inherited by Dallas.

Decision: The Court of Appeal (Vaughan Williams, Stirling and Cozens-Hardy LJJ) unanimously affirmed the first instance decision of Buckley J and held that Brooks-Jenkins had the prior claim to the legacy because he had given notice of his assignment to Beedell first. This was so despite the fact that Stuart had given notice as soon as he discovered that Beedell had been granted letters of administration, and that Stuart's failure to give notice earlier had in no way contributed to the creation of Brooks-Jenkins' equitable interest, which arose pursuant to the second assignment from Dallas.

Extracts: The extracts from the judgments of Buckley J and all three members of the Court of Appeal discuss the requirement of notice under the rule in *Dearle v Hall*.

Buckley J

[393] Between the date of the will in 1893 and of the death in 1902, ... Dallas of course had no property at all as regards this legacy. He had merely a possibility or expectancy, if the testator died without revoking his will, that he would be entitled (an event which happened), but he had no property at all. That an equitable incumbrance may be given upon a mere possibility or expectancy or upon future property, of course, is well settled. I read from ... the well-known sentence in Lord Macnaghten's judgment in *Tailby v Official*

Receiver: 'It has long been settled that future property, possibilities and expectancies are assignable in equity for value. The mode or form of assignment is [394] absolutely immaterial provided the intention of the parties is clear. To effectuate the intention an assignment for value, in terms present and immediate, has always been regarded in equity as a contract binding on the conscience of the assignor and so binding the subject-matter of the contract when it comes into existence, if it is of such a nature and so described as to be capable of being ascertained and identified'.[38] ... When you are dealing with a property such as this it is, of course, obvious that there is no legal holder of the fund, and that it is impossible to give notice to anybody. There is a considerable body of cases relating to property of this description, which arose in the old days before purchase in the army was abolished. An officer's commission was not his property which he could bind in any way, but it was something which, by virtue of the system which prevailed as to purchase, might in a contingent event be represented by money, and there was an expectancy or a possibility of a fund coming to him if he was gazetted out of the army. What happened in these cases was this. The money in question was paid into the name of the officer's army agents, and became the property of the officer at the moment when his retirement was gazetted. Down to that moment he had nothing at all beyond the expectancy to which I have referred ... In all those cases what was decided was this: Until the moment at which the fund in the army agent's hands became, by the gazetting of the officer's retirement, his property, there was no fund of which there was any legal holder at all. It became his on the gazetting, with the result that the notices given to the army agents before the gazetting were [395] perfectly useless and idle ... The previous notice was void altogether, because it was not given to a person who was the legal holder of the fund. But immediately upon the appearance of the *Gazette* the equitable incumbrancers, if they were wise, took care to serve the army agents with notice. The rule was that all notices received on the same day ranked pari passu as regards notice, and inter se took priority according to priority of date of the incumbrance ... From those cases it is obvious that two results follow — that where the subject of the equitable incumbrance is an expectancy or possibility, notice is necessary, and that priority goes according to the date of the receipt of the notice, or as between notices of even date, according to the priority of the date of the charge ...

[396] [T]he doctrine of notice rests upon the principle that the equitable assignee ought to take such steps as will prevent the assignor from retaining the apparent ownership of the fund; and, secondly (if it be a different proposition, although I think it is only an application of the former one), that he must take such steps as will give him a right in rem against the fund as distinguished from a right against the conscience of the assignor of the fund, and that that ought to be done by his taking possession of the fund to some extent — not necessarily to the full extent, but so far as possible. *Dearle v Hall*[39] is a case which has been very often criticized ... [it] is indisputable law, although many judges have said that they [397] will not extend it ...

[398] I pass on to consider what notice must be given, and to whom. As regards the person to whom notice must be given, ... it appears that it must be a notice given to a person who is 'bound by some contract or obligation, existing at the time when the notice

---

38. *Tailby v Official Receiver* (1888) 13 App Cas 523 at 543.
39. (1828) 38 ER 475.

reaches him, to receive and to pay over, or to pay over, if he has previously received, the fund'.[40] That was the whole **[399]** substratum of the earlier cases: that the notice given to the agent, when he was not bound by any contract or obligation, was altogether futile and useless. The only notice effectual was that which was given when, by the gazetting of the officer out of the army, the army agent became the trustee for him. The notice, therefore, must be given to a person bound by some contract or obligation. Next, the notice, if acquired in fact by the legal holder of the fund, is operative, even though it be obtained, not by direct notice from the incumbrancer, but under such circumstances as that, as a matter of business, the owner of the fund would be taken to have known it. I read this from Lord Cairns' judgment in *Lloyd v Banks*: 'If it can be shewn that in any way the trustee has got knowledge of that kind — knowledge which would operate upon the mind of any rational man, or man of business, and make him act with reference to the knowledge he has so acquired — then I think the end is attained, and that there has been fixed upon the conscience of the trustee, and through that upon the trust fund, a security against its being parted with in any way that would be inconsistent with the incumbrance which has been created'.[41] Further, suppose there are several trustees, notice to one of their number will be sufficient if he be not a trustee standing in such a position that it is his interest to conceal the notice, and this is none the less true because the question arises after that one who has received the notice is dead, and when the survivor and the new trustee have no knowledge. It was decided in *In re Wyatt*[42] — in the House of *Lords Ward v Duncombe*[43] — that an effective notice is not displaced by any change of the trustees; so that if notice be given, say, to all of the trustees, and they all cease to be trustees, and three other persons become trustees who have no notice, the original notice is good. But this last proposition is, it may be, subject to [an] exception ... **[400]** If ... the assignor be himself one of the trustees, and he is the only person who receives notice, then ... notice to him will not be sufficient. In *Browne v Savage* Kindersley VC says: 'In the case where the *assignor* is himself one of the trustees, he being the only one of the trustees who has any notice or knowledge of the assignment which he has made, if he should afterwards apply to another person to advance him a sum of money on an assignment of his interest, concealing the fact of the prior assignment, such proposed assignee could not, by any caution in making inquiry of all the trustees, discover the fact of the prior assignment; for it is the interest of the trustee, who is the proposed assignor, to conceal the prior assignment; and the other trustees know nothing about it'.[44] I pass on to consider who were the persons who had notice and who were the persons who ought to have had notice on the facts of the case before me. Now the first proposition which it will be necessary to deal with is this ... Dallas, the sole surviving executor, being himself the assignor, and of course knowing of all his own assignments, was he, when the testator died, a legal holder of the fund so that his knowledge operated in favour of all the equitable assignees as being, within *Lloyd v Banks*, knowledge which he had which would be effectual? The first question to deal with upon this is, What was the effect of [Dallas']

---

40. *Addison v Cox* (1872) LR 8 Ch App 76 at 79.
41. *Lloyd v Banks* (1868) LR 3 Ch App 488 at 491.
42. [1892] 1 Ch 188.
43. [1893] AC 369.
44. *Browne v Savage* (1859) 62 ER 244 at 246.

renunciation? Sect 79 of the statute 20 & 21 Vict c 77, and s 16 of 21 & 22 Vict c 95 are sections which deal, as regards the former with the case of renunciation, and as regards the latter with the case of death of the executor, or failure of the executor to appear and take probate when cited. As regards renunciation, in the case before me the statute provides that where a person renounces, 'the rights of such person in respect of the executorship shall wholly cease, and the representation to the testator and the administration of his effects shall and may, without any further renunciation, go, devolve, and be committed in like manner [401] as if such person had not been appointed executor'. Upon that first ground, as it seems to me, the executor who subsequently renounced, as the result of the renunciation stood from the first in such a position as that he was not for this purpose a legal holder of the fund. Leaving the statute and regarding the case upon general grounds, according to *Ward v Duncombe*[45] what you have to do is to give a notice to the person who has the disposal of the fund. You serve the legal holder because it is he who holds the purse-strings and keeps the money. Now it seems to me the executor who renounced never was a person who had the disposal of the fund. He could not have had the disposal of the fund except by intermeddling with the estate. If he intermeddles with the estate he cannot renounce. He therefore is a person who never had the disposition, and therefore is not the person to whom the notice ought to be given. Suppose the sole executor who had not proved was served with a notice, would it be his duty, when administration was subsequently granted to somebody else, to hand on that notice to the person who would then be legal holder of the fund, and would that have a retrospective operation as if it had been served on the date of the renunciation by the renouncing executor? I think not. The renouncing executor owes no duty to the estate. His position is this — that the testator has by his will nominated him to an office, and the tenure of that office no doubt comes to the executor, not by virtue of the probate, but by virtue of the will; but he is not bound to take the office. The testator cannot impose it upon him against his will, and if he refuses to take it then he is a person who refuses to have anything to do with the estate, and he then cannot be a person who owes to the estate the duty of handing on to a legal personal representative, when subsequently constituted, notices which in his hands were nothing at all. Again, apart from those grounds altogether, what was [Dallas'] position? He was sole surviving executor and assignor. Suppose that a notice to him under any circumstances could be effectual — I mean as being a service on a legal holder of a fund — this question then arises: Where [402] the sole legal holder is also the equitable assignor, is the knowledge which he necessarily possesses a knowledge which enures for the benefit of the equitable incumbrancer? It is but an application of the principle of *Browne v Savage* to say that that cannot be so.

Browne v Savage lays down that if you give notice to one of several trustees, he being himself the assignor, that will not avail. On all these grounds it seems to me that although [Dallas] had knowledge, the fact that he had knowledge was not notice for the purpose of protecting the equitable incumbrancer. Then, if he was not the person, who was the person to whom the notice could be given? The answer is easy. There came into existence for the first time a legal holder of this fund when on March 4, 1903, administration, with the will annexed, was granted to Mrs Beedell. I am not suggesting that in the meantime there was no legal holder at all. The legal ownership must be somewhere, but it was not

---

45. [1893] AC 369.

in [Dallas]. Whether it was in the Crown or the President of the Probate Division, as it would have been under the old law, I need not set myself to inquire. It was somewhere, no doubt, but it was not in [Dallas]. It was not in any person who was served with notice before March 4, 1903, when Mrs Beedell took out administration. She was the legal holder, and she was, in my judgment, the only person on whom notice could effectually be served. Substantially that determines all the questions that have been argued before me ... [405] I declare that the priority of these incumbrancers will be according to the dates of the notices given by them to [Beedell] after administration was granted, and that of course in the case of notices on the same day they will rank in priority of the respective charges.

Vaughan Williams LJ

[410] In my opinion the decision of Buckley J is quite right and ought to be affirmed ...

There could be [411] no effective notice given so as to effect priorities until the fund came into existence and there was a person who had control of the fund and to whom notice could be given. Therefore one begins with the proposition that there was no notice at all during the lifetime of the testator.

Then the next period we have to deal with is the period between the death of the testator and the renunciation of probate by ... Dallas. Now, with regard to that period, it is not necessary for us to decide whether there was a good notice, so as to affect priority, given to the executor named in the will, who subsequently renounced, before such renunciation, because it is plain on the authorities that if the person to whom the notice is given is himself the assignor, both in the case of the incumbrance first granted and also in the case of the later assignment, that cannot be an effective notice. The reason of that is this — that whatever view one takes of the principle upon which notice is allowed to affect priorities, it is common to all the theories of the principle upon which these notices are effective to alter priorities that the notice when given is given upon the hypothesis that the trustee or other person who legally dominates the fund will inform the person giving the notice whether there is any prior incumbrance in existence; and it is plain that in a case in which there is only one such trustee or person controlling the fund, and he has made the first assignment, it is futile to give him notice of the second assignment at all, because his obvious interest is to conceal from the puisne incumbrancer the first incumbrance he has made; for if the person proposing to make an advance were aware of the first incumbrance he would probably refuse to advance money on the security of a second assignment ...

[412] The result of the authorities, to my mind, is this — that, as notice to or knowledge of a sole assignor trustee is not an effective notice to operate on priorities, we may dismiss at once from this case all considerations of the knowledge of ... Dallas, the named executor who subsequently renounced. Even if there had been an express notice to him, it would not have been an operative notice for this purpose. Then, passing from that and inquiring when the next notice was given, we find that no other notice was given by any incumbrancer at all until after the grant of letters of administration to Mrs Beedell. Those letters of administration were granted to her on March 4, 1903, and notice was given to her by the Brooks-Jenkins incumbrancers on March 5, and any effective notice which was given by Stuart was given several days subsequent to that.

[413] In that state of things the question we have to answer here is, Ought the Brooks-Jenkins incumbrance which in point of date of creation is subsequent to the Stuart incumbrance to take priority of the Stuart incumbrance? The title possessed by the several incumbrancers is equitable only, and their equities would, in ordinary course, be in order of date; but the Brooks-Jenkins incumbrancers were the first to give notice of their incumbrances. Now, the ground upon which [Stuart's counsel] sought to argue that that notice alone ought not to give priority to any of those incumbrances was this: he said that the whole principle upon which notice is allowed to affect priorities is that those who have not given notice have been guilty of some neglect of duty. Now, if that be the true principle, it cannot be said that Stuart was guilty of any neglect of duty whatever. He could not have given notice during the lifetime of the testator. So far as … Dallas, the assignor and the named executor in the will, was concerned, Stuart could not have given an effective notice to him; and therefore the first time at which he could have given an effective notice was upon the grant of letters of administration. He could not tell when that was going to take place, and he could not prevent the Brooks-Jenkins incumbrancers from giving the first notice, for it was through Messrs Brooks, Jenkins & Co, their solicitors, that application was made for the letters of administration which were granted to Mrs Beedell.

Now, I agree … that there is no reason to attribute any negligence to Stuart; but the answer is that that is not the true principle to be applied. The true principle has been determined once and for all by the case of *Ward v Duncombe*. Now, it seems to me that that case decides that the principle which has been suggested by [Stuart's counsel] in his argument as the ground on which notice, when given, has the effect it is allowed to have in a question of priorities is not the true principle … [In *Ward v Duncombe*] Lord Macnaghten says [414] this: 'It may, perhaps, be doubted whether the views of Sir Thomas Plumer in *Dearle v Hall* were quite correctly appreciated in *Foster v Cockerell*,[46] which gives the go-by to all considerations founded upon the conduct of the parties. But however that may be, *Foster v Cockerell* unquestionably lays down that the rule known as the rule in *Dearle v Hall* is independent of any consideration of the conduct of the competing assignees, where the assignee second in date has no notice of the earlier assignment. Priority in such a case depends simply and solely on priority of notice'.[47]

I cannot imagine any words which could more clearly lay down the principle upon which these notices are supposed to operate. They operate independently of any consideration of conduct of the competing assignees, but simply and solely on priority of notice.

Stirling LJ

[415] The question to be determined here is whether the rule laid down in *Dearle v Hall* is applicable to the present case. Now, the rule established by *Dearle v Hall* is, in the words of Lord Macnaghten in *Ward v Duncombe*, 'That an assignee of an equitable interest in personal estate without notice of an existing prior assignment may gain priority simply

---

46. (1835) 5 ER 1315.
47. *Ward v Duncombe* [1893] AC 369 at 390.

by the act of giving notice to the person who has legal dominion over the fund before notice is given by the earlier assignee'.[48]

It has been contended before us that the rule ought not to be applied where the earlier assignee has not been guilty of any negligence in serving notice; but the passage already cited by my Lord from Lord Macnaghten's speech in *Ward v Duncombe* appears to me to entirely negative that argument. It is quite true, as has already been pointed out, that Lord Macnaghten went on to observe that it was difficult to state [416] exactly the principle upon which the rule in *Dearle v Hall* was established, and at least he warns those who have to apply that rule against extending it to a new case. Then the question we have to consider is whether this case is or is not covered by authority. It may be said at once that there is no case reported in the books entirely like the present in its facts; but, in my opinion, the army agents' cases really govern this case ...

[417] Then the point lastly made was this, that the priorities ought to be established by the fact that ... Dallas was executor, and that the case stands in the same position as where an incumbrancer who has given notice to a trustee who has since died or retired is held not to be prejudiced by the fact that another trustee is appointed who is not aware of the notice already given and receives fresh notice. Upon that point I ... only say that we are not now deciding whether notice to an executor who does not act and renounces is of any value whatever; but personally I should be very loth to hold that it is.

Cozens-Hardy LJ

[417] Since the case of *Ward v Duncombe* there is very little open to us to do beyond repeating that the rule in *Dearle v Hall* is in no way dependent upon the conduct of the assignees. It is also settled quite clearly that the rule applies [418] equally although there is no trust fund and no trustee in existence at the date of the several assignments. The army agents' cases are only intelligible on this principle. *Johnstone v Cox*[49] was a clear decision on this point ... Therefore it appears to me that there is only one point open to us. It is said that ... Dallas, as assignor, had knowledge (as of course he had) of his own incumbrance, and that the knowledge which he possessed of his own incumbrance, he being an executor named in the will, must be regarded as equivalent to a notice entitling the assignees to priority in order of the dates of the assignments. I cannot take that view. It appears to me that the knowledge of the assignor is quite a different thing from the notice that is given by an assignee to the person who has control of the fund. Under these circumstances it is not necessary to decide whether notice to an executor who renouncesand disclaims can have any effect or validity; but, speaking for myself, I should require a great deal of argument to induce me to assent to that proposition.

Comment
1. See Radan & Stewart at **7.37–7.41**.

---

48. *Ward v Duncombe* [1893] AC 369 at 384.
49. (1880) 16 Ch D 571, affirmed at (1881) 19 Ch D 17.

Priority between registered and unregistered interests in the Torrens system

---

7.6   Bahr v Nicolay (No 2) (1988) 164 CLR 604

Court: High Court of Australia

Facts: Mr and Mrs Bahr were the registered proprietors of Torrens title land (lot 340) in Western Australia. In 1980 they contracted to sell the land to Nicolay. The contract stipulated that Nicolay would lease the land back to the Bahrs for three years. It also stipulated in clause 6 that the Bahrs could repurchase the land from Nicolay at an agreed price at the end of the three-year period. Nicolay became registered proprietor and, in 1981, sold the land to Mr and Mrs Thompson. The Thompsons knew of the arrangement between the Bahrs and Nicolay and expressly acknowledged so in clause 4 of the contract of purchase from Nicolay. After the Thompsons became registered, they confirmed in writing to the Bahrs that they were required to sell back the land to them. Later the Thompsons changed their minds and sought to rely on the register to defeat the Bahrs' claim to the land. Any dishonest conduct by the Thompsons was found to have occurred after they had become registered proprietors.

Issue: The issue before the High Court was whether the Thompsons had an indefeasible title.

Decision: The High Court (Mason CJ, Wilson, Brennan, Dawson and Toohey JJ) unanimously found in favour of the Bahrs and held that the Thompsons' title to the land was not indefeasible. Mason CJ and Dawson J held that the Bahrs had priority over the Thompsons either because their conduct constituted fraud or because the Bahrs had *in personam* rights against them. Wilson and Toohey JJ held that there was no fraud by the Thompsons, but that the Bahrs had *in personam* rights against them. Brennan J did not consider the issue of fraud and held in favour of the Bahrs on the basis of *in personam* rights that they had against the Thompsons.

Extracts: The extracts from the joint judgment of Mason CJ and Dawson J and the joint judgment of Wilson and Toohey JJ discuss the operation of the principles of fraud and *in personam* rights in the context of Torrens title land.

Mason CJ and Dawson J

[612] This characterization of cl 4 lies at the heart of the [Thompsons'] [613] case: namely that mere notice of a prior unregistered interest does not amount to fraud within the meaning of s 68 [of the *Transfer of Land Act 1893* (WA)]. That section provides that, except in the case of fraud, the registered proprietor holds the land subject only to incumbrances notified on the certificate of title, save for exceptions not material to this case. Section 134 provides that, except in the case of fraud, no person taking a transfer of land shall be affected by actual or constructive notice of any trust or unregistered interest and that knowledge of any trust or unregistered interest 'shall not of itself be imputed as fraud'.

Sections 68 and 134 give expression to, and at the same time qualify, the principle of indefeasibility of title which is the foundation of the Torrens system of title. As the Judicial Committee observed in *Gibbs v Messer*:

> The object is to save persons dealing with registered proprietors from the trouble and expense of going behind the register, in order to investigate the history of their author's title, and to satisfy themselves of its validity.[50]

Neither the two sections nor the principle of indefeasibility precludes a claim to an estate or interest in land against a registered proprietor arising out of the acts of the registered proprietor himself.[51] Thus, an equity against a registered proprietor arising out of a transaction taking place after he became registered as proprietor may be enforced against him.[52] So also with an equity arising from conduct of the registered proprietor before registration,[53] so long as the recognition and enforcement of that equity involves no conflict with ss 68 and 134. Provided that this qualification is observed, the recognition and enforcement of such an equity is consistent with the principle of indefeasibility and the protection which it gives to those who deal with the registered proprietor on the faith of the register.

There is no fraud on the part of a registered proprietor in merely acquiring title with notice of an existing unregistered interest or in taking a transfer with knowledge that its registration will defeat such an interest.[54] The decision in *Waimiha Sawmilling* merely gives effect to s 134 by excluding from the statutory concept of fraud an acquisition of title with notice of any trust or unregistered interest. However, Lord Buckmaster in expressing the [614] reasons for the decision went rather further when he reproduced the following passage of the remarks of Lord Lindley in the earlier decision (*Assets Co Ltd v Mere Roihi*[55]): 'Fraud ... means actual fraud, dishonesty of some sort, not what is called constructive or equitable fraud'.[56] Lord Buckmaster went on to instance, as examples of fraud, the transfer whose object is to cheat a man of a known existing right and a deliberate and dishonest trick causing an interest not to be registered.[57]

These comments do not mean all species of equitable fraud stand outside the statutory concept of fraud. Far from it. In *Latec Investments Ltd v Hotel Terrigal Pty Ltd (In liq)*, Kitto J held that a collusive and colourable sale by a mortgage company to its subsidiary was a plain case of fraud. According to his Honour, '[t]here was pretence and collusion in the conscious misuse of a power', this being a 'dishonest course'.[58] Likewise, in *Loke Yew v Port Swettenham Rubber Co Ltd*, Lord Moulton instanced the case of an agent who has

---

50. *Gibbs v Messer* [1891] AC 248 at 254.
51. *Breskvar v Wall* (1971) 126 CLR 376 at 384–5.
52. *Barry v Heider* (1914) 19 CLR 197.
53. *Logue v Shoalhaven Shire Council* [1979] 1 NSWLR 537 at 563.
54. *Mills v Stokman* (1967) 116 CLR 61 at 78; *Waimiha Sawmilling Co v Waione Timber Co* [1926] AC 101.
55. [1905] AC 176 at 210.
56. *Waimiha Sawmilling Co v Waione Timber Co* [1926] AC 101 at 106.
57. *Waimiha Sawmilling Co v Waione Timber Co* [1926] AC 101 at 106–7.
58. *Latec Investments Ltd v Hotel Terrigal Pty Ltd (In liq)* (1965) 113 CLR 265 at 274.

purchased land on behalf of his principal but has taken the conveyance in his own name, and in virtue thereof claims to be the owner of the land, though he is in law a trustee for his principal.[59] It seems that his Lordship did not intend to make this illustration as an example of the statutory concept of fraud. His Lordship had earlier dealt with the issue of fraud and indefeasibility and was, when instancing the acquisition of title by an agent, propounding another answer based on the power and duty of the Court to rectify the register ... Despite this, the example given by Lord Moulton is in our view an instance of fraud within the meaning of s 68.

According to the decisions of this Court actual fraud, personal dishonesty or moral turpitude lie at the heart of the two sections and their counterparts.[60] However, from the [Bahrs'] point of view the examples may not travel quite far enough because the dishonesty which they exhibit is dishonesty on the part of the registered proprietor in securing his registration as proprietor ...

[615] For our part we do not see the illustrations given and the statements made in the cases as amounting to definitive pronouncements that fraud is confined to fraud in the obtaining of a transfer or in securing registration. The statements, viewed in their context, merely express the reasons why particular circumstances fall within the statutory exception. Nor do we see anything in the language or the purpose of s 68 which warrants such a restrictive interpretation ... The section restricts, in the interests of indefeasibility of title, rights which would exist otherwise at law or in equity. And granted that an exception is to be made for fraud why should the exception not embrace fraudulent conduct arising from the dishonest repudiation of a prior interest which the registered proprietor has acknowledged or has agreed to recognize as a basis for obtaining title, as well as fraudulent conduct which enables him to obtain title or registration? In the context of s 68 there is no difference between the false undertaking which induced the execution of the transfer in *Loke Yew* and an undertaking honestly given which induces the execution of a transfer and is subsequently repudiated for the purpose of defeating the prior interest. The repudiation is fraudulent because it has as its object the destruction of the unregistered interest notwithstanding that the preservation of the unregistered interest was the foundation or assumption underlying the execution of the transfer. For the same reason the subsequent repudiation by a transferee of property of a limited beneficial interest in that property [616] is fraudulent, when the transferee took the property on terms that the limited beneficial interest would be retained by the transferor. It is immaterial that the transferee 'may have been innocent of any fraudulent intent in taking the conveyance in absolute form'.[61]

What then was the purpose and effect of cl 4 of the agreement between [Nicolay] and the [Thompsons]? The matrix of circumstances in which the agreement was made throws up three significant factors. First, the making of an agreement between [Nicolay] and [the Thompsons] which would result in the destruction of the [Bahrs'] existing rights, or allow the destruction of those rights, by registration of a transfer in favour of the [Thompsons] in circumstances whereby the rights became unenforceable would expose [Nicolay] to liability for breach of contract ... Secondly, as we have seen, upon registration of such

---

59. *Loke Yew v Port Swettenham Rubber Co Ltd* [1913] AC 491 at 504.
60. See *Butler v Fairclough* (1917) 23 CLR 78 at 90; *Stuart v Kingston* (1923) 32 CLR 309 at 356.
61. *Bannister v Bannister* [1948] 2 All ER 133 at 136.

a transfer, the combined effect of ss 68 and 134 would, in the absence of fraud, bring about the destruction of the [Bahrs'] rights. Thirdly, at least until registration of such a transfer, the [Bahrs'] equitable interest under the 1980 agreement, being first in time, had priority over the interest of the [Thompsons] as purchasers under their agreement with [Nicolay].

Viewed in this setting, cl 4 of the later agreement was designed to do more than merely evidence the fact that the [Thompsons] had notice of the [Bahr's] rights. If that were the only purpose to be served by the acknowledgment it would achieve nothing. It would enable the [Thompsons] to destroy the [Bahrs'] interest and would leave [Nicolay] exposed to potential liability for breach of contract at the suit of the [Bahrs']. In the circumstances outlined it is evident that the purpose of cl 4 was to provide that the transfer of title to lot 340 was to be subject to the [Bahrs'] rights [to purchase the land from Nicolay] in the sense that those rights were to be enforceable against the [Thompsons].

At first glance it might seem that the words of cl 4 are inadequate to achieve this purpose. But an acknowledgment of an antecedent agreement in an appropriate context may amount to an agreement or undertaking to recognize rights arising under that antecedent agreement. And here the inferences to be drawn from the matrix of circumstances are so strong that they necessarily influence the interpretation of cl 4. These inferences provide a secure foundation [617] for imputing an intention to the parties and reading cl 4 as a reflection of that intention ...

[618] Granted that the purpose of cl 4 is as we have explained it, what is its legal effect? Is it simply an undertaking to perform the 1980 agreement if called upon to do so by the [Bahrs]? Contract scarcely seems to give sufficient effect to what the parties had in mind. A trust relationship is a more accurate and appropriate reflection of the parties' intention.

The [Bahrs] submitted that cl 4 creates a trust in favour of them as third parties ... However, in the absence of the manifestation of a clear intention to create a trust, the courts have been reluctant to hold that a trust exists ...

This reluctance to accept that the parties have created an express trust has induced the English courts to impose what has been described as a constructive trust in order to protect a prior interest from destruction on the registration of a later interest.[62] ...

On the other hand Fullagar J stated a contrary view in *Wilson v Darling Island Stevedoring & Lighterage Co Ltd*: 'It is difficult to understand the reluctance which courts have sometimes shown to infer a trust in such cases'.[63] His Honour was referring to contracts whereby a benefit is promised to a third party. We agree with his Honour's comment. If the inference to be drawn is that the parties intended to create or protect an interest in a third party and the trust relationship is the appropriate means of creating or protecting that interest or of giving effect to the intention, then [619] there is no reason why in a given case an intention to create a trust should not be inferred. The present is just such a case. The trust is an express, not a constructive, trust. The effect of the trust is that the [Thompsons] hold lot 340 subject to such rights as were created in favour of the [Bahrs] by the 1980 agreement.

---

62. See *Bannister v Bannister* [1948] 2 All ER 133; *Binions v Evans* [1972] Ch 359; *Lyus v Prowsa Ltd* [1982] 2 All ER 953.
63. *Wilson v Darling Island Stevedoring & Lighterage Co Ltd* (1956) 95 CLR 43 at 67.

Even if we had not reached this conclusion, we would not have regarded the registration of the transfer in favour of the [Thompsons] as destroying the [Bahrs'] rights. Having regard to the intention of the parties expressed in cl 4 of the later agreement, the subsequent repudiation of cl 6 of the 1980 agreement constituted fraud. The case therefore fell within the statutory exception with the result that the [Bahrs'] prior equitable interest prevails over the [Thompsons'] title, the [Thompsons] taking with notice of that interest.

Wilson and Toohey JJ

[629] [In this case] the real question is — having registered their interest under the provisions of the Act, did the [Thompsons] acquire a title which was indefeasible in the sense that it was no longer open to attack by the [Bahrs]? The question may be further refined by asking — having regard to ss 68 and 134 of the Act, was there in any relevant sense fraud on the part of the [Thompsons]? Unless there was such fraud, the [Thompsons] hold their title free of any interest the [Bahrs] have by reason of cl 6, subject to any claim in personam that may lie against the [Thompsons]. That is a matter to which we shall turn later in these reasons ...

[630] What then constitutes fraud for the purposes of ss 68 and 134? A convenient starting point is a passage in the judgment of the Privy Council in *Waimiha Sawmilling Co v Waione Timber Co*:

[631] If the designed object of a transfer be to cheat a man of a known existing right, that is fraudulent, and so also fraud may be established by a deliberate and dishonest trick causing an interest not to be registered and thus fraudulently keeping the register clear. It is not, however, necessary or wise to give abstract illustrations of what may constitute fraud in hypothetical conditions, for each case must depend upon its own circumstances. The act must be dishonest, and dishonesty must not be assumed solely by reason of knowledge of an unregistered interest.[64] ...

The emphasis in the authorities is on actual fraud on the part of [632] the registered proprietor. Such fraud may be found even though the registered proprietor has not himself made any representation. In *Latec Investments Ltd. v Hotel Terrigal Pty Ltd (In liq)*, Kitto J commented:

... we were invited to hold that nothing is fraud in the sense which is relevant under the *Real Property Act* unless it includes a fraudulent misrepresentation. The whole course of authority on this branch of the law is to the contrary. Moral turpitude there must be; but a designed cheating of a registered proprietor out of his rights by means of a collusive and colourable sale by a mortgagee company to a subsidiary is as clearly a fraud, as clearly a defrauding of the mortgagor, as a cheating by any other means.[65] ...

[636] Can it be said, using the language of *Waimiha Sawmilling Co v Waione Timber Co*, that the designed object of the transfer to the [Thompsons] was to cheat the [Bahrs] of a known existing right? Notwithstanding the various matters to which we have referred, we think the evidence falls short of establishing that case. The [Thompsons] agreed to

---

64. *Waimiha Sawmilling Co v Waione Timber Co* [1926] AC 101 at 106–7.
65. *Latec Investments Ltd v Hotel Terrigal Pty. Ltd (In liq)* (1965) 113 CLR 265 at 273–4.

buy lot 340 in the hope, even the expectation, that the [Bahrs] would not be able to buy [637] back lot 340. But the evidence does not justify a finding that it was their intention to ensure that the [Bahrs] did not do so. However it does establish that the [Thompsons] took a transfer of lot 340, knowing of cl 6, accepting an obligation to resell to the [Bahrs] and communicating that acceptance ... , but banking on the [Bahrs'] inability to find the $45,000 necessary to implement the clause. What are the consequences of that finding?

It is nearly a century since, in *Gibbs v Messer*, the Privy Council described the Torrens System in these terms:

> The object is to save persons dealing with registered proprietors from the trouble and expense of going behind the register, in order to investigate the history of their author's title, and to satisfy themselves of its validity. That end is accomplished by providing that every one who purchases, in bona fide and for value, from a registered proprietor, and enters his deed of transfer or mortgage on the register, shall thereby acquire an indefeasible right, notwithstanding the infirmity of his author's title.[66]

That statement still stands as an exposition of the nature and purpose of the Torrens System, though 'bona fide' must be equated with 'in the absence of fraud', and 'indefeasibility' is a word that does not appear in all the Torrens statutes of this country.

Nevertheless, in accepting the general principle of indefeasibility of title, the Privy Council in *Frazer v Walker* made it clear that 'this principle in no way denies the right of a plaintiff to bring against a registered proprietor a claim in personam, founded in law or in equity, for such relief as a court acting in personam may grant'.[67]

Sir Garfield Barwick, who was a member of the Privy Council in *Frazer v Walker*, commented in *Breskvar v Wall*:

> Proceedings may of course be brought against the registered proprietor by the persons and for the causes described in the quoted sections of the Act or by persons setting up matters depending upon the acts of the registered proprietor himself. These may have as their terminal point orders binding the registered proprietor to divest himself wholly or partly of the estate or interest vested in him by registration and endorsement of the certificate of title.[68]

This vulnerability on the part of the registered proprietor is not inconsistent with the concept of indefeasibility. The certificate of title is conclusive. If amended by order of a court it is, as [638] Barwick CJ pointed out, 'conclusive of the new particulars it contains'.[69]

Returning to *Frazer v Walker*, the Privy Council said of claims in personam:

> The principle must always remain paramount that those actions which fall within the prohibition of ss 62 and 63 may not be maintained.[70]

---

66. *Gibbs v Messer* [1891] AC 248 at 254.
67. *Frazer v Walker* [1967] 1 AC 569 at 585.
68. *Breskvar v Wall* (1971) 126 CLR 376 at 384–5.
69. *Breskvar v Wall* (1971) 126 CLR 376 at 385.
70. *Frazer v Walker* [1967] 1 AC 569 at 585.

The reference to ss 62 and 63 is a reference to the *Land Transfer Act* 1952 (NZ), roughly corresponding with ss 68 and 199 of the Act. The point being made by the Privy Council is that the indefeasibility provisions of the Act may not be circumvented. But, equally, they do not protect a registered proprietor from the consequences of his own actions where those actions give rise to a personal equity in another. Such an equity may arise from conduct of the registered proprietor after registration.[71] And we agree with Mahoney JA in *Logue v Shoalhaven Shire Council* that it may arise from conduct of the registered proprietor before registration.[72]

The evidence leads irresistibly to the following conclusions. The [Thompsons] understood through their agent ... that [Nicolay] would not sell lot 340 unless they agreed to be bound by the obligation in cl 6 which required [Nicolay] to resell to the [Bahrs]. The [Thompsons] bought lot 340 on the understanding common to vendor and purchasers that they were so bound and cl 4 was included to give effect to that understanding. Clause 4 may have been, of itself, insufficient for that purpose but the [Thompsons'] letter of 6 January 1982 and their two offers of 8 January 1982 put beyond doubt their acknowledgment of their obligation to the [Bahrs].

By taking a transfer of lot 340 on that basis, and the [Bahrs'] interest under cl 6 constituting an equitable interest in the land, the [Thompsons] became subject to a constructive trust in favour of the [Bahrs].[73] If it be the position that the [Bahrs'] interest under cl 6 fell short of an equitable estate, they none the less had a personal equity enforceable against the [Thompsons]. In either case ss 68 and 134 of the Act would not preclude the enforcement of the estate or equity because both arise, not by virtue of notice of them by the [Thompsons], but because of their acceptance of **[639]** a transfer on terms that they would be bound by the interest the [Bahrs] had in the land by reason of their contract with [Nicolay].

Comments

1. See Radan & Stewart at **7.78–7.97**.
2. The two joint judgments differ on the nature of the trust that arose as a result of the right of the Bahrs to repurchase the land from Nicolay. Mason CJ and Wilson J, at 619, said it was an express trust. Wilson and Toohey JJ, at 638, held that it was a constructive trust. It can be noted that Brennan J, at 655, also held that it was a constructive trust.
3. For analyses of this case in the context of the impact of *in personam* claims on indefeasibility see J G Tooher, 'Muddying the Torrens Waters with the Chancellor's Foot? *Bahr v Nicolay*' (1993) 1 *Australian Property Law Journal* 1 and L Stevens & K O'Donnell, 'Indefeasibility in Decline: the In Personam Remedies' in D Grinlinton (ed), *Torrens in the Twenty-First Century*, LexisNexis, Wellington, 2003, p 141.

---

71. *Barry v Heider* (1914) 19 CLR 197.
72. *Logue v Shoalhaven Shire Council* [1979] 1 NSWLR 537 at 563.
73. *Lyus v Prowsa Developments Ltd* [1982] 2 All ER 953; *Binions v Evans* [1972] Ch 359 at 368.

Priority and *in personam* rights under the Torrens system

7.7 Vassos v State Bank of South Australia [1993] 2 VR 316

Court: Supreme Court of Victoria

Facts: Peter Vassos and his children Tommy and Anne were the registered proprietors of Torrens title land in Flinders Street, Melbourne. The State Bank had a registered mortgage over the land as security for a loan of $130,000. Subsequently a substitute mortgage guaranteeing a loan of $500,000 to Tommy's business was registered in favour of the bank. However, the signatures of Peter and Anne to this mortgage were forged by Tommy. The bank was unaware of the forgery.

Issues: The issues before the Supreme Court were whether the bank's indefeasible title to the mortgage was defeated either on the statutory ground of fraud as set out in s 42 of the *Transfer of Land Act 1958* (Vic) or on the basis of an *in personam* right vested in Peter and Anne.

Decision: Hayne J in the Supreme Court held that the bank's indefeasible title was not defeated on either the grounds of fraud or *in personam* rights. As to the ground of fraud, his Honour noted clear authority to the effect that only fraud on the part of the registered proprietor of the relevant interest fell within the scope of fraud under the Torrens system. Because there was no such conduct on the part of the bank in this case, the claim against them based on fraud failed. As to the claim of *in personam* rights, his Honour held that even if the bank's conduct may have been somewhat careless, it was not unconscientious or unconscionable, and therefore did not give rise to any *in personam* claim against it. However, Hayne J went on to hold that Peter and Anne were entitled to be indemnified for the losses they would suffer as a result of his ruling on indefeasibility pursuant to indemnity provisions set out in s 110 of the *Transfer of Land Act*.

Extracts: The extracts from the judgment of Hayne J discuss the principles relating to *in personam* rights and their application to the facts of this case.

Hayne J

[329] In *Frazer v Walker* the Judicial Committee made it clear that the general principle that registration under Torrens System legislation confers on a registered proprietor a title to the interest in respect of which he is registered which is immune from all adverse claims save for those specifically excepted does not deny 'the right of a plaintiff to bring against a registered proprietor a claim in personam, founded in law or in equity, for such relief as a court acting in personam may grant'.[74] ...

This vulnerability to *in personam* proceedings is not inconsistent with indefeasibility. The certificate of title is conclusive but its registration does not protect the registered proprietor from the consequences of his own [330] actions where those actions give a personal equity in another.[75] ...

---

74. *Frazer v Walker* [1967] 1 AC 569 at 585.
75. *Bahr v Nicolay [No 2]* (1988) 164 CLR 604 at 637–8.

[331] [*Mercantile Mutual Life Insurance Co Ltd v Gosper*] also concerned a forged instrument. In 1982 Mrs Gosper gave a mortgage over a property that she owned and later varied that mortgage to increase the amount that it secured. In 1988 her husband applied for a loan from Mercantile Mutual Life Insurance Co which approved the loan on terms that the existing mortgage would be transferred to it and varied to take account of the additional loan. A transfer of mortgage and variation of mortgage were registered but it was later found out that Mr Gosper had forged all the signatures required of his wife in connection with the transfer and variation and had acted entirely without her knowledge or consent ...

[332] The majority of the [New South Wales Court of Appeal] (Kirby P and Mahoney JA) held that [Mrs Gosper] had a personal equity against [Mercantile Mutual] entitling [her] to compel discharge of the mortgage on payment of the amount secured by the original, genuine, mortgage but may have differed in their identification of how that equity arose. Mahoney JA considered that [Mercantile Mutual] had used [Mrs Gosper's] certificate of title in breach of obligations it owed [her] and that the use of the certificate in that way was a necessary step in securing registration of the forged variation of mortgage. His Honour held that where the registration of the forged instrument had been produced by such a breach by the new owner, that was sufficient to create a personal equity against the new owner.[76] Kirby P, while agreeing with this analysis, may be read as expressing a wider view: that [Mrs Gosper] should be restored to the position representing the legal relationship that existed before registration of the forged instrument because she then had an equity of redemption (and thus an equitable interest in the land) which should be protected because the forged instrument did not affect the position as between [herself] and [Mercantile Mutual].[77] However this may be, I consider that as Mahoney JA said: 'It is proper to accept that, on the existing state of the authorities, the mere fact of forgery of the instrument does not establish a "personal" equity'.[78]

Much turned in *Gosper's Case* on the fact that there had been a variation of a mortgage when on any view the original mortgage bound the mortgagor. The present case is very different.

I consider it of the first importance to recall that the bank's title as mortgagee here is not defeated by the fact of forgery. The bank acquired that title innocent of any fraud or knowledge of fraud. Its title is as mortgagee to secure all amounts owed by any of the mortgagors including amounts owed by any of the mortgagors as guarantors of [Tommy's business]. Of course two of the three mortgagors never assented to become surety for [Tommy's business] or to give the bank a mortgage as security for any such indebtedness but in no case where the signature of a mortgagor has been forged will that mortgagor have assented to pay the debt secured by the mortgage. If, as [Peter and Anne] contended, the fact of lack of assent of the mortgagor gives an *in personam* right to a discharge, then every mortgagor whose signature was forged would be entitled to compel the mortgagee to discharge the mortgage on the basis that the mortgagee was not entitled to demand any more than had been agreed to be paid and the 'mortgagor' had never agreed to pay anything. That flies in the face of indefeasibility of title for without any fault of any kind

---

76. *Mercantile Mutual Life Insurance Co Ltd v Gosper* (1991) 25 NSWLR 32 at 48–9.
77. *Mercantile Mutual Life Insurance Co Ltd v Gosper* (1991) 25 NSWLR 32 at 37.
78. *Mercantile Mutual Life Insurance Co Ltd v Gosper* (1991) 25 NSWLR 32 at 47.

on the part of the mortgagee he could always be compelled to discharge his security and his title obtained by registration could always be set aside at the suit of the defrauded party ...

The bare fact that a party has not assented to the transaction recorded in an instrument registered under Torrens system legislation does not, in my opinion, give that person a right enforceable by *in personam* action to have the transaction reversed. For my part I consider it is clear that more than **[333]** the bare fact of forgery (and thus an absence of assent) must be shown to found any *in personam* action of the kind spoken of in *Frazer v Walker* and subsequent cases.

As Mahoney JA points out in *Gosper's Case* there has been no comprehensive definition of 'personal' equity for these purposes.[79] Again as his Honour points out it may be possible to discern in the authorities two suggestions about the content of the expression 'personal equity' in this context: that the interest must not be inconsistent with the terms or policy of the legislation and that 'personal' equities arise only from acts of the new owner.[80] However whatever the limits may be on such 'personal' equities the very language used to describe the right and the reference to the remedies being '*in personam* remedies' is a clear reference to the remedies being available in circumstances where equity would act, ie, in cases which equity would classify as unconscionable or unconscientious. In the present case ... it may well be that the bank did not act without neglect but there is my view no material which would show that the bank acted unconscionably. There was no misrepresentation by it, no misuse of power, no improper attempt to rely upon its legal rights, no knowledge of wrongdoing by any other party. It obtained a mortgage, apparently regular on its face but which was in fact forged. Even if by making reasonable enquiries the bank could have discovered the fact of the forgery I do not consider that that fact alone renders its conduct unconscionable. I do not consider that [Peter and Anne] have any *in personam* right against the bank; all that they have shown is the mere fact of forgery of the instrument.

Comment

1. See Radan & Stewart at **7.101**.

Priority and the failure to lodge a caveat under the Torrens system

---

7.8 Person-to-Person Financial Services Pty Ltd v Sharari
[1984] 1 NSWLR 745

Court: Supreme Court of New South Wales

Facts: Tredgolde had a registered mortgage over Torrens title land. He also held the certificate of title as the registered mortgagee. Sharari took a subsequent mortgage

---

79. *Mercantile Mutual Life Insurance Co Ltd v Gosper* (1991) 25 NSWLR 32 at 45.
80. *Mercantile Mutual Life Insurance Co Ltd v Gosper* (1991) 25 NSWLR 32 at 45; *Breskvar v Wall* (1971) 126 CLR 376 at 384–5.

over the property, but his solicitor failed to have that mortgage registered. Furthermore, Sharari did not lodge a caveat to protect his unregistered mortgage. Subsequently, Person-to-Person took a mortgage over the property after being told by the owner of the land that Tredgolde had the only other mortgage over the property. Person-to-Person's search of the register revealed only Tredgolde's mortgage. Person-to-Person lodged a caveat in respect of its unregistered mortgage.

Issue: The issue before the Supreme Court was whether Sharari's unregistered mortgage had priority over Person-to-Person's subsequent unregistered mortgage. The critical factor in determining the priority dispute was whether Sharari's failure to lodge a caveat amounted to postponing conduct and thereby displaced the priority his interest otherwise had by being the first in time.

Decision: McLelland J in the Supreme Court ruled that Sharari was guilty of postponing conduct and that, therefore, Person-to-Person's unregistered mortgage had obtained priority over Sharari's unregistered mortgage.

Extracts: The extracts from the judgment of McLelland J discuss the principles relating to the circumstances in which a failure to lodge a caveat over Torrens title land constitute postponing conduct on the part of the holder of the first unregistered interest.

McLelland J

[746] As between two equitable interests in property, the earlier in time is entitled to priority unless the circumstances are such as to make it inequitable [747] as between the holders thereof that the earlier should have such priority. Such circumstances may be found where some act or omission by the holder of the earlier interest has led the other to acquire his interest on the supposition that the earlier did not exist. The omission relied on by [Person-to-Person] in the present case is the failure of [Sharari] either to register his mortgage or lodge a caveat in respect of his interest as mortgagee.

It is quite clear, as was held in *J & H Just (Holdings) Pty Ltd v Bank of New South Wales*,[81] that failure by the holder of an equitable interest to lodge a caveat in respect of that interest where a caveat might have alerted the acquirer of a subsequent equitable interest to the existence of the earlier interest of which he was unaware, does not necessarily result in the postponement of the earlier to the subsequent interest, but that case does not provide authority for the proposition that failure to lodge a caveat can never bring about the postponement of an earlier to a subsequent interest …

The effect of a failure by the holder of an equitable interest to lodge a caveat will depend upon the particular circumstances. A critical point of distinction between the circumstances under consideration in *Butler v Fairclough*[82] and those under consideration in *J & H Just (Holdings) Pty Ltd v Bank of New South Wales* is that the party whose conduct in failing to lodge a caveat was under consideration was in the former case an unregistered second mortgagee who did not have the certificate of title, and in the latter case an unregistered first mortgagee who did have the certificate of title …

---

81. (1971) 125 CLR 546.
82. (1917) 23 CLR 78.

[748] In the present case there is evidence before me, which I accept, to the effect that it is the settled practice of competent solicitors in New South Wales acting for second or subsequent mortgagees, to ensure either the prompt registration of the mortgage or lodgment of a caveat. The failure by [Sharari] through his solicitor to conform to this practice would naturally lead those who searched, such as [Person-to-Person], to believe that there was no outstanding second mortgage and it is my opinion that the failure of [Sharari], in the absence of registration of his mortgage, to lodge a caveat led [Person-to-Person] to acquire its mortgage on the supposition that no unregistered second mortgage [749] already existed, in circumstances which make it inequitable as between the parties that [Person-to-Person's] mortgage should have priority over that of [Sharari].

Comments

1. See Radan & Stewart at **7.106–7.118**.
2. In *Capital Finance Australia Ltd v Struthers* [2008] NSWSC 440 at [22], Hamilton J said:

   [T]he correct principle is that preference should be given to what is the better equity on an examination of the relevant circumstances. The failure to lodge a caveat in respect of the prior interest is just one of the circumstances to be considered in determining whether it is inequitable that the prior equitable owner retain that priority. Judges of this Court have subsequently held that, where there was a failure to caveat, evidence of search on behalf of the person with the subsequent interest and reliance by that person in acquiring his or her interest on the result of the search, those facts in the context of the overall circumstances of a case may lead to the postponement of the prior interest to the subsequent interest: see the decisions of McLelland J in *Person-to-Person* and of Bryson J in *Double Bay Newspapers Pty Ltd v A W Holdings Pty Ltd* (1996) 42 NSWLR 409].

7.9   Jacobs v Platt Nominees Pty Ltd [1990] VR 146

Court: Full Court of the Supreme Court of Victoria

Facts: Platt Nominees owned Torrens title land in Melbourne. Mr and Mrs Platt were the sole owners and directors of Platt Nominees. Their daughter, Mrs Jacobs, had an option to purchase the property from Platt Nominees. She had no reason to believe that her parents would sell the land to anybody else and, therefore, decided not to lodge a caveat. However, her parents decided to sell the land to Perpetual Trustee Co. Jacobs sought a declaration that she was entitled to have her option enforced by a decree of specific performance. Perpetual Trustees argued that its interest as purchaser of the property had priority over that of Jacobs and therefore sought a declaration that it was entitled to have its contract specifically enforced.

Issue: The issue before the Full Court was whether Jacobs' failure to caveat meant that her interest was postponed to that of Perpetual Trustees.

Decision: The Full Court (Crockett, King and Gobbo JJ) unanimously ruled in favour of Jacobs and held that her failure to lodge a caveat did not mean that her interest was postponed to that of Perpetual Trustees.

> **Extracts:** The extracts from the joint judgment of the Full Court discuss the principles relating to a priority dispute over competing unregistered interests in Torrens title land where the owner of the first interest has not lodged a caveat.

Crockett, King and Gobbo JJ

[149] In ... *Butler v Fairclough*: [Griffith CJ said]: 'A person who has an equitable charge upon the land may protect it by lodging [150] a caveat, which in my opinion operates as notice to all the world that the registered proprietor's title is subject to the equitable interest alleged in the caveat'.[83]

[This] statement was the subject of some reservation by at least four members of the High Court in *J & H Just (Holdings) Pty Ltd v Bank of New South Wales*. There a registered proprietor of land had executed a memorandum of mortgage in favour of the bank to secure an overdraft and had deposited the duplicate certificate of title with the bank. The bank did not register the memorandum or lodge a caveat. The proprietor later created a further mortgage in favour of another lender who had searched the title and found no evidence of any encumbrance. On his claim to be registered in priority to the bank, the court held the bank's priority had not been lost by its failure to lodge a caveat. Barwick CJ ... said: 'Whilst it may be true in some instances that "the register may bear on its face a notice of equitable claims", this is not necessarily so and whilst in some instances a caveat of which the lodgment is noted in the certificate of title may be "notice to all the world" that the registered proprietor's title is subject to the equitable interest alleged in the caveat this, in my opinion, is not necessarily universally the case. To hold that a failure by a person entitled to an equitable estate or interest in land under the *Real Property Act* to lodge a caveat against dealings with the land must necessarily involve the loss of priority which the time of the creation of the equitable interest would otherwise give, is not merely in my opinion unwarranted by general principles or by any statutory provision but would in my opinion be subversive of the well recognized ability of parties to create or to maintain equitable interests in such lands. Sir Owen Dixon's remarks in *Lapin v Abigail*[84] with which I respectfully agree, point in this direction'.[85] ...

[151] The decision in *J & H Just's Case* was distinguished by Gowans J in *Osmanoski v Rose*[86] on the basis that the statutory provisions in the New South Wales cases differed significantly from those in the Victorian Act. It was also said that the fact that the bank held the duplicate title was a further significant distinguishing feature. As to the first, we are of the view that the Victorian legislation is not so different that it provides a necessary reason for distinguishing *Just's Case* ...

As to the matter of the duplicate title, this was certainly important but it was discussed in the context of demonstrating a further reason why the caveat as a method of self-protection was not necessary. It does not bear out a proposition that the holder of the prior equitable interest is expected to give notice to the world. Indeed, the duplicate title

---

83. *Butler v Fairclough* (1917) 23 CLR 78 at 91.
84. (1930) 44 CLR 166, at 205.
85. *J & H Just (Holdings) Pty Ltd v Bank of New South Wales* (1971) 125 CLR 546 at 554.
86. [1974] VR 523.

affords no assistance to the subsequent holder for it only prevents registration; it does not prevent creation of the second equitable interest.

On one reading, the judgment [in *Osmanoski v Rose*] does not assert that mere failure to lodge a caveat without full consideration of all relevant circumstances can suffice to postpone the earlier equity. To the extent that it does, it is in our view in conflict with authority, in particular *Just's Case*. But it is only necessary to say at this point that *Just's Case* does not exclude the possibility that mere failure to lodge caveat may suffice providing all other relevant circumstances are considered ...

The last main authority on the question of competing equities namely, *Heid v Reliance Finance Corporation Pty Ltd*,[87] further confirms ... that all relevant circumstances must be considered ...

[159] It is now ... convenient to deal first with any postponement of [Jacobs'] prior equity on the basis of estoppel. This cannot ... sustain any postponement in the present case for two reasons. In the first place, the notion of a representation by [Jacobs] which created an assumption of fact relied upon by Perpetual to its detriment is wholly inapposite to the present case. The primary purpose of a caveat is, as was said in *Just's Case* to provide protection for the caveator not to give notice to the world. The practice of lodging caveats is at best that and not a duty, much less a duty to the world at large. In any event there was no settled practice proved that covered all options to purchase nor was it proved that there was a settled practice for unregistered transactions that conveyed that the prospective purchasers invariably searched the title with the relevant expectation before entering into any purchase. In addition, the existence of the obligations as to disclosure created by the changes to the *Sale of Land Act* further weakened the force of any argument as to the creation of any assumption. The doctrine of estoppel is more appropriate to the cases where parties armed the third party 'with the power of going into the world under false colours',[88] by arming him with title deeds and evidence of payment. That is not the situation here.

Secondly, the mere alteration of position cannot in our view sustain an estoppel in the present type of situation and, as there is no sufficient evidence of detriment, the estoppel argument cannot sustain any postponement of the prior equity.

The second method of deciding the postponement question rests on what may be conveniently described as the broad principle in the joint judgment of Mason and Deane JJ in *Heid's Case*. The starting point is that prima facie priority in time will decide the matter unless there be something 'tangible and distinct having grave and strong effect to accomplish the purpose'.[89] As was said in the joint judgment in *Heid's Case*: 'It will always be necessary to characterize the conduct of the holder of the earlier interest in order to determine whether, in all the circumstances, that conduct is such that, in fairness and in justice, the earlier interest should be postponed to the later interest'.[90] The joint judgment goes on to refer to negligence and estoppel as elements and to [160] warn that mere causal links may not suffice and that failure to lodge a caveat does not in itself involve the loss of priority, being only one of the circumstances to be considered.

---

87. (1983) 154 CLR 326.
88. *Dixon v Muckleston* (1872) LR 8 Ch App 155 at 160.
89. *Shropshire Union Railways and Canal Co v R* (1857) LR 7 HL 496 at 507.
90. *Heid v Reliance Finance Corporation Pty Ltd* (1983) 154 CLR 326 at 341.

In our view the significant circumstance in the present case was the fact that [Jacobs] had secured the option from her parents in such a way that it was inconceivable that her mother and father would join together to sell the motel in breach of the option. It was, in short, not reasonably foreseeable that her failure to lodge a caveat exposed herself or others to a risk of a later sale. In this setting her explanation that she did not want to upset her father by lodging a caveat was entirely consistent.

Comment
1. See Radan & Stewart at **7.106–7.118**.

8

CONFIDENTIAL INFORMATION

Introduction

8.1 This chapter deals with the doctrine of breach of confidence. The extracts outline the origins of the doctrine and its main elements, including the requirement of secrecy. The doctrine applies to a number of areas of activity and can be used to protect information that arises in personal relationships, commercial settings and in government. The doctrine has continued to expand in the twentieth and twenty-first centuries and is now the main common law source of privacy protection in Australia.

The extracts in this chapter discuss the following:

- the origins of the doctrine of breach of confidence and the source of the equitable jurisdiction: *Prince Albert v Strange* (1849) 47 ER 1302; *Morison v Moat* (1852) 68 ER 492; *Moorgate Tobacco Co Ltd v Philip Morris Ltd (No 2)* (1984) 156 CLR 414;
- the elements of the modern action for breach of confidence: *Coco v A N Clark (Engineers) Ltd* (1968) 1a IPR 587;
- the requirement of secrecy and necessity for the information to not have entered the public domain: *Australian Football League v Age Company Ltd* (2006) 15 VR 19;
- the application of the doctrine to trade secrets: *Del Casale v Artedomus (Aust) Pty Limited* [2007] NSWCA 172;
- the application of the doctrine to government secrets: *Commonwealth v John Fairfax & Sons Ltd* (1980) 147 CLR 39;
- the defence of public interest and iniquity: *Australian Football League v Age Company Ltd* (2006) 15 VR 19;
- the application of the doctrine of breach of confidence to protect privacy interests: *Australian Broadcasting Corporation v Lenah Game Meats Pty Ltd* (2001) 208 CLR 199.

8.2   Prince Albert v Strange (1849) 47 ER 1302

Court: High Court of Chancery

Facts: Queen Victoria and her husband, Prince Albert the Queen's Consort, made drawings and etchings together for their amusement. The royals had impressions made of the artwork which they gave to a printer, Brown, to produce. An employee of Brown, Middleton, took the impressions without permission and these had somehow come into the possession of three men: Strange, J T Judge and J A F Judge. Strange sought to

---

publicly display his copies of the etchings and print them in a descriptive catalogue. Prince Albert successfully sought an injunction to restrain the display and the publication of the catalogue. Strange appealed this decision to the Lord Chancellor.

Issue: The main issue was concerned with the basis on which an injunction could have been issued.

Decision: Lord Cottenham, the Lord Chancellor, decided that the Prince had a proprietary right in the unpublished artwork and that an injunction could issue to prevent publication. In addition to the proprietary basis, equity would also prevent publication in cases of breach of trust, breach of confidence or breach of contract.

Extracts: The extract from the judgment of Lord Cottenham discusses the reasons why equity will issue an injunction to prevent publication.

Lord Cottenham

[1310] It was said, by one of the learned counsel for [Strange], that the injunction must rest on the ground of property or breach of trust. Both appear to me to exist in this case. The property in an author or composer of any work, whether of literature, art or science, such work being unpublished and kept for his private use or pleasure cannot be disputed, after the many decisions in which that proposition has been affirmed or assumed. I say 'assumed,' because, in most of the cases which have been decided, the question was not as to the original right of the author, but whether what had taken place did not amount to a waiver of such right: as, in the case of letters, how far the sending of the letters; in the case of dramatic composition, how far the permitting performance; and, in the case of Abernethy's Lectures,[1] how far the oral delivery of the lecture had deprived the author of any part of his original right and property — a question which could not have arisen if there had not been such original right or property. It would be a waste of time to refer in detail to the cases on this subject.

If, then, such right and property exist in the author of such work, it must so exist exclusively of all other persons. Can any stranger have any right or title to, or interest in, that which belongs exclusively to another? And yet this is precisely what [Strange] claims, although, by a strange inconsistency, he does not dispute the general proposition as to [the Prince's] right and property; for he contends, that, admitting [the Prince's] right and property in the etchings in question, and, as incident to it, the right to prevent publication or exhibition of copies of them, yet he insists that some persons, having had access to certain copies ... and having from such copies composed a description and list of the originals, he ... is entitled to publish such list and description: that is, that he is entitled, against the will of the owner, to make such use of his exclusive property.

It being admitted that [Strange] could not publish a copy — that is, an impression — of the etchings, how in principle does a catalogue, list or description differ? A copy or impression

---

1. This case is reported as *Abernathy v Hutchison* (1824) 47 ER 1313.

of the etchings could only be a means of communicating knowledge and information of the original; and does not a list and description do the same? The means are different, but the object and effect are similar; for in both the object and effect is to make known to the public, more or less, the unpublished works and compositions of the author, which he is entitled to keep wholly for his private use and pleasure, and to withhold altogether, or so far as he may please, from the knowledge of others.

Cases of abridgments, translations, extracts and criticisms of published works, have no reference whatever to the present question. They all depend on the extent and right, under the Acts, with respect to copyright, and have no analogy to the exclusive right of the author in unpublished compositions, which depend entirely on the common law right of property. A clerk of Sir John Strange, having, whilst in his employ, made an abridgment of such of his manuscript cases as related to evidence, was restrained by Lord Hardwicke, in 1754, from publishing it, the cases themselves being then unpublished.

Upon the first question, therefore, that of property, I am clearly of opinion, that, the exclusive right and interest of [the Prince] in the compositions and works in question being established, and there being no right or interest whatever in [Strange], [the Prince] is entitled to the injunction of this Court to protect him against the invasion of such right and interest by [Strange], which the publication of any catalogue would undoubtedly be.

[1311] But this case by no means depends solely on the question of property; for a breach of trust, confidence or contract itself would entitle the [Prince] to the injunction. The [Prince's] affidavit states the private character of the work or composition, and negatives any licence or authority for publication (the gift of some of the etchings to private friends not implying any such licence or authority); and states distinctly the belief of the [Prince] that the catalogue, and the descriptive and other remarks therein contained, could not have been compiled, except by means of the possession of the several impressions of the etchings, surreptitiously and improperly obtained. To this case no answer is made, [Strange] saying only, that he did not at the time believe the etchings to have been improperly obtained, but not suggesting any mode by which they could have been properly obtained, so as to entitle the possessor to use them for publication.

If, then, these compositions were kept private, except as to some given to private friends, and some sent to Mr Brown, for the purpose of having certain impressions taken, the possession of [Strange], or of his partner Judge, must have originated in a breach of trust, confidence or contract in Brown, or some person in his employ, taking more impressions than were ordered, and retaining the extra number; or in some person to whom copies were given, which is not to be supposed, but which, if it were the origin of the possession of [Strange], would be equally a breach of trust, confidence or contract, as was considered in the case of *The Duke of Queensbury v Shebbeare*.[2] And upon the evidence on behalf of the [Prince], and the absence of any explanation on the part of [Strange], I am bound to assume that the possession of the etchings or engravings, on the part of [Strange] or Judge, has its foundation in a breach of trust, confidence or contract, as Lord Eldon did in the case of Mr. Abernethy's Lectures … and upon this ground, also, I think the [Prince's] title to the injunction sought to be discharged fully established.

---

2.   (1758) 28 ER 924.

8.3   Morison v Moat (1852) 68 ER 492

Court: High Court of Chancery

Facts: This case concerned a recipe for medicine — Morison's Vegetable Universal Medicine — which was invented by James Morison. James and Thomas Moat created a business partnership to manufacture and sell the medicine. The recipe was never patented. It was a condition of the partnership that Thomas never tell anyone about the recipe for the medicine. After many years the partnership was taken over by the sons of James (Alexander and John) and the son of Thomas (Crofton). The business was effectively run by Alexander and John. Crofton was the silent partner. The partnership later dissolved. Alexander and John continued to produce medicines using the original formula. It was discovered by Alexander and John that Crofton had also begun to manufacture and sell medicine which he called 'Morison's Universal Medicine by C W Moat'. It was believed that Thomas had, prior to his death, communicated the secret recipe to Crofton, in breach of the original partnership agreement.

Issue: The issue before the court was whether it was possible to prevent Crofton from exploiting the recipe, given that it was not property? Moreover, could it be possible that the recipe was an asset of the partnership and so open to all the ex-partners to exploit?

Decision: Sir G J Turner VC ordered a perpetual injunction to restrain Crofton Moat from using the recipe and selling it under the title of 'Morison's Universal Medicine' or 'Morison's Vegetable Universal Medicine'.

Extracts: The extract from the judgment of Sir G J Turner VC examines the equitable jurisdiction to restrain a breach of confidence and the basis of the agreement between James Morison and Thomas Moat which gave rise to this obligation.

Sir G J Turner VC

[498] [The Morisons'] case was rested in argument upon the ground that [Moat] had obtained this secret by breach of faith or of contract on the part of Thomas Moat. The subsidiary ground brought forward by the bill, of [Crofton Moat] selling his medicines under the original name and description, was relied upon rather in support of the case of breach of faith and of contract than as a separate and distinct ground for the interference of the Court. Upon that part of the case it is sufficient, therefore, to observe that there might be difficulty in maintaining it, at all events, until the [Morisons] should have established their right at law. The true question is whether, under the circumstances of this case, the Court ought to interpose by injunction, upon the ground of breach of faith or of contract. That the Court has exercised jurisdiction in cases of this nature does not, I think, admit of any question. Different grounds have indeed been assigned for the exercise of that jurisdiction. In some cases it has been referred to property, in others to contract, and in others, again, it has been treated as founded upon trust or confidence, meaning, as I conceive, that the Court fastens the obligation on the conscience of the

party, and enforces it against him in the same manner as it enforces against a party to whom a benefit is given the obligation of performing a promise on the faith of which the benefit has been conferred; but, upon whatever grounds the jurisdiction is founded, the authorities leave no doubt as to the exercise of it ...

[500] It was much pressed in argument, on the part of [Moat], that the effect of granting an injunction in such a case as the present would be to give the [Morisons] a better right than that of a patentee ... but what we have to deal with here is, not the right of the [Morisons] against the world, but their right against [Moat]. It may well be that the [Morisons] have no title against the world in general, and may yet have a good title against [Moat] ...

It does not appear to be disputed that James Morison was the inventor, and, down to the 23d of June 1830, the sole depository of the secret in question. Upon the 23d of June 1830 the partnership deed between him and Moat, and the two bonds, were executed; and the first question to be considered is, what was the effect of those instruments? It was contended, on the part of [Moat], that the effect of them was to constitute the secret an asset of the partnership; but, looking at the deed alone, apart from the bonds, I am much disposed to think it could not have that effect; and taking the deed, as I think it must be taken, in connexion with the bonds, I think it clear that it could not so operate. The question, I apprehend, is one of intention, like the question whether there is a partnership in mines, or only in the minerals which are raised and manufactured by parties working the mines; and this deed, I think, contains indications that the secret was not intended to belong to the partnership; for although it contemplated the introduction of new partners, and expressly provides for the communication of the secret by James Morison to Thomas Moat, it leaves it to the option of James Morison whether he will communicate the secret to persons introduced either by himself or by Moat, according as the word 'he' in the clause referred to may apply to one or the other (a point which is not material); and it is difficult to conceive that a secret which one partner had a discretion to withhold from others could be intended to be a partnership asset. Again, the clause as to accounts seems to look to matters which would properly and without difficulty be the subject of account, and not to such an asset as this secret would be. An account was to be taken upon a new partner coming in. Is it conceivable that, if this secret had been contemplated as an asset of the partnership, there would have been no provision as to what should then be done respecting it, no provision for valuing it, either then or at the termination of the partnership? But, however this question might have stood upon the deed alone, the bonds seem to me to conclude it; for, by Moat's bond, he is not to communicate the secret to any person whomsoever; and by Morison's bond he is not to communicate it except to persons whom he or Moat may introduce into the partnership, or for the purposes of the foreign trade; and how then could it be in the contemplation of the parties that it should be an asset of the partnership? in which case it would be liable to be sold when the partnership determined. The true effect of these instruments appears to me to be that Morison reserved to himself the secret against all the world except Thomas Moat. Morison had power to introduce partners into the concern; Moat had the like power with the concurrence of Morison, but not otherwise. It was entirely at the option of Morison whether he would communicate the secret to any partner introduced either by himself or by Moat. Moat was also bound not to reveal the secret to any person whatsoever.

8.4   Moorgate Tobacco Co Ltd v Philip Morris Ltd (No 2) (1984) 156 CLR 414

Court: High Court of Australia

Facts: Philip Morris Ltd (Philip Morris) was a company which was licensed to sell Kent cigarettes, which were produced by an American company, Loew's Theatres Inc (Loew's). Philip Morris also manufactured and marketed its own cigarettes in Australia under the name 'Marlboro Lights'. Before the licence agreement between them came to an end, Loew's and Philip Morris had negotiations regarding Loew's idea to sell new, low tar cigarettes known as 'Kent Golden Lights' or 'Kent Special Mild'. Those negotiations did not bear fruit and the licence agreement was completed. Loew's business in Australia was later acquired by Moorgate Tobacco Co Ltd (Moorgate), a company which was a member of the British and American Tobacco Group. Roughly three weeks after Moorgate purchased Loew's concerns, Philip Morris registered 'Golden Lights' as a trade mark in Australia. Moorgate claimed that Philip Morris' registration of the trade mark was a breach of contract, fiduciary duty, tort law and confidential information.

Issue: The issue before the High Court was whether there was a jurisdiction in equity to protect confidential information. Was the information confidential in nature and was there an equitable obligation which would prevent Philip Morris from exploiting the marketing idea?

Decision: The High Court (Gibbs CJ, Mason, Wilson, Deane and Dawson JJ) unanimously held that, while equity had a jurisdiction to protect confidential information, the information at hand did not have a 'quality of confidence'.

Extracts: The extract from the judgment of Deane J outlines the equitable jurisdiction and why he believed the information regarding the idea of marketing 'Golden Lights' cigarettes to not be confidential.

Deane J

[437] Moorgate relied in two distinct ways on the alleged confidentiality of certain of the information which Loew's communicated to Philip Morris. Firstly, it was said that that allegedly confidential information had been obtained by Philip Morris as a result of its having undertaken the fiduciary duty of acting for Loew's in relation to the proposed introduction of the new cigarette in the Australian market. If Philip Morris had acquired confidential information, by use or by reason of such a fiduciary position or of opportunity or knowledge resulting therefrom, it would, on well established principles, be precluded from using the information to its own advantage or to the detriment of Loew's. As has been said however, Moorgate has failed to establish that Philip Morris undertook any such fiduciary duty. Alternatively, it was submitted that the effect of the combination of the confidential nature of the relevant information and the circumstances in which it was communicated was that Philip Morris was under a duty, enforceable *in personam*

by equitable remedies, not to disclose or make use of the confidential information other than for the purposes for which it was communicated to it.[3]

It is unnecessary, for the purposes of the present appeal, to attempt to define the precise scope of the equitable jurisdiction to grant relief against an actual or threatened abuse of confidential information not involving any tort or any breach of some express or implied contractual provision, some wider fiduciary duty or some copyright or trade mark right. A general equitable jurisdiction to grant such relief has long been asserted and should, in my view, now be accepted.[4] Like most heads of exclusive equitable jurisdiction, its rational basis does not lie in proprietary right. It lies in the notion of an obligation of conscience arising from the circumstances in or through which the information was communicated or obtained. Relief under the jurisdiction is not available, however, unless it appears that the information in question has 'the necessary quality of confidence about it'[5] and that it is significant, not necessarily in the sense of commercially valuable,[6] but in the sense that the preservation of its confidentiality or secrecy is of substantial concern to [Moorgate]. That being so, the starting point of the alternative argument must be the identification of the relevant confidential information. Again, the argument breaks down at the threshold.

The allegedly confidential information is identified by Moorgate as being the 'marketing results, advertising, position paper and the knowledge that [Loew's] wanted to introduce the brand in Australia'. Putting to one side for the moment information about what Loew's desired or intended to do, examination of the designated material discloses that it consisted of the type of general information and argument that one would expect a company desiring to license the manufacture and marketing in Australia of a new type of cigarette under a 'line extension' of its parent mark to communicate to an 'arms-length' potential licensee which already manufactured and marketed a competing product. In particular, the evidence did not establish that any of the material was in fact regarded as confidential by Loew's or that Loew's at any time requested Philip Morris to treat or regard it as confidential. In argument, senior counsel for Moorgate tended to restrict the suggested confidential information to the information that Loew's wanted to introduce the new cigarettes in Australia under the brand mark 'Kent Golden Lights'. In that regard, however, the evidence established neither that any such information was communicated to Philip Morris nor that, if it had been, it was even accurate. All that the evidence indicated was that Loew's was anxious that Philip Morris agree to manufacture and market the new cigarettes, possibly under the name 'Kent Golden Lights', in Australia under an agreement which would provide for the payment by Philip Morris to Loew's of a royalty upon sales. It is probably implicit in the material in evidence that Loew's would have wished, in the event that Philip Morris was not interested, to obtain some other licensee but the evidence is quite silent as to whether Loew's ever had any desire or

---

3. See *Saltman Engineering Co Ltd v Campbell Engineering Co Ltd* (1947) 65 RPC 203 at 215; *Interfirm Comparison (Australia) Pty Ltd v Law Society of New South Wales* [1975] 2 NSWLR 104 at 117ff; *Talbot v General Television Corporation Pty Ltd* [1980] VR 224 at 230.

4. See *Commonwealth v John Fairfax & Sons Ltd* (1980) 147 CLR 39 at 50–2.

5. *Saltman Engineering Co Ltd v Campbell Engineering Co Ltd* (1947) 65 RPC 203 at 215 per Lord Greene MR.

6. *Duchess of Argyll v Duke of Argyll* [1967] Ch 302 at 329.

intention itself to manufacture or market the new product here. If the allegedly confidential information is restricted to the information that Loew's desired to obtain a licensee who would manufacture and market the new product in Australia, there was nothing in the evidence nor in the nature of that information that established that it was regarded by Loew's as confidential or that it was in fact confidential. In the result, the evidence failed to establish that any part of the designated information possessed the necessary element of confidentiality or secrecy or that the preservation of its confidentiality or secrecy was of substantial concern to Loew's. Indeed, senior counsel who then appeared for Moorgate expressly conceded, in his final address on the trial, that the information acquired by Philip Morris from Loew's in relation to the possible introduction of the new cigarettes in the Australian market was 'non-confidential'.

It should be mentioned that the claim that Philip Morris acted in abuse of confidential information appears to have been abandoned at first instance. Moorgate was, however, allowed to rely on the claim in the Court of Appeal apparently without objection by Philip Morris. That being so, I consider that Moorgate was entitled in this court to attack the decision which the Court of Appeal gave against it on the question. The failure to establish the confidentiality of the relevant information means, however, that that attack must fail. It is unnecessary to consider whether, if Philip Morris had been under an enforceable obligation to observe the confidentiality of any information that Loew's 'wanted to introduce the brand [Kent Golden Lights] in Australia', its application for registration of the mark 'Golden Lights' would have constituted a breach of that obligation.

Comments

1. See Radan & Stewart at **8.5–8.27**.
2. The judicial account of the origins of the doctrine greatly varies from contract, property and even tort. Most recently the English courts have described the doctrine as protecting human rights: *Campbell v Mirror Group Newspapers Ltd* [2004] 2 AC 457 at 473; *Mosley v News Group Newspapers Ltd* [2008] EWHC 1777 at [7].

The elements of the modern action for breach of confidence

8.5   Coco v A N Clark (Engineers) Ltd (1968) 1a IPR 587

Court: Chancery Division, High Court of Justice

Facts: Coco designed a moped engine. He approached A N Clark (Engineers) Ltd (Clark), a company situated on the Isle of Wight, about manufacturing his design. In the course of negotiations, Coco disclosed the designs. The negotiations failed. Soon after, Clark began to produce mopeds called the 'Clark Scamp' which appeared to be based on Coco's designs. Coco sought an injunction to stop Clark from producing the mopeds.

Issue: The issue before the court was whether Coco could satisfy the court that there had been a breach of an obligation of confidence which should be remedied with an injunction.

Decision: Megarry J held that although he was satisfied that the negotiations could have imparted an obligation of confidence, Coco had not proved that the information had a quality of confidence. Coco had not been able to show that the similarities between his engine and Clark's were achieved by using Coco's designs. Nor had Coco shown that his designs were so original in nature that they had a necessary quality of confidence. Clark agreed, in any event, to set aside a royalty for each engine sold, to be paid into a trust account while the proceedings were on foot, which would be kept secure until a final determination of the matter.

Extracts: The extract from Megarry J's judgment sets out the three elements of the modern action for breach of confidence.

Megarry J

The equitable jurisdiction in cases of breach of confidence is ancient; confidence is the cousin of trust. The Statute of Uses 1535 is framed in terms of 'use, confidence or trust' and a couplet, attributed to Sir Thomas More, Lord Chancellor avers that:

Three things are to be helpt in Conscience;

Fraud, Accident and things of Confidence.[7]

In the middle of the last century, the great case of *Prince Albert v Strange*[8] reasserted the doctrine. In the case before me, it is common ground that there is no question of any breach of contract, for no contract ever came into existence. Accordingly, what I have to consider is the pure equitable doctrine of confidence, unaffected by contract. Furthermore, I am here in the realms of commerce, and there is no question of any marital relationship such as arose in *Duchess of Argyll v Duke of Argyll*.[9] Thus limited, what are the essentials of the doctrine?

Of the various authorities cited to me, I have found *Saltman Engineering Co Ltd v Campbell Engineering Co Ltd*;[10] *Terrapin Ltd v Builders' Supply Co (Hayes) Ltd*[11] and *Seager v Copydex Ltd*[12] of the most assistance. All are decisions of the Court of Appeal. I think it is quite plain from the *Saltman* case that the obligation of confidence may exist where, as in this case, there is no contractual relationship between the parties. In cases of contract, the

---

7. See 1 Rolle's Abridgement 374.
8. (1849) 1 Mac & G 25.
9. [1967] Ch 302.
10. (1948) 65 RPC 203.
11. [1960] RPC 128.
12. [1967] 1 WLR 923; [1967] RPC 349.

primary question is no doubt that of construing the contract and any terms implied in it. Where there is no contract, however, the question must be one of what it is that suffices to bring the obligation into being; and there is the further question of what amounts to a breach of that obligation.

In my judgment, three elements are normally required if, apart from contract, a case of breach of confidence is to succeed. First, the information itself, in the words of Lord Greene MR in the *Saltman* case, must 'have the necessary quality of confidence about it'.[13] Secondly, that information must have been imparted in circumstances importing an obligation of confidence. Thirdly, there must be an unauthorised use of that information to the detriment of the party communicating it. I must briefly examine each of these requirements in turn.

First, the information must be of a confidential nature. As Lord Greene said in the *Saltman* case, 'something which is public property and public knowledge'[14] cannot per se provide any foundation for proceedings for breach of confidence. However confidential the circumstances of communication, there can be no breach of confidence in revealing to others something which is already common knowledge. But this must not be taken too far. Something that has been constructed solely from materials in the public domain may possess the necessary quality of confidentiality: for something new and confidential may have been brought into being by the application of the skill and ingenuity of the human brain. Novelty depends on the thing itself, and not upon the quality of its constituent parts. Indeed, often the more striking the novelty, the more commonplace its components. Mr Mowbray demurs to the concept that some degree of originality is requisite. But whether it is described as originality or novelty or ingenuity or otherwise, I think there must be some product of the human brain which suffices to confer a confidential nature upon the information: and, expressed in those terms, I think that Mr Mowbray accepts the concept.

The difficulty comes, as Lord Denning MR pointed out in the *Seager* case,[15] when the information used is partly public and partly private; for then the [591] recipient must somehow segregate the two and, although free to use the former, must take no advantage of the communication of the latter. To this subject I must in due course return. I must also return to a further point, namely, that where confidential information is communicated in circumstances of confidence the obligation thus created endures, perhaps in a modified form, even after all the information has been published or is ascertainable by the public; for the recipient must not use the communication as a spring board: see the *Seager* case.[16] I should add that, as shown by *Cranleigh Precision Engineering Ltd v Bryant*,[17] the mere simplicity of an idea does not prevent it being confidential.[18] Indeed, the simpler an idea, the more likely it is to need protection.

The second requirement is that the information must have been communicated in circumstances importing an obligation of confidence. However secret and confidential

---

13. *Saltman Engineering Co Ltd v Campbell Engineering Co Ltd* (1948) 65 RPC 203 at 215.
14. *Saltman Engineering Co Ltd v Campbell Engineering Co Ltd* (1948) 65 RPC 203 at 215.
15. *Seager v Copydex Ltd* [1967] 1 WLR 923 at 931.
16. *Seager v Copydex Ltd* [1967] 1 WLR 923 at 931, 933.
17. [1965] 1 WLR 1293.
18. *Cranleigh Precision Engineering Ltd v Bryant* [1965] 1 WLR 1293 at 1309, 1310.

CHAPTER 8: CONFIDENTIAL INFORMATION

the information, there can be no binding obligation of confidence if that information is blurted out in public or is communicated in other circumstances which negative any duty of holding it confidential. From the authorities cited to me, I have not been able to derive any very precise idea of what test is to be applied in determining whether the circumstances import an obligation of confidence. In the *Argyll* case, Ungoed-Thomas J concluded his discussion of the circumstances in which the publication of marital communications should be restrained as being confidential by saying, 'If this was a well-developed jurisdiction doubtless there would be guides and tests to aid in exercising it'.[19] In the absence of such guides or tests he then in effect concluded that part of the communications there in question would on any reasonable test emerge as confidential. It may be that that hard-worked creature, the reasonable man, may be pressed into service once more; for I do not see why he should not labour in equity as well as at law. It seems to me that if the circumstances are such that any reasonable man standing in the shoes of the recipient of the information would have realised that upon reasonable grounds the information was being given to him in confidence, then this should suffice to impose upon him the equitable obligation of confidence. In particular, where information of commercial or industrial value is given on a business-like basis and with some avowed common object in mind, such as a joint venture or the manufacture of articles by one party for the other, I would regard the recipient as carrying a heavy burden if he seeks to repel a contention that he was bound by an obligation of confidence: see the *Saltman* case.[20] On that footing, for reasons that will appear, I do not think I need explore this head further. I merely add that I doubt whether equity would intervene unless the circumstances are of sufficient gravity; equity ought not to be invoked merely to protect trivial tittle-tattle, however confidential.

Thirdly, there must be an unauthorised use of the information to the detriment of the person communicating it. Some of the statements of principle in the cases omit any mention of detriment; others include it. At first sight, it seems that detriment ought to be present if equity is to be induced to intervene; but I can conceive of cases where a plaintiff might have substantial motives for seeking the aid of equity and yet suffer nothing which could fairly be called detriment to him, as when the confidential information shows him in a favourable light but gravely injures some relation or friend of his whom he wishes to protect. The point does not arise for decision in this case, for detriment to [Coco] plainly exists. I need therefore say no more than that although for the purposes of this case I have **[592]** stated the propositions in the stricter form, I wish to keep open the possibility of the true proposition being that in the wider form.

Before I turn to the second main head, that of interlocutory relief, I should mention one point on the substantive law that caused me some difficulty during the argument. This is what may be called the 'spring board' doctrine. In the *Seager* case, Lord Denning quoted a sentence from the judgment of Roxburgh J in the *Terrapin* case, which was quoted and adopted as correct by Roskill J in the *Cranleigh* case.[21] It runs as follows:

---

19. *Duchess of Argyll v Duke of Argyll* [1967] Ch 302 at 330.
20. *Saltman Engineering Co Ltd v Campbell Engineering Co Ltd* (1948) 65 RPC 203 at 216.
21. *Cranleigh Precision Engineering Ltd v Bryant* [1965] 1 WLR 1293; [1966] RPC 81.

As I understand it, the essence of this branch of the law, whatever the origin of it may be, is that a person who has obtained information in confidence is not allowed to use it as a spring board for activities detrimental to the person who made the confidential communication, and spring board it remains even when all the features have been published or can be ascertained by actual inspection by any member of the public.[22]

Salmon LJ in the *Seager* case also states:

The law does not allow the use of such information even as a spring board for activities detrimental to the plaintiff.[23]

Quite apart from authority, I would recognise the principle enshrined in those words as being salutary. Nevertheless, I am not entirely clear how it is to be put into practical effect in every case. Suppose a case where there is a confidential communication of information which is partly public and partly private; suppose that the recipient of the information adds in confidence ideas of his own, improving the initial scheme; and suppose that the parties then part, with no agreement concluded between them. How is a conscientious recipient of the ideas to comply with the requirements that equity lays upon him? For in the words of Lord Denning in the *Seager* case, he

… must take special care to use only the material which is in the public domain. He should go to the public source and get it: or, at any rate, not be in a better position than if he had gone to the public source. He should not get a start over others by using the information which he received in confidence.[24]

Suppose that the only confidential information communicated is that some important component should be made of aluminium instead of steel and with significant variations in its design and dimensions. The recipient knows that this change will transform a failure into a success. He knows that, if he had persevered himself, he might have come upon the solution in a week or in a year. Yet he is under a duty not to use the confidential information as a spring board or as giving him a start.

What puzzles me is how, as a law-abiding citizen, he is to perform that duty. He could, I suppose, commission someone else to make the discovery anew, carefully abstaining from saying anything to him about aluminium or the design and dimensions which will achieve success; but this seems to me to be artificial in the extreme. Yet until this step is taken and the discovery made anew, he cannot make use of his own added ideas for the further improvement of the design which he had already communicated in confidence to the original communicator, ideas which would perhaps make a success into a triumph. He cannot build his superstructure as long as he is forbidden to use the foundations. Nor is the original communicator in a much better case. He is free to use his own original idea, which converted failure into success; but he cannot take advantage of the original recipient's further ideas, of which he knows, until such time as he or someone commissioned by him would, unaided by any confidence, have discovered them.

---

22. *Seager v Copydex Ltd* [1967] 1 WLR 923 at 931.
23. *Seager v Copydex Ltd* [1967] 1 WLR 923 at 933.
24. *Seager v Copydex Ltd* [1967] 1 WLR 923 at 931.

[593] For those who are not law-abiding and conscientious citizens there is, I suppose, a simple answer: ignore the duty, use the information, and then pay damages. This may be the course which Lord Denning envisaged in the *Seager* case: for after stating that the recipient should not get a start over others by using the confidential information, he continued:

> At any rate, he should not get a start without paying for it. It may not be a case for injunction or even for an account, but only for damages, depending on the worth of the confidential information to him in saving him time and trouble.[25]

I also recognise that a conscientious and law-abiding citizen, having received confidential information in confidence, may accept that when negotiations break down the only honourable course is to withdraw altogether from the field in question until his informant or someone else has put the information into the public domain and he can no longer be said to have any start. Communication thus imposes on him a unique disability. He alone of all men must for an uncertain time abjure this field of endeavour, however great his interest. I find this scarcely more reasonable than the artificiality and uncertainty of postponing the use of the information until others would have discovered it.

The relevance of the point, I think, is this. If the duty is a duty not to use the information without consent, then it may be the proper subject of an injunction restraining its use, even if there is an offer to pay a reasonable sum for that use. If, on the other hand, the duty is merely a duty not to use the information without paying a reasonable sum for it, then no such injunction should be granted. Despite the assistance of counsel, I feel far from assured that I have got to the bottom of this matter. But I do feel considerable hesitation in expressing a doctrine of equity in terms that include a duty which law-abiding citizens cannot reasonably be expected to perform. In other words, the essence of the duty seems more likely to be that of not using without paying, rather than of not using at all. It may be that in fields other than industry and commerce (and I have in mind the *Argyll* case) the duty may exist in the more stringent form; but in the circumstances present in this case I think that the less stringent form is the more reasonable. No doubt this matter may be canvassed and resolved at the trial; but on motion, in a case where both the probabilities and the evidence support the view that the fruits of any confidential communication were to sound in monetary compensation to the communicator, I should be slow to hold that it was right to enjoin the defendant company from making any use of the information …

[594] Having now considered the law, I can attempt to apply it to the facts of this case. With regard to the first main head, that of the substantive law, I feel no difficulty about the second condition. I think that the circumstances under which the information was given were plainly circumstances which imported an obligation of confidence. From the first, the whole object of the discussions was that [Clark] should manufacture a moped based on [Coco's] design, and [Coco] imparted his information with that object alone. I cannot think that the information was given under any circumstances save those of an

---

25. *Seager v Copydex Ltd* [1967] 1 WLR 923 at 932.

implied obligation to preserve any trade secrets that emerged. If the reasonable man is overworked, so is the officious bystander; but just as he provides a convenient touchstone for implied terms in contracts, so I think he may perform some useful function in relation to the implied obligation of confidence. If he had said to the parties at the outset, 'Do you not think that you ought to have an express agreement that everything you are discussing is confidential?', I think the parties would have testily suppressed him with a common 'But it obviously is'....

I turn to the first and third conditions. It is far less clear whether they are satisfied. How far is the information confidential in nature, and how far has [Clark] made an unauthorised use of any information that was confidential in nature? If there has been any such use, it clearly has been an unauthorised use to the detriment of [Coco]; but [Coco's] claim must fail if what [Clark] has without authority used to his detriment was not confidential in nature. [Coco] founds his case on what during the argument was described as a complex of confidential similarities between the two engines. [Clark] points to the fact that the components of the Scamp engine are available to anyone on the open market. Even the piston, designed by [Coco], is obtainable thus. [Coco's] engineering expert deposes to many resemblances between the two engines, under the heads of cylinder dimensions, combustion chamber, pistons, connecting rods, inlet and exhaust ports, flywheel magneto, carburettor, silencers and speed ratio. It will be seen that some of these items relate to design and others to the components used; and plainly the two engines enjoy a number of close and important similarities. But, as [counsel for Clark] pointed out with force, that is not enough. What matters is how far the Scamp achieves these similarities by drawing on confidential information imparted by [Coco] in confidence, and how far these factors had produced ... an engine which had any originality or other qualities that could provide information of a confidential nature. I remain in almost complete darkness as to the extent to which the ideas were common to the moped world. I have read the last paragraph of the expert's affidavit many times, and on each occasion it has conveyed to me doubt rather than conviction. When at the trial he gives evidence viva voce and is cross-examined, this matter may well be resolved one way or the other. I can only say that, on this motion, that evidence and the evidence of [Coco] have in my judgment fallen well short of what is requisite for interlocutory relief. Subject to one matter, I do not think that [Coco] has shown either a strong prima facie case for the existence of his right which is likely to succeed, or a prima facie case of infringement which is reasonably capable of succeeding.

Comments

1. See Radan & Stewart at **8.28**.
2. The trial of the matter never took place. The Scamp engine was only produced for one year. Production ceased in November 1968 and a receiver was appointed to Clark soon after. The company still survives today as Clark Masts Teksam Ltd, still trading on the Isle of Wight.

The requirement of secrecy and necessity for the information to not have entered the public domain

8.6 Australian Football League v Age Company Ltd (2006) 15 VR 19

Court: Supreme Court of Victoria

Facts: AFL players were contractually bound to undergo drug testing. The agreement between the players and the AFL stated that the first two positive drug tests would be kept confidential between the AFL and the player. The names of three AFL players who had tested positive to drugs were published on an internet discussion forum. An electronic newspaper article had also named the players to a limited group of subscribers for about five hours. A further publication of one of the players' names had occurred when a phone caller named the player on the 'Fox Footy' television program. The AFL and the players' association sought a permanent injunction on two newspapers to prevent them from publishing the names of the players.

Issue: The issue before the court was whether the transitory publication of the players' identities had destroyed the confidential nature of the information.

Decision: Kellam J found that the information had still not yet fully entered the public domain and remained confidential. A permanent injunction was ordered on the release of the players' identities.

Extracts: The extract from Kellam J's judgment analyses the authorities on secrecy and disclosure to the public.

Kellam J

[427] The law in relation to the public domain

Information will be confidential only if it is not 'public property and public knowledge'.[26] Put another way, information will not have the necessary quality of confidence about it if it is 'public knowledge, commonly known, publicly known, well known, public property ... or common knowledge'.[27]

The issue before me is whether the information the subject of confidentiality has received sufficient publicity to effectively destroy the purpose of confidentiality, and thus to make it pointless on the part of the court to restrain the further publication of confidential information.

---

26. *Saltman Engineering Company Ltd v Campbell Engineering Company Ltd* [1963] 3 All ER 413 at 415.
27. R Dean, *The Law of Trade Secrets and Personal Secrets*, 2nd ed, Lawbook Co, Sydney, 2002, p 80.

The submission of the [newspaper] as to the public domain

As stated above, the [newspaper] contend[s] that there is ample evidence of widespread public dissemination of the names of the three AFL players in the context of their having tested positive to illicit drugs when so tested. It is submitted that the court in such circumstances cannot sensibly restrain the media defendants from publishing what is, it is submitted, known publicly. The [newspaper] submit[s] that even where confidentiality has been destroyed wrongfully, if the information is in the public domain, then the confidentiality does not continue to exist. In this regard, the [newspaper] rel[ies] upon the statement of Lord Goff in *Attorney-General v Guardian Newspapers Ltd (No 2)* (the '*Spycatcher*' case) where his Lordship said:

> ... it is difficult to see how a confidant who publishes the relevant confidential information to the whole world can be under any further obligation not to disclose the information, simply because it was he who wrongfully destroyed its confidentiality. The information has, after all, already been so fully disclosed that it is in the public domain: how, therefore, can he thereafter be sensibly restrained from disclosing it? Is he not even to be permitted to mention in public what is now common knowledge? For his wrongful act, he may be held liable in damages, or may be required to make restitution; but, to adapt [sic] the words of Lord Buckmaster [in *Mustad's* case][28] the confidential information, as confidential information, has ceased to exist, and with it should go, as a matter of principle, the obligation of confidence.[29]

[428] The [newspaper] submit[s] that if the confidential information has entered the public domain then the information in question has lost any confidential quality it may have had previously. That is plainly so. It would be entirely pointless and indeed, would bring the administration of justice into disrepute, for the court to endeavour to restrain the publication of matters which are well known by a large number of members of the public. I do not understand the [AFL] to argue to the contrary. The real issue between the parties is whether the confidential material has entered the public domain. It is obvious from what I have set out above that the names of three players who have allegedly tested positive to illicit substances are known by a number of people in the community. However, the question of whether or not the information can be said to have passed into the public domain is a question of fact. As Gaudron J said in *Johns v Australian Securities Commission*:

> There is a question whether an obligation of confidence is extinguished because of subsequent publication to the world at large by third parties or, even, by the person who owed the duty in the first place. Again in that situation, it is sometimes said that the information has passed into the public domain. The question that then arises is, in essence, whether the information has lost its confidential quality. And as already pointed out, that is largely a question of fact.[30]

---

28. *O Mustad & Son v S Allcock & Co Ltd* [1964] 1 WLR 109.
29. *Attorney-General v Guardian Newspapers Ltd (No 2)* [1990] 1 AC 109 at 286–7.
30. (1993) 178 CLR 408 at 461–2.

In the *Spycatcher* case Lord Goff described the expression 'public domain' as meaning:

> ... no more than that the information in question is so generally accessible that, in all the circumstances, it cannot be regarded as confidential.[31]

A number of considerations have been regarded by the courts as being relevant to the question of whether information has entered the public domain. In determining whether the information should be regarded as being confidential the degree of accessibility has been seen to be an important factor. In *Franchi v Franchi*, Cross J said:

> Clearly a claim that the disclosure of some information would be a breach of confidence is not to be defeated simply by proving that there are other people in the world who know the facts in question besides the man as to whom it is said that his disclosure would be a breach of confidence and those to whom he has disclosed them.[32]

In that case, Cross J was dealing with a trade secret, but he used the following phrase which appears to me to be of general application:

> It must be a question of degree depending on the particular case, but if relative secrecy remains, the plaintiff can still succeed.[33]

Nevertheless, in *Woodward v Hutchins* a somewhat narrower interpretation of what is the public domain was applied. The Court of Appeal dealt with the claim for confidentiality by a rock group against their former press agent who had [429] published details of their private lives, including what Lord Denning MR described as 'a very unsavoury incident in a Jumbo Jet'. It was said by Lord Denning:

> But what is confidential? As Bridge LJ pointed out in the course of the argument, Mr Hutchins, as a press agent, might attend a dance which many others attended. Any incident which took place at the dance would be known to all present. The information would be in the public domain. There could be no objection to the incidents being made known generally. It would not be confidential information. So in this case the incident on this Jumbo Jet was in the public domain. It was known to all the passengers on the flight.[34]

However, in my view, the case of *Woodward v Hutchins* stands on its own facts, being that there was nothing in the defendant's engagement which required him to regard as being confidential the behaviour of members of the rock group in a public place.

The question of whether even limited publication would become known to an 'ever-widening group of people' has been regarded as an appropriate factor to be considered. In *Commonwealth v John Fairfax & Sons Ltd*, Mason J gave consideration to the issue of dissemination of confidential material in which as many as 100 volumes of books had been sold already.

---

31. *Attorney-General v Guardian Newspapers (No 2)* [1990] 1 AC 109 at 282.
32. (1967) RPC 149 at 152–3.
33. (1967) RPC 149 at 153.
34. *Woodward v Hutchins* [1977] 1 WLR 760 at 764.

He said:

> The sales of the book already made, including those made to Indonesia and the United
> States, the countries most likely to be affected by its contents, and the publication of the
> first instalment in the two newspapers, indicate that the detriment which the plaintiff
> apprehends will not be avoided by the grant of injunction. In other circumstances the
> circulation of about 100 copies of a book may not be enough to disentitle the possessor
> of confidential information from protection by injunction, but in this case it is likely
> that what is in the book will become known to an ever-widening group of people here
> and overseas, including foreign governments.[35]

However, in *G v Day*, Yeldham J gave consideration to circumstances where the confidential
information (disclosure of the plaintiff's name) on television on two occasions had taken
place. His Honour said:

> In the present case the references to the plaintiff on television were transitory and
> brief. His name was mentioned once only on each occasion. It was not recorded in
> any permanent form (other than in the script) and there is no suggestion that any
> reaction from any viewer was conveyed to the plaintiff. Probably his name would not
> be remembered by any who did not already know him. I regard these disclosures as
> being of a limited and impermanent nature. Any publication in a newspaper would, on
> the contrary, be in a permanent form for all its readers to note.[36]

Accordingly, it would appear that, as a general rule, the publication of confidential
information in widely-circulated print media would place information in the public
domain. However, there are few authorities dealing with the effect of publication of
confidential material on the internet. One **[430]** authority is *EPP Australia Pty Ltd v Levy*
where Barrett J gave consideration to the circumstances whereby the defendant's case was
that much of the material that the plaintiff sought to bring within a contractual restraint
of confidentiality was in the public domain. His Honour said:

> It is true that the names and contact details of a number of members are available on
> the internet. In fact, participants in the member to member segment of the programme,
> that is, members who use the programme not only as an advantageous buying tool but
> also as a selling and promotional mechanism targeting other members, receive, as part
> of their membership, inclusion in the EPP website with an online listing of their own
> business. Clearly, therefore, the particulars those members place on the website become
> available throughout the world to anyone with internet access. Rather than being kept
> confidential in any way, those particulars are subjected to processes intended to give
> them very wide publicity. The particulars, needless to say, identify by name and location
> the businesses of particular members.[37]

The circumstances to which Barrett J was referring in *EPP Australia Pty Ltd v Levy* were
that the plaintiff operated a business which involved the introduction of small businesses

---

35. *Commonwealth v John Fairfax & Sons Ltd* (1980) 147 CLR 39 at 50.
36. *G v Day* [1982] 1 NSWLR 24 at 40.
37. *EPP Australia Pty Ltd v Levy* [2001] NSWSC 482 at [15].

in need of goods and services to suppliers, who would be prepared to do business with those parties on terms more favourable than those that could be obtained through other channels. Members of the buying group paid a membership fee to the plaintiff in return for the privilege of access to the favoured buyer arrangements. Membership was sold through agents who were remunerated by way of an amount of money per member introduced. The defendants in the case were agents who had each entered into an agent's contract and a confidentiality deed. The agency was terminated. After the termination of their agency the defendants approached members of the plaintiff with proposals that those members do business with the defendants, or with their interests. The plaintiff commenced proceedings seeking damages and interlocutory injunctions in relation to the contracted obligations of confidentiality. In these circumstances his Honour said:

> It must be said at the outset that part of the information that the defendants have used is in the public domain. I regard everything which is accessible through resort to the internet as being in the public domain. It is true that someone can obtain that information only if they have access to a computer which has a modem which connects to an internet service provider who, for a fee, provides a connection to the internet. But those barriers are, in my view, no more challenging or significant in today's Australia complete with internet cafes, than those involved in access to a newspaper or television content, both of which should, according to precedent, be seen as involving the public domain.[38]

The submission of the [AFL] as to the public domain

However, the [AFL] submit[s] that there has been no more than limited speculation in the internet exchanges. In some parts they refer to many different players. Other parts acknowledge expressly the rumour-like nature of the postings. The [AFL and players] contend that the internet exchanges do not amount to the information being in the 'public domain'. They submit further that the information, even if published in some internet postings, is not common knowledge. It is argued that even if the names are known by some persons, there [431] is nevertheless much to protect, as is clear by the desire of the media to publish the information. The [AFL and players] submit that even if any of the published speculation has named one or more players who may have tested positive, whether coincidental or not, such publication has been limited.

They contend, first, that the publication of three names as part of the speculation that occurred when the *Sydney Morning Herald* was distributed electronically to a small number of organisations and then recalled is of no consequence. By itself, I accept that this publication would not be sufficient to say that the confidential information has entered the public domain.

The [AFL and players] contend further that the mention of a name on Fox Footy by a caller was momentary, speculative and heard by a limited audience only. There is no evidence before me as to the size of the audience but by itself, I accept that this incident would not be of such moment that it could be said that the information came into the public domain by reason thereof.

---

38. *EPP Australia Pty Ltd v Levy* [2001] NSWSC 482 at [20].

As to the dissemination of any confidential material within the AFL, the evidence before me is of limited oral discussion of one of the purported names by the chief executive of the players' association with the president of that association and discussion with the players named and one or more of their parents and/or their managers. There is no evidence before me of the extent of dissemination of gossip, speculation or information among the so-called 'AFL family'. There is evidence that some journalists have stated to Mr Gale and others that they have possession of information as to the names of the players who have twice tested positive. No such journalist gave evidence before me, however. There is no evidence before me that any such information has any documentary basis, and it is extremely difficult to discern whether such beliefs are based upon credible sources, or instead upon general gossip and speculation. I do not consider that the evidence in these regards is such as to say that the confidential information of the identity of any player who has tested positive under the IDP is in the public domain.

Conclusion as to whether or not the confidential information is in the public domain

The strongest argument as to the information being in the public domain is not that revealed by the above three possible sources of the release of the confidential information, being the *Sydney Morning Herald*, Fox Footy and inside the so-called 'AFL family'. Each of those sources disseminated information to a limited audience. There has been no dissemination to the public at large, being the readers of national newspapers, or the viewers of free to air television or by other mass media outlets. In my view, the strongest argument relates to the information referred to in the various internet postings, or alternatively, that in conjunction with the above three possible sources of release of confidential information.

The nature of the information appearing on the various internet sites referred to by Mr Poulton in his affidavit of 15 May 2006 bears some consideration. An analysis of the exhibits produced by Mr Poulton does show that the websites in question over the period of March and April of 2006 contain a large number of references to the issue of drug-testing by the AFL. However, much of what is placed upon the websites referred to by Mr Poulton, is speculation. For example, Ex AFL1 names three players about whom there is no suggestion before me of any positive test under the IDP. Some of the postings express the fact that they [432] are 'surmise'. There is surmise as to the club to which players who may have tested positive belong. One posting states, 'Only a guess based on which paper the report came from'. Exhibit AFL3 contains similar speculation by those posting the entries. Exhibit AFL4 contains a discussion about trading certain players at the end of the year. Some correspondents appear to treat the discussion as a genuine discussion about trading players. Others treat the discussion thread as an opportunity to speculate about who may have tested positive. Assertions are made to the effect that 'these are rumoured names'. Likewise, Ex AFL5, which refers to another website, contains statements from correspondents such as, 'I hope like hell it is (player X)' and 'Nothing like a bit of gossip'. Exhibit AFL10 contains the comment: 'The whole point of being on this site is having the freedom to post whatever nonsense we feel like.' Other of the exhibits to which Mr Poulton referred reveal similar sentiments to the effect that the information is gossip and speculation. On the other hand, there are several positive assertions as to the identity of the players who tested positive, but by an unnamed person or persons using a pseudonym. The question is whether such internet postings have put the confidential information into the public domain.

As stated above, Barrett J in *EPP v Levy* said in the circumstances of the case before him that he regarded 'everything which is accessible through resort to the internet as being in the public domain'.[39] However, it should be noted that Barrett J was referring to a website operated by a commercial entity which permitted members of a buying group to place the particulars of their businesses upon the website. The viewer of such a website would be entitled to treat the appearance of such particulars on the website as being information of at least some veracity and authority. Likewise, the reader of a newspaper, or the viewer of a television station, is entitled to treat a news report appearing therein as having at least some veracity and accountability. While it is true that this might vary according to the nature of the news media publishing the report, a reader or viewer knows that some entity, be it the reporter or publisher of a newspaper, or in the case of a radio or television station, the speaker, a producer or corporate owner is identifiable and accountable. For instance, the average member of the public is aware of the fact that a newspaper or television or radio station may be subject to the laws of defamation if it published wrongful information without good cause. No doubt the public is aware that other processes such as the control exercised by the Australian Press Council are applicable. The public regards information published by the print, television and radio media as being generally credible.

Can it be said, however, that a 'discussion forum' which enables opinions, gossip, trivia, rumour and speculation to be published as an assertion of fact by anonymous contributors places the information the subject of such discussion into the public domain? There can be little doubt that, as the High Court in *Dow Jones & Company Inc v Gutnick*[40] observed, the internet throws up many challenges for established principles of common law, but that does not mean that it can be a 'law free zone'. The fact is that anyone, be it a disgruntled employee, a journalist, or anyone else interested in propagating what might otherwise be confidential information can put information upon a discussion forum under an assumed name. Indeed, the lack of accountability is such that one person can [433] place such information upon a discussion forum, or for that matter on numerous discussion fora, in many different names. If speculation, gossip or even assertion from an anonymous source, thus being incapable of being verified or in any way held accountable, is to be regarded as the putting of information in the public domain, then the opportunity for the unethical, and the malicious, to breach confidentiality and then claim that there is no confidentiality is unrestrained. For example, an unethical intending publisher could, without having access to confidential information, speculate by use of an assumed name, as to what might be confidential. This speculation could be placed on a number of discussion fora under a number of pseudonyms and asserted to be fact. Could it then be asserted, as here, that the fact that the material has been the subject of assertion in 'chat rooms' means that confidentiality is lost?

---

39. *EPP Australia Pty Ltd v Levy* [2001] NSWSC 482 at [20].
40. (2002) 210 CLR 575 at 617–19.

In my view, the fact that such speculative gossip, innuendo and assertion by unknown persons has been placed on the websites of various discussion fora does not make confidential material lose its confidential nature. Obviously there are many users of the internet and an unknown, but no doubt significant, number of users of such websites as those referred to above might well have seen the names to which anonymous persons have referred in their postings. However, it is still in the realm of speculation. That is a vastly different proposition from the circumstances of publication of material by a newspaper, television station or other source of dissemination of news and other material such as radio or authorised websites conducted by such sources. Those sources are accountable for the information they publish and are, to an extent at least, trusted by the public to report material to that public accurately. On the evidence before me the public, and particularly that part of the public who use internet chat rooms have no such expectation of authenticity, veracity or otherwise of the information posted on such websites.

Comment

1. See Radan & Stewart at **8.30–8.36**.

The protection of trade secrets

8.7   Del Casale v Artedomus (Aust) Pty Limited
[2007] NSWCA 172

Court: Court of Appeal of New South Wales

Facts: Artedomus was a stone and ceramic importing company. It was the only importer in Australia of 'modica' stone, known also as 'Isernia', a special stone from the Ragusa region of Italy. The knowledge of the origins of the stone was kept a secret. Del Casale and Savini were directors and managers of Artedomus. They were aware that the origins of the stone were to be kept confidential. They later resigned and, as part of an agreement to sell their shareholdings in the company, they agreed that they would not compete with Artedomus or divulge 'commercially sensitive information'. They later used the information they had learned from working for Artedomus to find a supplier of the modica stone in Italy, and they used an already formed company, Stone Arc, to import the stone to Australia. At trial they were found to have breached confidence. A permanent injunction was issued to prevent them from using the confidential information and an account of profits was ordered.

Issue: The issue before the Court of Appeal was whether the information regarding the source of the stone was confidential.

Decision: The Court of Appeal (Hodgson, McColl and Campbell JJA) found that there was no breach of confidence, although the agreement not to compete with Artedomus had been breached. The injunction was lifted.

Extracts: The extract from the judgment of Hodgson JA discusses the issue of commercial confidences, especially in relation to employees.

Hodgson JA

Was the information such as would be protected without an agreement?

[29] In finding the information in this case was such as would be protected without any agreement, the primary judge relied on the persistence, time and effort devoted by Mr Schepsis [a director of Artedomus] to setting up the importation of modica stone from Sicily to Australia, the use of the name Isernia to conceal the source of the stone, the lengths to which Mr Schepsis and Artedomus went to maintain that concealment, and the difficulty of ascertaining without assistance the fact that Isernia was in fact modica stone. Mr Moses for the opponent submitted that the primary judge was not shown to be in error in so finding.

[30] Mr Ashhurst for the claimants submitted that, even if the information was confidential to the extent that an employee would have to treat it as confidential during employment and may be restrained by contract from using it after the employment has ended, it did not have the degree of confidentiality that would attract protection after the employment had ended in the absence of a contractual agreement. He pointed out that in *Wright v Gasweld*,[41] it was held that the information ascertained by trial and error over a number of years, that four particular Taiwanese suppliers, out of 3,000 suppliers of certain products, were reliable was not a trade secret that would attract equitable protection after employment had ended, in the absence of a contractual agreement; although by majority, it was held to be sufficiently confidential to be capable of protection by such an agreement.

[31] I find this question not an easy one to resolve. Although criteria for confidentiality were discussed in *Wright v Gasweld*, there is not in that case or in any of the cases to which we have been referred a clear elaboration of what would determine whether the confidentiality went beyond that which could be protected by agreement so as to be such as to continue to affect the employee after the employment had ended, without the need for an agreement. Another difficulty is that it is not entirely clear whether the implication of terms in the employment contract has any relevance to the issue; and it is not entirely clear whether equitable principles concerning confidential information apply in the case of employment in the same way as they apply in other areas where one party gives confidential information to another party, in circumstances of confidence, so as to give rise to an obligation of confidence that equity will enforce.

---

41. *Wright v Gasweld Pty Ltd* (1991) 22 NSWLR 317.

[32] In the first place, it is clear that a contract of employment generally includes an implied term imposing a duty of good faith on the employee, and that this [in] turn carries with it an obligation on the employee not to divulge confidential information or to use it in a way that could be detrimental to the employer.[42] The content of this duty will vary according to the position of the employee: generally, more senior employees, having access to more confidential information, will be subject to greater restraint than more junior employees.

[33] If this obligation is breached during employment, for example by copying customer lists or even deliberately memorising them so that they can be used after the employment comes to an end, that breach of contract may justify the grant of relief when the employee seeks to use that information after the employment has come to an end. There is no suggestion in this case that the claimants obtained confidential information, during their employment, in breach of this implied term.

[34] There is authority for the proposition that this implied term imposing a duty of good faith continues to operate after the employment comes to an end, albeit in a more restricted way.[43] I am doubtful that this is so as a general rule, at least in so far as it suggests there may be a remedy in contract that goes beyond such remedy as may be available on the basis of general equitable principles of confidentiality. It is clear that there can be terms of an employment contract that continue to operate after the employment comes to an end; but generally that will be because they are express terms which so provide. Implied terms may also operate in that way if the nature of the employment is such as to clearly require a term operating after the end of employment, as could be the case where a person is employed as an in-house professional adviser to whom confidential information is given for the purpose of obtaining professional advice, such as legal advice. Apart from such special cases, in my opinion the difficulty illustrated by the *Faccenda Chicken* case[44] of determining the extent of any obligation of confidentiality, extending after the end of employment, counts against such obligation being implied, either as an incident of the relationship or a matter of business efficacy.

[35] In my opinion, generally questions concerning an employee's obligation of confidentiality after employment has come to an end, in the absence of an express contract dealing with the matter, are best dealt with as part of the general law concerning confidentiality of information, both because it is very doubtful what, if any, term can be implied into a contract, and also because it is very unlikely that relief obtainable pursuant to any such implied term would go beyond relief obtainable on general equitable principles. There is the theoretical difference that damages may be obtainable for breach of contract; but this is unlikely to make the remedy available in contract more extensive than that based on general equitable principles, because it seems clear that compensation is available for breach of fiduciary duty (and thus probably is available for breach of a duty of confidentiality).[45] ...

---

42. *Robb v Green* [1895] 2 QB 315.
43. *Faccenda Chicken Ltd v Fowler* [1987] Ch 117 at 136.
44. *Faccenda Chicken Ltd v Fowler* [1987] Ch 117.
45. *Nocton v Lord Ashburton* [1914] AC 932; *Beach Petroleum v Kennedy* (1999) 48 NSWLR 1; *Cassis v Kalfus (No 2)* [2004] NSWCA 315.

[37] [I]n applying these general equitable principles to the particular case of post-employment use, by an ex-employee, of the confidential information of an employer obtained during employment, there are particular considerations which tend to qualify their operation. They are that very often an employee will necessarily through employment come to have knowledge which the employer would prefer not to have generally known, that often such knowledge will become part of the employee's know-how (which the employee should be able to use after employment ceases), that very often it is difficult or impossible to isolate from the employee's general know-how particular pieces of confidential information which the employee is not permitted to use while otherwise being free to use know-how generally, and that competition should not be prevented by preventing ex-employees using their know-how.

[38] Considerations such as these have led to a distinction being drawn, in cases such as *Faccenda Chicken* and *Wright v Gasweld*, between two classes of confidential information, one of which an ex-employee cannot use (even in the absence of contractual restrictions), and the other of which an ex-employee can use, at least unless there is a valid contractual restraint. There is some variation in the naming of these two classes. For example, there is a question whether both are properly called trade secrets, with the latter being a particular class of trade secrets which is also given the appellation 'know-how'; or whether only the former class should be called trade secrets. In either event, the latter class is often called 'know-how'.

[39] It is clear that information may be confidential, even if it is known to persons other than the person claiming confidentiality: it may be sufficient that the information is not freely available, particularly if it is not freely available to competitors of the employer. There is no challenge to what the primary judge said about this matter ... There is no real dispute that the information identified by the primary judge is confidential in the sense of falling into one of these classes; and the substantial question is whether it falls into the former class or latter class.

[40] In *Wright v Gasweld* ... Kirby P listed some factors that helped in determining whether information may be considered confidential.[46] That list has been expanded by R Dean, *The Law of Trade Secrets and Personal Secrets*[47] to include:

1. The extent to which the information is known outside the business.
2. The extent to which the trade secret was known by employees and others involved in the plaintiff's business.
3. The extent of measures taken to guard the secrecy of the information.
4. The value of the information to the plaintiffs and their competitors.
5. The amount of effort or money expended by the plaintiffs in developing the information.
6. The ease or difficulty with which the information could be properly acquired or duplicated by others.
7. Whether it was plainly made known to the employee that the material was [considered] by the employer as confidential.

---

46. *Wright v Gasweld* (1991) 22 NSWLR 317 at 334.
47. 2nd ed, 2002, Thomson, p 190.

8. The fact that the usages and practices of the industry support the assertions of confidentiality.
9. The fact that the employee has been permitted to share the information only by reason of his or her seniority or high responsibility.
10. That the owner believes these things to be true and that belief is reasonable.
11. The greater the extent to which the 'confidential' material is habitually handled by an employee, the greater the obligation of the confidentiality imposed.
12. That the information can be readily identified.

[41] In my opinion, the stronger these factors are in any particular case, the more likely it is that the particular information will be treated as a trade secret that the ex-employee is not entitled to use or divulge; but in my opinion, there is another factor or class of factors which is also extremely important to this question, namely the extent to which the particular information can be readily isolated from the employee's general know-how which the employee is entitled to use after the end of employment.

[42] In cases where the confidential information is of the nature of a secret formula or process, involving a number of elements such that independent discovery by enquiry or experiment is unlikely to occur, that confidential information can quite readily be distinguished from an employee's general know-how. In those cases, the courts are ready to restrain use of that information by an ex-employee.[48]

[43] However, where the confidential information is something that is ascertainable by enquiry or experiment, albeit perhaps substantial enquiry or experiment, and the know-how which the ex-employee is clearly entitled to use extends to knowledge of the *question* which the confidential information answers, it becomes artificial to treat the confidential information as severable and distinguishable from that know-how; and in that kind of case, courts have tended not to grant relief.

[44] In *E Worsley & Co Ltd v Cooper*, an ex-employee's knowledge of the sources of particular types of paper sold by the employer was treated in that way .... Morton J noted that the information in question was 'information which a determined and persistent trade rival, with sufficient skill and knowledge of the paper business, could have ascertained at the cost of considerable enquiries of considerable length'; and he went on to say that if a customer came to the ex-employee and asked if he could supply paper the same as a particular type of paper sold by the employer, it could not be wrong for the ex-employee to tell the truth and say he could.[49] I note however that it was not suggested in that case that the ex-employee had been warned during employment that this particular information was confidential.

[45] In *Balston Ltd v Headline Filters Ltd*, the relevant confidential information was knowledge of the satisfactory degree of dilution of a standard solvent for a particular purpose; and Scott J at 344 noted the hopeless artificiality of suggesting that the ex-employee should be required to carry out experiments to ascertain the satisfactory degree of dilution when he had that information from his employment.[50] The ex-employee could not be prevented from using his know-how to the effect that

---

48. See, for example, *Amber Size & Chemical Co Ltd v Menzel* [1913] 2 Ch 239.
49. *E Worsley & Co Ltd v Cooper* [1939] 1 All ER 290 at 308.
50. *Balston Ltd v Headline Filters Ltd* [1987] FSR 330 at 334.

the particular purpose could be served by the standard solvent diluted to some degree or other, so it was unrealistic in the extreme to suggest he could be prevented from using his recollection as to the satisfactory degree of dilution.

[46] Although the consideration was not spelt out precisely in this way in *Wright v Gasweld*, I think it was implicit in the view of Gleeson CJ,[51] Kirby P[52] and Samuels JA,[53] that the confidential information in that case was not such that the employee would be prevented from using it after the termination of employment, in the absence of a contract to that effect. The information in that case, that four suppliers in Taiwan of particular types of goods, out of a total of about 3,000 suppliers, had proved reliable, was very difficult to isolate from the ex-employee's general experience and know-how. The four suppliers could not be prevented from dealing with the ex-employee, nor would it be reasonable (without a contract to that effect) to preclude the ex-employee altogether from dealing with those suppliers; so again, there would be the artificiality of requiring the ex-employee to engage in some exercise of trial and error to ascertain reliable suppliers, in circumstances where the ex-employee already had the knowledge that these four suppliers were reliable.

[47] Before considering the circumstance of this case, I would note that this line of reasoning may justify a distinction being drawn in cases such as these between an ex-employee *using* this information as part of the know-how acquired from the employment, on the one hand, and *disclosing* it to other persons on the other hand. In *Worsley v Cooper*,[54] Morton J placed some reliance on the circumstance that the ex-employee in that case was merely using the information, not disclosing it; and he referred to statements to similar effect in the judgment of Joyce J in the Court of Appeal in *Herbert Morris Ltd v Saxelby*[55] and Bennet J in *United Indigo Chemical Co Ltd v Robinson*.[56] In my opinion, it may well be the case that equitable relief could be granted against an ex-employee *disclosing* confidential information in some cases where it would not be granted against the ex-employee *using* it.

[48] Turning to the circumstances of this case, it seems to me very difficult to separate out, from the general know-how in relation to stone acquired by Mr Del Casale and Mr Savini, as a severable piece of confidential information, the information that Isernia is modica stone. Certainly, subject to any contract that may have existed, they were entitled to compete with Artedomus in the stone business after their employment had come to an end, and they were entitled to obtain stone for that purpose from any source. They were entitled to go to a trade fair, and to look for suppliers of stone at that fair, including suppliers of stone similar to Isernia. What restraint of use of this particular piece of confidential information would require is that in doing so, they somehow blot out their knowledge that Isernia was modica stone and undertake the attempt to find similar stone under those artificial circumstances.

[49] The degree of confidentiality of the information in this case was quite high, having regard to the criteria mentioned above; but not it seems to me higher than that in

---

51. *Wright v Gasweld* (1991) 22 NSWLR 317 at 325–6.
52. *Wright v Gasweld* (1991) 22 NSWLR 317 at 334–5.
53. *Wright v Gasweld* (1991) 22 NSWLR 317 at 341.
54. [1939] 1 All ER 290 at 308–9.
55. [1915] 2 Ch 57 at 88.
56. (1939) 49 RPC 178 at 187.

Wright v Gasweld; and as I have explained, it does not seem to me that this information is information that can realistically be separated out from the general know-how in relation to the stone business acquired by Mr Del Casale and Mr Savini. It is to be remembered that they were not merely employees of Artedomus, but directors; but subject to the effect of s 183 of the *Corporations Act*, to which I will come, I do not think that makes any difference in principle to the considerations I have discussed: these considerations apply similarly to directors as to other very senior employees.

[50] For those reasons, in my opinion the primary judge was in error in finding that the information was confidential to the extent that its use would be prohibited after cessation of the employment and/or directorship of Mr Del Casale and Mr Savini, in the absence of express contractual restraint.

Comment

1. See Radan & Stewart at **8.47–8.57**.

Protection of government secrets

8.8   Commonwealth v John Fairfax & Sons Ltd (1980) 147 CLR 39

Court: High Court of Australia

Facts: John Fairfax & Sons Ltd were going to publish a book called *Documents on Australian Defence and Foreign Policy 1968–1975*, which contained Australian government documents on the Indonesian invasion of East Timor, the renegotiation of agreements for American military bases in Australia, the presence of the Soviet navy in the Indian Ocean, the ANZUS treaty and Australia's support of the Shah of Iran. Both *The Age* newspaper and the *Sydney Morning Herald* were to publish extracts. The government sought interlocutory injunctions to prevent publication on a number of grounds, including breach of copyright and breach of confidence. Before the publishers had received notice of the injunction several thousand copies of the newspapers which contained book excerpts had been distributed. A number of books had also been sold, some to the United States and Indonesian embassies.

Issue: The issue before the High Court was whether the doctrine of breach of confidence applied to governmental information.

Decision: The High Court (Mason J) granted the injunctions. The injunctions were not granted on the basis of breach of confidential information, but rather on the basis of breach of copyright.

Extracts: The extract from the judgment of Mason J discusses the test of public interest.

Mason J

[50] The [government] says that this case falls neatly within a fundamental principle of Equity. The principle is that the court will 'restrain the publication of confidential information improperly or surreptitiously obtained or of information imparted in confidence which ought not to be divulged'.[57] In conformity with this principle, employees who had access to confidential information in the possession of their employers have been restrained from divulging information to third parties in breach of duty and, if they have already divulged the information, the third parties themselves have been restrained from making disclosure or making use of the information.[58] The [government] had within its possession confidential information comprised in the documents published in the book. The probability is that a public servant having access to the documents, in breach of his duty and contrary to the security classifications, made copies of the documents available to Messrs [51] Walsh and Munster or to an intermediary who handed them to Messrs Walsh and Munster. In drawing this inference I am mindful that no claim is made that copies of the documents came into the possession of Messrs Walsh and Munster with the authority of the [government].

No attempt has been made to suggest that the [publishers] were unaware of the classified nature of the documents or of the [government's] claim that it had not authorized publication. The book records the security classification of many of the documents. Mr Pritchett made it clear to the defendants on Friday evening that on his view the material had been obtained without the plaintiff's authority, if not improperly.

Basic to the [government's] argument is the proposition that information which is not 'public property and public knowledge', in the words of Lord Greene MR in *Saltman Engineering Co Ltd v Campbell Engineering Co Ltd*,[59] is protected by the principle. Even unclassified government information would fall within the protection claimed, so long as it is not publicly known. According to the [government], no relevant distinction is to be drawn between the government and a private person. A citizen is entitled to the protection by injunction of the secrets of his or her private life, as well as trade secrets.[60] So, with the government, it is entitled to protect information which is not public property, even if no public interest is served by maintaining confidentiality.

However, the plaintiff must show, not only that the information is confidential in quality and that it was imparted so as to import an obligation of confidence, but also that there will be 'an unauthorised use of that information to the detriment of the party communicating it'.[61] The question then, when the executive government seeks the protection given by equity, is: What detriment does it need to show?

The equitable principle has been fashioned to protect the personal, private and proprietary interests of the citizen, not to protect the very different interests of the executive government. It acts, or is supposed to act, not according to standards of private interest, but in the public interest. This is not to say that equity will not protect

---

57. *Lord Ashburton v Pape* [1913] 2 Ch 469 at 475.
58. *Tipping v Clarke* (1843) 67 ER 157 at 393; *Lamb v Evans* [1893] 1 Ch 218 at 235.
59. (1948) 65 RPC 203 at 215.
60. *Argyll v Argyll* [1967] Ch 302.
61. *Coco v A N Clark (Engineers) Ltd* [1969] RPC 41 at 47.

information in the hands of the government, but it is to say that when equity protects government information it will look at the matter through different spectacles.

[52] It may be a sufficient detriment to the citizen that disclosure of information relating to his affairs will expose his actions to public discussion and criticism. But it can scarcely be a relevant detriment to the government that publication of material concerning its actions will merely expose it to public discussion and criticism. It is unacceptable in our democratic society that there should be a restraint on the publication of information relating to government when the only vice of that information is that it enables the public to discuss, review and criticize government action.

Accordingly, the court will determine the government's claim to confidentiality by reference to the public interest. Unless disclosure is likely to injure the public interest, it will not be protected.

The court will not prevent the publication of information which merely throws light on the past workings of government, even if it be not public property, so long as it does not prejudice the community in other respects. Then disclosure will itself serve the public interest in keeping the community informed and in promoting discussion of public affairs. If, however, it appears that disclosure will be inimical to the public interest because national security, relations with foreign countries or the ordinary business of government will be prejudiced, disclosure will be restrained. There will be cases in which the conflicting considerations will be finely balanced, where it is difficult to decide whether the public's interest in knowing and in expressing its opinion, outweighs the need to protect confidentiality.

Support for this approach is to be found in *Attorney-General v Jonathan Cape Ltd*, where the Court refused to grant an injunction to restrain publication of the diaries of Richard Crossman. Lord Widgery LCJ said:

> The Attorney-General must show (a) that such publication would be a breach of confidence; (b) that the public interest requires that the publication be restrained, and (c) that there are no other facts of the public interest contradictory of and more compelling than that relied upon. Moreover, the court, when asked to restrain such a publication, must closely examine the extent to which relief is necessary to ensure that restrictions are not imposed beyond the strict requirement of public need.[62]

Although this statement has been criticized on the ground that it is contrary to principle and unduly restricts the right of government to restrain disclosure,[63] [53] his Lordship was correctly elaborating the principle so as to take account of the special character of the government and defining the detriment which it needs to show.

How, then, does the claim for an injunction to restrain disclosure of confidential information stand? Mr Henderson has testified that publication of parts of the book would be detrimental to relations with foreign countries. He was not cross-examined on his opinion because this has been an interlocutory hearing. At a trial the soundness of his opinion would be strenuously contested.

---

62. *Attorney-General v Jonathan Cape Ltd* [1976] QB 752 at 770–1.
63. See M W Bryan, 'The Crossman Diaries — Developments in the Law of Breach of Confidence' (1976) 92 *Law Quarterly Review* 180.

Mr Pritchett did not state that the disclosure of any particular documents would be prejudicial to national defence. He said, however, that a number of documents in the book were Defence Department documents with a security classification ranging from 'TOP SECRET' downwards. According to the [government's] 'Protective Security Handbook', the classifications accorded to some of these documents indicate that disclosure would be prejudicial to national security. But in the absence of evidence from Mr Pritchett, I am not prepared to assume that publication of any of the documents will now prejudice national security, except perhaps in the limited sense suggested by Mr Henderson, that publication might make other countries less willing to provide information on a confidential basis.

There is the possibility that Mr Henderson and Mr Pritchett attach too much importance to the fact that documents are classified. Security classification is given to a document when it is brought into existence. Thereafter, it seems, there is no regular procedure for reconsidering the classification of documents, with the consequence that the initial classification lingers on long after the document has ceased to be a security risk. My impression is that, with one exception, the documents have not been reconsidered for classification since they were brought into existence.

The contents of some documents possibly suggest that disclosure of them would embarrass Australia's relations with other countries and consequently affect their willingness to make available defence and diplomatic information on a confidential basis. I have given particular attention to Ch 6 of the book and to ten passages in it identified by Mr Henderson. In some passages overseas political and diplomatic personalities are mentioned, information and attitudes are ascribed to them and comments, [54] some critical, are made about them. Some confidential reports or opinions of ambassadors of foreign countries are set out. Some of the ten passages appear in the East Timor material which the [publishers] intended to publish.

However, I am not persuaded that the degree of embarrassment to Australia's foreign relations which will flow from disclosure is enough to justify interim protection of confidential information. In any event, the question whether an injunction should be granted on this ground is resolved against the [government] by the publication that has taken, and is likely to take, place.

The sales of the book already made, including those made to Indonesia and the United States, the countries most likely to be affected by its contents, and the publication of the first instalment in the two newspapers, indicate that the detriment which the [government] apprehends will not be avoided by the grant of an injunction. In other circumstances the circulation of about 100 copies of a book may not be enough to disentitle the possessor of confidential information from protection by injunction, but in this case it is likely that what is in the book will become known to an ever-widening group of people here and overseas, including foreign governments.

Comment
1. See Radan & Stewart at **8.58–8.69**.

The defences of iniquity and the public interest

8.9 Australian Football League v Age Company Ltd (2006) 15 VR 419

Court: Supreme Court of Victoria

Facts: AFL players were contractually bound to undergo drug testing. The agreement between the players and the AFL was partially contained in the AFL Illicit Drugs Policy ('IDP') which stated that the first two positive drug tests would be kept confidential between the AFL and the player, whereas the third would be subject to disciplinary action, which was necessarily public. The names of three AFL players who had tested positive to drugs were published on an internet discussion forum. An electronic newspaper article had also named the players to a limited group of subscribers for about five hours. A further publication of one of the players' names had occurred when a phone caller named the player on the 'Fox Footy' television program. The AFL and the players' association sought a permanent injunction on two newspapers to prevent them from publishing the names of the players.

Issue: The issue before the court was whether the players' drug taking was inequitable behaviour which was not deserving of equity's protection. Another issue was whether it was in the public interest for the identities of the players to be made public.

Decision: Kellam J found that the players' drug taking was not inequitable behaviour. Equity could protect the confidence of the players' identities even though they had been involved in an illegal activity. Nor was there a public interest in making their identities known.

Extracts: The extract from the judgment of Kellam J reviews both defences of iniquity and public interest and discusses how they should be applied in Australia.

Kellam J

[433] The iniquity rule

The submission of the [newspaper] as to iniquity

The [newspaper] contend further that there is no confidence recognised by the law in circumstances of iniquity. Put another way, Mr Marks, of senior counsel for the [newspaper], contends that the information the AFL seeks to have remain confidential is information which reveals that AFL players have committed a criminal offence. He points out that in all States and Territories of Australia it is an offence to use and/ or possess 'a drug of dependence' or a 'prohibited drug' … Mr Marks [counsel for the newspaper] argues that the law in Australia is that information concerning a crime, wrong or misdeed of public importance will not be recognised by the law as being confidential. He submits that persons privy to such information cannot, by private agreement or otherwise, prevent its [434] disclosure by reverting to the equitable doctrine of breach of confidence. He submits that there is simply no confidence in equity as to the disclosure of an iniquity.

Mr Marks relies upon the early case of *Gartside v Outram*. In that case, in relation to a claim for confidentiality of a trade secret, the court held that an employee could not be made the object of confidential obligation where the obligation related to information concerning the fraudulent conduct of his employer. Wood V-C said:

> The true doctrine is, that there is no confidence as to the disclosure of iniquity.[64]

Mr Marks relies upon the statement of Lord Denning in *Initial Services Ltd v Putterill* where Lord Denning said:

> There may be cases where the misdeed is of such a character that the public interest may demand, or at least excuse, publication on a broader field, even to the press.[65]

However it should be observed that the introductory words of Lord Denning prior to the above statement contain a rider which appears in the following terms:

> The disclosure must, I should think, be to one who has a proper interest to receive the information. Thus it would be proper to disclose a crime to the police; or a breach of the Restrictive Trade Practices Act to the registrar.[66]

In *A v Hayden*,[67] Gibbs CJ gave consideration to the concept of iniquity. He referred[35] to the conclusion of Sheppard J in *Allied Mills Industries Pty Ltd v Trade Practices Commission*[68] who after a careful review of the authorities said:

> ... the public interest in the disclosure ... of iniquity will always outweigh the public interest in the preservation of private and confidential information.[69]

In relation to that conclusion the Chief Justice said:

> That is too broad a statement, unless 'iniquity' is confined to mean serious crime. The public interest does not, in every case, require the disclosure of the fact that a criminal offence, however trivial, has been committed.[70]

He said further:

> It is clear that a person who owes a duty to maintain confidentiality will not be allowed to escape from his obligation simply because he alleges that crimes have been committed and that it is in the public interest that he should disclose information relating to them.[71]

---

64. *Gartside v Outram* (1856) 26 LJ Ch 113 at 114.
65. *Initial Services Ltd v Putterill* [1968] 1 QB 396 at 406.
66. *Initial Services Ltd v Putterill* [1968] 1 QB 396 at 405–6.
67. (1984) 156 CLR 532.
68. (1981) 34 ALR 105 at 141.
69. *A v Hayden* (1984) 156 CLR 532 at 545.
70. *A v Hayden* (1984) 156 CLR 532 at 545–6.
71. *A v Hayden* (1984) 156 CLR 532 at 546.

In his submission, Mr Marks notes that Gibbs CJ made no reference to the rider attached by Lord Denning in *Initial Services Ltd* requiring the information to be imparted to someone with an appropriate interest in receiving it, before the [435] rule would apply. Mr Marks submits that there is an essential flaw in the rider attached to the rule by Lord Denning in *Initial Services Ltd*. He contends that if the information lacked the confidential character because it concerned iniquity, then it could not matter to whom it was disclosed. He submits that the identity and interest of the person receiving it could not affect the confidential character of the information. He argues that if it were otherwise, the information would have a different character of confidentiality depending upon who had possession of it. In this regard Mr Marks relies upon the judgment of Gummow J in *Corrs Pavey Whiting & Byrne v Collector of Customs (Vic)*. Gummow J, under a heading '*Gartside v Outram*: for what principle is it authority?' reviewed a number of the relevant authorities and said:

> From this consideration of *Gartside v Outram* I conclude that that case provides insufficient basis for any 'public interest defence' of the kind that, in its name, has been developed in the recent English authorities. The truth as to what *Gartside v Outram* decided is less striking and more readily understood in terms of basic principles. It is that any court of law or equity would have been extremely unlikely to imply in a contract between master and servant an obligation that the servant's good faith to his master required him to keep secret details of his master's gross bad faith to his customers.[72]

He went on to say that the principle, in equity, where there is no reliance on contractual confidence is:

> ... no wider than one that information will lack the necessary attribute of confidence if the subject-matter is the existence or real likelihood of the existence of an iniquity in the sense of a crime, civil wrong or serious misdeed of public importance, and the confidence is relied upon to prevent disclosure to a third party with a real and direct interest in redressing such crime, wrong or misdeed.[73]

Although this articulation of the rule by Gummow J appears similar indeed to that formulated in *Gartside v Outram*, together with the rider attached by Lord Denning in *Initial Services v Putterill*, Mr Marks relies upon a further statement of Gummow J that:

> It is no great step to say that information as to crimes, wrongs and misdeeds, in the sense I have described, lacks what Lord Green MR called 'the necessary quality of confidence': *Saltman Engineering Co Ltd v Campbell Engineering Co Ltd* (1948) 65 RPC 203 at 215.[74]

Mr Marks submits that it is clear from that statement that there is no confidence in the disclosure of iniquity and that if that is so, it is illogical to assert that there is any restriction upon anyone to whom such disclosure should be made.

---

72. *Corrs Pavey Whiting & Byrne v Collector of Customs (Vic)* (1987) 14 FCR 434 at 454–6.
73. *Corrs Pavey Whiting & Byrne v Collector of Customs (Vic)* (1987) 14 FCR 434 at 456.
74. *Corrs Pavey Whiting & Byrne v Collector of Customs (Vic)* (1987) 14 FCR 434 at 456.

The submission of the [AFL] as to iniquity

The submission of the [AFL] is that it is not enough that publication will disclose an iniquity. It is submitted that the disclosure of the iniquity must be necessary as a matter of public welfare, for example in the interests of the administration of justice. It is submitted further that, even where the so-called **[436]** iniquity rule has a sphere of operation, it overrides the confidence only in so far as the confidence would conceal the existence of the iniquity from those who have a real interest in receiving it.

Conclusion as to whether or not the iniquity rule permits publication by the [newspaper] of otherwise confidential material

Gurry, in considering the statement by Denning MR in *Initial Services Ltd* that disclosure of an iniquity must be made to one who has a proper interest in the disclosure, states as follows:

> This element of the defence can operate as an important control device to ensure that attempts are not made to justify capricious disclosures. It seems settled that the proper authority to whom information relating to crime should be disclosed is the police or the Director of Public Prosecutions. Where the misdeed is a breach of statutory duty, the statutory authority charged with administering the relevant legislation would have a 'proper interest' to receive the information. Where it is a civil wrong, the individual against whom the tort has been, or is intended to be, committed, is presumably the proper person to whom disclosure should be made. Thus in *Gartside v Outram* Wood V-C considered that disclosure of fraudulent business practices to the defrauded customers was justified.[75]
>
> If the event or practice affects the community as a whole, then there are grounds for justifying a general disclosure through, for example the media or by the publication of a book. In *Church of Scientology v Kaufman*[76] Goff J considered that the publication of a book exposing the malpractices of scientology, which affected, or had a potential effect on, the general public, was legitimate. [Some footnotes omitted.]

In my opinion, that statement set out in Gurry, although published more than 20 years ago, does reflect the state of the law in Australia at the present time.

In my view, the position advanced by Mr Marks that if information relates to an iniquity being a crime, wrong or misdeed of public importance it will not be recognised by the law as being confidential, is too wide. I accept the submission of the [AFL] that in order to rely upon the so-called iniquity rule so as to eradicate the protection that would otherwise be granted in equity in respect of confidential information, it is necessary for the person relying upon that defence to establish that:

(a) the proposed disclosure will in fact disclose the existence of or the real likelihood of the existence of an iniquity that is a crime, civil wrong or serious misdeed of public importance;[77]

(b) that the iniquity to be disclosed is of a character of public importance, in the sense that what is to be disclosed affects the community as a whole, or affects the public welfare; and

---

75. F Gurry, *Breach of Confidence*, 1984, Oxford University Press, Oxford, p 345.

76. [1973] RPC 635.

77. *AG Australia Holdings Ltd v Burton* (2002) 58 NSWLR 464 at 456.

(c) that the person who is seeking to protect the confidence is so doing in order to prevent disclosure to a third party with a real and direct interest in redressing the alleged crime, wrong or misdeed.[78]

In my view the disclosure of names of players who have tested positive to illicit drugs will not disclose any iniquity of a serious criminal nature. At the highest, such disclosure may establish that the players at some stage had traces [437] of illicit drugs in their urine and thus the information may be relevant to the possibility of, or the suggestion of, a crime having been committed by one of them. However, no crime, be it possession of or use of such illicit substance, could possibly be proved by such information alone.

Furthermore, even if the information can be said to disclose an iniquity, there is no suggestion that it is the intention of the [newspaper] to disclose such matters to a third party with a real interest in redressing any such possible crime. The [newspaper] seek[s] to disclose the information for the purposes of what might be described as an 'interesting story' for football fans and for other readers, and for no other purpose.

Public interest

The submission of the [newspaper] as to public interest

However, in addition to the iniquity argument, the [newspaper] contend[s] that they are entitled to publish the identity of AFL players who have twice tested positive under the IDP, because it can be inferred from the positive tests that they have used drugs and engaged in seriously wrongful conduct. It is argued that it is in the public interest that such seriously wrongful conduct not be hidden, and that young people should know both the identities of such players and their conduct and, furthermore, that it be appreciated by the public that such conduct by the players will not escape public scrutiny. It is submitted by Mr Marks that it is clear law that the disclosure of information which has been imparted in circumstances otherwise requiring an obligation of confidence can be justified when it is in the public interest so to do. Mr Marks concedes that the precise scope of the public interest exception is unclear upon the authorities, but he contends that in a case where the information sought to be kept confidential discloses anti-social and criminal conduct on the part of AFL players the public interest dictates that the [newspaper] ha[s] the right to publicise such disclosure. Mr Marks submits that a number of categories of disclosure of information, including breach of national security, crime, fraudulent or serious misdeeds, and breach of statute, are public interest exceptions well supported by authority. In relation to crimes and wrongful conduct he submits that the public interest defence is closely related to, but not the same as, the iniquity rule. He relies upon the statement of Lord Denning MR (with whom the other members of the Court of Appeal agreed) in *Fraser v Evans*:

> ... I do not look upon the word 'iniquity' as expressing a principle. It is merely an instance of just cause or excuse for breaking confidence. There are some things which may be required to be disclosed in the public interest, in which event no confidence can be prayed in aid to keep them secret.[79]

---

78. *Corrs Pavey Whiting & Byrne v Collector of Customs (Vic)* (1987) 14 FCR 434 at 456.
79. *Fraser v Evans* [1969] 1 QB 349.

The submission of the [AFL] as to public interest

The plaintiffs contend that there is no general public interest defence in the context of breach of confidence cases in equity. It is submitted that the public interest defence in English law is, to use the words of Gummow J, 'picturesque' but imprecise. It is argued that this is clear from the statement of Gummow J in **[438]** *Smith Kline & French Laboratories (Aust) Ltd v Secretary Department of Community Services and Health* when he said:

> ... I would accept ... that (i) an examination of the recent English decisions shows that the so-called 'public interest' defence is not so much a rule of law as an invitation to judicial idiosyncrasy by deciding each case on an ad hoc basis as to whether, on the facts overall, it is better to respect or to override the obligation of confidence; and (ii) equitable principles are best developed by reference to what conscionable behaviour demands of the defendant, not by 'balancing' and then overriding those demands by reference to matters of social or political opinion.[80]

As submitted by the [AFL], it is on this basis that in Australia the correct legal position is that there is no general public interest defence. However the [AFL] concede[s] that the issue is yet to be determined authoritatively in Australia. In this regard it is submitted in the alternative that even if a general public interest defence exists requiring the weighing up of competing interests, in this case there is a competing public interest which justifies the protection afforded in equity to the confidential information of the identity of players who have tested positive under the IDP. It is submitted that the argument advanced by the [newspaper], being that by reason of the 'reprehensible' nature of drug use, the media should be free to name AFL players who have twice tested positive to illicit substances, on the basis that those players are in a position to influence the lives of others, is not a tenable proposition. It is argued, first, that there is nothing preventing discussion and debate among members of the community in relation to drug taking in sport, the AFL's anti-doping code, the IDP, the fact that players have twice tested positive, or any related topic. It is argued that it is untenable to suggest that effective discussion or communication is stifled, or that the public interest is affected, because the public cannot satisfy its curiosity regarding the names of players who have twice tested positive under the IDP. It is argued that there are powerful reasons why confidentiality should be protected. Those reasons include the fact that there is an IDP, the aim and object of the IDP and its essential features, the fact that publication may well lead to the eradication of a balanced, health and welfare orientated, drug policy, resulting in less drug-testing than that which exists currently, with the result that young players and others will be deprived of the opportunity of early education and rehabilitation. Furthermore, it is argued by the [AFL] that publication of the identity of the players will serve only public curiosity. It is submitted that no public welfare or other interest will be served. The preservation of confidentiality has no impact upon freedom of discussion about the merits of the IDP, the issue of the use of illicit drugs, drugs in sport or any other related topic. Thus it is argued on behalf of the plaintiffs that there is no competing public interest which justifies the setting aside of the protection afforded in equity to the confidential information.

---

80. *Smith Kline & French Laboratories (Aust) Ltd v Secretary Department of Community Services and Health* (1990) 22 FCR 73 at 111.

Conclusion as to the question of whether or not the public interest is relevant to the publication of the names of the players

It is true that the existence of, and/or the extent of, any public interest defence to a breach of confidentiality is by no means clear and settled in Australia. It would appear that in the UK an approach of balancing public interest with the [439] interests served by confidentiality has developed. The decision in *Lion Laboratories Ltd v Evans* establishes that proposition. Griffiths LJ said:

> The first question to be determined is whether there exists a defence of public interest to actions for breach of confidentiality and copyright, and if so, whether it is limited to situations in which there has been serious wrongdoing by the plaintiffs — the so-called 'iniquity' rule.

> I am quite satisfied that the defence of public interest is now well established in actions for breach of confidence and, although there is less authority on the point, that it also extends to breach of copyright ...

> I can see no sensible reason why this defence should be limited to cases in which there has been wrongdoing on the part of the plaintiffs. I believe that the so-called iniquity rule evolved because in most cases where the facts justified a publication in breach of confidence, it was because the plaintiff had behaved so disgracefully or criminally that it was judged in the public interest that his behaviour should be exposed. No doubt it is in such circumstances that the defence will usually arise, but it is not difficult to think of instances where, although there has been no wrongdoing on the part of the plaintiff, it may be vital in the public interest to publish a part of his confidential information.[81]

It should be noted that there is no suggestion by the [newspaper] in the case before me that the [AFL has] been guilty of iniquitous behaviour. Rather, it is argued that it is the information which the plaintiffs seek to keep confidential that discloses iniquitous behaviour on the part of others.

In *David Syme & Company Ltd v General-Motors-Holden's Ltd*,[82] Samuels JA agreed with the notion that the public interest involved a balance between a countervailing public interest and the public interest in maintaining a right to confidentiality. He referred to the statement of Lord Denning MR in *Woodward v Hutchins*, that it:

> ... is a question of balancing the public interest in maintaining the confidence against the public interest in knowing the truth.[83]

Samuels JA said, however, that in determining whether or not the public interest outweighs the duty of the confidence, it is necessary to look to the character of the information which is sought to be disclosed and to compare it with the nature of the interest that it is argued requires revelation.[84]

---

81. *Lion Laboratories Ltd v Evans* [1985] QB 526 at 526.
82. (1984) 2 NSWLR 294 at 309.
83. *Woodward v Hutchins* [1977] 1 WLR 760 at 764.
84. *David Syme & Company Ltd v General-Motors-Holden's Ltd* [1984] 2 NSWLR 294 at 310.

This approach of balancing of interests received support from Kirby P in *Attorney-General (UK) v Heinemann Publishers Australia Pty Ltd*,[85] when he quoted with approval from the dissenting judgment of Lord Denning in *Schering Chemicals Ltd v Falkman*, that:

> ... In order to warrant a restraint, there must be a pressing social need for protecting the confidence sufficiently pressing to outweigh the public interest in freedom of the press.[86]

[440] However, the defence of public interest in those terms has been rejected by Gummow J on two occasions, the first being the 1987 case of *Corrs Pavey Whiting & Byrne v Collector of Customs (Vic)*, and secondly, in 1990, in *Smith Kline & French Laboratories (Aust) Ltd v Secretary Department of Community Services and Health*, where he said:

> My views upon the wisdom of adopting in Australia the English authorities in which the 'public interest' defence has been constructed in recent years, from what may be thought inadequate historical and doctrinal materials, have been expressed in *Corrs Pavey Whiting & Byrne v Collector of Customs (Vic)* at 451–458.[87]

In *Sullivan v Sclanders*, Gray J considered a number of the above authorities and said, in relation to the facts then before him:

> I ... conclude, upon review of the relevant material, that I can discern no case of iniquity. As a result, whether the iniquity rule or the balancing of public interest approach is applied the result is the same.
>
> However, as a matter of strict legal principle I consider the application of the iniquity rule to be the correct approach. Equitable principles are best developed by reference to what conscionable behaviour demands of the defendant rather than by balancing those demands with matters of public interest. This approach avoids the ad hoc judicial idiosyncrasy associated with deciding whether, on the facts overall, it is better to respect or override the obligation of confidence.[88]

Gray J went on to say:

> Even if the balancing of public interests is the correct approach, it was necessary for the learned judge to have considered whether any disgraceful or criminal behaviour was disclosed or whether some matter vital to the public interest required that the material be published.[89]

I have concluded already that there is insufficient evidence of iniquity of such a nature that 'makes legitimate the publication of confidential information ... so as to protect the community from destruction, damage or harm', to use the words used by Mason J in *Commonwealth v John Fairfax & Sons Ltd*.[90] I respectfully adopt the approach of Gummow J

---

85. (1987) 10 NSWLR 86 at 169.
86. *Schering Chemicals Ltd v Falkman* [1982] QB 1 at 32.
87. *Smith Kline & French Laboratories (Aust) Ltd v Secretary Department of Community Services and Health* (1990) 22 FCR 73 at 111.
88. *Sullivan v Sclanders* (2000) 77 SASR 419 at 427.
89. *Sullivan v Sclanders* (2000) 77 SASR 419 at 427.
90. (1980) 147 CLR 39 at 57.

in *Corrs Pavey Whiting & Byrne* and Gray J in *Sullivan v Sclanders* in relation to the narrower 'iniquity rule' on the basis that equity '[is] best developed by reference to what conscionable behaviour demands'.[91] However, if I am incorrect in this view, and even if the correct approach is the balancing of public interests, I would take the view that the balance falls in favour of the [AFL].

It is quite clear that the public interest disclosure must amount to more than public 'curiosity' or public 'prurience'. As Lord Wilberforce said in *British Steel Corporation v Granada Television Ltd*:

> ... there is a wide difference between what is interesting to the public and what it is in the public interest to make known.[92]

[441] In this regard, Raff J said in *Sullivan v Sclanders*:

> An important distinction needs to be drawn between matters that ought to be disclosed in the public interest, and those which are merely of public interest in the sense that many people would like to know them.[93]

Furthermore, as Griffiths LJ said in *Lion Laboratories Ltd v Evans*:

> The defendants have, in my view, made out a powerful case for publication in the public interest. In these circumstances I can see no alternative but to permit publication. It would surely be wrong to refuse leave to publish material that may lead to a reappraisal of a machine that has the potential for causing a wrongful conviction of a serious criminal offence.

> When the press raise the defence of public interest, the court must appraise it critically; but if convinced that a strong case has been made out, the press should be free to publish, leaving the plaintiff to his remedy in damages.

> I end with one word of caution: there is a world of difference between what is in the public interest and what is of interest to the public. This judgment is not intended to be a 'mole's charter'.[94]

In the case before me the [AFL] entered into an arrangement whereby players in the AFL competition could be tested for the use of illicit drugs outside of competition. The evidence put before me is to the effect that the IDP was developed as a result of a consultation between the plaintiffs and others including AFL medical officers, drug education and rehabilitation experts and the Australian Drug Foundation. Prior to the policy coming into effect the AFL had conducted statistical testing of players in relation to the use of illicit drugs such as cocaine, ecstasy and marijuana, and had established an increase in the low incidence of use of such drugs by players. The IDP was introduced because the AFL wished to prohibit the use of illicit drugs and 'increase education of the AFL playing group in relation to the dangers of illicit drugs and protect players from the risk of harm'

---

91. *Sullivan v Sclanders* (2000) 77 SASR 419 at 427.
92. [1981] AC 1096 at 1168.
93. *Sullivan v Sclanders* (2000) 77 SASR 419 at 426.
94. *Lion Laboratories Ltd v Evans* [1985] QB 526 at 553.

and, further, 'to increase education of the public at large in relation to the dangers of illicit drugs and to set a positive example'.[95] The advice given to the AFL was that a rehabilitative model of management involving education, counselling and monitoring treatment was appropriate to the discouragement of the use of illicit drugs ...

[442] No evidence was led before me as to the range of ages of persons playing in the AFL competition. No evidence was led before me as to the statistical analysis conducted by the AFL as to use of illicit drugs by players prior to the development of the IDP. However, it is common knowledge that players as young as 17 are involved in the AFL competition. It is common knowledge that players in the AFL come from a variety of backgrounds and in many cases from rural and indigenous communities. It is common knowledge that, at least in some States of Australia, players in the AFL competition achieve so-called 'celebrity status'. It is the common knowledge of any judge of this court that the use of the drugs which are circumscribed by the IDP are, regrettably, commonplace among young people in the general community of an age similar to at least some of those in the AFL player cohort. Taking into account the pressures of professional sport, the public scrutiny of players engaged in professional sport, the so-called 'celebrity status' of players, their age range and the background of many players in the AFL competition, it is not surprising that some players in the competition are either manipulated by others, or on occasions fall into temptation to use drugs of the nature of those used by many others in the community. On this basis, it appears to me that it can be well argued that the IDP has a sound basis. It can be well argued that a process which is designed to identify players who might use illicit [443] drugs and to endeavour to rehabilitate and educate them before exposing them to public scrutiny is a sensible approach. The emotional and financial damage that might be done to a young player who is detected to be in breach of the IDP, if his first or second breach for that matter were to become public, needs no further explanation. The fact that the confidentiality was implicit in the acceptance by the players of a significant infringement in their lives, that being that they are to be tested randomly in circumstances well beyond those regarded as being necessary by the World Anti-Doping Authority, is not without significance in consideration of the matter.

On the other hand, what is the public interest sought to be served by the publication of otherwise confidential material? The media is well aware of the terms of the IDP. I have no doubt that there is a public interest in discussion of the terms of the IDP. It may be that some would hold the view that the IDP is too lenient in relation to players who test positive. That debate can be had without the identification of players who have tested positive. It may be that some would regard the provision of confidentiality at all as being inappropriate. Any public interest in that debate can be had without the identification of any players who have tested positive. It may well be that there is a public interest in discussion of the manner in which the policy distinguishes between cannabinoids and other drugs. That is a debate which can be had in the absence of the knowledge of the identity of any player who has tested positive. The non-naming of the players who have tested positive does not in any legitimate way derogate from proper public discussion of these issues.

---

95. Clause 1.6 of the IDP.

In the end result, it appears to me that there is nothing other than the satisfaction of public curiosity in having the confidentiality of the names of those who have tested positive breached by being released. It may well be a wonderful front page story for the newspapers and a scoop for other sections of the media. No doubt photographs of any players concerned will be published and the issue will be productive of many words of journalistic endeavour. However, I can see nothing that is in the public welfare or in the interests of the community at large which can be served by the identification, and perhaps to a degree the vilification and shaming of those who agreed to be tested randomly pursuant to the terms of the IDP, on the basis that such testing would remain confidential until such time as there were to be three positive tests. Accordingly, even if there is a public interest defence to the claim of confidentiality made by the [AFL] I do not conclude that it outweighs the public interest in having the information remain confidential.

Comments
1. See Radan & Stewart at **8.96–8.106**.
2. This case is also discussed in this chapter at **8.6**.
3. The public interest test can also be satisfied in cases of danger to the public. In *W v Edgell* [1990] 1 All ER 835, a psychiatric report, commissioned to support an application for a forensic patient's release, was not found to be confidential. The patient had killed five people. The application for release had been withdrawn after the doctor's report as it was clear that the patient was not well enough to be released. The doctor was justified in forwarding a copy of his report to the government, given the risk that the patient represented to the safety of the public.

The application of the doctrine of breach of confidence to protect privacy interests

8.10   Australian Broadcasting Corporation v Lenah Game Meats Pty Limited (2001) 208 CLR 199

Court: High Court of Australia

Facts: Lenah operated a game meat processing business in Tasmania. Part of its work involved the killing and processing of brush tail possums in licensed abattoirs for the export market. Unknown trespassers entered into Lenah's property and installed hidden video cameras that filmed the slaughter and processing activities. The film was then supplied to an animal rights group, which passed it over to the ABC for public broadcasting. Lenah applied for, and obtained, interlocutory injunctions against the ABC and the animal rights group to restrain use of the film on the grounds that it had been unlawfully obtained and jeopardised Lenah's business.

Issue: The issue was whether the film footage was confidential.

Decision: The High Court (Gleeson CJ, Gaudron, Gummow, Hayne and Kirby JJ; Callinan J dissenting) found that the information was not confidential and refused to grant an injunction. The majority judges arrived at the decision by different routes.

Extracts: The extract from the judgment of Gleeson CJ discusses how equity can protect privacy interests in the doctrine of confidence.

Gleeson CJ

[221] It is not suggested that the operations that were filmed were secret, or that requirements of confidentiality were imposed upon people who might see the operations. The abattoir is, no doubt, regularly visited by inspectors, and seen by other visitors who come to the premises for business or private reasons. The fact that the operations are required to be, and are, licensed by a public authority, suggests that information about the nature of those operations is not confidential. There is no evidence that, at least before the events giving rise to this case, any special precautions were taken by the respondent to avoid its operations being seen by people outside its organisation. But, like many other lawful animal slaughtering activities, the respondent's activities, if displayed to the public, would cause distress to some viewers. It is claimed that loss of business would result. That claim is not inherently improbable. A film of a vertically integrated process of production of pork sausages, or chicken pies, would be unlikely to be used for sales promotion. In the present state of the evidence, the case has been argued on the basis, and all four judges in the Supreme Court have accepted, that the respondent will suffer some financial harm if the film is broadcast ...

[223] The Attorney-General of the Commonwealth, intervening, made the following submissions: (1) A court of equity has jurisdiction to grant an injunction to restrain the use of information where the information has been obtained by a trespasser, or by some other illegal, tortious, surreptitious or otherwise improper means and use of the information would be unconscionable. (2) The jurisdiction extends to ordering an injunction against any person to whom the information has been conveyed, whether or not that person is implicated in the trespass or other illegal, tortious, surreptitious or otherwise improper conduct. (3) In determining whether the use of the information would be unconscionable, the court should take account of all the circumstances of the case, including the competing public interests in preserving the rule of law, protecting private property and in otherwise protecting the relevant information, and the public interest in freedom of speech. (4) In all cases, the fact that the information was improperly obtained should weigh heavily against allowing the information to be used. (5) The onus of showing that the publication is in the public interest should rest on the person seeking to publish the improperly obtained information.

The arguments appeared to proceed upon the basis that the relevant information is what the processing of possums, as carried out by the respondent, looks, and sounds, like. The film was the means adopted by the trespassers for obtaining, recording, and communicating, that information. The film is their property; just as if a less well equipped intruder had used a note book, or a sketch pad, to record in written or pictorial form what was seen and heard. The slaughtering process is not confidential, and information about it was not obtained in circumstances of trust and confidence, or otherwise importing an obligation of good faith. The trespassers acted illegally, tortiously and surreptitiously, not merely to obtain the information, but to obtain it in a form calculated to facilitate its public display, and to maximise its potential impact upon those to whom it was ultimately conveyed. It is the conduct of the trespassers in obtaining and recording the information that is said to expose the appellant to restraint upon the use it may make of the product of that conduct ...

[224] It is clear that there was no relationship of trust and confidence between the respondent and the people who made, or received, the film. It is also clear that if, by information, is meant the facts as to the slaughtering methods used by the respondent, such information was not confidential in its nature. But equity may impose obligations of confidentiality even though there is no imparting of information in circumstances of trust and confidence. And the principle of good faith upon which equity acts to protect information imparted in confidence may also be invoked to 'restrain the publication of confidential information improperly or surreptitiously obtained'.[96] The nature of the information must be such that it is capable of being regarded as confidential. A photographic image, illegally or improperly or surreptitiously obtained, where what is depicted is private, may constitute confidential information. In *Hellewell v Chief Constable of Derbyshire*, Laws J said:

> If someone with a telephoto lens were to take from a distance and with no authority a picture of another engaged in some private act, his subsequent disclosure of the photograph would, in my judgment, as surely amount to a breach of confidence as if he had found or stolen a letter or diary in which the act was recounted and proceeded to publish it. In such a case, the law would protect what might reasonably be called a right of privacy, although the name accorded to the cause of action would be breach of confidence. It is, of course, elementary that, in all such cases, a defence based on the public interest would be available.[97]

I agree with that proposition, although, to adapt it to the Australian context, it is necessary to add a qualification concerning the constitutional freedom of political communication earlier mentioned. The present is at least as strong a case for a plaintiff as photography from a distance with a telephoto lens. But it is the reference to 'some private act' that is central to the present problem. The activities filmed were carried out on private property. They were not shown, or alleged, to be private in any other sense ...

[225] If the activities filmed were private, then the law of breach of confidence is adequate to cover the case. I would regard images and sounds of private activities, recorded by the methods employed in the present case, as confidential. There would be an obligation of confidence upon the persons who obtained them, and upon those into whose possession they came, if they knew, or ought to have known, the manner in which they were obtained.

By current standards, the manner in which the information in the present case was obtained was hardly sophisticated, and, if there were a relevant kind of privacy invaded,

---

96. *The Commonwealth v John Fairfax & Sons Ltd* (1980) 147 CLR 39 at 50.
97. *Hellewell v Chief Constable of Derbyshire* [1995] 4 All ER 473 at 476.

the invasion was not subtle. The law should be more astute than in the past to identify and protect interests of a kind which fall within the concept of privacy ...

But the lack of precision of the concept of privacy is a reason for [226] caution in declaring a new tort of the kind for which the respondent contends. Another reason is the tension that exists between interests in privacy and interests in free speech. I say 'interests', because talk of 'rights' may be question-begging, especially in a legal system which has no counterpart to the First Amendment to the United States Constitution or to the *Human Rights Act 1998* (UK). The categories that have been developed in the United States for the purpose of giving greater specificity to the kinds of interest protected by a 'right to privacy' illustrate the problem.[98] The first of those categories, which includes intrusion upon private affairs or concerns, requires that the intrusion be highly offensive to a reasonable person. Part of the price we pay for living in an organised society is that we are exposed to observation in a variety of ways by other people.

There is no bright line which can be drawn between what is private and what is not. Use of the term 'public' is often a convenient method of contrast, but there is a large area in between what is necessarily public and what is necessarily private. An activity is not private simply because it is not done in public. It does not suffice to make an act private that, because it occurs on private property, it has such measure of protection from the public gaze as the characteristics of the property, the nature of the activity, the locality, and the disposition of the property owner combine to afford. Certain kinds of information about a person, such as information relating to health, personal relationships, or finances, may be easy to identify as private; as may certain kinds of activity, which a reasonable person, applying contemporary standards of morals and behaviour, would understand to be meant to be unobserved. The requirement that disclosure or observation of information or conduct would be highly offensive to a reasonable person of ordinary sensibilities is in many circumstances a useful practical test of what is private.

It is unnecessary, for present purposes, to enter upon the question of whether, and in what circumstances, a corporation may invoke privacy. United Kingdom legislation recognises the possibility.[99] Some forms of corporate activity are private. For example, neither members of the public, nor even shareholders, are ordinarily entitled to attend directors' meetings. And, as at present advised, I see no reason why some internal corporate communications are any less private than those of a partnership or an individual. However, the foundation of much of what is protected, where rights of privacy, as distinct from rights of property, are acknowledged, is human dignity. This may be incongruous when applied to a corporation. The outcome of the present case would not be materially different if the respondent were [227] an individual or a partnership, rather than a corporation. The problem for the respondent is that the activities secretly observed and filmed were not relevantly private. Of course, the premises on which those activities took place were private in a proprietorial sense. And, by virtue of its proprietary right to exclusive possession of the premises, the respondent had the capacity (subject to the possibility of trespass or other surveillance) to grant or refuse permission to anyone who wanted to observe, and record, its operations. The same can be said of any landowner, but

---

98. Prosser, 'Privacy' (1960) 48 *California Law Review* 383; *Restatement of the Law Second, Torts*, §652A.

99. *R v Broadcasting Standards Commission; Ex parte British Broadcasting Corporation* [2001] QB 885 at 896–7.

it does not make everything that the owner does on the land a private act. Nor does an act become private simply because the owner of land would prefer that it were unobserved. The reasons for such preference might be personal, or financial. They might be good or bad. An owner of land does not have to justify refusal of entry to a member of the public, or of the press. The right to choose who may enter, and who will be excluded, is an aspect of ownership. It may mean that a person who enters without permission is a trespasser; but that does not mean that every activity observed by the trespasser is private.

It is necessary, then, to return to the principal arguments advanced on behalf of the respondent. The first point to note about these arguments is the manner in which the concept of unconscionability is employed. In the case of the argument put by [Lenah], the conduct (or threatened conduct) of the [ABC] in publishing a film known to have been taken as the result of a trespass is characterised as unconscionable. It does not matter whether, in order to justify that characterisation, it is thought necessary to add a reference to the harm likely to be suffered by [Lenah]; at this stage such harm is not in contest. Such unconscionability, if established, is then said to provide the ground in equity for the relief claimed in the action. In the case of the argument put by the Attorney-General, unconscionability is introduced as an additional element, apparently connecting the wrongful conduct of the trespassers in obtaining the film to the use of the information by the [ABC]. It is elaborated in proposition 3, stated above.

No doubt it is correct to say that, if equity will intervene to restrain publication of the film by the [ABC], the ultimate ground upon which it will act will be that, in all the circumstances, it would be unconscientious of the [ABC] to publish. But that leaves for decision the question of the principles according to which equity will reach that conclusion. The conscience of the [ABC], which equity will seek to relieve, is a properly formed and instructed conscience. The real task is to decide what a properly formed and instructed conscience has to say about publication in a case such as the present. If the Attorney-General is correct, it will take account of a number of factors additional to the circumstances in which the film was obtained, including (although this is not spelled out) what the [ABC] knew or ought to have known about those circumstances.

The necessary first step is to say that, subject to possible **[228]** qualifications of the kind set out in proposition 3, the circumstances in which the film was made, known as they now are to the [ABC], mean that the [ABC] is bound on conscience not to publish. That proposition is not self-evidently correct, and cannot be established by mere assertion. The [ABC] is in the business of broadcasting. I accept that, although a public broadcaster, its position is not materially different from a commercial broadcaster with whom it competes. In the ordinary course of its business it publishes information obtained from many sources, thereby contributing to the flow of information available to the public. The sources from which that information may come, directly or indirectly, cover a wide range of behaviour; some of it impeccable, some of it reprehensible, and all intermediate degrees. If the [ABC], without itself being complicit in impropriety or illegality, obtains information which it regards as newsworthy, informative, or entertaining, why should it not publish? It is, of course, subject to any relevant statute law, including criminal law, and to the law of defamation, breach of confidence, negligence, and any other potential liability in tort or contract. But we have arrived at this point in the argument because of the respondent's inability to point to any specific legal inhibition on publication. [Lenah] must explain why the [ABC] is bound in conscience not to publish; and, bearing in mind the consequences of such a conclusion for the free flow of information, it is not good enough to say that any person who fails to see this dictate of conscience is merely displaying moral obtuseness.

The step from the illegality of the behaviour of the trespassers to a conclusion that the [ABC] must not publish, even though the [ABC] was not party to the illegality, itself involves an important matter of principle: the extent to which the civil courts will lend their aid to the enforcement of the criminal law. There are, in a number of Australian jurisdictions, statutes which prohibit or regulate secret surveillance, and deal with the consequences of breaches, including the use that may be made by third parties of the products of such surveillance. Legislation of that kind was in issue, for example, in *John Fairfax Publications Pty Ltd v Doe*.[100] Some may think there ought to be legislation covering a case such as the present; but there is not. And it is only necessary to consider the complexity which such legislation, when enacted, takes, and the exceptions and qualifications that are built into it, to see the need for caution in embracing superficially attractive generalisations ...

[229] Next, reliance was placed upon the act of trespass. Again, the difficulty is to bridge the gap between the trespassers' tort and the [ABC]'s conscience.

There is judicial support for the proposition that the trespassers, if caught in time, could have been restrained from publishing the film. In *Lincoln Hunt Australia Pty Ltd v Willesee*[101] some representatives of a producer of material for television entered commercial premises, with cameras rolling, and harassed people on the premises. Their conduct amounted to trespass. Young J had to consider whether to restrain publication of the film. Because of the effrontery of the conduct of the defendants, he concluded this was a case for large exemplary damages, and that damages were an adequate remedy. On that ground, he declined an injunction. In accordance with settled practice, and principle, however, the first question he asked himself was as to the plaintiff's equity. Because of the ground on which he declined relief, he did not need to decide that question which, he said, took him 'into very deep waters'.[102] However, he expressed the following tentative opinion, which has been taken up in later cases:[103]

> In the instant case, on a prima facie basis I would have thought that there is a lot to be said in the Australian community where a [230] film is taken by a trespasser, made in circumstances as the present, upon private premises in respect of which there is some evidence that publication of the film would affect goodwill, that the case is one where an injunction should seriously be considered.[104]

If, in the present case, the [ABC] had been a party to the trespass, it would be necessary to reach a conclusion about the question which Young J thought should seriously be considered. I would give an affirmative answer to the question, based on breach of confidence, provided the activities filmed were private. I say nothing about copyright,

---

100. (1995) 37 NSWLR 81.
101. (1986) 4 NSWLR 457.
102. *Lincoln Hunt Australia Pty Ltd v Willesee* (1986) 4 NSWLR 457 at 461.
103. *Rinsale Pty Ltd v Australian Broadcasting Corporation* [1993] Aust Torts Reports 81–231 at 62,380; *Emcorp Pty Ltd v Australian Broadcasting Corporation* [1988] 2 Qd R 169 at 174; *Takhar v Animal Liberation SA Inc* [2000] SASC 400 at [75]–[80].
104. *Lincoln Hunt Australia Pty Ltd v Willesee* (1986) 4 NSWLR 457 at 464.

because that was not argued. But the case was one against the trespassers. That was why exemplary damages were available, and constituted a sufficient remedy.

A rather different case was *Donnelly v Amalgamated Television Services Pty Ltd*. Police, executing a search warrant, took a video recording of the plaintiff, in his underpants, in a bedroom. The video found its way into the hands of a television broadcaster. An action was brought to restrain publication of the video and for an interlocutory injunction. Hodgson CJ in Eq, in the orthodox manner, first considered whether the plaintiff had shown a serious question to be tried.[105] He said:

> If police, in exercising powers under a search warrant or of arrest, were to enter into private property and thereby obtain documents containing valuable confidential information, albeit not protected by the law concerning intellectual property, I believe they could in a proper case be restrained, at the suit of the owner of the documents, from later using that information to their own advantage, or to the disadvantage of the owner, or passing the information on to other persons for them to use in that way; and if other persons acquired such information from the police, knowing the circumstances of its acquisition by the police, then I believe those other persons could likewise be restrained. I believe the same applies to material obtained in that way which is gratuitously humiliating rather than confidential.[106]

A film of a man in his underpants in his bedroom would ordinarily have the necessary quality of privacy to warrant the application of the law of breach of confidence. Indeed, the reference to the gratuitously humiliating nature of the film ties in with the first of the four categories of privacy adopted in United States law, and the requirement that the intrusion upon seclusion be highly offensive to a reasonable person.

For reasons already given, I regard the law of breach of confidence as providing a remedy, in a case such as the present, if the nature of [231] the information obtained by the trespasser is such as to permit the information to be regarded as confidential. But, if that condition is not fulfilled, then the circumstance that the information was tortiously obtained in the first place is not sufficient to make it unconscientious of a person into whose hands that information later comes to use it or publish it. The consequences of such a proposition are too large.

Comments
1. See Radan & Stewart at **8.129–8.157**.
2. All the judges in this case recognised the potential for a new tort of privacy to be developed at common law. Since the case no higher appeal jurisdiction has found for such a tort (*Giller v Procopets* [2008] VSCA 236; *Kalaba v Commonwealth* [2004] FCA 763) but there is a District Court decision in which a tort was recognised: *Grosse v Purvis* [2003] QDC 151.

---

105. *Donnelly v Amalgamated Television Services Pty Ltd* (1998) 45 NSWLR 570 at 573.
106. *Donnelly v Amalgamated Television Services Pty Ltd* (1998) 45 NSWLR 570 at 575.

9

FIDUCIARY OBLIGATIONS

Introduction

9.1 This chapter is concerned with fiduciary obligations. Fiduciary obligations are ones of trust and confidence. The person in whom confidence is reposed within that relationship is referred to as the fiduciary. The person to whom fiduciary obligations are owed is called the beneficiary (or principal).

Fiduciary obligations are strict. A fiduciary in breach of their obligations is liable even where the fiduciary acted in good faith breach and where there is no proven loss to the principal. The obligations are negative, meaning that they forbid the fiduciary from acting in certain ways, but do not require the fiduciary to act positively in the interests of the principal.

The extracts in this chapter discuss the following:

- the definition of fiduciary obligations and how they can be determined: *Hospital Products Ltd v United States Surgical Corporation* (1984) 156 CLR 41;
- the strict nature of fiduciary duties: *Boardman v Phipps* [1967] 2 AC 46;
- the application of fiduciary principles to joint ventures: *United Dominions Corporation Ltd v Brian Pty Ltd* (1985) 157 CLR 1 at 12;
- the courts' approach to the imposition of fiduciary duties in the family context: *Paramasivam v Flynn* (1998) 90 FCR 489;
- the application of fiduciary duties to the doctor–patient relationship: *Breen v Williams* (1996) 186 CLR 71; and
- the application of fiduciary doctrine to indigenous peoples: *Bodney v Westralia Airports Corporation Pty Ltd* (2000) 109 FCR 178.

The definition of fiduciary obligations and how they can be determined

9.2 Hospital Products Ltd v United States Surgical Corporation (1984) 156 CLR 41

Court: High Court of Australia

Facts: Blackman negotiated an exclusive distributorship arrangement for Australia in relation to products manufactured by United States Surgical Corporation (USSC).

Blackman promised to use his best efforts to promote USSC products within Australia. Blackman's company, Hospital Products International Ltd (HPI), was soon after substituted as the distributor. Subsequently HPI, using USSC products as models, began to manufacture products that were essentially identical to those manufactured by USSC. HPI then terminated its arrangement with USSC and began to sell its own products to USSC customers. USSC argued that HPI owed it fiduciary obligations and that HPI's conduct amounted to a breach of fiduciary duties owed to it.

Issue: The main issue was whether HPI owed a fiduciary duty to USSC, in addition to any contractual duties.

Decision: A bare majority (Gibbs CJ, Wilson and Dawson JJ) held that there was no fiduciary relationship between the parties and that USSC's right to relief rested in a claim for damages for breach of contract. The majority considered that because the relationship between the parties was a commercial one entered into by equal parties at arm's length with the intention that both parties would gain a profit, it was inappropriate to find a fiduciary relationship between the parties. USSC had rights against HPL for breach of an implied contractual term that the distributor would use its best efforts to promote USSC products within Australia.

Extracts: In the first extract Gibbs CJ discusses the problems of defining when a fiduciary relationship exists. The second extract is from the judgment of Mason J. While Mason J was in the minority, his discussion of the definition of fiduciary relationships is highly instructive.

Gibbs CJ

[67] Fiduciary relationship

It is clear that HPI committed serious breaches of its obligation to use its best efforts to promote the sale of USSC's products, and that USSC is entitled to recover from HPI damages for these breaches. However, USSC contends that it was also owed by HPI a fiduciary obligation, the breach of which entitled USSC not merely to compensation but to 'restitution of property unconscientiously withheld';[1] and to the equitable remedies of equitable lien and constructive trust. A person who occupies a fiduciary position may not use that position to gain a profit or advantage for himself, nor may he obtain a benefit by entering into a transaction in conflict with his fiduciary duty, without the informed consent of the person to whom he owes the duty. This principle — some would prefer to say 'these principles' — has been described as 'inflexible'[2] and 'fundamental'[3] [68] and its nature and application have been discussed in a number of comparatively recent cases: by this Court in *Consul Development Pty Ltd v DPC Estates Pty Ltd*[4] and *Chan v Zacharia;*[5]

---

1. *Vyse v Foster* (1872) LR 8 Ch App 309 at 333.
2. *Birchnell v Equity Trustees, Executors and Agency Co Ltd* (1929) 42 CLR 384 at 408.
3. *Phipps v Boardman* [1967] 2 AC 46 at 123.
4. (1975) 132 CLR 373.
5. (1984) 154 CLR 178.

by the Judicial Committee in *NZ Netherlands Society 'Oranje' Inc v Kuys*[6] and *Queensland Mines Ltd v Hudson;*[7] by the Court of Appeal of New Zealand in *Coleman v Myers,*[8] and by the Supreme Court of Canada in *Canadian Aero Service Ltd v O'Malley.*[9] Clearly if HPI was under a fiduciary obligation to USSC it failed to fulfil it. The question however is whether any fiduciary relationship did exist between the parties.

The authorities contain much guidance as to the duties of one who is in a fiduciary relationship with another, but provide no comprehensive statement of the criteria by reference to which the existence of a fiduciary relationship may be established. The archetype of a fiduciary is of course the trustee, but it is recognized by the decisions of the courts that there are other classes of persons who normally stand in a fiduciary relationship to one another — e.g., partners, principal and agent, director and company, master and servant, solicitor and client, tenant-for-life and remainderman. There is no reason to suppose that these categories are closed. However, the difficulty is to suggest a test by which it may be determined whether a relationship, not within one of the accepted categories, is a fiduciary one.

In the present case McLelland J [the trial judge] said that there were two matters of importance in deciding when the court will recognize the existence of the relevant fiduciary duty. First, if one person is obliged, or undertakes, to act in relation to a particular matter in the interests of another and is entrusted with the power to affect those interests in a legal or practical sense, the situation is, in his opinion, analogous to a trust. Secondly, he said that the reason for the principle lies in the special vulnerability of those whose interests are entrusted to the power of another to the abuse of that power. The learned members of the Court of Appeal considered that the first of these statements needed a qualification which McLelland J had intended to suggest, namely that the undertaking to act in the interests of another meant that the fiduciary undertook not to act in his own interests; they said that the principle is that 'a fiduciary relationship exists where the facts of the case in hand establish that [69] in a particular matter a person has undertaken to act in the interests of another and not in his own'. They added that it is not inconsistent with this principle that a fiduciary may retain that character although he is entitled to have regard to his own interest in particular matters. Their conclusion was that in matters concerning the development of USSC's market in Australia for its surgical stapling products, and its protection from competition, HPI undertook to act in USSC's interest and not in its own.

I doubt if it is fruitful to attempt to make a general statement of the circumstances in which a fiduciary relationship will be found to exist. Fiduciary relations are of different types, carrying different obligations[10] and a test which might seem appropriate to determine whether a fiduciary relationship existed for one purpose might be quite inappropriate for another purpose. For example, the relation of physician and patient, and priest and penitent, may be described as fiduciary when the question is whether there is a presumption of undue influence, but may be less likely to be relevant when an

---

6. [1973] 2 All ER 1222.
7. (1978) 18 ALR 1.
8. [1977] 2 NZLR 225.
9. (1973) 40 DLR (3d) 371.
10. See *In re Coomber; Coomber v Coomber* [1911] 1 Ch 723 at 728–729; *Jenyns v Public Curator (Qld)* (1953) 90 CLR 113 at 132–133; and *Phipps v Boardman* [1967] 2 AC at 126.

alleged conflict between duty and interest is in question. Moreover, different fiduciary relationships may entail different consequences, as is shown by the discussion of the respective positions of a trustee and a partner in relation to the renewal of a lease.[11]

In the decided cases, various circumstances have been relied on as indicating the presence of a fiduciary relationship. One such circumstance is the existence of a relation of confidence, which may be abused.[12] However, an actual relation of confidence — the fact that one person subjectively trusted another — is neither necessary for nor conclusive of the existence of a fiduciary relationship; on the one hand, a trustee will stand in a fiduciary relationship to a beneficiary notwithstanding that the latter at no time reposed confidence in him, and on the other hand, an ordinary transaction for sale and purchase does not give rise to a fiduciary relationship simply because the purchaser trusted the vendor and the latter defrauded him.

Another circumstance which it is sometimes suggested indicates [70] the existence of a fiduciary relationship is inequality of bargaining power, but it is clear that such inequality alone is not enough to create a fiduciary relationship in every case and for all purposes. In any case, Mr Blackman was not in a position of dominance or advantage over USSC at the time the contract was made. Indeed, if there was any inequality in the situation of the parties, it might well be thought that USSC was in the stronger position. On the other hand, the fact that the arrangement between the parties was of a purely commercial kind and that they had dealt at arm's length and on an equal footing has consistently been regarded by this Court as important, if not decisive, in indicating that no fiduciary duty arose.[13] A similar view was taken in Canada in *Jirna Ltd v Mister Donut of Canada Ltd*.[14]

In *Reading v The King*, a case in which a soldier had obtained bribes by abuse of his position, Asquith L.J. said:

> A consideration of the authorities suggests that for the present purpose a 'fiduciary relation' exists (a) whenever the plaintiff entrusts to the defendant property, including intangible property as, for instance, confidential information, and relies on the defendant to deal with such property for the benefit of the plaintiff or for purposes authorized by him, and not otherwise ... and (b) whenever the plaintiff entrusts to the defendant a job to be performed, for instance, the negotiation of a contract on his behalf or for his benefit, and relies on the defendant to procure for the plaintiff the best terms available ...[15]

That decision was approved in the House of Lords although Lord Porter said that the words 'fiduciary relationship' in that setting were used in 'a wide and loose sense'.[16] The

---

11. See *In re Biss; Biss v Biss* [1903] 2 Ch 40 at 56–57, 61–62; *Griffith v Owen* [1907] 1 Ch 195 at 203–204, and *Chan v Zacharia* (1984) 154 CLR 178.
12. *Tate v Williamson* (1866) LR 2 Ch App 55 at 61; *Coleman v Myers* [1977] 2 NZLR at 325.
13. See *Jones v Bouffier* (1911) 12 CLR 579 at 599–600, 605; *Dowsett v Reid* (1912) 15 CLR 695 at 705; *Para Wirra Gold & Bismuth Mining Syndicate N L v Mather* (1934) 51 CLR 582 at 592; *Keith Henry & Co Pty Ltd v Stuart Walker & Co Pty Ltd* (1958) 100 CLR 342 at 351.
14. (1971) 22 DLR (3d) 639; affd (1973) 40 DLR (3d) 303.
15. [1949] 2 KB at 236.
16. *Reading v The King* [1951] AC 507 at 516.

first branch of Lord Asquith's statement has no application to the present case. It was submitted on behalf of USSC that that company had entrusted to HPI its actual and prospective business connexion and goodwill in Australia and had relied on HPI to protect and increase that goodwill for the benefit of USSC. I do not need to discuss the question whether product goodwill can be regarded as property capable of assignment by itself, for I find it impossible to [71] accept that HPI became a fiduciary in respect of USSC's goodwill. The contract did not oblige HPI to protect USSC's goodwill nor were representations made that it would be protected. HPI's relevant obligation was to use its best efforts to promote the sale of USSC's goods. However, apart from the agreement, in cl. 2 of the letter of 27 December 1978, to purchase Downs' inventory and use the dealership inventory of approximately $100,000 to $125,000 wholesale value, HPI was not obliged to purchase from USSC any particular quantity or value of products for distribution. Failure to make further purchases would only be a breach if it amounted to a failure to do all that could reasonably be expected to promote the sale of the products, and HPI's business circumstances and financial situation could be considered in deciding what was reasonable. There was no express provision as to the duration of the agreement; it was therefore terminable either at will or on reasonable notice. Although what HPI did would be likely to affect the market for USSC's goods in Australia, it is apparent that HPI had not given an undertaking to develop or protect the market since its obligation to buy the products for distribution was qualified by what was reasonable having regard to its own circumstances, and it was free to terminate the agreement at any time. Nor was USSC powerless in this situation; it also was free to terminate the agreement and make other arrangements for the distribution of its goods. The argument that a fiduciary relation was created with regard to the goodwill of the products in my opinion quite deserts the reality of the situation.

The second branch of Lord Asquith's statement, if regarded as enunciating a general rule divorced from its context, seems to me, with all respect, to be far too wide; the fact that there is a duty to be performed — a job to do — cannot in every case create a fiduciary obligation. I agree with the statement of Megarry VC in *Tito v Waddell (No 2)*[17] that the imposition of a statutory duty to perform certain functions cannot be said as a general rule to impose fiduciary obligations, and the same is true of contractual duties arising under ordinary commercial contracts.

Finally, I would refer to the opinion expressed by Dr Finn in his comprehensive work on *Fiduciary Obligations*, that, for the purposes of the conflict rule, a fiduciary is 'simply, someone who undertakes to act for or on behalf of another in some particular matter or matters'.[18] Even if it were meant that every agent is a fiduciary, the statement would be open to doubt.[19] [72] And if the statement is to be understood more widely it cannot be accepted without some qualification. Indeed Dr Finn appeared himself to qualify it when he went on to say:

---

17. [1977] Ch 106 at 229–230.
18. P D Finn, *Fiduciary Obligations*, Law Book Company, Sydney, 1977, p 201.
19. See *McKenzie v McDonald* [1927] VLR 134 at 144; *Phipps v Boardman* [1967] 2 AC 46 at 127, and cases cited by F E Dowdrick, 'The Relationship of Principal and Agent' (1954) 17 *The Modern Law Review* 24 at 31–32.

The finding of such an undertaking is simply a question of fact in each case. So if, for example, all that can be shown is that two people have dealt with each other only as principals neither will be the other's fiduciary.[20]

The test suggested by the Court of Appeal in the present case seems to me not inappropriate in the circumstances, although it must be remembered that any test can only be stated in the most general terms and that all the facts and circumstances must be carefully examined to see whether a fiduciary relationship exists.[21] However, if the Court of Appeal's test is applied, it is not satisfied, for in my opinion HPI did not undertake, whether by representation or contractual provision, to act solely in the interests of USSC and not in its own interests.

An examination of all the circumstances confirms in my opinion that the relationship between the parties was not a fiduciary one. It is true that USSC relied on HPI to promote the sale of its products and left it to HPI to determine how it should go about doing so, and that HPI had it in its power to affect USSC's interests beneficially or adversely. However, there are two features of the case, in particular, which together constitute an insuperable obstacle to the acceptance of USSC's contention that a fiduciary relationship existed between itself and HPI. In the first place, as I have said, the arrangement was a commercial one entered into by parties at arm's length and on an equal footing. It was open to USSC to include in its contract whatever terms it thought necessary to protect its position, for USSC acted in response to Mr. Blackman's request and was under no pressure either to make him a distributor in place of Downs or to accept an agreement on his terms; indeed USSC itself prepared the letter of agreement which its in-house counsel asked Mr. Blackman to sign. An ordinary commercial contract made in those circumstances, even as a result of fraud, is unlikely to give rise to fiduciary obligations. Secondly, it was of course clear that the whole purpose of the transaction from Mr. Blackman's point of view, as USSC knew, was that he, and later HPI, should make a profit. Further, as I have already explained, in the performance of the contract a conflict between the [73] interests of HPI and USSC was likely to arise, and any such conflict was not necessarily to be resolved in favour of USSC. How, in those circumstances, is it possible to say that HPI was under an obligation not to profit from its position, and not to place itself in a situation in which its duty and its interest might conflict? It is true, as Lord Wilberforce said in *New Zealand Netherlands Society 'Oranje' Incorporated v. Kuys*,[22] that a person 'may be in a fiduciary position quoad a part of his activities and not quoad other parts: each transaction, or group of transactions must be looked at'. His Lordship referred to *Birtchnell v Equity Trustees, Executors and Agency Co Ltd* where Dixon J said:

> The subject-matter over which the fiduciary obligations extend is determined by the character of the venture or undertaking for which the partnership exists, and this is to be ascertained, not merely from the express agreement of the parties ... but also from the course of dealing actually pursued by the firm.[23]

---

20. Finn, *Fiduciary Obligations*, note 18 above, p 201.
21. Cf *Phipps v Boardman* [1967] 2 AC 46 at 123, 127.
22. [1973] 2 All ER 1222 at 1225–1226.
23. *Birtchnell v Equity Trustees, Executors and Agency Co Ltd* (1929) 42 CLR 384 at 408.

Lord Wilberforce said that although these remarks were made in the context of a partnership the principle must be of general application, and it is clear that in the case of every fiduciary relationship it is critical to determine what is the subject of the fiduciary obligation. However, in the present case, there was, in my opinion, no part of the transaction to which a fiduciary obligation might sensibly be limited. HPI was entitled to make a profit from the entire conduct of the distributorship, and possible and actual conflicts between its interest and its duty might arise at any stage in the conduct of that business. It would commit a breach of its contractual obligations only if it acted unreasonably and thereby failed to use it best endeavours to promote the sale of the products. An obligation to act reasonably falls far short of that imposed by the rules of equity on a fiduciary, who can defeat a claim to account for profits acquired by reason of his fiduciary position and by reason of the opportunity resulting from it only on the ground that the profits were made with the knowledge and assent of the person to whom the fiduciary obligation was owed;[24] the equitable rules are exceedingly strict, as the decisions in *Regal (Hastings) Ltd v Gulliver*,[25] and *Phipps v Boardman* plainly illustrate. What is attempted in this case is to visit a fraudulent course of conduct and a gross breach of contract with equitable sanctions. It is not necessary to do so in order to vindicate commercial morality, for the ordinary remedies for damages for fraud and breach of contract were **[74]** available to USSC although it did not choose to pursue the former, but in any case the equitable doctrines sought to be invoked have no application to the present circumstances.

For these reasons I conclude that HPI did not stand in a fiduciary relation to USSC and that the only relief to which USSC was entitled in the circumstances of the case was an award of damages for breach of contract.

Mason J

[96] Was HPI a fiduciary?

Because distributor–manufacturer is not an established fiduciary relationship, it is important in the first instance to ascertain the characteristics which, according to tradition, identify a fiduciary relationship. As the courts have declined to define the concept, preferring instead to develop the law in a case by case approach, we have to distil the essence or the characteristics of the relationship from the illustrations which the judicial decisions provide. In so doing we must recognize that the categories of fiduciary relationships are not closed.[26]

The accepted fiduciary relationships are sometimes referred to as relationships of trust and confidence or confidential relations,[27] [namely] trustee and beneficiary, agent and principal, solicitor and client, employee and employer, director and company, and partners. The critical feature of these relationships is that the fiduciary undertakes or agrees to act for or on behalf of or **[97]** in the interests of another person in the exercise of a power or discretion which will affect the interests of that other person in a legal or

---

24. See *Phipps v Boardman* [1967] 2 AC 46 at 105.
25. [1967] 2 AC 134.
26. *Tufton v Sperni* [1952] 2 TLR 516 at 522; *English v Dedham Vale Properties Ltd* [1978] 1 All ER 382 at 398.
27. Cf *Phipps v Boardman* [1967] 2 AC 46 at 127.

practical sense. The relationship between the parties is therefore one which gives the fiduciary a special opportunity to exercise the power or discretion to the detriment of that other person who is accordingly vulnerable to abuse by the fiduciary of his position. The expressions 'for', 'on behalf of', and 'in the interests of' signify that the fiduciary acts in a 'representative' character in the exercise of his responsibility, to adopt an expression used by the Court of Appeal.

It is partly because the fiduciary's exercise of the power or discretion can adversely affect the interests of the person to whom the duty is owed and because the latter is at the mercy of the former that the fiduciary comes under a duty to exercise his power or discretion in the interests of the person to whom it is owed.[28] Thus a mere sub-contractor is not a fiduciary. Although his work may be described loosely as work which is to be carried out in the interests of the head contractor, the sub-contractor cannot in any meaningful sense be said to exercise a power or discretion which places the head contractor in a position of vulnerability.

That contractual and fiduciary relationships may co-exist between the same parties has never been doubted. Indeed, the existence of a basic contractual relationship has in many situations provided a foundation for the erection of a fiduciary relationship. In these situations it is the contractual foundation which is all important because it is the contract that regulates the basic rights and liabilities of the parties. The fiduciary relationship, if it is to exist at all, must accommodate itself to the terms of the contract so that it is consistent with, and conforms to, them. The fiduciary relationship cannot be superimposed upon the contract in such a way as to alter the operation which the contract was intended to have according to its true construction.

Because I take a different view about the terms of the contract I do not share the Court of Appeal's conclusion that HPI was under a fiduciary duty to carry on the entire distributorship business in the joint interests of USSC and HPI. That view, it seems to me, rested very heavily on the suggested promise to carry on the business for the common benefit of the parties and on the implied term that HPI would do nothing inimical to USSC's interests.

My conclusion that HPI was at liberty to make some business decisions by reference to its own interests, subject to the obligations arising under the best efforts promise and the other terms of the [98] contract express and implied, presents an overwhelming obstacle to the existence of the comprehensive fiduciary relationship found by the Court of Appeal. This is because HPI's capacity to make decisions and take action in some matters by reference to its own interests is inconsistent with the existence of a general fiduciary relationship. However, it does not exclude the existence of a more limited fiduciary relationship for it is well settled that a person may be a fiduciary in some activities but not in others.[29]

The appellant submits, mistakenly in my view, that the very existence of the best efforts promise is inconsistent with the co-existence of a fiduciary duty. True it is that

---

28. See generally Weinrib, 'The Fiduciary Obligation' (1975) 25 *University of Toronto Law Journal* 4–8.

29. *NZ Netherlands Society 'Oranje' Inc v Kuys* [1973] 2 All ER 1222 at 1225–1226; *Birtchnell v Equity Trustees, Executors and Agency Co Ltd* (1929) 42 CLR 384 at 408; *Phipps v Boardman* [1967] 2 AC 46 at 127.

a promise or a contractual term may be so precise in its regulation of what a party can do that there is no relevant area of discretion remaining and therefore no scope for the creation of a fiduciary duty.[30] Here, however, HPI enjoyed a substantial area of discretion in the exercise of its responsibility to promote the market in Australia for USSC surgical stapling products. The giving of a best efforts promise to promote that market did not relevantly limit the ambit of HPI's discretion in discharging that responsibility.

In considering whether a fiduciary duty, and if so, what fiduciary duty, was generated by that responsibility we have to take account of the following factors:

(1) there was a valuable market for USSC's products in Australia;
(2) USSC, by appointing HPI, entrusted HPI with the exclusive responsibility of promoting that market during the term of the distributorship which was determinable by either party on reasonable notice;
(3) the manner in which the market was to be promoted was left to HPI's general discretion, subject to the express and implied terms of the contract;
(4) the exercise of that discretion provided HPI with a special opportunity of acting to the detriment of the market for USSC's products, rendering USSC vulnerable to abuse by HPI of its position, USSC having no representation at all in Australia;
(5) in selling USSC's products to Australian customers HPI was not acting as agent for USSC;
(6) although HPI's actions would not alter or affect USSC's legal rights vis-a-vis others, its actions could and did affect adversely in a practical sense the market in Australia **[99]** for USSC's products and consequently its product goodwill in this country;
(7) in the circumstances mentioned in (1)–(6) above USSC relied on HPI to protect and promote USSC's product goodwill in Australia; and
(8) HPI's responsibility to protect and promote USSC's product goodwill was necessarily subject to the qualification of reasonableness attached to the best efforts promise.

Point (8) above presents an unusual problem. The classical illustrations of the fiduciary relationship are those in which the fiduciary is under a duty to act not in his own interests or solely in his own interests but in the interests of another or jointly in the interests of another and himself, e.g., a trustee and a partner. In the present case the nature of the distributorship relationship and the best efforts promise with its attendant standard of reasonableness necessarily entailed that HPI could make some business decisions by reference to its financial interests, without subordinating them to the promotion of the market for USSC's products, so long at any rate as HPI did not deliberately do something, or omit to do something, for the purpose of destroying or injuring that market. And, as we know, HPI when it entered into a contract to sell USSC's products to an Australian customer was not acting as trustee or agent for USSC. The contractual rights which arose against the customer were held by HPI in its own right and were not the subject of any trust in favour of USSC. HPI was entitled to recover and retain the purchase price for its own benefit, being under no duty to account to USSC.

---

30. *RH Deacon & Co Ltd v Varga* (1972) 30 DLR (3d) 653; affd (1973) 41 DLR (3d) 767.

But entitlement to act in one's own interests is not an answer to the existence of a fiduciary relationship, if there be an obligation to act in the interests of another. It is that obligation which is the foundation of the fiduciary relationship, even if it be subject to qualifications including the qualification that in some respects the fiduciary is entitled to act by reference to his own interests. The fiduciary duty must then accommodate itself to the relationship between the parties created by their contractual arrangements. And entitlement under the contract to act in a relevant matter solely by reference to one's own interests will constitute an answer to an alleged breach of the fiduciary duty. The difficulty of deciding under the contract when the fiduciary is entitled to act in his own interests is not in itself a reason for rejecting the existence of a fiduciary relationship, though it may be an element in arriving at the conclusion that the person asserting the relationship has not established that there is any obligation to act in the interests of another.

There has been an understandable reluctance to subject commercial transactions to the equitable doctrine of constructive trust and [100] constructive notice. But it is altogether too simplistic, if not superficial, to suggest that commercial transactions stand outside the fiduciary regime as though in some way commercial transactions do not lend themselves to the creation of a relationship in which one person comes under an obligation to act in the interests of another. The fact that in the great majority of commercial transactions the parties stand at arm's length does not enable us to make a generalization that is universally true in relation to every commercial transaction. In truth, every such transaction must be examined on its merits with a view to ascertaining whether it manifests the characteristics of a fiduciary relationship.

The disadvantages of introducing equitable doctrine into the field of commerce, which may be less formidable than they were, now that the techniques of commerce are far more sophisticated, must be balanced against the need in appropriate cases to do justice by making available relief in specie through the constructive trust, the fiduciary relationship being a means to that end. If, in order to make relief in specie available in appropriate cases it is necessary to allow equitable doctrine to penetrate commercial transactions, then so be it.[31] A preferable approach to an artificial narrowing of the fiduciary relationship — the gateway to relief in specie — is to define and delimit more precisely the circumstances in which the remedy by way of constructive trust will be granted.

There is a strong case for saying that because USSC entrusted HPI with the responsibility of protecting and promoting the market for USSC's products in Australia HPI was a fiduciary in protecting and promoting USSC's Australian product goodwill. In procuring orders for, making sales of and supplying USSC's products to Australian consumers HPI was acting in USSC's interests as well as its own. And by engaging in these activities HPI enhanced both USSC's local product goodwill and the goodwill of its own distributing business. By the sale of its products to its distributor here and by its sale of those products to Australian consumers under the name of 'Auto Suture' in circumstances in which the products were associated by consumers with USSC as manufacturer, USSC created a local product goodwill.[32] The [101] remarks of Latham CJ

---

31. See, for example, *Barclays Bank Ltd v Quistclose Investments Ltd* [1970] AC 567 and *Swiss Bank Corporation v Lloyds Bank Ltd* [1982] AC 584.
32. *Estex Clothing Manufacturers Pty Ltd v Ellis and Goldstein Ltd* (1967) 116 CLR 254 at 267–268, 270–271; *Imperial Tobacco Company of India Ltd v Bonnan* (1924) 41 RPC 441.

and Rich J in *Commissioner of Taxes (Q) v Ford Motor Co of Australia Pty Ltd*[33] indicate that goodwill cannot be assigned independently of the business with which it is associated, but they do not deny the existence of local product goodwill in a case such as the present. The difficulty of determining how much of the goodwill in Australia was local product goodwill of USSC and how much was goodwill of HPI's distributing business does not deny the separate existence in USSC of local product goodwill.

USSC, by entrusting HPI with a responsibility for protecting and promoting the market for USSC's products in Australia, effectively constituted HPI the custodian of its product goodwill in this country. Its responsibility in procuring orders, making sales and effecting deliveries of USSC's products in Australia armed HPI with a power and discretion to affect USSC's product goodwill. And in exercising this responsibility HPI had a special opportunity of acting to the detriment of USSC which was, accordingly, vulnerable to the abuse by HPI of its position.

HPI's position as custodian of USSC's product goodwill in Australia may be likened in a general way to that of a bailee whose duty it is to protect and preserve a chattel bailed to him. It has been well recognized, at least since the judgment of Jessel MR in *In re Hallett's Estate*,[34] that a bailee stands in a fiduciary relationship with his bailor when the bailor entrusts to the bailee goods to be held or dealt with by him for the benefit of the bailor or for certain limited purposes stipulated by the bailor.

In engaging in the activities which I have mentioned, activities related to the production and promotion of USSC's product goodwill, HPI was acting in its own interests as well as in the separate interests of USSC Although, as we have seen, it was entitled to prefer its own interests to the interests of USSC in some situations where those interests might come into conflict, this entitlement was necessarily subject to the requirement that HPI act bona fide and reasonably with due regard to the interests of USSC. In no circumstance could it act solely in its own interests without reference to the interests of USSC. This, as it seems to me, fixed HPI with the character of a fiduciary in relation to those activities mentioned, notwithstanding that in pursuing them HPI was also acting in its own interests and that it was carrying on the distributorship business generally for its own benefit and in no sense as a trustee for USSC. [102] This conclusion is largely founded on the general nature of the responsibility which, according to the contract, HPI undertook to discharge in pursuing the relevant activities, though the obligation not to compete and the obligation not to deliberately injure USSC's market were significant elements in that responsibility. And it is the general nature of that responsibility which distinguishes HPI from the mortgagee who is bound to exercise his power of sale in good faith. In exercising that power the mortgagee is acting in his own interests, subject to the requirement of good faith[35] and possibly that of reasonable care.[36] Even so, the mortgagee's duty in exercising the power is sometimes described as analogous to a fiduciary duty.[37]

---

33. (1942) 66 CLR 261 at 272.
34. (1880) 13 Ch D 696 at 708–709.
35. See *Kennedy v De Trafford* [1897] AC 180 at 185.
36. See *Australia and New Zealand Banking Group Ltd v Bangadilly Pastoral Co Pty Ltd* (1978) 139 CLR 195 at 222–225.
37. Sir Frederick Jordan, *Chapters on Equity in New South Wales*, 6th ed, University of Sydney, Sydney, 1947, p 113.

Comments

1. See Radan & Stewart at **9.1–9.21**.
2. Fiduciary relationships are characterised by many features including duties of loyalty, relationships of confidence, inequality of bargaining power, the exercise of unilateral discretion, dependency and vulnerability and undertakings to act in the interests of another. Professor Finn argued that all of these issues could be embodied in a doctrine of 'reasonable expectations', where the imposition of a fiduciary duty would be dependent on whether the principal had an objectively reasonable expectation that the fiduciary would act in the beneficiary's interest to the exclusion of their own personal interests: P D Finn, 'The Fiduciary Principle' in T G Youdan (ed), *Equity, Fiduciaries and Trusts*, Carswell, Toronto, 1989. Glover has argued that the question of what is 'reasonable' just replaces the older characteristics within an empty normative shell, which the judges will have to fill in with the old characteristics and/ or other values they hold dear. In that sense reasonable expectations is a limitation device rather than a rational test, much like 'reasonable foreseeability' in negligence: J Glover, *Equity, Restitution and Fraud*, LexisNexis Butterworths, Sydney, 2004, pp 32–33. See also P Parkinson, 'Fiduciary Obligations' in Parkinson (ed), *The Principles of Equity*, 2nd ed, Lawbook Co, Sydney, 2003, p 391.

The strict nature of fiduciary duties

9.3   Boardman v Phipps [1967] 2 AC 46

Court: House of Lords

Facts: Boardman was the solicitor for a family trust. He attended the annual general meeting of Lester & Harris Ltd, a company in which the trust had a substantial shareholding. Boardman and Tom Phipps, one of the beneficiaries under the trust, were unhappy with the state of the company. Together they planned to acquire shares in the company to take it over. Boardman was able to assess the viability of the takeover because of information about the company he gained whilst acting as solicitor for the trust. Boardman advised the beneficiaries of the trust of these plans and no objection was made by any of them; however, the trial judge determined that he had not provided the full picture of his interests in the transaction. He also had the consent of two of the three trustees; the third, being senile, was not advised of these plans.

The takeover was successful. The trust, Boardman and Tom Phipps all made substantial profits in relation to the shares they had personally acquired. John Phipps, one of the beneficiaries under the trust, sought an account of the profits made by Boardman and Tom Phipps on the grounds of breach of fiduciary duties.

Issue: The issue was whether Boardman and Tom Phipps should have to account for the profits made when the trust also profited greatly.

Decision: By a bare majority the House of Lords (Lord Cohen, Lord Hodson and Lord Guest) held that the information obtained by Boardman was trust property and that he had breached his fiduciary duties by investing his own money in the scheme. The fact that the trust profited from Boardman's endeavours was irrelevant. Boardman and Tom Phipps had not received the fully informed consent of all the trustees. Nor did they have the informed consent of all the beneficiaries.

Extracts: In this extract Lord Guest explains why Boardman was liable even though his actions were in good faith and benefited all the parties.

Lord Guest

[115] ... I do not for one moment suggest that there was anything dishonest or underhand in what Boardman did. He has obtained a clean certificate below and I do not wish to sully it. But the law has a strict regard for principle in ensuring that a person in a fiduciary capacity is not allowed to benefit from any transactions into which he has entered with trust property. If Boardman was acting on behalf of the trust, then all the information he obtained [during negotiations] became trust property. The weapon which he used to obtain this information was the trust holding and I see no reason why information and knowledge cannot be trust property. In *Hamilton v Wright*[38] Lord Brougham said:

> The knowledge which he acquires as trustee is of itself sufficient ground of disqualification, and of requiring that such knowledge shall not be capable of being used for his own benefit to injure the trust; the ground of disqualification is not merely because such knowledge may enable him actually to obtain an undue advantage over others.

In *Regal (Hastings) Ltd v Gulliver*[39] Viscount Sankey says:

> *Imperial Hydropathic Hotel Co Blackpool v Hampson*[40] makes no exception to the general rule that a solicitor or director, if acting in a fiduciary capacity, is liable to account for the profits made by him from knowledge acquired when so acting.

[116] *Aas v Benham*[41] is another case where the use of information by a person in a fiduciary capacity was challenged.

The position of a person in a fiduciary capacity is referred to in *Regal (Hastings) Ltd v Gulliver*[42] by Lord Russell of Killowen where he said:

> My Lords, with all respect I think there is a misapprehension here. The rule of equity which insists on those, who by use of a fiduciary position make a profit being liable

---

38. (1842) 9 Cl & F 111 at 124.
39. [1967] AC 134 at 139.
40. (1882) 23 Ch D 1.
41. [1891] 2 Ch 244.
42. [1967] AC 134 at 144–145.

to account for that profit, in no way depends on fraud, or absence of bona fides; or upon such questions or considerations as whether the profit would or should otherwise have gone to the plaintiff, or whether the profiteer was under a duty to obtain the source of the profit for the plaintiff, or whether he took a risk or acted as he did for the benefit of the plaintiff, or whether the plaintiff has in fact been damaged or benefited by his action. The liability arises from the mere fact of a profit having, in the stated circumstances, been made. The profiteer, however honest and well-intentioned, cannot escape the risk of being called upon to account.

Again Lord Russell quotes with approval from the judgment of the Lord Ordinary in *Huntington Copper Co. v Henderson*[43] to the following effect:

Whenever it can be shown that the trustee has so arranged matters as to obtain an advantage whether in money or money's worth to himself personally through the execution of his trust, he will not be permitted to retain, but be compelled to make it over to his constituent.

Lord Wright in the same case said:

That question can be briefly stated to be whether an agent, a director, a trustee or other person in an analogous fiduciary position, when a demand is made upon him by the person to whom he stands in the fiduciary relationship to account for profits acquired by him by reason of his fiduciary position, and by reason of the opportunity and the knowledge, or either, resulting from it, is entitled to defeat the claim upon any ground save that he made profits with the knowledge and assent of the other person.[44]

Again Lord Wright said:

The courts below have held that it does not apply in the present case, for the reason that the purchase of the shares by [the directors of a company], though made for their own advantage, and though the knowledge and opportunity which [117] enabled them to take the advantage came to them solely by reason of their being directors of the ... company, was a purchase which, in the circumstances, the [the directors] were under no duty to the [company] to make, and was a purchase which it was beyond the [directors'] ability to make, so that, if the [directors] had not made it, the [company] would have been no better off by reason of the [directors] abstaining from reaping the advantage for themselves. With the question so stated, it was said that any other decision than that of the courts below would involve a dog-in-the-manger policy. What the [directors] did, it was said, caused no damage to the [company] and involved no neglect of the [directors'] interests or similar breach of duty. However, I think the answer to this reasoning is that, both in law and equity, it has been held that, if a person in a fiduciary relationship makes a secret profit out of the relationship, the court will not inquire whether the other person is damnified or has lost a profit which otherwise he would have got. The fact is in itself a fundamental breach of the fiduciary relationship. Nor can the court adequately investigate the matter in most cases.

---

43. (1877) 4 R 294.
44. [1967] AC 134 at 154.

Applying these principles to the present case I have no hesitation in coming to the conclusion that [Boardman and Tom Phipps] hold the Lester & Harris shares as constructive trustees and are bound to account to the respondent. It is irrelevant that the trustees themselves could not have profited by the transaction. It is also irrelevant that [Boardman and Tom Phipps] were not in competition with the trustees in relation to the shares in Lester & Harris. [Boardman and Tom Phipps] argued that as the shares were not acquired in the course of any agency undertaken by the appellants they were not liable to account. Analogy was sought to be obtained from the case of *Aas v Benham*[45] where it was said that before an agent is to be accountable the profits must be made within the scope of the agency … That, however, was a case of partnership where the scope of the partners' power to bind the partnership can be closely defined in relation to the partnership deed. In the present case the knowledge and information obtained by Boardman was obtained in the course of the fiduciary position in which he had placed himself. The only defence available to a person in such a fiduciary position is that he made the profits with the knowledge and assent of the trustees. It is not contended that the trustees had such knowledge or gave such consent.

Comments
1. See Radan & Stewart at **9.6**.
2. See R Flannigan, 'The Strict Character of Fiduciary Liability' (2006) *New Zealand Law Review* 209.

The application of fiduciary duties to joint ventures

9.4   United Dominions Corporation Ltd v Brian Pty Ltd
(1985) 157 CLR 1

Court: High Court of Australia

Facts: The facts concerned a joint venture agreement for the development of land between United Dominions Corporation (UDC), Security Projects Ltd (SPL) and Brian Pty Ltd (Brian). The land in question was owned by SPL. The joint venture was largely financed by funds from UDC secured by a mortgage signed by SPL. The joint venturers provided the balance of funds for the development. The development realised a significant profit. However, UDC retained the profit. No distribution of profit was made to Brian. UDC's claim to what would otherwise have been Brian's share of profits was based upon a provision in the mortgage to SPL, referred to as the 'collateralisation clause', to the effect that the mortgage was security for *any* money that had been advanced to SPL. SPL was indebted to UDC in respect

---

45. [1891] 2 Ch 244.

of other projects apart from the joint venture. Brian was never informed of the existence of the collateralisation clause. Brian claimed that the clause breached fiduciary obligations owed to it by UDC and SPL.

Issue: The issue was whether the relationship of joint venture had given rise to fiduciary obligations.

Decision: The High Court (Gibbs CJ, Mason, Brennan, Deane and Dawson JJ) unanimously found that the joint venture had given rise to a fiduciary duty.

Extracts: In this extract from the joint decision of Mason, Brennan and Deane JJ, the judges examine the factors which led them to decide in favour of the existence of fiduciary obligations.

Mason, Brennan and Deane JJ

[10] The term 'joint venture' is not a technical one with a settled common law meaning. As a matter of ordinary language, it connotes an association of persons for the purposes of a particular trading, commercial, mining or other financial undertaking or endeavour with a view to mutual profit, with each participant usually (but not necessarily) contributing money, property or skill. Such a joint venture (or, under Scots' law, 'adventure') will often be a partnership. The term is, however, apposite to refer to a joint undertaking or activity carried out through a medium other than a partnership: such as a company, a trust, an agency or joint ownership. The borderline between what can properly be described as a 'joint venture' and what should more properly be seen as no more than a simple contractual relationship may on occasion be blurred. Thus, where one party contributes only money or other property, it may sometimes be difficult to determine whether a relationship is a joint venture in which both parties are entitled to a share of profits or a simple contract of loan or a lease under which the interest or rent payable to the party providing the money or property is determined by reference to the profits made by the other. One would need a more confined and precise notion of what constitutes a 'joint venture' than that which the term bears as a matter of ordinary language before it could be said by way of general proposition that the relationship between joint venturers is necessarily a fiduciary one.[46] The most [11] that can be said is that whether or not the relationship between joint venturers is fiduciary will depend upon the form which the particular joint venture takes and upon the content of the obligations which the parties to it have undertaken. If the joint venture takes the form of a partnership, the fact that it is confined to one joint undertaking as distinct from being a continuing relationship will not prevent the relationship between the joint venturers from being a fiduciary one. In such a case, the joint venturers will be under fiduciary duties to one another, including fiduciary duties in relation to property the subject of the joint venture, which are the ordinary incidents of the partnership relationship, though those fiduciary duties will be moulded to the character of the particular relationship.[47]

---

46. But cf per Cardozo CJ in *Meinhard v Salmon* 164 NE 545 (1928), at 546.
47. See generally *Birtchnell v Equity Trustees, Executors & Agency Co Ltd* (1929) 42 CLR 384 at 407–409.

In the present case, it is apparent that the relationship between the participants in the shopping centre venture was a fiduciary one at least from the time when the formal agreement was executed. Under the agreement, the participants were joint venturers in a commercial enterprise with a view to profit. Profits were to be shared. The joint venture property was held upon trust. The participants indemnified the managing participant (SPL) against losses. The policy of the joint enterprise was ultimately a matter for joint decision. Apart from the absence of any reference in the agreement to 'partnership' or 'partners', the relationship between the participants under the agreement exhibited all the indicia of, and plainly was, a partnership: It is true that UDC came to the joint venture in the role of prospective financier and, in so far as borrowings from it by the SPL group on behalf of the partnership were concerned, occupied the role of lender as well as that of partner. In so far as the property which was the subject of the joint venture was concerned however, the fact that UDC was a lender to SPL on behalf of the partnership did not absolve it from the ordinary fiduciary obligations of a partner.

It was submitted on behalf of UDC that no fiduciary relationship existed and no fiduciary duties arose between the prospective participants in the joint venture until the joint venture agreement was actually executed in July 1974. To the extent that that submission involves a general legal proposition that the relationship between prospective partners or joint venturers cannot be a fiduciary one until a formal agreement is executed, it is clearly [12] wrong. A fiduciary relationship can arise and fiduciary duties can exist between parties who have not reached, and who may never reach, agreement upon the consensual terms which are to govern the arrangement between them. In particular, a fiduciary relationship with attendant fiduciary obligations may, and ordinarily will, exist between prospective partners who have embarked upon the conduct of the partnership business or venture before the precise terms of any partnership agreement have been settled. Indeed, in such circumstances, the mutual confidence and trust which underlie most consensual fiduciary relationships are likely to be more readily apparent than in the case where mutual rights and obligations have been expressly defined in some formal agreement. Likewise, the relationship between prospective partners or participants in a proposed partnership to carry out a single joint undertaking or endeavour will ordinarily be fiduciary if the prospective partners have reached an informal arrangement to assume such a relationship and have proceeded to take steps involved in its establishment or implementation.

In the present case, the relationship between UDC, Brian and SPL had plainly assumed a fiduciary character prior to 24 October 1973 when SPL gave the first of the mortgages to UDC. By that time, the arrangements between the prospective joint venturers had passed far beyond the stage of mere negotiation. Each had, by then, agreed to be, and been accepted as, a participant in each of the proposed joint ventures, if both or either of them went ahead. Each had made or agreed to make financial contributions towards the costs of the project or projects in which it or he had agreed to participate. SPL was acting as agent for the proposed joint venturers in relation to the establishment of each of the joint ventures and as trustee of those funds with which it had already been entrusted. In so far as Brian was concerned, it was a fundamental element of the substratum of the fiduciary relationship that then existed that the subject land, which was being purchased with joint venture funds for joint venture purposes, would be held available to be devoted to any ensuing joint venture or joint ventures and that Brian, as an accepted joint venturer who had already made financial contribution towards the proposed hotel joint venture, was and would remain able to participate in the net profits in accordance with its share in the relevant joint venture. To transpose the words of Dixon J in *Birtchnell*, the participants in each of the then proposed joint ventures were 'associated for ... a [13] common end' and the relationship between them was 'based ... upon a mutual confidence' that they would 'engage in [the] particular ... activity or transaction for the joint advantage only.'[48] It matters not, for present purposes, whether that relationship is seen as that which may exist between prospective partners or joint venturers before the terms of any partnership or joint venture agreement have been settled or whether it is seen as a limited preliminary partnership or joint venture to investigate and explore the possibilities of an ultimate joint venture or ventures. On either approach, it was a fiduciary one.

That being so, the proposed participants in each joint venture were under fiduciary obligations to one another in relation to the proposed project at the time when the first of the mortgages was given and accepted. In particular, each participant was under a fiduciary duty to refrain from pursuing, obtaining or retaining for itself or himself any collateral advantage in relation to the proposed project without the knowledge and informed assent of the other participants. 'The subject-matter over which the fiduciary obligations' extended must be 'determined by the character of the venture or undertaking for which' the relationship between the prospective joint venturers existed.[49] It included the land which was the subject of the proposed joint ventures and whose purchase had been funded by moneys contributed by the prospective participants or borrowed by SPL for the purposes of the proposed ventures. By that mortgage, SPL and UDC combined to apply the property the subject of the proposed joint venture to their own collateral purposes in a manner which involved the obtaining of a collateral advantage for themselves and which was, both potentially and in the event, destructive of the whole interest of the other joint venturers including Brian. In combining to apply the property to their own collateral purposes and in giving and obtaining those collateral advantages without the knowledge or consent of Brian, SPL and UDC each acted in breach of its fiduciary duty to Brian.

Comments
1. See Radan & Stewart at **9.81–9.86**.
2. For more on the imposition of fiduciary duties in commercial contexts see S White, 'Commercial relationships and the burgeoning fiduciary principle' (2000) 9 *Griffith Law Review* 98.

---

48. (1929) 42 CLR 384 at 407–408.
49. Per Dixon J, *Birtchnell v Equity Trustees, Executors & Agency Co Ltd* (1929) 42 CLR 384 at 408, in a partnership context but equally applicable here.

The application of fiduciary duties in the familial context

9.5   Paramasivam v Flynn (1998) 90 FCR 489

Court: Full Federal Court

Facts: Paramasivam claimed to have been sexually abused by Flynn. Paramasivam alleged that this first happened when he was an 11-year-old child living in Fiji. Flynn later brought Paramasivam to Australia to live and acted as his guardian. Paramasivam claimed that the abuse occurred in Fiji and Australia until he reached the age of 21.

Paramasivam brought his claim several years after the alleged events occurred. Flynn argued that the limitation period had expired and that no claim could be brought. Personal injury claims must be commenced within six years of the event. However, in the *Limitation Act 1969* (NSW), there is no time limit for bringing claims for breach of fiduciary duty. At trial Gallop J held that there was no fiduciary duty, that the limitation period applied and that it was not 'just and reasonable' to extend the period of time for bringing the claims.

Issue: The issue on appeal was whether the claims could be dealt with as breaches of fiduciary duty, which would allow Paramasivam to avoid the limitation period.

Decision: The Full Court (Miles, Lehane and Weinberg JJ), in a unanimous decision, found that there was no basis for a claim of breach of fiduciary duty and upheld the trial judge's decision to strike out the application.

Extracts: This extract considers the applicability of fiduciary duties to novel situations such as claims against guardians for sexual abuse.

Miles, Lehane and Weinberg JJ

[504] Did the primary judge err in considering the strength of the equitable claim?

We have dealt with the general proposition that, on the authorities as they now stand, it is appropriate, on an application to extend time, to take into account as a relevant factor the strength or weakness of the appellant's case as it appears from material before the Court. In addition, however, to matters going generally to the relative strength of the appellant's case, his Honour gave particular consideration to the appellant's case based on breach of fiduciary duty; and his conclusion was that he was not persuaded that that case had real prospects of success.

We have already referred to the lack of detail, in the pleading, as to the material facts said to give rise to the relationship and to define the scope of the duties arising from it. Even disregarding that, however, in our view his Honour's conclusion was justified.

A relationship such as that alleged, of guardian and ward, may give rise to duties typically characterised as fiduciary — not to allow duty and interest to conflict and not to make an unauthorised profit within the scope of the relationship (although one might need to know more about the relationship than presently appears in order to ascertain the ambit of any such duties arising in this case). Similarly, it is likely to be a relationship giving rise to a presumption of undue influence affecting transactions, particularly but not exclusively voluntary transactions, entered into by the ward and conferring benefits on the guardian. Equally, of course, breach of a fiduciary duty, and breaches of other equitable obligations, are not remediable only by injunction or by a proprietary or restitutionary remedy: a plaintiff who has suffered loss resulting from breach of such a duty is entitled to compensation for that loss. There is no room for doubt about any of those propositions, and it is unnecessary to cite authority for them. Nevertheless, the judge was right in regarding the appellant's claim as, under Australian law, novel. That is so because of two of its aspects: the nature of the alleged breach and the kinds of loss or injury which the appellant claims to have suffered and for which he seeks equitable compensation.

In Anglo-Australian law, the interests which the equitable doctrines invoked by the appellant, and related doctrines, have hitherto protected are economic interests. If property is transferred or a transaction entered into as a result of undue influence, then the transaction may be set aside or, no doubt, the appellant may be compensated for loss resulting from the transaction; similarly if a transaction is induced by unconscionable conduct; so, in cases usually classified as involving fiduciary obligations not to allow interest to conflict with duty, the interests protected have been economic. If a fiduciary, within the scope of the fiduciary obligation, makes an unauthorised profit or takes for [505] himself or herself an unauthorised commercial advantage, then the person to whom the duty is owed has a remedy. With one exception, that is the context of, and the assumption underlying, all the recent discussions of fiduciary duty in the High Court.[50] The exception is *Breen v Williams*[51] where the appellant, seeking to rely on fiduciary duty to protect an interest of a rather different sort, namely the right of a patient to access medical records in the possession of a doctor, was held to fail. Much academic writing proceeds on the assumption that the interests protected by these equitable doctrines are economic.[52]

Of course, conduct such as that alleged against the respondent in this case can readily be described in terms of abuse of a position of trust or confidence, or even in terms of the undertaking of a role which may in some respects be representative and, within the scope of that role, allowing personal interest (in the form of self gratification) to displace a duty to protect the appellant's interests. But it should not be concluded, simply because the allegations can be described in those terms, that the appellant should succeed in an action for breach of fiduciary duty if the allegations are made good. What the apparent applicability of the descriptions illustrates is not only the incompleteness but also the imperfection of all the individual formulae which have at various times been suggested as

---

50. See, for example, *Hospital Products Ltd v United States Surgical Corporation* (1984) 156 CLR 41; *United Dominions Corporation Ltd v Brian Pty Ltd* (1985) 157 CLR 1; *Daly v Sydney Stock Exchange Ltd* (1986) 160 CLR 371; *Chan v Zacharia* (1984) 154 CLR 178.

51. (1996) 186 CLR 71.

52. See Cooter and Freedman, 'The Fiduciary Relationship: Its Economic Character and Legal Consequences' (1991) 66 *New York University Law Review* 1045; DeMott, 'Fiduciary Obligation and Intellectual Siege: Contemporary Challenges to the Duty to be Loyal' (1992) 30 *Osgoode Hall Law Journal* 470; and P D Finn, 'The Fiduciary Principle', in TG Youdan (ed), *Equity, Fiduciaries and Trusts*, Carswell, Toronto, 1989, pp 1–56.

encapsulating fiduciary relationship or duty. The principles can be understood only in the context of the way in which the courts have applied them. In that context the success of the appellant's fiduciary claims, in this case, would indeed be a novelty.

To say of a claim that it is a novelty is not necessarily to condemn it or to require the conclusion that it cannot succeed. It is sufficient to demonstrate this point merely to refer to the gradual extension, during this century, of the kinds of loss for which damages are recoverable in tort — particularly in negligence. But an advance must be justifiable in principle. Here, the conduct complained of is within the purview of the law of tort, which has worked out and elaborated principles according to which various kinds of loss and damage, resulting from intentional or negligent wrongful conduct, are to be compensated. That is not a field on which there is any obvious need for equity to enter and there is no obvious advantage to be gained from equity's entry upon it. And such an extension would, in our view, involve a leap not easily to be justified in terms of conventional legal reasoning.

On the appeal, the appellant relied heavily on *M(K) v M(H)*,[53] a decision of the Supreme Court of Canada. That case had to do with claims, both in tort and on the footing of fiduciary obligation, arising from alleged incest by the appellant's father. The Supreme Court held that the relationship of parent and child was fiduciary, giving rise to a fiduciary duty to protect the child's well-being and health; and that incest was a breach of that duty. The judgment of the Court was delivered by La Forest J, with whom the [506] other members of the Court agreed. His Lordship held that the relationship of parent and child fell clearly within the established formulations of circumstances giving rise to fiduciary relationships. There was no principle requiring the duties arising from such a relationship to be restricted to the protection of economic interests: in certain contexts, equity had recognised a parental duty to protect the economic interests of a child; but case law did not limit the range of obligations that might attach to the relationship; and:

> Indeed, the essence of the parental obligation in the present case is simply to refrain from inflicting personal injury upon one's child.[54]

With great respect, there can be no doubt that that is a fundamental aspect of a parent's obligation; and it is one which should be, and is, appropriately protected by law. It does not follow, however, that 'fiduciary' is the right label for it, still less that equitable intervention is necessary, appropriate or justified by any principled development of equity's doctrines.[55] It is, perhaps, significant that the question arose, in *M(K) v M(H)*, only in a context where — and, apparently, was raised only because — a limitation statute barred proceedings at law, but not in equity. That was the context, also, of the New South Wales case to which we shall now turn. We know of no other context in which such an extension of equitable principle has been suggested.

The New South Wales case is the decision of the Court of Appeal in *Williams*.[56] The plaintiff, who was of Aboriginal descent, claimed that her treatment, during her childhood,

---

53. (1992) 96 DLR (4th) 289.
54. *M(K) v M(H)* (1992) 96 DLR (4th) 289 at 327.
55. Compare P Parkinson, 'Fiduciary Law and Access to Medical Records' (1995) 17 *Sydney Law Review* 433 at 443.
56. *Williams v Minister, Aboriginal Land Rights Act 1983* (1994) 35 NSWLR 497.

by the Aborigines Welfare Board involved breaches of the Board's fiduciary duty as to her custody, maintenance and education. The Court held (by a majority) that the NSW Act did not apply directly to the equitable claim and should not be applied, in the circumstances, by analogy. Kirby P referred to *M(K) v M(H)* and said:

> I see no reason to conclude that the principles expressed by the Supreme Court of Canada would not be applicable in this jurisdiction. Nor is the vehicle of the equitable principles propounded (a claim by an alleged victim of incest) determinative or restrictive of the content of the principles ... The trial of Ms Williams' claim against the respondent, based upon her allegation of breach of fiduciary duty for which they are liable, is not disposed of by a refusal of the extension of time sought in respect of the tort claims by the application of s 60G(2) of the *Limitation Act 1969* (NSW).[57]

Priestley JA, who agreed with Kirby P in the result, took a considerably more cautious approach:

> To enable a properly satisfactory and fully explored answer to be given to [several of the questions] Mrs Williams wishes to raise, it seems to me desirable that Mrs Williams have the opportunity of putting all relevant evidence before the Court at a trial, rather than that the matters of significance which the case raises should be dealt with on the incomplete state of the evidence at present before the Court.

> These considerations have influenced my general agreement with the approach of Kirby P. That approach involves conclusions, favourable to Ms Williams, about the arguability of a number of issues. I have reached some of these conclusions only with hesitation and I recognise they may be vulnerable to a strict approach. However, this case seems to me pre-eminently [507] to be of the kind where a broad approach should be taken to questions of arguability of legal propositions which may be novel but which require careful consideration in the light of changing social circumstances.[58]

That case, however, preceded *Breen*.[59] *Breen* involved, factually, a quite different question: whether a doctor owed his patient a fiduciary duty to disclose a patient's medical records to her. The Court held that, though a doctor might commonly owe fiduciary duties to a patient, those duties did not include the one for which the appellant contended. In the course of their judgments, the members of the Court made clear their disagreement with several aspects of recent Canadian approaches to the development of the law relating to fiduciaries.[60] And it is notable that, in giving examples of circumstances in which a medical practitioner might be held in breach of a fiduciary duty owed to a patient, their Honours chose examples from the main stream. Thus, Dawson and Toohey JJ said:

> ... it is the law of negligence and contract which governs the duty of a doctor towards a patient. This leaves no need, or even room, for the imposition of fiduciary obligations. Of course, fiduciary duties may be superimposed upon contractual

---

57. *Williams v Minister, Aboriginal Land Rights Act 1983* (1994) 35 NSWLR 497 at 510.
58. *Williams v Minister, Aboriginal Land Rights Act 1983* (1994) 35 NSWLR 497 at 516.
59. *Breen v Williams* (1996) 186 CLR 71.
60. See per Brennan CJ, *Breen v Williams* (1996) 186 CLR 71 at 83, per Dawson and Toohey JJ 94, 95, per Gaudron and McHugh JJ 110–113 and per Gummow J at 132 and following.

obligations and it is conceivable that a doctor may place himself in a position with potential for a conflict of interest — if, for example, the doctor has a financial interest in a hospital or a pathology laboratory — so as to give rise to fiduciary obligations ... But that is not this case.[61]

Likewise, Gummow J:

> The issue here is not that which would arise, for example, where a medical practitioner had advised the patient to undergo treatment at a particular private hospital in which the practitioner had an undisclosed financial interest, or where the medical practitioner prescribed one of a number of equally suitable pharmaceutical drugs for the undisclosed reason that this assisted the practitioner to obtain undisclosed side-benefits from the manufacturer.[62]

There are also, in *Breen*, significant observations about the interrelationship between common law obligations and the fiduciary principle. For example, Gaudron and McHugh JJ said:

> In our view, there is no basis upon which this Court can hold that Dr Williams owed Ms Breen a fiduciary duty to give her access to the medical records. She seeks to impose fiduciary obligations on a class of relationship which has not traditionally been recognised as fiduciary in nature and which would significantly alter the already existing complex of legal doctrines governing the doctor-patient relationship, particularly in the areas of contract and tort. As Sopinka J remarked in *Norberg v Wynrib*:[63] 'Fiduciary duties should not be super imposed on these common law duties simply to improve the nature or extent of the remedy.'[64]

See also the observations of Gummow J, and the academic writing to which his Honour refers.[65]

All those considerations lead us firmly to the conclusion that a fiduciary claim, such as that made by the plaintiff in this case, is most unlikely to be upheld by Australian courts. Equity, through the principles it has developed [508] about fiduciary duty, protects particular interests which differ from those protected by the law of contract and tort, and protects those interests from a standpoint which is peculiar to those principles. The truth of that is not at all undermined by the undoubted fact that fiduciary duties may arise within a relationship governed by contract or that liability in equity may co-exist with liability in tort. To say, truly, that categories are not closed does not justify so radical a departure from underlying principle. Those propositions, in our view, lie at the heart of the High Court authorities to which we have referred, particularly, perhaps, *Breen*. It follows that Gallop J was justified in concluding that he was not persuaded that the appellant's claim based on breaches of fiduciary duty owed by the respondent to the appellant had real prospects of success.

---

61. *Breen v Williams* (1996) 186 CLR 71 at 93–94.
62. *Breen v Williams* (1996) 186 CLR 71 at 136.
63. [1992] 2 SCR 226 at 312; (1992) 92 DLR (4th) 449 at 481.
64. *Breen v Williams* (1996) 186 CLR 71 at 110.
65. *Breen v Williams* (1996) 186 CLR 71 at 125.

Comments

1. See Radan & Stewart at **9.68–9.80**.
2. For a traditional criticism of the expansion of fiduciary duties into novel categories see R P Meagher and A Maroya, 'Crypto-Fiduciary Duties' (2003) 26(2) *University of New South Wales Law Journal* 348.
3. For a discussion of fiduciary claims in sexual abuse cases see N Mullany, 'Civil actions for childhood abuse in Australia' (1999) 115 *Law Quarterly Review* 565.

The application of fiduciary duties to the doctor–patient relationship

9.6   Breen v Williams (1995) 186 CLR 71

Court: High Court of Australia

Facts: Breen had breast augmentation in 1977 with silicon breast implants. In 1978 she noticed that capsules had formed in her breasts and she sought the advice and treatment of Dr Williams. Years later she developed complications and she joined an American class action against the manufacturer of the implants, Dow Corning Corporation. That action was settled but Australian litigants needed to file their medical records with the United States District Court. She sought her medical records from Dr Williams. He agreed to provide them on the basis that Breen release him from any liability in relation to the treatment that he provided. Breen refused to do so and asserted that she had a right to access her medical records. That argument was based on many heads, including contractual rights, property rights and fiduciary duties.

Issue: The issue was concerned with whether the relationship between a patient and a doctor was a fiduciary relationship which gave rise to a right for patients to be able to demand production of their medical records.

Decision: The High Court (Brennan CJ, Dawson, Toohey, Gaudron, McHugh and Gummow JJ) unanimously found that there was no right to demand the access to the medical records which could be founded on breach of fiduciary duty, nor on any contractual or property rights.

Extracts: In this extract Gaudron and McHugh JJ examine the reason why the doctor–patient relationship is not wholly fiduciary in nature, and does not come with a fiduciary duty to provide medical records to patients.

Gaudron and McHugh JJ

Some aspects of the doctor–patient relationship exhibit characteristics that courts have used to find a fiduciary relationship. For example, from the most mundane consultation with a general practitioner through to the most complicated surgical procedure by a specialist surgeon, a patient is invariably dependent upon the advice and treatment of his or her doctor. Patients also invariably confide intimate personal details about themselves to their doctors. In some circumstances, the dependency of the patient or the provision of confidential information may make the relationship between a doctor and patient fiduciary in nature. But that does not mean that their **[108]** relationship would be fiduciary for all purposes. As Mason J pointed out in *Hospital Products*,[66] a person may stand in a fiduciary relationship to another for one purpose but not for others.

In *Birtchnell v Equity Trustees, Executors & Agency Co Ltd*[67] Dixon J said that in 'considering the operation of [fiduciary principles], it is necessary to [ascertain] the subject matter over which the fiduciary obligations extend'. In the present case, if Dr Williams owed a fiduciary duty to Ms Breen, the duties and obligations which arose from their fiduciary relationship could only come from those aspects of the relationship which exhibited the characteristics of trust, confidence and vulnerability that typify the fiduciary relationship.[68] They could only attach in respect of matters that relate to diagnosis, advice and treatment.

A consideration of the fundamental obligations of a fiduciary shows that Dr Williams owed no fiduciary duty to Ms Breen to give her access to the records that he had created. The law of fiduciary duty rests not so much on morality or conscience as on the acceptance of the implications of the biblical injunction that '[n]o man can serve two masters'.[69] Duty and self-interest, like God and Mammon, make inconsistent calls on the faithful. Equity solves the problem in a practical way by insisting that fiduciaries give undivided loyalty to the persons whom they serve. In *Bray v Ford*, Lord Herschell said:

> It is an inflexible rule of a Court of Equity that a person in a fiduciary position, such as the respondent's, is not, unless otherwise expressly provided, entitled to make a profit; he is not allowed to put himself in a position where his interest and duty conflict. It does not appear to me that this rule is, as has been said, founded upon principles of morality. I regard it rather as based on the consideration that, human nature being what it is, there is danger, in such circumstances, of the person holding a fiduciary position being swayed by interest rather than by duty, and thus prejudicing those whom he was bound to protect. It has, therefore, been deemed expedient to lay down this positive rule.[70]

In the present case, it is impossible to identify any conflict of interest, unauthorised profit or any loss resulting from any breach of duty.

Dr Cashman submitted that Dr Williams had a conflict of interest because in his letter to Ms Breen dated 10 August 1993 he offered to release the records subject to the condition that Ms Breen release him from any legal claims arising out of the treatment. Dr Cashman contended that this condition evidenced Dr Williams' desire to secure **[109]** 'a legal advantage out of the release of the information' which conflicted with his duty to act at all times in the best interests of the patient. Leaving aside the problem of identifying

---

66. (1984) 156 CLR 41 at 98.
67. (1929) 42 CLR 384 at 409.
68. *Daly v Sydney Stock Exchange Ltd* (1986) 160 CLR 371 at 377.
69. Matthew: 6:24.
70. [1896] AC 44 at 51–52; and see *Chan v Zacharia* (1984) 154 CLR 178 at 198–199.

the basis upon which this duty to act at all times in Ms Breen's best interests is grounded, this argument is without substance. If it were correct, it would lead to the anomalous result that no breach of fiduciary relationship would exist if the doctor unconditionally denied a request for reasonable access, but that a breach of fiduciary obligation would exist if the denial was conditional. This is unacceptable. Duty must precede breach. In *Tito v Waddell (No 2)*, Megarry V-C pointed out:

> If there is a fiduciary duty, the equitable rules about self-dealing apply: but self-dealing does not impose the duty. Equity bases its rules about self-dealing upon some pre-existing fiduciary duty: it is a disregard of this pre-existing duty that subjects the self-dealer to the consequences of the self-dealing rules. I do not think that one can take a person who is subject to no pre-existing fiduciary duty and then say that because he self-deals he is thereupon subjected to a fiduciary duty.[71]

In the present case, there was no breach of fiduciary duty in the conditional denial of access because there was no pre-existing duty on the part of Dr Williams to give access to the records.

It is also impossible to identify any profit that Dr Williams may have derived from the relationship beyond the payment of his authorised professional fees. Nor is the case one where Dr Williams seeks to make or has made a profit from confidential information that he obtained in the course of his relationship with Ms Breen.

The problem of reconciling the alleged fiduciary duty to act in the best interests of Ms Breen with other rights and obligations of Dr Williams and Ms Breen also makes it difficult to see how there could be a fiduciary duty to give access to records relating to her medical treatment. In *Hospital Products*, Mason J explained the relationship of fiduciary obligations and contractual rights and obligations as follows:

> That contractual and fiduciary relationships may co-exist between the same parties has never been doubted. Indeed, the existence of a basic contractual relationship has in many situations provided a foundation for the erection of a fiduciary relationship. In these situations it is the contractual foundation which is all important because it is the contract that regulates the basic rights and liabilities of the parties. The fiduciary relationship, if it is to exist at all, must accommodate itself to the terms of the contract so that it is consistent with, and conforms to, them. The fiduciary [110] relationship cannot be superimposed upon the contract in such a way as to alter the operation which the contract was intended to have according to its true construction.[72]

The right of access claimed by Ms Breen is not one given by the contract between her and Dr Williams. Nor can it arise from any undertaking, express or implied, by Dr Williams to act as the representative of Ms Breen because no such undertaking was given. Moreover, the contract between the parties gives her no right to or interest in the medical records. They remain the property of Dr Williams.[73] Furthermore, a fiduciary duty that Dr Williams would always act in Ms Breen's best interests, which is the foundation of the claim of a

---

71. [1977] Ch 106 at 230.
72. *Hospital Products Ltd v United States Surgical Corporation* (1984) 156 CLR 41 at 97.
73. *Estate of Finkle* 395 NYS 2d 343 (1977) at 344–345.

fiduciary obligation to provide access to the records, would conflict with the narrower contractual and tortious duty to exercise reasonable care and skill in the provision of professional advice and treatment that Dr Williams undertook.

In addition, Dr Williams is the owner of the copyright in the records. By federal law, ownership of the copyright gives Dr Williams a number of exclusive proprietary rights including the right to reproduce the records in any material form.[74] He is the beneficial owner of those rights. He does not hold them on trust for Ms Breen. In the absence of an undertaking, express or implied, on the part of Dr Williams to allow her to copy the records, it is difficult to see how Ms Breen could be allowed to copy the records even if she had a right of access to the records.

In our view, there is no basis upon which this Court can hold that Dr Williams owed Ms Breen a fiduciary duty to give her access to the medical records. She seeks to impose fiduciary obligations on a class of relationship which has not traditionally been recognised as fiduciary in nature and which would significantly alter the already existing complex of legal doctrines governing the doctor–patient relationship, particularly in the areas of contract and tort. As Sopinka J remarked in *Norberg v Wynrib*: 'Fiduciary duties should not be superimposed on these common law duties simply to improve the nature or extent of the remedy.'[75]

Dr Cashman relied strongly on the decision of the Supreme Court of Canada in *McInerney v MacDonald*[76] to support his contention that Dr Williams owed Ms Breen a fiduciary duty to give her access to the medical records. In *McInerney*, the Supreme Court held that a doctor owed a fiduciary duty to his or her patient to allow access to medical records, subject to certain conditions. La Forest J, who delivered the judgment of the Court, after holding that the doctor owes **[111]** a duty to his or her patient 'to act with utmost good faith and loyalty'[77] said:

> The fiduciary duty to provide access to medical records is ultimately grounded in the nature of the patient's interest in his or her records ... [I]nformation about oneself revealed to a doctor acting in a professional capacity remains, in a fundamental sense, one's own. The doctor's position is one of trust and confidence. The information conveyed is held in a fashion somewhat akin to a trust. While the doctor is the owner of the actual record, the information is to be used by the physician for the benefit of the patient. The confiding of the information to the physician for medical purposes gives rise to an expectation that the patient's interest in and control of the information will continue.[78]

Later his Lordship said:

> The trust-like 'beneficial interest' of the patient in the information indicates that, as a general rule, he or she should have a right of access to the information and that the physician should have a corresponding obligation to provide it. The patient's interest

---

74. *Copyright Act 1968* (Cth), s 31(1)(a)(i).
75. [1992] 2 SCR 226 at 312; (1992) 92 DLR (4th) 449 at 481.
76. [1992] 2 SCR 138; (1992) 93 DLR (4th) 415.
77. *McInerney v MacDonald* [1992] 2 SCR 138 at 148–149; (1992) 93 DLR (4th) 415 at 423.
78. *McInerney v MacDonald* [1992] 2 SCR 138 at 150; (1992) 93 DLR (4th) 415 at 424.

being in the information, it follows that the interest continues when that information is conveyed to another doctor who then becomes subject to the duty to afford the patient access to that information.[79]

However, in this country it is not possible to regard the doctor–patient relationship as one in which the doctor is under a general duty 'to act with utmost good faith and loyalty' to the patient. When a medical practitioner undertakes to treat or advise a patient on a medical matter, '[t]he law imposes on a medical practitioner a duty to exercise reasonable care and skill in the provision of professional advice and treatment',[80] not a general duty 'to act with the utmost good faith and loyalty'.

Secondly, with great respect to La Forest J, it does not help analysis of the legal issues in the present class of case to say that the information 'is held in a fashion somewhat akin to a trust' or that there is an expectation that the patient's 'control of the information will continue'. The information is not property.[81] Moreover, the only control that a patient has over the information that he or she has given to the doctor is to restrain its improper use.[82] Nor is there any trust of it. Equity does not require the doctor to record, account for or even remember the information. Nor can equity at the suit of the [112] patient prevent the doctor from destroying the records that contain the information. The records are the property of the doctor. He or she may be restrained from using the information in them to make an unauthorised profit or from disclosing that information to unauthorised persons. But otherwise the records are his or hers to save or destroy. The idea that a doctor who shreds the records of treatment of living patients is necessarily in breach of fiduciary duties owed to those patients is untenable.

Furthermore, the judgment of La Forest J does not deal with the fact that the medical records of a patient will often, perhaps usually, contain much more than the information that the patient has given to the doctor. In addition to any observations concerning the patient's condition and notes recording treatment and research, the records may contain comments by the doctor about the personality and conduct of the patient. They may also contain information concerning the patient that the doctor has obtained from other sources. The patient has no rights in relation to or control over any information that has not come from him or her. We can think of no legal principle that would give the patient even a faintly arguable case for access to information in the records that is additional to what the patient has given. If the relationship of doctor and patient was a status-based fiduciary relationship in which the doctor was under a general fiduciary duty in relation to all dealings concerning the patient, the patient might be entitled to access to all the information in his or her medical records. But there is no general fiduciary duty.

La Forest J said that the 'fiduciary duty to provide access to medical records is ultimately grounded in the nature of the patient's interest in his or her records'.[83] However, the patient has no legal rights in respect of significant parts of the information contained in

---

79. *McInerney v MacDonald* [1992] 2 SCR 138 at 152; (1992) 93 DLR (4th) 415 at 425.
80. *Rogers v Whitaker* (1992) 175 CLR 479 at 483.
81. *Federal Commissioner of Taxation v United Aircraft Corporation* (1943) 68 CLR 525 at 534–535.
82. *W v Egdell* [1990] Ch 359 at 389, 415, 419.
83. *McInerney v MacDonald* [1992] 2 SCR 138 at 150; (1992) 93 DLR (4th) 415 at 424.

medical records. If a patient has a legal right of access to medical records merely because he or she has given personal and confidential information to a doctor, it would seem to follow that journalists, accountants, bank officers and anybody else receiving personal and confidential information always had a fiduciary duty to give access to their records to the person who gave that information.[84]

Thirdly, the Canadian law on fiduciary duties is very different from the law of this country with respect to that subject. One commentator has recently pointed to the 'vast differences between Australia and [113] Canada in understanding of the nature of fiduciary obligations'.[85] One significant difference is the tendency of Canadian courts to apply fiduciary principles in an expansive manner so as to supplement tort law and provide a basis for the creation of new forms of civil wrongs.[86] The Canadian cases also reveal a tendency to view fiduciary obligations as both proscriptive and prescriptive.[87] However, Australian courts only recognise proscriptive fiduciary duties. This is not the place to explore the differences between the law of Canada and the law of Australia on this topic. With great respect to the Canadian courts, however, many cases in that jurisdiction pay insufficient regard to the effect that the imposition of fiduciary duties on particular relationships has on the law of negligence, contract, agency, trusts and companies in their application to those relationships.[88] Further, many of the Canadian cases pay insufficient, if any, regard to the fact that the imposition of fiduciary duties often gives rise to proprietary remedies that affect the distribution of assets in bankruptcies and insolvencies.

In this country, fiduciary obligations arise because a person has come under an obligation to act in another's interests. As a result, equity imposes on the fiduciary proscriptive obligations — not to obtain any unauthorised benefit from the relationship and not to be in a position of conflict. If these obligations are breached, the fiduciary must account for any profits and make good any losses arising from the breach. But the law of this country does not otherwise impose positive legal duties on the fiduciary to act in the interests of the person to whom the duty is owed.[89] If there was a general fiduciary duty to act in the best interests of the patient, it would necessarily follow that a doctor

---

84. The special circumstances of the case may, of course, create a fiduciary relationship which would require the journalist, accountant, bank officer or other person to reveal all relevant information to the person who gave the information. *Commonwealth Bank of Australia v Smith* (1991) 42 FCR 390 provides an example in the case of a bank officer. But none of these persons owes a fiduciary duty to give access to records merely because they have received confidential information.

85. P Parkinson, 'Fiduciary Law and Access to Medical Records: Breen v Williams' (1995) 17 *Sydney Law Review* 433 at 439–440.

86. P Parkinson, 'Fiduciary Law and Access to Medical Records: Breen v Williams' (1995) 17 *Sydney Law Review* 433 at 442–443; P D Finn, 'The Fiduciary Principle' in T G Youdan (ed), *Equity, Fiduciaries and Trusts*, Carswell, Toronto, 1989, pp 25–26.

87. See *J (LA) v J (H)* (1993) 102 DLR (4th) 177; P Parkinson, 'Fiduciary Law and Access to Medical Records: Breen v Williams' (1995) 17 *Sydney Law Review* 433 at 441.

88. P D Finn, 'The Fiduciary Principle' in T G Youdan (ed), *Equity, Fiduciaries and Trusts*, Carswell, Toronto, 1989, p 26.

89. See Parkinson, 'Fiduciary Law and Access to Medical Records: Breen v Williams', note 62 above, pp 441–442.

has a duty to inform the patient that he or she has breached their contract or has been guilty of negligence in dealings with the patient. That is not the law of this country.

In Australia, therefore, *McInerney* cannot be regarded as a persuasive authority. In this country a court cannot use the law of fiduciary duty to provide relief to Ms Breen which, if granted, would have the effect of imposing a novel, positive obligation on Dr Williams to maintain and furnish medical records to Ms Breen. It follows that Dr Williams does not owe Ms Breen any fiduciary duty to [114] give Ms Breen access to the medical records that relate to his treatment of her.

Comments

1. See Radan & Stewart at **9.94–9.98**.
2. For more on the application of fiduciary duties in the healthcare context see T M Carlin, 'Doctors as Fiduciaries — Revisiting the Past with an Eye on the Future' (2001) 9(1) *Journal of Law and Medicine* 95 and T A Faunce & S N Bolsin, 'Fiduciary Disclosure of Medical Mistakes: The Duty to Promptly Notify Patients of Adverse Health Care Events' (2005) 12 *Journal of Law and Medicine* 478.

The application of fiduciary duties to indigenous peoples

9.7   Bodney v Westralia Airports Corporation Pty Ltd (2000) 109 FCR 178

Court: Federal Court of Australia

Facts: Bodney was the representative of a group of Aboriginal Australians who were claiming native title over land which adjoined Perth airport. The land was owned by the Commonwealth and leased to the Westralia Airports Corporation. The land was owned under the Torrens system in fee simple. It was argued that the Crown owed fiduciary duties to the native title holders when disposing of the land to the Commonwealth.

Issue: The issue was whether the Crown could owe a fiduciary duty to indigenous Australians.

Decision: Lehane J decided that there were not enough facts upon which to prove the existence of a fiduciary duty being owed to the particular indigenous claimants in the case, although it was possible that such a claim might be successfully proven by others in later cases.

Extracts: In this extract Lehane J discusses the comparative law on fiduciary duties from the United States, Canada and New Zealand and compares it with the native title jurisprudence of Australia.

Lehane J

Fiduciary duty — constructive trust

[197] The submission that there was a constructive trust (or that one might be imposed) arising out of a breach of fiduciary duty was put by counsel for the second applicants ... [198] The facts alleged relate principally to general executive and legislative attitudes to relations with indigenous people from the time of settlement. There are, however, some more specific facts alleged. I have referred already to particular allegations as to the continuing exercise by the applicants and their predecessors of the rights which they assert in relation to the claim area. The other particular allegations, specific to the claim area, are these:

> 1.8 The Crown in right of the State of Western Australia, prior to the acquisitions taking place, had taken steps to protect the presence, occupation, use and enjoyment of the area by the native title parties and their predecessors by establishing areas within the area the subject to [sic] the acquisitions which were reserved from sale and were designated to be for the use and benefit of Aboriginal people; and such areas were used and occupied by the native title parties and their predecessors.

> 1.9 The Crown in right of the Commonwealth knew or, after reasonably diligent inquiry, was capable of knowing of the fact of the setting aside of such areas for the use and benefit of Aboriginal people and the occupation of those areas by Aboriginal people, whom they were capable of ascertaining by reasonably diligent inquiry were the native title parties or their predecessors.

...

The general allegations commence with a proclamation made by the first Governor, Captain James Stirling, which included the paragraph:

> And whereas the protection of Law doth of right belong to all People who come or be found within the Territory aforesaid I do hereby give notice that if any person shall be convicted of behaving in a fraudulent cruel or felonious manner to the Aboriginal race of inhabitants of this Country such person shall be liable to be prosecuted and tried for the offence as if the same had been committed against any others of His Majesty's subjects.

The allegations then refer to much colonial legislation, commencing from the 1840s (and largely long since repealed), making particular provision for indigenous people and their protection. The legislation related, for example, to restrictions on access to alcohol, to the provision of reserves and their [199] management and the provision of medical services and education. Particularly, the second applicant relied on the effect of s 70 of the *Constitution Act 1889* (WA) and certain provisions of the *Aborigines Act 1905* (WA). The former provision required the appropriation of an annual sum to be applied by the Aborigines Protection Board in promoting the welfare and education of Aborigines (and by s 73 of the *Constitution Act*, any bill to amend s 70 was to be reserved 'to the Governor for the signification of Her Majesty's pleasure thereon'). The provisions of the *Aborigines Act*, the effect of which is pleaded in the amended statement of facts, issues and contentions, established an Aborigines Department to exercise supervision and care over matters affecting the interests and welfare of Aborigines and to protect them against injustice, imposition and fraud; and provided for the establishment of reserves, their management and regulation and for the making of regulations for the control, care and education of Aborigines in institutions. Certain observations made in the Legislative Council in 1883 by the then Premier are referred to as well.

That history was said to show that the Crown had recognised or assumed general tutelary obligations in relation to Aboriginal people. That was said to have given rise to a 'fiduciary expectation': that is, that the Crown would act in the interests of the Aboriginal people and for the purpose of the relationship with them which it had assumed.[90] The Crown had asserted sovereignty over the Aboriginal people; it had adopted a protective role; it had power to abrogate their interests (and had performed acts in exercise of that power). Those circumstances, it was said, together with the creation of the 'fiduciary expectation', gave rise to fiduciary obligations on the part of the Crown. As well as general statements in the cases about circumstances giving rise to fiduciary duties, the second applicants relied on authorities in the United States, Canada and New Zealand, on the analysis in the judgment of Toohey J in *Mabo (No 2)*[91] and the discussion by Deane and Gaudron JJ[92] of the availability of equitable remedies, particularly the remedial constructive trust, to protect native title against the wrongful denial of it or wrongful interference with it. Recognising the obvious difficulty with a proposition that the Crown is obliged to exercise powers exclusively in the interests of Aboriginal people,[93] the second applicants contended (relying on United States and particularly Canadian authorities) for the existence of a duty which required, in the exercise of a power to dispose of land so as to extinguish native title, at least consultation with the owners of native title, the taking of their interests into account and, perhaps, reasonableness according to an objective standard.

A particular difficulty with the fiduciary case is, indeed, the level of generality at which the facts are pleaded. Ordinarily, the question whether fiduciary duties arise is decided having regard to the particular circumstances of particular relationships, or particular dealings, between particular people. Similarly, a constructive trust is imposed, ordinarily, because the circumstances of dealings between particular people make it unconscionable that one should, to the exclusion of the other, be permitted to assert a full beneficial title to particular property: one circumstance in which that may arise, of course, is where property has been acquired in breach of a fiduciary duty. Here, the claims are based mainly upon a general obligation, said to have been assumed by the Crown (and largely treating as immaterial any distinction between the Crown in right of one polity and the Crown in right of another) at and [200] following European settlement of Western Australia, to protect the indigenous people. It is that general obligation said to have been assumed, coupled with a power to injure the interests of indigenous people (for example, by granting land and thereby extinguishing native title) that is said to have given rise to a fiduciary duty which was breached where title to land was granted or assumed by

---

90. P D Finn, 'The Fiduciary Principle', in Youdan (ed), *Equity, Fiduciaries and Trusts* (1989), pp 46, 47.
91. At 199–205.
92. *Mabo v Queensland (No 2)* (1992) 175 CLR 1 at 112, 113.
93. *Wik Peoples v Queensland* (1996) 187 CLR 1 at 95–97.

the Crown without consultation with indigenous people who may have had rights in relation to it and without having particular regard to their interests. Those, in essence, were the propositions on which the argument concentrated. To the extent that facts relating to the particular land, or particular indigenous people said to have had rights in relation to it, are pleaded, again that has been done at a high level of abstraction and, as I have mentioned, there is undisputed evidence as to the extent to which any of the claim area was actually within lands which were, at any relevant times, reserved for particular purposes of Aboriginal people.

In *Thorpe v Commonwealth (No 3)*, Kirby J summarised the effect of authorities in the United States and Canada as follows (omitting references to authority):

> In the United States of America it has been held that a fiduciary relationship exists in certain circumstances between the United States and the Indian tribes. It would appear that such relationship was found on the basis that the tribes, as domestic dependent nations, had sought and received the protection of the United States, a more powerful government. A fiduciary duty with respect to the lands of indigenous peoples has also received a measure of acceptance in Canada. In the context of land surrendered to the Crown by Aboriginal groups, it has been held that a trust-like relationship was established. Indeed, in Canada it has been suggested that the Crown has a broader responsibility to act in a fiduciary way towards indigenous peoples arising out of the Crown's historical powers over, and assumption of responsibility for, such peoples within its protection. The recognition of Aboriginal rights within the Canadian Constitution has also been invoked as a foundation for a fiduciary relationship.[94]

In *Fejo* his Honour referred ... to the need to exercise care in the use of authorities from other jurisdictions:

> ... because of the peculiarities which exist in each of them arising out of historical and constitutional developments, the organisation of the indigenous peoples concerned and applicable geographical or social considerations.[95]

Nevertheless, counsel for the second applicants relied on authorities from other jurisdictions as indicating a basis for finding a fiduciary duty which transcended the particular local conditions and the particular legal frameworks of the various jurisdictions.

Counsel placed particular reliance on a series of Canadian authorities, the first of which is *Guerin v The Queen*.[96] *Guerin* itself involved a lease of Indian lands to a golf club. A statutory scheme regulating the disposal of Indian lands provided that those lands might be disposed of only by the Crown upon surrender by the Indian band concerned; the Crown, following surrender, negotiated for the disposal of the land on behalf of the band. In those circumstances, there is nothing surprising about the conclusion that the Crown, in negotiating a disposal in that capacity, undertook a fiduciary [201] duty to act in the interests of members of the band. As Dickson J explained the matter:

---

94. (1997) 71 ALJR 767 at 775.
95. *Fejo v Northern Territory* (1998) 195 CLR 96 at 148–149.
96. (1984) 13 DLR (4th) 321.

> The purpose of this surrender requirement is clearly to interpose the Crown between the Indians and prospective purchasers or lessees of their land, so as to prevent the Indians from being exploited. This is made clear in the Royal Proclamation itself, which prefaces the provision making the Crown an intermediary with a declaration that 'great Frauds and Abuses have been committed in purchasing Lands of the Indians, to the great Prejudice of our Interest and to the great Dissatisfaction of the said Indians ...' Through the confirmation in the *Indian Act* of the historic responsibility which the Crown has undertaken, to act on behalf of the Indians so as to protect their interests in transactions with third parties, Parliament has conferred upon the Crown a discretion to decide for itself where the Indians' best interests really lie ... This discretion on the part of the Crown, far from ousting, as the Crown contends, the jurisdiction of the Courts to regulate the relationship between the Crown and the Indians, has the effect of transforming the Crown's obligation into a fiduciary one.[97]

The language of the Proclamation quoted by his Lordship is reminiscent of language used in the Proclamation and some of the early legislation on which the second applicants rely. In the Canadian legislative scheme, however, the language was directed to abuses requiring the particular protection of laws which specifically interpose the Crown as intermediary for the purpose of protecting the interests of Aboriginal people in dealing with their land.

Two aspects of the later Canadian cases relied upon require caution in their use as authority directly applicable in Australia. One is the extent to which they depend upon a construction of particular statutes, most importantly s 35(1) of the *Constitution Act 1982* (Can). That section provides that the existing Aboriginal and treaty rights of the Aboriginal Peoples of Canada are thereby recognised and affirmed. Lamer CJC pointed out in *Delgamuukw v British Columbia* that: 'On a plain reading of the provision, s 35(1) did not create Aboriginal rights; rather, it accorded constitutional status to those rights which were "existing" in 1982.'[98] Nevertheless, it is evident that the 'constitutionalisation' of Aboriginal rights has had a significant influence on judicial decisions. So, in *R v Sparrow*, Dickson CJC and La Forest J, delivering the judgment of the Supreme Court of Canada, said this:

> There is no explicit language in the provision that authorises this court or any court to assess the legitimacy of any government legislation that restricts Aboriginal rights. Yet, we find that the words 'recognition and affirmation' incorporate the fiduciary relationship referred to earlier and so import some restraint on the exercise of sovereign power. Rights that are recognised and affirmed are not absolute. Federal legislative powers continue, including, of course, the right to legislate with respect to Indians pursuant to s 91(24) of the *Constitution Act 1867* [(Can)]. These powers must, however, now be read together with s 35(1). In other words, federal power must be reconciled with federal duty and the best way to achieve that reconciliation is to demand the justification of any government regulation that infringes upon or denies aboriginal

---

97. (1984) 13 DLR (4th) 321 at 340.
98. (1997) 153 DLR (4th) 193 at 249.

rights. Such scrutiny is in keeping with the liberal interpretive principle enunciated in [certain earlier authority], and the concept of holding the Crown to a high standard [202] of honourable dealing with respect to the aboriginal peoples of Canada as suggested by [*Guerin*].[99]

So, in *Delgamuukw* Lamer CJC discussed at length the way in which the Courts would consider whether particular measures or governmental acts were justified for the purposes of s 35(1). The relevant passage in his Lordship's judgment commences at 260. In all cases consultation is required and the consultation must be in good faith 'and with the intention of substantially addressing the concerns of the aboriginal peoples whose lands are at issue'.[100] Most cases will require something 'significantly deeper than mere consultation'. Some might require the 'full consent of an aboriginal nation'. The extent of the considerations which the Court would take into account appears in the following passage:

> The exclusive nature of aboriginal title is relevant to the degree of scrutiny of the infringing measure or action. For example, if the Crown's fiduciary duty requires that aboriginal title be given priority, then it is the altered approach to priority that I laid down in *R v Gladstone* (1996) 137 DLR (4th) 648 which should apply. What is required is that the government demonstrate ... 'both that the process by which it allocated the resource and the actual allocation of the resource which results from that process reflect the prior interest' of the holders of aboriginal title in the land. By analogy with *Gladstone*, this might entail, for example, that governments accommodate the participation of aboriginal peoples in the development of the resources of British Columbia, that the conferral of the fee simples for agriculture, and of leases and licences for forestry and mining reflect the prior occupation of aboriginal title lands, that economic barriers to aboriginal uses of their land (eg licensing fees) be somewhat reduced. This list is illustrative and not exhaustive.[101]

Those passages indicate also the other aspect of them which requires caution in their use as authority here. The law as to fiduciary obligations has developed in Canada in ways which are not reflected in developments in Australian law.[102]

Against that background, the United States authorities need not, I think, be discussed at length. Again several aspects of the United States legal context require caution in seeking directly to apply United States authority here. One is the limited sovereignty of Indian tribes recognised as 'domestic dependent nations'.[103] In *United States v Wheeler* Stewart J, delivering the opinion of the Court, described the position as follows:

---

99. (1990) 70 DLR (4th) 385 at 409.
100. (1997) 153 DLR (4th) 193 at 265.
101. (1997) 153 DLR (4th) 193 at 264.
102. *Breen v Williams* (1996) 186 CLR 71 at 82, 83, 92, 93, 110–114 and 137. See also the statements about the circumstances in which fiduciary obligations arise, and their content, at 113 per Gaudron and McHugh JJ and at 132–138 per Gummow J.
103. *Cherokee Nation v Georgia* (1831) 8 L Ed 25 at 31, 32.

The sovereignty that the Indian tribes retain is of a unique and limited character. It exists only at the sufferance of Congress and is subject to complete defeasance. But until Congress acts, the tribes retain their existing sovereign powers. In sum, Indian tribes still possess those aspects of sovereignty not withdrawn by treaty or statute, or by implication as a necessary result of their dependent status.[104]

No such sovereignty is recognised in Australia.[105] Secondly, the fiduciary or trust relationship recognised in relation to the Indian peoples of the United States appears to arise largely both from their position as domestic dependent nations [203] and from particular statutory regimes.[106] Thirdly, it appears that the law as to fiduciary duty, influenced perhaps by particular statutory contexts, has developed in the United States in ways that have not yet been reflected here.[107]

In New Zealand, the *Treaty of Waitangi 1840* done at Waitangi on 6 February 1840 has been described as 'major support' for a fiduciary duty.[108] [In *Te Runanga o Wharekauri Rekohu Inc v Attorney-General*] Cooke P, delivering the judgment of the Court, referred ... to the emerging relevance of fiduciary obligation, in a number of common law jurisdictions, in the context of relations with indigenous peoples; but the circumstances giving rise to such obligations, in jurisdictions other than New Zealand, were not a matter which called for analysis.[109]

Duties of the kind for which the second applicants contend have supported the judgment of Toohey J in *Mabo (No 2)*.[110] After referring to *Guerin*, his Honour said:

> ... if the Crown in right of Queensland has the power to alienate land the subject of the Meriam people's traditional rights and interests and the result of that alienation is the loss of traditional title, and if the Meriam people's power to deal with their title is restricted in so far as it is inalienable, except to the Crown, then this power and corresponding vulnerability give rise to a fiduciary obligation on the part of the Crown. The power to destroy or impair a people's interests in this way is extraordinary and is sufficient to attract regulation by Equity to ensure that the position is not abused. The fiduciary relationship arises, therefore, out of the power of the Crown to extinguish traditional title by alienating the land or otherwise; it does not depend on an exercise of that power.[111]

His Honour found further support for the existence of fiduciary obligation in the course of dealings by the Queensland Government with the Murray Islanders, the exercise of control or regulation by welfare legislation and the institution by legislation of

---

104. (1978) 435 US 313 at 323.
105. *Coe v Commonwealth* (1993) 68 ALJR 110 at 115; 118 ALR 193 at 200.
106. See, for example, *United States v Mitchell* 463 US 206 (1983) at 225–227; see also *United States v Creek Nation* 295 US 103 (1935) at 109, 110.
107. That is illustrated by a case on which the second applicants placed a considerable reliance, *Pyramid Lake Paiute Tribe of Indians v Morton* 354 F Supp 252 (1973), especially at 256–258.
108. *Te Runanga o Wharekauri Rekohu Inc v Attorney-General* [1993] 2 NZLR 301 at 306; see also *Te Runanganui o Te Ika Whenua Inc Society v Attorney-General* [1994] 2 NZLR 20 at 24.
109. *Te Runanga o Wharekauri Rekohu Inc v Attorney-General* [1993] 2 NZLR 301 at 306.
110. *Mabo v Queensland (No 2)* (1992) 175 CLR 1 at 199ff.
111. *Mabo v Queensland (No 2)* (1992) 175 CLR 1 at 203.

a form of local government. His Honour summarised his discussion of the content of the fiduciary obligation, as follows:

> A fiduciary has an obligation not to put himself or herself in a position of conflict of interests. But there are numerous examples of the Crown exercising different powers in different capacities. A fiduciary obligation on the Crown does not limit the legislative power of the Queensland Parliament, but legislation will be a breach of that obligation if its effect is adverse to the interests of the title holders, or if the process it establishes does not take account of those interests.[112]

A number of matters should be noted before proceeding further. One is that Toohey J made clear, his acceptance of the proposition that, if legislation reveals a clear and plain intention to extinguish traditional native title, it is effective to do so.[113] Secondly, the plaintiffs in *Mabo (No 2)*, though they claimed a declaration that there was a trust or fiduciary obligation, did not claim any specific relief for breach of fiduciary duty.[114] Thirdly, [204] none of the other judgments in *Mabo (No 2)* supports the existence of a fiduciary obligation of the kind discussed by Toohey J. Dawson J (who dissented) took the view that no such obligation could exist consistently with his view that 'upon annexation the lands comprising the Murray Islands became Crown lands and the Crown asserted the right to deal with those lands unimpeded by any recognition of, or acquiescence in, native title'.[115] Deane and Gaudron JJ did not refer to the possible existence of a fiduciary obligation. On the other hand, their Honours held that a wrongful extinguishment of native title might give rise to a claim for compensatory damages and (in the passage to which I have already referred) that equitable relief might also be available in appropriate cases, including 'the imposition of a remedial constructive trust framed to reflect the incidents and limitations of the rights under the common law native title'.[116] It seems, however, that their Honours contemplated that remedy being imposed in circumstances where there was an actual threatened interference with the enjoyment of rights derived from native title, where that title continued to exist: that is, had not been extinguished. Their Honours held that the Crown had power (for example by legislation in clear and unambiguous terms) wrongfully to extinguish native title by inconsistent grant. Such an extinguishment, being wrongful though effective, might give rise to an obligation to pay compensatory damages.[117]

Mason CJ, Brennan and McHugh JJ, however, did not agree, subject to the operation of the *Racial Discrimination Act*, that extinguishment of native title by inconsistent grant was wrongful or gave rise to a claim for compensatory damages. And in *Wik* Brennan CJ held, in relation to the exercise of powers of alienation under the *Land Act 1910* (Qld) (the 1910 Act) (and in language equally apposite to the Western Australian legislation):

---

112. *Mabo v Queensland (No 2)* (1992) 175 CLR 1 at 205.
113. *Mabo v Queensland (No 2)* (1992) 175 CLR 1 at 195.
114. *Mabo v Queensland (No 2)* (1992) 175 CLR 1 at 199, 200.
115. *Mabo v Queensland (No 2)* (1992) 175 CLR 1 at 167.
116. *Mabo v Queensland (No 2)* (1992) 175 CLR 1 at 113.
117. *Mabo v Queensland (No 2)* (1992) 175 CLR 1 at 111.

... indeed, the proposition that the Crown is under a fiduciary duty to the holders of native title to advance, protect or safeguard their interests while alienating their land is self-contradictory. The sovereign power of alienation was antipathetic to the safeguarding of the holders of native title. In conferring the power of alienation, Parliament imposed no guidelines to be observed in its exercise. The power was to be exercised as the Governor in Council saw fit. At the time when the 1910 Act conferred the power of alienation on the Governor in Council, native title was not recognised by the Courts. The power was not conditioned on the safeguarding or even the considering of the interests of those who would now be recognised as the holders of native title.[118]

And ..., his Honour held that the absence of fiduciary duty precluded the acceptance of a submission that a constructive trust should be imposed.[119]

In *Thorpe*, Kirby J considered the authorities and concluded:

The result is that whether a fiduciary duty is owed by the Crown to the indigenous peoples of Australia remains an open question. This Court has simply not determined it. Certainly, it has not determined it adversely to the proposition. On the other hand, there is no holding endorsing such a fiduciary duty, still less for the generality of the claim asserted in the first declaration in Mr Thorpe's writ.[120]

In my view, the foregoing discussion leads to two conclusions. One is that the authorities from other jurisdictions do not provide a firm basis for the assertion of a fiduciary duty of the kind for which the second applicants contend. The other is that the tendency of authority in the High Court [205] including, significantly, *Breen*, is against the existence of such a duty. That, of course, does not mean that circumstances will not arise in which the Crown has fiduciary duties, owed to particular indigenous people, in relation to the alienation of land over which they hold native title. Nor does it mean that where, in particular circumstances, a duty of that kind is breached (or a breach is threatened) a constructive trust might not appropriately be imposed. But the second applicants' pleading does not, in my view, allege facts which would establish a fiduciary duty, on the part either of the State or of the Commonwealth, requiring either the State or the Commonwealth not to participate as they did (or in the manner in which they did) in the transactions as a result of which the Commonwealth obtained title to the land incorporating the claim area.

In any event, however, the argument about fiduciary duty and constructive trust, and for that matter a good deal of the foregoing discussion, is in my view largely beside the point. The separate questions ask, principally, whether any native title to the various parts of the claim area has been extinguished by one, or by combinations, of the various transactions of which Mr Guthrie gave evidence. The proceeding itself is one in which a determination of native title is sought in relation to the claim area: such an application may result (*Native Title Act*, s 225) in a determination that native title does not exist in relation to an area, because any native title that may have existed has been

---

118. *Wik Peoples v Queensland* (1996) 187 CLR 1 at 83.
119. *Wik Peoples v Queensland* (1996) 187 CLR 1 at 97.
120. *Thorpe v Commonwealth (No 3)* (1997) 71 ALJR 767 at 776.

extinguished. Neither the separate questions nor the application in the proceeding invite, if the conclusion is reached that any native title has been extinguished, an inquiry into whether the extinguishment was wrongful or, if so, what remedies might be available and appropriate. None of the Australian authorities suggests that if the Crown, in accordance with plain and unambiguous legislation, grants or assumes an interest in land which confers rights inconsistent with the continued existence of native title, native title, in some form, persists. To the contrary, it is extinguished, and the act of extinguishment is effective even if it is wrongful. It may well be that the balance of authority does not favour the proposition that an act which extinguishes native title, carried out in accordance with legislation which in plain terms authorises it, is ever to be regarded as wrongful. But that, again, is beside the point: if wrongful, it is nevertheless effective. And, in my view, even if an act giving rise to extinguishment was wrongful, a proposition that the substance of native title nevertheless persisted, or might be revived, by medium of a constructive trust is irreconcilable with the clear statements of principle in *Fejo* ...

Comments
1. See Radan & Stewart at **9.99–9.106**.
2. For more on fiduciary duties and indigenous peoples see E Fox-Decent, 'Fashioning Legal Authority from Power: The Crown–Native Fiduciary Relationship' (2006) 4 *New Zealand Journal of Public International Law* 91, J I Reynolds, *A Breach of Duty: Fiduciary Obligations and Aboriginal Peoples*, Purich Publishers, Saskatoon, 2005 and R H Bartlett, *Native Title in Australia*, 2nd ed, LexisNexis Butterworths, Sydney, 2004.

10

UNDUE INFLUENCE

Introduction

10.1 This chapter deals with the principles pursuant to which a transaction may be held to have resulted from undue influence by one of the parties to it over the other. Undue influence can be established in three ways. First, a relationship of undue influence can be established on the facts of a particular case. Second, certain legal relationships are, *ipso facto*, ones where one party is presumed to have undue influence over the other. Third, the facts and circumstances of a particular relationship can lead to a finding that the relationship is one of undue influence. Once it is established that a relationship is one of undue influence, there is a presumption that any transaction entered into between the parties was the result of undue influence being exercised by the dominant party in the relationship. If the dominant party cannot rebut this presumption, the contract is voidable.

The cases extracted in this chapter discuss the following:

- the basic principles relating to undue influence: *Johnson v Buttress* (1936) 56 CLR 113;
- rebuttal of the presumption of undue influence: *Bester v Perpetual Trustee Co Ltd* [1970] 3 NSWR 30; and
- the place of undue influence in the context of a wife's guarantee of a lender's loan to her husband: *Yerkey v Jones* (1939) 63 CLR 649; *Garcia v National Australia Bank Limited* (1998) 194 CLR 395.

The principles of undue influence

10.2   Johnson v Buttress (1936) 56 CLR 113

Court: High Court of Australia

Facts: Buttress was the son of the late John Buttress and administrator with the will annexed of his father's estate. During his lifetime, John and his wife had befriended her distant relative Mary Johnson, a woman who later gave aid and comfort to John's wife during her terminal illness. John continued his friendship with Johnson after his wife's death and named her as the beneficiary in his will, to the exclusion of his son in whom he had lost confidence. John's only asset of any significance was a small cottage in the Sydney suburb of Maroubra in which he lived and from which he earned a small income from rent. At one point, he told Johnson he wished to transfer his house to her. They attended Johnson's solicitor's office where, after some routine questioning, John signed the relevant transfer documents in which consideration was expressed as 'natural love and affection'. The rest of John's family was unaware of the transfer of the cottage to Johnson or of the will he had made in her favour. Shortly before his death, John made a new will in which he named his niece Agnes Hart as the sole beneficiary. After his father's death, Buttress, as administrator, commenced proceedings to set aside the transfer to Johnson on the grounds of undue influence.

Issue: The issue before the High Court was whether the transfer from John to Johnson should be set aside on the grounds of undue influence.

Decision: The High Court (Latham CJ, Starke, Dixon, Evatt and McTiernan JJ) unanimously found in favour of John's son and set aside the transfer of the Maroubra cottage to Johnson. It held that an antecedent relationship of influence between John and Johnson had been established on the facts, which imposed on Johnson the burden to prove that John had freely exercised his independent will. Since she had failed to do this, the transfer had to be set aside.

Extracts: The extracts from the judgment of Latham CJ reflect the High Court's reasoning on the matters to be established where undue influence is alleged as a vitiating element. The extracts from the judgment of Dixon J set out the basic principles relevant to undue influence.

Latham CJ

[119] The jurisdiction of a court of equity to set aside gifts *inter vivos* which have been procured by undue influence is exercised where undue influence is proved as a fact, or where, undue influence being presumed from the relations existing between the parties, the presumption has not been rebutted. Where certain special relations exist undue influence is presumed in the case of such gifts. These relations include those of parent and child, guardian and ward, trustee and *cestui que trust*, solicitor and client, physician and patient and cases of religious influence. The relations mentioned, however, do not constitute an exhaustive list of the cases in which undue influence will be presumed from personal relations. Wherever the relation between donor and donee is such that the latter is in a position to exercise dominion over the former by reason of the trust and confidence reposed in the latter, the presumption of undue influence is raised.

Where such a relation of what may be called, from one point of view, dominion, and from another point of view, dependence, exists, the age and condition of the donor are irrelevant so far as raising the presumption of undue influence is concerned. It must be affirmatively shown by the donee that the gift was ... 'the pure, voluntary, well-understood act of the mind' of the donor.[1]

It may not be necessary in all cases to show that the donor received competent independent advice ... [120] But evidence that such advice has been given is one means, and the most obvious means, of helping to establish that the gift was the result of the free exercise of independent will; and the absence of such advice, even if not sufficient in itself to invalidate the transaction, would plainly be a most important factor in determining

---

1. *Huguenin v Baseley* (1807) 33 ER 526 at 535.

whether the gift was in fact the result of a free and genuine exercise of the will of the donor.

In the case of an illiterate or weak-minded person it will be more difficult for the donee to discharge the prescribed onus of proof than in other cases. The burden will be still heavier upon the donee where the donor has given him all or practically all of his property.[2] ...

[123] I apply to this case the words of *Sir John Leach* VC in *Griffiths v Robins*, ... altering only the pronouns to make the words more plainly applicable to the present case and omitting words referring to independent advice which later authorities ... have shown to be unnecessary as part of the rule of law:-

> He (the donor) had entire trust and confidence in her (the person who induced him to execute the deed of gift); and it may be stated that she was the person upon whose kindness and assistance he depended. She stood, therefore, in a relation to him which so much exposed him to her influence that she can maintain no deed of gift from him unless she can establish that it was the result of his own free will.[3]

Thus, in my opinion, the [facts of this case] show that though it has not been affirmatively proved against [Johnson] that she exercised undue influence, yet she has not displaced the presumption of undue influence which arises in the circumstances of this case. Thus the transaction cannot stand by reason of the general policy of the law directed to preventing the possible abuse of relations of trust and confidence.

Dixon J

[134] The basis of the equitable jurisdiction to set aside an alienation of property on the ground of undue influence is the prevention of an unconscientious use of any special capacity or opportunity that may exist or arise of affecting the alienor's will or freedom of judgment in reference to such a matter. The source of power to practise such a domination may be found in no antecedent relation but in a particular situation, or in the deliberate contrivance of the party. If this be so, facts must be proved showing that the transaction was the outcome of such an actual influence over the mind of the alienor that it cannot be considered his free act. But the parties may antecedently stand in a relation that gives to one an authority or influence over the other from the abuse of which it is proper that he should be protected. When they stand in such a relation, the party in the position of influence cannot maintain his beneficial title to property of substantial value made over to him by the other as a gift, unless he satisfies the court that he took no advantage of the donor, but that the gift was the independent and well-understood act of a man in a position to exercise a free judgment based on information as full as that of the donee. This burden is imposed upon one of the parties to certain well-known relations as soon as it appears that the relation existed and that he has obtained a substantial benefit from the other. A solicitor must thus justify the receipt of such a benefit from his client, a physician from his patient, a parent from his child, a guardian from his ward, and a man from the woman he has engaged to marry. The facts which must be proved in order

---

2. *Price v Price* (1852) 42 ER 571; *Inche Noriah v Shaik Allie Bin Omar* [1929] AC 127.
3. *Griffiths v Robins* (1818) 56 ER 480 at 480.

to satisfy the court that the donor was freed from influence are, perhaps, not always the same in these different relationships, for the influence which grows out of them varies in kind and degree. But while in these and perhaps one or two other relationships their very nature imports influence, the doctrine which throws upon the recipient the burden of justifying the transaction is confined to no fixed category. It rests upon a principle. It applies whenever one party occupies or assumes [135] towards another a position naturally involving an ascendancy or influence over that other, or a dependence or trust on his part. One occupying such a position falls under a duty in which fiduciary characteristics may be seen. It is his duty to use his position of influence in the interest of no one but the man who is governed by his judgment, gives him his dependence and entrusts him with his welfare. When he takes from that man a substantial gift of property, it is incumbent upon him to show that it cannot be ascribed to the inequality between them which must arise from his special position. He may be taken to possess a peculiar knowledge not only of the disposition itself but of the circumstances which should affect its validity; he has chosen to accept a benefit which may well proceed from an abuse of the authority conceded to him, or the confidence reposed in him; and the relations between him and the donor are so close as to make it difficult to disentangle the inducements which led to the transaction. These considerations combine with reasons of policy to supply a firm foundation for the presumption against a voluntary disposition in his favour. But, except in the well-recognized relations of influence, the circumstances relied upon to establish an antecedent relation between the parties of such a nature as to necessitate a justification of the transaction will be almost certain to cast upon it at least some measure of suspicion that active circumvention has been practised. This often will be so even when the case falls within the list of established relations of influence. Because of the presence of circumstances which might be regarded as presumptive proof of express influence, cases outside the list but nevertheless importing a special relationship of influence sometimes are treated as if they were not governed by the presumption but depended on an inference of fact. *Scrutton* LJ has remarked on the inclination of common law judges 'to rely more on individual proof than on general presumption, while considering the nature of the relationship and the presence of independent advice as important, though not essential, matters to be considered on the question whether the transaction in question can be supported'.[4] Further, when the transaction is not one of gift but of purchase or other [136] contract, the matters affecting its validity are necessarily somewhat different. Adequacy of consideration becomes a material question. Instead of inquiring how the subordinate party came to confer a benefit, the court examines the propriety of what wears the appearance of a business dealing. These differences form an additional cause why cases which really illustrate the effect of a special relation of influence in raising a presumption of invalidity are often taken to decide that express influence which is undue should be inferred from the circumstances.

Comment

1. See Radan & Stewart at **10.9, 10.13, 10.27–10.30, 10.32.**

---

4.   *Lancashire Loans Ltd v Black* [1934] 1 KB 380 at 404.

Rebutting the presumption of undue influence

10.3   Bester v Perpetual Trustee Co Ltd [1970] 3 NSWR 30

Court: Supreme Court of New South Wales

Facts: Bester, a young woman at the time she inherited her father's estate equally with her brother, was encouraged to make a settlement of her share soon after she turned 21. She was influenced by three much older men — the representative from her trustee company and her two uncles, one of whom was the solicitor who drafted the deed of settlement — to execute the deed on the basis that it was in her interest to protect the capital from access by other people. She was told that the assets would be placed beyond her control and in the hands of trustees, whose duty would be to keep the capital intact for the benefit of any future children. She was entitled to receive a modest income from the assets during her lifetime. The solicitor uncle referred her to an independent solicitor, Emanuel, who simply read the document to her and asked whether she had any questions about it. At the time of settlement, the applicant was 21 years of age, without parental guidance and possessed of extremely limited business experience. She understood the general import of the deed and felt that the three men who arranged it knew best what was in her interest. Many years later, after marrying and having no children, she sought a court order that the deed be set aside on the ground that she had been subjected to undue influence when the document was signed.

Issue: The issue before the Supreme Court was whether a deed of settlement could be rescinded for undue influence where the applicant was advised of the nature of the deed and was in receipt of advice from an independent source. The nature of the independent advice and the settlement itself were crucial to the establishment of undue influence.

Decision: Street J in the Supreme Court ruled that undue influence had been established by the degree of confidence placed by Bester in her uncles and trustee. It was also found that the deed had not been executed of her own free will because it was improvident (it placed the property irrevocably beyond her control) and because the advice she received was inadequate (it failed to point out there was no obligation to settle her inheritance, that individual terms of the deed could have been negotiated and that alternative strategies could have been explored). His Honour also rejected the argument that the settlement should not be set aside on the ground of laches.

Extracts: The extracts from the judgment of Street J focus on the requirements of undue influence and in particular on the nature of the independent advice that equity requires.

Street J

[35] The issue upon which success or failure turns in a case such as the present was crystallized by the Privy Council in *Kali Bakhsh Singh v Ram Gopal Singh*: '... whether the grantor thoroughly comprehended, and deliberately and of her own free will carried out, the transaction'.[5]

---

5.   *Kali Bakhsh Singh v Ram Gopal Singh* (1913) 30 TLR 138 at 139.

In determining whether or not this issue should be resolved for or against the plaintiff [Bester], there are a number of circumstances that are traditionally regarded as significant. One of these circumstances is the nature of the transaction itself. If it can be demonstrated that the transaction is, so far as the settlor is concerned, improvident, then that will be a powerful consideration pointing towards success on the part of a settlor seeking to set aside a settlement upon the ground that it was not thoroughly comprehended, and deliberately and of the settlor's own free will carried out. A leading case upon the significance of improvidence is the decision of James VC in *Everitt v Everitt*.[6] The improvidence associated with the transaction with which James VC was concerned was in some respects similar to the heads of the present settlement which are relied upon as demonstrating improvidence. Briefly, they may be summarized as being that [Bester] finally, irrevocably and absolutely placed her property beyond all recall so far as she was concerned when she executed this document. In return for whatever protection her property might have from incautious handling on [her] part ..., or unscrupulous intervention on the part of some third party, the settlement involves her foregoing every interest whatever in the property during her lifetime except the bare right to receive income, coupled with the prospect of some or all of the money being applied towards providing a residence for her, her husband, and her children, if she should have any. The absence of any power of revocation, absolute or qualified, the absence of any right to have resort to corpus, absolute or qualified, the absence of any right to intervene in the activities of the trustees, either in particular matters or in point of the selection of the trustees, are all factors which go, in my view, to justify this transaction being categorized as in some respects improvident.

Another of the *indicia* to which reference may legitimately be made in determining the critical issue of whether [Bester] thoroughly comprehended the transaction, and entered into it deliberately and of her own free will, is the presence or absence of independent advice having been tendered to her. Mr Emanuel was brought into the present transaction with the intention no doubt of his meeting this requirement. I am of the view, however, that such part as he played in connexion with this settlement could not fairly be described as meeting that degree of independent advice that [Bester], as a person subject to a relationship of influence, was entitled to receive. Mr Emanuel was, I accept, most careful to read the document through, and to invite questions of [Bester]. But it was not textual advice upon the engrossment which was of prime importance in this regard: rather, it was advice upon the more general topic of whether a settlement should be entered into at all, and, if so, the general nature of the settlement, which in my view ought to have been provided for [her]. The document had been completely engrossed, and, indeed, Mr Emanuel's certificate had been typed at the end of it before it was even shown to [her]. I accept [Bester's] **[36]** evidence that she had been advised as to what she should do before she went to Mr Emanuel and, further, that she did not, from her discussion with Mr Emanuel, gain any impression as to whether he was advising her in favour of, or against, the signing.

The need to provide meaningful advice in order to enable an independent choice to be made by a person in the position of [Bester] is of great importance. The purpose of obtaining advice is to enable the making of an independent choice. It may be that to an informed and

6.   (1870) LR 10 Eq Cas 405.

intelligent listener advice confined to explaining will enable an intelligent choice to be made to the effect that the document being explained is acceptable to the party being asked to execute it. But the mere fact that a document is explained, and that no questions are asked nor criticism made of it by the party to whom it is being explained, does not tend strongly in favour of the conclusion that this party made a deliberate and intelligent choice to adopt each and every one of the provisions contained in the document.

> **Comment**
> 1. See Radan & Stewart at **10.31**, **10.36**.

The wife's guarantee of her husband's loan

> ### 10.4   Yerkey v Jones (1939) 63 CLR 649
>
> **Court:** High Court of Australia
>
> **Facts:** Estyn Jones became interested in buying a three-acre parcel of land at Payneham in South Australia from Mr and Mrs Yerkey. The land had a house and other fixtures that made it suitable for his plan to run a poultry farm and breed dogs. His wife Florence Jones did not support her husband's idea. However, Estyn negotiated directly with Mr Yerkey and agreed to buy the property for £3500 by instalment payments on the condition that further security was provided. He had no property in his name but offered the property in which he and his wife lived at Walkerville, which was owned by Florence. He was taken to Yerkey's solicitor who drew up a letter to reflect the deal, which Estyn signed. It provided for a payment of £200 after two years and the balance of £3300 to be paid after the expiration of three years from the date of the contract. Florence Jones was to execute a second mortgage over her property at Walkerville for £1000, which would be included in the £3300 payment. Estyn did not tell his wife about this arrangement until a week later, upon which she firstly opposed and then reluctantly agreed to do as her husband had arranged. The mortgage was executed and the sale proceeded. Estyn Jones failed to develop the poultry farm and the property at Payneham deteriorated. Interest payments on the mortgage fell into arrears and Mr and Mrs Yerkey took legal action in accordance with their rights as mortgagees. Florence brought proceedings to have the mortgage over her Walkerville property set aside.
>
> **Issue:** The issue before the High Court was whether there was a presumption that a wife in such circumstances acts under the influence of her husband. It also had to decide whether Florence had acted under Estyn's influence when executing the mortgage.
>
> **Decision:** The High Court (Latham CJ, Rich, Dixon and McTiernan JJ) unanimously held in favour of the Yerkeys. It held that in cases where a wife confers a benefit upon her husband voluntarily, a presumption of undue influence does not arise. Although it may be possible for actual undue influence to be established in such cases, Florence Jones had failed to prove this on the facts in her case. The Yerkeys were able to enforce their mortgage over the Walkerville property.

> **Extracts:** The extracts from the judgment of Dixon J explain why the relationship of husband and wife is not one in which it is presumed that the husband has influence over the wife. They also detail the principles of equity that can be invoked by a wife who has guaranteed a loan made to her husband.

Dixon J

[675] In *In re Lloyds Bank Ltd; Bomze and Lederman v Bomze* the present Lord Chancellor (Lord *Maugham*), speaking of gifts by a wife to her husband, said that it is well settled that the relation is not one of those in which the doctrine of [undue influence] applies, but where there is evidence that a husband has taken unfair advantage of his influence over his wife or her confidence in him, it is not difficult for the wife to establish her title to relief.[7] The reason for excluding the relation of husband and wife from the category to which the presumption applies is to be found in the consideration that there is nothing unusual or strange in a wife from motives of affection or even of prudence conferring a large proprietary or pecuniary benefit upon her husband. The Court of Chancery was not blind to the opportunities of obtaining and unfairly using influence over his wife which a husband often possesses. But in the relations comprised within the category to which the presumption of undue influence applies, there is another element besides the mere existence of an opportunity of obtaining ascendancy or confidence and of abusing it. It will be found that in none of those relations is it natural to expect the one party to give property to the other. That is to say, the character of the relation itself is never enough to explain the transaction and to account for it without suspicion of confidence abused.

The distinction drawn between large gifts taken by a man from the woman to whom he is affianced, a case to which the presumption applies, and similar gifts by a wife to her husband, a case to which it does not apply, a distinction sometimes condemned, is explained by this consideration and also, perhaps, by the consideration that the rule is one of policy and, upon a balance, policy is against applying it to husband and wife. But while the relation of a husband to his wife is not one of influence, and no presumption exists of undue influence, it has never been divested completely of what may be called equitable presumptions of an invalidating tendency.

In the first place, there is the doctrine, which may now perhaps be regarded as a rule of evidence, that, if a voluntary disposition in favour of the husband is impeached, the burden of establishing that it was not improperly or unfairly procured may be placed upon him by proof of circumstances raising any doubt or suspicion. In the [676] second place, the position of strangers who deal through the husband with the wife in a transaction operating to the husband's advantage may, by that fact alone, be affected by any equity which as between the wife and the husband might arise from his conduct. In the third place, it still is or may be a condition of the validity of a voluntary dealing by the wife for the advantage of her husband that she really obtained an adequate understanding of the actual nature and consequences of the transaction.

It will be seen that all three of these matters must have a special importance when the transaction in question is one of suretyship and the wife without any recompense, except

---

7. *In re Lloyds Bank Ltd; Bomze and Lederman v Bomze* (1931) 1 Ch 289 at 302.

the advantage of her husband, saddles herself or her separate property with a liability for his debt or debts ...

[677] Of the three suggested rules or presumptions ... the existence of the first appears to be beyond question, but it is somewhat vague and indefinite. It may amount to no more than saying that the opportunities which a wife's confidence in her husband gives him of unfairly or improperly procuring her to become surety for his debts or to confer some other benefit upon him is recognized as a matter of fact and taken into account with other facts as a reason for calling upon him to explain or justify a given transaction.

The second of the three matters is connected with the rule established in the case of relations of influence. That rule is that where there is a relation of influence and the dominant party is the person by or through whom an instrument operating to his advantage is obtained from the other the instrument is voidable even as against strangers who have become parties to the instrument for value if they had notice of the existence of the relation of influence or of the circumstances giving rise to it ...

[678] Although the relation of husband to wife is not one of influence, yet the opportunities it gives are such that if the husband procures his wife to become surety for his debt a creditor who accepts her suretyship obtained through her husband has been treated as taking it subject to any invalidating conduct on the part of her husband even if the creditor be not actually privy to such conduct. It is evident, however, that in many cases, though it is the husband who obtains his wife's consent to act as guarantor or surety, yet the creditor or his agents will deal directly with the wife personally. It must then be a question how far an apparent or real comprehension on the part of the wife or advice or explanation received by her will prevent any earlier improper conduct on the part of the husband from operating to make the transaction voidable ...

[683] [T]he course of development which the rules of equity governing the voidability of instruments of suretyship entered into by married women for debts of their husbands have followed has left the state of the law somewhat indefinite, if not uncertain. To such transactions the same general principles are considered applicable as affect the validity of voluntary alienations of valuable property in favour of the husband, **[684]** but the application of these principles is necessarily qualified by considerations arising out of the position of the creditor as a third party giving value to the husband and possibly bona fide. It is almost needless to say that the equitable grounds for setting aside a voluntary disposition, while well understood, recognize the indefinite variation of form which unconscientious conduct may assume.

The difficulty, if not danger, thus created of attempting to state the conditions which must be fulfilled before a given kind of conduct or of unfairness amounts to an invalidating cause is greatly increased by the introduction of the consideration that the equity must be such as ought to prevail against the claims of the creditor as a possibly innocent third party. But it is clearly necessary to distinguish between, on the one hand, cases in which a wife, alive to the nature and effect of the obligation she is undertaking, is procured to become her husband's surety by the exertion by him upon her of undue influence, affirmatively established, and on the other hand, cases where she does not understand the effect of the document or the nature of the transaction of suretyship. In the former case the fact that the creditor, on the occasion, for example, of the actual execution of the instrument, deals directly with the wife and explains the effect of the document to her will not protect him. Nothing but independent advice or relief from the ascendancy of her husband over her judgment and will would suffice. If the creditor has left it to the husband to obtain his wife's consent to become surety and no more is done independently of the husband than to ascertain that she understands what she is doing, then, if it turns out that she is in fact acting under the undue influence of her husband, it seems that the transaction will be voidable at her instance as against the creditor. It is not clear how far the same principle is to be applied to a case where the wife is induced to become surety by the husband making some fraudulent or even innocent misrepresentation of fact which, though material, does not go to the nature and effect of the instrument or transaction. It may be said that the making of such a representation is no more to be anticipated by a creditor when a husband procures his wife's guarantee than when any other principal debtor procures a surety. On the other hand, the basal reason for binding the creditor with equities arising [685] from the conduct of the husband is that in substance, if not technically, the wife is a volunteer conferring an important advantage upon her husband who in virtue of his position has an opportunity of abusing the confidence she may be expected to place in him and the creditor relies upon the person in that position to obtain her agreement to become his surety. Misrepresentation as well as undue influence is a means of abusing the confidence that may be expected to arise out of the relation.

In the second case, that where the wife agrees to become surety at the instance of her husband though she does not understand the effect of the document or the nature of the transaction, her failure to do so may be the result of the husband's actually misleading her, but in any case it could hardly occur without some impropriety on his part even if that impropriety consisted only in his neglect to inform her of the exact nature of that to which she is willing blindly, ignorantly or mistakenly to assent. But, where the substantial or only ground for impeaching the instrument is misunderstanding or want of understanding of its contents or effect, the amount of reliance placed by the creditor upon the husband for the purpose of informing his wife of what she was about must be of great importance.

If the creditor takes adequate steps to inform her and reasonably supposes that she has an adequate comprehension of the obligations she is undertaking and an understanding of the effect of the transaction, the fact that she has failed to grasp some material part of the document, or, indeed, the significance of what she is doing, cannot, I think, in itself give her an equity to set it aside, notwithstanding that at an earlier stage the creditor relied upon her husband to obtain her consent to enter into the obligation of surety. The creditor may have done enough by superintending himself the execution of the document and by attempting to assure himself by means of questions or explanation that she knows to what she is committing herself. The sufficiency of this must depend on circumstances, as, for example, the ramifications and complexities of the transaction, the amount of deception practised by the husband upon his wife and the intelligence and business understanding of the woman. But, if the wife has been in receipt of the advice of a [686] stranger whom the creditor believes on reasonable grounds to be competent, independent and disinterested, then the circumstances would need to be very exceptional before the creditor could be held bound by any equity which otherwise might arise from the husband's conduct and his wife's actual failure to understand the transaction. If undue influence in the full sense is not made out but the elements of pressure, surprise, misrepresentation or some or one of them combine with or cause a misunderstanding or failure to understand the document or transaction, the final question must be whether the grounds upon which the creditor believed that the document was fairly obtained and executed by a woman sufficiently understanding its purport and effect were such that it would be inequitable to fix the creditor with the consequences of the husband's improper or unfair dealing with his wife.

Apart from the unwisdom or improvidence of the transaction into which he persuaded her, the facts of the present case do not show that Estyn Jones exercised any influence over his wife which could be considered undue or a ground for interference by a court of equity. His enthusiasm for a project or enterprise that it was foolish to embark upon was not shared by his wife, but it is impossible to believe that she did not understand as well as he that, if the purchase was to be made, whatever money was needed must be found by her. The discussion and difference of opinion between them related to the prudence of the venture and the probabilities of its success. When he committed himself or themselves to buy the bungalow and poultry-farm before she had yielded her consent, he may have done so with a view of presenting her with a *fait accompli* which she would not take the responsibility of rejecting. His statement that he had bound himself to get her to finance the purchase and that he would get into trouble if she refused contained no element of falsity. The nature and extent of the trouble into which she thought he would get if she rejected the transaction is not stated by her, and apparently she was faced with the fact that her husband had agreed to buy the property, all parties knowing that she must find the funds which the transaction might call for. [687] In placing his wife in this position, Estyn Jones no doubt did what he ought not to have done. But he created a situation with which his wife had to deal as she thought best in the interests of all concerned. She was not deluded, coerced or overborne. She was placed in a dilemma, a dilemma unfair to a woman, but not in a situation rendering the course she chose to take one from which afterwards she was entitled to be relieved. That which, according to the findings contained in the reasons given by [the trial judge], induced her to agree to the purchase and to take her part by giving a mortgage was her husband's persuasion in which, to his optimism as to the success of the venture and its consequent 'safety', he added the arguments, first, that he had agreed to purchase and was bound, secondly, that he would get into trouble if she refused to give the mortgage, thirdly, that the mortgage was a guarantee not falling due for three years and, fourthly, that if anything went wrong and she lost her house at Walkerville they would have the bungalow and poultry farm at Payneham.

[The Yerkeys] are not shown to have known that [Florence Jones] was definitely opposed to the transaction; they knew that it was not she but Estyn Jones who had the resources enabling them to become purchasers, and in that sense they relied upon him, as the person with whom they negotiated and contracted, to obtain his wife's security. But it was not a case where a husband having incurred a heavy indebtedness is relied upon by a creditor to obtain from his wife a guarantee which will improve the position of the creditor to the detriment of the wife, who will obtain no benefit except the satisfaction of relieving her husband for a time from one of his embarrassments.

It was a transaction in which on the one hand [the Yerkeys] were stating the terms on which they would sell their property and on the other Estyn Jones was negotiating for the acquisition of a home for himself and his wife and a new means of livelihood.

The difference might not be enough if Estyn Jones had obtained his wife's consent by undue influence or fraud. But, for the reasons I have given, the case appears to me to come down to the effect of a combination of matters, consisting in the inducements stated, [Florence Jones'] understanding of the transaction when she attended **[688]** for the purpose of executing the instrument of mortgage, the actual provisions it contained, the explanation she received and her final comprehension of the matter.

She went to the solicitors' office ... believing that she was to give a mortgage over her house at Walkerville for £1,000, forming part of the purchase money falling due in three years, and that the mortgage would operate as a guarantee, so that the burden would fall on her house if her husband then failed to find the £1,000.

The solicitors were instructed by [the Yerkeys] and acted solely on their behalf and in their interests. [The Yerkeys] in the course of their evidence said that they did not regard them as their solicitors any more than [the Jones'], and that this was made clear to Estyn Jones. [Florence Jones], however, did not say that she relied upon the solicitors as protecting her interests or acting on her behalf or that of her husband, and Estyn Jones gave no evidence to the effect that he considered the solicitors as in any way acting for him or his wife. I do not think that [Florence Jones] can be regarded as having signed the mortgage in reliance upon the advice or approval of the solicitors and as having mistakenly supposed that they were acting on behalf of herself or her husband. I do not think that such a case was made by her, and the suggestion arose only out of answers given in the cross-examination of [the Yerkeys] ...

[689] [Estyn Jones'] explanation of the mortgage appears to me to have been simple enough and complete enough to ensure that any woman of average intelligence would understand that she was making herself liable for interest on the £1,000 and that, if it was not paid, the principal might be called up and that she bound herself to pay it so that she might be sued and her property sold. As to the effect of the clauses directed to the exclusion of the principles of law by which a surety may be discharged from his obligations though the debt is not paid, probably the explanation was incomplete, and, if complete, it doubtless would have failed to produce any impression except a confused idea that some possibility of the mortgagee escaping was excluded. But, if the general nature and effect of an instrument such as a mortgage executed by a married woman is understood or on reasonable grounds the creditor or other party or his agents believes it to have been understood, it is no ground for setting it aside that some of its details or its possible consequences or applications are not comprehended, notwithstanding that the husband is the person who has obtained her consent to the transaction. This observation applies to the suggestion that, even though the £1,000 was paid under the mortgage, the contract might be cancelled for default in the rest of the purchase money and the payment applied to answer damages.

If [Florence Jones] grasped the points I have mentioned, I do not think that the provisions of the instrument involved a departure from the nature of the transaction, as she would understand it, sufficient to warrant a court of equity setting it aside. How far she did in fact understand her personal responsibility and the effect of default in interest in causing principal to become immediately payable is a question of fact upon which [the trial judge] took a view in her favour. But in my opinion the solicitor had no reason to suppose that she did not grasp the essentials of the transaction and on reasonable grounds [the Yerkeys] and their solicitor believed **[690]** that she had understood the substantial effect in all material respects, of the obligations she was undertaking. In my opinion [Florence Jones] failed to make out a case which under the principles I have discussed entitled her to equitable relief.

Comments

1. See Radan & Stewart at **10.53–10.70**.
2. For an analysis of this case, and later cases that have applied it, see B Collier, 'The Rule in Yerkey v Jones: Fundamental Principles and Fundamental Problems' (1996) 4 *Australian Property Law Journal* 1.

10.5   Garcia v National Australia Bank Ltd (1998) 194 CLR 395

Court: High Court of Australia

Facts: Jean and Fabio Garcia were a married couple and directors of a gold trading company, Citizens Gold Bullion Exchange Pty Ltd, which Fabio ran. Jean conducted her own physiotherapy practice. In 1979 they executed a mortgage over their matrimonial home in favour of the National Australia Bank (NAB) that secured all moneys they might owe to the bank, including sums owing under any future guarantees. Between 1985 and 1987 Jean signed four guarantees in favour of NAB, three of which guaranteed repayment to the bank of debts owed by Citizens Gold. After their marriage was dissolved in January 1990, the Family Court ordered that, subject to the NAB mortgage, Fabio was to transfer his interest in their home to Jean. Citizens Gold was later wound up. In June 1990, Jean sought declarations that the mortgage and the guarantees in respect of the Citizens Gold debts were void. She claimed that Fabio had misrepresented to her the nature and extent of the 1987 guarantee. Although she knew what she was signing, she had done so in the belief that the loan was limited to $270,000 and would be secured by the gold bullion, rather than the home.

The trial judge in the Supreme Court found that Jean had signed the guarantee on her husband's insistence and that she had done so with no advice. On the basis of the principles in *Yerkey v Jones*, the Supreme Court held that Jean was a volunteer because she had obtained no benefit under the transactions. As a result, she was not bound by any of the guarantees she had signed and owed no money to NAB under the mortgage in respect of her interest in the home before the making of the Family Court order. The Court of Appeal reversed the decision, deciding *Yerkey v Jones* no longer applied in New South Wales because it made outmoded assumptions about the position of married women. Jean appealed to the High Court.

Issue: The issue before the High Court was whether the Court of Appeal had erred in rejecting the principles in *Yerkey v Jones* as no longer applicable law.

Decision: The High Court (Gaudron, McHugh, Gummow, Kirby, Hayne and Callinan JJ) unanimously held in favour of Jean. With the exception of Kirby J, all of their Honours did so upon the basis that the principles in *Yerkey v Jones* represented good law in Australia. Accordingly, the guarantees were set aside as unconscionable transactions as they affected Jean.

Extracts: The extracts from the joint majority judgment of Gaudron, McHugh, Gummow and Hayne JJ support the view, derived from *Yerkey v Jones*, that a creditor with knowledge that the debtor has the benefit of a guarantee provided by his wife is deemed to have notice of undue influence. The separate judgment of Kirby J is extracted in so far as it reflects his view that this is not restricted to husband and wife situations, but to any relationship in which the creditor has notice that the guarantor manifests an emotional dependency on the debtor.

Gaudron, McHugh, Gummow and Hayne JJ

[403] The Court of Appeal held that it was not bound to follow *Yerkey v Jones*.[8] Sheller JA [in the Court of Appeal] concluded that what had been said to be the principle in *Yerkey v Jones* is 'a principle to which [Dixon J] only adhered' …

He [agreed with]:

> … doubts about a principle founded on the assumption that a married woman is ipso facto under a special disadvantage in any transaction involving her husband and that the husband is in this context the stronger party.[9]

Accordingly, Sheller JA concluded that 'the so-called principle in *Yerkey v Jones* should no longer be applied in New South Wales'.[10]

We consider the better view to be that the reasons for decision of Dixon J in *Yerkey v Jones* were not significantly different from the reasons of the other members of the Court …

[W]e consider that the principles spoken of by Dixon J in *Yerkey v Jones* are simply particular applications of accepted equitable principles which have as much application today as they did then.

Yerkey v Jones was said, in argument, to reflect outdated views of society generally and the role of women in society in particular. It was submitted that changes in Australian society since 1939, when *Yerkey v Jones* was decided, require that equitable rules move to meet these changed circumstances.

That Australian society, and particularly the role of women in that society, has changed in the last six decades is undoubted. But some things are unchanged. There is still a significant number of women in Australia in relationships which are, for many and varied reasons, marked by disparities of economic and other power between the [404] parties. However, the rationale of *Yerkey v Jones* is not to be found in notions based on the subservience or inferior economic position of women. Nor is it based on their vulnerability to exploitation because of their emotional involvement,[11] save to the extent that the case was concerned with actual undue influence.

So far as *Yerkey v Jones* proceeded on the basis of the earlier decision of Cussen J in *Bank of Victoria Ltd v Mueller*,[12] it is based on trust and confidence, in the ordinary sense of

---

8. (1939) 63 CLR 649.
9. *National Australia Bank Ltd v Garcia* (1996) 39 NSWLR 577 at 593.
10. *National Australia Bank Ltd v Garcia* (1996) 39 NSWLR 577 at 598.
11. *Barclays Bank plc v O'Brien* [1994] 1 AC 180 at 198; cf *Wilkinson v ASB Bank Ltd* [1998] 1 NZLR 674 at 689.
12. [1925] VLR 642.

those words, between marriage partners. The marriage relationship is such that one, often the woman, may well leave many, perhaps all, business judgments to the other spouse. In that kind of relationship, business decisions may be made with little consultation between the parties and with only the most abbreviated explanation of their purport or effect. Sometimes, with not the slightest hint of bad faith, the explanation of a particular transaction given by one to the other will be imperfect and incomplete, if not simply wrong ...

It may be that the principles applied in *Yerkey v Jones* will find application to other relationships more common now than was the case in 1939 — to long term and publicly declared relationships short of marriage between members of the same or of opposite sex — but that is not a question that falls for decision in this case. It may be that those principles will find application where the husband acts as surety for the wife but again that is not a problem that falls for decision here. This case concerns a husband and wife and it is to that relationship that the present decision relates, just as it is concerned only with the circumstance of the wife acting as surety for her husband. The resolution of questions arising in the context of other relationships may well require consideration of other issues ...

In his reasons for decision in *Yerkey v Jones*, Dixon J dealt with at least two kinds of circumstances: the first in which there is actual undue influence by a husband over a wife and the second, that dealt with in *Mueller*, in which there is no undue influence but there is a failure to explain adequately and accurately the suretyship transaction which the husband seeks to have the wife enter for the immediate economic benefit not of the wife but of the husband, or the **[405]** circumstances in which her liability may arise. The former kind of case is one concerning what today is seen as an imbalance of power. In point of legal principle, however, it is actual undue influence in that the wife, lacking economic or other power, is overborne by her husband and goes surety for her husband's debts when she does not bring a free mind and will to that decision. The latter case is not so much concerned with imbalances of power as with lack of proper information about the purport and effect of the transaction. The present appeal concerns circumstances of the latter kind rather than the former ...

[406] Dixon J was dealing with two kinds of case. In the former, the case of actual undue influence, as Dixon J says, explaining the effect of the document to the surety will not protect the creditor and '[n]othing but independent advice or relief from the ascendancy of her **[407]** husband over her judgment and will would suffice'. In the latter, '[i]f the creditor takes adequate steps to inform [the wife] and reasonably supposes that she has an adequate comprehension of the obligations she is undertaking and an understanding of the effect of the transaction, the fact that she has failed to grasp some material part of the document, or, indeed, the significance of what she is doing' cannot give her an equity to set the instrument aside.

The term 'unconscionable' does not appear in any of the judgments in *Yerkey v Jones* ...

In *Amadio*, Mason J said:

Historically, courts have exercised jurisdiction to set aside contracts and other dealings on a variety of equitable grounds. They include fraud, misrepresentation, breach of fiduciary duty, undue influence and unconscionable conduct. In one sense they all constitute species of unconscionable conduct on the part of a party who stands to receive a benefit under a transaction which, in the eye of equity, cannot be enforced because to do so would be inconsistent with equity and good conscience. But relief on the ground of 'unconscionable conduct' is usually taken to refer to the class of case in which a party makes unconscientious use of his superior position or bargaining power to the detriment of a party who suffers from some special disability or is placed in some special situation of disadvantage ... Although unconscionable conduct in this narrow sense bears some resemblance to the doctrine of undue influence, there is a difference between the two. In the latter the will of the innocent party is not independent and voluntary because it is overborne. In the former the will of the innocent party, even if independent and voluntary, is the result of the disadvantageous position in which he is placed and of the other party unconscientiously taking advantage of that position.[13]

It was submitted that *Yerkey v Jones* has been overruled by *Amadio* **[408]** or that the principles applied in *Yerkey v Jones* had been subsumed in principles applied in *Amadio*.

There are several answers to this contention. First, there is nothing in *Amadio* that suggests that it was intended to overrule *Yerkey v Jones* or to subsume the rules applied there in some broader principle enunciated in *Amadio*.

Secondly, far from anything said in *Amadio* suggesting that it was intended to mark out the boundaries of the whole field of unconscionable conduct, as Mason J said:

It goes almost without saying that it is impossible to describe definitively all the situations in which relief will be granted on the ground of unconscionable conduct.[14]

Thirdly, *Amadio* was a case of unconscionable conduct very different from the cases considered in *Yerkey v Jones*. In *Amadio* there was actual misconduct on the part of the son of the respondents which affected their entry into the mortgage and guarantee and the bank was on notice of that misconduct. There was no allegation of undue influence by the son with notice on the part of the bank (a situation corresponding to that in *Bank of New South Wales v Rogers*[15]), nor was the alleged case of undue influence on the part of the bank made out. What Mason J identified as '[t]he critical issue' was whether the plaintiffs were entitled to relief on the ground of unconscionable conduct. The transaction was not enforced against the respondents because it would have been unconscionable for the bank to do so. And it was unconscionable for the bank to enforce it because the bank's employee had shut his eyes to the vulnerability of the respondents and the misconduct of their son.

The principles applied in *Yerkey v Jones* do not depend upon the creditor having, at the time the guarantee is taken, notice of some unconscionable dealing between the husband as borrower and the wife as surety. *Yerkey v Jones* begins with the recognition that the surety is a volunteer: a person who obtained no financial benefit from the transaction, performance of the obligations of which she agreed to guarantee. It holds, in what we have called the first kind of case, that to enforce that voluntary transaction against her when in fact she did not bring a free will to its execution would be unconscionable. It holds further, in the second kind of case, that to enforce it against her if it later emerges that she did not understand the purport and effect of the transaction of suretyship would

---

13. *Commercial Bank of Australia Ltd v Amadio* (1983) 151 CLR 447 at 461, 474.
14. *Commercial Bank of Australia Ltd v Amadio* (1983) 151 CLR 447 at 461.
15. (1941) 65 CLR 42.

be unconscionable (even though she is a willing party to it) if the lender took no steps itself to explain its purport and effect to her or did not reasonably believe that its purport [409] and effect had been explained to her by a competent, independent and disinterested stranger. And what makes it unconscionable to enforce it in the second kind of case is the combination of circumstances that: (a) in fact the surety did not understand the purport and effect of the transaction; (b) the transaction was voluntary (in the sense that the surety obtained no gain from the contract the performance of which was guaranteed); (c) the lender is to be taken to have understood that, as a wife, the surety may repose trust and confidence in her husband in matters of business and therefore to have understood that the husband may not fully and accurately explain the purport and effect of the transaction to his wife; and yet (d) the lender did not itself take steps to explain the transaction to the wife or find out that a stranger had explained it to her.

To hold, as *Yerkey v Jones* did, that in those circumstances the enforcement of the guarantee would be unconscionable represents no departure from accepted principle. Rather, it:

> ... conforms to the fundamental principle according to which equity acts, namely that a party having a legal right shall not be permitted to exercise it in such a way that the exercise amounts to unconscionable conduct.[16]

It will be seen that the analysis of the second kind of case identified in *Yerkey v Jones* is not one which depends upon any presumption of undue influence by the husband over the wife. As we have said, undue influence is dealt with separately and differently. Nor does the analysis depend upon identifying the husband as acting as agent for the creditor in procuring the wife's agreement to the transaction. Rather, it depends upon the surety being a volunteer and mistaken about the purport and effect of the transaction, and the creditor being taken to have appreciated that because of the trust and confidence between surety and debtor the surety may well receive from the debtor no sufficient explanation of the transaction's purport and effect. To enforce the transaction against a mistaken volunteer when the creditor, the party that seeks to take the benefit of the transaction, has not itself explained the transaction, and does not know that a third party has done so, would be unconscionable ...

[410] [S]ome comparison can be drawn between the refusal to permit enforcement of the guarantee in the circumstances identified in *Yerkey v Jones* and the equally well recognised and long established principles which would preclude enforcement of a guarantee in some cases where the creditor has not disclosed to the intending surety some features of the transaction.[17]

We do not pause to attempt to specify what features of such a transaction should be identified by the creditor to the surety and we are not to be taken as suggesting that the principles dealt with in *Yerkey v Jones* are to be seen as no more than some particular application of these rules. Nevertheless, the intervention of equity in cases of that kind

---

16. *Legione v Hateley* (1983) 152 CLR 406 at 444.
17. *Commercial Bank of Australia Ltd v Amadio* (1983) 151 CLR 447 at 454–5; *Union Bank of Australia Ltd v Puddy* [1949] VLR 242; *Hamilton v Watson* (1845) 8 ER 1339; *Lee v Jones* (1864) 144 ER 194; *London General Omnibus Co Ltd v Holloway* [1912] 2 KB 72. See also *Behan v Obelon Pty Ltd* (1985) 157 CLR 326 at 329–30.

may also be seen as rooted in the conclusion that to permit enforcement of the guarantee against a mistaken surety (mistaken in that kind of case because the creditor should have, but did not, inform the surety of some particular fact) would be unconscionable.

No doubt these cases are no more than analogies. They are not to be treated as defining what is meant by 'unconscionable' or as, in some way, governing the present circumstances. They are, however, useful illustrations of why the enforcement of the guarantee in this case would be unconscionable.

As is implicit in what we have said, we prefer not to adopt the analysis made by Lord Browne-Wilkinson in *Barclays Bank Plc v* [411] *O'Brien* which proceeded from identifying 'the circumstances in which the creditor will be taken to have had notice of the wife's equity to set aside the transaction'.[18] Sir Anthony Mason has pointed out that 'constructive notice in *O'Brien* is used in order to ascertain whether a transaction about to be entered into is impeachable, not so as to fix a person who acquires an interest in the property with knowledge of an antecedent interest in property, that being the traditional function of constructive notice'.[19] Such an analysis may be required in ordering the priority of competing interests in property but in the present context it may well distract attention from the underlying principle: that the enforcement of the legal rights of the creditor would, in all the circumstances, be unconscionable.

We consider that the only question of notice that arises is whether the creditor knew at the time of the taking of the guarantee that the surety was then married to the creditor. Other questions of notice do not intrude.

As is apparent from what was said in *Yerkey v Jones* the creditor may readily avoid the possibility that the surety will later claim not to have understood the purport and effect of the transaction that is proposed. If the creditor itself explains the transaction sufficiently, or knows that the surety has received 'competent, independent and disinterested'[20] advice from a third party, it would not be unconscionable for the creditor to enforce it against the surety even though the surety is a volunteer and it later emerges that the surety claims to have been mistaken.

What then of the present case? The trial judge found that [Jean Garcia] did not understand the purport or effect of the transaction. She knew it was a guarantee but she thought it was a guarantee of limited overdraft accommodation to be applied only in the purchase of gold. Nor did she understand that her obligations under the guarantee were secured by the mortgage which she had given over her home. It being found that the bank took no step to explain the transaction to her and knew of no independent advice to her about it (there having been no such independent advice) the conclusion that [Jean Garcia] was entitled to succeed in her claim to set the transaction aside was inevitable if she was a volunteer.

The trial judge found that [Jean Garcia] was not 'directly involved' in Citizens Gold ... [412] Although [he] found that from time to time some benefit flowed to the family from the companies, he found that they were companies that were in the 'complete control' of [Fabio Garcia]. Taken as a whole, those findings demonstrate that [Jean Garcia] in

---

18. *Barclays Bank plc v O'Brien* [1994] 1 AC 180 at 195.
19. Sir Anthony Mason, 'The Impact of Equitable Doctrine on the Law of Contract' (1998) 27 *Anglo-American Law Review* 1 at 15.
20. *Yerkey v Jones* (1939) 63 CLR 649 at 686.

fact obtained no real benefit from her entering the transaction; she was a volunteer. The fact that she was a director of the company is nothing to the point if, as the trial judge's findings show, she had no financial interest in the fortunes of the company.

Kirby J

[413] The issues arising are ... :

1. Does the principle stated by Dixon J in *Yerkey* express a special rule of equity applicable to a case where a wife gives a guarantee of a debt for the benefit of her husband (or entities controlled by him) and where the wife's agreement to give the guarantee was obtained by undue influence, pressure or misrepresentation on the part of the husband or without an adequate understanding of the nature and effect of the transaction? Does that principle represent the holding of this Court or simply an opinion of Dixon J, never specifically endorsed by the Court as a binding rule? (The *Yerkey v Jones* point).
2. Whatever the status of the opinion of Dixon J in *Yerkey*, should any rule which *Yerkey* may have stated in 1939 now be regarded as obsolete and subsumed in the principles expressed in later decisions [414] such as *Amadio*? Should this be done having regard to changes in society affecting married women, their legal status, the expansion of the availability of financial credit to them and the desirability of avoiding reliance upon discriminatory criteria for the provision of equitable relief and the development of equitable doctrine? (The *Commercial Bank of Australia Ltd v Amadio* point).
3. If the equitable principle expressed by Dixon J in *Yerkey* is revealed as his individual opinion, is overruled as obsolete or now treated as absorbed in the broader doctrines of equity, does the exposition of such doctrine in *Amadio* sufficiently meet the particular problem of sureties who are emotionally vulnerable or dependent on the debtor? Or is a broader statement of equitable principle required than that expressed in *Amadio*? In particular, should this Court follow the decision of the House of Lords in *Barclays Bank Plc v O'Brien*[21] or some modified version of the principles there stated? (The *Barclays Bank Plc v O'Brien* point) ...

[419] As Sheller JA demonstrated in the Court of Appeal,[22] ... none of the other Justices constituting this Court in *Yerkey* expressly agreed in the opinion of Dixon J. Nor did they do so by implication in reasons suggesting the adoption of the same legal analysis.[23] ...

[420] Upon [proper] analysis, the opinion of Dixon J in *Yerkey* is neither expressly nor [421] impliedly a statement of a holding of this Court. Should it nonetheless, in light of its provenance, apparent durability and suggested continuing applicability now be accepted by the Court, as the majority think? In my opinion, it should not. ...

[430] I favour a re-formulation of the principle expressed by Lord Browne-Wilkinson in *O'Brien*. It is my view that the principle should be stated thus: Where a person has entered into an obligation to stand [431] as surety for the debts of another and the credit provider knows, or ought to know, that there is a relationship involving emotional

---

21. [1994] 1 AC 180.
22. *National Australia Bank Ltd v Garcia* (1996) 39 NSWLR 577 at 598.
23. Cf Fehlberg, 'Women in "Family" Companies: English and Australian Experiences' (1997) 15 *Company and Securities Law Journal* 348 at 355.

dependence on the part of the surety towards the debtor:[24] (1) the surety obligation will be valid and enforceable by the credit provider unless the suretyship was procured by the undue influence, misrepresentation or other legal wrong of the principal debtor; (2) if there has been undue influence, misrepresentation or other legal wrong by the principal debtor, unless the credit provider has taken reasonable steps to satisfy itself that the surety entered into the obligation freely and in knowledge of the true facts, the credit provider will be unable to enforce the surety obligation because it will be fixed with notice of the surety's right to set aside the transaction; (3) unless there are special exceptional circumstances or the risks are large, a credit provider will have taken such reasonable steps to avoid being fixed with constructive notice if it warns the surety (at a meeting not attended by the principal debtor) of the amount of the surety's potential liability, of the risks involved to the surety's own interests and advises the surety to take independent legal advice. Out of respect for economic freedom, the duty of the credit provider will be limited to taking reasonable steps only.[25]

In this way, equity is capable of affording a principle for relief in cases of this kind which (1) is expressed in non-discriminatory terms; (2) is addressed to the real causes of the vulnerability; and (3) recognises the credit provider's superior powers to insist that volunteers in a vulnerable position are afforded access to relevant information and, where necessary, independent advice. The House of Lords concluded in this general way in *O'Brien*. This Court should follow and adopt that decision. It is applicable to the circumstances of this case. The Court can properly do so without procedural unfairness to the Bank. The point was reserved and argued below. It was also debated at some length on the hearing of this appeal. No different evidentiary foundation is suggested by the wife. She merely sought the application of the applicable equitable principles to the facts as found by the primary judge ...

[434] When I turn to apply the principle in *O'Brien*, modified in the way that I have re-expressed it, I consider that (although for reasons different than he expressed), the orders of the primary judge were correct. The Bank knew, or could readily have discovered, that [435] Mrs Garcia reposed trust and confidence in her husband in relation to her financial affairs. Mrs Garcia was thus in a position of potential vulnerability to demands that she should act as a surety, even if the Bank had no reasonable means of knowing the details of the particular stresses of her personal relationship. Breakdown of personal relationships is sufficiently common in Australia to have alerted a credit provider, such as the Bank, to the potentiality of this surety's vulnerability. This is particularly so where (as here) a domestic home in which the borrower lived was put at risk by the surety arrangements. The Bank could readily, without unduly intrusive questions, have discovered the nature of the parties' relationship. It was already aware that they were cohabitees. Formalities and public declaration of their relationship (assuming the latter to be possible and appropriate) would not be necessary. Sufficient that basic questioning disclosed a transaction on its face of little or no specific advantage to the proposed surety and that such party stood at high risk in relation to the roof over her head.

---

24. In *Wilkinson v ASB Bank Ltd* [1998] 1 NZLR 674 at 691, the New Zealand Court of Appeal expressed the relationship as 'involving an emotional tie or dependency on the part of the guarantor towards the principal debtor'.

25. Price, 'Undue Influence: Nullus Finis Litium' (1998) 114 *Law Quarterly Review* 186 at 187–8.

Misrepresentation by Mr Garcia to his wife being established, together with constructive notice of the potential vulnerability of the wife, the Bank is unable to enforce the surety obligation against her because it is fixed with constructive notice of her right to set aside the transaction having regard to its failure to take reasonable steps to satisfy itself that she entered the obligation freely and with knowledge of the relevant facts. It is here that the principal weakness in the Bank's case is obvious. As the primary judge found, in this case the Bank's ordinary procedures were not followed. Mrs Garcia was given no advice or explanation of the documents which she was signing. Still less was she told to seek independent advice or that such evidence would be a pre-condition to the Bank's acceptance of her guarantee. The fact that she was a director of the company and that she presented as an 'intelligent articulate lady' in a professional position is certainly relevant. But it is not ultimately determinative. To the knowledge of the Bank, the home in which she lived was being placed in jeopardy. The Bank failed to insist that she was made fully aware of that risk. In such circumstances, there being no exceptional reasons to hold otherwise, the Bank was unable to enforce the surety obligation. Although the case is not clear cut and some of the evidence supported the Bank's arguments, I have concluded that the primary judge was right to hold as he did. Banks and other credit providers can protect themselves from this result. Most already do so.

The result to which I have come flows not from the fact that Mrs Garcia was a married woman in need of special protection, as such, from the law of equity. It flows from a broader doctrine by which equity protects the vulnerable parties in a relationship and ensures that in proper cases they have full information and, where necessary, independent advice before they volunteer to put at risk the major asset of their relationship for the primary advantage of those to whose pressure they may be specially vulnerable.

Comments
1. See Radan & Stewart at **10.58–10.65**.
2. For discussions of this case see E Stone, 'The Distinctiveness of *Garcia*' (2006) 22 *Journal of Contract Law* 170 and M Brown, 'The Bank, the Wife and the Husband's Solicitor' (2007) 14 *Australian Property Law Journal* 147.

11

UNCONSCIONABLE TRANSACTIONS

Introduction

11.1 This chapter deals with the principles pursuant to which a transaction is characterised as being unconscionable in equity. Such situations arise where one party to the transaction is found to have made an unconscientious use of his or her superior position or bargaining power to the detriment of the other party who suffers from some special disadvantage or disability. The circumstances in which unconscionable transactions arise are varied and cannot be definitively described. These principles have also been given statutory force, especially by the *Trade Practices Act 1974* (Cth).

The cases extracted in this chapter discuss the following:

- disadvantage due to intoxication and mental and physical weakness: *Blomley v Ryan* (1956) 99 CLR 362;
- disadvantage due to business inexperience and lack of understanding of English: *Commercial Bank of Australia Ltd v Amadio* (1983) 151 CLR 447;
- disadvantage due to romantic infatuation: *Louth v Diprose* (1992) 174 CLR 621;
- unconscionability and business regulation under s 51AA of the *Trade Practices Act 1974* (Cth): *Australian Consumer & Competition Commission v C G Berbatis Holdings Pty Ltd* (2003) 214 CLR 51; and
- the relationship between unconscionable transactions and undue influence: *Bridgewater v Leahy* (1998) 194 CLR 457.

Intoxication and mental and physical weakness

11.2   Blomley v Ryan (1956) 99 CLR 362

Court: High Court of Australia

Facts: Ryan was an elderly resident of New South Wales who was the owner of a grazing property near Goondiwindi known as Worrah. He had a pronounced alcohol dependency and participated in frequent bouts of drinking that often lasted for days at a time. Blomley was a Queenslander interested in purchasing Worrah. He, together with his agent and others, made numerous attempts in discussions with Ryan to convince him to sell Worrah for a total price of £25,000. Blomley's solicitor drafted a contract to that effect, which also provided for a £5 deposit and annual instalment payments over several years. After it was signed by the parties, Ryan refused to complete. When Blomley sought an order for specific performance, Ryan counter-claimed to have the contract set aside. He alleged that the purchase price was well below market value, the terms were extremely favourable to Blomley and that he had been rushed into the sale. He also claimed that Blomley was aware Ryan was, at the time the contract was formed, 'old, lacking in education, suffering from the effects of intoxication, mentally and physically weak, without proper advice, unable properly to protect himself and on unequal terms with [Blomley]'.

Issue: The issue before the High Court was whether the contract should be rescinded on the basis that the contract was an unconscionable bargain or whether Blomley was entitled to have it specifically enforced.

Decision: In a majority decision the High Court (McTiernan and Fullagar JJ; Kitto J dissenting) held that the contract should be rescinded on the basis that the contract was an unconscionable bargain.

Extracts: The extracts from the judgment of Fullagar J focus on the indicia of fraud as understood by equity and the circumstances in which transactions may be set aside on the ground that they are unconscionable bargains.

Fullagar J

[401] [This] case is not one of that comparatively rare class where a man's faculties, whether from age or natural infirmity or drink or any other cause, are so defective that he does not really know what he is doing — that his mind does not go with his deed. In such a case his instrument is void even at law — *non est factum* ... It is a case, I think, in which relief could be obtained by [Ryan], if at all, only in equity. And, when we look for the principle on which equity did grant relief in such cases, we find as so often in equity, only very wide general expressions to guide us. There was, I think, a typical difference in approach between equity and the common law. To the common law the transaction in question might be void or voidable, but the primary question was as to the reality of the assent of the person resisting enforcement of the contract. Equity traditionally looked at the matter rather from the point of view of the party seeking to enforce the contract [402] and was minded to inquire whether, having regard to all the circumstances, it was consistent with equity and good conscience that he should be allowed to enforce it ...

[404] The real effect of the cases on the subject was, I think, stated by Sir *William Grant* MR in *Cooke v Clayworth* ... The Master of the Rolls said:

I think a Court of Equity ought not to give its assistance to a person who has obtained an agreement, or deed, from another in a state of intoxication; and on the other hand ought not to assist a person to get rid of any agreement, or deed, merely upon the ground of his having been intoxicated at the time: *Dunnage v White*.[1] I say merely upon that ground; as, if there was, as Lord *Hardwicke* expresses it in *Cory v Cory*,[2] any unfair

1.   (1818) 36 ER 329.
2.   (1747) 27 ER 864.

advantage made of his situation, or as Sir *Joseph Jekyll* says in *Johnson v Medlicott*,[3] any contrivance or management to draw him in to drink, he might be a proper object of relief in a Court of Equity. As to that extreme state of intoxication, that deprives a man of his reason, I apprehend, that even at Law it would invalidate a deed, obtained from him while in that condition.[4]

This statement of equitable principle was referred to and acted upon in ... *Wiltshire v Marshall*. In the first of these cases specific performance was decreed. In the second a bill to set aside was dismissed. [This] is the only reported case I have succeeded in finding in which a transaction has actually been set aside by a court of equity on the ground that one party was intoxicated but not so far intoxicated as to make his deed void even at law. Sir *William Page Wood* VC put the principle on which he acted in this way. He said:

> And now, having shortly considered what is the state of the law upon this subject, the first thing I have to do is ... to determine ... whether it was so entered into as to display absence of judgment in the person making it, and a degree of unfairness in the person accepting it.[5]

The authorities which I have cited show, I think, that, when a court of equity is asked to refuse specific performance of, or to set aside, a contract at the instance of a party who says that he was drunk at the time of making it, the principles applied do not differ in substance from those applied in such cases as *Clark v Malpas*;[6] **[405]** *Fry v Lane*,[7] and the other cases cited by [the trial judge]. But they show also that cases in which an allegation of intoxication is a main feature are approached with great caution by courts of equity. This is, I think, not so much because intoxication is a self-induced state and a reprehensible thing, but rather because it would be dangerous to lend any countenance to the view that a man could escape the obligation of a contract by simply proving that he was 'in liquor' when it was made. So we find it said again and again that *mere* drunkenness affords no ground for resisting a suit to enforce a contract. Where, however, there is real ground for thinking that the judgment of one party was, to the knowledge of the other, seriously affected by drink, equity will generally refuse specific performance at the suit of that other, leaving him to pursue a remedy at law if he so desires. And, where the court is satisfied that a contract disadvantageous to the party affected has been obtained by 'drawing him in to drink', or that there has been real unfairness in taking advantage of his condition, the contract may be set aside.

One other general observation may be made before proceeding to the facts of the present case. The circumstances adversely affecting a party, which may induce a court of equity either to refuse its aid or to set a transaction aside, are of great variety and can hardly be satisfactorily classified. Among them are poverty or need of any kind, sickness, age, sex, infirmity of body or mind, drunkenness, illiteracy or lack of education, lack of assistance or explanation where assistance or explanation is necessary. The common characteristic

---

3. (1731) 24 ER at 998.
4. *Cooke v Clayworth* (1811) 34 ER 222 at 223.
5. *Wiltshire v Marshall* (1866) 14 LT (NS) 396 at 397.
6. (1862) 54 ER 1067; 45 ER 1238.
7. (1888) 40 Ch D 312.

seems to be that they have the effect of placing one party at a serious disadvantage *vis-à-vis* the other. It does not appear to be essential in all cases that the party at a disadvantage should suffer loss or detriment by the bargain. In *Cooke v Clayworth*, in which specific performance was refused, it does not appear that there was anything actually unfair in the terms of the transaction itself. But inadequacy of consideration, while never of itself a ground for resisting enforcement, will often be a specially important element in cases of this type. It may be important in either or both of two ways — firstly as supporting the inference that a position of disadvantage existed, and secondly as tending to show that an unfair use was made of the occasion. Where, as here, intoxication is the main element relied upon as creating the position of disadvantage, the question of adequacy or inadequacy of consideration is, I think, likely to be a matter of major, and perhaps decisive, importance. It will almost always, **[406]** I think, be:

> ... an important ingredient in considering whether a person did exercise any degree of judgment in making a contract, or whether there is a degree of unfairness in accepting the contract.[8] ...

[T]he wide discrepancy between price and value is not the only interesting feature of this transaction. There are two others. In the first place, the deposit on a contract of sale for £25,000 was £5. In the second place, the sale was on terms, which provided for payment of the price over a period of more than four years, and the rate of interest on unpaid purchase money was four per cent. The bank rate of interest current at the time was five per cent. It may be said that the deposit was a matter of small practical importance, but the only thing that can save it from being justly **[407]** described as ridiculous is the fact that a purchaser at so very low a price would be likely to move heaven and earth rather than default. It is obviously an additional abnormal element in the transaction itself, as is also, of course, the low rate of interest payable under the contract. The rate of interest was an important matter, because [Ryan] was proposing to 'retire', and presumably to live on the interest of his capital.

The learned trial judge found the explanation of this remarkable transaction in the facts that [Ryan] was an old man, whose health and faculties had been impaired by habitual drinking to excess over a long period, who was at the material time in the middle of a prolonged bout of heavy drinking of rum, and who was utterly incapable of forming a rational judgment about the terms of any business transaction. Having carefully read and considered the evidence, I agree with this view. His Honour also held that [Ryan's] condition must have been patent to [Blomley's] father, who acted as [his] agent, and to Stemm, who acted (ostensibly) as [Ryan's] agent, and that these persons took such an unfair advantage of that condition that a court of equity could not allow the contract to stand. I agree with this view also ...

[Blomley] himself, who is a young man, took little or no part in the proceedings at any stage: the negotiations were conducted by his father. Stemm, an employee of Dalgety & Co Ltd, acted as 'agent' for the sale of the property. Ostensibly he was acting in that capacity for [Ryan], to whom his firm would look for their commission. But it is obvious that he was, so to speak, 'in [Blomley's] camp' throughout: his concern was simply to procure a sale, and nothing seems to have been further from his mind than the idea that

---

8. *Wiltshire v Marshall* (1866) 14 LT 396 at 397.

it was his duty to obtain the best price he could for [Ryan], and generally to look after [Ryan's] interests ...

[409] His Honour expressed his general finding by saying that [Ryan's] condition was such that:

> ... he was incapable of considering the question of the sale of his property with any real degree of intelligent appreciation of the matters involved.[9]

More specifically he said that he had:

> ... no doubt that [Ryan's] drinking bout on this occasion extended from some little time before Saturday, 18th April until, at least, towards the end of the following week and that there were many occasions during this period when he was quite incapable ... of transacting the simplest forms of business.[10]

I take his Honour to have thought that on these 'occasions' any instrument signed by [Ryan] must have been held to be void even at law, and that throughout the period he was incapable of making an intelligent decision or forming a rationally considered judgment on a matter of business. During the night of the 20th to 21st he became again, as his Honour found, 'grossly intoxicated',[11] and early on the 21st he was 'barely sensible of what was going on around him',[12] though his condition 'may have improved a little'[13] during the drive (about forty miles) to Goondiwindi ...

[411] It was argued that [Ryan] had by conduct affirmed the contract after regaining a normal state of mind. It has been said that, in cases of this type, equity will not relieve unless there has been a prompt repudiation after a cessation of any vitiating circumstances. [Ryan] did not repudiate the contract until 22nd July. In the meantime he had bought another property, in which he proposed to reside, and he had allowed certain stock to be placed on 'Worrah' by [Blomley] or his father. But [the solicitor] had not supplied him with a copy of the contract, and I do not think, on the evidence, that he had any real understanding of the position until early in July, when he obtained a copy of the document ... [and] consulted a firm of solicitors at Moree. After obtaining their advice he acted promptly enough. His drinking bout continued for some days after 21st April, and [the trial judge] thought that at its conclusion he had, at the [412] best, only a hazy recollection of what had actually happened. When — to use his own expressive phrase — the 'booze got out of his system', he seems to have begun to think seriously about the position, but there is nothing to suggest that he was aware that the transaction might be successfully challenged, or even alive to what he had really done in April. In all the circumstances it would be wrong, in my opinion, to hold that there was any affirmation of the contract or any failure to repudiate in due time a transaction which, even when he became sober, he did not fully understand and appreciate until the document was in his hands ...

[A]fter full consideration of the whole case, I am satisfied that we have here an example of a thoroughly unconscionable transaction, which no court of equity could possibly

---

9. *Blomley v Ryan* (1955) 99 CLR 362 at 370.
10. *Blomley v Ryan* (1955) 99 CLR 362 at 368.
11. *Blomley v Ryan* (1955) 99 CLR 362 at 372.
12. *Blomley v Ryan* (1955) 99 CLR 362 at 373.
13. *Blomley v Ryan* (1955) 99 CLR 362 at 373.

enforce itself, or allow to be enforced at law. I would regard specific performance as out of the question, and to let the contract be enforced at law would, in this particular case, be, in effect, to allow the overreaching party to reap the full reward of his inequitable conduct. The appeal should, in my opinion, be dismissed.

Comment

1. See Radan & Stewart at **11.12**, **11.25–11.26**.

Business inexperience and lack of understanding of English

11.3 Commercial Bank of Australia Ltd v Amadio (1983) 151 CLR 447

Court: High Court of Australia

Facts: The Amadios were an elderly couple with limited English language skills. They were asked by their son Vincenzo to provide a mortgage over commercial premises they owned as further security for his business, Amadio Builders. He told them the mortgage was required for a six-month period and that their liability would be limited to $50,000. The mortgage in favour of the Commercial Bank in fact included a guarantee by the couple to secure the existing debts of the son's business and any future indebtedness without restrictions as to amount or time. The bank was well aware of the financial difficulties faced by the business but the couple was led to believe it was profitable. They signed the mortgage in their own home, in the presence of their son and a bank representative, Virgo, but without the benefit of an interpreter or independent legal advice. When the son's business went into liquidation, the bank made a demand on the Amadios. The couple then commenced action to set aside the mortgage and the bank counter-claimed for the amount owing.

Issue: The issue before the High Court was whether the mortgage entered into by the Amadios was an unconscionable bargain.

Decision: In a majority decision, the High Court (Gibbs CJ, Mason, Wilson and Deane JJ; Dawson J dissenting) held that the mortgage was an unconscionable bargain.

Extracts: The extracts from the judgments of Mason J and Deane J set out the High Court's formulation of the principles relevant to unconscionable bargains.

Mason J

[461] Historically, courts have exercised jurisdiction to set aside contracts and other dealings on a variety of equitable grounds. They include fraud, misrepresentation, breach of fiduciary duty, undue influence and unconscionable conduct. In one sense they all constitute species of unconscionable conduct on the part of a party who stands to receive a benefit under a transaction which, in the eye of equity, cannot be enforced because to do so would be inconsistent with equity and good conscience. But relief on the ground of 'unconscionable conduct' is usually taken to refer to the class of case in which a party makes unconscientious use of his superior position or bargaining power to the detriment

of a party who suffers from some special disability or is placed in some special situation of disadvantage … Although unconscionable conduct in this narrow sense bears some resemblance to the doctrine of undue influence, there is a difference between the two. In the latter the will of the innocent party is not independent and voluntary because it is overborne. In the former the will of the innocent party, even if independent and voluntary, is the result of the disadvantageous position in which he is placed and of the other party unconscientiously taking advantage of that position.

There is no reason for thinking that the two remedies are mutually exclusive in the sense that only one of them is available in a particular situation to the exclusion of the other. Relief on the ground of unconscionable conduct will be granted when unconscientious advantage is taken of an innocent party whose will is overborne so that it is not independent and voluntary, just as it will be granted when such advantage is taken of an innocent party who, though not deprived of an independent and voluntary will, is unable to make a worthwhile judgment as to what is in his best interest.

It goes almost without saying that it is impossible to describe definitively all the situations in which relief will be granted on the ground of unconscionable conduct. As Fullagar J said in *Blomley v Ryan*:

> [462] The circumstances adversely affecting a party, which may induce a court of equity either to refuse its aid or to set a transaction aside, are of great variety and can hardly be satisfactorily classified. Among them are poverty or need of any kind, sickness, age, sex, infirmity of body or mind, drunkenness, illiteracy or lack of education, lack of assistance or explanation where assistance or explanation is necessary. The common characteristic seems to be that they have the effect of placing one party at a serious disadvantage vis-à-vis the other.[14]

Likewise Kitto J spoke of it as 'a well-known head of equity' which —

> … applies whenever one party to a transaction is at a special disadvantage in dealing with the other party because illness, ignorance, inexperience, impaired faculties, financial need or other circumstances affect his ability to conserve his own interests, and the other party unconscientiously takes advantage of the opportunity thus placed in his hands.[15]

Deane J

[474] The jurisdiction of courts of equity to relieve against unconscionable dealing developed from the jurisdiction which the Court of Chancery assumed, at a very early period, to set aside transactions in which expectant heirs had dealt with their expectations without being adequately protected against the pressure put upon them by their poverty.[16] The jurisdiction is long established as extending generally to circumstances in which (i) a party to a transaction was under a special disability in dealing with the other party with the consequence that there was an absence of any reasonable degree of equality between them, and (ii) that disability was sufficiently evident to the stronger party to

---

14. *Blomley v Ryan* (1956) 99 CLR 362 at 405.
15. *Blomley v Ryan* (1956) 99 CLR 362 at 415.
16. See *O'Rorke v Bolingbroke* (1877) 2 App Cas 814 at 822.

make it prima facie unfair or 'unconscientious' that he procure, or accept, the weaker party's assent to the impugned transaction in the circumstances in which he procured or accepted it. Where such circumstances are shown to have existed, an onus is cast upon the stronger party to show that the transaction was fair, just and reasonable: 'the burthen of shewing the fairness of the transaction is thrown on the person who seeks to obtain the benefit of the contract'.[17]

The equitable principles relating to relief against unconscionable dealing and the principles relating to undue influence are closely related. The two doctrines are, however, distinct. Undue influence, like common law duress, looks to the quality of the consent or assent of the weaker party.[18] Unconscionable dealing looks to the conduct of the stronger party in attempting to enforce, or retain the benefit of, a dealing with a person under a special disability in circumstances where it is not consistent with equity or good conscience that he should do so. The adverse circumstances which may constitute a special disability for the purposes of the principles relating to relief against unconscionable dealing may take a wide variety of forms and are not susceptible to being comprehensively catalogues [sic] ...

[475] In most cases where equity courts have granted relief against unconscionable dealing, there has been an inadequacy of consideration moving from the stronger party. It is not, however, essential that that should be so.[19] Notwithstanding that adequate consideration may have moved from the stronger party, a transaction may be unfair, unreasonable and unjust from the viewpoint of the party under the disability. An obvious instance of circumstances in which that may be so is the case where the benefit of the consideration does not move to the party under the disability but moves to some third party involved in the transaction. Thus, it is established that the jurisdiction extends, in an appropriate case, to relieve a guarantor of the burden of a guarantee of existing and future indebtedness.[20] Such a guarantee is properly to be viewed in the terms enunciated by Cussen J in *Bank of Victoria Ltd v Mueller*:

> In the first place, it is obvious that a large benefit is conferred both on the creditor and the debtor, which, so far as any advantage to the guarantor is concerned, is voluntary, though no doubt 'consideration' exists so far as the creditor is concerned, so soon as forbearance is in fact given or advances are in fact made. It is, I think, to some extent by reference to the rule or to an extension of the rule that, in the case of a large voluntary donation, a gift may be set aside in equity if it appears that the donor did not really understand the transaction, that such a guarantee may be treated as voidable as between the husband and wife.[21]

Cussen J's above analysis was made in the context of a guarantee procured by a husband from his wife in favour of the husband's bank. There is, however, no basis in principle or

---

17. See per Lord Hatherley, *O'Rorke v Bolingbroke* (1877) 2 App Cas 814 at 823; *Fry v Lane* (1888) 40 Ch D 312 at 322; *Blomley v Ryan* (1956) 99 CLR 362 at 428–9.

18. See *Union Bank of Australia Ltd v Whitelaw* [1906] VLR 711 at 720; *Watkins v Combes* (1922) 30 CLR 180 at 193–4; *Morrison v Coast Finance Ltd* (1965) 55 DLR (2d) 710 at 713.

19. See *Blomley v Ryan* (1956) 99 CLR 362 at 405; *Harrison v National Bank of Australasia Ltd* (1928) 23 Tas LR 1; but cf *Lloyds Bank v Bundy* [1975] 1 QB 326 at 337 and *Cresswell v Potter* [1978] 1 WLR 255 at 257.

20. See *Owen and Gutch v Homan* (1853) 4 HL Cas 997 at 1034–5.

21. *Bank of Victoria Ltd v Mueller* [1925] VLR 642 at 649.

in policy for confining the process of reasoning therein contained to cases of the relief of female spouses. It is appropriate to the circumstances of the present case.

I turn to consider the question whether, at the time they executed the guarantee/ mortgage, Mr and Mrs Amadio were under a relevant disability in dealing with the bank. This question is best [476] approached by a comparison of the relative positions of the bank on the one hand and Mr and Mrs Amadio on the other.

The bank, for its part, was a major national financial institution. It was privy to the business affairs and financial instability of Amadio Builders. It was aware that that company had, for some time, been unable to meet its debts as they fell due. It was aware of the state of Amadio Builders' two overdrawn accounts with it and of past failures to observe agreed borrowing limits. It had actually suggested ... that Mr and Mrs Amadio enter into the mortgage transaction to secure Amadio Builders' indebtedness to it. It was aware of the contents of its own document which Mr Virgo presented to Mr and Mrs Amadio for their signature.

In contrast was the position of Mr and Mrs Amadio. Their personal circumstances have already been mentioned. They were advanced in years. Their grasp of written English was limited. They relied on Vincenzo for the management of their business affairs and believed that he and Amadio Builders were prosperous and successful. They were approached in their kitchen by the bank, acting through Mr Virgo, at a time when Mr Amadio was reading the newspaper after lunch and Mrs Amadio was washing dishes. They were presented with a complicated and lengthy document for their immediate signature. They had received no independent advice in relation to the transaction which that document embodied and about which they had learned only hours earlier from Vincenzo who, it is common ground in the present appeal, had misled them as regards the extent and duration of their potential liability under it. Apart from indicating that the guarantee/mortgage was unlimited in point of time, Mr Virgo made no personal attempt to explain it to them. Foolishly, but — in view of their limited grasp of written English and their knowledge that Mr Virgo came to them with the approval of their son — perhaps understandably, they did not attempt to read the document for themselves. They signed it in the mistaken belief that their potential liability was limited to a maximum of $50,000.

It is apparent that Mr and Mrs Amadio, viewed together, were the weaker party to the transaction between themselves and the bank. Their weakness may be likened to that of the defendant in *Blomley v Ryan* of whom McTiernan J said:

> His weakness was of the kind spoken of by Lord Hardwicke [in *Earl of Chesterfield v Janssen*][22] in defining the fraud characterised as taking surreptitious advantage of the weakness, [477] ignorance or necessity of another. The essence of such weakness is that the party is unable to judge for himself.[23]

That weakness constituted a special disability of Mr and Mrs Amadio in their dealing with the bank of the type necessary to enliven the equitable principles relating to relief against unconscionable dealing. Put more precisely, the result of the combination of their age, their limited grasp of written English, the circumstances in which the bank presented the

---

22. (1751) 28 ER 82 at 100.
23. *Blomley v Ryan* (1956) 99 CLR 362 at 392.

document to them for their signature and, most importantly, their lack of knowledge and understanding of the contents of the document was that, to adapt the words of Fullagar J quoted above, they lacked assistance and advice where assistance and advice were plainly necessary if there were to be any reasonable degree of equality between themselves and the bank.

The next question is whether the special disability of Mr and Mrs Amadio was sufficiently evident to the bank to make it prima facie unfair or 'unconscientious' of the bank to procure their execution of the document of guarantee and mortgage in the circumstances in which that execution was procured. In procuring it, the bank acted through Mr Virgo: his actions were the actions of the bank and his knowledge was the knowledge of the bank. His evidence indicates that he was not unacquainted with the personal circumstances of Mr and Mrs Amadio and their reliance on Vincenzo whom he described as the 'dominant member of the family'. He was aware of the inability of Amadio Builders to pay its debts as they fell due and must also have been aware of the potential consequences to Mr and Mrs Amadio of the unlimited guarantee in the document which he tendered to them for their immediate execution.

It has not been argued on behalf of the bank that Mr Virgo was so unaware of the circumstances in which Mr and Mrs Amadio executed the document that he was entitled to believe that the transaction was one where no advice, independent or otherwise, was called for. The argument for the bank has been to the effect that, at relevant times, Mr Virgo honestly and reasonably relied upon a representation made to him, by Vincenzo, that the latter had discussed the transaction with his parents, informed them of its nature and effect, explained it fully to them and duly obtained their consent to it.

The evidence that Vincenzo made any such representation to Mr Virgo is unimpressively sparse. Upon analysis, it consists of Mr Virgo's own evidence that he assumed that Mr and Mrs Amadio's 'agreement or offer to give this mortgage was a result of a family conference of some sort'. When it was suggested to him that there was nothing upon which he could base that [478] assumption apart from the fact that Vincenzo had told him that he had spoken to his parents about the transaction and that the bank could proceed with it, Mr Virgo answered:

> That is right. The whole thing had come to me as a fait accompli, not only from the bank's point of view but also having then been informed by Vincenzo that the matter had been agreed within the family and all that required to be done was for the execution of the document ...

It must, in fairness, be stressed that there is no suggestion that Mr Virgo or any other officer of the bank has been guilty of dishonesty or moral obliquity in the dealings between Mr and Mrs Amadio and the bank. The evidence does, however, demonstrate that there was no proper basis at all for any assumption that Mr and Mrs Amadio had received adequate advice from Vincenzo as to the effect of the document which Mr Virgo presented to them for their signature. Even if that were not the case, it would be difficult to accept as reasonable a belief that Vincenzo had successfully explained to his parents the content and effect of a document which embodied 18 separate covenants of meticulous and complicated legal wording in circumstances where, to Mr Virgo's knowledge, Vincenzo had himself never seen the document at the time when any such suggested explanation must have taken place. If there were otherwise room for doubt, what transpired when

Mr Virgo called on Vincenzo in his office and on Mr and Mrs Amadio in their kitchen makes clear that Mr Virgo simply closed his eyes to the vulnerability of Mr and Mrs Amadio and the disability which adversely affected them.

Mr Virgo gave evidence that Vincenzo did not trouble even to read the document before agreeing that Mr Virgo should take it to Mr and Mrs Amadio for execution. He also gave evidence that [479] Mr and Mrs Amadio did not read it. In other words, in a situation where it was apparent to him that advice and assistance were necessary, he knew that no one who might have rendered such advice and assistance to Mr and Mrs Amadio had even read the document to ascertain whether its terms imposed no greater potential liability upon [them] than that which they were prepared to undertake. In the circumstances, the only comment which either Mr or Mrs Amadio made as to the contents of the guarantee/ mortgage on the occasion when they executed it, namely Mr Amadio's comment that it was only for six months, was of unmistakable significance. That statement revealed that Mr Amadio and, it must be assumed, Mrs Amadio were seriously misinformed as to a basic term of the transaction. It would, at least by that stage, have been plain to any reasonable person, who was prepared to see and to learn, that he was put on inquiry. The stage had been reached at which the bank, through Mr Virgo, was bound to make a simple inquiry as to whether the transaction had been properly explained to Mr and Mrs Amadio. The bank cannot shelter behind its failure to make that inquiry. The case is one in which 'wilful ignorance is not to be distinguished in its equitable consequences from knowledge'.[24] Mr and Mrs Amadio's disability and the inequality between themselves and the bank must be held to have been evident to the bank and, in the circumstances, it was prima facie unfair and 'unconscientious' of the bank to proceed to procure their signature on the guarantee/mortgage. With that conclusion, the onus is cast upon the bank to show that the transaction was 'in point of fact fair, just, and reasonable'.[25]

Mr and Mrs Amadio were not wholly misinformed as to the terms and effect of the guarantee/mortgage. The learned trial judge found that they correctly understood that the document which they were signing was a guarantee supported by a mortgage of their Wicks Avenue land. In that regard, it is relevant to mention that the evidence discloses that Mr and Mrs Amadio had, on a number of previous occasions, provided a guarantee, supported by a mortgage of that land, to secure borrowing by a company associated with one or other of their sons. While it is true that Mr and Mrs Amadio were initially led to believe that the guarantee/mortgage was limited in duration to six months, they were disabused of that notion by the clear indication given by Mr Virgo, [480] prior to execution of the document, that the guarantee/mortgage was a 'continuing' one and unlimited in point of time. They executed the document to assist their son's company in obtaining credit from the bank. Acting on the basis of that execution, the bank extended Amadio Builders' overdraft limit and advanced further money to that company. If Mr and Mrs Amadio's potential liability had been limited to a maximum of $50,000, and if they had been informed as to the true financial position of Amadio Builders, it would be strongly arguable that the guarantee/mortgage could not properly be said either to have resulted from their special disability or to be other than fair, just and reasonable.

---

24. Per Lord Cranworth LC, *Owen and Gutch v Homan* (1853) 4 HL Cas 997 at 1035.
25. *Fry v Lane* (1888) 40 Ch D 312 at 321.

As has been said however, the guarantee/mortgage did not contain any such limit upon potential liability and Mr and Mrs Amadio were under a complete misapprehension as to the financial stability of the company whose indebtedness to the bank they were guaranteeing. The learned trial judge found that had they known of the financial troubles Amadio Builders was then experiencing, they would not have executed the guarantee/mortgage. That finding has not been challenged on the appeal. In the circumstances, the execution of the guarantee/mortgage by Mr and Mrs Amadio flowed from the position of special disability in which they were placed. From Mr and Mrs Amadio's point of view, the great difference between a potential liability of up to $50,000 under a guarantee of a financially successful company and a potential liability under a guarantee of a financially troubled company in whatever amount that company might become indebted to its bank requires little elaboration. The one would have been within their means to incur to assist their son. The other represented their potential financial ruin. In the circumstances in which it was procured, the guarantee/mortgage was unfair, unjust and unreasonable. Indeed, in fairness to the bank, I did not understand the contrary to be submitted on its behalf.

Relief against unconscionable dealing is a purely equitable remedy. The concept underlying the jurisdiction to grant the relief is that equity intervenes to prevent the stronger party to an unconscionable dealing acting against equity and good conscience by attempting to enforce, or retain the benefit of, that dealing. Equity will not, however, 'restrain a defendant from asserting a claim save to the extent that it would be unconscionable for him to do so. If this limitation on the power of equity results in giving to a plaintiff less than what on some general idea of fairness he might be considered entitled to, that cannot be helped'.[26] **[481]** Where appropriate, an order will be made which only partly nullifies a transaction liable to be set aside in equity pursuant to the principles of unconscionable dealing.[27] Where an order is made setting aside the whole of a transaction on the ground of unconscionable dealing, the order will, in an appropriate case, be made conditional upon the party obtaining relief doing equity.

While the matter was not raised in the bank's notice of appeal, I was, at one stage, inclined to think that the appropriate relief in the present case would be an order setting aside the guarantee/mortgage only to the extent to which it imposed upon Mr and Mrs Amadio a potential liability in excess of $50,000 or that any order wholly setting aside the guarantee/mortgage should be conditional upon Mr and Mrs Amadio paying to the bank the amount of $50,000 which represents the amount of the potential liability which they intended to undertake. Ultimately, I have come to the view that Mr and Mrs Amadio are entitled to have the whole transaction set aside unconditionally. It is true that it is not ordinarily encumbent upon a bank to bring to the attention of a potential guarantor of a customer's account details of a type which are ordinarily to be expected.[28] In the present case however, it was, as has been said, evident to the bank that Mr and Mrs Amadio stood in need of advice as to the nature and effect of the transaction into which they were entering. It is apparent that any such advice would have included the importance to a guarantor of ascertaining from the bank the state of the customer's account which was being guaranteed and any unusual features of the account. If such information had

---

26. Per Lord Greene MR, Wrottesley and Evershed LJJ in *Re Diplock* [1948] 1 Ch 465 at 532.
27. See *Bank of Victoria Ltd v Mueller* [1925] VLR 642 at 659 and the cases there cited.
28. See *Goodwin v National Bank of Australasia Ltd* (1968) 117 CLR 173 at 175.

been obtained by Mr and Mrs Amadio, they would not, on the evidence and in the light of the learned trial judge's finding, have entered into the guarantee/mortgage at all. The whole transaction should properly be seen as flowing from the special disability which was evident to the bank and as being unfair, unjust and unreasonable.

Comment
1. See Radan & Stewart at **11.4, 11.13–11.16, 11.21**.

Romantic infatuation

11.4   Louth v Diprose (1992) 175 CLR 621

Court: High Court of Australia

Facts: Diprose was a middle-aged solicitor who developed a relationship with Louth after their respective marriages had broken down. In 1982, Louth moved to Adelaide and took up residence in a house owned by her sister. Diprose followed her to Adelaide and continued the relationship. In 1985, Louth informed Diprose that the property was to be sold. She appeared upset and agitated by this development and at one point threatened suicide. Diprose agreed to purchase the house for Louth for almost $60,000 and she soon thereafter became registered proprietor of the property. In 1988, the relationship broke down and Diprose commenced proceedings in the Supreme Court of South Australia seeking a declaration that he was the property's beneficial owner. The trial judge held Diprose was so infatuated with Louth that the gift of the house had been made while he was in a state of emotional dependence. He also found that Louth had manufactured a crisis about her sister's house without justification, disingenuously threatened suicide and manipulated Diprose's feelings towards her. An order was made for the transfer of the property to Diprose.

Issue: The issue before the High Court was whether Diprose was in a state of special disadvantage or disability such as to satisfy the equitable principles of unconscionable dealings and so justify the order made in his favour.

Decision: The majority of the High Court (Mason CJ, Brennan, Deane, Dawson, Gaudron and McHugh JJ; Toohey J dissenting) held in favour of Diprose and upheld the trial judge's orders on the basis that Diprose was under a special disability in dealing with Louth, who had been guilty of unconscionable conduct.

Extracts: The extracts from the judgments of Brennan J and Deane J outline the High Court's reasoning in finding a special disadvantage in this case. The extracts from the dissenting judgment of Toohey J illustrate the view that courts should not take too liberal an approach to what could in any given circumstances constitute a 'special disability'.

Brennan J

[626] The jurisdiction of equity to set aside gifts procured by unconscionable conduct ordinarily arises from the concatenation of three factors: a relationship between the

parties which, to the knowledge of the donee, places the donor at a special disadvantage vis-à-vis the donee; the donee's unconscientious exploitation of the donor's disadvantage; and the consequent overbearing of the will of the donor whereby the donor is unable to make a worthwhile judgment as to what is in his or her best interest.[29] A similar [627] jurisdiction exists to set aside gifts procured by undue influence. In *Commercial Bank of Australia Ltd v Amadio*, Mason J distinguished unconscionable conduct from undue influence in these terms:

> In the latter the will of the innocent party is not independent and voluntary because it is overborne. In the former the will of the innocent party, even if independent and voluntary, is the result of the disadvantageous position in which he is placed and of the other party unconscientiously taking advantage of that position.[30]

Deane J identified the difference in the nature of the two jurisdictions:

> Undue influence, like common law duress, looks to the quality of the consent or assent of the weaker party ... Unconscionable dealing looks to the conduct of the stronger party in attempting to enforce, or retain the benefit of, a dealing with a person under a special disability in circumstances where it is not consistent with equity or good conscience that he should do so.[31]

Although the two jurisdictions are distinct, they both depend upon the effect of influence (presumed or actual) improperly brought to bear by one party to a relationship on the mind of the other whereby the other disposes of his property. Gifts obtained by unconscionable conduct and gifts obtained by undue influence are set aside by equity on substantially the same basis. In *White and Tudor's Leading Cases in Equity*,[32] the notes to *Huguenin v Baseley*[33] treat the principle applied in cases of unconscionable conduct as an extension of the principle applied in cases of undue influence:

> The principle upon which equity will give relief as against the persons standing in [the categories of confidential] relations to the donor, will be extended and applied *to all the variety of relations in which dominion may be exercised by one person over another.*[34]

The ground for setting aside a gift obtained by unconscientious exploitation of a donor's special disadvantage, as explained in *Amadio*, can be compared with the ground for setting aside a gift [628] obtained by undue influence, as explained by Dixon J in *Johnson v Buttress*:

> The basis of the equitable jurisdiction to set aside an alienation of property on the ground of undue influence is the prevention of an *unconscientious use of any special*

---

29. *Commercial Bank of Australia Ltd v Amadio* (1983) 151 CLR 447 at 461, 462, 474–5, 489; *Blomley v Ryan* (1956) 99 CLR 362 at 415.
30. *Commercial Bank of Australia Ltd v Amadio* (1983) 151 CLR 447 at 461.
31. *Commercial Bank of Australia Ltd v Amadio* (1983) 151 CLR 447 at 474.
32. 9th ed (1928), vol 1, pp 203ff.
33. (1807) 33 ER 526.
34. White and Tudor, *Leading Cases in Equity*, 9th ed (1928), vol 1, p 227; founded on *Dent v Bennett* (1839) 41 ER 105 at 108; *Smith v Kay* (1859) 11 ER 299 at 310–11.

capacity or opportunity that may exist or arise *of affecting the alienor's will or freedom of judgment* in reference to such a matter. The source of power to practise such a domination may be found in no antecedent relation but in a particular situation, or in the deliberate contrivance of the party. If this be so, facts must be proved showing that the transaction was *the outcome of such an actual influence over the mind of the alienor* that it cannot be considered his free act. But the parties may antecedently stand in a relation that gives to one an authority or influence over the other from the abuse of which it is proper that he should be protected. (Emphasis added).[35]

The similarity between the two jurisdictions gives to cases arising in the exercise of one jurisdiction an analogous character in considering cases involving the same points in the other jurisdiction.

The relationship

There are some categories of confidential relationships from which a presumption of undue influence arises when a substantial gift is made by one party to the relationship to the other — relationships such as solicitor and client, physician and patient, parent and child, guardian and ward, superior and member of a religious community. Public policy creates a presumption of undue influence in cases where the relationship falls into one of the recognised categories.[36] Those categories do not exhaust the cases in which it may be held that it is contrary to conscience for a donee to retain a gift. In cases where the relationship is not one of confidentiality, a gift may be impeached where the evidence shows that in fact it was procured by unconscionable conduct. Where a gift is impeached on the ground that it was obtained by unconscionable conduct consisting in an unconscionable exploitation of an antecedent relationship, the relationship is one in which one party stands in a position of special disadvantage vis-a-vis the other. Such relationships are infinitely various,[37] the common feature being that the donor is, to the knowledge of the donee, in a position of *special* disadvantage vis-a-vis the donee: that is to say, in matters in **[629]** which their interests do not coincide, the donor's capacity to make a decision as to his or her own best interest is peculiarly susceptible to control or influence by the donee. As Mason J said in *Amadio*:

> I qualify the word 'disadvantage' by the adjective 'special' in order to disavow any suggestion that the principle applies whenever there is some difference in the bargaining power of the parties and in order to emphasise that the disabling condition or circumstance is one which seriously affects the ability of the innocent party to make a judgment as to his own best interests, when the other party knows or ought to know of the existence of that condition or circumstance and of its effect on the innocent party.[38]

The relevant relationship may exist because of some weakness in the donor. Thus Fullagar J in *Blomley v Ryan* took as instances of weakness 'poverty or need of any kind,

---

35. *Johnson v Buttress* (1936) 56 CLR 113 at 134.
36. *Allcard v Skinner* (1887) 36 Ch D 145 at 171; *Inche Noria v Shaik Allie Bin Omar* [1929] AC 127 at 132–3; *Morley v Loughnan* [1893] 1 Ch 736 at 752.
37. *Blomley v Ryan* (1956) 99 CLR 362 at 405; *Commercial Bank of Australia Ltd v Amadio* (1983) 151 CLR 447 at 462.
38. *Commercial Bank of Australia Ltd v Amadio* (1983) 151 CLR 447 at 462.

sickness, age, sex, infirmity of body or mind, drunkenness, illiteracy or lack of education, lack of assistance or explanation where assistance or explanation is necessary'.[39] And McTiernan J said that '[t]he essence of such weakness is that the party is unable to judge for himself'.[40] It is unnecessary to show that the donee contributed to that weakness. In the present case, King CJ found —

> ... a relationship existed between [Diprose] and [Louth] which placed [Diprose] in a position of emotional dependence upon [Louth] and gave her a position of great influence on his actions and decisions. From the time they first met he was utterly infatuated by her. He had had unhappy domestic experiences and was anxious to lavish love and devotion upon a woman. He fell completely in love with [her].[41] ...

Given those findings, the relationship between [Diprose] and [Louth] was so different in degree as to be different in kind from the ordinary relationship of a man courting a woman. It was found that the personal relationship between them was such that [Diprose] was extremely susceptible **[630]** to influence by [Louth], as [she] knew ...

Exploitation of the donor's disadvantage

Equity intervenes 'whenever one party to a transaction is at a special disadvantage in dealing with the other party ... and the other party unconscientiously takes advantage of the opportunity thus placed in his hands'.[42] Citing this passage in *Amadio*, Dawson J said:

> What is necessary for the application of the principle is exploitation by one party of another's position of disadvantage in such a manner that the former could not in good conscience retain the benefit of the bargain.[43]

What his Honour said of a bargain can be said equally of a gift.

In the present case, King CJ made explicit findings of an unconscientious exploitation by [Louth] of [Diprose's] weakness:

> ... I am satisfied that she deliberately manufactured the atmosphere of crisis in order to influence [Diprose] to provide the money for the house. I am satisfied, moreover, that she played upon his love and concern for her by the suicide threats in relation to the house. She then refused offers of assistance short of full ownership of the house knowing that his emotional dependence upon her was such as to lead inexorably to the gratification of her unexpressed wish to have him buy the house for her. I am satisfied that it was a process of manipulation to which he was utterly vulnerable by reason of his infatuation.[44]

[631] *The donor's will and judgment*

When a donor who stands in a relationship of special disadvantage vis-à-vis a donee makes a substantial gift to the donee, slight evidence may be sufficient to show that the

---

39. *Blomley v Ryan* (1956) 99 CLR 362 at 405.
40. *Blomley v Ryan* (1956) 99 CLR362 at 392; see per Deane J in *Commercial Bank of Australia Ltd v Amadio* (1983) 151 CLR 447 at 476–7.
41. *Diprose v Louth (No 1)* (1990) 54 SASR 438 at 447–8.
42. Per Kitto J in *Blomley v Ryan* (1956) 99 CLR 362 at 415.
43. *Commercial Bank of Australia Ltd v Amadio* (1983) 151 CLR 447 at 489.
44. *Diprose v Louth (No 1)* (1990) 54 SASR 438 at 448.

gift has been procured by unconscionable conduct. Whether that finding should be made depends on the circumstances. In *Watkins v Combes*, Isaacs J said:

> It is not the law, as I understand it, that the mere fact that one party to a transaction who is of full age and apparent competency reposed confidence in, or was subject to the influence of, the other party is sufficient to cast upon the latter the onus of demonstrating the validity of the transaction. Observations which go to that extent are too broad.[45]

But where it is proved that a donor stood in a specially disadvantageous relationship with a donee, that the donee exploited the disadvantage and that the donor thereafter made a substantial gift to the donee, an inference may, and often should, be drawn that the exploitation was the effective cause of the gift. The drawing of that inference, however, depends on the whole of the circumstances.

In this case, [Louth] contends that, whatever view is taken of her conduct, the proper conclusion to be reached on the evidence is that [Diprose] made the gift to her simply because he wished to do so, imprudent though the gift may have been. If that be the right conclusion, so that the gift was not the result of unconscionable conduct on the part of [Louth], [Diprose] cannot recover the gift. As Lindley LJ pointed out in *Allcard v Skinner*:

> Courts of Equity have never set aside gifts on the ground of the folly, imprudence, or want of foresight on the part of donors. The courts have always repudiated any such jurisdiction ... It would obviously be to encourage folly, recklessness, extravagance and vice if persons could get back property which they foolishly made away with, whether by giving it to charitable institutions or by bestowing it on less worthy objects.[46] ...

[632] Once it is proved that substantial property has been given by a donor to a donee after the donee has exploited the donor's known position of special disadvantage, an inference may be drawn that the gift is the product of the exploitation. Such an inference must arise, however, from the facts of the case; it is not a presumption which arises by operation of law. The inference may be drawn unless the donee can rely on countervailing evidence to show that the donee's exploitative conduct was not a cause of the gift. At the end of the day, however, it is for the party impeaching the gift to show that it is the product of the donee's exploitative conduct. This is the final and necessary link in the chain of proof of unconscionable conduct leading to a decree setting aside the gift.

[Diprose] discharged that onus in the present case. That is implicit in the conclusion of King CJ:

> By reason of [Diprose's] infatuation and [Louth's] manipulation of it he was 'unable to make a worthwhile judgment as to what is in his best interest'.[47] [Louth] was well aware of that and her manufacture of an atmosphere of crisis where no crisis existed was dishonest and smacked of fraud. To my mind [Louth's] unconscientious use of her power over [Diprose] resulting from his infatuation, renders it unconscionable for her [633] to retain the benefit of such a large gift out of [his] limited resources.[48]

His Honour inferred that the gift was the product of [Louth's] 'manipulation' of [Diprose].

---

45. *Watkins v Combes* (1922) 30 CLR 180 at 193; and see per Starke J in *Harris v Jenkins* (1922) 31 CLR 341 at 367–8.
46. *Allcard v Skinner* (1887) 36 Ch D 145 at 183.
47. *Commercial Bank of Australia Ltd v Amadio* (1983) 151 CLR 447 at 461.
48. *Diprose v Louth (No 1)* (1990) 54 SASR 438 at 448.

The findings of fact made by King CJ were attacked both in the Full Court and before this court. The attack failed in the Full Court and ... the attack should fail here. I would dismiss the appeal.

Deane J

[637] It has long been established that the jurisdiction of courts of equity to relieve against unconscionable dealing extends generally to circumstances in which (i) a party to a transaction was under a special disability in dealing with the other party to the transaction with the consequence that there was an absence of any reasonable degree of equality between them and (ii) that special disability was sufficiently evident to the other party to make it prima facie unfair or 'unconscionable' that that other party procure, accept or retain the benefit of, the disadvantaged party's assent to the impugned transaction in the circumstances in which he or she procured or accepted it. Where such circumstances are shown to have existed, an onus is cast upon the stronger party to show that the transaction was fair, just and reasonable: 'the burthen of shewing the fairness of the transaction is thrown on the person who seeks to obtain' or retain the benefit of it.[49]

The adverse circumstances which may constitute a special disability for the purposes of the principle relating to relief against unconscionable dealing may take a wide variety of forms and are not susceptible of being comprehensively catalogued ...

[638] On the findings of the learned trial judge in the present case, the relationship between [Diprose] and [Louth] at the time of the impugned gift was plainly such that [Diprose] was under a special disability in dealing with [Louth]. That special disability arose not merely from [Diprose's] infatuation. It extended to [his] extraordinary vulnerability ... in the false 'atmosphere of crisis' in which he believed that the woman with whom he was 'completely in love' and upon whom he was emotionally dependent was facing eviction from her home and suicide unless he provided the money for the purchase of the house. [Louth] was aware of that special disability. Indeed, to a significant extent, she had deliberately created it. She manipulated it to her advantage to influence [Diprose] to make the gift of the money to purchase the house. When asked for restitution she refused. From [Diprose's] point of view, the whole transaction was plainly a most improvident one.

In these circumstances, the learned trial judge's conclusion that [Louth] had been guilty of unconscionable conduct in procuring and retaining the gift of $59,206.55 was not only open to him. In the context of his Honour's findings of fact, it was inevitable and plainly correct. On those findings, the case was not simply one in which [Diprose] had, under the influence of his love for, or infatuation with, [Louth], made an imprudent gift in her favour. The case was one in which [Louth] deliberately used that love or infatuation and her own deceit to create a situation in which she could unconscientiously manipulate [Diprose] to part with a large proportion of his property. The intervention of equity is not merely to relieve [Diprose] from the consequences of his own foolishness. It is to prevent his victimization.[50]

---

49. See per Lord Hatherley, *O'Rorke v Bolingbroke* (1877) 2 App Cas 814 at 823; *Fry v Lane* (1888) 40 Ch D 312 at 322; *Blomley v Ryan* (1956) 99 CLR 362 at 428–9; *Commercial Bank of Australia Ltd v Amadio* (1983) 151 CLR 447 at 474.
50. See *Allcard v Skinner* (1887) 36 Ch D 145 at 182; *Nichols v Jessup* [1986] 1 NZLR 226 at 227–9; *Commonwealth v Verwayen* (1990) 170 CLR 394 at 440.

Neither party has sought to challenge the relief which was granted on the basis of that conclusion on the ground that, as suggested by [the majority in the Full Court], it would have been more appropriate to make orders leading to the restitution of the moneys rather than to **[639]** make a declaration that [Louth] hold the house in trust for [Diprose]. Accordingly, the appeal should be dismissed ...

Toohey J

[651] Unconscionability and the present appeal

[T]here can be no doubt as to the strength of [Diprose's] feelings for [Louth] and the lengths, including the financial lengths, to which he was prepared to go to express those feelings. But equally, while [Louth] was content to accept the many benefits she received from [Diprose], there can be no doubt that she made her position in the relationship quite clear. It was [he] who continued to seek her out. She did not mislead him in regard to her position; she did not hold out any false hopes to him. They were both adults; each had been married before ([Diprose] twice); and [he] was a practising solicitor who must have appreciated fully the consequences that the law would ordinarily attach to the gifts he made to [Louth], including the money involved in the purchase of the Tranmere house. It was [his] idea to buy the house, not [hers] ...

[653] It is apparent ... that he bought the house for [Louth] because she 'had been through a lot of ... stress and problems' and because he 'wanted her to be secure'.[51] ... And, as is apparent from the evidence ... generally, he bought the house for her in the clear realisation that she would never marry him. As [the dissenting judge in the Full Court] pointed out in his judgment, [Diprose] took a number of steps in connection with the purchase of the house. He prepared the contract of sale, arranged Land Titles Office searches, obtained an application form under the First Home Owners Scheme and filled in the details, prepared the transfer and prepared the settlement statement. In other words, [he] did not commit himself by one impulsive or hasty act; he had plenty of time to consider what he was doing and what he did took place over a month ...

[T]he starting point is ... that there was a gift of the house to [Louth]. It was of course a very generous gift in the circumstances; it was a gift that [Diprose's] children might justifiably have resented; and it was a gift that **[654]** [he] himself might well have regretted and later did regret. But the law is clear:

> The mere fact that a transaction is based on an inadequate consideration or is otherwise improvident, unreasonable, or unjust is not in itself any ground on which this court can set it aside as invalid. Nor is such a circumstance in itself even a sufficient ground for a presumption that the transaction was the result of fraud, misrepresentation, mistake, or undue influence, so as to place the burden of supporting the transaction upon the person who profits by it. The law in general leaves every man at liberty to make such bargains as he pleases, and to dispose of his own property as he chooses. However improvident, unreasonable, or unjust such bargains or dispositions may be, they are binding on every party to them unless he can prove affirmatively the existence of one of the recognized invalidating circumstances, such as fraud or undue influence.[52] ...

---

51. *Diprose v Louth (No 2)* (1990) 54 SASR 450 at 479.
52. *Brusewitz v Brown* [1923] NZLR 1106 at 1109.

Although the concept of unconscionability has been expressed in fairly wide terms, the courts are exercising an equitable jurisdiction according to recognized principles. They are not armed with a general power to set aside bargains simply because, in the eyes of the judges, they appear to be unfair, harsh or unconscionable. This is in contrast to some legislation which 'permits the courts to exercise a broad discretion to control harsh, oppressive, unconscionable or unjust contracts'.[53] The equitable jurisdiction exists when one of the parties 'suffers from some special disability or is placed in some special situation of disadvantage'.[54] In some cases, for instance where there is unfamiliarity with written English as in *Amadio* or unintelligence and deafness as in *Wilton v Farnworth*,[55] the special situation of disadvantage may be readily apparent. But that is not the present case.

Comments
1. See Radan & Stewart at **11.17–11.20, 11.24**.
2. For a discussion of this case see L Sarmas, 'Storytelling and the Law: A Case Study of *Louth v Diprose*' (1994) 19 *Melbourne University Law Review* 701.

Unconscionability and business regulation: the *Trade Practices Act 1974* (Cth)

11.5 Australian Competition & Consumer Commission v C G Berbatis Holdings Pty Ltd (2003) 214 CLR 51

Court: High Court of Australia

Facts: Mr and Mrs Roberts were lessees of premises in a shopping centre and wanted to renew or extend their lease so that they could make an advantageous sale of their business. They were keen to do so as their daughter suffered from a serious illness and they felt unable to keep their business going and provide her with sufficient care. Their existing lease made no provision for renewal or extension and so the Roberts were required to negotiate with the lessors, C G Berbatis Holdings Pty Ltd (Berbatis). Berbatis agreed to the granting of a new lease, enabling the sale of the business by the Roberts but, as a condition of doing so, required the Roberts to abandon a legal claim against them based upon overcharging of centre management fees. The Roberts were uncomfortable about surrendering this claim, which other tenants in the centre were also making, believing it entitled them to approximately $50,000. However, they did so, secured the new lease and sold their business. The settlement of the tenants' claim subsequently showed that the Roberts would have received only a little under $3000 had they continued their participation in the claim.

The Roberts did not pursue any claim against Berbatis. Rather, it was the Australian Competition and Consumer Commission (ACCC), exercising its powers under the *Trade Practices Act 1974* (Cth), which commenced proceedings in the Federal Court

---

53. Cope, *Duress, Undue Influence and Unconscientious Bargains*, (1985), p 188.
54. *Commercial Bank of Australia Ltd v Amadio* (1983) 151 CLR 447 at 461.
55. (1948) 76 CLR 646.

seeking injunctive relief and a declaration that Berbatis had contravened the provisions of s 51AA(1) of the Act. That section stipulates: 'A corporation must not, in trade or commerce, engage in conduct that is unconscionable within the meaning of the unwritten law, from time to time, of the States and Territories'.

At first instance, French J found in favour of the ACCC, saying that the Roberts were at a 'special disadvantage' of a 'situational', rather than 'constitutional' nature; that is, their disability was not due to any particular personal characteristics of the kind observed in *Blomley v Ryan* or *Commercial Bank of Australia v Amadio*, but rather, that it arose from the position they were in and their keen desire to be rid of the business. In doing so, however, French J did not rely upon the daughter's illness as a factor. French J took the view that the provision of independent advice to Mrs Roberts was of little impact in overcoming the unconscionability arising from the Roberts' 'situational disadvantage'.

Issue: The issue before the High Court was whether Berbatis had engaged in unconscionable conduct by contravening s 51AA(1) of the Act.

Decision: The majority of the High Court (Gleeson CJ, Gummow, Hayne and Callinan JJ; Kirby J dissenting) held that Berbatis was not guilty of unconscionable conduct within the bounds of s 51AA(1).

Extracts: The extracts from the judgment of Gleeson CJ set out the majority view of the scope of unconscionability under the Act. The extracts from the dissenting judgment of Kirby J argue for a broader interpretation of unconscionability in this context.

Gleeson CJ

[62] Although he was concerned to make the point that ss 51AB and 51AC of the Act have a wider operation than s 51AA, senior counsel for the [ACCC] argued the case on the basis that the relevant form of unconscionable conduct in question was 'the knowing exploitation by one party of the special disadvantage of another'. He said that, by special disadvantage, he meant 'a disabling circumstance seriously affecting the ability of the innocent party to make a judgment in [that party's] own best interests'. Applied to a case such as the present, that approach is consistent with what the Act calls the unwritten law concerning unconscionable conduct, bearing in mind that the Act also allows for development of the law from time to time. It is also consistent with the legislative history of s 51AA. In the Second Reading speech when the legislation was introduced, it was said:

> Unconscionability is a well understood equitable doctrine, the meaning of which has been discussed by the High Court in recent times. It involves a party who suffers from some special disability or is placed in some special situation of disadvantage and an 'unconscionable' taking advantage of that disability or disadvantage by another. The doctrine does not apply simply because one party has made a poor bargain. In the vast majority of commercial transactions neither party would be likely to be in a position of special disability or special disadvantage, and no question of unconscionable conduct would arise. Nevertheless, unconscionable conduct can occur in commercial transactions and there is no reason why the Trade Practices Act should not recognise this.[56]

---

56. Australian House of Representatives, *Parliamentary Debates* (Hansard), 3 November 1992 at 24008.

The Explanatory Memorandum referred to the decisions of this Court in *Blomley v Ryan*[57] and *Commercial Bank of Australia Ltd v Amadio*.[58] Those decisions were considered more recently in *Bridgewater v Leahy*.[59]

These decisions mark out the area of discourse involved, and explain the approach of the [ACCC], which was accepted by [Berbatis]. It was also the approach taken by French J, and by the Full Court. In the context of s 51AA, with its reference to the unwritten [63] law, which is the law expounded in such cases as those mentioned above, unconscionability is a legal term, not a colloquial expression. In everyday speech, 'unconscionable' may be merely an emphatic method of expressing disapproval of someone's behaviour, but its legal meaning is considerably more precise …

In the present case, French J said that the lessees suffered from a 'situational' as distinct from a 'constitutional' disadvantage, in that it did not stem from any inherent infirmity or weakness or deficiency. That idea was developed somewhat in a joint judgment, to which French J was a party, in *Australian Competition and Consumer Commission v Samton Holdings Pty Ltd*, where it was said that, under the rubric of unconscionable conduct, equity will set aside a contract or disposition resulting from the knowing exploitation by one party of the special disadvantage of another, and then it was said:

> The special disadvantage may be constitutional, deriving from age, illness, poverty, inexperience or lack of education: *Commercial Bank of Australia Ltd v Amadio*. Or it may be situational, deriving from particular features of a relationship between actors in the transaction such as the emotional dependence of one on the other: *Louth v Diprose*; *Bridgewater v Leahy*.[60]

While, with respect to those who think otherwise, I would not assign the facts of *Bridgewater v Leahy* to such a category, the reference to emotional dependence of the kind illustrated by *Louth v Diprose*[61] as a form of special disadvantage described as 'situational' rather than 'constitutional' is understandable and acceptable, provided that such descriptions do not take on a life of their own, in substitution for the language of the statute, and the content of the law to which it refers. There is a risk that categories, adopted as a convenient method of exposition of an underlying principle, might be misunderstood, and come to supplant the principle. The stream of judicial exposition of principle cannot rise above the source; and there is nothing to suggest that French J intended that it should. A problem is that the words 'situation' and 'disadvantage' have ordinary meanings which, in [64] combination, extend far beyond the bounds of the law referred to in s 51AA; and, it may be added, far beyond the bounds of what was explained to Parliament as the purpose of the section.

One thing is clear, and is illustrated by the decision in *Samton Holdings* itself. A person is not in a position of relevant disadvantage, constitutional, situational, or otherwise, simply because of inequality of bargaining power. Many, perhaps even most, contracts are made between parties of unequal bargaining power, and good conscience does not

---

57. (1956) 99 CLR 362.
58. (1983) 151 CLR 447.
59. (1998) 194 CLR 457.
60. (2002) 117 FCR 301 at 318.
61. (1992) 175 CLR 621.

require parties to contractual negotiations to forfeit their advantages, or neglect their own interests ...

Unconscientious exploitation of another's inability, or diminished ability, to conserve his or her own interests is not to be confused with taking advantage of a superior bargaining position. There may be cases where both elements are involved, but, in such cases, it is the first, not the second, element that is of legal consequence. It is neither the purpose nor the effect of s 51AA to treat people generally, when they deal with others in a stronger position, as though they were all expectant heirs in the nineteenth century, dealing with a usurer.[62]

In the present case, there was neither a special disadvantage on the part of the lessees, nor unconscientious conduct on the part of the lessors. All the people involved in the transaction were business [65] people, concerned to advance or protect their own financial interests. The critical disadvantage from which the lessees suffered was that they had no legal entitlement to a renewal or extension of their lease; and they depended upon the lessors' willingness to grant such an extension or renewal for their capacity to sell the goodwill of their business for a substantial price. They were thus compelled to approach the lessors, seeking their agreement to such an extension or renewal, against a background of current claims and litigation in which they were involved. They were at a distinct disadvantage, but there was nothing 'special' about it. They had two forms of financial interest at stake: their claims, and the sale of their business. The second was large; as things turned out, the first was shown to be relatively small. They had the benefit of legal advice. They made a rational decision, and took the course of preferring the second interest. They suffered from no lack of ability to judge or protect their financial interests. What they lacked was the commercial ability to pursue them both at the same time.

Good conscience did not require the lessors to permit the lessees to isolate the issue of the lease from the issue of the claims. It is an everyday occurrence in negotiations for settlement of legal disputes that, as a term of a settlement, one party will be required to abandon claims which may or may not be related to the principal matter in issue. French J spoke of the lessors using '[their] bargaining power to extract a concession [that was] commercially irrelevant to the terms and conditions of any proposed new lease'. A number of observations may be made about that. Parties to commercial negotiations frequently use their bargaining power to 'extract' concessions from other parties. That is the stuff of ordinary commercial dealing. What is relevant to a commercial negotiation is whatever one party to the negotiation chooses to make relevant. And it is far from self-evident that when a landlord is considering a tenant's request to renew a lease, the existence of disputes between the parties about the current lease is commercially irrelevant to a decision as to whether, and on what terms, the landlord will agree to the request. The reasoning of French J appears to involve a judgment that it was wrong for the lessors to relate the matter of the lessees' claims to the matter of their request for a renewal of the lease. Why this is so was not explained. It formed a crucial part of the reasoning of French J and, in my view, cannot be sustained.

Reference was earlier made to counsel's submission that there was here a disabling circumstance affecting the ability of the lessees to make a judgment in their own best

---

62. *Commercial Bank of Australia Ltd v Amadio* (1983) 151 CLR 447 at 462.

interests. In truth, there was no lack of ability on their part to make a judgment about anything. Rather, there was a lack of ability to get their own way. That is a disability that affects people in many circumstances in commerce, and in life. It is not one against which the law ordinarily provides relief.

In the course of their reasoning on the contentions advanced by the appellant, and in distinguishing between driving a hard bargain and unconscionable conduct, the members of the Full Court, in a single [66] sentence, remarked that it could not be said that the will of the lessees was overborne, or that they did not act independently and voluntarily. In the context, I would not understand that to indicate that their Honours thought that unconscionability required duress. It was simply an observation of fact as to part of the context in which the issue of unconscionability arose.

Kirby J

[83] *The objects of the Act and of the section*: The object of the Act, as stipulated in s 2, is 'to enhance the welfare of Australians through the promotion of competition and fair trading and provision for consumer protection'. The introduction of statutory notions of unconscionable conduct into the Act was a recognition of the advantages of the 'unwritten law' doctrines in promoting fair trading. Such equitable categories developed in order to protect the integrity of the contracting process where a party is induced to act or enter a transaction due to weakness or illegitimate pressure, and does so without full information or appreciation of the extent or nature of the transaction or the way it affects that party's interests and choices. By enacting s 51AA, the Parliament adopted from the unwritten law the characterisation of conduct as unconscionable, and prohibited such conduct by corporations engaged in trade or commerce. The design of s 51AA was intended not to expand the notions of unconscionable conduct in the unwritten law but to allow the application in such circumstances of the flexible remedies available under the Act. Yet the very fact that such a provision would facilitate more cases coming before the courts than might otherwise be the case inevitably results in a closer elaboration of the concept of unconscionable conduct in new and different factual circumstances. The present is such a case.

A particular purpose of the inclusion of s 51AA in the Act was to afford more effective remedies to small operators in the marketplace, such as the Roberts. They already had access to remedies of an equitable character. However, in practice, where the stakes were comparatively low (as here) a corporation dealing with such a small player would normally be entitled to assume that it could take advantage of the comparative weakness of that player without any real fear that it would be rendered accountable in a court of law or equity ...

The proper approach to the section: In outlining his approach to the construction and application of s 51AA, the primary judge said, correctly in my view:

> Section 51AA prohibits corporations from engaging in conduct which is unconscionable within the meaning of the common law of Australia. The meaning of the term is found in the dictionary. Its [84] meaning is not altered by the unwritten law. What the unwritten law does presently is to confine its operation to certain classes of case. The reference in s 51AA to the 'meaning of the unwritten law' is a reference to the classes of case in which the unwritten law will award remedies for unconscionable conduct ...

There is no distinct rule which defines such conduct. The description embodied in the word 'unconscionable' ultimately refers to the normative characterisation of conduct by a judge having jurisdiction in the relevant class of case ... [T]he rules governing the relevant application of the term 'unconscionable conduct' and therefore the application of s 51AA are judge-made rules that can change from time to time. The development of doctrine which may alter that application may occur in the judgments of the courts of the States and Territories and of the High Court and of the Federal Court in the exercise of its accrued jurisdiction. This may also occur through the exercise of jurisdiction under s 51AA which itself if valid, will become a significant source of the unwritten law.[63]

The primary judge also observed that s 51AA 'uses the unwritten law to the extent that it provides for the characterisation of conduct as unconscionable and then prohibits such conduct'.[64] In terms of the type of conduct that would fit the description 'unconscionable within the meaning of the unwritten law', the primary judge made three pertinent observations: first, that as a general proposition the object of equity's intervention is to prevent behaviour contrary to conscience, however, this does not mean that the prohibition in s 51AA encompasses all conduct that would attract the intervention of equity;[65] secondly, that within the meaning of the 'unwritten law' the notion of unconscionable conduct has no 'technical meaning' and provides 'a standard determined by judicial decision-making rather than a rule';[66] and thirdly, that while the Explanatory Memorandum prepared in support of the clause in the Bill that became s 51AA of the Act specifically referred to the concept of unconscionable conduct explained in *Blomley* and *Amadio*, that 'may turn out to have been an unduly narrow selection of case law'.[67]

While the present appeal was substantially argued by reference to the principles of unconscionable dealing as elaborated in cases such as *Blomley* and *Amadio*, the reach of the section, in my view, goes further. Its full scope remains to be elaborated in this and future cases ...

[94] A prime purpose for bringing the notions of unconscionability into [95] the Act, and expressing them as relevant to business standards for Australian corporations engaged in trade and commerce, was to render those standards more effective by creating real sanctions and by affording novel remedies that might on occasion be invoked by the ACCC on behalf of small players. The ACCC is entitled under the Act to bring proceedings (as it did here) in its own name to enforce the rights of others. In this way, it was envisaged by the Parliament that test cases, such as that brought by the ACCC for the Roberts, would help to promote the object of fair trading and translate the principles of the legislation into corporate behaviour, thereby incorporating equitable notions into

---

63. *Australian Competition and Consumer Commission v C G Berbatis Holdings Pty Ltd [No 2]* (2000) 96 FCR 491 at 503–4.
64. *Australian Competition and Consumer Commission v C G Berbatis Holdings Pty Ltd [No 2]* (2000) 96 FCR 491 at 504.
65. *Australian Competition and Consumer Commission v C G Berbatis Holdings Pty Ltd [No 2]* (2000) 96 FCR 491 at 498.
66. *Australian Competition and Consumer Commission v C G Berbatis Holdings Pty Ltd [No 2]* (2000) 96 FCR 491 at 502.
67. *Australian Competition and Consumer Commission v C G Berbatis Holdings Pty Ltd [No 2]* (2000) 96 FCR 491 at 495.

practical day-to-day application. This point is reinforced by an examination of the kinds of remedies available for a contravention of s 51AA. In particular, recovery of damages under s 82 or pecuniary penalties under s 76 of the Act was not available.

In a passage cited [above], the primary judge commented on the relationship between the emerging case law interpreting and applying s 51AA of the Act, and the existing doctrines of the unwritten law. This is an issue that will warrant further examination. It may be that the different policies and concerns that motivate the provision of relief in equity and under the Act, would also translate into subtle differences in the characterisation of conduct as unconscionable. The concern of equity is limited to justice in the individual case given the potential for inadequate results by reason of some of the rules of the common law. Therefore, even if conduct otherwise exhibits the elements of unconscionable dealing as understood in equity, it may still not receive that characterisation if the traditional equitable remedies (such as setting aside the transaction for instance) are not appropriate in the circumstances of the case. The Act on the other hand provides a wider set of procedures and remedies (as this appeal illustrates) designed to enhance the 'educative and deterrent effect of [the] legislative prohibition'.[68] Given that such purposes would ordinarily be outside equity's contemplation, a contravention of the Act might yet be found although equitable relief would not lie.

It follows that this Court should approach a case such as the present, brought under the Act, recognising that its importance extends beyond the humble case of the Roberts. By upholding the rights of the Roberts — on the face of things small and objectively of limited significance [96] — a message is delivered that the Act is not to be trifled with. Unconscionable conduct, in the sense referred to in s 51AA of the Act, is to be avoided by corporations lest they find themselves on the receiving end of proceedings such as the ACCC brought on behalf of the Roberts. Uninstructed by the history and purpose of the Act, and remembering only the cases in equity from which the 'unwritten law' on unconscionable conduct is derived, a court might well view the present proceedings differently. But when the place of s 51AA in the Act, its history and its educative and deterrent purposes are remembered, the outcome reached by the primary judge can be better understood.

Comments

1. See Radan & Stewart at **11.44–11.54**.
2. In *Australian Competition and Consumer Commission v Samton Holdings Pty Ltd* (2002) 117 FCR 301 at 317–19, the Full Court of the Federal Court (Grey, French and Stone JJ) said the following in relation to s 51AA:

   Professor Finn (as he then was) [in Finn, 'Unconscionable Conduct' (1994) 8 *Journal of Contract Law* 37 at 38–9] … identified 'four not altogether distinct ways' in which the language of unconscionable conduct has been used in the case law: 1. As an organising idea informing specific equitable rules and doctrines which do not in terms refer to, or require, an explicit finding of unconscionable conduct — eg rules on stipulations as to time and notices to complete. 2. In relation to specific equitable doctrines of which estoppel, unilateral mistake, relief against forfeiture and undue

---

68. *Trade Practices Legislation Amendment Bill 1992* (Cth), Explanatory Memorandum at [44].

influence are examples. They are united by the idea that equity will prevent an unconscionable insistence on strict legal rights and are conditioned upon the explicit finding of unconscionable conduct in the persons against whom they are invoked. 3. In relation to the discrete doctrine of unconscionable dealing which concerns one species of unconscionable conduct. 4. In relation to unconscionable conduct founding a cause of action not mediated by any discrete doctrine.

Four classes of case attracting the application of the language of unconscionability are described in LBC, *Laws of Australia*, vol 35 (at 31 January 2002) Unfair Dealing 35.5 Notion of Unconscionability [1]–[38]: (i) Exploitation of vulnerability or weakness (ii) Abuse of position of trust or confidence (iii) Insistence upon rights in circumstances which make that harsh or oppressive (iv) Inequitable denial of legal obligations.

These are said to be supported by three broad standards: (i) That those in positions of strength or influence should not take advantage of another's relative weakness. (ii) That people should not, by appeal to strict legal rights, cause hardship to others by violating their reasonable expectations. (iii) That those in fiduciary positions should act only in the interests of those to whom those fiduciary duties are owed.

Under the rubric of unconscionable conduct, equity will: (i) Set aside a contract or disposition resulting from the knowing exploitation by one party of the special disadvantage of another. The special disadvantage may be constitutional, deriving from age, illness, poverty, inexperience or lack of education. Or it may be situational, deriving from particular features of a relationship between actors in the transaction such as the emotional dependence of one on the other. (ii) Set aside as against third parties a transaction entered into as the result of the defective comprehension by a party to the transaction, the influence of another and the want of any independent explanation to the complaining party. (iii) Prevent a party from exercising a legal right in a way that involves unconscionable departure from a representation relied upon by another to his or her detriment. (iv) Relieve against forfeiture and penalty. (v) Rescind contracts entered into under the influence of unilateral mistake.

Each of these categories of case (the list may not be exhaustive) involves the identification of unconscionable conduct, albeit its content and degree will vary according to the category. It is a term which has various shades of meaning according to its context. There are different thresholds of conduct in various categories, all of which may be described as unconscionable …

Ultimately the language of s 51AA requires identification of conduct able to be characterised as unconscionable in a sense known to the unwritten law. In the context of that law as it presently stands, unconscionable conduct is that which supports the grant of relief on the principles set out in specific equitable doctrines. Five categories of case are set out above … [T]he terms of the section are not limited to those categories. Although the section is confined by the parameters of the 'unwritten law', it is the unwritten law 'from time to time'. Neither the Explanatory Memorandum nor the Second Reading Speech can be treated as imposing qualifications which are not found in the words of s 51AA. On the other hand, equitable doctrine does not presently provide a remedy against conduct simply on the basis that it is unfair in the opinion of a judge. It cannot be applied to unconscionable conduct at large.

3. For analyses of this case and of the different views on the scope of s 51AA see R Bigwood, 'Australian Competition and Consumer Commission v C G Berbatis Holdings Pty Ltd: Curbing Unconscionability: Berbatis in the High Court of Australia' (2004) 28 Melbourne University Law Review 203 and B Horrigan, 'The Expansion of Fairness-Based Business Regulation — Unconscionability, Good Faith and the Law's Informed Conscience' (2004) 32 Australian Business Law Review 159.

Unconscionability and undue influence

11.6   Bridgewater v Leahy (1998) 194 CLR 457

Court: High Court of Australia

Facts: Bill York, a substantial pastoral property holder from Queensland, provided in his will for his wife and four married daughters. The daughters' share of his estate was subject to an option he had granted for $200,000 to his nephew and business partner, Neil York, with whom he had a close personal and working relationship. Bill relied on the much younger Neil to manage his farming interests. In 1988, Neil suggested to Bill that he be allowed to buy a portion of the land that was subject to the option for $150,000, being the amount Neil and his wife had obtained from the sale of their own property. Bill agreed, despite the fact that the portion of land in question had a market value of about $700,000. Bill's solicitor suggested the contract for sale reflect the larger purchase price, but that Bill execute a deed of forgiveness for the balance, being about $550,000. The solicitor did not advise Bill to seek independent legal advice, but did arrange for him to be medically examined before he signed the deed and the transfer documents. When Bill died in 1989, Neil exercised the option and purchased the remainder of the landholdings described in the will for $200,000. Bill's daughters, inheriting $50,000 each from their father's estate, commenced legal action against the estate's executor Leahy, initially by attacking the will and the option. When they failed at trial, they then challenged the deed of forgiveness on the ground that it had been induced by Neil's unconscionable conduct towards Bill. A majority of the Queensland Court of Appeal dismissed their appeal. The daughters then appealed to the High Court.

Issue: The issue before the High Court was whether Neil had acted in an unconscionable way towards Bill in the transactions for the transfer of land and the release of liability for payment of the balance of the purchase price.

Decision: The majority of the High Court (Gaudron, Gummow and Kirby JJ; Gleeson CJ and Callinan J dissenting) held that unconscionable conduct by Neil had been established on the facts because of his 'passive acceptance of a benefit in unconscionable circumstances'.

Extracts: The extracts from the joint majority judgment as well as the joint dissenting judgment reflect contrasting views on the extent to which unconscionability may be grounded on the passive acceptance of a benefit.

Gaudron, Gummow and Kirby JJ

[475] The [daughters] do not submit that the transfers and the deed are voidable by Bill's estate on the ground that, when they were executed, Bill was incapable of understanding their effect, in the sense of their general purport.[69] Further, this is not a case where the instruments are said to be void at law on the footing of non est factum. It is not alleged that Bill's faculties were so defective that 'he [did] not really [476] know what he [was] doing — that his mind [did] not go with his deed'.[70] The case with respect to the transfers and the deed is, like that identified by Fullagar J in *Blomley v Ryan*, one 'in which relief [can] be obtained by the [daughters], if at all, only in equity' ...

[T]his appeal turns upon what the [daughters] contend is the misconception in the reasons of the primary judge (uncorrected in the Court of Appeal) of the determinative equitable doctrine and the consequent misapplication of principle to the primary facts ...

The strength of the [daughters'] case in this Court is that, whilst there is little disagreement as to the primary facts, neither [the trial judge] nor the majority in the Court of Appeal correctly applied the relevant principles to those facts and, upon that false basis, drew inferences which are either irrelevant or incorrectly focused.

The challenge in this Court is not to concurrent findings of fact but to concurrent misapplication of principle to uncontentious primary facts ...

[477] It is apparent from the reasons of the primary judge that his Honour treated the fate of the case with respect to unconscionable dealing in a real sense as consequent upon the failure of the claim with respect to undue influence and that the failure of that claim in turn was linked with the initial holding with respect to the execution of the Will.

In addition to the distinction between the doctrine of undue influence as understood in courts of probate and courts of equity, it is appropriate to emphasise the distinction between the equitable doctrines concerned with undue influence and unconscionable dealings or conduct. On occasion, both doctrines may apply in the one [478] case. Each doctrine may be seen as a species of that genus of equitable intervention to refuse enforcement of or to set aside transactions which, if allowed to stand, would offend equity and good conscience. However, there are conceptual and practical distinctions between them and these were insufficiently expressed by the primary judge ...

Sir Anthony Mason, with reference to the well developed Australian body of authority on the subject, has contrasted the two doctrines as follows:

> My understanding of undue influence ... is that it denotes an ascendancy by the stronger party over the weaker party such that the relevant transaction is not the free, voluntary and independent act of the weaker party ... In other words, it is the actual or presumed impairment of the judgment of the weaker party that is the critical element in the grant of relief on the ground of undue influence ... Unconscionable conduct, as the term suggests, focuses more on the unconscientious conduct of the defendant. As a ground of relief in England unconscionable conduct has been confined largely to 'catching bargains' with expectant heirs and others in particular categories of disadvantage eg those who are illiterate ... In Australia, it has been recognised that unconscionable

---

69. *Gibbons v Wright* (1954) 91 CLR 423 at 449.
70. *Blomley v Ryan* (1956) 99 CLR 362 at 401.

conduct is a ground of relief which will be available 'whenever one party by reason of some condition or circumstance is placed at a special disadvantage vis-à-vis another and unfair or unconscientious [479] advantage is taken of the opportunity thereby created'.[71] Unconscionable conduct is also recognised in New Zealand as a ground of relief in these circumstances ...[72]

[485] The primary judge dealt with the absence of independent advice with respect to the steps taken by Bill ... [concluding] ... that he was 'satisfied that had Bill been independently advised by another lawyer, the end result would likely have been the same'. Such an approach to the matter is supported by some authority in this Court with respect to alleged undue influence.[73] There the focus is upon the quality of the assent of the disponor to the transaction.

Where the complaint is of unconscionable dealing, the point is rather different. As Manning J put it in *Re Levey; Ex parte Official Assignee*,[74] 'the Court does not allow any person to take advantage of any known weakness of the vendor' and the Court asks whether that party had 'the opportunity' of professional advice as to 'the [486] effect of what he [was] doing'. This denial of the opportunity to have 'the assistance of a disinterested legal adviser',[75] rather than speculation as to what might have followed had it been pursued, is an element in the unconscientious conduct in respect of which equity intervenes to deny the entitlement of the disponee to retain the property in question, unless the disponee shows the disposition to have been 'fair, just and reasonable'.[76] ...

[489] [Bill] said that he had often helped his daughters, buying a hairdressing salon in Chinchilla for June, land for Kevin and Shirley at Dulacca and a house for Desley in Cairns. Dealing with the reasons why Neil had been given the land, Bill said that Neil 'has worked hard', that Neil had stuck with him 'through thick and thin' and that he thought Neil was 'entitled to it'. Of his daughters, he said that they 'married blokes and they never helped me', that they had 'never worked on the place', 'never picked up sticks', had 'got their own jobs' and that he had 'never asked them to do anything for [him]' ...

[490] The position of disadvantage which renders one party subject to exploitation by another such that the benefit of an improvident disposition by the disadvantaged party may not in good conscience be retained may stem from a strong emotional dependence or attachment.[77] *Louth v Diprose* was such a case. In his judgment in the South Australian Full Court, a decision which was upheld in this Court, Jacobs ACJ said:

> It is an oversimplification to say that because the respondent acted as he did with his eyes open, and with a full understanding of what he was doing, he was not in a position of disadvantage, and therefore not the victim of unconscionable conduct.[78] ...

---

71. (1983) 151 CLR 447 at 462.
72. Sir Anthony Mason, 'The Impact of Equitable Doctrine on the Law of Contract' (1998) 27 *Anglo-American Law Review* 1 at 6–8.
73. *Linderstam v Barnett* (1915) 19 CLR 528 at 530–1; *Watkins v Combes* (1922) 30 CLR 180 at 197.
74. (1894) 15 NSWR (B&P) 30 at 36.
75. *Longmate v Ledger* (1860) 66 ER 67 at 69.
76. *Commercial Bank of Australia Ltd v Amadio* (1983) 151 CLR 447 at 474.
77. *Louth v Diprose* (1992) 175 CLR 621 at 626, 629–30, 637–8, 643.
78. *Diprose v Louth (No 2)* (1990) 54 SASR 450 at 453.

[491] We have referred to the primary judge's conclusion that Bill had 'the capacity then to know what he was doing and to make informed decisions about the disposition of his property'. That however is not an answer to the question whether, on the primary facts, the conclusion should have been reached that advantage was taken of Bill's disadvantaged position. Even with respect to the doctrine of undue influence, as distinct from that dealing with unconscionable conduct, equitable principles may be invoked to set aside a gift where a donor is perfectly competent to understand and intend what he or she did ...

[493] Relief

The relationship between Bill and Neil meant that, when Neil raised the question of using the proceeds of sale of the [land Neil sold], they were meeting on unequal terms. Neil took advantage of this position to obtain a benefit through a grossly improvident transaction on the part of his uncle.

In some cases, the equity that arises by reason of an unconscientious or unconscionable dealing of the nature with which this appeal is concerned may be satisfied only by setting aside that dealing in its entirety. The dealing may be embodied in the one instrument which contains several provisions or in several instruments. In other circumstances, of which this case is an example, the equity may be satisfied by orders setting aside some but not all of these instruments or some but not all of the provisions thereof.[79]

It is unconscionable for Neil and his wife to retain the benefit of the improvident transaction by asserting the forgiveness of the whole of the debt which would otherwise be owing to Bill's estate. On the findings of fact made by and available to him, the primary judge should have held that the deed should not be allowed to stand and be given its full effect; the Court of Appeal also should have intervened. A similar conclusion would have followed with respect to the transfers but for the complexities that would arise in the disentanglement of the transactions involved, including the absence of [Neil's father] and the mortgagee as parties to this litigation. In the circumstances of this case and [494] consistently with the framing of relief which, in Lord Blackburn's phrase, is 'practically just',[80] the [daughters], as representatives of Bill's estate, properly may elect that only the deed itself be set aside. However, in seeking equity, the estate must be prepared to do equity.[81] In particular, weight has to be given to [Bill's] wish significantly to benefit [Neil] which was expressed in ... the will ...

Although the present action was differently cast, the ultimate question it presents may be appreciated by considering what would be the outcome of an action by the estate to recover from Neil and Beryl the amount forgiven. In that situation and having regard to all the circumstances, would it be consistent with equity and good conscience for Neil and Beryl to plead the deed as to the full amount of the forgiveness? Would a response by the estate seeking rescission of the deed as to the whole of the forgiveness succeed?

Had the transfers been implemented and the will taken effect [495] according to its terms before the deed was executed, the residuary estate, dealt with in ... the will, would

---

79. See *Willis v Barron* [1902] AC 271 at 272–3; *Maguire v Makaronis* (1997) 188 CLR 449 at 474–5.
80. *Erlanger v New Sombrero Phosphate Company* (1878) 3 App Cas 1218 at 1278–9. See also *Vadasz v Pioneer Concrete (SA) Pty Ltd* (1995) 184 CLR 102 at 113–4.
81. *Vadasz v Pioneer Concrete (SA) Pty Ltd* (1995) 184 CLR 102 at 115; *Maguire v Makaronis* (1997) 188 CLR 449 at 474–5, 496–9.

have been augmented by recoupment from Neil and Beryl of the amount forgiven by the deed. The option in Neil's favour still would have operated but only in respect of the remaining interests of the estate in the [remaining land], together with the partnership interest and the interest in personal property.

As we have indicated earlier in these reasons, the consequence of an order setting aside the deed as to the whole of the forgiveness would be that the substantial amount so retrieved by the estate would fall wholly into the residue divisible under [the will] equally between Bill's daughters. The option provision would not apply to it. The interests of Bill's widow under … the will would be unaffected. What would Neil's position be under the will? The transfers withdrew from the estate what had been [Bill's] interests in the [remaining land]. The transfers are not set aside. [Bill] benefited to the extent of the $150,000 paid by Neil on the revised settlement date of 28 November 1988. Upon the present thesis, the exercise of the option in … [the will], in its remaining operation, would have yielded to Neil (as was in fact the case) assets valued at some $248,000 in exchange for the payment of $200,000. That would not reflect any significant level of benefaction to Neil by his uncle.

Had the transfers not been made and [the residuary estate clause in the will] been left to operate in its terms at Bill's death, then, in exchange for the $200,000 he later paid on exercise of the option, Neil would have received value in a sum greatly exceeding $248,000 which, as we have indicated, represented that which Neil acquired when he exercised the option after Bill's death. That further value would have been represented by the value at that time of the total consideration of $696,811 payable in accordance with the transfers for the acquisition of Bill's interests in the [remaining land]. However, as we indicated earlier, Neil had been prepared to pay and had paid $150,000 towards that $696,811. This payment by him should not now be left out of account.

The status quo with respect both to the deed and the transfers cannot be restored. The issue then is whether, in the situation presented by the setting aside of the deed but not the transfers, an allowance should be made by the estate in favour of Neil which qualifies what otherwise would be the full recoupment to the estate of the amount forgiven by the Deed. This was $546,811 of the purchase price under the Transfers of $696,811. Should the estate, as a term of the restoration of its rights to recover the debt, be required to make a provision in Neil's favour? Before an answer is given, regard must be paid to the subjection of the estate to claims under Pt 4 of the *Succession Act*.

If [the residuary estate clause in the will] had operated in Neil's favour, fully in accordance with its terms in respect of the whole of [Bill's] lands there indicated, [Bill's] daughters as well as his widow would have had their rights [496] against the estate under Pt 4 of the *Succession Act*, asserting that adequate provision had not been made from the estate for their proper maintenance and support. They might reasonably have expected substantial provision to be made by order in their favour. Nevertheless, if the widow and daughters had pursued the family provision application, regard would have to have been had to such evidence and submissions as were properly presented in opposition to their claims. In particular, some significant weight would have to have been given to Bill's wish to benefit his nephew by the means adopted in [the residuary estate clause] of the will. The result would have been to retain some provision in Neil's favour after the orders were made on the family provision application. This provision should be reflected in the terms now imposed upon the estate in setting aside the deed. There should be an allowance in favour of Neil and Beryl from the indebtedness which may be recouped from them by the estate as a consequence of the setting aside of the deed.

The matter should be returned to the Supreme Court to determine, in the absence of agreement in this respect between the parties and after hearing such further evidence (if any) as is allowed, the amount of such allowance ...

Gleeson CJ and Callinan J (dissenting)

[466] The relief primarily sought by the [daughters] would involve leaving intact the transfer of the land the subject of the 1988 transaction from Bill to Neil and Beryl York in consideration for $696,811 (a price which Neil never agreed to pay and Bill never intended to seek), together with the payment of $150,000, but cancelling the deed by which the balance of $546,811 was forgiven. The result would be to defeat the intentions of all the parties to the transaction. The [daughters], however, would be substantially better off than they would have been had the transaction never been entered into. Neil would be compelled to pay for the land transferred in 1988, not only an amount over and above that for which he was entitled to acquire that and other land under his option, (which he exercised), but also an amount over and above that which he offered to Bill York and which Bill York accepted ...

[469] The essence of the [daughters'] claim is that, in 1988, Neil York took unfair advantage of Bill York. His conduct, it is said, involved an unconscientious use of power arising out of the circumstances and condition of the parties to the transaction, of the kind considered in *Blomley v Ryan*.[82] On this approach, Bill York was a 'victimized party'.[83]

It would not be to the point had Bill York entered into a transaction which was unfair to his wife and daughters, if there were nothing more to it. The [daughters] based their argument upon what they said was a special disability on the part of Bill York, and an unconscientious taking advantage of such disability by Neil. That is the way their case was put, and it was to that proposition that the judgments in the courts below responded.

What was the special disability? The trial judge, and the majority in the Court of Appeal, found there was none. They found that Bill York knew and understood what he was doing in 1988, and that the transaction into which he entered gave effect to his long standing and firmly held wishes. They also pointed out that it is impossible to separate the 1988 transaction from the 1985 will, and that any characterisation of the dealings between Bill and Neil York in 1988 must take account of their common understanding of what was to take place on the death of Bill in relation to the subject lands. There is no evidence, and no finding in the courts below, that the 1988 transaction resulted from any apprehension on the part of Neil York, either that his uncle would alter his will to Neil's disadvantage, or that a successful challenge to the will might be made after Bill York's death. As was noted above, almost a year elapsed between the time when the 1988 transaction was first proposed and the time when it was completed; and this was when Bill York was aged about 84. [470] The transaction can scarcely be regarded as some kind of pre-emptive strike ...

The nature of the relevant disadvantage concerns the ability of the weaker, or victimised, party, to make an informed judgment as to his or her interests. This is made

---

82. *Blomley v Ryan* (1956) 99 CLR 362 at 386.
83. *Blomley v Ryan* (1956) 99 CLR 362 at 386.

clear in *Commercial Bank of Australia Ltd v Amadio*. Mason J, after referring to Fullagar J in *Blomley v Ryan* said:

> It is made plain enough ... that the situations mentioned are no more than particular exemplifications of an underlying general principle which may be invoked whenever one party by reason of some condition or circumstance is placed at a special disadvantage vis-à-vis another and unfair or unconscientious advantage is then taken of the opportunity thereby created. I qualify the word 'disadvantage' by the adjective 'special' in order to disavow any suggestion that the principle applies whenever there is some difference in the bargaining power of the parties and in order to emphasise that the disabling condition or circumstance is one which seriously affects the ability of the innocent party to make a judgment as to his own best interests, when the other party knows or ought to know of the existence of that condition or circumstance and of its effect on the innocent party.[84]

In the same case Deane J,[85] identifying the weakness which attracts the jurisdiction, referred to the statement of McTiernan J in *Blomley v Ryan* that the 'essence of such weakness is that the party is unable to judge for himself'.[86] ...

[471] The [daughters] have not demonstrated plain injustice or clear error of the kind referred to by Deane J. Rather, the findings of fact made in the courts below appear to be correct.

It is of interest to note the findings of fact at first instance in some of the leading cases on this topic. In *Wilton v Farnworth* a person who was 'markedly dull-witted and stupid'[87] was persuaded to sign over to another his interest in his wife's estate without having any idea of what he was doing. In *Blomley v Ryan* the defendant took advantage of the plaintiff's alcoholism to induce him to enter a transaction when his judgment was seriously affected by drink. In [472] *Amadio* the special disability of the guarantors included a limited understanding of English, pressure to enter in haste into a transaction they did not understand, and reliance upon their son. In *Louth v Diprose* the primary judge found that the donee, with whom the donor was 'utterly infatuated', had threatened suicide, manufactured a false atmosphere of personal crisis, and engaged in a process of manipulation to which the donor was vulnerable. The judge found that the donee's conduct 'smacked of fraud'.[88]

Of course, it is the principles enunciated in those cases, and not their particular facts, which are of importance. The facts, however, illustrate the practical content of the principles; and they are a long way removed from the facts of the present case. As to the principles expounded in the cases, the findings in the court below establish Bill York's independence of mind and capacity for judgment when he entered into the 1988 transaction; a transaction which can only be understood in a wider context, including the provisions of the 1985 will, and Bill York's long and firmly held intention that Neil York should succeed to his pastoral interests. The findings deny the existence of any

---

84. *Commercial Bank of Australia Ltd v Amadio* (1983) 151 CLR 447 at 462.
85. *Commercial Bank of Australia Ltd v Amadio* (1983) 151 CLR 447 at 476–7.
86. *Blomley v Ryan* (1956) 99 CLR 362 at 392.
87. *Wilton v Farnworth* (1948) 76 CLR 646 at 649.
88. *Louth v Diprose* (1992) 175 CLR 621 at 637.

special disability in Bill York, and they acquit Neil York of unconscientious conduct. It is not a sufficient answer to these concurrent findings of fact to suggest that the members of the courts below failed to address the correct issues. The issues were squarely before them and, in particular, the principles in *Amadio* were considered.

We do not accept that [the trial judge] failed to give separate and independent consideration to the claim which is presently in issue, and treated its failure as a necessary consequence of the failure of the challenges to the will. Rather, his Honour treated the will as an important part of the factual background to the 1988 transaction. In that he was correct. The reasoning of the majority in the Court of Appeal reflected an accurate appreciation and application of the relevant principles.

The claim based on unconscionability should fail.

Comments
1. See Radan and Stewart at **11.74–11.80**.
2. For discussions of this case see A Finlay, 'Can We See the Chancellor's Foot?: *Bridgewater v Leahy*' (1999) 14 *Journal of Contract Law* 265 and T Cockburn, 'The Boundaries of Unconscionability and Equitable Intervention: *Bridgewater v Leahy* in the High Court' (2000) 8 *Australian Property Law Journal* 1.

12

EQUITABLE ESTOPPEL

Introduction

12.1 This chapter deals with relief based upon equitable estoppel. Equitable estoppel brings together what have been traditionally seen as separate forms of estoppel in equity, namely, promissory estoppel and proprietary estoppel. Although both of these forms of estoppel are seen as species of equitable estoppel, there are distinctions between them, especially in the realm of the form of relief granted once the estoppel is established. With promissory estoppel relief is generally reliance-based, whereas with proprietary estoppel it is more often expectation-based.

The cases extracted in this chapter discuss the following:

- the nature and principled basis of equitable estoppel: *Waltons Stores (Interstate) Ltd v Maher* (1988) 164 CLR 387; *The Commonwealth of Australia v Verwayen* (1990) 170 CLR 394;
- the clarity of the representation and equitable estoppel: *Thorner v Major* [2009] 3 All ER 945;
- detriment as an element of equitable estoppel: *Je Maintiendrai Pty Ltd v Quaglia* (1980) 26 SASR 101; and
- relief based upon equitable estoppel: *Giumelli v Giumelli* (1999) 196 CLR 101.

The nature of equitable estoppel

12.2   Waltons Stores (Interstate) Ltd v Maher (1988) 164 CLR 387

Court: High Court of Australia

Facts: The Mahers owned commercial premises in Nowra which Waltons was interested in leasing. Waltons needed to relocate its business in Nowra to new premises and the Mahers' site was available. They agreed that the Mahers would demolish the existing premises and erect a new building to meet Waltons' requirements. A draft agreement for lease was sent to the solicitors for the Mahers and some amendments were discussed. Waltons' solicitors indicated that they expected their client's agreement to the alterations and said that they would let the Mahers know if the amendments were not acceptable. The Mahers' solicitors sent the amended lease, duly executed by the Mahers, to Waltons' solicitors 'by way of exchange'. The letter was not acknowledged by Waltons' solicitors until two months later. The Mahers began to demolish the existing premises, as time was critical if they were to complete the demolition and the

289

new construction in time for the start of the lease agreement. It was later established in court that Waltons knew what the Mahers were doing. However, after receiving the letter and executed lease, Waltons reconsidered its position and a few months later wrote to the Mahers' solicitors saying that the lease had not been executed by Waltons and that Waltons was not proceeding with it. The Mahers sued Waltons for damages for breach of contract on the basis that Waltons was estopped from denying the existence of the lease. They were successful at first instance and in the Court of Appeal in New South Wales. Waltons appealed to the High Court.

Issues: The issues before the High Court were whether Waltons could be estopped from denying the existence of a binding contract to take a lease of the Mahers' premises at Nowra and, if so, whether Waltons should be ordered to pay damages rather than to specifically perform the lease agreement

Decision: The High Court (Mason CJ, Wilson, Brennan, Deane and Gaudron JJ) unanimously dismissed Waltons' appeal and upheld the lower courts' order that damages be paid to the Mahers. Mason CJ and Wilson J, in a joint judgment, and Brennan J found for the Mahers on the basis of equitable estoppel. Deane and Gaudron JJ found for the Mahers on the basis of common law estoppel.

Extracts: The extracts below from the joint judgment of Mason CJ and Wilson J and the judgment of Brennan J reveal the main elements of equitable estoppel and its application to the facts of the case. They also discuss the availability of equitable estoppel in cases where there is no pre-existing contractual relationship between the parties. The judgment of Brennan J includes an often cited summary of the main elements of equitable estoppel.

Mason CJ and Wilson J

[399] Promissory estoppel certainly extends to representations (or promises) as to future conduct.[1] So far the doctrine has been mainly confined to precluding departure from a representation by a person in a pre-existing contractual relationship that he will not enforce his contractual rights, whether they be pre-existing or rights to be acquired as a result of the representation.[2] But Denning J in *Central London Property Trust Ltd v High Trees House Ltd*,[3] treated it as a wide-ranging doctrine operating outside the pre-existing contractual relationship ... In principle there is certainly no reason the doctrine should not apply so as to preclude departure by a person from a representation that he will not enforce a non-contractual right.[4]

[400] There has been for many years a reluctance to allow promissory estoppel to become the vehicle for the positive enforcement of a representation by a party that he would do

---

1. *Legione v Hateley* (1983) 152 CLR 406 at 432.
2. *Ajayi v R T Briscoe (Nigeria) Ltd* [1964] 3 All ER 556 at 559; *State Rail Authority of New South Wales v Heath Outdoor Pty Ltd* (1986) 7 NSWLR 170 at 193.
3. [1947] KB 130 at 134–5.
4. *Durham Fancy Goods Ltd v Michael Jackson (Fancy Goods) Ltd* [1968] 2 QB 839 at 847; *Attorney-General v Codner* [1973] 1 NZLR 545 at 553.

something in the future. Promissory estoppel, it has been said, is a defensive equity[5] and the traditional notion has been that estoppel could only be relied upon defensively as a shield and not as a sword. *High Trees* itself was an instance of the defensive use of promissory estoppel. But this does not mean that a plaintiff cannot rely on an estoppel. Even according to traditional orthodoxy, a plaintiff may rely on an estoppel if he has an independent cause of action, where in the words of Denning LJ in *Combe v Combe*, the estoppel 'may be part of a cause of action, but not a cause of action in itself'.[6]

But the [Mahers] ask us to drive promissory estoppel one step further by enforcing directly in the absence of a pre-existing relationship of any kind a non-contractual promise on which the representee has relied to his detriment. For the purposes of discussion, we shall assume that there was such a promise in the present case. The principal objection to the enforcement of such a promise is that it would outflank the principles of the law of contract. Holmes J expressed his objection to the operation of promissory estoppel in this situation when he said:

> It would cut up the doctrine of consideration by the roots, if a promisee could make a gratuitous promise binding by subsequently acting in reliance on it.[7]

Likewise, Sir Owen Dixon considered that estoppel cut across the principles of the law of contract, notably offer and acceptance and consideration.[8] And Denning LJ in *Combe v Combe*, after noting that 'The doctrine of consideration is too firmly fixed to be overthrown by a side-wind', said that such a promise could only be enforced if it was supported by sufficient consideration.[9] Moreover, it has been suggested that the enforcement of a promise given without consideration is by no means consistent with *Hoyt's Pty* **[401]** *Ltd v Spencer*[10] and *Maybury v Atlantic Union Oil Co Ltd*.[11]

There is force in these objections and it may not be a sufficient answer to repeat the words of Lord Denning MR in *Crabb v Arun District Council*: 'Equity comes in, true to form, to mitigate the rigours of strict law'.[12] True it is that in the orthodox case of promissory estoppel, where the promisor promises that he will not exercise or enforce an existing right, the elements of reliance and detriment attract equitable intervention on the basis that it is unconscionable for the promisor to depart from his promise, if to do so will result in detriment to the promisee. And it can be argued that there is no justification for applying the doctrine of promissory estoppel in this situation, yet denying it in the case of a non-contractual promise in the absence of a pre-existing relationship. The promise, if enforced, works a change in the relationship of the parties, by altering an existing legal

---

5. *Hughes v Metropolitan Railway Co* (1877) 2 App Cas 439 at 448; *Combe v Combe* [1951] 2 KB 215 at 219–20.
6. *Combe v Combe* [1951] 2 KB 215 at 220.
7. *Commonwealth v Scituate Savings Bank* (1884) 137 Mass 301 at 302.
8. Sir Owen Dixon, 'Concerning Judicial Method' (1956) 29 *Australian Law Journal* 468 at 475.
9. *Combe v Combe* [1951] 2 KB 215 at 220.
10. (1919) 27 CLR 133.
11. (1953) 89 CLR 507. See Finn, 'Equitable Estoppel' in Finn (ed), *Essays in Equity*, Law Book Co, Sydney, 1985, 59 at 75, and Greig and Davis, *The Law of Contract*, Law Book Co, Sydney (1987), pp 146–9, 175; but cf Seddon, 'A Plea for the Reform of the Rule in *Hoyt's Pty Ltd v Spencer*' (1978) 52 *Australian Law Journal* 372.
12. *Crabb v Arun District Council* [1976] Ch 179 at 187.

relationship in the first situation and by creating a new legal relationship in the second. The point has been made that it would be more logical to say that when the parties have agreed to pursue a course of action, an alteration of the relationship by non-contractual promise will not be countenanced, whereas the creation of a new relationship by a simple promise will be recognized.[13]

The direct enforcement of promises made without consideration by means of promissory estoppel has proceeded apace in the United States. The *Restatement on Contracts* 2d, § 90 states:

> (1) A promise which the promisor should reasonably expect to induce action or forbearance on the part of the promisee or a third person and which does induce such action or forbearance is binding if injustice can be avoided only by enforcement of the promise. The remedy granted for breach may be limited as justice requires.

This general proposition developed from the treatment in particular situations of promissory estoppel as the equivalent of consideration. Thus in *Allegheny College v National Chautauqua County Bank* Cardozo CJ said:

> [402] Certain ... it is that we have adopted the doctrine of promissory estoppel as the equivalent of consideration in connection with our law of charitable subscriptions.[14]

However, we need to view the development of the doctrine in the United States with some caution. There promissory estoppel developed partly in response to the limiting effects of the adoption of the bargain theory of consideration which has not been expressly adopted in Australia or England. It may be doubted whether our conception of consideration is substantially broader than the bargain theory,[15] though we may be willing to imply consideration in situations where the bargain theory as implemented in the United States would deny the existence of consideration. It is perhaps sufficient to say that in the United States, as in Australia, there is an obvious interrelationship between the doctrines of consideration and promissory estoppel, promissory estoppel tending to occupy ground left vacant due to the constraints affecting consideration.

The proposition stated in §90(1) of the *Restatement* seems on its face to reflect a closer connection with the general law of contract than our doctrine of promissory estoppel, with its origins in the equitable concept of unconscionable conduct, might be thought to allow. This is because in the United States promissory estoppel has become an equivalent or substitute for consideration in contract formation, detriment being an element common to both doctrines. None the less the proposition, by making the enforcement of the promise conditional on (a) a reasonable expectation on the part of the promisor that his promise will induce action or forbearance by the promisee and (b) the impossibility of avoiding injustice by other means, makes it clear that the promise is enforced in circumstances where departure from it is unconscionable. Note that the emphasis is on the promisor's reasonable expectation that his promise will induce action or forbearance, not on the fact that he created or encouraged an expectation in the promisee of performance of the promise.

---

13. D Jackson, 'Estoppel as a Sword' (1965) 81 *Law Quarterly Review* 223 at 242.
14. *Allegheny College v National Chautauqua County Bank* (1927) 246 NY 369 at 374.
15. *Australian Woollen Mills Pty Ltd v Commonwealth* (1954) 92 CLR 424 at 456.

Some recent English decisions are relevant to this general [403] discussion. *Amalgamated Property Co v Texas Bank*[16] in the Court of Appeal and *Pacol Ltd v Trade Lines Ltd*,[17] are instances of common law or conventional estoppel. However, the comment of Robert Goff J in *Texas Bank* at first instance is significant. His Honour observed:

> Such cases are very different from, eg, a mere promise by a party to make a gift or to increase his obligations under an existing contract; such promise will not generally give rise to an estoppel, even if acted on by the promisee, for the promisee may reasonably be expected to appreciate that, to render it binding, it must be incorporated in a binding contract or contractual variation, and that he cannot therefore safely rely upon it as a legally binding promise without first taking the necessary contractual steps.[18]

The point is that, generally speaking, a plaintiff cannot enforce a voluntary promise because the promisee may reasonably be expected to appreciate that, to render it binding, it must form part of a binding contract.

Crabb was an instance of promissory estoppel. It lends assistance to the view that promissory estoppel may in some circumstances extend to the enforcement of a right not previously in existence where the defendant has encouraged in the plaintiff the belief that it will be granted and has acquiesced in action taken by the plaintiff in that belief. There the defendants, knowing of the plaintiff's intention to sell his land in separate portions, encouraged the plaintiff to believe that he would be granted a right of access over their land and, by erecting gates and failing to disabuse him of his belief, encouraged the plaintiff to act to his detriment in selling part of the land without reservation of a right of way. This raised an equity in favour of the plaintiff which was satisfied by granting him a right of access and a right of way over the defendants' land. The Court of Appeal deduced from the circumstances an equity in the plaintiff to have these rights without having to pay for them. As Oliver J pointed out in *Taylors Fashions Ltd v Liverpool Victoria Trustees Co Ltd*,[19] the Court of Appeal treated promissory estoppel and proprietary estoppel or estoppel by acquiescence as mere facets of the same general principle, a point also made by Lord Denning MR in *Texas Bank*,[20] and seemingly accepted by the Privy Council in *Attorney-General (Hong Kong) v Humphreys Estate Ltd*.[21] In *Taylors Fashions*, Oliver J also remarked that what gave rise to the need for the court to intervene was the [404] defendants' unconscionable attempt to go back on the assumptions which were the foundation of their dealings.[22] Indeed, Scarman LJ in *Crabb* saw the question in terms of whether an equity had arisen from the conduct and relationship of the parties, concluding that the court should determine what was 'the minimum equity to do justice to the plaintiff'.[23]

---

16. [1982] QB 84.
17. [1982] 1 Lloyd's Rep 456.
18. *Amalgamated Investment & Property Co Ltd v Texas Commerce International Bank Ltd* [1982] QB 84 at 107.
19. [1982] QB 133 at 153.
20. [1982] QB 84 at 122.
21. [1987] 1 AC 114 at 123–4.
22. *Taylors Fashions Ltd v Liverpool Victoria Trustees Co Ltd* [1982] QB 133 at 153.
23. *Crabb v Arun District Council* [1976] Ch 179 at 193–194, 198. See also *Pascoe v Turner* [1979] 2 All ER 945 at 951.

The decision in *Crabb* is consistent with the principle of proprietary estoppel applied in *Ramsden v Dyson*.[24] Under that principle a person whose conduct creates or lends force to an assumption by another that he will obtain an interest in the first person's land and on the basis of that expectation the other person alters his position or acts to his detriment, may bring into existence an equity in favour of that other person, the nature and extent of the equity depending on the circumstances. And it should be noted that in *Crabb*, as in *Ramsden v Dyson*, although equity acted by way of recognizing a proprietary interest in the plaintiff, that proprietary interest came into existence as the only appropriate means by which the defendants could be effectively estopped from exercising their existing legal rights.

One may therefore discern in the cases a common thread which links them together, namely, the principle that equity will come to the relief of a plaintiff who has acted to his detriment on the basis of a basic assumption in relation to which the other party to the transaction has 'played such a part in the adoption of the assumption that it would be unfair or unjust if he were left free to ignore it'.[25] Equity comes to the relief of such a plaintiff on the footing that it would be unconscionable conduct on the part of the other party to ignore the assumption.

Before we turn to the very recent decision of the Privy Council in *Humphreys Estate* ... we should say something of equity's attitude to the enforcement of voluntary promises. So far equity has set its face against the enforcement of such promises and future representations as such. The support for the exercise of a general equitable jurisdiction to make good expectations created or encouraged by a defendant given by Lord Cottenham LC in *Hammersley v De Biel*,[26] affirmed by the House of Lords in that **[405]** case, was undermined by the insistence in *Jorden v Money*[27] on a representation of existing fact and destroyed by *Maddison v Alderson*.[28]

Because equitable estoppel has its basis in unconscionable conduct, rather than the making good of representations, the objection, grounded in *Maddison v Alderson*, that promissory estoppel outflanks the doctrine of part performance loses much of its sting. Equitable estoppel is not a doctrine associated with part performance whose principal purpose is to overcome non-compliance with the formal requirements for the making of contracts. Equitable estoppel, though it may lead to the plaintiff acquiring an estate or interest in land, depends on considerations of a different kind from those on which part performance depends. Holding the representor to his representation is merely one way of doing justice between the parties.

In *Humphreys Estate* the defendants representing the Hong Kong Government negotiated with a group of companies (HKL), which included the respondent Humphreys Estate, for an exchange whereby the Government would acquire eighty-three flats, being part of property belonging to HKL, and in exchange HKL would take from the Government a Crown lease of property known as Queen's Gardens and be granted the right to develop

---

24. (1866) LR 1 HL 129.
25. *Grundt v Great Boulder Pty Gold Mines Ltd* (1937) 59 CLR 641 at 675. See also *Thompson v Palmer* (1933) 49 CLR 507 at 547.
26. (1845) 8 ER 1312.
27. (1854) 10 ER 868.
28. (1883) 8 App Cas 467.

that property and certain adjoining property held by HKL. The negotiations did not result in a contract, though the exchange of properties was agreed in principle but subject to contract. The Government took possession of HKL's property and expended a substantial sum on it. HKL took possession of Queen's Gardens and demolished existing buildings and paid to the Government $103,865,608, the agreed difference between the value of the two properties. HKL withdrew from the negotiations and sued to recover the amount paid and possession of the first property. The defendants claimed that HKL was estopped from withdrawing from the agreement in principle. The Privy Council rejected this claim on the ground that the Government failed to show (a) that HKL created or encouraged a belief or expectation on the part of the Government that HKL would not withdraw from the agreement in principle and (b) that the Government relied on that belief or expectation.[29] Their Lordships observed:

> It is possible but unlikely that in circumstances at present [406] unforeseeable a party to negotiations set out in a document expressed to be 'subject to contract' would be able to satisfy the court that the parties had subsequently agreed to convert the document into a contract or that some form of estoppel had arisen to prevent both parties from refusing to proceed with the transactions envisaged by the document.[30]

The foregoing review of the doctrine of promissory estoppel indicates that the doctrine extends to the enforcement of voluntary promises on the footing that a departure from the basic assumptions underlying the transaction between the parties must be unconscionable. As failure to fulfil a promise does not of itself amount to unconscionable conduct, mere reliance on an executory promise to do something, resulting in the promisee changing his position or suffering detriment, does not bring promissory estoppel into play. Something more would be required. *Humphreys Estate* suggests that this may be found, if at all, in the creation or encouragement by the party estopped in the other party of an assumption that a contract will come into existence or a promise will be performed and that the other party relied on that assumption to his detriment to the knowledge of the first party. *Humphreys Estate* referred in terms to an assumption that the plaintiff would not exercise an existing legal right or liberty, the right or liberty to withdraw from the negotiations, but as a matter of substance such an assumption is indistinguishable from an assumption that a binding contract would eventuate. On the other hand the United States experience, distilled in the *Restatement* (2d, §90), suggests that the principle is to be expressed in terms of a reasonable expectation on the part of the promisor that his promise will induce action or forbearance by the promisee, the promise inducing such action or forbearance in circumstances where injustice arising from unconscionable conduct can only be avoided by holding the promisor to his promise.

The application of these principles to the facts of the present case is not without difficulty. The parties were negotiating through their solicitors for an agreement for lease to be concluded by way of customary exchange. *Humphreys Estate* illustrates the difficulty of establishing an estoppel preventing parties from refusing to proceed with a transaction expressed to be 'subject to contract'. And there is the problem identified in *Texas Bank*[31]

---

29. *Attorney-General of Hong Kong v Humphreys Estate Ltd* [1987] 1 AC 114 at 124.
30. *Attorney-General of Hong Kong v Humphreys Estate Ltd* [1987] 1 AC 114 at 127–8.
31. [1982] QB 84 at 107.

that a voluntary promise will not generally give rise to an estoppel because the promisee may reasonably be expected to appreciate that he cannot safely rely upon it. This problem is magnified in the present case where the parties were represented by their solicitors.

All this may be conceded. But the crucial question remains: was [407] [Waltons] entitled to stand by in silence when it must have known that [the Mahers] were proceeding on the assumption that they had an agreement and that completion of the exchange was a formality? The mere exercise of its legal right not to exchange contracts could not be said to amount to unconscionable conduct on the part of [Waltons]. But there were two other factors present in the situation which require to be taken into consideration. The first was the element of urgency that pervaded the negotiation of the terms of the proposed lease. As we have noted, [Waltons] was bound to give up possession of its existing commercial premises in Nowra in January 1984; the new building was to be available for fitting out by 15 January and completed by 5 February 1984. The ... solicitor [for the Mahers] had said to [Waltons'] solicitor on 7 November that it would be impossible for Maher to complete the building within the agreed time unless the agreement were concluded 'within the next day or two'. The outstanding details were agreed within a day or two thereafter, and the work of preparing the site commenced almost immediately.

The second factor of importance is that [the Mahers] executed the counterpart deed and it was forwarded to [Waltons'] solicitor on 11 November. The assumption on which [the Mahers] acted thereafter was that completion of the necessary exchange was a formality. The next their solicitor heard from [Waltons] was a letter from its solicitors dated 19 January, informing him that [Waltons] did not intend to proceed with the matter. It had known, at least since 10 December, that costly work was proceeding on the site.

It seems to us, in the light of these considerations, that [Waltons] was under an obligation to communicate with [the Mahers] within a reasonable time after receiving the executed counterpart deed and certainly when it learnt on 10 December that demolition was proceeding. It had to choose whether to complete the contract or to warn [the Mahers] that it had not yet decided upon the course it would take. It was not entitled simply to retain the counterpart deed executed by the respondents and do nothing. [Waltons'] inaction, in all the circumstances, constituted clear encouragement or inducement to [the Mahers] to continue to act on the basis of the assumption which they had made. It was unconscionable for it, knowing that [the Mahers] were exposing themselves to detriment by acting on the basis of a false assumption, to adopt a course [408] of inaction which encouraged them in the course they had adopted. To express the point in the language of promissory estoppel, the appellant is estopped in all the circumstances from retreating from its implied promise to complete the contract.

Brennan J

[416] Equitable estoppel ... does not operate by establishing an assumed state of affairs ... [A]n equitable estoppel is a source of legal obligation. It is not enforceable against the party estopped because a cause of action or ground of defence would arise on an assumed state of affairs; it is the source of a legal obligation arising on an actual state of affairs. An equitable estoppel is binding in conscience on the party estopped, and it is to be satisfied by that party doing or abstaining from doing something in order to prevent detriment to the party raising the estoppel which that party would otherwise suffer by having acted or

abstained from acting in reliance on the assumption or expectation which he has been induced to adopt. Perhaps equitable estoppel is more accurately described as an equity created by estoppel ...

[419] The element which both attracts the jurisdiction of a court of equity and shapes the remedy to be given is unconscionable conduct on the part of the person bound by the equity, and the remedy required to satisfy an equity varies according to the circumstances of the case ... Sometimes it is necessary to decree that a party's expectation be specifically fulfilled by the party bound by the equity; sometimes it is necessary to grant an injunction to restrain the exercise of legal rights either absolutely or on condition; sometimes it is necessary to give an equitable lien on property for the expenditure which a party has made on it. However, in moulding its decree, the court, as a court of conscience, goes no further than is necessary to prevent unconscionable conduct. What, then, is unconscionable conduct? An exhaustive definition is both impossible and unnecess-[420]-ary, but the minimum elements required to give rise to an equitable estoppel should be stated.

Some indication of what constitutes unconscionable conduct can be gleaned from the instances in which an equity created by estoppel has been held to arise. If cases of equitable estoppel are in truth but particular instances of the operation of the general principles of equity, there is little purpose in dividing those cases into the categories of promissory and proprietary estoppel which are not necessarily exhaustive of the cases in which equity will intervene ... I do not find it generally helpful to divide into classes the cases in which an equity created by estoppel has been held to exist. However, the familiar categories serve to identify the characteristics of the circumstances which have been held to give rise to an equity in the party raising the estoppel. In cases of promissory estoppel, the equity binds the holder of a legal right who induces another to expect that that right will not be exercised against him. In cases of proprietary estoppel, the equity binds the owner of property who induces another to expect that an interest in the property will be conferred on him. In cases where there has been an imperfect gift of property the equity binds the donor of the property when, after the making of the imperfect gift, he does something to induce the donee to act on the assumption that the imperfect gift is effective or on the expectation that it will be made effective.

In all cases where an equity created by estoppel is raised, the party raising the equity has acted or abstained from acting on an assumption or expectation as to the legal relationship between himself and the party who induced him to adopt the assumption or expectation. The assumption or expectation does not relate to mere facts, whether existing or future. (An assumption as to a legal relationship may be an assumption that there is no legal relationship, as in the cases where A builds on B's land assuming it to be his own.) [421] Though the party raising the estoppel may be under no mistake as to the facts, he assumes that a particular legal relationship exists or expects that a particular legal relationship will exist between himself and the party who induced the assumption or expectation. The assumption or expectation may involve an error of law. Thus a promissory or a proprietary estoppel may arise when a party, not mistaking any facts, erroneously attributes a binding legal effect to a promise made without consideration. But, if the party raising the estoppel is induced by the other party's promise to adopt an assumption or expectation, the promise must be intended by the promisor and understood by the promisee to affect their legal relations ...

[T]he basic object of the doctrine ... is to avoid the detriment which the promisee would suffer if the promisor fails to fulfil the promise. It ... is important to observe that the doctrine has no application to an assumption or expectation induced by a promise which is not intended by the promisor and understood by the promisee to affect their legal relations ...

[422] It follows that an assumption or expectation by one party which does not relate to what the other party is bound to do or not to do gives no foundation for an equitable estoppel, though the assumption or expectation relates to the prospect of the other party conducting himself in a particular way. The risk that the other party who, being free to conduct himself in whatever way he chooses, may choose to conduct himself in a way different from that assumed or [423] expected rests with the party who adopts the assumption or expectation.

Parties who are negotiating a contract may proceed in the expectation that the terms will be agreed and a contract made but, so long as both parties recognize that either party is at liberty to withdraw from the negotiations at any time before the contract is made, it cannot be unconscionable for one party to do so. Of course, the freedom to withdraw may be fettered or extinguished by agreement but, in the absence of agreement, either party ordinarily retains his freedom to withdraw. It is only if a party induces the other party to believe that he, the former party, is already bound and his freedom to withdraw has gone that it could be unconscionable for him subsequently to assert that he is legally free to withdraw.

It is essential to the existence of an equity created by estoppel that the party who induces the adoption of the assumption or expectation knows or intends that the party who adopts it will act or abstain from acting in reliance on the assumption or expectation. When the adoption of an assumption or expectation is induced by the making of a promise, the knowledge or intention that the assumption or expectation will be acted upon may be easily inferred. But if a party encourages another to adhere to an assumption or expectation already formed or acquiesces in the making of an assumption or the entertainment of an expectation when he ought to object to the assumption or expectation — steps which are tantamount to inducing the other to adopt the assumption or expectation — the inference of knowledge or intention that the assumption or expectation will be acted on may be more difficult to draw.

The unconscionable conduct which it is the object of equity to prevent is the failure of a party, who has induced the adoption of the assumption or expectation and who knew or intended that it would be relied on, to fulfil the assumption or expectation or otherwise to avoid the detriment which that failure would occasion. The object of the equity is not to compel the party bound to fulfil the assumption or expectation; it is to avoid the detriment which, if the assumption or expectation goes unfulfilled, will be suffered by the party who has been induced to act or to abstain from acting thereon.

If this object is kept steadily in mind, the concern that a general application of the principle of equitable estoppel would make non-contractual promises enforceable as contractual promises can be [424] allayed. A non-contractual promise can give rise to an equitable estoppel only when the promisor induces the promisee to assume or expect that the promise is intended to affect their legal relations and he knows or intends that the promisee will act or abstain from acting in reliance on the promise, and when the promisee does so act or abstain from acting and the promisee would suffer detriment by his action or inaction if the promisor were not to fulfil the promise. When these elements are present, equitable estoppel almost wears the appearance of contract, for the action or inaction of the promisee looks like consideration for the promise on which, as the promisor knew or intended, the promisee would act or abstain from acting. Lord Westbury in *Dillwyn v Llewelyn*, assimilated the relationship arising from equitable estoppel to the relationship arising in contract:

> If A puts B in possession of a piece of land, and tells him, 'I give it to you that you may build a house on it', and B on the strength of that promise, with the knowledge of A, expends a large sum of money in building a house accordingly, I cannot doubt that the donee acquires a right from the subsequent transaction to call on the donor to *perform that contract* and complete the imperfect donation which was made. (Emphasis added.)[32] ...

[425] But there are differences between a contract and an equity created by estoppel. A contractual obligation is created by the agreement of the parties; an equity created by estoppel may be imposed irrespective of any agreement by the party bound. A contractual obligation must be supported by consideration; an equity created by estoppel need not be supported by what is, strictly speaking, consideration. The measure of a contractual obligation depends on the terms of the contract and the circumstances to which it applies; the measure of an equity created by estoppel varies according to what is necessary to prevent detriment resulting from unconscionable conduct.

In *Combe v Combe* Denning LJ limited the application of promissory estoppel, as he expounded the doctrine, to ensure that it did not displace the doctrine of consideration. His Lordship's solution of the problem was to hold that the promise should not itself be a cause of action, but merely the foundation of a defensive equity ...

The remedy offered by promissory estoppel has been limited to preventing the enforcement of existing legal rights. In *Crabb v Arun District Council* Lord Denning MR said that if a person:

> ... by his words or conduct, so behaves as to lead another to believe that he will not insist on his strict legal rights — knowing or intending that the other will act on that belief — and he does so act, that again will raise an equity in favour of the other; and it is for a court of equity to say in what way the equity may be satisfied.[33]

If the object of the principle were to make a promise binding in equity, the need to preserve the doctrine of consideration would require a limitation to be placed on the remedy. But there is a logical difficulty in limiting the principle so that it applies only to promises to suspend or extinguish existing rights. If a promise by A not to enforce an existing right against B is to confer an equitable right on B to compel fulfilment of the promise, why should B be denied the same protection in similar circumstances if the promise is intended to create in B a new legal right against A? There is no logical distinction to be drawn between a change in legal relationships [426] effected by a promise which extinguishes a right and a change in legal relationships effected by a promise which creates one. Why should an equity of the kind to which *Combe v Combe* refers be regarded as a shield but not a sword? ...

---

32. *Dillwyn v Llewelyn* (1862) 45 ER 1285 at 1286.
33. *Crabb v Arun District Council* [1976] Ch 179 at 188.

Moreover, unless the cases of proprietary estoppel are attributed to a different equity from that which explains the cases of promissory estoppel, the enforcement of promises to create new proprietary rights cannot be reconciled with a limitation on the enforcement of other promises. If it be unconscionable for an owner of property in certain circumstances to fail to fulfil a non-contractual promise that he will convey an interest in the property to another, is there any reason in principle why it is not unconscionable in similar circumstances for a person to fail to fulfil a non-contractual promise that he will confer a non-proprietary legal right on another? It does not accord with principle to hold that equity, in seeking to avoid detriment occasioned by unconscionable conduct, can give relief in some cases but not in others.

If the object of the principle of equitable estoppel in its application to promises were regarded as their enforcement rather than the prevention of detriment flowing from reliance on promises, the courts would be constrained to limit the application of the principles of equitable estoppel in order to avoid the investing of a non-contractual promise with the legal effect of a contractual promise. In *Ajayi v R T Briscoe (Nigeria) Ltd*, the Privy Council sought to qualify the enforceability of a non-contractual promise in this way:

> The principle, which has been described as quasi estoppel and perhaps more aptly as promissory estoppel, is that when one party to a contract in the absence of fresh consideration agrees not to enforce his rights an equity will be raised in favour of the other party. This equity is, however, subject to the qualifications (1) that the other party has altered his position, (2) that the promisor can resile from his promise on giving reasonable notice, which need not be a formal notice, giving the promisee a reasonable opportunity of resuming his position, (3) the promise only becomes final and irrevocable if the promisee cannot resume his position.[34]

The qualifications proposed bring the principle closer to a principle the object of which is to avoid detriment occasioned by [427] non-fulfilment of the promise. But the better solution of the problem is reached by identifying the unconscionable conduct which gives rise to the equity as the leaving of another to suffer detriment occasioned by the conduct of the party against whom the equity is raised. Then the object of the principle can be seen to be the avoidance of that detriment and the satisfaction of the equity calls for the enforcement of a promise only as a means of avoiding the detriment and only to the extent necessary to achieve that object. So regarded, equitable estoppel does not elevate non-contractual promises to the level of contractual promises and the doctrine of consideration is not blown away by a side wind. Equitable estoppel complements the tortious remedies of damages for negligent misstatement or fraud and enhances the remedies available to a party who acts or abstains from acting in reliance on what another induces him to believe.

As an element in unconscionable conduct is the inducing of the other party to adopt an assumption or expectation as to the parties' legal relations, the question arises whether silence is capable of inducing the adoption of the assumption or expectation ...

Clearly an assumption or expectation may be adopted not only as the result of a promise but also in certain circumstances as the result of encouragement to adhere to an

---

34. *Ajayi v R T Briscoe (Nigeria) Ltd* [1964] 3 All ER 556 at 559.

assumption or expectation already formed or as the result of a party's failure to object to the assumption or expectation on which the other party is known to be conducting his affairs. In the present [428] case the question is whether Waltons, knowing that Mr Maher was labouring under the belief that Waltons was bound to the contract, was under a duty to correct that belief. The evidence was capable of supporting an inference that Waltons knew the belief under which Mr Maher was labouring when Waltons became aware that Mr Maher was doing the work specified in the deed. Waltons deliberately refrained from correcting what Waltons must have regarded as an erroneous belief. Was it Waltons' duty to do so? ...

Silence will support an equitable estoppel only if it would be inequitable thereafter to assert a legal relationship different from the one which, to the knowledge of the silent party, the other party assumed or expected. What would make it inequitable to depart from such an assumption or expectation? Knowledge that the assumption or expectation could be fulfilled only by a transfer of the property of the person who stays silent, or by a diminution of his rights or an increase in his obligations. A person who knows or intends that the other should conduct his affairs on such an assumption or expectation has two options: to warn the other that he denies the correctness of the assumption or expectation when he knows that the other may suffer detriment by so conducting his affairs should the assumption or expectation go unfulfilled, or to act so as to avoid any detriment which the other may suffer in reliance on the assumption or expectation. It is unconscionable to refrain from making the denial and then to leave the other to bear whatever detriment is occasioned by non-fulfilment of the assumption or expectation.

In my opinion, to establish an equitable estoppel, it is necessary for a plaintiff to prove that (1) the plaintiff assumed or expected that a particular legal relationship then existed between the plaintiff and the defendant or expected that a particular legal relationship would exist between them and, in the latter case, that the defendant would not be free to withdraw from the expected legal relationship; (2) the [429] defendant has induced the plaintiff to adopt that assumption or expectation; (3) the plaintiff acts or abstains from acting in reliance on the assumption or expectation; (4) the defendant knew or intended him to do so; (5) the plaintiff's action or inaction will occasion detriment if the assumption or expectation is not fulfilled; and (6) the defendant has failed to act to avoid that detriment whether by fulfilling the assumption or expectation or otherwise. For the purposes of the second element, a defendant who has not actively induced the plaintiff to adopt an assumption or expectation will nevertheless be held to have done so if the assumption or expectation can be fulfilled only by a transfer of the defendant's property, a diminution of his rights or an increase in his obligations and he, knowing that the plaintiff's reliance on the assumption or expectation may cause detriment to the plaintiff if it is not fulfilled, fails to deny to the plaintiff the correctness of the assumption or expectation on which the plaintiff is conducting his affairs.

This is such a case, as a brief recapitulation of the facts will show. The terms of the proposed contract had been agreed between the solicitors and set out in the counterpart deed executed and delivered to Waltons' solicitor by way of exchange. In the days immediately following ... receipt [by Waltons' solicitor] of the executed counterpart deed, Waltons could properly have had the document returned and could have withdrawn from the negotiations. But the counterpart deed was not returned; it was retained presumably on the terms on which it had been delivered, ie, by way of exchange. The retention of the counterpart deed and the absence of any demur as to the schedule of finishes or terms of the deed was tantamount to a promise by Waltons that it would complete the exchange. That would not have sufficed to raise an equitable estoppel unless the Mahers acted on the promise to their detriment. But, after Waltons knew that Mr Maher had commenced work and (as it must have known) that Mr Maher had done so in the expectation that Waltons would execute and deliver the original deed, Waltons remained silent in order to have the benefit of the proposed contract if and when Waltons should decide to execute and deliver the original deed. As Waltons (by its solicitor) knew that Mr Maher (by his solicitor) had said that he would commence the work only if an agreement was concluded, Waltons must have known that Mr Maher either assumed that the contract had been made or expected that it would be made and that Waltons was not free to withdraw. Waltons intended that Mr Maher should continue to build the store in reliance on that assumption or expectation. Then, if not before, the time had come for Waltons to elect between terminating the negotiations or allowing Mr Maher to continue on [430] the footing that Waltons was bound to enter into the proposed contract. Waltons' silence induced Mr Maher to continue either on the assumption that Waltons was already bound or in the expectation that Waltons would execute and deliver the original deed as a matter of obligation. It was unconscionable for Waltons subsequently to seek to withdraw after a substantial part of the work was complete, leaving the Mahers to bear the detriment which non-fulfilment of the expectation entailed. Having elected to allow Mr Maher to continue to build, it was too late for Waltons to reclaim the initial freedom to withdraw which Waltons had in the days immediately following 11 November. As the Mahers would suffer loss if Waltons failed to execute and deliver the original deed, an equity is raised against Waltons. That equity is to be satisfied by treating Waltons as though it had done what it induced Mr Maher to expect that it would do, namely, by treating Waltons as though it had executed and delivered the original deed. It would not be appropriate to order specific performance if only for the reason that the detriment can be avoided by compensation. The equity is fully satisfied by ordering damages in lieu of specific performance.

Comments

1. See Radan & Stewart at **12.20–12.46**.
2. In relation to the first of Brennan J's six elements of equitable estoppel, a broader view was taken by Priestley JA in *Austotel Pty Ltd v Franklins Selfserve Pty Ltd* (1989) 16 NSWLR 582 at 610, where his Honour indicated that it was enough if the relying party assumed that 'a promise [would] be performed'. An example where the representor's behaviour is outside any existing or expected legal relationship, and which might come within Priestley JA's formulation, is where A promises to pay B $200 within 10 days.
3. For discussions of this case see E Clark, 'The Swordbearer Has Arrived: Promissory Estoppel and *Waltons Stores (Interstate) v Maher*' (1987–1989) 9 *University of Tasmania Law Review* 68, C N H Bagot, 'Equitable Estoppel and Contractual Obligations in the Light of *Waltons v Maher*' (1988) 62 *Australian Law Journal* 926.

12.3 The Commonwealth of Australia v Verwayen (1990) 170 CLR 394

Court: High Court of Australia

Facts: Verwayen was one of a number of Royal Australian Navy servicemen who were injured in the 1964 collision between HMAS *Voyager* and HMAS *Melbourne* during combat exercises near Jervis Bay. At various times after the collision, the Commonwealth reiterated publicly that it would not contest liability or raise the limitations defence in the event of personal injury claims arising from the accident. In such cases, the only issue was seen to be assessment of damages. Verwayen sued the Commonwealth for negligence about 20 years after the event. Two years later, the Commonwealth policy in relation to the *Voyager* collision changed and it amended its defence to Verwayen's claim, contesting liability and objecting that his action was out of time.

Issue: The issue before the High Court was whether the Commonwealth was estopped from relying on its defences or whether it had waived the benefit of its statutory right to plead the limitation period.

Decision: The majority of the High Court (Deane, Dawson, Toohey and Gaudron JJ; Mason CJ, Brennan and McHugh JJ dissenting) held that the Commonwealth was either estopped from raising the defences because of its conduct or that it had waived its right to rely on either defence.

Extracts: The extracts from the dissenting judgment of Mason CJ reflect the view that, although estoppel by conduct may have been established, an order for costs in Verwayen's favour would be sufficient, since a complete denial of the Commonwealth's right to defend the action would have been disproportionate to any detriment suffered by Verwayen. The extracts from the judgment of Deane J, which outline the main principles of estoppel by conduct, illustrate the view that the Commonwealth's conduct raised an equity in Verwayen's favour, which could be satisfied only by holding the Commonwealth to the state of affairs it had promised.

Mason CJ

[409] That brings me to estoppel, a label which covers a complex array of rules spanning various categories. There are the divisions between common law and equitable estoppel, between estoppel by conduct and estoppel by representation, and the distinction between present and future fact. There are titles such as promissory estoppel, proprietary estoppel and estoppel by acquiescence. Yet all of these categories and distinctions are intended to serve the same fundamental purpose, namely 'protection against the detriment which would flow from a party's change of position if the assumption (or expectation) that led to it were deserted'.[35]

At common law the principle of estoppel by conduct or representation ('estoppel in pais') provided that protection by preventing the party estopped from unjustly

---

35. *Waltons Stores (Interstate) Ltd v Maher* (1988) 164 CLR 387 at 419.

departing from an assumption of fact which his conduct had caused another party to adopt or accept for the purpose of their legal relations.[36] But it was well established that, in order to support an estoppel by conduct, the representation (or assumption) must be a representation of an existing fact, a promise or representation of intention to do something being insufficient for that purpose.[37]

The principle of estoppel by conduct or representation applied in equity, as at common law, though in equity the principle was [410] known as equitable estoppel.[38] And in equity it was also well settled that the representation (or assumption) must be of an existing fact, not of future fact or mere intention. That is what *Jorden v Money* decided, despite the fact, as Bowen LJ pointed out in *Edgington v Fitzmaurice*, that 'the state of a man's mind is as much a fact as the state of his digestion'.[39] This limitation upon the principle of estoppel was seemingly founded upon the notion that to hold a person to an assumption which his conduct has caused another to adopt or accept was tantamount to enforcing a voluntary promise in the absence of consideration. The need to avoid this consequence was an important aspect of the majority reasoning in *Jorden v Money*.

However, neither the decision nor the reasoning in that case can now be sustained. Promissory estoppel, recognized by this Court in *Legione v Hateley*,[40] has undermined the idea that voluntary promises cannot be enforced in the absence of consideration. What is more, promissory estoppel has an extensive area of operation now that it is acknowledged that the doctrine is not confined to pre-existing contractual relationships.[41] Furthermore, the acceptance of the doctrine of promissory estoppel has been accompanied by a recognition that the distinction between present and future fact is unsatisfactory and produces arbitrary results instead of serving any useful purpose.[42] Indeed, the difference between the majority and Lord St Leonards in *Jorden v Money* was a striking illustration of the arbitrary nature of the distinction.

In conformity with the fundamental purpose of all estoppels to afford protection against the detriment which would flow from a party's change of position if the assumption that led to it were deserted, these developments have brought a greater underlying unity to the various categories of estoppel. Indeed, the consistent trend in the modern decisions points inexorably towards the emergence of one overarching doctrine of estoppel rather than a [411] series of independent rules.

One obstacle to the existence of a single overarching doctrine is a suggested difference in the nature of estoppel by conduct on the one hand and equitable estoppel (including promissory estoppel) on the other and in the character of the protection which they respectively provide. Traditionally, estoppel by conduct has been classified as a rule of

---

36. *Grundt v Great Boulder Pty Gold Mines Ltd* (1937) 59 CLR 641 at 657, 674; *Thompson v Palmer* (1933) 49 CLR 507 at 547; *Waltons Stores (Interstate) Ltd v Maher* (1988) 164 CLR 387 at 397–9, 413–5, 443, 458.

37. *Yorkshire Insurance Co v Craine* [1922] 2 AC 541 at 553.

38. *Jorden v Money* (1854) 5 HLC 185 at 210, 212–3; *Thompson v Palmer* (1933) 49 CLR 507 at 519–20, 547, 558; *Waltons Stores (Interstate) Ltd v Maher* (1988) 164 CLR 387 at 447–8.

39. (1885) 29 Ch D 459 at 483.

40. (1983) 152 CLR 406.

41. *Waltons Stores (Interstate) Ltd v Maher* (1988) 164 CLR 387 at 399–406.

42. *Moorgate Ltd v Twitchings* [1976] QB 225 at 242; *Waltons Stores (Interstate) Ltd v Maher* (1988) 164 CLR 387 at 398–9, 450–1, 452; *Foran v Wight* (1989) 168 CLR 385 at 411–3, 433–7.

evidence, available where there is a cause of action, to prevent a person from denying what he previously represented, and has not itself constituted a cause of action.[43] Being an evidentiary principle, estoppel by conduct achieved, and could only achieve, the object of avoiding the detriment which would be suffered by another in the event of departure from the assumed state of affairs by holding the party estopped to that state of affairs. The rights of the parties were ascertained and declared by reference to that state of affairs. On the other hand, equity was more flexible. Equity was concerned, not to make good the assumption, but to do what was necessary to prevent the suffering of detriment. To do more would sit uncomfortably with a general principle whose underlying foundation was the concept of unconscionability. So, in *Waltons Stores*, a majority of this Court concluded that equitable estoppel entitled a party only to that relief which was necessary to prevent unconscionable conduct and to do justice between the parties. Mason CJ and Wilson J referred[44] to the statement of Scarman LJ in *Crabb v Arun District Council*,[45] that the court should determine what was 'the minimum equity to do justice to the plaintiff'. He went on to state: 'Holding the representor to his representation is merely one way of doing justice between the parties'[46] ...

[412] It follows that, as a matter of principle and authority, equitable estoppel will permit a court to do what is required in order to avoid detriment to the party who has relied on the assumption induced by the party estopped, but no more. In appropriate cases, that will require that the party estopped be held to the assumption created, even if that means the effective enforcement of a voluntary promise. To that extent there is an overlap between equitable estoppel generally and estoppel by conduct in its traditional form. But since the function of equitable estoppel has expanded and it has become recognized that an assumption as to future fact may ground an estoppel by conduct at common law as well as in equity, it is anomalous and potentially unjust to allow the two doctrines to inhabit the same territory yet produce different results. Moreover, as I have already indicated, the fact that estoppel by conduct has expanded beyond its evidentiary function into a substantive doctrine means that there is no longer any justification for insisting on the making good of assumptions in every case.

In any event, there is a very strong case for saying that equity had discarded earlier the notion that the purpose of the rules of estoppel by conduct was to make good the relevant assumption. As Professor Finn points out in his essay 'Equitable Estoppel' ... 'the language of expectations [was] forsaken entirely for that of "equities"' in *Crabb v Arun District Council*.[47] Lord Denning MR had qualified the language of expectations in *ER Ives Investment Ltd v High*, by stating that the 'court will not allow [the] expectation to be defeated *when it would be inequitable so to do*' (emphasis added).[48] That qualification, made repeatedly in cases which can be traced back to the Privy Council's statement in *Plimmer v Mayor of Wellington* that 'the Court must look at the circumstances in each case to decide

---

43. *Grundt v Great Boulder Pty Gold Mines Ltd* (1937) 59 CLR 641 at 658; *Low v Bouverie* [1891] 3 Ch 82 at 101, 105.
44. *Waltons Stores (Interstate) Ltd v Maher* (1988) 164 CLR 387 at 404.
45. [1976] Ch 179 at 198.
46. *Waltons Stores (Interstate) Ltd v Maher* (1988) 164 CLR 387 at 405.
47. Finn, 'Equitable Estoppel' in Finn (ed), *Essays in Equity*, Law Book Co, Sydney (1985) at 68.
48. *ER Ives Investment Ltd v High* [1967] 2 QB 379 at 394–3.

in what way the equity can be satisfied',[49] has transformed the basis of the equitable principles of estoppel.[50]

[413] In these circumstances, it would confound principle and common sense to maintain that estoppel by conduct occupies a special field which has as its hallmark function the making good of assumptions. There is no longer any purpose to be served in recognizing an evidentiary form of estoppel operating in the same circumstances as the emergent rules of substantive estoppel. The result is that it should be accepted that there is but one doctrine of estoppel, which provides that a court of common law or equity may do what is required, but not more, to prevent a person who has relied upon an assumption as to a present, past or future state of affairs (including a legal state of affairs), which assumption the party estopped has induced him to hold, from suffering detriment in reliance upon the assumption as a result of the denial of its correctness. A central element of that doctrine is that there must be a proportionality between the remedy and the detriment which is its purpose to avoid. It would be wholly inequitable and unjust to insist upon a disproportionate making good of the relevant assumption.[51]

The assumption may be one as to a legal as well as to a factual state of affairs. There is simply no reason to restrict the assumption to a factual matter as there was at the time when the rules of estoppel by conduct were evidentiary. It has already been recognized that an equitable estoppel may relate at least to a matter of mixed fact and law.[52] Moreover, the distinction between assumptions as to fact and assumptions as to law is artificial and elusive.[53] So it would be productive only of confusion and arid technicality to restrict the operation of the doctrine so as to exclude from its scope an assumption as to a purely legal state of affairs. It is therefore not surprising that long ago the Judicial Committee recognized that a representation as to the legal effect of an agreement can give rise to an estoppel.[54] ...

[416] It remains only to determine what relief is appropriate to satisfy the estoppel which [Verwayen] has successfully raised in this case. When a court approaches the task of ascertaining the minimum relief necessary to 'do justice' between the parties, it is not correct to make an assessment of the moral rectitude of the actions of the parties in a manner divorced from a consideration of the legal consequences and attributes of those actions. Thus it must be borne in mind that a voluntary promise is generally not enforceable and that pleadings are susceptible of amendment. The breaking of a promise, without more, is morally reprehensible, but not unconscionable in the sense that equity will necessarily prevent its occurrence or remedy the consequent loss. In the same way, with estoppel, something more than a broken promise is required.

---

49. *Plimmer v Mayor of Wellington* (1884) 9 App Cas 699 at 714.
50. Finn, 'Equitable Estoppel' in Finn (ed), *Essays in Equity*, 1985, at 62–71.
51. See also the conclusion of Lord Denning MR in *Amalgamated Investment & Property Co Ltd v Texas Commerce International Bank Ltd* [1982] QB 84 at 122.
52. *Waltons Stores (Interstate) Ltd v Maher* (1988) 164 CLR 387 at 415–6, 420–1, 452; *Foran v Wight* (1989) 168 CLR 385 at 433–5.
53. See the discussion of Oliver J in *Taylors Fashions Ltd v Liverpool Trustees Co* [1982] QB 133 at 150–1.
54. *Sarat Chunder Dey v Gopal Chunder Laha* (1892) LR 19 Ind App 203; *Calgary Milling Co Ltd v American Surety Co of New York* [1919] 3 WWR 98; see also *Amalgamated Investment & Property Co Ltd v Texas Commerce International Bank Ltd* [1982] QB 84 at 106–7.

Each case is one of degree. Reliance upon an assumption for an extended period may give rise to an estoppel justifying a court in requiring that the assumption be made good. The same result may follow from substantial and irreversible detriment suffered in reliance upon the assumption or from detriment which cannot satisfactorily be compensated or remedied. In the present case the detriment suffered by [Verwayen] in reliance on the assumption induced by the Commonwealth appears to be of a more limited nature. The procedure adopted for the determination of this case in the Supreme Court means that we have no finding or evidence of the detriment, flowing from his reliance upon the assumption, which [Verwayen] would suffer from the Commonwealth's pleading of the limitation defence or the *Groves* defence. It must be assumed, however, that that detriment would include significant expense and inconvenience. However, as far as [Verwayen's] emotional condition is concerned, it is sheer speculation to suggest that his reliance on the Commonwealth's actions after commencement of the action caused any deterioration of that condition. Evidence of detriment must be affirmatively demonstrated; this is not a case involving the exercise of judicial discretion.[55]

The question then is whether an order for costs is a sufficient recompense for [Verwayen] in respect of the detriment suffered by him. An order for costs has traditionally been regarded as a sufficient adjustment to meet prejudice in terms of expense and inconvenience occasioned by the pleading of new defences and I am not persuaded that principle or circumstance call for any different **[417]** answer in the present case. There is no material before the Court to justify a conclusion that [Verwayen] commenced his action on the basis of any express or implied representation on the part of the Commonwealth. [Verwayen's] solicitors inquired of the Secretary of the Department of Defence in September 1984 whether he would agree to waive the Statute of Limitations and admit liability. The relevant Minister replied on 29 October 1984, stating that the matter had been referred for consideration to the Australian Government Solicitor. The statement of claim was issued on 2 November 1984. It can hardly be said that these circumstances establish the existence of an assumption on the part of [Verwayen] that liability was not in issue. Indeed, the Minister's letter alerted [his] solicitors to the fact that, although the defences had not been pleaded when the question had previously arisen, the Commonwealth still saw fit to refer the question for legal advice on this occasion. If anything, this suggests the absence of a definite and unambiguous policy at the time when [Verwayen] commenced his action.

To hold the Commonwealth to its representations, thereby depriving it of defences which were available to it by statute or the general law, would be a disproportionate response to the detriment suffered by [Verwayen] in reliance upon the assumption that the defences would not be pleaded. True it is that the representations reflected a deliberate policy decision made by government at ministerial level at least. That circumstance gave the representations the quality of apparent reliability and went to the issue of reliance. But the apparent reliability of the representations does not enlarge the nature or scope of the detriment which [Verwayen] has suffered in reliance on the representations following the denial of the assumption generated by them. Likewise, the fact that the Commonwealth is the party against whom an estoppel is pleaded is not in this case a point of distinction. It was

---

55. Cf *Murray v Munro* (1906) 3 CLR 788 at 796; *Ketteman v Hansel Properties Ltd* [1987] AC 189 at 220.

not argued that any special rule of estoppel applies to assumptions induced by government, either so as to expand or so as to contract the field of operation of the doctrine ...

Deane J

[431] The relationship between promissory estoppel and estoppel by conduct

In *Waltons Stores (Interstate) Ltd v Maher*,[56] and *Foran v Wight*,[57] I attempted to explain the reasons which induced me to conclude that promissory estoppel should be seen not as a separate and distinct doctrine which operates only in equity but as an emanation of the general doctrine of estoppel by conduct which had been explained by Dixon J in *Thompson v Palmer*[58] and *Grundt v Great Boulder Pty Gold Mines Ltd*.[59] I do not regard [432] myself as constrained to depart from that conclusion by what was said in other judgments in those two cases. The support to be found in some of those other judgments for insistence upon a difference in nature between promissory estoppel and estoppel by conduct has, however, caused me to reconsider the question of the relationship between the two. That reconsideration has not caused me to abandon the view that promissory estoppel is but one aspect of a general doctrine of estoppel by conduct which should, under a modern Judicature Act system with merged availability of remedies, be seen as operating indifferently in both law and equity. It has, however, made me more conscious of the force of contrary views. It has also made me conscious of the inadequacy of what I wrote in earlier judgments.

The principle of promissory estoppel can be traced, particularly through the judgment of Denning J in *Central London Property Trust Ltd v High Trees House Ltd*,[60] and, in this country, through the majority judgments in *Legione v Hateley*,[61] to *Hughes v Metropolitan Railway Co*[62] and *Birmingham and District Land Co v London and North Western Railway Co*.[63] Lord Cairns LC in *Hughes*[64] and Bowen LJ in *Birmingham*[65] referred to the relevant principle in terms appropriate to a doctrine of estoppel: a party who has induced another party to act on the assumption that contractual rights will not be enforced 'will not be allowed to enforce' those rights 'where it would be inequitable having regard to the dealings which have thus taken place between the parties' (per Lord Cairns LC) or 'without at all events placing the parties in the same position as they were before' (per Bowen LJ). In the *High Trees Case*,[66] Denning J, no doubt influenced by statements of high authority to the effect that the general doctrine of estoppel by conduct did not extend to assumptions of future fact or conduct,[67] was at pains to distance the principle which he recognized

---

56. (1988) 164 CLR 387 at 447–53.
57. (1989) 168 CLR 385 at 433–7.
58. (1933) 49 CLR 507 at 547.
59. (1937) 59 CLR 641 at 674–7.
60. [1947] KB 130 at 133–5.
61. (1983) 152 CLR 406.
62. (1877) 2 App Cas 439.
63. (1888) 40 Ch D 268.
64. (1877) 2 App Cas 439 at 448.
65. (1888) 40 Ch D 268 at 286.
66. [1947] KB 130 at 134.
67. See, in particular, *Chadwick v Manning* [1896] AC 231 at 238.

from that general doctrine. He referred to four cases in which it had been held that the circumstances gave rise to an estoppel[68] and insisted that they were 'not cases of estoppel in the strict sense' but 'promises **[433]** — promises intended to be binding, intended to be acted on, and in fact acted on'. However, his Lordship went on to identify the operation of the principle in terms which acknowledged its essential similarity to the operation of the doctrine of estoppel by conduct: 'The courts have not gone so far as to give a cause of action in damages for the breach of such a promise, but they have refused to allow the party making it to act inconsistently with it. It is in that sense, and that sense only, that such a promise gives rise to an estoppel.' In *Combe v Combe*,[69] Denning LJ took a firm step towards the assimilation of 'the principle stated in the *High Trees* case' with the general doctrine of estoppel by conduct. In what could pass as a succinct statement of the operation of that general doctrine, he pointed out that the *'principle does not create new causes of action'* but *'only* prevents a party from insisting upon his strict legal rights, when it would be unjust to allow him to enforce them, having regard to the dealings which have taken place between the parties' (emphasis added).

A number of obstacles lay in the path of the acceptance of promissory estoppel as an emanation of estoppel by conduct. For one thing, there was, as has been indicated, strong authority for the proposition that the doctrine of estoppel by conduct did not extend to a representation about future facts or conduct. For another, the ancestry of old equity cases encouraged the perception that the principle of promissory estoppel was an exclusively equitable one, notwithstanding that investigation of the sentences immediately following the oft-quoted passage from Bowen LJ's judgment in *Birmingham* discloses that his Lordship expressly disavowed any suggestion that the principle enunciated by Lord Cairns LC in *Hughes' Case* was not 'a principle that was recognised by Courts of Law as well as of Equity'.[70]

In so far as promissory estoppel relates to an assumption about future fact or conduct, it can, of course, be distinguished from other instances of estoppel, including equitable estoppel, based upon assumptions about existing facts or legal entitlement. That distinction no doubt explains the tendency in cases immediately following the *High Trees Case* to treat promissory estoppel as somehow different in principle from other instances of estoppel. It does not, however, of itself necessarily indicate any difference in nature or principle between promissory estoppel, other aspects of **[434]** equitable estoppel and the general doctrine of estoppel by conduct. In that regard it is relevant to recall that Dixon J's classic expositions of the doctrine of estoppel by conduct in *Thompson v Palmer* (an equity suit in pre-Judicature Act New South Wales) and *Grundt* (a claim in the Western Australian Warden's Court involving, inter alia, questions of trespass and conversion) would seem to have been predicated upon the assumption that the doctrine operated consistently at law and in equity and were worded in terms which, with the possible exception of one reference to 'assumption of fact' (in *Grundt*[71]), are appropriate to encompass an assumption about future facts or conduct.

---

68. See *Fenner v Blake* [1900] 1 QB 426 at 428–9; *In re Wickham* (1917) 34 TLR 158 at 159; *Re William Porter & Co Ltd* [1937] 2 All ER 361 at 363–4; *Buttery v Pickard* [1946] WN 25 at 26.
69. [1951] 2 KB 215 at 219.
70. *Birmingham and District Land Co v London and North Western Railway Co* (1888) 40 Ch D 268 at 286.
71. (1937) 59 CLR 641 at 674.

Obviously, the operation in equity of any doctrine of estoppel may be described in words which would be inappropriate to describe its operation at law. In particular, it is commonplace to speak of promissory estoppel as of itself giving rise to 'an equity'. Precisely the same comment could, however, be made about the operation of any form of estoppel by conduct (including representation and acquiescence) in equity. I turn to explain why that is so.

The phrase 'an equity' can be used in the narrow sense of referring to an immediate right to positive equitable relief. The word 'equity' was used in that sense in the standard pre-Judicature Act submission (as if it were a plea or demurrer) in equity in New South Wales to the effect that the plaintiff had 'no equity' entitling him or her to invoke equitable jurisdiction. Used in that sense, the phrase does not encompass the entitlement of a 'promisee' under a promissory estoppel. A promissory estoppel does not, *of itself*, give rise to any right to traditional equitable relief at all, let alone a right to claim compensation under the statutes which conferred power upon equity courts to award compensatory damages. As has been seen, Denning LJ, in *Combe v Combe*, stressed that promissory estoppel 'does not create new causes of action where none existed before' but simply 'prevents a party from insisting upon his strict legal rights'. Subsequently in his judgment, his Lordship pointed out that '[s]eeing that the principle *never* stands alone as giving a cause of action in itself, it can *never* do away with the necessity of consideration when that is an essential part of the cause of action' (emphasis added).[72] His Lordship's statements in that regard accord with earlier and subsequent authority.

[435] The phrase 'an equity' can, however, be used in a broader and less precise sense to refer to any entitlement or obligation ('the equities') of which a court of equity will take cognizance. In that sense, the phrase can be used to refer to a 'defensive equity' such as 'laches, acquiescence or delay' or a mere set-off or to an interest or entitlement which does not of itself found equitable relief. It is in that broader and less precise sense that it is permissible to speak of the operation of estoppel in equity as giving rise to 'an equity'. This use of the phrase 'an equity' in relation to the operation of promissory estoppel can be illustrated by reference to cases in the Supreme Court of New South Wales where, until 1972 when a Judicature Act system was first introduced, old phraseology was preserved and the distinction between 'an equity' which of itself founded a claim for relief and 'an equity' which did not remained of critical importance in some circumstances ...

[436] The judgments of the members of the Full Court of the Supreme Court of New South Wales in the abovementioned cases need to be qualified or amended in the light of subsequent recognition of the extent to which estoppel generally, and promissory estoppel in particular, can establish an ingredient of an action, whether at law or in equity, for relief framed on the basis of the assumed state of affairs. However, the New South Wales judgments correctly identify the only basis upon which it can properly be said that promissory estoppel of itself gives rise to 'an equity'. That equity is, as the cases on promissory estoppel seem to me to make plain, an entitlement in equity proceedings to preclude departure by the other party from the assumed state of affairs if departure would, in all the circumstances, be unconscionable. The content of the estoppel will, of course, vary according to the nature of the assumption. In particular, the assumption may extend only to observance of the assumed state of affairs until after the expiry of reasonable notice

---

72. *Combe v Combe* [1951] 2 KB 215 at 220.

of intended departure. Alternatively, the circumstances may be such [437] that insistence upon strict adherence to the assumed state of affairs would go beyond, and even conflict with, what the requirements of good conscience would demand. In such a case, equitable relief may be available only on a more restricted basis (see below). Nonetheless, the point remains that promissory estoppel does not *of itself* give rise to any entitlement to relief in equity. In that regard, promissory estoppel conforms with 'the true proposition of law, that, while a party cannot in terms found a cause of action on an estoppel, he may, as a result of being able to rely on an estoppel, succeed on a cause of action on which, without being able to rely on that estoppel, he would necessarily have failed'.[73] ...

[439] I would prefer to read Lord Denning's statement [in *Moorgate Ltd v Twitchings*] that a court of equity will look to the circumstances 'to see in what way the equity can be satisfied'[74] (and to similar statements by his Lordship and others in other cases) as referring to the need to identify the minimum content of the assumed state of affairs from which the doctrine of estoppel precludes departure and the appropriate relief to which the relevant party is entitled pursuant to ordinary equitable principles operating on that assumed state of affairs. That construction of his Lordship's comment would make it consistent with his emphasis, in the *High Trees* and other cases, upon the proposition that promissory estoppel does not give rise to any cause of action. If, contrary to that reading of his Lordship's comment, Lord Denning was suggesting (as his and Scarman LJ's judgments in *Crabb v Arun District Council*,[75] would seem to indicate) that estoppel by conduct of itself operates in equity to give rise to an equity in the form of some imprecise cause of action for whatever relief might seem fair in the circumstances, I am respectfully unable to accept that as an accurate statement of the operation of the doctrine. That is not, of course, to deny either the flexibility of equitable remedies when equitable principle entitles a party to relief framed on the basis of the assumed state of affairs or the need in an appropriate case to modify relief where the circumstances are such that it would represent a denial rather than a vindication of equity to preclude any departure at all from the assumed state of affairs. It is simply to recognize the basic proposition that estoppel does not of itself provide a cause of action either in law or in equity. A fortiori, estoppel does not of itself provide an independent cause of action in equity for non-traditional equitable relief in the form of compensatory damages, under Lord Cairns' Act or subsequent statutory provisions, for the detriment caused by a departure from an otherwise unenforceable promise as to future conduct. If it did, promissory estoppel could no longer be said to provide a basis upon which ordinary principles of law, including the doctrine of consideration, would operate.[76] To the [440] contrary, it would directly confound the doctrine of consideration and, in a case of promissory estoppel where consideration had moved from the promisee but compensatory damages for detriment sustained exceeded damages for loss of bargain, simply override the law of contract.

Once it is accepted that the general doctrine of estoppel by conduct extends to representations about future facts (including conduct) and that the operation of promissory

---

73. Per Brandon LJ, *Amalgamated Investment & Property Co Ltd v Texas Commerce International Bank Ltd* [1982] 1 QB 84 at 131–2.

74. *Moorgate Ltd v Twitchings* [1976] QB 225 at 242.

75. [1976] Ch 179 at 187–90, 193.

76. See *Combe v Combe* [1951] 2 KB 215 at 220.

estoppel in equity conforms with the operation of estoppel by conduct in law and equity, there is no reason in principle for refusing to accept promissory estoppel as but an emanation of the general doctrine of estoppel by conduct. In pre-Judicature Act times when, to the 'discredit [of] our jurisprudence', cases could arise in which courts of law and equity applied 'different rules of right and wrong to the same subject matter',[77] the confinement of a developing doctrine to one or other of law and equity may well have been unavoidable. It is not so, however, in a modern system where the law represents the fusion and interaction of both disciplines and is administered by courts of both law and equity. Oliver J in *Taylors Fashions* and Robert Goff J (at first instance) in the *Texas Bank Case* have convincingly explained why it is undesirable to seek to restrict equitable estoppel to certain defined categories such as promissory estoppel, proprietary estoppel and estoppel by acquiescence. For the reasons which I indicated in *Waltons Stores*[78] when read in the context of what I have written above, it appears to me that the courts of this country should recognize a general doctrine of estoppel by conduct which encompasses the various categories of 'equitable estoppel' and which operates throughout a fused system of law and equity.

Unconscientious conduct

The doctrine of estoppel by conduct is founded upon good conscience. Its rationale is not that it is right and expedient to save persons from the consequences of their own mistake. It is that it is right and expedient to save them from being victimized by other people.[79] The notion of unconscionability is better described than defined. **[441]** As Lord Scarman pointed out in *National Westminster Bank Plc v Morgan*, definition 'is a poor instrument when used to determine whether a transaction is or is not unconscionable: this is a question which depends upon the particular facts of the case'.[80] The most that can be said is that 'unconscionable' should be understood in the sense of referring to what one party 'ought not, in conscience, as between [the parties], to be allowed' to do.[81] In this as in other areas of equity-related doctrine, conduct which is 'unconscionable' will commonly involve the use of or insistence upon legal entitlement to take advantage of another's special vulnerability or misadventure in a way that is unreasonable and oppressive to an extent that affronts ordinary minimum standards of fair dealing. That being so, the question whether conduct is or is not unconscionable in the circumstances of a particular case involves a 'real process of consideration and judgment'[82] in which the ordinary processes of legal reasoning by induction and deduction from settled rules and decided cases are applicable but are likely to be inadequate to exclude an element of value judgment in a borderline case such as the present.

Relief in a case of estoppel by conduct

There could be circumstances in which the potential damage to an allegedly estopped party was disproportionately greater than any detriment which would be sustained

---

77. See the Report of the Common Law Commissioners, etc, quoted in *NSW Rutile Mining Co v Eagle Metal* [1960] SR (NSW) 495 at 505.
78. (1988) 164 CLR 387 at 447, 453.
79. Cf *Allcard v Skinner* (1887) 36 Ch D 145 at 182.
80. *National Westminster Bank Plc v Morgan* [1985] AC 686 at 709.
81. See Story, *Commentaries on Equity Jurisprudence*, 2nd Eng ed (1892), par 1219; *Thompson v Palmer* (1933) 49 CLR 507 at 537.
82. See *Harry v Kreutziger* (1978) 95 DLR (3d) 231 at 240.

by the other party to an extent that good conscience could not reasonably be seen as precluding a departure from the assumed state of affairs if adequate compensation were made or offered by the allegedly estopped party for any detriment sustained by the other party. An obvious example would be provided by a case in which the party claiming the benefit of an estoppel precluding a denial of his ownership of a million dollar block of land owned by the allegedly estopped party would sustain no detriment beyond the loss of one hundred dollars spent on the erection of a shed if a departure from the assumed state of affairs were allowed. In such a case, the payment of, or a binding [442] undertaking to pay, adequate compensation would preclude a finding of estoppel by conduct. In other cases, particularly cases involving an assumption about a future state of affairs, the circumstances may be such that any significant detriment would be avoided altogether if the party affected were given reasonable notice of the intended departure. In such a case, the estoppel may only preclude departure from the assumed state of affairs otherwise than after such reasonable notice has been given. Even in a case where an estoppel by conduct is established and would prima facie operate to preclude departure from the assumed state of affairs, the circumstances may be such that to grant unqualified relief on that basis would exceed any requirements of good conscience and be unduly oppressive of the other party. 'Of all doctrines, equitable estoppel' — and, I would add, equitable relief based on the assumed state of affairs — 'is surely one of the most flexible'.[83]

There is clear support in the cases and learned writings for the view that, in this as in other fields, equitable relief must be moulded to do justice between the parties and to prevent a doctrine based on good conscience from being made an instrument of injustice or oppression. That being so, it should be accepted that the prima facie entitlement to relief based on the assumed state of affairs must, under a doctrine which is of general application in a system where equity prevails, be qualified if it appears that that relief would exceed what could be justified by the requirements of conscientious conduct and would be unjust to the estopped party. In some such cases, an appropriate qualification may be a requirement that the party relying upon the estoppel do equity.[84] In other cases, the relief to which the party relying upon the estoppel would be entitled upon the assumed state of affairs will merely represent the outer limits within which the jurisdiction of a modern court to mould its relief to suit the circumstances of a particular case should be exercised in a manner which will do true justice between the parties. In some such cases the appropriate order may be one which places the party entitled to the benefit of the estoppel 'in the same position as [he or she was] before'.[85] In others, the appropriate order may be an order for compensatory damages.

[443] To acknowledge the fact that the relief appropriate to a case of estoppel by conduct may vary according to the circumstances is not to suggest that relief is to be framed on an unprincipled basis. Prima facie, the operation of an estoppel by conduct is to preclude departure from the assumed state of affairs. It is only where relief framed

---

83. See *Amalgamated Investment & Property Co Ltd v Texas Commerce International Bank Ltd* [1982] 1 QB 84 at 103; *Taylors Fashions Ltd v Liverpool Trustees Co* [1982] 1 QB 131 at 153.
84. See *Amalgamated Investment & Property Co Ltd v Texas Commerce International Bank Ltd* [1982] 1 QB 84 at 108–9.
85. *Birmingham and District Land Co v London and North Western Railway Co* (1888) 40 Ch D 268 at 286.

on the basis of that assumed state of affairs would be inequitably harsh, that some lesser form of relief should be awarded. Moreover, while the relief awarded should be appropriate to the circumstances of the particular case, the courts should not adopt an arbitrary or idiosyncratic approach to the determination of what is in fact appropriate. In particular, it is permissible to recognize prima facie categories of cases in which it will not be inequitable to award relief framed on the basis of the assumed state of affairs. It is arguable that one such category should consist of cases in which an employer deliberately and with full knowledge of relevant circumstances induces an employee injured by the negligence of the employer or a co-employee to act to his or her detriment by pursuing an action for compensatory damages on the basis that the employer will not take advantage of unmeritorious technical defences to resist liability. It is not, however, necessary to pursue that question for the purposes of the present case.

The content and operation of the general doctrine of estoppel by conduct

It is undesirable to seek to define exhaustively and in the abstract the content or operation of any general legal doctrine. Inevitably, there will be unforeseen and exceptional cases. Ordinarily, there will be borderline areas in which the interaction of the doctrine with other doctrines will be uncertain. Most important, it is part of the genius of the common law that development on a case-by-case basis enables its adaptation to meet changing circumstances and demands.

On the other hand, the conceptual foundations of a legal doctrine constitute an essential basis of judicial decision in a borderline case such as the present. Those conceptual foundations can only be identified by reference to the essential content and operation of the doctrine. It is, for that reason, desirable that I identify in a general way what I see as the conceptual foundation and essential operation of the doctrine of estoppel by conduct which has, during this century, emerged as a coherent body of substantive and consistent principle. To a significant extent, I do so in words taken (without specific acknowledgment) from the judgments of others in earlier **[444]** cases. For ease of subsequent reference (in this judgment) I shall use numbered paragraphs.

1. While the ordinary operation of estoppel by conduct is between parties to litigation, it is a doctrine of substantive law the factual ingredients of which fall to be pleaded and resolved like other factual issues in a case. The persons who may be bound by or who may take the benefit of such an estoppel extend beyond the immediate parties to it, to their privies, whether by blood, by estate or by contract. That being so, an estoppel by conduct can be the origin of primary rights of property and of contract.

2. The central principle of the doctrine is that the law will not permit an unconscionable — or, more accurately, unconscientious — departure by one party from the subject matter of an assumption which has been adopted by the other party as the basis of some relationship, course of conduct, act or omission which would operate to that other party's detriment if the assumption be not adhered to for the purposes of the litigation.

3. Since an estoppel will not arise unless the party claiming the benefit of it has adopted the assumption as the basis of action or inaction and thereby placed himself in a position of significant disadvantage if departure from the assumption be permitted, the resolution of an issue of estoppel by conduct will involve an examination of the relevant belief, actions and position of that party.

4. The question whether such a departure would be unconscionable relates to the conduct of the allegedly estopped party in all the circumstances. That party must have played such a part in the adoption of, or persistence in, the assumption that he would be guilty of unjust and oppressive conduct if he were now to depart from it. The cases indicate four main, but not exhaustive, categories in which an affirmative answer to that question may be justified, namely, where that party: (a) has induced the assumption by express or implied representation; (b) has entered into contractual or other material relations with the other party on the conventional basis of the assumption; (c) has exercised against the other party rights which would exist only if the assumption were correct; (d) knew that the other party laboured under the assumption and refrained from correcting him when it was his duty in conscience to do so. [445] Ultimately, however, the question whether departure from the assumption would be unconscionable must be resolved not by reference to some preconceived formula framed to serve as a universal yardstick but by reference to all the circumstances of the case, including the reasonableness of the conduct of the other party in acting upon the assumption and the nature and extent of the detriment which he would sustain by acting upon the assumption if departure from the assumed state of affairs were permitted. In cases falling within category (a), a critical consideration will commonly be that the allegedly estopped party knew or intended or clearly ought to have known that the other party would be induced by his conduct to adopt, and act on the basis of, the assumption. Particularly in cases falling within category (b), actual belief in the correctness of the fact or state of affairs assumed may not be necessary. Obviously, the facts of a particular case may be such that it falls within more than one of the above categories.

5. The assumption may be of fact or law, present or future. That is to say it may be about the present or future existence of a fact or state of affairs (including the state of the law or the existence of a legal right, interest or relationship or the content of future conduct).

6. The doctrine should be seen as a unified one which operates consistently in both law and equity. In that regard, 'equitable estoppel' should not be seen as a separate or distinct doctrine which operates only in equity or as restricted to certain defined categories (eg acquiescence, encouragement, promissory estoppel or proprietary estoppel).

7. Estoppel by conduct does not of itself constitute an independent cause of action. The assumed fact or state of affairs (which one party is estopped from denying) may be relied upon defensively or it may be used aggressively as the factual foundation of an action arising under ordinary principles with the entitlement to ultimate relief being determined on the basis of the existence of that fact or state of affairs. In some cases, the estoppel may operate to fashion an assumed state of affairs which will found relief (under ordinary principles) which gives effect to the assumption itself (eg where the defendant in an action for a declaration of trust is estopped from denying the existence of the trust).

8. The recognition of estoppel by conduct as a doctrine operating consistently in law and equity and the prevalence of equity in a Judicature Act system combine to give the whole doctrine a degree of flexibility which it might lack if it were an exclusively common law doctrine. In particular, the prima facie entitlement to relief based upon

the assumed state of affairs will be qualified in a case where such relief would exceed what could be justified by the **[446]** requirements of good conscience and would be unjust to the estopped party. In such a case, relief framed on the basis of the assumed state of affairs represents the outer limits within which the relief appropriate to do justice between the parties should be framed …

[I]n my view, … subject to any necessary amendments to the pleadings being allowed and made … the Commonwealth is estopped from disputing its liability to Mr Verwayen for damages for the injuries he sustained while in its service.

Comments

1. See Radan & Stewart at **12.28–12.60**.
2. Although Brennan J's formulation of the relevant principles of equitable estoppel in *Waltons Stores (Interstate) Ltd v Maher*[86] has been most commonly cited and applied in subsequent decisions, the Court of Appeal in Victoria expressed a preference in *New Zealand Pelt Export Company Ltd v Trade Indemnity New Zealand Limited* [2004] VSCA 163 for Deane J's formulation of principles in this case. Nettle JA (Ormiston JA and Hansen AJA agreeing) said, at [98]–[99]:

   One possibly significant difference between the two formulations is that [in *Waltons Stores v Maher*] Brennan J considered that it was a requirement that the party to be estopped should know or intend the other party act in reliance on the assumption or expectation. [In *Verwayen*] Deane J considered it was enough that the party to be estopped clearly ought to have known that the other party would be induced by the estopped party's conduct to adopt, and act on the basis of the assumption or expectation. But for present purposes I doubt that it matters …

   I add, however, that if it were necessary to make a choice, there are at least three reasons to prefer Deane J's formulation. In the first place, it is more consistent with the observations of Mason CJ and Wilson J in *Waltons Stores v Maher*, that the principle which underlies *High Trees* estoppel is that the courts will grant relief to a plaintiff who has acted to his detriment on the basis of a basic assumption in relation to which the other party has played such a part in the adoption of the assumption that it would be unfair or unjust if left free to ignore it. That view accords with the broad general ground of estoppel that where one of two innocent parties must suffer, the loss should fall on him by whose indiscretion it was occasioned. Secondly, as the joint judgment of Mason CJ. and Wilson J in *Waltons Stores v Maher* demonstrates, the principle which underlies *High Trees* estoppel is the same principle as underlies the kind of estoppel exemplified in *Ramsden v Dyson*;[87] and the better view is that in such a case the party to be estopped need not know of the full extent of his or her legal rights — it is sufficient that he or she ought to have appreciated what they were. Parity of reasoning suggests that it may be sufficient in a case of *High Trees* estoppel that the party to be estopped ought to have known that the other party would be induced by the estopped party's conduct to adopt and act on the basis of an assumption or expectation. Thirdly, the source of the idea that actual knowledge

---

86. (1988) 164 CLR 387 at 428–9.
87. (1866) LR 1 HL 129.

is an essential requirement seems to be the judgment of Lord Denning in *Crabb v Arun District Council*,[88] and while his Lordship did say in that case that it was necessary that the party to be estopped know and intend that the other party act on the basis of the relevant assumption, his Lordship based his judgment on the speech of Lord Cairns in *Hughes v Metropolitan Railway Co*, and Lord Cairns did not speak in terms of knowledge or intent. The crucial passage of his speech was as follows: ' ... if parties who have entered into definite and distinct terms involving certain legal results — certain penalties or legal forfeiture — afterwards by their own act or with their own consent enter upon a course of negotiation which has the effect of leading one of the parties to suppose that the strict rights arising under the contract will not be enforced, or will be kept in suspense, or held in abeyance, the person who otherwise might have enforced those rights will not be allowed to enforce them where it would be inequitable having regard to the dealings which have thus taken place between the parties. My Lords, I repeat that I attribute to the Appellant no intention here to take advantage of, to lay a trap, but it appears to me that both parties by entering upon the negotiation which they entered upon, made it an inequitable thing that the exact period of six months dating from the month of October should afterwards be measured out as against the Respondent as the period during which the repairs must be executed'.[89]

3. For discussions of this case see A Robertson, 'Satisfying the Minimum Equity: Equitable Estoppel Remedies after Verwayen' (1996) 20 *Melbourne University Law Review* 805 and A Robertson, 'Towards a Unifying Purpose for Estoppel' (1996) 22 *Monash University Law Review* 1.

Clarity of the representation and equitable estoppel

12.4   Thorner v Major [2009] 3 All ER 945

Court: House of Lords

Facts: Peter Thorner was a man of few words who kept to himself and was not given to 'direct talking'. He owned Steart Farm in Somerset. Although he had six siblings, he was not close to any of them. However, he was close to his cousin Jimmy and Jimmy's son, David. When Peter's wife died in 1976, David began to help Peter with the physical and administrative work for Steart Farm. David's contribution was extensive and continued until Peter's death in 2005. David was not paid for the work he did. In the 1980s David began to hope that he would inherit the farm. Hope turned into expectation when, in 1990, Peter gave David a Prudential Bonus Notice in relation to two policies on Peter's life. Peter told David that it was for death duties when he died. Subsequently, Peter

---

88. [1976] Ch 179.
89. *Hughes v Metropolitan Railway Co* (1877) 2 App Cas 439 at 448.

made statements that could only be interpreted to suggest that David would continue with the farm after Peter's death. In 1997 Peter made a will leaving the farm to David. However, he destroyed the will in the following year after falling out with one of the other beneficiaries mentioned in it. Peter died without leaving a will.

Issue: The issue before the House of Lords was whether Steart Farm passed on intestacy to Peter's siblings or whether David had a claim to it based upon the principles of proprietary estoppel.

Decision: The House of Lords (Lords Hoffmann, Scott of Foscote, Rodger of Earlsferry, Walker of Gestingthorpe and Neuberger of Abbotsbury) unanimously held that David had a claim to Steart Farm based upon the principles of proprietary estoppel. In so doing, the House of Lords overruled the earlier Court of Appeal decision and restored the decision of the trial judge in this case.

Extracts: The extracts from the speeches of Lord Walker of Gestingthorpe and Lord Neuberger of Abbotsbury discuss the requirements of clarity of the representation and the certainty of the description of the property in relation to a claim based upon proprietary estoppel and how these principles applied to the facts of this case.

Lord Walker of Gestingthorpe

[956] My Lords, this appeal is concerned with proprietary estoppel … [957] [M]ost scholars agree that the doctrine is based on three main elements, although they express them in slightly different terms: a representation or assurance made to the claimant; reliance on it by the claimant; and detriment to the claimant in consequence of his (reasonable) reliance …

This appeal raises two issues. The first and main issue concerns the character or quality of the representation or assurance made to the claimant. The other (which could be regarded as a subsidiary part of the main issue, but was argued before your Lordships as a separate point) is whether, if the other elements for proprietary estoppel are established, the claimant must fail if the land to which the assurance relates has been inadequately identified, or has undergone a change (in its situation or extent) during the period between the giving of the assurance and its eventual repudiation …

[964] [On the first issue] [t]here is some authority for the view that the 'clear and unequivocal' test does not apply to proprietary estoppel. That … view has been expressed in at least the past three editions of Treitel *Law of Contract*. The current edition by Mr Edwin Peel, in a passage comparing promissory and proprietary estoppel, states:

> … promissory estoppel arises only out of a representation or promise that is 'clear' or 'precise and unambiguous'. Proprietary estoppel, on the other hand, can arise where there is no actual promise: eg where one party makes improvements to another's land under a mistake and the other either knows of the mistake or seeks to take unconscionable advantage of it.[90]

---

90. Treitel, *Law of Contract*, 12th ed, 2007, para 3–144.

The present appeal is not of course a case of acquiescence (or standing-by). David does not assert that he can rely on money which he has spent on the farm, or improvements which he has made to it. His case is based on Peter's assurances to him. But if all proprietary estoppel cases (including cases of acquiescence or standing-by) are to be analysed in terms of assurance, reliance and detriment, then the landowner's conduct in standing by in silence serves as the element of assurance. As Lord Eldon LC said over 200 years ago in *Dann v Spurrier*:

> ... this Court will not permit a man knowingly, though but passively, to encourage another to lay out money under an erroneous opinion of title; and the circumstance of looking on is in many cases as strong as using terms of encouragement.[91]

I would prefer to say (while conscious that it is a thoroughly question-begging formulation) that to establish a proprietary estoppel the relevant assurance must be clear enough. What amounts to sufficient clarity, in a case of this sort, is hugely dependent on context. I respectfully concur in the way Hoffmann LJ put it in *Walton v Walton* (in which the mother's 'stock phrase' to her son, who had worked for low wages on her farm since he left school at fifteen, was 'You can't have more money and a farm one day'). Hoffmann LJ stated:

> The promise must be unambiguous and must appear to have been intended to be taken seriously. Taken in its context, it must have been a promise which one might reasonably expect to be relied upon by the person to whom it was made.[92]

Hoffmann LJ enlarged on this:

> But in many cases of promises made in a family or social context, there is no intention to create an immediately binding contract. There are several reasons why the law is reluctant to assume that there was. One which is relevant in this case is that such promises are often subject to unspoken and ill-defined qualifications. Take for example the promise in this case. When it was first made, Mrs Walton did not know what the future might hold. Anything might happen which could make it quite inappropriate for the farm to go to the plaintiff.

> [965] But a contract, subject to the narrow doctrine of frustration, must be performed come what may. This is why Mr Jackson, who appeared for the plaintiff, has always accepted that Mrs Walton's promise could not have been intended to become a contract.

> But none of this reasoning applies to equitable estoppel, because it does not look forward into the future and guess what might happen. It looks backwards from the moment when the promise falls due to be performed and asks whether, in the circumstances which have actually happened, it would be unconscionable for the promise not to be kept.[93] ...

---

91. *Dann v Spurrier* (1802) 32 ER 94 at 95.
92. *Walton v Walton*, 14 April 1994, unreported, CA at [16].
93. *Walton v Walton*, 14 April 1994, unreported, CA at [19]–[21].

In this case the context, or surrounding circumstances, must be regarded as quite unusual. The [trial] judge heard a lot of evidence about two countrymen leading lives that it may be difficult for many city-dwellers to imagine — taciturn and undemonstrative men committed to a life of hard and unrelenting physical work, by day and sometimes by night, largely unrelieved by recreation or female company. The [trial] judge seems to have listened carefully to this evidence and to have been sensitive to the unusual circumstances of the case.

I respectfully consider that the Court of Appeal did not give sufficient weight to the advantage that the trial judge had in seeing and hearing the witnesses ... To my mind the [trial] judge did find ... that Peter's assurances, objectively assessed, were intended to be taken seriously and to be relied on ... I do not think that there was sufficient reason for the Court of Appeal to reverse the trial judge's careful findings and conclusion. I do not share the Court of Appeal's apparent apprehension that floodgates might be opened, because cases like this are fairly rare, and trial judges realise the need to subject the evidence (whether as to assurances, as to reliance or as to detriment) to careful, and sometimes sceptical, scrutiny ...

[In relation to the second issue] [i]n my opinion it is a necessary element of proprietary estoppel that the assurances given to the claimant (expressly or impliedly, or, in standing-by **[966]** cases, tacitly) should relate to identified property owned (or, perhaps, about to be owned) by the defendant. That is one of the main distinguishing features between the two varieties of equitable estoppel, that is promissory estoppel and proprietary estoppel ... The latter ... must relate to *identified property* (usually land) owned (or, perhaps, about to be owned) by the defendant ...

In this case the deputy judge made a clear finding of an assurance by Peter that David would become entitled to Steart Farm. The first, 'watershed' assurance was made in 1990 at about the time that Peter made an advantageous sale of one field for development purposes, and used part (but not the whole) of the proceeds to buy more agricultural land, so increasing the farm to the maximum at about 582 acres (some merely tenanted by Peter) which Peter farmed in 1992. Both Peter and David knew that the extent of the farm was liable to fluctuate (as development opportunities arose, and tenancies came and went). There is no reason to doubt that their common understanding was that Peter's assurance related to whatever the farm consisted of at Peter's death ...

[Counsel for Peter's personal representatives] relied on some observations by my noble and learned friend Lord Scott of Foscote in *Yeoman's Row Management Ltd v Cobbe*,[94] pointing out that in *Ramsden v Dyson*, Lord Kingsdown referred to 'a *certain* interest in land'[95] (my emphasis). But, as Lord Scott noted, Lord Kingsdown immediately went on to refer to a case where there was uncertainty as to the terms of the contract (or, as it may be better to say, in the assurance) and to point out that relief would be available in that case also. All the 'great judges' to whom Lord Kingsdown referred thought that even where there was some uncertainty an equity could arise and could be satisfied, either by an interest in land or in some other way.

In any event, for the reasons already mentioned, I do not perceive any real uncertainty in the position here. It is possible to imagine all sorts of events which might have

---

94. [2008] 4 All ER 713 at [18]–[21].
95. *Ramsden v Dyson* (1866) LR 1 HL 129 at 170.

happened between 1990 and 2005. If Peter had decided to sell another field or two, whether because of an advantageous development opportunity or because the business was pressed for cash, David would have known of it, and would no doubt have accepted it without question (just as he made no claim to the savings account which held that part of the proceeds of **[967]** the 1990 sale which Peter did not roll over into land). If Peter had decided in 2000 to sell half the farm in order to build himself a retirement home elsewhere (an unlikely hypothesis) David might well have accepted that too ... But it is unprofitable, in view of the retrospective nature of the assessment which the doctrine of proprietary estoppel requires, to speculate on what might have been.

Lord Neuberger of Abbotsbury

[968] David's contention that he is entitled to the freehold of Steart Farm is, and was at first instance and in the Court of Appeal, founded squarely on proprietary estoppel, whose main elements are often summarised as being, in brief, assurance, reliance and detriment ... The issues in the present case really focus on the quality or nature of the assurance required before a proprietary estoppel can be established ...

The conclusion reached by the Court of Appeal ... rests on the proposition that a statement by A that he will leave certain property on his death to B could have one of two meanings. It might constitute an assurance that this is what A is binding himself to do; in other words, it might be a commitment by A to leave the property to B. Or it might be no more than a statement of A's current intention, which can be subject to change with the passage of time, with or without a change of circumstances ... **[969]** The Court of Appeal's reasoning was that, as a statement must be a 'clear and unambiguous' assurance to found an estoppel, a claim such as that raised in this case could only succeed if it could be established that the statement relied on was clearly expressed so as to have the former, not the latter, meaning ...

[I]t seems to me ... that, if the statements were reasonably understood by David to have the effect which the [trial] judge found, namely an assurance, and David reasonably acted on that understanding to his detriment, then what Peter intended is not really germane. That is supported by a consistent line of authority.[96] It may be that there could be exceptional cases where, even though a person reasonably relied on a statement, it might be **[970]** wrong to conclude that the statement-maker was estopped, because he could not reasonably have expected the person so to rely. However, such cases would be rare, and, in the light of the facts found by the deputy judge, it has not been, and could not be, suggested that this was such a case ...

Perhaps more importantly, the meaning to be ascribed to words passing between parties will depend, often very much, on their factual context. This is particularly true in a case such as this, where a very taciturn farmer, given to indirect statements, made remarks obliquely referring to his intention with regard to his farm after his death ...

[971] It should be emphasised that I am not seeking to cast doubt on the proposition ... that there must be some sort of an assurance which is 'clear and unequivocal' before it can be relied on to found an estoppel. However, that proposition must be read as

---

96.   *Crabb v Arun DC* [1976] Ch 179 at 187, 188; *Sidney Bolsom Investment Trust Ltd v E Karmios & Co (London) Ltd* [1956] 1 QB 529 at 540–541; *Taylors Fashions Ltd v Liverpool Victoria Trustees Co Ltd, Old and Campbell Ltd v Liverpool Victoria Friendly Society* [1982] QB 133 at 151–152.

subject to three qualifications. First, it does not detract from the normal principle ... that the effect of words or actions must be assessed in their context. Just as a sentence can have one meaning in one context and a very different meaning in another context, so can a sentence, which would be ambiguous or unclear in one context, be a clear and unambiguous assurance in another context ...

Secondly, it would be quite wrong to be unrealistically rigorous when applying the 'clear and unambiguous' test. The court should not search for ambiguity or uncertainty, but should assess the question of clarity and certainty practically and sensibly, as well as contextually. Again, this point is underlined by the authorities ... which support the proposition that, at least normally, it is sufficient for the person invoking the estoppel to establish that he reasonably understood the statement or action to be an assurance on which he could rely.

Thirdly, ... there may be cases where the statement relied on to found an estoppel could amount to an assurance which could reasonably be understood as having more than one possible meaning. In such a case, if the facts otherwise satisfy all the requirements of an estoppel, it seems to me that, at least normally, the ambiguity should not deprive a person who reasonably relied on the assurance of all relief: it may well be right, however, that he should be accorded relief on the basis of the interpretation least beneficial to him ...

[972] Before turning to that second issue, I should add that, even if Peter's 'implicit statement' may have been revocable, as the Court of Appeal thought, I should not be taken as accepting that it would necessarily follow that, once the statement had been maintained by Peter and acted on by David for a substantial period, it would have been open to Peter freely to go back on it. It may be that he could not have done so, at least without paying David appropriate compensation, unless the change of mind was attributable to, and could be justified by, a change of circumstances. It seems to me that it would be arguable that, even assuming that the 'implicit statement' was not irrevocable, if, say in 2004, Peter had changed his mind, David would nonetheless have been entitled to equitable relief, in the light of his 14 or more years of unpaid work on the farm ...

Based on the reasoning of my noble and learned friend, Lord Scott of Foscote in *Yeoman's Row Management Ltd v Cobbe*,[97] [Peter's personal representatives] contend that the identity of the property the subject of the assurance or statement relied on to found a proprietary estoppel must be 'certain'. Accordingly, they argue, even if David would otherwise make good his proprietary estoppel claim, it must fail because the property the subject of the alleged estoppel in this case is not certain enough.

So far as the relevant facts of this case are concerned, the extent of the land owned and farmed by Peter varied. When he inherited Steart Farm in 1976, it comprised about 350 acres of freehold low-lying pasture and rough grazing. In 1990, he sold a large field for development, and used the proceeds to buy more land, so that, by 1992, he owned 463 acres, and the farm included another 120 acres which Peter rented. By 1998, he was farming only some 160 [973] acres of that land himself, having let out the remainder on farm business tenancies. As at the date of his death, Peter was in the process of negotiating a sale of some six acres to developers.

---

97. *Yeoman's Row Management Ltd v Cobbe* [2008] 4 All ER 713 at [18]–[20], [28].

In *Cobbe*'s case, Mr Cobbe devoted considerable time, effort, and expertise to obtaining planning permission for land owned by Yeoman's Row. Although they reached an oral 'agreement in principle', the parties had decided not to enter into a contract, but Mr Cobbe went ahead on the basis, as appreciated by Yeoman's Row, that he expected them to do so once planning permission was obtained. Initially, this was also the intention of Yeoman's Row, but their intention changed about three months before planning permission was obtained, although they did not tell Mr Cobbe until afterwards. Mr Cobbe's estoppel claim failed (although he was entitled to a quantum meruit payment). As I see it, Mr Cobbe's claim failed because he was effectively seeking to invoke proprietary estoppel to give effect to a contract which the parties had intentionally and consciously not entered into, and because he was simply seeking a remedy for the unconscionable behaviour of Yeoman's Row.

In the context of a case such as *Cobbe*'s, it is readily understandable why Lord Scott considered the question of certainty was so significant. The parties had intentionally not entered into any legally binding arrangement while Mr Cobbe sought to obtain planning permission: they had left matters on a speculative basis, each knowing full well that neither was legally bound. There was not even an agreement to agree (which would have been unenforceable), but, as Lord Scott pointed out, merely an expectation that there would be negotiations. And, as he said, an 'expectation dependent upon the conclusion of a successful negotiation is not an expectation of an interest having [sufficient] certainty'.[98]

There are two fundamental differences between that case and this case. First, the nature of the uncertainty in the two cases is entirely different. It is well encapsulated by Lord Walker's distinction between 'intangible legal rights' and 'the tangible property which he or she expects to get', in *Cobbe*'s case.[99] In that case, there was no doubt about the physical identity of the property. However, there was total uncertainty as to the nature or terms of any benefit (property interest, contractual right, or money), and, if a property interest, as to the nature of that interest (freehold, leasehold, or charge), to be accorded to Mr Cobbe.

In this case, the extent of the farm might change, but, on the [trial] judge's analysis, there is, as I see it, no doubt as to what was the subject of the assurance, namely the farm as it existed from time to time. Accordingly, the nature of the interest to be received by David was clear: it was the farm as it existed on Peter's death. As in the case of a very different equitable concept, namely a floating charge, the property the subject of the equity could be conceptually identified from the moment the equity came into existence, but its precise extent fell to be determined when the equity crystallised, namely on Peter's death.

Secondly, the analysis of the law in *Cobbe*'s case was against the background of very different facts. The relationship between the parties in that case was entirely arm's length and commercial, and the person raising the estoppel was a highly experienced businessman. The circumstances were such that the parties could well have been expected to enter into a contract, however, although they discussed contractual terms, they had consciously chosen not to do so. They had intentionally left their legal relationship to

98. *Yeoman's Row Management Ltd v Cobbe* [2008] 4 All ER 713 at [18].
99. *Yeoman's Row Management Ltd v Cobbe* [2008] 4 All ER 713 at [68].

be negotiated, and each of them knew that neither of them was legally bound. [974] What Mr Cobbe then relied on was 'an unformulated estoppel ... asserted in order to protect [his] interest under an oral agreement for the purchase of land that lacked both the requisite statutory formalities ... and was, in a contractual sense, incomplete'.[100]

In this case, by contrast, the relationship between Peter and David was familial and personal, and neither of them, least of all David, had much commercial experience. Further, at no time had either of them even started to contemplate entering into a formal contract as to the ownership of the farm after Peter's death. Nor could such a contract have been reasonably expected even to be discussed between them. On the [trial] judge's findings, it was a relatively straightforward case: Peter made what were, in the circumstances, clear and unambiguous assurances that he would leave his farm to David, and David reasonably relied on, and reasonably acted to his detriment on the basis of, those assurances, over a long period.

In these circumstances, I see nothing in the reasoning of Lord Scott in *Cobbe*'s case which assists [Peter's personal representatives] in this case. It would represent a regrettable and substantial emasculation of the beneficial principle of proprietary estoppel if it were artificially fettered so as to require the precise extent of the property the subject of the alleged estoppel to be strictly defined in every case. Concentrating on the perceived morality of the parties' behaviour can lead to an unacceptable degree of uncertainty of outcome, and hence I welcome the decision in *Cobbe*'s case. However, it is equally true that focusing on technicalities can lead to a degree of strictness inconsistent with the fundamental aims of equity ...

[975] Accordingly, the notion that, where the promise relates to 'the farm', which is a readily recognisable entity at any one time, there is no reason why it should not apply to that entity as it exists at the date 'the promise falls due to be performed', ie as at Peter's death.

Of course, there may be cases where the facts justify a different conclusion either because the promise had a different meaning at the time it was made, or because intervening events justify giving it a different effect — or even no effect. However, such considerations do not apply in this case. The farm did increase in size, but this had largely happened by 1992, which was only two years after the principal statement on which the estoppel relies; and 13 years elapsed thereafter, during which that statement, together with subsequent statements by Peter, were relied on by David. Further, the increase in the farm's size was achieved largely by Peter buying more land with money obtained through the sale for development of a much smaller area of the farm. In any event, there is no suggestion that Peter had any wish or moral obligation to leave the farm or any part of it to anyone other than David.

It is true that in none of the statements relied on by David made express reference to Steart Farm, but the deputy judge interpreted them as having that meaning, and ... there is no basis for interfering with that conclusion. On the contrary: on the facts of this case, it seems to me to have been an eminently sensible conclusion. Indeed, that point is a neat illustration of the fundamental importance of context to the questions of how a particular statement or action would have been understood, and whether it was 'clear and unambiguous'.

---

100. *Yeoman's Row Management Ltd v Cobbe* [2008] 4 All ER 713 at [18].

Comments
1. See Radan & Stewart at **12.19, 12.23–12.25**.
2. For a discussion of this case see N Piška, 'Hopes, Expectations and Recoverable Promises in Proprietary Estoppel' (2009) 72 *Modern Law Review* 998; J Uguccioni, 'The Resurrection of Proprietary Estoppel' [2009] *Lloyd's Maritime & Commercial Law Quarterly* 436.

Detriment and equitable estoppel

12.5   Je Maintiendrai Pty Ltd v Quaglia (1980) 26 SASR 101

Court: Full Court of the Supreme Court of South Australia

Facts: The Quaglias (the tenants) operated a hairdressing salon in premises leased from shopping centre proprietor Je Maintiendrai Pty Ltd (the landlord). The three-year lease provided for a monthly rental of $278, to be increased annually on the basis of consumer price index rises. Some time after the lease term commenced, the parties had further discussions and the landlord company agreed to accept a reduced monthly rental of $240 for the remainder of the term. Quaglia paid the reduced rent as agreed, but then attempted to vacate before the lease term had expired. When the landlord discovered the Quaglias' plans, it demanded payment of arrears of $2392, claimed to be the difference between the paid rent and the rental provided for in the lease. Its action was denied by a trial judge in the Local Court who held it was estopped from claiming arrears because of the reduced rental promise. The landlord appealed to the Full Court.

Issue: The issue before the Full Court was whether estoppel was applicable in circumstances where the promise to accept a reduced rent was made by the landlord in the absence of consideration from the tenant.

Decision: The majority of the Full Court (King CJ and White J; Cox J dissenting) rejected the landlord's appeal. It held that although the promisor/landlord had the right to resile from its gratuitous promise in respect of future payments, it could not recover arrears where the promisee/tenant established injustice by way of detriment suffered. The tenants' detriment was the debt accumulated, by way of unpaid rent, in reliance on the landlord's promise.

Extracts: The extracts from the judgment of King CJ highlight the requirement of proving a detriment suffered by the promisee for estoppel to be operative.

King CJ

[102] The issue on this appeal is whether [the landlord], having told [the tenants] that their rent was reduced, is estopped from recovering from [them] as arrears of rent the additional amount which would have been due under the lease but for the reduction ...

The [landlord's] promise to reduce the rent has no contractual force because it was made without consideration. The acceptance of a sum which is less than that legally due is not binding and does not extinguish liability for the balance unless there is fresh consideration.[101] The evidence does not disclose fresh consideration. The [tenants'] case therefore rests upon an estoppel to which the facts are alleged to give rise.

Few areas of law have given rise to more controversy in the last few decades than the area of promissory estoppel. There is a question as to whether the very notion of estoppel based upon promise or statement of future intention has any place in our law. It appears to run directly counter to the decision of the House of Lords in *Jorden v Money*.[102] That case appeared to decide that to found an estoppel a representation of existing fact was required as contrasted with a mere expression of future intention. **[103]** Yet twenty-three years after *Jorden v Money*, Lord Cairns LC in *Hughes v Metropolitan Railway Co* was able to say:

> ... it is the first principle upon which all Courts of Equity proceed, that if parties who have entered into definite and distinct terms involving certain legal results — certain penalties or legal forfeiture — afterwards by their own act or with their own consent enter upon a course of negotiation which has the effect of leading one of the parties to suppose that the strict rights arising under the contract will not be enforced, or will be kept in suspense, or held in abeyance, the person who otherwise might have enforced those rights will not be allowed to enforce them where it would be inequitable having regard to the dealings which have thus taken place between the parties.[103]

The principle of equity expressed by Lord Cairns in that passage was applied by the Court of Appeal in *Birmingham and District Land Company v London and North Western Railway Co*. Bowen LJ, referring to the principle enunciated by Lord Cairns, said:

> It seems to me to amount to this, that if persons who have contractual rights against others induce by their conduct those against whom they have such rights to believe that such rights will either not be enforced or will be kept in suspense or abeyance for some particular time, those persons will not be allowed by a Court of Equity to enforce the rights until such time has elapsed, without at all events placing the parties in the same position as they were before.[104]

The notion of promissory estoppel was given a modern formulation and a new impetus by the decision of Denning J ... in *Central London Property Trust Ltd v High Trees House Limited*, where it was said to be the 'natural result of the fusion of law and equity'.[105] The doctrine has been expounded by Lord Denning in a number of subsequent cases. It has been recognized and confirmed by the House of Lords.[106] In *Woodhouse Ltd v Nigerian Produce Ltd* Lord Hailsham recognized the doctrine as 'an expanding doctrine' which raised

---

101. *Foakes v Beer* (1884) 9 App Cas 605.
102. (1854) 10 ER 868.
103. *Hughes v Metropolitan Railway Co* (1877) 2 App Cas 439 at 448.
104. *Birmingham and District Land Company v London and North Western Railway Co* (1889) 40 Ch D 268 at 286.
105. *Central London Property Trust Ltd v High Trees House Limited* [1947] KB 130 at 134.
106. *Tool Metal Manufacturing Co Ltd v Tungsten Electric Co Ltd* [1955] 1 WLR 761.

'problems of coherent expression which have never been systematically explored'.[107] The doctrine has received recognition in New Zealand.[108]

The learned authors of the third Australian edition of Cheshire and Fifoot on the *Law of Contract* (1974) maintain that the High Court has rejected the doctrine and that promissory estoppel forms no part of the law of Australia. The learned authors rely, in support of that contention, on *Albert House Ltd (In Voluntary Liquidation) v Brisbane City Council*.[109] ...

[104] I do not think that [that] case can be regarded as a rejection of the doctrine of promissory estoppel. The learned authors of Cheshire and Fifoot also rely upon the Privy Council case *Chadwick v Manning*.[110] This was an appeal from a decree made by the Chief Judge in Equity in the Supreme Court of New South Wales in a suit to restrain a guarantor from proceeding at law to enforce an indemnity against his co-guarantor on the ground that the co-guarantor had altered his position on the faith of a representation that the indemnity would not be enforced. The Privy Council held that there had been no such representation, but also held, endorsing *Jorden v Money*, that a representation as to intention as distinct from existing fact could not found [105] an estoppel. The latter holding is inconsistent, however, with the subsequent Privy Council case of *Ajayi v R T Briscoe (Nigeria) Ltd*.[111]

In [that case] the Privy Council clearly and unequivocally recognized estoppel arising from promise or statement of intention, as part of the law, although it did not find the necessary conditions to be present in that case. I think that until the question is dealt with by the High Court, this Court should treat the formulation of the principle in *Ajayi's case* as authoritative. In that case the Privy Council formulated the principle as follows:

> Their lordships are of opinion that the principle of law as defined by Bowen LJ has been confirmed by the House of Lords in the case of the *Tool Metal Manufacturing Co Ltd v Tungsten Electric Co Ltd*,[112] where the authorities were reviewed, and no encouragement was given to the view that the principle was capable of extension so as to create rights in the promises for which he had given no consideration. The principle, which has been described as quasi estoppel and perhaps more aptly as promissory estoppel, is that when one party to a contract in the absence of fresh consideration agrees not to enforce his rights an equity will be raised in favour of the other party. This equity is, however, subject to the qualification (1) that the other party has altered his position, (2) that the promisor can resile from his promise on giving reasonable notice, which need not be a formal notice, giving the promisee a reasonable opportunity of resuming his position, (3) the promise only becomes final and irrevocable if the promisee cannot resume his position.[113]

---

107. *Woodhouse Ltd v Nigerian Produce Ltd* [1972] AC 741 at 758.
108. *Commissioner of Inland Revenue v Morris* [1958] NZLR 1126; *McCathie v McCathie* [1971] NZLR 58 especially at 71.
109. (1968) 42 ALJR 158.
110. [1896] AC 231.
111. [1964] 3 All ER 556.
112. [1955] 2 All ER 657.
113. *Ajayi v R T Briscoe (Nigeria) Ltd* [1964] 3 All ER 556 at 559.

It is clear from the above formulation that there can be no estoppel unless the promisee has altered his position on the faith of the promise. Lord Denning maintains that it is sufficient that the promisee has acted upon the promise and that in the case of promissory estoppel, unlike estoppel by representation, detriment to the promisee is unnecessary.[114] The rule in the case of estoppel by representation of an existing fact is clear. The representor is estopped only if the representee would suffer a detriment in the event of the representor being permitted to set up rights against the representee inconsistent with the representation. The principle upon which estoppel in pais is founded, as expressed by Dixon J in *Grundt v Great Boulder Gold Mines Pty Ltd*, 'is that the law should not permit an unjust departure by a party from an assumption of fact which he has caused another party to adopt or accept for the purpose of their legal relations'.[115] The principle upon which estoppel arising from a promise or statement of intention is founded, as expressed by Lord Cairns LC in *Hughes v Metropolitan Railway Co*, is that 'the person who otherwise might have enforced those rights will not be allowed to enforce them where it would be inequitable having regard to the dealings which have thus taken [106] place between the parties'.[116] The basic principle underlying both types of estoppel is, I apprehend, the same. It rests upon the injustice to the representee or promisee of allowing the representor or promisor, in the circumstances which exist, to depart from the representation or promise. If the representee or promisee will suffer no detriment as a consequence of the other party resiling from his position and asserting his strict legal rights, it is difficult to see where the injustice of permitting him to do so would lie. I can see no valid reason for making a distinction between these two types of estoppel in this respect. In my opinion, a person who promises or states his intention to another not to enforce or insist upon his legal rights is not estopped from resiling from that position and reverting to the strict legal position, unless his doing so would result in some detriment and therefore some injustice to that other.

In the present case there was an intimation that the rent legally due under the lease was reduced. This clearly amounts to a promise not to enforce the legal right to the difference between the reduced amount and the amount legally due. It is not disputed that [the landlord] was entitled to revert to the strict legal position as to future payments upon giving due notice. The claim in the action relates to the difference between the reduced amount and that legally due from the time the intimation was given and the time when it was clear that [the landlord] required payment in full. Whether on the facts [the landlord] might have been permanently estopped does not therefore fall for decision. What must be decided is whether, if [the landlord] were allowed to recover the arrears, [the tenants] would suffer a detriment which renders it unjust that [the landlord] should be permitted to do so.

The learned trial Judge found that [the tenants] would suffer a detriment as a result of being faced with a lump sum liability. I quote his reasons:

> That it is often easier for people to make small periodical payments than to find a lump sum is obvious, and there is no need to point to the use by many people of instalment credit facilities, on which extra costs are incurred in respect of the credit charges, to

---

114. *W J Alan Ltd v El Nasr Export and Import Co* [1972] 2 QB 189.
115. *Grundt v Great Boulder Gold Mines Pty Ltd* (1937) 59 CLR 641 at 674.
116. *Hughes v Metropolitan Railway Co* (1877) 2 App Cas 439 at 448.

pay for houses, goods or services. Where, as in the present case [the landlord] has agreed to forego, and not merely to defer, the receipt of part of the future payments contractually due he cannot, without prejudicing [the tenant], subsequently demand as a lump sum all the money which would have been paid by past instalments had [the landlord] not agreed to accept less. In the present case, instead of having to find a comparatively small sum of money every month, which [the tenants] were, though not without difficulty, able to do, they were in fact, after almost eighteen months of being lulled to sleep, suddenly faced with a demand to pay a large sum of accumulated 'arrears'...

[107] The evidence as to detriment is sparse. The [tenants'] case would be stronger if there were evidence of financial hardship or embarrassment as a result of the debt accumulating or, as in *Holt v Markham*,[117] that the money had been spent in other ways and that [they] were unable to pay, at any rate without difficulty or inconvenience. It would be stronger if there were evidence that they had conducted their affairs differently as a result of the reduction, for example that they had refrained from exploring the possibility of selling the business and assigning the lease. The sparsity of evidence of detriment has caused me to consider anxiously whether the learned Judge's conclusion can be supported. In the end I have reached the conclusion that we should not disturb it. The [tenants] conducted a small business. There was some evidence of their financial position and the learned trial Judge heard it given. He was in a better position than is this Court to judge whether the accumulation of arrears of this magnitude would be a detriment to [the tenants], and to assess whether any significance was to be attached to [the tenants'] failure to say so expressly. I think that we should accept the conclusion which he reached.

Comment

1. See Radan & Stewart at **12.41–12.44**.

Relief based upon equitable estoppel

12.6   Giumelli v Giumelli (1999) 196 CLR 101

Court: High Court of Australia

Facts: The Giumelli family partnership ran an orchard business on two properties in Western Australia. One of the sons, Robert, worked on the properties without wages but received free board and pocket money, his earnings being credited in the partnership accounts. Over time, his parents made certain promises to him in relation to one of the properties, Dwellingup. First, they promised him part of the property for his unpaid work on the family business and for his work on improving the property.

---

117. [1923] 1 KB 504.

Second, they promised that, if he built a house on the property, it would belong to him. He did so before he married, bearing the cost of $47,000 but with a $25,000 advance from the partnership. Third, they promised after he married that, if he stayed on the Dwellingup property instead of taking up an offer to relocate and work with his father-in-law, they would subdivide the property and give him a portion with the house and an orchard. Robert stayed on the property, but after his marriage ended he entered into a relationship with a woman of whom his parents disapproved. They told him he would have to choose between the property and the woman. He remarried and left Dwellingup, which was subsequently occupied and further improved by one of the other brothers. Robert started action to wind up the partnership, and later claimed that his parents held the Dwellingup property in trust to transfer the promised lot to him.

The trial judge found in his favour on the basis that he suffered a detriment by spending money in reliance on the second promise. But there was no detriment arising from the third promise because, by staying on Dwellingup, he continued to contribute to the partnership assets and to his own earnings. Robert appealed to the Full Court of the Supreme Court of Western Australia, which found that he had indeed suffered a detriment in reliance on the third promise. The court ordered the parents to subdivide the property to create the promised lot and transfer it to him. Robert's parents appealed to the High Court.

Issues: The first issue before the High Court was whether the doctrine of equitable estoppel could provide a remedy on the basis of expectation loss in order to enforce the promises that induced the conduct detrimental to Robert when he relied on them. If so, the court was then required to determine whether the appropriate remedy could be in the form of an award of a money sum rather than specific relief such as an order that the property be transferred to Robert.

Decision: The High Court (Gleeson CJ, McHugh, Gummow, Kirby and Callinan JJ) unanimously granted Robert monetary compensation to the value of the property that should have been transferred to him by his parents. This was based not on actual detriment or reliance loss, but on his lost expectation.

Extracts: The extracts from the joint judgment of the majority (Kirby J gave a short and separate concurring judgment) outline the reasoning that informed the High Court's decision.

Gleeson CJ, McHugh, Gummow and Callinan JJ

[112] In the present case, the constructive trust is proprietary in nature. It attaches to the Dwellingup property. Such a trust does not necessarily impose upon the holder of the legal title the various administrative duties and fiduciary obligations which attend the settlement of property to be held by a trustee upon an express trust for successive interests. Rather, the order made by the Full Court is akin to orders for

conveyance made by Lord Westbury LC in *Dillwyn v Llewelyn*[118] and, more recently, by McPherson J in *Riches v Hogben*.[119]

In these cases, the equity which founded the relief obtained was found in an assumption as to the future acquisition of ownership of property which had been induced by representations upon which there had been detrimental reliance by the plaintiff. This is a well recognised variety of estoppel as understood in equity and may found relief which requires the taking of active steps by the defendant ...

[113] The relief granted by the Full Court indicates that the equity of [the Giumellis] was more than a 'defensive equity'. This phrase was used by Deane J in *The Commonwealth v Verwayen*[120] to denote laches, acquiescence or delay or a mere set-off. Further, by obliging [the Giumellis] to execute a conveyance, the equity established by [Robert] did more than prevent [the Giumellis] from insisting upon their strict legal rights as present owners. On the other hand, [Robert] did not establish an immediate right to positive equitable relief as understood in the same sense that a right to recover damages may be seen as consequent upon a breach of contract.

The present case fell within the category identified by the Privy Council in *Plimmer v Mayor of Wellington*[121] where 'the Court must look at the circumstances in each case to decide in what way the equity can be satisfied'. Before a constructive trust is imposed, the court should first decide whether, having regard to the issues in the litigation, there is an appropriate equitable remedy which falls short of the imposition of a trust.[122] At the heart of this appeal is the question whether the relief granted by the Full Court was appropriate and whether sufficient weight was given by the Full Court to the various factors to be taken into account, including the impact upon relevant [114] third parties, in determining the nature and quantum of the equitable relief to be granted.

In their notice of appeal, [the Giumellis] seek the dismissal of [Robert's] claim. However, in their written and oral submissions, they accept that, at least in respect of what was identified as the second promise, [Robert] had an equity to some relief. They submit that this fell short of an order for a subdivision and the conveyance of the promised lot ...

[117] In ... respect [of the detriment Robert suffered by relying on the third promise], we prefer the conclusions reached by Rowland J and Ipp J in the Full Court. Rowland J approached the matter on the [118] footing that, even if it be conceded that Robert had not suffered an appreciable loss of income by remaining in the partnership, the detriment suffered by him was the loss of the property which he worked to improve, not to obtain immediate income from that exercise but to gain the proprietary interest.[123] For that, Robert gave up the opportunity of a different career path. Ipp J pointed out that the reasoning of the primary judge placed no weight upon the circumstance that the partnership had no security of tenure and did not own the real estate.[124] ...

---

118. (1862) 45 ER 1285 at 1287.
119. [1985] 2 Qd R 292 at 302.
120. *The Commonwealth of Australia v Verwayen* (1990) 170 CLR 394 at 435.
121. (1884) 9 App Cas 699 at 714.
122. *Bathurst City Council v PWC Properties Pty Ltd* (1998) 157 ALR 414 at 425–6; *Napier v Hunter* [1993] AC 713 at 738, 744–5, 752.
123. *Giumelli v Giumelli* (1996) 17 WAR 159 at 166.
124. *Giumelli v Giumelli* (1996) 17 WAR 159 at 174.

[The trial judge] determined the appropriate measure of relief by reference to his findings as to the second promise. His Honour's findings with respect to the third promise led to the dismissal of that aspect of the case from consideration …

[119] In his supplementary reasons, the primary judge said that the compensation to which Robert was entitled in respect of the second promise was that sum which would place him in the position he would be in if he owned the house on the land on which it was situated and was able now to realise that asset. The relief sought on the pleadings did not independently extend to loss of rent from the house from the date of Robert's exclusion and this was not a matter which could be taken into account 'in the award of equitable compensation for loss of the house and the land on which it stands'.

His Honour did not make any order which would have had the effect of charging upon the Dwellingup property, or the promised lot, or any portion thereof, the amount for which he entered judgment and interest thereon …

[120] The Full Court differed from the primary judge with respect to the third promise. This extended to the promised lot. That being so, the consideration by the Full Court of the appropriate relief was not confined to the house and the land to which it was a fixture. [The Giumellis] challenge the width of the specific relief granted by the Full Court. In particular, they emphasise that an order for the creation and conveyance of the promised lot went beyond any 'reversal' of the detriment occasioned by [Robert] in reliance upon the third promise. They submit that it was not open to the Full Court, in a case such as the present, to grant relief which went beyond the reversal of such detriment. In that regard, [the Giumellis] claim decisive support from the decision in *Verwayen*. However, in our view and consistently with the course of Australian authority since *Verwayen*, that decision is not authority for any such curtailment of the relief available in this case. Rather, there is much support in the judgments for a broader view of the present matter.

Detriment

In their submissions, [the Giumellis] stress the need to limit the measure of equitable relief lest the requirement for consideration to support a contractual promise be outflanked and direct enforcement be given to promises which did not give rise to legal rights. However, in *Verwayen*, Dawson J, after pointing out that at common law the role of estoppel was largely as a rule of evidence, stated that in equity its role has been vastly expanded to raise questions of substance. His Honour continued:

> At the same time, the discretionary nature of the relief in equity [121] marks a further reason why the fear of the common law that promissory estoppel would undermine the doctrine of consideration is unwarranted.[125] …

[125] The circumstances of the case

However, [the Giumellis] correctly challenge the Full Court order on other grounds. Before making an order designed to bring about a conveyance of the promised lot to [Robert], the Full Court was obliged to consider all the circumstances of the case. These circumstances included the still pending partnership action, the improvements to the promised lot by family members other than Robert, both before and after his residency there, the breakdown in family relationships and the continued residence on the promised

---

125. *The Commonwealth of Australia v Verwayen* (1990) 170 CLR 394 at 454.

CHAPTER 12: EQUITABLE ESTOPPEL

lot of [his brother] Steven and his family. It will be recalled that Steven is a party to the partnership action but not to the present action.

When these matters are taken into account, it is apparent that the order made by the Full Court reflected what in *Verwayen* was described as the prima facie entitlement of Robert. However, qualification was necessary both to avoid injustice to others, particularly Steven and his family, and to avoid relief which went beyond what was required for conscientious conduct by Mr and Mrs Giumelli. The result points inexorably to relief expressed not in terms of acquisition of title to land but in a money sum. This would reflect, with respect to the third promise, the approach taken by [the trial judge] when giving relief in respect of the second promise.

Conclusion
Whilst the holding of the Full Court with respect to the third promise should be upheld, the Full Court erred in the measure of relief which it granted in respect of the promised lot. This is a case for the fixing of a money sum to represent the value of the equitable claim of [Robert] to the promised lot. It will be necessary for the matter to be remitted to a judge of the Supreme Court to take that step. The amount so ascertained, with interest, should be charged upon the whole of the Dwellingup property. There will be no requirement of a subdivision of the promised lot as part of the remedy.

Comments
1. See Radan & Stewart at **12.47–12.55**.
2. For discussions of this case see J Edelman, 'Remedial Certainty or Remedial Discretion in Estoppel after *Giumelli*' (1995) 15 *Journal of Contract Law* 179 and F Burns, '*Giumelli v Giumelli* Revisited: Equitable Estoppel, the Constructive Trust and Discretionary Remedialism' (2001) 22 *Adelaide Law Review* 123.

13

RELIEF AGAINST FORFEITURE

Introduction

13.1 This chapter deals with the circumstances in which a person stands to lose some interest in property because of his or her breach of contract or as a result of the contract being terminated for some other reason. In such circumstances, that person's interest may be protected by a court pursuant to principles relating to relief against forfeiture. The jurisdiction to relieve against forfeiture is underpinned by the principle of unconscientiousness. In broad terms, relief against forfeiture relates to circumstances involving fraud, accident, mistake or surprise. Important illustrations where such relief arises include contracts for the sale of land and contracts for the lease of land.

The cases extracted in this chapter discuss the following:

- the basis of equitable jurisdiction to relieve against forfeiture: *Shiloh Spinners Ltd v Harding* [1973] AC 691;
- the operation of relief against forfeiture principles in cases of contracts terminated following a breach of an essential time stipulation: *Legione v Hateley* (1983) 152 CLR 406; *Tanwar Enterprises Pty Ltd v Cauchi* (2003) 217 CLR 315; and
- the nature of the remedies available where a right to relief against forfeiture is established: *On Demand Information plc v Michael Gerson (Finance) plc* [2003] 1 AC 368.

Jurisdiction to relieve against forfeiture

13.2   Shiloh Spinners Ltd v Harding [1973] AC 691

Court: House of Lords

Facts: In 1961, Shiloh assigned its leasehold interest in a section of land comprising two adjoining properties upon which a mill was situated. The assignment contained covenants to the effect that the assignee and its successors in title would observe certain fencing requirements and undertake works as required for the support of buildings on that part of the land that remained in the possession of Shiloh. It was also stipulated that Shiloh had the right to re-enter the land and retake possession in the event of failure to observe the covenants. The right to re-enter was not registered as a land charge under statute. In 1965, the assignee in turn assigned its interest to the demolition contractor Harding, who had notice of the covenants. Harding proceeded to demolish most of the buildings on his premises and, in the process, breached the covenants in the lease.

Shiloh commenced proceedings to re-enter the land, which Harding opposed and in response to which he sought relief against forfeiture.

Issues: The issues before the House of Lords included whether a right of re-entry for breach of covenants in an assigned lease is an equitable right; whether such a right is registrable; whether it is enforceable against a successor in title; and whether the court had jurisdiction it should exercise in such cases.

Decision: The House of Lords (Lords Wilberforce, Pearson, Simon of Glaisdale and Kilbrandon and Viscount Dilhorne) unanimously allowed Shiloh's appeal. Their Lordships held that the court had the requisite equitable jurisdiction in cases involving breaches of leasehold covenants for repair.

Extracts: The extracts from the speeches of Lord Wilberforce and Lord Simon of Glaisdale provide useful summaries of the nature and extent of the court's jurisdiction in equity to relieve against forfeiture.

Lord Wilberforce

[722] There cannot be any doubt that from the earliest times courts of equity have asserted the right to relieve against the forfeiture of property. The jurisdiction has not been confined to any particular type of case. The commonest instances concerned mortgages, giving rise to the equity of redemption, and leases, which commonly contained re-entry clauses; but other instances are found in relation to copyholds, or where the forfeiture was in the nature of a penalty. Although the principle is well established, there has undoubtedly been some fluctuation of authority as to the self-limitation to be imposed or accepted on this power. There has not been much difficulty as regards two heads of jurisdiction. First, where it is possible to state that the object of the transaction and of the insertion of the right to forfeit is essentially to secure the payment of money, equity has been willing to relieve on terms that the payment is made with interest, if appropriate, and also costs.[1] Yet even this head of relief has not been uncontested: Lord Eldon LC in his well-known judgment in *Hill v Barclay*[2] expressed his suspicion of it as a valid principle, pointing out, in an argument which surely has much force, that there may be cases where to oblige acceptance of a stipulated sum of money even with interest, at a date when receipt had lost its usefulness, might represent an unjust variation of what had been contracted for.[3] Secondly, there were the heads of fraud, accident, mistake or surprise, always a ground for equity's intervention, the inclusion of which entailed the exclusion of mere inadvertence and a fortiori of wilful defaults.

Outside of these there remained a debatable area in which were included obligations in leases such as to repair and analogous obligations concerning the condition of property, and covenants to insure or not to assign. As to covenants to repair and cases of waste, cases can be quoted before the 19th century in which relief was granted.[4] There were

---

1. *Peachy v Duke of Somerset* (1721) 93 ER 626 and cases there cited.
2. (1811) 33 ER 1037.
3. See also *Reynolds v Pitt* (1812) 34 ER 468.
4. See *Webber v Smith* (1689) 23 ER 676 and *Nash v Earl of Derby* (1705) 23 ER 948.

hostile pronouncements. In *Wadmam v Calcroft*[5] both Sir William Grant MR and Lord Eldon LC are found stating it to be clear that relief cannot be given against the breach of other covenants — ie than covenants to pay rent.

It was soon after that the critical divide or supposed divide occurred, between the liberal view of Lord Erskine LC in *Sanders v Pope* and the strict view of Lord Eldon LC in *Hill v Barclay*. The latter case came to be followed as the true canon; the former was poorly regarded in Lincoln's Inn, but it is important to observe where the difference lay. This was not, as I understand it, in any disagreement as to the field in which relief might be granted, for both cases seem to have accepted that, in principle, relief from forfeiture might be granted when the covenant was to lay out a sum of money on property: but rather on whether equity would relieve against a wilful breach. The breach in *Sanders v Pope* was of this kind but Lord Erskine LC said:

> If the covenant is broken with the consciousness, that it is broken, that is, if it is wilful, not by surprise, accident, or ignorance, still if it is [723] a case, where full compensation can be made, these authorities say, not that it is imperative upon the court to give the relief, but that there is a discretion.[6]

To this Lord Eldon LC answers:

> ... with regard to other cases, [namely, waste or omitting repairs] the doctrine I have repeatedly stated is all wrong, if it is to be taken, that relief is to be given in case of a wilful breach of covenant.[7]

The emphasis here, and the root of disagreement, clearly relates to wilful breaches, and on this it is still Lord Eldon LC's view which holds the field.

The suggestion that relief could not be granted against forfeiture for breach of other covenants was not one that followed from either case: relief was so granted in *Bargent v Thomson*.[8] Equally in *Barrow v Isaacs & Son*, a case of a covenant against underletting without consent, a high water mark of the strict doctrine, the emphasis is not so much on the nature of the breach which may or may not be relieved against, but on the argument that it is enough to show that compensation can be given:

> ... it was soon recognised that there would be great difficulty in estimating the proper amount of compensation; and, since the decision of Lord Eldon LC in *Hill v Barclay* it has always been held that equity would not relieve, merely on the ground that it could give compensation, upon breach of any covenant in a lease except the covenant for payment or rent.[9]

We are not bound by these decisions, certainly not by every shade of opinion they may reflect, but I am entirely willing to follow them in their main lines.

As regards the present appeal it is possible to disengage the following considerations. In the first place there should be put on one side cases where the court has been asked to relieve against conditions contained in wills or gifts inter vivos. These raise considerations

---

5. (1804) 32 ER 768.
6. *Sanders v Pope* (1806) 33 ER 108 at 112.
7. *Hill v Barclay* (1811) 34 ER 238 at 241.
8. (1864) 66 ER 792.
9. *Barrow v Isaacs & Son* [1891] 1 QB 417 at 425.

of a different kind from those relevant to contractual stipulations. Secondly, no decision in the present case involves the establishment or recognition directly or by implication of any general power — that is to say, apart from the special heads of fraud, accident, mistake or surprise — in courts exercising equitable jurisdiction to relieve against men's bargains. Lord Eldon LC's firm denial of any such power in *Hill v Barclay* does not call for any revision or review in this case. Equally there is no need to qualify Kay LJ's proposition in *Barrow v Isaacs & Son* (cited above). I would fully endorse this: it remains true today that equity expects men to carry out their bargains and will not let them buy their way out by uncovenanted payment. But it is consistent with these principles that we should reaffirm the right of courts of equity in appropriate and limited cases to relieve against forfeiture for breach of covenant or condition where the primary object of the bargain is to secure a stated result which can effectively be attained when the matter comes before the court, and where the forfeiture provision is added by way of security for the production of that result. The word 'appropriate' involves consideration of the conduct of the applicant for relief, in particular whether his default was wilful, of the gravity of the breaches, and of the disparity **[724]** between the value of the property of which forfeiture is claimed as compared with the damage caused by the breach.

Both as a matter of history and by the nature of things, different considerations apply to different covenants. As regards covenants to pay rent, in spite of Lord Eldon LC's reservations, the matter has, subject to qualifications which need not be discussed, been taken over by statute ... The same is true of covenants to insure and other covenants in leases. I shall consider shortly the implications of the legislation as regards other covenants than those expressly mentioned. As regards covenants to repair and analogous covenants concerning the condition of property, other than those now dealt with by Act of Parliament, it is not necessary to overrule *Hill v Barclay* any more than it was necessary for Lord Eldon LC to do more than to distinguish *Sanders v Pope*. Lord Eldon LC's decision was in fact based partly upon the circumstance that he was concerned with a wilful default and partly upon the impossibility of speculating whether the later doing of the repairs would compensate the landlord: such considerations remain relevant. Where it is necessary, and, in my opinion, right, to move away from some 19th century authorities, is to reject as a reason against granting relief, the impossibility for the courts to supervise the doing of work. The fact is a reality, no doubt, and explains why specific performance cannot be granted of agreements to this effect but in the present context it can now be seen (as it was seen by Lord Erskine LC in *Sanders v Pope*) to be an irrelevance: for what the court has to do is to satisfy itself, ex post facto, that the covenanted work has been done, and it has ample machinery, through certificates, or by enquiry, to do precisely this. This removes much of the support from one of the more formidable authorities, viz: the majority judgment in *Bracebridge v Buckley*.[10]

There remain two other arguments which cannot be passed over. First it is said that the strict view (that there should be no relief except under the two classical headings) has been endorsed in this House in *Hughes v Metropolitan Railway Co*. There is no substance in this. The basis of decision in this House was that the landlord's notice was suspended in operation by acquiescence, so that there was no effective breach. The opinion invoked is that of Lord Cairns LC, in which there appears this portion of a sentence:

---

10. (1816) 146 ER 68.

[I]t could not be argued, that there was any right of a court of equity, ... to give relief in cases of this kind, by way of mercy, or by way of merely of saving property from forfeiture, ...[11]

— words which have only to be re-read to show that they are no sort of denial of the jurisdiction now invoked.

Secondly, a point of more difficulty arises from the intervention of Parliament in providing specific machinery for the granting of relief against forfeiture of leases.[12] This, it is said, negatives an intention that any corresponding jurisdiction should [725] exist outside the case of leases. I do not accept this argument. In my opinion where the courts have established a general principle of law or equity, and the legislature steps in with particular legislation in a particular area, it must, unless showing a contrary intention, be taken to have left cases outside that area where they were under the influence of the general law. To suppose otherwise involves the conclusion that an existing jurisdiction has been cut down by implication, by an enactment moreover which is positive in character (for it amplifies the jurisdiction in cases of leases) rather than negative. That legislation did not have this effect was the view of Kay LJ in *Barrow v Isaacs & Son*, when he held that covenants against assigning — excluded from the Conveyancing Act 1881 — were left to be dealt with according to the ordinary law.[13] ...

The present case, in my opinion, falls within the class of case in which it would be possible for a court of equity to intervene. When [Shiloh] assigned a portion of their leased property, retaining the rest, which adjoined and was supported by the portion assigned, they had an essential interest in securing adequate protection for their buildings, in having the entire site fenced, in preventing unauthorised access through the assigned property. The covenants were drafted accordingly. The power of re-entry was inserted by way of reinforcement of the contractual obligation which it must have been perceived might cease to be enforceable as such. Failures to observe the covenants having occurred, it would be right to consider whether the assignor [Shiloh] should be allowed to exercise his legal rights if the essentials of the bargain could be secured and if it was fair and just to prevent him from doing so. It would be necessary, as stated above, to consider the conduct of the assignee [Harding], the nature and gravity of the breach, and its relation to the value of the property which might be forfeited. Established and, in my opinion, sound principle requires that wilful breaches should not, or at least should only in exceptional cases, be relieved against, if only for the reason that the assignor should not be compelled to remain in a relation of neighborhood with a person in deliberate breach of his obligations.

In this light should relief have been granted? [Harding's] difficulty is that the Vice-Chancellor, who heard the witnesses and went into all the facts, clearly took the view that the case was not one for relief. I should be reluctant, in any event, except on clear conviction to substitute a different view of my own. But I have examined in detail the evidence given, the correspondence over a period of four years, the photographs and plans of the site. All this material establishes a case of clear and wilful breaches of more

---

11. *Hughes v Metropolitan Railway Co* (1877) 2 App Cas 439 at 448.
12. See *Law of Property (Amendment) Act 1859* (22 & 23 Vict c 35), *Common Law Procedure Act 1852*, *Law of Property Act 1925*, *Leasehold Property (Repairs) Act 1938* and other statutes.
13. *Barrow v Isaacs & Son* [1891] 1 QB 417 at 430.

than one covenant which, if individually not serious, were certainly substantial: a case of continuous disregard by [Harding] of [Shiloh's] rights over a period of time, coupled with a total lack of evidence as to [Harding's] ability speedily and adequately to make good the consequences of his default, and finally a failure to show any such disproportion between the expenditure required and the [726] value of the interest involved as to amount to a case of hardship. In my opinion the case is not, on established principles, one for relief.

Lord Simon of Glaisdale

[726] The last hundred years have seen many examples of relaxation of the stance of regarding contractual rights and obligations as sacrosanct and exclusive of other considerations: though these examples do not compel equity to follow — certainly not to the extent of overturning established authorities — they do at least invite a more liberal and extensively based attitude on the part of courts which are not bound by those authorities. I would therefore myself hold that equity has an unlimited and unfettered jurisdiction to relieve against contractual forfeitures and penalties. What have sometimes been regarded as fetters to the jurisdiction are, in my view, [727] more properly to be seen as considerations which the court will weigh in deciding how to exercise an unfettered jurisdiction.[14] Prominent but not exclusive among such considerations is the desirability that contractual promises should be observed and contractual rights respected, and even more the undesirability of the law appearing to condone flagrant and contemptuous disregard of obligations. Other such considerations are how far it is reasonable to require a party who is prima facie entitled to invoke a forfeiture or penalty clause to accept alternative relief (eg, money payment or re-instatement of premises) and how far vindication of contractual rights would be grossly excessive and harsh having regard to the damage done to the promisee and the moral culpability of the promisor. (I do not intend this as an exhaustive list.) It is these internal considerations which may limit the cases where courts of equity will relieve against forfeiture, rather than any external confine on jurisdiction.

Lastly, there being, in my judgment, jurisdiction to relieve against re-entry in the present case, how should it be exercised? ... The proper attitude of an appellate court to the review of a discretionary jurisdiction has frequently been stated. Perhaps the locus classicus is the speech of Viscount Simon LC in *Blunt v Blunt*, in which the rest of the House concurred ... He said:

> This brings me to a consideration of the circumstances in which an appeal may be successfully brought against the exercise of the divorce court's discretion. If it can be shown that the court acted under a misapprehension of fact in that it either gave weight to irrelevant or unproved matters or omitted to take into account matters that are relevant, there would, in my opinion, be ground for an appeal. In such a case the exercise of discretion might be impeached, because the court's discretion will have been exercised on wrong or inadequate materials, but, as was recently pointed out in this House in another connexion in *Charles Osenton v Johnston*: 'The appellate tribunal is not at liberty merely to substitute its own exercise of discretion for the discretion already exercised by the judge. In other words, appellate authorities ought not to reverse the

---

14. Cf *Blunt v Blunt* [1943] AC 517; *Kara v Kara and Holman* [1948] P 287 at 292.

order merely because they would themselves have exercised the original discretion, had it attached to them, in a different way. But if the appellate tribunal reaches the clear conclusion that there has been a wrongful exercise of discretion in that no weight, or no sufficient weight, has been given to relevant considerations … then the reversal of the order on appeal may be justified.'[15] *Osenton's* case was one in which the discretion being exercised was that of deciding whether an action should be tried by an official referee, and the material for forming a conclusion was entirely documentary and [728] was thus equally available to the appellate court. The reason for not interfering, save in the most extreme cases, with the judge's decision under section 4 of the Matrimonial Causes Act 1937 is of a far stronger character, for the proper exercise of the discretion in such a matter largely depends on the observation of witnesses and on a deduction as to matrimonial relations and future prospects which can best be made at the trial.[16]

Viscount Simon LC did not, in my view, intend in any way to suggest that it was enough to justify an appellate court in interfering with the exercise of a discretion that the appellate court would give different weight to the various considerations which the court exercising the jurisdiction must have had in mind: that would be to substitute the appellate court's discretion for that of the court charged with the exercise of the discretion, since it is generally of the essence of a discretionary jurisdiction that there are a number of conflicting considerations to be weighed, to which different minds could reasonably attach different weight. It is only if there has been misdirection (in fact or in law) or if the exercise of the discretion is 'plainly wrong' (which means, I think, that no reasonable tribunal could exercise the discretion in such a way) that the appellate court is entitled to interfere.

> **Comment**
> 1. See Radan & Stewart at **13.2–13.4**.

Forfeiture and essential time stipulations

> ### 13.3   Legione v Hateley (1983) 152 CLR 406
>
> **Court:** High Court of Australia
>
> **Facts:** By a contract dated 14 July 1978 Mr and Mrs Hateley agreed to purchase land from Mr and Mrs Legione for $35,000 payable by a deposit of $6000 and the balance on 1 July 1979. Mr and Mrs Hateley were to pay interest at 8 per cent from 1 July 1978. The contract also provided for a rate of interest of 14 per cent if there was default in payment. Time was expressed to be of the essence. However, neither party could enforce their rights unless they gave a written notice to the other requiring them to remedy their default within 14 days (condition 5). The Hateleys paid the deposit, went into possession and, unbeknown to the Legiones, built a house on the land. On 29 June

---

15. *Charles Osenton v Johnson* [1942] AC 130 at 138.
16. *Blunt v Blunt* [1943] AC 517 at 526–7.

1979 they sought a three-month extension to pay the balance of the purchase price. That request was refused. On 26 July 1979 the Legiones served a notice pursuant to condition 5 of the contract requiring the Hateleys to remedy their defaults by paying the balance of the purchase price and interest.

On 9 August the Hateleys' solicitor telephoned the Legiones' solicitor and spoke to the secretary of the partner of the firm who was handling the matter. The solicitor's version of what was said during that conversation was as follows: 'I told Miss Williams that my client had arranged bridging finance from the ANZ Bank. I told her that the bank required approximately a week in which to carry out their usual title searches, but they would be ready to settle on [17 August]. Miss Williams said to me, "I think that'll be all right, but I'll have to get instructions"'. On 14 August 1979 the Legiones' solicitors delivered to the Hateleys' solicitors a letter stating that the contract had been rescinded pursuant to the notice. On the next day the Hateleys tendered the balance of the purchase price. This was rejected. The Hateleys then sued the Legiones for specific performance of the contract. In response, the Legiones sought a declaration to the effect that the contract had been rescinded. Mr Hateley died and the action for specific performance was continued by Mrs Hateley. Mrs Hateley argued that if the Legiones' notice of rescission was held to be valid, she was entitled to relief against forfeiture of her interest under the contract in the land and the improvements erected upon it.

Issues: The issues before the High Court were whether the statements made by the secretary for the Legiones' solicitor on 9 August 1979 amounted to an estoppel that precluded the Legiones from treating the contract as rescinded and, if no such estoppel arose, whether Mrs Hateley was entitled to relief against forfeiture.

Decision: On the issue of estoppel, a majority of the High Court (Mason, Deane and Brennan JJ; Gibbs CJ and Murphy J dissenting) held that the secretary's statements did not give rise to an estoppel. On the relief against forfeiture issue, a majority (Gibbs CJ, Mason, Murphy and Deane JJ; Brennan J dissenting) held that the principles relating to relief against forfeiture were relevant to a case such as this and remitted the case to the Victorian Supreme Court for determination on the facts.

Extracts: The extracts from the joint judgments of Gibbs CJ and Murphy J, and Mason and Deane JJ, discuss the principles of relief against forfeiture in the context of breach of an essential time stipulation.

Gibbs CJ and Murphy J

[423] There is no doubt that when the purchasers executed the contract and paid the deposit the beneficial ownership of the land passed to them subject to the payment of the purchase money. The effect of cl 15 of the copyright conditions of sale was to deprive the [424] purchasers of their interest in the land once a notice had been given under that clause and the default in payment to which the notice referred had not been remedied within the time limited in the notice. In saying that we of course assume, contrary to our own opinion, that no estoppel had occurred. In these circumstances it is manifest that the condition brought about a forfeiture of the purchasers' interest in the land.

In *Shiloh Spinners Ltd v Harding* Lord Wilberforce said:

> There cannot be any doubt that from the earliest times courts of equity have asserted the right to relieve against the forfeiture of property. The jurisdiction has not been confined to any particular type of case. The commonest instances concerned mortgages, giving rise to the equity of redemption, and leases, which commonly contained re-entry clauses; but other instances are found in relation to copyholds, or where the forfeiture was in the nature of a penalty. Although the principle is well established, there has undoubtedly been some fluctuation of authority as to the self-limitation to be imposed or accepted on this power. There has not been much difficulty as regards two heads of jurisdiction. First, where it is possible to state that the object of the transaction and of the insertion of the right to forfeit is essentially to secure the payment of money, equity has been willing to relieve on terms that the payment is made with interest, if appropriate, and also costs ... Secondly, there were the heads of fraud, accident, mistake or surprise, always a ground for equity's intervention, the inclusion of which entailed the exclusion of mere inadvertence and a fortiori of wilful defaults.[17]

Later, after discussing some of the authorities, his Lordship went on:

> But it is consistent with these principles that we should reaffirm the right of courts of equity in appropriate and limited cases to relieve against forfeiture for breach of covenant or condition where the primary object of the bargain is to secure a stated result which can effectively be attained when the matter comes before the court, and where the forfeiture provision is added by way of security for the production of that result.[18] ...

[425] In the light of those statements of principle it is difficult to see any reason why the power of courts of equity to relieve against forfeiture should not be available in a case such as the present ...

[429] A court of equity will grant specific performance notwithstanding a failure to make a payment within the time specified by the contract if there is nothing to render such an order inequitable. The fact that time for the performance of the stipulated obligation is of the essence of the contract generally makes the grant of specific performance inequitable in such a case. However, if it is just to relieve against the forfeiture which is incurred when the vendor retains payments already made under the contract, it is difficult to see why it should be unjust to relieve the purchaser against the forfeiture of the interest in the property that results in exactly the same circumstances. No doubt, where the parties have chosen to make time of the essence of the contract the grant of relief against forfeiture as a preliminary to an order for specific performance will be exceptional. Nevertheless on principle we can see no reason why such an order should not be made if it will not cause injustice but will on the contrary prevent injustice. If relief against the forfeiture is granted, the objection to the grant of specific performance is removed.

In the present case the circumstances revealed by the existing evidence indicate that it would be unjust for the vendors to insist on the forfeiture of the purchasers' interest in the land. Important among those circumstances is the fact that the purchasers have erected on the land a house of considerable value and if the contract is rescinded the vendors will receive an ill-merited windfall. Further there are the facts that the purchase moneys were

---

17. *Shiloh Spinners Ltd v Harding* [1973] AC 691 at 722.
18. *Shiloh Spinners Ltd v Harding* [1973] AC 691 at 723.

tendered only four days after the notice expired, and that the late payment was explained by the terms of the letter from the vendors' solicitors. The breach by the purchasers was neither wilful nor apparently serious. To enforce the legal rights of the vendors in these circumstances would be to exact a harsh and excessive penalty for a comparatively trivial breach. However, an opportunity should be given to the vendors to establish whether they have suffered damage as a result of the purchasers' failure. Moreover it will be necessary for the court to consider what terms should be imposed on the purchasers as a condition of the grant of relief. Clearly they should be required to pay the balance of the purchase price and interest, although at what rate will be a matter that requires consideration. Whether the purchasers should in addition be required to pay anything in respect of damages or costs depends on the evidence and argument that may be adduced.

Mason and Deane JJ

[440] We turn to [Hateley's] submission that she is entitled to relief against the forfeiture of her interest in the land ...

[441] Two Privy Council decisions are daunting obstacles confronting [Hateley's] case. [*Steedman v Drinkle*[19] and *Brickles v Snell*[20]] stand seemingly as authority for the proposition that specific performance, even by way of relief against forfeiture, is never ordered when a stipulation as to time, which is of the essence of the contract, has not been observed. However, three years before those decisions, the Privy Council in *Kilmer v British Columbia Orchard Lands Ltd*[21] had ordered specific performance of a contract by way of relief against forfeiture at the suit of the purchaser, notwithstanding that the vendor had elected to treat the contract as at an end following the purchaser's default in making due payment of an instalment of the purchase price, the contract containing a provision that time was to be of the essence.

The principle which the Judicial Committee applied in *Kilmer's Case* had been enunciated in *In re Dagenham (Thames) Dock Co; Ex parte Hulse*, where the Court of Appeal in Chancery ... held that a provision in a contract entitling the vendor to rescind for late payment, forfeit instalments of purchase price already paid and retake possession, time being of the essence of the contract, was a penalty against which relief should be granted by requiring completion on terms that the purchaser pay the balance of the purchase price with interest for late payment. Mellish LJ expressed the principle in this way:

> ... where there is a stipulation that if, on a certain day, an agreement remains either wholly or in any part unperformed — in which case the real damage may be either very large or very trifling — there is to be a certain forfeiture incurred, that stipulation is to be treated as in the nature of a penalty.[22]

James LJ spoke of it as 'an extremely clear case of a mere penalty for non-payment of the purchase-money', agreeing that it was a penalty from which the company was entitled to be relieved on payment of the residue of the purchase money with interest.[23]

---

19. [1916] 1 AC 275.
20. [1916] 2 AC 599.
21. [1913] AC 319.
22. *In re Dagenham (Thames) Dock Co; Ex parte Hulse* (1873) LR 8 Ch App 1022 at 1025.
23. *In re Dagenham (Thames) Dock Co; Ex parte Hulse* (1873) LR 8 Ch App 1022 at 1025.

In *Kilmer's Case* in the judgment prepared by Lord Macnaghten ... the views of James and Mellish LJJ were repeated and applied. Their Lordships said:

> It seems to be even a stronger case, for the penalty, if enforced according to the letter of the agreement, becomes more and more severe as the agreement approaches completion, and the money liable to confiscation becomes larger.[24]

[442] *Kilmer's Case* was explained in *Steedman v Drinkle* and *Brickles v Snell* as a case in which the vendor had waived the due payment of the overdue instalment so that the purchaser's breach of contract was not a breach of an essential condition. Unfortunately *Kilmer's Case* does not easily lend itself to this explanation. Waiver was one of the arguments advanced in support of the appeal. It was not, however, reflected in the judgment, where their Lordships set out the provision making time of the essence in respect of payment of instalments and forfeiting all instalments paid in the event of any delay in payment and noted that the relevant payment was by the terms of the agreement to be made on or before 14 June 1910, that it was extended to 7 July 1910, and that on 9 July the vendor declared that the deal was off. In the absence of any reference in the judgment to a waiver of time being of the essence — and there is no reference — it is difficult to conclude that the judgment turned upon any finding to that effect. Indeed, the report contains no reference to material which could sustain the conclusion that there had been a waiver of the essentiality of prompt payment. The extension of the time for payment from 14 June to 7 July would not involve such a waiver. So much had been decided in *Barclay v Messenger*,[25] more recently followed by this Court in *Tropical Traders Ltd v Goonan*[26] where Kitto J, with whom Taylor and Menzies JJ agreed, accepted the explanation of *Kilmer's Case* offered in *Steedman v Drinkle* and *Brickles v Snell* ...

Much earlier Dixon J in *McDonald v Dennys Lascelles Ltd* had questioned the correctness of the traditional explanation of *Kilmer's Case*. He said that the view adopted in the *Dagenham (Thames) Dock Case*:

> ... seems to have been that relief should be granted, not against the forfeiture of the instalments, but against the forfeiture of the estate under a contract which involved the retention of the purchase money: and this may have been the ground upon which Lord Moulton proceeded in [*Kilmer's Case*], notwithstanding the explanation of that case given in *Steedman v Drinkle* and *Brickles v Snell*.[27]

Apart from *Steedman v Drinkle* and *Brickles v Snell*, statements in the judgments in *Mehmet v Benson*,[28] and in *Petrie v* [443] *Dwyer*,[29] appear to support the proposition that specific performance of a contract cannot be obtained by a purchaser once the contract has been rescinded in consequence of his breach of an essential term ...

The question has not been raised as an issue in recent times, no doubt because the doctrine enunciated in *Steedman v Drinkle* and *Brickles v Snell* has been thought to hold

---

24. *Kilmer v British Columbia Orchard Lands Ltd* [1913] AC 319 at 325.
25. (1874) 43 LJ Ch 449 at 456.
26. (1964) 111 CLR 41 at 53–5.
27. *McDonald v Dennys Lascelles Ltd* (1933) 48 CLR 457 at 478.
28. (1965) 113 CLR 295 at 307–8, 309, 314–15.
29. (1954) 91 CLR 99 at 104–5.

the field. However, Farwell J in *Mussen v Van Diemen's Land Co* expressed the opinion that specific performance, with or without compensation, would be ordered at the suit of a purchaser wherever possible, so long as he was able and willing to complete. He said:

> There are no doubt cases where there has been a failure to pay the instalments and to complete the contract, and the purchaser has then come forward and said: 'I am here and now ready and willing to complete the contract and to pay the price originally stipulated by the contract and to carry out its terms', and then the Court has said that it is inequitable and against conscience that the vendor should refuse specific performance and claim to retain the money already paid. That is because the Court has said that if the plaintiff is willing to carry out his contract, notwithstanding the fact that temporarily at any rate he was unable to do so, if he is willing and able to carry out his contract, it being the primary intention of the parties that the sale should take place, it would be against conscience for the defendant to say: 'I will not give effect to the primary intention of the parties, but I will refuse to complete, and I will retain the money which has been paid to me'.[30] ...

[444] Underlying the approach taken in the *Dagenham (Thames) Dock Case* and *Kilmer's Case* is an expansive view of the equitable jurisdiction to relieve against forfeiture. This in turn conforms to the fundamental principle according to which equity acts, namely that a party having a legal right shall not be permitted to exercise it in such a way that the exercise amounts to unconscionable conduct.

It has been thought by some that the equitable jurisdiction to relieve against penalties and forfeitures is a branch of the jurisdiction to relieve in cases of accident. This view has been strongly contested on the ground that the correct foundation of the jurisdiction was expressed by Lord Macclesfield LC in *Peachy v Duke of Somerset*:

> The true ground of relief against penalties is from the original intent of the case, where the penalty is designed only to secure money, and the Court gives him [the obligee] all that he expected or desired.[31]

The principle as expressed by Lord Macclesfield was modified and extended by Lord Thurlow LC who, in *Sloman v Walter*, expressed it in this way:

> The rule, that where a penalty is inserted merely to secure the enjoyment of a collateral object, the enjoyment of the object is considered as the principal intent of the deed, and the penalty only as accessional, and, therefore, only to secure the damage really incurred, is too strongly established in equity to be shaken.[32]

It is, however, doubtful whether these comments, appropriate as they may have been to relief against penalties, were intended to apply with equal force to all cases of relief against forfeiture. There is more to be said for the view that when the equitable jurisdiction is invoked to relieve against a forfeiture which is not in the nature of a penalty, equity looks to unconscionable conduct, as Farwell J indicated in *Mussen's Case*, in the passage already quoted, especially when unconscionable conduct is associated with fraud, mistake, accident or surprise.

---

30. *Mussen v Van Diemen's Land Co* (1938) Ch 253 at 263–4.
31. *Peachy v Duke of Somerset* (1721) 93 ER 626 at 630.
32. *Sloman v Walter* (1783) 28 ER 1213 at 1214.

[445] A penalty, as its name suggests, is in the nature of a punishment for non-observance of a contractual stipulation; it consists of the imposition of an additional or different liability upon breach of the contractual stipulation. On the other hand, forfeiture involves the loss or determination of an estate or interest in property or a proprietary right, eg, a lease, in consequence of a failure to perform a covenant. When non-payment of rent or a fine is made the occasion for forfeiture of an estate or interest in property it may be proper to treat the forfeiture as being similar in character to a penalty because it is designed to ensure payment of the rent or fine. There is, however, a real distinction between 'penalty' and 'forfeiture' and it is unfortunate that the terms have been frequently used in a way which blurs it. The claims made by the purchasers in *Steedman v Drinkle* and *Brickles v Snell* were for relief against the 'forfeiture' of instalments of purchase money. The relevant contracts, like the modern contract of sale, permitted the vendor to 'forfeit' instalments of purchase money. In this situation, despite the use of the word 'forfeit', relief is granted on the footing that the contractual provision entitling the vendor to retain the instalments is in substance a penalty, or in the nature of a penalty, because it is designed to ensure payment of the entire purchase price and it exceeds the damage which he suffers by reason of the purchaser's default.

[Hateley's] claim here is of a different kind to that involved in *Steedman v Drinkle* and *Brickles v Snell*. She seeks relief against forfeiture of her equitable interest as purchaser under a binding contract for sale. Forfeiture of the purchaser's interest, usually the consequence of the vendor's rescission for breach of an essential term, occurs under the general law regulating the rights of vendor and purchaser. Such a forfeiture is to be distinguished from a contractual forfeiture which is designed to ensure performance of a principal obligation. True it is that condition 5 expressly regulated the vendor's right of rescission in the present case and provided for rescission on non-compliance with the prescribed notice on expiration of the time limited. However, the presence of this contractual stipulation, which merely regulates the vendor's common law right to rescind, does not alter the essential character of the forfeiture of the purchaser's interest which occurs when rescission takes place. No doubt the risk of forfeiture is a strong inducement to completion of the contract, that being the primary intention of the parties, but it [446] is incorrect to describe the rescission for which condition 5 provides and the forfeiture of the purchaser's interest which it entails as a penalty or as being in the nature of a penalty.

In this Court [in *Brown v Heffer*[33]] it has been said that the purchaser's equitable interest under a contract of sale is commensurate only with her ability to obtain specific performance of the contract. On this view the loss of [Hateley's] equitable interest, from which she presently seeks to be relieved, was occasioned by her failure to comply with an essential condition of the contract, payment of the balance of the purchase price on 10 August 1979, the date fixed for completion by [the Legiones'] rescission notice, time being of the essence by virtue of condition 5. Upon the expiration of the time fixed by the notice the contract came to an end.

A competing view — one which has much to commend it — is that the purchaser's equitable interest under a contract for sale is commensurate, not with her ability to obtain specific performance in the strict or primary sense, but with her ability to protect her

---

33. (1967) 116 CLR 344 at 349.

interest under the contract by injunction or otherwise.[34] If this view were to be adopted and applied, [Hateley's] inability to obtain specific performance in the primary sense would not entail the loss of her equitable interest. She would retain that interest so long as she was entitled to make out a case for relief against forfeiture.

However, for the purposes of this case we are prepared to accept the correctness of the statement in *Brown v Heffer*. It then becomes necessary to look behind the authorities to the reasons which have been put forward to sustain the view that rescission in consequence of breach of an essential term is an absolute bar to relief against forfeiture of the purchaser's interest. Before doing so, we should make one comment on the authorities. *Steedman v Drinkle* and *Brickles v Snell* deny the exercise, rather than the existence, of jurisdiction to relieve against forfeiture of the purchaser's interest under a contract when he is in breach of an essential term and the contract has been brought to an end. If the purchaser in this situation fails to obtain relief it is because he is unable to bring **[447]** himself within the principles according to which relief is granted or refused, not because there is an absence of jurisdiction to grant him relief.

The rule that relief is never granted in respect of forfeiture by operation of law has no application to a forfeiture which occurs in consequence of a voluntary act done in the exercise of a legal right for, as we have seen, it is against such an act that relief is ordinarily granted. In this case rescission was the consequence of [Hateley's] non-compliance with a notice given by the [Legiones] in exercise of the right conferred by condition 5. However, condition 5 does not affect the intrinsic character of rescission — essentially it is a voluntary act done by way of exercise of a legal right bringing about a legal consequence, the termination of the contract. Of course, if relief be granted against the vendor's voluntary act, the legal consequence flowing from that act — the rescission — is displaced and the purchaser's equitable interest is either continued or renewed.

Next there is the problem presented by the suggested unavailability of specific performance. Relief against forfeiture of the purchaser's interest under a contract for sale ordinarily involves an order for specific performance of the contract against the vendor, subject to compensation, that is, to the imposition of such terms as will fairly compensate him for insistence on completion of the contract in the altered circumstances occasioned by the purchaser's breach. The critical question then is: Should specific performance ever be ordered when the purchaser is in breach of an essential condition? The argument in favour of a negative answer is forceful. If parties expressly or impliedly stipulate that performance of a term is essential to their bargain then it would ordinarily be unjust to the innocent party to require him to complete notwithstanding a breach of that term. Generally speaking equity expects men to carry out their bargains and 'will not let them buy their way out by uncovenanted payment'.[35] Nor will it remake the parties' contract simply because it transpires that as things have happened one party has made a bad bargain.

But if there be fraud, mistake, accident, surprise or some other element which would make it unconscionable or inequitable to insist on forfeiture of the purchaser's interest under the contract because he has not performed in strict accordance with its terms there is no injustice to the innocent party in granting relief against forfeiture by means

---

34. *Tailby v Official Receiver* (1888) 13 App Cas 523 at 546–9.
35. *Shiloh Spinners Ltd v Harding* [1973] AC 691 at 723.

of specific performance with or without compensation. **[448]** *Cheney v Libby* provides an illustration of an unconscionable rescission. There the Court ordered specific performance of a contract for the sale of land, time being of the essence, when the purchaser had failed on the due date to pay an instalment of purchase price in dollars, the stipulated mode of payment. The purchaser had been misled by the vendor's conduct into thinking that another form of payment would be accepted because it had been accepted by the vendor in the past. Once he knew the vendor refused to accept the payment, the purchaser promptly tendered payment in dollars, though the due date for payment had passed. The Court said:

> Even where time is made material, by express stipulation, the failure of one of the parties to perform a condition within the particular time limited, will not in every case defeat his right to specific performance, if the condition be subsequently performed, without unreasonable delay, and no circumstances have intervened that would render it unjust or inequitable to give such relief. The discretion which a court of equity has to grant or refuse specific performance, and which is always exercised with reference to the circumstances of the particular case before it, may, and of necessity must, often be controlled by the conduct of the party who bases his refusal to perform the contract upon the failure of the other party to strictly comply with its conditions.[36]

After noting that forfeiture of the contract would enable the vendor 'to take advantage of his own wrong',[37] the Court went on to say that the provisions of the contract — 'cannot be applied where the efficient cause of the failure of the party seeking specific performance to comply strictly and literally with the contract was the conduct of the other party'.[38]

The foregoing discussion indicates that the Judicial Committee in *Steedman v Drinkle* and *Brickles v Snell* gave more weight to the value of enforcing contracts according to their strict terms and less attention to the fundamental principle which underlies the exercise of the equitable jurisdiction to relieve against forfeiture than we are disposed to give them. That the Judicial Committee did so is readily understandable because in the early part of this century overriding importance attached to the concept of freedom of contract and to the need to hold parties to their bargains. These considerations, though still important, should not be allowed to override competing **[449]** claims based on long standing heads of justice and equity. The result of the two decisions was to enunciate an inflexible rule that specific performance will never be granted where there is a breach of an essential condition, thereby diminishing the utility of the remedy in cases of relief against forfeiture. A preferable course is to adjust the availability of the remedy so that it becomes an effective instrument in situations in which it is necessary to relieve against forfeiture of the purchaser's interest under a contract for sale. The rule would then be expressed by saying that it is only in exceptional circumstances that specific performance will be granted at the instance of a purchaser who is in breach of an essential condition.

Whether the exceptional circumstances exist in a given case hinges on the existence of unconscionable conduct. It is impossible to define or describe exclusively all the situations

---

36. *Cheney v Libby* (1890) 134 US 68 at 78.
37. *Cheney v Libby* (1890) 134 US 68 at 79.
38. *Cheney v Libby* (1890) 134 US 68 at 80.

which may give rise to unconscionable conduct on the part of a vendor in rescinding a contract for sale. None the less it may be said that where the conduct of the vendor, though not creating an estoppel or waiver, has effectively caused or contributed to the purchaser's breach of contract there is ground for exercising the jurisdiction to relieve. And if it also appears that the object of the rescission is not to safeguard the vendor from adverse consequences which he may suffer as a result of the contract remaining on foot, but merely to take unconscientious advantage of the benefits which will fortuitously accrue to him on forfeiture of the purchaser's interest under the contract, there will be even stronger ground for the exercise of the jurisdiction.

In the ultimate analysis the result in a given case will depend upon the resolution of subsidiary questions which inevitably arise. The more important of these are: (1) Did the conduct of the vendor contribute to the purchaser's breach? (2) Was the purchaser's breach (a) trivial or slight, and (b) inadvertent and not wilful? (3) What damage or other adverse consequences did the vendor suffer by reason of the purchaser's breach? (4) What is the magnitude of the purchaser's loss and the vendor's gain if the forfeiture is to stand? (5) Is specific performance with or without compensation an adequate safeguard for the vendor?

Comment

1. See Radan & Stewart at **13.17–13.18**.

13.4 Tanwar Enterprises Pty Ltd v Cauchi (2003) 217 CLR 315

Court: High Court of Australia

Facts: Separate contracts for the purchase of three adjoining parcels of land for $4.5m were entered into by Tanwar in October 1999. Tanwar paid $450,000 by way of total deposit on the contracts. Each contract specified the completion date as 28 February 2000, although this was not expressed as being of the essence. The completion dates were later amended to August of that year. As Tanwar was not in a position to complete by that time, Cauchi and others (the vendors) served termination notices on 20 August but, after protracted negotiations between the parties, a deed was entered into in early June 2001 nominating the new and essential completion date of 25 June. The deed made it clear that failure to complete by the agreed time would result in forfeiture of deposit. On the completion date, Tanwar's incoming mortgagees informed the parties that they would not be able to proceed with settlement until the following day. On 26 June, Tanwar gave notice to Cauchi that it was in a position to complete. Cauchi responded by issuing notices of termination the same day. Tanwar sought declarations that the terminations were invalid and orders for relief against forfeiture and specific performance.

Issue: The issue before the High Court was whether Cauchi had validly terminated the contracts of sale and whether Tanwar as purchaser was entitled to relief.

Decision: The High Court (Gleeson CJ, McHugh, Gummow, Hayne, Heydon, Kirby and Callinan JJ) unanimously rejected Tanwar's appeal. The court held that the vendors were entitled to exercise their contractual rights to terminate since they had not contributed to Tanwar's breach. Also, relief on the ground of accident was not available to Tanwar because the possibility of breach was reasonably within its contemplation.

Extracts: The extracts from the joint judgment of Gleeson CJ, McHugh, Gummow, Hayne and Heydon JJ focus on what is required to establish unconscientious reliance on essential time stipulations, thereby precluding relief against forfeiture.

Gleeson CJ, McHugh, Gummow, Hayne and Heydon JJ

[326] In submissions, extensive reference was made to the decision in *Legione*.[39] That case made it plain that the principles identified as promissory or equitable estoppel may operate to preclude the enforcement of contractual rights and so may estop a party from treating the contract in question as terminated for failure to meet an essential time stipulation. The division of opinion within the Court turned upon the question whether a particular telephone conversation was sufficient to found the necessary estoppel; in particular, whether the conversation contained a representation of the necessary clarity to the effect that observance of the time stipulation was not insisted upon. The majority (Mason, Brennan and Deane JJ) held that the terms of the conversation did not meet the necessary standard. The facts of the present appeal supply no foundation for an estoppel against reliance by [Cauchi] upon the essential time stipulation in the 2001 Deeds.

In *Legione*,[40] the Court also received written submissions upon a further question. This was identified as being whether the purchasers should be relieved against 'the forfeiture' brought about by the notice of rescission. Pursuant to the contract, the purchasers had been entitled to go into possession on payment of the deposit. They had done so and had built a house on the land before the due date for completion which was nearly twelve months after the date of the contract.

The 'forfeiture point' had not been pursued to any degree at the trial in *Legione* and the order made by this Court was that the case be remitted to the Supreme Court of Victoria for the determination of that issue.[41] The conclusion reached by Mason and Deane JJ had been that the Supreme Court had the necessary jurisdiction to relieve against forfeiture and that there was a serious question to be tried in the exercise of that jurisdiction.[42] Gibbs CJ and Murphy J concurred in the order giving effect to that conclusion.[43] Brennan J dissented.

Subsequently, in the joint judgment of five members of the Court in *Ciavarella v Balmer*, it was held that there was no evidence to found any estoppel against termination of the contract for sale of land. An application to amend the notice of appeal in this Court so as to claim relief against forfeiture was refused. The Court described as [327] follows the circumstances which had led to the order of remittal in *Legione*:

---

39. *Legione v Hateley* (1983) 152 CLR 406.
40. *Legione v Hateley* (1983) 152 CLR 406 at 411.
41. *Legione v Hateley* (1983) 152 CLR 406 at 459.
42. *Legione v Hateley* (1983) 152 CLR 406 at 450.
43. *Legione v Hateley* (1983) 152 CLR 406 at 429–30.

[T]he material in evidence strongly indicated unconscionable conduct on the part of the vendor in seeking to insist on the rescission of the contract in circumstances where the statement of the vendor's solicitors had helped lull the purchaser into a belief that the vendor would accept completion provided it took place within a few days and where the consequence of rescission was that the vendor would reap the benefit of the very valuable improvements which the purchaser had effected to the property.[44]

In the present appeal, there is nothing to suggest that [Cauchi] lulled Tanwar into any relevant false sense of security. To the contrary, the terms of the 2001 Deeds strikingly demonstrated an attitude by [Cauchi] which would keep Tanwar on edge.

What then remains to support any case of unconscientious reliance by the vendors upon their legal right to terminate? It is convenient at this stage to consider the decision in *Stern*.[45]

Stern

The dispute concerned an instalment contract made in 1969 under which the last instalment would be paid in 1983. Time was made of the essence, after various vicissitudes, by notice given in 1979. Completion did not take place when specified and, in response to an action for an order for possession, the purchasers cross-claimed for specific performance and relief against forfeiture of their estate and interest in the land. By majority (Deane, Dawson and Gaudron JJ), the Court upheld the order of the New South Wales Court of Appeal.[46] This ordered relief against forfeiture and specific performance on terms including an inquiry as to the balance of the purchase money still owing and the interest to be payable thereon.

Deane and Dawson JJ said that 'the contract as it was carried into effect was essentially an arrangement whereby the appellants undertook to finance the respondents' purchase upon the security of the land' so that 'there was a close and obvious parallel between it and a purchase with the aid of a mortgage'.[47] The contracts between Tanwar and [Cauchi] do not share that characteristic.

Gaudron J, the third member of the majority in *Stern*, doubted whether the instalment contract there in question was in substance part of a security transaction.[48] Her Honour decided the appeal on a wider footing. This was that a decree of specific performance would secure all that the vendors had bargained for, whereas to deny that [328] remedy would prejudice the purchasers. A house had been built on the land, the land had increased in value and the balance unpaid was a relatively insignificant amount.[49] These circumstances, to which the vendors had not contributed, made it unconscionable for the vendors to insist on their contractual rights.

On the other hand, Mason CJ (in the minority as to the outcome) stressed that this was not a case like *Legione* where the conduct of the vendors had led to, caused, or contributed

---

44. *Ciavarella v Balmer* (1983) 153 CLR 438 at 453.
45. *Stern v McArthur* (1988) 165 CLR 489.
46. *McArthur v Stern* (1986) 5 NSWLR 538 at 558.
47. *Stern v McArthur* (1988) 165 CLR 489 at 528.
48. *Stern v McArthur* (1988) 165 CLR 489 at 540; cf *Union Eagle Ltd v Golden Achievement Ltd* [1997] AC 514 at 522.
49. *McArthur v Stern* (1988) 165 CLR 489 at 540–1.

to, the breach of contract by the purchasers.[50] At bottom, the case put by Tanwar depends upon acceptance of the view of the equity jurisdiction taken by Gaudron J at the expense of that preferred by Mason CJ. The view of Mason CJ should be accepted.

Mason CJ and *Stern*

In *Legione*, Mason and Deane JJ instanced 'fraud, mistake, accident, [and] surprise' as elements which may make it inequitable to insist on termination of a contract for failure to observe its strict terms.[51] Subsequently, in *Stern*,[52] Mason CJ took *Legione* and *Ciavarella* as establishing that the court will not readily relieve against loss of a contract for sale validly rescinded by the vendor for breach of an essential condition; and, in particular, equity was not authorised 'to reshape contractual relations into a form the court thinks more reasonable or fair where subsequent events have rendered one side's situation more favourable'.[53] That latter proposition is at odds with the approach by Gaudron J in *Stern*, to which reference has been made earlier in these reasons ... but, nevertheless, it should be accepted as an accurate statement of the law. The result, as indicated above, is that Tanwar's case on the appeal is significantly weakened.

Mason CJ dissented as to the outcome in *Stern*, but this was to a significant degree because of the view he took of the nature of the particular contract in question and the denial of an analogy drawn, particularly by Deane and Dawson JJ,[54] to a mortgage transaction. To the extent that what Mason CJ said in *Stern* represented a development (or, perhaps, a contraction) of what had been put in the earlier cases, then it is to be preferred.

In *Stern*,[55] Mason CJ also stated that equity intervenes only where the vendor has, by the vendor's conduct, caused or contributed to a circumstance rendering it unconscionable for the vendor to insist upon its legal rights. That helps explain why mere supervening events and changes in the relevant circumstances are insufficient. But it should be [329] noted that cases falling within the heads of mistake or accident will not necessarily be the result of activity by the vendor. In addition, his Honour spoke in *Stern*[56] of the circumstances being 'exceptional' to attract equitable intervention. That also emphasised the insufficiency of subsequent events which are adverse to the interests of one side. However, the term 'exceptional' is apt to be misunderstood, and it will be necessary to return to it later in these reasons under the heading 'The present appeal'.

Subsidiary questions?

In *Legione*, Mason and Deane JJ had concluded their analysis of what they saw as the relevant principles by saying as follows:

> In the ultimate analysis the result in a given case will depend upon the resolution of subsidiary questions which inevitably arise. The more important of these are: (1) Did the conduct of the vendor contribute to the purchaser's breach? (2) Was the purchaser's

---

50. *McArthur v Stern* (1988) 165 CLR 489 at 503–4.
51. *Legione v Hateley* (1983) 152 CLR 406 at 447–8.
52. *Stern v McArthur* (1988) 165 CLR 489 at 502–3.
53. *McArthur v Stern* (1988) 165 CLR 489 at 503.
54. *McArthur v Stern* (1988) 165 CLR 489 at 528.
55. *McArthur v Stern* (1988) 165 CLR 489 at 502–3.
56. *McArthur v Stern* (1988) 165 CLR 489 at 502–3.

breach (a) trivial or slight, and (b) inadvertent and not wilful? (3) What damage or other adverse consequences did the vendor suffer by reason of the purchaser's breach? (4) What is the magnitude of the purchaser's loss and the vendor's gain if the forfeiture is to stand? (5) Is specific performance with or without compensation an adequate safeguard for the vendor?[57]

Tanwar relies upon those five 'subsidiary questions'. It accepts that the first question should be answered unfavourably because the conduct of [Cauchi] did not contribute to Tanwar's breach. However, Tanwar says that its breach was trivial or slight, or inadvertent, that [Cauchi] … suffered but nominal damage and no adverse consequences, that specific performance would be an adequate safeguard for [Cauchi's] interests … and that [Cauchi] stood to gain the advantages flowing from the expenditure by Tanwar in obtaining the development approvals, together with the increase in value of the land which apparently occurred between the date of the contracts and the termination.

With respect to the third, fourth and fifth 'subsidiary questions' posed in *Legione* by Mason and Deane JJ, [Cauchi] respond that Tanwar entered into arrangements with the proposed second mortgagees dependent upon the arrival of funds from Singapore on the last day when settlement was required under the 2001 Deeds, and that notions of trivial or inadvertent breach must be considered in that light. With respect to the alleged increase in value, [Cauchi], correctly, emphasise that the first of the comparative dates is not 19 October 1999, but 5 June 2001, the date of the 2001 Deeds. This postdated the obtaining of the development approvals on 18 February [330] 2000. In any event, there had been no valuation evidence to found any specific finding respecting increase in value due to those consents or to other market forces. No such finding had been made. However, it was accepted that the benefit of the approvals would, with termination, accrue to [Cauchi]. But that was an inevitable outcome bargained for when the 2001 Deeds had been negotiated.

The 'interest' of Tanwar

[Cauchi] also challenge the doctrinal basis for treating as determinative of Tanwar's appeal these five 'subsidiary questions'. The vendors are correct in doing so.

What was said by Mason and Deane JJ in *Legione* respecting the 'subsidiary questions' must be treated with care. That to which the questions are said to be 'subsidiary' is the basic issue presented earlier in their joint judgment. This is expressed as:

> … the respondent's submission that she is *entitled to relief against the forfeiture of her interest in the land* upon terms that she pay to the appellants the amount of $30,188.24 that was tendered to them on 15 August 1979 and not accepted, being the balance of the purchase moneys under the contract.[58] (Emphasis added.)

But what, if any, was the interest in the land enjoyed by Tanwar as purchaser? If there was such an interest, did it attract the exercise of the jurisdiction to relieve against forfeiture? What is the relationship between, on the one hand, the attitude of equity respecting forfeiture, and, on the other hand, the attitude of equity respecting the observance of express time stipulations?

---

57. *Legione v Hateley* (1983) 152 CLR 406 at 449.
58. *Legione v Hateley* (1983) 152 CLR 406 at 440.

Without answers to these questions, the significance for this appeal of the basic issue expressed in *Legione*, and thus the relevance of the five 'subsidiary questions', cannot be assessed. But the answers are to be supplied only by a patient examination of several fundamentals, the understanding of which by equity courts has changed across time.

One commences by identifying the 'interest' of a purchaser in the land the subject of an uncompleted contract. In *Lysaght v Edwards*,[59] Sir George Jessel MR described the position of the vendor at the moment of entry into a contract of sale as 'something between' a bare trustee for the purchaser and a mortgagee who in equity is entitled to possession of the land and a charge upon it for the purchase money; in particular, the vendor had the right in equity to say to the purchaser '[e]ither pay me the purchase-money, or lose the estate'. This way of looking at the relationship in equity between vendor and purchaser before completion appeared also in the works of eminent [331] writers of the period in which the Master of the Rolls spoke.[60] Later, Kitto J[61] and Brennan J[62] preferred to treat what was said in *Lysaght* as indicating that 'to an extent' the purchaser acquired the beneficial ownership upon entry into the contract.

This analogical reasoning in turn suggested (i) the purchaser had before completion an equitable estate in the land which would be protected against loss consequent upon termination of the contract by the principles developed in equity for relief against forfeiture and (ii) in the same way as failure to redeem a mortgage upon the covenanted date for repayment did not destroy the equity of redemption without the proper exercise of a power of sale[63] or a foreclosure suit in equity,[64] failure to complete the contract on the due date did not bar the intervention of equity to order specific performance.

But what, on this way of looking at the matter, was the significance of a contractual stipulation specifying a date for completion as essential? The treatment by the English equity judges of this subject developed in the course of the nineteenth century, as Justice Lindgren has detailed in his extrajudicial writing on the subject.[65] While Lord Thurlow would have pushed the mortgage analogy to the extreme that a time stipulation in equity could never be essential unless there was something in the nature of the subject matter of the contract, such as its fluctuating or depreciating value,[66] to give it that quality, his view was doubted by Lord Eldon in *Seton v Slade*[67] and rejected by Sir Lloyd Kenyon MR in *Mackreth v Marlar*.[68]

If the express contractual stipulation fixing time as an essential matter was not to be disregarded, how did that attitude stand with the analogy drawn from the relief against

---

59. (1876) 2 Ch D 499 at 506.
60. Maitland, *Equity*, 2nd ed rev (1936), pp 314–5; Pomeroy, *A Treatise on the Specific Performance of Contracts* (1879), §§315, 322, 389; Williams and Lightwood, *A Treatise on the Law of Vendor and Purchaser of Real Estate and Chattels Real*, 4th ed (1936), vol 1, pp 59–60.
61. *Haque v Haque [No 2]* (1965) 114 CLR 98 at 124.
62. *KLDE Pty Ltd v Commissioner of Stamp Duties (Q)* (1984) 155 CLR 288 at 301.
63. *Latec Investments Ltd v Hotel Terrigal Pty Ltd (In liq)* (1965) 113 CLR 265 at 274–5.
64. Maitland, *Equity*, 2nd ed rev (1936), pp 182–3.
65. *Time in Performance of Contracts*, 2nd ed (1982), [210]–[222].
66. Hanbury, *Modern Equity*, 8th ed (1962), pp 85–6.
67. (1802) 32 ER 108.
68. (1786) 29 ER 1156.

forfeiture cases? The answer given by Pomeroy,[69] with reference to [*Dagenham*],[70] was that equity would relieve the purchaser from the operation of an essential time stipulation, 'and from the forfeiture', if the provision was inserted as a penalty to **[332]** secure completion of the contract at the purchaser's risk of loss of the equitable interest in the land under the executory contract.

That reasoning, together with the authority of *Dagenham*, was relied upon in the majority judgments in *Legione*.[71] What the Court of Appeal in Chancery decided in *Dagenham*, and on what facts and grounds, is not fully apparent from the abbreviated report.[72] But it must be remembered that in *Dagenham* there had been forfeiture of a payment of half the purchase price, so that it was not surprising that the forfeiture was treated as penal.[73]

It should be added that, in *Dagenham*, as in *Stern* and other instalment contract cases, there would have existed an equitable lien securing for the purchaser the payments so made.[74] It has been held in this Court that the lien may be enforceable even though there may be a good defence to a claim to specific performance of the contract.[75] It is the payment and retention of the moneys, not the availability of specific performance, which is critical.[76] But there remains the question, unnecessary to decide here, whether the lien of the purchaser necessarily is lost upon termination of the contract for breach by the purchaser of an essential time stipulation.[77]

At all events, the analogies drawn over a century ago in *Lysaght*[78] with the trust and the mortgage are no longer accepted. Jacobs J observed in *Chang v Registrar of Titles* that:

> [w]here there are rights outstanding on both sides, the description of the vendor as a trustee tends to conceal the essentially contractual relationship which, rather than the relationship of trustee and beneficiary, governs the rights and duties of the respective parties.[79]

Subsequently, in *Kern Corporation Ltd v Walter Reid Trading Pty Ltd*, Deane J said:

> [I]t is both inaccurate and misleading to speak of the unpaid vendor under an uncompleted contract as a trustee for the purchaser.[80]

---

69. Pomeroy, *A Treatise on the Specific Performance of Contracts* (1789), §391.
70. *In re Dagenham (Thames) Dock Co; Ex parte Hulse* (1873) LR 8 Ch App 1022.
71. *Legione v Hateley* (1983) 152 CLR 406 at 426, 441.
72. See Harpum, 'Relief Against Forfeiture and the Purchaser of Land' [1984] *Cambridge Law Journal* 134 at 147–8.
73. Lang, 'Forfeiture of Interests in Land' (1984) 100 *Law Quarterly Review* 427 at 434–5.
74. *Hewell v Court* (1983) 149 CLR 639 at 663–4.
75. *Hewell v Court* (1983) 149 CLR 639 at 650, 664.
76. *Rose v Watson* (1864) 33 LJ Ch (NS) 385 at 389–90.
77. Harpum, 'Relief Against Forfeiture and the Purchaser of Land' [1984] *Cambridge Law Journal* 134 at 139.
78. *Lysaght v Edwards* (1876) 2 Ch D 499 at 506.
79. *Chang v Registrar Titles* (1976) 137 CLR 177 at 190.
80. *Kern Corporation Ltd v Walter Reid Trading Pty Ltd* (1987) 163 CLR 164 at 192.

In *Stern*, Gaudron J points out,[81] consistently with authority in this **[333]** Court,[82] that the 'interest' of the purchaser is commensurate with the availability of specific performance. That availability is the very question in issue where there has been a termination by the vendor for failure to complete as required by the essential stipulation. Reliance upon the 'interest' therefore does not assist; it is bedevilled by circularity ...

The five 'subsidiary questions' stated by Mason and Deane JJ in *Legione*,[83] and set out above, reflect the treatment by Lord Wilberforce in *Shiloh Spinners Ltd v Harding* (a lease case) of the 'appropriate' considerations guiding the exercise of equity's jurisdiction to relieve against forfeiture for breach of covenants added by way of security for the production of a stated result. His Lordship said:

> The word 'appropriate' involves consideration of the conduct of the applicant for relief, in particular whether his default was wilful, of the gravity of the breaches, and of the disparity between the value **[334]** of the property of which forfeiture is claimed as compared with the damage caused by the breach.[84]

However, the end sought to be protected, on the analysis by Mason and Deane JJ in *Legione*, was the interest of the purchaser in the land. That 'interest', being for its existence dependent upon the administration of the very remedy in issue, does not suffice ...

It is sufficient for present purposes to observe that, where the issue, as in Tanwar's appeal, concerns alleged unconscientious reliance by vendors upon their contractual right to terminate, it does not assist to found the equity of the purchaser upon the protection of rights to injunctive relief acquired under a contract the termination of which has taken place. Whilst the contracts here were on foot, breach thereof by [Cauchi] would have been restrained. But there was no relevant breach of contract by **[335]** [Cauchi], and the contracts were terminated in exercise of a contractual right to do so.

The present appeal

What Lord Wilberforce in *Shiloh Spinners* called 'the special heads of fraud, accident, mistake or surprise'[85] identify in a broad sense the circumstances making it inequitable for [Cauchi] to rely upon their termination of Tanwar's contracts as an answer to its claim for specific performance. No doubt the decided cases in which the operation of these 'special heads' is considered do not disclose exhaustively the circumstances which merit this equitable intervention. But, at least where accident and mistake are not involved, it will be necessary to point to the conduct of the vendor as having in some significant respect caused or contributed to the breach of the essential time stipulation. Tanwar's situation falls beyond that pale. The statement by Mason CJ in *Stern*[86] respecting the

---

81. *McArthur v Stern* (1988) 165 CLR 489 at 537.
82. *Brown v Heffer* (1967) 116 CLR 344 at 349; *Legione v Hateley* (1983) 152 CLR 406 at 456–7; *Bahr v Nicolay [No 2]* (1988) 164 CLR 604 at 612, 645–6. See also the warning by Stamp LJ in *Berkeley v Poullett* [1977] 1 EGLR 86 at 93 against error caused by putting 'the cart before the horse', to which Austin J referred in *Chief Commissioner of Stamp Duties (NSW) v Paliflex Pty Ltd* (1999) 47 NSWLR 382 at 390.
83. *Legione v Hateley* (1983) 152 CLR 406 at 449.
84. *Shiloh Spinners Ltd v Harding* [1973] AC 691 at 723–4.
85. *Shiloh Spinners Ltd v Harding* [1973] AC 691 at 723.
86. *McArthur v Stern* (1988) 165 CLR 489 at 502–3.

insignificance of subsequent events for which the vendors were in no way responsible is fatal to the main thrust of Tanwar's case.

It should be made clear that what is said above does not support any proposition that the circumstances must be 'exceptional' before equity intervenes. In their joint judgment in *Stern*,[87] Deane and Dawson JJ, with reference to what had been said by Mason and Deane JJ in *Legione*, said, in a passage which puts the point of present significance:

> Mason and Deane JJ were not saying that there must be unconscionable conduct of an exceptional kind before a case for relief can be made out. Rather, what was being said was that a court will be reluctant to interfere with the contractual rights of parties who have chosen to make time of the essence of the contract. The circumstances must be such as to make it plain that it is necessary to intervene to avoid injustice or, what is the same thing, to relieve against unconscionable — or, more accurately, unconscientious — conduct.[88]

Thus, it remains for Tanwar to show that it is against conscience for [Cauchi] to set up the termination of the contracts. In the present appeal, as already has been indicated, there was no representation by [Cauchi] which could found any estoppel. Nor has Tanwar asserted that there was any mistake in any relevant sense.

In *Ciavarella*,[89] the order for remittal made in *Legione* was seen to have been made on the footing that there were already in the evidence indications that the vendors in *Legione* had helped to lull the [336] purchasers into the belief that they would accept completion provided it occurred within a few days. To relieve in those circumstances would be an exercise of the jurisdiction with respect to 'surprise'. That, as remarked earlier in these reasons, cannot be asserted in the present case.

The second matter which Mason and Deane JJ emphasised in *Legione* was the possibility that a case might be made out in the Supreme Court that the vendors were seeking to reap the benefits of the very valuable improvements to the property which the purchasers had effected whilst in possession under the contract.[90] It is not clear from their Honours' remarks whether the reaping of the benefit of the improvements as a consequence of termination of itself would be sufficient to deny insistence by the vendors upon their rescission. It is not readily apparent how that circumstance alone could be sufficient. The contract in *Legione* had permitted the purchasers to enter into possession and any improvements they then made were at risk of the operation of the contractual provisions for termination.

Accident

In its extremity, Tanwar then founds upon the jurisdiction to relieve against the consequences of 'accident'.

In *Legione*,[91] Mason and Deane JJ referred to authorities disputing the treatment of cases of relief against penalties and forfeitures as instances of relief against accident. The jurisdiction with respect to accident was recognised at a time before the development of

---

87. *McArthur v Stern* (1988) 165 CLR 489 at 526.
88. *Legione v Hateley* (1983) 152 CLR 406 at 449.
89. *Ciavarella v Balmer* (1983) 153 CLR 438 at 453.
90. *Legione v Hateley* (1983) 152 CLR 406 at 449; *Ciavarella v Balmer* (1983) 153 CLR 438 at 453.
91. *Legione v Hateley* (1983) 152 CLR 406 at 444.

any settled body of equitable principles. The point is well made by Professors Keeton and Sheridan:

> 'Accident' was a vague term which covered many situations, in their nature unforeseen, and it could, in particular situations, shade off into fraud. The law of mistake, particularly in relation to contracts and conveyances, is included under this head, and it led in turn to the development of the equitable rules governing the rectification of contracts and other instruments, and the rescission of documents of all kinds.[92]

What then remains as the subject matter of accident in modern equity? In *Baird v BCE Holdings Pty Ltd*,[93] Young J referred to various writings on the subject which distinguish mistake as supposing an operation of the will of the agent in producing the event, albeit by reason of erroneous impressions on the mind. Spence, writing in 1846, said that the kinds of accidents or cases of extremity which might be relieved against were only to be ascertained from an examination of [337] the cases.[94] He instanced forfeiture and penalties. Other instances include the accidental diminution of assets in the hands of an executor, lost evidence and the defective execution of powers of appointment,[95] all far from the present case.

However, the learned writers on the subject emphasise and put to one side those situations where the event which has come to pass is one for which an express exculpatory provision might have been made, but was not sought or was not agreed to, and where to relieve against its consequences after it has occurred would deprive the other party to the contract of an essential right.[96] In particular, equity will not relieve where 'the possibility of the accident may fairly be considered to have been within the contemplation of the contracting parties'.[97] Story wrote:

> And this leads us naturally to the consideration of those cases of accident in which no relief will be granted by Courts of Equity. In the first place, in matters of positive contract and obligation created by the party (for it is different in obligations or duties created by law), it is no ground for the interference of equity that the party has been prevented from fulfilling them by accident, or that he has been in no default, or that he has been prevented by accident from deriving the full benefit of the contract on his own side ... The reason is, that he might have provided for such contingencies by his contract if he had so chosen; and the law will presume an intentional general liability where he has made no exception. (Footnotes omitted.)[98]

It is here that the circumstances leading up to, and the terms of, the 2001 Deeds are of critical importance. [Cauchi] withdrew the earlier notices of termination in return for the assumption by Tanwar of obligations to complete couched in unqualified terms. The

---

92. *Equity*, 3rd ed (1987), p 38.
93. (1996) 40 NSWLR 374 at 385–6.
94. *The Equitable Jurisdiction of the Court of the Chancery* (1846), vol 1, p 628.
95. *Snell's Equity*, 30th ed (2000), pp 603–6.
96. Bispham, *The Principles of Equity*, 6th ed (1903), §§175, 176; Merwin, *The Principles of Equity and Equity Pleading* (1895), §419.
97. Smith, *Principles of Equity*.
98. *Commentaries on Equity Jurisprudence*, 13th ed (1886), vol 1, §101.

obligation in the 2001 Deeds to settle by the stipulated time was not made subject to the availability of Tanwar's finance on that day. That there might be a failure by a third party to provide the finance was reasonably within the contemplation of Tanwar. The failure by Tanwar to avail itself of the advantages it obtained by negotiating the 2001 Deeds and by keeping the contracts on foot had the effect of exposing Tanwar again to the exercise by [Cauchi] of their rights to terminate the contracts.[99] Equity does not intervene to prevent the effective exercise of those rights. The claim by Tanwar for relief against the [338] consequences of the failure in the timely provision of the second mortgage does not succeed.

Comment

1. See Radan & Stewart at **13.11–13.16**.

Remedies for relief against forfeiture

13.5   On Demand Information Plc v Michael Gerson (Finance) Plc [2003] 1 AC 369

Court: House of Lords

Facts: On Demand Information (ODI) entered into four agreements with Gerson Finance (GF) for the leasing of video and editing equipment. The leases provided for 36-month terms, upon the expiration of which ODI could continue the leases for consecutive 12-month periods with payments up-front. The leases also allowed ODI to sell the equipment to a third party and retain 95 per cent of the proceeds of sale by way of a rebate of rentals. However, it was explicitly stated that appointment of a receiver to the lessee amounted to repudiatory breach, entitling GF to terminate the leases and claim a termination payment. When ODI went into receivership, GF purported to terminate the leases, two of which had expired. The receiver attempted to sell off part of ODI's business as a going concern. One potential bidder made purchase conditional upon transfer of the leases. The receiver offered to GF more than 5 per cent of the value of the equipment as consideration for its consent to the sale, but GF refused to consent. ODI brought an action for relief against forfeiture, but the receiver proceeded to obtain an interim order allowing sale of the equipment, with proceeds held in escrow until resolution of the forfeiture action.

Issue: The issue before the House of Lords was whether the court had jurisdiction in equity to grant relief in the case of finance leases after the sale of the goods that were the subject of the lease.

Decision: The House of Lords (Lords Nicholls of Birkenhead, Browne-Wilkinson, Hobhouse of Woodborough, Millett and Scott of Foscote) unanimously allowed the appeal by ODI. It was held that, although sale of the goods under a finance lease brought to an end the lessee's claim to the remedy of relief against forfeiture, ODI as

---

99. See *Cameron v UBS AG* (2000) 2 VR 108 at 115–6.

lessee under the finance lease did not lose its substantive rights in the property to which relief would have been aimed. A court could grant the most appropriate remedy (in this case 95 per cent of the proceeds of sale) in the plaintiff's favour, provided that relief against forfeiture would have been ordered before the sale.

Extracts: The extracts from the speech of Lord Millett are indicative of their Lordships' view that a court has considerable flexibility in terms of the remedy to be ordered in cases which do, or did, give rise to a right to relief against forfeiture.

Lord Millett

[381] [W]hile the proceeds of sale are merely a substitute for the property in question, the sale inevitably affects the nature of the remedy which the court can grant. The subject matter of the proceedings, and therefore of the order which the court will ultimately make at trial, is no longer property but money. In the paradigm case, where the ownership of the property is in dispute, the court can no longer make a declaration of title, or order the party in possession to give possession to the other, or give specific relief in relation to the property. After the property has been sold no such relief is possible. Instead, orders which the court would otherwise have made are replaced by orders for payment out of the money (if in court) or declarations of entitlement to give a good receipt for the money (if in an escrow account).

It is self-evident that the court cannot make an order granting relief from forfeiture of a lease after the lease has been determined otherwise than by the forfeiture in question. [The order for sale] did not in itself make it impossible for the court to grant relief from forfeiture; this remained possible until the moment the equipment was sold. But the sale brought the leases to an end independently of the antecedent forfeiture against which relief was sought.

But the fact that by the time the case was heard the court could no longer give the lessee the particular relief claimed in the writ does not mean that it was bound to dismiss its claim. If (i) the lessee would have been entitled to the relief claimed in the writ immediately before the sale and (ii) the only reason that the court could not grant that relief was that the equipment had since been sold pursuant to an order of the court which was not intended to affect the parties' rights, then it should give effect to those rights by making whatever order in relation to the proceeds of sale best reflects them. This is not to ignore the fact that the equipment had been sold or to grant relief as if it had not been sold, but to recognise that the sale was not to affect the parties' substantive rights, and that substantive rights can be given effect in more than one way.

The error in the approach of the deputy judge and the majority of the Court of Appeal, if I may say so, lies in the description of the lessee's right as a right to relief from forfeiture. But that was merely a means to an end. It was the remedy, appropriate in the circumstances obtaining at the date of the writ, which the lessee sought in order to secure commercially valuable rights. Those rights included the right to retain 95% of the proceeds of a sale made under clause 12 of the leases, that is to say a sale made after bringing the leases to an end by notice. It was no longer an appropriate or possible [382] remedy when the case came before the court. The reason it was no longer appropriate or possible was that the equipment had been sold, not pursuant to clause 12 but to an order of the court which was intended so far as possible to preserve the parties' rights. The question was how to give effect to those rights, once they had been determined, by an order in relation to the proceeds of sale. The sale brought an end to the lessee's claim to a particular remedy, viz, relief from forfeiture, but not to the rights to which such a remedy would have responded, and substituted a claim to payment out of the fund.

I do not think there is any real difficulty in formulating an appropriate order in this case. Had it been possible to grant relief from forfeiture immediately before the equipment was sold, it would have been on terms that all outstanding rentals were paid and that the administrative receivers should guarantee payment of future rentals. No sale could have taken place until the leases were brought to an end by notice, and accordingly some further secondary rentals would inevitably have become payable. The equipment would have to be sold at the best available price, now agreed to have been £251,617. These are all matters which should be taken into account in deciding the proportions in which the parties are entitled to the moneys in the escrow account.

I would allow the appeal and, failing agreement between the parties, remit the case to the Chancery Division to make such orders as may be necessary to give effect to the judgment of the House.

Comment
1. See Radan & Stewart at **13.39**.

14

PENALTIES

Introduction

14.1 This chapter examines the law on penalties. The paradigm case in which the question of a penalty arises is where there is a clause in a contract that stipulates the sum of money to be paid by the contract breaker to the other party as compensation for the breach of contract. The clause is enforceable if the sum stipulated is a genuine pre-estimate of the damage suffered by the innocent party. However, if it is not, it is a penalty and is not enforceable.

The cases extracted in this chapter discuss the following:

- the classic principles relating to the law of penalties: *Dunlop Pneumatic Tyre Company Ltd v New Garage and Motor Ltd* [1915] AC 79; *Ringrow Pty Ltd v BP Australia Pty Ltd* (2005) 224 CLR 656; and
- penalties in the context of hire purchase transactions: *Esanda Finance Corporation Limited v Plessnig* (1989) 166 CLR 131.

The principles relating to penalties

14.2 Dunlop Pneumatic Tyre Company Ltd v New Garage and Motor Ltd [1915] AC 79

Court: House of Lords

Facts: Dunlop contracted to sell tyres, covers and tubes to New Garage which, in turn, sold these items to the public. Pursuant to clause 2 of its contract with Dunlop, New Garage agreed not to sell the goods to the public below certain set prices. Clause 5 of the contract stipulated that New Garage would pay, as liquidated damages, £5 for each tyre, cover or tube that was sold in breach of clause 2. New Garage breached clause 2 of the contract by selling tyres and tubes below the stipulated prices. Dunlop sought to enforce clause 5 of the contract.

Issue: The issue before the House of Lords was whether clause 5 was a penalty or a valid liquidated damages clause.

Decision: The House of Lords (Lords Dunedin, Atkinson, Parker of Waddington and Parmoor) unanimously held that clause 5 was not a penalty.

> **Extracts:** The extracts from the speech of Lord Dunedin set out what has become the classic statement on the law differentiating penalties from enforceable liquidated damages clauses.

Lord Dunedin

[86] My Lords, we had the benefit of a full and satisfactory argument, and a citation of the very numerous cases which have been decided on this branch of the law … I do not think it advisable to attempt any detailed review of the various cases, but I shall content myself with stating succinctly the various propositions which I think are deducible from the decisions which rank as authoritative:-

1. Though the parties to a contract who use the words 'penalty' or 'liquidated damages' may prima facie be supposed to mean what they say, yet the expression used is not conclusive. The Court must find out whether the payment stipulated is in truth a penalty or liquidated damages. This doctrine may be said to be found passim in nearly every case.
2. The essence of a penalty is a payment of money stipulated as in terrorem of the offending party; the essence of liquidated damages is a genuine covenanted pre-estimate of damage.[1]
3. The question whether a sum stipulated is penalty or liquidated damages is a question of construction to be decided [87] upon the terms and inherent circumstances of each particular contract, judged of as at the time of the making of the contract, not as at the time of the breach.[2]
4. To assist this task of construction various tests have been suggested, which if applicable to the case under consideration may prove helpful, or even conclusive. Such are:
    (a) It will be held to be a penalty if the sum stipulated for is extravagant and unconscionable in amount in comparison with the greatest loss that could conceivably be proved to have followed from the breach …
    (b) It will be held to be a penalty if the breach consists only in not paying a sum of money, and the sum stipulated is a sum greater than the sum which ought to have been paid. This though one of the most ancient instances is truly a corollary to the last test. Whether it had its historical origin in the doctrine of the common law that when A promised to pay B a sum of money on a certain day and did not do so, B could only recover the sum with, in certain cases, interest, but could never recover further damages for non-timeous payment, or whether it was a survival of the time when equity reformed unconscionable bargains merely because they were unconscionable … is probably more interesting than material.
    (c) There is a presumption (but no more) that it is a penalty when 'a single lump sum is made payable by way of compensation, on the occurrence of one or more or all of several events, some of which may occasion serious and others but trifling damage'.[3]

---

1. *Clydebank Engineering and Shipbuilding Co v Don Jose Ramos Yzquierdo y Castaneda* [1905] AC 6.
2. *Public Works Commissioner v Hills* [1906] AC 368; *Webster v Bosanquet* [1912] AC 394.
3. *Lord Elphinstone v Monkland Iron and Coal Co* (1886) 11 App Cas 332 at 342.

On the other hand:

(d) It is no obstacle to the sum stipulated being a genuine pre-estimate of damage, that the consequences of the breach are such **[88]** as to make precise pre-estimation almost an impossibility. On the contrary, that is just the situation when it is probable that pre-estimated damage was the true bargain between the parties.[4]

Turning now to the facts of the case, it is evident that the damage apprehended by [Dunlop] owing to the breaking of the agreement was an indirect and not a direct damage. So long as they got their price from [New Garage] for each article sold, it could not matter to them directly what [New Garage] did with it. Indirectly it did. Accordingly, the agreement is headed 'Price Maintenance Agreement' and the way in which [Dunlop] would be damaged if prices were cut is clearly explained in evidence by Mr Baisley, and no successful attempt is made to controvert that evidence. But though damage as a whole from such a practice would be certain, yet damage from any one sale would be impossible to forecast. It is just, therefore, one of those cases where it seems quite reasonable for parties to contract that they should estimate that damage at a certain figure, and provided that figure is not extravagant there would seem no reason to suspect that it is not truly a bargain to assess damages, but rather a penalty to be held in terrorem.

The argument of [New Garage] was really based on two heads. They overpressed, in my judgment, the dictum of Lord Watson in *Lord Elphinstone's Case*,[5] reading it as if he had said that the matter was conclusive, instead of saying, as he did, that it raised a presumption, and they relied strongly on the case of *Willson v Love*.[6]

Now, in the first place, I have considerable doubt whether the stipulated payment here can fairly be said to deal with breaches, 'some of which' — I am quoting Lord Watson's words — 'may occasion serious and others but trifling damage'. As a mere matter of construction, I doubt whether clause 5 applies to anything but sales below price. But I will assume that it does. None the less the mischief, as I have already pointed out, is an indirect mischief, and I see no data on which, as a matter **[89]** of construction, I could settle in my own mind that the indirect damage from selling a cover would differ in magnitude from the indirect damage from selling a tube; or that the indirect damage from a cutting-price sale would differ from the indirect damage from supply at a full price to a hostile, because prohibited, agent. You cannot weigh such things in a chemical balance. The character of the agricultural land which was ruined by slag heaps in *Elphinstone's Case* was not all the same, but no objection was raised by Lord Watson to applying an overhead rate per acre, the sum not being in itself unconscionable.

I think *Elphinstone's Case*, or rather the dicta in it, do go this length, that if there are various breaches to which one indiscriminate sum to be paid in breach is applied, then the strength of the chain must be taken at its weakest link. If you can clearly see that the loss on one particular breach could never amount to the stipulated sum, then you may

---

4. *Clydebank Engineering and Shipbuilding Co v Don Jose Ramos Yzquierdo y Castaneda* [1905] AC 6 at 11; *Webster v Bosanquet* [1912] AC 394 at 398.
5. (1886) 11 App Cas 332 at 342.
6. [1896] 1 QB 626.

come to the conclusion that the sum is penalty. But further than this it does not go; so, for the reasons already stated, I do not think the present case forms an instance of what I have just expressed.

Comments

1. See Radan & Stewart at **14.15–14.17**.
2. In reference to Lord Dunedin's comment, at 86, that 'the essence of liquidated damages is a genuine covenanted pre-estimate of damage', Jackson J said in *Alfred McAlpine Capital Projects Ltd v Tilebox Ltd* [2005] EWHC 281 (TCC) at [48]:

   Although many authorities use or echo the phrase 'genuine pre-estimate', the test does not turn upon the genuineness or honesty of the party or parties who made the pre-estimate. The test is primarily an objective one, even though the court has some regard to the thought processes of the parties at the time of contracting.

14.3 Ringrow Pty Ltd v BP Australia Pty Ltd (2005) 224 CLR 656

Court: High Court of Australia

Facts: BP entered into a contract for the sale of a service station site at Lansvale to Ringrow, the company that operated the service station as franchisee. The contract provided for the execution of two further agreements upon sale. One was a BP 'privately owned site agreement', which provided that Ringrow would operate under the BP brand and sell only BP fuel. Breach by Ringrow entitled BP to terminate the agreement and claim liquidated damages calculated by reference to BP's expected profits over the balance of the term. The other agreement was a deed of option that allowed BP to re-purchase the site on termination of the first agreement at a predetermined price based on site market value without accounting for goodwill. It was agreed that exercise of the option by BP negated any claim for damages. Ringrow breached the agreement by purchasing fuel from another provider. BP exercised its option to repurchase the property and Ringrow claimed the option deed was void because it amounted to a penalty.

Issue: The issue before the High Court was whether the terms of the option deed operated as a penalty for breach of the BP site agreement.

Decision: The High Court (Gleeson CJ, Gummow, Kirby, Hayne, Callinan and Heydon JJ) unanimously rejected Ringrow's appeal and held the deed was not a penalty in the circumstances of the case.

Extracts: The extracts from the joint judgment of the High Court reflect its position that the principles of law on penalties require evidence of an advantage that is oppressively disproportionate in relation to the benefits flowing from a genuine pre-estimate of damage. They also affirm the view that courts will look to uphold commercial agreements freely entered into between parties at arm's length.

Gleeson CJ, Gummow, Kirby, Hayne, Callinan and Heydon JJ

[662] The law of penalties, in its standard application, is attracted where a contract stipulates that on breach the contract-breaker will pay an agreed sum which exceeds what can be regarded as a genuine pre-estimate of the damage likely to be caused by the breach.

The starting point for [Ringrow] was the following passage[7] in Lord Dunedin's speech in *Dunlop Pneumatic Tyre Co Ltd v New Garage and Motor Co Ltd*:

2. The essence of a penalty is a payment of money stipulated as in terrorem of the offending party; the essence of liquidated damages is a genuine covenanted pre-estimate of damage …

3. The question whether a sum stipulated is penalty or liquidated damages is a question of construction to be decided upon the terms and inherent circumstances of each particular contract, judged of as at the time of the making of the contract, not as at the time of the breach …

4. To assist this task of construction various tests have been suggested, which if applicable to the case under consideration may prove helpful, or even conclusive. Such are:

   (a) It will be held to be penalty if the sum stipulated for is extravagant and unconscionable in amount in comparison with the greatest loss that could conceivably be proved to have followed from the breach …

   (b) It will be held to be a penalty if the breach consists only in not paying a sum of money, and the sum stipulated is a sum greater than the sum which ought to have been paid …

   (c) There is a presumption (but no more) that it is penalty when 'a single lump sum is made payable by way of compensation, on the occurrence of one or more or all of several events, some of which may occasion serious and others but trifling damage'.[8]

[663] Neither side in the appeal contested the foregoing statement by Lord Dunedin of the principles governing the identification, proof and consequences of penalties in contractual stipulations. The formulation has endured for ninety years. It has been applied countless times in this and other courts. In these circumstances, the present appeal afforded no occasion for a general reconsideration of Lord Dunedin's tests to determine whether any particular feature of Australian conditions, any change in the nature of penalties or any element in the contemporary market-place[9] suggest the need for a new formulation. It is therefore proper to proceed on the basis that *Dunlop Pneumatic Tyre Co Ltd v New Garage and Motor Co Ltd* continues to express the law applicable in this country, leaving any more substantial reconsideration than that advanced, to a future case where reconsideration or reformulation is in issue …

[667] *The argument of proportionality.* The next argument advanced by [Ringrow] to be examined is its argument that para 4(c) of the passage from Lord Dunedin's speech rested on a concept of proportionality which the option deed contravened in calling for a

---

7. *Dunlop Pneumatic Tyre Co Ltd v New Garage and Motor Co Ltd* [1915] AC 79 at 86–7.
8. *Lord Elphinstone v Monkland Iron and Coal Co* (1886) 11 App Cas 332 at 342.
9. See, for example, *AMEV-UDC Finance Ltd v Austin* (1986) 162 CLR 170 at 190.

reconveyance of BP Lansvale after termination of the [site agreement] rather than a lease for the balance of the five year term of the [site agreement]. It must be rejected for three reasons.

First, neither *Dunlop Pneumatic Tyre Co Ltd v New Garage and Motor Co Ltd* nor any other authority[10] supports the 'proportionality' doctrine which [Ringrow] advocated. The principles of law relating to penalties require only that the money stipulated to be paid on breach or the property stipulated to be transferred on breach will produce for the payee or transferee advantages significantly greater than the advantages which would flow from a genuine pre-estimate of damage. Among the different words which have been used to describe how extensive the difference must be before the transaction creates a penalty are the words employed by Mason and Wilson JJ in *AMEV-UDC Finance Ltd v Austin* — a 'degree of disproportion'[11] sufficient to point to oppressiveness. But their Honours were not asserting any doctrine of the kind relied on by [Ringrow], which would rest on a disproportion between the innocent party's commercial interests and the promise extracted to protect them. That type of idea underlies the law relating to contracts in restraint of trade, which recognises certain interests which it is legitimate for a covenantee to seek to protect by a covenant in restraint of the covenantor's trade, so long as the covenant is not wider than is reasonably necessary to protect those interests.[12] Such an idea is not, however, part of the law relating to penalties. Mason and Wilson JJ initially made the point that an agreed sum should only be 'characterised as a penalty if it is out of all proportion to damage likely to be suffered as a result of breach'.[13] Later their Honours referred to proportionality as follows:

> [668] [E]quity and the common law have long maintained a supervisory jurisdiction, not to rewrite contracts imprudently made, but to relieve against provisions which are so unconscionable or oppressive that their nature is penal rather than compensatory. The test to be applied in drawing that distinction is one of degree and will depend on a number of circumstances, including (1) the degree of *disproportion* between the stipulated sum and the loss likely to be suffered by the plaintiff, a factor relevant to the oppressiveness of the term to the defendant, and (2) the nature of the relationship between the contracting parties, a factor relevant to the unconscionability of the plaintiff's conduct in seeking to enforce the term. The courts should not, however, be too ready to find the requisite degree of *disproportion* lest they impinge on the parties' freedom to settle for themselves the rights and liabilities following a breach of contract.[14] (Emphasis added.)

Nothing in either passage supports the need to inquire into whether there is proportionality between the impugned provision and the legitimate commercial interests of the party relying on it.

---

10. [Ringrow] also relied on *Pigram v Attorney-General for the State of New South Wales* (1975) 132 CLR 216 at 227 and *O'Dea v Allstates Leasing System (WA) Pty Ltd* (1983) 152 CLR 359 at 369, 383, 399.
11. *AMEV-UDC Finance Ltd v Austin* (1986) 162 CLR 170 at 193.
12. See, for example, *Butt v Long* (1953) 88 CLR 476 at 486.
13. *AMEV-UDC Finance Ltd v Austin* (1986) 162 CLR 170 at 190.
14. *AMEV-UDC Finance Ltd v Austin* (1986) 162 CLR 170 at 193–4. [Ringrow] relied on the approval given to this and the preceding passage by Wilson and Toohey JJ in *Esanda Finance Corporation Ltd v Plessnig* (1989) 166 CLR 131 at 139.

The same is true of other judicial uses of the expression 'proportion' in the penalty context. Thus in *Lord Elphinstone v Monkland Iron and Coal Co* Lord Herschell LC, in examining the validity of a covenant by which lessees who had been given a right to place slag on the land leased to them covenanted to pay the lessor £100 per acre for all land not levelled and soiled within a particular period, said:

> The agreement does not provide for the payment of a lump sum upon the non-performance of any one of many obligations differing in importance. It has reference to a single obligation, and the sum to be paid bears a strict proportion to the extent to which that obligation is left unfulfilled. There is nothing whatever to shew that the compensation is [inordinate] or extravagant in relation to the damage sustained.[15]

This reasoning did not require there to be a strict proportion; it merely relied, as a step towards the conclusion that the compensation was not inordinate or extravagant, on the fact that the compensation bore a strict proportion to the unfulfilled obligation.

Secondly, for this Court to take the unusual step of recognising the proportionality doctrine advocated by [Ringrow] notwithstanding its lack of support in authority might, depending on how it was formulated, involve the overruling of cases on the penalty doctrine which have not up to now been doubted. There are likely to be instances in which the courts, applying received principles, would find **[669]** that no penalty existed, but would decide the case in favour of the contract-breaker if there were a proportionality doctrine.

It must be concluded that the proportionality doctrine does not exist in this context and should not be recognised. Although [Ringrow] presented the proportionality doctrine as part of the received law on penalties, in truth its closest analogy is with the restraint of trade doctrine. The problem is that the proportionality doctrine contradicts the rules on penalties without satisfying the requirements of the restraint of trade doctrine.

Thirdly, consideration of the purpose of the law of penalties shows why this must be so. The law of contract normally upholds the freedom of parties, with no relevant disability, to agree upon the terms of their future relationships. As Mason and Wilson JJ observed in *AMEV-UDC Finance Ltd v Austin*:

> [T]here is much to be said for the view that the courts should return to ... allowing parties to a contract greater latitude in determining what their rights and liabilities will be, so that an agreed sum is only characterised as a penalty if it is out of all proportion to damage likely to be suffered as a result of breach.[16]

Exceptions from that freedom of contract require good reason to attract judicial intervention to set aside the bargains upon which parties of full capacity have agreed. That is why the law on penalties is, and is expressed to be, an exception from the general rule. It is why it is expressed in exceptional language. It explains why the propounded penalty must be judged 'extravagant and unconscionable in amount'. It is not enough that it should be lacking in proportion. It must be 'out of all proportion'. It would therefore be a reversal of longstanding authority to substitute a test expressed in terms of mere disproportionality. However helpful that concept may be in considering other legal questions, it sits uncomfortably in the present context.

---

15. *Lord Elphinstone v Monkland Iron and Coal Co* (1886) 11 App Cas 332 at 345.
16. *AMEV-UDC Finance Ltd v Austin* (1986) 162 CLR 170, 190.

Comments
1. See Radan & Stewart at **14.16**.
2. For a discussion of this case see E Peden & J W Carter, 'Agreed Damages Clauses — Back to the Future?' (2006) 22 *Journal of Contract Law* 189.

Penalties and hire purchase transactions

14.4   Esanda Finance Corporation Limited v Plessnig (1989) 166 CLR 131

Court: High Court of Australia

Facts: Plessnig ran a small business in the transport industry and entered into a hire purchase arrangement with Esanda for the hire of a used prime mover. The cash sale price of the vehicle was $44,000 which, when repaid over 36 monthly instalments, amounted to approximately $67,000 inclusive of charges. Because the business was unable to keep up regular repayments, Plessnig arranged for return of the prime mover, which Esanda sold for $27,000. Esanda then obtained judgment against Plessnig for $13,000 pursuant to the hire purchase agreement, which specified the damages recoverable by the finance company in case of default by the hirer. Plessnig argued that the amount recovered under the contract amounted to a penalty.

Issue: The issue before the High Court was whether the amount recoverable under the hire purchase agreement compensated Esanda for its loss or penalised Plessnig for the breach.

Decision: The High Court (Wilson, Brennan, Deane, Toohey and Gaudron JJ) unanimously held in favour of Esanda on the basis that the default and recovery terms of the agreement did not represent a penalty.

Extracts: The extracts from the joint judgment of Wilson and Toohey JJ review some relevant authorities in respect of the test to be used in deciding whether liquidated damages clauses are penal in nature. The extracts from the judgment of Brennan J raise the problem of liquidated damages clauses that effectively permit recovery of expectation damages, but his Honour nevertheless accepts that Esanda's loss upon termination for non-repudiatory breach was properly taken into account in deciding whether the recoverable amount was a penalty.

Wilson and Toohey JJ

[138] The question for decision in this case is a narrow one. It is whether cl 6 of the agreement, in authorizing in the event of a termination of the contract in consequence of the hirer's default the recovery by the owner of an amount determined in accordance with cl 5, is penal rather than compensatory in character. We are not concerned with the characterization of a clause which provides for the payment of a

sum of money on the happening of a specified event other than a breach of contractual duty, a question which was [139] considered in *Export Credits Guarantee Department v Universal Oil Products Co.*[17]

The Court has considered the doctrine of penalties on a number of occasions in recent years.[18] In considering whether a term of a contract is penal in character rather than a genuine pre-estimate of damage, Mason and Wilson JJ observed in [*AMEV-UDC Finance Ltd v Austin*] that the test:

> … is one of degree and will depend on a number of circumstances, including (1) the degree of disproportion between the stipulated sum and the loss likely to be suffered by the plaintiff, a factor relevant to the oppressiveness of the term to the defendant, and (2) the nature of the relationship between the contracting parties, a factor relevant to the unconscionability of the plaintiff's conduct in seeking to enforce the term.[19]

Earlier in their reasons their Honours had discussed the first of these circumstances. After referring to the decisions of the House of Lords in *Clydebank Engineering and Shipbuilding Co v Don Jose Ramos Yzquierdo y Castaneda*[20] and *Dunlop Pneumatic Tyre Co Ltd v New Garage and Motor Co Ltd*,[21] they said:

> In both these decisions, in conformity with the doctrine's historic antecedents, the concept is that an agreed sum is a penalty if it is 'extravagant, exorbitant or unconscionable'.[22] This concept has been eroded by more recent decisions which, in the interests of greater certainty, have struck down provisions for the payment of an agreed sum merely because it may be greater than the amount of damages which could possibly be awarded for the breach of contract in respect of which the agreed sum is to be paid.[23] These decisions are more consistent with an underlying policy of restricting the parties, in case of breach of contract, to the recovery of an amount of damages no greater than that for which the law provides. However, there is much to be said for the view that the courts should return to the *Clydebank* and *Dunlop* concept, thereby allowing parties to a contract greater latitude in determining what their rights and liabilities will be, so that an agreed sum is only characterized as a penalty if it is out of all proportion to damage likely to be suffered as a result of breach.[24]

[140] A similar view was expressed in *Elsley v J G Collins Insurance Agencies Ltd*, where Dickson J, in delivering the judgment of the Supreme Court of Canada, said:

> It is now evident that the power to strike down a penalty clause is a blatant interference with freedom of contract and is designed for the sole purpose of providing relief against

---

17. [1983] 2 All ER 205.
18. *IAC (Leasing) Ltd v Humphrey* (1972) 126 CLR 131; *O'Dea v Allstates Leasing System (WA) Pty Ltd* (1983) 152 CLR 359; *AMEV-UDC Finance Ltd v Austin* (1986) 162 CLR 170.
19. *AMEV-UDC Finance Ltd v Austin* (1986) 162 CLR 170 at 193.
20. [1905] AC 6.
21. [1915] AC 79.
22. *Clydebank Engineering and Shipbuilding Co v Don Jose Ramos Yzquierdo y Castaneda* [1905] AC 6 at 10–11, 17; *Dunlop Pneumatic Tyre Co Ltd v New Garage and Motor Co Ltd* [1915] AC 79 at 87.
23. See *Cooden Engineering Co Ltd v Stanford* [1953] 1 QB 86 at 98.
24. *AMEV-UDC Finance Ltd v Austin* (1986) 162 CLR 170 at 190.

oppression for the party having to pay the stipulated sum. It has no place where there is no oppression.[25]

As *O'Dea*[26] and *AMEV-UDC* show, the fact that the 'recoverable amount' payable by [Plessnig] under cl 6 is payable upon termination of the agreement consequent upon breach, rather than in respect of the breach alone, does not mean that the clause escapes the scrutiny of the law relating to penalties. But it does mean that in determining whether the 'recoverable amount' is a genuine pre-estimate of loss or a penalty, 'relevant loss is not restricted to the loss flowing immediately and merely from the actual breach of contract; it includes the loss of the benefit of the contract resulting from the election to terminate for breach ...'[27] [Plessnig's] submission to the contrary must be rejected.

Brennan J

[143] One of the tests stated by Lord Dunedin in *Dunlop Pneumatic Tyre Co Ltd v New Garage and Motor Co Ltd* to assist in ascertaining whether a stipulated sum is a penalty is whether the sum 'is extravagant and unconscionable in amount in comparison with the greatest loss that could conceivably be proved to have followed from the breach'. To apply this test, it is necessary to identify the breach prescribed by the clause which imposes the supposed penalty and to ascertain the measure of loss which might follow from that breach. If the stipulated sum is payable on the occurrence of any breach of the contract, whether serious or trifling in its consequences, there is a presumption that the sum is a penalty.

By cl 6 of the parties' hire-purchase contract, the owner (Esanda) is authorized in the event of any breach by the hirer (Plessnig) to retake possession of the goods hired, and thereby to terminate the hiring and to recover 'as liquidated damages' a sum calculated by the formula prescribed by cl 5 and described as 'the recoverable amount'. The recoverable amount includes an amount which compensates the owner for his loss of instalments of rental which would have become payable if the hiring had not been terminated. Rental instalments are expressed to be 'payable during the hiring' and the hirer agrees to pay the rent until the hiring is determined: cl 2. The right to be paid those instalments is therefore lost on the termination of the hiring. But is the owner's right to be paid future rental instalments lost because of the hirer's breach, which may be a trifling breach, or because of the owner's election to terminate the hiring? Under the general law a party who breaches a condition in a contract or who commits a fundamental breach of or repudiates a contract — a party who commits what I shall call a repudiatory breach — is exposed to the loss of all his future contractual rights and to liability to compensate an innocent party for loss of his bargain; but a non-repudiatory breach does not expose the party in default to that liability in the absence of a stipulation in [144] that behalf. If a hire-purchase contract confers on the owner a contractual right to terminate the hiring for any breach, that right is distinct from and cumulative upon the owner's general law right to terminate the contract for a repudiatory breach. In such a case the source of the right to terminate the hiring is the contract. A stipulation which confers the right

---

25. *Elsley v J G Collins Insurance Agencies Ltd* (1978) 83 DLR (3d) 1 at 15.
26. *O'Dea v Allstates Leasing System (WA) Pty Ltd* (1983) 152 CLR 359.
27. *AMEV-UDC Finance Ltd v Austin* (1986) 162 CLR 170 at 197; see also at 181, 194, 205–6, 210.

to terminate the hiring for any breach does not transform the non-essential terms into conditions and therefore the contract may remain on foot after the hiring is terminated. Whether a term which is commercially non-essential can be elevated effectively to the level of a condition by appropriate drafting is a problem which does not now arise.[28]

In this Court, no clear opinion has emerged as to the effect for the purpose of the law of penalties of a loss suffered by an innocent party in consequence of his exercise of a contractual power to terminate for breach of a non-essential term. In *AMEV-UDC Finance Ltd v Austin*, a hirer of equipment defaulted in paying an instalment of rent on the due date whereupon the owner, in exercise of a contractual power, terminated the hiring and demanded payment of a sum calculated in accordance with a contractual formula: the whole unpaid balance of the total rent payable under the hiring agreement subject to certain adjustments representing the difference between the residual value of the equipment specified in the agreement and the sale price of the equipment. The hirer was found not to have repudiated the agreement. As the clause entitling the owner on termination of the hiring to the whole unpaid balance of the total rent without discount was held to impose a penalty,[29] the issue for determination was whether the owner was entitled to no more than the instalments unpaid at the date of termination together with interest as damages for the hirer's breach or whether the owner was entitled to enforce the hirer's contractual obligation to pay up to the amount of any loss sustained by the owner in consequence of the termination of the hiring. A sharp division of opinion appeared in the answers given by the majority (Gibbs CJ, Mason and Wilson JJ) and by the minority (Deane and Dawson JJ). The majority held that the owner was entitled only to the former relief: the minority held that the owner was entitled to the latter relief.

Gibbs CJ, agreeing with the decision of the English Court of Appeal in *Financings Ltd v Baldock*,[30] which had held the [145] owner's damages for non-repudiatory breach to be limited to instalments in arrears at the date of termination with interest, said:

> The ratio of that part of the decision was that where there has been no repudiation by the hirer, and the owner has exercised his power to determine the hiring because the hirer was in arrears with his payments, any loss occurring after the determination will have resulted, not from the hirer's breach of contract in being late in his payments, but from the owner's election to determine the hiring ... Very similar reasoning was accepted by this Court in *Shevill v Builders Licensing Board*,[31] a case in which a lessor exercised a power of re-entry when the lessee fell into arrears in the payment of rent.[32]

Mason and Wilson JJ said:

> The point is that when the lessor terminates pursuant to the contractual right given to him for breach by the lessee, the loss which he can recover for non-fundamental breach is limited to the loss which flows from the lessee's breach. The lessor cannot recover the loss which he sustains as a result of his termination because that loss is attributable

---

28. See *Lombard North Central Plc v Butterworth* [1987] QB 527.
29. See *O'Dea v Allstates Leasing System (WA) Pty Ltd* (1983) 152 CLR 359.
30. [1963] 2 QB 104.
31. (1962) 149 CLR 620.
32. *AMEV-UDC Finance Ltd v Austin* (1986) 162 CLR 170 at 175.

to his act, not to the conduct of the lessee. It is otherwise in the case of fundamental breach, breach of an essential term or repudiation.[33]

In rejecting a submission that equity would condition the granting of relief against a penalty by requiring the guilty party to compensate the innocent party for loss incurred consequent on termination for non-fundamental breach, their Honours said:

> ... it would now be inconsistent with modern authority for equity to condition its relief by imposing on the obligor a liability to pay damage which flows, not from the obligor's breach of contract, but from the obligee's act in exercising his contractual right to terminate for non-fundamental breach.[34]

If, for the purpose of applying the *Dunlop* test, regard is had solely to the damages which the majority in *AMEV-UDC* held to flow from the hirer's breach, a stipulation for liquidated damages to be paid by a hirer on termination of the hiring for non-repudiatory breach which imposes a liability to pay for losses flowing from the termination should be treated as imposing a penalty. However, a further examination of *AMEV-UDC* shows that a majority of the Court said that that is not the law. Deane J, in dissent, held that the loss against which the supposed penalty was **[146]** to be measured to determine whether it was in truth a penalty included the loss sustained upon termination. His Honour, accepting the explanation for this proposition advanced by the majority in *Cooden Engineering Co Ltd v Stanford*,[35] said:

> In essence, that explanation is that, at least for the purposes of the rules relating to penalties, the loss sustained by reason of the exercise of a contractual right to terminate upon breach in a case such as the present is to be seen as flowing from the breach. The point was clearly made by Hodson LJ in *Cooden* when he expressed his difficulty in seeing 'the validity of the distinction between a claim to receive payment of a sum of money because of a right to determine arising from breach of contract and a claim to receive payment of the same sum by reason of breach of contract giving a right to determine'.[36] In that context and notwithstanding the support for the contrary view which can be found in some cases, I am unable to accept that the common law would found upon that very distinction between breach and termination to reduce the extent to which a penalty clause can be enforced below the actual amount of the loss sustained upon termination for breach.[37]

Dawson J, also in dissent, perceived a logical but not a legal distinction between loss flowing from non-repudiatory breach and loss flowing from termination pursuant to a contractual power, observing:

> Moreover, if, as is logical but is not done, the provision for loss upon termination of the agreement were to be compared in amount with the loss flowing from a breach not amounting to a repudiation, it would almost certainly be markedly more and for that

---

33. *AMEV-UDC Finance Ltd v Austin* (1986) 162 CLR 170 at 186.
34. *AMEV-UDC Finance Ltd v Austin* (1986) 162 CLR 170 at 191.
35. [1953] 1 QB 86.
36. *Cooden Engineering Co Ltd v Stanford* [1953] 1 QB 86 at 96–7.
37. *AMEV-UDC Finance Ltd v Austin* (1986) 162 CLR 170 at 204.

reason a penalty even though a genuine pre-estimate of the lessor's damage upon the exercise of his contractual right to terminate the agreement. It is not done because the result is obviously unsatisfactory, but I shall return to that point shortly.[38]

And:

... if a provision stipulating a payment by way of accelerated rent or the like upon repossession is to be regarded as payable upon breach rather than upon termination of the agreement for the purpose of characterizing it as a penalty and if upon the provision being characterized as a penalty the only recovery permitted is for the breach and not for the loss of the bargain (assuming no repudiation), there can be no justification for having regard to the loss arising from termination in determining whether the provision is a genuine pre-estimate of damage or a penalty.[39]

[147] Yet, his Honour said, 'that is what is done'. If that is so, losses flowing not from the breach alone but from the termination as well are taken into account in determining whether a pecuniary liability is a penalty. Mason and Wilson JJ expressed, albeit obiter, a view which bears out Dawson J's observation. First, their Honours did not regard termination as an event supervening on an antecedent breach and, on that account, to place post-termination loss outside the purview of the law relating to penalties. Their Honours said:

If the option [to terminate] is exercised on the occasion of the hirer's breach of contract, it accords with principle and authority to say that the sum is payable in respect of the breach of contract and is a penalty, unless it is a genuine pre-estimate of the damage.[40]

Although their Honours held that losses caused by the termination of the contract were not to be included in the owner's damages, they thought it right to take them into account in determining whether a pecuniary liability imposed by the contract is a penalty. Their Honours said:

Our rejection of the appellant's arguments should not be taken as throwing any doubt on the right of the owner or the lessor to recover his actual loss on his early termination of a hire-purchase agreement or chattel lease, pursuant to a contractual right, for the hirer's non-fundamental breach, under a correctly drawn indemnity provision.[41]

In the light of these observations, I take the law to accept an incongruity in holding that an owner's damages at law for a non-repudiatory breach are limited to losses caused by the breach alone while holding that a clause which imposes a liability on the hirer to pay the losses caused by exercise of a power to terminate a hiring upon breach is not a penalty. It may be appropriate to reconsider this incongruity in some later case and, if that is done, it may well be necessary to canvass the correctness of some earlier decisions of this Court. For the moment I adopt, in common with the other members of the Court, the view that the owner's loss consequent upon the termination of the hiring for non-repudiatory breach

---

38. *AMEV-UDC Finance Ltd v Austin* (1986) 162 CLR 170 at 213.
39. *AMEV-UDC Finance Ltd v Austin* (1986) 162 CLR 170 at 215.
40. *AMEV-UDC Finance Ltd v Austin* (1986) 162 CLR 170 at 184–5.
41. *AMEV-UDC Finance Ltd v Austin* (1986) 162 CLR 170 at 194.

is to be taken into account in determining whether the recoverable amount prescribed by cl 5 is a penalty. It is implicit in this view that a contractual power to terminate a hiring is not itself a penalty though the fact of termination is relevant to the determination whether a pecuniary liability then imposed on the hirer is a penalty.[42] Depending on the circumstances, the [148] exercise of such a contractual power might be oppressive to the hirer and productive of a windfall profit for the owner. This consideration draws attention to equity's jurisdiction to grant relief against the unconscionable exercise of legal rights to which reference will presently be made. For the moment, assuming that the power to terminate the hiring for a non-repudiatory breach is effectively exercised, the question is whether the amount of [Plessnig's] liability imposed pursuant to cl 6 is extravagant or unconscionable in comparison with the greatest losses that could conceivably be proved to have followed the breach *and* the termination.

The 'recoverable amount' prescribed by cl 5 is a balance struck by debiting [Plessnig] with certain items and crediting him with others. The items debited consist in 'the total rent ... and all other moneys payable for the full period of hire (including ... costs of repossession storage maintenance and selling expenses)', from which are deducted all moneys paid by [Plessnig], the wholesale value of the goods repossessed and 'a rebate of charges calculated in accordance with Clause 13 hereof': cl 5. The cl 13 rebate represents the interest or terms charges attributable to the portion of the original hiring period which is still to go at the time of termination. On termination of the hiring, [Esanda] loses the right to receive future rental instalments and may incur costs in repossessing, storing, maintaining and selling the goods the subject of the contract, but [it] acquires possession of the goods and a discharge of [Plessnig's] option to purchase them. [Esanda's] loss on termination is the balance of the 'cash price' which it has outlaid to acquire the hired goods (see cll 1 and 2 and the 'Hirer's Declaration' embodied in the 'Offer to Hire') to the extent to which it has not been recouped, unrecouped interest earned and administration charges incurred up to the time of termination and the costs associated with repossessing and selling the hired goods less the value of the repossessed goods. If the loss is recovered on termination, [Esanda's] capital is available for alternative investment and its outgoings are covered. Clauses 5 and 13 contain a formula which so quantifies the recoverable amount as to equate it with the net loss suffered by [Esanda], assuming that the value of the goods which [it] repossesses and sells to a third party is properly set at 'the best wholesale price reasonably obtainable for them in their then condition as at the time of ... taking possession of them': cl 5(b). As [Esanda] is a finance company which outlays money to acquire goods selected by [a] hirer and is not a retailer of goods, the best wholesale price obtainable on repossession cannot be said to be an extravagant and unconscionable under-estimate of [149] what [it] is likely to obtain if it sells the goods after termination of the hiring ...

[150] If a clause which requires the hirer to pay the owner for losses occasioned by termination for breach under a contractual power is not a penalty provision, the reason must be that the court regards that clause and the clause authorizing the owner to terminate the hiring, to repossess and sell the goods and to recover the net losses then outstanding as provisions to secure the owner's interests as a moneylender, as well as to secure the due performance of the hirer's obligations. The right to recover post-termination losses is needed

---

42. *O'Dea v Allstates Leasing System (WA) Pty Ltd* (1983) 152 CLR 359.

to secure the owner's return of the money lent with interest and the recoupment of the owner's costs and expenses. The owner's rights to terminate the hiring, to repossess and sell the goods and to recover the recoverable amount can hardly be supported as a stipulation for the payment of a genuine pre-estimate of damage caused by any non-repudiatory breach of the hirer's obligations, but they can be seen to be security for the due performance of the hirer's obligations *and* the protection of the owner's interests as a [151] moneylender. In other words, if it be right to uphold a stipulation for the payment of post-termination losses as a stipulation for the payment of liquidated damages, the corollary is that the transaction be treated in much the same way as a chattel mortgage and the contractual power to terminate, repossess and sell be treated merely as security for the repayment of the moneys lent with interest and recoupment of the owner's costs and expenses.

If a hire-purchase contract is so regarded, equity may grant the hirer relief against an exercise by an owner of its contractual right to terminate, repossess and sell the hired goods in the event of a non-repudiatory breach of the contract because the contractual right may be seen as a penalty designed to secure money and a court of equity can give the owner all that he is entitled to as a moneylender ... In *BICC Plc v Burndy Corporation*, it was held that there is jurisdiction in equity to grant relief against forfeiture of a possessory or proprietary interest in personal property[43] and those are the kinds of interests held by a hirer who has committed no repudiatory breach. Under the general law, the hirer is entitled to continued possession of the goods and, if payment of rental instalments entitles him to purchase the goods, he acquires a proprietary interest in the property which is susceptible of protection in equity. Though he has no legal title to the goods until he has fulfilled the conditions prescribed by the contract ... his contractual right to acquire the title by fulfilling those conditions may be protected. It is neither necessary nor possible to state exhaustively the circumstances in which equity will intervene to protect a hirer's possessory or proprietary interests against an exercise of the owner's contractual rights. The circumstances will be identified more clearly as the jurisdiction to grant relief is argued and exercised in particular cases. This is not one of them. For the moment, it is sufficient to note that there are two factors which are of general relevance. First, the deliberation and seriousness of the [152] hirer's breach and, secondly, the likelihood of the owner, by exercise of its contractual rights, making a windfall profit which the owner is not contractually required to account for to the hirer.

In the present case, [Plessnig] did not seek relief against the exercise by [Esanda] of its contractual rights. Had [he] done so, it is unlikely [he] would have succeeded. [Plessnig] had defaulted in the payment of four successive monthly rental instalments and, at the time of repossession, $7,048.46 of a total sum of $31,939.26 which had become payable was outstanding. [Esanda] gave [Plessnig] a reasonable opportunity to make good [the] default but [he] did not take that opportunity. The goods — a prime mover — were sold for $27,000 which was insufficient to meet the unpaid balance of [Esanda's] outlays, interest, charges and expenses. A recoverable amount of $9,300.42 became due. This amount, together with interest at 15 per cent per annum under cl 4(c), was the basis of [Esanda's] claim in the action.

In the Full Court of the Supreme Court of South Australia [Esanda's] award was reduced to the instalments in arrears, $7,048.46 together with interest, solely on the ground that

---

43. *BICC Plc v Burndy Corporation* [1985] Ch 232 at 251–2.

cl 6 imposed a penalty. Once it is accepted that it is right to have regard to [Esanda's] losses on termination in determining whether the recoverable amount is 'extravagant and unconscionable', [Plessnig's] attack on cl 6 is limited to two points: the adoption of the best wholesale price rather than the retail price as the amount to be credited to [Plessnig] in calculating the recoverable amount and the absence of any liability on the part of [Esanda] to account to [Plessnig] for any surplus over the amount due under cl 5 resulting from the sale of the goods repossessed. For the reasons given, neither of these points stamps the recoverable amount with the character of a penalty. Having failed to sustain [the] attack on cl 6, [Plessnig] must be held liable to pay the recoverable amount.

Comment
1. See Radan & Stewart at **14.18–14.19**.

15

INTRODUCTION TO TRUSTS

Introduction

15.1   This chapter is concerned with the concept of the trust and how it relates to other types of legal relationship. The essential nature of the trust features a separation of the legal ownership of property from the beneficial entitlement to that property. There are three elements to a trust:

1. *the trustee* — a legal person who holds a vested legal title (or a vested equitable title) in the property, subject to fiduciary duties;
2. *trust property* — property in real or personal form which is identified or ascertainable and capable of being held on trust. The trust property can be legal or equitable property; and
3. *the beneficiary* (sometimes referred to as the *cestui que trust* in older cases, or the *object* of the trust in modern cases) — a person, or group of persons, who hold a beneficial equitable estate in the property and on whose behalf the trustee must act.

Trusts occur in many contexts and it can be sometimes difficult to determine whether a relationship is a trust relationship or something else. The cases extracted in this chapter examine some of these situations and discuss:

- the relationship between trust and contract: *Gosper v Sawyer* (1985) 160 CLR 548;
- the relationship of trusts and fiduciary duties: *Visnic v Sywak* (2009) 257 ALR 517;
- the relationship between trust and agency: *Olma v Amendola* [2004] SASC 274;
- the relationship between trusts, charges and conditional dispositions: *Countess of Bective v Federal Commissioner of Taxation* (1932) 47 CLR 417;
- the relationship between trust and debt: *Barclays Bank Ltd v Quistclose Investments Ltd* [1970] AC 567; and
- the relationship between trust and personal equitable obligations: *Hammond v Hammond* [2007] NSWSC 106.

Contracts and trusts

15.2   Gosper v Sawyer (1985) 160 CLR 548

Court: High Court of Australia

Facts: Ross Sawyer was an employee at the Shell refinery. When he became an employee he was required to join the Shell Australia Contributory Pension Fund ('the Fund') which was a compulsory superannuation scheme. He was injured at work and later was made redundant. The Fund had made a determination that he was not totally and permanently incapacitated and the amount he received ended up being less than what he contributed, after taking inflation into account. In 1983, Sawyer sought an order from the New South Wales Industrial Commission to review the terms of Funds under s 88F(1) of the *Industrial Arbitration Act 1940* (NSW). This section allowed the Commission to review contracts which were harsh, unconscionable or oppressive.

Unfortunately for Sawyer, the Fund and all the trustees were based in Victoria. They were eventually served in Victoria but only made conditional appearances before the Commission to say that they had not been properly served and that the Commission had no jurisdiction.

A Supreme Court judge, Cahill J, found that the Commission did have jurisdiction and could serve the claim on the trustees even though they were in Victoria. Part of Cahill J's reasons were based on s 11(1)(b) of the *Service and Execution of Process Act 1901* (Cth). This section allowed courts to proceed with 'contract' claims against defendants who were interstate, as long as the claim originated in the court's jurisdiction and had been properly served.

Issue: The issue was whether Sawyer's claim concerning the trust fund was a 'contract' claim in terms of s 11(1)(b) of the *Service and Execution of Process Act 1901* (Cth).

Decision: The High Court (Gibbs CJ, Mason, Wilson, Deane and Dawson JJ) found that the Commission did not have jurisdiction. A claim concerning a superannuation trust was not a contract claim that came under s 11(1)(b) of the *Service and Execution of Process Act 1901* (Cth).

Extracts: The following extracts from the two joint decisions (one from Gibbs CJ, Wilson and Dawson JJ, the other from Mason and Deane JJ) examine the question of whether an action to challenge the provisions of a trust can be considered as a contract claim.

Gibbs CJ, Wilson and Dawson JJ

[559] In the present case the contract of employment between Shell and Mr Sawyer was entered into in the State of New South Wales. It was submitted on behalf of Mr Sawyer that the relief sought in the present proceedings was by way of affecting that contract, since, by the contract of employment, the employee was obliged to become a member of the Fund and accordingly to be bound by the trust deed. However, the relief sought against the trustees was not by way of affecting the contract of employment, to which, of course, they were not parties; what was sought was relief affecting the trust deed, as the words of the notice of motion show. It was submitted, in the alternative, that the relationship of the employee and the trustees under the trust deed was itself a 'contract' within s 11(1)(b). A wide meaning has been given to 'contract' in s 11(1)(b); it has been held that it extends to 'an implied or constructive contract for which an action in

the nature of *assumpsit* would at common law have been available'[1] **[560]** or, in other words, to 'implied, constructive or fictitious contracts, without consensual element, but for purposes of the old forms of action, at any rate, deemed to amount to contract — cases where *assumpsit* or an *indebitatus* count would have been available at common law'.[2] It seems incongruous to have to determine the meaning of s. 11(1)(b) by reference to forms of action made obsolete by the *Judicature Acts*, but if that is an appropriate course it would not assist Mr Sawyer in the present case. It does not need the authority of Bullen and Leake[3] to establish that an application to avoid or vary a trust deed could not possibly have been made by an action of assumpsit or on an indebitatus count. Even if s 11(1)(b) is given its widest possible meaning, and if 'contract' in that provision includes, not only quasi-contracts, but such things as judgments and statutes under which fixed sums of money are payable, it cannot include discretionary trusts, except perhaps in the case where the trustee has admitted that he holds trust money as that of the beneficiary.[4] It is quite impossible to regard an application to avoid or vary the deed of trust in the present case as an application seeking relief in respect of a contract within s 11(1)(b). Moreover, even if the trust deed could be held to be a contract, it was not made or entered into in New South Wales.

Mason and Deane JJ

[567] Section 88F(1) provides, for present purposes, that the Commission may, on any one or more of a number of identified grounds, make an order or award declaring void or varying 'any contract or arrangement or any condition or collateral arrangement relating thereto whereby a person performs work in any industry'. There are three contracts or arrangements in the present case which it might be argued came within those words. The first is the contract between Shell and Mr Sawyer under which Mr Sawyer was obliged to become a member of the Fund. That was the actual contract of employment between Shell and Mr Sawyer and was, at least while it was current, plainly a 'contract ... whereby a person performs work in any industry'. None of the appellants was, however, a party to that contract and it has not been argued that they are joined as necessary or proper parties to proceedings against Shell to have it varied or declared void. The second is the 'arrangement' between Mr Sawyer and the appellants or their predecessors as trustees pursuant to which Mr Sawyer became a member of the Fund. It might be argued that that was a 'collateral arrangement' relating to the employment contract. The third is the 'arrangement', which is embodied in the terms of the trust deed and pursuant to which the Fund was established and upon the terms and conditions of which its assets are held and are to be applied. It is also arguable that that was such a 'collateral arrangement'.

Examination of the material before the Court, particularly the notice of motion which constituted the initiating process before the Commission and Mr Sawyer's supporting affidavit, indicates that the relief sought in the purported application pursuant to s. 88F is,

---

1. See *Victoria v Hansen* [1960] VR 582 at 586.
2. *Wilson Electric Transformer Co Pty Ltd v Electricity Commission (NSW)* [1968] VR 330 at 332.
3. Bullen & Leake, *Precedents of Pleadings*, 3rd ed, 1868, pp 35–57.
4. See Bullen & Leake, *Precedents of Pleadings*, note 3 above, p 47.

in so far as it is brought against the appellants, in respect of the third only of those possible contracts or arrangements. The relief which the notice of motion seeks is particularized as an order or award declaring void or varying 'an arrangement and/or a condition or collateral arrangement relating thereto between the applicant of the one part and the respondents of the other part *being* the Shell Australia Contributory Pension Fund' (emphasis added). The main grounds on which relief is sought are that the provisions of the Fund or some of them are 'unfair, harsh, unconscionable [568] and/or against the public interest' or have operated, so far as [Mr Sawyer] is concerned, in a manner which is unfair, harsh, unconscionable and/or against the public interest'. What Mr Sawyer seeks, as against the appellants, is an order varying the effect of the actual trust deed to increase the amount which he became entitled to be paid from the Fund upon the termination of his employment. In that regard, it is clear enough that the relief sought in the notice of motion is not 'in respect of' the limited arrangement between Mr Sawyer and the then trustees pursuant to which Mr Sawyer became a member of the Fund. That arrangement is neither specifically mentioned nor made the subject of attack. To the contrary, Mr Sawyer relies upon his membership of the Fund as a basis for his claim to have the provisions of the trust deed governing it varied so that he will be entitled to receive more from the Fund.

It follows that the application against the [Trustees] (as distinct from Shell) must be seen as related only to the third of the above-mentioned possible contracts or arrangements, namely, to the arrangement embodied in the terms of the trust deed governing the Fund whose provisions are alleged, in the notice of motion, to be and to have operated in a manner which is 'unfair, harsh, unconscionable and/or against the public interest'. That being so, the critical question is whether, assuming that they be otherwise competent, proceedings seeking to have the provisions of that trust deed varied or avoided pursuant to s. 88F are, within s 11(1)(b) of the *Service and Execution of Process Act*, proceedings seeking, 'in respect of' a 'contract' which was 'made or entered into within' New South Wales, 'relief ... by way of enforcing, rescinding, dissolving, annulling, or otherwise affecting such contract'.

The word 'contract' in s 11(1)(b) should not be given a narrow or technical meaning. It should be construed as extending both to the ordinary contract constituted by offer and acceptance and to imputed or quasi contracts.[5] The words 'enforcing, rescinding, dissolving, annulling, or *otherwise affecting*' (emphasis added) indicate that the scope of the section is not confined to traditional causes of action in contract any more than it is confined to actions for relief in respect of consensual contracts. More particularly, the words of the section are apt to refer to proceedings to have a contract declared void or varied by a court in the exercise of some special statutory jurisdiction such as that conferred by s. 88F of the Act.

The origins and nature of contract and trust are, of course, quite different. There is however no dichotomy between the two. The contractual relationship provides one of the most common bases for [569] the establishment or implication and for the definition of a trust. Conversely, the trust, particularly the resulting and constructive trust, represents one of the most important means of protecting parties in a contractual relationship and

---

5. Cf *Bowling v Cox* [1926] AC 751 at 754–755.

of vindicating contractual rights. An action to vary the terms of a trust could, in some cases, properly be seen as an action affecting a contract pursuant to whose terms the trust was established and governed. The mere fact that the purported proceedings under s. 88F in the present case related to provisions of the trust deed pursuant to which the [trustees] held the Fund does not necessarily mean that those proceedings could not also be an action 'affecting' a 'contract' for the purposes of s 11(1)(b) of the *Service and Execution of Process Act*.

If it were possible to isolate the trust relationship between the appellants and Mr Sawyer and to see it as a separate and independent relationship arising under the contract or arrangement pursuant to which Mr Sawyer became a member of the Fund, it would be arguable that the various provisions of the trust deed regulating the rights and obligations of the appellants and Mr Sawyer were properly to be regarded as a 'contract' for the purposes of s 11(1)(b). It is not, however, possible to isolate the provisions of the trust deed in their operation with respect to Mr Sawyer from the same provisions in their operation with respect to the other members of the Fund. There is but one fund which is held upon the one set of trusts contained in the one trust deed. It is not possible to divide the fund or the provisions of the trust into a separate fund or a separate set of trusts for each individual member. That being so, and notwithstanding that some of the provisions of the trust deed are framed in terms of contract, there are difficulties in the proposition that the provisions of the trust deed governing the Fund could properly be seen as an overall 'contract' in any relevant sense. It is not necessary to express a final view in that regard however, since it is plain that any such overall 'contract' could not properly be held to have been made in New South Wales: the trust deed was made and the Fund was established in Victoria; by its express terms (cl. 34), the trust deed is 'in all respects governed by the law of Victoria'; the Fund is administered and remains situate in Victoria.

The only relevant contracts or arrangements made in New South Wales were the contract of employment between Mr Sawyer and Shell and, arguably, the limited contract or arrangement pursuant to which Mr Sawyer became a member of the Fund. It has been seen that the purported proceedings by Mr Sawyer against the appellants under s. 88F do not seek 'in respect of' those contracts 'relief … by way of enforcing, rescinding, dissolving, annulling, or otherwise [570] affecting' such contracts. Even if the purported proceedings against the appellants under s. 88F can properly be regarded as proceedings 'in respect of' and 'affecting' a 'contract' embodying the overall terms and conditions upon which the appellants held the Fund, the case does not come within s 11(1)(b) in that any such 'contract' was not 'made or entered into within' New South Wales.

Comments

1. See Radan & Stewart at **15.22–15.29**.
2. Complexities arise in contracts created by the parties for the benefit of a third person. According to the doctrine of privity, only the contracting parties can sue for breach of such a contract. Third party beneficiaries are unable to sue on the contract: *Woodar Investment Development Ltd v Wimpey Construction UK Ltd* [1980]

1 All ER 571. However, if it can be argued that the contract creates a trust of the contractual rights then it might be argued that the third party can enforce the contract as a beneficiary: *Winterton Constructions Pty Ltd v Hambros Australia Ltd* (1991) 101 ALR 363 at 370. The question of whether contractual rights are held on trust is answered by examining the words of the agreement: *McLellan v Sharantelli Pty Ltd* [2000] VSC 174. The intention must be to create a trust, and not just an intention to benefit a third party: *Dalton v Ellis; Estate of Bristow* [2005] NSWSC 1252. It isn't necessary for the contracting parties to expressly recognise the existence of a trust for one to be imposed: *Kowalski v MMAL Staff Superannuation Fund Pty Ltd (ACN 064 829 616) (No 3)* [2009] FCA 53 at [92].

3. See C H Tham, 'Trust, not Contract: Restoring Trust in the *Contracts (Rights of Third Parties) Act*' (2005) 21 *Journal of Contract Law* 107.

Trusts and fiduciary obligations

15.3   Visnic v Sywak (2009) 257 ALR 517

Court: The Court of Appeal of New South Wales

Facts: Visnic argued that his accountant, Sywak, held a number of shares in four different companies on trust for him. This claim was upheld at trial by Brereton J, who ordered that the shares be transferred into Visnic's name. Brereton J also ordered that the companies be wound up as the transfer of the shares left the companies deadlocked. Visnic argued that Sywak had also breached other fiduciary duties. Visnic sought orders for equitable damages and/or an account of profits for any benefits which had been received by Sywak during the time he was in control of the companies. Brereton J refused to make those orders. Visnic appealed.

Issue: The issue for the Court of Appeal was whether the remedies for breach of fiduciary duty should be ordered in addition to the orders to transfer the shares back to Visnic.

Decision: The Court of Appeal (Spigelman CJ, Campbell and Macfarlan JJA) upheld the trial judge's decision not to order an account of profits and equitable compensation. The court drew a distinction between breach of fiduciary duty and breach of trust. While there had been a breach of trust, it was not clear that there was a breach of any fiduciary duty in relation to a conflict between interest and duty. Nor could it be said that any profit made by Sywak was sufficiently connected (in a causal sense) to the refusal to hand back the shares.

Extracts: This extract from Spigelman CJ's judgment examines the differences in remedies available for breach of trust and breach of fiduciary duty.

Spigelman CJ

[519] The judgments of Brereton J

With respect to the matters which remained in issue, Brereton J said in his first judgment:

[123] The plaintiff has sought an order that it be referred to an Associate Judge to inquire into and certify the damages allegedly suffered by reason of the first defendant's breaches of fiduciary duty, and that the first defendant be directed to file an affidavit accounting for his dealings with the assets and income of the four corporations. I accept that, at least, in respect of the negotiations with the Business Associates, and as the legal owner of shares of which Mr Visnic was a beneficiary, that Mr Sywak was a fiduciary. However, the Statement of Claim identifies no damage resulting from a breach of fiduciary duty, other than depriving Mr Visnic of his shareholdings. It seems to me that the only damage that could have been occasioned to Mr Visnic is loss of the dividend that he might otherwise have received, but there is no evidence that dividends were declared or paid during the relevant period. Accordingly, as presently advised, it seems to me that there is not the necessary evidence of some damage that would be required to refer the matter for an inquiry. The orders that I have already pronounced will restore to him his shareholding. If there has been some breach by Mr Sywak of some obligation owed by him to any of the companies — whether as their accountant or as a director — prima facie, that is a matter for the liquidator to pursue. Lest I have overlooked something in this respect, however, I will reserve liberty to apply if it is desired to pursue an inquiry as to damages.[6]

I have indicated at [3] the order for an inquiry which [Visnic] sought by notice of notion consequent upon this judgment. In his second judgment his Honour said:

[3] At the outset, I make some observations about some of the concepts referred to in paragraph 123 of my previous judgment. First, I accepted that, in some limited respects — namely, the negotiations with the business associates and as legal owner of shares of which Mr Visnic was a beneficiary — that Mr Sywak was a fiduciary. Secondly, I recorded that there appeared to be no evidence, nor even allegation, of damage resulting from any breach of fiduciary duty, other than Mr Visnic being deprived of his shareholdings. Thirdly, I identified a possibility that there might have been some breach [520] by Mr Sywak of some obligation owed by him to the companies (as distinct from to Mr Visnic), which would be a matter for the liquidator to pursue.[7]

His Honour referred to relevant authorities.[8] His Honour concluded:

[13] At least for the purposes of what has to be decided on this application, the following may be drawn from the cases to which I have so far referred. First, equity requires a fiduciary to restore to the trust estate anything lost from it as a result of a

---

6. *Visnic v Sywak* [2007] NSWSC 701 at [123].
7. *Visnic v Sywak* [2008] NSWSC 427 at [13]–[15].
8. *Re Dawson (dec'd); Union Fidelity Trustee Co Ltd v Perpetual Trustee Co Ltd* [1966] 2 NSWR 211; *Hill v Rose* [1990] VR 129; *Canson Enterprises Ltd v Boughton & Co* [1991] 3 SCR 534; *Chan v Zacharia* (1984) 154 CLR 178.

breach of duty. Secondly, a fiduciary is obliged to account for benefits or gains made by the fiduciary from a breach of duty to the person to whom the relevant fiduciary obligation was owed. Thirdly, while the obligation to make equitable compensation is not constrained to the same extent as liability to pay damages in common law by considerations of causation and foreseeability, nonetheless there must be some common sense connection between the loss or the profit and the breach in question.

[14] Returning then to the present case, the only fiduciary duties which I accepted in my previous judgment were (1) in connection with the negotiations with the business associates and (2) as trustee of those shares that Mr Sywak held on trust for Mr Visnic. The only breach of such duty that I found — and indeed, the only breach of fiduciary duty which has been suggested in the present argument — was that Mr Sywak deprived Mr Visnic of his shareholding. I identified the possibility that, as well as the property in the shareholdings themselves, a dividend might have been declared or paid in respect of Mr Visnic's shares from which Mr Sywak benefited, but there was no evidence that any such dividend has been declared or paid during the relevant period; that has not changed, and there remains no evidence that dividends were declared or paid during the relevant period. In those circumstances, it seems to me now, as it seemed to me then, that restitution to the trust estate of the property of which it was deprived by the breach of the trust will be effected by the orders, already made, declaring trusts in respect of the shareholdings and requiring their transfer to Mr Visnic.

[15] On the present application, however, it has been argued that there are additional benefits in respect of which Mr Sywak ought to be liable to account: in particular, to take the highest and least controversial of them, payments made or authorised by him from the assets of at least one of the companies to his personal superannuation fund which, for present purposes, I shall assume were made for his own benefit. Mr A W Street SC informs me, and I do not doubt, that there was some evidence of such a payment in the substantive proceedings, and I proceed on that basis. Assuming, as I do, that such payments were made by Mr Sywak, then it may well be that they were in breach of an obligation owed by him to the companies as a director of those companies or as accountant for those companies. But applying the test referred to by McLachlin J in *Canson Enterprises Pty Ltd v Boughton & Co*, they do not seem to me to be losses that, on any common sense view of causation, were caused by the relevant breach, namely, depriving Mr Visnic of his shareholdings; indeed, they seem to me to be entirely unconnected with and outside the scope of that breach. They arose from a different breach of a different duty, one owed to the companies; not the breach of the particular duties that, I have found, were owed by Mr Sywak to Mr Visnic.

[13] His Honour emphasised the significance of the distinction between a breach of duty owed to a shareholder and a breach of duty owed to a company, referring to *Prudential Assurance Co Ltd v Newman Industries Ltd (No 2) (Prudential Assurance (No 2))*.[9] His Honour then said:

[17] ... However, the proposition that in a case where the relevant obligation is owed to the company, any corresponding liability to account is also owed to the company,

---

9.   [1982] Ch 204.

can [521] be tested by asking what would be the position in the present case if the company had creditors. Assuming, as I do, that Mr Sywak has received benefits from one or more of the companies, then Mr Street suggested that the remedy would be a liability to account for one half of those benefits to Mr Visnic. If the company had creditors, plainly the obligation would be to return the whole — not one half — of the benefit to the company, so that it could be applied first for the benefit of the creditors and then division between the shareholders. Thus, it seems to me plain that, in respect of such breaches, where the duty breached, if any, was one that was owed to the company, the obligation to account is one that lies to the company and not to Mr Visnic.

[18] Again, the position can be tested by speculating that if, notwithstanding the breach that I have found in respect of Mr Visnic's shareholding, Mr Sywak had acted properly as a director, there would be no liability to account in respect of the payments into the superannuation fund. On the other hand, if he had not taken Mr Visnic's shares, but authorised the payments to be made to the superannuation fund, there would still be a liability to account to the company, regardless of the absence of any breach of duty to Mr Visnic.

[19] All these considerations point firmly to the conclusion that the matters about which it is now suggested Mr Sywak ought be required to account to Mr Visnic are matters in respect of which he is obliged to account, if at all, to the company and not to Mr Visnic.

[20] For those reasons, I am of the view that, even were there no other obstacle to the grant of the relief sought, Mr Visnic is not entitled on the merits to the inquiry which he seeks. In short, so far as the breaches of fiduciary obligation owed to him are concerned, no damage or profit such as would attract an inquiry has been identified over and beyond the depreciation of his shares which will be remedied by the restitution to him of the shareholding, which has already been decreed. So far as it is suggested that there is a liability to account in respect of other amounts received by Mr Sywak, any liability to account is owed, if at all, to the relevant company and not to Mr Visnic.

[21] The same result is supported by two other considerations. The first is that, in reserving liberty to apply for an inquiry, I had expressed the qualification 'at least' in the second sentence of paragraph 123 — lest it might be established on further argument that Mr Sywak's fiduciary obligations to Mr Visnic went further than those which I accepted — and the qualifications 'it seems to me' and 'as presently advised' in the fourth and fifth sentences — which were intended to reflect the circumstance that the identification of damage for the purposes of an inquiry had not been addressed in the submissions at the substantive hearing, and that I wished to afford Mr Visnic an opportunity to point to anything further in respect of damage that I might have overlooked in the course of preparing the judgment. I did not contemplate that evidence not before the court at the time of the final hearing would be received on the liberty to apply; but as I have said, I accept that there was evidence before me insofar as the payment to the superannuation fund is concerned, and at least in that respect the present application would not have been precluded by the absence of requisite evidence. Nonetheless, what I had in mind was that I might be persuaded that Mr Sywak's fiduciary obligations were more extensive, or that my attention might be drawn to evidence of damage that I might have overlooked in respect of the breaches then found. Evidence and argument

on the present application has not persuaded me on either of those matters to a different position.

[22] Secondly, it is also of some relevance, as Mr M R Aldridge SC points out, that whereas Mr Sywak, in the principal proceedings, proposed that he be afforded an opportunity to buy out Mr Visnic pursuant to *Corporations Act 2001* (Cth), s 233(1)(d) — albeit acknowledging that that would be a much less likely result if, as eventuated, my conclusion was that the shareholdings were in equity equal — Mr Visnic pressed for a winding up order and resisted any suggestion that Mr Sywak should be afforded the opportunity of obtaining alternative remedy. Mr Visnic might have sought, but did not seek, an order under s 233(1)(g) authorising him to institute, prosecute, defend or **[522]** discontinue proceedings in the name and on behalf of any of the companies. This also tells against now allowing him a remedy in the nature of a derivative action in these proceedings.

[23] This result will not leave Mr Visnic without a remedy. First, insofar as breaches of duty to the company are established, the liquidator can pursue them. There is some evidence that the liquidator is investigating those matters, although it obviously cannot be foretold to what extent the liquidator will pursue them. Secondly, if the liquidator does not do so, then Mr Visnic may bring a derivative action pursuant to *Corporations Act* s 236 and s 237, subject to obtaining the leave of the court to do so.[10]

His Honour dismissed [Visnic's] notice of motion. This order disposed of a notice of motion, filed on behalf of [Sywak], seeking that [Visnic's] notice of motion be struck out.

As will appear further below, I agree with his Honour's reasons.

The 'sufficient connection' issue

His Honour's rejection of [Visnic's] case turned on the proposition that no connection had been established between the particular breach of fiduciary duty, which his Honour had found to have occurred, and any matter into which an inquiry for purposes of determining an account of profits was said to be required.

In [123] of his Honour's first judgment which I have set out at [10] above, and to which his Honour made further direct reference at [14] and [21] of his second judgment, set out at [12] and [13] above, his Honour identified two relevant fiduciary duties. Nothing was said to flow from the first, namely the business associates' negotiations, which was a reference to the process by which [Visnic] and [Sywak] acquired their interests in two of the four corporations from the original joint venturers with [Visnic]. It is unnecessary to refer to this matter further. The submissions focused, and focused only, on the beneficial entitlement to the shares in each of the four corporations.

I note that in [123] of his first judgment, his Honour referred to these two particular fiduciary duties in a context where he found that 'at least' these had been breached. His Honour had before him pleadings and submissions which may have suggested the existence of some other kind of fiduciary relationship, for example, with respect to the management of the affairs of the corporation. However, nothing of that character was pressed before his Honour. No additional fiduciary relationship was suggested to

---

10. *Visnic v Sywak* [2008] NSWSC 427 at [17]–[23].

exist in the submissions to this court. There is, as I have said, no appeal from the first judgment.

As set out at [12] above, Brereton J identified in [15] of his second judgment that, in the case of one corporation, there was evidence that [Sywak] had caused funds of that corporation to be paid into his personal superannuation fund. His Honour had before him, prior to the second judgment, additional evidence including the claim made in the winding-up by [Sywak] which, of course, came after his Honour's appointment of a liquidator in the first judgment.

With respect to each of the four corporations, [Sywak] made claims to the liquidator as to funds advanced by him on behalf of those corporations. In these claims he accepted that amounts had to be deducted by reason of payments, in each case, made to him from the funds of the corporation. It does appear that there was evidence in the case of each corporation of a character which, if [Visnic] was otherwise entitled to enforce the remedy of account, [523] could constitute profits for purposes of that remedy. As noted above, his Honour proceeded on the basis that there were such, albeit only with respect to the payment of superannuation funds. It is unnecessary to consider, for present purposes, all of the matters to which [Visnic] referred in this respect. The analysis below applies to each of them.

What is required is the identification of a link between the particular breach of fiduciary duty found to have occurred and a 'profit' capable of being identified. This linkage is often referred to in terms of 'causation'. However, it is more appropriate to use the terminology of the joint judgment of the High Court in *Maguire v Makaronis* (*Maguire*).[11] What is required is 'a sufficient connection (or "causation") between breach of duty and the profit derived'.[12]

The issue before this court is whether there is a 'sufficient connection' between the particular breach found and any matter into which an order for accounts could be said to relevantly inquire. The necessity for such a link, to which it may be convenient, albeit somewhat inaccurate, to refer to as a requirement of causation, has been expressed on a number of occasions in different but equivalent terminology.

The joint judgment in *Maguire* above said:

Where the plaintiff seeks recovery of a profit, the necessary connection has been identified in this court by asking whether the profit was obtained 'by reason of [the defendant's] fiduciary position or by reason of his taking advantage of opportunity or knowledge derived from his fiduciary position'.[13]

The joint judgment in *Warman* said:

A fiduciary must account for a profit or benefit if it was obtained either (1) when there was a conflict or possible conflict between his fiduciary duty and his personal interest, or (2) by reason of his fiduciary position or by reason of his taking advantage of opportunity or knowledge derived from his fiduciary position.[14]

---

11. (1997) 188 CLR 449.
12. *Maguire v Makaronis* (1997) 188 CLR 449 at 468.
13. *Maguire v Makaronis* (1997) 188 CLR 449 at 468 quoting *Warman International Ltd v Dwyer* (1995) 182 CLR 544 at 557.
14. *Warman International Ltd v Dwyer* (1995) 182 CLR 544 at 557.

[Visnic] suggested that an issue raised on this appeal is whether, notwithstanding the reliance on proposition (2) of *Warman* in *Maguire*, proposition (1) can be relied upon as an alternative basis for a 'sufficient connection'.

There are cases in which proposition (1) will apply. This is not such a case. In my opinion, neither proposition applies in this case. [Sywak] held property in trust. The only breach indicated by his Honour's reasons was the refusal to transfer the legal interest when called upon to do so. There is no sufficient connection with any benefit suggested to have been received by [Sywak] from the corporations for purposes of directing an inquiry which could identify and quantify any such a benefit.

Brereton J proceeded on the basis that if a sufficient connection had been suggested to exist between the appropriation of the shareholding and some other benefit to [Sywak], he may have made the orders sought. His Honour gave the example of the payment of a dividend. Other examples of a 'sufficient connection' could be identified, for example, if the shareholding had been used in order to carry into effect a members' voluntary winding-up with a subsequent distribution of assets. His Honour was unable to identify any such connection, nor was any specific matter of this character relied upon in this court.

[524] In oral submissions in this court, [Visnic] suggested that there was a sufficient connection because the appropriation of [Visnic's] shares enabled [Sywak] to control the company and, thereby, make the contested payments.

There may be cases in which appropriation of a shareholding can be said to be sufficiently linked to conduct of the person who, thereby, controls the company. There was no such finding, nor evidence that this was such a case. This court should not make such a finding for the first time. It is quite inconsistent with the case that [Visnic] advanced below.

[Visnic's] case below was that he had always believed that he was entitled to half the shares. Nevertheless, [Sywak] conducted the financial affairs of each company without any relevant intervention, it appears, from [Visnic]. [Sywak] was the accountant of each company and financial matters had been delegated to him.

The primary focus of [Visnic's] submissions was to the effect that his Honour's finding with respect to the deprivation of [Visnic's] interests in the shares should be characterised as a finding that there existed a conflict of interest and duty. [Visnic] submitted that when the matter is characterised at this level of generality, in view of the high public interest which is to be vindicated by enforcing the rights of beneficiaries, his Honour's findings should be taken to establish a sufficient connection for purposes of an inquiry into the extent to which a conflict of interest and duty had manifested itself in the affairs of the four corporations by [Sywak].

[Visnic's] contention that, upon establishing a breach with respect to a particular fiduciary relationship, he was entitled to proceed on the basis that there was a general finding of a conflict of interest and duty should be rejected. When determining what relief is appropriate, it is always necessary to focus upon the particular fiduciary relationship which has been established.

[Visnic's] contention is an example of the fallacy exposed in the frequently cited passage of Fletcher Moulton LJ in *Re Coomber*:

... Fiduciary relations are of many different types ... and the courts have again and again, in cases where there has been a fiduciary relation, interfered and set aside acts which, between persons in a wholly independent position, would have been perfectly valid. Thereupon in some minds there arises the idea that if there is any fiduciary relation whatever any of these types of interference is warranted by it. They conclude that every kind of fiduciary relation justifies every kind of interference. Of course that is absurd. The nature of the fiduciary relation must be such that it justifies the interference. There is no class of case in which one ought more carefully to bear in mind the facts of the case ... than cases which relate to fiduciary and confidential relations and the action of the court with regard to them.[15]

The legal incidents of a person who holds property in trust for another constitute a distinct, well developed body of rules. They cannot be subsumed as merely one example of rules or principles applicable to every relationship to which the appellation fiduciary may be applicable. As the learned authors of *Jacobs' Law of Trusts in Australia* put it: 'The trust is a fiduciary relation, but every fiduciary relation is not a trust',[16] and: 'Trustees and fiduciaries owe different [525] duties, which are breached in different ways, and breaches give rise to different remedies at the suit of different plaintiffs'.[17]

[Visnic's] analysis involves an inappropriately 'high level of abstraction'.[18]

His Honour made no finding that the relevant breach was a conflict of interest and duty. His Honour's reasoning is to the effect that the legal title to the shares had been acquired by [Sywak], but the beneficial title had remained with [Visnic]. As Brereton J said at [14] of his reasons, set out at [12] above: 'The only breach of such duty that I found ... was that Mr Sywak deprived Mr Visnic of this shareholding'. Another way of expressing this breach of a duty is as a failure to transfer the legal title on demand.

In any event, [Visnic's] submissions involve an impermissible elision. Even if there was breach in the sense of a conflict of interest and duty with respect to the shares, that did not involve any breach which would permit an inquiry into whether there had been any other conflicts of that character in conduct which can be seen to be related to the original breach in some way or another. That proposition goes well beyond the bounds of a 'sufficient connection'.

Comment

1. See Radan & Stewart at **15.30–15.31**.

---

15. [1911] 1 Ch 723 at 728–9.
16. J D Heydon and M J Leeming, *Jacobs' Law of Trusts in Australia*, LexisNexis Butterworths, 7th ed, Sydney, 2006 at [202].
17. Heydon & Leeming, *Jacobs' Law of Trusts in Australia*, note 16 above, at [208]. See also *Maguire v Makaronis* (1997) 188 CLR 449 at 473.
18. *Lumbers v W Cook Builders Pty Ltd (in liq)* (2008) 232 CLR 635; *Friend v Brooker* (2009) 255 ALR 601.

Trust and agency

15.4   Olma v Amendola [2004] SASC 274

Court: Full Court of the Supreme Court of South Australia

Facts: Mr and Mrs Amendola were immigrants of Italian descent. After coming into a sum of money from a compensation claim the Amendolas gave $75,000 to Olma (an elderly friend of the couple) after she had offered to take the money and invest on the Amendolas' behalf. The Amendolas argued that the money was held on trust and that interest earned over the period should be accounted for by Olma. Olma argued that she was a gratuitous bailee and that, although she had to repay the original amount, she was not bound to pay back any interest. She argued alternatively that the agreement was a form of *mutuum* or quasi-bailment, where a person borrows personalty for consumption, with an obligation to later replace the personalty with an equivalent amount. The trial judge found that the money was held on trust and ordered interest to be paid. Olma appealed that decision.

Issue: The issue was whether the arrangement between the parties was a trust or a bailment.

Decision: The Full Court (Duggan, Besanko and Anderson JJ) found that the relationship was a trust.

Extracts: In this extract Besanko J examines the characteristics of the relationships of trust and bailment.

Besanko J

1. Interest on the sum of $75,000.00

[42] The [trial] Judge found that the cheque for $75,000.00 was given to [Olma] in August 1985 for the purpose of investment and that the arrangement was that the $75,000.00 would be divided into a tranche of $50,000.00 which would be invested for ten years and a tranche of $25,000.00 which would be invested at call.

[43] [Mr Amendola's] evidence was to the effect that there were representations by [Olma] as to the interest rate which she could earn on the money, whereas [Olma's] evidence was to the effect that [Mr Amendola] said that he did not want interest, that all he wanted to do was hide the money and have it returned after ten years. As I have said, the Judge found that the evidence fell short of establishing an express agreement as to interest and in reaching that conclusion the Judge took into account, as he was entitled to do, the fact that there was no reason why [Olma] would have guaranteed a minimum rate of return as there was nothing in the transaction for her. On the other hand, the Judge found that the [Amendolas] did not forego a right to interest as asserted by [Olma] and in reaching that conclusion the Judge took into account the likelihood that the [Amendolas] would have gratuitously abandoned an annual entitlement to interest of more than $8,000.00. The Judge said it defied commonsense that they would have done

so. [Olma] launched a strong attack on this observation of the Judge. She submitted that the Judge did not act by reference to the evidence, but rather by reference to his own notions of what commonsense demanded. Not only was that wrong as a matter of principle said [Olma], but it was certain to lead to error in the circumstances of this case having regard to the following matters:

1. [Mr Amendola] was accustomed to keeping large sums of cash in his house.
2. [Mr Amendola] wanted to hide the money either because he did not want it to affect the pension he collected, or because he was concerned that if others knew he had the money his daughter might be subjected to threats.

…

[44] [Olma] submitted that the Judge should have found either that there was an express agreement between the parties that [Olma] would not be liable to account for interest, or that there was no agreement about interest and in the circumstances the relationship between the parties was properly characterised as one of bailment or quasi bailment (*mutuum*) rather than trust.

[45] I pause to say something about the submission that the relationship between the parties was one of bailment or quasi bailment.

[46] Two obvious points may be noted at the outset. First, neither party submitted that [Olma] was to be rewarded for the obligations she undertook. Secondly, neither party submitted that the goods in this case, that is, the cheque for $75,000.00 was to be returned to the [Amendolas] in specie. In her written outline on appeal, [Olma] submitted that the relationship was properly characterised as a gratuitous bailment of the *mutuum* category, alternatively it was properly characterised as mandate or deposit. The submission that the relationship was one of mandate or deposit was not pressed during oral submissions on the appeal and it was said that the relationship was one of *mutuum*. In any event in my opinion, the relationship was clearly not one of mandate or deposit. In the case of mandate and deposit, property in the goods does not pass.[19] In the circumstances of this case, it is clear that the legal title in the funds was to pass.

[47] *Mutuum* may be described as a loan of goods for consumption whereby the borrower incurs an obligation to return not the goods that he was given, but the equivalent in quality and quantity. If I borrow a cup of sugar from my neighbour I am obliged to return not the same sugar but rather the equivalent amount in quality and quantity. Goods which may be the subject of a *mutuum* are referred to as fungibles, that is, goods of such a nature that one unit or portion can be replaced by another. *Mutuum* is to be distinguished from a *commodatum* which is a gratuitous loan of goods which are to be returned to the lender. In other words, property in the goods does not pass in the case of a *commodatum* whereas property in the goods does pass in the case of a *mutuum*. *Mutuum* is said to be a form of quasi-bailment. It is not a relationship of bailment.[20]

[48] There are only a few cases dealing with the relationship of *mutuum*. There is a discussion of the distinction between *commodatum* and *mutuum* and the effect of a

---

19. R P Meagher and W M C Gummow, *Jacobs' Law of Trusts in Australia*, 6th ed, Butterworths, Sydney, 1997 at [209].
20. *Chapman Bros v Verco Bros & Co Ltd* (1933) 49 CLR 306, *Halsbury's Laws of England*, vol 2 at [1534].

promise unsupported by consideration by the bailor or quasi-bailor to leave the goods with the bailee or quasi-bailee for a certain period of time in *Parastatidis v Kotaridis*.[21] There is a discussion of the question whether the relationship of *mutuum*, which was recognised in Roman law, is recognised in English law in *Comptroller-General of Customs v Woodlands Enterprises Pty Ltd*.[22] I also refer to the illuminating discussion of the effect of the Roman law on the English law of bailment by Emmett J.[23] [49] I am prepared to assume, without deciding, that a relationship of *mutuum* is recognised in English law. Where the goods are money, contracts of bailment are rare.[24] A relationship of *mutuum* is likely to be very rare.[25] The circumstances surrounding the handing over of money to be replaced later by an equivalent sum of money will often give rise to a loan or a trust, rarely I would think, a relationship of *mutuum*.

[50] I return now to the criticisms of the Judge's reasoning. To approach the matter by ignoring the evidence and finding an obligation to account for interest by reference to what the notion of commonsense suggests would be an error, but that is not how the Judge approached the matter. The Judge was able to find on the evidence that the money was given to [Olma] for her to invest and that the sum of $50,000.00 was to be invested for ten years and the sum of $25,000.00 was to be invested at call. The Judge was unable to make a finding that [Olma] said that she would obtain and pay a particular rate of interest. In assessing whether he should accept [Olma's] evidence that [Mr Amendola] said he did not want interest, the Judge was entitled to consider whether that was likely as a matter of common experience or commonsense bearing in mind the following matters established by the evidence ...

[51] I do not think that there is any error in such an approach.

[52] It is true that a good deal of evidence given by the parties was unsatisfactory and that the onus was on the [Amendolas] to prove their case. However, it was open to the Judge on the evidence to find that the money was given to [Olma] for the purpose of investment, and that of the sum of $75,000.00, the sum of $50,000.00 was to be invested for ten years and the sum of $25,000.00 at call. The fund was to remain the [Amendolas'] property. I think the conclusion of the Judge that in those circumstances there was a trust was correct. On occasions there will be difficulty in distinguishing between a trust relationship and other forms of relationship, but I do not think that this is such a case. [Olma] was given the sum of $75,000.00 for the purpose of investing the money on behalf of the [Amendolas].

Comment

1. See Radan & Stewart at **15.37–15.41**.

---

21. [1978] VR 449.
22. (1995) 128 FLR 113.
23. Emmett, 'Roman Traces in Australian Law' (2001) 20 *Australian Bar Review* 205.
24. N Palmer, *Bailment*, Law Book Company, Sydney, 1979 at pp 105–109.
25. *Brambles Security Services Ltd v Bi-Lo Pty Ltd* (1992) Aust Tort Rep 81-161.

Trusts, charges and conditional dispositions

15.5 Countess of Bective v Federal Commissioner of Taxation (1932) 47 CLR 417

Court: High Court of Australia

Facts: The Countess of Bective's first husband died leaving a sum of money on trust for their infant daughter. The trust required the trustees to give the Countess the net annual income from the fund until the child reached 15 years of age. The money had to be spent on the child's maintenance, education and support. The Commissioner of Taxation had included this annual sum in the Countess' assessable income.

Issue: The issue was whether the sum paid to the Countess as guardian was to be enjoyed by her beneficially, and therefore treated as her income.

Decision: The High Court (sitting with Dixon J as the sole judge) decided that the Countess had been wrongly assessed and that the gift was not part of her assessable income.

Extracts: In this extract Dixon J describes different types of conditional gifts.

Dixon J

[418] When a provision is made by way of gift, testamentary or inter vivos, directing a payment to one person and expressing a purpose beneficial to another or others, it may receive one or other of at least four different interpretations.

(1) The expression of the purpose may be taken as but a statement of the donor's motive or of his expectation. If so, the first person takes the gift absolutely and incurs no legal or equitable obligation to fulfil the purpose.[26]

(2) The purpose may be so stated as to amount to a condition upon and subject to which the first person takes the gift beneficially. By accepting it the donee incurs an equitable duty to perform the [419] condition which is annexed to the gift. If the condition requires a money payment, it must be made whether the property given is or is not adequate for the purpose.[27]

(3) The first person may take the gift beneficially, but the statement of the purpose, particularly if it involves the payment of money, may operate as an equitable charge thereon in favour of the other or others. Bequests and devises to parents for the maintenance and benefit of their children are from their very nature peculiarly

---

26. Examples of such a construction will be found in *Benson v Whittam* (1831) 58 ER 246; *Thorp v Owen* (1831) 58 ER 246; *Webb v Wools* (1852) 61 ER 343; *Byne v Blackburn* (1858) 53 ER 811 at 812; *Scott v Key* (1865) 55 ER 907 (as to the one-third of the estate); *Lambe v Eames* (1871) LR 6 Ch 597; *Mackett v Mackett* (1872) LR 14 Eq 49.

27. See per Lord Cairns in *Attorney-General v Wax Chandlers Co* (1873) LR 6 HL 1 at 19; *Messenger v Andrews* (1828) 38 ER 885.

susceptible of this interpretation. 'Where a fund is bequeathed to a parent, subject to a trust to maintain and educate his children, the surplus will belong to the parent; it is a gift subject to a charge.'[28] It is a construction which, as no exact account of expenditure upon maintenance is required in equity, may be considered to effectuate the intention of a husband who devises or bequeaths property to his wife for the purpose of maintaining their children. His widow is enabled to apply the income towards their joint upkeep as a family and to continue a common establishment. If a testamentary gift is made to a parent for the benefit both of himself and of his children, it appears from the decided cases that such a construction is usually adopted. Whenever a gift is made to one person beneficially, subject to his paying money to another, the provision takes effect as a charge, notwithstanding that words of condition are used, unless an intention clearly appears that it should operate by way of condition. The second object of the disposition thus obtains proprietary and not merely personal rights and is not left in danger of losing the intended benefit through the donee's electing to reject the gift with its attendant condition, rather than to accept it cum onere. Of the decided cases upon dispositions stating a purpose that includes the maintenance or benefit of children, the greater number gives to the provision an operation, which, under one description or another, amounts to a gift subject to a charge. It is, I think, the substantial effect of the view adopted in *Hamley v Gilbert*.[29] **[420]**

(4) The direction to pay the first person may be regarded as conferring no beneficial interest upon him, and, whether he receives it strictly in the character of a trustee or in some other character such as guardian, the expression of the purpose may amount to a statement of objects to which he is bound to apply the fund. Gifts providing for the maintenance of children appear to have received this interpretation in *Wetherell v Wilson*;[30] *In re Yates; Yates v Wyatt*[31] and perhaps in *Leach v Leach*[32] and *In re Morgan*.[33]

But an obligation to apply moneys in the maintenance of children or others does not involve the liability which arises from an ordinary trust. It is a general rule that guardians of infants, committees of the person of lunatics, and others who are entrusted with funds to be expended in the maintenance and support of persons under their care are not liable to account as trustees. They need not vouch the items of their expenditure, and, if they

---

28. G Spence, *The Equitable Jurisdiction of the Court of Chancery*, V & R Stevens and G S Norton, London, 1849, vol II, p 466.

29. (1821) 37 ER 885 at 887; *Berkeley v Swinburne* (1834) 58 ER 723; *Woods v Woods* (1836) 1 40 ER 429 at 432; *Hadow v Hadow* (1838) 59 ER 426 at 428; *Gilbert v Bennett* (1839) 59 ER 658; *Raikes v Ward* (1842) 66 ER 1106 at 1108; *Thorp v Owen* (1843) 67 ER 252; *Longmore v Elcum* (1843) 63 ER 160 at 163–4 (reservation by Knight Bruce VC of the question whether the children took under the equivalent of a charge or as joint tenants); *Crockett v Crockett* (1848) 41 ER 1057 at 1060; *Browne v Paull* (1850) 61 ER 36 at 40–41; *Carr v Living* (1860) 54 ER 514; *Berry v Briant* (1862) 2 62 ER 521 at 523 (as to two-thirds of the estate); *Scott v Key* (1865) 55 ER 907; *In re Booth; Booth v Booth* (1894) 2 Ch 282; *In re G (Infants)* (1899) 1 Ch 719 at 724–5. See also per Lord Selborne in *Cunningham v Foot* (1878) 3 App Cas 974 at 1002 and Chitty J in *Re Oliver; Newbald v Beckitt* (1890) 62 LT 533 at 535.

30. (1836) 48 ER 237.

31. (1901) 2 Ch 438.

32. (1843) 60 ER 118.

33. (1883) 24 Ch D 114.

fulfil the obligation of maintenance in a manner commensurate with the [421] income available to them for the purpose, an account will not be taken. Often the person to be maintained is a member of a family enjoying the advantages of a common establishment; always the end in view is to supply the daily wants of an individual, to provide for his comfort, edification and amusement, and to promote his happiness. It would defeat the very purpose for which the fund is provided, if its administration were hampered by the necessity of identifying, distinguishing, apportioning and recording every item of expenditure and vindicating its propriety. Although these considerations furnish an independent foundation for the general rule, yet, after all, it is a doctrine regulating the application of moneys payable under an instrument, whether a will, a settlement or an order of a Court of equity, and the operation of the doctrine must depend upon the provisions contained in the instrument, both express and implied. But the effect of the instrument will often be governed by the circumstances to which it was intended to apply, and, in particular, by a consideration of the nature of the actual abode, the condition of the household and the state of the family of the infant or other person to be maintained. Courts of equity have not disguised the fact that the general rule gives to a parent or guardian dispensing the fund an opportunity of gaining incidental benefits, but the nature and extent of the advantages permitted must depend peculiarly upon the intention ascribed to the instrument. *Brown v Smith*[34] describes conditions which may be contemplated by an order of the Court, and they are material also to the meaning and operation of other instruments providing for maintenance. Statements to be found in some authorities that any surplus remaining after adequate maintenance has been provided belongs to the person having the care of the infant or of the lunatic cannot be safely used unless careful attention is given to the scope and purpose of the instrument under which the moneys arise and the conditions to which its operation is directed ...

A guardian is not permitted to receive moneys for maintenance without liability to account except upon the condition that he discharges his duty adequately to maintain and not otherwise. Upon his default the Court will administer the fund or intercept the payments and has jurisdiction to order an account or an inquiry.[35] Where, however, the condition is performed the Court does not inquire whether the money has been completely expended or whether the recipient has spent small sums for his personal benefit, but, nevertheless, it [423] remains an allowance to a person in a fiduciary capacity and for a definite purpose ...

In the present case the question is not whether the taxpayer is a trustee for the purpose of assessment. The trustees of the instrument certainly come, if she does not, within the meaning of the definition of 'trustee'. The question is whether the payments to her form part of her assessable income. The income of the trust fund appears to have been included in the taxpayer's assessment upon the view that she took it beneficially, the statement of the purpose contained in the provision for maintenance amounting to

---

34. (1878) 10 Ch D 377 at 380–2.
35. *In re Oldfield* (1828) 2 Molloy 294; *Leach v Leach* (1843) 60 ER 120; *Browne v Paull* (1850) 61 ER 40; *Re Dalton* (1852) 42 ER 554 at 557; *Castle v Castle* (1857) 44 ER 759 at 762; *Carr v Living* (1860) 54 ER 514 at 515; *Hora v Hora* (1863) 55 ER 300; *In re Weld* (1882) 20 Ch D 451 at 457; *In re Morgan* (1883) 24 Ch D 114 at 116–7; *In re Evans; Welch v Channell* (1884) 26 Ch D 58 at 64; *Macrae v Harness* (1910) 103 LT 629 at 631.

no more than an expression of the donor's motive, or of his expectation. Its inclusion [424] in her assessable income could be supported, if the statement of the purpose were understood as annexing to a gift to her a condition which she was bound to perform. Possibly, it might be supported also if the provision were construed as a gift of income to the taxpayer subject to a charge for maintenance. But if either of these two constructions were adopted, a corresponding deduction should be allowed for expenditure upon maintenance, a deduction which would not, of course, necessarily amount to the same sum. On the other hand, if she is not an object intended to be benefited at all by the provision for maintenance, the payments ought not, in my opinion, to be included as assessable income of the taxpayer, although, if it appeared that she had appropriated to her own use an unexpended surplus after discharging her duty of maintaining her daughter, that surplus would be taxable as part of her income.

The instrument providing for maintenance is an indenture. None of the circumstances in which it was made appears, and its meaning and operation must be ascertained, so to speak, in the abstract. It is expressed to be made between the father, who is referred to as 'the settlor' of the one part and the trustees of the other part. The property settled consists of shares in two trading companies. The instrument begins with a recital of the settlor's desire to make provision in manner thereinafter appearing for his daughter, who is referred to as 'the beneficiary'. The first of the trusts declared operates until the beneficiary reaches fifteen years of age and contains the provision for maintenance out of which this appeal arises. Before stating its terms, it is convenient to describe the trusts to operate thereafter. When the beneficiary attains the age of fifteen the income of the trust is to be paid or applied by the trustees at their discretion to the beneficiary for her maintenance, education and benefit until she attains the age of twenty-one. Thereafter the trustees stand possessed of corpus and income for the beneficiary absolutely. If she die[s] before attaining full age leaving a child or children who attain full age, or, being daughters, marry, the trust is for such child or children absolutely. But if the beneficiary die[s] before attaining full age without leaving any child who obtains a vested interest, then the trust is for the taxpayer [425] for life and after her death for the children then living of the settlor as tenants in common.

By the terms of the first trust of the instrument, the trustees are required until the beneficiary attains the age of fifteen years to pay to the taxpayer the net annual income of the trust at such time and in such manner as the trustees shall determine for the maintenance, education and support of the beneficiary, and, in the event of the death of the taxpayer before the beneficiary attains that age, to pay the net annual income to the guardian or guardians of the beneficiary in manner aforesaid for the maintenance, support and education of the beneficiary, and the trustees are to be under no obligation to see to the application of the net annual income by the taxpayer, or by the guardian or guardians. It is to be noticed that, excluding this clause from consideration, the only provision contained in the settlement in favour of the taxpayer is a limitation over upon the entire failure of the trusts declared in favour of the daughter of the settlor and her possible children. The recital and the description of the daughter as 'the beneficiary' establish that she was the object of the settlement. The provision, which, upon her daughter's reaching the age of fifteen, terminates the taxpayer's dispensation and requires the trustee to undertake the payment or application of the income to the beneficiary for her maintenance, education and benefit, suggests that no other reason than the tenderness of the girl's age actuated the settlor in directing payment to her mother or her guardian until that time. In the clause containing this direction there is no difference in the forms of expression used in requiring the trustees to pay the income to the taxpayer and in requiring them to pay it to the guardian if the taxpayer should die. Upon these grounds, I conclude that the taxpayer is not a beneficial object of the provision for maintenance, but is chosen, as is the guardian after her death, as an appropriate person to dispense the income belonging to the child for her benefit. In establishing this conclusion I think the taxpayer has discharged the burden of showing that the assessment was wrong in including the entire sum received by the taxpayer under the settlement as her assessable income. But, in the absence of any information as [426] to the taxpayer's actual expenditure upon the purpose for which she receives the income, I shall do no more than remit the assessment to the Commissioner.

Comments

1. See Radan & Stewart at **15.71–15.79**.
2. The Countess of Bective was originally Elsie (later 'Elise') Florence Tucker, a Sydney typist. She married Sir Rupert Turner Havelock Clarke, the 2nd Baronet of Rupertswood, when she was 22 years old and when he was 53. She was Sir Rupert's second wife. Sir Rupert died in 1926. In 1928 Elise married Terence Geoffrey Thomas Taylour, who was at that time the Earl of Bective, and later, the 5th Marquess of Headford. During the Second World War she was an advocate for the creation of an Australian women's land army and air force. She died on 16 May 1972.

   The Baronetcy of Rupertswood is the only Australian hereditary title. It was created by Queen Victoria when she made Sir Rupert's father, Sir William John Clarke, the 1st Baronet for his charitable work in Victoria.

   The infant beneficiary mentioned in the case was Elizabeth Elsie Faith Clarke, who was born in 1924. She now lives in Norfolk, England.

Trust and debt

15.6   Barclays Bank Ltd v Quistclose Investments Ltd
[1970] AC 567

Court: House of Lords

Facts: Rolls Razor Ltd (Rolls Razor), under the control of the colourful and notorious entrepreneur John Bloom, advertised and, on hire purchase terms, sold cheap twin-tub washing machines directly to the public. In due course it became heavily indebted to Barclays Bank (the bank). Rolls Razor borrowed money from Quistclose Investments Ltd (Quistclose), a company controlled by Bloom. The money was sent to the bank for deposit in a special bank account with a covering letter, dated 15 July 1964, in which Rolls Razor stated that the money 'will only be used to meet the dividend' to be paid to its shareholders and which had been previously been approved by Rolls Razor. However, a few days later while Bloom was holidaying in Bulgaria and before the dividend was paid, Rolls Razor went into voluntary liquidation. The collapse of Rolls Razor meant that the dividend could not be paid as the shareholders now became postponed to Rolls Razor's ordinary creditors. The bank claimed the money was available as a set-off against Rolls Razor's indebtedness to it. Quistclose sought to retrieve the money and claimed that the bank had no right to use the loan funds as a set-off.

Issues: The issue before the House of Lords was whether the loan funds from Quistclose were, in these circumstances, held on trust for Quistclose or whether they were part of Rolls Razor's assets on liquidation. If it was the former, and the bank had notice of the trust, the bank had no claim to any of the loan funds.

Decision: The House of Lords (Lords Reid, Morris of Borth-y-Gest, Guest, Pearce and Wilberforce) unanimously ruled in favour of Quistclose. The loan to Rolls Razor from Quistclose was for a mutually agreed purpose that failed and, as a consequence, Rolls Razor held the loan funds on trust for Quistclose. The bank, having knowledge of all relevant facts, was held to be constructive trustee of the funds for Quistclose. In coming to its decision in this case the House of Lords made it clear that one set of facts can give rise to the co-existence of a debt and a trust.

Extracts: The extract from the speech of Lord Wilberforce, with whom the other Law Lords agreed, discusses the idea of a loan for a special purpose which creates a trust with primary and secondary arms.

Lord Wilberforce

[579] Two questions arise, both of which must be answered favourably to [Quistclose] if they are to recover the money from the bank. The first is whether, as between [Quistclose] and Rolls Razor Ltd the terms on which the loan was made were such as to impress on the sum of £209,719 8s 6d a trust in their favour in the event of the dividend not being paid. The second is whether, in that event, the bank had such notice of the trust or of the circumstances giving rise to it as to make the trust binding on them.

It is not difficult to establish precisely on what terms the money was advanced by [Quistclose] to Rolls Razor Ltd. There is no doubt that [580] the loan was made specifically in order to enable Rolls Razor Ltd to pay the dividend. There is equally, in my opinion, no doubt that the loan was made only so as to enable Rolls Razor Ltd to pay the dividend and for no other purpose. This follows quite clearly from the terms of the letter of Rolls Razor Ltd to the bank of July 15, 1964, which letter, before transmission to the bank, was sent to [Quistclose] under open cover in order that the cheque might be (as it was) enclosed in it. The mutual intention of [Quistclose] and of Rolls Razor Ltd, and the essence of the bargain, was that the sum advanced should not become part of the assets of Rolls Razor Ltd, but should be used exclusively for payment of a particular class of its creditors, namely, those entitled to the dividend. A necessary consequence from this, by process simply of interpretation, must be that if, for any reason, the dividend could not be paid, the money was to be returned to [Quistclose]: the word 'only' or 'exclusively' can have no other meaning or effect.

That arrangements of this character for the payment of a person's creditors by a third person, give rise to a relationship of a fiduciary character or trust, in favour, as a primary trust, of the creditors, and secondarily, if the primary trust fails, of the third person, has been recognised in a series of cases over some 150 years.

In *Toovey v Milne* part of the money advanced was, on the failure of the purpose for which it was lent (viz, to pay certain debts), repaid by the bankrupt to the person who had advanced it. On action being brought by the assignee of the bankrupt to recover it, the plaintiff was nonsuited and the nonsuit was upheld on a motion for a retrial. In his judgment Abbott CJ said:

> I thought at the trial, and still think, that the fair inference from the facts proved was that this money was advanced for a special purpose, and that being so clothed with a specific trust, no property in it passed to the assignee of the bankrupt. Then the purpose having failed, there is an implied stipulation, that the money shall be repaid. That has been done in the present case; and I am of opinion that that repayment was lawful, and that the nonsuit was right.[36]

The basis for the decision was thus clearly stated, viz, that the money advanced for the specific purpose did not become part of the bankrupt's estate. This case has been repeatedly followed and applied.[37] ... In [*In re Rogers*], the money provided by the third party had been paid to the creditors before the bankruptcy. Afterwards the trustee in bankruptcy sought to recover it. It was held that the money was advanced to the bankrupt for the special purpose of enabling his creditors to be paid, was impressed with a trust for the purpose and never became the property of the bankrupt. Lindley LJ[38] decided the case on principle but said that if authority was needed it would be found in *Toovey v Milne* and other cases. Bowen LJ[39] said that the money came to the bankrupt's hands impressed with a trust and did not become the property of the bankrupt [581] divisible amongst his creditors, and the judgment of Kay LJ[40] was to a similar effect.

These cases have the support of longevity, authority, consistency and, I would add, good sense. But they are not binding on your Lordships and it is necessary to consider such arguments as have been put why they should be departed from or distinguished.

It is said, first, that the line of authorities mentioned above stands on its own and is inconsistent with other, more modern, decisions. Those are cases in which money has been paid to a company for the purpose of obtaining an allotment of shares.[41] I do not think it necessary to examine these cases in detail, nor to comment on them, for I am satisfied that they do not affect the principle on which this appeal should be decided.

---

36. *Toovey v Milne* (1819) 106 ER 514 at 515.
37. See *Edwards v Glyn* (1859) 121 ER 12; *In Re Rogers, Ex p Holland and Hannen* (1891) 8 Morr 243; *In re Drucker (No 1)* [1902] 2 KB 237; *In re Hooley, Ex parte Trustee* [1915] HBR 181.
38. *In Re Rogers, Ex p Holland and Hannen* (1891) 8 Morr 243 at 248.
39. *In Re Rogers, Ex p Holland and Hannen* (1891) 8 Morr 243 at 248.
40. *In Re Rogers, Ex p Holland and Hannen* (1891) 8 Morr 243 at 249.
41. See *Moseley v Cressey's Co* (1865) LR 1 Eq 405; *Stewart v Austin* (1866) LR 3 Eq 299; *In re Nanwa Gold Mines Ballantyne v Nanwa Gold Mines Ltd* [1955] 1 WLR 1080.

They are merely examples which show that, in the absence of some special arrangement creating a trust ..., payments of this kind are made on the basis that they are to be included in the company's assets. They do not negative the proposition that a trust may exist where the mutual intention is that they should not be included.

The second, and main, argument for the [bank] was of a more sophisticated character. The transaction, it was said, between [Quistclose] and Rolls Razor Ltd was one of loan, giving rise to a legal action of debt. This necessarily excluded the implication of any trust, enforceable in equity, in [Quistclose's] favour: a transaction may attract one action or the other, it could not admit of both.

My Lords, I must say that I find this argument unattractive. Let us see what it involves. It means that the law does not permit an arrangement to be made by which one person agrees to advance money to another, on terms that the money is to be used exclusively to pay debts of the latter, and if, and so far as not so used, rather than becoming a general asset of the latter available to his creditors at large, is to be returned to the lender. The lender is obliged, in such a case, because he is a lender, to accept, whatever the mutual wishes of lender and borrower may be, that the money he was willing to make available for one purpose only shall be freely available for others of the borrower's creditors for whom he has not the slightest desire to provide.

I should be surprised if an argument of this kind — so conceptualist in character — had ever been accepted. In truth it has plainly been rejected by the eminent judges who from 1819 onwards have permitted arrangements of this type to be enforced, and have approved them as being for the benefit of creditors and all concerned. There is surely no difficulty in recognising the co-existence in one transaction of legal and equitable rights and remedies: when the money is advanced, the lender acquires an equitable right to see that it is applied for the primary designated purpose (see *In Re Rogers* where both Lindley and Kay LJJ explicitly recognised this): when the purpose has been carried out (ie, the debt paid) the lender has his remedy against the borrower in debt: if the primary purpose cannot be carried out, the question arises if a secondary purpose (ie, repayment to the lender) has been agreed, expressly or by implication: if it has, the remedies of equity may be invoked to give effect to it, if it has not (and **[582]** the money is intended to fall within the general fund of the debtor's assets) then there is the appropriate remedy for recovery of a loan. I can appreciate no reason why the flexible interplay of law and equity cannot let in these practical arrangements, and other variations if desired: it would be to the discredit of both systems if they could not. In the present case the intention to create a secondary trust for the benefit of the lender, to arise if the primary trust, to pay the dividend, could not be carried out, is clear and I can find no reason why the law should not give effect to it.

I pass to the second question, that of notice ... I am prepared, for this purpose, to accept, by way of assumption, the position most favourable to the bank, ie, that it is necessary to show that the bank had notice of the trust, or of the circumstances giving rise to the trust, at the time when they received the money, viz, on July 15, 1964, and that notice on a later date, even though they had not in any real sense given value when they received the money or thereafter changed their position, will not do. It is common ground, and I think right, that a mere request to put the money into a separate account is not sufficient to constitute notice. But on July 15, 1964, the bank, when they received the cheque, also received the covering letter of that date … ; previously there had been the telephone conversation between [a director of Rolls Razor Ltd and a manager of the bank] … From these there is no doubt that the bank was told that the money had been provided on loan by a third person and was to be used only for the purpose of paying the dividend. This was sufficient to give them notice that it was trust money and not assets of Rolls Razor Ltd: the fact, if it be so, that they were unaware of the lenders' identity (though [Quistclose's] name as drawers was on the cheque) is of no significance. I may add to this, as having some bearing on the merits of the case, that it is quite apparent from earlier documents that the bank were aware that Rolls Razor Ltd could not provide the money for the dividend and that this would have to come from an outside source and that they never contemplated that the money so provided could be used to reduce the existing overdraft. They were in fact insisting that other or additional arrangements should be made for that purpose. As was appropriately said by Russell LJ,[42] it would be giving a complete windfall to the bank if they had established a right to retain the money.

Comments

1. See Radan & Stewart at **15.53–15.65**.
2. Lord Wilberforce spoke of the need for there to be a mutual intention between the lender and borrower for the co-existence of a trust and debt to arise. However, in *Re Kayford Ltd* [1975] 1 All ER 604 at 607, it was held that the intention of either would be sufficient. In that case only the recipient of the money had the intention that the money be held on trust if the purpose for which the money was paid failed. This is discussed in Radan & Stewart at **16.26–16.29**.
3. For analysis of the case see W Swadling (ed), *The Quistclose Trust: Critical Essays*, Hart Publishing, Oxford, 2004.
4. John Bloom's marketing of washing machines was a key event in revolutionising the retailing of household durables in Britain in the late 1950s and early 1960s. As Anthony Sampson has observed: 'His enterprise compelled his conservative rivals to abandon the gentlemanly pursuit of small markets with large profit-margins in favour of the more risky but lucrative pursuit of mass markets with small margins': A Sampson, *Anatomy of Britain Today*, Hodder & Stoughton, London, 1965, p 558. In relation to Bloom's career following the collapse of Rolls Razor, Robert Stevens writes as follows: 'He ran a number of clubs, including the Crazy Horse Saloon in the West End of London, where he had a notorious affair with a waitress, the implausibly named Miss Lovebody. He appears to have been forced out by a gangster, Jo Wilkins. In 1972, he opened a chain of Merrie England restaurants around Los Angeles. His house was raided by the FBI, and in March 1979 he was

---

42. *Quistclose Investments Ltd v Rolls Razor Ltd (in Liquidation)* [1968] Ch 540 at 563.

given a suspended sentence for making pirated video copies of the film *Star Wars*. He then left for Majorca, where he opened a bar/restaurant. Here the trail goes cold': R Stevens, 'Rolls Razor Ltd' in W Swadling (ed), *The Quistclose Trust: Critical Essays*, Hart Publishing, Oxford, 2004, p 7. Bloom's own account of his life is found in J Bloom, *It's No Sin to Make a Profit*, W H Allen, London 1971.

5. The *Quistclose* trust is a difficult creature to classify: see Radan & Stewart at **15.60–15.65**. Various theories at classification include an express trust with two limbs, a resulting trust, or a transfer with a personal obligation attached: see J Glister, 'The Nature of Quistclose Trust: Classification and Reconcilitation' (2004) 63 *Cambridge Law Journal* 632. Glister, at 633, states:

> … these theories as to the nature of the *Quistclose* trust are not necessarily mutually exclusive and that there is no single 'right answer': the finding of an express trust in one *Quistclose*-type situation would not preclude the finding of a resulting trust in another. As mentioned above, classification and an analysis of the parties' agreement necessarily inform each other: depending on that agreement it may in any given situation be more appropriate to categorise the relationship as that of express trust, resulting trust, or of no trust at all.

Trusts and personal equitable obligations

15.7   Hammond v Hammond [2007] NSWSC 106

Court: Supreme Court of New South Wales

Facts: Donald John Hammond died in 2005. He was divorced but had three adult children: Luke, Chere and John. John was a person with Down's Syndrome and was cared for by his mother Sabina, Donald's ex-wife.

Donald made a holographic will, which is a will which is entirely handwritten and signed (but not witnessed). Probate was granted to Donald's brother, Terry, who received the bulk of the estate. Part of the will read:

> To my children Luke, Chere & John I bequeath to each the sum of $100 (one hundred dollars) each. They never concerned themselves about me when alive so I consider in death they should not worry. I loved them dearly & I cannot understand why they treated me so brutally. The remainder of my estate is to go to my brother on the condition that he ensures John my youngest son never wants for anything. I further request that in caring for John his mother Sabina will never have access to any of my money. I will not place a caveat on Terry regarding the family home. Dad never wanted it to be sold — I leave the decision to Terry. I may see you all in paradise. Love Don XXX.

Donald's estate was worth approximately $650,000. The three children had lodged family provisions claims to seek a greater part of the estate. The claims involving Luke and Chere were settled, but questions remained about the entitlements of John.

Issue: The issue was whether Terry was under a personal equitable obligation to provide for John so that he 'never wanted for anything'.

Decision: Young CJ in Eq reviewed the authorities and came to a tentative conclusion that there was a personal equitable obligation imposed by the holographic will on Terry to provide for John. However, counsel were asked to provide further submissions before Young CJ made a final determination.

Extracts: In the extract Young CJ examines the authorities relating to the creation of personal equitable obligations.

Young CJ in Eq

[10] The basic question to be asked in this case with respect to the first stage is whether the provision for [John] in the will that his uncle Terry is under an enforceable equitable obligation to ensure that John never wants for anything is a proper provision for John.

[11] The High Court in *Singer v Berghouse*[43] said:

> The determination of the first stage in the two-stage process calls for an assessment of whether the provision (if any) made was inadequate for what, in all the circumstances, was the proper level of maintenance etc appropriate for the applicant having regard, amongst other things, to the applicant's financial position, the size and nature of the deceased's estate, the totality of the relationship between the applicant and the deceased, and the relationship between the deceased and other persons who have legitimate claims upon his or her bounty.

[12] The condition imposed on [Terry] could not be said to constitute a trust. The question is whether it is sufficient to amount to an enforceable equitable condition. That is not a condition of forfeiture but a condition which a court of equity would, in order to govern the conscience of [Terry], enforce by way of injunction or an order for equitable compensation.

[13] *Jacobs' Law of Trusts*[44] truly says:

> There is also the class of case where the condition relates to the enjoyment of the property by the donee after accepting it. In such cases, the gift may be construed as imposing a personal equitable obligation on the donee to make the necessary payment to such other person ... In so far as the gift is construed as imposing a personal equitable obligation on the donee, it is directly enforceable in equity by that other person, who,

---

43. (1994) 181 CLR 201 at 209–10.
44. Heydon & Leeming, *Jacobs' Law of Trusts in Australia*, note 16 above, at [234].

unlike a cestui que trust or chargee, has no rights in rem against the property, but, unlike a mere chargee, has a personal right against the donee ...

[14] *Jacobs* says:[45]

It is submitted that in the case of such a personal equitable obligation the rights of the obligee could, paradoxically, in some circumstances be greater than those of a cestui que trust or mere chargee, in that the donee of the property could be required to perform the obligation even if it cost the donee more than the value of the property.

[15] The situation appears to be that [Terry] seems to have accepted the property and the obligation to care for John. I use the word 'seems' because there was very little argument put to me about whether the condition in the will amounted to an equitable personal obligation. What was put to me was that the moral obligation of the defendant to care for John was sufficient provision. In the last part of the cross-examination and in re-examination, [Terry] said that he was committed to providing money for John provided that Ms Sabina Hammond, John's mother, was nowhere near the funds passing from the estate to John. [Terry] said that was what was in the will. In re-examination he was asked whether he had received any application on behalf of John for the payment or the use of any of the monies of the estate. He answered 'No' and then was asked:

Q — If bona fide representations were put to you, of either receipts or invoices would you consider them and if appropriate pay them?

A — Most certainly, if they were considered necessary to John I would have paid them.

He also indicated that although he felt there would be some difficulties in he and Sabina Hammond agreeing on many matters, he would be prepared to discuss John's problems or needs with her.

[16] In my view the mere fact that [Terry] was under a moral obligation to John would not be proper provision for John because circumstances could easily change and relationships sour. However, it would seem to me that if there was an equitable personal obligation on [Terry] to use the money, then proper provision would have been made for John because virtually the whole estate, or even after the orders in favour of the other children a substantial portion of the estate, would be protected. Indeed, I would agree with what *Jacobs*[46] says and that is, that if [Terry] accepted the property it may well be that he would be obliged to pay out for John even more than the value of the estate.

[17] The question then is whether the so-called condition in the will amounts to a binding equitable personal obligation.

[18] The leading Australian case is the decision of Harvey J in *Gill v Gill*.[47]

[19] In that case the defendant had been given by the testator the testator's farm at Dumaresq Island on the Manning River 'on condition that he keep the homestead as a home and provide board and residence for his sisters'. Harvey J said and following that the question before him was whether the condition was too vague and uncertain to be enforced.[48] However, he distinguished between conditions of forfeiture where the court

---

45. Heydon & Leeming, *Jacobs' Law of Trusts in Australia*, note 16 above, at [238].
46. Heydon & Leeming, *Jacobs' Law of Trusts in Australia*, note 16 above, at [238].
47. (1921) 21 SR (NSW) 400.
48. (1921) 21 SR (NSW) 400 at 406.

requires certainty so it is possible at any given moment to say where the estate is vested and conditions in equity setting out a personal obligation. In the latter class of case there is a personal obligation that flows from the equitable doctrine that a person cannot approbate and reprobate under the same instrument. In such a case there is no higher degree of certainty than that required for the creation of a trust. His Honour considered that in *Gill's case* he should declare the equitable obligation but was not satisfied that any loss had been suffered by the plaintiff as at that point of time.

[20] The nature of these conditions was considered by Brennan J in a dissenting judgment, though one which is non controversial so far as principle is concerned, in *Muschinski v Dodds*[49] and following. In that case a de facto couple purchased a piece of real estate at Picton. The woman put in the majority of the purchase money, but the man promised to put in the proceeds of his divorce settlement which were thought to be substantial (but in fact were not) and do certain work. Brennan J said:

> A condition annexed to a gift may be either of two kinds: a condition involving a forfeiture for non-fulfilment or a condition creating merely a personal obligation to fulfil it. A donee who takes a gift to which a condition of the latter kind is annexed incurs an equitable obligation to perform the condition ... A condition which creates a personal obligation may be enforced in equity by an order for compensation or, where appropriate, by a decree of specific performance ...[50]

...

[22] The nature of these conditions was again examined by White J in *Re Boning*.[51] So far as is relevant for the present case, the gift was to Greenpeace Australia Ltd upon condition that the monies be used for Greenpeace International activities. Her Honour found that this was an enforceable equitable condition.

[23] The key problem in the instant case is whether the words 'on condition that he ensures John ... never wants for anything' are sufficiently certain to be enforced by the court as an equitable personal obligation. It is clear from the cases, particularly *Gill v Gill*, that the degree of certainty required is not as great as when one is dealing with a condition of forfeiture. However, there are boundaries which have been noted in *Gill v Gill* as the same as that required for the creation of a trust. One needs therefore to go to the cases to see more precisely where the boundary is to be drawn.

[24] Many of the reported cases (and there are not many reported cases in this area) deal with situations where the condition was that the donee pay money to a third party so, in *Re Hodge*[52] the testatrix gave her estate to her husband on condition that he pay an annuity to her sister; see also *Rees v Engelbach*.[53]

[25] In *Re Williames*[54] the English Court of Appeal had to deal with a will where the testator gave his real property to a series of life tenants on condition that they effect repairs. His widow was the first life tenant and it was admitted that she failed to keep

---

49. (1985) 160 CLR 583 at 599.
50. (1985) 160 CLR 583 at 605.
51. [1997] 2 Qd R 12.
52. [1940] Ch 260.
53. (1871) LR 12 Eq 225.
54. (1885) 54 LT 105.

the premises in repair, but it was argued that she was not liable for permissive waste. However, Kay J at first instance and the Court of Appeal held that it was a condition; she had accepted the gift and she had to pay.

[26] In *Re Moore*[55] the gift was to the executor 'in trust for my sisters Margaret ... Caroline ... and Helen ... on condition that they will support Maria Moore ... They are hereby enjoined to take care of my nephew John ... as may seem best in the future'.

[27] Kay J held that the condition to support Maria Moore was sufficiently definite. However, when contrasted with the condition to Maria Moore, the words of the second condition, 'as may seem best in the future' were too vague.

[28] That case is to be contrasted with a case referred to by Kay J, namely *Broad v Bevan*.[56] The will there provided:

> I give and bequeath unto my daughter Ann ... the sum of £5 a year for her life ... I also order and direct my son Joseph to take care of and provide for my said daughter Ann during her life.

[29] Joseph was the executor and residuary legatee. It was argued that as the amount to be paid by Joseph to take care of and provide for Ann was uncertain, the direction that Joseph take care of Ann failed. However, Plumer MR referred the matter to the Master to enquire what would have been the proper maintenance for Ann and, the Master having certified it was six shillings per week, he made an order in that amount. This was confirmed by Lord Gifford MR.

[30] In *Abraham v Alman*[57] the will provided that Isaac Jacobs was to have £60 per year, but was to provide for two of the testator's granddaughters, Sarah and Esther. The tutor for Sarah and Esther moved that the administrator be directed to pay them such sum as might be considered adequate for their maintenance. Lord Gifford MR held that the benefaction was too uncertain and distinguished *Broad v Bevan* on the basis that *Broad v Bevan* involved a direction that the donee take care of and provide for the plaintiff.

[31] In *Batt v Anns*[58] the will provided that the testator left his illegitimate son, Thomas under the protection of his wife, Ann, to be by her apprenticed and taken care of, and to be provided for to the best of her judgment, as long as the said Ann remains unmarried. It was held by the Lord Chancellor that the son was entitled to maintenance out of the testator's estate if the estate were sufficient and ordered an enquiry as to its sufficiency. See also *Jackson v Hamilton*.[59]

[32] The cases were considered in New Zealand in *Re SBH*.[60] The testator, an American, had bigamously married another woman in Bermuda whilst his first wife was still alive. In his will he made the following provision for his bigamous wife (whom he had by then divorced):

---

55. (1886) 55 LJ Ch 418.
56. (1823) 38 ER 198.
57. (1826) 38 ER 196.
58. (1841) 11 LJ Ch 52.
59. (1846) 9 Irish Equity R 430; 3 Jo & Lat 702.
60. [1936] NZLR 756.

I wish my trustees to make such provision for her maintenance as the exigencies of the funds will permit and requiring the beneficiaries to contribute to her support.

[33] Ostler J said:

If the will had merely provided for the maintenance of CMH, then I think the bequest would have been good upon the principle that *id certum est quod certum reddi protest*: see *Broad v Bevan; Jackson v Hamilton*; and *Batt v Anns*; but in this case, assuming the word 'wish' is a word of direction, the duty cast upon the trustee is not to make provision for her maintenance out of the estate, but to make such provision for her maintenance as the exigencies of the fund will permit.[61]

His Honour held that that was too uncertain.

[34] The case is to my mind a borderline one.

...

[36] In the instant case, the matter was heard as part of a running list of *Family Provision Act* applications. Despite the fact that experienced counsel appeared on both sides, and despite the fact that I raised the matter of a *Gill v Gill* condition during closing submissions, no submissions were put to me on the point at all.

[37] My analysis of the authorities indicates to me that it is more likely than not that the present will does express an enforceable *Gill v Gill* condition. However, I do not wish to come to a final decision on the point without giving counsel time to have the matter further argued or to make further written submissions if they or either of them so wish.

[38] If the condition is a proper *Gill v Gill* condition and enforceable, the next question is whether [Terry] has accepted the gift. If he has accepted the gift (and as I indicated earlier it seems that he has), then if *Jacobs* is correct ... then [Terry] is bound to support John even over and above the estate assets.

[39] If the condition is an enforceable *Gill v Gill* condition and the gift has been accepted by [Terry], then there has been no failure to provide for John as he has as much out of the estate as he can get (subject to the legacies to be given by consent order to his siblings which his counsel does not oppose). Accordingly, he has not jumped the first hurdle of the two-stage process and the Family Provision Act proceedings must be dismissed. I would think, however (again without having heard counsel) that I would do so without an order for costs.

[40] If there has not been an acceptance of the gift, then as there is no residue clause, presumably there would be a partial intestacy with the result, I think, that the estate would pass to the three children in equal shares, so that each would get something like $210,000. This is more than Luke and Chere were prepared to take by way of settlement so that their proceedings would presumably have to be dismissed. The question would then be whether $210,000 was sufficient provision for the plaintiff John.

[41] My current thinking, and in this I have been assisted by submissions of counsel, is that even that amount would have been insufficient. Accordingly, I would then have to go to the second stage of the two-stage process.

---

61. [1936] NZLR 756 at 758.

[42] My present thinking is that [Terry]'s answer that no-one has ever asked him to meet any of John's needs is insufficient and that unless [Terry] sets up a regime whereby there could be a fair bona fide consideration of John's needs under which regime John had an enforceable right to receive maintenance, then I would need to set up a system such as that set up under the *Protected Estates Act* 1983 whereby the Protective Commissioner, or some other skilful person, would manage a fund on behalf of John.

[43] Having seen Sabina Hammond in the witness box, my present feeling is that it would not be an appropriate order to put her in control of the funds. I realise that she is a mother and has a mother's affection for John; I realise too that the testator's desire that she have nothing to do with the money may well have been based on the conflicts that arose between the testator and his former wife during their marriage and I know, too, that when one is dealing with a protected person, the fact that the carer may also benefit from the benefaction is usually not a relevant matter.[62] However, the way in which Sabina Hammond's evidence came across was that it would be too dangerous to allow her to have untrammelled control of John's money.

[44] So far as Sabina Hammond's views that a house in Bondi might be purchased for something like $600,000 for John and herself to live in, it would seem on any view of the evidence that this, because of lack of funds, can only be a pipe dream.

[45] Accordingly, in my view, if the matter were to stop here the proper thing to do would be to conclude that John has an enforceable equitable right for maintenance from Terry. Accordingly, he has not been left without proper support. His application should be dismissed with no order as to costs and orders made for the provision for Luke and Chere as per the settlement. I would probably also be prepared to make an order declaring the superannuation funds as notional property.

[46] However, because [counsel had not argued these issues] I will merely publish these reasons and stand the matter over until 1 March 2007 for mention in case counsel wish to argue the matter further, orally or in writing.

Comment
1. See Radan & Stewart at **15.74–15.76**.

---

62. See *Bective (Countess) v Federal Commissioner of Taxation* (1932) 47 CLR 417.

16

CREATION OF EXPRESS TRUSTS

Introduction

16.1 This chapter primarily deals with the issues concerning the creation of express trusts. Express trusts can be created in three main ways:

1. by *declaration*, where a titleholder expresses his or her intention to hold their property on trust for another;
2. by *transfer*, where title is transferred to a person with instructions that it be held on trust for another; the transfer can occur either via an *inter vivos* transaction (a settlement) or *post mortem* (by will); and
3. by *direction*, where the beneficiary of an existing trust directs the trustee to hold his or her interest on trust for another.

Equity requires that trusts be able to satisfy the three certainties, which are concerned with intention, subject matter and beneficiaries. Trusts may also have to satisfy the statutory requirements for writing. The extracts in this chapter discuss the following:

* the test for certainty of intention to create a trust: *Shortall v White* [2007] NSWCA 372;
* the test for certainty of subject matter: *White v Shortall* (2006) 68 NSWLR 650;
* the test for certainty of beneficiaries: *In Re Baden's Deed Trusts; McPhail v Doulton* [1971] AC 424; and
* the requirements for writing: *Pascoe v Boensch* (2008) 250 ALR 24.

Certainty of intention

16.2   Shortall v White [2007] NSWCA 372

Court: Court of Appeal of New South Wales

Facts: Alan Shortall and Louise White were in a de facto relationship which ended in 2003. After the relationship ended they continued to see each other and were friends. White was concerned about her financial future. Shortall promised that he would transfer 220,000 shares in a company called Unitract into her name. Shortall was entitled to 1.5 million shares in the company but they were being held in escrow (meaning that he would not get full beneficial ownership until a later time). Later, after a counselling session, Shortall confirmed the commitment in writing, but on the basis that White would sign a cheque to him worth $20,000. White provided the cheque and Shortall wrote a letter which said:

> THIS LETTER IS TO CONFIRM THAT I AM HOLDING IN TRUST FOR YOU 222,000 UNITRACT SHARES. THESE SHARES WILL BE TRANSFERRED TO YOUR NAME AND CONTROL AT ANY TIME THAT YOU REQUEST AFTER 1/AUGUST/2003. IN THE CASE OF MY DEATH, THE ABOVE TRANSFER OF 222,000 UNITRACT, TO YOUR NAME, WILL BE AUTHORISED BY MY EXECUTOR, STEVEN SHORTALL

Shortall later denied any obligation to transfer the shares. White argued that the statement had created a trust of the shares, but Shortall countered by saying that he had no intention to create a trust. It was also argued that the trust failed the test for certainty of subject matter: see **16.3**. At trial, Campbell J found that a trust had been intended and created. Shortall appealed that decision.

Issue: The issue before the Court of Appeal was whether Shortall had intended a trust to be created.

Decision: Handley AJA found that the test for certainty of intention had been satisfied. Hodgson and Santow JJA agreed with Handley AJA.

Extracts: In this extract Handley JA outlines the test of certainty of intention and states that in cases of agreements to create a trust which are supported by consideration, the test of certainty should be objective.

Handley JA

[24] The appellant's related point was that there was no trust because he did not intend to create one. The Judge found that the test in this case was subjective relying on the majority decision in *Commissioner of Stamp Duties (Qld) v Jolliffe*[1] that no form of words will create a trust contrary to the real intention of the person alleged to have created it. The opening of the savings bank account in that case 'in trust' for the depositor's wife was, and on the evidence, remained a unilateral voluntary transaction of which the wife knew nothing. The principle applied by the majority, despite the vigorous dissent of Isaacs J, may be accepted as properly applicable where the transaction is unilateral and the beneficiary and others are not informed: compare *Kauter v Hilton*[2] and *T Choithram International S A v Pagarini*.[3]

[25] The transaction evidenced by the letter of 17 March was of an entirely different character. It represented the outcome of discussions earlier that day between the parties, and the letter evidencing the trust was handed to the beneficiary. The transaction was for value and it created a contract. In cases such as the present one would think, on principle,

---

1. (1920) 28 CLR 178 at 181.
2. (1953) 90 CLR 86, 100.
3. [2001] 1 WLR 1, 6, 12.

that the contract rule would apply and the intention to create a trust or otherwise would be judged objectively.

[26] The respondent filed a notice of contention by leave to contend that the Judge erred in holding that the test of intention was subjective. The cases cited in support of that contention by Mr Perram SC for [White] support it although they dealt with trusts of a different character. In *Trident General Insurance Co Ltd v McNiece Bros Pty Ltd*,[4] which concerned a trust of a promise in a policy of indemnity insurance, Mason CJ and Wilson J said:

> ... the courts will recognise the existence of a trust when it appears from the language of the parties, construed in its context, including the matrix of circumstances, that the parties so intended. We are speaking of express trusts, the existence of which depends on intention. In divining intention from the language the parties have employed the courts may look to the nature of the transaction and the circumstances, including commercial necessity, in order to infer or impute intention.

[27] In the same case Deane J said:

> ... equity's requirement of an intention to create a trust will be at least prima facie satisfied if the terms of the contract expressly or impliedly manifest that intention as the joint intention of both promisor and promisee.[5]

[28] These principles have been applied in other situations where the parties were in a contractual relationship. Thus in *Walker v Corboy*[6] the Court of Appeal had to determine whether a farm produce agent held the net proceeds of sale on trust for his principal, or was merely the principal's debtor. In *Re Australian Elizabethan Theatre Trust*[7] Gummow J applied those principles in determining whether a Quistclose trust had been created.

[29] Thus both principle and authority support the application of an objective test to determine whether an alleged settlor intended that a bilateral transaction should create a trust.

Comments

1. See Radan & Stewart at **16.4–16.29**.
2. The judgment of Hadley AJA mentions the case of *Commissioner of Stamp Duties v Joliffe* (1920) 28 CLR 178. In this case a husband opened a bank account, purportedly on trust, for his wife. Later his wife died and death duties became payable on the proceeds of the account. The husband denied that his real intention was to create a trust. A majority of the High Court (Knox CJ and Gavan Duffy J) found that words of declaration could not create a trust contrary to the true intention of the creator. As such the trust was not valid even though express words of trust were used. The case illustrates that a voluntary, unilateral transaction will be judged on a subjective text of intention, as opposed to the objective one used in *White v Shortall*.

---

4. (1988) 165 CLR 107 at 121.
5. (1988) 165 CLR 107 at 147.
6. (1990) 19 NSWLR 382.
7. (1991) 30 FCR 491.

Certainty of subject matter

16.3   White v Shortall (2006) 68 NSWLR 650

Court: Supreme Court of New South Wales

Facts: The facts are set out above at **16.2**. Shortall had recorded his promise to hold 220,000 shares in a company called Unitract on trust. White argued that the declaration was valid and binding. Shortall argued that the declaration failed the test of certainty of subject matter as the precise numbering of the shares had not been specified.

Issue: The issue discussed in this extract was whether the test for certainty of subject matter had been satisfied.

Decision: Campbell J found that the test had been satisfied. When the matter was appealed Campbell J's finding was left undisturbed by the Court of Appeal.

Extracts: In this extract Campbell J reviews the authorities on the test for certainty of subject matter, including material from the United Kingdom, United States and Australia.

Campbell J

[676] There is no doubt that a share can be held on trust. Lord Shaw said in *Lord Strathcona Steamship Co Ltd v Dominion Coal Co Ltd*:

> The scope of the trusts recognized in equity is unlimited. There can be a trust of a chattel or of a chose in action, or of a right or obligation under an ordinary legal contract, just as much as a trust of land.[8]

At the time the letter of 17/18 March 2003 was written, the defendant was registered as the holder of 1.5 million ordinary shares in Unitract. Mr Curtin submits that it is impossible to have a trust of some only of the shares of a particular class registered in the name of a particular shareholder.

In *Kauter v Hilton*,[9] Dixon CJ, Williams J and Fullagar J reiterated: '... the established rule that in order to constitute a trust the intention to do so must be clear and that it must also be clear what property is subject to the trust and reasonably certain who are the beneficiaries'. Those 'three certainties' that are necessary for the existence of a trust arise from the sort of thing that an express trust is.

Mr Curtin submits that in the present case, trust property is not adequately identified by saying that it is 222,000 of the 1.5 million shares that the defendant held in Unitract. Rather, the defendant submits, before one can identify the property with certainty, it is necessary to be able to state *which* 222,000 shares were held on trust, and *which* were the remaining shares that were not held on trust.

---

8.   [1926] AC 108 at 124.
9.   (1953) 90 CLR 86 at 97.

Hunter v Moss

On 21 December 1993, the English Court of Appeal (Dillon LJ, Mann LJ and Hirst LJ) delivered an ex tempore judgment in *Hunter v Moss*.[10] That case concerned a company that had 1,000 issued shares, all of one class. The defendant held 950 of those shares. The Court of Appeal treated the trial judge as having in substance found that the defendant had declared that he held 50 of those 950 shares on trust for the **[677]** plaintiff. The Court did not accept a submission that that purported trust was ineffective because its subject matter was uncertain. Thus, *Hunter v Moss* is directly against the contention that Mr Curtin puts.

However, Mr Curtin points out that, as a decision of the English Court of Appeal, *Hunter v Moss* is not binding on me, and is useful only to the degree of the persuasiveness of its reasoning: *Cook v Cook*.[11] He submits that the reasoning in *Hunter v Moss* is not persuasive, and the conclusion it arrived at mistaken in principle.

The reception accorded to *Hunter v Moss*

Very promptly after the decision in *Hunter v Moss* was delivered, Professor Hayton (as his Honour then was) criticised it as erroneous.[12] Professor Hayton later repeated that criticism in other publications.[13]

Professor Hayton is not the only critic of the decision. Professor Birks, in an article predominantly devoted to the Privy Council decision in *Re Goldcorp Exchange Ltd (in receivership)*[14] says in passing, 'One inference is that the Court of Appeal's decision in *Hunter v Moss* must be wrong.'[15] HAJ Ford and WA Lee, [accept] Professor Hayton's criticisms, at least in a situation where no value has been given for the purported creation of the trust.[16] ... Ockelton, ... criticises *Hunter v Moss*, saying ... 'My claim to ownership, whether legal or beneficial, is a nonsense unless I can say what it is that I own and, in consequence, that you don't.'[17] *Hunter v Moss* is also criticised [by] PJ Clarke ...[18]

JD Heydon and MJ Leeming, in *Jacobs' Law of Trusts in Australia*, says:

> ... if there is no property upon which the trust can take effect, or if it is so described by the settlor that it cannot be identified, there can be no trust. For example, if a testator leaves a $1,000 to A and requests that if anything of it remains at A's death, it be left to the Sydney Hospital 'what remains of it' is too vague a description to enable the court to enforce any trust in respect of it. Likewise, where the subject matter is

---

10. [1994] 3 All ER 215.
11. (1986) 162 CLR 376.
12. D Hayton, 'Uncertainty of Subject-Matter of Trusts' (1994) 110 *Law Quarterly Review* 335.
13. J Underhill and D Hayton, *Law Relating to Trusts and Trustees*, 16th ed, London, Butterworths LexisNexis, 2003, at pp 78–79; Hayton and Marshall, *Commentary and Cases on the Law of Trusts and Equitable Remedies*, 12th ed, 2005 at para 3–82–3–85.
14. [1995] 1 AC 74.
15. Peter Birks, 'Proprietary Restitution: An Intelligible Approach' (1995) 9 (2) *Trust Law International* 43 at 45.
16. H A J Ford and W A Lee, *Principles of the Law of Trusts*, Thomson Lawbook Co, 2007, at [4130].
17. M Ockelton, 'Share and Share Alike?' (1994) 53 *Cambridge Law Journal* 448 at 450.
18. P J Clarke, 'Land Law and Trusts' (1994) 241 *All England Reports Review* at 249–251.

an undifferentiated portion of a parcel of shares (*Herdegen v Federal Commissioner of Taxation* (1988) 84 ALR 271), or of a deposit in a bank account (*Re Appleby's Estate* (1930) 25 Tas LR 126). (Some citations omitted)[19]

In that same paragraph, *Jacobs'* refers to *Hunter v Moss* as a 'strongly criticised decision'. ... However, the decision in *Hunter v Moss* has its defenders. Jill Martin ... deals with some of the criticisms of *Hunter v Moss* in a fashion.[20] **[678]** ... Support also comes from Professor R Goode ...[21]... GE Dal Pont and DRC Chalmers ... supported *Hunter v Moss*, concluding that specific items need not be identified or separated from any pre-existing bulk held by the settlor where intangibles such as shares, money or debt are the subject matter of the trust.[22]

...

[689] Construction of the declaration of trust

The declaration of trust that the defendant made is, in substance, that, of those shares in Unitract that he held, 222,000 of them were held in trust for the plaintiff. In my view, that is, in substance, that 220,000 of the shares he held were on trust for the plaintiff, and the rest were on trust for himself. The trust in relation to the rest of the shares is the type of trust that one infers must have been intended, if the trust that definitely was intended concerning the 220,000 shares is to operate. The declaration of trust left him free to deal with the parcel of 1.5 million shares as he pleased, provided that it was not reduced below 220,000, provided that any encumbrances on the shareholding were such that at least 222,000 were left unencumbered, and provided that the plaintiff was entitled to call for the transfer of 222,000 shares at any time after 1 August 2003. If there were to be any declaration of dividend or return of capital prior to the time that the plaintiff had the 220,000 shares transferred to her, the plaintiff would be entitled to receive an appropriate proportionate part of the dividend or return of capital. When I say 'an appropriate proportionate part' I refer to the fact that the quantum of a dividend or return of capital is necessarily calculated by reference to the number of shares held by a shareholder at a particular date. The plaintiff would be entitled to a proportion of the amount of a dividend or return of capital equal to 220,000 divided by the total number of shares in Unitract held by the defendant at that particular date.

Once a finding has been made that there was an intention to hold 220,000 shares on trust, that intention needs to be given effect to in the way that is appropriate to the kind of property that is being talked about. Given the types of rights that are involved in holding shares in a company, the way that rights of a shareholder need not be identified only in terms of owning particular identified shares, how identification of individual shares can be unimportant for a transfer of some of the shares in a shareholding, and

---

19. J D Heydon and M J Leeming, *Jacobs' Law of Trusts in Australia*, LexisNexis Butterworths, 7th ed, Sydney, 2006, p 67.

20. Jill Martin, 'Certainty of Subject Matter: A Defence of Hunter v Moss' (1996) 60 *The Conveyancer and Property Lawyer* 223. Martin substantially repeats in J E Martin, *Hanbury and Martin, Modern Equity*, London, Sweet and Maxwell, 17th ed, 2005 at [3–023].

21. R Goode, 'Are Intangible Assets Fungible?' (2003) *Lloyd's Maritime and Commercial Law Quarterly* 379.

22. G E Dal Pont and D R C Chalmers, *Equity and Trusts in Australia*, 3rd ed, Lawbook Co, Sydney, 2004 at [16.65].

how these particular shares in Unitract were in any event not numbered and were held as an undifferentiated balance in a share register, there is nothing in the nature of the trust property that is inconsistent with recognising the validity of the trust. To recognise the trust is not to perfect an imperfect gift — because there is no transfer of any property involved in a declaration of trust, but rather the declarer of the trust states the terms on which, henceforth, he will hold certain property that he already holds.

A trust of this kind is not analogous to a simple trust, where a single and discrete item of property is held on a bare trust for a single beneficiary. Rather, it is a trust of a fund (the entire shareholding of 1.5 million shares) for two different beneficiaries (the plaintiff and the defendant himself), where powers of management are necessarily involved in the trust (to sell or encumber, within limits that such dealings do not impinge on the plaintiff's rights), and **[690]** where duties on the trustee would arise as a matter of law (for example, to deal with any dividends and capital distributions by distributing them in the appropriate proportions). It is because the trust is construed as being of the entire shareholding that it is not necessary for the plaintiff to be able to point to some particular share and be able to say 'That share is mine'. It is because of this feature of the trust that the defendant declared that an attempt to draw an analogy with cases concerning whether property passes in items of goods when the goods are not appropriated to the contract ... fails — because in those cases, identification of the individual items in which property has passed is essential if the property in them is to pass ... It does not require there to be identification of particular shares in which the beneficiary has the beneficial interest. Given the nature of shares in a company, it is perfectly sensible to talk about an individual having a beneficial interest in 222,000 shares out of a parcel of 1.5 million, even if it is not possible to identify individual shares that are held on trust.

Indeed, ... the test for validity of a trust is not dependent on a beneficiary being able to identify particular property that is held on trust for him or her. In many discretionary trusts, the only interest that a particular beneficiary can claim to have at a particular time is the vested interest subject to defeasance (and sometimes contingent as well) that a taker in default of appointment has.[23] Because of the powers of management that the trustee of such a trust often has, it is often not possible for the taker in default of appointment to be able to point to any of the assets of the trust and say simply 'that asset is mine'. All that such a person can do is point to an asset and say 'that asset is mine, provided the trustee does not sell it before the vesting date, provided the trustee does not make an appointment of it to someone else, and provided any other contingencies that there are before I take an interest vested in possession happen'. In the present case, one can identify the property that is subject to the trust (the entire shareholding) one can identify the trustee (the defendant), and one can identify the beneficiaries (the plaintiff as to 220,000 shares, the defendant as to the rest). That is all that is needed for a valid trust.

Cases consistent with, though not decisive of, validity of the trust

It is of some relevance that one of the ways in which equity imposes a remedy for breach of trust, when trust property has become mixed with non-trust property that is indistinguishable from it, is by recognising a trust of the mixed fund, so that the wronged

---

23. Cf *Stein v Sybmore Holdings Pty Ltd* (2006) 64 ATR 325 at 330.

beneficiary can recover the equivalent of the trust property from the mixed fund, in specie. *Brady v Stapleton*[24] was such a case. When bankruptcy was looming following a large judgment to recover unpaid income-tax, Mr Coward transferred various property (including shares) to people likely to be well disposed to him. The trial judge, Clyne J, found:

> ... that Coward was the head and front of a daring and scandalous scheme designed to swindle the Commissioner of Taxation, that he was actively assisted **[691]** in this scheme by his wife and his brother-in-law (Brady) and that [three other named people] were inert participants in the scheme.[25]

One such transfer was of six different parcels of shares in Canadian Pacific Tobacco Co Ltd, totalling in all 32,280 shares, to Brady. Brady at all times held 1300 shares in that company, that he owned beneficially. Brady then transferred 17,000 shares to Coward's wife. Having found that Brady held all the shares that were transferred to him as trustee for Coward, Clyne J ordered Brady to pay the trustee in bankruptcy a sum of monetary compensation. The trustee in bankruptcy appealed against that order, seeking an order that shares be transferred to him in specie. Dixon CJ and Fullagar J ... explained the problem they had to solve:

> ... it may be taken that Mrs Coward took the 17,000 shares with notice of the facts from which the trust affecting Brady's shares arose, and therefore with notice of the trust. But the difficulty is that it is impossible to identify, among the shares held by Mrs Coward and Brady, any particular shares as being the 32,280 shares which are subject to the trust for the bankrupt. The strong probability that this difficulty is not fortuitous does not seem to help towards a solution of the problem. It was this impossibility of identification which led Clyne J to refuse the orders which the trustee now seeks.[26]

Even so, the High Court granted a remedy in specie. Dixon CJ and Fullagar J ... referred to the judgment of Mellish LJ in *Re International Contract Co*,[27] and said:

> ... where it is possible to give effect to the rights of a *cestui que trust* by simply taking out so much money or so many bonds or so many shares, the *cestui que trust* may elect whether he will take property in specie out of the mass or have a charge on the mass.

> [the true distinction observed by equity] ... is well illustrated by the contrast between the case ... where a trustee has mixed trust money with his own and bought a horse, and the case where he has mixed trust bonds with bonds of his own. Yet a horse is an 'indistinguishable mass' in one sense, and the bonds are an 'indistinguishable mass' in almost the opposite sense. The horse is an 'indistinguishable mass' in the sense that it is not practicable to attribute one part of him to the trust fund and another part of him to the trustee's own funds. The bonds are an 'indistinguishable mass' in the sense that there is no practical reason for differentiating one bond from another and it is quite

---

24. (1952) 88 CLR 322.
25. *Brady v Stapleton* (1952) 88 CLR 322 at 329.
26. *Brady v Stapleton* (1952) 88 CLR 322 at 336.
27. (1872) 7 Ch App 485.

possible to take out so many bonds as will suffice to make good the trust fund. The real distinction which equity draws is between the case where it is, and the case where it is not, practicable to give effect to the rights of the *cestui que trust* by appropriating to him a specific severable part of the available property.[28]

I recognise that recognising a trust by way of a remedy is not the same as declaring a trust in the first place. However, that it is possible for equity to recognise a trust of a particular number of shares out of a larger parcel, by way of remedy, is at the least consistent with it being possible for a person, out of court, to declare such a trust.

Milroy v Lord[29] is another case that is at least consistent with it being possible to hold part of a shareholding on trust. It concerned a purported assignment of part of the shareholding of an intending donor. The only reason why the purported assignment was not held to be an effective declaration of trust was as a matter of construction. If it was fundamentally impossible to declare oneself trustee of part of one's holding of shares, one would expect that ground to have been relied upon as well.

[692] United States authorities
United States courts have seen no difficulty in recognising the validity of a trust of a specified number of shares out of a larger holding of shares.

In *Rollestone v National Bank of Commerce*[30] Ragland J in the Supreme Court of Missouri construed a statement of the holder of more than one million shares in a particular company as being a declaration of trust of 10,000 of those shares. He referred to the settlor's shares:

> ... all of which were exactly alike in kind and value. There was no earmark by which any one of them could be distinguished from the others, so as to give it additional value or importance. They were like grain of a uniform quality, wherein one bushel is of the same kind and value as another ... the words '10,000 shares of capital stock' embodied, therefore, an accurate description of definite property rights in the corporation. A certificate of the same number of shares would have evidenced nothing more.[31]

DiLucia v Clemens[32] is a decision of the Superior Court of Pennsylvania (Cirillo President Judge, Brosky J and Beck J). The holder of more than 25,000 shares in a corporation declared a trust of 2000 of them. This was valid[33] because:

> ... the identity of the shares was clear and the description sufficient because the shares were fungible. It is immaterial that no specific shares were isolated and held in trust.
>
>> It is the identity of the [trust] fund, not of the pieces of coin or banknotes, that controls. ... Where the agent has mingled his own property with that of the principal, the latter may reclaim from the admixture an amount equal to his own, although it may not be the same

---

28. *Brady v Stapleton* (1952) 88 CLR 322 at 338–339.
29. (1862) 45 ER 1185 (the principle in which was approved by the High Court in *Corin v Patton* (1990) 169 CLR 540 at 549).
30. 252 SW 394 (1923).
31. 252 SW 394 (1923) at 398.
32. 541 A 2d 765 (1988).
33. 541 A 2d 765 (1988) at 767.

identical property ... and where a trustee has mingled trust funds with his own, and afterwards takes sums from the common mass for his own use, it will be presumed, so long as the mass is as large as the original trust funds, that the sum so taken was his own and not the trust fund's: *Vosburgh's Estate* 279 Pa 329, 333, 123 A. 813, 815 (1924).

The only United States decision that I located which came to a different conclusion was *Busch v Truitt*,[34] a decision of the District Court of Appeal, Second District, Division Two, California. A man owned over 17,000 shares in the capital of the company, all of which were held in escrow. He wrote a letter acknowledging that there were '1380 shares of escrowed stock that I owe you as of this date'. The trial judge had held that there was an effective trust. The District Court of Appeal reversed that decision and held ... that failure to identify the specific trust fund meant that there was no trust. All the cases cited in support of that conclusion were Californian ones.

That decision of the District Court of Appeal was in effect reversed by *Busch v Truitt*,[35] a decision of the Supreme Court of California, in Bank. Even though the ruling of the Supreme Court of California was 'the judgment is affirmed',[36] it is apparent from the reasons (which incorporate by reference the reasons given in *Kroger v Truitt*), and also from the fact that the judgment opens by stating that it is an appeal from the *trial* judge, that the judgment that was affirmed was that of the trial judge, not that of the District Court of Appeal.

Both *Busch v Truitt* and *Kroger v Truitt* arose from the activities of the president of a corporation that was encountering financial difficulties. The corporation had issued some stock that was freely transferable, and some **[693]** 'escrow' stock that could be sold only with permission of a public authority. The president held escrow stock. The president's way of dealing with the corporation's financial difficulties was to 'borrow' from shareholders unrestricted stock, promise to replace that unrestricted stock with escrow stock, and sell the unrestricted stock. The president died before these promises were performed. At the time of his death, he owned enough of the escrow stock to perform all these promises. His widow was his administratrix and sole beneficiary. She entered an agreement with the various people who had been promised stock, compromising their claims, and that agreement was approved by the probate Court. She later did not perform that agreement, so far as some of the promisees were concerned. Busch and Kroger were two promisees who did not receive stock, and who sued the executrix. Both succeeded before the trial judge. While the litigation involved questions other than the validity of the trust, in the course of the reasons in the Supreme Court of California, in Bank in *Kroger v Truitt*, Shenk J (with whom Gibson CJ, and Edmonds J, Carter J, Traynor J, Schauer J and Spence J concurred) said:

... the statement of the foregoing facts and supported findings ... are sufficient to establish the creation of the trust in the decedent's lifetime and to identify the stock held for the purpose of discharging the obligations.[37]

---

34. 160 P 2d 925 (1945).
35. 163 P 2d 735 (1945).
36. 163 P 2d 735 (1945) at 739.
37. 163 P 2d 735 (1945) at 737.

One of the arguments of the administratrix was that, even if there had been an express trust in the lifetime of the deceased, the litigation against her was defeated because the litigation had not been brought within the four-year period after the death of the deceased that was required by the relevant statute of limitations. The reason that Shenk J gave ... for that argument failing was that by the action of the administratrix in 'entering into a written agreement whereby she promised to transfer a certain number of shares to each of the persons named therein', and obtaining the approval of the probate Court to that agreement:

> ... she indicated with reasonable certainty her intention to hold the specified shares of stock for the purpose of transferring them to designated beneficiaries. Civ. Code, §2221. The written agreement approved by the probate Court and given in part for the $43,500 received by the administratrix was effective to create an express trust to hold the shares released for the benefit of the former owners of stock loaned to the decedent. There is no contention that the action was filed too late if the agreement of August 12, 1942, created an express trust.[38]

Thus, the reasoning of the Supreme Court of California, in Bank, in *Kroger v Truitt*, and hence also in *Busch v Truitt* involved on two separate occasions a recognition of the validity of a trust of a certain number of shares out of a larger shareholding.

That leaves the decision of the District Court of Appeal in *Busch v Truitt* with no standing as an authority. I have not found any United States decision that applies the District Court of Appeal decision in *Busch v Truitt*. Thus it seems not to represent the present United States law on whether it is possible to have a trust of some of the shares in a larger holding.

The tendency of the United States courts to look to the substance of the settlor's intention in deciding whether there is sufficient certainty of subject matter of a trust is illustrated by *Bay Biscayne Co v Baile*,[39] a decision of the Supreme Court of Florida. There, $1000 cash, a note for $1000, and 15 promissory notes, drawn by three different debtors, for a total face value of $19,400 were all handed to a trustee, on the basis that securities to the amount of $15,000 face value would be selected by the trustee **[694]** and guaranteed by the settlor, with the selected securities to be held in trust to pay the former housekeeper of the settlor $1200 per annum, with the trustee to have power to substitute the securities by notes or securities satisfactory to the settlor. The court held ... that the fact that the trustee never selected securities did not prevent a valid trust arising:

> It is claimed that, because Mr Baile did not select $15,000 of the securities from the $19,400, the trust was never completed. We cannot agree with this construction of the trust agreement. This was merely a matter of detail which could not affect the trust which had already been established. This was left for the trustee to do, and certainly it cannot be said that the trustee by some improper act or omission upon his part could destroy the trust.[40]

---

38. 163 P 2d 735 (1945) at 738.
39. 75 So 860 (1917).
40. 75 So 860 (1917) at 869.

I mention these United States decisions not because every aspect of the reasoning would be applicable in the Australian legal system, but as comfort that the same result as *Hunter v Moss* has been arrived at in another significant common law system, and also because some of them are mentioned in the only Australian authority that refers, even indirectly, to the present problem.

Herdegen v Federal Commissioner of Taxation

Herdegen v Federal Commissioner of Taxation[41] is a decision of Gummow J as a judge of first instance in the Federal Court of Australia. It concerns the liability of a husband and wife who had been shareholders in a company, and who were assessed as liable to pay vendor shareholder recoupment tax. That was the tax imposed upon the former shareholders of companies that went out of existence with unpaid company tax and/or undistributed profits tax, as part of certain tax schemes. The legislation imposing the tax on the former shareholders created an exception to liability for the tax if the former shareholders had held their shares as 'bare trustees'.

Mr and Mrs Herdegen claimed that they had the benefit of that exception. Of the 100 issued shares in the company, Mr Herdegen held 59 and Mrs Herdegen held 41. The shares in the company were numbered. The trust was alleged to arise from a conversation (deposed to in par 9 of a particular affidavit) in which Mr Herdegen said that he suggested that the shares be held as to 25 for himself and his wife, as to 38 for (A, one of the people he was talking to), and as to 37 for (B, another of the people he was talking to), and from evidence that Mr Herdegen had always regarded the assets of himself and his wife as 'our joint asset'.

There was also some oral evidence from Mr Herdegen that, later, he had had a conversation with his wife in which she assented to his suggestion that … 'I should hold [A's 38] shares in trust [and] you should hold [B's] 37 shares in trust out of your share[s].' However cross-examination set out … on that evidence left it in a condition where no trial judge could accept it. As well, Mr Herdegen had sworn to two inconsistent views about how he regarded, at the time a particular affidavit was sworn, the shares as held on trust.

Gummow J concluded:

> In these circumstances, I am quite unable to be satisfied that Mr Herdegen has shown there was (a) an oral declaration of trust by Mr Herdegen that he held 38 of his 59 shares in Onedin Investments on trust for [A], or alternatively, such a declaration in favour of Transia, (b) an oral declaration of trust by Mr Herdegen 'as agent for Mrs Herdegen' that she held 37 of her 41 shares in Onedin Investments on trust for [B], or, alternatively, an oral declaration to this effect by Mr Herdegen, without prior authority of Mrs Herdegen, but later ratified by her in **[695]** the discussion of which they gave evidence. That is how the applicants' cases were put in counsel's written submissions.

> (I should add that with respect to the 38 shares allegedly held on trust by Mr Herdegen, no attempt was made to indicate how they were selected from among the parcel of 59 shares numbered 1–10 and 52–100. The same is true of Mrs Herdegen's shares. As to whether such specific identification was essential to establish certainty of subject matter,

---

41. (1988) 84 ALR 271.

or whether the shares might be treated as fungible for this purpose, the authorities appear to be unsettled: *Rollestone v National Bank of Commerce* (1923) 252 SW 394 at 398; *Busch v Truitt* (1945) 160 P 2d 925 at 928; affd 163 P 2d 739. I am also prepared to assume without deciding that it would in law have been competent for Mr Herdegen to declare a trust for his wife in the way contended for by the applicants.)

What emerges from the evidence quite clearly is a failure by Mr Herdegen to focus his attention upon the distinction between the separate ownership of himself and his wife and the allocation of distinct parcels of shares between particular beneficiaries, and to frame accordingly the words relied upon to give effect to any intention to declare trusts. He may well have believed in May 1979 that what had been achieved was the creation of trusts of shares in Onedin Investments in favour of [A] and [B]. But that would not be sufficient. The whole vice in the applicants' cases is indeed manifest in par (9) of Mr Herdegen's affidavit which puts the applicants' case in its most favourable light.[42]

Reading his Honour's reasoning process as a whole, it seems that the deficiency that he saw, in identification of the subject matter of the trusts, was that he could not be satisfied that there had been an intention expressed that the 38 shares intended to be held for A were to come from the shareholding of Mr Herdegen, or from the shareholding of Mrs Herdegen, and likewise he could not be satisfied that there had been an intention expressed that the 37 shares intended to be held for B would come from the shareholding of Mr Herdegen, or from the shareholding of Mrs Herdegen.

I do not overlook the fact that, when introducing his discussion of whether there were valid trusts, Gummow J had said:

Counsel for the applicants submitted that for the purposes of s 5(5), there might be a trust (and a 'bare' trust) binding a vendor, although it was not possible for the vendor to establish which shares of a parcel held by the vendor were held for which of several beneficiaries. Thus, it was said that Mr Herdegen held 38 of his 59 shares in Onedin Investments on bare trust within the meaning of s 5(5), although he might not be able to establish which of the 59 shares were so held and for whom they were held, as between [A], Transia or [B].

In my view, this cannot be so. The trust asserted is an express non-purpose trust of personalty of the traditional type and without any of the complexities that arise in defining the nature of the rights of beneficiaries under the modern discretionary trust (as to which see *Gartside v IRC*[43]). Even if it were a discretionary trust, the class comprising the objects of the exercise of the trustee's discretion still would have to be certain of identification in the sense of the authorities (as notably explained in *McPhail v Doulton*[44]). And, in any event, there must be certainty also as to the property bound by the trust (*FCT v Clarke*[45]; *Scott on Trusts*, 4th ed (1987), §76, 77).

---

42. *Herdegen* (1988) 84 ALR 271 at 279.
43. [1968] AC 553.
44. [1971] AC 424.
45. (1927) 40 CLR 246 at 283–285.

In the present case, each applicant propounds a trust of which he or she was trustee. Their counsel rather tended to approach the matters as if there was one trust with co-owners declaring themselves trustees of jointly owned assets. That thinking tends to obscure the issues. Further, if there is the necessary certainty in identity of trustee, subject matter and beneficiary, then in any given case it will be necessary for those propounding the express trust to establish on the part of the alleged settlor the presence of the necessary intention to constitute a trust.[46]

[696] It occurs to me that a person who read in isolation the first paragraph I have quoted from par 277, and of the statement 'In my view this cannot be so' might think that that was a denial that it was possible for Mr Herdegen to hold 38 of his 59 shares on trust for A, when he had not identified which 38 shares were so held. However, that reading would be incorrect. The proposition that Gummow J is denying is (in part) that Mr Herdegen held 38 of his 59 shares on a *bare* trust ...

If the correct way of regarding what Mr Herdegen had done was that he had declared himself a trustee of 38 of his 59 shares, that is a trust of his 59 shares that would be partly for the benefit of the beneficiary, and partly for the benefit of Mr Herdegen himself. Such a trust of the 59 shares is not a bare trust.

Further, the proposition that Gummow J is denying is that Mr Herdegen held 38 of his 59 shares on a bare trust, in a particular factual situation namely that he is not able to establish (i) which of the 59 shares were so held, and (ii) for whom, out of the potential beneficiaries, they were so held. Gummow J is not denying that it was possible for Mr Herdegen to hold 38 of his 59 shares on trust for some specified person.

...

The passage from the judgment of Gummow J ... expressly leaves open the question of whether it is possible to have a valid trust of a particular number of shares from a larger parcel. Thus, reading his Honour's reasons as a whole, they leave open the question of whether under Australian law it is possible to have a valid trust of a particular number of shares from a larger parcel.

One might get the impression, from the citation by Gummow J of [the American cases, *Rollestone* and *Busch v Truitt*] ... that the two American cases referred to left the law on that topic in an unsettled state. As I have endeavoured to show above, the outcome of *Busch v Truitt* on appeal to the Supreme Court of California is consistent with the decision in *Rollestone*, and the United States authorities on the topic do not appear to be unsettled. However, when the decision in *Herdegen* leaves open the question whether, as a matter of Australian law, it is possible to have a trust of a particular number of shares from a larger parcel, it is of no particular importance whether or not one got that impression.

It follows from this discussion that I do not, with respect, agree with the view expressed in *Jacobs' Law of Trusts in Australia*[47] that *Herdegen* is authority for the proposition that an undifferentiated portion of a parcel of shares is a subject matter too vague for the Court

---

46. *Herdegen* (1988) 84 ALR 271 at 277.
47. Heydon & Leeming, *Jacobs' Law of Trusts in Australia*, above note 19, at p 67 [NB the reference in the official version is wrongly attributed to p 167].

to enforce any trust in respect of, unless one uses 'undifferentiated' with a very particular shade of meaning.

Comment
1. See Radan & Stewart at **16.30–16.40**.

Certainty of objects

16.4   McPhail v Doulton [1971] AC 424

Court: House of Lords

Facts: Betram Baden created a trust fund for the employees and former employees of Mathew Hall & Co Ltd. The deed said:

> The trustees shall apply the net income of the fund in making at their absolute discretion grants to or for the benefit of any of the officers and employees or ex-officers or ex-employees of the company or to any relatives or dependants of any such persons in such amounts at such times and on such conditions (if any) as they think fit and any such grant may at their discretion be made by payment to the beneficiary or to any institution or person to be applied for his or her benefit and in the latter case the trustees shall be under no obligation to see to the application of the money.

Bertram later died and the trustees approached the court to determine the question of whether the trust was valid. The trustees included Peter Doulton, Alexander Pearson, Arthur Hoskins and Denis Clancey. The defendants included (among others) representative of Betram's estate — Robert McPhail, Enid Baden (Bertram's widow) and Raymond Baden.

Issue: The issue was whether the gift was a trust or a power. If it was a trust, the next issue was what the test for certainty of objects should be. There were two alternatives:

- list certainty, which required the trustee to be able to list all the beneficiaries when the trust was created; and

- criterion certainty, which required the trustee to be able to apply criteria to determine whether or not a person was within the class of beneficiaries.

Decision: A majority of the House (Lord Reid, Viscount Dilhorne and Lord Wilberforce; Lord Hodson and Lord Guest dissenting) found that disposition was a trust and that the test for certainty should be criterion certainty.

Extracts: In this extract, Lord Wilberforce reviews the authorities on the differences between trusts and powers and on the applicable test of certainty of objects.

Lord Wilberforce

In this House, the [representatives of the estate] contend, and this is the first question for consideration, that the provisions of clause 9 (a) constitute a trust and not a power. If that is held to be the correct result, both sides agree that the case must return to the Chancery Division for consideration, on this footing, whether this trust is valid. But here comes a complication. In the present state of authority, the decision as to validity would turn on the question whether a complete list (or on another view a list complete for practical purposes) can be drawn up of all possible beneficiaries. This follows from the Court of Appeal's decision in *Inland Revenue Commissioners v Broadway Cottages Trust*[48] as applied in later cases by which, unless this House decides otherwise, the Court of Chancery would be bound. The [trustees] invite your Lordships to review this decision and challenge its correctness. So the second issue which arises, if clause 9 (a) amounts to a trust, is whether the existing test for its validity is right in law and, if not, what the test ought to be.

Before dealing with these two questions some general observations, or reflections, may be permissible. It is striking how narrow and in a sense artificial is the distinction, in cases such as the present, between trusts or as the particular type of trust is called, trust powers, and powers. It is only necessary to read the learned judgments in the Court of Appeal to see that what to one mind may appear as a power of distribution coupled with a trust to dispose of the undistributed surplus, by accumulation or otherwise, may to another appear as a trust for distribution coupled with a power to withhold a portion and accumulate or otherwise dispose of it. A layman and, I suspect, also a logician would find it hard to understand what difference there is.

[449] It does not seem satisfactory that the entire validity of a disposition should depend on such delicate shading, and if one considers how in practice reasonable and competent trustees would act, and ought to act, in the two cases, surely a matter very relevant to the question of validity, the distinction appears even less significant. To say that there is no obligation to exercise a mere power and that no court will intervene to compel it, whereas a trust is mandatory and its execution may be compelled, may be legally correct enough but the proposition does not contain an exhaustive comparison of the duties of persons who are trustees in the two cases. A trustee of an employees' benefit fund, whether given a power or a trust power, is still a trustee and he would surely consider in either case that he has a fiduciary duty: he is most likely to have been selected as a suitable person to administer it from his knowledge and experience, and would consider he has a responsibility to do so according to its purpose. It would be a complete misdescription of his position to say that, if what he has is a power unaccompanied by an imperative trust to distribute, he cannot be controlled by the court unless he exercised it capriciously, or outside the field permitted by the trust ... Any trustee would surely make it his duty to know what is the permissible area of selection and then consider responsibly, in individual cases, whether a contemplated beneficiary was within the power and whether, in relation to other possible claimants, a particular grant was appropriate.

---

48. [1955] Ch 20.

Correspondingly a trustee with a duty to distribute, particularly among a potentially very large class, would surely never require the preparation of a complete list of names, which anyhow would tell him little that he needs to know. He would examine the field, by class and category; might indeed make diligent and careful inquiries, depending on how much money he had to give away and the means at his disposal, as to the composition and needs of particular categories and of individuals within them; decide upon certain priorities or proportions, and then select individuals according to their needs or qualifications. If he acts in this manner, can it really be said that he is not carrying out the trust?

Differences there certainly are between trust (trust powers) and powers, but as regards validity, should they be so great as that in one case complete, or practically complete, ascertainment is needed, but not in the other? Such distinction as there is would seem to lie in the extent of the survey which the trustee is required to carry out: if he has to distribute the whole of a fund's income, he must necessarily make a wider and more systematic survey than if his duty is expressed in terms of a power to make grants. But just as, in the case of a power, it is possible to underestimate the fiduciary obligation of the trustee to whom it is given, so, in the case of a trust (trust power), the danger lies in overstating what the trustee requires to know or to inquire into before he can properly execute his trust. The difference may be one of degree rather than of principle ... [T]rusts and powers are often blended, and the mixture may vary in its ingredients.

With this background I now consider whether the provisions of clause 9 (a) constitute a trust or a power. I do so briefly because this is not a matter on which I or, I understand, any of your Lordships have any **[450]** doubt. Indeed, a reading of the judgments of Goff J and of the majority in the Court of Appeal leave the strong impression that, if it had not been for their leaning in favour of possible validity and the state of the authorities, these learned judges would have found in favour of a trust. Naturally read, the intention of the deed seems to me clear: clause 9 (a), whose language is mandatory ('shall'), creates, together with a power of selection, a trust for distribution of the income, the strictness of which is qualified by clause 9 (b), which allows the income of any one year to be held up and (under clause 6 (a)) either placed, for the time, with a bank, or, if thought fit, invested. Whether there is, in any technical sense, an accumulation seems to me in the present context a jejune inquiry: what is relevant is that clause 9 (c) marks the difference between 'accumulations' of income and the capital of the fund: the former can be distributed by a majority of the trustees, the latter cannot. As to clause 10, I do not find in it any decisive indication. If anything, it seems to point in favour of a trust, but both this and other points of detail are insignificant in the face of the clearly expressed scheme of clause 9. I therefore agree with Russell LJ and would to that extent allow the appeal, declare that the provisions of clause 9 (a) constitute a trust and remit the case to the Chancery Division for determination whether on this basis clause 9 is (subject to the effects of section 164 of the Law of Property Act, 1925) valid or void for uncertainty.

This makes it necessary to consider whether, in so doing, the court should proceed on the basis that the relevant test is that laid down in *Inland Revenue Commissioners v Broadway Cottages Trust*[49] or some other test.

---

49. [1955] Ch 20.

That decision gave the authority of the Court of Appeal to the distinction between cases where trustees are given a *power* of selection and those where they are bound by a *trust* for selection. In the former case the position, as decided by this House, is that the power is valid if it can be said with certainty whether any given individual is or is not a member of the class and does not fail simply because it is impossible to ascertain every member of the class.[50] But in the latter case it is said to be necessary, for the trust to be valid, that the whole range of objects (I use the language of the Court of Appeal) should be ascertained or capable of ascertainment.

The [trustees] invited your Lordships to assimilate the validity test for trusts to that which applies to powers. Alternatively they contended that in any event the test laid down in the *Broadway Cottages case* was too rigid, and that a trust should be upheld if there is sufficient practical certainty in its definition for it to be carried out, if necessary with the administrative assistance of the court, according to the expressed intention of the settlor. I would agree with this, but this does not dispense from examination of the wider argument. The basis for the *Broadway Cottages* principle is stated to be that a trust cannot be valid unless, if need be, it can be executed by the court, and (though it is not quite clear from the judgment where argument ends and decision begins) that the court can only execute it by ordering an equal distribution in which every beneficiary shares. So it is necessary to examine the authority and reason for this supposed rule as to the execution of trusts by the court.

[451] Assuming, as I am prepared to do for present purposes, that the test of validity is whether the trust can be executed by the court, it does not follow that execution is impossible unless there can be equal division.

As a matter of reason, to hold that a principle of equal division applies to trusts such as the present is certainly paradoxical. Equal division is surely the last thing the settlor ever intended: equal division among all may, probably would, produce a result beneficial to none. Why suppose that the court would lend itself to a whimsical execution? and as regards authority, I do not find that the nature of the trust, and of the court's powers over trusts, calls for any such rigid rule. Equal division may be sensible and has been decreed, in cases of family trusts, for a limited class, here there is life in the maxim 'equality is equity', but the cases provide numerous examples where this has not been so, and a different type of execution has been ordered, appropriate to the circumstances.

Mosely v Moseley[51] is an early example, from the time of equity's architect, where the court assumed power (if the executors did not act) to nominate from the sons of a named person as it should think fit and most worthy and hopeful, the testator's intention being that the estate should not be divided. In *Clarke v Turner,*[52] on a discretionary trust for relations, the court decreed conveyance to the heir-at-law judging it 'most reputable for the family that the heir-at-law should have it'. In *Warburton v. Warburton,*[53] on a discretionary trust to distribute between a number of the testator's children, the House of Lords affirmed a decree of Lord Keeper Wright that the eldest son and heir, regarded

---

50. *In re Gulbenkian's Settlements* [1970] AC 508.
51. (1673) Fin 53.
52. (1694) Free Ch 198.
53. (1702) 4 Bro PC 1.

as necessitous, should have a double share, the court exercising its own discretionary judgment against equal division.

These are examples of family trusts but in *Richardson v Chapman*,[54] the same principle is shown working in a different field. There was a discretionary trust of the testator's 'options' (namely, rights of presentation to benefices or dignities in the Church) between a number of named or specified persons, including present and former chaplains and other domestics, also 'my worthy friends and acquaintance, particularly the Reverend Dr. Richardson of Cambridge'. The House of Lords (reversing Lord Keeper Henley) set aside a 'corrupt' presentation and ordered the trustees to present Dr. Richardson as the most suitable person. The grounds of decision in this House, in accordance with the prevailing practice, were not reported, but it may be supposed that the reported argument was accepted that where the court sets aside the act of the trustee, it can at the same time decree the proper act to be done, not by referring the matter to the trustee's discretion, but by directing him to perform as a mere instrument the thing decreed.[55] This shows that the court can in a suitable case execute a discretionary trust according to the perceived intention of the truster. It is interesting also to see that it does not seem to have been contended that the trust was void because of the uncertainty of the words 'my worthy friends and acquaintance'. There was no doubt that Dr. Richardson came within the designation.

In the time of Lord Eldon, the Court of Chancery adopted a less flexible practice: in *Kemp v Kemp*[56] Sir Richard Arden MR, commenting on *Warburton v Warburton*[57] ('a very extraordinary' **[452]** case), said that the court now disclaims the right to execute a power (ie, a trust power) and gives the fund equally. But I do not think that this change of attitude, or practice, affects the principle that a discretionary trust can, in a suitable case, be executed according to its merits and otherwise than by equal division. I prefer not to suppose that the great masters of equity, if faced with the modern trust for employees, would have failed to adapt their creation to its practical and commercial character. Lord Eldon himself, in *Morice v Bishop of Durham*[58] laid down clearly enough that a trust fails if the object is insufficiently described or if it cannot be carried out, but these principles may be fully applied to trust powers without requiring a complete ascertainment of all possible objects. His earlier judgment in the leading, and much litigated, case of *Brown v Higgs*[59] shows that he was far from fastening any rigid test of validity upon trust powers. After stating the distinction, which has ever since been followed, between powers, which the court will not require the donee to execute, and powers in the nature of a trust, or trust powers, he says of the latter that if the trustee does not discharge it, the court will, *to a certain extent*, discharge the duty in his room and place. To support this, he cites *Harding v Glyn*,[60] an early case where the court executed a discretionary trust for 'relations' by distributing to the next-of-kin.

---

54. (1760) 7 Bro PC 318.
55. (1760) 7 Bro PC 318 at 326–327.
56. (1801) 5 Ves Jr 849.
57. (1702) 4 Bro PC 1.
58. (1805) 10 Ves Jr 522.
59. (1803) 8 Ves Jr 561.
60. (1739) 1 Atk 469.

I dwell for a moment upon this point because, not only was *Harding v Glyn* described by Lord Eldon [in *Brown v Higgs*[61]] as having been treated as a clear authority in his experience for a long period, but the principle of it was adopted in several nineteenth-century authorities. When the *Broadway Cottages Trust* case came to be decided in 1955, these cases were put aside as anomalous,[62] but I think they illustrate the flexible manner in which the court, if called on, executes trust powers for a class. At least they seem to prove that the supposed rule as to equal division does not rest on any principle inherent in the nature of a trust. They prompt me to ask why a practice, or rule, which has been long followed and found useful in 'relations' cases should not also serve in regard to 'employees', or 'employees and their relatives', and whether a decision which says the contrary is acceptable.

I now consider the modern English authorities, particularly those relied on to show that complete ascertainment of the class must be possible before it can be said that a discretionary trust is valid.

In re HJ Ogden[63] is not a case which I find of great assistance. The argument seems to have turned mainly on the question whether the trust was a purpose trust or a trust for ascertained objects. The latter was held to be the case and the court then held that all the objects of the discretionary gift could be ascertained. It is weak authority for the requirement of complete ascertainment.

The modern shape of the rule derives from *In re Gestetner Settlement*,[64] where the judgment of Harman J., to his later regret established the distinction between discretionary powers and discretionary trusts. The focus of this case was upon powers. The judgment first establishes a distinction between, on the one hand, a power collateral, or appurtenant, or other powers 'which do not impose a trust on the conscience of the donee',[65] and on the other hand a trust imposing [453] a duty to distribute. As to the first, the learned judge said: 'I do not think it can be the law that it is necessary to know of all the objects in order to appoint to one of them.'[66] As to the latter he uses these words: 'It seems to me there is much to be said for the view that he must be able to review the whole field in order to exercise his judgment properly.'[67] He then considers authority on the validity of powers, the main stumbling-block in the way of his own view being some words used by Fry J in *Blight v Hartnoll*[68] ... and I think it worth while quoting the words of his conclusion. He says:

> The settlor had good reason, I have no doubt, to trust the persons whom he appointed trustees; but I cannot see here that there is such a duty as makes it essential for these trustees, before parting with any income or capital, to survey the whole field, and to consider whether A is more deserving of bounty than B. That is a task which was and

---

61. (1803) 8 Ves Jr 561 at 570.
62. See [1955] Ch 20 at 33–35.
63. [1933] Ch 678.
64. [1953] Ch 672.
65. [1953] Ch 672 at 684.
66. [1953] Ch 672 at 684.
67. [1953] Ch 672 at 685.
68. (1881) 19 Ch D 294 at 301.

which must have been known to the settlor to be impossible, having regard to the ramifications of the persons who might become members of this class.

If, therefore, there be no duty to distribute, but only a duty to consider, it does not seem to me that there is any authority binding on me to say that this whole trust is bad. In fact, there is no difficulty, as has been admitted, in ascertaining whether any given postulant is a member of the specified class. Of course, if that could not be ascertained the matter would be quite different, but of John Doe or Richard Roe it can be postulated easily enough whether he is or is not eligible to receive the settlor's bounty. There being no uncertainty in that sense, I am reluctant to introduce a notion of uncertainty in the other sense, by saying that the trustees must worry their heads to survey the world from China to Peru, when there are perfectly good objects of the class in England.[69]

Subject to one point which was cleared up in this House in *In re Gulbenkian's Settlements*, all of this, if I may say so, seems impeccably good sense, and I do not understand the learned judge to have later repented of it. If the judgment was in any way the cause of future difficulties, it was in the indication given — not by way of decision, for the point did not arise — that there was a distinction between the kind of certainty required for powers and that required for trusts. There is a difference perhaps but the difference is a narrow one, and if one is looking to reality one could hardly find better words than those I have just quoted to describe what trustees, in either case, ought to know. A second look at this case, while fully justifying the decision, suggests to me that it does not discourage the application of a similar test for the validity of trusts.

So I come to [the *Broadway Cottages case*]. This was certainly a case of trust, and it proceeded on the basis of an admission, in the words of the judgment, 'that the class of "beneficiaries" is incapable of ascertainment'. In addition to the discretionary trust of income, there was a trust of capital for all the beneficiaries living or existing at the terminal date. This necessarily **[454]** involved equal division and it seems to have been accepted that it was void for uncertainty since there cannot be equal division among a class unless all the members of the class are known. The Court of Appeal applied this proposition to the discretionary trust of income, on the basis that execution by the court was only possible on the same basis of equal division. They rejected the argument that the trust could be executed by changing the trusteeship, and found the relations cases of no assistance as being in a class by themselves. The court could not create an arbitrarily restricted trust to take effect in default of distribution by the trustees. Finally they rejected the submission that the trust could take effect as a power: a valid power could not be spelt out of an invalid trust.

My Lords, it will have become apparent that there is much in this which I find out of line with principle and authority but before I come to a conclusion on it, I must examine the decision of this House in *In re Gulbenkian's Settlements*[70] on which the [representatives of the estate] placed much reliance as amounting to an endorsement of the *Broadway Cottages case*. But is this really so? That case was concerned with a power of appointment

---

69. [1953] Ch 672 at 688–9.
70. [1970] AC 508.

coupled with a gift over in default of appointment. The possible objects of the power were numerous and were defined in such wide terms that it could certainly be said that the class was unascertainable. The decision of this House was that the power was valid if it could be said with certainty whether any given individual was or was not a member of the class, and did not fail simply because it was impossible to ascertain every member of the class. In so deciding, their Lordships rejected an alternative submission, to which countenance had been given in the Court of Appeal, that it was enough that one person should certainly be within the class. So, as a matter of decision, the question now before us did not arise or nearly arise. However, the opinions given were relied on, and strongly, as amounting to an endorsement of the 'complete ascertainment' test as laid down in the *Broadway Cottages case*.

My Lords, I comment on this submission with diffidence, because three of those who were party to the decision are present here today, and will express their own views. But with their assistance, and with respect for their views, I must endeavour to appraise the [argument of representatives of the estate]. My noble and learned friend Lord Reid's opinion can hardly be read as an endorsement of the *Broadway Cottages case*. It is really the opinion of my noble and learned friend Lord Upjohn which has to be considered. Undoubtedly the main part of that opinion, as one would expect, was concerned to deal with the clause in question, which required careful construction, and with the law as to powers of appointment among a numerous and widely defined class. But having dealt with these matters the opinion continues with some general observations. I have considered these with great care and interest: I have also had the advantage of considering a detailed report of the argument of counsel on both sides who were eminent in this field. I do not find that it was contended on either side that the [*Broadway Cottages case*] was open to criticism — neither had any need to do so. The only direct reliance upon it appears to have been to the extent of the fifth proposition appearing on p. 31 of the report, which was relevant as referring to powers, but does not touch this case. It is consequently not surprising that my noble and learned friend Lord [455] Upjohn nowhere expresses his approval of this decision and indeed only cites it, in the earlier portion, in so far as it supports a proposition as to powers. Whatever dicta therefore the opinion was found to contain, I could not, in a case where a direct and fully argued attack has been made on the *Broadway Cottages case*, regard them as an endorsement of it and I am sure that my noble and learned friend, had he been present here, would have regarded the case as at any rate open to review. In fact I doubt very much whether anything his Lordship said was really directed to the present problem. I read his remarks as dealing with the suggestion that trust powers ought to be entirely assimilated to conditions precedent and powers collateral. The key passage is where he says:[71]

> Again the basic difference between a mere power and a trust power is that in the first case trustees owe no duty to exercise it and the relevant fund or income falls to be dealt with in accordance with the trusts in default of its exercise, whereas in the second case the trustees must exercise the power and in default the court will. It is briefly summarised in *Halsbury's Laws of England*:

---

71. [1970] AC 508 at 525.

... the court will not exercise or compel trustees to exercise a purely discretionary power given to them; but the court will restrain the trustees from exercising the power improperly, and, if it is coupled with a duty, the court can compel the trustees to perform their duty.[72]

It is a matter of construction whether the power is a mere power or a trust power and the use of inappropriate language is not decisive.[73]

So, with all respect to the contrary view, I cannot myself see how, consistently with principle, it is possible to apply to the execution of a trust power the principles applicable to the permissible exercise by the donees (even if trustees) of mere powers; that would defeat the intention of donors completely.

But with respect to mere powers, while the court cannot compel the trustees to exercise their powers, yet those entitled to the fund in default must clearly be entitled to restrain the trustees from exercising it save among those within the power. So the trustees or the court must be able to say with certainty who is within and who is without the power. It is for this reason that I find myself unable to accept the broader proposition advanced by Lord Denning MR and Winn LJ, mentioned earlier, and agree with the proposition as enunciated in *In re Gestetner Settlement*[74] and the later cases.

The reference to 'defeating the intention of donors completely' shows that what he is concerned with is to point to the contrast between powers and trusts which lies in the facultative nature of the one and the mandatory nature of the other, the conclusion being the rejection of the 'broader' proposition as to powers accepted by two members of the Court of Appeal. With this in mind it becomes clear that the sentence so much relied on by the [representatives of the estate] will not sustain the weight they put on it. This is:

The trustees have a duty to select the donees of the donor's bounty from among the class designated by the donor; he has not entrusted [456] them with any power to select the donees merely from among known claimants who are within the class, for that is constituting a narrower class and the donor has given them no power to do this.[75]

What this does say, and I respectfully agree, is that, in the case of a trust, the trustees must select from the class. What it does not say, as I read it, or imply, is that in order to carry out their duty of selection they must have before them, or be able to get, a complete list of all possible objects.

So I think that we are free to review the *Broadway Cottages case*. The conclusion which I would reach, implicit in the previous discussion, is that the wide distinction between the validity test for powers and that for trust powers is unfortunate and wrong, that the rule recently fastened upon the courts by [the *Broadway Cottages case*] ought to be discarded, and that the test for the validity of trust powers ought to be similar to that accepted by

---

72. 3rd ed, Vol 30, 1959 at p 241, [445].
73. *Wilson v Turner* (1883) 22 Ch D 521 at 525.
74. [1953] Ch 672.
75. [1970] AC 508 at 524.

this House in *In re Gulbenkian's Settlements* for powers, namely, that the trust is valid if it can be said with certainty that any given individual is or is not a member of the class. ...

Assimilation of the validity test does not involve the complete assimilation of trust powers with powers. As to powers, I agree with my noble and learned friend Lord Upjohn in *In re Gulbenkian's Settlements* that although the trustees may, and normally will, be under a fiduciary duty to consider whether or in what way they should exercise their power, the court will not normally compel its exercise. It will intervene if the trustees exceed their powers, and possibly if they are proved to have exercised it capriciously. But in the case of a trust power, if the trustees do not [457] exercise it, the court will: I respectfully adopt as to this the statement in Lord Upjohn's opinion ... I would venture to amplify this by saying that the court, if called upon to execute the trust power, will do so in the manner best calculated to give effect to the settlor's or testator's intentions. It may do so by appointing new trustees, or by authorising or directing representative persons of the classes of beneficiaries to prepare a scheme of distribution, or even, should the proper basis for distribution appear by itself directing the trustees so to distribute. The books give many instances where this has been done, and I see no reason in principle why they should not do so in the modern field of discretionary trusts ... Then, as to the trustees' duty of inquiry or ascertainment, in each case the trustees ought to make such a survey of the range of objects or possible beneficiaries as will enable them to carry out their fiduciary duty ... A wider and more comprehensive range of inquiry is called for in the case of trust powers than in the case of powers.

Two final points: first, as to the question of certainty. I desire to emphasise the distinction clearly made and explained by Lord Upjohn [in *In re Gulbenkian's Settlements*[76]] between linguistic or semantic uncertainty which, if unresolved by the court, renders the gift void, and the difficulty of ascertaining the existence or whereabouts of members of the class, a matter with which the court can appropriately deal on an application for directions. There may be a third case where the meaning of the words used is clear but the definition of beneficiaries is so hopelessly wide as not to form 'anything like a class' so that the trust is administratively unworkable or in Lord Eldon's words one that cannot be executed.[77] I hesitate to give examples for they may prejudice future cases, but perhaps 'all the residents of Greater London' will serve. I do not think that a discretionary trust for 'relatives' even of a living person falls within this category.

Comments

1. See Radan & Stewart at **16.41–16.76**.
2. *McPhail v Doulton* was concerned with a discretionary trust. In a fixed trust the beneficiaries must be identifiable in such a way as to allow the court to draw up a complete list of the beneficiaries at the time their beneficial interests come into

---

76. [1970] AC 508 at 524.
77. *Morice v Bishop of Durham* (1805) 10 Ves Jr 522 at 527.

effect: *Kinsela v Caldwell* (1975) 132 CLR 458; *Re Gulbenkian's Settlements* [1970] AC 508. For example, in *Lempens v Reid* [2009] SASC 179, a gift to 'such of them my friends who resided with me from overseas' failed as the deceased had not provided any information as to who these people were and all attempts at discovering them had been unsuccessful.

Trusts and the requirements for writing

16.5   Pascoe v Boensch (2008) 250 ALR 24

Court: Full Court of the Federal Court of Australia

Facts: The Boenschs were a married couple who had become divorced in 1998. They were the registered owners as joint tenants of land at Rydalmere in Sydney. As part of their divorce settlement, it was agreed that the woman would transfer her joint tenancy to her ex-husband, if he would declare that the property would then be held on trust for their children. The man and woman declared in writing in 1999 that the property was being held for the benefit of the 'Boensch family' and that the woman would transfer her interest in the property to the man so that it could be held on trust. The transfer was signed by the woman but never registered as the mortgagee bank would not agree to its registration unless the man agreed to refinance his mortgage. Mr Boensch became bankrupt in 2005 and the trustee in bankruptcy argued that the memorandum had been ineffective to create a trust as it did not satisfy the requirements of writing.

Issue: The issue for the court was whether the declaration of trust satisfied the requirements of writing, as set out in s 23C(1)(b) of the *Conveyancing Act 1919* (NSW).

Decision: The Full Court (Finn, Dowsett and Edmonds JJ) found that the requirements for writing had been satisfied and that a trust had been validly created.

Extracts: In this extract the Full Court discusses the impact of s 23C and whether it has been satisfied. The extract also contains examination of the three certainties and whether they have been satisfied.

Finn, Dowsett and Edmonds JJ

The Conveyancing Act

[12] While the requirements of s 23C cast an uncertain shadow over this appeal, it is unnecessary that we embark upon any detailed consideration of the interrelationship of its component parts. It is appropriate, though, that we make the following comment. Section 23C(1)(b) of that Act requires [amongst other things that] any declaration of trust respecting any interest in land to be manifest and proved by some writing signed by the declarant. This subparagraph — which imposes an evidentiary requirement — clearly applies to the memorandum, if it is to be an [28] effective declaration of trust.

What it requires is that the writing admits the trust and satisfies the 'three certainties' of intention, subject-matter and object (to which we refer below).[78] Additionally, though, because the memorandum, if effective, disposed of an existing equitable interest, it needed as well to satisfy the requirements of s 23C(1)(c) of the Conveyancing Act. The writing requirement of that subparagraph — which deals with the disposition of an equitable interest or a subsisting trust and which imposes a validity requirement — has the objects of preventing hidden oral transactions in equitable interests and of enabling trustees to ascertain who in truth are the beneficiaries.[79] But the subparagraph does not require the writing to set out the terms of the trust or the fact that a trust exists.[80]

When answering the separate question, his Honour referred in passing to the need for a declaration of trust in relation to land to be in writing to satisfy the provisions of s 23C(1)(b) of the Conveyancing Act. No reference was made to the need to comply with s 23C(1)(c). The appellant seems neither at first instance nor on the appeal to have put in issue any alleged non-compliance with either s 23C(1)(b) or, for that matter, s 23C(1)(c) of the Act, although it is noted in his written submissions on the appeal that compliance with both provisions was necessary. This failure, to put it neutrally, has rather blurred what in the circumstances are the appropriate principles of interpretation to be applied in interpreting the memorandum, if indeed the relevant inquiry as to Mr Boensch's intention is limited to construing that manifest in that document in its setting.

Because of the view we take of the memorandum, we are content to deal with it for the purposes of the preliminary question on the basis that it attracts the requirements both of s 23C(1)(b) — as is implicit in the Federal Magistrate's decision — and s 23C(1)(c), which the respondents contend has clearly been satisfied. We would note, though, that in the circumstances, if subpara (1)(b) is satisfied, so also will be subpara (1)(c).

The decision below

The Federal Magistrate did not accept that the memorandum was a sham. He accepted that at the time the memorandum was signed Mr and Ms Boensch were the legal owners of the property but that Ms Boensch held her interest on trust for Mr Boensch, who had, in consequence, the entire beneficial interest in the property. In consequence, subject to satisfying the writing requirements of s 23C(1)(b) of the Conveyancing Act, Mr Boensch could declare himself to be trustee of that interest. The Federal Magistrate considered that by the memorandum of trust he constituted himself trustee of that interest for his children.

We would note his Honour accepted Mr Boensch's evidence when it was challenged in cross-examination.

The appeal

While there are six grounds of appeal now relied upon, the appeal in substance concerns the question whether in the circumstances Mr Boensch satisfied the various requirements necessary to be complied with to constitute a voluntary trust of his beneficial interest by way of declaration in favour of his two children.

---

78. See *Hagan v Waterhouse* (1991) 34 NSWLR 308 at 385–6.
79. *Vandervell v Inland Revenue Cmrs* [1967] 2 AC 291 at 311.
80. Compare *Re Tyler, Graves v King* [1967] 3 All ER 389 at 392.

[29] By way of preface we would observe that no challenge has been made to the Federal Magistrate's finding that the memorandum was not a sham. We would also note again that no explicit challenge is made to the sufficiency of the memorandum for Conveyancing Act purposes, if in fact a trust was constituted by the declaration.

For the purposes of this appeal, it is necessary to refer briefly to certain elementary principles of trust law relating to the voluntary constitution of a trust by way of declaration. We emphasise both 'voluntary' and 'declaration' for the reason that where valuable consideration is given for the creation of a trust somewhat different principles can apply if the trust is not fully constituted at the time of the declaration.

(i)   Essential to the voluntary creation of any express trust, whether arising by declaration or transfer, is that the trust itself satisfies the three certainties outlined by Lord Langdale in *Knight v Knight*;[81] that is, there must be certainty of intention to create a trust; certainty as to the subject-matter of the trust; and certainty as to the objects (or beneficiaries) of the trust: on the three certainties.[82] The first and third of these have been put in issue in the appeal.

(ii) Though there is no required formula to be used to create a trust[83] the declarant must manifest an intention *presently* to create a relationship in respect to property which the law characterises as a trust.[84] The intention must be one actually had[85] and it must be to create an immediately operative trust.[86] An intention that the trust be constituted at a later date will be ineffective to create a trust either at the time of the declaration or at that later date. The ultimate onus of proving the intention to create a trust rests on the parties seeking to propound it.[87]

(iii) The requirement that there be certainty as to the beneficiaries of a trust is tied to the supervision and control that courts exercise over trusts: a court might be called upon to administer a trust or to direct the distribution of it to some person or persons. For present purposes it is sufficient to note that, if a trust was declared in the memorandum, it was a fixed trust and, in consequence, the beneficiaries of it must be ascertained or else ascertainable when their interests are to vest.[88]

Turning now to the appeal itself, it is to be acknowledged that there were occasional infelicities in his Honour's choice of language which in turn have founded grounds of appeal, but which on any fair reading of the Federal Magistrate's reasons were of no operative significance in his ultimate decision. At [10] and [18] of his reasons the memorandum of trust was inexactly described in the language of 'gift': compare ground of appeal 1. It was also described erroneously (at [9]) as a 'Deed', which it clearly was not:

---

81.   (1840) 3 Beav 148 at 173.
82.   See generally H A J Ford and W A Lee, *Principles of the Law of Trusts*, Lawbook Co, Sydney, 1983, Chs 2, 4 and 5; G E Dal Pont and D R C Chalmers, *Equity and Trusts in Australia*, 4th ed, Lawbook Co, Sydney, 2007, Ch 17.
83.   *Richards v Delbridge* (1874) LR 18 Eq 11 at 14.
84.   *Re Armstrong (decd)* [1960] VR 202.
85.   *Commissioner of Stamp Duties (Qld) v Jolliffe* (1920) 28 CLR 178.
86.   *Harpur v Levy* (2007) 16 VR 587.
87.   *Hyhonie Holdings Pty Ltd v Leroy* [2004] NSWCA 72 at [45].
88.   See *Kinsela v Caldwell* (1975) 132 CLR 458 at 461.

compare ground of appeal 3. Equally the transfer signed by Ms Boensch was described incorrectly as a deed of transfer: at [11]; and see ground of appeal 5. We need say no more [30] about these grounds. They have no bearing on the proper disposition of the appeal and counsel for the appellant has accepted as much.

There are three more substantial issues raised by the appellant.

The first challenges the Federal Magistrate's conclusion that there was an intention presently to declare a trust. It runs down two courses. It is said, initially, that properly construed the document discloses an intention to constitute a trust in the future. Illustrative of this, it is said, is the condition precedent in the memorandum to the constitution of the trust that Ms Boensch transfer her share of ownership to Mr Boensch. Alternatively, it is said that there is such ambivalence, ambiguity and uncertainty in what is conveyed by the memorandum — characteristics not clarified by the evidence — that it cannot be said that Mr Boensch has discharged the onus of proving he had an actual intention to constitute a trust.[89]

The second and third issues coalesce. It is contended that Mr Boensch has not identified with certainty the interests to be taken by the beneficiaries of the trust and in any event there is no certainty as to who are the beneficiaries: 'the Boensch family' or the named children.

The respondents contend that no proper challenges have been made to the Federal Magistrate's findings of primary fact. In any event, though, it is contended that in light of the evidence and his Honour's unchallenged acceptance of Mr Boensch's evidence about his immediate intention to create a trust, the appeal must be rejected.

Consideration

We begin with the trite observation that, while Mr Boensch's intention, if any, to constitute a trust and the terms of it are to be divined from the language used in the memorandum, the court may in construing it have regard to the surrounding circumstances known to Mr Boensch and to the purpose and object of the transaction.[90] As we will indicate below, context is of no little importance in this matter. Importantly, Mr Boensch's actual intention and the terms actually intended may properly be inferred from all the circumstances if they can properly be said to be nonetheless manifest on the proper construction of the memorandum itself.[91] We would note in passing that, in the setting of the Conveyancing Act, at least, intention cannot be presumed or imputed: for the difference between inferring and imputing intention.[92]

---

89. Compare *Hyhonie Holdings Pty Ltd v Leroy* [2004] NSWCA 72.

90. See *Trident General Insurance Co Ltd v McNiece Bros Pty Ltd* (1988) 165 CLR 107 at 121; *Herdegen v FCT* (1988) 84 ALR 271 at 277. See also Dal Pont & Chalmers, *Equity and Trusts in Australia*, note 72 above, p 459. On the convergence of principles of construction in relation to resort to 'context' or 'surrounding circumstances', see *Lion Nathan Australia Pty Ltd v Coopers Brewery Ltd* (2005) 223 ALR 560 at [78]–[79].

91. See *Trident General Insurance Co Ltd v McNiece Bros Pty Ltd* (1988) 165 CLR 107.

92. See *Hawkins v Clayton* (1988) 164 CLR 539 at 570.

[29] To appreciate what is conveyed by the memorandum of trust it is important to understand the context and the circumstances of its making. We would note the following:

(i)   Mr and Ms Boensch were at the time of the creation of the document only recently divorced. They had two infant children, aged 9 and 7.
      On separation Mr and Ms Boensch entered into an agreement for shared custody of the children, child support and the division of property. Prior to the making of the property settlement consent orders, Mr Boensch **[31]** had a number of conversations with Ms Boensch in which he spoke of the need to make provision for the support of their children and to give them a start for life.

(iii) The Federal Magistrate accepted Mr Boensch's evidence of his concern on learning that a new partner in a future relationship with him may be able to make a claim on the Rydalmere property. If such a claim was made he would not then be in a position to make his intended gift to his children to give them a start in life; nor would he be able to finance his 50% child support contribution.

(iv) In talking to others at the time about his concern, he was made aware of the trust concept. This led to his being led to a person who, as his Honour found, was not a solicitor but who prepared the memorandum. Mr Boensch located a justice of the peace who witnessed their signing of a copy of the memorandum.

Considered in this context and bearing in mind that the memorandum was not a professionally prepared one, its burden in our view is tolerably clear. Putting to one side the third paragraph (which deals with Ms Boensch), the remaining three paragraphs considered together disclose an intention on Mr Boensch's part — and his is the only relevant intention — to create a fixed trust of the Rydalmere property for his children and, we would infer, an actual intention that at some time in the future the property could be resettled by him as trustee on the children on terms more advantageous to them than those of the minimalist trust manifest in the memorandum.

Our reasons for arriving at this view can be stated shortly. The matrimonial environment leading to the signing of the memorandum and the age of the children at the time occasioned, on the evidence, an immediate concern in Mr Boensch for the future of the children. Further, he became aware that if he retained his interest in the property, it could, in the context of his entering into a new relationship, become vulnerable to a claim by a new partner. That vulnerability, we would comment, would remain for as long as he retained an interest in the property but would not if he divested himself of it in favour of his children.

Mr Boensch clearly attributed an immediate and solemn significance to the memorandum. Otherwise his having it witnessed by a justice of the peace seems inexplicable. The document speaks of something thereby being 'created for the benefit of the Boensch family'. Considered in context, this observation is properly to be interpreted as referring to a beneficial effect for all of the family; that is, himself, Ms Boensch and the children from the creation of the trust for the children. The benefit to the parents was that flowing from provision being made for their infant children and, in Mr Boensch's case, the elimination of his 'concern' as to a possible consequence that might ensue from any new relationship into which he might enter. In light of that concern we consider it unlikely in the circumstances that he intended to retain any interest in the property.

The circumstances make it wholly improbable that he intended to confer some proprietary benefit on his wife. The benefit to the children was self-evident.

It is said that this use of the description 'the Boensch family' is itself illustrative of uncertainty in the memorandum for the reason that in cross-examination he said that as at August 1999 he did not know 'what Boensch family comprises at this point'. That answer was given in a confused and [32] confusing passage of cross-examination. The context suggests that Mr Boensch may well have considered that he was being asked a technical, perhaps legal, question as to who comprised the Boensch family consequent upon the divorce. It was this he could not answer.

The trust property is certainly described. The intended beneficiaries are the two infants. Without there being any explicit provision as to the quantum of their respective interests in the entirety of the beneficial interest in the property, it is to be inferred that they were to take equally.

Such conduct of Mr Boensch after the declaration and before the July 2003 judgment against him, in relation to his dealing with the property or by way of communication of the fact of its existence, is slight but serves more to confirm than to falsify the conclusion we have reached. We would, though, acknowledge that some of the actions he took, such as claiming the 'rates' of the property as a business deduction, were inappropriate. Nonetheless, there was evidence that he communicated to others from whom he sought professional or other services, or who leased the property, that he was, and was acting as, trustee of the Boensch Trust. We attribute no real significance to any of this subsequent conduct. While much of it may have been of relevance if the question of a sham, that is, of no real intention, was in question, it is probably for the most part inadmissible in the present matter as being self-serving to Mr Boensch's case .... The balance, such as it is, which was not self-serving, has little probative value. In any event, we are satisfied that the memorandum considered in context speaks for itself.

The third paragraph of the memorandum is obviously surplusage for present purposes. Mr Boensch, as owner of the entire beneficial interest in the property, could at any time have called upon Ms Boensch to cause her legal title to be transferred to him. She had in fact already executed and given Mr Boensch a transfer of her title. The paragraph itself had no bearing at all on the constitution of the trust intended by Mr Boensch. It related only to the question who might for the future be the trustee of that trust. That is not a matter of any significance in the preliminary question.

Comment
1. See Radan & Stewart at **16.86–16.101**.

17

VARIATION AND TERMINATION OF TRUSTS

Introduction

17.1 This chapter deals with the principles governing the variation and termination of trusts. Variation can occur via a provision in the trust deed, through the exercise of the inherent jurisdiction of the court or through statutory powers contained in trusts legislation.[1] Trusts can be terminated for various reasons, including illegality, public policy or because the trust offends the rule against perpetuities.

The cases extracted in this chapter discuss the following:

- the variation of trusts under trustee legislation: *Stein v Sybmore Holdings* [2006] NSWSC 1004;
- the effect of illegality on trusts: *Nelson v Nelson* (1995) 184 CLR 538;
- the effect of public policy on trusts: *Ellaway v Lawson* [2006] QSC 170; and
- the rule against perpetuities: *Nemesis Australia Pty Ltd v Commissioner of Taxation* (2005) 225 ALR 576.

The variation of trusts under trustee legislation

17.2   Stein v Sybmore Holdings Pty Ltd [2006] NSWSC 1004

Court: Supreme Court of New South Wales

Facts: Morrie Stein created a discretionary family trust in 1978 to provide for his wife, children and grandchildren. The trustee was Sybmore Holdings Pty Ltd ('Sybmore') which was a family company controlled by Morrie and his wife. By the time of this litigation the trust assets were between $13m and $14m. Morrie's two children Tanya and Ian were aged 35 and 29 years, respectively, were unmarried and without children.

The deed originally provided for the trust assets to be distributed on 23 December 2007 ('the vesting date'). Morrie was concerned that if he was required to distribute

---

1.   See *Trustee Act 1925* (ACT) s 81; *Trustee Act 1925* (NSW) s 81; *Trustee Act 1936* (SA) s 59B; *Trustee Act 1898* (Tas) s 47; *Trustee Act 1958* (Vic) s 63; *Trustees Act 1962* (WA) s 89.

the funds the beneficiaries would face substantial tax liabilities. The beneficiaries all agreed that it would be better for them to postpone the vesting day until well into the future. The effect of delaying vesting did raise some potential for disadvantage. Delay would postpone the chance for beneficiaries to access the capital of the funds. Delay would also increase the chance of more beneficiaries being born, diluting the fund. However, the beneficiaries believed that there would be an overall benefit to postponing vesting.

Morrie made an application to the court to have the vesting day varied.

Issue: The issue for the court was whether the variation could be authorised under s 81 of the *Trustee Act 1925* (NSW).

Decision: Campbell J found that the variation could be authorised to a date not later than 31 March 2058.

Extracts: In this extract, Campbell J discusses the power of the court under the section to authorise variations of trusts.

Campbell J

Section 81

[24] Section 81 *Trustee Act 1925* (NSW) provides:

(1) Where in the management or administration of any property vested in trustees, any sale, lease, mortgage, surrender, release, or disposition, or any purchase, investment, acquisition, expenditure, or transaction, is in the opinion of the Court expedient, but the same cannot be effected by reason of the absence of any power for that purpose vested in the trustees by the instrument, if any, creating the trust, or by law, the Court:

(a) may by order confer upon the trustees, either generally or in any particular instance, the necessary power for the purpose, on such terms, and subject to such provisions and conditions, including adjustment of the respective rights of the beneficiaries, as the Court may think fit, and

(b) may direct in what manner any money authorised to be expended, and the costs of any transaction, are to be paid or borne as between capital and income.

(2) The provisions of subsection (1) shall be deemed to empower the Court, where it is satisfied that an alteration whether by extension or otherwise of the trusts or powers conferred on the trustees by the trust instrument, if any, creating the trust, or by law is expedient, to authorise the trustees to do or abstain from doing any act or thing which if done or omitted by them without the authorisation of the Court or the consent of the beneficiaries would be a breach of trust, and in particular the Court may authorise the trustees:

(a) to sell trust property, notwithstanding that the terms or consideration for the sale may not be within any statutory powers of the trustees, or within the terms of the instrument, if any, creating the trust, or may be forbidden by that instrument,

(b) to postpone the sale of trust property,

(c) to carry on any business forming part of the trust property during any period for which a sale may be postponed,

(d) to employ capital money subject to the trust in any business which the trustees are authorised by the instrument, if any, creating the trust or by law to carry on.

...

(4) The powers of the Court under this section shall be in addition to the powers of the Court under its general administrative jurisdiction and under this or any other Act.

Present property rights in the trust property

[25] In circumstances where Tanya and Ian are both alive and without children the effect of cl 3(c) of the Trust Deed is that the income of any year is held on trust for Tanya and Ian in equal shares, except to the extent that the Trustee decides to appoint that income to someone else under Clause 3(a), or accumulate it under Clause 3(b). In the language of property law, under Clause 3(a) and (b) there is a power to appoint the income, and under Clause 3(c) there is a gift over to Tanya and Ian in default of appointment. Where there is a power to appoint property amongst members of a class, and a gift over in default of appointment, the takers in default have a vested, but defeasible, interest in the property.[2]

[26] In similar fashion, Clause 6 of the Trust Deed gives Tanya and Ian as Residuary Beneficiaries a vested but defeasible interest in the capital of the Trust. The interest of, say, Tanya in the capital is a contingent interest, because it is contingent on her surviving until the Vesting Day. It is defeasible because if the Trustee appoints the property to someone else, under the power of appointment contained in Clause 6 or 7, it will no longer flow to her as a taker in default of appointment. Even so, such a defeasible contingent interest in the capital is a right of property, which is vested in interest but not in possession.

[27] Mr and Mrs Stein, Ian and Tanya are all potential objects of the Trustee's power of appointment

• of income, under Clause 3,

• of capital on the Vesting Day, under Clause 6, and

• of capital prior to the Vesting Day, under Clause 7.

Being a potential object of a power of appointment is not enough to confer any rights of property in the assets which can be appointed. Thus it is only Tanya and Ian who have any present rights of property in the Trust assets.

---

2. Geraint Thomas, *Thomas on Powers*, 1998, at pp 2–67, 2–75, and 2–79; *Hartigan Nominees Pty Ltd v Rydge* (1992) 29 NSWLR 405 at 426–7 per Mahoney JA (with whom Kirby P agreed).

Effect of extension of the vesting day on beneficial interests in the trust fund

[28] If the date by which the Vesting Day must occur is delayed for several decades, and if, say, Ian dies before the Vesting Day, but Tanya remains alive, the effect of the extension of the Vesting Day will be to change the beneficial interests in the Trust Fund from what they are now. In particular, if Ian leaves a child or children, that child or children will as a result come to have a vested but defeasible interest in half of the capital, while if Ian dies without children Tanya will come to have a vested but defeasible interest in the whole of the capital. If Ian dies before the Vesting Day leaving a child or children, that child or children will also acquire corresponding rights in the income. Other possible events, concerning who dies, who remains alive, and who has children, will result in other changes to the beneficial interests in the Trust Fund from what those beneficial interests are now. Does the fact that there will be these changes in beneficial interest mean that s 81 cannot be used to empower the Trustee to extend the date by which the Vesting Day must occur?

[29] In *Audio Visual Copyright Society Ltd v Australian Record Industry Assn Ltd*[3] Simos J considered a situation where the collecting society for copyright royalties for sound recordings and cinematograph films held royalties on trust for various copyright owners entitled to them. It had distributed part, but not all, of the royalties received by it during certain accounting periods amongst the people it understood to be the copyright owners for whom it held those royalties in trust. A decision of the High Court established that owners of the copyright in sound recordings incorporated in the soundtracks of cinematograph films were entitled to be paid part of the royalties that the Society had collected. The collecting society had not previously distributed royalties to owners of that species of copyright, as it had believed it had no obligation to do so. The Society sought the Court's approval to distribute those royalties relating to past accounting periods which had not already been distributed on the basis that the scheme of allocation which had applied before the High Court's decision continued. Simos J said:

> ... s 81 of the Trustee Act does not authorise the Court to empower the plaintiff to distribute royalties relating to prior accounting periods, which are currently undistributed, on the basis of the old scheme of allocation, because to do so would, in my opinion, have the effect of altering the beneficial interests of the relevant beneficiaries, and it is common ground that s 81 cannot be validly used to confer a power which produces such a result.[4]

[30] *Jacobs' Law of Trusts in Australia* appears to draw from that statement of Simos J a general proposition that *'section 81 gives no power to alter the beneficial interests of the beneficiaries'.*[5]

[31] I do not, with respect, think any such general proposition can be drawn from it.

[32] Simos J's reasoning in para [76] was closely tied to the facts of the case before him. Immediately before para [76] his Honour had set out at length the reasons why the

---

3. (1999) 152 FLR 142.
4. *Audio Visual Copyright Society Ltd v Australian Record Industry Assn Ltd* (1999) 152 FLR 142 at 162.
5. J D Heydon & M J Leeming, *Jacobs' Law of Trusts in Australia*, 5th ed, LexisNexis Butterworths, Sydney, 2006, p 373.

Society sought the particular approval that it sought. As I read para [76], his Honour was not purporting to state any general principles. In any event, as appears from the words '*as is common ground*', the application of s 81 does not seem to have been the subject of a real contest. For both these reasons, I do not regard para [76] of his Honour's judgment as establishing any general principle. If, however, the proposition that Jacobs states is inherent in his Honour's decision, I would respectfully disagree with it.

[33] The correct position, in my view, is that sometimes section 81 can be used in a way that alters beneficial interests.

[34] Section 81(1)(a) expressly states that the power it confers extends to '*adjustment of the respective rights of the beneficiaries*'. Those words are not found in the corresponding English section.[6] They have the effect of making the NSW section wider than the English section.[7]

[35] As well, there is authority that sometimes section 81 can justify a transaction which has the effect of altering beneficial interests. In *Re AS Sykes (dec'd) and the Trustee Act*[8] Helsham J recognised that s 81(1)(a) might permit alteration of beneficial interests in certain circumstances. In *NM Superannuation Pty Ltd v Hughes*[9] McLelland CJ in Eq said:

> The conferring on a trustee under s 81 of a power to effect a dealing or transaction in the management or administration of the trust on the ground of expediency may, in some cases, involve or require some incidental or consequential adjustment of the respective rights of beneficiaries …

See also, to similar effect, *Re Cosaf Pty Ltd*;[10] *Arakella Pty Ltd v Paton*.[11] Thus, the fact that extension of the Vesting Day will be likely to alter who ultimately has beneficial interests in the trust fund is not necessarily fatal to this application.

[36] In *Riddle v Riddle*[12] Dixon J said that the powers given by s 81 were not intended to be restricted by any implications. In my view, the correct approach to s 81 involves application of the words of the section, without preconceptions about the type of transaction that it applies to. That includes without any preconception that it cannot be used in a way that alters beneficial interests.

Structure of section 81

[37] It is clear enough that applying section 81 requires one to:

– identify a '*sale, lease, mortgage, surrender, release, or disposition, or any purchase, investment, acquisition, expenditure or transaction*' (which I will refer to as a '*dealing*') that is proposed
– enquire whether that dealing is in the opinion of the Court expedient

---

6. *Trustee Act 1925* (Eng) s 57.
7. *Ku-Ring-Gai Municipal Council v The Attorney-General* (1954) 55 SR (NSW) 65 at 73–74 per Roper CJ in Eq, Brereton and Maguire JJ.
8. [1974] 1 NSWLR 597 at 601.
9. Supreme Court of NSW, 5 March 1996 unreported, BC 9600423 at 8–9.
10. Supreme Court of NSW, Young J, 18 December 1992 unreported.
11. (2004) 60 NSWLR 334 at 355–361.
12. (1952) 85 CLR 202 at 214.

[38] However, considering section 81 just as a piece of prose, there is a syntactic ambiguity about the role that the phrase *'in the management or administration of any property vested in trustees'* plays in the section. One possibility is that *'in the management or administration of any property vested in trustees'* is an adjectival phrase that describes the particular dealing in question, so that the section requires that dealing to be one which is entered in the process of management or administration of property vested in trustees.

[39] Another possibility is that *'in the management or administration of any property vested in trustees'* is an adverbial phrase that qualifies *'expedient'*. On that reading, the opening words of s 81(1) mean the same as:

> Where any sale, lease, mortgage, surrender, release or disposition, or any purchase, investment, acquisition, expenditure or transaction, is in the opinion of the Court expedient in the management or administration of any property vested in trustees, but the same cannot be effected ...

[40] On that reading, the only expediency that is relevant to the section is expediency that is for the purpose of, or advances, the management or administration of any property vested in trustees.

[41] In *Ku-Ring-Gai Municipal Council v The Attorney-General*[13] Roper CJ in Eq, Brereton and Maguire JJ said:

> In order to invoke the provisions of s 81 it *must* be shown that a question has arisen in the management or administration of property vested in a trustee and that the making of an order such as the section authorises is expedient — that is, expedient in the management or administration of the property.

and later on the same page:

> The expediency to be considered under s 81 *must* be expediency in the management or administration of the actual property held upon trust ... (emphases added)

[42] This decision binds me to hold that the second of the possible syntactic roles of *'in the administration of any property vested in trustees'* is the correct one.

[43] As well, though, there is a requirement, derived by a process of construction that I cannot see, but that I am bound to follow, that *'a question has arisen in the management or administration of property vested in a trustee'*. In applying that requirement, a *'question'* must be the same as a problem, rather than a topic concerning which there is real doubt. It could not possibly have been the intention of the legislature that s 81 would not be available if it was perfectly obvious that trustees did not have power to enter a particular dealing, so that there was no question about it, in the sense of it being a matter of real doubt.

[44] I turn to consider whether the various elements of s 81 are made out.

---

13. (1954) 55 SR (NSW) 65 at 74.

Any ... transaction

[45] Of the types of dealing listed in s 81(1), in the phrase beginning *'any sale, lease ...'*, the only noun capable of applying to the present situation is *'transaction'*. *'Transaction'*, in s 81, extends to amendment of the Trust Deed.[14]

[46] Thus the type of power that Mr Stein seeks to have conferred on the Trustee is within the scope of s 81.

Is in the opinion of the court expedient

[47] In *Riddle v Riddle* Williams J said:

> The section is couched in the widest possible terms. The sole question is whether it is expedient in the interest of the trust property as a whole that such an order should be made.

And:

> The ordinary natural grammatical meaning of 'expedient' is 'advantageous', 'desirable', 'suitable to the circumstances of the case'.[15]

[48] The type of expediency which can be considered is not completely open-ended. As Dixon J said in *Riddle* 'Expediency means expediency in the interest of the beneficiaries.'[16]

[49] In *Re Craven's Estate* Farwell J said:

> It cannot mean that however expedient it may be for one beneficiary if it is inexpedient from the point of view of the other beneficiaries concerned the Court ought to sanction the transaction. In order that the matter may be one which is in the opinion of the Court expedient, it must be expedient for the trust as a whole.[17]

[50] The application of a test of *'expedient for the trust as a whole'* can encounter some difficulties in the context of a discretionary trust like the present one, which of its nature involves the trustee having a power to completely cut out some of the potential objects of the trust. The wording of s 81 does not actually say that an exercise of power is expedient only if it is expedient for the trust as a whole. Williams J was the only judge in the majority in *Riddle* who adopted such a test. I would prefer to leave out any such gloss on the statute.

[51] In deciding whether it is expedient to give the Trustee the power it seeks, I do not rely upon the evidence that Mr Stein's original intentions for this trust miscarried in the drafting. I would accept that, both in deciding what is expedient and in exercising

---

14. *Re Philips New Zealand Ltd* [1997] 1 NZLR 93; *Re Bowmil Nominees Pty Ltd (as trustee of the Williamson Superannuation Fund)* [2004] NSWSC 161 at [16] per Hamilton J; *James N Kirby Foundation v Attorney General (NSW)* (2004) 213 ALR 366 at 370 [16] per White J.
15. (1952) 85 CLR 202 at 220, 221–2.
16. (1952) 85 CLR 202 at 214.
17. [1937] Ch 431 at 436.

discretion about whether to confer power to enter a particular dealing transaction, it is proper to take into account whether that dealing transaction advances the objectives of the Trust. But I am in some uncertainty about whether, when a Trust has been declared in writing, the objectives of the Trust are to be found by inquiry into the subjective motivations of the person who caused it to be set up. In those circumstances, and when taking Mr Stein's subjective intentions into account would not affect the outcome of the case, I think it better not to take Mr Stein's subjective intentions into account.

[52] When I talk about whether a proposal is one that would *advance the objectives of the Trust* in the context of deciding whether a proposal is expedient, I do not mean whether it is completely within the scope of the Trust deed. After all, the whole purpose of s 81 is to enable power to be conferred to enter dealings that, if the Court did not make an order, would *not* be within power.

[53] However, there is a more general sense in which one can tell, from the terms of the trust deed and the sort of context of social institutions and laws within which it was made, whether the conferring of power to carry out a particular dealing or type of dealing will involve a departure from the spirit of the settlor's intention. It has some analogy to the way in which the court, in deciding whether to settle a cy près scheme, decides whether there was a general charitable intention. It involves trying to ascertain whether a departure from the strict letter of administering the trust is a departure in some respect that is an important part of the settlor's intention, or a departure in a matter of inessential detail. The type of trust that is involved could be relevant here. A simple trust, to invest and pay income to or for the benefit of a nominated person, could probably not be altered, by the making of an order under s 81, to the same extent as could a more complex trust, like a family discretionary trust, or a superannuation trust. In the latter type of trusts, it is within the spirit of the settlor's intention that there can be changes, within a certain ambit, in the beneficial interests in the trust property — whether by the exercise of a trustee's discretion, or by conferring discretions on someone other than a trustee, as happens with the opportunity for a member of a superannuation fund to nominate, from time to time, who will receive benefits. In the latter type of trusts, there is a well-understood context of law (often tax law) which the trusts are clearly intended to take advantage of — it is often not difficult to conclude that keeping advantages of that type is within the spirit of the settlor's intentions, or if that context of law were to change, it might be possible to conclude that it was within the spirit of the settlor's intention the trust should accommodate itself to whatever the new law was.

[54] Even without taking Mr Stein's subjective intentions into account, I am satisfied that it is expedient to confer on the Trustee the power that Mr Stein seeks. It is well within the scope of the purpose of the trust, ascertained from the trust instrument alone, that it aims to provide benefits after the death of Mr Stein (as the use of the word 'widow' in the list of Specified Beneficiaries demonstrates), and also to provide for his grandchildren and more remote issue. An extension of the Vesting Day would facilitate that objective. The Trust Deed itself establishes possibilities of flexible distribution of assets among members of the Stein family, and extension of the Vesting Day would enable that flexibility to continue to operate. The possibility of flexible distribution is no mere accident of the trust deed. Rather, part of the context in which the trust deed needs to be understood is that it is common for people who have more assets than they need for their own survival to seek to benefit close family members, without giving up control of the assets. Another

part of the context in which the trust deed needs to be understood is that there has been for decades a system of income taxation in which a natural person is taxed on a basis whereby the first tranche of income in a year is tax-free, and successive tranches are taxed at increasingly higher rates — thus directing income from a discretionary trust in any year to the potential beneficiary who has a marginal rate of tax below the top rate will lessen the overall tax paid by the family unit. Maintaining flexibility to distribute both capital and income among members of Mr Stein's family over generations provides one basis upon which I find that the conferring of the power would be expedient.

[55] As well, the minimisation of the capital gains tax and stamp duty on the trust property provides a separate basis upon which the conferring of the power is expedient.

[56] I also take into account that the wife and children of Mr Stein support the proposal, for sensible reasons. They together make up all the people who are presently potential objects of the powers of appointment in the Trust Deed. Tanya and Ian are the only people who have present rights of property in the Trust fund. Tanya and Ian are also, on present indications, the people who would acquire property rights vested in both interest and possession if the Vesting Day were to remain unaltered and the power of appointment of capital were not exercised.

[57] That they support the proposal is not a separate reason why the exercise of the power is expedient. After all, s 81 says that it is the opinion of the Court as to expediency, not the opinion of the beneficiaries or potential beneficiaries, which matters. Rather, the fact that they support the proposal, and their reasons for supporting it, provide me with comfort that my conclusion that it is expedient to confer the power is right.

In the management or administration of property vested in trustees

[58] In the present case, the Trust fund is clearly 'property vested in trustees'.

[59] I enquire first whether a question has arisen 'in the management or administration of' that property. Management or administration of property includes taking steps to preserve the property, and taking steps to make the property financially productive. In my view, planning to minimise the impact of tax and duties on the trust property advances both those objectives and so is part of the administration of trust property. As well, the management or administration of property vested in trustees includes transferring part or all of it from time to time to those who have become entitled to it.

[60] In the present case the Trustee wants to continue to hold the Trust property past 2007, and to pay its income to whichever of the potential income recipients it decides, in the same fashion as it has done since 1978. It wants to avoid capital gains tax and stamp duty being payable on any of the trust property. However it cannot do any of these things because the present provisions defining the Vesting Day require distribution no later than 23 December 2007. That is, it seems to me, a problem that has arisen in the management or administration of the trust property.

[61] I next inquire whether the expediency which I have found is one that advances the management or administration of the property that is vested in trustees. Conferring on the Trustee power to go on providing benefits from the Trust to members of the Stein family, in the flexible way in which the Trust has been able to since 1978, enables the management or administration of the Trust property to continue past 23 December 2007, and in that way advances the management or administration of that property.

Minimising the tax and duty on the Trust property has the effect that the Trust property is better managed and administered, and in that way the management or administration of that property is advanced. It is established that s 81 can be used to empower a trustee to carry out a scheme the sole purpose of which is to minimise the taxation liabilities which fall on the trust property: *Re AS Sykes (dec'd) and the Trustee Act.*[18]

[62] Thus, both tests that *Ku-Ring-Gai Council* require to be satisfied for the element '*in the management or administration of property vested in trustees*' in s 81 have been satisfied.

Cannot be affected by reason of the absence of any power

[63] The express power of variation contained in cl 18 of the Trust Deed specifically excepts the making of a variation to the Vesting Day. Thus, there is an absence of power under the instrument creating the Trust. The trustees have no power, under the general law, to extend the Vesting Day. The power the absence of which s 81(1) is concerned with is a power *vested in the trustees* by the instrument creating the trust or by law — hence it is not necessary to decide whether anyone else (such as the Court, in its inherent jurisdiction) has any power to authorise conferring the power on the trustees.

[64] This element of s 81 is satisfied.

May by order confer

[65] Because the section says the Court *may* confer the power, it creates a discretion, which needs to be exercised. However there would be a considerable, and perhaps total, overlap between factors that established expediency, and the factors that led a Court to decide that as a matter of discretion it was appropriate to exercise the power under s 81. I can at present think of only one circumstance in which a Court would be likely to hold that it was expedient, in the sense section 81 uses that word, for a particular dealing to be entered into, that the trustee lacked power to enter that dealing, but that in the exercise of its discretion it would not give power for that dealing to take place. That is if there was some means other than the making of an order under s 81 by which the same practical objective could be achieved as would be achieved if power to enter the dealing were conferred.

[66] One possible means by which the practical objective that I have held is expedient could be achieved, without making an order conferring power to vary the Vesting Day, is if it were possible to rectify the trust deed so that it contained a later Vesting Day.

[67] A trust deed can be rectified if it is shown not to accord with the intentions of the person or persons who declared the trust.[19] I am satisfied that the Trust Deed is not what Mr Stein wanted (assuming it is his intention that matters, or that his intention should be attributed to the settlor). However rectification requires not only proof that the document executed was not what was intended, but also proof of what *was* intended, with sufficient certainty to enable the Court to make an order which states the words that need to be deleted from, and/or included in, the instrument to give effect to the actual

---

18. [1974] 1 NSWLR 597.
19. *Commissioner of Stamp Duties (NSW) v Carlenka Pty Ltd* (1995) 41 NSWLR 329; I C F Spry, *Equitable Remedies* (2001), p 614.

intention.[20] That order is then endorsed on the instrument that is to be rectified.[21] Even if I inferred that Mr Hay had the same intention as Mr Stein, I am not satisfied that there is cogent enough proof of what *was* required to enable an order to be drafted. Hence the Deed cannot be rectified.

[68] In the circumstances of this case, power to amend the Trust Deed to extend the Vesting Day ought, as a matter of discretion, be granted.

Subject to such provisions and conditions ... as the court may think fit

[69] It would probably be a wrong exercise of discretion to confer on the Trustee a power to amend the Vesting Day in a way which allowed the Trust to continue for a period which would be longer than the permissible perpetuity period, measured from the date of creation of the Trust. However, after discussion with counsel for the applicant, the power which the plaintiff now seeks does not have any such problem. No other limitation on the power is called for.

[70] In these reasons I have relied on section 81(1) alone. Counsel for the plaintiff also relied on section 81(2). I note that in *Riddle* Williams J said that '*subsection (2) widens, if it is possible so to do, the jurisdiction of the Court beyond that conferred by subs (1)*'.[22] In light of the conclusion I have reached it is not necessary to consider section 81(2) any further.

[71] In all these circumstances I will make orders of the general kind that is asked.

Comment

1. See Radan & Stewart at **17.8–17.21**.

The effect of illegality on trusts

17.3   Nelson v Nelson (1995) 184 CLR 538

Court: High Court of Australia

Facts: Bettie Nelson provided the purchase money for the purchase of a house at 5 Bent Street, Petersham in Sydney. The property was registered in the names of her son, Peter, and daughter, Elizabeth. The reason for placing the property in her children's names was to enable her to buy another house with a subsidised loan under the Defence Service Homes Act 1918. The subsidy was only available to people who did not already own a house. Two years later she purchased another house in Paddington using the subsidised loan. To receive the subsidy she falsely declared that she did not have any interest in another house.

The Bent Street house was sold in 1990. The proceeds from sale reaped a net gain of $232,509. Her daughter claimed that she was entitled to half of these proceeds. Bettie

---

20. *Seton's Judgments and Orders,*1912, pp 1638–1643.
21. *Seton's Judgments and Orders,*1912, pp 1638–1643; *Re Jay-O-Bees Pty Ltd (in liq); Rosseau Pty Ltd (in liq) v Jay-O-Bees Pty Ltd (in liq)* [2004] NSWSC 818; (2004) 50 ACSR 565 at [74].
22. (1952) 85 CLR 202 at 219.

and Peter argued that the money was held on resulting trust for Bettie, as she had provided the entirety of the purchase moneys for the house.

Issue: The issue was whether Bettie's illegal conduct in claiming the subsidy on a second home disentitled her from claiming the protection of a resulting trust.

Decision: The High Court (Deane, Dawson, Toohey, McHugh and Gummow JJ) unanimously found that the resulting trust was not destroyed by her illegal behaviour.

Extracts: In this extract, Deane and Gummow JJ discuss alternative approaches to illegality and reject the notion that illegality should automatically meant that equity should refuse to become involved.

Deane and Gummow JJ

Illegality — the submissions

[549] The claim of illegality in the present case presents two distinctive features. First, the rights which Mrs Nelson asserts and the remedies she seeks are equitable. Secondly, the source of the alleged illegal purpose is in statute.

This is not a case where, independently of statute, the creation or performance of a trust or the observance of any condition imposed by the terms of the trust is said to offend a head of public policy. Nor is it a case of a contract to create an express trust where it is contended that the constitution of the trust by the conveyance of the legal title from the settlor to the trustee would be illegal.

Rather, the question is whether a joint owner of the legal title to land is able to resist, by reason of illegality, the assertion of a beneficial title arising as a resulting trust.

The accounting by the second respondents to the first appellant, Mrs Nelson, of the proceeds of sale as Mrs Nelson's beneficial entitlement on its face does not involve the doing of any illegal act. Nevertheless, a source of 'illegality' may be public policy as to acts associated with or in furtherance of illegal purposes. In turn, this may involve consideration of the purposes a statute seeks to serve. Accordingly, there is a large and miscellaneous class of trusts which are held invalid on the ground that their enforcement would be against public policy, even though enforcement would not involve any criminal act by the trustee; likewise, provisions contained in an express trust may be illegal on the same grounds even though the trust itself does not fail for illegality.

The first respondent, the joint holder of the legal title, submits that (i) a court of equity will never enforce an equitable proprietary interest at the suit of a party to an illegality, rather, it will let the loss lie where it falls; (ii) further, the claimant must fail if the making good of the claimant's case necessarily involves disclosure of the illegal purpose; [550] (iii) in this case rebuttal of the presumption of advancement requires disclosure of an unlawful purpose, thus precluding the setting up by Mrs Nelson of the resulting trust in her favour; and (iv) the only relevant recognised exception to the operation of these principles applies where the claimant has not carried the illegal purpose into effect, whereas in the present case the purpose was carried into effect with the purchase of the Kidman Lane property. As we will endeavour to explain, these submissions should not be accepted.

Counsel for the appellants contends that the Defence Services Homes Act 1918 (Cth) ('the Act'), both before and after the 1988 amendments, did not expressly or impliedly prohibit the transaction the subject of the present action, namely the purchase by Mrs Nelson of the Bent Street property in the names of her children. Still less did it expressly or impliedly prohibit the enforcement by Mrs Nelson of what she maintains is the trust in her favour over the proceeds of sale. Therefore, it is submitted, the issue of illegality must depend upon a refusal to enforce the resulting trust on a ground of public policy derived from the statute. The appellants deny there is such a policy which operates in this way.

Illegality and statute

In a case where principles of illegality operate, the result is to impugn the plaintiff's rights, legal and equitable. It is true that, on occasion, the courts, in refusing to order reconveyance to the plaintiff of property transferred to further a purpose forbidden by statute, have said that the plaintiff lacks clean hands. An example is *Groves v Groves*[23] where land had been so conveyed to give a property qualification to the transferee; but Alexander CB also said that the illegal object of the conveyance required refusal to interfere 'consistently with law and equity'. In some cases the doctrine as to parties in pari delicto has been treated as the common law 'counterpart' to the equity maxim, so that the two concepts are interchangeable.[24]

However, in cases of illegality, it is not merely a question, as is involved with the operation of the maxim that he who comes to equity must come with clean hands, of denying the plaintiff equitable remedies, for example, specific performance of a contract, whilst leaving the plaintiff to the remedy at law, for example, damages for breach of contract. The distinction between the operation of the equity maxim, as a discretionary defence to a claim to equitable relief, and the notion of illegality has been drawn by Professor Pettit. Writing as [551] contributor to the title 'Equity' in Halsbury and with citation of much authority, he says:

> Where the transaction is itself unlawful it is not necessary to have recourse to this principle. In equity, just as at law, no suit lies in general in respect of an illegal transaction, but this is on the ground of its illegality, not by reason of the plaintiff's demerits.[25]

In the United States, the same point is expressed by Professor Dobbs in his work *Law of Remedies*:

> The first step in analysis of a putative unclean hands defense is to determine whether the defense really appeals to (or seeks to generate) a rule of law grounded in legal policy

---

23. (1829) 3 Y and J 163 at 174 [148 ER 1136 at 1141].
24. *Byron v Clay* (1989) 867 F 2d 1049 at 1052 (7th Cir); *Dillon v Dean* (1990) 551 NYS 2d 547 at 549; cf *Tinsley v Milligan* [1994] 1 AC 340 at 356–357.
25. *Halsbury's Laws of England*, vol 16 (Reissue), 1993, p 751. Professor Pettit also makes the point in his article, 'He who comes into Equity must come with Clean Hands' (1990) 54 *The Conveyancer and Property Lawyer* 416 at 422.

and applicable to a describable class of cases. For example, the defense might really be the defense that the plaintiff is attempting to enforce an illegal contract. If this is the case, the term 'unclean hands' should be dropped altogether and the analysis should proceed on the basis of the rule of law in issue.[26]

In *Loughran v Loughran*, Brandeis J distinguished between illegality, 'a substantive defence', and the equitable 'doctrine of clean hands'.[27]

It is well settled that, in a case where the contention is that an express trust fails for illegality because performance of the trust or of a provision thereof involves commission of an act rendered illegal by statute, the extent of the illegality and its consequences turn upon construction of the statute.

In *Orr v Ford*,[28] ss 91 and s 296 of the *Land Act 1962 (Q)* were interpreted as rendering certain selections held by a trustee liable to forfeiture by the Minister but as not touching the lawfulness or enforceability of the equitable interest of the beneficiary of a trust of the selection unless and until there was a forfeiture. That was not to deny that the policy of the statute was directed against the holding of selections on trust.

Difficult questions may arise in relating the alleged illegality in the constitution or performance of the trust to what, upon its true construction, is the operation of the statute in question. Authorities in contract law such as *Vita Food Products Inc v Unus Shipping Co* [552] *Ltd*[29] and *Yango Pastoral Co Pty Ltd v First Chicago Australia Ltd*[30] suggest the drawing of a distinction between (i) an express statutory provision against the making of a contract or creation or implication of a trust by fastening upon some act which is essential to its formation, whether or not the prohibition be absolute or subject to some qualification such as the issue of a licence; (ii) an express statutory prohibition, not of the formation of a contract or creation or implication of a trust, but of the doing of a particular act; an agreement that the act be done is treated as impliedly prohibited by the statute and illegal; and (iii) contracts and trusts not directly contrary to the provisions of the statute by reason of any express or implied prohibition in the statute but which are 'associated with or in furtherance of illegal purposes'. The phrase is that of Jacobs J in *Yango*.[31]

Examples in the third category include cases where the mode of performance adopted by the party carrying out the contract contravenes statute, although the contract was capable of performance without such contravention.[32]

---

26. Dan Dobbs, *Law of Remedies* vol 1, 1993, at 2.4(2).
27. (1934) 292 US 216 at 228–229. Other United States authorities which draw the distinction between illegality and unclean hands appear in *In re Torrez* (1987) 827 F 2d 1299 at 1301, fn 4 (9th Cir).
28. (1989) 167 CLR 316.
29. [1939] AC 277 at 293.
30. (1978) 139 CLR 410 at 429–430, 432–433. See also *McCarthy Bros Pty Ltd v Dairy Farmers' Co-operative Milk Co Ltd* (1945) 45 SR (NSW) 266; *J C Scott Constructions v Mermaid Waters Tavern Pty Ltd* [1984] 2 Qd R 413; *Buckland v Massey* [1985] 1 Qd R 502 at 507; *Hurst v Vestcorp Ltd* (1988) 12 NSWLR 394 at 445; *Farrow Mortgage Services Pty Ltd (In liq) v Edgar* (1993) 114 ALR 1.
31. (1978) 139 CLR 410 at 432; see also at 430, per Mason J.
32. *St John Shipping Corporation v Joseph Rank Ltd* [1957] 1 QB 267 at 282; *Ashmore, Benson, Pease and Co Ltd v Dawson Ltd* [1973] 1 WLR 828 at 832–833; [1973] 2 All ER 856 at 859–860; cf *North v Marra Developments Ltd* (1981) 148 CLR 42 at 59–60.

In this last class of case, the courts act not in response to a direct legislative prohibition but, as it is said, from 'the policy of the law'. The finding of such policy involves consideration of the scope and purpose of the particular statute. The formulation of the appropriate public policy in this class of case may more readily accommodate equitable doctrines and remedies and restitutionary money claims than is possible where the making of the contract offends an express or implied statutory prohibition.[33]

In earlier times, effect was given to what the courts perceived to be 'the equity of the statute'.[34] This doctrine had the support of the common law judges led by Sir Edward Coke, who looked back to a time before the rise of the doctrine of parliamentary sovereignty and the subjection to it of the common law.[35] The notion of the equity [553] of the statute operated in two ways. First, the policy of the statute, as so perceived, might operate upon additional facts, matters and circumstances beyond the apparent reach of the terms of the statute. In addition, cases within the terms of the statute but not within its mischief might be placed outside its operation. Bentham gave the following, ironical description of this development:

> The best-imagined provision might perhaps have done more mischief than good unless moulded into form by the prudence of the judge. On the one hand, the obligative part was not wide enough to embrace the mischief: on the other hand, the qualificative parts were not wide enough to yield shelter to innocence or to afford the necessary range to power.[36]

Further, it was said that, although courts of equity did not differ from those of law in the exposition of statutes, they did so in the remedies given and the manner of applying them.[37] Thus, as was pointed out in Fonblanque,[38] the Chancellors devised the principle (still familiar[39]) that equity will not allow a statute made for the prevention of fraud to be converted into the instrument of fraud, and also developed the doctrine of part performance. Again, Chancery would order delivery up of a security given for a usurious and thus illegal consideration only upon terms that the plaintiff pay the defendant what was bona fide due to the defendant. It will be necessary to refer again to the usury cases later in these reasons.

The doctrine of the equity of the statute has analogies in civil law systems. It is said that the search for the statute's equity 'has become indispensable for civil code readers'.[40]

---

33. *Farrow Mortgage Services* (1993) 114 ALR 1 at 13.
34. John Comyns, *Digest of the Laws of England*, vol 5, 'Parliament', 1800, at R 13, R 15; Matthew Bacon, *New Abridgement of the Law* 1832, in Gwillim and Dodd (eds), vol 7, 'Statute', 458–459; Edward Wilberforce, *Statute Law*, 1881, pp 238–243; Samuel Thorne, 'The Equity of a Statute and Heydon's Case' (1936) 31 *Illinois Law Review* 202.
35. Gerald Postema, *Bentham and the Common Law Tradition*, 1986, p 17.
36. Jeremy Bentham, *Of Laws in General*, Hart (ed), 1970, p 239.
37. *Bosanquett v Dashwood* (1734) 25 ER 648 at 649.
38. *A Treatise of Equity*, 5th ed, vol 1, 1820, pp 25–26.
39. See, for example, *Cadd v Cadd* (1909) 9 CLR 171 at 187; *Organ v Sandwell* [1921] VLR 622 at 630; *Wratten v Hunter* [1978] 2 NSWLR 367 at 369–370.
40. Shael Herman, 'The "Equity of the Statute" and Ratio Scripta: Legislative Interpretation among Legislative Agnostics and True Believers' (1994) 69 *Tulane Law Review* 535 at 538.

However, the doctrine of the equity of the statute attracted the ire of Bentham. He described it as a further branch of customary law which struck its roots into the substance of the statute law and infected statute law 'with its own characteristic obscurity, uncertainty and confusion'.[41] The doctrine fell deeply into disfavour in England and the United States, with the rise of legal positivism in the last century.[42] Nevertheless, the doctrines developed in equity survived. In the legal system as a whole [554] there remained, and indeed entered the statute law itself, particular applications, developed by the eighteenth century judges, of the broader concept of the equity of the statute. One such instance in the modern law of bankruptcy is the avoidance of preferences. This was first devised by Lord Mansfield, as it was said, 'without any positive enactment'[43] and as a protection or furtherance of the policy disclosed by the existing statute law.

The third class of illegality, represented by many modern authorities, may be seen as a survival of an earlier school of statutory interpretation. Further, various decisions of Lord Mansfield and Lord Eldon,[44] to which reference is still made in contemporary authorities and to which it will be necessary to refer in these reasons, must be understood with this background in mind.

A fundamental principle of the common law has been said to be that a court will not lend its aid to a plaintiff who founds a course of action upon an immoral or illegal act, particularly where both parties are equally in fault. These propositions are generally treated as following from the judgment of Lord Mansfield in *Holman v Johnson*.[45] One issue which underlies various submissions in the present case is the extent to which those propositions, with the qualifications to them which have developed in the law of contract, apply to a plaintiff who comes to equity seeking to enforce a resulting trust.

It should be noted that *Holman v Johnson* was a case in which the making and performance of the contract in question appears not to have been directly contrary to the provisions of statute. The allegation was that the contract was associated with or in furtherance of illegal purposes in the sense of the phrase later used by Jacobs J in *Yango*. The case came before the King's Bench in banc on a rule to show cause why a new trial should not be granted. The rule was discharged. The buyer was sued for the price of tea under

---

41. Jeremy Bentham, *Of Laws in General*, Hart (ed), 1970, p 240. Other examples from Bentham's writings are collected in Theodore Sedgwick, *A Treatise on the Rules which govern the Interpretation and Construction of Statutory and Constitutional Law*, 1874, p 251.

42. Theodore Sedgwick, *A Treatise on the Rules which govern the Interpretation and Construction of Statutory and Constitutional Law*, 1874, pp 263–265; Henry Hardcastle, *A Treatise on the Construction and Effect of Statute Law*, 1901, pp 113–115.

43. *Humphery v McMullen* (1868) 7 SCR (NSW) 84 at 89–90; *Muntz v Smail* (1909) 8 CLR 262 at 292–296; Robert Weisberg, 'Commercial Morality, the Merchant Character, and the History of the Voidable Preference' (1986) 39 *Stanford Law Review* 48–55.

44. *Holman v Johnson* (1775) 98 ER 1120; *Muckleston v Brown* (1801) 31 ER 934; *Curtis v Perry* (1802) 31 ER 1285; *Ex parte Yallop* (1808) 33 ER 677; *Ex parte Houghton* (1810) 34 ER 97.

45. (1775) 98 ER 1120.

a contract made in France for sale and delivery in that country. The buyer's defence was that the tea was to be smuggled into England without payment of duty and that the seller had been aware of this. It was held that there had been no contravention of the relevant English revenue laws. The seller had no concern in the smuggling scheme and the circumstance that the seller had knowledge of the illegal purpose of the defendant in buying [555] the tea from him did not render the contract sufficiently associated with or in furtherance of that illegal purpose.[46] What has largely gone unnoticed in the later decisions is that Lord Mansfield held that the facts of *Holman v Johnson* did not fall within the principles as to illegality which he propounded, so that recovery in fact was allowed to the seller.[47]

The importance in a case such as this of ascertaining what two Canadian scholars have called 'the underlying purpose' of relevant legislation[48] is borne out by the course of authority dealing with both express and implied or resulting trusts. Brief mention should be made of express trusts.

Upon its true construction a statute itself may prohibit the creation of an express trust. It may do so in direct terms or by forbidding the taking of a step necessary for the formation of such a trust, such as a transfer of the legal title. The prohibition may be absolute,[49] or subject to a condition or approval. An example of the latter[50] is provided by s 19 of the *Aboriginal Land Rights (Northern Territory) Act 1976* (Cth), which imposes special requirements upon dealings by a Land Trust with any estate or interest in land vested in it.

Another example, closer to the present litigation whilst not involved in it, was provided by s 35 of the Act. This was included in Pt VI (ss 28–38B). Part VI, together with Pt III (ss 16A–18A), Pt IV (ss 19–19B) and Pt V (ss 20–27B), were repealed, with effect from 19 December 1988, by s 10 of the *Defence Service Homes Amendment Act 1988* (Cth) (the Amendment Act). These provisions thus were in force at the time of the acquisition of the Bent Street property in 1987. Section 25 forbade the making of advances by the Defence Service Homes Corporation (the Corporation) except upon the security of a mortgage to the Corporation of the interest in the property of the borrower. Section 35(1) provided that, so long as any land was subject to a mortgage in accordance with the statute, a transfer of the land 'or of any estate or interest therein' would not 'have any force or effect' unless made with the consent in writing of the Corporation.

---

46. Cf *Neal v Ayers* (1940) 63 CLR 524 at 528–529, 532.
47. As Professor Palmer points out in *The Law of Restitution*, 1978, vol 2, par 8.4.
48. Peter Maddaugh and John McCamus, *The Law of Restitution*, 1990, p 345.
49. For example, *Veterans' Entitlements Act 1986* (Cth) s 125; *Superannuation Act 1990* (Cth) s 41; *Social Security Act 1991* (Cth) ss 66, 128, 170, 220, 280, 339, 387, 571, 654, 724, 757, 806, 870, 976, 1052, 1061W.
50. See also reg 41 of the former *Banking (Foreign Exchange) Regulations* made under the *Banking Act 1945* (Cth) and continued under the *Banking Act 1959* (Cth). Regulation 41 was considered in *Sykes v Stratton* [1972] 1 NSWLR 145 at 157, 160.

It was held that the creation of an express trust was a transfer within the meaning of the provision.[51] However, in a series of decisions it also was held that, if the property in question had been sold and the rights of the Corporation fully satisfied, there was nothing in the [556] statute which prevented the trust, the operation of which had been temporarily denied by it, attaching to the proceeds of sale,[52] and that upon discharge of the mortgage held by the Corporation a trust previously denied force and effect might bind the land itself.[53] These decisions were upon the old s 35, contravention of which was not alleged in this case. However, they also are consistent with the broader proposition that, as the statute then stood, the interest which it sought to protect was that of the Corporation in the moneys advanced. It will be necessary to return to that proposition later in these reasons when consideration has been given to other provisions of the Act.

Contract and trust

Counsel for ... Elizabeth Nelson, contend that what they identified as the principles of property law applicable in the present case are not displaced or qualified by principles of illegality discerned from the underlying purpose or policy of the statute in question. Rather, counsel submits, the position as regards trusts was simpler than that in contract. Equity would never enforce an equitable proprietary interest at the suit of a party to an illegality, and Mrs Nelson was such a party. Further, the unlawful purpose had been carried into effect and Mrs Nelson could not displace the presumption of advancement in favour of her daughter unless that illegal purpose was disclosed. The result, on the submissions, would be that equity would leave the loss to lie where it fell, upon Mrs Nelson.

These submissions seek to draw a false line between the legal institutions of contract and trust. Lord Wilberforce observed that there was surely no difficulty in recognising the co-existence in the one transaction of legal and equitable rights and remedies.[54] In *Gosper v Sawyer*, Mason and Deane JJ said:

> The origins and nature of contract and trust are, of course, quite different. There is however no dichotomy between the two. The contractual relationship provides one of the most common bases for the establishment or implication and for the definition of a trust. Conversely, the trust, particularly the resulting and constructive trust, represents one of the most important means of protecting parties in a contractual relationship and of vindicating contractual rights.[55]

Further, many express trusts, particularly those created or manifested in writing, contain conditions, precedent or subsequent, to which the same principles of public policy apply whether perceived through the lens of contract or trust. Thus, in *Permanent Trustee Co Ltd v* [557] *Dougall*,[56] Harvey CJ in Eq held that a condition in a will aimed at preventing any

---

51. *Maurice v Lyons* (1969) 89 WN (Pt 1) (NSW) 385 at 393–394; [1969] 1 NSWR 307 at 315.
52. *Horton v Public Trustee* [1977] 1 NSWLR 182.
53. *Olsen v Olsen* [1977] 1 NSWLR 189.
54. *Barclays Bank Ltd v Quistclose Investments Ltd* [1970] AC 567 at 581.
55. (1985) 160 CLR 548 at 568–569.
56. (1931) 34 SR (NSW) 83 at 85.

beneficiary becoming a lessee or licensee of a hotel was invalid on the ground of public policy, being a condition absolutely in restraint of trade.[57]

However, that is not to say that the case is necessarily treated in the same fashion where, on the one hand, it is a question of recovery of moneys paid under, or damages for breach of, an illegal contract and, on the other, a particular equitable remedy is sought to give effect to an allegedly illegal trust.

The first respondent's submissions rely upon the apparently pervasive effect of the dictum of Lord Mansfield in *Holman v Johnson* that: '[n]o Court will lend its aid to a man who founds his cause of action upon an immoral or an illegal act.'[58] That dictum, as well as the proposition 'let the estate lie where it falls', has been applied not only, for example, to actions in tort for damages for conversion as in *Bowmakers Ltd v Barnet Instruments Ltd*,[59] and for moneys had and received,[60] but also in suits to enforce resulting trusts, as in *Palaniappa Chettiar v Arunasalam Chettiar.*[61]

We turn to consider these propositions as the first respondent would have them apply to this appeal, commencing with that dealing with reliance upon illegality.

There are several difficulties with the acceptance of such a principle as determinative of a case such as the present. First, it has been held in England that the outcome turns upon whether what immediately is in issue is the rebuttal of a resulting trust by demonstrating that what was intended was a gift, or the rebuttal of a presumption of advancement by demonstrating that a gift was not intended. The distinction may be considered by an example where Blackacre is purchased with the money of A but transferred by the vendor on completion to B, who is the child of A. Authority in England, provided by *Tinsley v Milligan*,[62] is that A cannot rely on evidence of his own illegality to rebut the presumption that a gift in favour of B was intended. On the other hand, if A purchases Blackacre in the name of B, the relationship between them being such that there is no presumption of advancement, A may enforce the resulting trust in A's favour because there is no **[558]** necessity to prove the reason for the conveyance into the name of B and thus no need to rely on A's illegality.[63]

---

57. See also *Church Property Trustees, Diocese of Newcastle v Ebbeck* (1960) 104 CLR 394.
58. (1775) 98 ER 1120 at 1121.
59. [1945] KB 65 at 70; see also *Thomas Brown and Sons Ltd v Fazal Deen* (1962) 108 CLR 391 at 411.
60. *Kiriri Cotton Co Ltd v Dewani* [1960] AC 192.
61. [1962] AC 294 at 303. See also *Singh v Ali* [1960] AC 167 at 177; *Blackburn v YV Properties Pty Ltd* [1980] VR 290 at 291, 299–300; *Tinsley v Milligan* [1994] 1 AC 340 at 366, 367, 374–375; cf *Payne v McDonald* (1908) 6 CLR 208 at 211.
62. [1994] 1 AC 340 at 366, 367, 374–375.
63. *Tinsley v Milligan* [1994] 1 AC 340 at 367, 368–369, 375–376. The distinction is discussed in various commentaries upon *Tinsley v Milligan*, including S H Goo, 'Let the Estate Lie Where It Falls' (1994) 45 *Northern Ireland Legal Quarterly* 378; R A Buckley, 'Social Security Fraud as Illegality' (1994) 100 *Law Quarterly Review* 3; N Cohen, 'The Quiet Revolution in the Enforcement of Illegal Contracts' (1994) *Lloyds Maritime and Commercial Law Quarterly* 163; Hugh Stowe, 'The "Unruly Horse" has Bolted: Tinsley v Milligan' (1994) 57 *Modern Law Review* 441; A Berg, 'Illegality and Equitable Interests' (1993) *Journal of Business Law* 513. See also Nelson Enonchong, 'Illegality: The Fading Flame of Public Policy' (1994) 14 *Oxford Journal of Legal Studies* 295 at 299.

These results depend on the form in which a particular legal proceeding is cast and, unusually for equity, are achieved at the expense of substance. Further, they may operate indiscriminately and thus lead to harsh consequences as between particular parties. It is true, as Lord Mansfield pointed out in *Holman v Johnson* that 'if the plaintiff and defendant were to change sides, and the defendant was to bring his action against the plaintiff, the latter would then have the advantage of it'.[64] But that consideration only heightens the lack of attraction of such a proposition in the court of equity. Furthermore, it in turn encourages a quest for mitigation by the drawing of further fine distinctions and exceptions whereby recovery will be permitted.

A second approach to the matter is to let the loss lie where it falls, the policy being one to encourage observance of the law by threat of a sharp and broad sword. This view commended itself to the minority in *Tinsley v Milligan*. It was said, again with reference to Lord Mansfield in *Holman v Johnson*, that:

> [i]t is important to observe that, as Lord Mansfield made clear, the principle is not a principle of justice; it is a principle of policy, whose application is indiscriminate and so can lead to unfair consequences as between the parties to litigation. Moreover the principle allows no room for the exercise of any discretion by the court in favour of one party or the other.[65]

Reliance also was placed by the minority[66] upon what was seen as the authoritative source of principle in equity provided by the decision of Lord Eldon LC in *Muckleston v Brown*.[67] It will be necessary further to consider this case, together with *Cottington v Fletcher*.[68]

The outcome in *Tinsley v Milligan* indicates that adoption of one approach rather than the other may lead to opposite results. As we have indicated, on this appeal the first respondent relies upon both as operating in her favour. She submits (and the Court of Appeal so [559] decided) that Mrs Nelson can only rebut the presumption of advancement by revealing her purpose of obtaining a subsidised loan by concealment and, further, that the loss should be left to fall upon Mrs Nelson.

In our view, neither of these approaches is to be adopted in the present case. Two factors are of paramount importance. First, as the appellants submit and we would accept, the question of illegality is bound up with the view taken of the underlying policy of the Act. To quote a United States scholar, 'if illegality consists in the violation of a statute, courts will give or refuse relief depending upon the fundamental purpose of the statute'.[69] Secondly, what is sought are equitable remedies in aid of an alleged trust and equity is equipped to attain a result which eschews harsh extremes.

The range and flexibility of equitable remedies assist in achieving an appropriate result in the particular case; this means, in the words of one commentator, '[t]he old common

---

64. (1775) 98 ER 1120 at 1121.
65. [1994] 1 AC 340 at 355.
66. *Holman v Johnson* [1994] 1 AC 340 at 356.
67. (1801) 31 ER 934.
68. (1740) 26 ER 498.
69. George Clark, *Equity, An Analysis and Discussion of Modern Equity Problems*, 1928 reprint, par 401.

law idea of all or nothing will no longer have to apply'.[70] Accordingly, unlike the common law, equity may impose terms upon a party seeking administration of equitable remedies. Further, equity has not subscribed to any absolute proposition that the consequence of illegality, particularly where what is involved is contravention of public policy manifested by statute, is that neither side may obtain any relief, so that the matter lies where it falls. Rather, in various instances equity has taken the view that it may intervene, albeit with the attachment of conditions, lest there be 'no redress at all against the fraud nor any body to ask it'.[71]

Let the loss lie where it falls?

Cottington v Fletcher and *Muckleston v Brown* require attention, given the reliance placed upon them for a general proposition that, in a case of illegality, equity lets the loss lie where it falls. In particular, remarks of Lord Eldon in *Muckleston* have been treated as controlling authority as to the attitude of equity to illegality in trust law.[72]

One must begin with the decision of Lord Hardwicke LC in *Cottington v Fletcher*. The litigation arose at a time when there was in force extensive legislation which imposed serious civil disabilities upon those professing the Roman Catholic faith. The plaintiff held an advowson as patron, that is to say, he held, as an incorporeal hereditament, the right to present a priest to a particular church and [560] benefice in the Church of England.[73] However, the plaintiff was an adherent of the Roman Catholic faith. He assigned the advowson to the first defendant for the term of ninety-nine years intending that the defendant hold the advowson on trust for him so as to avoid the operation of legislation[74] which vested in the Universities of Oxford and Cambridge the presentation of livings otherwise in the gift of Roman Catholics. The plaintiff then conformed to the Church of England and brought a bill in Chancery seeking reassignment by the first defendant of the balance of the term. In the meantime, the first defendant, upon the recommendation of the plaintiff, had presented the second defendant to the living. To the bill, the first defendant pleaded the *Statute of Frauds 1677* (Eng), saying that there was no written declaration of trust. The first defendant also admitted that he had held as express trustee, but only to make the appointment of the second defendant. The consequence was an admission that there was a resulting trust for the plaintiff after the performance of that presentment.

Lord Hardwicke overruled the plea of the *Statute of Frauds* because it was coupled with these admissions. Furthermore, the trust which was so admitted was not rendered void by the legislation. This vested the interest in the two Universities only upon the purported presentment. The plaintiff had conformed to the Church of England before the presentment of the second defendant. The Lord Chancellor went on to say that the

---

70. John Wade, 'Restitution of Benefits Acquired Through Illegal Transactions' (1945) 95 *University of Pennsylvania Law Review* 261 at 304.

71. *Turton v Benson* (1718) 24 ER 488 at 489.

72. *Tinsley v Milligan* [1994] 1 AC 340 at 356, 365, 372, following *Gascoigne v Gascoigne* [1918] 1 KB 223 at 226–227. See also *Singh v Ali* [1960] AC 167 at 177; *Preston v Preston* [1960] NZLR 385 at 404; *Blackburn v YV Properties Pty Ltd* [1980] VR 290 at 296; *Munro v Morrison* [1980] VR 83 at 88.

73. See *Halsbury's Laws of England*, vol 14, 1993, 'Ecclesiastical Law', par 776.

74. Including the *Presentation of Benefices Act 1605* (Eng) and the *Presentation of Benefices Act 1713* (UK).

result might have been different if, rather than having made these admissions, the first defendant had demurred. For it would then simply have appeared from the bill itself that the plaintiff had assigned the advowson in trust for himself in order to avoid the operation of the legislation. The case thus turned upon the operation of statute upon express and resulting trusts.

In *Muckleston v Brown* Lord Eldon was dealing with an alleged testamentary secret trust of real estate for charitable purposes at a time when the *Charitable Uses Act 1735*[75] assisted the interests of the heir at law by hampering, through a registration procedure, devises of land for charitable purposes. The heirs at law of the testator brought a bill contending that the testator had devised certain estates to the defendants on terms that they be held on an intended trust for charitable purposes. The defendants demurred to the discovery sought by the bill. Their objection was based upon the nature of the discovery sought, so that they were entitled to have the decision on the point in the first instance before the defendants were required to plead.[76] The Lord Chancellor held that the plaintiffs were claiming entitlement [561] under a resulting trust upon failure of the trust of the land for charitable purposes, a trust 'against the policy of the law', and that the trustees were required to answer. In particular, it was no answer for the trustees to resist discovery on the footing that it exposed them to penalty or forfeiture. Primacy had to be given to the proposition that that which was liable to be forfeited was a trust against a policy of the law manifested by the Mortmain legislation.[77]

Cottington was cited. Lord Eldon appeared to prefer the view that, in *Cottington*, even though the trust was admitted, the better view would have been that equity should have declined to interfere. The plaintiff had stated in the bill that he had been guilty of 'a fraud upon the law', namely 'to evade, to disappoint, the provision of the Legislature, to which he is bound to submit'. He had come to equity to be relieved against the consequences of his own act, and the defendants were implicated in that dishonesty. In such circumstances, equity should say, 'Let the estate lie, where it falls'. However, Lord Eldon went on, that was not the case before him.

These authorities, when so understood, appear as responses to certain statutory regimes which controlled the litigation. They do not provide authority for any general proposition as to the attitude taken by equity in any case where an issue of illegality in relation to a trust arises by reason of a contravention of the policy of a particular statute. As one might expect from such situations, equity eschews any broad generalisations in favour of concentrating upon the specific situation which has arisen, in the light of the relevant statutory provisions.

Equitable relief and illegality

In *Smith v Jenkins*,[78] Windeyer J declared that the maxim ex turpi causa non oritur actio should be confined to the law of contracts and conveyances. The decreasing significance

---

75. 9 Geo II c 36, repealed by the *Mortmain and Charitable Uses Act 1888* (UK). The *Mortmain Acts* were never in force in Australia: *Balfour v Public Trustee* [1916] VLR 397 at 404–405.
76. James Wigram, *Points in the Law of Discovery*, 1840, pp 20–32.
77. *Muckleston v Brown* (1801) 31 ER 934 at 942.
78. (1970) 119 CLR 397 at 411–414.

of the maxim in the law of tort, especially negligence, may be traced in subsequent decisions of this Court.[79]

Story[80] stated that, in general, although not universally, equity followed the rule of law as to participants in a common crime where parties were concerned in illegal transactions. However, Story continued:

> But in cases where the agreements or other transactions are repudiated on account of their being against public policy, the circumstance that the relief is asked by a party who is particeps criminis is not in equity material. The reason is that the public [562] interest requires that relief should be given, and it is given to the public through the party.

One such class of case, well recognised in this Court,[81] was identified by Ashburner as that of 'repentance before anything done to carry out illegal purpose'.[82] Another concerns recovery of money or other property which, whilst tainted by illegality, was induced by fraud of one of the parties or was the product of a breach of fiduciary duty owed by one party to the other.[83]

Ashburner also refers to a group of decisions identified as cases of public policy. He, like Pomeroy,[84] refers to marriage brokage contracts and to the decisions holding that money paid thereunder may be recovered. Pomeroy and Story[85] discuss cases of borrowers coming to equity seeking relief against contracts declared void by the old statutes against usury,[86] saying that equity would interfere but on terms that the plaintiff pay the defendant what was really and bona fide due, after deduction of the usurious interest; if the plaintiff did not make such an offer, the defendant might demur to the bill and it would be dismissed. Story goes on to say:

---

79. *Jackson v Harrison* (1978) 138 CLR 438; *Gala v Preston* (1991) 172 CLR 243; cf *Thomas Brown and Sons Ltd v Fazal Deen* (1962) 108 CLR 391 at 411. See also *Hardy v Motor Insurers' Bureau* [1964] 2 QB 745 at 767.

80. Joseph Story, *Equity Jurisprudence*, 1908, Bigelow (ed), vol 1, Ch 7, par 298.

81. The authorities in this court are collected in *Martin v Martin* (1959) 110 CLR 297 at 305. The authorities include *Payne v McDonald* (1908) 6 CLR 208 and *Perpetual Executors and Trustees Association of Australia Ltd v Wright* (1917) 23 CLR 185, the reasoning in which was accepted by the English Court of Appeal in *Tribe v Tribe* [1996] Ch 107.

82. Walter Ashburner, *Principles of Equity*, 1933, p 472.

83. *George v Greater Adelaide Land Development Co Ltd* (1929) 43 CLR 91 at 99–100; *Abdurahman v Field* (1987) 8 NSWLR 158 at 162–163; *Weston v Beaufils [No 2]* (1994) 50 FCR 476 at 499–500.

84. *Pomeroy's Equity Jurisprudence*, 1941, vol 3, par 941. See also John Wade, 'Restitution of Benefits Acquired Through Illegal Transactions' (1945) 95 *University of Pennsylvania Law Review* 261 at 297–301; Peter Maddaugh and John McCamus, *The Law of Restitution*, 1990, pp 354–355, 366–374.

85. Joseph Story, *Equity Jurisprudence*, 1908, Bigelow (ed), vol 1, Ch 7, par 301.

86. Repealed in 1854 by 17 and 18 Vict c 90 (*Usury Laws Repeal Act 1854* (UK)). This repealed 11 statutes in force in England commencing 37 Hen VIII c 9 (1545) and ending with 13 and 14 Vict c 56 (1850). Collectively known as the usury laws, these forbade the exaction of interest above statutory rates.

The ground of this distinction is, that a Court of Equity is not positively bound to interfere in such cases by an active exertion of its powers; but it has a discretion on the subject, and may prescribe the terms of its interference, and he who seeks equity at its hands may well be required to do equity. And it is against conscience that the party should have full relief, and at the same time pocket the money loaned, which may have been granted at his own mere solicitation. For then a statute made to prevent fraud and oppression would be made the instrument of fraud.[87]

Of course, the usury laws are gone, and marriage brokage cases little heard of. But much modern regulatory legislation concerns [563] financial dealings, and, in any event, what is of present importance are the fundamental reasons for, not the occasions of, equitable intervention. In that regard, reference should be made to the decision of Jacobs J in *Money v Money [No 2]*.[88] His Honour referred to the jurisdiction of equity to order delivery up of instruments, such as bonds, negotiable instruments or deeds, upon which a party otherwise could sue at law, where there was an illegal consideration and such consideration did not appear on the face of the document.[89] Jacobs J went on to identify a further principle of equity that, even though a transaction might be tainted with illegality on the ground that its performance is contrary to public policy, equity will interfere on further grounds of public policy if the transaction ought not to be allowed to stand even where the plaintiff is particeps criminis. After referring to what is said on the subject by Story,[90] his Honour continued:[91]

> It seems to me that it is only by such a principle that the cases in Equity on, for instance, marriage brokage contracts can be explained. In *Hall v Potter*,[92] the House of Lords granted relief even though the marriage had actually taken place. In *Hermann v Charlesworth*,[93] Collins MR referred to the broader point of view of the Courts of Equity and dealt with many of the authorities.[94] It would not seem that this approach is limited to marriage brokage contracts but it extends to other agreements such as those which involve a fraud upon the legislature: *Vauxhall Bridge Co v Spencer (Earl)*.[95]

But, in these cases, no doubt the operation of the particular statute will be critical. That is illustrated by the money lending legislation considered by the Privy Council in *Kasumu v Baba-Egbe*[96] and by this Court in *Mayfair Trading Co Pty Ltd v Dreyer*.[97] These are best understood as cases in which the legislation precluded the money lender from recovering any compensation for the loan which had been made by it, with the result that it was not

---

87. Joseph Story, *Equity Jurisprudence*, 1908, Bigelow (ed), vol 1, Ch 7, par 301.
88. [1966] 1 NSWR 348.
89. *Money v Money [No 2]* [1966] 1 NSWR 348 at 351. See also Baker and Langan (eds), *Snell's Equity*, 1990, p 32.
90. Joseph Story, *Equity Jurisprudence*, 1908, Bigelow (ed), vol 1, Ch 7, par 301.
91. *Money v Money [No 2]* [1966] 1 NSWR 348 at 352.
92. (1695) Show Parl Cas 76 [1 ER 52].
93. [1905] 2 KB 123.
94. *Hermann v Charlesworth* [1905] 2 KB 123 at 133 et seq.
95. (1821) 37 ER 774 at 775.
96. [1956] AC 539.
97. (1958) 101 CLR 428.

open for such compensation to be recoverable by means of the imposition of a term upon equitable relief sought by the borrower.[98]

In *Kasumu*, the borrower brought an action seeking delivery under [564] the mortgage documents and the Privy Council rejected the contention of the money lender that such relief, being equitable, should be granted only on terms that the principal amount of the mortgage be repaid. The money lender had failed to comply with the requirements of the relevant statute which had provided that, in those circumstances, the money lender 'shall not be entitled to enforce any claim in respect of any transaction in relation to which the default shall have been made'. Hence, the Privy Council held that the imposition of a requirement of repayment, as a condition of equitable relief, would constitute a claim in respect of a transaction within the very terms of the statutory prohibition.

As will become apparent, the scheme of the present Act is quite different. Its policy may be satisfied by the imposition of an appropriate term concerning the subsidy received by Mrs Nelson as the price for the relief she seeks to enforce by the resulting trust.

Resulting trusts and statutory illegality

The intersection between the institution of the resulting trust and the principles of illegality is identified by Scott as follows:

> Although a resulting trust ordinarily arises where A purchases property and takes title in the name of B, A may be precluded from enforcing the resulting trust because of the illegality of his purpose. If A cannot recover the property, B keeps it and is thereby enriched. The question in each case is whether the policy against the unjust enrichment of the grantee is outweighed by the policy against giving relief to the payor who has entered into an illegal transaction.[99]

However, where the illegality flows from statute, the matter is not at large in the manner suggested above. Rather it is a question of the impact of the statute itself upon the institution of the resulting trust. As the matter is put by White and Tudor[100] in their notes to *Dyer v Dyer*:[101]

> There will be no resulting trust if the policy of an Act of Parliament would be thereby defeated.

The position was further explained by Griffith CJ in *Garrett v L'Estrange*,[102] in giving the judgment of the Court:

> It was laid down by Lord Eldon a long time ago ... that there can not be a resulting trust contrary to the provisions of an Act of Parliament. The suggestion of an implication of law contrary to a positive law is indeed a contradiction in terms. This contention is, [565] therefore, negatived by the same considerations which negative the alleged express trust.

---

98. *Pavey and Matthews Pty Ltd v Paul* (1987) 162 CLR 221 at 226, 261–262, 269–270.

99. Scott and Fratcher, *Law of Trusts*, 1989, par 444.

100. White and Tudor, *Leading Cases in Equity*, 1928, vol 2, p 757.

101. (1788) 30 ER 42.

102. (1911) 13 CLR 430 at 435. See also *Preston v Preston* [1960] NZLR 385 at 405; *Orr v Ford* (1989) 167 CLR 316 at 328.

The decision of Lord Eldon to which the Chief Justice referred was *Ex parte Houghton*.[103] This case and Lord Eldon's earlier decision in *Ex parte Yallop*[104] concerned resulting trusts said to arise by payment of purchase money where there was a device to avoid ship registry laws. In *Yallop*, the Lord Chancellor said:

> These two Acts of Parliament (stat 26 Geo III c 60; stat 34 Geo III c 68) were drawn upon this policy; that it is for the public interest to secure evidence of the title to a ship from her origin to the moment, in which you look back to her history; how far throughout her existence she has been British-built, and British-owned; and it is obvious, that, if, where the title arises by act of the parties, the doctrine of implied trust in this Court is to be applied, the whole policy of these Acts may be defeated; as neutrals may have interests in a ship, partly British-owned; and the means of enforcing the Navigation Laws depend upon knowing from time to time, who are the owners, and, whether the ship is British-owned, and British-built. Upon that the Legislature will not be content with any other evidence than the registry; and requires the great variety of things, prescribed by these Acts. They go so far as to declare, that notwithstanding any transfer, any sale, or any contract, if the purpose is not executed in the mode and form, prescribed by the Act, it shall be void to all intents and purposes. The consequence, established by positive and repeated decisions, is, that upon a contract for the purchase of a ship, which it may be supposed, might have been executed without public mischief, though by force of that contract and by operation of Law the purchaser would be the owner in Equity from the moment of the purchase, and the vendor from that moment would be devested [sic] of all interest, yet it is decided, that these Acts are so imperative, that, if they rest upon the contract, it cannot be said of a ship, as of an estate, that by operation of Law, and by force of the contract, the ownership is changed; and if the money had been paid, the decision would be upon the same principle; and it must be recovered by another form of proceeding.[105] ...

In *Worthington v Curtis*,[106] a contract between a father and an insurance company for the issue of a policy on the life of his child was considered illegal and void under the *Life Assurance Act 1774* (UK).

[566] The child died and the insurer paid the money assured by the policy to the father as administrator of the child's estate. It was held that, although as between the insurer and the company the policy was illegal and void, as between the father and the estate the father was entitled to retain the money for his own benefit, the presumption of advancement being rebutted by the evidence that the policy was effected for the benefit of the parent. Accordingly, the administrator of the estate could not resist the claim of the beneficiary to money in his hands, on the footing that the money was the product of a contract rendered illegal and void by statute. The question of title to the proceeds of the policy was insufficiently connected with that to which the legislation had been directed.

---

103. (1810) 34 ER 97.
104. (1808) 33 ER 677.
105. (1808) 33 ER 677 at 680. In *Curtis v Perry* (1802) 31 ER 1285 at 1288, Lord Eldon had left open the question of the effect of these statutes upon implied trusts.
106. (1875) 1 Ch D 419.

Recent United States decisions deal with legislation of a similar nature to that with which this appeal is concerned. They do so in a manner consistent with the older authorities. *In re Torrez*[107] concerned federal laws which limited the right to receipt of federally subsidised irrigation water to landowners of parcels not exceeding a particular acreage. If a farmer had a holding in excess of the acreage limitation, the result was loss of eligibility for irrigation water for the excess acreage. Mr and Mrs Torrez were already receiving their maximum allotment of subsidised water before they purchased additional land in the names of their son and daughter-in-law. The son and daughter-in-law wished to sell the property in order to finance a reorganisation of their affairs under Ch 11 of the federal bankruptcy law. The issue was whether they were at liberty to do so and, in particular, whether the illegality of the purpose of their parents in putting the property in their names was destructive of a resulting trust in favour of the parents. The Court of Appeals held that the resulting trust was enforceable. It referred to various relevant factors under the law of California, as follows:

> These factors include the completed nature of the transaction, such that the public can no longer be protected by invocation of the rule that illegal agreements are not to be enforced; the absence of serious moral turpitude on the part of the party against whom the defense is asserted; the likelihood that invocation of the rule will permit the party asserting the illegality to be unjustly enriched at the expense of the other party; and disproportionality of forfeiture as weighed against the nature of the illegality.[108]

Their Honours went on to refer to previous statements to the effect that one who takes title to land in the name of another 'for the purpose of defrauding the government cannot enforce a resulting trust **[567]** in his favour'.[109] The Court of Appeals then referred to the decision of the California Court of Appeal in *Hainey v Narigon*.[110] It had been held there that it was wrong to impose a resulting trust upon property purchased by the plaintiff in the name of the defendant pursuant to an agreement between them which permitted the plaintiff to subvert the loan requirements of the federal Veterans Administration legislation.[111] The California Court of Appeal held that, because the agreement violated the federal statute and regulations governing loans to veterans and was contrary to public policy, the plaintiff was not entitled to enforce the trust; a lien was imposed on the property in favour of the plaintiff but only for the net amount of his financial investment in it.

In *In re Torrez* the Court of Appeals distinguished *Hainey* in the following passage:

> Essential to *Hainey* was the fact that the applicable statutes and regulations explicitly prohibited assignment of benefits conferred upon a veteran in connection with the VA guarantee of home loans for veterans ... Here, no prohibitions exist against the acquisition of excess land; instead, federal regulations provide merely for the loss of eligibility for receipt of water upon such acquisition ... Similarly lacking in *Hainey* were

---

107. (1987) 827 F 2d 1299 (9th Cir).
108. *In re Torrez* (1987) 827 F 2d 1299 at 1301 (9th Cir).
109. *In re Torrez* (1987) 827 F 2d 1299 at 1302 (9th Cir). Reference was made to the Restatement Trusts, 2d, §444, pp 405–406. See also Scott and Fratcher, *Law of Trusts*, 1989, par 444.
110. (1966) 55 Cal Rptr 638.
111. 38 USCA §3704 as renumbered in 1991 by Pub L 102-83 par 5(a), (c)(1).

the problems of disproportionality of forfeiture to illegality, given the court's grant of a lien to plaintiff in the amount of his investment in the property notwithstanding his illegal conduct.[112]

The Court of Appeals then dealt with the public policy consideration that recognition of a resulting trust would give judicial sanction to a continuing fraudulent scheme against the federal government. The Court pointed out[113] that the government was entitled, under the legislation, to deny eligibility for subsidised water in respect of the excess acreage, saying that any public policy objections might adequately be addressed by administrative proceedings under those provisions.

Against the background traced above we accept the submission for the appellants that the crucial step is to identify the relevant public policy, beginning with the provisions of the Act, before and after the amendments made in 1988. The Bent Street property was purchased before the commencement of those amendments but it was after their [568] commencement that the application for subsidy was lodged on 25 July 1989 and the subsidy towards the purchase of the Kidman Lane property was procured.

The scheme of the Act and the facts of the case

We have already referred to s 35 as it stood before its repeal. Nothing turns upon it directly for the purposes of this case. There was no 'transfer', being the purported creation of a trust in respect of any property in which the Corporation already held an interest as described in the section.

As we have indicated, Pts III, IV, V and VI of the Act were repealed with effect from 19 December 1988. Part V (ss 20–27B) had been headed 'Advances on mortgage for purposes of homes'. Section 20 empowered the Corporation to make an advance to an eligible person on the prescribed security, to enable that person, among other things, to purchase a dwelling-house together with the land on which it was erected. The maximum advance was $25,000 (s 21). With an exception not presently relevant, no advance was to be made to any person unless the Corporation was satisfied that (i) the dwelling-house in question was intended to be used by the person as a home for himself and his dependants and (ii) neither the person nor the person's spouse was the owner of any other dwelling-house (s 23). If at any time, in the opinion of the Corporation, any money advanced had not been applied for the purpose for which it was advanced, the Corporation might, by notice in writing, call in the whole or part of that amount (s 27(1)) and remedies were given for the recovery of that amount by the Corporation (s 27(2)).

Section 32A empowered the Corporation to call up, by notice in writing, the whole of the moneys secured under the mortgage on the relevant property, making the moneys due and payable, if, at the time of the making of the advance, a person had declared 'that the person was not the owner of any dwelling-house' or 'that the wife or husband of the person was not the owner of any dwelling-house' other than the one to which the

---

112. *In re Torrez* (1987) 827 F 2d 1299 at 1302. See also as to resulting trusts and the Veterans Administration housing laws, *Johnson v Johnson* (1987) 237 Cal Rptr 644.
113. *In re Torrez* (1987) 827 F 2d 1299 at 1302.

advance related and it subsequently had come to the knowledge of the Corporation that the declaration was untrue. In this way, ss 23 and 32A were linked.

The scheme of the Act changed in 1988 with the Amendment Act. This implemented an agreement (the Agreement) made 9 November 1988 between the Commonwealth of Australia and the Bank.[114] Section 16 of the Amendment Act inserted the Agreement as Sch 1 to the Act. Clause 11 of the Agreement provided for payment by the Commonwealth of an interest subsidy to the Bank upon 'Subsidised Advances' made by the Bank. The term 'Subsidised Advances' was defined in cl 1 of the Agreement as including an advance made by the [569] Bank in accordance with a certificate of entitlement issued by the Commonwealth to an entitled applicant.

These provisions were implemented by amendments to the Act. In place of Pts III, IV, V and VI, new Pts III (ss 15–23), IV (ss 24–30), V (ss 31–37) and VI (ss 38–38H) were inserted. Section 15(1)(b) provides that a person may apply to the Secretary for a certificate of entitlement in relation to a subsidy on a subsidised advance that the person may seek from the Bank. The certificate of entitlement shall specify the maximum amount determined under s 25, in respect of which subsidy is payable, and the rate of interest payable on the advance (s 17). The rate of interest upon an initial advance is 6.85 per cent per year (s 31). Section 18(1)(b) obliges the Secretary not to issue a certificate of entitlement unless satisfied that the person is not the owner of any dwelling-house other than the dwelling-house in respect of which the advance is payable. The $25,000 received upon the Kidman Lane purchase was the maximum amount for which subsidy was payable.

The Secretary may, by notice of cancellation, cancel the subsidy from the date specified in the notice if the Secretary is satisfied that a certificate of entitlement in relation to the advance was issued as a result of a false statement made by the person to whom it was issued, or where the person was not entitled to the certificate (s 26(1)).

Where a subsidy has ceased to be payable under s 26 for either of the above reasons, the Secretary may, by notice in writing, require payment to the Commonwealth of the amount specified in the notice in the manner and within the period specified in the notice (s 29(1)). The amount in the notice might be the whole or such part of the amount of subsidy as the Secretary determined to be reasonable (s 29(2)). Where a person has failed to comply with a notice, the amount specified in the notice may be recovered from the person in a court of competent jurisdiction as a debt due to the Commonwealth (s 29(4)). Section 30 states:

(1) The Secretary may, on behalf of the Commonwealth, by instrument in writing:
   (a) write off an amount that a person has been required to pay to the Commonwealth under section 29;
   (b) waive the right of the Commonwealth to recover from a person the whole or part of an amount that the person has been required to pay to the Commonwealth under that section; or

---

114. The agreement is analysed in *Westpac Banking Corporation v Commissioner of Stamp Duties (Qld)* [1994] 2 Qd R 212 at 218–223.

(c) allow a person who has been required to pay an amount to the Commonwealth under section 29 to pay that amount by such instalments as are specified in the instrument.

(2) A decision under subsection (1) takes effect:

(a) on the day specified in the notice, being the day on which the decision is made or any day before or after that day; or

(b) if no day is so specified — on the day on which the decision is made.

Decisions under s 26, and those requiring payment under s 29, are [570] 'reviewable decisions' within the meaning of the definition in s 4. The consequence is that they attract the operation of the system of internal review and review by the Administrative Appeals Tribunal pursuant to ss 43 and 44 of the Act.

Reference also should be made to certain provisions of the *Crimes Act 1914* (Cth) which were in force at all material times. It is not suggested by counsel for the first respondent that any of the parties to the litigation had rendered themselves liable for prosecution under those provisions. Rather, he draws attention to them in connection with what he describes as the wide operation of the Act itself. He submits that these provisions showed that the legislature had not left the Act without attendant criminal sanctions for contravention.

The provisions in question are ss 29A, 29B, 29D and 86. Section 86 creates conspiracy offences, s 29A deals with false pretences and s 29D defrauding the Commonwealth or a public authority under the Commonwealth. Section 29B should be set out in full. It states:

Any person who imposes or endeavours to impose upon the Commonwealth or any public authority under the Commonwealth by any untrue representation, made in any manner whatsoever, with a view to obtain [sic] money or any other benefit or advantage, shall be guilty of an offence.

Penalty: Imprisonment for 2 years.

On the other hand, counsel for the appellants points to these provisions in support of the proposition that the purpose of the Act is sufficiently served by such penalties and that the denial of the resulting trust would cause prejudice to a person in the position of Mrs Nelson without furthering the objects of the legislation. Reference is made to the statement in *Archbolds (Freightage) Ltd v S Spanglett Ltd*,[115] adopted by Jacobs J in *Yango*,[116] that the purpose of a statute may sufficiently be served by the penalties prescribed for the offender.[117] It then is submitted that the imposition of the additional sanction, the inability of the first appellant to enjoy the proceeds of what otherwise is her beneficial ownership of the Bent Street property, would not be an appropriate adjunct to the scheme for which the Act provides.

That submission should be accepted. Further, the relevant provisions of the legislation, before and after the Amendment Act, show its purpose to be the provision of public

---

115. [1961] 1 QB 374 at 390.

116. (1978) 139 CLR 410 at 432–433.

117. Cf Bell, 'Conceptions of Public Policy' in Cane and Stapleton (eds), *Essays for Patrick Atiyah*, 1991, pp 94–97.

moneys to facilitate the purchase of housing by eligible persons, but on the footing that the eligible person not own another dwelling. The means by which that purpose has been effected have changed from secured loan to interest subsidy [571] in respect of an advance by the Bank. But it has consistently been the scheme of the legislation that, if the public moneys are misapplied, they are made recoverable by the Corporation or the Commonwealth. However, as the cases on the former s 35 demonstrate, the interest of the Corporation or the Commonwealth in the dwelling or proceeds of sale thereof is co-extensive with the funds provided by it; if they be restored then effect may be given to a trust in respect of the balance of the equitable interest in the dwelling or the proceeds of sale thereof.

A question in the present case thus arises as to whether the trust in respect of the proceeds of sale which Mrs Nelson asserts in her favour is tainted by illegality because of its association with or furtherance of a purpose which is contrary to the policy of the law as indicated by the scheme of the Act. If that be so, the question then is whether the consequence is that (i) no relief is available to Mrs Nelson, or (ii) relief may be granted but upon terms apt to make good the concern of the Commonwealth which was denied by the grant of the subsidy in respect of Kidman Lane whilst, as she always intended, Mrs Nelson was beneficial owner of the Bent Street property.

In our view, the answer to the first question is in the affirmative. The findings in the Supreme Court show that the title to Bent Street was taken in the name of the children, with the intention that Mrs Nelson be the beneficial owner so as to put her in an advantageous position later to obtain, if she so wished, financial assistance under the Act by concealing the true state of affairs.

It may have been that a change of heart upon which she had acted before she sought to enforce the resulting trust may have meant that the trust was never more than incipiently illegal. But that issue does not arise. The purpose was implemented with the obtaining of the subsidy for the Kidman Lane purchase. Mrs Nelson still holds this property. The litigation concerns ownership of the fund from the later sale of the Bent Street property. Given this state of affairs, the question remains as to what are the limitations upon the relief obtainable by Mrs Nelson.

In our view, as the price of obtaining the relief she seeks for the recognition and enforcement of a resulting trust in respect of the whole of the balance of the proceeds of sale of the Bent Street property, Mrs Nelson must be prepared to do equity according to the requirements of good conscience. That may involve consideration of more than the interests of the parties to the litigation. Here, good conscience calls for the taking by Mrs Nelson of steps sufficient to satisfy the demands of the underlying policy of the Act.

This requires denial to Mrs Nelson of the benefit in respect of the purchase of the Kidman Lane property which she has obtained by her unlawful conduct. This would appear to us to be a sum representing the present value of the difference, over the term of the loan agreement dated 30 August 1989, for the advance by the Bank to Mrs Nelson of $25,000, between the subsidised interest rate and that rate which, upon [572] its usual terms, the Bank would have charged Mrs Nelson on an advance of $25,000 over the same period and for the same purpose.

That sum should be in the same amount as that which the Commonwealth might properly specify in a notice given to Mrs Nelson under s 29 of the Act.

If Mrs Nelson were to tender to the Commonwealth that amount which the Commonwealth might properly have specified in a notice given under s 29 of the Act, it is to be presumed that the Commonwealth would accept it. In particular, it is to be presumed that the amount would not be written off by the Commonwealth under par (a) of s 30(1) and that there would be no waiver under par (b) of the right of the Commonwealth to recover the amount of the subsidy.

The state of the record before this Court does not enable us to compute the sum we have mentioned (the Benefit Sum). The solicitors for the first appellant and for the first respondent should be given the opportunity to agree that amount, after such consultation with the Commonwealth and the Bank as they may be advised. If that agreement is not reached on or before 30 November 1995, any party should have liberty to apply to this Court. It would appear, in that event, to be necessary to refer the proceeding to the Equity Division of the Supreme Court for a finding as to the amount of the Benefit Sum. The Judge or Master dealing with the matter then might admit such further evidence as might be necessary to dispose of the matter.

If the agreement mentioned is reached, then declarations made in this Court should take effect finally to dispose of the case without further litigation in the Supreme Court.

What is required is the formulation of, and acceptance by Mrs Nelson of, a term upon the relief to which she is otherwise entitled which denies to her the benefit she obtained by her unlawful conduct and provides for the payment to the Commonwealth of the Benefit Sum.

Comments

1. See Radan & Stewart at **17.8–17.21**.
2. Since *Nelson v Nelson*, the courts have upheld transactions which hid beneficial interests to gain access to the first home buyers grant: *Robins v Robins* [2006] WASC 301. Trusts have also been upheld when people were seeking to avoid land tax and minimise capital gains tax: *Tesoriero v Tesoriero* [2007] NSWSC 54. These transactions were not struck down for illegality as the legislative schemes were not aimed at making such trusts unenforceable and the underlying policy of the statutes did not require equity to strike them down.

Trusts and public policy

17.4   Ellaway v Lawson [2006] QSC 170

Court: Supreme Court of Queensland

Facts: Mary Knight died on 6 July 2005. The beneficiaries under her will were Mary's daughters, Mrs Lawson and Mrs Ellaway. The will appointed Mrs Lawson as executrix.

Under clause 3(c)(ii), Mrs Ellaway was not to receive her interest until she either divorced her husband or he was dead. Mrs Ellaway sought to have the condition struck out on the basis that it was contrary to public policy.

Issue: The issue was whether the clause encouraged Mrs Ellaway to divorce, and in that sense, was against public policy.

Decision: Douglas J found that the tendency of the clause was not against public policy.

Extracts: In this extract, Douglas J reviews the authorities on public policy and conditions which encourage divorce.

Douglas J

[2] Mrs Lawson receives her share immediately but by cl 3(c)(ii) of the will, Mrs Ellaway does not receive her bequest 'until such time as ... (she) ... either —

(i)   divorces her current husband; or

(ii)   her current husband dies ...'

[3] If the gift does not take effect there is a gift over to a Catholic Parish church which was served, and responded through the Archdiocese, but did not appear on the hearing of the application.

[4] The applicant contends that the limitation imposed by the will on Mrs Ellaway's receipt of the bequest is void as being contrary to public policy. The respondent's executrix, Mrs Lawson, argues that the High Court decision in *Ramsay v Trustees Executors and Agency Co Ltd*[118] requires me to determine this issue in favour of the will as it stands and to dismiss the application.

[5] It is clear that the testatrix wished to prevent her son-in-law from benefiting from a bequest to her daughter. That conclusion stems from the terms of the will. I was also presented with evidence dealing with Mrs Knight's wishes in respect of that issue. There was no objection to my receiving it, although Mr Mullins SC for the respondent executrix, who swore the relevant affidavit, submitted that, in the ordinary case, such extrinsic evidence would not be admissible where the words of limitation are clear. He submitted that these words were clear but that the admissibility of such evidence was not free from doubt on a review of the relevant authorities.[119] Latham CJ said that the question must be decided without evidence in *Ramsay*.[120] Mr Mullins also submitted that the evidence in the affidavit led at least to the conclusion that Mrs Knight was not motivated by a wish to see her daughter divorced or her son-in-law dead but by a wish to ensure that her daughter's financial interests were protected.

[6] It seems to me that such evidence is unlikely to be useful in the ordinary case and I was not assisted in the construction of this clause by the evidence led here. My view about the usefulness of the evidence is also influenced by the approach of the majority in the High Court in *Ramsay*, which was to examine objectively the tendency of the clause attacked to ascertain whether it was contrary to public policy.

[7] Such an approach was applied by Lowe J at first instance in the Victorian Supreme Court in *In re Ramsay*.[121] There the will provided that the estate be held by trustees:

---

118. (1948) 77 CLR 321.

119. See *Re Caborne* [1943] Ch 224 at 228; *Re Thompson* [1939] 1 All ER 681 and *Re Johnson's Will Trusts* [1967] 1 Ch 387 at 394.

120. (1948) 77 CLR 321 at 327.

121. [1948] VLR 347.

... to pay the income of my estate to my son George Binnie Ramsay for such period and so long as he shall remain married to his present wife Irene Ramsay and on the termination of such period in trust for my said son absolutely provided however that should my said son predecease his said wife during such period my estate shall go to my said nephew Robert Ramsay and my sister Mary Marshall Baillieu in equal shares.

[8] His Honour analysed the relevant test usefully at 349–350. He concluded, in reliance on a statement of Lord Atkin in *Fender v St John-Mildmay*,[122] that, if a court was inquiring whether the tendency of a gift was such as to make it invalid, that tendency could only be established if the 'generality of mankind will be induced by a gift of the kind in question to act in the way which is against the policy of the law'. Having analysed the likely consequences in that case, he concluded, when dealing with the tendency of the clause to encourage a divorce:

I find it almost impossible to suppose that a wife whose husband is enjoying the income of a fund from which she will benefit while she is his wife and who must know that her conduct will probably result in her losing that benefit and her injured husband getting the corpus of the estate, would ordinarily be willing to terminate it.[123]

[9] His approach proved influential when the matter went on appeal to the High Court. Latham CJ said:[124]

I agree with *Lowe J* — and the contrary has not been argued upon this appeal — that the provision in this particular case was intended (so far as intention is important) to secure an income to the son during the marriage, and to prevent his wife obtaining any interest, either directly under the father's will, or indirectly through her husband's will, in the corpus. There is nothing illegal in such an intention — it is simply a case of a testator choosing his beneficiaries.

What then is the tendency of the provision as affecting the conduct of the son? In applying the principle which was called in argument 'the tendency test', what is to be considered is the general tendency of the provision, and not the particular circumstances or characteristics of the persons concerned: see *Re Wallace; Champion v Wallace*.[125] The learned judge applied the test as stated by Lord Atkin in *Fender v St. John-Mildmay*[126] in his consideration of the validity of an agreement for marriage to take place after a decree nisi should be made absolute. The agreement was attacked as tending to lead to immorality in the form of irregular sexual relations during the period before the decree was made absolute. Lord *Atkin* said:[127] — 'But assuming, as we must, that the harmful tendency of a contract must be examined, what is meant by tendency? It can only mean, I venture to think, that taking that class of contract as a whole the contracting parties will generally, in a majority of cases, or at any rate in a considerable number

---

122. [1938] AC 1 at 13.
123. [1948] VLR 347 at 351.
124. (1948) 77 CLR 321 at 326–329.
125. [1920] 2 Ch 274 at 278.
126. [1938] AC 1.
127. [1938] AC 1 at 13.

of cases, be exposed to a real temptation by reason of the promises to do something harmful, ie, contrary to public policy; and that it is likely that they will yield to it. All kinds of contracts provide motives for improper actions, e.g., benefits deferred until the death of a third party, and contracts of insurance. To avoid a contract it is not enough that it affords a motive to do wrong: it must surely be shown that such a contract generally affords a motive and that it is likely to be effective.'

The appellant contends that this rule was properly applied in the case of *Re Caborne; Hodge v Smith*.[128] This decision of *Simonds* J was the basis of the appellant's argument. In that case the court considered the validity of a provision which was different in form, but was identical in substance with that to be found in the present case. The only difference was that there was an absolute gift in the first instance to a son of a testatrix which was cut down to a gift of income if his then wife was still alive and married to him. It was held[129] that this provision could fairly be represented 'as a direct encouragement, either himself to commit those acts which would enable his wife to proceed against him [for divorce]', or to take advantage of his wife's offences. The decision was that the provision was void.

The question whether a case falls within the prohibited class must be determined by a consideration of its general tendency, as Lord *Atkin* said, to provide a temptation and an estimate of the risk that persons would yield to that temptation.

...

In spite of what is said in *Re Caborne*[130] I can see no adequate reason for presuming that it can be said generally of beneficiaries under a will that they would be likely to use wrongful methods in order to obtain a divorce so as to get money. The question is whether such provisions would, in general, present a temptation to a man to destroy his marriage by improper means to which it would be likely that he would yield. The fact that it would be known that he would obtain a pecuniary advantage by bringing his marriage to an end would in itself be an element which would deter most persons from setting out to destroy their own marriages. Some persons, however, would not be influenced by consideration of what might be called social sanctions as distinct from moral considerations, but, on as good a judgment as I can form on the matter, I am not prepared to adopt the view of mankind which was applied in *Re Caborne*.[131] The result of that view would be that if a father had a married daughter and provided in his will for the payment of an allowance to her if her husband died before her or if she were unfortunate enough to be divorced from him, the provision would be invalid because it would tempt her to terminate her marriage in order to get the allowance. Where certain grounds exist a person is entitled under the law to a divorce. In the present case the mere existence of the provision in question in the father's will would lead a court to scrutinize very carefully the evidence in any divorce proceedings to which the son was a party. In my opinion it is not to be assumed that persons will, notwithstanding all

---

128. [1943] Ch 224.
129. [1943] Ch 224 at 229.
130. [1943] Ch 224.
131. [1943] Ch 224.

deterrents, do unlawful or corrupt acts in order to obtain a divorce so as to get money. The argument of the appellant in this case asks the court to determine the validity of the challenged provision by reference to what may not unfairly be described as 'highly improbable contingencies'.

[10] Similarly Starke J said:[132]

A disposition by will is contrary to public policy if it is injurious to public interests or has a tendency to injure public interests (*Fender v St John-Mildmay*[133]). Some provisions are recognized as harmful in themselves, for instance, provisions in general restraint of marriage or provisions requiring the separation of husband and wife. Others have a tendency to injure the public interests of which *Egerton v Brownlow*[134] is an example. But it must be a general tendency to injure public interests; to do something harmful to public interests having regard to human nature and not the character of particular individuals. The tendency must be 'substantial and serious', 'a real temptation ... to do something harmful, ie contrary to public policy'[135] and one to which parties are likely to succumb.

The question whether such a tendency exists is one of law for the court and depends upon the provisions of the will and any relevant surrounding circumstances. It is clear that the testator desired to exclude his son's wife, so far as he could, from any benefit from his estate. But testators frequently, I am afraid, cut off their children with the proverbial penny for marrying against their will. Dispositions of this character, unjust though they may be, do not infringe any rule of public policy. But what are the harmful tendencies of the present will? It was not seriously suggested that the general tendency of the will would operate as an inducement to the son to get rid of his wife by criminal means. Such a suggestion would be 'fanciful and unreal' and has even been described as 'ridiculous'. But it was contended that the general tendency of the will would operate as a direct encouragement to the son either to commit matrimonial offences which would enable his wife to divorce him or to take advantage of his wife's offences. It is not, as Lord *Atkin* observed,[136] contrary to public policy that married persons should be divorced. The contention ignores, I think, the moral standards and conduct of decent and ordinary members of the community and concludes that these standards would be wholly insufficient to withstand the temptation of the pecuniary advantage arising under the terms of the will. It should be observed that the termination of the marriage by means of divorce could not be achieved without the active participation of the wife in the proceedings. And if the husband and wife acted in concert to procure a divorce they might easily defeat their ends and lay themselves open to a charge of conspiracy. The contention that the provisions of the will have a tendency to induce departure from the standards of ordinary moral and decent persons for a pecuniary advantage is, I think, unreal and fanciful.

---

132. (1948) 77 CLR 321 at 330–331.
133. [1938] AC 1.
134. (1853) 10 ER 359.
135. [1938] AC 1 at 13.
136. [1938] AC 1 at 17.

So far I cannot think that the public interests are in any way impaired or harmfully affected by the terms of the will.

Next it was contended that the provisions of the will are contrary to public policy because they tend to weaken the *consortium vitae* of matrimony — the matrimonial relations of husband and wife, to foster inharmonious relations between husband and wife.

This contention is also, I think, unreal and fanciful. I cannot accept the view that the provisions of the will expose persons to the temptation of destroying or weakening the serenity, comfort and affections of their home life for the pecuniary advantages provided in the will. The contention envisages a standard of morality and conduct so strange that I dismiss the notion that ordinary and decent members of the community might by reason of the provisions of the will destroy or weaken the *consortium vitae* of matrimony.

But the case of *Re Caborne; Hodge v Smith*[137] was relied upon. It is not identical in terms with the present will but I agree that in effect it is indistinguishable from the present case and is contrary to the view I have expressed. The case is not binding upon this Court and, with respect, I am unable to adopt the conclusion there reached. To adopt Lord *Atkin's* phrase it affords 'another instance of the horrid suspicions to which high minded men are sometimes prone'.[138] The 'unruly horse',[139] public policy, got away, I am afraid, with the learned judge and carried him off the course.

[11] See also McTiernan J.[140] Dixon and Williams JJ dissented and Dixon CJ did not repent his dissent in *Church Property Trustees, Diocese of Newcastle v Ebbeck*[141] but, in my view, *Ramsay* does create a significant hurdle to the success of the applicant's submissions.

[12] The passages I have extracted show that the High Court in *Ramsay* did not follow the English decision in *Re Caborne; Hodge v Smith*.[142] That decision was applied in the later English decision *In re Johnson's Will Trusts*[143] where, in that jurisdiction, the law has taken a different course. Mr Cameron sought to distinguish *Ramsay* on the basis that, first, there is a positive obligation on his client either to divorce her husband, or to hope that he predeceases her and, secondly, because she takes no income from the bequest pending the occurrence of the conditions attacked. He also submits that the separate subclauses dealing with divorce and death are not separable from each other.

[13] It does not seem to me to be correct to say that there is any obligation on Mrs Ellaway to divorce her husband. Nor would I have thought that the condition that she not take the bequest until her current husband dies could be attacked. As Latham CJ said in *Ramsay*:

---

137. [1943] 1 Ch 224.
138. [1938] AC 1 at 16.
139. [1938] AC 1 at 10.
140. (1948) 77 CLR 321 at 333–335.
141. (1960) 104 CLR 394 at 403.
142. [1943] Ch 224.
143. [1967] Ch 387.

There is no doubt that in the case of some persons a gift of this character would have a tendency to bring about a divorce. In exactly the same way there is no doubt that in the case of some persons the gift of property to A for life and then to B would lead B to kill or to try to kill A so as to accelerate his interest. But normal human beings do not kill others to get property, and it has never been held that gifts coming into operation upon the death of a person are unlawful as providing encouragement to murder.[144]

[14] If it were appropriate to sever the clause about divorce from the clause dealing with death then I expect that I could do it, cf Williams J in dissent in *Ramsay*.[145]

[15] I am slightly more troubled by the fact that, in this will, there is no provision for the applicant to receive any income from the bequest during the continuance of her marriage. Factually, at least, that could provide a greater incentive to divorce than existed in *Ramsay*. The reasons from the majority decisions extracted above, however, are expressed in general terms in decrying the likely effect of pecuniary advantage on people's willingness to divorce lawfully. On questions of principle, as this is at least to some extent, there is little merit in reducing a test to be applied in a variety of circumstances to an examination of the precise financial incentive likely to encourage a happily married person to divorce. It should not be a question of debating over the figure for which one will forego one's spouse.

[16] On the other hand, changing attitudes to divorce since *Ramsay*, reflected in the far greater proportion of marriages that end in divorce and the diminished difficulty of establishing the grounds for divorce brought about by statutory changes since 1948, may suggest that the public policy issues no longer loom so large in allowing provisions such as these to be attacked. Generally speaking, those changes may support an argument that it is no longer forbidden to provide for the possible dissolution of a marriage contract, which the policy of the law was said to be 'to preserve intact and inviolate'.[146] It is not necessary for me to go down that path. Even if it were, there is still significant support for marriage as an institution and little to support the view that any increase in the number of divorces is socially desirable. Again, it is still necessary to establish the statutory grounds for a divorce to be granted by the Courts having jurisdiction under the Family Law Act 1975 (Cth).

[17] Another reason for rejecting the argument that this provision is void as against public policy may arise from the provisions of the Succession Act 1981 (Qld) permitting application to be made to this Court, where adequate provision has not been made from an estate for the proper maintenance and support of the deceased person's spouse, child or dependant, for better provision to be made; see s 41. In other words, there is a statutory method of ameliorating the effect of a will that may fail to make adequate provision for a person in the applicant's position so why use the blunt instrument of public policy to attack the clause when a more precise tool has been provided by Parliament? That is recognised by the form of this application which seeks such relief as an alternative.

---

144. (1948) 77 CLR 321 at 327.
145. (1948) 77 CLR 321 at 337.
146. See *H v W* (1857) 69 ER 1157 at 1159, relied on by Dixon J in *Ramsay* at 332 and see Windeyer J in *Ebbeck* at 414–415.

[18] Principally, it is my view, however, that the tendency of the clause is not itself illegal or void as against public policy, and that the decision in *Ramsay* requires the dismissal of this application.

Comments

1. See Radan & Stewart at **17.59–17.73**.
2. Racist conditions have traditionally not been found to be against public policy. In *Kay v South Eastern Sydney Area Health Service* [2003] NSWSC 292, the testatrix (who wrote her own will) gave a gift on trust as follows:

   I give The Children's Hospital at Randwick $10,000 for treatment of White [underlined twice] babies.

   It was argued that the condition was against public policy and that the condition could be struck off. Young J disagreed and found that the condition was an integral part of the gift which could not be removed. Both the *Racial Discrimination Act 1975* (Cth), s 8 and the *Anti-Discrimination Act 1977* (NSW), s 55, expressly provided that any charitable disposition was not subject to legislative control. On that basis Young J found that there was no public policy against a racist condition. The gift was a valid charitable gift and on that basis could be upheld.

The rule against perpetuities

17.5   Nemesis Australia Pty Ltd v Commissioner of Taxation (2005) 225 ALR 576

Court: Federal Court of Australia

Facts: Nemesis Australia Pty Ltd ('Nemesis') was a trustee of the Steve Hart Family Trust ('SHFT'). In the years 1995, 1997, 1998 and 1999 it made a number of distributions of income from the trust to three other related trusts which were controlled by corporate trustees. The corporate trustees were beneficiaries under the SHFT.

Nemesis was assessed as being liable for taxation on the amounts which had been distributed. The Commissioner argued that the distributions had not been effective as they offended the rule against perpetuities. This was because the SHFT had a vesting period of 80 years from the date it was created. The related trusts were created later, and consequently their vesting periods were also later, vesting outside of the 80-year period set by the Steve Hart Family Trust.

Issue: The issue for the court was whether the dispositions to the related trusts offended the rule against perpetuities. If they did, a further issue arose as to whether that automatically meant that the dispositions were ineffective.

Decision: Tamberlin J found that the dispositions were valid. There was a chance that the powers of appointment in the related trusts would be exercised within the perpetuity period and on that basis the legislation allowed for the court to 'wait and see' whether the powers were exercised within time. Tamberlin J found that the effect of the wait and see provisions was that the disposition must be treated as if it were not subject to the rule until such time as it becomes established that the vesting must occur outside the perpetuity period.

Extracts: In this extract Tamberlin J reviews the perpetuities legislation and discusses how it modifies the common law rule.

Tamberlin J

[581] The Property Law Act 1974 (Qld) (the Property Act) relevantly provides as follows:

208 *Powers of appointment*

    (1)   For the purposes of the rule against perpetuities a power of appointment *shall be treated as a special power* unless —

        (a) in the instrument creating the power it is expressed to be exercisable by 1 person only; and

        (b) *it could* at all times during its currency when that person is of full age and capacity *be exercised by the person so as immediately to transfer to* or *otherwise vest in the person the whole of the interest governed by the power* without the consent of any other person or compliance with any other condition, not being a formal condition relating only to the mode of exercise of the power.

    ...

209 *Power to specify perpetuity period*

    (1)   Except as otherwise provided in this part where the instrument by which any disposition is made so provides the *perpetuity period applicable* to the disposition under the rule against perpetuities instead of being of any other duration *shall be such number of years not exceeding 80 as is specified in the instrument as the perpetuity period* applicable to the disposition.

    (2)   Subsection (1) shall not have effect where the disposition is made in exercise of a special power of appointment but where a period is specified under that subsection in the instrument creating such a power the period shall apply in relation to any disposition under the power as it applies in relation to the power itself.

    (3)   If no period of years is specified in an instrument by which a disposition is made as the perpetuity period applicable to the disposition but a date certain is specified in the instrument as the date on which the disposition shall vest the instrument shall, for the purposes of this section, be deemed to specify as the perpetuity period applicable to the disposition a number of years equal to the number of years from the date of the taking effect of the instrument to the specified vesting date.

210 *Wait and see rule*

(1) Where apart from the provisions of this section and of section 213 a disposition *would be void* on the ground that the interest disposed of *might not become vested until too remote a time* the disposition shall be treated *until* such time (if any) *as it becomes established that the vesting must occur, if at all, after the end of the perpetuity period* as if the disposition were not subject to the rule against perpetuities, and its becoming so established shall not affect the validity of anything previously done in relation to the interest disposed of by way of advancement, application of intermediate income or otherwise.

... (emphasis added)[147]

[582] Rule against perpetuities

As pointed out by the Queensland Law Reform Commission in its 1971 report entitled 'On the Law Relating to Perpetuities and Accumulations', the rule against perpetuities performs a useful social function in limiting the power of members of generations past from tying up property in such a form as to prevent its being freely disposed of in the present or the future.

The common law rule and its operation were summarised by the Privy Council in *Air Jamaica Ltd v Charlton*:[148]

> ... no interest is valid unless it must vest, if it vest at all, within a period of a life in being, the date of the gift plus 21 years. The rule is applied remorselessly. A gift is defeated if, *by any possibility, however remote*, it may vest outside the perpetuity period. It is not saved by the fact that, in the event, it vests inside the period ...
>
> The rule against perpetuities also applies to the administrative trusts and powers of the trustee. Such powers must not be capable of being exercised outside the perpetuity period, and they may be void even if all trusts to which they are attached are valid. Where, therefore, there is a trust for A for life with remainder to his widow for life, then the trustees are given a power to sell or lease land comprised in the settlement, the power is void ab initio because it is capable of being exercised at any time during the widow's life, and she may survive A by more than 21 years (emphasis added).

Accordingly, a disposition to vest within the life of A plus 22 years would be void under the above rule.

It is well settled that the rule against perpetuities is not a rule of construction but a peremptory command of law.[149] In the present case, the applicable rule is set out in s 209(1) and provides that the perpetuity period applicable to a disposition under the rule against perpetuities shall be such number of years, not exceeding 80, as is specified

---

147. For related legislation in other jurisdictions see *Perpetuities and Accumulations Act 1985* (ACT) s 9; *Perpetuities Act 1984* (NSW) s 8(1); *Law of Property Act 2000* (NT) s 184; *Perpetuities and Accumulations Act 1992* (Tas) s 9; *Perpetuities and Accumulations Act 1968* (Vic) s 6; *Property Law Act 1969* (WA) s 103. The rule has been abolished in South Australia: *Law of Property Act 1936* (SA) s 61.

148. [1999] 1 WLR 1399 at 1408–9.

149. See J C Gray, *The Rule against Perpetuities*, 1942, p 629.

as the perpetuity period in the instrument. As noted, the relevant date specified in the SHFT deed is 80 years and it terminates on 31 May 2061. The other trusts for the trustee beneficiaries have vesting dates ranging from 1 March 2072–16 February 2074, which are all outside the 80-year period specified in the SHFT deed.

The rule against perpetuities does not apply to *general* powers of appointment. This is because a person who is entitled to exercise a general power of appointment is treated in law as the owner of property since he or she can, with the 'stroke of a pen', become the owner. In these circumstances, the power to appoint includes a power to appoint oneself, which is equivalent to beneficial ownership. On the other hand, a *special* power of appointment is not equivalent to beneficial ownership. In *Jacobs' Law of Trusts in Australia*[150] the distinction is stated in these terms:

> A person may ... by a settlement inter vivos have vested in him a power to appoint property of the ... settlor to third parties. This is a *special* power of appointment and is to be distinguished from a *general* power of appointment under which the donee of the power may appoint the property to any person absolutely, *including himself*. In the case of general powers no question of trusts arises. This is because there are no particular parties in whose interests equity might intervene, the object of the power being the whole of mankind (emphasis added).

In *Re Gulbenkian's Settlement Trusts; Whishaw v Stephens*,[151] Lord Reid pointed out that:

> [583]   [W]hen a power is given to trustees *as such,* it appears to me the situation must be different. A settlor ... who entrusts a power to his trustees must be relying on them in their fiduciary capacity so they cannot simply push aside the power and refuse to consider whether it ought in their judgment to be exercised. And they cannot give money to a person who is not within the classes of persons designated by the settlor ... (emphasis added).

Special or general power

The principles concerning the classification of a power as either a general or a special power require a liberal and practical approach to be taken.

In the present case, the power under the SHFT deed is for the benefit of a limited class of beneficiaries. It is true that the class of beneficiaries is very wide. However, this is not determinative. In this case, the power to designate beneficiaries expressly excludes certain persons, including the trustee, and, therefore, is not a general power.

[Nemesis] contends that the power of appointment in the SHFT deed is general because it is a hybrid power and s 208 does not apply because the trustee of the SHFT can vary the deed to allow itself to be added as a beneficiary. [Nemesis]'s argument is that, by taking these steps, the trustee could vary the trust to invest in itself the whole of the interest without the consent of any other person.

For a number of reasons, s 208 does apply in the present case. First, the variation steps have not been taken and no variation has been made by the trustee. Therefore, at the

---

150. R P Meagher and W M C Gummow, *Jacobs' Law of Trusts in Australia*, 5th ed, Butterworths, Sydney, 1986, p 38.
151. [1970] AC 508 at 518.

relevant time, the trustee was obliged to appoint income among a specified class. Second, the variation clause in the SHFT deed does not allow the trustee to end the trust by obtaining the trust property for itself. Third, any power must be exercised for the benefit of the beneficiaries and an appointment by the trustee to itself by effecting a variation could not be seen to be for the benefit of the beneficiaries. Finally, even if such steps were available to the trustee, the power must be such that the trustee can immediately, without the consent of any other person or compliance with any other condition, appoint to itself. In the present case, this cannot be done. Steps must be taken by the trustee and consents are required. Accordingly, the power in the present case, in its nature and by reason of its exclusions and provisions, is properly characterised as a special power of appointment. If, contrary to my conclusion, the view were taken that the power of appointment in the SHFT deed was a general power, s 208 of the Property Act operates, in my opinion, to deem it to be a special power.

Reading back

The commissioner submits that in the present case the deeds of the other trusts must be read in conjunction with, and as part of, the principal deed, namely, the SHFT deed. Under the SHFT deed, the nominated trustee beneficiaries are appointed in their capacity *as trustees*. There is no appointment to them as specified persons. The appointment is to each trustee as trustee of a particular trust. Therefore, any income distributed to the trustee in that capacity is controlled by the vesting date specified in the deed of settlement of that trust. This means that, for example, if a trust fund is appointed in 2060, several weeks before the vesting date specified in the SHFT deed, that fund becomes subject to the provisions of the later trust deed and the vesting date under the SHFT deed will extend to the date specified as the vesting date under the later trust deed and, [584] therefore, breach the 80-year requirement. Accordingly, reading the deeds of the other trusts together with the SHFT deed, there is a breach of the perpetuity period from the moment when the deeds of the other trusts, which provide for vesting outside the perpetuity period specified under the SHFT deed, are executed.

This submission is supported by the decision in *Re Pilkington's Will Trusts*.[152] In this case, the trustees purported to exercise a special power for the benefit of an infant beneficiary by resettling the trust property upon themselves on terms of new trusts for her benefit. The House of Lords held that the new trusts must be read as if they had been created by the settlor of the existing settlement, at the time of the existing settlement, and, when tested against the rule against perpetuities in that situation, they failed. The principle is stated by Viscount Radcliffe (with whom Lords Hodson, Jenkins and Devlin agreed) in the following terms:

> It is not in dispute that, if the limitations of the proposed settlement are to be treated as if they had been made by the testator's will and as coming into operation at the date of his death, there are trusts in it which would be *void ab initio* as violating the perpetuity rule. They postpone final vesting by too long a date.[153]

---

152. [1964] AC 612.
153. [1964] AC 612 at 641.

The substitution of a new trust does not alter this position. Viscount Radcliffe continued:

> ... I think that the important point for the purpose of the rule against perpetuities is that the new settlement is only effected by the operation of a fiduciary power which itself 'belongs' to the old settlement.[154]

From its inception, the SHFT had as its beneficiaries the trustees of the other trusts. Accordingly, it is appropriate to read back into the SHFT deed the vesting dates provided for in the deeds of the other trusts, with the consequence that there is a breach of the 80-year period in the use of each of the other trusts. In this case, the effect of the specification in the other trusts of the vesting date outside the 80-year period is that the rule against perpetuities is infringed and the appointments are void under s 209.

The dates of the deeds are as follows. Under the SHFT deed, the date of the making of the deed is 1 June 1981 and the vesting date is 31 May 2060. Under the HFT No 2 deed, the date of the making of the deed is 2 March 1993 and the vesting date is 1 March 2072. Under the HFT No 3 deed, the date of the making of the deed is 28 August 1993 and the vesting date is 27 August 2072.

J H C Morris and W Barton Leach[155] express the principle as follows:

> A *special* power of appointment *is not equivalent to beneficial ownership.* Therefore the appointees must be capable of taking under the instrument creating the power; and the perpetuity period starts from the date when the power is created, not from the date when it is exercised. Otherwise, property could be appointed from settlement to settlement in perpetuity without ever coming under the control of an absolute owner. The appointment is 'read back' into the instrument creating the power, as if the donee were filling in blanks in the donor's instrument (emphasis added).

Wait and see rule

Section 210(1) of the Property Act provides that, where a disposition would be void on the ground that the interest disposed of *might* not become vested until too remote a time, the disposition *shall* be treated until such time as **[585]** it becomes *established* that the vesting *must occur*, if at all, after the end of the perpetuity period as if the disposition were not subject to the rule against perpetuities.

Nemesis says that, even if s 209 of the Property Act applies in the present case, there is no breach of the rule against perpetuities because of the 'wait and see' rule in s 210.

At common law and under s 210, the 'wait and see' rule is designed to enable the court to look at what actually occurs before the expiry of the perpetuity period and the circumstances as they have unfolded in order to determine whether there has been a vesting within the perpetuity period. If, in fact, the interest is vested prior to the expiry of the perpetuity period, notwithstanding that a longer period is provided for in the trust deed, the trust may be valid. The trust would then not infringe the rule against perpetuities. Accordingly, s 210 was introduced to remedy what was seen as

---

154. [1964] AC 612 at 642.
155. J H C Morris and W Barton Leach, *The Rule Against Perpetuities*, 1956, p 140.

a deficiency in the common law rule, namely, that the common law was concerned with possible or hypothetical, and not actual, events. Under the common law rule, the disposition of an interest is void if, at the date of creation, it could *by any possibility* vest outside the perpetuity period. This rule was criticised by the Queensland Law Reform Commission because it may in fact happen that, at the time at which the question of validity is contested, the contingencies have already been satisfied within the perpetuity period.

The commissioner submits that s 210 has no operation to save the appointment in the present case because there is no relevant element of contingency. Counsel submits that this is not a case of a disposition that 'might not become vested until too remote a time' because it is certain from the date the deed is executed that the settlor had made a positive determination that the income must vest, if at all, within a period which was longer than the relevant perpetuity period. This is not a case, for example, where one looks at the actual circumstances at the end of a life in being at the age of the beneficiaries to see whether they will take within 21 years from the death of the life in being. The breach of the perpetuity period in the present case arises by reason of the reading back of the vesting dates in the deeds of the other trusts to the original SHFT deed, because it can be seen that, immediately upon the deeds of the other trusts coming into effect, the period provided for in those deeds *must* exceed the 80-year period so that there is an infringement of s 209. There was no uncertain contingency about which to wait and see, such as a life in being which could be within a wide spectrum of possible duration. By way of contrast, in *Re Thomas Meadows & Co Ltd and Subsidiary Companies (1960) Staff Pension Scheme Rules*,[156] where the 'wait and see' rule was applied, there was no specification that the vesting date was outside the perpetuity period.

Under the 'wait and see' rule, one waits to see whether the event happens within the perpetuity period. If it does, it is a valid exercise, and if it does not, it is invalid. The commissioner submits that if the 'wait and see' rule applied in the present circumstances, the perpetuity period of 80 years would be meaningless because, on this approach, every discretionary trust, even one expressed to be for 100 years, would be valid for at least 80 of those years. Accordingly, since a new trust could be set up before the end of the 80-year period providing for a distribution within a further 80 years, the trust property could be rolled over indefinitely.

[586] In the present case, it is, in my view, possible that the trustee of each trust might *not* exercise the discretion conferred by the other trust deeds to advance the vesting date to a date within the perpetuity period as set out in the SHFT deed. It can, therefore, be said that the interest disposed of *might* not become vested until too remote a time. However, s 210 also provides that where a disposition might be void on the basis that it might not become vested until too remote a time, the disposition must be treated as valid until such time as it is *established* that the vesting *must* occur after the end of the perpetuity period, as if the disposition were not subject to the restriction. Therefore, in my view, s 210 operates to validate a disposition and anything done in relation to the interest disposed of by way of the application of intermediate income.

---

156. [1971] 1 Ch 278 at 285.

The intention of the 'wait and see' rule is to avoid the draconian consequences which otherwise flow from the rigid application of the rule against perpetuities. It applies in the present case because under each of the relevant trust deeds the trustees possess a discretionary power *to advance* the vesting date. The definition of 'vesting date' in each of the deeds includes a provision that the expression 'vesting date' shall mean the specified date or an *earlier* date nominated by the trustees in their sole and unfettered discretion. Such power includes the nomination of an earlier date within the 80-year period under the SHFT deed.

Until the expiration of the 80-year period provided for in the SHFT deed, it is not possible to say that the vesting *must* occur after the end of the original 80-year period. Accordingly, everything done within that period is valid.

Consequently, in the present case, any possible breach of the rule against perpetuities within the perpetuity period specified in the SHFT deed must be treated as a valid disposition. For this reason, the submission advanced for the commissioner must fail. In my view, the integers of s 210 are made out in the present case, namely:

- the interest disposed of under the SHFT *might* not become vested until too remote a time;
- that disposition must be treated until such time as *it becomes established that the vesting must* occur outside the perpetuity period *as if the disposition were not subject to the rule.*

Both these integers having been satisfied in this case, the rule against perpetuities has no application and the dispositions are not nullities. Accordingly, the commissioner's basis of claim must fail.

Consequence of invalidity

In view of my conclusion in relation to s 210 and the operation of the 'wait and see' rule, none of the income dispositions are invalid for breach of the 80-year rule, and it is necessary to wait and see what in fact happens within the 80-year period before it can be established that the fund must vest outside the period.

I will, nevertheless, briefly express my conclusions in relation to the consequences of invalidity on the basis that the appointments of income are to be treated as invalid. If the rule applies to invalidate dispositions under the SHFT deed, then the income for the relevant years in relation to those default beneficiaries who renounced their entitlement would come within s 99 A. I accept the submission for the commissioner on this point that, as between the trustee and the beneficiaries who have disclaimed, the disclaimers made by them operate [587] retrospectively so that they must be treated as never entitled to the income for the purposes of s 97 of the Income Tax Assessment Act 1936 (Cth) in respect of the relevant income years.[157]

> **Comment**
> 1. See Radan & Stewart at **17.84–17.106**.

---

157. See *Ramsden v FCT* (2004) ATC 4659; [2004] FCA 632.

18

CHARITABLE TRUSTS

Introduction

18.1 Charitable trusts are express trusts, which exist for a purpose rather than for identifiable beneficiaries. The purposes must be ones that fall within the definition of charity. The extracts in this chapter deal with the following issues:

- the definition of charity: *Commissioner for Special Purposes of the Income Tax v Pemsel* [1891] AC 531;
- trusts for the relief of poverty: *Ballarat Trustees Executors & Agency Co v Federal Commissioner of Taxation* (1950) 80 CLR 350;
- trusts for the advancement of education: *Oppenheim v Tobacco Securities Co Ltd* [1951] AC 297;
- trusts for the advancement of religion: *Commissioner of Taxation v Word Investments* (2008) 236 CLR 204;
- trusts for purposes otherwise beneficial to the community: *Incorporated Council of Law Reporting (Qld) v Federal Commissioner of Taxation* (1971) 125 CLR 659; and
- the *cy-près* doctrine: *Attorney-General (NSW) v Perpetual Trustee Co Ltd* (1940) 63 CLR 209.

The definition of charity

18.2 Commissioner for Special Purposes of the Income Tax v Pemsel [1891] AC 531

Court: House of Lords

Facts: A trust of land had been created in 1813 which devoted one-half of the rent and profits from the land to the Moravian Church (known also as the 'Protestant Episcopal Church' or the 'United Brethren') for its work in 'heathen lands'. Another quarter was devoted to maintaining, supporting and educating the children of the priests and missionaries in the Church. The remaining quarter was devoted to establishing and maintaining 'choir-houses' in the United Kingdom (accommodation for members of the Church who were single).

Pemsel was the treasurer of the Church. He sought an allowance for the income tax that had been paid by the Church on the basis that it was a charitable institution. The Commissioner refused. Pemsel brought a writ of mandamus to force the Commissioner to grant the allowance. The action failed at trial before Lord Coleridge CJ and Grantham J but succeeded on appeal before the Court of Appeal (Lord Esher MR, Lopes and Fry LJJ). By the time of the appeal to the House of Lords the Commissioner had accepted the charitable status of the grants for education and housing, but still resisted recognising the charitable status of the gift to the Church for work overseas.

Issue: The issue was whether the gift of rent and profits for use in missionary work overseas was a charitable purpose.

Decision: The majority (Lord Watson, Lord Herschell, Lord Macnaghten and Lord Morris; Lord Halsbury LC and Lord Bramwell dissenting) found that the disposition was charitable.

Extracts: In this extract Lord Macnaghten discusses the meaning of 'charity'.

Lord Macnaghten

[580] That according to the law of England a technical meaning is attached to the word 'charity,' and to the word 'charitable' in such expressions as 'charitable uses,' 'charitable trusts,' or 'charitable purposes,' cannot, I think, be denied. The Court of Chancery has always regarded with peculiar favour those trusts of a public nature which, according to the doctrine of the Court derived from the piety of early times, are considered to be charitable. Charitable uses or trusts form a distinct head of equity. Their distinctive position is made the more conspicuous [581] by the circumstance that owing to their nature they are not obnoxious to the rule against perpetuities, while a gift in perpetuity not being a charity is void. Whatever may have been the foundation of the jurisdiction of the Court over this class of trusts, and whatever may have been the origin of the title by which these trusts are still known, no one I think who takes the trouble to investigate the question can doubt that the title was recognised and the jurisdiction established before the *Act of 43 Elizabeth* (*Statute of Elizabeth*)[1] and quite independently of that Act. The object of that statute was merely to provide new machinery for the reformation of abuses in regard to charities. But by a singular construction it was held to authorize certain gifts to charity which otherwise would have been void. And it contained in the preamble a list of charities so varied and comprehensive that it became the practice of the Court to refer to it as a sort of index or chart. At the same time it has never been forgotten that the 'objects there enumerated,' as Lord Chancellor Cranworth observes, 'are not to be taken as the only objects of charity but are given as instances.'[2] Courts of Law, of course, had nothing to do with the administration of trusts. Originally, therefore, they were not concerned with charities at all. But after the passing of the *Act 9 Geo 2*, commonly known as the *Statute of Mortmain*, which avoided in certain cases gifts to 'uses called charitable uses,' alienations and dispositions to charitable uses sometimes came under

---

1. *Charitable Gifts Act 1601* (Eng).
2. *London University v Yarrow* (1857) 1 De G & J 72 at 79.

the cognizance of Courts of Law, and those Courts, as they were bound to do, construed the words 'charitable uses' in the sense recognised in the Court of Chancery, and in the *Statute of Elizabeth*, as their proper meaning. I have dwelt for a moment on this point, because it seems to me that there is a disposition to treat the technical meaning of the term 'charity' rather as the idiom of a particular Court than as the language of the law of England. And yet of all words in the English language bearing a popular as well as a legal signification I am not sure that there is one which more unmistakeably has a technical meaning in the strictest sense of the term, that is a meaning clear and distinct, peculiar to the law as [582] understood and administered in this country, and not depending upon or coterminous with the popular or vulgar use of the word.

...

[583] No doubt the popular meaning of the words 'charity' and 'charitable' does not coincide with their legal meaning; and no doubt it is easy enough to collect from the books a few decisions which seem to push the doctrine of the Court to the extreme, and to present a contrast between the two meanings in an aspect almost ludicrous. But still it is difficult to fix the point of divergence, and no one as yet has succeeded in defining the popular meaning of the word 'charity.' The learned counsel for the Crown did not attempt the task. Even the paraphrase of the Master of the Rolls is not quite satisfactory. It would extend to every gift which the donor, with or without reason, might happen to think beneficial for the recipient; and to which he might be moved by the consideration that it was beyond the means of the object of his bounty to procure it for himself. That seems to me much too wide. If I may say so without offence, under conceivable circumstances, it might cover a trip to the Continent, or a box at the Opera. But how does it save Moravian missions? The Moravians are peculiarly zealous in missionary work. It is one of their distinguishing tenets. I think they would be surprised to learn that the substantial cause of their missionary zeal was an intention to assist the poverty of heathen tribes. How far then, it may be asked, does the popular meaning of the word 'charity' correspond with its legal meaning? 'Charity' in its legal sense comprises four principal divisions: trusts for the relief of poverty; trusts for the advancement of education; trusts for the advancement of religion; and trusts for other purposes beneficial to the community, not falling under any of the preceding heads. The trusts last referred to are not the less charitable in the eye of the law, because incidentally they benefit the rich as well as the poor, as indeed, every charity that deserves the name must do either directly or indirectly. It seems to me that a person of education, at any rate, if he were speaking as the Act is speaking with reference to endowed charities, would include in the category educational and religious charities, as well as charities for the relief of the poor. Roughly speaking, I think he would exclude the fourth division. Even [584] there it is difficult to draw the line. A layman would probably be amused if he were told that a gift to the Chancellor of the Exchequer for the benefit of the nation was a charity. Many people, I think, would consider a gift for the support of a lifeboat a charitable gift, though its object is not the advancement of religion, or the advancement of education, or the relief of the poor. And even a layman might take the same favourable view of a gratuitous supply of pure water for the benefit of a crowded neighbourhood. But after all, this is rather an academical discussion. If a gentleman of education, without legal training, were asked what is the meaning of 'a trust for charitable purposes,' I think he would most probably reply, 'That sounds like a legal phrase. You had better ask a lawyer.'

Comments

1. See Radan & Stewart at **18.6–18.10**.
2. Once a charitable purpose has been identified a charitable trust must also provide a benefit to the public. The benefit must be for the entire public or for a significant proportion of it: *Re Compton* [1945] Ch 123. This is discused below in the extract from *Oppenheim v Tobacco Securities Co Ltd* [1951] AC 297.
3. The fact that a charitable trust makes a profit does not rob it of charitable status: *Re Resch's Will Trusts; Le Cras v Perpetual Trustee Co Ltd* [1969] 1 AC 514. In *Tasmanian Electronic Commerce Centre Pty Ltd v Commissioner of Taxation* (2005) 219 ALR 647, the promotion of digital commerce and the provision of aid to businesses for that purpose was deemed to be charitable. Heerey J, at 662, said:

   > Once it is accepted that assistance to business and industry can provide a public benefit of the kind which the law recognises as charitable, a proposition which does not seem to be in dispute in the present case, I do not see how the fact that individual businesses may benefit can be a disqualifying factor. On the contrary, if business in general is assisted, it seems inevitable that some firms at least will become profitable, or more profitable, as a result of that assistance. There would be no point in the exercise if this were not the case. It would be an odd result if an institution established to benefit business could only qualify as a charity if the recipients of its benefits made losses or did no more than break even.

   This issue is discussed more fully below in the extract from *Commissioner of Taxation v Word Investments* (2008) 236 CLR 204.
4. Efforts to reform the definition of charity have so far not met with much success in Australia. Small changes were introduced in the *Extension of Charitable Purpose Act 2004* but recently the Henry Review of taxation has recommended introducing more widespread reform: Commonwealth of Australia, *Australia's Future Tax System Consultation Paper* (Canberra: Treasury, 2008).

Trusts for the relief of poverty

18.3   Ballarat Trustees Executors & Agency Co v Federal Commissioner of Taxation (1950) 80 CLR 350

Court: High Court of Australia

Facts: Henry Angus Cameron left a sum of money to the St Andrew's Presbyterian Hospital Cathedral Place Melbourne to be used to pay the medical fees of those who were in the opinion of the Board of Management of the Hospital 'deserving people who [were] unable to pay any fees or such fees as private patients'.

Estate tax was levied on the amount gifted to the hospital by the Commissioner of Taxation. The trustee of the estate appealed that decision and argued that s 8 (5) of the

Estate Duty Assessment Act 1914–1942 said that gifts to hospitals for the relief of persons in 'necessitous circumstances' were exempt from tax.

Issue: The issue was whether the gift was a gift for the relief of poverty, and, in that sense, a gift for persons in 'necessitous circumstances'.

Decision: The High Court (Kitto J sitting alone) found that the gift was not for persons in necessitous circumstances as the Board might decide to use the funds to waive fees for people who might not be able to pay, but who may nevertheless not be poor.

Extracts: In this extract Kitto J attempts to define what it means to be poor for the law of charity.

Kitto J

[354] There are two classes of persons for whose relief the trust fund in this case is to be established and maintained, namely: (1) persons who are, in the opinion of the Board, deserving people who are unable to pay any fees; and (2) persons who are, in the opinion of the Board, deserving people who are unable to pay such fees as private patients in St Andrew's Hospital are usually required to pay. The income of the trust fund may be applied, consistently with the will, for the benefit of either or both of these classes and it follows, in my opinion, that the trust fund is not entitled to the exemption provided by s 8 (5), unless persons of the second of these classes are persons in necessitous circumstances in the sense I have mentioned.

It should be stated here that both parties to this appeal were willing to assume that the purposes to which the trust fund is devoted by the will are valid charitable purposes, if not as being for the relief of poverty, at least as being within the fourth class mentioned by Lord Macnaghten in *Commissioners for Special Purposes of Income Tax v. Pemsel*.[3] Accordingly the commissioner, while not admitting that monies applied for the benefit of the second class of persons mentioned in clause 10 of the will would be applied for the relief of poverty, did not contend that the disposition of the trust fund was invalid; and the appellant did not contend that by virtue of s. 131 of the *Property Law Act 1928* the trust fund was to be regarded as applicable exclusively for the benefit of the first class of persons mentioned in clause 10 of the will.

The question therefore comes down to this: whether persons can be said to be in necessitous circumstances if nothing is known of their financial position except that, when in need of hospital attention, they are unable to pay such fees as patients at St Andrew's Hospital are usually required to pay. It is true that it is the Board's opinion, and not the fact, as to the inability to pay such fees which is made by the will the test of eligibility; but it must be assumed, I think, for the purposes of s 8 (5) that the opinion of a responsible Board entrusted with a fiduciary duty to form a proper opinion will coincide with the fact.

---

3. (1891) AC 531; cf *Re Chown; Teele v University of Melbourne* (1939) VLR 443; *Perpetual Trustee Co v St Luke's Hospital* (1939) 39 SR (NSW) 408; 56 WN 181.

The amount of the fees charged at St Andrew's may vary from time to time; but it is sufficient, I think, to consider the existing situation. The trust fund cannot be for the relief of persons in necessitous circumstances, unless it be true to say that under [355] present-day conditions a person can be described as in necessitous circumstances if, for want of more ample means than he has, he must go for hospital treatment either to a free public hospital or to an intermediate hospital less expensive than St Andrew's.

The expression 'necessitous circumstances' is not defined by the Act, nor has it been judicially interpreted in its present or a comparable context. It does not admit of definition in terms so precise as to provide a yardstick for the determination of every case which may arise. Yet it is an expression which is familiar in common speech, not as limited to cases of abject penury, but as conveying the notion which the Oxford Dictionary endeavours to express as 'having little or nothing to support oneself by; poor, needy; hard up.' None of these words or phrases can be selected as by itself precisely defining the expression. 'There are degrees of poverty less acute than abject poverty or destitution, but poverty nevertheless'[4] and 'necessitous circumstances' refers in my opinion to some degree of poverty. 'In such matters one must often be guided to a great degree by one's own experience in the use of terms'.[5] Approaching the matter in that way, I should say that a person is in necessitous circumstances if his financial resources are insufficient to enable him to obtain all that is necessary, not only for a bare existence, but for a modest standard of living in the Australian community. Such an attempted explanation of the expression is perhaps hardly less vague than the expression itself; but it serves to bring out what I think is important in this case, namely, that s 8 (5) refers to inability to afford what may fairly be regarded as necessities for persons living in Australia, as distinguished from things which are merely desirable advantages.

On this view of the matter, I should not be prepared to apply the expression 'in necessitous circumstances' to that class of persons in Australia who enjoy a modestly comfortable existence and yet are unable to afford hospital treatment at a cost equal to the fees charged at St. Andrew's. There is a considerable margin between necessitous circumstances and affluence, and in my opinion within that margin fall many cases of inability to afford as much for hospital treatment as a privately-conducted hospital like St Andrew's has to charge under modern conditions, even though not carried on for profit.

Evidence was given by Mr McFerran to the effect that free public hospitals in Melbourne have been unable to accept all the patients [356] who have desired to enter them, and that this has been the situation ever since the testator's death in 1947. I have no difficulty in believing that this is correct. It was said on behalf of the appellant that in consequence of this situation persons who cannot afford to pay fees such as are charged at St Andrew's cannot secure hospital accommodation and therefore are in necessitous circumstances. I do not think that this contention should be accepted. Consistently with the will, the income of the trust fund may be used to pay St Andrew's fees for persons who could have gained admission to free public hospitals. Moreover the trust created by the will is perpetual, and the present inadequacy of public hospital accommodation may well be merely temporary. But in any case the question is not whether the persons for whose benefit the income of

---

4. *Lemm v Federal Commissioner of Taxation* (1942) 66 CLR 399 at 410, per Williams J.
5. *Perpetual Trustee Co Ltd v Federal Commissioner of Taxation* (1931) 45 CLR 224 at 233, per Dixon J.

the trust fund will be applied would be unable to secure admission to public hospitals; it is whether persons whose financial resources are inadequate to enable them to pay the fees usually charged at St Andrew's can be said on that account alone to answer the description of persons in necessitous circumstances. I do not think that they can.

Comments
1. See Radan & Stewart at **18.47–18.53**.
2. The relief of poverty also covers trusts for the aged and the impotent. Examples of such trusts include: trusts for the elderly, *City of Hawthorn v Victorian Welfare Association* [1970] VR; trusts for orphans, *Attorney-General (NSW) v Perpetual Trustee Co Ltd* (1940) 63 CLR 209; trusts for 'crippled children', *The Cram Foundation v Corbett-Jones* [2006] NSWSC 495; trusts for the blind, *Re Inman (dec'd)* [1965] VR 238; and trusts for single mothers ('who have erred once but not twice'), *Re Wyld* [1932] SASR 298.

Trusts for the advancement of education

18.4   Oppenheim v Tobacco Securities Co Ltd [1951] AC 297

Court: House of Lords

Facts: John and Elizabeth Phillips created a trust and appointed Tobacco Securities Co Ltd to be the trustee. The income was to be used by the trustees to provide for the education of children of employees or former employees of British-American Tobacco or any of its subsidiary or allied companies. At the time of the litigation the number of employees of British-American Tobacco and its allied companies was in excess of 110,000 people.

Issue: The trust was created in perpetuity so could only be valid if it was charitable. The issue was whether the trust could satisfy the requirement for being in the pubic interest.

Decision: Lord Simonds, Lord Normand, Lord Oaksey and Lord Morton of Henryton, (Lord MacDermott dissenting) decided that the trust failed because it could not be considered to satisfy the requirement for being in the public interest as all the beneficiaries were named by reference to an employment relationship.

Extracts: In this extract Lord Simonds discusses why the test of public benefit requires that beneficiaries not be chosen by reference to a blood relationship or contractual relationship.

Lord Simonds

Before I turn to the authorities I will make some preliminary observations. It is a clearly established principle of the law of charity that a trust is not charitable unless it is directed to the public benefit. This is sometimes stated in the proposition that it must benefit the community or a section of the community. Negatively it is said that a trust is not charitable if it confers only private benefits. In the recent case of *Gilmour v Coats*[6] this principle was reasserted. It is easy to state and has been stated in a variety of ways, the earliest statement that I find being in *Jones v Williams*,[7] in which Lord Hardwicke LC, is briefly reported as follows: 'Definition of charity: a gift to a general public use, which extends to the poor as well as to the rich ...'. With a single exception, to which I shall refer, this applies to all charities. We are apt now to classify them by reference to Lord Macnaghten's division in *Income Tax Commissioners v Pemsel*,[8] and, as I have elsewhere pointed out, it was at one time suggested that the element of public benefit was not essential except for charities falling within the fourth class, 'other purposes beneficial to the community'. This is certainly wrong except in the anomalous case of trusts for the relief of poverty with which I must specifically deal. In the case of trusts for educational purposes the condition of public benefit must be satisfied. The difficulty lies in determining what is sufficient to satisfy the test, and there is little to help your Lordships to solve it.

[306] If I may begin at the bottom of the scale, a trust established by a father for the education of his son is not a charity. The public element, as I will call it, is not supplied by the fact that from that son's education all may benefit. At the other end of the scale the establishment of a college or university is beyond doubt a charity. 'Schools of learning and free schools and scholars of universities' are the very words of the preamble to the *Statute of Elizabeth*. So also the endowment of a college, university or school by the creation of scholarships or bursaries is a charity and none the less because competition may be limited to a particular class of persons. It is upon this ground, as Lord Greene MR, pointed out in *In re Compton*,[9] that the so-called Founder's Kin cases can be rested. The difficulty arises where the trust is not for the benefit of any institution either then existing or by the terms of the trust to be brought into existence, but for the benefit of a class of persons at large. Then the question is whether that class of persons can be regarded as such a 'section of the community' as to satisfy the test of public benefit. These words 'section of the community' have no special sanctity, but they conveniently indicate first, that the possible (I emphasize the word 'possible') beneficiaries must not be numerically negligible, and secondly, that the quality which distinguishes them from other members of the community, so that they form by themselves a section of it, must be a quality which does not depend on their relationship to a particular individual. It is for this reason that a trust for the education of members of a family or, as in *In re Compton*,[10] of a number of families cannot be regarded as charitable. A group of persons may be numerous but, if the nexus between them is their personal relationship to a single propositus or to several propositi, they are neither the community nor a section of the community for charitable purposes.

I come, then, to the present case where the class of beneficiaries is numerous but the difficulty arises in regard to their common and distinguishing quality. That quality

6. [1949] AC 426.
7. (1767) 2 Amb 651.
8. [1891] AC 531 at 583.
9. [1945] Ch 123 at 136.
10. [1945] Ch 123.

is being children of employees of one or other of a group of companies. I can make no distinction between children of employees and the employees themselves. In both cases the common quality is found in employment by particular employers. The latter of the two cases by which the Court of Appeal held itself to be bound, *In re Hobourn Aero Components Ld.'s Air Raid Distress Fund,*[11] is a direct authority for saying that such a common quality does not constitute its possessors a section of the public for charitable purposes. In the former case, **[307]** *In re Compton,*[12] Lord Greene MR, had by way of illustration placed members of a family and employees of a particular employer on the same footing, finding neither in common kinship nor in common employment the sort of nexus which is sufficient. My Lords, I am so fully in agreement with what was said by Lord Greene in both cases and by my noble and learned friend, then Morton LJ, in the *Hobourn* case,[13] that I am in danger of repeating without improving upon their words. No one who has been versed for many years in this difficult and very artificial branch of the law can be unaware of its illogicalities, but I join with my noble and learned friend in echoing the observations which he cited[14] from the judgment of Russell LJ, in *In re Grove-Grady*[15] and I agree with him that the decision in *In re Drummond*[16] 'imposed a very healthy check upon the extension of the legal definition of "charity"'. It appears to me that it would be an extension, for which there is no justification in principle or authority, to regard common employment as a quality which constitutes those employed a section of the community. It must not, I think, be forgotten that charitable institutions enjoy rare and increasing privileges, and that the claim to come within that privileged class should be clearly established. With the single exception of *In re Rayner,*[17] which I must regard as of doubtful authority, no case has been brought to the notice of the House in which such a claim as this has been made, where there is no element of poverty in the beneficiaries, but just this and no more, that they are the children of those in a common employment.

Learned counsel for the appellant sought to fortify his case by pointing to the anomalies that would ensue from the rejection of his argument. For, he said, admittedly those who follow a profession or calling, clergymen, lawyers, colliers, tobacco-workers and so on, are a section of the public; how strange then it would be if, as in the case of railwaymen, those who follow a particular calling are all employed by one employer. Would a trust for the education of railwaymen be charitable, but a trust for the education of men employed on the railways by the Transport Board not be charitable? and what of service of the Crown whether in the civil service or the armed forces? Is there a difference between soldiers and soldiers of the King? My Lords, I am not impressed by this sort of argument and will consider on its merits, if the occasion should arise, the case where the description of the occupation and the

11. [1946] Ch 194.
12. [1945] Ch 123.
13. [1946] Ch 194.
14. [1946] Ch 194 at 208.
15. [1929] 1 Ch 557 at 582.
16. [1914] 2 Ch 90.
17. 89 L J (Ch) 369.

employment is in effect the same, where in a word, if you know what a man does, you [308] know who employs him to do it. It is to me a far more cogent argument, as it was to my noble and learned friend in the *Hobourn* case,[18] that if a section of the public is constituted by the personal relation of employment, it is impossible to say that it is not constituted by 1,000 as by 100,000 employees, and, if by 1,000, then by 100, and, if by 100, then by 10. I do not mean merely that there is a difficulty in drawing the line, though that too is significant: I have it also in mind that, though the actual number of employees at any one moment might be small, it might increase to any extent, just as, being large, it might decrease to any extent. If the number of employees is the test of validity, must the court take into account potential increase or decrease, and, if so, as at what date?

I would end, my Lords, where I began, by saying that I concur in the reasoning of the Court of Appeal in the *Hobourn* case,[19] but there are certain points in the argument for the appellant about which I should say a few words. It was urged by counsel for the Attorney-General, who was allowed to address the House, that there was here a valid charitable trust created, since there was no private person who could sue to enforce the trust. I am not persuaded that this would be so, if the trust were otherwise enforceable. But in any case the test is not a valid one. If this trust is charitable, the Attorney-General can sue to enforce it: it does not follow that it is charitable because no one else can sue to enforce it. I would also, as I have previously indicated, say a word about the so-called 'poor relations' cases. I do so only because they have once more been brought forward as an argument in favour of a more generous view of what may be charitable. It would not be right for me to affirm or to denounce or to justify these decisions: I am concerned only to say that the law of charity, so far as it relates to 'the relief of aged, impotent and poor people' (I quote from the statute) and to poverty in general, has followed its own line, and that it is not useful to try to harmonize decisions on that branch of the law with the broad proposition on which the determination of this case must rest. It is not for me to say what fate might await those cases if in a poverty case this House had to consider them. But, as was observed by Lord Wright in *Admiralty Commissioners v Valverda*, while 'this House has no doubt power to overrule even a long established course of decisions of the courts provided it has not itself determined the question', yet 'in general this House will adopt this course only in plain cases where serious inconvenience or injustice would follow from perpetuating an erroneous construction or ruling of law.'[20] I quote with respect those [309] observations to indicate how unwise it would be to cast any doubt upon decisions of respectable antiquity in order to introduce a greater harmony into the law of charity as a whole.

Comment

1. See Radan & Stewart at **18.54–18.53**.

---

18. [1946] Ch 194.
19. [1946] Ch 194.
20. [1938] AC 173 at 194.

Trusts for the advancement of religion

18.5   Commissioner of Taxation v Word Investments
(2008) 236 CLR 204

Court: High Court of Australia

Facts: The Wycliffe Bible Translators ('Wycliffe') were a charitable group who sought to spread Christianity through the translation of the Bible into other languages. The organisation had been endorsed as a tax-exempt charity. Wycliffe had set up a separate company called Word Investments Ltd ('Word') which operated a funeral home business and an investment scheme. Word operated on a profit basis but all profits were paid to the charitable purposes of Wycliffe. The Federal Commissioner of Taxation refused to classify Word as an exempt charity.

Issue: The issue was whether Word was a charitable institution even though it was operated for profit.

Decision: Gummow, Hayne, Heydon and Crennan JJ (Kirby J dissenting) found that the company was charitable.

Extracts: In this extract the majority discusses the issue of whether Word's purposes were to advance religion.

Gummow, Hayne, Heydon and Crennan JJ

[214] *First issue: are Word's objects confined to charitable purposes?*

The primary argument. The Commissioner submitted that Word's objects were not confined to religious or charitable purposes. The Commissioner accepted that where the question was whether property was held by a trustee on trust for charitable purposes, the character of the trust as a trust for charitable purposes was not affected by the power of the trustee to invest the assets, or use them to carry on businesses, with a view to profit. But the Commissioner submitted that where the question was not whether the property was held by a trustee on trust for charitable purposes, but rather was whether an institution not holding its property as trustee, but owning it absolutely, was to be characterised as a charitable institution, its power to use its assets in business with a view to profit, and its utilisation of that power, was [215] crucial. The Commissioner submitted that if an entity claiming to be a charitable institution made a profit 'as an incidental activity, or as concomitant and ancillary to the conduct' of the entity's charitable activities, it would not cease to be a charitable institution. But he said that if the profit-generating activity went beyond the incidental or the ancillary, the institution was not charitable. The Commissioner relied on the following statement by Gibbs J (Barwick CJ, Menzies and Walsh JJ concurring) in *Stratton v Simpson*:[21]

---

21. (1970) 125 CLR 138 at 159–160.

It is established that 'an institution is a charitable institution if its main purpose is charitable although it may have other purposes which are merely concomitant and incidental to that purpose or in other words if each of its objects is either charitable in itself or should be construed as ancillary to other objects which themselves are charitable.[22] If however the non-charitable purpose is not merely incidental or ancillary to the main charitable purpose, the institution will not be charitable.[23]The Commissioner submitted that the main object of Word was not religious but was 'to engage in investment and trading activities for the purpose of raising funds for Wycliffe and other similar organisations'. The Commissioner submitted that the 'basic function' of Word was to conduct businesses, and the making of profits and the distribution of them to charitable institutions like Wycliffe were merely incidental to the conducting of businesses.

The Commissioner relied on a statement of Starke J that where the stated objects in a memorandum of association are 'of a mixed character and the memorandum does not make it clear which are its main or dominating characteristics', it was necessary to examine the activities of the company.[24] The Commissioner additionally relied on the following statement of Williams J in the same case about the Royal Australasian College of Surgeons:[25]

[I]n order to determine what is the main or dominant purpose of the College, it is a mistake to examine the objects contained in the memorandum in [a] disjunctive fashion. They should be examined in conjunction with one another and in the light of the circumstances in which the College was formed and of the manner in which the College is fulfilling the purposes for which it was incorporated.

The Commissioner further relied on *Roman Catholic Archbishop of Melbourne v Lawlor*.[26] That case concerned an attempted bequest to [216] an archbishop and three bishops 'to establish a Catholic daily newspaper'. The particular point which the Commissioner desired to extract from the case was put succinctly by Starke J thus: 'The objects and purposes of a Catholic newspaper are not, and can by no means be, confined to strictly charitable purposes.'[27]

Finally, the Commissioner relied on the following statement of Rand and Locke JJ in the Supreme Court of Canada in *Dames du Bon Pasteur v The King*:

We have today many huge foundations yielding revenues applied solely to charitable purposes; they may consist, as in one case, of a newspaper business; even if these foundations themselves carried on their charitable ministrations, to characterise them as charitable institutions merely because of the ultimate destination of the net

---

22. *Congregational Union of NSW v Thistlethwayte* (1952) 87 CLR 375 at 442, 450.
23. *Oxford Group v Inland Revenue Commissioners* [1949] 2 All ER 537; *In re Harpur's Will Trusts* [1962] Ch 78 at 87.
24. *Royal Australasian College of Surgeons v Federal Commissioner of Taxation* (1943) 68 CLR 436 at 448.
25. *Royal Australasian College of Surgeons v Federal Commissioner of Taxation* (1943) 68 CLR 436 at 452.
26. (1934) 51 CLR 1.
27. (1934) 51 CLR 1 at 25.

revenues, would be to distort the meaning of familiar language; and to make that ultimate application the sole test of their charitable quality would introduce into the law conceptions that might have disruptive implications upon basic principles not only of taxation but of economic and constitutional relations generally. If that is to be done, it must be by the legislature.[28]

The central authorities. It must be said at the outset that the Commissioner relied on authorities coming from a range of fields and on a range of issues — whether land was being used exclusively or wholly for charitable purposes so as to enjoy immunity from rates;[29] whether a bequest for a particular purpose was for charitable purposes;[30] whether a gift for charitable and non-charitable purposes, the whole gift being capable of devotion to the latter, was charitable;[31] will construction cases;[32] and cases about whether, for example, a building was exempt from rates on the ground that it was used exclusively for the religious work of a religious organisation.[33] The primary relevant line of authority, however, is that which is concerned with the predecessor to ss 50–5, 50–50 and 50–110 of the *Income Tax Assessment Act 1997 Cth* (the *1997 Act*), namely s 23(e) of the *Income Tax Assessment Act 1936* (Cth) (the *1936 Act*).[34] The Commissioner did rely on this line of authority.[35] The principal statements made in it were made **[217]** about companies in an age in which the ultra vires doctrine existed and in which it was mandatory for companies to state their objects in a memorandum of association. In that age, a failure by a company to comply with its objects could have deleterious consequences for third parties dealing with the company. It is not now mandatory for companies to state their objects in a memorandum of association, and the ultra vires doctrine no longer exists.[36] But there is no reason to suppose that the tests laid down in the s 23(e) line of cases no longer apply in relation to the *1997 Act* to companies like Word, which state objects in a memorandum. That is, it is necessary to examine the objects, and the purported effectuation of those objects in the activities, of the institution in question. In examining the objects, it is necessary to see whether its main or predominant or dominant objects, as distinct from its concomitant or incidental or ancillary objects, are charitable.[37]

---

28. [1952] 2 SCR 76 at 92.
29. *Salvation Army (Victoria) Property Trust v Fern Tree Gully Corporation* (1952) 85 CLR 159; *Scottish Burial Reform & Cremation Society Ltd v Glasgow Corporation* [1968] AC 138.
30. *Roman Catholic Archbishop of Melbourne v Lawlor* (1934) 51 CLR 1.
31. *Re Smith* [1967] VR 341 at 346; *Executor Trustee & Agency Co of South Australia Ltd v Australasian Conference Association Ltd* [1954] SASR 151 at 159–160.
32. *Stratton v Simpson* (1970) 125 CLR 138.
33. *Dames du Bon Pasteur v The King* [1952] 2 SCR 76; see also *Oxfam v Birmingham City District Council* [1976] AC 126.
34. It provided that the 'income of a religious ... charitable institution' was to be exempt from income tax.
35. *Royal Australasian College of Surgeons v Federal Commissioner of Taxation* (1943) 68 CLR 436 at 447–448, 450–451, 452; *Incorporated Council of Law Reporting (Qld) v Federal Commissioner of Taxation* (1971) 125 CLR 659 at 670–672.
36. See *Companies (Victoria) Code*, ss 66C, 67, 68. See now *Corporations Act 2001* (Cth), ss 124, 125.
37. *Royal Australasian College of Surgeons v Federal Commissioner of Taxation* (1943) 68 CLR 436 at 447, 448, 450, 452.

The distinction between purposes and objects. In *H A Stephenson & Son Ltd (In liq) v Gillanders, Arbuthnot & Co* Dixon J drew the following distinction:

> When the question is whether a particular transaction binds the company, or is extra vires, the well-known principle may not apply by which, in considering whether a company should be wound up because the substratum of its constitution has failed, its true, main, dominant or paramount purpose is ascertained and general clauses are understood as subsidiary, as conferring powers not independent but subserving the main end. In the one case the ultimate question is whether it is just and equitable that the company should be wound up, and, for its determination, general intention and common understanding among the members of the company may be important. In the other case the question is one of corporate capacity only, and this must be ascertained according to the true meaning of the memorandum interpreted by a fair reading of the whole instrument.

While the distinction may lack precise correspondence with the modern law since the abolition of the ultra vires doctrine, it applies precisely to companies like Word, which have a memorandum of association with an objects clause.[38]

What are the objects of Word? However, it is not necessary in this appeal to seek to distinguish between the main, predominant or dominant object and other objects. That is because Word has only one group of objects — a group of objects of advancing religious charitable [218] purposes. All other 'objects' which may seem to be outside that group are on their true construction either objects within that group, or powers to carry out objects within that group.

Clause 3 of Word's memorandum of association is too lengthy to quote, but it opens with the words: 'The object [sic] for which the company is established are ...' It suffices to quote the first three objects:

(a) (i) To proclaim preach teach enunciate expound and to propagate evangelise continue carry forward expand and increase the Christian Religion both in Victoria and throughout the rest of the world by all means whether oral printed visual audible mechanical or otherwise.

    (ii) To provide train maintain and send forth teachers preachers and lecturers who subscribe to the basis of belief of the member of the Company contained in Clause 8 hereof.[39]

    (iii) To co-operate with encourage and provide assistance both financial and otherwise for Evangelical Missionary Organisations and Evangelical Missionaries operating or to become operative in Victoria or elsewhere throughout the world.

The memorandum declares that the objects specified 'shall be regarded as independent objects'. Clause 3(a) of the memorandum sets out seventeen matters. Clause 3(a)(xvii), which gives a power to acquire equipment for the purposes of Word stands apart from the other sixteen matters and is of the same kind as those set out in sub-cll 3(b)–(ak). Among the other sixteen matters set out in cl 3(a) are numerous purposes, which, whether considered by themselves or in the context of cl 3, are plainly charitable (eg, sub-cl

---

38. (1931) 45 CLR 476 at 487.
39. Clause 8 sets out seven propositions comprising a declaration of faith.

3(a)(i)). There are other purposes in cl 3(a) which, considered by themselves, are not charitable, for example, cl 3(a)(iv), which provides: 'To hold rallies and other meetings in Victoria and when occasion arises through the rest of the world.' However, when the sixteen purposes enumerated in cl 3(a)(i)–(xvi) are read as a whole, each of them on its true construction states a charitable purpose — a purpose of advancing religion in a charitable sense. Those which taken separately are beyond that purpose are to be read down as being within it. Clauses 3(a)(xvii) and (c)–(ak) need to be read in the light of cl 3(b) which provides: 'To carry on any business or activity which may seem to the Company capable of being conveniently carried on in connection with the objects for which this Company is established.' This suggests that for the most part it is cl 3(a) which states the company's purposes, not cl 3(b)–(ak), which perform another function. That suggestion is confirmed by the radical difference between the matters listed in cl 3(a)(i)–(xvi) and the matters listed in cl 3(a)(xvii) and (b)–(ak). The former can truly be described as purposes, while the latter are not to be construed as purposes at all, but rather as powers.

[219] The most specific of the arguments advanced by the Commissioner for the conclusion that the objects for which Word's profits might be applied were not limited to religious or other charitable purposes centred on three provisions of the memorandum. One was cl 3(k) of the memorandum: 'To subscribe and make payments to any fund for religious charitable *or* benevolent objects of any description' (emphasis added). The second was cl 3(u):

> To set aside out of the profits of [Word] such sums as the Board of Directors thinks proper as reserved, for maintaining the whole or any part of [Word;s] property or for meeting contingencies and for any other purposes connected with the business of [Word] or any part thereof and the Board of Directors may invest the sums so set aside in the business of [Word] or in such securities as the Board of Directors selects.

The third was the incorporation by cl 3(aj) of cl 7 of the Third Schedule to the *Companies Act 1961* (Vic) which conferred a power 'to subscribe or guarantee money for charitable *or* benevolent objects, *or* for any exhibition, *or* for any public, general, *or* useful object' (emphasis added).

So far as cl 3(u) is concerned, a power to retain profits conferred on directors of a company which has charitable purposes cannot negate its character as a charitable institution. Its exercise, while it may delay the moment when assets are applied to charitable purposes, also increases the chance that more assets will eventually be so applied. So far as cl 3(k) and cl 7 of the Third Schedule are concerned, they do not create purposes. They confer powers only. Those powers do not authorise conduct which does not further the charitable purposes of Word.

The Commissioner's reliance on *Roman Catholic Archbishop of Melbourne v Lawlor* was misplaced. In that case Rich J, Starke J and Dixon J held that a gift by will of personal property 'to establish a Catholic daily newspaper' extended beyond charitable purposes. Gavan Duffy CJ and Evatt J, and McTiernan J, held that it did not. The question whether the 'purposes' stated in cl 3(a)(xvii) and (b)–(ak) are in truth purposes or merely powers is quite different from the question in *Lawlor's* case. It is true that the question whether all the purposes stated in cl 3(a) are charitable purposes and no more bear some analogy with that discussed in *Lawlor's* case, but it is clear that when the purposes in cl 3(a)(i)–(xvi) are read together they are all charitable purposes.

It is therefore necessary to reject the Commissioner's arguments so far as they submitted that Word had a 'commercial object of profit from the conduct of its business' which was 'an end in itself' and was not merely incidental or ancillary to Word's religious purposes. Word endeavoured to make a profit, but only in aid of its charitable purposes. To point to the goal of profit and isolate it as the relevant purpose is to create a false dichotomy between characterisation of an institution as commercial and characterisation of it as charitable.

[220] *Circumstances of Word's formation.* In addition to what flows from the construction to be given to the memorandum of association, it is necessary to take into account the circumstances in which Word was formed.[40] The Administrative Appeals Tribunal found that the founders of Word 'had a clear intention that its function was to raise funds for the benefit of [Wycliffe] and/or similar religious organisations'. Among the evidence supporting that finding was the assertion of Mr Ross Wilkerson, a director of both Word and Wycliffe, that the 'intention in establishing [Word] was to create a fundraising auxiliary primarily to support the religious activities of [Wycliffe] and the propagation of Christian religion'. He also said that Word 'was established as a financial support company for Wycliffe'. He further said that Word 'regards itself as a supporting arm of Wycliffe and the directors of [Word] have a close interest and involvement in the work of Wycliffe'; that Wycliffe recommends people to be directors of Word; and that the two companies share offices and staff. There was also evidence of David Cummings, who had served with Wycliffe Bible Translators (International) from 1957 (ie before Word was incorporated). He said that the group who founded Word had three points in mind:

1. That interested friends of Wycliffe might lend [Word] money, for the board of [Word] to invest, so that any profits would then go directly to the work of Bible translation and its affiliate activities such as Church Planting (establishing an initial core group of worshippers), training of pastors, literacy work, publishing the translated scriptures and recruiting nationals to be involved in translation work and preaching the gospel.

2. It was a way of highlighting the need for funding for the religious work of Wycliffe and an avenue for friends to have a vehicle to see their investment directly helping the religious work of Wycliffe Bible Translators and its workers.

3. The [Word] board then gave itself to finding the most profitable ways it could use the money, lent or given from the interested Christian public, that would gain the best income on the invested moneys. It was the intention that most (if not all) of the interest would be channeled into the religious work of Wycliffe or its members, with the balance of interest being returned to investors.

Word's activities. In *Royal Australasian College of Surgeons v Federal Commissioner of Taxation* McTiernan J said that whether the appellant in that case fulfilled the description of a scientific institution depended less on the fact that it could direct its efforts to scientific objects than 'what it does in pursuit of each of them'.[41] The [221] inquiry, so far as it is directed to activities, must centre on whether it can be said that the activities are

---

40. *Royal Australasian College of Surgeons v Federal Commissioner of Taxation* (1943) 68 CLR 436 at 452 per Williams J (circumstances in which the College was formed).

41. (1943) 68 CLR 436 at 450. See also at 448–449 per Starke J; at 452 per Williams J.

carried on in furtherance of a charitable purpose. So far as the actual activities of Word in furtherance of its purposes are relevant, it is plain that, subject to the Commissioner's contentions in relation to the second and third issues,[42] the funds paid out by Word were paid to bodies fulfilling charitable purposes. The activities of Word in raising funds by commercial means are not intrinsically charitable, but they are charitable in character because they were carried out in furtherance of a charitable purpose.

The *Dames du Bon Pasteur* case. The short answer to the Commissioner's reliance on *Dames du Bon Pasteur v The King*[43] is that Word's position does not depend on the mere fact that its revenues are applied solely to charitable purposes, but on the related fact that those are its sole purposes. Unlike the society in that case as viewed by the majority of the Supreme Court of Canada, Word is not a company with both charitable and non-charitable purposes which carried on commercial businesses and incidentally conferred benefits on charity; Word is a company having purposes which are solely charitable and which carried on commercial businesses only in order to effectuate those purposes.

Christian Enterprises Ltd v Commissioner of Land Tax (NSW). The Commissioner relied on the opinions of Nagle J at trial[44] and Walsh JA (Asprey JA concurring) on appeal in *Christian Enterprises Ltd v Commissioner of Land Tax (NSW)*.[45] Christian Enterprises Ltd was a company limited by guarantee. Its primary objects were either religious or raising funds for religious purposes. Its objects were expressed to include commercial objects, but these were expressed to be for the purposes of carrying out the primary objects. The Commissioner of Land Tax assessed it as liable for land tax, and rejected its claims that it was exempt as a 'charitable institution' pursuant to s 10(1)(d) of the *Land Tax Management Act 1956* (NSW) or a 'religious society' pursuant to s 10(1)(e). Nagle J said that in view of the religious purposes, it could be said that the company was being carried on for charitable purposes, but held that it was not a charitable *institution*: it was not enough to constitute an institution that seven individuals with charitable intentions formed themselves into a company.[46] He also held that it was not a religious society. In the Court of Appeal, Walsh JA and Asprey JA (Wallace P dissenting) agreed on the first point, but disagreed on the second. Contrary to the Commissioner's submissions in the present appeal, Walsh JA (like Nagle J) did not construe the phrase 'charitable institution' as a single **[222]** composite expression, but saw it as having two integers — one to do with objects which were charitable, the second to do with 'institutional' characteristics. Thus he said: 'the religious objects of the company must be regarded as charitable objects. But I do not think it was an "institution".'[47] Walsh JA went on to deny that every company with charitable objects was a charitable institution. The Commissioner submitted in this appeal that the 'authorities and dictionary references discussed by Nagle J and Walsh JA suggest that for an entity to be a "charitable institution" it must possess a public character, purpose or object'. The authorities and dictionary references do not in fact suggest this. Walsh JA summarised an argument of counsel which assumed that the word 'institution'

---

42. Discussed below at 224–228.
43. [1952] 2 SCR 76 at 92; see above at 216.
44. [1967] NSWR 653.
45. [1968] 2 NSWR 99.
46. [1967] NSWR 653 at 657.
47. [1968] 2 NSWR 99 at 104.

included 'a notion of something which has a public character or serves a public purpose', but he rejected the argument which made that assumption.[48] If Walsh JA, despite that rejection, was intending to adopt counsel's assumption, the Commissioner did not explain why Word's purpose of advancing religion — a charitable purpose having, ex hypothesi, benefit to the public, and carried out on a substantial basis financially speaking — caused it to lack a public character or not to serve a public purpose. Although Nagle J and Walsh JA discussed examples of what was and what was not an institution, as did the Privy Council in the main case they relied on, *Minister of National Revenue v Trusts and Guarantee Co Ltd*,[49] neither they nor the Privy Council explicitly offered any test for the meaning of 'institution'. In that case the Canadian settlor had settled a fund to be used 'for the benefit of the aged and deserving poor' of the town of Colne in Lancashire, but there was no 'charitable institution' as required for exemption from Canadian income tax; the trust was 'an ordinary trust for charity'[50] and there was no 'institution' 'in the sense in which boards of trade and chambers of commerce are institutions'.[51] Accordingly, this case can readily be distinguished, since it concerned a gift to a trustee on trust for charitable purposes as distinct from an 'institution' not holding property on trust, but owning it outright and having charitable objects. *Christian Enterprises Ltd v Commissioner of Land Tax (NSW)*, too, can be distinguished: unlike Word, the company had not begun to carry out its purposes, but it only engaged in the preparatory acts of investing funds for a short time before buying land on which it planned to build, but had not yet built, houses for resale.[52] In contrast, Word's activities in pursuance of its purposes have been carried on for years.

[223] For these reasons, *Christian Enterprises Ltd v Commissioner of Land Tax (NSW)* does not support the Commissioner's position in this appeal.

Glebe Administration Board v Commissioner of Pay-roll Tax (NSW). The Commissioner also relied on *Glebe Administration Board v Commissioner of Pay-roll Tax (NSW)*.[53] It was there held that the wages paid by the Board, a body corporate constituted under the *Church of England (Bodies Corporate) Act 1938* (NSW), were not exempt from pay-roll tax on the ground that the exemption given by the *Pay-roll Tax Act 1971* (NSW), s 10(b), for wages paid by 'a religious ... institution' was not applicable. A majority of the Court of Appeal of the Supreme Court of New South Wales (Priestley JA, McHugh JA concurring) viewed the Board as 'a statutory corporation doing commercial work within limitations fixed by reference to religious principles'[54] and construed s 10(b) as not being aimed at 'exempting from liability to pay-roll tax wages paid to persons substantially engaged in commercial activity'.[55]

That case, then, is a decision about a particular statute different from the one under consideration in this appeal, and a decision about a different entity. In contrast to the

---

48. [1968] 2 NSWR 99 at 104.
49. [1940] AC 138.
50. [1940] AC 138 at 148, 150.
51. [1940] AC 138 at 149.
52. [1967] NSWR 653 at 654.
53. (1987) 10 NSWLR 352.
54. (1987) 10 NSWLR 352 at 365.
55. (1987) 10 NSWLR 352 at 373.

view which the Court of Appeal took of the Board in that case, the correct view in this case is that Word was using its powers to employ commercial methods to raise money for its purposes: it was not doing commercial work within limitations fixed by reference to religious principles.

A final argument. The Commissioner sought leave to rely on an argument not put before the Full Court that the conduct by Word of its investment arm alone prevented it from being a charitable institution. That leave should be granted, but the argument should be rejected for the reasons stated above.

Conclusion. Nothing in the authorities or arguments relied on by the Commissioner suggests that Word is not an 'institution' in the senses approved in *Stratton v Simpson*:[56]

> '... an establishment, organisation, or association, instituted for the promotion of some object, especially one of public utility, religious, charitable, educational etc'[57] ... 'an undertaking formed to promote some defined purpose ...' or 'the body (so to speak) called into existence to translate the purpose as conceived in the mind of the founders into a living and active principle.'[58]

[224] Accordingly, subject to the Commissioner's other arguments, it is to be concluded that Word is a charitable institution.

A caveat. To avoid doubt in future, it should be noted that it would not be enough that the purpose or main purpose of an institution were charitable if in fact it ceased to carry out that purpose. Just like the former s 23(g)(iii) of the *1936 Act*, so the former s 23(e) of that Act, and item 1.1 in the table in the present s 50–5 of the *1997 Act*, being provisions in the legislation exempting tax on annual income, have 'a periodic operation'; the statute 'directs the inquiry to a particular time, namely, the year of income so that consideration must be given not only to the purpose for which the [institution] was established but also the purpose for which it is currently conducted.'[59] It was not submitted that Word had acted outside its purposes; rather it was submitted that it had acted inside them, but that they were non-charitable for the reasons advanced in relation either to the first issue or the second. That contention has been rejected so far as it applies to the first issue and is rejected below in relation to the second issue.

Second issue: can an institution be charitable where it does not engage in charitable activities beyond making profits which are directed to charitable institutions which do engage in charitable activities?

The Commissioner's arguments. The Commissioner submitted that: 'this is the first occasion on which a court in Australia has determined that an entity that does not itself engage in any significant charitable activities but, rather, conducts an investment, trading or other commercial activity for profit (albeit not for the benefit of its members) is a charitable institution, or is otherwise charitable in nature, because under its constitution it was required to, and does, distribute its profits to one or more charitable institutions.'

---

56. (1970) 125 CLR 138 at 158 per Gibbs J (Barwick CJ, Menzies and Walsh JJ concurring).
57. Quoting *The Shorter Oxford English Dictionary.*
58. Quoting *Mayor of Manchester v McAdam* [1896] AC 500 at 511 per Lord Macnaghten.
59. *Cronulla Sutherland Leagues Club Ltd v Federal Commissioner of Taxation* (1990) 23 FCR 82 at 96 per Lockhart J. See also *Federal Commissioner of Taxation v Triton Foundation* (2005) 147 FCR 362 at 370–371 [20], and the discussion at 237 below.

The Commissioner submitted that the courts below had been wrong to make that determination. It was for the purposes of this submission that the Commissioner relied on the activities of Word. The Commissioner's point was that while, for example, it was an object of Word to 'proclaim … the Christian Religion', it did not in fact do so. All it did was raise money from commercial activities and hand it to other bodies so that they could proclaim the Christian religion. It submitted that there was no nexus between the profit and the effectuation of a charitable purpose. There were too many intermediate steps — '[Word] determining to distribute, rather than retain for its own [225] purposes, the profit, determining to whom a distribution is to be made and making the distribution'.

Resolution. It is implicit in the Commissioner's argument that there is a distinction between two cases. One case would arise where a company limited by guarantee which had religious charitable objects organised itself into two divisions, one of which employed the company's assets to make profits, the other of which spent the profits on those objects. A second case would exist where a company limited by guarantee had the same objects and made the same profits, but gave them to other organisations which spent them on those objects. On the Commissioner's argument, the first company is a charitable institution, but the second is not. It would not reflect credit on the law if the distinction implicit in the Commissioner's argument were sound. The English Court of Appeal, dismissing an appeal from Slade J, rejected a similar argument in *Inland Revenue Commissioners v Helen Slater Charitable Trust Ltd*[60] (admittedly in a different statutory context) in holding that the income of one company having charitable objects was 'applied for charitable purposes' when it was paid to another company with almost identical objects. Oliver LJ said, in giving the judgment of Waller LJ, himself and Fox LJ, that:

> … where the trusts on which the funds are held envisage the accomplishment of the charitable purpose by a payment to some other organisation, I cannot for my part see why such a payment is not an application of the funds … I entertain no doubt whatever that, as a general proposition, funds which are donated by charity 'A', pursuant to its trust deed or constitution, to charity 'B' are funds which are 'applied' by charity 'A' for charitable purposes.[61]

Strictly speaking, that case (like this) was not one in which funds were held on trust, but was one in which one company owned assets and had certain purposes. But in this case, like that, the objects included advancing charitable purposes by assisting other organisations,[62] and the Commissioner does not dispute that the payments which Word makes are within its purposes. And the present case is stronger than that case, for in that case the funds advanced were retained by the recipient company and not expended on charitable purposes, whereas in the present case the income paid to Wycliffe and like bodies is expended on charitable purposes. One submission advanced by Mr Andrew Park QC for the successful taxpayer in that case may be noted:

> The Crown's wide submission that money subject to charitable trusts is not 'applied for charitable purposes' unless actually expended in the field, is revolutionary, unworkable

---

60. [1982] Ch 49.
61. *Inland Revenue Commissioners v Helen Slater Charitable Trust Ltd* [1982] Ch 49 at 56.
62. See cl 3(a)(iii), quoted above at 218.

and unacceptable in practice. There are innumerable charities, both large and [226] small, in this country which operate on the basis of raising funds and choosing other suitable charitable bodies to donate those funds to ... If the Crown's wide argument is correct, many charitable bodies would be losing a recognised entitlement to tax relief and may, moreover, cease to be regarded as charitable.[63]

It is likely that the position in Australia is similar.

In *Baptist Union of Ireland (Northern) Corporation Ltd v Commissioners of Inland Revenue* MacDermott J said:

> ... the charitable purpose of a trust is often, and perhaps more often than not, to be found in the natural and probable consequences of the trust rather than in its immediate and expressed objects.

> Similarly, the charitable purposes of a company can be found in a purpose of bringing about the natural and probable consequence of its immediate and expressed purposes, and its charitable activities can be found in the natural and probable consequence of its immediate activities.[64]

For those reasons the second issue must be resolved against the Commissioner.

Comment

1. See Radan & Stewart at **18.29–18.41** and **18.60–18.72**.

Trusts for purposes otherwise beneficial to the community

18.6   The Incorporated Council of Law Reporting of the State of Queensland v Federal Commissioner of Taxation (1971) 125 CLR 659

Court: High Court of Australia

Facts: The Incorporated Council of Law Reporting of the State of Queensland ('the Council') had been created solely for the purpose of producing law reports in Queensland. All profits were required to be put back into law reporting and into law libraries. The Federal Commissioner of Taxation decided that the Council was not a charitable institution and refused it favourable tax treatment.

Issue: The issue was whether not-for-profit law reporting could fall within the fourth category of charity.

---

63. [1982] Ch 49 at 52.
64. (1945) 26 TC 335 at 348.

Decision: The High Court (Barwick CJ, McTiernan and Windeyer JJ) found that the Council's activities were charitable as they benefited the public and came within the spirit and intendment of the Preamble to the Statute of Elizabeth.

Extracts: In this extract Barwick CJ explains why the Council's activities were not educational, and why they did fall within the fourth category.

Barwick CJ

However much a student may and should profit by reading the law reports, the purpose of their production cannot, in my opinion, be held to be educational. Further, in my opinion, their function for the judiciary is informative rather than educational.

But is the Council nonetheless, a 'charitable institution' within the meaning of s. 23 (e) of the *Income Tax and Social Services Contribution Assessment Act 1936* (Cth) (the Act). If its purposes are charitable, it will be such an institution for the nature of the institution inheres in the purposes it is created to and does pursue. There is no need in this connexion to consider what is the main purpose of the Council as, in my opinion, it has in substance but one purpose, namely the production of law reports, both in the form of weekly or periodical notes and of annual volumes. Clause 3 (d) though expressed as an object is really related to the disposal of the income of the Council: but it qualifies the purpose of producing law reports in that it negatives private gain as a part of that purpose. The application of the net proceeds of the pursuit of its purpose in producing law reports does not in itself in my opinion relevantly form a purpose of the Council, though that application bears upon the ultimate conclusion whether or not the Council is a charitable institution.

The Act attempts no definition of charity or of what for its purposes will be charitable. But having regard to the decision of the *Privy Council in Chesterman v Federal Commissioner of Taxation*[65] it must be taken that whether or not the institution is relevantly charitable will be determined according to the principles upon which the Court of Chancery would act in connexion with an alleged charity. That means that the indications contained in the preamble to the *Statute of Elizabeth 1601* and the classifications in Lord Macnaghten's speech in Commissioner for *Special Purposes of Income Tax v Pemsel (Pemsel's Case)*[66] are to be observed in deciding whether or not the institution is charitable for the purposes of the Act.

The reported cases may in some instances afford a guide by analogy to the decision whether a particular trust, or a particular purpose is charitable. In addition, the many dicta found in the reasons for judgment in such cases, though by no means of one accord, provide valuable assistance in resolving such a question. But in the long run, it seems to me, it is a matter of judgment whether the trust or purpose fairly falls within the equity, or as it is sometimes said, 'within the spirit and intendment' of the preamble to the *Charitable Uses Act 1601* (Imp.). This is clearly **[667]** so in Australia and it would appear still to be so in England where that preamble appears to have been repealed by the operation of the *Charities Act 1960* (UK).[67]

---

65. (1925) 37 CLR 317.
66. [1891] AC 531 at 583.
67. See generally Keeton, *Law of Trusts*, 1971, pp 163, 164; S G Maurice and D B Parker, *Tudor on Charities*, 1967, p 1 et seq.

The instances given in that preamble are not exhaustive. Charity is not limited to activities eiusdem generis with those instances, if indeed a genus is really to be found in them. But the preamble does give an indication and, it would seem, a definitive indication, of what will be charitable, whether in point of trust or of purpose. Lord Macnaghten in *Pemsel's Case*[68] extracted from this indication four heads or categories of charity of which the first three heads or categories are capable of more certain application than the last category, which is the one with which the Court must be concerned in this case.

The question here is whether the production not for private gain of law reports, recording the decisions of a superior court in a judicial system in which the decision of an earlier case may itself in terms or by analogy, or in association with other such decisions determine the result of a later case, is a purpose beneficial to the community within the scope of the fourth head of charity as expressed in *Pemsel's Case*.[69]

Not every purpose beneficial to the community is a charitable purpose but only those which are within the equity of the preamble to the *Statute of Elizabeth*. The purpose must not merely be beneficial: it must also be charitable.[70] In this connexion however we are reminded by Lord Wrenbury in *Chesterman v Federal Commissioner of Taxation*[71] that 'the word "charitable" in the Elizabethan sense is large and more comprehensive than the other words in the context'.

I do not find it necessary in this case to pursue the question whether Lord Macnaghten's formulation of this fourth head of charity extended or merely re-expressed Sir Samuel Romilly's phrase 'objects of general public utility' which he used in argument in *Morice v Bishop of Durham*;[72] see the speech of Lord Reid in *Inland Revenue Commissioners v Baddeley*.[73]

[668] Here, as I shall shortly point out, the benefit of the production of law reports is not limited to any section of the community but accrues to the community as a whole. Nor need the Court, in my opinion, in this case, for reasons I shall later express, seek for analogy to the production of law reports in the circumstances of some authoritatively decided case.

It is important, and indeed crucial for the resolution of the question posed in the case to recall the function which the reports of decided cases, particularly by superior courts, performs in our system of law. Foster J. in his reasons for judgment in *Incorporated Council of Law Reporting for England and Wales v Attorney-General*[74] quotes extensively, and for present purposes most helpfully, from the reports made in 1849 and in 1853 by the Society for Promoting the Amendment of the Law. In that case, his Lordship had before him an account by Professor Goodhart of the history of what Professor Goodhart called 'judge-made law' to which, though not formally before this Court, reference may properly be made as an exact

---

68. [1891] AC 531.
69. [1891] AC 531.
70. See *In re Macduff; Macduff v Macduff* [1896] 2 Ch 451; *Attorney-General. National Provincial and Union Bank of England* [1924] AC 262; *Williams' Trustees v Inland Revenue Commissioners* [1947] AC 447 and *In re Strakosch, deceased; Temperley v Attorney-General* [1948] Ch 37.
71. [1926] AC 128 at 132; (1925) 37 CLR 317 at 320.
72. (1805) 32 ER 947 at 951.
73. [1955] AC 572 at 608.
74. [1971] Ch 626 at 638–641.

and useful summary of the development of the law reports and of the place they occupy in the administration of the law. The facts to which the professor refers are historical and, in my opinion, of that notoriety which brings them within judicial notice. The extracts which his Lordship has included in his reasons for judgment make unnecessary any extensive reference by me to the function of the law reports in our system of law.

In Queensland the only available reports of the decisions of the Supreme Court of Queensland are those produced by the Council. Without them it would not be possible to ascertain what in any particular field of law had been decided without a time-consuming search of court records, assuming that the reasons given in decided cases are kept by the offices of the Court not as part of the formal record of the case but as archival material. For myself I doubt whether such reasons, particularly when orally expressed, have always been so kept. But such research is not practicable in the exigencies of the daily administration of the law. Thus, in my opinion, it can confidently be said that in modern times without the availability of law reports in book form the law could not be adequately administered. Justice according to law would be in danger of being supplanted by justice according to whim which is in reality a contradiction in terms. Thus the production of law reports is, in my opinion, clearly beneficial to the whole community because of the universal importance of maintaining the socially sustaining fabric of the law.

[669] Yet it must be considered whether that benefit is charitable in the Elizabethan sense. Out of certain of the instances given in the preamble to the Act of 1601 a broad concept emerges of the kind of object of public utility which will satisfy the quality of charity. Any notion that that concept is of an eleemosynary nature is seen to be untenable by some of those very instances themselves, e.g. the repair of bridges, havens, causeways, seabanks and highways and the setting out of soldiers. Further, these instances seem to regard the provision of some of the indispensables of a settled community as charitable. The ability to move from place to place and to do so without let of rivers and streams, protection of the land from the ravage of the sea, security against enemies, are fundamentals of the society seen to be within the concept of charitable public benefit as much as assistance to the needy and as education of the generations. Consistently with the spirit and width of this concept of charity the promotion of agriculture is seen to be charitable[75] and even the promotion of horticulture.[76] Agriculture partakes of that fundamental social quality which can give a charitable nature to a trust or purpose relating thereto which is beneficial to the community. So it would seem does horticulture. On occasions, a benefit of that kind to a section of the public less than the whole community by the trust or purpose may be enough: but, as I mentioned before, I am not here concerned with such a case. The sustenance of the law is a benefit of a material kind which enures for the benefit of the whole community. Is not its administration, with regularity, and with as much consistency as a system based on human judgment can attain, as socially fundamental as the instances which I have taken from the preamble? Surely it is. Though perhaps not now universally accepted because no doubt not properly understood, it is true that the society cannot exist as such if it is not based upon and protected by justice under law: and nurtured by obedience to law. As I have said, justice under law requires, according to the

---

75. *Inland Revenue Commissioners v Yorkshire Agricultural Society* [1928] 1 KB 611.
76. *Re Pleasants* (1923) 39 TLR 675.

system of law which we have entrenched in Australia, and I think enhanced, the ready availability of reports of the decisions of the superior courts.

Thus, to my mind, without seeking any analogy in cases which have gone before, the production of law reports of a superior court is within the equity and the spirit and intendment of the preamble and thus capable of forming a charitable purpose.

All that remains is to add the lack of private gain by the members of the Council. That the Council itself should profit by the [670] production of the law reports cannot prevent the Council being a charitable institution. Indeed, the very fact that the Act exempts the income of a charitable institution concedes that such an institution may derive profits from its activities.

Here there are two significant matters. First, the memorandum of association forbids any distribution of the profits of the Council to or amongst its members. No doubt the presence of such a provision was material to the incorporation of the Council as a company limited by guarantee. Second, the actual distributions of the Council's profits have been confined to grants to the libraries of the Supreme Court of Queensland. Those libraries are themselves important adjuncts to the administration of the law. They facilitate the very purpose the production of the law reports is designed to achieve. They do so none the less because their holdings are not available to every member of the public but only to those with or seeking training in the law. Indeed they are available to all those groups of the community who in general can profit by their use. The application of the profits of the Council to the support of the Supreme Court libraries is itself, in my opinion, an application to charity.

In sum, we have here an incorporated body, an institution, not carried on for private gain which produces reports of the decisions of the Supreme Court of Queensland in book or magazine form. The production of such law reports is its sole purpose. In my opinion, that purpose is within the equity, or the spirit and intendment of the preamble to the *Statute of Elizabeth* and, being of general public benefit, is charitable. This conclusion is reinforced by but does not to my mind depend upon the circumstances that the reports which the Council produce are the only reports available of the decisions of the Supreme Court of Queensland and that the only distribution of profits made by the Council is by way of grant to the funds of the libraries of the Supreme Court of Queensland.

In my opinion, the question asked in the case stated should be answered in the affirmative.

Comments
1. See Radan & Stewart at **18.73–18.97**.
2. Trusts in the fourth category must be of benefit to the community and fall within the spirit of the Preamble to the Statute of Elizabeth. Three years after *Incorporated Council of Law Reporting*, in *Royal National Agricultural and Industrial Association v Chester* (1974) 3 ALR 486, the High Court found that a trust for the breeding and racing of pigeons was not charitable because there was no analogous charitable purpose in the Preamble. Arguments based on the use of pigeons to help military and civilian communication efforts and breeding for improving scientific knowledge all failed. When one compares both cases it is hard to see why one succeeded and the other failed. Clearly the analogical reasoning employed is not always predictable.

The *cy-près* doctrine

18.7 Attorney-General (NSW) v Perpetual Trustee Co Ltd (1940) 63 CLR 209

Court: High Court of Australia

Facts: Annie Reid McDonell died leaving her farm, Milly Milly at West Wyalong, to 'Perpetual Trustee Co for a training farm for orphan lads being Australians'. Unfortunately, the farm was not suitable for being run as a training farm. There was not enough accommodation and there was not enough money to run the farm and pay for the boys' clothing, food and maintenance, or for medical, dental or other incidental expenses.

Issue: The issue was whether Annie's intention for Milly Milly to be used as a training farm was a specific intention or whether she had expressed a general charitable intention. If the intention was specific it was impossible to perform and the gift would fail and pass to residuary beneficiaries in the will. If the intention was a general charitable intention, the fact that the farm could not be used for training was not fatal to the gift. A *cy-près* scheme could be ordered (whereby a court official might arrange to do something with the farm, such as sell it, and give the proceeds to a similar training farm).

Decision: Rich, Dixon, Evatt and McTiernan JJ (Latham CJ and Starke J in dissent) found that there was a general charitable intention of training orphan Australian boys in farming which could be satisfied by ordering a *cy-près* scheme.

Extracts: In this extract, Dixon and Rich JJ discuss the approach to finding a general charitable intention in a gift.

Dixon and Evatt JJ

[222] No one denies that to train orphans as farmers is a charitable purpose for which a trust may be validly created. The matter in question is whether, because it has been found impossible to use Milly Milly itself as a place of training, the trust declared in the will fails entirely, so that the property is undisposed of.

A charitable trust is a trust for a purpose, not for a person. The objects of ordinary trusts are individuals, either named or answering a description, whether presently or at some future time. To dispose of property for the fulfilment of ends considered beneficial to the community is an entirely different thing from creating equitable estates and interests and limiting them to beneficiaries. In this fundamental distinction sufficient reason may be found for many of the differences in treatment of charitable and ordinary trusts. As a matter of reason, if not of history, it explains the differences between the interpretation placed on declarations or statements of [223] charitable purposes and the construction and effect given to limitations of estates and interests. Estates and interests are limited with a view of creating precise and definite proprietary rights, to the intent that property shall devolve according to the form of the gift and not otherwise. Whatever conditions are expressed or implied in such limitations are therefore as a rule construed as essential to the creation or vesting of the estate or interest unless an intention to the contrary appears. But to interpret charitable trusts in the same manner would be to ignore the conceptions upon which such trusts depend.

In the first place, the law of trusts does not enable a testator or settlor to control and direct the future use of his property as an independent power but only as a means to an end. His directions are not enforced simply because he has given them by an instrument in proper form and independently of the nature and description of the remoter purposes they are found to subserve. If they do not concern the creation, devolution or enjoyment of estates or interests, they are enforced only when they answer some purpose of a defined class allowed by law as tending to the public benefit.[77] The reason why the specific directions given by an instrument declaring a charitable trust receive effect is because they tend to a purpose falling within the legal description of charity. The existence of that purpose is, therefore, the foundation of a valid trust. In the next place, the very idea of a trust for a purpose beneficial to the community involves the distinction between ends and means. If property is devoted to an abstract end or purpose, the details of its application or use must be considered as a means to the end. Where the trust instrument does not leave such matters to the administration of the trust but formulates an elaborate plan or scheme or gives particular directions, there is reason in the view that the exact plan or directions are not of the essence of the disposition. In the third place, as the purpose of the trust need not, and, indeed, most usually does not, involve the expenditure or consumption of corpus, continuity and [224] indefiniteness of duration form a common characteristic of charitable trusts. This characteristic would be lost or imperilled by a construction of specific directions making them essential to the operation of the trust, in spite of all the unforeseen changes which time brings.

The settled rule has therefore a foundation in reason as well as in historical considerations. That rule was expressed by Lord Eldon in words that have often been quoted:

> 'I consider it now established,' he said, 'that although the mode, in which a legacy is to take effect, is in many cases with regard to an individual legatee considered as of the substance of the legacy, where a legacy is given so as to denote that charity is the legatee, the court does not hold that the mode is of the substance of the legacy; but will effectuate the gift to charity, as the substance; providing a mode for that legatee to take, which is not provided for any other legatee.'[78]

> 'The principle on which the doctrine rests appears to be, that the court treats charity in the abstract as the substance of the gift, and the particular disposition as the mode, so that in the eye of the court the gift notwithstanding the particular disposition may not be capable of execution subsists as a legacy which never fails and cannot lapse.'[79]

---

77. See (1931) 31 *Law Quarterly Review* 361; (1937) 53 *Law Quarterly Review* 26–35; (1938) 54 *Law Quarterly Review* 258, and *Hobart Savings Bank v Federal Commissioner of Taxation* (1930) 43 CLR 364 at 375.

78. *Mills v Farmer* (1815) 34 ER 595 at 596.

79. *Mayor of Lyons v Advocate-General of Bengal* (1876) 1 App Cas 91 at 113 per Sir Montague E Smith.

The doctrine is said to have reached its full development before the principle of resulting trusts was understood. But at the close of the eighteenth century, greater regard was given to the interests of the heir at law. In *Attorney-General v Whitechurch* Lord Alvanley said:

> The doctrine of cy-pres, which has been so much discussed in this court, and by which I understand the rule to execute the charitable intention as nearly as possible, however wildly and extravagantly it has been acted upon in former cases, is by late decisions, particularly since the Statute[80] administered in this way. The court will not administer a charity in a different manner from that pointed out, unless they see, that though it cannot be literally executed, another mode may be adopted, by which it may be carried into effect in substance without infringing upon the rules of law.[81]

[225] A distinction in trusts declared for charitable purposes has thus come to exist which, however clear in conception, has proved anything but easy of application. It is the distinction between, on the one hand, cases in which every element in the description of the trust is indispensable to the validity and operation of the disposition and, on the other hand, cases where a further and more general purpose is disclosed as the true and substantial object of the trust, which may therefore be carried into effect at the expense of some part of the particular directions given by the trust instrument.

If there are insuperable objections, either of fact or of law, to a literal execution of a charitable trust it at once becomes a question whether the desires or directions of the author of the trust, with which it is found impracticable to comply, are essential to his purpose. If a wider purpose forms his substantial object and the directions or desires which cannot be fulfilled are but a means chosen by him for the attainment of that object, the court will execute the trust by decreeing some other application of the trust property to the furtherance of the substantial purpose, some application which departs from the original plan in particulars held not essential and, otherwise, keeps as near thereto as may be. The question is often stated to be whether the trust instrument discloses a general intention of charity or a particular intention only. But, in its application to cases where some particular direction or directions have proved impracticable, the doctrine requires no more than a purpose wider than the execution of a specific plan involving the particular direction that has failed. In other words 'general intention of charity' means only an intention which, while not going beyond the bounds of the legal conception of charity, is more general than a bare intention that the impracticable direction be carried into execution as an indispensable part of the trust declared.

Cases arising from illegality, impracticability or failure of some part of the express directions contained in a charitable trust are almost infinite in their variety. Sometimes the trust is expressed as a detailed scheme which the settlor or testator has elaborated. Such a scheme may be found entirely impracticable or on the other hand the impracticability may be confined to a small part, the failure of which would not defeat or change the operation of what [226] is left. Sometimes the trust is expressed without any elaboration of detail and yet some particular element involved in the description of the purposes of the trust is found to be the source of an impracticability. The present case is one of this

---

80. The *Georgian Mortmain Act 9 Geo II* c 36.
81. (1796) 30 ER 937 at 938–939.

class. For it is the use of Milly Milly itself as a training farm which causes the difficulty, to the training of lads on a farm, nor the finding of Australian orphans who are both lads and are willing to be trained in farming. In applying the general doctrine to such varying cases it is inevitable that different considerations will govern the result and that the principle and the modes of reasoning will be stated in different forms. The problem will at times present itself as that of distinguishing between an immediate and a remoter purpose and of deciding whether the remoter is dominant or essential and the immediate subordinate or accidental. At other times it will appear as a question whether the existence of a main or paramount purpose is manifested notwithstanding that the declaration of the charitable trust takes the form of a direction to carry out a detailed plan. Upon some trusts the question may arise as one of severability, that is, whether so much of the provision as is impracticable is interdependent with or independent of and severable from the rest. Upon others, as a question whether a complete gift to an ultimate charitable purpose has not been made with directions superadded or annexed for the purpose of carrying it into effect, directions the failure of which leave the primary gift unaffected.[82] Yet again the matter may wear the appearance of a question whether part of the description of the trust, or a specific direction, amounts to a condition precedent to the trust taking effect.[83]

The truth is that the time-honoured distinction between essential and accidental characteristics is at the root of the test provided by the modern law for ascertaining whether a trust for charitable purposes, found incapable of literal execution according to its tenor, is nevertheless to be administered cy-pres. In other departments of the law, however, similar distinctions are in use. Analogies may **[227]** be seen in the question whether a contractual provision is of the essence; whether a term is a condition or a warranty; in the question whether invalid provisions of a statutory enactment or other instrument are severable or form part of an indivisible whole; in the question whether a law is mandatory or directory, and perhaps in the question whether the substantial purpose of creating a special power of appointment was to ensure a benefit to the objects so that they take in default of its exercise by the donee.

In determining whether a wider charitable intention is the substantial purpose of the express directions by which the trust is constituted, the court is guided by the trust instrument and the conclusion is commonly said to depend on a question of construction. No doubt the terms of the document, together with any extrinsic circumstances admissible in aid of construction, form the materials for ascertaining whether the specific directions were animated by a wider charitable purpose which amounted to the true or substantial object of the trust. The process of extracting from such materials an intention implicit in the transaction which they evidence is properly called interpretation. But the construction of the language in which the trust is expressed seldom contributes much towards a solution. More is to be gained by an examination of the nature of the charitable trust itself and what is involved in the author's plan or project. In distinguishing between means and ends, between the dominant and the subsidiary, between the substance and

---

82. See, *In re Monk* (1927) 2 Ch at 211 per Sargant LJ and *In re Wilson* (1913) 1 Ch at 320–321 per Parker J.
83. Cf, *In re Monk* (1927) 2 Ch at 205 per Lord Hanworth MR.

the form, an understanding of the relative importance in fact of the component parts of the plan or purpose expressed in the trust is a first step towards forming an opinion of the respective values they possessed in the view of the testator or settlor. His forms of expression are by no means to be neglected. In the arrangement of his ideas and his use of terms the importance which he attached to the particular and to the general respectively may appear. The decided cases show that slight indications have at times been treated as enough to warrant a conclusion in favour of a wider charitable intention.

Almost all charitable trusts expressed with any particularity must tend towards some more general purpose. But to find that the trust as expressed is designed to achieve some further and [228] wider end of a charitable nature is one thing. To find that the secondary and wider end is the dominant object to which the property is devoted is another and a further step. This step cannot be taken unless, from the nature of the trust, the provisions of the instrument and any circumstances which may legitimately be taken into account, the existence of such an intention may reasonably be inferred. For no definite presumption has been established in favour of a general charitable intention. At the same time the court leans, it is said, in favour of charity and is ready to infer a general intention. But little is therefore required as a ground for treating a wider purpose as the essential object of the trust.

The precise question raised by the present case is perhaps somewhat out of the common run. For it depends, not upon the impracticability of particular directions formulated by a testator as part of a scheme or plan which he has elaborated, but on the unsuitability of the specific property devised and bequeathed for purposes which are otherwise quite practicable and, though well defined, are stated with an avoidance of embarrassing particularity.

The testatrix in her disposition of Milly Milly has sufficiently stated her intention of advancing a charitable purpose, a purpose which may be said to consist in four ingredients or elements, viz., (a) the training (b) of orphan (c) lads (d) in farming. But she has stated that intention in a direction that her Milly Milly property shall be held by her trustees for a training farm for orphan lads (being Australians). It is of course clear that she regarded Milly Milly as suitable for such a purpose. But the question is whether this consideration is of the essence or is to be treated as subsidiary to the main purpose to which she devoted the land. Ought she to be regarded as meaning that the actual use of Milly Milly as the place where the boys were to be trained was an indispensable condition of her disposition? Or is the guiding purpose the training of Australian orphan lads in farming pursuits and did her choice fall on Milly Milly as an appropriate means? In other words was she devoting Milly Milly to the furtherance of the beneficial purpose or was her real object a solicitude for the retention and utilization of Milly Milly? It must be borne in mind that although the form of the gift shows that the testatrix regarded Milly Milly as suitable [229] for the purpose of a training farm, yet it is clear that it possessed no features giving it any special suitability and distinguishing it from other grazing or farming lands; and there is nothing either in the language of the will or in the surrounding circumstances to suggest that the testatrix chose Milly Milly for any better reason than that, of the assets of which she was disposing by will, Milly Milly provided the most suitable means of giving effect to her intentions. The failure of her issue and the presence in her will of other charitable bequests form a sufficient foundation for the inference that her testamentary dispositions were based on a desire to devote much of her property to the general benefit of the community and to negative any idea that she may have been actuated less by a wish to advance the useful end to which she devoted the property, than by some desire to conserve Milly Milly intact, a desire, to suppose a possible example, that it might continue as an enduring memorial to herself or her husband. Again she was not the framer of any particular scheme of training centering on Milly Milly. She left the means of carrying out her general purpose at large. Nevertheless she devoted the land unconditionally and once for all to the purpose. Suppose that it had been found practicable at first to use the lands as a training farm but after some time, perhaps many years, changing conditions had made it no longer feasible. Could she be taken to intend that a trust should in that event result in favour of her next of kin? Then after all Milly Milly is the subject of the trust and the purpose is the object for which it is held in trust. When property is made the subject of interminable trusts for purposes, an intention is not lightly to be inferred that in no contingencies is its form to be changed.

In questions of this kind the significance and application of rules and doctrines necessarily expressed in abstract and general terms is, we think, evidenced by the course of judicial decisions. It is true that it is not easy to find cases like the present. *In re Packe*[84] which was relied upon for the next of kin, does not appear to us at all like it. For there the will made it clear that the executors were to look for a society which would undertake the conduct of the 'retreat' with the money which the testatrix appropriated [230] for that purpose. Nor does *In re Taylor*[85] resemble it, where the testamentary gift was obviously inspired by no other intention than to advance a plan which in his lifetime the testator thought he had put into execution but which was entirely invalid. On the other hand, the Victorian case of *Re Wiseman's Trusts*[86] is more in point. The ground of the decision of Hood J in favour of a cy-pres application of the property is summarized in two sentences relevant to the present case:

> The declared design of the deed is to provide a home for neglected children. No virtue can be ascribed to the particular locality provided for that home, nor to any special rules and regulations relating thereto.[87]

But the general trend of the case law over a long period of time appears to us to be against holding that the use of Milly Milly in specie formed an indispensable part of the gift. The gift, in our opinion, ought to be regarded as dominated by a more general charitable purpose.

We think the appeal should be allowed. The decree appealed against should be varied by omitting therefrom the declarations that in making the disposition of Milly Milly the testatrix has not expressed a general charitable intention and that the said property passes as on an intestacy of the testatrix and by substituting therefor a declaration that the trusts declared in respect of Milly Milly should be executed cy-pres and that a scheme ought to be settled. With that declaration the cause should be remitted to the Supreme Court to be dealt with according to law.

---

84. (1918) 1 Ch 437.
85. (1888) 58 LT 538; 4 TLR 302.
86. (1915) VLR 439.
87. (1915) VLR 439 at 443.

Comments

1. See Radan & Stewart at **17.84–17.106**.
2. Milly Milly still exists as a homestead on Sandy Creek near West Wyalong, south of Lake Cowal in New South Wales. The locals have a 'Miss Milly Milly' pageant which is open to both sexes, and it has been reported that 'some of the blokes [give] the sheilas a run for their money for the coveted Miss Milly Milly Crown': ABC NSW Country Hour (http://www.abc.net.au/rural/nsw/stories/s1018970.htm) (accessed 4 April 2010).

19

RESULTING TRUSTS

Introduction

19.1 A resulting trust is a trust that arises because equity presumes that a trust was intended to be created. Because resulting trusts arise in the absence of an expressed intention to create a trust they are sometimes referred to as 'implied' trusts.

There are two types of resulting trust:

1. *Automatic resulting trusts* which arise when there has been a failure of an express trust, or, alternatively, where there is a surplus of trust property after a trust has been terminated. In these situations the remaining trust property is held on resulting trust for the creator of the trust because it is presumed that the creator intended to receive any leftover beneficial interest; and

2. *Presumed resulting trusts* which arise because contributions have been made to the purchase of property but the contributor has not been given a legal title that is equivalent to that contribution. In such a transaction, equity presumes that the equivalent legal title is held on trust for the contributor. This category of resulting trusts also includes resulting trusts which arise when property has been voluntarily transferred to a person who has not provided consideration.

The extracts in this chapter deal with the following issues:

* automatic resulting trusts: *Re Gillingham Bus Disaster Fund* [1958] Ch 300;
* presumed resulting trusts and the presumption of advancement: *Calverley v Green* (1984) 155 CLR 244;
* the presumption of joint tenancy in the purchase of the matrimonial home: *Trustees of the Property of Cummins (a bankrupt) v Cummins* (2006) 227 CLR 278.

Automatic resulting trusts

19.2   Re Gillingham Bus Disaster Fund [1958] Ch 300

Court: Chancery Division

Facts: In 1951, there was a bus crash which killed 24 Royal Marines cadets and injured several more. The local mayors of Gillingham, Rochester and Chatham wrote a letter to a daily newspaper which asked the public to contribute to a fund which was to be used to pay for the funeral expenses, the care expenses of the surviving cadets, and 'then to such worthy cause or causes in memory of the boys who lost their lives, as the Mayors may determine'. Nearly £9000 was collected from known donors and anonymous donors. The trustees spent £2368 in defraying funeral expenses and caring for the surviving cadets with disabilities but the trustees were unsure about what to do with the surplus.

Issue: The issue was what the trustees should do with the surplus. If the trust was charitable the surplus might be able to be used under a *cy-près* scheme. If not, the funds may have to be repaid to the donors under a resulting trust or be given to the Crown as *bona vacantia*.

Decision: Harman J found that the trust was not charitable. The funeral and care expenses of this particular group of boys was not a charitable use. Nor was the idea that the Mayors could use the funds for 'worthy causes' as this could include both charitable and non-charitable objects. Given the trust was not charitable it was not possible to order a *cy-près* scheme.

Harman J then found that a resulting trust arose, given that the purpose of the trust had failed. The resulting trust would mean that the surplus would be held on trust by the trustees for the donors. The fact that it would be difficult to identify the donors did not prevent the resulting trust from arising.

Extracts: In this extract Harman J weighs up the issue of whether the surplus is held on resulting trust or whether it goes to the Crown.

Harman J

[310] I have already decided that the surplus of this fund now in the hands of the plaintiffs as trustees ought not to be devoted to charitable purposes under a cy pres scheme. There arises now a further question, namely, whether, as the Treasury Solicitor claims, this surplus should be paid to the Crown as bona vacantia, or whether there is a resulting trust in favour of the subscribers, who are here represented by the Official Solicitor. The general principle must be that where money is held upon trust and the trusts declared do not exhaust the fund it will revert to the donor or settlor under what is called a resulting trust. The reasoning behind this is that the settlor or donor did not part with his money absolutely out and out but only sub modo to the intent that his wishes as declared by the declaration of trust should be carried into effect. When, therefore, this has been done any surplus still belongs to him. This doctrine does not, in my judgment, rest on any evidence of the state of mind of the settlor, for in the vast majority of cases no doubt he does not expect to see his money back: he has created a trust which so far as he can see will absorb the whole of it. The resulting trust arises where that expectation is for some unforeseen reason cheated of fruition, and is an inference of law based on after-knowledge of the event.

Counsel for the Crown admitted that it was for him to show that this principle did not apply to the present case. Counsel for the subscribers cited to me *In Re Abbott*.[1] In

---

1.   [1900] 2 Ch 326.

that case a fund had been subscribed for the relief of two distressed ladies who had been defrauded of their patrimony. There was no instrument of trust. When the survivor of them died the trustees had not expended the whole of the moneys subscribed and the summons asked whether this surplus resulted to the subscribers or whether it was payable to the personal representatives of the two ladies. Stirling J had no difficulty in coming to the conclusion that the ladies were not intended to become the absolute owners of the fund and therefore their personal representatives had no claim. It was never suggested in this case that any claim by the Crown to bona vacantia might arise. A similar result was reached in *In Re Hobourn Aero Components Air Raid Distress Fund*,[2] where the judge found that though the objects of the fund were charitable no general charitable intent was shown in the absence of any element of public benefit and decided that the money belonged [311] to the subscribers upon a resulting trust. Here again no claim was made on behalf of the Crown that the surplus constituted bona vacantia.

I was referred to two cases where a claim was made to bona vacantia and succeeded. The first of these was *Cunnack v Edwards*.[3] This was a case of a society formed to raise a fund by subscriptions and so forth from the members to provide for widows of deceased members. Upon the death of the last widow of a member it was found that there was a surplus. It was held by the Court of Appeal that no question of charity arose, that there was no resulting trust in favour of the subscribers, but that the surplus passed to the Crown as bona vacantia. A L Smith LJ said this:

> But it was argued that the proper implication is that when the society itself came to an end, as it has done, there was then a resulting trust of what might happen to be in the coffers of the society in favour of all the personal representatives of those who had been members since the year 1810, and Chitty J has so held. Now it was never contemplated that the society would come to an end; but, on the contrary, provision was made for the introduction of new members for its perpetual existence; and the existing members had power to alter and revise the rules, so that, if it was found that the society was too affluent, provision might be made as to what was to be done with what money might not be wanted. As the member paid his money to the society, so he divested himself of all interest in this money for ever, with this one reservation, that if the member left a widow she was to be provided for during her widowhood. Except as to this he abandoned and gave up the money for ever. The case of *Smith v Cooke*,[4] in which it was held there was no resulting trust, shows the principle applicable to such a point. In my opinion this case cannot be likened to that of a man providing a fund by way of trust for the payment of an annuity to his widow during her life, and making no provision for the fund when the widow died and her interest therein ceased, in which case there would be a resulting trust, because the implication in such a case would be that the settlor intended that when the trust came to an end the fund should revert to his representatives, he not having provided to whom it should then go. In such a case there would be no abandonment of the fund as in the present case. In my opinion there was no resulting trust [312] in favour of all those members who had ever subscribed to the fund.[5]

---

2. [1946] Ch 86.
3. [1896] 2 Ch 679; 12 TLR 614.
4. [1891] AC 297.
5. [1896] 2 Ch 679 at 683.

Rigby LJ said:

> The members were not cestuis que trust of the funds or of any part thereof, but persons who, under contracts or quasi-contracts with the society, secured for valuable consideration certain contingent benefits for their widows which could be enforced by the widows in manner provided by the Acts. Any surplus would, according to the scheme of the rules, be properly used up (under appropriate amendments of the rules) either in payment of larger annuities or in reduction of contributions. It is true that no such alterations were made, and it is now too late so to distribute the funds; but I do not think that such omission can give to the contracting parties any benefit which they did not bargain for.[6]

The ratio decidendi seems to have been that having regard to the constitution of the fund no interest could possibly be held to remain in the contributor who had parted with his money once and for all under a contract for the benefit of his widow. When this contract had been carried into effect the contributor had received all that he had contracted to get for his money and could not ask for any more.

A similar result was reached in the case of *Smith v Cooke*,[7] cited by A L Smith LJ,[8] though it does not appear from the report what the result was. Another case cited to me was *Braithwaite v Attorney-General*.[9] Here again it was held that there was no room for a resulting trust and the claim to bona vacantia succeeded. The opponents there, it appears, were the last two surviving annuitants. Their claim was rejected on the ground that they had had or were having everything for which the contract provided. The claim of the Attorney-General on behalf of charity was rejected, it being held that there was no charity. A different result was reached by Kekewich J in *In Re Buck*,[10] but it was on the ground that the society was a charity and the money was therefore directed to be applied cy pres.

In addition there were cited to me the three hospital cases: *In Re Welsh Hospital (Netley) Fund;*[11] *In Re Hillier's Trusts*[12] and *In Re Ulverston and District New Hospital Building Trusts*.[13] [313] In the first of these cases P O Lawrence J held that all subscribers to the hospital must be taken to have parted with their money with a general intention in favour of charity. This was the only contest in the case, between the subscribers on the one hand and charity on the other. In *Hillier's* case Upjohn J, at first instance, found that certain categories of subscribers were entitled to have their money back but that others, namely, those who had contributed to collections at entertainments and so forth, had no such right.[14] The Court of Appeal varied this order and declared that the whole fund should go to charity but without prejudice to the right of any individual to prove that he

---

6. [1896] 2 Ch 679 at 689.
7. [1891] AC 297.
8. [1896] 2 Ch 679 at 683.
9. [1909] 1 Ch 510; 25 TLR 333.
10. [1896] 2 Ch 727.
11. [1921] 1 Ch 655.
12. [1954] 1 WLR 9 at 700 (CA); [1953] 2 All ER 1547; [1954] 2 All ER 59 (CA).
13. [1956] Ch 622; [1956] 3 All ER 164.
14. [1954] 1 WLR 9.

had no general intention but only the particular intention in favour of one hospital.[15] In the *Ulverston*[16] case the Court of Appeal decided that the whole fund had been collected with only one object and not for general charitable purposes and that, so far as money had been received from identifiable sources, there was a resulting trust. No claim to bona vacantia was there made, and Jenkins LJ, in explaining the position in *In Re Hillier's Trusts*,[17] said this:

> I appreciate that anonymous contributors cannot expect their contributions back in any circumstances, at all events so long as they remain anonymous. I appreciate also the justice of the conclusion that anonymous contributors must be regarded as having parted with their money out-and-out, though I would make a reservation in the case of an anonymous contributor who was able to prove conclusively that he had in fact subscribed some specified amount to the fund. If the organisers of a fund designed exclusively and solely for some particular charitable purpose send round a collecting box on behalf of the fund, I fail to see why a person who had put £5 into the box, and could prove to the satisfaction of the court he had done so, should not be entitled to have his money back in the event of the failure of the sole and exclusive charitable purpose for which his donation was solicited and made.[18]

Jenkins LJ, in the course of his judgment, threw out the suggestion that donations from unidentifiable donors might in such a case be treated as bona vacantia.[19]

It was argued for the Crown that the subscribers to this fund must be taken to have parted with their money out and out, and that there was here, as in *Cunnack v Edwards*[20] and *Braithwaite v Attorney-General*,[21] **[314]** no room for a resulting trust. But there is a difference between those cases and this in that they were cases of contract and this is not. Further, it seems to me that the hospital cases are not of great help because the argument centred round general charitable intent, a point which cannot arise unless the immediate object be a charity. I have already held there is no such question here. In my judgment the nearest case is the *Hobourn* case,[22] which, however, is no authority for the present because no claim for bona vacantia was made.

In my judgment the Crown has failed to show that this case should not follow the ordinary rule merely because there was a number of donors who, I will assume, are unascertainable. I see no reason myself to suppose that the small giver who is anonymous has any wider intention than the large giver who can be named. They all give for the one object. If they can be found by inquiry the resulting trust can be executed in their favour. If they cannot I do not see how the money could then, with all respect to Jenkins LJ, change its destination and become bona vacantia. It will be merely money held upon a trust for which no beneficiary can be found. Such cases are common and where it is known that

---

15. [1954] 1 WLR 9 at 711.
16. [1956] Ch 622.
17. [1954] 1 WLR 9 at 700.
18. [1956] Ch 622 at 633.
19. [1956] Ch 622 at 633.
20. [1896] 2 Ch 679.
21. [1909] 1 Ch 510.
22. [1946] Ch 86.

there are beneficiaries the fact that they cannot be ascertained does not entitle the Crown to come in and claim. The trustees must pay the money into court like any other trustee who cannot find his beneficiary. I conclude, therefore, that there must be an inquiry for the subscribers to this fund.

Comments

1. See Radan & Stewart at **19.15–19.19**. The matter was appealed by the Attorney-General but only on the issue of whether the trust was charitable. The Court of Appeal upheld the finding of Harman J and there was no discussion of resulting trusts: *Gillingham Bus Disaster Fund* [1959] Ch 62.

2. Automatic resulting trusts will also arise in cases when an attempt to create an express trust has failed. After an express trust fails, equity imposes a resulting trust by presuming an intention on the part of the creator for the trust property to revert back to the creator. In *Twinsectra Ltd v Yardley* [2002] 2 AC 164 Lord Millet described the *Quistclose* trust (from *Barclays Bank Ltd v Quistclose Investments Ltd* [1970] AC 567) as an example of this type of resulting trust. Both the Queensland and New South Wales Courts of Appeal have looked favourably on this approach but neither completely adopted the analysis: *Quince v Varga* [2008] QCA 376 and *Salvo v New Tel Ltd* [2005] NSWCA 281. See Radan & Stewart at **15.60–15.63**.

Presumed resulting trusts and the presumption of advancement

19.3   Calverley v Green (1984) 155 CLR 244

Court: High Court of Australia

Facts: Arthur Calverley and Dianne Green had been in a longstanding de facto relationship and lived as husband and wife for more than 10 years. In the early years of the relationship they lived in Arthur's house but they eventually decided to buy a new house to live in. Arthur had difficulty in obtaining finance on his own, but finance was eventually approved on the basis that he and Dianne would be jointly and severally liable under a mortgage. However, it was agreed that the repayments of that mortgage would be made by Arthur. A deposit of $9000 was paid by Arthur from the proceeds of the sale of his house and the balance was raised from the mortgage. The parties were registered as joint tenants.

On dissolution of the relationship, Dianne claimed her half share in the house. It was held at first instance that she had no beneficial interest in the property because the sole reason for naming her a joint tenant was to obtain finance. The Court of Appeal reversed that decision and found that the parties were joint owners in both law and equity.

Issue: The issue was whether the property should be split 50:50 as a reflection of their legal interests as joint tenants or whether a resulting trust should arise which would reflect their contributions to the purchase price. Another issue arose in relation to the presumption of advancement and whether that presumption should be applied to de facto relationships.

Decision: A majority of the High Court (Gibbs CJ, Mason, Brennan and Deane JJ; Murphy J dissenting) found that the woman's liability under the mortgage was a contribution to the purchase price of the house. Therefore, a resulting trust was presumed which reflected the respective contributions of the parties to the purchase price. Within the majority Mason, Brennan and Deane JJ found that there was no presumption of advancement that operated in the context of de facto relationships. Gibbs CJ felt that the presumption could arise in de facto relationships but that it had been rebutted by the actual intentions of the parties.

Extracts: In these extracts from Gibbs CJ's judgment and Mason and Deane JJ's joint judgment, their Honours discuss the presumptions of resulting trust and advancement and how these presumptions work in the context of de facto relationships.

Gibbs CJ

[246] Where a person purchases property in the name of another, or in the name of himself and another jointly, the question whether the other person, who provided none of the purchase money, acquires a beneficial interest in the property depends on the intention of the purchaser. However, in such a case, unless there is such a relationship between the purchaser and the other person as gives rise to a presumption of advancement, ie, a presumption that the purchaser intended to give the other a beneficial interest, it is presumed that the purchaser did not intend the other person to take beneficially. In the absence of evidence to rebut that presumption, there arises a resulting trust in favour of the purchaser. Similarly, if the purchase money is provided by two or more persons jointly, and the property is put into the name of one only, there is, in the absence of any such relationship, presumed to be a resulting trust in favour of the other or others. For the presumption to apply the money must have been provided by the purchaser in his character as such — not, eg, as a loan. Consistently with these principles it has been held that if two persons have contributed the purchase money in unequal shares, and the property is purchased in their joint names, there is, again in the absence of a relationship that gives rise to a presumption of advancement, a presumption that the property is held by the purchasers in trust for themselves as tenants in common in the proportions in which they contributed the purchase [247] money.[23]

As I have indicated, the general rule that in the situations mentioned it is presumed that a resulting trust arises in favour of the purchaser, or in favour of two purchasers in the proportions in which they contributed the purchase money, is subject to the exception created by the presumption of advancement. 'It is called a presumption of advancement but it is rather the absence of any reason for assuming that a trust arose or in other words that the equitable right is not at home with the legal title';[24] in other words, it is 'no more than a circumstance of evidence which may rebut the presumption of resulting trust'.[25]

---

23. *Robinson v Preston* (1858) 4 K & J 505 at 510 [70 ER 211 at 213]; *Ingram v Ingram* [1941] VLR 95 and *Crisp v Mullings* [1976] EG 730 (a decision of the English Court of Appeal).
24. *Martin v Martin* (1959) 110 CLR 297 at 303.
25. *Pettitt v Pettitt* [1970] AC 777 at 814.

The presumption arises when a husband makes a purchase in the name of his wife, or a father in the name of his child or other person to whom he stands in loco parentis. The authorities have denied that it arises where a wife makes a purchase in the name of her husband,[26] or a mother in the name of her child[27] or where the purchase is taken in the name of a sister,[28] nephew,[29] son-in-law[30] or grandchild,[31] unless the purchaser is in loco parentis to the nominee. The principle on which these decisions have been rested is not altogether satisfactory. Lord Eldon said in *Murless v Franklin* that the presumption of advancement arises 'where the purchaser is under a species of natural obligation to provide for the nominee'.[32] In *Bennet v Bennet*[33] Jessel MR also said that the presumption arises from the existence of an obligation on the one person to make a provision for the other; he went on to say that 'the presumption of gift arises from the moral obligation to give;[34] later he referred to it as a 'moral legal obligation ... [an] obligation according to the rules of equity'.[35] Isaacs J in *Scott v Pauly*, seems to have thought that in a case where the purchaser is the father the presumption of advancement

> ... is an inference which the Courts of [248] equity in practice drew from the mere fact of the purchaser being the father, and the head of the family, under the primary moral obligation to provide for the children of the marriage, and in that respect differing from the mother.[36]

However, *Soar v Foster* is authority for the proposition that the existence of a moral obligation to support the person in whose name the purchase is taken is not enough to give rise to a presumption of advancement. In that case the purchaser had gone through a form of marriage with his deceased wife's sister after the passing of Lord Lyndhurst's Act which rendered null and void all marriages within the prohibited degrees of consanguinity or affinity; thereafter they cohabited together and treated each other as man and wife. It was submitted that if the purchaser had a moral obligation to prove for the other party, that could raise a presumption of advancement.[37] Page Wood VC rejected the submission. He said:

> Then how does the inference arise that the purchase was intended as a provision for the Defendant? Not upon the ground of his being under a moral obligation to provide for the Defendant, for that argument would be equally applicable, if, instead of an invalid

---

26. *Mercier v Mercier* [1903] 2 Ch 98.
27. *Bennet v Bennet* (1879) 10 Ch D 474; *Scott v Pauly* (1917) 24 CLR 274 at 282; *Pickens v Metcalf and Marr* [1932] NZLR 1278.
28. *Noack v Noack* [1959] VR 137 at 140.
29. *Russell v Scott* (1936) 55 CLR 440.
30. *Knight v Biss* [1954] NZLR 55.
31. *Soar v Foster* (1858) 4 K & J 152 at 157 [70 ER 64 at 66].
32. (1818) 1 Swans 13 at 17 [36 ER 278 at 280].
33. (1879) 10 Ch D 474 at 476.
34. (1879) 10 Ch D 474 at 477.
35. (1879) 10 Ch D 474 at 478.
36. (1917) 24 CLR 274 at 282.
37. (1858) 4 K & J 152 at 156–157 [70 ER 64 at 66].

marriage of this description, the case had been one of bigamy by a person representing himself to be unmarried. In such a case there would be a clear moral duty incumbent upon the person supposed to provide for a woman whom he had so grossly deceived. The same argument would apply to a case of mere cohabitation without any form of marriage whatever. Any moralist would say that a man was bound to make provision for the woman with whom he had so cohabited. But it would be impossible for this Court to hold, if in either of the cases supposed an investment had been made by the man in the names of himself and the woman, that, upon the mere ground of his being under such moral obligation, the purchase could be presumed to have been intended by him as a provision of advancement.[38]

The principle upon which the presumption of advancement rests does not seem to me to have been convincingly expounded in the earlier authorities, nor do the two presumptions, of a resulting trust and advancement, together always lead to a result which coincides with that which one would expect to occur in ordinary human experience. For example, a lady who placed deposits, each of £150, in the names of her niece and nephew, aged respectively two and six years, would not ordinarily be thought to intend that the infants should hold the deposits as trustees for her, but that is the result to **[249]** which the authorities led Northcroft J in *In re Muller; Cassin v Mutual Cash Order Co Ltd*.[39]

In *Wirth v Wirth*[40] Dixon CJ put the law on a more rational basis. That was not a case of a purchase in the name of another, but one of a voluntary transfer by an existing owner. The question whether a resulting trust is presumed in the latter case is not without complications, but it is unnecessary to discuss it here. Dixon CJ who accepted, or at least was content to assume, the correctness of the view expressed by Cussen J in *House v Caffyn*,[41] that if the land is under the Torrens system there is a presumption of a resulting trust, went on to hold, following *Moate v Moate*,[42] that a transfer of property by a prospective husband to his intended wife in contemplation of the marriage for which they had contracted raised a presumption of advancement. Dixon CJ said:

> While the presumption of advancement doubtless in its inception was concerned with relationships affording 'good' consideration, it has in the course of its growth obtained a foundation or justification in the greater prima facie probability of a beneficial interest being intended in the situations to which the presumption has been applied.[43]

He referred to *Soar v Foster*[44] but noted that in *Murdock v Aherne*[45] Molesworth J seems to have regarded the relation between a man and a woman whom the man had bigamously married and who knew it as within the presumption of advancement. Dixon CJ went on to say:

---

38. (1858) 4 K & J 152 at 161 [70 ER 64 at 67–68].
39. [1953] NZLR 879.
40. (1956) 98 CLR 228.
41. [1922] VLR 67 at 78.
42. [1948] 2 All ER 486.
43. (1956) 98 CLR 228 at 237.
44. (1858) 4 K & J 152 [70 ER 64].
45. (1878) 4 VLR (E) 244 at 249.

No doubt in *Moate v Moate* Jenkins J applied the presumption of advancement where it had not hitherto been applied. But the application was not inconsistent with any decided case and it accords with reason. To say that a transfer of property to an intended wife made in contemplation of the marriage raised a presumption of a resulting trust but a similar transfer made immediately after the celebration of the marriage raised a presumption of advancement involves almost a paradoxical distinction that does not accord with reason and can find a justification only on the ground that the doctrine depends in categories closed for historical reasons. That is not characteristic of doctrines of equity.[46]

Neither of the other members of the Court in that case found it necessary to decide whether there was a presumption of advancement when the property was transferred to the intended wife. However, the principle as stated by Dixon CJ is intelligible and is **[250]** likely to lead to a just result and should in my opinion be accepted. The presumption should be held to be raised when the relationship between the parties is such that it is more probable than not that a beneficial interest was intended to be conferred, whether or not the purchaser owed the other a legal or moral duty of support. It is true that this may require a reconsideration of the correctness of the actual results reached in some of the earlier cases, but to regard that as a barrier to acceptance of the principle would be to treat the established categories as frozen in time. As Dixon CJ said, that would not be characteristic of the doctrines of equity.

It then becomes necessary to apply the principle enunciated by Dixon CJ in *Wirth v Wirth*[47] to the case in which a man purchases property in the name of a woman with whom he is living in a de facto relationship. I do not regard *Napier v Public Trustee (WA)*[48] as concluding the question in favour of the view that a presumption of advancement can never arise in such a case. In that case Aickin J, with whom Mason, Murphy and Wilson JJ agreed, said that it is 'well established that no presumption of advancement arises in favour of a de facto wife'.[49] However, the question was not argued in that case and it was not necessary to decide it for the purposes of the decision; I left the question open. The question is whether the relationship which exists between two persons living in a de facto relationship makes it more probable than not that a gift was intended when property was purchased by one in the name of the other. The answer that will be given to that question will not necessarily be the same as that which would be given if the question were asked concerning a man and his mistress who were not living in such a relationship. The relationship in question is one which has proved itself to have an apparent permanence, and in which the parties live together, and represent themselves to others, as man and wife. It is true that in some cases a person may maintain a de facto relationship for the very purpose of preventing the other party to the relationship from obtaining any right or claim to property, but the question now asked arises only when the party has taken the deliberate step of purchasing property in the name of the other. Once one rejects the test applied in *Soar v Foster* as too narrow, and rejects any notion of moral disapproval, such as is suggested in *Rider v Kidder*[50] as inappropriate to the resolution of disputes as

---

46. (1956) 98 CLR 228 at 238.
47. (1956) 98 CLR 228.
48. (1980) 55 ALJR 1; 32 ALR 153.
49. (1980) 55 ALJR 1 at 3; 32 ALR 153 at 158.
50. (1805) 10 Ves 360 [32 ER 884].

to property in the twentieth century, it seems natural to conclude that a man who puts property in the [251] name of a woman with whom he is living in a de facto relationship does so because he intends her to have a beneficial interest, and that a presumption of advancement is raised. Cases such as *Soar v Foster*, where the relationship was based on an invalid marriage ceremony, or *Murdock v Aherne*, where the relationship was founded on a bigamous marriage, would be a fortiori. For these reasons I consider that there was a presumption of advancement in the present case.

However, both the presumption of advancement, and the presumption of a resulting trust, may be rebutted by evidence of the actual intention of the purchaser at the time of the purchase.[51] Where one person alone has provided the purchase money it is her or his intention alone that has to be ascertained. In the present case however both purchasers contributed the purchase money. The amount of $18,000 borrowed under the mortgage was provided equally by the parties, for it was lent to them jointly, on terms which made them jointly and severally liable for its repayment, and, having thus been borrowed, was applied by them in part payment of the purchase price. Where there are two purchasers, who have contributed unequal proportions, but have taken the purchase in their joint names, the intentions of both are material. Even if the parties had no common intention, the intentions of each may be proved, for the purpose of proving or negating that one intended to make a gift to the other.

The evidence does show that [Calverley] had no intention to confer a beneficial interest on [Green] — it rebuts the presumption of advancement. When a purchase was contemplated, the question was whether [Calverley] could afford it. [Calverley] made no suggestion that the property be put in joint names until he experienced difficulty in obtaining finance. When he made the suggestion, he said that the finance company required the purchase to be in the joint names. It can be concluded, on the balance of probabilities, that [Calverley] did not intend to confer any beneficial interest on [Green]. The presumption of advancement thus being rebutted, it is presumed that [Green] held her one-half interest in the property on a resulting trust in favour of [Calverley], the extent of the trust being measured by the proportion of the purchase money which [Calverley] provided. Since [Calverley] already has a one-half legal interest in the property, the trust is in respect of so much of his proportionate [252] beneficial interest as exceeds one-half — to that extent [Green] holds her legal one-half in trust for [Calverley], so that [Calverley] has in all a beneficial interest in the proportion which his contribution bears to the total purchase price. The question, however, then arises whether [Green] holds any greater interest in trust for [Calverley] — that depends on whether when she took the legal title she intended to create a further trust in his favour. The evidence does not show that [Green] intended to confer any beneficial interest on [Calverley]. She may have regarded her signature to the mortgage documents as an empty formality, but if a bystander had asked her whether she intended that [Calverley] should own the land beneficially, even if he paid nothing under the mortgage, and she were obliged to pay the whole mortgage debt with interest, it is most unlikely that she would have replied in the affirmative. So far as the evidence shows, she formed no intention at all as to the beneficial ownership of the property, and it has not been established that she intended to hold any part of her interest in trust for [Calverley].

---

51. *Charles Marshall Pty Ltd v Grimsley* (1956) 95 CLR 353 at 364–365.

In other words, the evidence negatives an intention on the part of [Calverley] to confer a beneficial interest on [Green] and it does not reveal that [Green] had an actual intention that the land should be held beneficially by [Calverley] in any greater proportion than that in which he had contributed to the purchase price. [Calverley] may have had an actual intention that he should be beneficially entitled to the whole of the property, but his intention can only affect the question whether a resulting trust arises. In so far as no resulting trust arose in [Calverley]'s favour, a trust could arise in respect of the legal interest of [Green] only if she intended that [Calverley] should have a beneficial interest greater than that to which the resulting trust entitled him. The result in my opinion is that the evidence is sufficient to rebut a presumption of advancement, but not sufficient to rebut the presumption of a resulting trust.

The extent of the beneficial interests of the respective parties must be determined at the time when the property was purchased and the trust created. The fact that the mortgage debt was repaid by [Calverley] is therefore not relevant in determining the extent of the interests of the parties in the land, although it may be relevant on an equitable accounting between the parties. The parties each contributed $9,000 of the amount borrowed, and it appears that the remainder of the price, $9,250, was provided by [Calverley], although the evidence on that point is unsatisfactory and there is no distinct finding on the question. If [Calverley] did provide the [253] whole of the deposit, [Green]'s proportionate interest in the land was 9,000/27,250.

The learned members of the Court of Appeal approached the matter by taking as their starting point the fact that [Green] had a legal half interest in the property and then inquiring whether the evidence revealed that she had agreed, or had formed an intention, to hold her interest on trust for [Calverley]. They found that there was no such agreement or indication of intention. However, this approach gave no effect to the presumption that the property was held on a resulting trust in favour of the parties in the proportions in which they had contributed to the purchase price.

...

Mason and Brennan JJ

[257] The first question is whether [Green] was a contributor to the purchase price of the property, as the Court of Appeal found, or whether she was not, as Rath J found. [Calverley]'s payment of the instalments due under the memorandum of mortgage, in accordance with the arrangement made between the parties, may be thought to be, or to be the equivalent of, the provision pro tanto of the purchase price of the property. After all, the only moneys which were actually paid out of what the parties had owned before settlement of the contract for the purchase of the Baulkham Hills property or out of what they had earned thereafter had come out of [Calverley]'s pocket. The property was purchased on the basis that the purchasers should pay it off over twenty years, a basis familiar to many home buyers. It is understandable but erroneous to regard the payment of mortgage instalments as payment of the purchase price of a home. The purchase price is what is paid in order to acquire the property; the mortgage instalments are paid to the lender from whom the money to pay some or all of the purchase price is borrowed. In this case, the price was $27,250, of which $18,000 was borrowed from the mortgagee by [Green] and [Calverley] jointly. The balance was paid by [Calverley] out of his own funds,

being part of the proceeds of the sale of the Mount Pritchard property. Thus [Green] and [Calverley] both contributed to the purchase price of the Baulkham Hills property. They mortgaged that property to secure the performance of their joint and several obligation to repay principal and to pay interest. The payment of instalments under the mortgage was not a payment [258] of the purchase price but a payment towards securing the release of the charge which the parties created over the property purchased. We would agree with the view expressed by the English Court of Appeal in *Crisp v Mullings*, a case in which the material facts are not distinguishable from the present:

> The situation, in our view, is that the defendant does not establish that he alone provided the purchase-price, any more than he would have, had the whole price been provided by a joint mortgage; and the resulting trust of the whole is therefore not established.[52]

As both parties contributed to the purchase price, there could not be a resulting trust in favour of [Calverley] alone. It follows that the Court of Appeal was right to allow the appeal from Rath J. Then the Court of Appeal went on to hold that the legal estate prevailed unless there were an express trust created in favour of [Calverley] when the parties acquired the legal estate in the Baulkham Hills property. That was too large a step to take, for it was necessary to consider another equitable presumption which arises from the unequal contribution of the purchase price and which governs the present case unless some opposing presumption displaces it or the other facts of the case rebut or qualify it. Unless an equitable presumption of a trust is displaced by a counter-presumption or it is rebutted or qualified by evidence of the intention of the party paying the purchase price or of the common intention of the parties who contribute that price, the presumption determines the conclusion to be reached.[53] Once it was found that both parties had contributed to the purchase price, the conclusion had to conform to the relevant equitable presumption unless it was displaced, rebutted or qualified. When two or more purchasers contribute to the purchase of property and the property is conveyed to them as joint tenants the equitable presumption is that they hold the legal estate in trust for themselves as tenants in common in shares proportionate to their contributions unless their contributions are equal.[54]

[259] This is the basic presumption, though it may be displaced in appropriate cases by the presumption of advancement or, perhaps, qualified by an inference of the kind espoused by Lord Upjohn in *Pettitt v Pettitt*. His Lordship said:

> ... where both spouses contribute to the acquisition of a property, then my own view (of course in the absence of evidence) is that they intended to be joint beneficial owners and this is so whether the purchase be in the joint names or in the name of one. This is the result of an application of the presumption of resulting trust. Even if the property

---

52. [1976] EG 730 at 733.
53. *Stewart Dawson & Co (Vict) Pty Ltd. v Federal Commissioner of Taxation* (1933) 48 CLR 683 at 689–691; *Carkeek v Tate-Jones* [1971] VR 691 at 695–696.
54. Notes to *Lake v Gibson* (1729) 21 ER 1052 and *Lake v Craddock* (1732) 24 ER 1011 in Frederic White, *White and Tudor's Leading Cases in Equity*, 1928, vol 2, 882; *Rigden v Vallier* (1751) 26 ER 1219 at 1221; *Robinson v Preston* (1858) 70 ER 211 at 213; *Aveling v Knipe* (1815) 34 ER 580 at 582; *Hill v Hill* (1874) 8 IR Eq 140.

be put in the sole name of the wife, I would not myself treat that as a circumstance of evidence enabling the wife to claim an advancement to her, for it is against all the probabilities of the case unless the husband's contribution is very small.[55]

In some instances, the drawing of such an inference might work to the disadvantage of a wife who holds a legal interest in property greater than a joint tenancy and who would otherwise be entitled to rely upon the presumption of advancement to assert as large a beneficial interest as the legal interest which she holds. It is not necessary now to consider whether the founding of a joint beneficial tenancy in husband and wife upon their inferred intention 'is the result of an application of the presumption of resulting trust'. What is presently material is whether it is appropriate to draw the inference that the parties intended that they should have beneficially a joint tenancy in the Baulkham Hills property — an interest corresponding with the interest vested in them at law.

It may be conceded that Lord Upjohn's inference reflects the notion that both spouses may contribute to the purchase of assets during the marriage (as they often do nowadays) and that they would wish those assets to be enjoyed together during their joint lives and to be enjoyed by the survivor when they are separated by death. Such an inference is appropriate only as between parties to a lifetime relationship (like the presumption of advancement of a wife.[56] The exclusive union for life which is undertaken by both spouses to a valid marriage, though defeasible and oftentimes defeated, remains the foundation of the legal [260] institution of marriage[57] though it is no necessary element of the relationship of de facto husband and wife. The term 'de facto husband and wife' embraces a wide variety of heterosexual relationships; it is a term obfuscatory of any legal principle except in distinguishing the relationship from that of husband and wife. It would be wrong to apply either the presumption of advancement or Lord Upjohn's inference to a relationship devoid of the legal characteristic which warrants a special rule affecting the beneficial ownership of property by the parties to a marriage. The presumption could not arise nor the inference be drawn in favour of [Green] in this case, which must be decided in the light of the basic presumption. Therefore, it is unnecessary now to decide whether Lord Upjohn's inference should qualify the presumption of advancement in favour of a wife, but it can be said that the antiquity of the presumption of advancement does not preclude the elevation of such an inference to the level of a presumption to be applied where the absence of the spouses' common intention leaves room for its operation. The doctrines of equity are not ossified in history.[58]

Where the contributors to the purchase price are not husband and wife, the taking of a conveyance in their joint names is less likely to support an inference that they intend the right of survivorship to govern their beneficial interests. In a case where a man and woman are cohabiting though unmarried there is no presumption, either of equity or human experience, that they intend their relationship to have the same consequences upon their individual property rights as marriage has upon the property rights of spouses. An assumption that the parties to such an arrangement intend to maintain independent

---

55. [1970] AC 777 at 815.
56. *Carkeek v Tate-Jones* [1971] VR 691 at 695–696.
57. *Hyde v Hyde and Woodmansee* (1866) LR 1 P & D 130 at 133; *Khan v Khan* [1963] VR 203 at 204.
58. Cf *Wirth v Wirth* (1956) 98 CLR 228 at 238.

control of money and property and to retain a testamentary power to dispose of assets in which they have an interest is more likely to coincide with reality than an assumption of joint ownership. The provisions of ss 79 and 80 of the *Family Law Act 1975* (Cth) now furnish a further ground for not applying the special rules governing the title to property in the case of spouses in order to resolve property disputes between parties who have cohabited but who have not married. On dissolution of a marriage, ss 79 and 80 confer a discretionary power upon the Family Court of Australia to alter the property interests of the parties to the marriage if it is just and equitable to do so. On the termination of an association between a man and a woman who are not married to [261] each other, no discretionary power may be exercised and the jurisdiction of the courts of equity is simply to declare the proprietary rights of the parties — a jurisdiction which a court of equity is not at liberty to exceed either in the case of husband and wife or in the case of a man and woman who are not married.[59] Therefore, special rules affecting the title to property of husband and wife can have no application in the present case.

The next question is whether the equitable presumption applicable when unequal contributors to the purchase price who are not spouses and who take a conveyance to themselves as joint tenants is rebutted or qualified by the circumstances. The equitable presumption can be rebutted or qualified by evidence of a contrary intention common to the contributors of the purchase price. When a common intention is in issue, it is not ordinarily to be found in an uncommunicated state of mind; it is to be inferred from what the parties do or say.

It may be that evidence of a sole purchaser's own state of mind at the time of the purchase can be received from him when the court is seeking to ascertain his intention[60] but in the search for the common intention of two or more purchasers at that time, light will rarely be shed by evidence of their uncommunicated states of mind. Lord Diplock's speech in *Gissing v Gissing* contains the principle ordinarily to be applied:

> As in so many branches of English law in which legal rights and obligations depend upon the intentions of the parties to a transaction, the relevant intention of each party is the intention which was reasonably understood by the other party to be manifested by that party's words or conduct notwithstanding that he did not consciously formulate that intention in his own mind or even acted with some different intention which he did not communicate to the other party. On the other hand, he is not bound by any inference which the other party draws as to his intention unless that inference is one which can reasonably be drawn from his words or conduct. It is in this sense that in the branch of English law relating to constructive, implied or resulting trusts effect is given to the inferences as to the intentions of parties to a transaction which a reasonable man would draw from their words or conduct and not to any subjective intention or absence of intention which was not [262] made manifest at the time of the transaction itself. It is for the court to determine what those inferences are.[61]

---

59. See *Wirth v Wirth* (1956) 98 CLR 228 at 231–232 per Dixon CJ; *Hepworth v Hepworth* (1963) 110 CLR 309 at 317 per Windeyer J.
60. *Martin v Martin* (1959) 110 CLR at 304–305.
61. [1971] AC 886 at 906.

The Court of Appeal correctly took the time of the acquisition of the Baulkham Hills property as the material time for determining the beneficial interests of the parties. The evidentiary material from which the court might have drawn an inference as to the intention of the parties included their acts and declarations before or at the time of the purchase, or so immediately after it as to constitute a part of the transaction. Evidence of those acts and declarations were admissible either for or against the party who did the act or made the declaration, but any subsequent declarations would have been admissible only as admissions against interest.[62] In some cases it is possible to treat the concurrence of one party with the other's payment of the mortgage instalments as an admission of the former's exclusive interest, but the circumstance attending the payment of mortgage instalments is no more than one of the relevant facts. Another relevant fact is the relationship between the parties at the time. In the present case there was evidence of both of those facts. The Court of Appeal, having regard to those facts, inter alia, found that there was no common intention between [Green] and defendant that [Green] was to hold her interest in trust for [Calverley]. Nor did they find any other common intention. Their Honours held that the legal interests of the parties must prevail. The error in this approach is not in the refusal to find a common intention but in the failure first to apply the presumption that comes into play when the legal owners who are unequal contributors to the purchase price are not shown to have a common intention inconsistent with a tenancy in common in shares proportionate to their contributions. Applying the relevant presumption, the Court of Appeal should have held the parties to be equitable tenants in common in the Baulkham Hills property in proportion to the contribution each made to the purchase price. That proportion has not been precisely ascertained. The matter will have to be remitted to the Supreme Court to determine that proportion if the parties are unable to agree upon it.

As there was no agreement made after the purchase to alter the equitable interests acquired when the property was purchased, the payments made under the mortgage work no alteration in those interests. This case cannot be likened to *Bloch v Bloch*[63] where **[263]** the relevant property which the parties intended to acquire was seen to be not the title to land subject to mortgage but the land freed of the mortgage.[64] In such a case the price paid to free the land of mortgage as well as the price paid for the title to the land itself must be taken into account in determining the parties' beneficial interests. Mortgage payments may quantify the parties' interests under a resulting trust of a property acquired as a mortgage-free investment, but they would rarely quantify the interests of parties under a resulting trust of a house property acquired as a home to live in. If it is right to regard the payment of the mortgage instalments as having been made by [Calverley] out of his own funds and on his own account — that is, if he made those payments not intending [Green] ultimately to have the benefit of those payments — [Calverley] may be entitled to contribution from [Green] for her share of the payments and to an equitable charge to secure the making of her contribution.[65] That question was not argued on the appeal. Neither has any argument

---

62. *Shephard v Cartwright* [1955] AC 431 at 445; *Charles Marshall Pty. Ltd. v Grimsley* (1956) 95 CLR 353 at 365.
63. (1981) 37 ALR 55.
64. (1981) 55 ALJR at 706; 37 ALR at 64.
65. See *Ingram v Ingram* [1941] VLR 95 at 102.

been raised to assert the existence of a beneficial interest under a constructive trust arising after the transaction of purchase was closed and overriding the beneficial interests then acquired. In Canada and in some cases in England, the device of the constructive trust has been invoked 'to give relief to a wife who cannot prove a common intention or to a wife whose contribution to the acquisition of property is physical labour rather than purchase money'.[66] It is unnecessary to consider whether in some future case the device of a constructive trust might be relied on where property beneficially owned in particular proportions is maintained or enhanced by work done or contributions made in different proportions. If such a question arises in a contest between parties to a marriage it may be necessary to consider the extent to which the device is available in the equitable jurisdiction when ss. 79 and 80 of the *Family Law Act* confer a statutory jurisdiction to alter proprietary interests and that jurisdiction may be exercised to give relief to a party to a marriage who has made a non-pecuniary contribution to the purchase of property.

We would allow the appeal and set aside the judgment of the Court of Appeal except for its orders allowing the appeal from Rath J and setting aside his Honour's order. We would stand the **[264]** matter over until 12 February 1985 in order to give the parties an opportunity to agree, in the light of this judgment, upon an order which might finally dispose of the issues outstanding between them. If no agreement is reached, it will be necessary to remit the matter to the Supreme Court of New South Wales to proceed in accordance with this judgment. In that event, it would be open to the Supreme Court to consider, as Mahoney JA suggested, whether [Calverley] is entitled to any relief against [Green] in respect of his payments of the mortgage instalments.

Comment

1. See Radan & Stewart at **19.54–19.52**.

The presumption of joint tenancy in the purchase of the matrimonial home

---

19.4   Trustees of the Property of Cummins (a bankrupt) v Cummins (2006) 227 CLR 278

Court: High Court of Australia

Facts: Mr Cummins, a barrister, had become bankrupt after failing to pay income tax for nearly 45 years. He and his wife had purchased a house in 1970. Mr Cummins had contributed 23.7 per cent to the purchase price and Mrs Cummins had contributed 76.3 per cent. In 1987 Mr Cummins transferred his legal and beneficial interests in the matrimonial home to his wife. No consideration had been paid for by Mrs Cummins, although there was a contract, stamp duty had been paid and a valuer's report had

---

66. Per Laskin J (as he then was) in *Murdoch v Murdoch* (1973) 41 DLR (3d) 367 at 388; and see *Rathwell v Rathwell* (1978) 83 DLR (3d) 289 and *Pettkus v Becker* (1980) 117 DLR (3d) 257.

been paid for by her. Mr Cummins argued that the main purpose for doing this was to limit his exposure to professional negligence liability, as he claimed to fear the possibility that barristers would lose their immunity from negligence. The trustee in bankruptcy argued that the main purpose in transferring the home was to avoid the Commonwealth government's considerable claims for unpaid income tax.

The High Court found that the transaction was void as its main purpose was to avoid creditors. The High Court found that where a husband and a wife purchase a matrimonial property it will generally be inferred that the property will be held equally between them irrespective of the contributions that were made. Equally, if the property has been registered in joint names, equity will not interfere with that joint tenancy by creating disproportionate shares reflecting their contributions.

Issue: Once the High Court found the transfer to be void, the issue arose as to how the property should be divided. The property could be divided up 50:50 between Mrs Cummins and the trustee in bankruptcy to reflect the legal title. Alternatively, the property could be divided up in accordance with the proportionate contributions made by Mr and Mrs Cummins to the purchase of the home, which would leave the trustee with 23.7 per cent and Mrs Cummins with 76.3 per cent.

Decision: The High Court (Gleeson CJ, Gummow, Hayne, Heydon and Crennan JJ in a joint decision) found that the resulting trust analysis should be rejected and that the house should be split 50:50 between the trustee and Mrs Cummins.

Extracts: The extract contains a discussion of resulting trust principles and of the presumption of advancement and the High Court's reasons for not employing a resulting trust between married couples who register as joint tenants of the matrimonial home.

Gleeson CJ, Gummow, Hayne, Heydon and Crennan JJ

[297] The ownership of the Hunters Hill property

... [T]he generally accepted principles in this field, affirmed for Australia by *Calverley v Green*,[67] were expressed as follows in that case by Gibbs CJ:

> [I]f two persons have contributed the purchase money in unequal shares, and the property is purchased in their joint names, there is, again in the absence of a relationship that gives rise to a [298] presumption of advancement, a presumption that the property is held by the purchasers in trust for themselves as tenants in common in the proportions in which they contributed the purchase money.[68]

Further, the presumption of advancement of a wife by the husband has not been matched by a presumption of advancement of the husband by the wife.[69] The 'presumption of

---

67. (1984) 155 CLR 242.
68. (1984) 155 CLR 242 at 246–247.
69. (1984) 155 CLR 242 at 268 per Deane J.

advancement', where it applies, means that the equitable interest is at home with the legal title, because there is no reason for assuming that any trust has arisen.[70]

The subject matter of the August transactions with respect to the Hunters Hill property was identified in the transfer as 'all that the [sic] interest of the Transferor as joint tenant of and in the land above described'. The following remarks by Professor Butt in his work, *Land Law*, are in point:

> Strictly speaking, joint tenants do not have proportionate shares in the land. However, a joint tenant is regarded as having a *potential* share in the land commensurate with that of the other joint tenants. Where there are two joint tenants, that potential share is one-half; where there are three joint tenants, it is one-third; and so on. This potential share the joint tenant can deal with unilaterally during his or her lifetime.[71]

Hence the significance of the valuation which was obtained and the identification in the transfer of a consideration of $205,250, being one-half of the valuation.

What was there to conclude in August 1987 that the face of the register did not represent the full state of the ownership of the Hunters Hill property, and that the ownership as joint tenants was at odds with, and subjected to, the beneficial ownership established by trust law?

No part of the purchase price of $205,250 was paid by Mrs Cummins and the August 1987 transfer was voluntary, as explained earlier in these reasons. However, Mrs Cummins did pay the ad valorem stamp duty on the contract and the valuer's fee. There is force in the submission for the Trustees that it is unlikely these steps would have been taken by Mrs Cummins and that the August transaction with respect to the Hunters Hill property would have been cast in the way that it was had she believed that she already held approximately a two-thirds beneficial interest. At all events, these matters suggest that in August 1987 the parties were proceeding on the conventional basis that the equitable estate was at home with the registered estate of joint tenancy.[72] There is no necessary inconsistency between this conventional basis as to the nature of the ownership being dealt with in August 1987 and the later conventional basis on which the litigation was conducted, namely that the [299] consideration stipulated was not paid and that the property interest, ascertained as just described, was being dealt with on a voluntary basis.

It is important for a consideration of the issues concerning the operation, if any, of the principles respecting resulting trusts that the registered title was that of joint tenants rather than tenants in common. The severance effected in August 1987 had the effect of putting to an end the incident of survivorship.

The dislike by equity of survivorship and of what Deane J described as 'the gamble of the tontine'[73] was the expression of its preference for proportionate carriage of benefit and burden; equity reacted against the operation of chance to produce a result at odds with

---

70. (1984) 155 CLR 242 at 267 per Deane J.
71. (2001), 222 (footnote omitted).
72. See *Con-Stan Industries of Australia Pty Ltd v Norwich Winterthur Insurance (Australia) Ltd* (1986) 160 CLR 226 at 244–245.
73. *Corin v Patton* (1990) 169 CLR 540 at 573.

proportionate distribution between claimants. In *Corin v Patton*[74] Deane J said that there were two aspects of joint tenancy which attracted the operation of overriding equitable doctrine, based upon notions of good conscience and actual or presumed intention. They were:

> (i) the equality of the interests of joint tenants, regardless of intention or contribution, in the undivided rights constituting ownership of the relevant property, and (ii) the right of accretion by survivorship until there is a sole owner of the whole.[75]

Deane J added:

> Where legal joint tenancy persists, severance in equity must involve the creation of some distinct beneficial interests, that is to say, the creation of a trust for the joint tenants themselves as tenants in common in equal shares or for different beneficiaries or beneficial shares.[76]

In *Malayan Credit Ltd v Jack Chia-MPH Ltd*,[77] Lord Brightman, in delivering the advice of the Privy Council, considered an argument that, in the absence of an expressed agreement, persons who take as joint tenants at law hold as tenants in common in equity only in three classes of case. The first was the provision of purchase money in unequal shares, where the beneficial interest is held to reflect those unequal shares; the second, security taken jointly by parties who advance the loan moneys in unequal shares; and the third, partnership property.[78] The Privy Council held that the circumstances in which, in the absence of express agreement, equity may presume joint tenants at law to be tenants in common in equity of the beneficial interest of property were not limited in this way.

[300] In the circumstances of *Malayan Credit,* the Privy Council inferred from '[a]ll the circumstances'[79] that, since the commencement of a lease of property for the business purposes of the joint lessees, they had held beneficial interests in the lease as tenants in common in unequal shares representing the distinct and differing areas of the leased premises they occupied. Upon the sale of the leasehold premises, the net proceeds were to be divided not equally but in accordance with these proportions. This manifested the precept that among merchants the right of survivorship has no place.[80]

Among the features taken into account in *Malayan Credit*[81] as pointing in equity unmistakably towards a tenancy in common in unequal shares were the facts that, after the grant of the lease, the parties had paid stamp duties and survey fees in the same unequal shares and that the rental service charges had been paid in the same way.

---

74. (1990) 169 CLR 540.
75. (1990) 169 CLR 540 at 573.
76. (1990) 169 CLR 540 at 573.
77. [1986] AC 549 at 559–560.
78. See John McGhee, *Snell's Equity*, 2005, pp 103–104; Frederic White, *White and Tudor's Leading Cases in Equity*, 1928, vol 2, pp 881–893.
79. [1986] AC 549 at 561.
80. *Buckley v Barber* (1851) 6 Ex 164 at 179 [155 ER 498 at 504] per Parke B.
81. [1986] AC 549 at 561.

In *Malayan Credit*, there was, of course, no scope for any 'competing' presumption of advancement seen in family relations cases. In *Charles Marshall Pty Ltd v Grimsley*[82] and subsequently in *Calverley v Green*[83] this Court was concerned with family dealings in property: shares in the first case and improved land in the second case.

In *Charles Marshall*, the plaintiffs were daughters of the donor and the Court said that the presumption of an intention of advancement, that they be made beneficial as well as legal owners of the shares, might be rebutted by evidence manifesting a contrary intention. Dixon CJ, McTiernan, Williams, Fullagar and Taylor JJ said of the rebuttal of presumptions by manifestation of a contrary intention:

> Apart from admissions the only evidence that is relevant and admissible comprises the acts and declarations of the parties before or at the time of the purchase (in this case before or at the time of the acquisition of the shares by allotment) or so immediately thereafter as to constitute a part of the transaction.[84]

However, as *Malayan Credit*[85] illustrates, whilst evidence of subsequent statements of intention, not being admissions against interest, are inadmissible, evidence of facts as to subsequent dealings and of surrounding circumstances of the transaction may be received.[86]

[301] What then was the 'transaction' to which attention must be directed in determining whether, subsequent admissions or conventional assumptions or arrangements apart, the registered title to the Hunters Hill property acquired by Mr and Mrs Cummins was not at variance with an equitable title? The Hunters Hill property, at the time of their registration as joint proprietors on 10 August 1970, was vacant land. The purchase moneys were contributed, as explained earlier in these reasons, in the proportions 76.3 per cent (Mrs Cummins) and 23.7 per cent (Mr Cummins). A mortgage over the Hunters Hill property executed by Mr and Mrs Cummins in favour of the Commonwealth Savings Bank of Australia on 16 July 1971 secured an advance to them jointly of $8,000 on a covenant that they would erect and complete within six months of that date a dwelling house at a cost of not less than $33,500. The tax return by Mrs Cummins for the year ended 30 June 1971 but lodged by her tax agent in 1972 showed the Hunters Hill property as her place of residence.

The 'transaction' to which attention must be directed, in the sense given in *Charles Marshall* respecting the principles of resulting trusts, is a composite of the purchase of the Hunters Hill property followed by construction of a dwelling house occupied as the matrimonial home for many years preceding the August transactions. The relevant facts bearing upon, and helping to explain, the nature of the joint title taken on registration on 10 August 1970 include the other elements in that composite. To fix merely upon the unequal proportions in which the purchase moneys were provided for the calculation of the beneficial interests in the improved property which was dealt with subsequently in

---

82. (1956) 95 CLR 353.
83. (1984) 155 CLR 242.
84. (1956) 95 CLR 353 at 365.
85. [1986] AC 549 at 559–560.
86. Frederic White, *White and Tudor's Leading Cases in Equity*, 1928, vol 2, p 882.

August 1987 would produce a distorted and artificial result, at odds with practical and economic realities.[87] Looked at in this way, this is not a case which requires consideration of the authorities where an equitable lien or charge secures expenditure on improvements made but no beneficial interest in the land is conferred.[88]

Calverley v Green concerned the beneficial ownership of an improved property acquired as joint tenants by a man and a woman who had lived together for about ten years as husband and wife. The decision of this Court was that the presumption that they held the registered title in trust for themselves in shares proportionate to their contributions was not rebutted by the circumstances of the case. Mason and Brennan JJ[89] referred to the statement by Lord Upjohn in *Pettitt v Pettitt*[90] that, where spouses contribute to the acquisition of a property then, in the absence of contrary evidence, it is to be taken that they intended to be joint beneficial owners. Their Honours said that Lord Upjohn's remarks reflected the notion that both spouses may contribute to the purchase of assets through their marriage 'as they [302] often do nowadays'[91] and that they would wish those assets to be enjoyed together for their joint lives and by the survivor when they were separated by death. However, Mason and Brennan JJ considered such an inference to be appropriate only between parties to a lifetime relationship, being the exclusive union for life undertaken by both spouses to a valid marriage, though defeasible and oftentimes defeated.[92]

It is unnecessary for the purposes of the present case to express any concluded view as to the perception by Mason and Brennan JJ of the particular and exclusive significance to be attached to the status of marriage in this field of legal, particularly equitable, discourse. It is enough to note that, as Dixon CJ observed fifty years ago in *Wirth v Wirth*,[93] in this field, as elsewhere, rigidity is not a characteristic of doctrines of equity. The reasoning of the Privy Council in *Malayan Credit*[94] is an example of that lack of rigidity.

In the present case, Sackville J referred in the second judgment to the operation of statute law to produce divergent outcomes in particular classes of case.[95] In particular, his Honour referred to the regimes established by the *Family Law Act 1975* (Cth), s 79, and, in New South Wales, by the *Property (Relationships) Act 1984* (NSW).[96] The New South Wales statute provides for the declaration of title or rights in respect of property held by either party to a 'domestic relationship'. That term is broadly defined in s 5 as extending beyond the already broad definition of de facto relationship in s 4. The extent to which these

---

87. Cf the remarks of Lord Diplock in *Gissing v Gissing* [1971] AC 886 at 906.
88. See *Giumelli v Giumelli* (1999) 196 CLR 101 at 119–120 [31]–[32].
89. (1984) 155 CLR 242 at 259.
90. [1970] AC 777 at 815.
91. (1984) 155 CLR 242 at 259.
92. (1984) 155 CLR 242 at 259.
93. (1956) 98 CLR 228 at 238.
94. [1986] AC 549.
95. (2003) 134 FCR 449 at 462–463.
96. See also *Property Law Act 1958* (Vic), Pt IX; *Property Law Act 1974* (Qld), Pt 19; *De Facto Relationships Act* (NT); *Domestic Relationships Act 1994* (ACT); *De Facto Relationships Act 1996* (SA); *Family Court Act 1997* (WA), Pt 5A; *Relationships Act 2003* (Tas).

statutory innovations may bear upon further development of the principles of equity is a matter for another day.[97]

The present case concerns the traditional matrimonial relationship. Here, the following view expressed in the present edition of Professor Scott's work respecting beneficial ownership of the matrimonial home should be accepted:

It is often a purely accidental circumstance whether money of the husband or of the wife is actually used to pay the purchase price to the vendor, where both are contributing by money or labor to the various expenses of the household. It is often a matter of chance whether the family expenses are incurred and discharged or services are rendered in the maintenance of the home before or after the [303] purchase.[98]

To that may be added the statement in the same work:

Where a husband and wife purchase a matrimonial home, each contributing to the purchase price and title is taken in the name of one of them, it may be inferred that it was intended that each of the spouses should have a one-half interest in the property, regardless of the amounts contributed by them.[99]

That reasoning applies with added force in the present case where the title was taken in the joint names of the spouses. There is no occasion for equity to fasten upon the registered interest held by the joint tenants a trust obligation representing differently proportionate interests as tenants in common. The subsistence of the matrimonial relationship, as Mason and Brennan JJ emphasised in *Calverley v Green*[100] supports the choice of joint tenancy with the prospect of survivorship. That answers one of the two concerns of equity, indicated by Deane J in *Corin v Patton*[101] which founds a presumed intention in favour of tenancy in common. The range of financial considerations and accidental circumstances in the matrimonial relationship referred to by Professor Scott answers the second concern of equity, namely the disproportion between quantum of beneficial ownership and contribution to the acquisition of the matrimonial home.

In the present litigation, the case for the disinclination of equity to intervene through the doctrines of resulting trusts to displace the incidents of the registered title as joint tenants of the Hunters Hill property is strengthened by further regard to the particular circumstances. Solicitors acted for Mr and Mrs Cummins on the purchase in 1970. The conveyance was not uneventful. The contract was dated 14 April 1970 and was settled on 27 July 1970, but only after the issue by the solicitors for the vendor on 10 July of a notice to complete. It is unrealistic to suggest that the solicitor for the purchasers, Mr and Mrs Cummins, did not at any point advise his clients on the significance of taking title as joint tenants rather than as tenants in common. Secondly, use of the valuation obtained in 1987 to fix what was shown as the purchase price for the acquisition by

---

97. *Esso Australia Resources Ltd v Federal Commissioner of Taxation* (1999) 201 CLR 49 at 59–63 [18]–[28].
98. Scott, *The Law of Trusts* (1989), vol 5, §454, p 239.
99. Scott, *The Law of Trusts* (1989), vol 5, §443, pp 197–198. (Footnote omitted.)
100. (1984) 155 CLR 242 at 259.
101. (1990) 169 CLR 540 at 573.

Mrs Cummins of the interest of her husband is consistent, as already indicated, with the conventional basis of their dealings which treated the matrimonial home as beneficially owned equally.

Comments

1. See Radan & Stewart at **19.50–19.54**.

2. The presumption of joint tenancy raised in *Cummins* is not irrebuttable. In *Sui Mei Huen v Official Receiver for Official Trustee in Bankruptcy* (2008) 248 ALR 1 the Full Federal Court found that it can be displaced by an express or constructive agreement between a husband and wife concerning their interests. In this case there was an express agreement between the married couple that the man would surrender his interest in the house in exchange for the woman's promise that she would pay all future outgoings and mortgage payments and that she would make no further claims on him under the *Family Law Act 1975* (Cth) or for maintenance and support. The Full Court found that this had created a constructive trust of the man's legal half-interest in the property in favour of the wife. The *Cummins* presumption of joint tenancy had been rebutted and the agreement was enforceable against the ex-husband. Later, when the husband became bankrupt, the agreement also bound the trustee in bankruptcy.

20

TRUSTEES

Introduction

20.1 Trustees have a number of rights, powers and duties. Trustees' rights, powers and duties are framed by the trust document, the rules of equity and statute. The extracts in this chapter deal with the following issues:

- the trustee's right to indemnity: *Nolan v Collie* (2003) 7 VR 287;
- the trustee's duty to provide information: *McDonald v Ellis* (2007) 72 NSWLR 605; and
- the trustee's duty to consider the exercise of their trust powers: *Karger v Paul* [1984] VR 161.

The trustees' right to indemnity

20.2   Nolan v Collie (2003) 7 VR 287

Court: Court of Appeal of Victoria

Facts: This was a long-running case which involved two families: the Nolans and the Collies. The Nolans owned a family company called Merlaw Pty Ltd ('Merlaw'). It operated as the trustee for the Prudent Trust, a discretionary trust where the beneficiaries were members of the Nolan family. One of its main trust assets was an office building called Jolimont Terrace ('Jolimont').

The Nolans had an interest in another company called Terramont Pty Ltd ('Terramont'), which they shared with the Collie family. Terramont was the trustee of two discretionary trusts: the Terranol Trust (the beneficiaries of which were Mrs Nolan and the Nolan children) and the Terracol Trust (the beneficiaries of which were Mrs Collie and the Collie children).

In 1984 Merlaw entered into a contract to sell Jolimont to Terramont. It was agreed that as part of the sale Merlaw would remain registered as owner and that Terramont would pay the outstanding mortgage payments on the property. It was also agreed that these sums would come equally from the Nolan and Collie families. This agreement created a constructive trust of the property with Merlaw (as vendor) holding the property on constructive trust for Terramont (as purchaser). This trust is referred to in the judgment below as the 'purchase trust'.

The mortgage was refinanced in 1987 with the ANZ. A new mortgage was executed and registered over the property. Unfortunately, the bank mistakenly created an 'all moneys' mortgage which meant that the property became security for all of the debts of Merlaw, whether they were related to the Prudent Trust or not. In 1990 the ANZ decided to sell the property because Merlaw's debts to it exceeded $1m. The debts incurred by Merlaw as trustee for the Prudent Trust were fully paid out but the surplus went to pay its other debts as well. Terramont's interest in the land was not recognised and nothing was paid to it out of the proceeds. Merlaw later became insolvent.

The Collie family successfully sued Merlaw for breaching the constructive trust by offering Jolimont as security for all of Merlaw's debts. The Collies also argued that Merlaw had a right of indemnity as trustee to call upon the Prudent Trust assets to satisfy this claim, as Merlaw had been acting as trustee of the Prudent Trust when it breached constructive trust in favour of Terramont. The Collies then argued that they could be subrogated to Merlaw's position and make a claim on the assets of the Prudent Trust.

At trial Warren J found that Merlaw did have a right to indemnity from the trust assets and that the Collie family's claims could be subrogated to its position. This was because Jolimont was an asset of the Prudent Trust and Merlaw had mortgaged it in its capacity as trustee of the Prudent Trust. Merlaw had a right to indemnity because the mortgage liability had been 'properly incurred'.

The Nolans appealed and argued that the mortgage liability had arisen because of a breach of the purchase trust and this meant that it had not been 'properly incurred'.

Issue: The issue was whether Merlaw was entitled to be indemnified by the Prudent Trust in relation to its decision to grant the mortgage over Jolimont. This hinged on the question of whether the mortgage liabilities had been 'properly incurred'.

Decision: The Victorian Court of Appeal upheld the trial decision and found that Merlaw could be indemnified. It found that the test for trustees' indemnity should be whether the trustee's liabilities were 'not improperly incurred'. This was taken to exclude expenses which are incurred in circumstances of bad faith, without power or in the absence of reasonable care and diligence. The court found that while there was a lack of care in Merlaw's action it had not acted sufficiently heinously to be denied indemnity.

Extracts: In this extract Ormiston JA discusses the formulation of the test for trustees' indemnity and the conflicting authorities on what the test should be.

Ormiston JA

[302] First, ... it is necessary to deal with an argument mentioned briefly in counsel's outline and examined in greater detail in oral argument, to the effect that there was no right of indemnity in Merlaw because the obligation in question had not been 'properly incurred' in the administration of the relevant trust. The simple assertion for which counsel contended in the first place was based, as I would understand it,

on the premise that the relevant trust was the 'purchase [303] trust'. If that be so, so it was argued, a liability arising out of a breach of trust could not, ex hypothesi, be characterised as one which had been properly incurred in the administration of that trust. Clearly the breach caused compensable loss to the principal 'beneficiary' of the purchase trust, namely Terramont as purchaser, and there could be no basis for an indemnity in that respect. One may accept, whatever be the correct criterion for determining indemnifiable expenses and liabilities of a trustee, that that proposition, so far as it went, was correct.

For reasons which I have already attempted to explain, the real issue in the present case as to the nature of expenditure and liabilities entitling a trustee to indemnity from the trust assets is its application to the assets of the Prudent Trust and Merlaw's entitlement to make a claim against those assets. This issue was raised to a degree in oral argument, consistent with the [Nolans]' pleadings, to the effect that any liability to pay compensation, if it were in fact incurred in the course of acting as trustee for the Prudent Trust, was incurred while Merlaw was acting improperly in the role of that trustee. In addition it was argued that the acts giving rise to Merlaw's liability to the plaintiff in the first action were not performed for the benefit of the Prudent Trust's beneficiaries.

The assumed legal premise for these contentions, especially the primary contention, was that the trustee's right of indemnification against the trust estate is confined to liabilities and expenses which have been properly incurred in the carrying out of the trust. That test, at least at one time, seemed to be expressed in terms uniformly accepted.[1] Such an approach seemed, until a few years ago, also largely accepted by the two principal texts in this country on the law of trusts, as well as the standard English texts.[2] In very recent times, however, doubt has been cast on that simple proposition, in particular by the New South Wales Court of Appeal in *Gatsios Holdings Pty Ltd v Mick Kritharas Holdings Pty Ltd*.[3] In the course of his judgment Spigelman CJ said:

> The use of such terminology as conduct being 'proper' or 'reasonable', cannot be regarded as a test of when a trustee is entitled to receive indemnity for outgoings incurred [in] the course of execution of the trust. Such terminology generally records a conclusion which has been reached on other grounds.[4]

Meagher JA, in considering 'the limits to be placed on this right to indemnification', said:

> [O]ne must in principle incline to the view that if the activity in question had been fraudulent the law would withhold the right to indemnification ... I find it difficult

---

1. See, for example, *Re Beddoe* [1893] 1 Ch 547 at 558; *Vacuum Oil Co Pty Ltd v Wiltshire* (1945) 72 CLR 319 at 335 and *RWG Management Ltd v Commissioner for Corporate Affairs* [1985] VR 385 at 394, 396 per Brooking J.
2. See H A J Ford & W A Lee, *Principles of the Law of Trusts*, Looseleaf edition, LawBook Company, Sydney, 1996+, Ch 14, para 14040 (before the cumulative supplement No 7 of September 2002) and R P Meagher and W M C Gummow, *Jacobs' Law of Trusts in Australia*, 6th ed, Butterworths, Sydney, 1997, pp 628 [2102] and 631–2 [2105].
3. (2002) ATPR 41-864.
4. (2002) ATPR 41-864 at [8].

to formulate any other limitations. United States authorities ... might be read as establishing either or both these propositions: (a) that the activity in respect of which indemnity is claimed must be 'reasonable', and (b) that the activity must be 'proper'.[5]

[304] In my view, neither such limitation exists in Australian law. As to the former, it is in the circumstances, meaningless ... As to the latter, it is almost as meaningless to endeavour to apply some hypothetical standard of propriety in ordinary commercial life, absent fraud and crime.

As to what is the appropriate test, Mason P said that in substance he agreed with Meagher JA, but that he preferred to express no view on the issue whether a trustee's right depended on whether the conduct had been reasonable or proper, commenting only that '[t]he terms are notoriously open-ended', but cautioning that he 'would need to be persuaded that they are meaningless in the present situation'. Conceding that they embodied 'judgments to be made in context', he observed that '[s]ome outer limit needs to be drawn in order to recognise that certain types of grossly improper frolics by trustees will put them outside the presently uncertain boundary of the right now in question'.[6]

With the greatest of respect, it is by no means clear why a majority of their Honours in *Gatsios Holdings* seemed to sanction so significant a departure from accepted principle as to leave the trustee's right largely unconstrained.[7] It is possible that their views were prompted by the fact that the claim there in question resulted from a judgment obtained in an action in tort, which has always posed problems in relation to questions of indemnification. The form of their Honours' discussion tends to make it unlikely that their intention was so limited,[8] nor does it seem that the case depended, as it might have, on the terms of the trust deed, which appear to have been expressed benevolently towards the trustees.[9] Again with respect, the majority's views would appear to leave this important area of trust law rudderless and in a state where mischievous trustees might seize upon an almost unfettered right to indemnity as justifying improper depredations of trust funds, contrary to their obligation not to abuse their position by making it 'a means of profit or benefit' to themselves.[10]

To my way of thinking the conventionally stated test as to expenses 'properly incurred' is merely a convenient shorthand to describe those restraints applicable to trustees who would seek to look to trust funds for the payment of their expenses and other trust liabilities. It also has the advantage of succinctly expressing the notion of propriety as underpinning a trustee's relationship with the trust estate and the beneficiaries. One must

---

5. (2002) ATPR 41-864 at [47].
6. (2002) ATPR 41-864 at [42].
7. The decision of the court was in favour of indemnification. One of their Honours, indeed, has been in part responsible for the passages cited from *Jacobs' Law of Trusts* from the second edition in 1967 to the sixth edition in 1997.
8. Meagher JA's reference to 'this right' in [47] refers back to the same expression in [46] of his judgment, but the question there posed was whether 'this right' 'extends to reimbursement ... for damages ... for torts'.
9. (2002) ATPR 41-864 at [48].
10. R P Meagher and W M C Gummow, *Jacobs' Law of Trusts in Australia*, 6th ed, Butterworths, Sydney, 1997, [1742].

not forget, moreover, that in *Re Beddoe*, seen as one of the leading authorities, Lindley LJ explained that in cases of doubt the trust estate should bear the trustee's costs,[11] and that: 'The words "properly incurred" in the ordinary form of order[12] are equivalent to "not improperly incurred"'. The proposition was converted[13] by another respected judge, Bowen LJ, who was perhaps more familiar with courts of common law, into 'a proposition in which the word "properly" means reasonably as well as **[305]** honestly incurred'. His Lordship added that, while trustees ought not to bear expenses and liabilities personally 'on account of mere errors in judgment which fall short of negligence or unreasonableness', nevertheless 'mere bona fides is not the test'.[14]A L Smith LJ concurred[15] with the other members of the court.

Re Beddoe or the principles stated therein has been cited and applied in Australia on numerous occasions. In the High Court it was used in *National Trustees Executors & Agency Co of Australasia Ltd v Barnes*[16] as the basis for Rich ACJ and Williams J to support the proposition that a trustee is entitled to be indemnified out of the trust estate 'against all his proper costs, charges and expenses incident to the execution of the trust'. Starke J, who approached the matter slightly differently, nevertheless espoused a proposition that a trustee had a right to be recouped as of right all that he had 'expended properly' in that role.[17] Subsequently, in a judgment in which Dixon J formed part of the majority, his Honour said in *Vacuum Oil Co* that, where an executor has acted under appropriate authority, the executor had a 'right to be indemnified out of the assets in respect of liabilities he has incurred in the proper performance of his duties or exercise of his powers'.[18]

In two later cases in the High Court principles as to the indemnification of trustees were stated without specific reference to the 'proper' incurring of costs or expenses but in terms which would not deny the applicability of the rule, especially having regard to the reliance on the authorities referred to above in support of the propositions discussed in those later cases. In *Octavo Investments Pty Ltd v Knight*[19] the majority (Stephen, Mason, Aickin and Wilson JJ) referred on four occasions to *Vacuum Oil Co* with approval and without in any way suggesting that the test as to proper incurrence no longer applied. Likewise in *Commissioner of Stamp Duties (NSW) v Buckle*[20] the High Court again referred with approval to the passage cited above from *Vacuum Oil Co* and also to *Re Beddoe* itself, without there being any suggestion that the tests laid down in those cases were no longer apposite.

---

11. [1893] 1 Ch 547 at 558 at 558.
12. See, for example, Form 1 in *Seton's Forms of Judgments and Orders*, 1912, Vol II, pp 1126 and 1131–2.
13. *Re Beddoe* [1893] 1 Ch 547 at 558 at 562.
14. *Re Beddoe* [1893] 1 Ch 547 at 558 at 562.
15. *Re Beddoe* [1893] 1 Ch 547 at 558 at 566.
16. (1941) 64 CLR 268 esp at 277 per Williams J, which was concurred in by Rich ACJ.
17. *National Trustees Executors & Agency Co of Australasia Ltd v Barnes* (1941) 64 CLR 268 at 274.
18. (1945) 72 CLR 319 at 335 at 335. It should be noted that Dixon J, although not expressly citing *Re Beddoe*, explicitly referred to 'liabilities' as such, although the word seems to have been used in its widest sense.
19. (1979) 144 CLR 360.
20. (1998) 192 CLR 226.

The decision in *Gatsios Holdings* seems to have provoked a substantial rewriting of the relevant part of Ford and Lee's ch 14, especially para 14040,[21] reflecting a scepticism as to the applicability of a test of indemnification for expenses and liabilities upon the basis of those which are 'properly incurred'. In particular they seem unsure as to the appropriate test for liabilities in tort and they perceive that a different test may be applicable to indemnities sought by trust companies with no genuine assets other than those held on trust.[22] They now formulate, in slightly revised terms, the necessary conditions for satisfying a court that liabilities have been properly incurred by requiring that the trustee must have acted (a) within power; (b) with the degree of care and diligence that a person of ordinary prudence would exercise in the conduct of her or his affairs; and (c) in good faith. The first test may merely reflect an obvious requirement and the second and third are adaptations of the test of Bowen LJ in *Re Beddoe*, except **[306]** that the term 'reasonably' is adapted in reliance on the terms used in the judgment of Brooking J in *RWG Management*,[23] although his Honour had used the terms 'reasonable diligence and care'. With great respect, I am by no means confident that, in using the term 'reasonably', Bowen LJ was intending to pose so stringent a test as has now been suggested, for he also observed 'that trustees ought not to be visited with personal loss on account of mere errors in judgment ...'.[24] Likewise, and also with great respect, the test stated by Brooking J should be seen as intended as no more than a shorthand for the conventional statement of a trustee's duty.

Perhaps the rule will not pose difficulties where the issue relates merely to costs and expenses, although even in that area it has frequently been said that trustees should not be deprived of their right of reimbursement unless they have clearly been shown to have acted improperly, with the onus resting on those who seek to deny the right. But the rule relating to indemnification also applies to the incurring of liabilities and, by necessity, a considerable proportion of those must be incurred where in some way a trustee has been found to have acted in error. Doubtless liability in tort poses its own particular problems, as the cases, especially *Gatsios Holdings*, demonstrate. With respect, I would prefer therefore, at least for the time being, to confine what was said in that case to liabilities in tort incurred by trustees and the circumstances in which they should be so indemnified.

The answer to what now seems to be a degree of confusion as to the nature of costs, expenses and liabilities for which a trustee can seek indemnification may well lie in the simple proposition of Lindley LJ in *Re Beddoe* to the effect that the words 'properly incurred' are equivalent to the words 'not improperly incurred', a proposition so abundantly obvious that it tends to obscure some of the complications which have been overlooked from time to time. In my opinion the use of the negative is intended to show that what is 'proper' and 'improper' must be answered by reference to the circumstances and in particular by reference to the duty with which a trustee was obliged to comply or the power which a trustee is intending to exercise. The content of trustees' duties vary

---

21. H A J Ford & W A Lee, *Principles of the Law of Trusts*, Looseleaf edition, LawBook Company, Sydney, 1996+, Ch 14, para 14040.
22. H A J Ford & W A Lee, *Principles of the Law of Trusts*, Looseleaf edition, LawBook Company, Sydney, 1996+, 92–3 of the 7th Supplement of September 2002.
23. [1985] VR 385 at 396.
24. *Re Beddoe* [1893] 1 Ch 547 at 558 at 562.

considerably, as do the obligations taken on when a power is exercised. A significant number of trustees' duties requires strict compliance so that failure to comply with that duty will necessarily lead to the conclusion that a particular cost, expense or liability has not been properly incurred. On the other hand, the more day to day functions of a trustee in the management of a trust require only that the trustee 'exercise the same care as an ordinary, prudent person of business would exercise in the conduct of that business were it his or her own'.[25] The proposition is derived from a number of well-known authorities such as *Speight v Gaunt*;[26] *Austin v Austin*[27] and *Fouche v The Superannuation Fund Board*.[28] That test has been accepted for many years as providing an objective but not over-strict standard and it has been stated on many occasions that it does not require a subjective standard of diligence and care which an individual trustee might exercise in the management of his or her [307] own affairs, but only the objective standard of the 'ordinary prudent' business person taking on the role of a trustee.[29] In my opinion it was that latter obligation to which Bowen LJ was referring in *Re Beddoe*, so that to rely on what his Lordship said there may be misleading, even allowing for the fact that it has frequently been taken as expressing Lindley LJ's test in different terms. But that case was concerned solely with the costs of litigation and Bowen LJ's comments were confined explicitly to 'costs, charges, and expenses'.[30] 'Reasonably' must therefore be understood in the context of the particular duty which is in issue.

On the other hand, expenses and liabilities may be incurred where a trustee is engaged in activities which extend beyond mere management. The trustee may then be held to account far more strictly, in all senses. Conventionally a contrast is drawn with the performance of what have been called proscriptive and prescriptive duties such as the duty to keep and render accounts, the duty not to allow a conflict between duty and interest and the duty not to obtain an unauthorised benefit from the trust.[31] Again it seems to have been accepted that a higher standard is demanded, subject to any statutory provisions, when making investments on behalf of the trust.[32] For present purposes one may mention only one further strict duty recently described in the High Court as the duty 'to adhere to the terms of his trust in all things great and small, important, and seemingly unimportant'.[33] The fact that such breaches can now be excused under s 67 of the *Trustee Act 1958* was there noted by the High Court as indicating merely the strictness of the obligation and the need for legislation to relieve trustees who breached it. It would follow

---

25. *Breen v Williams* (1996) 186 CLR 71 at 137 per Gummow J.
26. (1883) 9 App Cas 1 at 19 per Lord Blackburn.
27. (1906) 3 CLR 516 at 525 per Griffith CJ.
28. (1952) 88 CLR 609 at 641 per Dixon, McTiernan and Fullagar JJ.
29. R P Meagher and W M C Gummow, *Jacobs' Law of Trusts in Australia*, 6th ed, Butterworths, Sydney, 1997, [1718].
30. *Re Beddoe* [1893] 1 Ch 547 at 558 at 562.
31. H A J Ford & W A Lee, *Principles of the Law of Trusts*, Looseleaf edition, LawBook Company, Sydney, 1996+, [9010].
32. *Re Whiteley* (1886) 33 Ch D 347 at 355 per Lindley LJ; and see H A J Ford & W A Lee, *Principles of the Law of Trusts*, Looseleaf edition, LawBook Company, Sydney, 1996+, [9020] and R P Meagher and W M C Gummow, *Jacobs' Law of Trusts in Australia*, 6th ed, Butterworths, Sydney, 1997, [1802].
33. *Youyang Pty Ltd v Minter Ellison Morris Fletcher* (2003) 212 CLR 484 at 498, [33], quoting Augustine Birrell QC in *The Duties and Liabilities of Trustees*, 1896, p 22.

that expenses or liabilities incurred as a result of a breach of that duty must ordinarily be characterised as improperly incurred, without regard to the reasonableness of the trustee's acts. It is obvious that there would be other breaches of these stricter duties which would lead to expenses and liabilities which were incapable of indemnification because each could be said to have been improperly incurred.

A test, therefore, based on whether a cost, expense or liability has been 'properly incurred' takes on some meaning, even if the answer depends on an analysis of the act which gives rise to the particular cost, expense or liability and the duty whose performance or breach may have led to that consequence. Naturally the vast majority of costs and expenses will not arise out of any breach of trust but will be merely incurred in the ordinary day to day management of it, but some will arise out of breaches of trust many of which will lead to a denial of indemnification because the relevant breach of duty will be characterised as having been improperly incurred. There will remain, nevertheless, some breaches of duty giving rise to expenses and liabilities about which that cannot be said automatically, so that one must examine those particular breaches individually in the context of the stated duty or power. I would therefore hesitate to agree with [308] the restated tests in Ford and Lee[34] which require that every properly incurred liability has to satisfy the triple test stated above.[35] The negative test is the relevant test, that is to allow indemnification for what has not been shown to have been improperly incurred. Thus it may be shown that a particular act is either outside the relevant power, done in bad faith, or exercised with an absence of the care and diligence that a person of ordinary prudence should exercise. I believe that, if carefully read, the judgment of Brooking J in *RWG Management* merely expresses the possibility that impropriety may be established in a variety of different ways according to the nature of the duty or power exercised by a trustee. It would follow that the test of 'reasonableness' is primarily concerned with the standard of ordinary diligence and care required in the management of trust affairs which might be expected of a trustee as objectively but not over-zealously enforced. That is why Bowen LJ insisted that in matters of management and the like 'mere errors of judgment' should not deny the right to indemnification but, with the greatest of respect, his insistence on a test of unreasonableness goes beyond what equity would demand. So far as costs and expenses are concerned, at least those which are the subject of taxation as 'indemnity costs', no question of reasonableness applies in the first instance as to the nature of the costs and expenses which the trustee may claim (at least in ordinary cases), but the test of reasonableness is imposed on the quantum of the amount claimed by a trustee which the Taxing Master should properly allow. Otherwise I reiterate what I have said above at 306.

The present case, like many others, involves a liability arising out of what might otherwise seem to be a relatively mundane performance of a trustee's duties, namely, the providing of a security, effectively to preserve a sale. The trustee's error was, as was clearly found in the earlier case by Byrne J, a mere slip which came about because of the speed whereby the parties sought to effectuate their intentions and which led to an explicit holding that there was no fraud involved on the part of the trustee. Of course

---

34. H A J Ford & W A Lee, *Principles of the Law of Trusts*, Looseleaf edition, LawBook Company, Sydney, 1996+, [14040].

35. See 305.

it could be said that the trustee acted negligently in the sense that it did not ensure that the mortgagee's rights were not confined to the debt arising out of the transaction relating to the Jolimont property, so that, by mistake, it made the security available to satisfy all of Merlaw's liabilities to the ANZ bank. It is arguable that the transaction was not carried out with the degree of care and diligence that a person of ordinary prudence would exercise in the conduct of his or her affairs, but I think, nevertheless, that such an analysis cannot here determine whether a trustee can fairly seek indemnification from the assets of a trust in circumstances where something has happened to go wrong.

No direct authority was cited which would govern the case in issue, but in my opinion this was not the type of case where the degree of want of prudence was such as to deprive the trustee Merlaw of the right to look to the trust estate to satisfy a liability of the kind here incurred. In other words it has not been shown that the trustee acted improperly. There was no question raised that the transaction was unauthorised or was not entered into in good faith, for, as I have explained before, the object of the trustee, at least in part, was to ensure that the contract might proceed to completion, which would certainly not come about if the purchaser was forced into defaulting on its obligations. The only error seems to have been a 'mere error of judgment', in allowing the mortgage, intended to [309] cover the debt arising from the purchase by Terramont of Jolimont, to be security for liabilities to the ANZ bank beyond those incurred with respect to that property. Incautiously, but not deliberately, as Byrne J held, the mortgage signed by Mr Nolan on behalf of Merlaw urgently just before Christmas permitted the ANZ bank to apply the proceeds of any sale of the mortgaged asset in discharge of all or any of Merlaw's liabilities to the bank, including, because of its generality, liabilities incurred by Merlaw in relation to the Prudent Trust other than those arising out of the contract relating to the subject land. Signing a mortgage in that form was clearly inappropriate and prejudicial to the parties interested in Jolimont, in particular Terramont and the interests standing behind it, but in substance it caused no prejudice directly to the Prudent Trust, save that it exposed Merlaw to the action which was successfully brought by the Collie interests and heard by Byrne J, which has led to the liability to make compensation to that purchaser. Indeed, apart from exposing Merlaw to that liability, the transaction was beneficial to that company in that, by chance and not by design, it provided additional security for all Merlaw's trust obligations owed to the ANZ bank. In broad terms close on $400,000 of its liabilities to the bank were satisfied by the reduction of its overdraft to that extent.

It may be regretted that her Honour did not examine why the liabilities here in question were not improperly incurred within the meaning of the authorities, but, so far as I can ascertain, little if anything was raised in argument before her on this issue. It was, however, entirely proper for Merlaw as trustee to seek to carry out its obligations under the sale that it had made of the Jolimont property to Terramont and to allow the title to be mortgaged a second time, this time to the ANZ bank, to ensure completion by the purchaser. Its careless expansion of the liabilities secured by the mortgage did not directly harm the Prudent Trust; on the contrary, in the way just described, it provided additional security to support that trust's many liabilities, albeit that it prejudiced the purchaser. Having regard to my conclusion already stated that it was appropriate that a mortgage over the Jolimont land should be entered into in support of the contract of sale and what would otherwise be properly intended to ensure the purchaser's position under that contract, it is hard to characterise the oversight relating to the extent of liabilities secured as being more than a mere error of judgment which had no immediate harmful effect on the Prudent Trust. I did not understand the [Nolans] to be arguing that he effectuated a breach of the Prudent Trust on behalf of Merlaw when he executed the mortgage on its behalf, but one may accept counsel's submissions to the effect that the trustee's acts were 'improper' as tending to the same conclusion, in that they were intended to support the contention that Merlaw had not acted properly in the performance of the trust.

In my opinion, notwithstanding that error which led to the successful action against Merlaw for breach of the purchase trust, I consider that this act on the part of Merlaw was not sufficiently heinous to deny it the right to indemnification from the Prudent Trust, inasmuch as it has not been shown to have been improperly incurred within the (largely) accepted meaning of that expression. If one were to accept the 'ordinary, prudent business person' test, the entry into the mortgage satisfied that test, as properly understood, and the extension of the security was, in the circumstances, a mere oversight and error of judgment.[36] It is not necessary to examine further the decision in *Gatsios Holdings*, which may **[310]** fairly be confined to liabilities arising out of torts,[37] nor the constant problems, commented upon so frequently in judgments[38] and especially in the textbooks, which arise because impersonal corporations, other than those under the strict control of the *Trustee Companies Act 1984*, are permitted to act as trustees of, in particular, trading trusts.

A second basis for a right of indemnity is the fact that the impugned act benefited the Prudent Trust estate. According to the authorities such benefit entitles a trustee to claim indemnification even if it cannot establish that a liability was properly incurred. As Brooking J expressed it in *RWG Management*: 'A trustee is, however, entitled to be indemnified in respect of a liability improperly incurred to the extent to which, acting in good faith, he has benefited the trust estate.'[39] For this proposition he relied on *Vyse v Foster*[40] and *Jesse v Lloyd*,[41] as well as Scott on Trusts.[42] See also Ford and Lee.[43]

The [Nolans] denied that the Prudent Trust obtained any benefit from the mortgage transaction. [They] primarily contended that there was no legal or logical connection between the incorrectly drafted mortgage and the Prudent Trust, in that Merlaw was seeking only to advance the interests of the parties to the Purchase Trust and in particular those who stood behind Terramont. For reasons already stated at length one cannot isolate the transactions in that way. Merlaw was the vendor and it was selling an asset

---

36. It is conceivable that, but for its registration, the mortgage might have been rectified for mistake.
37. It should be noted that less than a year later, in *Kirwan v Cresvale Far East Ltd* (2002) 44 ACSR 21; 21 ACLC 371 the NSW Court of Appeal again adopted *Re Beddoe*, though referring to the 'reasonable and honest' test of Bowen LJ, as well as the test laid down in *Barnes*: see at [259] per Giles JA with whom Meagher JA concurred.
38. See, for example, *Australian Securities Commission v AS Nominees Ltd* (1995) 62 FCR 504 at 516–18 per Finn J.
39. [1985] VR 385 at 396.
40. (1872) LR 8 Ch App 309; (1874) LR 7 HL 318.
41. (1883) 48 LT 656.
42. A Scott, *The Law of Trusts*, 1967, vol III, paras 244–8 and 268. See now 1987, vol 3A, paras 245.1 and 269–269.3.
43. H A J Ford & W A Lee, *Principles of the Law of Trusts*, Looseleaf edition, LawBook Company, Sydney, 1996+, 14050.

of the Prudent Trust. The fact that the vendor's beneficial interest in the land was by then relatively small in value (seemingly only $10,000 of the purchase moneys remained payable) was of no consequence, for the parties had not completed the sale and Merlaw had functions yet to carry out under the terms of that contract so as to vest full ownership in Terramont and to receive the balance of the purchase moneys.

Nor is it easy for the [Nolans] to make out a case that the Prudent Trust and its beneficiaries received no benefit. After all it was Merlaw's gains by reason of the proceeds of sale of Jolimont being applied to satisfy all of Merlaw's other liabilities to the ANZ bank which in effect formed the basis for the Collie interests' recovery of compensation in the action heard by Byrne J. There must have been a corresponding, if not identical, benefit to the beneficiaries of the Prudent Trust. That benefit was the use of the proceeds of the mortgagee's sale to reduce Merlaw's liabilities generally to the bank and not merely to reduce the much lesser liability relating only to the Jolimont land which the mortgage was intended to secure. The precise figure of the benefit (as such) was not identified, to my recollection, but it must have been the extent to which the Prudent Trust's liabilities were reduced in excess of the debt relating solely to Jolimont, which should have been the only amount secured by the mortgage. The primary amount of compensation for that element recovered in the first action (and which is the [311] subject of the other appeal to this court) should broadly represent one-half of the benefit obtained by the Prudent Trust and its beneficiaries, the other half being referable to Terranol and the Nolan interests. It may be somewhat less than the liability presently in issue, but it is unnecessary to pursue the question in detail, as I have already concluded that the liability was not improperly incurred by the respondent trustee, Merlaw.

Comments

1. See Radan & Stewart at **20.20–20.32**.
2. In addition to a right to indemnity trustees have an additional right of exoneration that allows them to draw directly on trust assets to discharge their duties, as opposed to paying out of their own funds and seeking reimbursement: *Savage v Union Bank of Australia Ltd* (1906) 3 CLR 1170.
3. The trustee's right to indemnification is an equitable property right that is effective against third parties in any priority dispute over the trust property: *Octavo Investments Pty Ltd v Knight* (1979) 144 CLR 360.

The trustees' duty to provide information and the beneficiary's right to it

20.3   McDonald v Ellis (2007) 72 NSWLR 605

Court: Court of Appeal of New South Wales

Facts: Harold Baker died on 16 December 1977. One of the major assets of the will was 'Tamahine', a block of flats at 21 Baden Street, Coogee in Sydney. Harold left a beneficial interest in the flats on trust to his widow, Marie Baker, for life, and then to his daughter, Roxanne Ellis, for life. After Roxanne's death the property was to go to Harold's grandchildren: one-half to John Ellis, one-quarter to Narelle McDonald and the remaining quarter to Margaret Bedford. Marie and Roxanne were appointed as trustees under the will. Marie had died many years before the litigation and Roxanne had appointed John to be a co-trustee with her in 1998. Roxanne was diagnosed with Alzheimer's disease in 2003. By the time of the litigation she was unable to make decisions for herself and she lived in a nursing home.

After Roxanne's incapacity John effectively took over as sole trustee. John and Narelle's relationship had deteriorated. John had not provided Narelle with any information on the state of the trust. She asked the court to order the production of the trust accounts.

Issue: The issue was whether a fixed beneficiary had a right to access the trust records.

Decision: Bryson AJ ordered that the accounts be produced. His Honour found that Narelle did have a right to be given information about the trust accounts.

Extracts: In this extract Bryson JA discusses the nature of the trustee's duty to provide information to the beneficiaries and finds that the right of fixed beneficiaries is based on their proprietary rights and is not based on the court's power to administer trusts.

Bryson AJ

[612] The administration of the trust is the responsibility of [Roxanne] as a trustee. If records of hers show how the net annual income is calculated or derived, she is obliged in her character as trustee to make those records available to beneficiaries. [Roxanne] participated in trust affairs in two capacities, as a trustee and also as a beneficiary. It could be said that when income is paid to her, it does not pass out of the hands of the trustees. She is a trustee and (although it is unauthorised that one trustee and not both should hold trust funds) the funds in her hands remain within the Court's control. The possibility is clear that [Roxanne], or attorneys acting on her behalf under power, may have documents relating to the trust property and its management. [John] referred in evidence to tax returns on behalf of [Roxanne] which show the income, [613] which raises the possibility that there may be lists of repair expenditures and depreciation schedules in those tax returns. As she is one of the trustees, such documents are within the range of documents to the inspection of which [Narelle] is entitled.

It is the duty of trustees to keep accounts and be in a position to produce them, and the defendants and particularly [John] have not done this. The need to prepare estate accounts on a proper basis is not something arising out of [Narelle]'s claim, nor is it something to be undertaken only to satisfy her. Preparing accounts is an ordinary duty of trustees to which the trustees, and particularly [John], should have attended in the past. In a relatively small and uncomplicated trust, where all interested are closely related and there is no conflict, informality might cause no concern and the trouble and expense of preparing accounts might be thought of as unwarranted. In the present case, where [Narelle] has, in effect, been claiming a right to see accounts for years and her claim has been disputed, it has been rash of [John] not to prepare and retain estate accounts. At one point I thought that it may still be possible to avoid the trouble and expense of preparing estate accounts if [Narelle] should regard the information in the managing agents' statements as sufficient to answer her enquiries and concerns. I sought during argument to promote some such arrangement but I had no success as [John]'s counsel maintained the position that these documents were confidential and [Narelle] should not see them.

The principal basis on which [Narelle]'s claim was resisted was that the way in which estate affairs are conducted and the net annual income is derived are not matters in which [Narelle] as a remainderman has any interest. In the development of this argument, it was contended to the effect that [Narelle] has no interest in the trust under which the trustees now pay net annual income to [Roxanne]; that the trust for the remaindermen including [Narelle] is a different trust. This is not a correct view of the dispositions in the Will. When dealing with the block of flats, the Will creates one trust of the block of flats with successive interests, and the remaindermen including [Narelle] now have present interests in the block of flats, vested in interest although not in possession. The remaindermen have at the present time an economic interest in the state of repair of the block of flats. Whether it is in or out of repair, whether some need for renovation at a future time is coming into being and whether there are any reserves or provisions, are factors affecting the money value of rights which the remaindermen now own.

There is no discretionary trust. The interests of [Narelle] and of other beneficiaries do not depend on any discretion of the trustees, or of anybody else. This sets to one side, as unimportant for disposition of this case, case law and principles relating to the protection of the discretionary decisions of trustees from disclosure. Decisions of trustees exercising choices in the performance of management duties, such as a decision whether or not to carry out some repair or other, or whether or not to make a provision for a class of repairs in the future, are not the discretions to which that body of case law relates.

Until recently, judicial authority established in a clear way that a beneficiary with a vested interest in trust property, even though that interest was not yet vested in possession, had a right to information about the estate property, including a right to see estate accounts and the right to inspect the property. This apparently clear position was disturbed by observations in the judgment [614] of the Privy Council delivered by Lord Walker of Gestingthorpe in *Schmidt v Rosewood Trust Ltd*.[44]

The Judicial Committee's concluded view is indicated at two passages, the first:

> Their Lordships consider that the more principled and correct approach is to regard the right to seek disclosure of trust documents as one aspect of the court's inherent jurisdiction to supervise, and if necessary to intervene in, the administration of trusts. The right to seek the court's intervention does not depend on entitlement to a fixed and transmissible beneficial interest. The object of a discretion (including a mere power) may also be entitled to protection from a court of equity, although the circumstances in which he may seek protection, and the nature of the protection he may expect to obtain, will depend on the court's discretion ... (and their Lordships referred to authority).[45]

---

44. [2003] 2 AC 709 at 734–735.
45. [2003] 2 AC 709 at 729.

Their Lordships said:

> Their Lordships have already indicated their view that a beneficiary's right to seek disclosure of trust documents, although sometimes not inappropriately described as a proprietary right, is best approached as one aspect of the court's inherent jurisdiction to supervise, and where appropriate intervene in, the administration of trusts. There is therefore in their Lordships' view no reason to draw any bright dividing line either between transmissible and non-transmissible (that is, discretionary) interests, or between the rights of an object of a discretionary trust and those of the object of a mere power (of a fiduciary character). The differences in this context between trusts and powers are (as Lord Wilberforce demonstrated in *In re Baden*[46]) a good deal less significant than the similarities. The tide of Commonwealth authority, although not entirely uniform, appears to be flowing in that direction.
>
> However the recent cases also confirm (as had been stated as long ago as *In re Cowin*[47] in 1886) that no beneficiary (and least of all a discretionary object) has any entitlement as of right to disclosure of anything which can plausibly be described as a trust document. Especially when there are issues as to personal or commercial confidentiality, the court may have to balance the competing interests of different beneficiaries, the trustees themselves and third parties. Disclosure may have to be limited and safeguards may have to be put in place. Evaluation of the claims of a beneficiary (and especially of a discretionary object) may be an important part of the balancing exercise which the court has to perform on the materials placed before it. In many cases the court may have no difficulty in concluding that an applicant with no more than a theoretical possibility of benefit ought not to be granted any relief.[48]

When considering the case law it is important to bear in mind something I have already alluded to, that [Narelle] in the present case has a vested interest in the trust property and is not in the position of the object of a discretionary trust who may or may not, according to some future decision or contingency, come to have an interest. This is a basal consideration because the claim of a person with a vested interest is related to property rights and is a claim to information about the person's own property. This is no less so because the title of the property is equitable. A claim by the object of a discretionary trust has a less clear and compelling basis. If their Lordships' conclusions were followed, it would be necessary to depart from the state of opinion which I regard as clearly established in New South Wales and to do so for reasons which do not touch on the case of a beneficiary with a vested interest making a claim for documents the characterisation of which as trust documents cannot be doubted.

The clarity of the position existing prior to *Schmidt v Rosewood Trust Ltd* is borne out by an analysis of earlier authority. The first case to which counsel **[615]** referred me was *Walker v Symonds*.[49] This complex case related to liability of trustees for default by a co-trustee. The facts included a release given by the beneficiary without adequate information. In the course of argument Lord Eldon LC said:

---

46. [1971] AC 424, 448–449.
47. 33 Ch D 179.
48. [2003] 2 AC 709 at 734.
49. (1818) 3 Swans 1; 36 ER 751.

It is the duty of trustees to afford to their *cestui que trust* accurate information of the disposition of the trust-fund; all the information of which they are, or ought to be, in possession: a trustee may involve himself in serious difficulty, by want of the information which it was his duty to obtain.[50]

In *Re Tillott; Lee v Wilson*, Chitty J said: 'The general rule, then, is what I have stated, that the trustee must give information to his *cestui que trust* as to the investment of the trust estate.'[51] His Lordship made orders under which the trustee was required to give the beneficiary authority for the bank in which the trust fund was deposited to tell the beneficiary whether the trust fund was encumbered. In that case the beneficiary held a vested interest in a share of the trust estate contingently on the death of his mother; his interest was not discretionary.

In *Re Dartnall; Sawyer v Goddard*,[52] the English Court of Appeal directed trustees to give a beneficiary a list of investments of the testator's estate. The beneficiary was entitled to share of a fund expectant on the death of a tenant for life. Most judicial attention was given to costs questions. In the course of decision, Lord Halsbury:

In the first instance the application made on behalf of the plaintiff for particulars of the trust estate and the investment thereof was, in my opinion, a just and proper one, and ought to have been granted. I see no reason why the trustees should not have granted it.[53]

Lindley LJ said: 'in strict right the plaintiff was entitled to the further information which she asked for.'[54]

O'Rourke v Darbishire[55] relates to discovery, but two Law Lords made *obiter dicta* expressing in general terms what by then was clearly understood to be the right of beneficiaries with respect to trust documents. These dicta, cited in *Re Londonderry's Settlement; Peat v Walsh*[56] by Harman LJ, appear to contemplate a beneficiary with a vested interest. Lord Wrenbury, in *O'Rourke v Darbishire* spoke of the right of access to documents as a property right and said:

The beneficiary is entitled to see all the trust documents because they are trust documents and because he is a beneficiary. They are in this sense his own. Action or no action, he is entitled to access to them. This has nothing to do with discovery. The right to discovery is a right to see someone else's documents. The proprietary right is a right to access to documents which are your own.[57]

The entitlement of a beneficiary to see trust documents was considered in much greater detail by the Court of Appeal in *Re Londonderry's Settlement*. The Court of Appeal

---

50. (1818) 3 Swans 1 at 58; 36 ER 751 at 772.
51. [1892] 1 Ch 86 at 88.
52. [1895] 1 Ch 474.
53. [1895] 1 Ch 474 at 478.
54. [1895] 1 Ch 474 at 479.
55. [1920] AC 581.
56. [1965] 1 Ch 918 at 932.
57. [1920] AC 581 at 626–627.

variously considered the effect of the beneficiary's entitlements being discretionary; what documents are trust documents for this purpose; and the influence both of confidentiality and of the exemption of trustees from disclosure of their consideration of discretions. The conflict of principles was stated by Harman LJ.[58] Harman LJ also referred to the difficulty of defining the obligations of trustees 'in the air' and not in relation to a particular document which the Court has seen.[59] His Lordship pointed out the shortcomings of general observations such as those in *O'Rourke v Darbishire*.[60] He treated a right to disclosure of trust documents as the ordinary rule and the principle which protects trustees' discretionary deliberations from disclosure as overriding the ordinary rule, [616] stating that: 'In my opinion such documents are not trust documents in the proper sense at all.'[61] Danckwerts LJ and Salmon LJ reached the same conclusion for reasons separately stated. Salmon LJ stated common characteristics of trust documents, without a comprehensive definition.[62]

It should I think be said of *Re Londonderry's Settlement* that the Court of Appeal gave protection to the trustees' considerations of the exercise of a discretion to appoint interest in the trust on the basis of acknowledgement that consideration started with the beneficiary having a right to disclosure. The fact that the beneficiary's entitlement depended on a favourable exercise of discretion did not influence this right.

In *Randall v Lubrano*[63] Holland J made a clear and emphatic statement of a beneficiary's right to know what the trust property is and how it has been and is being administered by the trustee. In that case the interest of the beneficiaries was discretionary, and all objects of the discretionary trust joined in seeking a remedy. I know from my having been in practice at the time, that the judgment of Holland J created a wide impression and dispelled resistance by trustees which it was not then unusual to encounter, although in retrospect it is difficult to see what its basis can have been. I see no encouragement for that view in *Re Londonderry's Settlement*. It is surprising that *Randall v Lubrano* was not reported at the time.

In *Spellson v George*, Powell J stated his view of the law, and of the basis in principle of the law:

> At the risk of being regarded as overly simplistic, it is as well to start with the fundamental proposition that one of the essential elements of a private trust, be it a discretionary trust or some other form of trust, is that the trustee is subject to a personal obligation to hold, and to deal with, the trust property for the benefit of some identified, or identifiable, person or group of persons.[64] It is, so it seems to me, a necessary corollary of the existence of that obligation that the trustee is liable to account to the person, or group of persons for whose benefit he holds the trust property,[65] and, that being so, the

---

58. [1965] 1 Ch 918 at 928–929.
59. [1965] 1 Ch 918 at 931.
60. [1965] 1 Ch 918 at 933.
61. [1965] 1 Ch 918 at 933.
62. [1965] 1 Ch 918 at 938.
63. (2009) 72 NSWLR 621.
64. See, for example, R P Meagher and W M C Gummow, *Jacobs' Law of Trusts in Australia*, 5th ed, Butterworths, Sydney, 1986, pp 8–9, [108]–[111].
65. See, for example, *Manning v Federal Commissioner of Taxation* (1928) 40 CLR 506 at 509 per Knox CJ.

trustee is obliged not only to keep proper accounts and allow a *cestui que trust* to inspect them, but he must also, on demand, give a *cestui que trust* information and explanations as to the investment of, and dealings with, the trust property.[66]

This being the essential nature of the position of a trustee, and the liability to account being an essential ingredient in it, it seems to me that it is inescapable that the *cestuis que trust*, or any one of the *cestuis que trust*, have, or has, a correlative right to approach the Court for its assistance in enforcing the personal obligation of the trustee, and, in particular, in enforcing the trustee's obligation to account.[67]

His Honour went on to state, with reasons and references to authority, his view that the same right is available to a person whose status is only that of a potential object of the exercise of a discretionary power.

Hartigan Nominees Pty Ltd v Rydge[68] related to the beneficiary's claim to see a memorandum of wishes provided by the instigator (not the settlor) of a discretionary trust for the use of trustees in exercising their powers. This case exposed the difficulties of identifying what are referred to as 'trust documents'. The beneficiary's interest was, as the object of a discretionary trust, potentially but not yet entitled if there should be a **[617]** favourable exercise of the trustees' discretion. The solicitor for the trustees had given the explanation that no distribution could be made because '... there is no provision in Sir Norman's memorandum which would entitle the trustees to make any payment to you at this time' (at 408E). The facts were unlike those in *Re Londonderry's Settlement* in that there had been reference to the memorandum in an explanation given on behalf of the trustees. For reasons extensively stated, Kirby P (who dissented) did not regard *Re Londonderry's Settlement* as a decision which should be followed. The majority, Mahoney JA and Sheller JA, did not take this view, although their reasons went far beyond a simple application of *Re Londonderry's Settlement*. The difficulty in the appeal and the division of opinion related to the application of the right of a beneficiary, including a discretionary beneficiary, to obtain information and inspect trust documents to the memorandum and to the trustees' discretionary decisions. Mahoney JA did not unqualifiedly endorse the extension of the right to all persons who are only possible beneficiaries under a discretionary trust or are one of a large number of possible beneficiaries (431E–432F), and discussed the difficulties of the limits of trust documents in this context (432F–433B). Mahoney JA's judgment contains a wide general and (I would respectfully say) orthodox survey of the law in this field. Sheller JA also made a wide survey. It should I think be said that the majority judgments do not depart from *Re Londonderry's Settlement*. Those judgments illustrate a number of difficulties which do not bear on the present case.

In my opinion, judges at first instance in New South Wales should treat the majority judgments in *Hartigan Nominees* as authoritative. While not all matters susceptible of doubt are settled, the starting point, at which the beneficiary is entitled to see trust

---

66. See, for example *Re Tillott; Lee v Wilson* [1892] 1 Ch 86 at 88; Ford and Lee, *Principles of the Law of Trusts,* 1983, pp 404 et seq; R P Meagher and W M C Gummow, *Jacobs' Law of Trusts in Australia*, 5th ed, Butterworths, Sydney, 1986, p 391; P Pettit, *Equity and the Law of Trusts,* 1974, p 330.
67. (1987) 11 NSWLR 300 at 315F–316C.
68. (1992) 29 NSWLR 405.

documents and have information about trust property, and that entitlement has a proprietary basis, is not open to question. The facts in the present case do not raise even the potential difficulties which might be thought to exist where the entitlement of the beneficiary is contingent or subject to a discretionary decision, or involve a decision of trustees which might raise a conflicting principle.

The subject under decision in *Schmidt v Rosewood Trust Ltd* was the appellant's claim for fuller disclosure of trust accounts and information about trust assets in which the appellant claimed discretionary interests or expectations in right of himself and of his deceased father. Under 'Disclosure to discretionary beneficiaries: the recent cases',[69] the Judicial Committee made a wide survey of case law, including New South Wales case law, and stated its general agreement with the approach adopted in the judgments of Kirby P and Shelley JA in *Hartigan Nominees*. The judgment of Kirby P, to which their Lordships referred at some length, was of course a dissenting decision and reached its conclusion on the basis of the beneficiary's right of inspection without examining or indeed referring to judicial decisions; the conclusion based itself instead on agreement with a view expressed by H A J Ford and W A Lee in *Principles of the Laws of Trust*,[70] which included this sentence: 'The equation of the right to inspect trust documents with the beneficiary's equitable propriety of rights gives rise to unnecessary and undesirable consequences.' The consequences referred to included doubts cast on the rights of beneficiaries who cannot claim to have an equitable proprietary interest in trust assets, such as the beneficiaries of discretionary trusts. This was, I must respectfully say, a slight basis indeed for discarding an established right of beneficiaries with vested interests to [618] inspection of documents of such primary importance as the accounts of the trustees. A decision that all access to trust documents should be in the discretion of the Court is a drastic solution to whatever problems might be perceived in supposing a proprietary basis for discretionary interests, and whatever problems may be perceived in delimiting which documents should be treated as trust documents and in protecting from access documents access to which involves some conflicting principle. Their Lordships alluded, twice but briefly, to the reasons given by Sheller JA which addressed difficulties relating to discretionary interests, not vested interests.

The views expressed in *Schmidt v Rosewood Trust Ltd* by the Privy Council on appeal from the Isle of Man, while they should be considered with respect, are not possibly a binding or authoritative source for a rule of law which would render the entitlement of [Narelle] in these proceedings to access the documents, to information, in short to accounts, a discretionary one.[71] There may be room for the view, on which the Privy Council acted, that such an entitlement is discretionary in the case of a beneficiary who is no more than the object of a discretionary trust and does not have the benefit of a favourable exercise of the trustee's discretion. The weight of opinion in New South Wales the other way on that issue is strong, but [Narelle]'s position in the present case is even stronger, as her entitlement is not discretionary but rather vested in interest.

---

69. [2003] 2 AC 709 at 729.
70. H A J Ford & W A Lee, *Principles of the Law of Trusts*, 2nd edition, LawBook Company, Sydney, 1990, p 425.
71. See *Cook v Cook* (1986) 162 CLR 376 at 390.

Their Lordships' conclusion[72] would make the beneficiary's right to seek disclosure of trust documents an aspect of the Court's inherent jurisdiction to supervise and, where appropriate, intervene in the administration of trusts. Although the reasons say that that right is 'sometimes not inappropriately described as a proprietary right', it is plain that their Lordships did not treat the right as a proprietary right.

The history of equity and the nature of its remedies mean that the treatment of equitable interests as proprietary, and the development of rules based on that treatment, can never be entirely logical or satisfactory; but if this is perceived as a problem, it is an inherent problem and should not be regarded as a basis for discarding a well-established rule.

An *obiter dictum* in the Privy Council about trust law in the Isle of Man has in my opinion very little claim to be followed at first instance in New South Wales where a different view has been accepted. The Privy Council does not exercise appellate authority over the courts of New South Wales, and its decisions made since its appellate power was abolished in 1986 have not had binding force in New South Wales. Still less have the Judicial Committee's *obiter dicta*. As with other decisions which are not binding, its claim to be followed depends upon the extent to which the views expressed are persuasive.

The opinion of Lord Walker does not, to my reading, identify any error in earlier opinion, or state any respect in which it might be said to be significantly unsatisfactory. No earlier judicial decisions adopting the basis on which the Privy Council reset the law were referred to, nor were any text writers. Nor to my reading were any significant policy considerations favouring departure from the previous rules set out. The only matter indicated was an opinion that the rule enounced was a better rule. It was not explained, with any significant reasoning, why it was a better rule. In my opinion it is not a better rule, because it introduces discretion and promotes resistance and debate in substitution for a rule which is relatively concrete. The tendency will be that only the determined and litigious beneficiary will find out about his own **[619]** affairs. Where there is a judicial discretion, there is room for litigious debate about the exercise of the discretion. There is no certainty on so elementary a matter as whether or not a beneficial owner is entitled to information about property in which the beneficial owner has an equitable interest. In the previous rule, in my interpretation, equity followed the law in treating as proprietary an equitable entitlement to trust property. Treating the equitable interest as proprietary brings with it an entitlement to information, unless there is a conflict with some other principle which equity must recognize, such as the principle protecting the trustee's discretionary considerations. Treating the entitlement to information as an aspect of the Court's discretionary exercise of its supervising power over trusts is a departure from the relatively concrete concept of equitable interests in trust property which has been adopted for some centuries.

In *Avanes v Marshall*[73] Gzell J after review of authorities, including recent authorities in Australia in which reference has been made to *Schmidt*, expressed the view that the approach in *Schmidt* should be adopted by Australian courts. I respectfully do not agree. It might be that the approach of *Schmidt* is appropriate where the interest of the

---

72. [2003] 2 AC 709 at 734.
73. (2007) 68 NSWLR 595 at 599 [15].

beneficiary is no higher than those of the potential objects of a discretionary trust, although opinion in New South Wales is otherwise. However that maybe, in the present case where [Narelle]'s right is already vested in interest, it would be a departure from clearly established opinion in New South Wales not to treat the claim to information as based on a proprietary interest, or to withhold enforcement of it except so as to enforce some competing entitlement, such as that of the trustees considered in *Re Londonderry's Settlement*, which required such departure.

On the facts of the present case, there is nothing in the nature of a discretionary ground on which any withholding of [Narelle]'s entitlement to information could reasonably be based. While I repeatedly sought in the course of argument to establish what discretionary ground was relied upon, nothing was referred to higher than [Roxanne]'s objection to any information about her affairs being given to [Narelle], expressed to [John] some years ago before incapacity overtook her. This is in the nature of a claim of confidentiality, but it is not supported by any underlying reason of greater strength than her expressed wish that [Narelle] should not know her affairs. A person who accepts benefits under a trust of which there are other beneficiaries does so on the basis that other beneficiaries also have rights in the trust, including rights to information. I characterise what is put forward as a claim to privacy, and not as a claim to confidentiality; in substance nothing was advanced as a reason for the Court to enforce [Roxanne]'s confidentiality by withholding the rights of some other person. There is no competing principle such as protection of the position of trustees in the exercise of discretion, which was protected in *Re Londonderry's Settlement*.

Notwithstanding my repeated enquiries, counsel was not able to refer to any adverse impact on the interests of [Roxanne] or of anyone else, or any particular harm that would be done by giving [Narelle] the information she seeks. Counsel informed me that the information contained in the managing agents' documents relating to the maintenance which has taken place is not itself the subject of any claim that it should not be produced. Production to [Narelle] herself of those documents was resisted because they disclose [Roxanne]'s income, for which confidentiality is claimed. This is not a case where [620] confidentiality relates to the interest of a third party. [Roxanne], when taking advantages under the trust, necessarily also incurs any disadvantage to her, actual or perceived, which arises out of administration of the trust.

On behalf of [John] it was contended, to the effect that it was shown by communications in correspondence, that [Narelle]'s case was presented as justified by or based on a concern to see that the interests of [Roxanne] are properly protected, that she receives income, what income it is that she receives and how her income is disbursed. It is clear that [Narelle] in correspondence by her former solicitor did put forward in strong terms a concern relating to [Roxanne]'s interests as the ground on which she claimed relief. However, it is in my opinion plain, as discussion elsewhere in this judgment shows, that [Narelle] had a right herself to see the trust documents and obtain information about the trust asset. A wish to protect the interests of her mother is not a ground on which she could base a claim, but her claim is well based on her own interests, and the presence of the other asserted basis in correspondence does not justify resistance to her claim. Advance by [Narelle] of grounds which were unnecessary, or even quite wrong, in support of a claim which she has on other grounds cannot prejudice that claim or dispose the Court against granting it on those other grounds.

Correspondence on behalf of the second defendant asserted readiness to give [Narelle] information about expenditures on maintenance of the block of flats:

> We take the position that a beneficiary's entitlement to view estate accounts extends only to the interest the beneficiary has in relation to the estate. For instance a beneficiary who receives a specific legacy is not entitled to be given the accounts that relate to residue. Similarly our clients are willing to satisfy your client that her interest in remainder is maintained but will not provide details of the income and outgoings on the trust property to which the income beneficiary is entitled. Accordingly we will provide to you a statement from the managing agents acting out that there are no outstanding rates or taxes on the property, the report obtained from the structural engineer and the certification relating to the fire rating of the property. If your client requires a valuation of her interest, please confirm that she will meet the cost of obtaining it and that the provision of this information will satisfy your client's concerns.

[Narelle] did not accept this limitation on the information to be given to her, either before or at the hearing. In my view there is no justification for limiting information to be furnished to [Narelle] in this way. Notwithstanding the position taken in that letter, it was maintained on behalf of [John] during the hearing, and in final submissions, to the effect that [Narelle] does not and cannot have any interest in aspects of management, including maintenance, because she as a remainderman has very limited rights of recourse against the trustee with respect to maintenance.

Whether or not such rights exist and whether or not the trustees have incurred any liability in respect of such rights, and the condition of the block of flats, are questions which it is not necessary to consider fully and to answer for the purpose of disposing of Claim 1. In my view those questions should only be addressed and answered when and if the Court is presented with a live issue relating to some clearly expressed and comprehensible basis upon which it is said that the trustees ought to be charged with some liability. Decision on the responsibility of trustees can only be addressed on a clear basis. An attempt to give answers in the abstract may fail to meet the difficulties presented by **[621]** some actual attempted impeachment of the trustees, when and if one ever eventuates.

[John]'s counsel contended that the present litigation is an exercise in futility because [Narelle] is not entitled to compel the life tenant or the trustee to repair the premises, let alone make a capital investment, and cannot compel the creation of a sinking fund. It would indeed be surprising if [Narelle] obtained an order compelling the trustees to take any such course, even more so, the life tenant. Any judicial remedy is much more likely to take the form of imposing liability for some failure on the part of the trustees.

Comments

1. See Radan & Stewart at **20.52–20.77**.
2. Trust documents have been defined as those documents which are in the possession of trustees as trustees and which contain information about the trust which the beneficiaries are entitled to know: *Re Londonderry's Settlement; Peat v Walsh* [1965] Ch 918. This notoriously circular definition has been found to include financial accounts, profit and loss statements of investment companies and, on occasion, the

names and addresses of other beneficiaries. Legal advice may be a trust document but courts may refuse disclosure if the documents have been prepared for litigation against a beneficiary: *Gray v BNY Trust Co of Australia Ltd* [2009] NSWSC 789.

The trustees' duty to consider the exercise of their trust powers

20.4   Karger v Paul [1984] VR 161

Court: Supreme Court of Victoria

Facts: Rose Mary Smith died on 21 December 1977. The will appointed her husband, Alfred, and her solicitor, Bernard Paul, as trustees of her estate. Clause 3 of the will gave the trustees a power to transfer all of the capital of the trust to Alfred, during his lifetime. The power could be used in the trustees' 'absolute and unfettered discretion'. The will also provided for any residue of the estate to go to Rose's cousin, Rita Karger, on Alfred's death.

Around the time of the grant of probate Alfred requested the solicitor to transfer all the property in his ownership. This was done. Alfred died soon after. His will left all of his property to Barbara Karasinski.

Rita was upset at having missed out on getting anything from Rose's will. She challenged the decision to transfer the property into Alfred's name. She sued Bernard, alleging that Alfred and Bernard had acted dishonestly and in bad faith. Rita said that they acted without any fair and proper consideration as to whether they should transfer the property to Alfred. She also sued Barbara alleging that she knew of these breaches of trust when she took the property.

Issue: The issue was whether the trustees' decision to exercise their discretion in Alfred's favour could be examined by the court as to whether it was a breach of trust.

Decision: McGarvie J found that a trustee's exercise of a wide discretionary power was not examinable unless there was evidence of bad faith, a lack of real and genuine consideration or the presence of ulterior purpose. If the trustee gave reasons those reason might also be examined.

Extracts: In this extract McGarvie J discusses the grounds upon which the court could review the decision of a trustee.

McGarvie J

[163] ... The discretionary power given to the trustees by [Clause 3], was a power, upon the request of Mr Smith, in their absolute and unfettered discretion to pay or transfer the whole or part of the capital of the estate to him. In my opinion the effect of the authorities is that, with one exception, the exercise of a discretion in these terms will not be examined or reviewed by the courts so long as the essential component parts of

the exercise of the particular discretion are present. Those essential component parts are present if the discretion is exercised by the trustees in good faith, upon real and genuine consideration and in accordance with the purposes for which the discretion was conferred. The exception is that the validity of the trustees' reasons will be examined and reviewed if the trustees choose to state their reasons for their exercise of discretion.

[164] In this context I consider that the test of acting honestly is the same as the test of acting in good faith.[74] It was argued for the plaintiff that gross negligence may of itself amount to an absence of good faith. I do not agree. Honest blundering and carelessness do not of themselves amount to bad faith.[75] Again I do not agree with the argument for the plaintiff that there is any conceptual territory which lies between good faith and bad faith. An act which falls short of good faith is done in bad faith.

For the plaintiff it was submitted that in this case the Court should examine whether the trustees gave fair and proper consideration to the exercise of the discretion and that the plaintiff should succeed in the action if they did not. In my view, in this case it is open to the Court to examine the evidence to decide whether there has been a failure by the trustees to exercise the discretion in good faith, upon real and genuine consideration and in accordance with the purposes for which the discretion was conferred. As part of the process of, and solely for the purpose of, ascertaining whether there has been any such failure, it is relevant to look at evidence of the inquiries which were made by the trustees, the information they had and the reasons for, and manner of, their exercising their discretion. However, it is not open to the Court to look at those things for the independent purpose of impugning the exercise of discretion on the grounds that their inquiries, information or reasons or the manner of exercise of the discretion, fell short of what was appropriate and sufficient. Nor is it open to the Court to look at the factual situation established by the evidence, for the independent purpose of impugning the exercise of the discretion on the grounds that the trustees were wrong in their appreciation of the facts or made an unwise or unjustified exercise of discretion in the circumstances. The issues which are examined by the Court are limited to whether there has been a failure to exercise the discretion in good faith, upon real and genuine consideration and in accordance with the purposes for which the discretion was conferred. In short, the Court examines whether the discretion was exercised but does not examine how it was exercised.

I regard it as an inherent requirement of the exercise of any discretion that it be given real and genuine consideration. To borrow a phrase from a passage quoted in *Partridge v The Equity Trustees Executors and Agency Co Ltd*[76] there must be the 'exercise of an active discretion'. It has been held that when the occasion for the exercise of a discretionary power has arisen, trustees, while not bound to exercise the discretion, are bound to consider whether it ought in their judgment to be exercised.[77] I think that it goes without saying that they must give real and genuine consideration. It seems to me that it is in this sense only that the Court can examine whether the trustees gave 'proper' consideration to the exercise of the discretion. The language used in this area has not

---

74. Compare *R v Holl* (1881) 7 QBD 575 at 580–1 per Bramwell LJ.

75. *Jones v Gordon* [1877] 2 AC 616 at 628–9 per Lord Blackburn.

76. (1947) 75 CLR 149 at 164.

77. *Klug v Klug* [1918] 2 Ch 67; *In re Gulbenkian's Settlement* [1970] AC 508 at 518.

always been distinguished by its precision.[78] The courts will examine whether a discretion has been exercised irresponsibly, capriciously or wantonly.[79] This is another way of saying that there may be an examination as to whether trustees have exercised their discretion on real and genuine consideration.[80]

[165] It is an established general principle that unless trustees choose to give reasons for the exercise of a discretion, their exercise of the discretion can not be examined or reviewed by a court so long as they act in good faith and without an ulterior purpose.[81] For reasons given above, I would add the further requirement, so obvious that it is often not mentioned, that they act upon real and genuine consideration. In the context, it was in that sense that Lord Truro LC used the expression 'with a fair consideration' in *Re Beloved Wilkes' Charity*.[82] In the case of an absolute and unrestricted discretion such as the discretion in the present case, the general principle is given unqualified operation.[83] The operation of the principle is discussed in *Jacobs' Law of Trusts in Australia*.[84]

The policy which underlies the principle was discussed by Lord Truro LC in *Re Beloved Wilkes' Charity*. In *Re Londonderry's Settlement*, Harman LJ explained the principle as follows:

> … trustees exercising a discretionary power are not bound to disclose to their beneficiaries the reasons actuating them in coming to a decision. This is a long-standing principle and rests largely, I think, on the view that nobody could be called upon to accept a trusteeship involving the exercise of a discretion unless, in the absence of bad faith, he was not liable to have his motives or his reasons called in question either by the beneficiaries or by the court. To this there is added a rider, namely, that if trustees do give reasons, their soundness can be considered by the court.[85]

In the same case Salmon LJ said:

> Whether or not the court, if it knew all the facts known to the trustees, would have acted as they did, again I do not know — nor is it material. The settlement gave the absolute discretion to appoint to the trustees and not to the courts. So long as the trustees exercise this power … bona fide with no improper motive, their exercise of the power cannot be challenged in the courts — and their reasons for acting as they did are, accordingly, immaterial. This is one of the grounds for the rule that trustees are not obliged to disclose to beneficiaries their reasons for exercising a discretionary power. Another ground for this rule is that it would not be for the good of the beneficiaries as a whole, and yet another that it might make the lives of trustees intolerable should such

---

78. See Hardingham and Baxt, *Discretionary Trusts*, 1975, 92.
79. *Lutheran Church of Australia South Australia District Incorporated v Farmers Co-operative Executors and Trustees Ltd* (1970) 121 CLR 628 at 639.
80. *Pilkington v Inland Revenue Commissioners* [1964] AC 612 at 641; [1962] 3 All ER 622.
81. *Re Beloved Wilkes' Charity* (1851) 42 ER 330; *Duke of Portland v Topham* (1864) 11 HLC 31; 11 ER 1242.
82. (1851) 42 ER 330 at 333.
83. *Gisborne v Gisborne* (1877) 2 App Cas 300 at 305 per Lord Cairns LC; *Tabor v Brooks* (1878) 10 Ch D 273; *Craig v National Trustees Executors and Agency Company of Australia Ltd* [1920] VLR 569.
84. (1977) 300–302.
85. [1965] Ch 918 at 928–9.

an obligation rest on them.[86] Nothing would be more likely to embitter family feelings and the relationship between the trustees and members of the family, were trustees obliged to state their reasons for the exercise of the powers entrusted to them. It might indeed well be difficult to persuade any persons to act as trustees were a duty to disclose their reasons, with all the embarrassment, arguments and quarrels that might ensue, added to their present not inconsiderable burdens.[87]

[166] It was argued for the plaintiff that the exception applied [to] her, because the trustees' reasons had been give[n] by Mr Paul in evidence. I do not accept that. It would defeat the policy which underlies the principle if beneficiaries could, by alleging lack of good faith against the trustees in an action and for practical purposes thus virtually obliging them to disclose in evidence the way they went about exercising the discretion, obtain a right to examination and review of the discretion which they would otherwise not have. The exception to the principle seems to proceed on the basis that if trustees of their own volition disclose their reasons they are treated as waiving their immunity and inviting examination and review of the reasons.

It was submitted for the plaintiff that it was open to the Court to examine and review whether the trustees had given 'fair consideration' to the exercise of their discretion. In particular it was argued that from the terms of the will and the circumstances of the case it was to be implied that Mrs Karger was to be given a fair opportunity of making representations to them before they exercised the discretion. It was put that this was necessary to ensure that the inquiries of the trustees were adequate. I do not consider that the implication is to be made. I see no good reason for importing rules of natural justice into the exercise of discretion by the trustees of the will. Such an implication is not necessary. The trustees of the will did not exercise their power in a type of situation where a right to make representations upon its exercise is normally afforded.[88] In any event the insufficiency of inquiries by the trustees is not a ground on which the exercise of discretion by the trustees can be examined and reviewed. As the expression 'fair consideration' correctly describes the ground on which the trustees' exercise of discretion can be examined and reviewed, only if it is used with the meaning equivalent to 'real and genuine consideration' there is no advantage in using it.

The principle I apply does not imply that there are not standards with which trustees should comply in the process of exercising their discretion. The approach which trustees should adopt in exercising particular discretionary powers has been elaborated in some of the cases.[89] When trustees disclose their reasons, making those reasons examinable, they are examined to see whether they satisfy the standard of being valid reasons. The principle which I apply is that, apart from cases where the trustees disclose their reasons, the exercise of an absolute and unfettered discretion is examinable only as to good faith, real and genuine consideration and absence of ulterior purpose, and not as to the method and manner of its exercise.

---

86. *Re Beloved Wilkes' Charity* (1851) 3 Mac and G 440; *Re Gresham Life Assurance Society; Ex parte Penney* (1872) 8 Ch App 446.
87. [1965] Ch 918 at 936–7. See also at 935–6 per Danckwerts LJ.
88. Cf *Charlton v Members of the Teachers Tribunal* [1981] VR 831 at 844NN5.
89. For example, *Re Hay's Settlement Trusts* [1982] 1 WLR 202 at 208–10 per Megarry VC; [1981] 3 All ER 786.

Comments

1. See Radan & Stewart at **20.108–20.115**.
2. Trustees cannot fetter the exercise of their discretionary powers in advance: *Thacker v Key* (1869) LR 8 Eq 408; *In Re Vestey's Settlement* [1951] Ch D 209. If the trustee makes resolutions or agreements which fetter their discretion they will be unenforceable: *Moore v Clench* [1875] 1 Ch D 447; *Fitzwood Pty Ltd v Unique Goal Pty Ltd (in liq)* (2001) 188 ALR 566 (aff'd on appeal: [2002] FCAFC 285).

21

BENEFICIARIES

Introduction

21.1 This chapter is concerned with the nature of interests held by beneficiaries. The extracts in this chapter deal with:

- the nature of beneficial interests in exhaustive and non-exhaustive discretionary trusts: *Secretary, Department of Families, Housing, Community Services and Indigenous Affairs v Elliott* (2009) 174 FCR 387;
- the nature of beneficial interests in unit trusts and the rule in *Saunders v Vautier*: *CPT Custodian Pty Ltd v Commissioner of State Revenue* (2005) 224 CLR 98;
- the nature of interests in discretionary trusts in proceedings under the *Family Law Act 1975* (Cth): *Kennon v Spry* (2008) 238 CLR 366.

The nature of beneficial interests in exhaustive and non-exhaustive discretionary trusts

21.2   Secretary, Department of Families, Housing, Community Services and Indigenous Affairs v Elliott (2009) 174 FCR 387

Court: Full Federal Court of Australia

Facts: The Elliott family consisted of Paul, his wife Emily and their daughter. Paul's father had created a discretionary trust in his will where the income of the trust could be used for the Elliotts' benefit. Any future children and grandchildren were also included as possible beneficiaries.

The will provided that the trustees had a discretion as to whether they should accumulate the trust income or distribute it to one or more of the beneficiaries each year.

Paul and Emily were pensioners. Centrelink had means-tested their pensions and included their interests under the discretionary trust in the means-testing. Under s 1207V(2) of the *Social Security Act 1991* (Cth) the trust assets could be attributed to them if the aggregate of their beneficial interests in the capital or income of the trust was 50 per cent or more. Centrelink, after included Paul and Emily's interests in the means-test, cancelled their pensions. The Social Security Appeals Tribunal overturned this decision but it was then affirmed by the Administrative Appeals Tribunal. A further appeal to the Federal Court led to Kenny J reinstating the pensions and that decision was appealed to the Full Federal Court.

Issue: The issue was whether the Elliotts had an interest in the discretionary trust which amounted to control for the purposes of the Social Security Act.

Decision: The Full Federal Court (Black CJ, Stone and Edmonds JJ) found that the beneficiaries did not have any right to income or capital until chosen by the trustee. As such, they had no legal or practical capacity to control the trust. Nor was there any interest which could be added to the interests of associates to equal more than 50 per cent of the beneficial interest. The decision by Centrelink to deny pensions to the beneficiaries was overturned.

Extracts: In this extract Black CJ, Stone and Edmonds JJ discuss the different kinds of beneficial interests that can exist in discretionary trusts. Their Honours also examine the effect on beneficial interests of trusts which dictate that income earned by the trust must be distributed (an exhaustive trust) and trusts where income may be accumulated (a non-exhaustive trust).

Black CJ, Stone and Edmonds JJ

[393] Analysis

The issue of whether a person who is a beneficiary or object, whether as to income or capital or both under a discretionary trust, has an 'interest' in that trust or the income thereof, invariably described as a 'beneficial interest', has been addressed in a number of cases over the last 120 years in different statutory contexts. In every case, the answer or conclusion arrived at has depended on two matters:

1. The nature of the discretionary trust in relation to the beneficiary or object; whether the trust is exhaustive with respect to the class of which the beneficiary or object is a member in the sense that the trustee is bound to distribute to one or more of the class or whether the trust is non-exhaustive by reason that the trustee has, in the case of income, a power to accumulate, or, in the case of corpus, there is a gift over in default of exercise of the discretion; and whether the relevant class is, at the relevant time, still open or closed; and [394]
2. the statutory context in which the issue arises; in particular whether the mechanism of the statute cannot operate unless the precise extent of the interests can be identified.

In respect of the first matter — the nature of the discretionary trust in relation to the beneficiary or object — at least four kinds of trust have been identified:

1. exhaustive trust with a closed class of beneficiaries;
2. exhaustive trust with an open class of beneficiaries;
3. non-exhaustive trust with a closed class of beneficiaries; and
4. non-exhaustive trust with an open class of beneficiaries.

Provided there is, at or during the relevant point or period of measurement, more than one member of the class, it is impossible to measure the extent of an individual beneficiary's interest in the trust whether the trust is of a kind which falls within (1), (2), (3) or (4). On the other hand, if the trust is of a kind that falls within (1) or (2), it will be possible, in relation to income, although perhaps not in relation to corpus in the case of trust (2), to measure the collective interests of all existing members of the class. This is, perhaps, best articulated by what Lord Reid said in *Gartside v Inland Revenue Commissioners*:

> I think that this idea of a group or class right must have arisen in this way. Where the trustees are *bound* to distribute the whole income among the discretionary beneficiaries and have no power to retain any part of it or use any part of it for any other purposes, you cannot tell what any one of the beneficiaries will receive until the trustees have exercised their discretion. But you can say with absolute certainty that the individual rights of the beneficiaries when added up or taken together will extend to the whole income. You can have an equation $x + y + z = 100$ although you do not yet know the value of x or y or z. And that may lead to important results where the trust is of that character. But that is not this case.[1] (Emphasis added.)

On the other hand, if the trust falls within (3), and certainly if it falls within (4), it will not be possible to measure the collective interests of all existing members of the class for the reason that the power to accumulate might be exercised. This is not to say that the members of the class have no rights; as French J said in *Australian Securities and Investments Commission v Carey*:[2]

> I accept that there are some rights enjoyed, even by the beneficiaries of a non-exhaustive discretionary trust with an open class of beneficiaries. They include the right to inspect the trust documents[3] and the right to require the trustee to provide information about management of the trust fund.[4] There is also a right to enforce the proper management of the trust by the trustee.[5]

But those rights are not, in any relevant sense, capable of measurement.

As to the second matter of statutory context, an illustration of the different conclusions that flow from different statutory contexts is *Attorney-General v Heywood*[6] and *Attorney-General v Farrell*[7] on the one hand and *Gartside*[8] on the other. The difference is summed up in the judgment of Lord Wilberforce in *Gartside*:

> *Attorney-General v Heywood* was decided in 1887 upon s 38(2)(c) of the *Customs and Inland Revenue Act 1881*, when what was levied was a stamp duty on property included in an account. The *1881 Act* defined various categories of **[395]** property to be included in an account, viz., property included in a gift made within three months of the death, property held on joint tenancy, and (under paragraph (c)) settled property in which a

---

1. [1968] AC 553 at 606.
2. 153 FCR 509 at [30].
3. *Re Londonderry's Settlement* [1965] Ch 918.
4. *Spellson v George* (1987) 11 NSWLR 300; *Hartigan Nominees Pty Ltd v Rydge* (1992) 29 NSWLR 405.
5. *Commissioner of Stamp Duties (Qld) v Livingston* (1964) 112 CLR 12; *Re Atkinson* [1971] VR 612.
6. (1887) LR 19 QBD 326.
7. [1931] 1 KB 81.
8. [1968] AC 553.

limited interest was reserved to the settlor or over which the settlor reserved a power of revocation. *Attorney-General v Heywood* was concerned with a voluntary settlement under which the trustees had a discretion to apply income, during the settlor's life, for a class including the settlor, and it was held by a Divisional Court that section 38(2)(c) applied. The judgment of Wills J contains the following passage:

> The word 'interest' is capable of different meanings, according to the context in which it is used or the subject-matter to which it is applied. If the contention for the defendants is right nobody has any interest in the property settled, and yet the whole fund was to be held for the benefit of three classes of persons — the husband, the wife, and the children; and the sum of the benefits conferred on all these three classes taken together, being the sum of three nothings amounts to nothing, whereas, on the other hand, it must necessarily comprehend the whole interest in the fund. This is simply a *reductio ad absurdum*. The application of the word 'interest' is not confined to a vested or a necessarily contingent interest. The Act was meant to cast a wider net than such a construction would imply.

When this decision was followed in *Attorney-General v Farrell*, section 38(2)(c) of the Act of 1881 (as amended in 1889) had been incorporated by the unhappy technique of reference into section 2(1)(c) of the *Finance Act, 1894* — 'as if therein enacted'. This case, too, was concerned with a settlement which contained a discretionary trust of income for the settlor and other persons. The Court of Appeal, not without hesitation, held that duty was payable and that *Attorney-General v Heywood* ought to be followed. Lord Hanworth MR expressed himself as unwilling to dissent from a case which had stood for so long and been acted upon: Greer LJ considered that but for *Attorney-General v Heywood* the case would have presented great difficulty. Romer LJ both applied and approved the previous decision.

The appellants invited your Lordships to overrule these cases. The Crown supported them and urged that they should be treated as governing the meaning of 'interest' in the present case. I see no need to take either course. Perhaps *Attorney-General v Farrell* could have been decided the other way on the ground that once section 38(2)(c) had been embodied in the *Finance Act, 1894*, s 2(1), the word 'interest' in the earlier section should be given a meaning similar to that which it bears in paragraphs (b) and (d), each of which involved the conception of extent. But this was not done and one can appreciate why not. For section 38(2)(c) is concerned, broadly, with the case of persons who settle their property, yet wish to benefit from it so long as they live. To tax them in such a case is perfectly understandable, however large or small the reserved benefit may be and whether it is defined in extent or undefined. No definition is necessary, because the measure of the charge is the whole value of the property. So naturally no reference is made to 'extent' — the mere fact of reservation is enough. I think, therefore, that the decisions in principle are acceptable. But — this is the other limb — acceptance of them does not carry the present case. In section 2(1)(b) of the *Finance Act, 1894* (and the same is true of section 2(1)(d)), a duty is imposed the quantum of which is related to the extent of the interest and I see no difficulty in saying that the element of extent is relevant under the two sections but not under the third: the distinction is both made in the language and is necessary if the tax is to work.[9]

---

9. [1968] AC at 619–621.

The different conclusions that flow from different statutory contexts are similarly exemplified in the judgments of the House of Lords, in a case subsequent to *Gartside*,[10] namely, *Leedale v Lewis*.[11] There the statute called for the apportionment of capital gains made by **[396]** non-resident trustees where resident beneficiaries had 'interests' in the settled property, with the apportionment to be made 'in such manner as is just and reasonable between' them. The persons in question only had discretionary interests in the settled property. In concluding that such discretionary beneficiaries had 'interests in settled property' for the purposes of s 42(2) of the *Finance Act 1965* (UK), Lord Fraser of Tullybelton said:

> Accordingly I agree with the Court of Appeal that the present case is not like *Gartside v Inland Revenue Commissioners* [1968] AC 553, where the mechanism of the statute could not be operated unless the precise extent of the interests could be identified.[12]

And Lord Wilberforce said:

> The key question is as to the meaning of the word 'interests' in section 42(2) of the *Finance Act 1965*, the alternatives being whether this word refers only to such interests as can be assigned a value, or whether it is a word of more general significance capable of covering any interest, quantifiable or non-quantifiable, of a beneficiary under a trust. That either of these is a possible meaning in fiscal legislation is made clear (a) by the general observations of Lord Reid in *Gartside v Inland Revenue Commissioners*[13] (see also those of Stephen J and Wills J in *Attorney-General v Heywood*[14]) and (b) by a comparison of the cases just cited. In *Heywood*, which arose under section 38 of the *Customs and Inland Revenue Act 1881*, and where the question was whether the settlor had reserved 'an interest' by including himself among a discretionary class of beneficiaries, the word 'interest' was given the more general meaning. To require that it meant something to which an ascertainable value could be assigned would, it was held, be contrary to the scheme of the statute. In *Gartside*, on the other hand, which arose under section 43 of the *Finance Act 1940*, and where the question was whether estate duty would be charged in respect of the determination of a discretionary interest, this House held that the word must bear the narrower meaning because the statute necessarily required ascertainment of the quantum of the interest. In *Gartside* I expressed the opinion, from which the other members of the House did not dissent, that these two cases could stand together. The word 'interest' is one of uncertain meaning and it remains to be decided on the terms of the applicable statute which, or possibly what other, meaning the word may bear.

> The appellant contends for the narrower meaning, and can find some support in section 42 of the Act of 1965. There is the reference to 'values' in subsection (2). There is subsection (3) which, he contends, sets out a code for assigning values to discretionary interests in income or capital — an exclusive code within one of whose provisions a case must fall if a charge to tax in respect of a discretionary trust is to arise. There is, thirdly, the reference, in subsection (2), to a life interest or an interest in reversion,

---

10. [1968] AC 553.
11. [1982] 1 WLR 1319.
12. [1982] 1 WLR 1319 at 1327.
13. [1968] AC 533 [sic] at 603.
14. (1887) 19 QBD 326.

but, in my opinion this does not survive a first critical look: the reference is clearly illustrative and nothing more.

The two main arguments are by no means negligible, but they are, in my opinion, greatly outweighed by those on the other side. I simply state them, as they impressed me; they are developed in discussion in the Court of Appeal's judgment.

1. The initial words of subsection (2) are 'any beneficiary'. Unless clearly directed otherwise, I would assume that 'persons having interests' was correlative to these words. Discretionary objects are clearly 'beneficiaries', so I would suppose them also to be included in 'persons having interests'.
2. The apportionment to be made under the subsection is mandatory. The amount of the gains — ie, the whole amount — must be apportioned in [397] the relevant year of assessment. This can only be done if discretionary objects, who may be the only 'beneficiaries' in that year, can be the objects of apportionment.
3. The words, in subsection (2), 'in such manner as is just and reasonable' and 'as near as may be, according to the respective values of those interests' suggest a broad rather than an actuarial approach in which all relevant considerations may be taken into account. They permit, inter alia, consideration of the settlor's letter of intent which shows, at least, that the settlement was to be regarded as for the benefit of the grandchildren, not of the settlor's two children.
4. That subsection (3) represents an exclusive code is in my opinion not supported by the form of the section. On the contrary, the structure of it suggests that subsection (2) is the main and general charging provision, subsection (3) being auxiliary and confined to particular cases.

These considerations together convince me that an apportionment in respect of 'interests' under a discretionary trust can, indeed must, be made.[15]

In the present case, the trusts as to both income and capital in cl 5(b) of the Will (together with cl 7(b)(i)) are non-exhaustive with an open class of beneficiaries. The beneficial interests of the existing beneficiaries both individually and collectively are incapable of measurement, but that is the very thing which s 1207V(2)(d) mandates before that 'control test' requirement is satisfied. In this regard, it is a statutory provision akin to that considered in *Gartside*[16] and unlike those considered in *Heywood*;[17] *Farrell*[18] and *Leedale*.[19]

Conclusion

The primary judge was very much alive to this issue. At [47] of her Honour's reasons she wrote:

I accept that, as the Secretary submitted, the word 'aggregate' in par 1207V(2)(d) is used in its ordinary sense, signifying '[t]o gather into one whole or mass; to collect together,

---

15. [1982] 1 WLR 1319 at 1329.
16. [1968] AC 553.
17. (1887) 19 QBD 326.
18. [1931] 1 KB 81.
19. [1982] 1 WLR 1319.

assemble; to mass'.[20] Paragraph (d) of subs 1207V(2) presupposes, however, that there are in fact 'beneficial interests in the corpus or income of the trust' that are capable of aggregation. If neither the individual nor his or her associates hold any such beneficial interests, then the paragraph cannot apply.

The wide definition of 'interest' contended for by the appellant inevitably fails in the face of the statutory requirement of aggregation.

For the foregoing reasons, s 1207V(2)(d) cannot apply to the trust constituted by cl 5(b) of the Will and as the appellant relied on no other requirement of the control test in s 1207V(2), the appeal must be dismissed with costs as taxed or agreed.

Comment

1. See Radan & Stewart at **21.1–21.5**.

The interests of beneficiaries in unit trusts and the rule in *Saunders v Vautier*

21.3   CPT Custodian Pty Ltd v Commissioner of State Revenue (2005) 224 CLR 98

Court: High Court of Australia

Facts: This case concerned unit trusts over land where the units were held by two companies, CPT Custodian Pty Ltd ('CPT') and Karingal 2 Holdings Pty Ltd ('Karingal'). The trust land was held at Glen Waverley, Keilor Downs, Cranborne Park and Mildura and all the lots contained shopping centres. CPT and Karingal operated as trustees of two of the unit trusts. Under one of the trusts, CPT held half of the units. In the other trust both companies (through related corporations) effectively held all the units.

The unit trust deeds conferred an equal interest in the trust property but dictated that the unit holders lacked any interest in any particular part of the trust fund. Unit holders were entitled to periodic distributions of income. Both the trustee and the manager were given a right to be paid fees and a right to be indemnified from the trust fund for those fees.

The issue that arose was whether the companies should be treated as the 'owners' of the properties under s 3(1) of the *Land Tax Act 1958* (Vic). That section defined an 'owner' to be 'every person entitled to any land for any estate of freehold in possession'. The Commissioner argued that the individual units each provided fixed and ascertainable rights which conferred a proprietorial interest in the trust property which was akin to 'ownership'. The Commissioner also argued that if a unit holder held all the units of the trust then they were fully entitled to the beneficial interests of the trust and the trust property became

---

20. See *Oxford English Dictionary*.

'vested in possession'. The Commissioner also argued that in such a situation, the beneficiary was entitled to terminate the trust under the rule in *Saunders v Vautier* (1841) 49 ER 282. This would perfect the title which, again, indicated a form of ownership.

Issue: The issue was whether the ownership of all the units in a unit trust amounted to a form of ownership.

Decision: The High Court (Gleeson CJ, McHugh, Gummow, Callinan and Heydon JJ) did not agree with the Commissioner and neither company was found to be entitled to 'freehold in possession'. The High Court found that the ownership of units did not necessarily confer an equitable interest in the property. The mere existence of a trust relationship did not automatically mean that unit holders had to be vested with a proprietorial interest in the trust fund.

The High Court also rejected the argument that the companies had ownership because they had the right to terminate the trusts under the rule in *Saunders v Vautier*. The right to terminate had not been exercised and the mere fact that such a power might be used did not mean that equity ought to regard it as having been used.

The High Court also found that the mere fact that a person may hold all the units in a trust did not meant that they were the 'owner' of the trust fund. All the beneficial interests in the unit trusts were still subject to the rights of the trustee and manager to be reimbursed and indemnified from the trust property.

Extracts: In this extract the High Court discusses the rights of unit holders in the trust and the rule in *Saunders v Vautier*.

Gleeson CJ, McHugh, Gummow, Callinan and Heydon JJ

[109] ... Something now should be said respecting the task of statutory construction which was presented to Nettle J [the trial judge] and then to the Court of Appeal. There were two steps to be taken. They were correctly identified in the submissions by the taxpayers to the Court of Appeal.[21] The first step was to ascertain the terms of the trusts upon which the relevant lands were held. The second was to construe the statutory definition to ascertain whether the rights of the taxpayers under those trusts fell within that definition.

In taking those steps, a priori assumptions as to the nature of unit trusts under the general law and principles of equity would not assist and would be apt to mislead. All depends, as Tamberlin and Hely JJ put it in *Kent v SS Maria Luisa [No 2]*,[22] upon the terms of the particular trust. The term 'unit trust' is the subject of much exegesis by commentators.[23]

---

21. (2003) 8 VR 532 at 539–540.
22. (2003) 130 FCR 12 at 33.
23. See Ford, 'Unit Trusts' (1960) 23 *Modern Law Review* 129; Ford, 'Public Unit Trusts', in Austin and Vann (eds), *The Law of Public Company Finance*, 1986, at 397; Sin, *The Legal Nature of the Unit Trust*, 1997; Thomas and Hudson, *The Law of Trusts*, 2003, Ch 51.

However, 'unit trust', like 'discretionary [110] trust',[24] in the absence of an applicable statutory definition, does not have a constant, fixed normative meaning which can dictate the application to particular facts of the definition in s 3(a) of the *Land Tax Act 1958 (Vic)* (the Act).[25]

To approach the case, as both Nettle J and the Court of Appeal appear to have done in response to submissions by the Commissioner, by asking first whether, as was said to be indicated by *Costa & Duppe Properties Pty Ltd v Duppe*[26] the holder of a unit 'in a unit trust' has 'a proprietary interest in each of the assets which comprise the entirety of the trust fund', and answering it in the affirmative,[27] did not immediately assist in construing the definition of owner in the Act. That definition does not speak of ownership of proprietary interests at large, but of entitlement to any estate of freehold in possession.

In *Schmidt v Rosewood Trust Ltd*[28] the Privy Council recently stressed that the right to seek the intervention of a court of equity to exercise its inherent authority to supervise and, if necessary, to intervene in the administration of trusts, 'does not depend on entitlement to a fixed and transmissible beneficial interest'. In a sense, the Commissioner's submissions tend to prove too much.[29] In any event, as Lord Wilberforce emphasised in *Gartside v Inland Revenue Commissioners*[30] it is one thing to identify rights protected by a court of equity, and another to identify an interest which has 'the necessary quality of definable extent which must exist before it can be taxed'. In the present case, the 'definable extent' is that specified by the definition in the Act. No doubt, unit holders accurately may be said to have had rights protected by a court of equity, but that does not require the conclusion that in the statutory sense they were 'owners' of the land held on the trusts in question.[31]

The trust deeds

The relevant trust deeds were not in identical form. However, their relevantly salient features appear sufficiently from a consideration of the Keilor Downs Deed (the Deed) to which the Court was taken at the hearing of the appeals.

At all material times the Trustee of the trusts of the Deed was CPT. The parties to the Deed were CPT and a party defined as 'the Manager', in which the management of the Fund was vested [111] exclusively (cll 2.5, 16.2). The Fund was vested in the Trustee upon trust for the Unit Holders (cll 2.4, 26.3). Both the Trustee (cl 23.2) and the Manager

---

24. *Chief Commissioner of Stamp Duties (NSW) v Buckle* (1998) 192 CLR 226 at 234 [8].
25. Section 102D(1) of the *Income Tax Assessment Act 1936* (Cth), for the purposes of Pt III, Div 6B, defines a 'unit' in relation to a 'prescribed trust estate' as including 'a beneficial interest, however described, in any of the income or property of the trust estate'. Nothing for these appeals turns upon the income tax legislation.
26. [1986] VR 90.
27. (2003) 8 VR 532 at 539.
28. [2003] 2 AC 709 at 729.
29. Cf *Schmidt v Rosewood Trust Ltd* [2003] 2 AC 709 at 729.
30. [1968] AC 553 at 617–618.
31. Cf *Kent v SS Maria Luisa [No 2]* (2003) 130 FCR 12 at 34–35.

(cl 23.1) were entitled to fees in significant amounts to be paid out of the Fund, and also to monthly reimbursement from the Fund of their costs, charges and expenses (cl 23.5).

The beneficial interest in the Fund was divided into units, each said to confer an equal interest in all property for the time being held by the Trustee upon the trusts of the Deed, but excluding that part of the Fund credited to a distribution account for distribution to unit holders (cl 3.2). But no unit conferred 'any interest in any particular part of the Trust Fund or any investment' and each unit had 'only such interest in the Trust Fund as a whole as [was] conferred on a Unit under the provisions contained in [the Deed]' (cl 3.2).[32] Unit holders were not entitled to require the transfer of any property comprised in the Fund, save as provided by the Deed (cl 28.13) but, by agreement with the Manager, distributions in specie might be made upon determination of the Fund (cl 15.5.5). A unit holder was not entitled to lodge a caveat claiming an estate or interest in any investment, being realty (cl 7.1.3).[33] Unit holders were bound by the terms of the Deed as if parties to it (cl 8). The Deed contemplated that all units might be held beneficially by a single unit holder (cl 29.4).

Clause 20 provided for the distribution to unit holders of periodic income entitlements, and cl 15 for the realisation of the Fund upon its determination and distribution of the proceeds among unit holders. In the circumstances detailed in cl 14 the Manager was obliged to repurchase units which would then be cancelled or be available for resale by the Manager.[34]

The Commissioner's submissions

Counsel for the Commissioner, with reference to provisions such as those of the Deed just described, submitted in this Court that (i) as a matter of general law, because the trust deeds conferred upon each unit holder fixed and ascertainable rights, in relation to the distribution of income and capital, and not depending upon the exercise of discretion, the trust deeds conferred upon each unit holder an equitable estate or interest in each asset from time to time comprising the trust fund; (ii) no other person or class had any such rights or interests; and (iii) these equitable estates or interests answered the statutory [112] requirement in the definition of owner of entitlement to land for any estate of freehold in possession.

The Commissioner added that the position was no different where there was a sub-trust, with a unit holder holding units in a unit trust, the trustee of which in turn held units in a land-holding trust. Such a position arose in the 1996 and 1997 land tax years with respect to the Keilor Downs Plaza Land and in 1997 with respect to the

---

32. Clause 5 of the Cranbourne Park Unit Trust Deed stated that 'each Unit Holder shall not be entitled to any particular asset, investment, or property of whatever kind of the Fund'.
33. It is unnecessary to enter upon the question whether such a negative stipulation would be enforced in equity, given the policy of the law perceived from the scope and purpose of the Torrens system legislation: *Nelson v Nelson* (1995) 184 CLR 538; *Fitzgerald v FJ Leonhardt Pty Ltd* (1997) 189 CLR 215. See, generally, Campbell, 'Contracting Around the Right to Caveat', in Grinlinton (ed), *Torrens in the Twenty-First Century*, 2003, p 203.
34. Cf *MSP Nominees Pty Ltd v Commissioner of Stamps* (SA) (1999) 198 CLR 494.

Cranbourne Park Shopping Centre Land. The Commissioner's submissions respecting sub-trusts cannot succeed if the primary propositions (i), (ii) and (iii) fail.

Propositions (i) and (ii) may be put to one side and attention first given to proposition (iii) which is the critical issue posed by the taxing law itself. It then is necessary to return to *Glenn v Federal Commissioner of Land Tax*[35] and what was said there respecting the similar definition of owner in the *Land Tax Assessment Act 1910* (the 1910 Act).

Glenn v Federal Commissioner of Land Tax[36]

In that case, Griffith CJ said of an argument for the Revenue that it was:

> ... based on the assumption that whenever the legal estate in land is vested in a trustee there must be some person other than the trustee entitled to it in equity for an estate of freehold in possession, so that the only question to be answered is who is the owner of that equitable estate. In my opinion, there is a prior inquiry, namely, whether there is any such person. If there is not, the trustee is entitled to the whole estate in possession, both legal and equitable.[37]

That statement was a prescient rejection of a 'dogma' that, where ownership is vested in a trustee, equitable ownership must necessarily be vested in someone else because it is an essential attribute of a trust that it confers upon individuals a complex of beneficial legal relations which may be called ownership.[38] The current state of authority, exemplified by *Federal Commissioner of Taxation v Linter Textiles Australia Ltd (In liq)*[39] bears out what was said in *Glenn* by Griffith CJ. General remarks in *Chief Commissioner of Stamp Duties (NSW) v ISPT Pty Ltd*,[40] a case referred to extensively in *Arjon Pty Ltd v Commissioner of State Revenue (Vic) (2)*,[41] may be at odds with what was said in *Glenn* to the extent that they go beyond construction of the particular New South Wales stamp duty legislation, but it is unnecessary to pursue the question here.

In *Glenn*, Griffith CJ construed the statutory expression 'estate in possession' as denoting 'an estate of which some person has the present right of enjoyment', saying that land tax being an annual tax, **[113]** 'the "owner" of the land is the person who is in the present enjoyment of the fruits which presumably afford the fund from which it is to be paid'.[42] Where a trust for accumulation was in operation, those who thereafter were to take the trust estate were not entitled to an 'estate of freehold in possession' and were not 'owners'. The Chief Justice continued:

> In my opinion, therefore, when the equitable rights created by a will, which may be as diverse as the testator thinks fit, are such that the beneficial enjoyment of property by

---

35. (1915) 20 CLR 490.
36. (1915) 20 CLR 490.
37. (1915) 20 CLR 490 at 497.
38. See Harris, 'Trust, Power and Duty' (1971) 87 *Law Quarterly Review* 31 at 47.
39. (2005) 220 CLR 592 at 606 [30]. See also *Kent v SS Maria Luisa [No 2]* (2003) 130 FCR 12 at 32–33.
40. (1998) 45 NSWLR 639 at 654.
41. (2003) 8 VR 502 at 515–517.
42. (1915) 20 CLR 490 at 496–497.

a particular object of his bounty cannot begin until the expiration of a determinate or indeterminate period, there is no present estate in possession in that property in any person other than the trustees of the will. In one sense, perhaps, the persons who are for the time being entitled to share in the fruits of the land may collectively be called the equitable owners, but that point is not material to the present case.[43]

Thereafter, this Court decided that it followed from *Glenn* that, while 'in one sense' those between whom a testamentary estate would be appropriated at the end of a stipulated period of accumulation of income were equitable owners of land included in the estate, they were not taxable as owners under the 1910 Act.[44]

In the present case, Nettle J, who was upheld on this issue by the Court of Appeal, applied to the definition of owner in s 3(a) of the Act the reasoning in *Glenn*. His Honour rejected the submission for the Commissioner, in essence renewed in this Court, that the entitlements of the unit holders made each unit holder an 'owner' in the relevant sense. His Honour was correct in doing so.

Hallmark of the unit trust?

To a significant degree the proposition advanced by the Commissioner and encapsulated in proposition (iii) set out above depended upon what in propositions (i) and (ii) was treated as the hallmark of any unit trust. The alleged hallmark is that, unlike shareholders with respect to the property of the company, unit holders do have beneficial interests in the assets of the trust; no other persons or class of persons has such an interest and, if not with the unit holders, where else rests the beneficial interest?

Similar reasoning is manifest in what was said in *Duppe*[45] concerning the interest of each unit holder in the three parcels of land comprising the assets of the unit trust considered in that case. That trust deed (in cll 7, 8) contained provisions in similar form to cl 3.2 of the Deed considered above. The issue in *Duppe* was whether each unit holder had an estate or interest in land within the meaning of s 89(1) of the *Transfer of Land Act 1958 (Vic)*, which was necessary to support a caveat. Brooking J, in answering that question in the affirmative, said:

> If there is a proprietary interest in the entirety, *there must be* a proprietary interest in each of the assets of which the entirety is composed.[46] (Emphasis added.)

However, in *Gartside*, Lord Wilberforce had said:

> It can be accepted that 'interest' is capable of a very wide and general meaning. But the wide spectrum that it covers makes it all the more necessary, if precise conclusions are to be founded upon its use, to place it in a setting: Viscount Radcliffe, delivering the Board's judgment in *Commissioner of Stamp Duties (Qld) v Livingston*[47] shows how this

---

43. (1915) 20 CLR 490 at 498.
44. *Union Trustee Co of Australia Ltd v Federal Commissioner of Land Tax* (1915) 20 CLR 526 at 531.
45. [1986] VR 90.
46. [1986] VR 90 at 96.
47. (1964) 112 CLR 12 at 28–29; [1965] AC 694 at 719.

word has to do duty in several quite different legal contexts to express rights of very different characters and that to transfer a meaning from one context to another may breed confusion.[48]

In *Livingston* itself, Viscount Radcliffe had observed that:

> ... the terminology of our legal system has not produced a sufficient variety of words to represent the various meanings which can be conveyed by the words 'interest' and 'property'. Thus propositions are advanced or rebutted by the employment of terms that have not in themselves a common basis of definition.[49]

When *Livingston* had been before this Court, Fullagar J and Kitto J each had spoken to similar effect.[50] Hence, perhaps, the development of the 'dogma' respecting concurrent and exhaustive legal and beneficial interests which has been referred to earlier in these reasons and which was decisively discounted by the Privy Council in *Livingston*. Terms are used here which lack a universal contemporary or historical meaning, divorced from the context, particularly any statutory context in which they are employed.[51]

It is unnecessary for the instant appeals to determine whether *Duppe* correctly decided the requirements in Victoria for a caveatable interest. But what was said there provides, after *Gartside* and *Livingston*, and more recently *Linter Textiles*,[52] no authority of the general significance assumed for it by the submissions here by the Commissioner.

[115] However, something must be said here respecting the decision of this Court in *Charles v Federal Commissioner of Taxation*.[53] That case was referred to extensively in *Duppe*[54] as the most important authority for the purposes of that case. Charles was said by the Commissioner to be consistent with the analysis urged in the Commissioner's submissions on the present appeals.

The significant conclusions expressed by Dixon CJ, Kitto and Taylor JJ in Charles appear in a passage where, after emphasising that a share in a company confers upon the holder no legal or equitable interest in the assets of the company, they continued:

> But a unit *under the trust deed before us* confers a proprietary interest in all the property which for the time being is subject to the trust of the deed;[55] so that the question whether moneys distributed to unit holders under the trust form part of their income or of their capital must be answered by considering the character of those moneys in the hands of the trustees before the distribution is made.[56] (Emphasis added.)

---

48. [1968] AC 553 at 617.
49. (1964) 112 CLR 12 at 22; [1965] AC 694 at 712.
50. *Livingston v Commissioner of Stamp Duties (Qld)* (1960) 107 CLR 411 at 438 per Fullagar J; at 450 per Kitto J.
51. See Speed, 'Beneficial Ownership' (1997) 26 *Australian Tax Review* 34.
52. (2005) 220 CLR 592. See also the remarks of Aickin J in *DKLR Holding Co (No 2) Pty Ltd v Commissioner of Stamp Duties (NSW)* (1982) 149 CLR 431 at 463.
53. (1954) 90 CLR 598.
54. [1986] VR 90 at 95.
55. *Baker v Archer-Shee* [1927] AC 844.
56. (1954) 90 CLR 598 at 609.

The reference by the Court in Charles to the first of the Archer-Shee cases[57] cannot attribute to that decision a general significance which today, in the light of the more recent authorities to which reference has been made above, it does not have. Lady Archer-Shee held a life interest in the income of the residuary estate of her father. The will was in simple form, with one tenant for life and no other object of the trust to be considered.[58] The contrast between that situation and the trusts with which Karingal and CPT are concerned will be readily apparent. No one, as Kitto J later pointed out, doubted that Lady Archer-Shee had a beneficial interest in the income.[59] But, did the moneys paid by the trustees to her account answer the statutory description of income of Lady Archer-Shee 'arising … from'[60] the stocks and shares in which the residuary estate was invested? Lord Wrenbury held that the answer was 'yes' because she had 'an equitable right in possession to receive during her life' the dividends, subject to deduction for the costs, charges and expenses of the trustees, and for United States tax.[61]

The deed considered in Charles divided the beneficial interest in the trust fund into units (cll 6, 7), and the trustees were bound to make half-yearly distributions to unit holders, in proportion to their respective numbers of units, of the 'cash produce' which had been [116] received by the trustees (cll 13A, 13B).[62] Karingal and CPT rightly stress that the deeds with which this litigation is concerned were differently cast and in terms which do not support any direct and simple conclusion respecting proprietary interests of unit holders such as that reached in *Charles*.

The interest of a unit holder under the deed

On this issue, remarks by Nettle J are in point and conclusive. His Honour said:

> It may well be that the income of the fund as finally constituted and distributed will include all of the rents and profits generated by a particular parcel of land within the fund. But it is distinctly possible that it will not. Each of the deeds gives power to the trustee to provide out of receipts for future and contingent liabilities; to apply receipts in the purchase of any property or business; to invest receipts in authorised investments and to deal with and transpose such investments; and the only right of the unit holder is to a proportionate share of the income of the fund for the year.

> The Commissioner contends that the trustees' powers of disposition and transposition make no difference. He submits that insofar as receipts from particular properties may be applied in making payments other than to a unit holder, they must be seen as made on behalf of the unit holder and in that sense as received by the unit holder. He says that it is in principle no different to the case of a simple trust of land with only

---

57. *Baker v Archer-Shee* [1927] AC 844; *Archer-Shee v Garland* [1931] AC 212.
58. See the remarks of Viscount Sumner [1927] AC 844 at 853.
59. *Livingston v Commissioner of Stamp Duties (Qld)* (1960) 107 CLR 411 at 450.
60. See the speech of Lord Wrenbury [1927] AC 844 at 863.
61. See [1927] AC 844 at 866.
62. (1954) 90 CLR 598 at 600, 606–607. See also the capital growth unit trust considered in *Read v The Commonwealth* (1988) 167 CLR 57 at 61, the terms of which were said by Mason CJ, Deane and Gaudron JJ to confer upon a unit holder a beneficial interest in the trust assets.

one beneficiary, under the terms of which the trustee is entitled to apply receipts in the payment of obligations and in the making of provisions in connection with the management of the land. The Commissioner contends that in such a case there can be no doubt that the beneficiary would be liable to tax as 'owner'. But I think there is a difference. In the case of a simple trust of the kind instanced by the Commissioner the entitlement of the trustee to apply part of the receipts in defined ways determines the amount of the income which the beneficiary has a right to receive. Contrastingly, in a case of a complex unit trust of the kind with which I am concerned, the entitlement of the trustee to apply receipts in defined ways informs the nature of the income that the unit holders have a right to receive: not a total of all of the receipts derived from each asset the subject of the fund but rather such if any income as may be derived from the product of the application of gross receipts in various ways.[63] (Footnotes omitted.)

[117] The Commissioner referred to s 45 of the Act as essential to his case. Section 45 provides, among other things, for the separate assessment of each 'joint owner' of land in respect of the individual interest of that owner in the land (s 45(3)). The term 'joint owners' is so defined in s 3(1) as to identify persons 'who own land jointly or in common, whether as partners or otherwise'. The 1910 Act contained a definition in those terms. It is apparent from the reasoning of Knox CJ in *Terry v Federal Commissioner of Taxation*,[64] a case upon the 1910 Act, that in order to be a joint owner the person in question must jointly occupy the same position with regard to entitlement for an estate of freehold in possession (ie, as 'owner' in the defined sense) as an individual would occupy in his own person. That requirement means that the notion of joint ownership in s 45 cannot overcome the failure of the Commissioner's case with respect to the definition of owner in s 3 of the Act.

Further, the units are discrete bundles of rights; each unit is not held in joint ownership with the totality of issued units. It appeared to be conceded in argument by the Commissioner that unit holders did not hold any land as joint tenants. However, they were said necessarily to own together the whole of the beneficial ownership which, on the Commissioner's case, must subsist. The Commissioner further submitted that this ownership, however understood, was within the closing words of the definition of 'joint owners', namely, 'or otherwise'.

There are two answers to these submissions. First, the concluding words are no more than part of the phrase 'whether as partners or otherwise', and do not lessen the requirement for ownership jointly or in common. Secondly, as already demonstrated, the assumption respecting beneficial ownership is misplaced.

The sole owner of all issued units

There remains the distinction upon which turned the outcome in the Court of Appeal. The distinction was drawn with reference to the reasons in *Arjon* where Phillips JA stated:

... where the trust deed itself declares that the trust fund as a whole is vested in all the unit holders together and there is but one person holding all the issued units, it seems

---

63. (2002) 51 ATR 190 at 205.
64. (1920) 27 CLR 429 at 434–435.

to me to follow that that sole unit holder must be regarded as in equity entitled to an interest, vested in possession, in all of the trust assets.[65]

Earlier in his reasons, his Honour had said of the sole unit holder:

> As the only person beneficially interested in the assets, it also has the power to bring the trust to an end at will and to require the transfer to it of the assets (even if only after satisfying any claim that the trustee might have to reimbursement or recoupment for [118] expenses incurred as trustee).[66]

This meant that the unit holder of all issued units had more than the accumulation of the rights attaching to each of the units considered severally. In particular, with a reference to *Saunders v Vautier*,[67] Phillips JA said that:

> ... quite apart from the terms of the trust deed, the holder of all of the units will ordinarily have the power to bring the trust to an end and, if it so chooses, appropriate the trust assets to itself.[68]

Karingal and CPT challenge these propositions and deny that the holder of all of the issued units was in a position to bring to an end the relevant unit trusts. The issue of statutory construction concerning the phrase 'entitled to any land for any estate of freehold in possession' in the definition in the Act of 'owner' must not be overlooked whilst pursuing any inquiry respecting *Saunders v Vautier*. The operation of the rule attributed to that case was taken by the Court of Appeal to override the complex stipulations of the Deed respecting its determination. The result was apparently that, because at each relevant 31 December there was an unrealised potential for the holder of all of the issued units to put the trusts to an end, the unit holders were on that date entitled to an estate of freehold in possession within the meaning of the statutory definition.

Saunders v Vautier is a case which has given its name to a 'rule' not explicitly formulated in the case itself, either by Lord Langdale MR (at first instance) or by Lord Cottenham LC (on appeal). In Anglo-Australian law the rule has been seen to embody a 'consent principle' recently identified by Mummery LJ in *Goulding v James*[69] as follows:

> The principle recognises the rights of beneficiaries, who are sui juris and together absolutely entitled to the trust property, to exercise their proprietary rights to overbear and defeat the intention of a testator or settlor to subject property to the continuing trusts, powers and limitations of a will or trust instrument.

A different view was taken long ago by the United States Supreme Court. In *Shelton v King*[70] the Court repeated what had been said by Miller J in 1875 when speaking for

---

65. (2003) 8 VR 502 at 520.
66. (2003) 8 VR 502 at 515.
67. (1841) 49 ER 282; affd (1841) 41 ER 482.
68. (2003) 8 VR 502 at 515.
69. [1997] 2 All ER 239 at 247.
70. (1913) 229 US 90.

the Supreme Court in *Nichols v Eaton*.[71] He saw no reason in the principles of public policy concerning frauds upon creditors, restraints upon alienation, the prevention of perpetuities and of excessive accumulations, or in the necessary incidents of equitable estates, which supported a rule of the width engrafted upon the law (then comparatively recently) by the English Court of Chancery as a limitation upon effecting the intent of [119] testators and settlors.[72] However that may be, there is force for Anglo-Australian law in the statement that the rule in *Saunders v Vautier* gives the beneficiaries a Hohfeldian 'power' which correlates to a 'liability' on the part of the trustees, rather than a 'right' correlative to a 'duty'. This is because, in the words of Professor J W Harris:

> [b]y breaking up the trust, the beneficiaries do not compel the trustees to carry out any part of their office as active trustees; on the contrary, they bring that office to an end.[73] (Footnote omitted.)

Whilst the reasoning of the Court of Appeal respecting the special case of the holder of all issued units depended largely upon the rule in *Saunders v Vautier*, in oral argument in this Court the Commissioner said that, in effect, here the rule was a red herring. The rule was but a corollary of the beneficial ownership for which the Commissioner contended in his earlier submissions; this did not depend upon the exercise of the entitlement to terminate the trust.

The submissions respecting the beneficial ownership by each unit holder have been rejected earlier in these reasons. The trusts exemplified in the Deed recognised (cl 29.4) that all issued units might be in the one beneficial ownership, but the trusts were drawn in terms conferring individual rights attached to each unit. They were not drawn to provide a single right of a cumulative nature so that the whole differed from the sum of the parts. There could be no such single right unless held jointly or in common, but the Deed was not cast in such terms.[74]

There is a further consideration. The facts of the present cases do not, in any event, answer the modern formulation of the rule in *Saunders v Vautier*, stated as follows in *Thomas on Powers*:

> Under the rule in *Saunders v Vautier*,[75] an adult beneficiary (or a number of adult beneficiaries acting together) who has (or between them have) an absolute, vested and indefeasible interest in the capital and income of property may at any time require the transfer of the property to him (or them) and may terminate any accumulation.[76]

Lightman J said in *Don King Productions Inc v Warren*[77] that the rule only applies if, as was not so there, the beneficiaries were entitled to wind up the trust and require the trustee to assign to them the subject matter of the trust.

---

71. (1875) 91 US 716 at 725.
72. See further *Claflin v Claflin* (1889) 20 NE 454; A Scott, *The Law of Trusts*, 1989, vol 4, §337.3; Sin, *The Legal Nature of the Unit Trust,* 1997, pp 114–120.
73. 'Trust, Power and Duty' (1971) 87 *Law Quarterly Review* 31 at 63.
74. Cf *Gartside v Inland Revenue Commissioners* [1968] AC 553 at 605.
75. (1841) 4 Beav 115 [49 ER 282]; affd *Saunders v Vautier* (1841) Cr & Ph 240 [41 ER 482].
76. Thomas, *Thomas on Powers*, 1998, p 176.
77. [2000] Ch 291 at 321; affd [2000] Ch 291 at 324ff.

[120] Notwithstanding these references to beneficiaries, the repositories of the power to override the terms of a trust by bringing to an end its further administration have been variously identified. For example, it has been asked to whom do the trustees owe their duties of administration? Looking at the testamentary trusts considered in *Glenn*, Isaacs J considered the scope of the duties of the trustees and asked whether the trusts were exclusively for the benefit of the appellants.[78] The appellants' interests in the residuary estate were subject to the payment of annuities to the widow of the testator for her life and to his unmarried daughters until marriage.[79] Isaacs J concluded:

> The trustees have prior duties to other legatees having definite interests, and the strict performance of those duties requires the trustees to retain possession of the property, to receive the profits, and to deal with them otherwise than by paying them to the appellants ... It is obvious, therefore, that the principle of *Saunders v Vautier*[80] cannot apply, for the trusts are not exclusively for the appellants' benefit.[81]

More recently, in *Sir Moses Montefiore Jewish Home v Howell and Co (No 7) Pty Ltd*,[82] Kearney J treated the power to achieve immediate payment of the trust property as reposed in the entire range of persons entitled to call for the due administration of the trust in question.

But that approach to the rule in *Saunders v Vautier* would not meet the case of the Deed considered in this litigation. In the Deed, the Manager covenanted with the Trustee (cl 23.4) to ensure that there were at all times sufficient readily realisable assets of the Trust available for the Trustee to raise the fees to which the Manager and the Trustee were entitled under cll 23.1 and 23.2 respectively. These stipulations made the Trustee and the Manager interested in due administration of the trusts of the Deed, in the sense identified by Kearney J in *Moses Montefiore*. Put somewhat differently, the unit holders were not the persons in whose favour alone the trust property might be applied by the trustee of the Deed.[83]

The classic nineteenth century formulation by the English courts of the rule in *Saunders v Vautier* did not give consideration to the significance of the right of the trustee under the general law to reimbursement or exoneration for the discharge of liabilities incurred in administration of the trust. In *Wharton v Masterman*,[84] Lord Davey approached the rule in *Saunders v Vautier* from the [121] viewpoint of the law respecting accumulations of income for an excessive period; if no person had any interest in the trust other than the legatee, the legatee might put an end to the accumulation which was exclusively for the benefit of that person and as a result there was no effective or enforceable direction for any accumulation.[85] However, his Lordship's discussion of the authorities[86] does indicate

---

78. (1915) 20 CLR 490 at 504.
79. (1915) 20 CLR 490 at 495.
80. (1841) 4 Beav 115 [49 ER 282]; affd (1841) Cr & Ph 240 [41 ER 482].
81. (1915) 20 CLR 490 at 504.
82. [1984] 2 NSWLR 406 at 410–411.
83. See *Blair v Curran* (1939) 62 CLR 464 at 498, 501; Thomas, *Thomas on Powers*, 1998, p 380.
84. [1895] AC 186.
85. [1895] AC 186 at 198–200.
86. [1895] AC 186 at 200–201.

that the rule in *Saunders v Vautier* could not apply if, by reason of the charging of legacies on the fund and accumulations, the persons seeking to put an end to the accumulations were 'only entitled to an undetermined and uncertain surplus (if any) which might be left of the fund after payment of the legacies'.[87]

In the present case, the unsatisfied trustees' right of indemnity was expressed as an actual liability in each of the relevant accounts at each 31 December date and rendered applicable the sense of the above words of Lord Davey. Until satisfaction of rights of reimbursement or exoneration, it was impossible to say what the trust fund in question was.[88]

There is a further, and related, point. This is suggested by remarks of Tamberlin and Hely JJ in *Kent v SS Maria Luisa [No 2].*[89] It is one thing to say, as in *Wharton v Masterman*,[90] that a court of equity will not enforce a trust for accumulations in which no person has an interest but the legatee, and another to determine for a statutory purpose that there is a presently subsisting interest in all of the trust assets at a particular date (midnight on 31 December of the immediately preceding year) because of what could thereafter be done in exercise of a power of termination of the trust in question but at that date had not been done. Equity often regards as done that which ought to be done, but not necessarily that which merely could be done. In any event, what is at stake here is the operation of statutory criteria upon general law concepts of equitable ownership.

Comment

1. See Radan & Stewart at **21.7–21.15**.

Discretionary trusts and family law

21.4 Kennon v Spry (2008) 238 CLR 366

Court: High Court of Australia

Facts: Dr ICF Spry, the well-known equity barrister, created a trust orally in 1968, and later recorded in writing in 1981. Dr Spry was the settlor and trustee. The trust was a discretionary trust where the beneficiaries were all the issue of Dr Spry's father and their spouses. In 1983 Dr Spry removed himself as a beneficiary to limit possible liabilities under land tax. When his marriage came into difficulties in 1998 he executed a document which removed himself and his wife as capital beneficiaries. Dr Spry and his wife separated in 2001. In 2002, he created four trusts for his daughters and he exercised his discretion as trustee to apply all the income and capital from the primary

---

87. [1895] AC 186 at 201.
88. *Chief Commissioner of Stamp Duties (NSW) v Buckle* (1998) 192 CLR 226 at 246 [48].
89. (2003) 130 FCR 12 at 35–36.
90. [1895] AC 186 at 198.

trust into the trusts for his daughters. He also transferred a number of shares into the daughters' trusts. Later that year he appointed Kennon as joint trustee, with himself, of the four trusts to the daughters. Mrs Spry made an application to the Family Court seeking to set aside the 1998 document which had removed her as a beneficiary, and the later transactions that benefited the daughters. At trial, Strickland J found in favour of Mrs Spry and set aside the transactions using s 106B of the *Family Law Act 1975* (Cth). Strickland J ordered that Dr Spry pay the wife a sum of over $2m. The Full Court dismissed an appeal and the matter then went on appeal to the High Court.

Issue: The relevant issue was whether the rights of Dr Spry and Mrs Spry were 'property of the marriage' within the meaning of s 79 of the *Family Law Act 1975* (Cth).

Decision: A majority of the High Court found that the trial decision and the decision of the Full Family Court should be upheld (French CJ, Gummow, Hayne and Keifel JJ; Heydon J dissenting). French CJ found that Dr Spry's powers of appointment over the trustee meant that he had control of the trust property. His Honour found that trust property coupled with the trustee's power was property of the marriage. Equally, French CJ also found that Mrs Spry's rights to be appointed and her equitable right to due consideration were property of the marriage. Gummow and Hayne JJ also found that the wife's right to be considered by the trustee was property of the marriage.

Extracts: The extract from the judgment of French CJ and the joint judgment of Gummow and Hayne JJ discusses the reasons for treating the rights under a discretionary trust as 'property' for the purposes of the Family Law Act.

French CJ

[385] ... Dr Spry created the Trust. He was the settlor. He so designated himself in cl 1 of the 1981 Instrument. He appointed himself as trustee. He assumed the power to appoint and remove further trustees. He did so, according to the terms of the 1981 Instrument, in his personal capacity. The power to vary the Trust he conferred upon himself [386] personally as 'the settlor'. That power was not constrained by fiduciary duties.[91] It was, however, limited so as not to authorise an increase in his rights to the beneficial enjoyment of the fund. Under the terms of the Trust neither he nor any of the other 'beneficiaries' had any rights to the beneficial enjoyment of the fund or any portion of it except upon his decision as trustee to apply all or any of it to himself or one or more of the other beneficiaries pursuant to cl 6. While the character of the Trust remained unchanged and Dr Spry remained as trustee there was, as counsel for Mrs Spry submitted, no beneficial interest in possession in any of the objects of the Trust including Dr Spry.

The Trust fell within the genus of 'discretionary trust', a term which has 'no fixed meaning and is used to describe particular features of certain express trusts'.[92] Absent an

---

91. On the other hand, a trustee exercising such a power would owe a fiduciary duty to the beneficiaries: *Lock v Westpac Banking Corporation* (1991) 25 NSWLR 593 at 609 per Waddell CJ in Eq.
92. *Chief Commissioner of Stamp Duties (NSW) v Buckle* (1998) 192 CLR 226 at 234 [8].

obligation on the part of the trustee to apply any of the income or capital of the Trust to any of the beneficiaries at any time it answered the description 'purely discretionary'[93] or 'non-exhaustive'.[94] The class of beneficiaries was 'open'. It extended to the spouses from time to time of the issue of [Dr Spry's father,] Charles Chambers Fowell Spry and further issue of that issue, including persons unborn when the Trust was created, and their spouses from time to time.

As sole trustee of the Trust Dr Spry had the legal title. He was the only person entitled in possession to the assets. His power as trustee to apply the income or capital under the terms of the Trust was not a species of property according to the general law[95] but his legal title was.

Absent a specific application of Trust capital or income to one of the objects of the Trust, there was no equitable interest in its assets held by anyone. There did not need to be. In *Glenn v Federal Commissioner of Land Tax*[96] Griffith CJ declined to accept 'the assumption that whenever the legal estate in land is vested in a trustee there must be some person other than the trustee entitled to it in equity'.[97] The Privy Council, in similar vein, pointed out in *Commissioner of Stamp Duties (Qld) v Livingston*[98] that the law does not require for all [387] purposes and at every moment in time, the separate existence of two different kinds of estate or interest in property, the legal and the equitable.

In *CPT Custodian Pty Ltd v Commissioner of State Revenue (Vic)*[99] the Court described the observation of Griffith CJ in *Glenn* as 'a prescient rejection of a "dogma" that, where ownership is vested in a trustee, equitable ownership must necessarily be vested in someone else because it is an essential attribute of a trust that it confers upon individuals a complex of beneficial legal relations which may be called ownership'.[100]

Against that background it is necessary to consider the question at the heart of the present appeals, namely whether Dr Spry or his wife or both of them had, prior to 1998, interests in or in relation to the assets of the Trust that could answer the description of 'property of the parties to the marriage' in s 79(1).

The assets of the trust as property

The word 'property' is used in different ways in different statutory contexts. There have been, for example, many cases in which the question has arisen whether and when the objects of a discretionary trust have 'property' interests for the purpose of revenue legislation.[101]

Section 79(1) of the *Family Law Act 1975* (Cth) (the Act) and the non-exhaustive definition of property in s 4(1) of the Act had their antecedent in s 86(1) of the *Matrimonial*

93. *Federal Commissioner of Taxation v Vegners* (1989) 90 ALR 547 at 552; 20 ATR 1645 at 1649.
94. Thomas and Hudson, *The Law of Trusts*, 2004, p 184.
95. *O'Grady v Wilmot* [1916] 2 AC 231 at 270.
96. (1915) 20 CLR 490.
97. (1915) 20 CLR 490 at 497.
98. (1964) 112 CLR 12 at 22; [1965] AC 694 at 712–713.
99. (2005) 224 CLR 98.
100. (2005) 224 CLR 98 at 112 [25].
101. See generally Hardingham and Baxt, *Discretionary Trusts*, 1984, pp 134–141.

Causes Act 1959 (Cth). The collocation 'property to which the parties are, or either of them is, entitled (whether in possession or reversion)' can be traced back to its gendered ancestor in s 45 of the *Matrimonial Causes Act 1857 (UK)* which applied to the property of an adulterous wife.

Section 79 confers a wide discretionary power to vary the legal interests in any property of the parties to a marriage or either of them and to make orders for a settlement of property in substitution for any interest in the property. It is subject to the limitation that it validly applies only with respect to a claim based on circumstances arising out of the marriage relationship.[102] The word 'property', appearing in the section, construed by reference to its ancestry in matrimonial causes statutes, has been given a wide meaning. In 1977 the Full Court of the Family Court said:

> The word has also been comprehensively defined in statutes both State and Imperial relating to married women's property. We do not propose to instance those definitions here, but in *Jones v* [388] *Skinner*[103] Langdale MR said: 'Property is the most comprehensive of all terms which can be used inasmuch as it is indicative and descriptive of every possible interest which the party can have.' This is a definition which commends itself to us as being descriptive of the nature of the concept of 'property' to which it is intended that the Family Law Act 1975 should relate and over which the Family Court of Australia should have jurisdiction to intervene when disputes arise in relation to the property of spouses as between themselves or when the court is asked to exercise the powers conferred upon it under Pt VIII or its injunctive powers under s 114 so far as they are expressed to relate to a property of the party to a marriage.[104]

In *Kelly [No 2]*[105] the Full Court of the Family Court did not think the word wide enough to cover the assets of a trust in which the relevant party to the marriage was neither settlor nor appointor nor beneficiary and over which he or she had no control.[106] The Court was concerned, inter alia, with the assets of a family company and family trust which were under the 'de facto control' of the husband. The assets could be taken into consideration as a 'financial resource' of the husband within the meaning of s 75(2)(b) of the Family Law Act. The trust assets, however, did not fall within the description of the 'property' of the husband for the purposes of s 79 because 'the husband could not assert any legal or equitable right in respect of them'.[107] That was a case in which the husband had neither a legal nor a beneficial interest.

In *Ashton*[108] a husband who had been the trustee of a family trust replaced himself as trustee with a company but continued as sole appointor. He was not a beneficiary but received income from the trust. It was conceded that he was 'in full control of the assets of the trust'.[109] The evidence made clear that he applied the assets and income from them

---

102. *Dougherty v Dougherty* (1987) 163 CLR 278 at 286 per Mason CJ, Wilson and Dawson JJ.
103. (1835) 5 LJ Ch 87 at 90.
104. *In Marriage of Duff* (1977) 29 FLR 46 at 55–56.
105. *In Marriage of Kelly [No 2]* (1981) 7 Fam LR 762.
106. (1981) 7 Fam LR 762 at 764, 768.
107. (1981) 7 Fam LR 762 at 768.
108. *In Marriage of Ashton* (1986) 11 Fam LR 457.
109. (1986) 11 Fam LR 457 at 461.

as he wished and for his own benefit.[110] The Full Court held that '[n]o person other than the husband has any real interest in the property or income of the trust except at the will of the husband'.[111] Special leave to appeal from that decision was refused by the High Court on 5 December 1986 (Gibbs CJ, Wilson and Brennan JJ).[112]

Where the husband was not entitled to be a trustee but was sole appointor and also a beneficiary, the Full Court of the Family Court in **[389]** Goodwin upheld a finding that 'the trust property was, in reality, the property of the husband'[113] and in so doing applied as a statement of principle the perhaps unremarkable proposition that:

> [T]he question whether the property of the trust is, in reality, the property of the parties or one of them … is a matter dependent upon the facts and circumstances of each particular case including the terms of the relevant trust deed.[114]

In that case the husband had the sole power of appointment of the trustee which was a creature under his control and he was a beneficiary to whom the trustee could make payments exclusive of other beneficiaries as the husband saw fit.[115]

Although a settlor is taken to transfer to the trustee the property in respect of which he or she creates a trust, there may be retained a right to take a benefit under it. Prior to the 1983 Deed Dr Spry as sole trustee had the 'absolute discretion' to apply all or any part of the income and/or capital of the fund to himself as one of the 'beneficiaries'. On the basis of that power, and consistently with authority including the decisions of the Full Court referred to above, the assets of the Trust would properly have been regarded as his property as a party to the marriage for the purposes of s 79. But the coexistence of the power together with Dr Spry's status as a beneficiary does not define a necessary condition of that conclusion.

By the 1983 Deed Dr Spry removed himself as a beneficiary of the Trust. In terms the 1983 Deed provided that he 'releases and abandons all and any beneficial interest … in the trust fund or income'. This left him, however, in possession of the assets, with the legal title to them and to the income which they generated unless and until he should decide to apply any of the capital or income to any of the continuing beneficiaries. The question remains whether the Trust fund was part of the 'property of the parties to the marriage' at that time within the meaning of s 79.

Counsel for Mrs Spry submitted that when the primary judge determined the proceedings the assets of the Trust were the property of a party to the marriage as Dr Spry was the only person entitled in possession to them. On that basis the Family Court had the power to make the order it did. No object in the Trust had any fixed or vested entitlement. Dr Spry was not obliged to distribute to anyone. The default distribution (cl 7) gave male beneficiaries other than Dr Spry no more than a contingent remainder.

---

110. (1986) 11 Fam LR 457 at 461.
111. (1986) 11 Fam LR 457 at 462.
112. See also *In Marriage of Davidson [No 2]* (1990) 101 FLR 373 for a similar conclusion on a similar trust deed.
113. *In Marriage of Goodwin* (1990) 101 FLR 386 at 392.
114. (1990) 101 FLR 386 at 392.
115. (1990) 101 FLR 386 at 392.

None had a vested interest subject to divestiture. The application of s 79, as a matter of construction, to the Trust assets was said to be supported by a number of considerations. Among these was the 'true character' of the Trust as a vehicle for 'Dr and Mrs Spry and their children'.

[390] In response, counsel for Dr Spry submitted that his legal title, absent any beneficial interest, did not justify treating the Trust property as his own. A policy question was said to be raised. It would be 'inappropriate' for the Court to treat the assets of a trust as a trustee's property where the trustee had no interest under the trust. The Court was invited to consider the implications of Mrs Spry's submissions for the case of a trustee with no personal relationship to the beneficial objects of the trust. The Family Court, it was said, must take the property of a party to the marriage as it finds it. It cannot ignore the interests of third parties nor the existence of conditions or covenants limiting the rights of the party who owns the property. In this connection reference was made to *Ascot Investments Pty Ltd v Harper*.[116]

In my opinion, the argument advanced on behalf of Mrs Spry should be accepted save that it is the Trust assets, coupled with the trustee's power, prior to the 1998 Instrument, to appoint them to her and her equitable right to due consideration, that should be regarded as the relevant property. It should be accepted that, in the unusual circumstances of this case and but for the 1998 Instrument and the 18 January 2002 Dispositions, s 79 would have had effective application to the Trust assets. Dr Spry was the sole trustee of a discretionary family trust and the person with the only interest in those assets as well as the holder of a power, inter alia, to appoint them entirely to his wife. This is perhaps not quite the same as the second argument advanced on behalf of Mrs Spry which is accepted by Gummow and Hayne JJ in their joint judgment. But the distinction may not amount to a difference. Even on the second argument the power of appointment and the right to due consideration, absent a legal estate upon which they can operate, are meaningless.

The terms 'dry legal title' or 'dry legal estate or interest' have sometimes been used to describe the legal estate in property held on trust.[117] The term describes a legal title divorced from any powers or duties. Under the general law such a title could not be treated as property of the trustee. But where a statute is involved the matter is one of interpretation. Even under the general law, where the legal title is associated with substantial powers or duties, the 'dry' metaphor may not be appropriate.[118]

The word 'property' in s 79 is to be read as part of the collocation 'property of the parties to the marriage'. It is to be read widely and conformably with the purposes of the *Family Law Act*. In the case of a non-exhaustive discretionary trust with an open class of beneficiaries, [391] there is no obligation to apply the assets or income of the trust to anyone. Their application may serve a wide range of purposes. In the present case, prior to the 1998 Instrument those purposes could have included the maintenance or enrichment of Mrs Spry.

---

116. (1981) 148 CLR 337 at 354 per Gibbs J.
117. *Molloy v Federal Commissioner of Land Tax* (1937) 58 CLR 352 at 360; *Burke v Dawes* (1938) 59 CLR 1 at 21; *Perpetual Trustee Co Ltd v Commissioner of Stamp Duties (NSW)* (1941) 64 CLR 492 at 510; *Re Australian Elizabethan Theatre Trust* (1991) 30 FCR 491 at 501.
118. *Minnesota v United States* (1939) 305 US 382 at 386 fn 1.

Where property is held under such a trust by a party to a marriage and the property has been acquired by or through the efforts of that party or his or her spouse, whether before or during the marriage, it does not, in my opinion, necessarily lose its character as 'property of the parties to the marriage' because the party has declared a trust of which he or she is trustee and can, under the terms of that trust, give the property away to other family or extended family members at his or her discretion.

For so long as Dr Spry retained the legal title to the Trust fund coupled with the power to appoint the whole of the fund to his wife and her equitable right, it remained, in my opinion, property of the parties to the marriage for the purposes of the power conferred on the Family Court by s 79. The assets would have been unarguably property of the marriage absent subjection to the Trust.

An exercise of the power under s 79 requiring the application of the assets of the Trust in whole or in part in favour of Mrs Spry would, prior to the 1998 Instrument, have been consistent with the proper exercise of Dr Spry's powers as trustee and would have involved no breach by him of his duty to the other beneficiaries.

As to the position of the other beneficiaries, it has long been accepted that in some circumstances the Family Court has power to make an order which will indirectly affect the position of a third party. That acceptance, which predated the enactment of Pt VIIIAA of the *Family Law Act*, is reflected in the judgment of Gibbs J in *Ascot Investments Pty Ltd v Harper*.[119] That case concerned the validity of an order in favour of a wife made by the Family Court requiring directors of a company not completely controlled by the husband to register a transfer of shares into her name. It is in that context that the passage relied upon by Dr Spry is to be understood:

> Except in the case of shams, and companies that are mere puppets of a party to the marriage, the Family Court must take the property of a party to the marriage as it finds it. The Family Court cannot ignore the interests of third parties in the property, nor the existence of conditions or covenants that limit the rights of the party who owns it.[120]

The articles of the company in that case gave to its directors a discretion to register or refuse to register a transfer of any shares in the company. The Family Court was found to have no power to direct them as to the manner in which their discretion should be exercised. Giving full effect to the generality of the passage quoted from the judgment of [392] Gibbs J, the case does not stand against the proposition that s 79 would apply in the circumstances of this case where the only property interests are those of the trustee who is a party to the marriage, and where no other beneficiary has any legal or equitable interest apart from a right to due consideration and administration. That, of course, is a right which is a relevant consideration informing the exercise of the Court's discretion as is any indirect effect upon a third party's rights.[121]

The preceding conclusion does not involve some general extension of s 79 which would require that it be hedged about with protective discretions of uncertain application to prevent its intrusion into trust arrangements affecting assets foreign or extraneous to

---

119. (1981) 148 CLR 337 at 354.
120. (1981) 148 CLR 337 at 355 per Gibbs J.
121. *R v Dovey; Ex parte Ross* (1979) 141 CLR 526 at 534 per Gibbs J, Barwick CJ and Mason J agreeing.

those acquired by the parties to the marriage in their own right. So if the husband were trustee of a charitable trust or executor of the will of a friend or client the mere legal title to the assets of such trusts, because of their origins and character, could not be regarded as part of the husband's property as a party to the marriage within the meaning of the *Family Law Act*. Importantly, in such a trust there could be no power of appointment to his wife and no corresponding equitable right enjoyed by her. The question of a trust involving a combination of purposes and family and extraneous assets does not arise.

The characterisation of the assets of the Trust, coupled with Dr Spry's power to appoint them to his wife and her equitable right to due consideration, as property of the parties to the marriage is supported by particular factors. It is supported by his legal title to the assets, the origins of their greater part as property acquired during the marriage, the absence of any equitable interest in them in any other party, the absence of any obligation on his part to apply all or any of the assets to any beneficiary and the contingent character of the interests of those who might be entitled to take upon a default distribution at the distribution date.

....

[393] The rights to due consideration and due administration as 'property'

Each of the beneficiaries had the right to compel the trustee to consider whether or not to make a distribution to him or her and a right to the proper administration of the Trust.[122] In *Gartside v Inland Revenue Commissioners*, Lord Wilberforce put it thus:

> No doubt in a certain sense a beneficiary under a discretionary trust has an 'interest': the nature of it may, sufficiently for the purpose, be spelt out by saying that he has a right to be considered as a potential recipient of benefit by the trustees and a right to have his interest protected by a court of equity. Certainly that is so, and when it is said that he has a right to have the trustees exercise their discretion 'fairly' or 'reasonably' or 'properly' that indicates clearly enough that some objective consideration (not stated explicitly in declaring the discretionary trust, but latent in it) must be applied by the trustees and that the right is more than a mere spes. But that does not mean that he has an interest which is capable of being taxed by reference to its extent in the trust fund's income: it may be a right, with some degree of concreteness or solidity, one which attracts the protection of a court of equity, yet it may still lack the necessary quality of definable extent which must exist before it can be taxed.[123]

The rights to consideration and to due administration are in the nature of equitable choses in action. There has been considerable judicial discussion about the nature of a beneficiary's right to due administration in the case of the residuary legatee of an unadministered deceased estate and members of superannuation funds whose benefits have not vested. The residuary legatee has an equitable right,[124] 'a chose in action, capable of being invoked for any purpose connected with the proper administration of [the] estate'.[125] Such a right has been treated as property for the purposes of the *Bankruptcy*

---

122. *Gartside v Inland Revenue Commissioners* [1968] AC 553 at 617.
123. [1968] AC 553 at 617–618; see also *Sainsbury v Inland Revenue Commissioners* [1970] Ch 712 at 725.
124. *Livingston v Commissioner of Stamp Duties (Qld)* (1960) 107 CLR 411 at 444 per Fullagar J.
125. *Commissioner of Stamp Duties (Qld) v Livingston* (1964) 112 CLR 12 at 27; [1965] AC 694 at 717.

Act 1966 (Cth).[126] In the case of a residuary legatee the right to due administration is connected to a real expectancy of an interest in the property. The same is true for the members of a superannuation fund although vesting of a benefit may be many years in the future. However, the right to due administration taken by itself in relation to a superannuation fund was described by the Full Court of the Family Court in 1986, in a brief consideration of the question, as 'an empty present right of no relevance'.[127]

In *Evans*[128] the majority in the Full Court of the Family Court found that consideration of the right to due administration of a superannuation fund offered 'no solution as to how realistically to make practical orders under s 79 about that "property" until it is in fact received'.[129] The case concerned a future entitlement to benefits from a superannuation fund. Nygh J drew the analogy between the unvested interest in a superannuation fund protected by a right of due administration and 'the interest which a potential beneficiary has in the proper administration of a trust'.[130]

The beneficiary of a non-exhaustive discretionary trust who does not control the trustee directly or indirectly has a right to due consideration and to due administration of the trust but it is difficult to value those rights when the beneficiary has no present entitlement and may never have any entitlement to any part of the income or capital of the trust.

Gummow and Hayne JJ, in their joint reasons, characterise Mrs Spry's right with respect to the due administration of the Trust as part of her property for the purposes of the *Family Law Act*. I respectfully agree with their Honours that prior to the 1998 Instrument the equitable right to due administration of the Trust fund could be taken into account as part of the property of Mrs Spry as a party to the marriage. So too could her equitable entitlement to due consideration in relation to the application of the income and capital. In so agreeing, however, I acknowledge, consistently with the observations of the Full Court in *Hauff* and *Evans*, that it is difficult to put a value on either of these rights though a valuation might not be beyond the actuarial arts in relation to the right to due consideration.

Dr Spry's power as trustee to apply assets or income of the Trust to Mrs Spry prior to the 1998 Instrument was, as pointed out by Gummow and Hayne JJ, able to be treated for the purposes of the *Family Law Act* as a species of property held by him as a party to the marriage, albeit subject to the fiduciary duty to consider all beneficiaries. This is so even though it may not be property according to the general law. So characterised for the purposes of the *Family Law Act* it had an attribute in common with the legal estate he had in the [395] assets as trustee. He could not apply them for his own benefit but that did not take them out of the realm of property of a party to the marriage for the purposes of s 79. In so far as Gummow and Hayne JJ rely upon the property comprised by Dr Spry's power as trustee and Mrs Spry's equitable rights prior to 1998, I agree that these property rights were capable of providing a basis for the orders which Strickland J made. I do so, as already indicated, by considering that power and the equitable rights, in conjunction with Dr Spry's legal title to the Trust assets, without which the power and the rights were meaningless.

---

126. *Official Receiver in Bankruptcy v Schultz* (1990) 170 CLR 306 at 314.
127. *In Marriage of Hauff* (1986) 10 Fam LR 1076 at 1081.
128. *In Marriage of Evans* (1991) 104 FLR 130.
129. (1991) 104 FLR 130 at 139.
130. (1991) 104 FLR 130 at 144.

Mrs Spry's right to due consideration as an object of the Trust could also be taken into account in determining whether it was just and equitable to make an order under s 79 on the basis that the assets of the Trust were property of the marriage. As noted in the preceding section the equitable entitlement of the children and other existing beneficiaries to due consideration could also be taken into account in making that judgment. There is no reason to suggest that his Honour did not do so appropriately.

Conclusions

The assets of the Trust, coupled with Dr Spry's power to appoint them to his wife and her right to due consideration, were, until the 1998 Instrument, the property of the parties to the marriage for the purposes of s 79. The fact that Dr Spry removed himself as a beneficiary by the 1983 Deed does not affect that conclusion. Because the 1998 Instrument effectively disposed of Mrs Spry's equitable right to be considered in the application of the Trust fund, and having regard to the trial judge's conclusions about the purpose of the instrument, the order setting it aside was an appropriate exercise of the Family Court's power under s 106B. Mrs Spry's equitable right could then be considered as part of the property of the parties to the marriage.

Gummow and Hayne JJ

'With respect to the property of the parties to the marriage'

[396] ... The phrase in para (ca) 'with respect to the property of the parties to the marriage or either of them' should be read in a fashion which [397] advances rather than constrains the subject, scope and purpose of the legislation. In particular, as statements by this Court[131] illustrate, the term 'property' is not a term of art with one specific and precise meaning. It is always necessary to pay close attention to any statutory context in which the term is used.[132] In particular it is, of course, necessary to have regard to the subject matter, scope and purpose of the relevant statute.

The questions that arise in these matters raise a dispute about construction of the Act. That dispute is not resolved by considering only the ways in which the term 'property' may be used in relation to trusts of the kinds described as 'discretionary trusts'. As Binnie J, writing for the Supreme Court of Canada, has recently said[133] (albeit in a different statutory context):

> The task is to interpret [the relevant statutes] in a purposeful way having regard 'to their entire context, in their grammatical and ordinary sense harmoniously with the scheme of the Act, the object of the Act, and the intention of Parliament'.[134]

And as Binnie J also said, because an interest (in that case, a fishing licence):

---

131. These include *Yanner v Eaton* (1999) 201 CLR 351 at 365–367 [17]–[19], 388–389 [85]–[86]; *Zhu v Treasurer (NSW)* (2004) 218 CLR 530 at 577 [135].

132. *Australian Securities and Investments Commission v Carey [No 6]* (2006) 153 FCR 509 at 518–519 [29]; *Saulnier v Royal Bank of Canada WBLI Inc* [2008] 3 SCR 166 at 178 [16].

133. *Saulnier v Royal Bank of Canada WBLI Inc* [2008] 3 SCR 166 at 178 [16].

134. Sullivan, *Sullivan and Driedger on the Construction of Statutes*, 2002, p 1.

may not qualify as 'property' for the general purposes of the common law does not mean that it is also excluded from the reach of the statutes. For particular purposes Parliament can and does create its own lexicon.[135]

[91] Section 4(1) of the Act provides:

property, in relation to the parties to a marriage or either of them, means property to which those parties are, or that party is, as the case may be, entitled, whether in possession or reversion.

Shortly after the commencement of the Act, the Full Court in *In Marriage of Duff*[136] considered that definition and said that an understanding of the term 'property' in a comprehensive sense:

... commends itself to us as being descriptive of the nature of the concept of 'property' to which it is intended that [the Act] should relate and over which the Family Court of Australia should have jurisdiction to intervene when disputes arise in relation to the property of spouses as between themselves or when the court is asked to exercise the powers conferred upon it under Pt VIII or its injunctive powers under s 114 so far as they are expressed to relate to a property of the party to a marriage. [398]

We are of the view that the intention of s 79 is to enable the court to take into account and assess all the property of the parties upon being asked by either of them to make an order altering the interests of the parties in the property. We are further of the view that when s 4 defines property as being 'property to which the parties are entitled whether in possession or reversion' the words 'whether in possession or reversion' are not intended to indicate that the kind of property with which this Act can deal must be property to which a party is entitled in possession or reversion but rather the phrase 'whether in possession or reversion' is, as a matter of grammar, an adverbial phrase which qualifies the word 'entitled'. The phrase means that the entitlement to the property may be either in possession or reversion, ie the phrase is descriptive of the entitlement and not of the property and it removes any fetter upon the court in dealing with property under this Act by limiting the nature of the entitlement thereto to entitlement in possession.

...

[408] Reference was made earlier in these reasons to the comprehensive sense in which the term 'property' is defined in s 4(1) of the Act.[137] And it will also be recalled that the 'property' which may be the subject of orders under s 79(1) of the Act is 'the property of *the parties* to the marriage or *either of them*' (emphasis added). The right of the wife with respect to the due administration of the Trust was included in her property for the purposes of the Act. The submissions by Mr Gleeson to this effect should be accepted. The submissions to the contrary by Mr Myers should not be accepted. And in considering what is the property of the *parties* to the marriage (as distinct from what might be identified as the property of the husband) it is important to recognise not only that the right of the wife was accompanied at least by the fiduciary duty of the husband to

---

135. *Saulnier v Royal Bank of Canada WBLI Inc* [2008] 3 SCR 166 at 178 [16].
136. (1977) 29 FLR 46 at 55–56.
137. See *Kennon v Spry* (2008) 238 CLR 366 at 397.

consider whether and in what way the power should be exercised, but also that, during the marriage, the power could have been exercised by appointing the whole of the Trust assets to the wife. Observing that the husband could not have conferred the same benefit on himself as he could on his wife denies only that he had property in the assets of the Trust, it does not deny that part of the property of the parties to the marriage, within the meaning of the Act, was his power to appoint the whole of the property to his wife and her right to a due administration of the Trust.

...

[411] The conclusion reached by the trial judge (erroneously) that the husband could have applied the whole or part of the Trust fund to or for *his* own benefit is inconclusive of the outcome. The jurisdiction being exercised by the Family Court was, as earlier indicated, jurisdiction over 'proceedings between the parties to a marriage *with respect to the property of the parties to the marriage or either of them*'[138] (emphasis added). What matters in this case is that once the 1998 Instrument and the 2002 Instrument were set aside by the s 106B orders, the property of the parties to the marriage or either of them was to be identified as including the right of the wife to due administration of the Trust, accompanied by the fiduciary duty of the husband, as trustee, to consider whether and in what way the power should be exercised. And because, during the marriage, the husband could have appointed the whole of the Trust fund to the wife, the potential enjoyment of the *whole* of that fund was 'property of the parties to the marriage or either of them'. Furthermore, because the relevant power permitted appointment of the whole of the Trust fund to the wife absolutely, the value of that property was the value of the assets of the Trust. In deciding what orders should be made under ss 79 and 80 of the Act, the value of that property was properly taken into account. Wrongly attributing its value to the husband is irrelevant to the ultimate orders made.

Comments

1. See Radan & Stewart at **21.18–21.25**.
2. After the decision Dr Spry liquidated his assets and the assets of the daughters' trusts, realising over $4.4m. In a restaurant conversation with two of his daughters he threatened to 'disappear' and he said that as a last resort he would burn the money and go to gaol rather than give Mrs Spry her share. One of the daughters later went to Dr Spry's house and discovered over $4.4m in cash. She rang Mrs Spry and they removed the money whereafter it was deposited in the trust account of Mrs Spry's solicitor. Enforcement proceedings were commenced. After Dr Spry agreed to some of the money being released to the wife (in exchange for some funds being released to him for legal expenses) Coleman J ordered that the amounts in trust be used to satisfy the outstanding sums to Mrs Spry (plus interest), with the rest being released to Dr Spry (apart from a sum to be used to pay costs). Dr Spry appealed that decision and said that the moneys were trust moneys which belonged beneficially to his daughters. The Full Court of the Family Court (May, Boland and O'Ryan JJ) upheld the orders of Coleman J: *Stephens v Stephens (Enforcement)* [2009] FAMCAFC 240.

---

138. Section 4(1) definition of 'matrimonial cause', para (ca).

22

DECLARATIONS

Introduction

22.1 This chapter deals with the principles governing the granting of declarations. A declaration is a non-coercive order granted by a court that states with finality the true nature of the law or the rights, duties and interests of the applicant under it.

The cases extracted in this chapter discuss the following:

- the availability of mere declaratory relief: *Forster v Jododex Pty Ltd* (1972) 127 CLR 421;
- the availability of declaratory relief for breaches of public rights: *Australian Conservation Foundation Inc v Commonwealth of Australia* (1980) 146 CLR 493; and
- the availability of declaratory relief in criminal proceedings: *Sankey v Whitlam* (1978) 142 CLR 1.

Mere declaratory relief

22.2   Forster v Jododex Australia Pty Ltd (1972) 127 CLR 421

Court: High Court of Australia

Facts: Jododex was granted an exploration licence pursuant to the *Mining Act 1906* (NSW) by the NSW Minister of Mines for a 12-month period. Several six-month extensions were also granted to Jododex after it had applied successfully to renew the licence. It transpired that Forster had also obtained authorities to enter parts of the land to which Jododex's licence applied for the purpose of mineral exploration. A mining warden began an investigation into the processing of Forster's applications during the final renewal term of Jododex's licence. Before the investigation had been completed, Jododex began proceedings in equity seeking a declaration that Forster could not be granted an authority to enter because Jododex had in existence a valid exploration licence. Street J in the Supreme Court of New South Wales granted the declaration. Forster then appealed to the High Court.

Issue: One of the principal issues before the High Court was whether the Supreme Court, in its equitable jurisdiction, had the power to make declarations in respect of a matter that was at the same time being investigated by a mining warden imbued with statutory powers for that purpose.

Decision: The High Court (McTiernan, Walsh, Gibbs, Mason and Stephen JJ) unanimously held that Street J had the jurisdiction to grant the declaration even though the warden also had the power to determine the matter in dispute. However, only a majority of the High Court (McTiernan, Mason and Stephen JJ; Walsh and Gibbs JJ dissenting) affirmed the order made by Street J. The division of opinion here was over whether Jododex had a valid exploration licence on the relevant date. If it did not, there was no scope for Street J to have granted the declaration. The majority of the High Court held that Jododex had a licence on the relevant time, whereas the minority held that it did not.

Extracts: The extracts from the judgment of Gibbs J discuss the jurisdiction of the court to grant declaratory relief, including mere declaratory relief.

Gibbs J

[433] The jurisdiction of a judge of the Supreme Court of New South Wales sitting in equity to make a declaration of right was when the proceedings were instituted and when the decree was made conferred by s 10 of the *Equity Act*, 1901 (as amended) (NSW). To understand the effect of that section in its most recent form [434] it is necessary to trace its history. Originally it reproduced s 50 of the *Chancery Procedure Act* 1852 (UK) which, according to the decisions which interpreted it, enabled a declaratory decree to be made only if there was a right to some consequential relief which, if asked for, might have been granted by the court, or, in certain cases, by some other court.[1] The power of the court was extended in England ... and by the *Administration of Justice Act* 1924 (NSW) s 10 was amended so that it substantially reproduced the words of [the English rule]. However, New South Wales had not then adopted the *Judicature Act* procedure and common law and equity were separately administered within the Supreme Court; this, indeed, remained the position until after the decree was made in the present proceedings. It was held by Harvey CJ in Eq in *Tooth & Co Ltd v Coombes* that:

> ... the subject matter of this section is 'a suit in equity' a well known form of procedure, viz: a suit for equitable relief or relating to equitable rights and titles.[2]

This restrictive view, that s 10 conferred on a judge sitting in equity jurisdiction to make a declaration of right only in proceedings for equitable relief or relating to equitable rights or titles, was adopted by this Court, although not without dissent.[3] However, in 1965, s 10 was further amended. Sub-section (1) of that section then read as follows:

> In addition to the jurisdiction which is otherwise vested in it, the Court shall have jurisdiction to make binding declarations of right whether or not any consequential relief is or could be claimed, and whether or not the suit in which the declaration is sought is a suit for equitable relief or a suit which relates to equitable rights or titles.

> No suit shall be open to objection on the ground that a merely declaratory decree is sought thereby.

1.   *Walsh v Alexander* (1913) 16 CLR 293 at 304–5.
2.   *Tooth & Co Ltd v Coombes* (1925) 42 WN (NSW) 93 at 94.
3.   *David Jones Ltd v Leventhal* (1927) 40 CLR 357.

Sub-section (2) provided, inter alia:

> Without limiting the generality of the jurisdiction conferred by subsection one of this section, the Court may by decree or order declare - ...
>
> (b) the interests, powers, rights and liabilities or duties of any persons arising under – ...
>
> [435] (vii) any Act or any ordinance, rule, regulation or other instrument having effect under any Act or by reason of any executive, ministerial or administrative act done or purporting to be done in pursuance of any Act or of any such ordinance, rule, regulation or other instrument.

This was the form of the section at the date of the decree. Although, at the date when the amending Act of 1965 was passed, law and equity were still separately administered in the Supreme Court of New South Wales, it cannot, in my opinion, be doubted that the object of the amendment to s 10 in 1965 was to free the Equity Court from the restrictions that had been held to exist in *Tooth & Co Ltd v Coombes* and the cases that had followed that decision. The very words of Sir John Harvey, which had been repeatedly quoted in subsequent decisions, are used in the section. In *Hume v Munro*, Williams J had said:

> In my opinion the principles laid down in the English decisions relating to the construction of [the English rule], apply to s 10, subject to any limitation that flows from the fact that the court of equity only has jurisdiction where equitable relief is sought or the right or title relied on is equitable.[4]

The amendment to s 10 removed this limitation. Thereafter the power of a judge sitting in equity in New South Wales to grant declaratory relief was as wide as that given to a judge of the High Court in England by [the English rule]. In *Salmar Holdings Pty Ltd v Hornsby Shire Council* Mason JA ... said:

> The jurisdictional limitations on the power to grant declaratory relief are, therefore, no more extensive than the limitations applicable to the power to grant declaratory relief exercisable by a court under a judicature system.[5]

I fully agree with these remarks as to the effect of s 10 in its amended form. The detailed provisions of sub-s (2) were, I think, unnecessary to achieve this result, but they do support this conclusion.

The jurisdiction to make a declaration is a very wide one. Indeed, it has been said that, 'under [the English rule], the power of the Court to make a declaration, where it is a question of defining the rights of two parties, is almost unlimited; I might say only limited by its own discretion'.[6] However, the jurisdiction may be [436] ousted by statute, although the right of a subject to apply to the court for a determination of his rights will not be held to be excluded except by clear words.[7] In the present case it was submitted

---

4. *Hume v Monro* (1941) 65 CLR 351 at 369.
5. *Salmar Holdings Pty Ltd v Hornsby Shire Council* [1971] 1 NSWLR 192 at 202.
6. *Hanson v Radcliffe Urban District Council* [1922] 2 Ch 490 at 507.
7. *Pyx Granite Co Ltd v Ministry of Housing and Local Government* [1960] AC 260 at 286.

that the Act reveals an intention that the decision of a warden to grant or refuse an authority to enter should not be subject to review in proceedings for a declaration under s 10 of the *Equity Act*.

With all respect, I find it difficult to see any reason why the Court should have lacked jurisdiction to declare that Jododex held the right which it claimed, namely the right of the holder of an exploration license validly renewed. There is no provision in the Act that gives to any other tribunal exclusive jurisdiction to decide the question whether a person is the holder of a valid exploration license, or that otherwise withdraws the determination of that question from the jurisdiction of the Supreme Court. Section 183 of the Act provides that:

> No proceedings under this Act shall be removable by certiorari or otherwise into the Supreme Court.

That section obviously has no application to the present case, where no proceedings are sought to be removed. It has been held in the Supreme Court of New South Wales that prohibition will not lie against the grant by a warden of an authority to enter upon private lands.[8] The reason given was that the warden when so acting is not a court, but prohibition may be directed to bodies other than courts if they perform quasi-judicial functions.[9] However, it is not here necessary to consider whether the actual decision reached in *Ex parte Phillips*[10] was correct. The Supreme Court of New South Wales has also held that when a warden grants or refuses an application for an authority to enter, there are no 'proceedings' within s 168 of the Act and there is consequently no jurisdiction to state a case for the decision of the Supreme Court.[11] On the other hand, mandamus will lie to a warden who fails to hear and determine according to law an application for an authority to enter.[12] However, these decisions, which **[437]** indicate that one procedure is available and another is not to review the decision of a warden who grants or refuses an authority to enter, seem to me to have no relevance to the present question. There is nothing in the provisions considered in those cases that indicates a clear intention to exclude the power of the court to make a declaratory order. The Act does not provide a specific remedy to which the holder of an exploration license who seeks to establish the rights which it gives him is bound to resort. It was submitted that when s 10 of the *Equity Act* was amended in 1965 the legislature did not intend by those general provisions to alter the effect of the special provisions of the *Mining Act*, which was the subject of considerable authority. The purpose of amending s 10 was to provide a more extensive remedy of a general kind, and there is no possible justification for reading the section as though it contained words excepting from its operation cases arising under the *Mining Act*. Some reliance was placed by [Forster] upon *Toowoomba Foundry Pty Ltd v The Commonwealth*[13] where it was held that the decision of an independent tribunal

---

8. *Ex parte Phillips* (1906) 23 WN (NSW) 145, followed in *Ex parte Miller* (1907) 7 SR (NSW) 214.
9. *R v Connell; Ex parte Hetton Bellbird Collieries Ltd* (1944) 69 CLR 407 at 429.
10. (1906) 23 WN (NSW) 145.
11. *Wake v Murphy* (1916) 16 SR (NSW) 523; *Wallamaine Colliery Pty Ltd v Cam & Sons Pty Ltd* [1961] SR (NSW) 195; *Keogh v Heffernan* [1961] SR (NSW) 535.
12. *Wade v Burns* (1966) 115 CLR 537.
13. (1945) 71 CLR 545.

acting under a statute or regulation cannot be challenged in an action claiming only a declaration that the decision is invalid. Since, in the present case, the warden has made no decision, *Toowoomba Foundry Pty Ltd v The Commonwealth* is distinguishable, and it is unnecessary to consider whether that case is consistent with later decisions of the House of Lords.[14] It is true that the purpose of Jododex in seeking a declaration was to forestall a possible contrary decision by the warden, but that does not mean that the validity of any proceeding by the warden is challenged in these proceedings.[15]

It is neither possible nor desirable to fetter the broad discretion given by s 10 by laying down rules as to the manner of its exercise. It does, however, seem to me that the Scottish rules summarized by Lord Dunedin in *Russian Commercial and Industrial Bank v British Bank for Foreign Trade Ltd*, should in general be satisfied before the discretion is exercised in favour of making a declaration:

> The question must be a real and not a theoretical question; the person raising it must have a real interest to raise it; he [438] must be able to secure a proper contradictor, that is to say, some one presently existing who has a true interest to oppose the declaration sought.[16]

Beyond that, however, little guidance can be given. As Lord Radcliffe said in *Ibeneweka v Egbuna*:

> After all, it is doubtful if there is more of principle involved than the undoubted truth that the power to grant a declaration should be exercised with a proper sense of responsibility and a full realisation that judicial pronouncements ought not to be issued unless there are circumstances that call for their making. Beyond that there is no legal restriction on the award of a declaration.[17]

In the present case the question whether Jododex held a valid exploration license was in no way hypothetical. Jododex had a real interest to establish the validity of the license and thus ensure that the warden would not grant the authorities to enter which [Forster] sought. [Forster] had a real interest to contest Jododex's claim which if upheld must result in the refusal of [Forster's] applications. If it be assumed, contrary to the decided cases, that Jododex could have obtained prohibition if the warden had wrongly granted [Forster's] applications, the existence of the alternative remedy would not require the Court to refuse to make a declaration. In the first place, a declaration would be a more satisfactory remedy than prohibition, being quicker, simpler and attended by less doubts. Even if this were not so, it seems to me, on principle, that a plaintiff should not necessarily be refused one form of relief because another is available in the same court.[18]

---

14. Such as *Vine v National Dock Labour Board* [1957] AC 488 and *Pyx Granite Co Ltd v Ministry of Housing and Local Government* [1960] AC 260.
15. See *Mutual Life and Citizens' Assurance Co Ltd v Attorney-General (Cth)* (1961) 106 CLR 48 at 54.
16. *Russian Commercial and Industrial Bank v British Bank for Foreign Trade Ltd* [1921] 2 AC 438 at 448.
17. *Ibeneweka v Egbuna* [1964] 1 WLR 219 at 225.
18. See *Pyx Granite Co Ltd v Ministry of Housing and Local Government* [1960] AC 260 at 290.

Comments

1. See Radan & Stewart at **22.7–22.9**.
2. For a discussion of the historical background in New South Wales to the emergence of the jurisdiction to grant mere declaratory relief see P Radan, 'The Emergence of the Jurisdiction to Grant Mere Declaratory Relief in New South Wales' (2006) 1 *Journal of Equity* 41.

Declarations and interferences with public rights

22.3 Australian Conservation Foundation Inc v Commonwealth of Australia (1980) 146 CLR 493

Court: High Court of Australia

Facts: A development company sought approval from the Commonwealth Government to establish and operate a resort at Farnborough in central Queensland. It also sought Reserve Bank approval for the borrowing of funds for the project from overseas. Federal regulations required the company to publish a draft environmental impact statement for public comment, in respect of which the Australian Conservation Foundation (ACF) lodged a submission. The responsible Minister in the government announced foreign exchange approval soon thereafter, and the developer published a final environmental impact statement. The ACF began proceedings in the High Court, seeking declarations and other orders challenging the approvals given for the project under the relevant foreign exchange and administrative regulations. The government applied for the proceedings to be struck out for lack of standing. A single judge in the High Court refused the application and the ACF appealed.

Issue: The issue before the High Court was whether the ACF had standing to seek declarations as a public interest group rather than as an entity whose private rights had been infringed.

Decision: The majority of the High Court (Gibbs, Stephen and Mason JJ; Murphy J dissenting) ruled that the ACF did not have standing to seek declaratory relief.

Extracts: The extracts from the judgment of Gibbs J reflect the majority High Court view that the ACF, as a private entity, has no standing 'to prevent the violation of a public right or to enforce the performance of a public duty' and discuss the standing requirements in relation to infringements of public rights.

Gibbs J

[526] It is quite clear that an ordinary member of the public, who has no interest other than that which any member of the public has in upholding the law, has no standing to sue to prevent the violation of a public right or to enforce the performance of a public duty. There is no difference, in this respect, between the making of a declaration and the grant of an injunction. The assertion of public rights and the prevention of public

wrongs by means of those remedies is the responsibility of the Attorney-General, who may proceed either ex officio or on the relation of a private individual. A private citizen who has no special interest is incapable of bringing proceedings for that purpose, unless, of course, he is permitted by statute to do so.

The rules as to standing are the same whether the plaintiff seeks a declaration or an injunction. In *Boyce v Paddington Borough Council*, Buckley J stated the effect of the earlier authorities as follows:

> A plaintiff can sue without joining the Attorney-General in two cases: first, where the interference with the public right is [527] such as that some private right of his is at the same time interfered with ...; and, secondly, where no private right is interfered with, but the plaintiff, in respect of his public right, suffers special damage peculiar to himself from the interference with the public right.[19]

The rule thus stated received the approval of the House of Lords in *London Passenger Transport Board v Moscrop*.[20] However in *Attorney-General; Ex rel McWhirter v Independent Broadcasting Authority*, Lord Denning MR suggested that an individual member of the public can apply for a declaration or an injunction 'if the Attorney-General refuses leave in a proper case, or improperly or unreasonably delays in giving leave, or his machinery works too slowly'.[21] In *Gouriet v Union of Post Office Workers*[22] the House of Lords disapproved of this dictum and, after a full consideration of the authorities, rejected the notion that the question of standing is one that lies within the discretion of the court, and reaffirmed that a private individual has standing to seek a declaration or an injunction to enforce a public right or prevent a public wrong only in the cases mentioned in *Boyce v Paddington Borough Council*. The general principle stated in *Gouriet v Union of Postal Workers*, that a private person, who is in the same situation as any other member of the public, has no standing to claim either an injunction or a declaration to enforce a public right or duty, has been consistently applied in this Court.

Although the general rule is clear, the formulation of the exceptions to it which Buckley J made in *Boyce v Paddington Borough Council* is not altogether satisfactory. Indeed the words which he used are apt to be misleading. His reference to 'special damage' cannot be limited to actual pecuniary loss, and the words 'peculiar to himself' do not mean that the plaintiff, and no one else, must have suffered damage. However, the expression 'special damage peculiar to himself' in my opinion should be regarded as equivalent in meaning to 'having a special interest in the subject matter of the action'. The words appear to have been understood in this sense by Viscount Maugham in *London Passenger Transport Board v Moscrop*,[23] and by Lord Wilberforce and Lord Edmund-Davies in *Gouriet v Union of Post Office Workers*.[24] In this Court, the law was stated in a way that supports that view in *Anderson v The Commonwealth*. In that case, the plaintiff [528] claimed that an agreement between the Commonwealth and a State restricting the importation of

---

19. *Boyce v Paddington Borough Council* [1903] 1 Ch 109 at 114.
20. [1942] AC 332; esp at 344–5.
21. *Attorney-General; Ex rel McWhirter v Independent Broadcasting Authority* [1973] QB 629 at 649.
22. [1978] AC 435.
23. [1942] AC 332 at 345.
24. [1978] AC 435 at 482, 514.

sugar into the Commonwealth was illegal and invalid. He alleged that he was interested in the matter as a member of the public. It was held that he had no locus standi. In a joint judgment delivered by Gavan Duffy CJ, Starke and Evatt JJ, it was said:

> But the Agreement made by the Commonwealth, and its prohibition, affect the public generally and the plaintiff has no interest in the subject matter beyond that of any other member of the public: he has no private or special interest in it. Great evils would arise if every member of the Commonwealth could attack the validity of the acts of the Commonwealth whenever he thought fit; and it is clear in law that the right of an individual to bring such an action does not exist unless he establishes that he is 'more particularly affected than other people'.[25]

Again, more recently, the majority of this Court applied a similar test in *Robinson v Western Australian Museum*.[26] Although, in some cases ... the formula of *Boyce v Paddington Borough Council* is, naturally enough, repeated, the broad test of special interest is, in my opinion, the proper one to apply ...

[530] I would not deny that a person might have a special interest in the preservation of a particular environment. However, an interest, for present purposes, does not mean a mere intellectual or emotional concern. A person is not interested within the meaning of the rule, unless he is likely to gain some advantage, other than the satisfaction of righting a wrong, upholding a principle or winning a contest, if his action succeeds or to suffer some disadvantage, other than a sense of grievance or a debt for costs, if his action fails. A belief, however strongly felt, that the law generally, or a particular law, should be observed, or that conduct of a particular kind should be prevented, does not suffice to give its possessor locus standi. If [531] that were not so, the rule requiring special interest would be meaningless. Any plaintiff who felt strongly enough to bring an action could maintain it.

It is quite clear that when the rule is thus understood, the Foundation has no special interest in the preservation of the environment at Farnborough, and of course none in [the developer's] exchange control transactions. Counsel for the Foundation sought to show an interest in two alternative ways — first, because of the nature of the Foundation and its objects and, secondly, because of the fact that it had sent written comments when the draft environmental impact statement was made available for public comment. The fact that the Foundation is incorporated with particular objects does not strengthen its claim to standing. A natural person does not acquire standing simply by reason of the fact that he holds certain beliefs and wishes to translate them into action, and a body corporate formed to advance the same beliefs is in no stronger position. If it is the fact that some members of the Foundation have a special interest — and it is most unlikely that any would have a special interest to challenge the exchange control transaction — it would not follow that the Foundation has locus standi, for a corporation does not acquire standing because some of its members possess it.

The fact that the Foundation had sent written comments which [the developer] was required to take into account in revising its draft environmental impact statement did not give the Foundation standing to bring the present action. A person who is concerned

---

25. *Anderson v The Commonwealth* (1932) 47 CLR 50 at 51–2.
26. (1977) 138 CLR 283 at 292–3, 301–3, 327–8.

enough about proposed action to furnish his comments on it does not necessarily have any interest in the proposed action in the relevant sense. The fact that the Foundation sent the written comments, as permitted by the administrative procedures, is logically irrelevant to the question whether it has a special interest giving it standing. That fact would only have some significance in relation to this question if the administrative procedures revealed an intention that a person who sent written comments thereby acquired further rights. As I have endeavoured to show, that is not the case. In support of this branch of the argument, we were referred to *Sinclair v Maryborough Mining Warden*. In that case, a **[532]** person who had been an objector on the hearing of certain applications before a mining warden sought, and in this Court obtained, mandamus requiring the warden to hear the application and objections according to law. The objector had no special interest, but represented a section of the public. However, it was not in question that he had a right to have his objection heard before the warden. Barwick CJ said:

> The appellant, having been an objector before the warden, had a right to have the hearing of the application conducted, and the warden consider the application and the objections and make his recommendation according to law. If the application has not been so heard and determined, he is a proper party to seek a mandamus to compel the hearing to be had according to law ...[27]

That passage clearly brings out the point of distinction between that case and the present — there the objector had a right which he was entitled to enforce; here, the person submitting the written comments had no further right.

Comment
1. See Radan & Stewart at **22.22–22.24**.

Declarations in criminal proceedings

22.4   Sankey v Whitlam (1978) 142 CLR 1

Court: High Court of Australia

Facts: Sankey, a private citizen, laid informations in 1975 against the former Prime Minister of Australia Gough Whitlam and three former senior ministers of his Cabinet and Executive Council. He alleged they had conspired to act unlawfully during office by borrowing money from overseas in contravention of Commonwealth law and by deceiving the Governor-General about the temporary nature of the loan. Proceedings began in the Queanbeyan Court of Petty Sessions and went to the NSW Court of Appeal on interlocutory matters concerning, among other things, production of documents in relation to which various parties, including the Commonwealth, claimed privilege. When it was decided in the Court of Petty Sessions that Crown privilege attached to certain key documents, Sankey joined the magistrate and the Commonwealth to the proceedings seeking declarations that the documents should be produced and used in

---

27. *Sinclair v Maryborough Mining Warden* (1975) 132 CLR 473 at 478.

the committal proceedings against Whitlam and the others. Whitlam sought declarations by cross-claim that the laws alleged to have been breached were not laws within the relevant meaning of the Crimes Act, that borrowing funds from overseas could not amount to an unlawful purpose under that Act, and that documents in respect of which privilege had not been claimed should not be admitted into evidence in any event. The cross-applications came before the High Court.

Issue: The issue before the High Court was whether it had the power to grant declarations at the request of an informant in committal proceedings and, if it did, whether it should exercise its discretion in the case at hand.

Decision: The High Court (Gibbs ACJ, Stephen, Mason, Jacobs and Aickin JJ) unanimously held that it had the power to grant declaratory relief and that ministerial certification of the privileged nature of subpoenaed documents was not conclusive. It established that the court had the power to inspect the documents and, after doing so in this case, the court dismissed the claims for privilege in relation to most of them.

Extracts: The extracts from the judgments of Gibbs ACJ and Stephen J define the ambit of the court's power to grant declarations in criminal proceedings.

Gibbs ACJ

[20] It is well established that the power of the court to make a declaration, under a provision such as s 75 of the *Supreme Court Act*, 1970 (NSW), as amended, or O 26, r 19 of the Rules of this Court, is a very wide one.[28] It is clear enough that the power of the court is not excluded because the matter as to which a declaration is sought may fall for decision in criminal proceedings. Indeed in *Dyson v Attorney-General*,[29] which is one of the foundations of the law on this subject, it was held that the court had power to make [21] a declaration that the plaintiff was not under any obligation to comply with the requisitions contained in a notice sent to him by the Commissioners of Inland Revenue, notwithstanding that neglect to comply with the notice was an offence ... Since that time there have been many cases in which the courts have made declarations in relation to questions which could have fallen for decision in criminal proceedings ... [I]t is enough for me to refer to only two of them. In *Munnich v Godstone Rural District Council*[30] it was held that the fact that the question of law which was in issue in that case had already arisen in criminal proceedings and had been decided adversely to the plaintiff was no bar to the making of the declaration which the plaintiff sought. In this Court, in *IXL Timbers Pty Ltd v Attorney-General (Tas)*, Windeyer J made a declaration on a question of constitutional law that arose in a pending prosecution, although he expressed the view that it would have been preferable if the matter had proceeded before the magistrate and been brought to this Court on appeal if necessary.[31]

Most of the cases in which declarations have been made in matters which could have been, or were, the subject of criminal proceedings were cases where the criminal

---

28. *Forster v Jododex Aust Pty Ltd* (1972) 127 CLR 421 at 435–6.
29. [1911] 1 KB 410 especially at 422.
30. [1966] All ER 930 at 933, 935, 939.
31. *IXL Timbers Pty Ltd v Attorney-General (Tas)* (1963) 109 CLR 574 at 575–6.

offence consisted of a breach of a regulatory provision, such as a failure to comply with an administrative requirement, a planning provision or a by-law. It has accordingly been suggested that a distinction should be drawn between offences involving moral turpitude — mala in se — and breaches of statutory and administrative regulations and prohibitions — mala quia prohibita — and that it is only in the latter case that a declaration will be made.[32] There is however no authority that would deny to the courts the power to make a declaration in matters which could be or have been the subject of proceedings for crimes involving moral turpitude, and it would be most unsatisfactory to make the power of the court depend upon so arbitrary and uncertain a test, although the nature of the criminal conduct alleged to have been committed or contemplated will no doubt be one of the circumstances to be considered in deciding in what manner the discretion of the court should be exercised. Some of the cases to which I shall later refer provide illustrations of circumstances in which there would be power to [22] make declarations which would have the effect of interfering with criminal proceedings in respect of offences which involve serious criminality in the ordinary sense.

It seems that the question whether a declaratory judgment may be made in relation to pending committal proceedings has arisen only in New South Wales. The discussion of the question in the courts of that State often begins with the decision in *Ex parte Cousens; Re Blacket*.[33] In that case the defendant, who was charged with treason allegedly committed in Japan and was brought before an examining magistrate, sought prohibition to restrain the magistrate from further proceeding on the ground that the courts of New South Wales had no jurisdiction to adjudicate upon the charge. Prohibition was refused, and it appears that the ground of the decision — or at least one of the grounds — was that the Supreme Court has no power to interfere by a prerogative writ with a magistrate conducting committal proceedings, because such proceedings are executive in their nature. However I am, with respect, unable to agree that it is involved in this decision that the Supreme Court has no power to make a declaration which will affect the conduct of committal proceedings. The two sorts of relief are governed by different principles, and if the decision of a magistrate is immune from review by means of the prerogative writs it does not follow that a declaration cannot be made in relation to the subject matter of the proceedings — so much is recognized in the judgment of Walsh J in *Forster v Jododex Aust Pty Ltd*.[34] On the other hand, if prohibition does lie, a declaration can nevertheless be made, for the existence of an alternative remedy is no bar to the making of a declaration, but merely a matter to be weighed by the court in the exercise of its discretion. For these reasons I do not consider it necessary in the present case to consider whether *Ex parte Cousens; Re Blacket* was correctly decided.

As Jordan CJ pointed out in *Ex parte Cousens; Re Blacket*: 'In substance, a committing magistrate determines nothing, except that in his opinion a prima facie case has been made out for committing the accused for trial'.[35] The Attorney-General, in deciding whether or not to present an indictment, will not be bound by the decision of the magistrate as to whether a prima facie case has been made out. These circumstances,

---

32. See Zamir, *The Declaratory Judgment* (1962), pp 215–24.
33. (1946) 47 SR (NSW) 145.
34. (1972) 127 CLR 421 at 428.
35. *Ex parte Cousens; Re Blacket* (1946) 47 SR (NSW) 145 at 147.

however, seem to me to be irrelevant to the question whether the court has power to make a declaration **[23]** which will affect the conduct of committal proceedings. The word 'right', in the expression 'declarations of right' in s 75 of the *Supreme Court Act*, 1970 (NSW) and O 26, r 19 is used in a sense that is wide and loose. It includes what might more precisely be described as privileges, powers and immunities. And the power to make a declaration extends to enable a plaintiff to have it declared that he is under no duty or liability to the defendant — that was established by *Guaranty Trust Co of New York v Hannay & Co*[36] as well as by *Dyson v Attorney-General*.[37] There is no reason in principle why a declaration should not be made that committal proceedings have been invalidly instituted or wrongly continued against the person seeking the declaration. For example, if the courts of New South Wales had no jurisdiction to entertain the charge brought against the defendant in *Ex parte Cousens; Re Blacket* it would in my opinion have been within the power of the Supreme Court to make a declaration accordingly. Another example is provided by *Reg v Schwarten; Ex parte Wildschut*.[38] In that case the Full Court of Queensland issued prohibition to a magistrate to restrain him from wrongly proceeding with the hearing of a committal proceeding in respect of a charge of manslaughter which had been commenced by another magistrate. Whether or not prohibition lay in such a case, the court could in my opinion have made an appropriate declaration.

Not all judges in New South Wales have shared the view of the majority of the Court of Appeal in *Connor v Sankey*[39] or have regarded the decision in Ex parte Cousens; Re Blacket as authority preventing the making of declarations in relation to the conduct of committal proceedings. In *Bacon v Rose*[40] Street CJ held that if it had been established that committal proceedings had been begun without the prior approval of the Minister, which was made by statute a condition precedent to the institution of proceedings for the offence in question, he could and would have made a declaration to that effect. In the event, however, he found that the plaintiff had not made out her entitlement to the declaration sought. In *Willesee v Willesee*[41] Holland J made a declaration that the plaintiff (who was charged with assault) was entitled, under the First Offenders (Women) Act, 1918 (NSW) to have the hearing of committal proceedings conducted in private and otherwise in accordance with the provisions of that Act. On the other hand **[24]** in *Acs v Anderson*[42] the Court of Appeal upheld a decision of Holland J who had refused, in his discretion, to make a declaration that the liquidator of a company had power to waive professional privilege claimed by a solicitor called to give evidence at committal proceedings of instructions given to him by persons acting on behalf of the company. The majority of the Court of Appeal left open the question whether a declaration could have been obtained in such a case. Finally in *Bourke v Hamilton*[43] Needham J held that if it were demonstrated that the evidence taken on behalf of the prosecution at committal

---

36. [1915] 2 KB 536.
37. [1911] KB 410.
38. [1965] Qd R 276.
39. [1976] 2 NSWLR 570.
40. [1972] 2 NSWLR 793.
41. [1974] 2 NSWLR 275.
42. [1975] 1 NSWLR 212.
43. [1977] 1 NSWLR 470.

proceedings was not such as would have enabled a magistrate correctly applying the law to have formed the opinion that a prima facie case had been made out, he had power to make a declaration and would be prepared to exercise the power. However after reviewing the evidence he was not satisfied that it had been established that no charge could properly result in the committal of the plaintiffs for trial and he declined to make a declaration.

Of these cases *Bacon v Rose* and *Willesee v Willesee* present little difficulty. In the former case it was claimed that the plaintiff was exposed to proceedings that had been wrongly brought, and in the latter that the proceedings were being conducted in a manner contrary to that provided by statute. There was in these cases clear power to grant a declaration. In both cases the question involved was principally one of law and the decision of that question was determinative, in the first case, of whether the proceedings should continue and, in the second case, of whether they should be conducted in public or in private. In these circumstances there were good reasons for exercising the discretionary power of the court by granting a declaration. Similar considerations apply to the cross-claim brought by Mr Whitlam for the declarations as to the Financial Agreement 1927. If the provisions of that Agreement are not a 'law of the Commonwealth' within s 86(1)(c) of the *Crimes Act*, the charges against [him] under that section cannot be sustained. In my opinion the court has power to declare that a charge brought against an accused person is one not known to the law, since the accused has a 'right' not to be exposed to proceedings that have no legal substance. Of course in exercising its discretion the court will have regard to the power of the examining magistrate to commit the accused for trial for an offence different from that charged in the information (see **[25]** *Justices Act*, ss 30, 41) but in the present case the circumstances are such that it is quite improbable that evidence given on committal proceedings on the charge under s 86(1)(c) could make out a prima facie case of any other offence (except possibly that of conspiracy which is already charged).

The question whether the power to grant declaratory relief extends to enable the court to declare that particular evidence is admissible or inadmissible, or that the evidence led by an informant is sufficient to make out a prima facie case, is a much more difficult one, because it is not so clear, in such cases, that the plaintiff has any 'right', even within the widest sense of that word, in respect of which he can seek relief. Grave doubts on this point were expressed by Hutley JA (with whom Moffitt P agreed) in *Acs v Anderson*,[44] but I need not consider whether there would be power to grant declaratory relief in all such cases. In my opinion it would be within power to grant a declaration of the kind sought by Mr Sankey in the present case. It seems to me that when an informant has properly required the production on subpoena of an admissible document, and the Commonwealth has objected to the production of the document on the ground that the public interest requires that it should not be disclosed, it is possible to regard the Commonwealth as asserting, against the informant as well as against the court, a 'right' to withhold production of the document, and that in those circumstances the court has power to grant declaratory relief if the objection is held to be untenable. The same reasoning would not justify the making of a declaration that documents for which privilege was not claimed should not be admitted, but as will appear I need not decide whether it would be proper to make a declaration in such a case.

---

44. [1975] 1 NSWLR 212 at 215–7.

In any case in which a declaration can be and is sought on a question of evidence or procedure, the circumstances must be most exceptional to warrant the grant of relief. The power to make declaratory orders has proved to be a valuable addition to the armoury of the law. The procedure involved is simple and free from technicalities; properly used in an appropriate case the use of the power enables the salient issue to be determined with the least possible delay and expense. But the procedure is open to abuse, particularly in criminal cases, and if wrongly used can cause the very evils it is designed to avoid. Applications for declarations as to the admissibility of evidence may in some cases be made by an accused person for purposes of delay, or by a prosecutor to impose an additional burden on the accused, but [26] even when such an application is made without any improper motive it is likely to be dilatory in effect, to fragment the proceedings and to detract from the efficiency of the criminal process. I am not intending to criticize those concerned with the conduct of *Bourke v Hamilton*,[45] or to show any disrespect for the careful judgments delivered in that matter — indeed I have derived much assistance from them — when I say that that case provides an example of the way in which criminal proceedings may be needlessly protracted if they are interrupted by an application for a declaration — in the end the declaration sought was refused but the proceedings had been delayed for the space of almost a year. The present case itself is another regrettable example of the delay that can be caused by departures from the normal course of procedure. For these reasons I would respectfully endorse the observations of Jacobs P (as he then was) in *Shapowloff v Dunn*,[46] that a court will be reluctant to make declarations in a matter which impinges directly upon the course of proceedings in a criminal matter. Once criminal proceedings have begun they should be allowed to follow their ordinary course unless it appears that for some special reason it is necessary in the interests of justice to make a declaratory order. Although these remarks may be no more than mere 'administrative cautions',[47] I nevertheless consider that if a judge failed to give proper weight to these matters it could not be said that he had properly exercised his discretion.

Stephen J

[78] The declaratory relief

Counsel for one of the defendants, Dr Cairns, made two distinct submissions each of which raised in quite different ways the utility and propriety of the procedure adopted in this case, the seeking of declaratory relief in relation to rulings by a magistrate in committal proceedings. The first submission was that the various subpoenas duces tecum issued by the magistrate at the instance of [Sankey] and which have given rise to the question of Crown privilege should be treated as in fact addressed to the Crown in right of the Commonwealth or to persons entitled to its immunities. So regarded, s 26 of the *Justices Act*, 1902 (NSW) does not, it is said, authorize the issue of such subpoenas or, if it does, it goes beyond power.

This submission was not made before the magistrate, is not the subject of any claim to relief either in [Sankey's] summons or in the cross-claim and is not relied upon by counsel for the Commonwealth, the party most directly affected. It has been said that there are

---

45. [1977] 1 NSWLR 470.
46. [1973] 2 NSWLR 468 at 470.
47. See *Ibeneweka v Egbuna* [1964] 1 WLR 219 at 224.

procedural and practical advantages which justify the institution of these proceedings. If there be such advantages, they may very readily be dissipated if, regardless of what has gone before, any party may canvass matters extraneous to the substance of the declaratory relief which is sought. This Court has heard lengthy argument upon Crown privilege for documents the production of which was sought by the issue of subpoenas. That argument has all proceeded upon the assumption, unchallenged in the committal proceedings, that the subpoenas were properly issued. I do not consider it appropriate now to embark upon the course of inquiry which this present submission, unsupported though it is by any express prayer for relief, would require. Accordingly I do no more than note that it was made.

The second submission urged on behalf of Dr Cairns is that the Supreme Court of New South Wales lacks jurisdiction to give declaratory relief in the circumstances of this case; alternatively that as a matter of discretion no declaratory relief should be granted. On the question of jurisdiction I go directly to the [79] authoritative statement of Gibbs J in *Forster v Jododex Aust Pty Ltd*. Omitting his Honour's citation of authorities, the passage runs as follows:

> The jurisdiction to make a declaration is a very wide one. Indeed, it has been said that, 'under O XXV, r 5, the power of the Court to make a declaration, where it is a question of defining the rights of two parties, is almost unlimited; I might say only limited by its own discretion': ... However, the jurisdiction may be ousted by statute, although the right of a subject to apply to the court for a determination of his rights will not be held to be excluded except by clear words.[48]

The passage has quite recently been relied upon by Needham J in *Bourke v Hamilton*.[49] His Honour's detailed review of those recent decisions in the New South Wales Supreme Court in which the use of declaratory relief in connexion with committal proceedings has been considered makes it unnecessary for me to traverse that ground. I need, I think, do not more than apply, as did Needham J, what was said by Gibbs J in the *Jododex Case* to the case in hand. That [Sankey] was entitled to institute the committal proceedings is unquestioned, s 13(a) of the *Crimes Act* 1914 (Cth) confers that right and to the extent that it does so it reflects the position at common law. It has always been the position, subject only to occasional statutory exceptions, that it is 'the right of any member of the public to lay an information and to prosecute an offence'.[50] As Lord Wilberforce observed in *Gouriet v Union of Post Office Workers*, 'All citizens have sufficient interest in the enforcement of the law to entitle them to take this step',[51] that is, to institute a prosecution ... Having the carriage of the prosecution, [Sankey] then caused subpoenas duces tecum to be issued and served. Again he had a clear right to do so — s 85E of the *Crimes Act* 1914 (Cth) and s 26 of the *Justices Act*, 1902 (NSW). When objections to compliance with those subpoenas were raised, based upon claims to Crown privilege, that immediately affected [Sankey] in the exercise of the rights to which I have referred. That the rights which [he] is asserting are not concerned with the defence of his own person or property is no reason to deny

---

48. *Forster v Jododex Aust Pty Ltd* (1972) 127 CLR 421 at 435–6.
49. [1977] 1 NSWLR 470.
50. *Lund v Thompson* [1959] 1 QB 283 at 285.
51. *Gouriet v Union of Post Office Workers* [1978] AC 435 at 482.

them recognition. They are **[80]** entitled to such recognition and there is, accordingly jurisdiction to make declarations such as are sought.

That proper sense of responsibility to which Lord Radcliffe refers in *Ibeneweka v Egbuna*[52] when he reminds us that 'judicial pronouncements ought not be issued unless there are circumstances which call for their making', will not, in my view, be lacking if this Court, in exercise of its discretion, determines to use the jurisdiction it possesses. I would, with respect, adopt the words of Walsh J in the *Jododex Case* when he said, 'I think that we ought not now to decide that the questions of law upon which the parties are in dispute should be left unresolved in these proceedings'.[53] If there be any merit in these proceedings it surely lies in the opportunity they afford of resolving once and for all questions of law first raised years ago in the magistrate's court at Queanbeyan and which have ever since troubled the parties and the courts. It being a matter of discretion, this Court should, in the particular circumstances of this case, grant such declaratory relief as the parties are entitled to. In many like cases an exercise of discretion in the contrary sense may be called for so as to avoid interference with the due and orderly administration of the law and with the proper exercise by magistrates of their functions in committal proceedings. The past history of this case, to which sufficient reference has already been made, is such that these considerations, often proper to be taken into account and which may even prove decisive, are here of little if any weight. In conclusion on the question of discretion, it is, of course, relevant that in these proceedings it is no mere question of the admissibility of evidence in any ordinary sense that is in issue.

In addition to declaratory relief [Sankey] in his summons sought mandatory orders. These were not, however, pressed in argument and should not, in the circumstances, be made.

Comment

1. See Radan & Stewart at **22.35–27.38.**

---

52. [1964] 1 WLR 219 at 224 at 225.
53. *Forster v Jododex Aust Pty Ltd* (1972) 127 CLR 421 at 428.

23

SPECIFIC PERFORMANCE

Introduction

23.1 This chapter deals with the availability of the remedy of specific performance to enforce a contract. Like all equitable remedies, specific performance is discretionary. A plaintiff has no right to equitable relief simply because a breach of contract has occurred. The court can refuse specific performance on the basis that it has no jurisdiction to hear the claim or it can refuse to grant the order in the exercise of its discretion. In either case, if specific performance is refused, the plaintiff is confined to pursuing his or her claim for damages at common law.

The cases extracted in this chapter discuss the following:

- the refusal to order specific performance on the jurisdictional ground that the plaintiff is adequately compensated by an order for damages at common law: *Beswick v Beswick* [1968] AC 58;
- the refusal to order specific performance on the discretionary ground that the contract is one of personal services: *C H Giles & Co Ltd v Morris* [1972] 1 All ER 960;
- the refusal to order specific performance on the discretionary ground that compliance with the order would require the constant supervision of the court: *Co-operative Insurance Society Ltd v Argyll Stores (Holdings) Ltd* [1998] AC 1;
- the refusal to order specific performance on the discretionary ground that the plaintiff is not ready, willing and able to perform his or her obligations under the contract: *Mehmet v Benson* (1965) 113 CLR 295; and
- whether the payment of money is a sufficient act of part performance: *Khoury v Khouri* (2006) 66 NSWLR 241.

The inadequacy of common law damages

23.2   Beswick v Beswick [1968] AC 58

Court: House of Lords

Facts: Peter Beswick, a coal merchant, entered into a contract with his nephew John Beswick for the sale of Peter's business. The business was to be transferred to John in exchange for, among other things, a weekly payment to Peter for the rest of his life and, after his death, the payment of an annuity to Peter's wife Ruth. When Peter died, John made only one payment to Ruth. She took legal action as administratrix of Peter's estate (she could not sue in her own name because of the privity of contract rule) claiming payment of arrears of the annuity and an order for specific performance of the continuing obligation to pay the annuity.

Issue: The issue before the House of Lords was whether damages would be an inadequate remedy for a plaintiff in cases involving non-payment of a contractual debt to a third party. If so, the decree of specific performance would be available to Ruth.

Decision: The House of Lords (Lords Reid, Hodson, Guest, Pearce and Upjohn) unanimously held that because damages were nominal in this case, they were an inadequate remedy, and ordered specific performance of the contract.

Extracts: The extracts from the speeches of Lords Reid, Hodson and Upjohn outline the court's reasoning on the issue of specific performance as a valid alternative to nominal damages in such cases.

Lord Reid

[72] Applying what I have said to the circumstances of the present [73] case, [Ruth] in her personal capacity has no right to sue, but she has a right as administratrix of her husband's estate to require [John] to perform his obligation under the agreement. He has refused to do so and he maintains that [her] only right is to sue him for damages for breach of his contract. If that were so, I shall assume that he is right in maintaining that the administratrix could then recover only nominal damages because his breach of contract has caused no loss to the estate of her deceased husband. If that were the only remedy available the result would be grossly unjust. It would mean that [John] keeps the business which he bought and for which he has only paid a small part of the price which he agreed to pay. He would avoid paying the rest of the price, the annuity to [Ruth], by paying a mere 40s damages.

Lord Hodson

[81] [I]t was argued [at one time] that specific performance would not be granted where the remedy at law was adequate and so should not be ordered. The remedy at law is plainly inadequate, as was pointed out by the Court of Appeal,[1] as (1) only nominal damages can be recovered; (2) in order to enforce a continuing obligation it may be necessary to bring a series of actions whereas specific performance avoids multiplicity of action. Again, it was said that the courts will not make an order which cannot be enforced. This argument also fell by the wayside for plainly the order can be enforced by the ordinary methods of execution …

The peculiar feature of this case is that [Ruth] is not only the personal representative of the deceased but also his widow and the person beneficially entitled to the money claimed. Although the widow cannot claim specific performance in her personal capacity, there is no objection to her doing so in her [82] capacity as administratrix, and when the moneys are recovered they will be in this instance held for the benefit of herself as the person for whom they are intended.

---

1. *Beswick v Beswick* [1966] 3 All ER 1 at 14.

The authorities where the remedy of specific performance has been applied in such circumstances as these are numerous … It is to be noticed that the learned counsel engaged in this and other cases never took the point now relied on that the personal representative of the contracting party could not enforce a contract such as this. As I understood the argument, for [John] it was contended that the personal representative could not obtain specific performance as the estate had nothing to gain, having suffered no loss. There is no authority which supports this proposition and I do not think that it has any validity.

Lord Upjohn

[102] I incline to the view that on the facts of this case damages are nominal for it appears that [Peter] died without any assets save and except the agreement which he hoped would keep him and then his widow for their lives. At all events let me assume that damages are nominal. So it is said nominal damages are adequate and the remedy of specific performance ought not to be granted. That is, with all respect, wholly to misunderstand that principle. Equity will grant specific performance when damages are inadequate to meet the justice of the case.

But in any event quantum of damages seldom affects the right to specific performance. If X contracts with Y to buy Blackacre or a rare chattel for a fancy price because the property or chattel has caught his fancy he is entitled to enforce his bargain and it matters not that he could not prove any damage.

In this case the court ought to grant a specific performance order all the more because damages *are* nominal. [John] has received all the property; justice demands that he pay the price and this can only be done in the circumstances by equitable relief. It is a fallacy to suppose that [Ruth] is thereby obtaining additional rights; [the administratrix] is entitled to compel [John] to carry out the terms of the agreement …

My Lords, in my opinion the Court of Appeal were clearly right to grant a decree of specific performance.

Comment
1. See Radan & Stewart at **23.29–23.31**.

Contracts for personal services

23.3   C H Giles & Co Ltd v Morris [1972] 1 All ER 960

Court: Chancery Division of the High Court of England and Wales

Facts: Invincible Policies Ltd, a firm of insurance brokers whose shares were owned by Morris and others, agreed with Giles' company for certain capital restructuring and reorganisation issues, as well as the sale of certain shares. One of the terms of the contract specified that Giles would be appointed under a service agreement as managing director of Invincible Policies for a five-year term. Morris and his fellow shareholders later disagreed over some matters and Giles' appointment did not proceed. He took

---

legal action against Morris and the others seeking specific performance of the contract. During the proceedings, and on legal advice, the parties consented to an order for specific performance of, among other things, the service agreement with Giles. But the board of Invincible Policies refused to appoint Giles because he lacked insurance experience. When Giles and his company again took action, Morris and the others argued they were wrongly advised, and that it would be wrong for the court to enforce a contract for personal services in circumstances where they would have to terminate the contract and face a claim for damages from Giles.

Issue: The main issue before the Chancery Division was whether an order for specific performance could be made in relation to a contract that included an obligation involving personal services.

Decision: Megarry J held that the order in the present case simply required the execution of the agreement. Just because the agreement contained an obligation to sign a contract for personal services, which would otherwise not be specifically enforceable, did not mean that the obligation to sign such a contract could not be specifically enforced.

Extracts: The extracts from the judgment of Megarry J outline the principles relating to granting a specific performance order where a contract for personal services is involved.

Megarry J

[967] What I have to consider is whether the presence in the agreement of [a subclause], providing for Mr Giles to enter into a service agreement with Invincible in the form of the draft annexed to the contract, prevents the court from decreeing specific performance of the entire agreement, including that subclause. It will be observed that there is no question of [Giles' company] seeking to enforce any order of the court which will compel any of [Morris and the others] to carry out, either as employer or employee, any personal services. The order made is an order to procure 'the execution by the Company of the engrossment' of the service agreement. The question is whether such an order falls within the principle that the court will not decree specific performance of a contract for personal services.

On the face of it the answer must be No. There is no question of the execution of the decree requiring constant superintendence by the court of a continuous series [968] of acts ... All that the decree requires in this respect is the procuring of a single act, namely, the execution of the service agreement. When that has been done, the question of any breach of the service agreement and any remedies for that breach is one between Invincible and Mr Giles, and not between Invincible and [Giles' company]. Invincible, too, is a party neither to the contract nor to the action.

The distinction between an order to perform a contract for services and an order to procure the execution of such a contract seems to me to be sound both in principle and on authority. I do not think that the mere fact the contract to be made is one of which the court would not decree specific performance is a ground for refusing to decree that the contract be entered into ...

[969] The reasons why the court is reluctant to decree specific performance of a contract for personal services (and I would regard it as a strong reluctance rather than a rule) are … more complex and more firmly bottomed on human nature. If a singer contracts to sing, there could no doubt be proceedings for committal if, ordered to sing, the singer remained obstinately dumb. But if instead the singer sang flat, or sharp, or too fast, or too slowly, or too loudly, or too quietly, or resorted to a dozen of the manifestations of temperament traditionally associated with some singers, the threat of committal would reveal [970] itself as a most unsatisfactory weapon; for who could say whether the imperfections of performance were natural or self-induced? To make an order with such possibilities of evasion would be vain; and so the order will not be made. However, not all contracts of personal service or for the continuous performance of services are as dependent as this on matters of opinion and judgment, nor do all such contracts involve the same degree of the daily impact of person on person. In general, no doubt, the inconvenience and mischief of decreeing specific performance of most of such contracts will greatly outweigh the advantages, and specific performance will be refused. But I do not think that it should be assumed that as soon as any element of personal service or continuous services can be discerned in a contract the court will, without more, refuse specific performance. Of course, a requirement for the continuous performance of services has the disadvantage that repeated breaches may engender repeated applications to the court for enforcement. But so may many injunctions; and the prospects of repetition, although an important consideration, ought not to be allowed to negative a right. As is so often the case in equity, the matter is one of the balance of advantage and disadvantage in relation to the particular obligations in question; and the fact that the balance will usually lie on one side does not turn this probability into a rule. The present case … requires not the performance of personal services or any continuous series of acts, but merely … the execution of an agreement which contains a provision for such services or acts.

Comment

1. See Radan & Stewart at **23.39–23.41**.

Constant court supervision of an order for specific performance

---

23.4   Co-operative Insurance Society Ltd v Argyll Stores (Holdings) Ltd [1998] AC 1

Court: House of Lords

Facts: The Co-operative Insurance Society (CIS) granted Argyll a 35-year lease to operate a supermarket in a unit of a shopping centre. The lease contained a term to the effect that Argyll was to keep the premises open for retail trade during the usual hours of business in that area. The supermarket was the anchor tenant, being the largest shop in the centre and the greatest attraction. About 15 years into the lease, Argyll undertook a major review of its business operations and decided to close a number of supermarkets, including the one in the CIS shopping centre. CIS urged Argyll to keep trading until a

---

suitable assignee could be found and even offered to negotiate a temporary discount on the rental. However, Argyll unilaterally closed the supermarket and stripped out the fixtures and fittings. CIS brought an action against Argyll for specific performance of the contractual term requiring the premises to be kept open. In the alternative, it sought damages.

Issue: The issue before the House of Lords was whether specific performance could be ordered of a term in a lease requiring the carrying on of a business.

Decision: The House of Lords (Lords Browne-Wilkinson, Slynn of Hadley, Hoffmann, Hope of Craighead and Clyde) unanimously held in favour of Argyll and refused the application for specific performance of the lease.

Extracts: The extracts from the speech of Lord Hoffmann emphasise that obligations of an ongoing nature contain the risk of repeated litigation and constant court supervision, making specific performance an inappropriate remedy.

Lord Hoffmann

[11] The [trial] judge refused to order specific performance. He said that there was on the authorities a settled practice that orders which would require a defendant to run a business would not be made. He was not content, however, merely to follow authority. He gave reasons why he thought that specific performance would be inappropriate. Two such reasons were by way of justification for the general practice. An order to carry on a business, as opposed to an order to perform a 'single and well-defined act', was difficult to enforce by the sanction of committal. And where a business was being run at a loss, specific relief would be 'too far-reaching and beyond the scope of control which the court should seek to impose'. The other two related to the particular case. A resumption of business would be expensive ... and although Argyll had knowingly acted in breach of covenant, it had done so 'in the light of the settled practice of the court to award damages'. Finally, while the assessment of damages might be difficult, it was the kind of exercise which the courts had done in the past ...

Specific performance is traditionally regarded in English law as an exceptional remedy, as opposed to the common law damages to which a successful plaintiff is entitled as of right. There may have been some element of later rationalisation of an untidier history, but by the 19th century it was orthodox doctrine that the power to decree specific performance was part of the discretionary jurisdiction of the Court of Chancery to do justice in cases in which the remedies available at common law were inadequate. This is the basis of the general principle that specific performance will not be ordered when damages are an adequate remedy ... The cases in which [a plaintiff] is confined to a claim for damages are regarded as the exceptions ... The principles upon which English judges exercise the discretion to grant specific performance are reasonably well settled and depend upon a number of considerations, mostly of a practical nature, which are of very general application ...

[12] The practice of not ordering a defendant to carry on a business is not entirely dependent upon damages being an adequate remedy. In *Dowty Boulton Paul Ltd*

v Wolverhampton Corporation, Sir John Pennycuick V-C refused to order the corporation to maintain an airfield as a going concern because:

> It is very well established that the court will not order specific performance of an obligation to carry on a business.[2]

He added:

> It is unnecessary in the circumstances to discuss whether damages would be an adequate remedy to the company.[3]

Thus the reasons which underlie the established practice may justify a refusal of specific performance even when damages are not an adequate remedy.

The most frequent reason given in the cases for declining to order someone to carry on a business is that it would require constant supervision by the court. In *J C Williamson Ltd v Lukey and Mulholland*, Dixon J said flatly:

> Specific performance is inapplicable when the continued supervision of the court is necessary in order to ensure the fulfilment of the contract.[4] ...

The judges who have said that the need for constant supervision was an objection to such orders were no doubt well aware that supervision would in practice take the form of rulings by the court, on applications made by the parties, as to whether there had been a breach of the order. It is the possibility of the court having to give an indefinite series of such rulings in order to ensure the execution of the order which has been regarded as undesirable.

Why should this be so? A principal reason is that, as Megarry J pointed out in [*C H Giles & Co Ltd v Morris*,[5]] ... the only means available to the court to enforce its order is the quasi-criminal procedure of punishment for contempt. This is a powerful weapon; so powerful, in fact, as often to be unsuitable as an instrument for adjudicating upon the disputes which may arise over whether a business is being run in accordance with the terms of the court's order. The heavy-handed nature of the enforcement mechanism is a consideration which may go to the exercise of the court's discretion in other cases as well, but its use to compel the running of a business is perhaps the paradigm case of its disadvantages and it is in this context that I shall discuss them.

[13] The prospect of committal or even a fine, with the damage to commercial reputation which will be caused by a finding of contempt of court, is likely to have at least two undesirable consequences. First, the defendant, who ex hypothesi did not think that it was in his economic interest to run the business at all, now has to make decisions under a sword of Damocles which may descend if the way the business is run does not conform to the terms of the order. This is, as one might say, no way to run a business. In this case the Court of Appeal made light of the point because it assumed that, once the defendant had been ordered to run the business, self-interest and compliance with the order would thereafter go hand in hand. But, as I shall explain, this is not necessarily true.

---

2.   *Dowty Boulton Paul Ltd v Wolverhampton Corporation* [1971] 1 WLR 204 at 211.
3.   *Dowty Boulton Paul Ltd v Wolverhampton Corporation* [1971] 1 WLR 204 at 212.
4.   *J C Williamson Ltd v Lukey and Mulholland* (1931) 45 CLR 282 at 297–8.
5.   [1972] 1 All ER 960.

Secondly, the seriousness of a finding of contempt for the defendant means that any application to enforce the order is likely to be a heavy and expensive piece of litigation. The possibility of repeated applications over a period of time means that, in comparison with a once-and-for-all inquiry as to damages, the enforcement of the remedy is likely to be expensive in terms of cost to the parties and the resources of the judicial system.

This is a convenient point at which to distinguish between orders which require a defendant to carry on an activity, such as running a business over a more or less extended period of time, and orders which require him to achieve a result. The possibility of repeated applications for rulings on compliance with the order which arises in the former case does not exist to anything like the same extent in the latter. Even if the achievement of the result is a complicated matter which will take some time, the court, if called upon to rule, only has to examine the finished work and say whether it complies with the order. This point was made in the context of relief against forfeiture in *Shiloh Spinners Ltd v Harding*. If it is a condition of relief that the tenant should have complied with a repairing covenant, difficulty of supervision need not be an objection. As Lord Wilberforce said:

> … what the court has to do is to satisfy itself, ex post facto, that the covenanted work has been done, and it has ample machinery, through certificates, or by inquiry, to do precisely this.[6]

This distinction between orders to carry on activities and orders to achieve results explains why the courts have in appropriate circumstances ordered specific performance of building contracts and repairing covenants.[7] It by no means follows, however, that even obligations to achieve a result will always be enforced by specific performance. There may be other objections, to some of which I now turn.

One such objection, which applies to orders to achieve a result and a fortiori to orders to carry on an activity, is imprecision in the terms of the order. If the terms of the court's order, reflecting the terms of the obligation, cannot be precisely drawn, the possibility of wasteful litigation over compliance is increased. So is the oppression caused by the defendant having to do things under threat of proceedings for contempt. The less **[14]** precise the order, the fewer the signposts to the forensic minefield which he has to traverse. The fact that the terms of a contractual obligation are sufficiently definite to escape being void for uncertainty, or to found a claim for damages, or to permit compliance to be made a condition of relief against forfeiture, does not necessarily mean that they will be sufficiently precise to be capable of being specifically enforced. So in *Wolverhampton Corporation v Emmons*, Romer LJ said that the first condition for specific enforcement of a building contract was that

> … the particulars of the work are so far definitely ascertained that the court can sufficiently see what is the exact nature of the work of which it is asked to order the performance.[8] …

Precision is of course a question of degree and the courts have shown themselves willing to cope with a certain degree of imprecision in cases of orders requiring the achievement

---

6. *Shiloh Spinners Ltd v Harding* [1973] AC 691 at 724.
7. See *Wolverhampton Corporation v Emmons* [1901] 1 KB 515 (building contract) and *Jeune v Queens Cross Properties Ltd* [1974] Ch 97 (repairing covenant).
8. *Wolverhampton Corporation v Emmons* [1901] 1 KB 515.

of a result in which the plaintiffs' merits appeared strong; like all the reasons which I have been discussing, it is, taken alone, merely a discretionary matter to be taken into account … It is, however, a very important one.

I should at this point draw attention to what seems to me to have been a misreading of certain remarks of Lord Wilberforce in *Shiloh Spinners Ltd v Harding*. He pointed out, as I have said, that to grant relief against forfeiture subject to compliance with a repairing covenant involves the court in no more than the possibility of a retrospective assessment of whether the covenanted work has been done. For this reason, he said:

Where it is necessary, and, in my opinion, right, to move away from some 19th century authorities, is to reject as a reason against granting relief, the impossibility for the courts to supervise the doing of work.[9]

This is plainly a remark about cases involving the achievement of a result, such as doing repairs, and, within that class, about making compliance a condition of relief against forfeiture. But in *Tito v Waddell (No 2)*[10] Sir Robert Megarry V-C took it to be a generalisation about specific performance and, in particular, a rejection of difficulty of supervision as an objection, even in cases of orders to carry on an activity. Sir Robert Megarry V-C regarded it as an adoption of his own views (based, as I have said, on incomplete analysis of what was meant by difficulty of supervision) in *C H Giles & Co Ltd v Morris*. In the present case, Leggatt LJ took this claim at face value.[11] In fact, Lord Wilberforce went on to say that impossibility of supervision 'is a reality, no doubt, and explains why **[15]** specific performance cannot be granted of agreements to this effect …'[12] Lord Wilberforce was in my view drawing attention to the fact that the collection of reasons which the courts have in mind when they speak of difficulty of supervision apply with much greater force to orders for specific performance, giving rise to the possibility of committal for contempt, than they do to conditions for relief against forfeiture. While the paradigm case to which such objections apply is the order to carry on an activity, they can also apply to an order requiring the achievement of a result.

There is a further objection to an order requiring the defendant to carry on a business, which was emphasised by Millett LJ in the Court of Appeal. This is that it may cause injustice by allowing the plaintiff to enrich himself at the defendant's expense. The loss which the defendant may suffer through having to comply with the order (for example, by running a business at a loss for an indefinite period) may be far greater than the plaintiff would suffer from the contract being broken …

It is true that [Argyll] has, by his own breach of contract, put himself in … an unfortunate position. But the purpose of the law of contract is not to punish wrongdoing but to satisfy the expectations of the party entitled to performance. A remedy which enables him to secure, in money terms, more than the performance due to him is unjust. From a wider perspective, it cannot be in the public interest for the courts to require someone to carry on business at a loss if there is any plausible alternative by which the other party can be given compensation. It is not **[16]** only a waste of resources but yokes the parties together

---

9. *Shiloh Spinners Ltd v Harding* [1973] AC 691 at 724.
10. [1977] Ch 106 at 322.
11. *Co-operative Insurance Society Ltd v Argyll Stores (Holdings) Ltd* [1996] Ch 286 at 292–3.
12. *Shiloh Spinners Ltd v Harding* [1973] AC 691 at 724.

in a continuing hostile relationship. The order for specific performance prolongs the battle. If the defendant is ordered to run a business, its conduct becomes the subject of a flow of complaints, solicitors' letters and affidavits. This is wasteful for both parties and the legal system. An award of damages, on the other hand, brings the litigation to an end. The defendant pays damages, the forensic link between them is severed, they go their separate ways and the wounds of conflict can heal.

The cumulative effect of these various reasons, none of which would necessarily be sufficient on its own, seems to me to show that the settled practice is based upon sound sense. Of course the grant or refusal of specific performance remains a matter for the judge's discretion. There are no binding rules, but this does not mean that there cannot be settled principles, founded upon practical considerations of the kind which I have discussed, which do not have to be re-examined in every case, but which the courts will apply in all but exceptional circumstances ...

[19] I think that no criticism can be made of the way in which [the trial judge] exercised his discretion. All the reasons which he gave were proper matters for him to take into account. In my view the Court of Appeal should not have interfered and I would allow the appeal and restore the order which he made.

Comments

1. See Radan & Stewart at **23.42–23.52**.
2. For a discussion of this case see P Radan, 'Specific Performance of a Lease Obligation to Operate a Business' (1997) 71 *Australian Law Journal* 740 and A Phang, 'Specific Performance — Exploring the Roots of Settled Practice' (1998) 61 *Modern Law Review* 421.
3. In *Diagnostic X-Ray Services Pty Ltd v Jewel Food Stores Pty Ltd* (2001) 4 VR 632, Beach J in the Supreme Court of Victoria dealt with a case very similar in its facts to *Co-operative Insurance Society v Argyll Stores*. The anchor tenant operated a supermarket and petrol station, but it closed the petrol station. Beach J granted an interlocutory mandatory injunction (in effect an order for specific performance) requiring the tenant to operate the petrol station. His Honour said that there were exceptional circumstances justifying such an order, namely: (i) the petrol station was an adjunct to the supermarket; (ii) there was no pressing urgency to sell the supermarket and petrol station; (iii) the tenant was seeking to sell the petrol station; (iv) the tenant had acted unilaterally in closing the petrol station; and, (v) significant detriment would result to other tenants in the centre. Beach J, at 636–7, also said:

   In *Argyll*, in holding that the settled practice of the courts is not to grant a mandatory injunction requiring the carrying on of a business, much emphasis was placed on the fact that the grant of such an injunction would require constant supervision by the court. In my opinion, it is highly doubtful that that can be said in the present case. [Jewel Food Stores] operated the petrol station quite successfully over the last seven years. If it is ordered to continue to do so, there is no valid reason why it cannot, and without the supervision of the court.

The requirement that the plaintiff be ready, willing and able

23.5   Mehmet v Benson (1965) 113 CLR 295

Court: High Court of Australia

Facts: Mehmet entered into an instalment contract for the purchase of a half share in land from Benson for £16,000. Settlement was delayed until payment of the final instalment, with possession in the interim given to Mehmet. An initial deposit of £3000 was payable followed by a further instalment two months later in the same amount. Thereafter, the balance of the purchase price was to be paid by way of annual instalments of £1500 each plus interest. The contract provided for time to be of the essence and there was an express right given to Benson to rescind or terminate the contract in the event Mehmet failed to comply or otherwise breached it. It also provided that Benson would retain his rights as vendor even if an extension of time was granted. In the event of default, the whole contract price became immediately due and payable. Mehmet paid the deposit and first instalment of £1500, but he then fell into arrears and negotiated settlement of the balance with Benson, making good a portion of the arrears. Eventually, he was declared bankrupt. Benson served a notice of rescission on the basis of Mehmet's earlier failure to make an instalment payment on time and to forfeit the instalment payments already made. After Mehmet was discharged from bankruptcy, he sought specific performance of the contract.

Issue: The issue before the High Court was whether Mehmet, in order to obtain an order for specific performance, was ready, willing and able to perform the contract.

Decision: The High Court (Barwick CJ, McTiernan and Windeyer JJ) unanimously held that, as Mehmet was, at the time of the hearing, ready willing and able to perform the contract, there was no reason to refuse the application for specific performance. The fact that he would not have satisfied this requirement at the time when he was an undischarged bankrupt did not matter.

Extracts: The extracts from the judgments of Barwick CJ and Windeyer J illustrate that a court should look for the substance, rather than the technical form, of a plaintiff's readiness to perform the terms of a contract.

Barwick CJ

[307] The question as to whether or not [Mehmet] has been and is ready and willing to perform the contract is one of substance not to be resolved in any technical or narrow sense. It is important to bear in mind what is the substantial thing for which the parties contract and what on the part of [Mehmet] in a suit for specific performance are his essential obligations. Here the substantial [308] thing for which [Benson] bargained was the payment of the price: and, unless time be and remain of the essence, he obtains what he bargained for if by the decree he obtains his price with such ancillary orders as recompense him for the delay in its receipt. To order specific performance in this case would not involve the court in dispensing with anything for which [Benson] essentially contracted.

Of course, [Mehmet] must not by his unreadiness or unwillingness to perform have disowned his obligation to do so, or abandoned his rights to the benefit of the contract. But it is the essential terms of the contract which he must be ready and willing to perform. He seeks a transfer of the interest in land, the subject of the contract: the counterpart obligation is the payment of the price. In considering the question of [Mehmet's] readiness and willingness in this respect in this case there are many factors. His default in paying the instalments of the price, whilst not conclusive, is amongst these factors. For a substantial period [Mehmet] was under the disability of an available act of bankruptcy, of which no doubt [Benson] might have sought to profit but did not. The concession of the plaintiff in *Jennings' Trustee v King*[13] that so long as it is available, an act of bankruptcy must prevent a purchaser from succeeding in specific performance, because he cannot make an effective payment in return for the conveyance, is justified by the two cases to which Harman J in that case refers. But neither of these cases, nor any others which I have been able to discover, would justify the conclusion that after the act of bankruptcy had ceased to be available, and in default of any effective action by the other party to bring the contract to an end meantime, a purchaser otherwise entitled to succeed must be denied specific performance because during the period the act of bankruptcy was available he was unable to complete.

Windeyer J

[314] It is necessary that the plaintiff in an action for specific performance should allege in his pleading and prove at the hearing his readiness and willingness to perform the contract on his part: and readiness involves an ability to perform it.[14] At the date when the suit is commenced the plaintiff must then be in a position to say that he is ready and willing to do at the proper time in the future whatever in the events that have happened the contract requires that he do.[15] And he must show too that he has performed or been ready and willing to perform the terms of the contract on his part. But if, notwithstanding earlier breaches, the contract remained on foot, then [315] it seems to me a plaintiff is not necessarily barred from having a decree for specific performance if those breaches, not having resulted in a valid rescission, can be made good by the payment of interest … [I]t is I think sufficient that the plaintiff in a purchaser's suit should allege that he is presently ready and willing and offers to pay the purchase money and that it is not strictly necessary in every case for him to go further. If some conditions had earlier been waived in the plaintiff's favour and therefore not complied with, it is inappropriate to allege that he was always ready and willing to perform them. It were better in such a case to allege that, save in so far as performance of any condition was waived or excused by the defendant, the plaintiff had performed, or been always ready and willing to perform, the contract on his part according to its terms. However that may be, I do not think that in this case [Mehmet] should have been refused specific performance because he did not prove all that he alleged. The case is difficult and unusual. I would, however, allow the appeal and substitute for the decree of the Supreme Court a decree for specific

---

13. [1952] 1 Ch at 909.
14. *Ellis v Rogers* (1884) 29 Ch D 661 at 667; *McDonald v McMullen* (1908) 25 WN (NSW) 142; *Alam v Preston* (1938) 38 SR (NSW) 475; *Bando v Goldberg* (1944) 62 WN (NSW) 87; *King v Poggioli* (1923) 32 CLR 222 at 247.
15. See *Fullers' Theatres Ltd v Musgrove* (1923) 31 CLR 524 at 549.

performance. But, as I am not convinced that [Mehmet] is now ready and willing to complete the contract, I think there should be a proviso to meet the situation if he should prove to be unready promptly to complete the contract by payment in full. To that end [Benson] should be expressly enabled to apply to the Supreme Court to fix a date for completion. If [Mehmet] is not then ready to complete, the Supreme Court could make a decree for rescission. In the view I take it is unnecessary to consider in detail the terms on which his Honour granted relief against forfeiture. But I see no reason for thinking that, specific performance having been refused, relief on those terms ought not to have been given, or that terms similar in general effect would be inappropriate if [Mehmet] proves unready to complete. I would allow the appeal and dismiss the cross-appeal.

> **Comment**
> 1. See Radan & Stewart at **23.62–23.64**.

Payment of money and the doctrine of part performance

> ### 23.6   Khoury v Khouri (2006) 66 NSWLR 241
>
> **Court:** Court of Appeal of New South Wales
>
> **Facts:** In 1988 the siblings Marina and Peter Khoury purchased a house in Bass Hill. The purchase was facilitated by a loan from the Commonwealth Bank which was secured by a mortgage over the property. In 1992 Peter orally agreed to hold his share in the house on trust for his brother Bechara Khouri and to transfer that share to his brother when called upon to do so. In return Bechara agreed to pay Peter $30,000 and to pay Peter's share of the loan repayments to the Commonwealth Bank. Bechara paid the $30,000 as agreed. About the same time Marina agreed to transfer her share of the house to Bishop Gibran, a family friend and the Bishop of the Antiochan Orthodox Church Diocese of Australia. In return Bishop Gibran paid Marina $70,000 and agreed to take over responsibility for her share of the loan payments to the Commonwealth Bank. Shortly after this agreement, Bechara reached agreement with Bishop Gibran by which Bechara paid the Bishop $70,000, and in return the Bishop agreed to make repayments of the loan to the Commonwealth Bank that Bechara had agreed to make pursuant to his earlier oral agreement with Peter. Bechara made the payment to the Bishop, who then made payments over the ensuing years in reduction of the loan to the Commonwealth Bank. In 1996, Marina and her husband borrowed money from the Arab Bank. Part of the loan was used to pay out the amount then outstanding on the loan to the Commonwealth Bank. The other part of the loan was used to repurchase the share of the house she had earlier sold to Bishop Gibran. The loan from the Arab Bank was secured by a mortgage over the Bass Hill property, with Peter acting as a guarantor on the loan. In 2002 Bechara demanded that his share of the house be transferred to him by Peter.
>
> **Issue:** The issue before the Court of Appeal was whether Bechara's payments of $30,000 to Peter and $70,000 to Bishop Gibran were sufficient acts of part performance upon which it could ground an order for specific performance in favour of Bechara.

> **Decision:** The Court of Appeal (Handley, Hodgson and Bryson JJA) unanimously held that the payments of money by Bechara were not sufficient acts of part performance.
>
> **Extracts:** The extracts from the judgment of Bryson JA, who gave the main judgment in this case, discuss the requirements of the doctrine of part performance and in particular the extent to which payments of money can be acts of part performance.

Bryson JA

[262] Case law ... shows that part performance was treated as a ground for specific performance in 1686, 10 years after the enactment of the *Statute of Frauds*,[16] and was relied on in several cases early in the 18th century ...

[263] The judicial approach to the meaning and effect of the *Statute of Frauds* may well have been influenced by the recital with which it opens: 'For prevention of many fraudulent practices, which are commonly endeavoured to be upheld by perjury and subornation of perjury; (2) be it enacted ...'. This recital establishes the purpose of the Statute clearly, and could support the view that if evidence shows that the transaction is genuine in some other way than by writing, the Statute was not intended to apply to it. If this was part of the reasoning of Seventeenth-Century Chancery judges, they are not known to have articulated it.

In *Last v Rosenfeld*, Hope J gave this account, which has the evident approval of the High Court in *Theodore v Mistford Pty Ltd*:[17]

> No sooner had the *Statute of Frauds* been enacted in 1677 than the courts set about relieving persons of its effect in cases where it was thought that the legislation could not have been intended to apply. In general terms, it was said that the courts would not allow the *Statute of Frauds* to be made an instrument of fraud, and that it did not prevent the proof of the fraud. No doubt, as was said by Selborne LC in *Maddison v Alderson*[18] in relation to one of the principles that was developed in this way, namely, the doctrine of part performance, this summary way of stating the principle, however true it may be when properly understood, is not an adequate explanation, either of the precise grounds, or of the established limits, of the relevant doctrine. The general approach indicated by this summary statement did, however, spread into a number of fields where a statute requires writing ...[19]

The modern foundation of the doctrine is the decision of the House of Lords in *Maddison v Alderson*. The speech of Lord Selborne LC has become a starting point for later consideration. His Lordship's speech includes these observations:

> ... That equity has been stated by high authority to rest upon the principle of fraud: 'Courts of Equity will not permit the statute to be made an instrument of fraud'. By this it cannot be meant that equity will relieve against a public statute of general policy in cases admitted to fall within it; and I agree ... that this summary way of stating the

---

16. *Butcher v Stapely* (1685) 23 ER 524.
17. (2005) 221 CLR 612 at 623–4.
18. (1883) 8 App Cas 467 at 474.
19. *Last v Rosenfeld* [1972] 2 NSWLR 923 at 927.

principle (however true it may be when properly [264] understood) is not an adequate explanation, either of the precise grounds, or of the established limits, of the equitable doctrine of part performance. In a suit founded on such part performance, the defendant is really 'charged' upon the equities resulting from the acts done in execution of the contract, and not (within the meaning of the statute) upon the contract itself. If such equities were excluded, injustice of a kind which the statute cannot be thought to have had in contemplation would follow. Let the case be supposed of a parol contract to sell land, completely performed on both sides, as to everything except conveyance; the whole purchase-money paid; the purchaser put into possession; expenditure by him (say in costly buildings) upon the property; leases granted by him to tenants. The contract is not a nullity; there is nothing in the statute to estop any Court which may have to exercise jurisdiction in the matter from inquiring into and taking notice of the truth of the facts. All the acts done must be referred to the actual contract, which is the measure and test of their legal and equitable character and consequences ... The line may not always be capable of being so clearly drawn ... but it is not arbitrary or unreasonable to hold that when the statute says that no action is to be brought to charge any person upon a contract concerning land, it has in view the simple case in which he is charged upon the contract only, and not that in which there are equities resulting from res gestae subsequent to and arising out of the contract. So long as the connection of those res gestae with the alleged contract does not depend upon mere parol testimony, but is reasonably to be inferred from the res gestae themselves, justice seems to require some such limitation of the scope of the statute, which might otherwise interpose an obstacle even to the rectification of material errors, however clearly proved, in an executed conveyance, founded upon an unsigned agreement.[20]

While extensively reviewing case law Lord Selborne LC said:

The doctrine, however, so established has been confined by judges of the greatest authority within limits intended to prevent a recurrence of the mischief which the statute was passed to suppress. The present case, resting entirely upon the parol evidence of one of the parties to the transaction, after the death of the other, forcibly illustrates the wisdom of the rule, which requires some evidentia rei to connect the alleged part performance with the alleged agreement. There is not otherwise enough in the situation in which the parties are found to raise questions which may not be solved without recourse to equity. It is not enough that an act done should be a condition of, or good consideration for, a contract, unless it is, as between the parties, such a part execution as to change their relative positions as to the subject-matter of the contract ... [I]t may be taken as now settled that part payment of purchase-money is not enough; and judges of high authority have said the same even of payment in full. Some of the reasons which have been given for that conclusion are not satisfactory; the best explanation of it seems to be, that the payment of money is an equivocal act, not (in itself), until the connection is established by parol testimony, indicative of a contract concerning land. I am not aware of any case in which the whole purchase-money has been paid without delivery of possession, nor is such a case at all likely to happen. All the authorities [show] that the acts relied upon as part performance must be unequivocally, and in their own nature, referable to some such agreement as that

---

20. *Maddison v Alderson* (1883) 8 App Cas 467 at 474–6.

[265] alleged ... The acts of part performance, exemplified in the long series of decided cases in which parol contracts concerning land have been enforced, have been (almost, if not quite, universally) relative to the possession, use, or tenure of the land. The law of equitable mortgage by deposit of title deeds depends upon the same principles.[21]

Lord Selborne LC reviewed many of the very numerous cases on part performance. They show that judicial opinion has not been completely uniform but from the earliest times there was unreadiness to give the *Statute of Frauds* its full literal effect. The readiness of the Court to give effect to equities arising upon conduct in performance of the contract does not provide a full or satisfactory exposition of unreadiness to treat part payment of the purchase money as an act of part performance; but as recognised by Lord Selborne that attitude to part payment was as well established by judicial authority as the doctrine of part performance itself ...

Consideration of part performance in the High Court of Australia has not produced any relaxation or departure from *Maddison v Alderson*. In *McBride v Sandland*, Isaacs J and Rich J ... [266] said:

(4) It must have been in fact done by the party relying on it on the faith of the agreement, and further the other party must have permitted it to be done on that footing.[22]

This is a very stringent requirement. Their Honours also said that it remained to be shown:

(7) That the act was done under the terms of that agreement by force of that agreement.[23]

Their Honours did not refer to the standing of part payment as an act of part performance, as their consideration was limited to the facts of that case.

The High Court again considered part performance in *Cooney v Burns*, where there was not in fact a payment. Knox CJ said '... It is settled that payment of part of the purchase-money is not of itself and apart from other circumstances — eg, delivery of possession — a sufficient act of part performance to take a case out of the statute'.[24]

In *JC Williamson Ltd v Lukey & Mulholland*, which related to an oral agreement for a five-year lease, the decision did not turn solely on part performance, but also involved suitability of the agreement for specific performance. Dixon J said, 'Equitable relief is obtainable, notwithstanding the *Statute of Frauds*, by a party who in pursuance of his contract has done acts of performance consistent only with some such contract subsisting ...'[25] and this appears to allude to Lord Selborne in *Maddison v Alderson*. Dixon J also said 'The acts of part performance must be such as to be consistent only with the existence of a contract between the parties, and to have been done in actual performance of that which in fact existed'.[26]

Regent v Millett, was a case in which the vendor, in an oral contract for sale, permitted the purchaser to take possession, and this was treated as an act of part performance,

---

21. *Maddison v Alderson* (1883) 8 App Cas 467 at 478.
22. *McBride v Sandland* (1918) 25 CLR 69 at 79.
23. *McBride v Sandland* (1918) 25 CLR 69 at 79.
24. *Cooney v Burns* (1922) 30 CLR 216 at 222–3.
25. *J C Williamson Ltd v Lukey & Mulholland* (1931) 45 CLR 282 at 297.
26. *J C Williamson Ltd v Lukey & Mulholland* (1931) 45 CLR 282 at 300.

although there was no contractual obligation to take possession. Justice Gibbs, in an ex tempore judgment with which other members of the Court agreed, said:

> ... it was submitted that a narrower test should be adopted and that it was necessary to establish 'such a performance as must necessarily imply the existence of the contract' — to use the words of Lord O'Hagan in *Maddison v Alderson*. However, the test suggested by the Earl of Selborne LC in that case, that the acts relied upon as part performance 'must be unequivocally, and in their own nature, referable to some such agreement as that alleged', has been consistently accepted as a correct statement of the law. It is enough that the acts are unequivocally and in their own nature referable to some contract of the general nature of that alleged (see *McBride v Sandland*).[27]

Justice Gibbs also adopted an expression in Dr. Williams' text '... The change of possession of land has been described as "the act of part performance par excellence"'.[28]

In *Waltons Stores (Interstate) Ltd v Maher*, Brennan J said:

> In order that acts may be relied on as part performance of an unwritten contract, they must be done under the terms and by force of that contract and they must be unequivocally and in their nature referable to some contract of the general nature of that alleged: *Regent v Millett*. The **[267]** acts which were held to amount to part performance were done by the Mahers to develop their own property, and the development was clearly for a commercial purpose. But, in my respectful opinion, those acts are not unequivocally and in their nature referable to an agreement for the lease of the Mahers' land.[29]

This passage is a restatement in classic terms of a formulation which has been repeatedly approved in the High Court, and has not received any disapprobation.

In *Steadman v Steadman*, the House of Lords, in a case about a complicated agreement for settlement of maintenance and property disputes between husband and wife, treated a payment of £100 arrears of maintenance, which was required by a term of the agreement, as an act of part performance so as to enable specific enforcement of another term under which the wife was to surrender her interest in the matrimonial home for another payment of money which had not been made. Law Lords in the majority expressed dissatisfaction with the general rule that payment of money cannot constitute an act of part performance of a parol contract for disposition of an interest in land. Lord Reid said:

> Normally the consideration for the purchase of land is a sum of money and there are statements that a sum of money can never be treated as part performance. Such statements would be reasonable if the person pleading the statute tendered repayment of any part of the price which he had received and was able thus to make restitutio in integrum. That would remove any 'fraud' or any equity on which the purchaser could properly rely. But to make a general rule that payment of money can never be part

---

27. *Regent v Millett* (1976) 133 CLR 679 at 682–3.
28. James Williams, *The Statute of Frauds Section Four in the Light of its Judicial Interpretation*, Cambridge, 1932, Ch 7.
29. *Waltons Stores (Interstate) Ltd v Maher* (1988) 164 CLR 387 at 432.

performance would seem to me to defeat the whole purpose of the doctrine and I do not think that we are compelled by authority to do that.[30]

Lord Simon of Glaisdale said that the reasons for the rule did not justify it 'as framed so absolutely'.[31] Lord Salmon was of the view that payments may be 'acts from which the nature of the contract can be deduced', while saying:

> It is no doubt true that often it is impossible to deduce even the existence of any contract from payment ... Nevertheless the circumstances surrounding a payment may be such that the payment becomes evidence not only of the existence of the contract under which it was made but also of the nature of that contract. What the payment proves in the light of its surrounding circumstances is not a matter of law but a matter of fact.[32]

Viscount Dilhorne said that his Lordship found it difficult to say on what principle the conclusion excluding payments of money from part performance had been reached.[33] Lord Morris of Borth-y-Gest dissented. Later legislative changes in the United Kingdom seem to make it unlikely that the House of Lords will again consider such a question.

In *Australian and New Zealand Banking Group Ltd v Widin*, the Full Court of the Federal Court of Australia applying the *Conveyancing Act* treated part performance as authoritatively expounded in *Maddison v Alderson*, and was of the view that there were acts of part performance in that case without resort to treating payment as an act of part performance. Justice Hill made an extremely comprehensive review and concluded, 'It may be possible to reconcile what is said in *Steadman* with the orthodox approach taken by the High Court to date and while there is much to be said for the adoption in Australia of *Steadman*, these are matters for the High Court rather than an intermediate Court of Appeal'.[34]

[268] I take the same view. In the present case there are no acts of ownership such as taking possession, paying rates or paying for the upkeep or improvement of the property, or receipt of rent or profits, or any other act at all. Acts of part performance have been almost universally closely related to possession and use or tenure of the land itself, such as where a purchaser is put into possession by the vendor, or allowed to take possession by the vendor, or where the purchaser carries out improvements. They have not necessarily been acts which the contract requires to be done. Acts on the land can much more readily be seen as unequivocally referable to the contract than payments of money. The anomaly of not recognising payment as an act of part performance is clear ...

The whole law of part performance is established by judicial authority, and discerning underlying principle is an obscure process ... Unless authoritatively directed to do otherwise, my view is that the Court of Appeal should apply the doctrine of part performance as it has received it, according to the terms in which it has been recognised in decisions of the High Court of Australia. The unavailability of payments as acts of part performance is part of what has been so received.

---

30. *Steadman v Steadman* [1976] AC 536 at 541.
31. *Steadman v Steadman* [1976] AC 536 at 565.
32. *Steadman v Steadman* [1976] AC 536 at 570.
33. *Steadman v Steadman* [1976] AC 536 at 555.
34. *Australian and New Zealand Banking Group Ltd v Widin* (1990) 26 FCR 21 at 37.

Payment may be relevant for other reasons yet not be treated as an act of part performance for the operation of s 54A [of the *Conveyancing Act*]. It is always necessary to prove the terms of the oral agreement, and the acts done in relation to the contract and its performance, including all payments made, can be put in evidence to show that there was an oral agreement as well as to show that there has been part performance. Payments are also relevant as part of the material upon which the Court is to act in deciding to award specific performance, which has a discretionary element, and is done in a way which resolves the whole controversy and sees to performance of outstanding obligations of each party.

Observations in *Steadman v Steadman* disapproving of excluding payments as acts of part performance are not altogether uniform. If the observations of Lord Salmon are applied, it cannot, in my opinion, be said that the series of payments to the Bishop are evidence either of the existence of the contract between Bechara and Peter, or of the nature of that contract. On no view was the arrangement between Bechara and the Bishop and the series of payments referable, let alone unequivocally referable, to the agreement between Bechara and Peter. That agreement required Bechara to do something quite different, to pay the instalments to the Commonwealth Bank, not to rely on a different arrangement which he made with the Bishop and to act on that other arrangement; and no less so if the fact is, as the trial judge inferred, that the Bishop did things which brought about the same result as performance of the contract would have done. Whether or not payments could qualify as acts [269] of part performance, these payments to the Bishop, and the arrangement with the Bishop for the Bishop to pay the instalments, have no claim at all for consideration as acts unequivocally referable to the contract as found or to a transaction of that kind. However that leaves the payment of the $30,000 for consideration; if there were no rule excluding payments, this payment would seem to fulfil every requirement for an act of part performance. As the law is, neither can be regarded, and s 54A stands in the way of Bechara's obtaining any relief in judicial proceedings, whether the declaratory order which he obtained, or any other relief.

Comment
1. See Radan & Stewart at **23.74–23.86**.

24

INJUNCTIONS

Introduction

24.1 This chapter deals with the principles governing the granting of injunctive relief. Generally, injunctions can be granted only if there is an infringement of some right belonging to the plaintiff. The exception to this rule is where an injunction is granted in relator proceedings. Injunctions can require positive conduct to be undertaken by the defendant — a mandatory injunction. However, more commonly, an injunction will restrain the defendant from engaging in some conduct — a prohibitory injunction. Injunctions can be granted before the dispute between the parties is resolved, with an interlocutory injunction, or following a full hearing of all the relevant facts, with a perpetual injunction. Injunctions can be granted in support of rights derived from the common law, equity or statute.

The cases extracted in this chapter discuss the following:

- the need for a plaintiff to have some right in need of protection before an injunction can be granted: *Australian Broadcasting Corporation v Lenah Game Meats Pty Limited* (2001) 208 CLR 199;
- the principles governing the granting of mandatory injunctions: *Redland Bricks Ltd v Morris* [1970] AC 652;
- the principles governing the granting of interlocutory injunctions: *Australian Broadcasting Corporation v O'Neill* (2006) 227 CLR 57;
- the granting of injunctions to restrain breaches of negative contractual stipulations: *Warner Bros Pictures Inc v Nelson* [1937] 1 KB 209;
- the granting of injunctions to enforce statutory rights: *Cooney v The Council of the Municipality of Ku-Ring-Gai* (1963) 114 CLR 582; and
- the principles governing relator proceedings: *The Attorney-General, on the Relation of Daniels, Steward and Wells v Huber, Sandy, and Wichmann Investments Pty Ltd* (1971) 2 SASR 142.

The plaintiff's right and the availability of injunctive relief

24.2 Australian Broadcasting Corporation v Lenah Game Meats Pty Limited (2001) 208 CLR 199

Court: High Court of Australia

Facts: Lenah operated a game meat processing business in Tasmania. Part of its work involved the killing and processing of brush tail possums in licensed abattoirs for the export market. Unknown trespassers entered into Lenah's property and installed hidden video cameras that filmed the slaughter and processing activities. The film was then supplied to an animal rights group, which passed it over to the ABC for public broadcasting. Lenah applied for, and obtained, interlocutory injunctions against the ABC and the animal rights group to restrain use of the film on the grounds that it had been unlawfully obtained and jeopardised Lenah's business.

Issue: The issue before the High Court was whether an injunction should be granted in favour of Lenah to prevent the ABC from distributing, publishing or copying the film.

Decision: The High Court (Gleeson CJ, Gaudron, Gummow, Hayne and Kirby JJ; Callinan JJ dissenting) allowed the ABC's appeal and refused to grant an injunction. The majority judges arrived at the decision by different routes, expressed in the various judgments.

Extracts: The extracts below from the judgment of Gleeson CJ, and the joint judgment of Gummow and Hayne JJ, reflect existing authority that, for an injunction to be granted, equity's auxiliary jurisdiction requires an established legal cause of action and its exclusive jurisdiction requires a recognised equitable basis for intervention. Although courts may determine the equitable bases for intervention, unconscionability alone will generally not suffice. The extracts from the judgment of Kirby J reflect his view that the power to grant an injunction is founded on the court's statutory powers and requires neither a legal cause of action nor an equitable basis for intervention. His decision to refuse the application for an injunction was based upon an implied constitutional right of freedom of political expression.

Gleeson CJ

[216] The nature of the jurisdiction

Sir Frederick Jordan, in his *Chapters on Equity in New South Wales*, said:

> The purpose of an interlocutory injunction is to keep matters in statu quo until the rights of the parties can be determined at the hearing of the suit.[1]

That is a sufficient description of the purpose for which the Supreme Court of Tasmania might properly have granted an interlocutory injunction in the present case. It is not a complete description of the circumstances in which an interlocutory injunction may be granted. But it covers this case. [Lenah] claimed a right, which it sought to have vindicated by a permanent injunction, to prevent [the ABC] from publishing or broadcasting any of the [217] material on the video tape which had come into its possession. Subject to any argument as to whether damages were an adequate remedy, there was a probability that such right would be rendered worthless if, before the final hearing, [the ABC] broadcast the material as and when it pleased. In order to preserve the subject matter of the dispute, and to prevent the practical destruction of the right claimed by [Lenah] before the action could be heard on a final basis, the Supreme Court had power to grant an interlocutory injunction. The immediate source of that power was s 11 of the *Supreme Court Civil Procedure Act* 1932 (Tas). Power of that nature has a long history, and is exercised according to principle,

---

1. Frederick Jordan, 6th ed (1947) at 146.

not unguided discretion. I agree with what is said by Gummow and Hayne JJ as to the relevant principles. For present purposes, what is most significant is that the justice and convenience of granting an interlocutory injunction, in a case such as the present, is to be found in the purpose for which the power exists.

The corollary of the proposition stated by Sir Frederick Jordan is that a plaintiff seeking an interlocutory injunction must be able to show sufficient colour of right to the final relief, in aid of which interlocutory relief is sought. Lord Cottenham LC in *Great Western Railway Co v Birmingham & Oxford Junction Railway Co* formulated the issue as whether 'this bill states a substantial question between the parties'.[2] In *McCarty v North Sydney Municipal Council*, the Chief Judge in Equity described the proposition that a plaintiff seeking an interlocutory injunction must show at least a probability that he will succeed in establishing his title to the relief sought at the final hearing as 'so well established that no authority is really needed in support of it'.[3]

We are not concerned in the present case with forms of relief, such as the Mareva order, or anti-suit injunctions, which have expanded the boundaries of this area of jurisprudence. Nor are we concerned with some special statutory jurisdiction. [Lenah] claims a right and seeks to have it vindicated by a permanent injunction. It claims to be entitled to restrain [the ABC], permanently, from making use of a video. The justice and convenience of imposing interim restraint, pending the hearing of the final action, if it exists, lies in the need to prevent the practical destruction of that right before there has been an opportunity to have its existence finally established.

In *Castlemaine Tooheys Ltd v South Australia*, Mason ACJ summarised the principles governing the grant or refusal of **[218]** interlocutory injunctions in both private law and public law litigation. He said:

> In order to secure such an injunction the plaintiff must show (1) that there is a serious question to be tried or that the plaintiff has made out a prima facie case, in the sense that if the evidence remains as it is there is a probability that at the trial of the action the plaintiff will be held entitled to relief; (2) that he will suffer irreparable injury for which damages will not be an adequate compensation unless an injunction is granted; and (3) that the balance of convenience favours the granting of an injunction.[4]

Underwood J held that the respondent failed to satisfy either (1) or (2).

A dispute arose in the course of argument as to 'whether interlocutory injunctive relief to prevent publication can be granted without any underlying cause of action to be tried'. In the context of the present case, this is puzzling. There could be no justification, in principle, for granting an interlocutory injunction here other than to preserve the subject matter of the dispute, and to maintain the status quo pending the determination of the rights of the parties. If [Lenah] cannot show a sufficient colour of right of the kind sought to be vindicated by final relief, the foundation of the claim for interlocutory relief disappears.

In a context such as the present, a proposition that [Lenah] has a 'free-standing' right to interlocutory relief is a contradiction in terms. This is demonstrated, not

---

2. *Great Western Railway Co v Birmingham & Oxford Junction Railway Co* (1848) 41 ER 1074 at 1076.
3. *McCarty v North Sydney Municipal Council* (1918) 18 SR (NSW) 210 at 211–2.
4. *Castlemaine Tooheys Ltd v South Australia* (1986) 161 CLR 148 at 153.

only by the purpose for which interlocutory relief is granted, but by the form of the relief. The Full Court granted the injunction sought 'until further order'. A more usual form of interlocutory injunction would be 'until the hearing of the action or further order', but the effect is the same. If there were a 'free-standing' right to injunctive relief, why would the injunction be limited in time? If there is no serious question to be tried because, upon examination, it appears that the facts alleged by [Lenah] cannot, as a matter of law, sustain such a right, then there is no subject matter to be preserved. There is then no justice in maintaining the status quo, because that depends upon restraining [the ABC] from doing something which, by hypothesis, [Lenah] has no right to prevent.

Unconscionability is a concept that may be of importance in considering the nature and existence of the claimed right which a plaintiff seeks to vindicate. It is a matter that requires examination in the present case. But, in these circumstances, it cannot be used to conjure up a right to interlocutory relief where there is no right to final relief. If [Lenah] cannot demonstrate that there is at least a serious question as to whether [the ABC] is free to keep the video and to use it as it thinks fit, how could conscience require or justify temporary restraint upon the use of the video by [the ABC]? If there is no serious question to be tried in the action, how can it be [219] unconscientious to keep and use the video in the meantime? Unconscionability has a role to play in the present case; but that role is in the evaluation of the claim to final relief. Such an evaluation became necessary at the interlocutory stage because it was contended that [Lenah] had no equity.

The extent to which it is necessary, or appropriate, to examine the legal merits of a plaintiff's claim for final relief, in determining whether to grant an interlocutory injunction, will depend upon the circumstances of the case. There is no inflexible rule. It may depend upon the nature of the dispute. For example, if there is little room for argument about the legal basis of a plaintiff's case, and the dispute is about the facts, a court may be persuaded easily, at an interlocutory stage, that there is sufficient evidence to show, prima facie, an entitlement to final relief. The court may then move on to discretionary considerations, including the balance of convenience ...

Gummow and Hayne JJ

[239] Interlocutory injunctions

Section 10 of the *Supreme Court Civil Procedure Act* 1932 (Tas) (the Supreme Court Act) provides for the concurrent administration by the Supreme Court of law and equity, but with the rules of equity to prevail in any conflict or variance between those rules and the rules of the common law (s 11(10)). Sub-section (7) of s 10 provides that the Court shall grant either absolutely or on terms all such remedies as any of the parties may be entitled to in respect of every legal or equitable claim brought forward in the proceeding 'so that, as far as possible, all matters in controversy between the parties may be completely and finally determined, and all multiplicity of legal proceedings concerning any of those matters avoided'.

Section 11 of the Supreme Court Act then deals with miscellaneous matters. Sub-section (12) of s 11 reads:

A mandamus or an injunction may be granted or a receiver appointed by an interlocutory order of the Court or a judge thereof in all cases in which it shall appear to the Court or judge to be just and convenient that such order should be made; and any such order may be made either unconditionally or upon such terms and conditions as the Court or judge shall think just; and if, whether before, or at, or after the hearing of any cause or matter, an application is made for an injunction to prevent any threatened or apprehended waste or trespass, the injunction may be granted if the Court or judge thinks fit, whether the person against whom the injunction is sought is or is not in possession under any claim of title or otherwise, or (if out of possession) does or does not claim a right to do the act sought to be restrained under any colour of title, and whether the estates claimed by both or by either of the parties are legal or equitable.

This provision closely follows the terms of s 25(8) of the *Supreme Court of Judicature Act 1873* (UK) (the Judicature Act). That is not surprising. The Tasmanian legislature enacted the Supreme Court Act **[240]** with the expressed objective of adopting the system established in England by the Judicature Act.

Lenah fixes upon the phrase in s 11(12) 'in all cases in which it shall appear to the Court or judge to be just and convenient' as indicating all that has to be shown to enliven the power to award an interlocutory injunction. However, the terms which introduce that phrase, 'injunction' and 'receiver', are legal terms of art. The point was made by Lindley LJ, early in the operation of the Judicature system. In *Holmes v Millage* his Lordship said:

> Although injunctions are granted and receivers are appointed more readily than they were before the passing of the Judicature Acts, and some inconvenient rules formerly observed have been very properly relaxed, yet the principles on which the jurisdiction of the Court of Chancery rested have not been changed. [5]

More recently, in *The 'Siskina'*, Lord Diplock declared:

> Since the transfer to the Supreme Court of Judicature of all the jurisdiction previously exercised by the court of chancery and the courts of common law, the power of the High Court to grant interlocutory injunctions has been regulated by statute. That the High Court has no power to grant an interlocutory injunction except in protection or assertion of some legal or equitable right which it has jurisdiction to enforce by final judgment, was first laid down in the classic judgment of Cotton LJ in *North London Railway Co v Great Northern Railway Co*,[6] which has been consistently followed ever since.[7]

Where interlocutory injunctive relief is sought in some special statutory jurisdiction which uses the term 'injunction' to identify a remedy for which it provides, that term takes its colour from the statutory regime in question.[8] Nor should the references in the authorities to legal or equitable rights obscure the significant and traditional use of the injunction in the administration of public trusts, being trusts for charitable purposes,

---

5. *Holmes v Millage* [1893] 1 QB 551 at 557.
6. *North London Railway Co v Great Northern Railway Co* (1883) 11 QBD 30 at 39–40.
7. *'Siskina' (Owners of Cargo Lately Laden on Board) v Distos Compania Naviera SA* [1979] AC 210 at 256.
8. *Cardile v LED Builders Pty Ltd* (1999) 198 CLR 380 at 394.

and in ensuring the observance of public law at the suit of the Attorney-General, with or without a relator, or at the suit of a person with a sufficient interest.

[241] Further, as was pointed out in *Cardile v LED Builders Pty Ltd*,[9] the injunctive remedy is still the subject of development in courts exercising equitable jurisdiction. This is true in public law, as *Enfield City Corporation v Development Assessment Commission*[10] illustrates. The treatment of the requirement for a legal right that is proprietary in nature, and of negative stipulations, referred to in *Cardile*,[11] are other examples. In addition, as the general law develops in such fields as the economic torts and the protection of confidential information, there is an increase in the scope of the legal and equitable rights for which an injunctive remedy may be available. Similar development of equity is to be observed in England. Lord Millett has said that in England equity is not only 'now fully awake' and 'on the march again', but '[i]ndeed it is rampant'.[12] However, his Lordship also emphasised that 'the essential basis for principled advance' lies in 'analytical exposition of traditional doctrine'.[13]

The basic proposition remains that where interlocutory injunctive relief is sought in a Judicature system court, it is necessary to identify the legal (which may be statutory)[14] or equitable rights which are to be determined at trial and in respect of which there is sought final relief which may or may not be injunctive in nature.[15] In *Muschinski v Dodds*, Deane J said that an equitable remedy 'is available only when warranted by established equitable principles or by the legitimate processes of legal reasoning, by analogy, induction and deduction, from the starting point of a proper understanding of the conceptual foundation of such principles'.[16]

Remarks by Windeyer J in *Colbeam Palmer Ltd v Stock Affiliates Pty Ltd*[17] are also in point. His Honour referred to the circularity involved in saying that, because a court of equity should enjoin interference with the economic or commercial interests of the plaintiff, those interests were proprietary in nature and that it was upon protection of those proprietary interests that the intervention of the court was to be based. Further, in *Moorgate Tobacco Co Ltd v Philip* [242] *Morris Ltd [No 2]*,[18] Deane J, delivering the judgment of the Court, set out a passage from the judgment of Dixon J in *Victoria Park Racing and Recreation Grounds Co Ltd v Taylor*, which included the following:

> But courts of equity have not in British jurisdictions thrown the protection of an injunction around all the intangible elements of value, that is, value in exchange, which may flow from the exercise by an individual of his powers or resources whether in the organisation of a business or undertaking or the use of ingenuity, knowledge,

---

9. (1999) 198 CLR 380 at 395.
10. (2000) 199 CLR 135.
11. *Cardile v LED Builders Pty Ltd* (1999) 198 CLR 380 at 395.
12. Foreword, *Snell's Equity*, 30th ed, 2000.
13. Foreword, *Snell's Equity*, 30th ed, 2000.
14. *Fejo v Northern Territory* (1998) 195 CLR 96 at 123; *Truth About Motorways Pty Ltd v Macquarie Infrastructure Investment Management Ltd* (2000) 200 CLR 591 at 628.
15. *Cardile v LED Builders Pty Ltd* (1999) 198 CLR 380 at 395–6.
16. *Muschinski v Dodds* (1985) 160 CLR 583 at 615.
17. (1968) 122 CLR 25 at 34.
18. (1984) 156 CLR 414 at 444–5.

skill or labour. This is sufficiently evidenced by the history of the law of copyright and by the fact that the exclusive right to invention, trade marks, designs, trade name and reputation are dealt with in English law as special heads of protected interests and not under a wide generalisation.[19]

Equally, courts of equity will not always grant injunctions against a party profiting from an illegal activity of some other person. That, too, is a 'wide generalisation' which provides an insufficient basis for identifying whether relevant equitable principles are engaged ...

Kirby J

[270] *Conclusion: injunctive power available*: I accept the need for care in providing injunctive relief. However, the cases collected by Callinan J demonstrate that no narrow view has been adopted as to the meaning of the expression 'a serious question to be tried'. Sometimes (as here) when the interlocutory injunction is sought, the *seriousness* of the matter will be plain but the precise *question* to be formulated may not yet be entirely clear. In such circumstances, it may **[271]** sometimes follow that, in its discretion, a court will refuse the interlocutory injunction. It might do so not being convinced that it is 'just and convenient that such order should be made'.[20] Or it might conclude that damages will, in the circumstances, be an adequate remedy.[21] But to deny a court, such as the Supreme Court, acting under a provision such as s 11(12) of the *Supreme Court Civil Procedure Act* the *power* to grant an injunction in such a case is a proposition I reject. The words of the statute and the status and function of that Court deny such a conclusion. Had such an approach been taken by earlier courts, there would have been no Mareva injunctions, no Anton Piller orders and many cases at the boundaries of injunctive remedies might have been differently decided.

The equitable foundation for injunctive relief

Equity meeting new needs: It is a commonplace that equity is a living force and that it responds to new situations. It must do so in ways that are consistent with equitable principles. If it were to fail to respond, it would atrophy. Where an attempt is made to restrain the use of information that has come into the hands of a party, the basis for the exercise of equitable jurisdiction does not lie, as such, in the proprietary rights of that party over the object containing the information. It lies, in the words of Deane J in *Moorgate Tobacco Co Ltd v Philip Morris Ltd [No 2]* 'in the notion of an obligation of conscience arising from the circumstances in or through which the information was communicated or obtained'.[22]

Equity and modern media: Commonly, claims for injunctive relief in such cases will involve assertions that publication, in the particular circumstances, would amount to an actionable breach of confidence. Where such a cause of action can be shown to be reasonably arguable, an applicant for an interlocutory injunction will be well on the way to securing such relief. However, it is not only in circumstances where confidential

---

19. *Victoria Park Racing and Recreation Grounds Co Ltd v Taylor* (1937) 58 CLR 479 at 509.
20. *Supreme Court Civil Procedure Act* s 11(12).
21. *Lincoln Hunt Australia Pty Ltd v Willesee* (1986) 4 NSWLR 457 at 458.
22. *Moorgate Tobacco Co Ltd v Philip Morris Ltd [No 2]* (1984) 156 CLR 414 at 438.

information has been 'improperly or surreptitiously [272] obtained or ... imparted in confidence [so that it] ought not to be divulged'[23] that courts have restrained such publication. Australian courts have responded to new circumstances that have involved serious affronts to conscience.

Such circumstances will arise in a case where information which lacks the quality of confidence has nevertheless been obtained illegally, tortiously, surreptitiously or otherwise improperly. In such cases the preservation of the confidentiality or secrecy of the information may be of substantial concern to the applicant for relief.[24] The jurisdiction to restrain the use of confidential information has long been exercised against third parties who have received the information from someone else. By extension, such jurisdiction may now be exercised, in a case where the information in question has been obtained illegally, tortiously, surreptitiously or improperly, even where the possessor is itself innocent of wrongdoing. The reason for providing the relief is to uphold the obligation of conscience and to prevent publication in circumstances where such publication would be unconscionable ...

[275] *Remedial law and modern relevance*: I do not believe that the approaches adopted by the experienced judges in the cases mentioned depart from the broad statutory power afforded to Supreme Courts in Australia to grant interlocutory injunctions. Nor do I believe that they depart from a sound application of equitable principles in modern conditions. To remain relevant to meet the new situations presented by the operations of modern media obtaining and using the fruits of criminal and wrongful acts of others, equity is capable of adaptation. Special considerations govern the provision of injunctive relief where the information in question concerns the activities of public bodies or governmental information. In such cases it is necessary for courts to wear 'different spectacles'.[25] However, in respect of other information, in determining whether its use would be unconscionable, a court would be obliged to take into account all of the circumstances of the case including competing public interests. Such public interests [276] include both upholding the integrity of private property and personal rights[26] and defending freedom of speech and expression.[27]

To hold that a superior court in Australia lacks the power to grant an interlocutory injunction to restrain a media defendant from broadcasting information acquired illegally, tortiously, surreptitiously or otherwise improperly simply because it was only a receptacle and not directly involved in the wrongful acquisition of the information would involve an unjustifiable abdication of the large powers afforded to such courts by their enabling statutes.[28] It would also involve a needless departure from a consistent line of decisional authority in Australia, given over the past twenty years. It would inflict

---

23. *Lord Ashburton v Pape* [1913] 2 Ch 469 at 475, cited in *The Commonwealth v John Fairfax & Sons Ltd* (1980) 147 CLR 39 at 50.

24. *Moorgate Tobacco Co Ltd v Philip Morris Ltd [No 2]* (1984) 156 CLR 414 at 438.

25. *The Commonwealth v John Fairfax & Sons Ltd* (1980) 147 CLR 39 at 51.

26. *Lincoln Hunt Australia Pty Ltd v Willesee* (1986) 4 NSWLR 457 at 465; *Emcorp Pty Ltd v Australian Broadcasting Corporation* [1988] 2 Qd R 169 at 176; *Rinsdale Pty Ltd v Australian Broadcasting Corporation* [1993] Aust Torts Rep ¶81-231 at 62,381.

27. *Summertime Holdings Pty Ltd v Environmental Defender's Office Ltd* (1998) 45 NSWLR 291.

28. See, for example, *Supreme Court Civil Procedure Act* s 11(12).

an undue narrowing on the availability of interlocutory injunctions to meet modern circumstances. Those circumstances occasionally demand the provision of such relief where the use of the information is shown to be unconscionable and other remedies are judged to be inadequate. It would impose on the practice of Australian courts a needless inflexibility when the applicable principles (as well as actual experience) show that such courts are well able to balance the competing interests at stake.

I see no reason why this Court should adopt such a narrow position in this branch of the law of remedies. I see every reason why it should not. Least of all should it adopt a narrow approach out of deference to judicial remarks written long before the features of the modern media and mass communications existed as they do today ... The power of modern media, so important for the freedoms enjoyed in Australia, can sometimes be abused. When that happens, the courts are often the only institutions in our society with the power and the will to provide protection and redress to those who are gravely harmed. Apart from the other cases where a cause of action can be shown to sustain the grant of an interlocutory injunction, in my view a court, such as the Supreme Court, has the statutory power to grant an injunction to restrain the use of information which has been obtained by a trespasser or by some other illegal, tortious, surreptitious or improper means where the use of such information would be unconscionable.

Comments
1. See Radan & Stewart at **24.6–24.9**.
2. For an analysis of this case see G Taylor & D Wright, '*Australian Broadcasting Corporation v Lenah Game Meats* — Privacy and Possums: An Analysis of the High Court's Decision' (2002) 26 *Melbourne University Law Review* 707.

Mandatory injunctions

24.3   Redland Bricks Ltd v Morris [1970] AC 652

Court: House of Lords

Facts: Morris' market garden was located on land that sloped down towards land used by Redland Bricks for earth and clay excavation. About 60 feet away from Morris' boundary, Redland Bricks had caused a deep pit to fill with water. Part of Morris' land slipped onto the adjoining land and continued to be undermined by the water over a period of months. This was despite actions taken by Redland Bricks to back-fill the area and to prevent further slippage. Morris began legal action seeking liquidated damages to recover costs incurred and injunctions to stop Redland Bricks from further eroding the land through excavation without putting steps in place to prevent damage. An order was also sought for the restoration of support to Morris' land. A single judge awarded £325 damages, an injunction to stop further undermining of the land without providing support and a mandatory injunction for Redland Bricks to restore support to Morris' land within six months. Redland Bricks appealed to the Court of Appeal and then to the House of Lords.

Issue: The main issue before the House of Lords was whether a mandatory injunction was justified in the circumstances. It was argued that damages represented adequate compensation and that Redland Bricks was put at risk because the order did not specify what it was actually required to do to comply with the order.

Decision: The House of Lords (Lords Reid, Morris of Borth-y-Gest, Hodson, Upjohn and Diplock) unanimously allowed the appeal by Redland Bricks.

Extracts: The extracts from the speech of Lord Upjohn discuss the elements required for the granting of a mandatory injunction.

Lord Upjohn

[665] My Lords, quia timet actions are broadly applicable to two types of cases: first, where the defendant has as yet done no hurt to the plaintiff but is threatening and intending (so the plaintiff alleges) to do works which will render irreparable harm to him or his property if carried to completion. Your Lordships are not concerned with that and those cases are normally, though not exclusively, concerned with negative injunctions. Secondly, the type of case where the plaintiff has been fully recompensed both at law and in equity for the damage he has suffered but where he alleges that the earlier actions of the defendant may lead to future causes of action. In practice this means the case of which that which is before your Lordships' House is typical, where the defendant has withdrawn support from his neighbour's land or where he has so acted in depositing his soil from his mining operations as to constitute a menace to the plaintiff's land. It is in this field that undoubted jurisdiction of equity to grant a mandatory injunction, that is an injunction ordering the defendant to carry out positive works, finds its main expression, though of course it is equally applicable to many other cases. Thus, to take the simplest example, if the defendant, the owner of land, including a metalled road over which the plaintiff has a right of way, ploughs up that land so that it is no longer usable, no doubt a mandatory injunction will go to restore it; damages are not a sufficient remedy, for the plaintiff has no right to go on the defendant's land to remake his right of way.

The cases of *Isenberg v East India House Estate Co Ltd*[29] and *Durell v Pritchard*[30] have laid down some basic principles, and your Lordships have been referred to some other cases which have been helpful. The grant of a mandatory injunction is, of course, entirely discretionary and unlike a negative injunction can never be 'as of course'. Every case must depend essentially on its own particular circumstances. Any general principles for its application can only be laid down in the most general terms:

1. A mandatory injunction can only be granted where the plaintiff shows a very strong probability on the facts that grave damage will accrue to him in the future. As Lord Dunedin said in 1919 it is not sufficient to say 'timeo'.[31] It is a jurisdiction to be exercised sparingly and with caution but, in the proper case, unhesitatingly.

---

29. (1863) 46 ER 637.
30. (1865) 1 Ch App 244.
31. *Attorney-General for the Dominion of Canada v Ritchie Contracting and Supply Co* [1919] AC 999 at 1005.

2. Damages will not be a sufficient or adequate remedy if such damage does happen. This is only the application of a general principle of equity; it has nothing to do with Lord Cairns' Act or *Shelfer's* case.[32]

[666]

3. Unlike the case where a negative injunction is granted to prevent the continuance or recurrence of a wrongful act the question of the cost to the defendant to do works to prevent or lessen the likelihood of a future apprehended wrong must be an element to be taken into account:
   (a) where the defendant has acted without regard to his neighbour's rights, or has tried to steal a march on him or has tried to evade the jurisdiction of the court or, to sum it up, has acted wantonly and quite unreasonably in relation to his neighbour he may be ordered to repair his wanton and unreasonable acts by doing positive work to restore the status quo even if the expense to him is out of all proportion to the advantage thereby accruing to the plaintiff;
   (b) but where the defendant has acted reasonably, though in the event wrongly, the cost of remedying by positive action his earlier activities is most important for two reasons. First, because no legal wrong has yet occurred (for which he has not been recompensed at law and in equity) and, in spite of gloomy expert opinion, may never occur or possibly only on a much smaller scale than anticipated. Secondly, because if ultimately heavy damage does occur the plaintiff is in no way prejudiced for he has his action at law and all his consequential remedies in equity.
   So the amount to be expended under a mandatory order by the defendant must be balanced with these considerations in mind against the anticipated possible damages to the plaintiff and if, on such balance, it seems unreasonable to inflict such expenditure upon one who for this purpose is no more than a potential wrongdoer then the court must exercise its jurisdiction accordingly. Of course, the court does not have to order such works as upon the evidence before it will remedy the wrong but may think it proper to impose upon the defendant the obligation of doing certain works which may upon expert opinion merely lessen the likelihood of any further injury to the plaintiff's land ...

4. If in the exercise of its discretion the court decides that it is a proper case to grant a mandatory injunction, then the court must be careful to see that the defendant knows exactly in fact what he has to do and this means not as a matter of law but as a matter of fact, so that in carrying out an order he can give his contractors the proper instructions ...

[667] My Lords, I shall apply these principles or conditions to this case, and I can do so very shortly.

1 As a matter of expert evidence supported by the further slip of land during the hearing it is obvious that this condition, which must be one of fact in each case, is satisfied and, indeed, is not disputed.

2 Damages obviously are not a sufficient remedy, for no one knows whether any further damage will occur and, if so, upon what scale — upon the expert evidence it might be very substantial.

---

32. *Shelfer v City of London Electricity Lighting Co* [1895] 1 Ch 287.

3 [Redland Bricks] have not behaved unreasonably but only wrongly. Upon the facts of this case the judge, in my opinion would have been fully justified in imposing on [Redland Bricks] an obligation to do some reasonable and not too expensive works which might have a reasonable chance of preventing further damage. He did not do so and it is not surprising that in the county court this was not further explored. Alternatively he might have given leave to apply for a mandatory injunction.

4 But in making his mandatory order in my opinion the judge totally disregarded this necessary and perfectly well settled condition. The terms of the order imposed on [Redland Bricks] an absolutely unqualified obligation on them to restore support without giving them any indication of what was to be done. The judge might have ordered [Redland Bricks] to carry out the remedial works described by [Morris'] expert in his evidence though it would have to be set out in great detail. I could have understood that, but as it was thought to cost £30,000 that would have been most unreasonable and would have offended principle 3, but the order in fact imposed went much further; it imposed an unlimited and unqualified obligation on [Redland Bricks], and I do not know how they could have attempted to comply with it. The expenditure of the sum of £30,000 which I have just mentioned would not necessarily have complied with it for though it would in all probability have prevented any further damage it was not guaranteed to do so and that is what in effect the mandatory order of the learned judge required. My Lords, in my opinion that part of the order of the county court judge cannot stand and the appeal must be allowed.

Comment

1. See Radan & Stewart at **24.20–24.25**.

Interlocutory injunctions

24.4 Australian Broadcasting Corporation v O'Neill
(2006) 227 CLR 57

Court: High Court of Australia

Facts: The ABC contracted with a former police officer and a documentary film company for the production of a program for television. It contained information and allegations concerning O'Neill, a convicted child killer, linking him with other murders and the notorious unsolved disappearance in 1966 of three siblings known as the Beaumont children. The ABC's planned screening of the film in 2005 was preceded by considerable publicity about O'Neill, conveying clear imputations that he was a 'multiple murderer'. This included defamatory statements by senior police officers, newspaper articles and a display of the film at the Hobart Film Festival. However, there were no current or intended criminal charges against O'Neill in relation to any of the matters raised against him publicly. O'Neill sought an interlocutory injunction in the Supreme Court of Tasmania to stop the ABC from screening the film on television.

> **Issue:** The issue before the High Court was whether the general principles for determining a discretionary grant of interlocutory injunctions to restrain wrongs were applicable to interlocutory applications to restrain publication of allegedly defamatory material.
>
> **Decision:** The majority of the High Court (Gleeson CJ, Gummow, Hayne and Crennan JJ; Kirby and Heydon JJ dissenting) allowed the ABC's appeal and refused interlocutory relief.
>
> **Extracts:** The extracts from the joint judgment of Gleeson CJ and Crennan J indicate that the granting of injunctions depends on whether there is a serious question to be tried on entitlement to relief, whether there is a likelihood of injury for which damages would not be adequate, and whether the balance of convenience favours the granting of an injunction. The extracts from the joint judgment of Gummow and Hayne JJ highlight the importance of the authority of *Beecham Group Ltd v Bristol Laboratories Pty Ltd*.

Gleeson CJ and Crennan J

[66] In his widely quoted judgment in *Bonnard v Perryman*,[33] in which Lord Esher MR, and Lindley, Bowen and Lopes LJJ concurred, Lord Coleridge CJ explained why 'the subject matter of an action for defamation is so special as to require exceptional caution in exercising the jurisdiction to interfere by injunction before the trial of an action to prevent an anticipated wrong' and why, when there is a plea of justification, it is generally wiser, in all but exceptional cases, to [67] abstain from interference until the trial and determination of the plea of justification. First, there is the public interest in the right of free speech. Secondly, until the defence of justification is resolved, it is not known whether publication of the matter would invade a legal right of the plaintiff. Thirdly, a defence of justification is ordinarily a matter for decision by a jury, not by a judge sitting alone as in an application for an injunction. Fourthly, the general character of the plaintiff may be an important matter in the outcome of a trial; it may produce an award of only nominal damages.

In one respect, what Lord Coleridge CJ said, in its application to this case, requires qualification. His Lordship was dealing with a context in which truth of itself amounted to justification. Here, in the state of the law at the time of the proceedings [before the trial judge and the Full Court], [the ABC] needed the added element of public benefit. Subject to that significant matter, what his Lordship said is directly in point. The general public interest in free speech is involved. The trial judge was prepared to accept that there was a strong possibility that the imputations could be shown to be true. The defence of justification remains unresolved. [O'Neill's] general character, or if the difference be material, reputation, is such that, even if he succeeded at trial, the damages awarded for the publication the subject of the interlocutory application could well be nominal.

Lord Coleridge CJ's conclusion was that 'it is wiser in this case, as it generally and in all but exceptional cases must be, to abstain from interference until the trial'.[34] That form of expression does not deny the existence of a discretion. Inflexibility is not the hallmark of a jurisdiction that is to be exercised on the basis of justice and convenience. Formulations

---

33. [1891] 2 Ch 269 at 284.
34. *Bonnard v Perryman* [1891] 2 Ch 269 at 285.

of principle which, for purposes of legal analysis, gather together considerations which must be taken into account may appear rigid if the ultimate foundation for the exercise of the jurisdiction is overlooked. Nevertheless, so long as that misunderstanding is avoided, there are to be found, in many Australian decisions, useful reminders of the principles which guide the exercise of discretion in this area. One of the best known statements of principle is that of Walsh J, before he became a member of this Court, in *Stocker v McElhinney [No 2]* ... [C]iting *Bonnard v Perryman,* he said:

(1) Although it was one time suggested that there was no power in the court, under provisions similar to those contained in [the Act governing procedure in the Supreme Court of New South Wales] to grant an interlocutory injunction, in cases of defamation, it is settled that the power exists in such cases.

(2) In such cases, the power is exercised with great caution, and [68] only in very clear cases.

(3) If there is any real room for debate as to whether the statements complained of are defamatory, the injunction will be refused. Indeed, it is only where on this point, the position is so clear that, in the judge's view a subsequent finding by a jury to the contrary would be set aside as unreasonable, that the injunction will go.

(4) If, on the evidence before the judge, there is any real ground for supposing that the defendant may succeed upon any such ground as privilege, or of truth and public benefit, or even that the plaintiff if successful, will recover nominal damages only, the injunction will be refused.[35]

The principles were discussed, for example, in *Chappell v TCN Channel Nine Pty Ltd*[36] (a decision referred to by Crawford J in a passage quoted above), *National Mutual Life Association of Australasia Ltd v GTV Corporation Pty Ltd,*[37] and *Jakudo Pty Ltd v South Australian Telecasters Ltd.*[38] As Doyle CJ said in the last-mentioned case, in all applications for an interlocutory injunction, a court will ask whether the plaintiff has shown that there is a serious question to be tried as to the plaintiff's entitlement to relief, has shown that the plaintiff is likely to suffer injury for which damages will not be an adequate remedy, and has shown that the balance of convenience favours the granting of an injunction. These are the organising principles, to be applied having regard to the nature and circumstances of the case, under which issues of justice and convenience are addressed. We agree with the explanation of these organising principles in the reasons of Gummow and Hayne JJ, and their reiteration that the doctrine of the Court established in *Beecham Group Ltd v Bristol Laboratories Pty Ltd*[39] should be followed. In the context of a defamation case, the application of those organising principles will require particular attention to the considerations which courts have identified as dictating caution. Foremost among those considerations is the public interest in free speech. A further consideration is that, in the defamation context, the outcome of a trial is especially likely to turn upon issues that are, by hypothesis, unresolved. Where one such issue is justification, it is commonly

---

35. *Stocker v McElhinney [No 2]* [1961] NSWR 1043 at 1048.
36. (1988) 14 NSWLR 153.
37. [1989] VR 747.
38. (1997) 69 SASR 440 at 442–3.
39. (1968) 118 CLR 618.

an issue for jury decision. In [69] addition, the plaintiff's general character may be found to be such that, even if the publication is defamatory, only nominal damages will be awarded ...

Gummow and Hayne JJ

[81] Interlocutory injunctions

The relevant principles in Australia are those explained in *Beecham Group Ltd v Bristol Laboratories Pty Ltd.* This Court (Kitto, [82] Taylor, Menzies and Owen JJ) said that on such applications the court addresses itself to two main inquiries and continued:

> The first is whether the plaintiff has made out a prima facie case, in the sense that if the evidence remains as it is there is a probability that at the trial of the action the plaintiff will be held entitled to relief ... The second inquiry is ... whether the inconvenience or injury which the plaintiff would be likely to suffer if an injunction were refused outweighs or is outweighed by the injury which the defendant would suffer if an injunction were granted.[40]

By using the phrase 'prima facie case', their Honours did not mean that the plaintiff must show that it is more probable than not that at trial the plaintiff will succeed; it is sufficient that the plaintiff show a sufficient likelihood of success to justify in the circumstances the preservation of the status quo pending the trial. That this was the sense in which the Court was referring to the notion of a prima facie case is apparent from an observation to that effect made by Kitto J in the course of argument.[41] With reference to the first inquiry, the Court continued, in a statement of central importance for this appeal:

> How strong the probability needs to be depends, no doubt, upon the nature of the rights [the plaintiff] asserts and the practical consequences likely to flow from the order he seeks.[42]

For example, special considerations apply where injunctive relief is sought to interfere with the decision of the executive branch of government to prosecute offences. Again, in *Castlemaine Tooheys Ltd v South Australia*,[43] Mason ACJ, in the original jurisdiction of this Court, said that '[i]n the absence of compelling grounds' it is the duty of the judicial branch to defer to the enactment of the legislature until that enactment is adjudged ultra vires, and dismissed applications for interlocutory injunctions to restrain enforcement of the law under challenge.

Various views have been expressed and assumptions made respecting the relationship between the judgment of this Court in *Beecham* and the speech of Lord Diplock in the subsequent decision, [83] *American Cyanamid Co v Ethicon Ltd.*[44] It should be noted that both were cases of patent infringement and the outcome on each appeal was the grant of an interlocutory injunction to restrain infringement. Each of the judgments

---

40. *Beecham Group Ltd v Bristol Laboratories Pty Ltd* (1968) 118 CLR 618 at 622–3.
41. *Beecham Group Ltd v Bristol Laboratories Pty Ltd* (1968) 118 CLR 618 at 620.
42. *Beecham Group Ltd v Bristol Laboratories Pty Ltd* (1968) 118 CLR 618 at 622.
43. (1986) 161 CLR 148 at 155–6.
44. [1975] AC 396.

appealed from had placed too high the bar for the obtaining of interlocutory injunctive relief.

Lord Diplock was at pains to dispel the notion, which apparently had persuaded the Court of Appeal to refuse interlocutory relief, that to establish a prima facie case of infringement it was necessary for the plaintiff to demonstrate more than a 50 per cent chance of ultimate success. Thus Lord Diplock remarked:

> The purpose sought to be achieved by giving to the court discretion to grant such injunctions would be stultified if the discretion were clogged by a technical rule forbidding its exercise if upon that incomplete untested evidence the court evaluated the chances of the plaintiff's ultimate success in the action at 50 per cent or less, but permitting its exercise if the court evaluated his chances at more than 50 per cent.[45]

In *Beecham*, the primary judge, McTiernan J, had refused interlocutory relief on the footing that, while he could not dismiss the possibility that the defendant might not fail at trial, the plaintiff had not made out a strong enough case on the question of infringement.[46] Hence the statement by Kitto J in the course of argument in the Full Court that it was not necessary for the plaintiff to show that it was more probable than not that the plaintiff would succeed at trial.

When *Beecham* and *American Cyanamid* are read with an understanding of the issues for determination and an appreciation of the similarity in outcome, much of the assumed disparity in principle between them loses its force. There is then no objection to the use of the phrase 'serious question' if it is understood as conveying the notion that the seriousness of the question, like the strength of the probability referred to in *Beecham*, depends upon the considerations emphasised in *Beecham*.

However, a difference between this Court in *Beecham* and the House of Lords in *American Cyanamid* lies in the apparent statement by Lord Diplock that, provided the court is satisfied that the plaintiff's claim is not frivolous or vexatious, then there will be a serious question to be tried and this will be sufficient. The critical statement by his Lordship is '[t]he court no doubt must be satisfied that the claim is not frivolous or vexatious; in other words, that there is a serious question to be tried'.[47] That was followed by a proposition which appears to reverse matters of onus:

> So *unless* the material available to the court at the hearing of the [84] application for an interlocutory injunction *fails to disclose* that the plaintiff has any real prospect of succeeding in his claim for a permanent injunction at the trial, the court should go on to consider whether the balance of convenience lies in favour of granting or refusing the interlocutory relief that is sought. (Emphasis added.)[48]

Those statements do not accord with the doctrine in this Court as established by *Beecham* and should not be followed. They obscure the governing consideration that the requisite strength of the probability of ultimate success depends upon the nature of the rights asserted and the practical consequences likely to flow from the interlocutory order sought.

---

45. *American Cyanamid Co v Ethicon Ltd* [1975] AC 396 at 406.
46. *Beecham Group Ltd v Bristol Laboratories Pty Ltd* (1968) 118 CLR 618 at 619.
47. *American Cyanamid Co v Ethicon Ltd* [1975] AC 396 at 407.
48. *American Cyanamid Co v Ethicon Ltd* [1975] AC 396 at 408.

The second of these matters, the reference to practical consequences, is illustrated by the particular considerations which arise where the grant or refusal of an interlocutory injunction in effect would dispose of the action finally in favour of whichever party succeeded on that application. The first consideration mentioned in *Beecham*, the nature of the rights asserted by the plaintiff, redirects attention to the present appeal.

Comment
1. See Radan & Stewart at **24.28–24.51**.

Injunctions and negative contractual stipulations

24.5   Warner Bros Pictures Inc v Nelson [1937] 1 KB 209

Court: King's Bench Division of the High Court of England and Wales

Facts: In 1934 Nelson, an actress professionally known as Bette Davis, entered into a one-year contract with Warner Bros. The contract also provided that Warner Bros could extend the arrangement with Nelson until 1942 by exercising options set out in it. The contract contained a restraint of trade clause by which Nelson agreed that 'she [would] not, during [the term of the contract] render any services for or in any other phonographic, stage or motion picture production or productions, or business of any other person or engage in any other occupation without the written consent of [Warner Bros] being first had and obtained'. In 1936 Nelson breached this provision by contracting to make a film in England without having obtained the consent of Warner Bros. Warner Bros sought an injunction to enforce the restraint of trade clause. There was no issue between the parties as to the validity of the restraint of trade clause.

Issue: The issue before the King's Bench Division was whether, in the circumstances of the case, it was appropriate to grant the injunction.

Decision: Branson J granted the injunction, but limited its application to a maximum of three years.

Extracts: The extracts from the judgment of Branson J set out and apply the principles relating to injunctive relief in aid of negative contractual stipulations.

Branson J

[214] I turn then to the consideration of the law applicable to this case on the basis that the contract is a valid and enforceable one. It is conceded that our Courts will not enforce a positive covenant of personal service; and specific performance of the positive covenants by the defendant to serve the plaintiffs is not asked in the present case. The practice of the Court of Chancery in relation to the enforcement of negative covenants is stated on the highest authority by Lord Cairns LC, in the House of Lords in *Doherty v Allman*. His Lordship says:

My Lords, if there had been a negative covenant, I apprehend, according to well settled practice, a **[215]** Court of Equity would have had no discretion to exercise. If parties, for valuable consideration, with their eyes open, contract that a particular thing shall not be done, all that a Court of Equity has to do is to say, by way of injunction, that which the parties have already said by way of covenant, that the thing shall not be done; and in such case the injunction does nothing more than give the sanction of the process of the Court to that which already is the contract between the parties. It is not then a question of the balance of convenience or inconvenience, or of the amount of damage or of injury — it is the specific performance, by the Court, of that negative bargain which the parties have made, with their eyes open, between themselves.[49]

That was not a case of a contract of personal service; but the same principle had already been applied to such a contract by Lord St Leonards, in *Lumley v Wagner*. The Lord Chancellor used the following language:

Wherever this Court has not proper jurisdiction to enforce specific performance, it operates to bind men's consciences, as far as they can be bound, to a true and literal performance of their agreements; and it will not suffer them to depart from their contracts at their pleasure, leaving the party with whom they have contracted to the mere chance of any damages which a jury may give. The exercise of this jurisdiction has, I believe, had a wholesome tendency towards the maintenance of that good faith which exists in this country to a much greater degree perhaps than in any other; and although the jurisdiction is not to be extended, yet a Judge would desert his duty who did not act up to what his predecessors have handed down as the rule for his guidance in the administration of such an equity.[50] ...

[Nelson], having broken her positive undertakings in the contract without any cause or excuse which she was **[216]** prepared to support in the witness-box, contends that she cannot be enjoined from breaking the negative covenants also. The mere fact that a covenant, which the Court would not enforce, if expressed in positive form, is expressed in the negative instead, will not induce the court to enforce it ... The Court will attend to the substance and not to the form of the covenant. Nor will the Court, true to the principle that specific performance of a contract of personal service will never be ordered, grant an injunction in the case of such a contract to enforce negative covenants if the effect of so doing would be to drive the defendant either to starvation or to specific performance of the positive covenants.[51] ...

[In] [t]he case of *Rely-a-Bell Burglar & Fire Alarm Co Ltd v Eisler* ... Russell J ... said ...:

It was said on the other side that there were points of distinction. It was said that the covenants in those two cases were so framed that the servant, if the covenants were enforced, could make his living neither by serving nor by carrying on business independently; whereas in the present case the covenant only prohibited **[217]** serving. Therefore, it was said, he was still free to start in business on his own account, and it could not be said, if an injunction were granted in the terms of the covenant, that he

---

49. *Doherty v Allman* (1878) 3 App Cas 709 at 719.
50. *Lumley v Wagner* (1852) 42 ER 687 at 693.
51. See *Whitwood Chemical Co v Hardman* [1891] 2 Ch 416 at 427.

would be forced to remain idle and starve. That distinction seems to me somewhat of a mockery. It would be idle to tell this defendant, a servant employed at a wage, that he must not serve anybody else in that capacity, but that the world was still open to him to start business as an independent man. It seems to me that if I were to restrain this man according to the terms of the covenant, he would be forced to remain idle and starve.[52] ...

The conclusion to be drawn from the authorities is that, where a contract of personal service contains negative covenants the enforcement of which will not amount either to a decree of specific performance of the positive covenants of the contract or to the giving of a decree under which the defendant must either remain idle or perform those positive covenants, the Court will enforce those negative covenants; but this is subject to a further consideration. An injunction is a discretionary remedy, and the Court in granting it may limit it to what the Court considers reasonable in all the circumstances of the case ...

[219] The case before me is, therefore, one in which it would be proper to grant an injunction unless to do so would in the circumstances be tantamount to ordering the defendant to perform her contract or remain idle or unless damages would be the more appropriate remedy.

With regard to the first of these considerations, it would, of course, be impossible to grant an injunction covering all the negative covenants in the contract. That would, indeed, force [Nelson] to perform her contract or remain idle; but this objection is removed by the restricted form in which the injunction is sought. It is confined to forbidding [Nelson], without the consent of [Warner Bros], to render any services for or in any motion picture or stage production for anyone other than [Warner Bros].

It was also urged that the difference between what [Nelson] can earn as a film artiste and what she might expect to earn by any other form of activity is so great that she will in effect be driven to perform her contract. That is not the criterion adopted in any of the decided cases. [Nelson] is stated to be a person of intelligence, capacity and means, and no evidence was adduced to show that, if enjoined from doing the specified acts otherwise than for [Warner Bros], she will not be able to employ herself both usefully and remuneratively in other spheres of activity, though not as remuneratively as in her special line. She will not be driven, although she may be tempted, to perform the contract, and the fact that she may be so tempted is no objection to the [220] grant of an injunction. This appears from the judgment of Lord St Leonards in *Lumley v Wagner*, where he used the following language:

It was objected that the operation of the injunction in the present case was mischievous, excluding the defendant J Wagner from performing at any other theatre while this Court had no power to compel her to perform at Her Majesty's Theatre. It is true, that I have not the means of compelling her to sing, but she has no cause of complaint, if I compel her to abstain from the commission of an act which she has bound herself not to do, and thus possibly cause her to fulfil her engagement. The jurisdiction which I now exercise is wholly within the power of the court, and being of opinion that it is a proper case for interfering, I shall leave nothing unsatisfied by the judgment I pronounce. The effect too of the injunction, in restraining J Wagner from

---

52. *Rely-a-Bell Burglar & Fire Alarm Co Ltd v Eisler* [1926] Ch 609 at 615.

singing elsewhere may, in the event — [that is a different matter] — of an action being brought against her by the plaintiff, prevent any such amount of vindictive damages being given against her as a jury might probably be inclined to give if she had carried her talents and exercised them at the rival theatre: the injunction may also, as I have said, tend to the fulfilment of her engagement; though, in continuing the injunction, I disclaim doing indirectly what I cannot do directly.[53] ...

[221] Then comes the question as to the period for which the injunction should operate ... [T]he Court should make the period such as to give reasonable protection and no more to [Warner Bros] against the ill effects to them of [Nelson's] breach of contract. The evidence as to that was perhaps necessarily somewhat vague. The main difficulty that [Warner Bros] apprehend is that [Nelson] might appear in other films whilst the films already made by them and not yet shown are in the market for sale or [222] hire and thus depreciate their value. I think that if the injunction is in force during the continuance of the contract or for three years from now, whichever period is the shorter, that will substantially meet the case.

The other matter is as to the area within which the injunction is to operate. The contract is not an English contract and the parties are not British subjects. In my opinion all that properly concerns this Court is to prevent the defendant from committing the prohibited acts within the jurisdiction of this court, and the injunction will be limited accordingly.

Comments

1. See Radan & Stewart at **24.57–24.71**.
2. Although Nelson lost her case against Warner Brothers, she emerged victorious in terms of her future career as is seen in the following extract from Ed Sikov, *Dark Victory, The Life of Bette Davis*, Henry Holt & Co, New York, 2007, pp 96–7:

   Interviewed at her hotel in Rottingdean, Davis, wearing blue beach pajamas and smoking a cigarette, called her defeat 'a sock in the teeth'. 'I'm a bit bewildered', she went on. 'I didn't make any plans for a hundred percent defeat. I thought at least that it would have been a partial victory for me and for everybody else with one of these body-and-soul contracts. Mind you, I didn't fight it as a test case for the whole film industry. I fought it for myself and for my career ... Instead of getting increased freedom, I seem to have provided — at my own expense — an object lesson for other would-be 'naughty young ladies' ...

   The episode turned out not to be the total loss Davis felt it to be at the time. It provided her with vital publicity, the key element of which was precisely that it was not dictated by Warner Bros' publicity department. She had despised not only the apparent indifference of her casting but also the way she had been marketed. She hated the early fashion shoots, the dyeing of her hair, the cereal ads ... Even Warners' best promotions for Davis were in some ways more damaging to her psyche than her worst scripts because they tried to sell her as being someone she wasn't. So although she lost the case, by taking such a belligerent stance against Warners in the full,

---

53. *Lumley v Wagner* (1852) 42 ER 687 at 693.

bright glare of the English-speaking press, she adroitly bypassed the studio's publicity machine and created a new persona for herself on her own terms: a strong-willed independent thinker as confrontational as any man.

It worked. Not only did Warners give her better, more suitable scripts upon her return to Burbank, but the studio's publicists began to exploit her pugnacious, ready-to-erupt persona themselves — to the studio's advantage as well as to Davis's. Contentiousness became her legacy. As the *Economist* put it on the occasion of her death, 'The two cigarettes lit by Paul Henreid in *Now, Voyager* — one for him, one for her — were as nothing compared to the two fingers she gave to the head of the studio, Jack Warner, in the high court in London in 1936'.

3. The decision in *Lumley v Wagner* discussed in this case is the starting point for the development of principles relating to the granting of injunctions in cases of this type. For an illuminating analysis of the context in which *Lumley v Wagner,* and the related cases of *Lumley v Gye* [1853] 118 ER 749 and (1854) 23 LT 66 dealing with the tort of interference with contractual relations are discussed, see S Waddams, 'Johanna Wagner and the Rival Opera Houses' (2001) 117 *Law Quarterly Review* 431.

Injunctions to enforce statutory rights

24.6   Cooney v The Council of the Municipality of Ku-Ring-Gai (1963) 114 CLR 582

Court: High Court of Australia

Facts: Ku-Ring-Gai Council took action against Cooney and others to restrain her from using premises in a residential area of Turramurra as a reception place. It had issued a proclamation to stop her from engaging in a trade or business without its consent, namely, providing refreshments and entertainment at social functions for which she was reimbursed. The Council contended it had validly used its statutory power not only for the establishment of residential areas but also to proclaim land that had previously been used for the conduct of trades as 'residential districts'. Cooney disputed the validity of the proclamation, denied that it had in any event been infringed and argued the court lacked jurisdiction to grant an injunction for breach of the proclamation since it had no proprietary right in the land in question.

Issue: One of the principal issues before the High Court was whether it had the jurisdiction to grant an injunction in favour of a council to restrain breaches of planning regulations.

Decision: The majority of the High Court (Kitto, Taylor, Menzies and Windeyer JJ; Dixon CJ dissenting) rejected Cooney's appeal. It held that the court's equitable jurisdiction extended to the granting of injunctions despite lack of a proprietary interest and that the powers it obtained from its enabling statutes conferred upon it a right of enforcement.

Extracts: The extracts from the judgment of Menzies J are indicative of the High Court's reasoning, which had the effect of expanding the equitable jurisdiction of the court to grant injunctions to local government against planning breaches without the necessity for relator suits on the fiat of the Attorney-General.

Menzies J

[603] The authority relied upon to show that the jurisdiction to grant injunctions is not available in such a case as this was *Attorney-General (ex relatione Lumley) and Lumley v T S Gill & Son Pty Ltd*[54] where the Full Court of the Supreme Court of Victoria decided that the advantage to the general public at large resulting from a by-law which made it an offence punishable by fine for a person to build a factory on land within a residential area was not such an advantage as a Court of Equity would protect by injunction. The basis of this decision was that, whereas to warrant an injunction for its protection some positive interest analogous to a right of property had to be established, the benefits or advantages to the public arising from the by-law were equated with those arising from a restrictive covenant in gross not enforceable by injunction rather than with those arising from a covenant restricting the use of land and creating something in the nature of a servitude appurtenant to other land enforceable by injunction. This decision was referred to by this Court in *Ramsay v Aberfoyle Manufacturing Co (Australia) Pty Ltd*[55] but, except in the judgments of Starke and *McTiernan* JJ, the question was not decided whether the limitation recognized in *Gill's Case* should be accepted. Starke J thought the principle asserted 'confines the jurisdiction within too narrow limits and runs counter to a body of authority that ought not to be disregarded'.[56] McTiernan J said the principles there stated 'are unexceptionable'[57] and that the decided cases 'exhibit no tendency to make equity the handmaid of the criminal [604] law'.[58] Whatever was the position in 1927, it is now apparent from a line of cases in New South Wales and in England that courts have granted injunctions or mandatory orders to protect benefits or advantages of the kind considered in *Gill's Case* and even any benefits or advantages that could not be regarded as having any resemblance at all to proprietary rights. Some of the New South Wales cases are *Council of the Shire of Hornsby v Danglade*[59] (mandatory order to compel demolition and removal of buildings erected contrary to Council's orders and ordinances under Local Government Act); *Warringah Shire Council v Moore*[60] (injunction to restrain defendant carrying out alterations to a building not approved by Council as provided by Local Government Act); *Lake Macquarie Shire Council v Morgan*[61] (injunction to restrain defendant's breach of cl 13 (d) of *Local Government Ordinance* 48 by engaging in trade or business in a public reserve without Council's permission); *Ku-ring-gai Municipal Council*

---

54. [1927] VLR 22.
55. (1935) 54 CLR 230.
56. *Ramsay v Aberfoyle Manufacturing Co (Australia) Pty Ltd* (1935) 54 CLR 230 at 247.
57. *Ramsay v Aberfoyle Manufacturing Co (Australia) Pty Ltd* (1935) 54 CLR 230 at 261.
58. *Ramsay v Aberfoyle Manufacturing Co (Australia) Pty Ltd* (1935) 54 CLR 230 at 260.
59. (1929) 29 SR (NSW) 118.
60. (1942) 15 LGR (NSW) 44.
61. (1948) 17 LGR (NSW) 22.

v Edwards[62] (injunction to restrain defendant from erecting a building not in conformity with the Council's approved plan and conditions attached thereto); *Greater Wollongong City Council v Jones*[63] (injunction to restrain defendant's user of land in a way the *Local Government Act* prohibits); *Waverley Municipal Council v Parker*[64] (injunction to restrain defendant altering a building in contravention of Local Government Act); and *Cumberland County Council v Corben*[65] (injunction to restrain defendants' user of land contrary to prohibitions contained in Planning Scheme Ordinance). Some of the English cases decided since 1927 are *Attorney-General v Sharp*[66] (injunction to restrain defendant from plying for hire of omnibus without licence contrary to statute); *Attorney-General v Premier Line Ltd*[67] (declaration of plaintiff's entitlement to an injunction to restrain defendant running road service without licence as required by statute); *Attorney-General v Bastow*[68] (injunction to restrain defendant's user of land as caravan site contrary to notice served under Town and Country Planning Act); *Attorney-General v Smith*[69] (injunction to restrain defendants from developing land as caravan site without permission pursuant to Town and Country Planning Act); and *Attorney-General v Harris*[70] (injunction to restrain defendant from selling flowers from stalls near cemetery in manner constituting a statutory **[605]** offence). It would, I think, be contrary to the trend of authority since 1927 to accept now the limitation adopted in *Gill's Case* upon the jurisdiction of a Court of Equity to grant injunctions. Prohibitions and restrictions such as those under consideration are directed towards public health and comfort and the orderly arrangement of municipal areas and are imposed, not for the benefit of particular individuals, but for the benefit of the public or at least a section of the public, *viz* those living in the municipal area. It seems to me that one object of endowing municipal councils with the capacity to take proceedings which the Attorney-General, representing the public generally, might take to secure the observance of provisions made by or under the *Local Government Act* ... was to enable councils to take the kind of proceedings which the Council has taken here and in proper cases to obtain injunctions to ensure the observance of such laws. A proper case is, I think, made out when it appears that some person bound by what may be described as a municipal law imposing a restriction or prohibition upon the use of land in portion of a municipal area for the public benefit or advantage has broken, and will, unless restrained, continue to break that law for his or her own advantage and to the possible disadvantage of members of the public living in the locality. The wide discretion of the Court is an adequate safeguard against abuse of a salutary procedure.

Comment

1. See Radan & Stewart at **24.73**.

---

62. [1957] SR (NSW) 379.
63. (1955) 1 LGRA 342.
64. (1960) 5 LGRA 241.
65. (1960) 77 WN (NSW) 650.
66. [1931] 1 Ch 121.
67. [1932] 1 Ch 303.
68. [1957] 1 QB 514.
69. [1958] 2 QB 173.
70. [1961] 1 QB 74.

Relator proceedings

24.7   The Attorney-General, on the Relation of Daniels, Steward and Wells v Huber, Sandy, and Wichmann Investments Pty Ltd (1971) 2 SASR 142

Court: Full Court of the Supreme Court of South Australia

Facts: The Attorney-General of South Australia brought an action at the relation of members of the public (Daniels and others) seeking an injunction to stop the 'Oh! Calcutta' theatrical revue. It was alleged that the production would involve indecent behaviour in a 'public place' by way of nudity and simulated sexual acts on stage that would breach police offences legislation. The producers of the show (Huber and others) made admission to the show subject not only to payment, but also age restrictions and signed acknowledgments from patrons, arguing the musical would not be performed in a public place. They also argued the court did not have jurisdiction to grant an interlocutory injunction in such a case.

Issue: The principal issue before the Full Court was whether its equitable jurisdiction allowed it to grant an interlocutory injunction in a case that involved possible breaches of statute.

Decision: The majority of the Full Court (Walters and Wells JJ; Bray CJ dissenting) found in favour of Daniels and others, holding that it was within the jurisdiction of the Supreme Court to adjudicate an application by the Attorney-General to restrain breaches of the law and to grant an injunction to stop activities that would involve such breaches.

Extracts: The extracts below from the judgments of Bray CJ and Walters J, respectively, outline the minority and majority views of the Full Court about the nature and exercise of the court's equitable jurisdiction in relation to injunctions.

Bray CJ

[160] [I]n more recent times injunctions have been issued to restrain the commission of summary offences, breaches of by-laws and the like, and injunctions have been made in libel actions ... [T]he argument for [the producers] in this case really involves the proposition that a court of equity, or it might be more accurate to say a superior court administering both law and equity, can issue an injunction to restrain the commission of any crime whenever it sees fit in the exercise of its discretion to do so, at least when the plaintiff is the Attorney-General and whether in a relator action or otherwise ...

[161] In the strict sense I do not think it can be said that the Court has no jurisdiction to grant an interlocutory injunction in a case like this, or in any action at all properly commenced in the Court, if it appears just and convenient so to do. But it does not follow at all that the Court ought now for the first time in the long history of the Anglo-Saxon legal system, apart from the decision of Little J in Victoria in *Attorney-General of Victoria v Lido Savoy Pty Ltd and Others* delivered on 23rd February, 1970 when the performance of 'Oh, Calcutta' in Victoria was restrained, to grant an interlocutory injunction to restrain the

commission of an offence against decency or morality when no civil right of anyone, and no interest remotely resembling a civil right of any individual, is involved and no interference with the material health, comfort, convenience or pocket of any particular person or persons or of the public at large is alleged. In my opinion it ought not to do so. It is not convenient to do so. And in cases like this it is not, in my view, just to do so either ...

[163] In *Attorney-General v Mercantile Investments Ltd* the Attorney-General of New South Wales applied for an injunction to restrain the promotion or conduct of an alleged lottery. It was refused. Harvey J, as he then was, said:

> I think it may be stated generally that the Court of Equity has power to intervene at the suit of the Attorney-General, and to grant an injunction against the commission of any threatened wrongful act which is a menace to the general rights of the public which are of a proprietary nature, such as the user of a highway, or which is likely to cause injury to the members of the public in general capable of being assessed in individual cases in terms of money, such as nuisances from noise, smell, or filth, *ie*, injuries to the health or comfort of the general public. I doubt whether the Court would ever interfere where the only injury alleged is to the moral well-being of the public, even though that injury is prohibited by Act of Parliament under a penalty. It may be said that this is a very sordid view to take of the jurisdiction of a Court presided over by the keeper of the King's conscience, and it may be that even in some cases of mere moral injury forbidden by statute the Court might intervene on some ground of urgency or danger of immediate consequences, but if so this Court should be very slow to interfere on behalf of the public in any case except where the members of the public require protection from some wrongful act from which they cannot protect themselves.[71]

Again, he said:

> I do not think this is of the class of cases in which this Court ought to be asked to exercise its discretionary jurisdiction by injunction. There is no injury to any proprietary rights and no personal damage to the health or comfort of any individual, and the people can protect themselves by refusing to contribute their money to the lottery. If an injunction were to be issued in this case where would it lead to? Sunday traders, keepers of disorderly houses, publicans committing breaches of the Liquor Act, bookmakers betting in 'places' contrary to the Games, Wages and Betting Houses Act could all be dealt with under the jurisdiction of this Court to punish for contempt.[72]

And his Honour upheld the demurrer which alleged that the court had no jurisdiction to grant the injunctions sought ...

[164] In *Ramsay v Aberfoyle Manufacturing Co (Australia) Pty Ltd* the High Court by majority upheld the refusal of an injunction to restrain the building of a factory in breach of the provisions of a by-law. It may be again that the actual decision in that case would be different now in view of the later authorities, but the learned Judges expressed themselves at large and in a manner very pertinent, in my view, to this case. Latham CJ said:

> Upon this principle a Court of equity would, in cases where the Attorney-General is a party, have a most extensive and hitherto unprecedented field of authority in securing

---

71. *Attorney-General v Mercantile Investments Ltd* (1920) 21 SR (NSW) 183 at 187.
72. *Attorney-General v Mercantile Investments Ltd* (1920) 21 SR (NSW) 183 at 189.

observance of the law. Obedience to any ordinary public statute is a matter of concern to the public, but in my opinion the general interest of the public in the observance of the law is not in itself sufficient to justify the Court in granting an injunction at the suit of the Attorney-General.[73] ...

[165] In *Attorney-General v Twelfth Night Theatre*[74] Hart J refused, in the exercise of his discretion, an injunction to restrain the use of certain words in a play and there was no occasion to explore the general question of whether a court of equity would interfere in such a case at all ...

If this is a case in which an interlocutory injunction can go, I can see nothing to stop a civil court in the exercise of its discretion from restricting the commission of any future act which it is alleged will constitute a criminal offence if it is committed. All the consequences mentioned by Harvey J in the *Mercantile Investment Case* would follow; and it would be a cause of some surprise that the authorities had not previously hit on this easy way of closing down brothels, sly-grog shops and gambling dens. The processes of a criminal trial with all its safeguards for the rights of accused persons could be short-circuited in this way. This may be tolerable in cases of carrying on business in residential zones, selling flowers from the footpath and plying for hire without a licence, particularly where it has proved profitable to continue the forbidden activity despite repeated finings; but surely it ought not to be done where conviction involves substantial penalties and the imputation of moral turpitude, at least in cases where no civil right or material interest of any particular individual or individuals is alleged to be involved or even any material interest of the public at large. If the offence sought to be restrained was indictable, as indeed it is possible here that [the producers] if this play is performed would be parties to an indictable misdemeanour, though that is not alleged in the pleadings in this case, how could the right to a jury trial be denied to a defendant who claimed that what he proposed to do did not constitute any offence at all? It cannot make any difference, surely, that instead his guilt may have to be proved beyond reasonable doubt in a court of summary jurisdiction instead of before a jury. If this injunction stands I view with apprehension the invasion of the civil courts by bands of self-appointed moral vigilantes using the name of the Attorney-General, as by constitutional practice they would be entitled to do if they showed him a prima-facie case, seeking to restrain the publication of books and periodicals, the showing of films, the opening of art exhibitions, the performance of plays and, for all I know, the holding of public meetings and the delivery of speeches. I think the door should be firmly shut now.

If there is an exception in a case where the public cannot protect themselves against a clear and urgent threatened moral danger, a possibility referred to by Harvey J in the *Mercantile Investment Case*, then this is not such a case; all the public have to do is stay away from the theatre. I would, however, with respect, doubt the existence of such an exception. The law has other ways of dealing with such dangers and, despite minor [166] exceptions, the dominant tradition of the English law has always been to deal with offenders or potential offenders retrospectively for what they have done, not prospectively for what they might be going to do.

I can conceive that there might be an exception where the defendant acquiesces in the procedure. He might prefer to get the determination of a civil court about the legality of

---

73. *Ramsay v Aberfoyle Manufacturing Co (Australia) Pty Ltd* (1935) 54 CLR 230 at 234.
74. [1969] Qd R 319.

what he proposes to do instead of running the risk of criminal prosecution after he has done it. But this is not such a case ...

[170] In other words [Daniels and others] are using the name of the nominal respondent to ask the Court to do something which he has power to do for himself in his official capacity without reference to the Court and which he has disclaimed the intention of doing unless and until a performance demonstrates that he ought to do it. I must say that if there were no other considerations in the case at all I think that that is a reason why an interlocutory injunction should not be granted.

With all respect to the views of Devlin J, as he then was, in *Attorney-General v Bastow*,[75] I do not agree that a relator action in the name of the Attorney-General is to be treated just as if it were an action brought by the Attorney-General of his own motion and that the very nature of a relator action means that he has surveyed all the ways in which the law might be enforced and come to the conclusion that the most effective way is to ask the court for an injunction. I agree, with respect, with the description of a relator action by Dixon AJ, as he then was, in *Attorney-General v T S Gill & Son Pty Ltd*:

> Now, the action by the Attorney-General at the relation of a private person is founded upon this view — that the acts complained of are not a violation of a private right of the person desiring to litigate, but are a violation of some public duty which the Crown is entitled to complain of, and a relator comes forward and applies to the Attorney-General, *in his quasi-judicial capacity*, for a fiat permitting the relator to sue out a writ in the Attorney-General's name. The function of the Attorney-General is to consider whether, in all the circumstances, the relator shows a peculiar grievance or injury to him by reason of the violation of a public right, or whether in some other respect he is particularly interested in that supposed violation of public right. In that 'case' *it is the duty of the Attorney-General, although a duty of im* [171] *perfect obligation,* assuming he is satisfied that there is a probable violation of a public duty, to issue his fiat enabling the relator to seek in the courts the appropriate remedy in the name of the Attorney-General.[76] (The italics are mine).

It seems to me that once the Attorney-General is satisfied that there is a probable violation of a public duty — and perhaps also that the relator has shown some peculiar grievance or interest in himself, though I doubt whether that was done here — he is under a quasi-judicial duty, though a duty of imperfect obligation, to issue his fiat; and that the issue of the fiat in such a case means no more than that he is so satisfied and is not to be taken as expressing any opinion at all that the grant of an interlocutory injunction is the most effective way of enforcing the law against the particular defendant ...

Walters J

[174] Whilst the Attorney-General must ... show that the public are affected, he stands on a different footing from an individual, since it is his duty to enforce the law. He need not show actual injury to anyone. He can come to the court to demand compliance with statute law on the part of any subject. The extent of his right to intervene and call the attention of the court to a breach of the statute was adumbrated as long ago as 1879, when Baggallay LJ said in *Attorney-General v Great Eastern Railway Co*:

---

75. [1957] 1 QB 514.
76. *Attorney-General v T S Gill & Son Pty Ltd* [1926] VLR 414 at 416.

It is in the interest of the public that the law should in all respects be respected and observed, and if the law is transgressed, *or threatened to be transgressed*, ... it is the duty of the Attorney-General to take the necessary steps to enforce it, nor does it make any difference [175] whether he sues *ex officio*, or at the instance of relators.[77] (The italics are mine) ...

Whether the Attorney-General should or should not undertake any action on behalf of the public is for him to decide, but when, in the exercise of his discretion, he elects to bring a suit in order to assert public rights and to secure obedience to the law, it is for the court to say whether the action is maintainable and whether he is entitled to the redress which he seeks ...

[180] It may well be that the extent to which a prosecution will probably attain some or all of the objectives of a suit in equity to restrain an apprehended illegal act, and the availability and effectiveness of the statutory remedy, are matters to be considered in determining whether a court should exercise its equitable jurisdiction and grant an injunction against future breaches of the law. But as a general rule, I think that it is equally proper to call into operation the processes of a civil law and the equitable powers of the court to prevent anticipated illegal acts, as it is to punish the offences thereby constituted after they have been committed. Moreover, the prosecution of statutory offences will involve no sanction other than the penalties provided, and, more often than not, the penalties imposed for the infringements will be fines, without any really effective preventive result. A defendant can still continue to act as he has done previously, and, if I may apply to the present case the language of Farwell J (at first instance) in *Attorney-General v Sharp*: 'The fines imposed are so much, and the business which the defendant does is so much; and it may well be that he can bear the burden of the fines which are imposed upon him and yet continue to make a profit by his business while neglecting to observe the directions and regulations which are imposed by the Act'.[78] On the other hand, one who ignores the general threat of a summary prosecution for infringement of a statute will not casually regard an injunction and the consequences of disobedience to it. And a statute ordinarily does not provide any direct means of preventing future or anticipated offences as an injunction will necessarily do.

For the foregoing reasons, I have come to the conclusion that neither the fact that the apprehended acts will constitute offences punishable by statute, nor the fact that a plain remedy for infringement of the law is afforded by the statute, can take away any of the jurisdiction which a court of equity might otherwise exercise. It is my opinion also that where there is evidence that a statute will in the future be openly, repeatedly, continuously, persistently and intentionally violated, a detriment to the public will result, and that the Attorney-General is entitled to call upon this Court to exercise its equitable jurisdiction and to determine whether [181] it is proper for an injunction to go in order to enforce obedience to the law ...

Before leaving the question of jurisdiction, I propose to deal shortly with the objection that the proceedings in this Court to enjoin the apprehended illegal acts will deprive [Daniels and others] of, or at least encroach upon, their rights to have the alleged illegality of those acts pronounced upon in accordance with the ordinary processes of the criminal

---

77. *Attorney-General v Great Eastern Railway Co* (1879) 11 Ch D 449 at 500.
78. *Attorney-General v Sharp* [1931] 1 Ch 121 at 124.

law, that is, by trial on a summary prosecution. In this connection, however, I think that a distinction must be drawn between crimes, which are definitely criminal and *mala in se*, and anti-social acts, which are made quasi-criminal by statute. In the case of the former, an enjoining of the act would be inappropriate, but in the case of the latter, it is my view that a completely different situation obtains. By an injunction to restrain quasi-criminal acts, the prospective offender is not convicted and punished for a crime by the injunction. The purpose of the injunction is to stay the arm of the prospective wrong-doer; to prevent either 'an act which tends in its nature to injure the public' or 'an illegal act of a public nature', and to suppress what the law declares to be an offence.

In the present case, it seems to me that a denial of a trial on a summary prosecution would be no more oppressive than the procedure by which a person who threatens to commit a breach of the peace is required to enter into a recognizance and to find sureties to keep the peace. I do not think it can be claimed that because an intended quasi-criminal act is punishable as such, a civil court is therefore deprived of its jurisdiction in equity, merely for the reason that there is a denial of, or some entrenchment upon, the right of trial on a summary prosecution ...

[185] [I]n a case such as that which is before us, the Court must attempt to judge the current standards of decency on the basis of what is known to be — as far as it can be known to the average person — the standards of modesty of ordinary men and women, unaffected in its reasoning, on the one hand, by the views of those who advocate an unrestricted licence for any particular section of the public to see, hear and experience what they wish to, and, on the other, by the views of those who attempt by their so-called garrulity to define traditional community standards. How far the provisions of the existing law may accord with some aspects of modern thinking, it is no part of the duty of this Court to inquire; the sole matter for consideration is whether the impugned behaviour will offend against requirements of the law as it now stands, the criteria being laid down in the tests which I have discussed ...

[186] Having arrived at the conclusion that if 'Oh! Calcutta' were presented, a large number of acts of indecent behaviour will occur at each performance, I think that the production will involve open, repeated, continuous, deliberate and persistent violations of the law, and that a detriment to the public interest will necessarily ensue. To my mind, the ordinary processes of the criminal law are incapable of redressing this sort of wrong-doing, and I think the present case is one in which this Court should intervene and, by the exercise of its equitable jurisdiction, restrain the apprehended illegal acts. I concede that nudity *per se*, when portrayed upon the stage, may not be indecent in some circumstances. And I am disposed also to concede that the indecent act of any one performer, of itself, may be quite insufficient to warrant the interposition of this Court. But in the view I take, where there is a series of individual indecent acts of several performers, openly, deliberately and persistently carried out and intended to be repeated or continued, the combined effect of those acts causes appreciable and serious injury to the public interest, and produces a final result which should be enjoined.

Comment
1. See Radan & Stewart at **24.76–24.79**.

25

MAREVA AND ANTON PILLER ORDERS

Introduction

25.1 This chapter deals with orders to protect the court's jurisdiction against defendants who threaten to dissipate or secrete their assets or evidence in order to evade the consequences of judicial process. The Mareva order does this by freezing a defendant's assets pending the hearing and determination of a plaintiff's cause of action against the defendant. The Anton Piller order does this by preventing the defendant from destroying evidence relating to the plaintiff's case. Both orders are usually granted only in exceptional circumstances.

The cases in this chapter discuss the following:

- the jurisdictional basis for Mareva orders: *Jackson v Sterling Industries Limited* (1987) 162 CLR 612;
- the principles governing the grant of Mareva orders: *Cardile v LED Builders Pty Limited* (1999) 198 CLR 380;
- the principles governing the grant of Anton Piller orders: *Anton Piller KG v Manufacturing Process Limited* [1975] 1 Ch 55; and
- the obligations of plaintiffs and their representatives in executing Anton Piller orders: *Celanese Canada Inc v Murray Demolition Corporation* (2006) 269 DLR (4th) 193; *Long v Specifier Publications Pty Ltd* (1998) 44 NSWLR 545.

Jurisdictional basis for Mareva orders

25.2 Jackson v Sterling Industries Limited (1987) 162 CLR 612

Court: High Court of Australia

Facts: Sterling Industries purchased two taverns from a company controlled by Jackson for $2.8m. After some time, it brought an action against the vendor company and Jackson under section 52 of the *Trade Practices Act 1974* for misleading and deceptive statements about the profitability of the sold businesses. When Jackson was reported to be divesting himself of assets, Sterling obtained court orders that resulted in him and his company providing undertakings to refrain from doing so. A further company controlled by Jackson then obtained loans totalling $4.3m, with the funds ultimately being diverted and released to Jackson himself. He claimed that he was then defrauded of the moneys in a diamond purchase scam. The police charged him with fraudulent misappropriation. At this point, Sterling Industries applied for a court order in relation to the section 52 proceedings, seeking payment into court by Jackson and the vendor company of $3m as security for anticipated judgment moneys.

Issue: The issue before the High Court was whether a Mareva injunction could be used not only to preserve assets but also to require a defendant to provide security as a condition of being allowed to defend an action.

Decision: The majority of the High Court (Mason CJ, Wilson, Brennan, Deane and Dawson JJ; Toohey and Gaudron JJ dissenting) found in favour of Jackson and his company. The majority ruled that where an asset preservation order purports to do more than just restrain a party from disposing of assets, it can only do so within the scope of the purpose to which the order is directed. The provision of security for a plaintiff does not fall within the scope of an order's legitimate purpose.

Extracts: The extracts from the judgment of Deane J and the joint judgment of Wilson and Dawson JJ illustrate the majority's views about the nature of Mareva injunctions, their proper use and their jurisdictional sources.

Deane J

[622] There may have been a time when it would have been strongly arguable that the making of an interlocutory order to preserve assets of a defendant pending the determination of proceedings against him could not properly have been seen as 'appropriate' to be made by a court in relation to the exercise of the jurisdiction to entertain the substantive proceedings. If that be so, that time has passed. Orders preventing a defendant from disposing of his assets so as to create a situation in which any judgment obtained against him would not be satisfied may be of comparatively recent development. They have, however, become an accepted incident of the jurisdiction of superior courts throughout most of the common law world. In this country, the jurisdiction to make such orders, commonly referred to as 'Mareva injunctions', has been progressively asserted and exercised by the Supreme Courts of Victoria, New South Wales, Western Australia, Queensland, the Australian Capital Territory and South Australia.

Initially, injunctive orders to preserve assets were made to prevent a non-resident defendant from removing assets from the territorial limits of a court's jurisdiction so as to frustrate the effectiveness of any judgment that might be obtained. In due course, it was perceived that a general interlocutory power to make orders preventing a defendant from disposing of his assets so as to defeat any judgment obtained in an action was an incident of the substantive jurisdiction to entertain the action and was not confined to the case where the defendant was a non-resident. That general power has been held to encompass an order requiring the disclosure by a defendant of his assets;[1] an order for the delivery up (to a named solicitor) of [623] designated assets which were not specifically

---

1. See *Bekhor Ltd v Bilton* [1981] QB 923; *TDK Tape Distributor v Videochoice Ltd* [1986] 1 WLR 141.

in issue in the proceedings;[2] and, an order restraining a local company from disposing of or dealing with assets which were outside the jurisdiction at least where they had been within the jurisdiction when the action commenced.[3] Arguably, it extends to the making of an ancillary order after judgment to protect the efficacy of execution.[4] As a general proposition, it should now be accepted in this country that 'a Mareva injunction can be granted ... if the circumstances are such that there is a danger of [the defendant's] absconding, or a danger of the assets being removed out of the jurisdiction or disposed of within the jurisdiction, or otherwise dealt with so that there is a danger that the plaintiff, if he gets judgment, will not be able to get it satisfied'.[5] ...

To some extent, the general power of the English High Court of Justice to grant a Mareva injunction was initially seen as based on the provisions of s 45(1) of the *Supreme Court of Judicature (Consolidation) Act* 1925 (UK). That general power should, however, now be accepted as an established part of the armoury of a court of law and equity to prevent the abuse or frustration of its process in relation to matters coming within its jurisdiction. That being so, the power to grant such relief in relation to a matter in which the Federal Court has jurisdiction is comprehended by the express grant to that Court by s 23 of the *Federal Court of Australia Act* of power, in relation to such matters, 'to make orders of such kinds, including interlocutory orders, and to issue, or direct the issue of, writs of such kinds, as the Court thinks appropriate'. Indeed, even in the absence of the provisions of s 23, the Federal Court would have possessed power to make such orders in relation to matters properly before it, as an incident of the general grant to it as a superior court of law and equity of the jurisdiction to deal with such matters.

Wilson and Dawson JJ

[616] We agree with Deane J. Since the first appearance of the remedy, the power to grant a Mareva injunction has been a matter of debate. It was initially seen to be derived from the power of the English High Court to 'grant ... an injunction ... by an interlocutory order in all cases in which it appears to the court to be just or convenient so to do'.[6] Section 23 of the *Federal Court of Australia Act* 1976 (Cth) gives to the Federal Court a comparable power, in relation to matters in which it has jurisdiction, 'to make orders of such kinds, including interlocutory orders ... as the Court thinks appropriate'.

[617] It is not without difficulty that reliance has been placed upon statutory provisions of this kind because, according to accepted doctrine, they permit interlocutory relief in relation to the disposition of property only in aid of some existing legal or equitable right, not a mere chose in action.[7] Initially the Mareva injunction was of limited scope being available only against a foreign defendant with movable assets within the jurisdiction

---

2. See *CBS United Kingdom Ltd v Lambert* [1983] Ch 37.
3. See *Hospital Products Ltd v Ballabil Holdings Ltd* [1984] 2 NSWLR 662; on appeal (1985) 1 NSWLR 155.
4. See *Stewart Chartering Ltd v C & O Managements SA* [1980] 1 WLR 460.
5. *Rahman (Prince Abdul) v Abu-Taha* [1980] 3 All ER 409 at 412.
6. *Supreme Court of Judicature (Consolidation) Act 1925* (UK); *Nippon Yusen Kaisha v Karageorgis* [1975] 3 All ER 282; *Mareva Compania Naviera SA v International Bulkcarriers SA* [1975] 2 Lloyd's Rep 509.
7. See *Pivovaroff v Chernabaeff* (1978) 16 SASR 329; *Ex parte BP Exploration Co (Libya) Ltd; Re Hunt* [1979] 2 NSWLR 406.

which, unless restrained, he was likely to remove. Some broader rationale was needed both to explain and fashion the eventual extension of the remedy to defendants resident within the jurisdiction and to the dissipation of assets within the jurisdiction for the purpose of defeating any judgment.[8] It was to be found in the notion that the purpose of the Mareva injunction was to prevent the abuse of the process of the court by the frustration of its remedies.[9] The enactment in England of s 37(3) of the *Supreme Court Act* 1981 (UK), which confirmed the Mareva injunction in its extended form, rendered somewhat academic further debate in England upon the foundation of the remedy.

However, if the power of a court to grant injunctions of the Mareva type and associated relief is to be found in its capacity to prevent the abuse of its process, then it is as much to be found in its inherent power as in any statutory power to grant such relief as is 'just or convenient' or 'appropriate'. Thus it was that in *Riley McKay Pty Ltd v McKay*[10] the New South Wales Court of Appeal found the power to grant relief of the Mareva type in s 23 of the *Supreme Court Act* 1970 (NSW). Section 23 provides that the 'Court shall have all jurisdiction which may be necessary for the administration of justice in New South Wales'. No relevant distinction is to be drawn between the inherent power of the Court and that bestowed by the section although, as the Court of Appeal pointed out, the section confirms the inherent power without increasing it.

One important result of viewing the Mareva injunction in this way is to emphasize the limits of the remedy. Its use must be necessary to prevent the abuse of the process of the court. As **[618]** Ackner LJ pointed out in *A J Bekhor & Co Ltd v Bilton*,[11] the Mareva injunction represents a limited exception to the general rule that a plaintiff must obtain his judgment and then enforce it. He cannot beforehand prevent the defendant from disposing of his assets merely because he fears that there will be nothing against which to enforce his judgment nor can he be given a secured position against other creditors. The remedy is not to be used to circumvent the insolvency laws.

In the Federal Court the power to grant a Mareva injunction may also be found in an inherent or, more correctly, implied power as well as in s 23 of the *Federal Court of Australia Act*. It is an implied power because of the statutory nature of the Court. Notwithstanding that the Federal Court is declared by s 5(2) of the *Federal Court of Australia Act* to be a superior court of record and a court of law and equity, there are limits upon its functions which differentiate it from other Australian superior courts ...

[619] It has been a criticism of the Mareva doctrine that it constitutes an enlargement rather than the fulfilment of a court's function. The criticism has not generally prevailed but it serves to emphasize the limited scope of the Mareva injunction. It exists not to create additional rights but to enable a court to protect its process from abuse in relation to the enforcement of its orders. It is neither a species of anticipatory execution nor does it give a form of security for any judgment which may ultimately be awarded. For the reasons given by Deane J, the orders made by the Federal Court went beyond the proper limits of the remedy and this appeal must be allowed.

---

8. See *Barclay-Johnson v Yuill* [1980] 1 WLR 1259 at 1264–6; *Rahman (Prince Abdul) v Abu-Taha* [1980] 1 WLR 1268 at 1272.

9. *Iraqi Ministry of Defence v Arcepey Shipping Co SA (The 'Angel Bell')* [1981] QB 65 at 72.

10. [1982] 1 NSWLR 264.

11. [1981] QB 923 at 941–2.

Requirements for a Mareva order

25.3 Cardile v LED Builders Pty Limited (1999) 198 CLR 380

Court: High Court of Australia

Facts: The Cardiles were the shareholders of Eagle Homes Pty Ltd, which ran a housing construction business. Eagle Homes was sued in the Federal Court by LED for infringement of copyright in relation to unauthorised use of LED's building plans. Before judgment was granted to LED, Eagle Homes declared a dividend of $400,000 to the Cardiles, who incorporated a new company called Ultra Modern Pty Ltd, which commenced operations using new building plans under the business name 'Eagle Homes'. A further dividend of $800,000 was declared in the Cardiles' favour by the Eagle Homes company. LED elected for an account of profits following upon its judgment in the infringement action and applied for Mareva orders against the judgment debtor Eagle Homes, the Cardiles and Ultra Modern Pty Ltd.

Issue: The issue before the High Court was whether a Mareva order could be granted against a third party in proceedings in which the third party has not been shown to have an interest in the assets of the judgment debtor.

Decision: The High Court (Gaudron, McHugh, Gummow, Kirby and Callinan JJ) unanimously held in favour of the Cardiles on the basis that the orders against them were too broad and transgressed the caution with which Mareva orders should be dispensed.

Extracts: The extracts from the joint majority judgment of Gaudron, McHugh, Gummow and Callinan JJ provide a succinct summary of the criteria to be met in relation to the granting of Mareva orders generally and, specifically, against third parties.

Gaudron, McHugh, Gummow and Callinan JJ

[393] None of the authorities cited to this Court went so far as to support an order of the width of that made in the Full Court. As the argument proceeded upon the grounds of appeal to which we have referred, several matters became apparent. One was that the English authorities appear to have developed to a stage where what is identified as the *Mareva* injunction or order lacks any firm doctrinal foundation and is best regarded as some special exception to the general law. Another was that, whilst it is undesirable that asset preservation orders of the *Mareva* variety be left as a sui generis remedy with no doctrinal roots, the term 'injunction' is an inappropriate identification of that area of legal discourse within which the *Mareva* order is to be placed. The third was the point encapsulated in the joint judgment of this Court in *CSR Ltd v Cigna Insurance Australia Ltd*:

The counterpart of a court's power to *prevent* its processes being abused is its power to *protect* the integrity of those processes once set in motion.[12]

The integrity of those processes extends to preserving the efficacy of the execution which would lie against the actual or prospective judgment debtor.[13] The protection of the administration of justice which this involves may, in a proper case, extend to asset preservation orders against third parties to the principal litigation. This appeal concerns the identification of such proper cases.

In *Jackson v Sterling Industries Ltd*,[14] Deane J referred to the armoury of a court of law and equity to prevent the abuse or frustration of its process in relation to matters coming within its jurisdiction. By this means, the risk of the stultification of the administration of justice is diminished. Once the source of power is recognised, then, whatever may be the limitations with respect to inferior courts, in the case of the Federal Court the power will be seen to be comprehended by the express grant in s 23 of the Federal [394] Court Act. In *National Australia Bank Ltd v Bond Brewing Holdings Ltd*,[15] Mason CJ, Brennan and Deane JJ described as mistaken any proposition that *Mareva* relief could only be obtained against the defendant to an action if there were a positive intention to frustrate any judgment. However, the presence in s 23 of the expression 'as the Court thinks appropriate' points to the requirement to develop principles governing the exercise of the power in such a fashion as to avoid abuse. This need, as indicated above, is at the heart of the present appeal. Meeting that need is not facilitated, and may be impeded, by continued attempts to force what has become known as the *Mareva* order into the mould of interlocutory injunctive relief as administered under that description by courts of equity.

The remedy of injunction
In that regard, further reference should now be made to the development of the injunctive remedy, to the strain placed upon it by its use to identify new statutory remedies and to its misapplication to identify either the nature of or the juridical foundation for the *Mareva* order.

The term 'injunction' is used in numerous statutes to identify a particular species of order, the making of which the law in question provides as part of a new regulatory or other regime, which may be supported by penal provisions. Notable examples in statutes presently in force nationally are found in s 80 of the *Trade Practices Act* 1974 (Cth), s 114 of the *Family Law Act* 1975 (Cth), s 1324 of the *Corporations Law* (Cth) and s 170NG of the *Workplace Relations Act* 1996 (Cth). These provisions empower courts to give a remedy in many cases where none would have been available in a court of equity in the exercise of its jurisdiction, whether to protect the legal (including statutory) or equitable rights of the plaintiff, the administration of a trust for charitable purposes, or the observance of public law at the suit of the Attorney-General, with or without a relator, or at the suit of a person with a sufficient interest.

In these situations, the term 'injunction' takes its content from the provisions of the particular statute in question. In other laws, for example Div 2 (ss 43–65) of Pt III of

---

12. *CSR Ltd v Cigna Insurance Australia Ltd* (1997) 189 CLR 345 at 391 (original emphasis).
13. *Jackson v Sterling Industries Ltd* (1987) 162 CLR 612 at 623, 638.
14. (1987) 162 CLR 612 at 623.
15. (1990) 169 CLR 271 at 277.

the *Proceeds of Crime Act* 1987 (Cth), where the term 'restraining order' is used, remedies having some characteristics of injunctions as understood in courts of equity are given their own particular statutory designation.[16]

[395] With respect to the power of a court of equity,[17] it is appropriate, for present purposes, to bear in mind several matters. First, not all mandatory orders are injunctive in nature. An order for the return of a specific chattel or the restoration of a fund to the party entitled to it is not an injunction as ordinarily understood.[18] Nor is the injunction the only interlocutory remedy which should be supported by an undertaking as to damages. Secondly, the contempt power extends to third parties who, whilst not themselves bound by an order, so conduct themselves as to obstruct the course of justice.[19] Thirdly, the injunctive remedy is still the subject of development in courts exercising equitable jurisdiction. Thus, whilst once there may have been an absolute requirement that, negative covenants aside, before an injunction might be granted in aid of a legal or statutory right, the right must be proprietary in nature, in modern cases, including, in this Court, *Bradley v The Commonwealth*,[20] there has been no advertence to such a requirement. Again, in this Court, the view once taken that an injunction should issue to restrain breach of a negative stipulation, without weighing the usual discretionary considerations, has been discounted as an overstatement.[21] The use of the anti-suit injunction, at least if granted in aid of contractual rights and obligations, is another example of development of traditional doctrine.[22]

However, in England, it is now settled by several decisions of the House of Lords[23] that the power stated in Judicature legislation — that the court may grant an injunction in all cases in which it appears to the court to be just and convenient to do so — does not confer an unlimited power to grant injunctive relief. Regard must still be had to [396] the existence of a legal or equitable right which the injunction protects against invasion or threatened invasion, or other unconscientious conduct or exercise of legal or equitable rights.[24] The situation thus confirmed by these authorities reflects the point made by

---

16. See also the use of the term 'order' in ss 80A and 87A of the *Trade Practices Act 1974* (Cth) to identify respectively the powers conferred upon courts to compel the disclosure of information or publication of advertisements, and to prohibit payment or transfer of moneys or other property.

17. Section 5(2) of the *Federal Court Act* provides that the Federal Court is a superior court of record and is a court of law and equity.

18. *Doulton Potteries Ltd v Bronotte* [1971] 1 NSWLR 591 at 596; *CSR Ltd v Cigna Insurance Australia Ltd* (1997) 189 CLR 345 at 390.

19. *Seaward v Paterson* [1897] 1 Ch 545 at 555; *Z Ltd v A-Z and AA-LL* [1982] QB 558 at 572, 578–9.

20. (1973) 128 CLR 557.

21. *Dalgety Wine Estates Pty Ltd v Rizzon* (1979) 141 CLR 552 at 560, 573–4.

22. See *CSR Ltd v Cigna Insurance Australia Ltd* (1997) 189 CLR 345 at 392.

23. *Bremer Vulkan Schiffbau und Maschinenfabrik v South India Shipping Corporation* [1981] AC 909 at 979–80, 992; *South Carolina Insurance Co v Assurantie Maatschappij 'De Zeven Provincien' NV* [1987] AC 24 at 40; *Pickering v Liverpool Daily Post and Echo Newspapers Plc* [1991] 2 AC 370 at 420–1.

24. The common injunction, whereby the Court of Chancery manifested its primacy, in some respects, over the courts of common law, was directed to maintaining what was then the structure of the English legal system and, thus, to the administration of justice in a broad sense having some affinity to the ends furthered by asset preservation orders of the *Mareva* variety.

Ashburner that 'the power of the court to grant an injunction is limited by the nature of the act which it is sought to restrain'.[25]

Further, the injunction remains a discretionary remedy in a particular sense of that term. In *Bristol City Council v Lovell*, Lord Hoffmann observed:

> The reason why an injunction is a discretionary remedy is because it formed part of the remedial jurisdiction of the Court of Chancery. If the Chancellor considered that the remedies available at law, such as damages, were inadequate, he could grant an injunction to give the plaintiff more effective relief. If he did not think that it was just or expedient to do so, he could leave the plaintiff to his rights at common law. The discretion is therefore as to the remedy which the court will provide for the invasion of the plaintiff's rights.[26]

Whilst s 23 of the Federal Court Act empowers the Federal Court to make 'orders of such kinds, including interlocutory orders ... as the Court thinks appropriate', the Federal Court is not thereby authorised to grant injunctive relief where jurisdiction is acquired under another statute which provides an exhaustive code of the available remedies and that code does not authorise the grant of an injunction. Nor does s 23 provide authority for the granting of an injunction where, whether under the general law or by statute, otherwise there is no case for injunctive relief. In *Patrick Stevedores Operations No 2 Pty Ltd v Maritime Union of Australia*,[27] the Federal Court entertained the common law claims in conspiracy either in the accrued jurisdiction or as an associated matter within the meaning of s 32 of the Federal Court Act.

In delivering the advice of the majority of their Lordships in **[397]** *Mercedes Benz AG v Leiduck*, Lord Mustill outlined the development over twenty years of the remedy associated with the orders made in *Mareva Compania Naviera SA v International Bulkcarriers SA*.[28] His Lordship observed that: '[a]midst all the burdensome practicalities theory has been left behind'.[29] Lord Mustill went on to outline three rationalisations which could be found in the English authorities, all of them unsatisfactory. One, later discredited by the House of Lords' decisions to which reference has already been made, was that the statutory power in Judicature systems to grant injunctive relief where just or convenient was relatively unlimited. Another was that, although framed as an injunction, the relief was a species of attachment, giving the claimant some rights of a proprietary nature in the assets in question and some advantage over other creditors of the defendant. Whilst not going that far in legal form, *Mareva* orders restricting dealings with assets do have characteristics of injunctive relief to enforce what are known in commerce as negative pledge agreements. However, the rationale of the *Mareva* order as a species of pre-judgment attachment has been discredited by authorities which Lord Mustill collected.[30] That left, in his Lordship's view, the *Mareva* injunction as 'a special exception to the general law'.[31]

---

25. *Principles of Equity*, 2nd ed (1933), p 335.
26. *Bristol City Council v Lovell* [1998] 1 All ER 775 at 782.
27. (1998) 195 CLR 1 at 29; *PCS Operations Pty Ltd v Maritime Union of Australia* (1998) 153 ALR 520 at 524–5.
28. [1975] 2 Lloyd's Rep 509.
29. *Mercedes Benz AG v Leiduck* [1996] AC 284 at 299.
30. *Mercedes Benz AG v Leiduck* [1996] AC 284 at 300.
31. *Mercedes Benz AG v Leiduck* [1996] AC 284 at 301.

In the *Mareva* case itself, Lord Denning MR had classified relief as injunctive on the footing that it went in aid of a legal right, namely the right of the plaintiff to be paid the debt owing, even before the establishment of that right by the getting of judgment for it.[32] However, as Bray CJ observed in *Pivovaroff v Chernabaeff*,[33] such a position was foreclosed by the long-standing decision of Lord Hatherley LC in *Mills v Northern Railway of Buenos Ayres Co*.[34] That decision had been taken as settled authority for the proposition, expressed by Joyce:

> A simple contract creditor of a company (having no mortgage or other security, and not having taken out execution) cannot sustain a bill to restrain the company from dealing with their assets as they please, on the ground that they are diminishing the fund for payment of his debt.[35]

The remedies sought in *Mills* had included an injunction to restrain the [398] payment of any dividend to shareholders until provision had been made for paying the creditor's debt. There had been prima facie evidence that the plaintiff was a creditor and had been unpaid for years. Thus, the plaintiff had made out, at least at the interlocutory level, the existence of his legal right. However, there being no security for the debt, the right was not, as then was considered important, proprietary in nature. Moreover, the contractual right itself would, on recovery of judgment, merge in the judgment. The substance of the relief sought by the plaintiff was anticipatory relief in aid of those rights that would at that later stage attach to the judgment debt.

However, to deny injunctive relief in those circumstances did not mean that in comparable situations the court was powerless. In Australia, it has since been determined by the Appeal Division of the Supreme Court of Victoria[36] and assumed by this Court[37] that circumstances may arise in which the appointment of a receiver of the assets of a company which is not expressly alleged to be insolvent may be justified in pending litigation even on the application of a plaintiff who claims to be an unsecured creditor ...

Further, there may be an equity which supports the appointment of a receiver (or the retention of a receiver appointed at an interlocutory stage) as part of the machinery for effecting final relief.[38] Such a receiver is not appointed merely because, in the circumstances of the case, this would be a more convenient mode of obtaining satisfaction of a judgment than the usual modes of execution provided by the common law or by statute.

Nevertheless, in speaking for the Court of Appeal in *Harris v Beauchamp Brothers*, Davey LJ emphasised that, in a suit by a judgment creditor 'to impeach an assignment or conveyance as fraudulent upon creditors', the court would, as ancillary to the principal relief sought in a proper case, appoint a receiver to preserve the property until the hearing

---

32. *Mareva Compania Naviera SA v International Bulkcarriers SA* [1975] 2 Lloyd's Rep 509 at 510.
33. (1978) 16 SASR 329 at 338–9.
34. (1870) LR 5 Ch App 621.
35. *The Law and Practice of Injunctions in Equity and at Common Law* (1872), vol 2 at 923.
36. *National Australia Bank Ltd v Bond Brewing Holdings Ltd* [1990] 1 VR 386 at 543–6.
37. *National Australia Bank Ltd v Bond Brewing Holdings Ltd* (1990) 169 CLR 271 at 276.
38. *Chitty's Archbold's Practice of the Queen's Bench Division of the High Court of Justice*, 14th ed (1885), vol 2 at 914; *Ashburner's Principles of Equity*, 2nd ed (1933) at 353–4.

of that impeachment suit. Davey LJ also indicated that, if a defendant threatened and intended fraudulently to make away with assets which otherwise might be taken in execution, the court would interfere.[39] On the other hand, execution of a **[399]** judgment might be enjoined on equitable grounds which could not have been entertained as a defence to the action in which the judgment was recovered.[40]

Finally, before judgment and in cases of an equitable debt or demand, courts of equity … may, by order in the nature of a writ of ne exeat colonia, prevent a defendant quitting the country without giving adequate bail or security. Dixon J in *Glover v Walters* said that the order is made where: 'real ground appears for believing that the defendant is seeking to avoid the jurisdiction or for apprehending that if the defendant is allowed to depart the plaintiff will lose his debt or be prejudiced in his remedy'.[41]

In these various ways, the courts developed doctrines and remedies, outside the injunction as understood in courts of equity, to protect the integrity of its processes once set in motion. The *Mareva* order for the preservation of assets should be seen as a further development. There is no harm in the use of the term *Mareva* to identify that development, provided the source of the remedy is kept in view when considering the form of the remedy in each particular case. An anterior question will be whether there is another interlocutory remedy among those considered above which will be suitable to meet the case in hand but be less extensive in scope.

The doctrinal basis of the Mareva order

In Australia, that view of the matter has been urged for many years. It is seen in the most recent statement of principle in this Court concerning the jurisdiction of the Federal Court to grant a Mareva order. In *Patrick Stevedores Operations No 2 Pty Ltd v* **[400]** *Maritime Union of Australia*, in their joint judgment, Brennan CJ, McHugh, Gummow, Kirby and Hayne JJ said:

> *Interlocutory relief*
>
> The powers of the Federal Court under s 23 of its Act are powers 'to make orders of such kinds, including interlocutory orders, as it "thinks appropriate"', as Deane J noted in *Jackson v Sterling Industries Ltd*.[42] He added: 'Wide though that power is, it is subject to both jurisdictional and other limits. It exists only "in relation to matters" in respect of which jurisdiction has been conferred upon the Federal Court. Even in relation to such matters, the power is restricted to the making of the "kinds" of order, whether final or interlocutory, which are capable of properly being seen as "appropriate" to be made by the Federal Court in the exercise of its jurisdiction.' One limitation on the powers of the Federal Court to grant interlocutory injunctions is that those powers must be exercised for the purpose for which they are conferred. In a later passage of the judgment of Deane J in *Jackson v Sterling Industries Ltd*, his Honour said a power to prevent the abuse or frustration of a court's process should be accepted 'as an established part of the armoury of a court of law and equity' and that 'the power to grant such relief in relation to a matter

---

39. *Harris v Beauchamp Brothers* [1894] 1 QB 801 at 810–11.
40. *Hughes v Metropolitan Railway Co* (1877) 2 App Cas 439 (equitable estoppel); *High v Bengal Brass Co and Bank of NSW* (1921) 21 SR (NSW) 232 (equitable set-off).
41. *Glover v Walters* (1950) 80 CLR 172 at 176.
42. (1987) 162 CLR 612 at 622.

in which the Federal Court has jurisdiction is comprehended by the express grant to that Court by s 23 of the *Federal Court of Australia Act*'.[43] But, his Honour observed, orders must be framed 'so as to come within the limits set by the purpose which [the order] can properly be intended to serve'.[44] The *Mareva* injunction is the paradigm example of an order to prevent the frustration of a court's process but other examples may be found. The moulding of an interlocutory injunction must depend upon the circumstances of each case. As Brennan J observed in *Jackson v Sterling Industries Ltd*: 'A judicial power to make an interlocutory order in the nature of a *Mareva* injunction may be exercised according to the exigencies of the case and, the schemes which a debtor may devise for divesting himself of assets being legion, novelty of form is no objection to the validity of such an order'.[45] The general principle which informs the **[401]** exercise of the power to grant interlocutory relief is that the court may make such orders, at least against the parties to the proceeding against whom final relief might be granted, as are needed to ensure the effective exercise of the jurisdiction invoked. The Federal Court had jurisdiction to make interlocutory orders to prevent frustration of its process in the present proceeding.[46]

Subject to two matters to which we shall come, this passage should be accepted as a correct statement of principle. The first matter is that, in that passage, the attention of the Court was directed to orders against parties to the proceedings and against whom final relief was sought. In that situation, the focus is the frustration of the court's process. If relief is available against non-parties, the focus must be the administration of justice. The second matter is that, to avoid confusion as to its doctrinal basis, it is preferable that references to '*Mareva* orders' be substituted for 'injunctions'.

In Australia, for many years, *Mareva* orders have been made in aid of the exercise of the specific remedies provided for execution against judgment debtors. Such orders are not interlocutory as they may operate after the recovery of final judgment, yet they are impermanent in the sense that they preserve assets and assist and protect the use of methods of execution and do not substitute for them.[47] In respect of their operation after, as well as before, the making of orders for final relief, the Mareva order should, in general, be supported by an undertaking as to damages.

Here, Ultra Modern and Mr and Mrs Cardile are third parties in respect of LED's action against Eagle Homes. The effective exercise of the jurisdiction in such litigation may call for asset preservation orders against third parties who may hold or otherwise be interested in (in the sense we explain further in these reasons) assets of the judgment debtor or potential judgment debtor or who may be obliged to contribute to the property of such a judgment debtor to help satisfy the judgment.

Third parties

In this litigation, as has been mentioned, final judgment on LED's claim against Eagle Homes for a money sum is still pending. The [Cardiles] correctly submit that the statement

---

43. *Jackson v Sterling Industries Ltd* (1987) 162 CLR 612; (1987) 162 CLR 612 at 623. See also *Jago v District Court (NSW)* (1989) 168 CLR 23 at 74.
44. *Jackson v Sterling Industries Ltd* (1987) 162 CLR 612 at 625.
45. *Jackson v Sterling Industries Ltd* (1987) 162 CLR 612 at 621.
46. *Patrick Stevedores Operations No 2 Pty Ltd v Maritime Union of Australia* (1998) 195 CLR 1 at 32.
47. See *Jackson v Sterling Industries Ltd* (1987) 162 CLR 612 at 626, 633, 637; *Deputy Commissioner of Taxation v Winter* (1988) 92 FLR 327 at 328–31.

of principle in *Patrick Stevedores* provides no basis for the making of an order against a non-party such as Ultra Modern which is not answerable or liable in some way to a party (plaintiff or defendant) in a proceeding where judgment has not been obtained or execution recovered, or not holding, controlling or capable of disposing of the property of a party in that **[402]** proceeding. This proposition, negative in character, should be accepted.

In its response here and in the Full Court of the Federal Court, LED relies on a decision of Kiefel J in *Tomlinson v Cut Price Deli Pty Ltd*. There, her Honour referred to the making of orders in aid of an injunction 'where the third party has become mixed up in the [challenged] transaction'.[48] In using that language, her Honour was no doubt conscious of the reference to the intermingling of affairs by Hope JA in *Coxton Pty Ltd v Milne*[49] and by Hoffmann LJ in *Mercantile Group (Europe) AG v Aiyela*[50] to the wife of the judgment debtor becoming 'mixed up' in the arrangements of the judgment debtor. But in the application before her Honour there was a large body of evidence to support a strongly arguable case that the third party had used, and was using, the property and business of the potential judgment debtor in order to prevent access to them by the applicant. And again, in *Aiglon Ltd v Gau Shan Co Ltd*,[51] there was evidence of a quite different kind and quality as to asset stripping in favour of a non-party from that which has been adduced here.

These cases were not mere cases of a mixing or intermingling of affairs and are distinguishable from this case. In using expressions such as 'mixing' or 'intermingling', their Honours and his Lordship were doing no more than describing the deliberate blurring, and attempts at the transferring, of property rights and interests that the evidence in those cases established on a sufficient basis for the grant of the relief. There was nothing novel in that approach to determination of the appropriate remedy.

LED's stance in this appeal is that it is not essential that the court's processes in support of which the *Mareva* relief is sought be confined to those set in motion upon a cause of action. That followed, it is submitted, from a passage in the speech of Lord Mustill in *Channel Tunnel Group Ltd v Balfour Beatty Construction Ltd*,[52] to which Hoffmann LJ referred in *Mercantile Group (Europe) AG v Aiyela*[53] in holding that the wife of the judgment debtor should be restrained from disposing of assets although no action had been brought against her. Lord Mustill said that the right to an interlocutory injunction which is incidental to, and dependent on, the enforcement of a substantive right usually, although not invariably, takes the shape of a cause of action. However, we do not think that his Lordship was **[403]** suggesting that an order might be made against a non-party not amenable in some way ultimately to some coercive process requiring it to disgorge, or in some other way to participate in the satisfaction of, a judgment against a party.

LED argues that its substantive rights are the final injunctive orders already made by Davies J against Eagle Homes following the determination of the issue of liability upon LED's actions for copyright infringement. Even if this be accepted for present purposes,

---

48. *Tomlinson v Cut Price Deli Pty Ltd*, unreported; Federal Court of Australia; 23 June 1995 at 11.
49. Unreported; Court of Appeal of NSW; 20 December 1985.
50. [1994] QB 366 at 375.
51. [1993] 1 Lloyd's Rep 164.
52. [1993] AC 334 at 362.
53. [1994] QB 366 at 375–6.

LED still has the problem, which in our opinion the evidence does not resolve in its favour, of showing that recourse may be had to [the Cardiles] to satisfy LED's prospective money judgment against Eagle Homes.

As LED submits, the development of this ancillary jurisdiction to grant *Mareva* orders has been an evolving process and the courts have approached the different factual situations as they have arisen 'flexibly'. There is a temptation to use the term 'flexible' to cloak a lack of analytical rigour and to escape the need to find a doctrinal and principled basis for orders that are made. There are significant differences between an order protective of the court's process set in train against a party to an action, including the efficacy of execution available to a judgment creditor, and an order extending to the property of persons who are not parties and who cannot be shown to have frustrated, actually or prospectively, the administration of justice. It has been truly said that a Mareva order does not deprive the party subject to its restraint either of title to or possession of the assets to which the order extends. Nor does the order improve the position of claimants in an insolvency of the judgment debtor. It operates in personam and not as an attachment. Nevertheless, those statements should not obscure the reality that the granting of a *Mareva* order is bound to have a significant impact on the property of the person against whom it is made: in a practical sense it operates as a very tight 'negative pledge' species of security over property, to which the contempt sanction is attached. It requires a high degree of caution on the part of a court invited to make an order of that kind. An order lightly or wrongly granted may have a capacity to impair or restrict commerce just as much as one appropriately granted may facilitate and ensure its due conduct.

We agree with the tenor of what was said with particular respect to *Mareva* relief before judgment by the Court of Appeal of New South Wales (Mason P, Sheller JA, Sheppard A-JA) in *Frigo v Culhaci*:

[404] [A *Mareva* order] is a drastic remedy which should not be granted lightly … A [*Mareva* order] is an interlocutory order which, if granted, imposes a severe restriction upon a defendant's right to deal with his or her assets. It is granted at the suit of a plaintiff whose status as a creditor is in dispute and who need not be a secured creditor. Its purpose is to preserve the status quo, not to change it in favour of the plaintiff. The function of the order is not to 'provide a plaintiff with security in advance for a judgment that he hopes to obtain and that he fears might not be satisfied; nor is it to improve the position of the plaintiff in the event of the defendant's insolvency'[54] … Many authorities attest to the care with which courts are required to scrutinise applications for [*Mareva* orders] … [55]

Another reason, unfortunately rarely adverted to in the cases, for care in exercising the power to grant a *Mareva* order is that there may be difficulties associated with the quantification and recovery of damages pursuant to the undertaking if it should turn out that the order should not have been granted. These matters were the subject of discussion by Aickin J in *Air Express Ltd v Ansett Transport Industries (Operations) Pty Ltd*.[56] A further question to which a *Mareva* order gives rise is the identification of the events to trigger its

---

54. *Abella v Anderson* [1987] 2 Qd R 1 at 2–3.
55. *Frigo v Culhaci*, unreported, 17 July 1998, at 10–11.
56. (1979) 146 CLR 249 at 260 et seq; affd (1981) 146 CLR 306.

dissolution or an entitlement to damages. So far as this is possible, some attention to that question should be given at the time that the order is framed in the first instance.

Discretionary considerations generally also should carefully be weighed before an order is made. Has the applicant proceeded diligently and expeditiously? Has a money judgment been recovered in the proceedings? Are proceedings (for example, civil conspiracy proceedings) available against the third party? Why, if some proceedings are available, have they not been taken? Why, if proceedings are available against the third party and have not been taken and the court is still minded to make a *Mareva* order, should not the grant of the relief be conditioned upon an undertaking by the applicant to commence, and ensure so far as is possible the expedition of, such proceedings? It is difficult to conceive of cases where such an undertaking would not be required. Questions of this kind may be just as relevant to the decision to grant *Mareva* relief as they are to a decision to dissolve it. These are matters to which courts should be alive. As will appear, they are matters which should have been considered by the Full Court in this case.

We have indicated our acceptance of a negative proposition put by [405] [the Cardiles]. However, we consider that the general proposition for which [they] contend — that the grant of *Mareva* relief against the third party should be limited to cases in which the third party holds or is about to hold or dissipate or further dissipate property beneficially owned by the defendant in the substantive proceedings — is too narrowly expressed. Nevertheless, it will be a rare case in which *Mareva* relief will be granted if such a situation does not exist.

We do not accept an example suggested by LED as an answer to [the Cardiles'] general proposition. LED contends that, if [the Cardiles'] proposition be correct, a third party to whom a defendant makes a fraudulent gift to render useless the judgment against him would be immune from *Mareva* relief, whereas a third party trustee would not, because the third party taking the fraudulent gift would have no right in law or in equity to retain it. The former would be amenable to a claim pursuant to s 37A of the *Conveyancing Act*, or process by a trustee in bankruptcy, or a liquidator, and susceptibility to that process may in our opinion be sufficient to support the grant of *Mareva* relief. The fact that such relief takes effect in personam, and may be distinguished from an equitable or other proprietary remedy such as tracing, does not mean that the availability of such remedies is irrelevant to a consideration whether that relief should be granted. Indeed the contrary is the case. The availability of a proprietary remedy may, in our opinion, in some cases be sufficient to constitute a substantive right in aid of which *Mareva* relief in personam might go.

The matters referred to above show that the general power of superior courts which is comprehended by the express grant in s 23 of the Federal Court Act is a broad one. But, as the statements of Deane J in *Jackson v Sterling Industries Ltd*[57] make clear, orders made pursuant to that section (and under the general power) must be capable of properly being seen as appropriate to the case in hand.

What then is the principle to guide the courts in determining whether to grant *Mareva* relief in a case such as the present where the activities of third parties are the object sought to be restrained? In our opinion such an order may, and we emphasise the word 'may', be appropriate, assuming the existence of other relevant criteria and discretionary

---

57. (1987) 162 CLR 612 at 622, 625.

factors, in circumstances in which: (i) the third party holds, is using, or has exercised or is exercising a power of disposition over, or is otherwise in possession of, assets, including 'claims and expectancies',[58] of the judgment debtor or potential judgment debtor; or (ii) some process, ultimately enforceable by the courts, is or may be available to the judgment creditor as a consequence of a judgment against that actual or potential judgment debtor, pursuant to which, whether by appointment of a liquidator, trustee in bankruptcy, **[406]** receiver or otherwise, the third party may be obliged to disgorge property or otherwise contribute to the funds or property of the judgment debtor to help satisfy the judgment against the judgment debtor.

It is that principle which we would apply to this case. Its application is a matter of law, although discretionary elements are involved.

Comment
1. See Radan & Stewart at **25.15–25.32**.

Requirements for an Anton Piller order

25.4   Anton Piller KG v Manufacturing Process Limited [1975] 1 Ch 55

Court: Court of Appeal of England and Wales

Facts: Anton Piller KG (AP) was a German manufacturer of generators and electric motors that designed a frequency converter for the computer industry. Manufacturing Process Ltd (MP) was a company that distributed and sold AP's products in Britain. As its agent, it had access to AP's intellectual property. Two executives of MP defected, alleging that the company was communicating with AP's competitors in Germany and supplying them with the design and specifications of its new frequency converter. They were in possession of communication between the companies that seemed to corroborate their claims. AP executives were concerned that the launch of a new type of frequency converter would be jeopardised by the communications and sought to restrain MP from infringing their copyright, using their confidential information or making copies of their machines. They also sought an order for entry to MP's premises to inspect, copy or remove its communications and documents.

Issue: The issue before the Court of Appeal was whether AP was entitled to orders restraining infringement of copyright as well as allowing access to MP's records.

Decision: The Court of Appeal (Lord Denning MR, Ormrod and Shaw LLJ) unanimously supported AP's application.

Extracts: The extracts from the judgments of Lord Denning MR and Ormrod LJ highlight the reasoning behind Anton Piller orders and the requirements that need to be met.

---

58. The phrase used by Deane J in *Jackson v Sterling Industries Ltd* (1987) 162 CLR 612 at 625.

Lord Denning MR

[60] Let me say at once that no court in this land has any power to issue a search warrant to enter a man's house so as to see if there are papers or documents there which are of an incriminating nature, whether libels or infringements of copyright or anything else of the kind. No constable or bailiff can knock at the door and demand entry so as to inspect papers or documents. The householder can shut the door in his face and say 'Get out'. That was established in the leading case of *Entick v Carrington*.[59] None of us would wish to whittle down that principle in the slightest. But the order sought in this case is not a search warrant. It does not authorise [AP's] solicitors or anyone else to enter [MP's] premises against their will. It does not authorise the breaking down of any doors, nor the slipping in by a back door, nor getting in by an open door or window. It only authorises entry and inspection by the permission of [MP] ... But it does do this: it brings pressure on [MP] to give permission. It does more. It actually orders them to give permission — with, I suppose, the result that if they do not give permission, they are guilty of contempt of court.

This may seem to be a search warrant in disguise. But it was fully considered in the House of Lords 150 years ago and held to be legitimate. The case is *United Company of Merchants of England, Trading to the East Indies v Kynaston*. Lord Redesdale said:

> The arguments urged for the Appellants at the Bar are founded upon the supposition, that the Court has directed a forcible inspection. This is an erroneous view of the case. The order is to permit; and if the East India Company should refuse to permit inspection, they will be guilty of a contempt of the court .... It is an order operating on the person requiring the defendants to permit inspection, not giving the authority of force, or to break open the doors of their warehouse.[60]

The case was not, however, concerned with papers or things. It was only as to the value of a warehouse; and that could not be obtained without an inspection. But the distinction drawn by Lord Redesdale affords ground for thinking that there is jurisdiction to make an order that the defendant 'do permit' when it is necessary in the interests of justice.

Accepting such to be the case, the question is in what circumstances ought such an order be made. If the defendant is given notice beforehand and is able to argue the pros and cons, it is warranted by that case in the House of Lords and by [Rules of the Supreme Court]. But it is a far stronger thing to make such an order ex parte without giving him [61] notice. This is not covered by the Rules of the Supreme Court and must be based on the inherent jurisdiction of the court. There are one or two old precedents which give some colour for it, *Hennessey v Rohmann, Osborne & Co*[61] and *Morris v Howell*,[62] an Irish case. But they do not go very far. So it falls to us to consider it on principle. It seems to me that such an order can be made by a judge ex parte, but it should only be made where it is essential that the plaintiff should have inspection so that justice can be done between

---

59. (1765) 95 ER 807.
60. *United Company of Merchants of England, Trading to the East Indies v Kynaston* (1821) 4 ER 561 at 564–5.
61. *Hennessey v Rohmann, Osborne & Co* [1877] WN 14.
62. *Morris v Howell* (1888) 22 LR Ir 77.

the parties: and when, if the defendant were forewarned, there is a grave danger that vital evidence will be destroyed, that papers will be burnt or lost or hidden, or taken beyond the jurisdiction, and so the ends of justice be defeated; and when the inspection would do no real harm to the defendant or his case.

Nevertheless, in the enforcement of this order, the plaintiffs must act with due circumspection. On the service of it, the plaintiffs should be attended by their solicitor, who is an officer of the court. They should give the defendants opportunity of considering it and of consulting their own solicitor. If the defendants wish to apply to discharge the order as having been improperly obtained, they must be allowed to do so. If the defendants refuse permission to enter or to inspect, the plaintiffs must not force their way in. They must accept the refusal, and bring it to the notice of the court afterwards, if need be on an application to commit.

[The order] serves to tell the defendants that, on the evidence put before it, the court is of opinion that they ought to permit inspection — nay, it orders them to permit — and that they refuse at their own peril. It puts them in peril not only of proceedings for contempt, but also of adverse inferences being drawn against them; so much so that their own solicitor may advise them to comply. We are told that in two at least of the cases such an order has been effective. We are prepared, therefore, to sanction its continuance, but only in an extreme case where there is a grave danger or property being smuggled away or of vital evidence being destroyed.

Ormrod LJ

I agree with all that Lord Denning MR has said. The proposed order is at the extremity of this court's powers. Such orders, therefore, will rarely be made, and only when there is no alternative way of ensuring that justice is done to the applicant.

[62] There are three essential pre-conditions for the making of such an order, in my judgment. First, there must be an extremely strong prima facie case. Secondly, the damage, potential or actual, must be very serious for the applicant. Thirdly, there must be clear evidence that the defendants have in their possession incriminating documents or things, and that there is a real possibility that they may destroy such material before any application inter partes can be made.

The form of the order makes it plain that the court is not ordering or granting anything equivalent to a search warrant. The order is an order on the defendant in personam to permit inspection. It is therefore open to him to refuse to comply with such an order, but at his peril either of further proceedings for contempt of court ... Great responsibility clearly rests on the solicitors for the applicant to ensure that the carrying out of such an order is meticulously carefully done with the fullest respect for the defendant's rights, as Lord Denning MR has said, of applying to the court, should he feel it necessary to do so, before permitting the inspection.

In the circumstances of the present case, all those conditions to my mind are satisfied, and this order is essential in the interests of justice.

Comment

1. See Radan & Stewart at **25.38–25.40**.

Plaintiff's obligations in executing an Anton Piller order

25.5   Celanese Canada Inc v Murray Demolition Corporation (2006) 269 DLR (4th) 193

Court: Supreme Court of Canada

Facts: Celanese Canada (CC) brought proceedings against Canadian Bearings Ltd (CB) for alleged theft and unauthorised use of its intellectual property, being information about certain technologies concerning the construction of vinyl acetate facilities. It was claimed the discovery of the information was made during the demolition of one of CC's plants. An Anton Piller order had been issued in CC's favour during the course of those proceedings. At the time the order was being executed, CB alleged that the contents of a sealed envelope were removed without authority. They contained a compact disc with privileged communications between CB and its legal advisers, the contents of which were electronically copied and stored by CC's representatives. CB brought proceedings to restrain CC's lawyers from further acting in the main suit.

Issue: The issues before the Supreme Court were (i) to determine which party in the proceedings bore the onus of proof in regard to any prejudice arising from disclosure of privileged communications, and (ii) to decide on the proper test for assessing the professional obligations of counsel in such cases.

Decision: The Supreme Court (McLachlin CJ, Bastarache, Binnie, LeBel, Deschamps, Fish and Charron JJ) unanimously upheld the appeal by CB. It held that the onus is on the recipient of the disputed information to rebut the legal presumption that the information would be used at trial.

Extracts: The extracts from the judgment of the court, delivered by Binnie J, address the steps to be taken by recipients of privileged information and their legal representatives pursuant to the making of Anton Piller orders.

Binnie J

[197] An *Anton Piller* order bears an uncomfortable resemblance to a private search warrant. No notice is given to the party against whom it is issued. Indeed, defendants usually first learn of them when they are served and executed, without having had an opportunity to challenge them or the evidence on which they were granted. The defendant may have no idea a claim is even pending. The order is not placed in the hands of a public authority for execution, but authorizes a private party to insist on entrance to the premises of its opponent to conduct a surprise search, the purpose of which is to seize and preserve evidence to further its claim in a private dispute. The only justification for such an extraordinary remedy is that the plaintiff has a strong *prima facie* case and can demonstrate that on the facts, absent such an order, there is a real possibility relevant evidence will be destroyed or otherwise made to [198] disappear. The protection of the party against whom an *Anton Piller* order is issued ought to be threefold: a carefully drawn order which identifies the material to be seized and sets out safeguards to deal, amongst

other things, with privileged documents; a vigilant court-appointed supervising solicitor who is independent of the parties; and a sense of responsible self-restraint on the part of those executing the order ... Inadequate protections had been written into the order. Those which had been provided were not properly respected ...

[205] *Anton Piller* orders have been available in Canada for close to 30 years. Unlike a search warrant they do not authorize forcible entry, but expose the target to contempt proceedings unless permission to enter is given ...

[206] With easier access to such orders, there has emerged a tendency on the part of some counsel to take too lightly the very serious responsibilities imposed by such a draconian order. It should truly be exceptional for a court to authorize the massive intrusion, without advance notice, of a privately orchestrated search on the privacy of a business competitor or other target party ...

[207] Experience has shown that despite their draconian nature, there is a proper role for *Anton Piller* orders to ensure that unscrupulous defendants are not able to circumvent the court's processes by, on being forewarned, making relevant evidence disappear. Their usefulness is especially important in the modern era of heavy dependence on computer technology, where documents are easily deleted, moved or destroyed. The utility of this equitable tool in the correct circumstances should not be diminished. However, such orders should only be granted in the clear recognition of their exceptional and highly intrusive character and, where granted, the terms should be carefully spelled out and limited to what the circumstances show to be necessary. Those responsible for their implementation should conform to a very high standard of professional diligence. Otherwise, the moving party, not its target, may have to shoulder the consequences of a botched search ...

[208] There are four essential conditions for the making of an *Anton Piller* order. First, the plaintiff must demonstrate a strong *prima facie* case. Second, the damage to the plaintiff of the defendant's alleged misconduct, potential or actual, must be very serious. Third, there must be convincing evidence that the defendant has in its possession incriminating documents or things, and fourthly it must be shown that there is a real possibility that the defendant may [209] destroy such material before the discovery process can do its work ...

Both the strength and the weakness of an *Anton Piller* order is that it is made *ex parte* and interlocutory: there is thus no cross-examination on the supporting affidavits. The motions judge necessarily reposes faith in the candour and complete disclosure of the affiants, and as much or more so on the professional responsibility of the lawyers participating in carrying out its terms ...

[210] *Anton Piller* orders are often conceived of, obtained and implemented in circumstances of urgency. They are generally time-limited ... Despite the urgency, the more detailed and standardized the terms of the order the less opportunity there will be for misunderstandings or mischief ...

Unless and until model orders are developed by legislation or recommended by law societies pursuant to their responsibility for professional conduct, the following guidelines for preparation and [211] execution of an *Anton Piller* order may be helpful, depending on the circumstances:

(1) **Basic Protection for the Rights of the Parties**
    (i)   The order should appoint a supervising solicitor who is independent of the plaintiff or its solicitors and is to be present at the search to ensure its integrity.

The key role of the independent supervising solicitor was noted by the motions judge in this case 'to ensure that the execution of the Anton Piller order and everything that flowed from it, was undertaken as carefully as possible and with due consideration for the rights and interests of all involved'. He or she is 'an officer of the court charged with a very important responsibility regarding this extraordinary remedy'.

(ii) Absent unusual circumstances the plaintiff should be required to provide an undertaking and/or security to pay damages in the event that the order turns out to be unwarranted or wrongfully executed.

(iii) The scope of the order should be no wider than necessary and no material shall be removed from the site unless clearly covered by the terms of the order.

(iv) A term setting out the procedure for dealing with solicitor–client privilege or other confidential material should be included with a view to enabling defendants to advance claims of confidentiality over documents before they come into the possession of the plaintiff or its counsel, or to deal with disputes that arise … [212]

(v) The order should contain a limited use clause (ie, items seized may only be used for the purposes of the pending litigation).

(vi) The order should state explicitly that the defendant is entitled to return to court on short notice to (a) discharge the order; or (b) vary the amount of security.

(vii) The order should provide that the materials seized be returned to the defendants or their counsel as soon as practicable.

(2) **The Conduct of the Search**

(i) In general the order should provide that the search should be commenced during normal business hours when counsel for the party about to be searched is more likely to be available for consultation. [213]

(ii) The premises should not be searched or items removed except in the presence of the defendant or a person who appears to be a responsible employee of the defendant.

(iii) The persons who may conduct the search and seize evidence should be specified in the order or should specifically be limited in number.

(iv) On attending at the site of the authorised search, plaintiff's counsel (or the supervising solicitor), acting as officers of the court should serve a copy of the statement of claim and the order and supporting affidavits and explain to the defendant or responsible corporate officer or employee in plain language the nature and effect of the order.

(v) The defendant or its representatives should be given a reasonable time to consult with counsel prior to permitting entry to the premises.

(vi) A detailed list of all evidence seized should be made and the supervising solicitor should provide this list to the defendant for inspection and verification at the end of the search and before materials are removed from the site.

(vii) Where this is not practicable, documents seized should be placed in the custody of the independent supervising solicitor, and defendant's counsel should be given a reasonable opportunity to review them to advance solicitor–client privilege claims prior to release of the documents to the plaintiff.

(viii) Where ownership of material is disputed, it should be provided for safekeeping to the supervising solicitor or to the defendant's solicitors.

(3) Procedure Following the Search

(i) The order should make it clear that the responsibilities of the supervising solicitor continue beyond the search itself to deal with matters arising out of the search, subject of course to [214] any party wishing to take a matter back to the court for resolution.

(ii) The supervising solicitor should be required to file a report with the court within a set time limit describing the execution, who was present and what was seized.

(iii) The court may wish to require the plaintiff to file and serve a motion for review of the execution of the search returnable within a set time limit such as 14 days to ensure that the court automatically reviews the supervising solicitor's report and the implementation of its order even if the defendant does not request such a review ...

[218] In my view, the present proceeding should not be seen as punitive in any way. I accept, as did the courts below, that [CC's legal representatives did not] set out to obtain access to, or to gain some advantage from privileged material. Their problem stems from carelessness and an excessively adversarial approach in circumstances that called for careful restraint in recognition of the exceptional position of responsibility imposed by the unilateral and intrusive nature of an *Anton Piller* order. The protection of solicitor–client confidences is a matter of high importance. On the present state of the record, [CB] can have no confidence that the privileged material to which [CC's legal representatives] obtained access will not be used to their prejudice.

Comment

1. See Radan & Stewart at **25.41–25.42**.

25.6   Long v Specifier Publications Pty Ltd
(1998) 44 NSWLR 545

Court: Court of Appeal in New South Wales

Facts: Long was a solicitor who acted for parties in the purchase of a publishing business. Litigation ensued upon the breakdown of the transaction, which included at one point the making of an Anton Piller order in favour of Long's clients. The order was made subject to a condition that Long undertake to make an inventory of goods that were removed from named premises and to 'remain at all times in charge' of them. He gave undertakings in those terms to the court. Long's record of the removed goods was perfunctory and he abandoned control of them by passing the property over to a third party. He was subsequently found guilty of contempt of court in the Equity Division of the Supreme Court for breach of undertakings and fined $15,000. Long appealed to the Court of Appeal.

Issue: The issues before the Court of Appeal were whether the Supreme Court had erred in holding that Long had acted in contempt of court on the facts and whether the fine was excessive.

Decision: The Court of Appeal (Meagher, Handley and Powell JJA) unanimously rejected Long's appeal. It held that Long's obligation to make an inventory required the making of a detailed list identifying each removed document and item, which he did not do. It also found Long's undertaking to remain in charge of the seized goods required him to remain in possession of them.

Extracts: The extracts from the judgment of Powell JA underline the nature of Anton Piller orders and the obligations of legal representatives who are entrusted with directing and controlling their execution.

Powell JA

[547] Reduced to its essentials, an Anton Piller order is an order that the defendant to whom, or to which, it is directed, should permit the persons specified in the order to enter upon his, or its, premises, and to inspect, take copies of, and to remove, specified material, or classes of material, indicating, where appropriate, documents, articles or other forms of property. It is an extraordinary remedy, designed to obtain, and to preserve, vital evidence pending the final determination of the plaintiff's claim in the proceedings, in a case in which it can be shown that there is a high risk that, if forewarned, the defendant, would destroy, or hide, the evidence, or cause it to be removed from the jurisdiction of the court. For this reason, such orders are invariably made ex parte.

Such orders derived their name from the decision of the Court of Appeal in *Anton Piller KG v Manufacturing Processes Ltd*,[63] the jurisprudential basis for their being made being said to be the inherent jurisdiction of the court to ensure that justice be done between the parties to the proposed litigation. As what is sought to be achieved by the making of such an order is the preservation of evidence which, more probably than not, otherwise would be destroyed or at least hidden or [548] spirited away, the cases in which, if the conditions to which I will later refer are fulfilled, such orders are most commonly made are those alleging breach of copyright, or alleged misuse of confidential information.

Although, superficially, the primary order made in such cases might appear to be a search warrant, it must be emphasised that this is not so. On the contrary, the order is a mandatory order operating in personam on the defendant requiring him to permit a nominated person, either alone or accompanied by others, to enter, search, and, where appropriate, to take copies of, or remove, documents or other property. Two consequences flow from this, they being, first, that, if permission is refused, entry and search may not lawfully be had or made; and, secondly, that, if the defendant, having been duly served with an order, refuses permission, be liable to be dealt with for contempt.

Since such an order is an extraordinary remedy, and since an ex parte order should be no greater in extent than is necessary for the purpose, the primary order should, as a minimum, specify, or deal with, the following:

(1) the particular person or persons — whether by name or description — and the maximum number of such persons, to be permitted to enter;

(2) the premises to which entry is to be permitted;

---

63. [1976] Ch D 55.

(3) the times between which entry is to be permitted;

(4) the particular purposes, as for example:

    (a) to search for, inspect and copy, material alleged to infringe copyright or to constitute or to contain confidential information;

    (b) to remove identified material, it being noted that, as a general rule, removal should be permitted only where, under copyright law, or under the general law, the material in question is the property of the plaintiff, or the order provides, first, for the preparation of a detailed list of the items being removed — the defendant being given an adequate opportunity to check the list — for the return of documents the subject of the list once copies have been made and, when there is any dispute as to the title to the items removed, providing for the safe custody of the items not to be returned, pending the return of any originating process.

As well, the order should provide for the defendant to have an opportunity to consider and to take legal advice in respect of it, before being obliged to comply with it, and there should be reserved to the defendant liberty to apply on very short notice to discharge the order. Further, the originating process should, in any event, be made returnable on short notice consistent with the defendant having an adequate opportunity to obtain legal advice and to prepare to apply to discharge, or to oppose the continuation of, the order and any associated relief.

As has been said in a number of the reported authorities, and as the facts giving rise to the present appeal attest, the *Anton Piller* procedure lends itself all too readily to abuse. It was what [Sir Donald Nicholls V-C] clearly enough regarded as the totally unsatisfactory manner in which the order which had originally been made by Millett J ... in *Universal Thermosensors Ltd* [549] *v Hibben* had been executed which led Sir Donald Nicholls V-C in his judgment to record:

(1) *Anton Piller* orders normally contain a term that before complying with the order the defendant may obtain legal advice, provided this is done forthwith. This is an important safeguard for defendants, not least because *Anton Piller* orders tend to be long and complicated, and many defendants cannot be expected to understand much of what they are told by the solicitor serving the order. But such a term, if it is to be of use, requires that in general *Anton Piller* orders should be permitted to be executed only on working days in office hours, when a solicitor can be expected to be available. In the present case Mrs Hibben was alone in her house, with her children in bed. She was brought to the door in her night attire at 7.15 am and told by a stranger knocking on the door that he had a court order requiring her to permit him to enter, that she could take legal advice forthwith, but otherwise she was not permitted to speak to anyone else at all. But how could she get legal advice at that time in the morning? She rang her solicitor's office but, predictably, there was no response.

(2) There is a further feature of the situation to which I have just alluded which must never be allowed to occur again. If the order is to be executed at a private house, and it is likely that a woman may be in the house alone, the solicitor serving the order must be, or must be accompanied by, a woman. A woman should not be subjected to the alarm of being confronted without warning by a solitary strange man, with no recognisable means of identification, waving some unfamiliar papers and claiming

an entitlement to enter her house and, what is more, telling her she is not allowed to get in touch with anyone (except a lawyer) about what is happening.

(3) In the present case a dispute arose about which documents were taken away, and from which of the premises visited. Understandably, those who execute these orders are concerned to search and seize and then get away as quickly as possible so as to minimise the risk of confrontation and physical violence. Nevertheless, in general *Anton Piller* orders should expressly provide that, unless this is seriously impracticable, a detailed list of the items being removed should be prepared at the premises before they are removed, and that the defendant should be given an opportunity to check this list at the time.

(4) *Anton Piller* orders frequently contain an injunction restraining those on whom they are served from informing others of the existence of the order for a limited period. This is to prevent one defendant from alerting others to what is happening. There is an exception for communication with a lawyer for the purpose of seeking legal advice. In the present case that injunction was expressed to last for a whole week. That is far too long. I suspect something went awry with the drafting of the order in this case.

(5) In the present case there was no officer or employee of TPL or Emco present when their offices and workshops were searched and documents and components taken away. This is intolerable. Orders should provide that, unless there is good reason for doing otherwise, the order should not be executed at business premises save in the presence of a responsible officer or representative of the company or trader in question.

(6) The making of an *Anton Piller* order in this case can be seen to be [550] justified by what was discovered. But it is important not to lose sight of the fact that one thing which happened was that Mr James carried out a thorough search of all the documents of a competitor company. This is most unsatisfactory. When *Anton Piller* orders are made in this type of case consideration should be given to devising some means, appropriate to the facts of the case, by which this situation can be avoided.

(7) *Anton Piller* orders invariably provide for service to be effected by a solicitor. The court relies heavily on the solicitor, as an officer of the court, to see that the order is properly executed. Unhappily, the history in the present case, and what has happened in other cases, show that this safeguard is inadequate. The solicitor may be young and have little or no experience of *Anton Piller* orders. Frequently he is the solicitor acting for the plaintiff in the action, and however diligent and fair minded he may be, he is not the right person to be given a task which to some extent involves protecting the interests of the defendant. I think there is force in some of the criticisms set out in the invaluable article by Professor Dockray and Mr Hugh Laddie QC.[64] It seems to me that the way ahead here, pursuing one of the suggestions made in that article, is that when making *Anton Piller* orders judges should give serious consideration to the desirability of providing, by suitable undertakings and otherwise: (a) that the order should be served, and its execution should be supervised, by a solicitor other than a member of the firm of solicitors acting for the plaintiff in the action; (b) that he or she should be an experienced solicitor having some familiarity with the workings of *Anton Piller* orders, and with judicial observations on this subject; (c) that the solicitor should prepare a written

64. Dockray & Laddie, 'Piller Problems' (1990) 106 *Law Quarterly Review* 601.

report on what occurred when the order was executed; (d) that a copy of the report should be served on the defendants; and (e) that in any event and within the next few days the plaintiff must return to the court and present that report at an inter partes hearing, preferably to the judge who made the order. As to (b), I can see advantages in the plaintiff being required to include in his evidence, put to the judge in support of his application for an *Anton Piller* order, details of the name of the solicitor and of his experience.

Of course this procedure would add considerably to the cost of executing an *Anton Piller* order. The plaintiff would have to be responsible for paying the fees of the solicitor in question, without prejudice to a decision by the court on whether ultimately those costs should be borne in whole or in part by the defendant. But it must be appreciated, and certainly it is my view, that *in suitable and strictly limited cases, Anton Piller* orders furnish courts with a valuable aid in their efforts to do justice between two parties. Especially is this so in blatant cases of fraud. It is important therefore that these orders should not be allowed to fall into disrepute. If further steps are necessary to prevent this happening, they should be taken. If plaintiffs wish to take advantage of this truly Draconian type of order, they must be prepared to pay for the safeguards experience has shown are necessary if the interests of defendants are fairly to be protected.[65]

Comment
1. See Radan & Stewart at **25.41–25.42**.

---

65. *Universal Thermosensors Ltd v Hibben* [1992] 3 All ER 257 at 275–6.

26

EQUITABLE COMPENSATION AND DAMAGES

Introduction

26.1 This chapter deals with the availability of two monetary remedies in equity. The first is equitable compensation, a remedy available exclusively in relation to breaches of equitable obligations such as breaches of trust or other fiduciary obligations. The second is equitable damages which can, pursuant to the Australian equivalents of *Lord Cairns' Act*, be awarded in addition to, or in lieu of, an order for specific performance or an injunction.

The cases extracted in this chapter explore the following:

- the general principles governing the assessment of equitable compensation: *Re Dawson (deceased); Union Fidelity Trustee Co Ltd v Perpetual Trustee Co Ltd* [1966] 2 NSWR 211;
- the relevance of the principle of contributory negligence in the assessment of equitable compensation: *Pilmer v Duke Group Ltd (In Liq)* (2001) 207 CLR 165;
- the question of whether exemplary damages can be awarded in claims for equitable compensation: *Harris v Digital Pulse Pty Ltd* (2003) NSWLR 298; and
- the assessment of equitable damages awarded pursuant to the Australian equivalents of *Lord Cairns' Act*: *Wentworth v Woollahra Municipal Council* (1982) 149 CLR 672; *Johnson v Agnew* [1980] AC 367.

Assessment of equitable compensation

26.2 Re Dawson (deceased); Union Fidelity Trustee Co Ltd v Perpetual Trustee Co Ltd [1966] 2 NSWR 211

Court: Supreme Court of New South Wales

Facts: Dawson was one of the executors and beneficiaries of his father's estate, which involved complex administration of properties and interests in New Zealand and New South Wales. The residuary beneficiaries of the father's estate were Dawson, his two brothers and their children. At one point, when administration of the New Zealand estate was in the hands of Dawson's attorneys, a sum of £4700 was received from the sale of a portion of the estate assets in New Zealand. Dawson arranged for the withdrawal of that amount from the estate account for the purpose of lending the moneys to two companies in New South Wales in which the extended Dawson family had an interest. Because of regulatory restrictions on the transfer of money from New Zealand to New South Wales, Dawson arranged for cash to be handed to a person who was to deliver it to New South Wales by presumably unlawful means. That person absconded with the entire amount. When Dawson himself later died, the trustees of his father's estate (Perpetual) retained an amount from Dawson's one-third share to recoup the moneys lost from the head estate through his breach of trust together with additional funds sufficient to cover exchange and interest. Dawson's trustees (Union) began proceedings to determine the amounts that Perpetual could retain.

Issues: The issues before the Supreme Court were to decide whether the sum of £4700 payable by Dawson's estate was to be paid in New Zealand or Australian currency, and to determine the appropriate interest to be calculated on that amount.

Decision: Street J held that Dawson's estate had to repay to the head estate a sum calculated at the rate of exchange prevailing at the time of restoration, not at the time of breach of trust. This involved a higher exchange and interest rate prevailing at the time the money had to be repaid.

Extracts: The extracts from the judgment of Street J discuss the principles for determining the amount of equitable compensation payable by a defaulting trustee in relation to the restitution of the trust property and interest.

Street J

[213] (a) Currency ...

[216] The ... obligation to make restitution, which courts of equity have from very early times imposed on defaulting trustees and other fiduciaries is of a more absolute nature than the common law obligation to pay damages for tort or breach of contract ... [T]he distinction between common law damages and relief against a defaulting trustee is strikingly demonstrated by reference to the actual form of relief granted in equity in respect of breaches of trust. The form of relief is couched in terms appropriate to require the defaulting trustee to restore to the estate the assets of which he deprived it. Increases in market values between the date of breach and the date of recoupment are for the trustee's account: the effect of such increases would, at common law, be excluded from the computation of damages; but in equity a defaulting trustee must make good the loss by restoring to the estate the assets of which he deprived it notwithstanding that market values may have increased in the meantime. The obligation to restore to the estate the assets of which he deprived it necessarily connotes that, where a monetary compensation is to be paid in lieu of restoring assets, that compensation is to be assessed by reference to the value of the assets at the date of restoration and not at the date of deprivation. In this sense the obligation is a continuing one and ordinarily, if the assets are for some reason not restored *in specie*, it will fall for quantification at the date when recoupment is to be effected, and not before ...

Authority for the form of relief being such as to require an actual restoration to the estate or to place it monetarily in the same position as if there had been an actual restoration is not lacking. In *Kellaway v Johnson*[1] Lord Langdale MR, in 1842 ordered trustees, who had in 1799 committed a breach of trust by selling £3000 consols, to replace the moiety of the £3000 consols to which the beneficiaries before the Court were entitled. In *Phillipson v Gatty* trustees in 1838 wrongfully sold £2347 consols for £2183. This matter came before Vice-Chancellor Wigram in 1848 and ... he said: 'Then comes another material question — are the trustees to replace the stock, or the money produced by the sale? ... My opinion is, that the trustees must replace the stock'.[2] The form of decree ... required the trustees to recoup to the estate sufficient to enable £2347 consols to be purchased. To the same effect is a decision of Kay J, in *Re Massingberd's Settlement; Clark v Trelawny*. There trustees in 1875 acting in excess of their powers of sale sold trust assets consisting of consols and bank annuities. It is stated in the headnote (although not mentioned in the report) that in 1875 these securities stood at much lower value than their value at the time of hearing. The defaulting trustees were ordered to purchase replacement ... Kay J, said: 'Where the sale itself was breach of trust, where the conversion of an investment was a thing not authorised, then it appears to me to follow inevitably that the cestui que trust may have his option either to take cash with four per cent interest, or to make the trustees liable for the amount of proper investment which they have sold — that is, to make them replace the proper investment'.[3] Kay J's reference to requiring [217] the trustees to replace the proper investment included requiring them to make good intermediate income which would have been derived from retention of the assets in the proper investment. This is made clear in the form of order made in that case ... This order declared the trustees liable to make good the consols sold together with dividends to which the beneficiaries before the Court were entitled, and ordered them to purchase in the names of the then trustees replacement consols and to submit to being charged in the accounts with cash equal to the dividends which would have been derived from the consols so far as those dividends were an issue in the proceedings before the Court ...

(b) Rate of Interest

In circumstances such as the present this Court has jurisdiction to impose upon the part in default an obligation to pay interest upon the moneys lost to the estate through his breach.[4] ...

[218] There does not appear to be any universal and inflexible principle which dictates the rate of interest to be applied in any given instance ...

The Court's jurisdiction in selecting the appropriate rate of interest is exercisable solely for compensatory purposes. Although orders for interest may in some cases appear to have the effect of penalising defaulting trustees, the Court does not, in ordering interest and in selecting a rate, attempt in any way to impose a punishment upon the defaulter.[5]

Comment
1. See Radan and Stewart at **26.2, 26.6–26.12**.

---

1.   (1842) 49 ER 601.
2.   *Phillipson v Gatty* (1848) 68 ER 213 at 219.
3.   *Re Massingberd's Settlement; Clark v Trelawny* (1890) 59 LJ Ch 107 at 108.
4.   *Nixon v Furphy* (1926) 26 SR (NSW) 409.
5.   *Vyse v Foster* (1872) LR 8 Ch App 309 at 333.

Contributory negligence and equitable compensation

26.3   Pilmer v Duke Group Ltd (In Liq)
(2001) 207 CLR 165

Court: High Court of Australia

Facts: The gold mining company Kia Ora Gold Corp NL (later named Duke Group Ltd) arranged for a company takeover of Western United Ltd, a company in which many of Kia Ora's directors held an interest. Securities legislation required the preparation of a report by 'independent qualified persons' to Kia Ora shareholders whose approval at a general meeting was required for the takeover to proceed. A firm of chartered accountants with a history of dealings with both companies was engaged by Kia Ora to prepare the independent report. In their report, the accountants verified that the price to be paid for the shares in Western United was fair and reasonable. This was not so, with the result that Kia Ora paid around $26m for shareholdings worth only $6m, enabling huge personal profits to be made by the Kia Ora directors who held shares in Western United. Kia Ora was subsequently placed into liquidation, and the liquidator sought to recover its loss by bringing an action against Pilmer and others, representing the partners of the accountancy firm that prepared the report. The accountants appealed to the High Court against a finding of breach of fiduciary duty and the calculation of damages.

Issue: The main issues before the High Court were whether the accountants owed a fiduciary duty to Kia Ora, and whether Kia Ora's conduct, and contribution to its own loss, could be taken into account when assessing equitable damages for breach of fiduciary duty.

Decision: The majority of the High Court (McHugh, Gummow, Hayne and Callinan JJ; Kirby J dissenting) held in favour of the accountants and agreed that they owed no fiduciary duty to Kia Ora. It also rejected the argument that Kia Ora's contribution to its own loss could constitute a complete or partial defence to liability on the part of the accountants.

Extracts: The extracts from the majority's joint judgment elaborate on the view that damages for breach of fiduciary duties are to be assessed on equitable principles rather than on common law elements of tort or contract. Kirby J's dissenting judgment, based on an acceptance of the accountants' fiduciary duty to Kia Ora, considers the effect of contributing fault on equitable compensation.

McHugh, Gummow, Hayne and Callinan JJ

[201] Various judgments in this Court[6] establish that, in Australia, the measure of compensation in respect of losses sustained by reason of breach of duty by a trustee or

---

6.   *Bennett v Minister of Community Welfare* (1992) 176 CLR 408 at 426–7; *Maguire v Makaronis* (1997) 188 CLR 449 at 467–5, 488–95; *McCann v Switzerland Insurance Australia Ltd* (2000) 203 CLR 579 at 587–8, 621–3.

other fiduciary is determined by equitable principles and that these do not necessarily reflect the rules for assessment of damages in tort or contract. In the present case, the Full Court, but for a reduction by reason of 'contributing fault' on the part of Kia Ora, would have awarded the same amount as equitable compensation for breach of fiduciary duty by [Pilmer] as it awarded for their breach of contract. In this appeal the occasion does not arise to consider whether, matters of 'contributing fault' aside, the measure of equitable compensation may not have been greater than the damages awarded in contract, or whether the fate which in this Court has befallen the award in contract would necessarily have precluded an award of equitable compensation if there had been a relevant breach of fiduciary duty.

With respect to [the question of] 'contributing fault', it is sufficient to say that the decision in *Astley v Austrust Ltd* indicates the severe conceptual difficulties in the path of acceptance of notions of contributory negligence as applicable to diminish awards of equitable compensation for breach of fiduciary duty. *Astley* affirms:

> At common law, contributory negligence consisted in the failure of a plaintiff to take reasonable care for the protection of his or her person or property. Proof of contributory negligence defeated the plaintiff's cause of action in negligence.[7]

Contributory negligence focuses on the conduct of the plaintiff, fiduciary law upon the obligation by the defendant to act in the interests of the plaintiff. Moreover, any question of apportionment [202] with respect to contributory negligence arises from legislation, not the common law. *Astley* indicates that the particular apportionment legislation of South Australia which was there in question did not touch contractual liability. The reasoning in *Astley* would suggest, a fortiori, that such legislation did not touch the fiduciary relationship ...

Kirby J

[228] 'Contributing fault' and equitable compensation

... [229] In a thorough review of authority ... [230] the Full Court finally accepted the principle of 'contributing fault'. As I read its reasons, it did not (as perhaps it might have done) subsume the considerations pertinent to such a deduction within a more general analysis of the issue of causation, or a different analysis by reference to general equitable notions of apportionment.[8] Instead, boldly, the Full Court embraced the idea of 'contributing fault'. It did so knowing full well that this was a contentious conclusion ...

[T]here are, as the joint reasons point out, severe 'conceptual difficulties' in the path of adopting a principle derived by analogy from contributory negligence to diminish awards of equitable compensation for the breach of fiduciary obligations. The foundation of the difficulty is explained by Gummow J, writing extracurially, in an essay to which I referred in *Maguire*:

> While negligence is concerned with the taking of reasonable [231] care, a fiduciary traditionally has more expected of him. His duty is one of undivided and unremitting

---

7. *Astley v Austrust Ltd* (1999) 197 CLR 1 at 11.
8. Referred to in *Maguire v Makaronis* (1997) 188 CLR 449 at 494.

loyalty. The fiduciary acts in a 'representative' capacity in the exercise of his responsibility. One must fear that introduction of concepts of contributory negligence into that setting inevitably will work a subversion of fundamental principle.[9]

To the same effect, Justice Handley has said:

Equity has not hitherto considered that a beneficiary is bound to protect himself against his fiduciary. The relationship is not at arm's length and the beneficiary is entitled to place trust and confidence in the fiduciary. The basis for a finding of contributory negligence is therefore lacking.[10]

Whatever might have been my inclination to explore the notion adopted by the Full Court prior to *Astley v Austrust Ltd*,[11] I regard the holding in that case as a splash of cold water, discouraging any creative instinct in this connection. There, after all, the Court was considering the development of an apportionment principle within the four walls of the common law and the applicable statute. A majority of the Court concluded that no such development was available. Damages for breach of contract could therefore not be reduced under apportionment legislation expressed in terms of 'contributory negligence' whether or not the plaintiff had, or could also have, sued in tort. In the face of that decision and the repeated recognition by this Court that, in Australia, the substantive rules of equity have retained their identity as part of a separate and coherent body of principles,[12] the attempt to push common law notions of contributory negligence, as now modified by statute, into equitable remedies collapses in the face of insurmountable obstacles.

Having come to this conclusion, the foundation for the Full Court's deduction for the 'contributing fault' of Kia Ora disappears. It is not, therefore, necessary to consider the factual complaints of Kia Ora about the conduct attributed to it by the Full Court, on the basis of which such 'contributing fault' was found to exist. Kia Ora objected that, in so far as the Full Court had relied on the conduct of some or all of its directors to establish 'contributing fault' on its part, this was misconceived. For Kia Ora, the issue was [Pilmer's] separate breach of fiduciary duty. That breach could not be minimised by reason of breaches on the part of others. Such arguments simply lend [232] force to the comments, stated above, concerning the danger of deflecting attention from the purposes of equitable relief, once breaches of fiduciary duties are found.

Comments
1. See Radan & Stewart at **26.20–26.24**.
2. For an analysis of this case see A Lynch, 'Equitable Compensation for Breach of Fiduciary Duty: Causation and Contribution — The High Court Dodges a Fusion Fallacy in *Pilmer*' (2001) 21 *Australian Bar Review* 173.

---

9. Gummow, 'Compensation for Breach of Fiduciary Duty' in Youdan (ed), *Equity, Fiduciaries and Trusts* (1989) 57, at 86 (footnotes omitted), referred to in *Maguire v Makaronis* (1997) 188 CLR 449 at 489.
10. Handley, 'Reduction of Damages Awards' in Finn (ed), *Essays on Damages* (1992) 113 at 127.
11. (1999) 197 CLR 1. It has taken legislative intervention to overcome that decision: see Young, 'Current Issues: Contributory Negligence' (2001) 75 *Australian Law Journal* 213 at 215.
12. *Maguire v Makaronis* (1997) 188 CLR 449 at 489.

Exemplary damages and equitable compensation

26.4   Harris v Digital Pulse Pty Ltd (2003) NSWLR 298

Court: Court of Appeal of New South Wales

Facts: Digital Pulse conducted an information technology and web design business. It employed Harris in its marketing section and Eden in web design. The contracts of employment provided expressly that employees would not compete with their employer. During the course of their employment with Digital Pulse, the two employees started their own business and engaged in work and projects for existing and potential clients of Digital Pulse. This was done secretly and in competition to their employer. When discovered, Harris was dismissed and Eden resigned. Digital Pulse commenced proceedings against both men for breach of contract and breach of fiduciary duties to their employer, seeking compensation, account of profits and exemplary damages.

Issue: The issue before the Court of Appeal was whether a court exercising equitable jurisdiction for breach of fiduciary duty had the requisite jurisdiction to award exemplary damages.

Decision: A majority of the Court of Appeal (Spigelman CJ and Heydon JA; Mason P dissenting) held that the New South Wales Supreme Court has no jurisdiction to order a punitive monetary award for breach of fiduciary duty arising from contract.

Extracts: The extracts from the majority judgments of Spigelman CJ and Heydon JA highlight the majority's views. The extracts from the dissenting judgment of Mason P argue that there is no bar to equity awarding exemplary damages in appropriate cases of wilful fiduciary breach.

Spigelman CJ

[305] Our law is not based on a single code of civil obligations from which specific rights and duties can be deduced. Our legal tradition is much messier than that. Each of tort, contract and equity, constitute distinct bodies of doctrine with their own history. There is an interaction between each area of law and the lines are often blurred, but they remain distinct bodies of doctrine.

The separation of equity and common law is of greater strength in Australian jurisprudence than appears to have become the case in other nations with similar traditions, including Canada and, it appears, New Zealand. This may be [306] due to the force and influence of extra-judicial writings on equity based on university lectures delivered by practitioners who became judges ... [and] perhaps particularly [in] New South Wales where the judicature system was not adopted until 1970, [and which] has its own tradition in equity jurisprudence based on these publications and the education of generations of Australian lawyers ...

The heart of the 'fusion fallacy' — as it has come to be called in Australia — is the proposition that the joint administration of two distinct bodies of law means that

697

the doctrines of one are applicable to the other. That is no more true of equity and common law than it was and is true of tort and contract within the common law context. That is not to say that one body of law does not influence the other. It is only to say that they remain conceptually distinct.

In *Norberg v Wynrib*, in a passage quoted with approval in a four judge joint judgment of the High Court in *Pilmer v Duke Group Ltd (in Liq)*,[13] McLachlin J, as her Ladyship then was, said:

> The foundation and ambit of the fiduciary obligation are conceptually distinct from the foundation and ambit of contract and tort. Sometimes the doctrines may overlap in their application, but that does not destroy their conceptual and functional uniqueness.[14]

Equitable remedies, including equitable compensation have elements that may be seen to be more punitive or deterrent than common law remedies available in similar factual situations. This may occur, for example, by reason of the application of different rules of liability, principles of causation or tests for remoteness. The integrity of equity as a body of law is not well served by adopting a common law remedy developed over time in a different remedial context on a different conceptual foundation. The fact that exemplary damages are awarded in tort is, in my opinion, not a basis for asking 'Why not?' in equity ...

[308] In his reasons for preferring the tort analogy, in my opinion, Mason P has given insufficient weight to the historical development of the law of tort which was closely connected with the development of criminal law. Many torts constituted crimes and accordingly, civil litigation raised issues of public interest, particularly involving a breach of the peace. In such a context it was entirely appropriate that considerations of punishment and deterrence arose in the context of actions in tort.

As Windeyer J said in *Uren v John Fairfax & Sons Pty Ltd*:

> Compensation is the dominant remedy if not the purpose of the law of torts today. But fault still has a place in many forms of wrongdoing. And the roots of tort and crime in the law of England are intermingled. Some things that today are seen as anomalies have roots that go deep, too deep for them to be easily uprooted.[15]

As Heydon JA notes, with further references, there was no such historical 'intermingling' between crime and either contract or equity.

To the extent that reasoning by analogy at this level of generality is appropriate, I believe that the contract analogy is more appropriate. Reasoning [309] of the highest authority has described the imposition of fiduciary obligations in terms of 'undertaking' and 'agreement', albeit imputed by operation of law. Furthermore, I find the extra judicial writings of Finn J, one of Australia's most significant scholars on fiduciary law, to be persuasive when he identifies an expectation interest on the part of a beneficiary and states it in terms reminiscent of contract law ...

[310] The fiduciary duties in the present case are derived from the existence of the contract of employment. The 'undertaking or agreement' of the employees to act in the interests of the employer, and the employer's 'entitlement to expect' that that will occur

---

13. (2001) 207 CLR 165 at 196.
14. *Norberg v Wynrib* [1992] 2 SCR 226 at 272.
15. (1966) 117 CLR 118, 149–50.

— imputed to the relationship by equity — is much closer to a contractual relationship than it is to circumstances creating obligations in tort. If argument by analogy of this kind is appropriate, I prefer the contract analogy.

Where, as here, the essential basis of the fiduciary duties is a contractual relationship this Court should not develop for the first time a remedy which is not available in the law of contract. This analysis does carry with it the corollary that the refusal to develop the law should be confined to cases of the character now before the Court, as identified above. There may be other cases in equity in which a tort analogy is more appropriate.

Heydon JA

[391] It is not the law of New South Wales that law and equity were fused when the judicature system was created by the *Supreme Court Act* 1970, s 57–s 63 and the *Law Reform (Law and Equity) Act* 1972, s 5–s 7. There was no 'fusion of two systems of principle but of the courts which administer the two systems'.[16] This corresponds with Windeyer J's approval in *Felton v Mulligan*[17] of the celebrated dictum in ... *Ashburner's Principles of Equity* ... that 'the two streams of jurisdiction, though they run in the same channel, run side by side and do not mingle their waters'.[18] ...

[416] If on the other hand it is necessary that the law be changed, consideration must be given whether an intermediate appellate court is the correct agent of that change.

If an entitlement in trial or intermediate appellate courts to grant exemplary damages for equitable wrongs arises because it is permissible to fashion and mould equitable remedies to meet the justice of the particular case, what other remedies are possible? Presumably it is not possible for those courts to grant remedies which High Court cases have ruled out. Thus it is not possible to grant both equitable compensation and an account of profits without compelling the plaintiff to elect between them, because there is High Court authority compelling election.[19] But can other remedies not opposed by distinct High Court authority be granted? ...

[419] As to Sir George Jessel MR's account of the development of equity in *Re Hallett's Estate*, it is true that the rules of equity have changed from time to time, and true that individual Chancellors — and Masters of the Rolls, Lord Keepers and Vice Chancellors — have effected these changes. It is also true that the rules can be changed in future. But those deeds of single judges were done when there was no appellate jurisdiction in the House of Lords, or very limited access to it, at a time before modern parliamentary democracy had developed, and members of parliaments consisted largely of wealthy men who in turn supported Cabinets composed largely of aristocratic oligarchs whom it was difficult to interest in the details of private law. What individual judges did in those constitutional and forensic conditions is not a sound guide to what modern Australian courts, at least at levels below the High Court, can do. A single equity judge in the time of Sir George Jessel MR had the power, the competence, the authority and the capacity to

---

16. *O'Rourke v Hoeven* [1974] 1 NSWLR 622 at 626.
17. (1971) 124 CLR 367 at 392.
18. D Brown, ed, *Ashburner's Principles of Equity*, 2nd ed (1933), 18.
19. *Warman International Ltd v Dwyer* (1995) 182 CLR 544. See also *Tang Man Sit v Capacious Investments Ltd* [1996] 1 AC 514 at 521.

compel acceptance from other judges which only the High Court has now, at least where the change goes beyond the application of existing principles in a new way or marginal extensions of the law ...

Sir George Jessel MR's judicial life coincided with the time when democracy in a modern form was beginning and the responsiveness of Parliament to social or legal ills was starting to develop. It was a time when the judiciary was small, highly skilled and united. It is now large, less skilled, and far from entirely united. For courts below the High Court to act in the manner of the single judges sitting in Chancery who made modern equity is to invite the spread of a wilderness of single instances, a proliferation of discordant and idiosyncratic opinions, and ultimately an anarchic 'system' operating according to the forms, but not the realities, of law.

Mason P (dissenting)

[325] **Appellants' submission that the award of exemplary damages involved a 'fusion fallacy'**

[Digital Pulse] did not suggest that the fused administration of law and equity[20] had any bearing on the issue. [Harris] submitted, however, that to uphold Palmer J would involve a 'fusion fallacy'.

Meagher, Gummow & Lehane describe the fusion fallacy as a particular type of error in legal reasoning which leads to an unsound result:

> The fusion fallacy involves the administration of a remedy, for example, common law damages for breach of fiduciary duty, not previously available either at law or in equity, or the modification of principles in one branch of the jurisdiction by concepts which are imported from the other and thus are foreign, for example, by holding that the existence of a duty of care in tort may be tested by asking whether the parties concerned are in fiduciary relations.[21] ...

But paucity of reasoning is not the badge of a fusion fallacy as defined in the passage from Meagher, Gummow & Lehane quoted above. Rather, the vice is stated in more categorical terms, by reference to novelty ('the administration of a remedy ... not previously available either at law or in equity') or borrowing ('the modification of principles in one branch of the jurisdiction by concepts which are imported from the other and *thus* are foreign' — my emphasis).

With respect to the learned authors of Meagher, Gummow & Lehane, this fusion fallacy concept is itself fallacious and historically unsound.

Meagher, Gummow & Lehane's example of a fusion fallacy based on novelty is 'common law damages for breach of fiduciary duty'. At one level, Meagher, Gummow & Lehane's proposition is self-evident, but in the same breath it is quite circular. 'Common law damages' is by definition a common law remedy and 'breach of fiduciary duty' is by definition an equitable wrong. Never the twain shall meet, if one assumes a priori the inability of one historical system to incorporate ideas from the other or to allow remedies to cross over by discriminating and at times partial adoption.

---

20. *Supreme Court Act 1970*, s 57.
21. R P Meagher, J D Heydon & M J Leeming, *Meagher, Gummow and Lehane's Equity: Doctrines and Remedies* (4th ed, 2002), 54 [2-105].

Meagher, Gummow & Lehane's second category of fusion fallacy (borrowing) has justly been described by Professor Tilbury as a concept that is **[326]** 'not peculiar to the law of remedies, but permeates all branches of the law'.[22]

No one to my knowledge advocates incorporation or borrowing by direct force of the enactment of the *Judicature Act* 1873 (UK) or its Australian counterparts. That would be a fusion fallacy of a very different sort, because there is much authority supporting the proposition that the fusion effected by the statute was of an administrative and procedural character. In Ashburner's famous metaphor: '... the two streams of jurisdiction, though they run in the same channel, run side by side and do not mingle their waters.'[23]

Like all metaphors this needs to be understood in context. But I shall not tarry over it, because Meagher, Gummow & Lehane's 'fusion fallacy' bogey is quite different in nature. In terms, it condemns law and equity to the eternal separation of two parallel lines, ignoring the history of the two 'systems' both before and after the passing of the *Judicature Act* (UK). And it treats the permission of the statute to fuse administration as if it were an enacted prohibition against a judge exercising the fused administration from applying doctrines and remedies found historically in one 'system' in a case whose roots may be found in the other 'system'.

Both 'Equity' and 'Common Law' had adequate powers to adopt and adapt concepts from each other's system well before the passing of the *Judicature Act* (UK), and nothing in that legislation limits such powers. They are of the very essence of judicial method which was and is part of the armoury of every judge in every 'common law' jurisdiction.

Neither system consistently and automatically ignored the other before the *Judicature Act* (UK); and there is even less justification for suggesting otherwise since the fusion of the administration of law and equity. I emphasise the words 'consistently and automatically'.

Meagher, Gummow & Lehane themselves offer many examples of the common law importing equitable doctrines.[24] Gummow J has recently added others.[25] Equity has returned the compliment, and examples are usually collected under the rubrics of the maxim 'equity follows the law' or equity's 'concurrent jurisdiction'. *AMEV-UDC Finance Ltd v Austin*,[26] to which Spigelman CJ refers, shows that in the area of penalties equity chose to follow the common law and, with the advent of the Judicature System, allow a discordant stream of equitable doctrine to 'wither on the vine' (see per Mason and Deane JJ at 191) in the interests of coherence in the law generally.

The borrowings from one system by another have never been slavish and were by no means universal or unconditional. Until the *Judicature Act* (UK), plaintiffs could fail completely if they knocked at the wrong door. Or they could find that one 'branch' was only able to address part of the matter in issue. There were also many areas where a common law remedy could not be engrafted upon an equitable right, and vice versa. But this was not because it was self-evidently fallacious for law or equity to develop in that manner. Rather, it was because the particular borrowing was not made.

---

22. Michael Tilbury, *Civil Remedies: Volume One — Principles of Civil Remedies* (1990), 10 [1017].
23. W Ashburner, *Principles of Equity* (2nd ed, 1933), 18.
24. R P Meagher, J D Heydon & M J Leeming, *Meagher, Gummow and Lehane's Equity: Doctrines and Remedies*, 4th ed, 2002, 25 [1-205].
25. See *Roxburgh v Rothmans of Pall Mall Australia Ltd* (2001) 185 ALR 335 at [84].
26. (1986) 162 CLR 170.

In some jurisdictions, such as Canada and New Zealand, there has been greater liberality in borrowing and adopting. *Day v Mead*[27] may have gone further than an Australian court is prepared to go ...

[327] At times, innovation seemed the hallmark of one or both systems (that is, Equity and Common Law). At other times, each proclaimed itself to have reached a state of self-satisfied rigidity. Sir Frederick Jordan's view about the rules of equity having become settled[28] would surprise an observer of the High Court post-1987 or thereabouts.

Since fusion of administration, judges have tended to use similar forms of judicial method whether administering law, equity or both. Of course, some judges have been readier to break new ground than others. Be that as it may, the fused administration of the two systems that occurred in England over 125 years ago has produced generations of judges who had understanding of both 'common law' and 'equity' and who practised in both fields. Barristers often specialised, but appellate courts were populated with former denizens of both 'systems'. Inevitably and appropriately, *unnecessary* barriers of separation have been broken down. Analogies have been drawn between rules operating in the two systems in the interests of coherence and simplicity. Distinctions with nothing but history to support them have, at times, been deliberately ironed out or conveniently overlooked as doctrines are passed from generation to generation.

Maitland forecast that: 'The day will come when lawyers will cease to inquire whether a given rule be a rule of equity or a rule of common law: suffice it that it is a well-established rule administered by the High Court of Justice'[29] ...

[328] For present purposes, it is sufficient to observe that this process continues, at times haltingly. Sometimes fusion has ceased to be visible, as with the various remedies for breach of contract. At times, false fears of fusion fallacies have caused hesitation or stumbling. At other times, concepts and remedies deriving from one system have been properly rejected as unsuitable for adoption by another ...

I do not assert that the Judicature system itself justifies the award of exemplary damages for breach of an equitable obligation. And I acknowledge that the reasoning in *Aquaculture Corporation*[30] is open to the interpretation that this was the manner in which the Court reasoned (see also the remarks of Cooke P, concerning exemplary damages, in *Attorney-General for the United Kingdom v Wellington Newspapers Ltd*[31]).

As will appear, my reasons (generally following those of Palmer J) are closely based on notions of consistency and coherence.

But before I leave [Harris'] charge of 'fusion fallacy' I state my entire agreement with the following remarks of Professor Tilbury:

[1019] But the further conclusion, inherent in the fluvial metaphor and explicit in the 'fusion fallacy', that in a fused jurisdiction it is impossible, for all time, to have a 'fused law' is both a non-sequitur and hard to justify in principle and policy. It is a non-sequitur because the proposition that the Judicature Acts do not *authorize* fusion of

---

27. [1987] 2 NZLR 443.
28. Frederick Jordan, 'Chapters in Equity in New South Wales' in Fredrick Jordan, *Select Legal Papers* (1983), 15.
29. F W Maitland, *Equity: A Course of Lectures* (1947), 20.
30. *Aquaculture Corporation and Cook v Evatt (No 2)* [1992] 1 NZLR 676.
31. [1988] 1 NZLR 129, 175 at 172.

principles, cannot lead to the conclusion that such a fusion is *prohibited*. In short, there is no fallacy. Fusion can, and does, take place independently of the Acts. Indeed, constant administration alone suggests such an interaction of the rules of law and of equity as to make fusion of principle inevitable. Further, it is submitted that, both in principle and in policy, it is desirable that the jurisdictional origins of rules of law become less and less important as those rules are adapted to changing social realities by courts in fused jurisdictions, where the relationship of those rules inter se and their overall purposes in the legal system as a whole can be better appreciated. After all, what can be done with rules is much more **[329]** important than where they came from. It is no answer to say that progeny must be legitimate, for this merely begs the question. As Lord Radcliffe, delivering the advice of the Judicial Committee, said in *Kasumu v Baba-Egbe*:[32] 'It must be admitted that, now that all courts endeavour to give effect to the rules of both systems with predominance for equity in the case of conflict, a distinction which is based entirely on the nature or history of the remedy sought does not seem a very satisfactory basis for a material difference in the resulting positions (of the parties)'.[33]

More recently, and to the same effect, are the words of Deane J.[34] And see by analogy *Hawkins v Clayton* per Deane J:

[I]t is necessary for care to be taken to avoid the risk that a consciousness of past separateness of common law and equitable doctrines may lead to a tendency to discount the full substantive effects of their fusion. Knowledge of the origins and development of the common law and equity and an awareness of the ordinary and continuing distinctness of controlling equitable principles are prerequisites of a full understanding of the content of a fused system of modern law. To ignore the substantive effects of the interaction of doctrines of law and equity within that fused system in which unity, rather than conflict, of principle is now to be assumed is, however, unduly to preserve the importance of past separation and continuing distinctness as a barrier against the orderly development of a simplified and unified legal system which fusion was intended to advance.[35]

This is not, of course, to argue for the wholesale fusion of law and equity, nor indeed that such a fusion has occurred. It is simply to assert that where piecemeal fusion does take, or has taken, place, it ought not to be rejected out of hand on the basis of a backward-looking argument that such a development would not have been possible before 1875.

To place aside the case law about equitable compensation and to rebut the charge of 'fusion fallacy' does not establish the legitimacy of the novel remedy awarded by Palmer J. To that I now turn ...

[337] A primary maxim is equity's claim that it will not suffer a wrong to be without a remedy. This is not an excuse for a 'naked power of improvisation'.[36] But it remains a beacon of intent. The concept captured in the maxim has at times induced boldness in

---

32. [1956] AC 539 at 550.
33. Michael Tilbury, *Civil Remedies: Volume One Principles of Civil Remedies* (1990) pp 11–12.
34. *Waltons Stores v Maher* (1988) 164 CLR 387 at 447.
35. *Hawkins v Clayton* (1988) 164 CLR 539 at 584.
36. R P Meagher, J D Heydon & M J Leeming, *Meagher, Gummow and Lehane's Equity: Doctrines and Remedies*, 4th ed, 2002, 86 [3-025].

the development of equity. The twentieth century saw new remedies being fashioned by equity to further institutions and relationships under equity's protection or in aid of the common law. These include the Mareva order, the Anton Piller order, injunctions in aid of the criminal law and the remedial constructive trust and lien ...

[341] Courts have traditionally been bold in such areas,[37] equity particularly so. Equity has always claimed to have the capacity to fashion and mould its remedies to meet the needs of the case.[38] Within its auxiliary jurisdiction, equity intervenes *because of* the deficiencies and inadequacies of the common law. Why should equity turn coy in its exclusive jurisdiction? Equity is usually noted for its flexibility and boldness, not its timidity. If it is accepted, as I think it must, that the stripping of profits will (on occasions) represent an inadequate means of enforcing common decency, why should equity stand proudly apart from the common law in withholding the discretionary remedy of exemplary damages in an otherwise appropriate case?

Judges should not be deterred by fear of a false 'fusion fallacy' charge. They should act boldly, remembering (in Lord Jessel MR's words) that the rules of equity 'have been established from time to time — altered, improved, and refined from time to time'.[39]

Comments

1. See Radan & Stewart at **26.27–26.34**.
2. For a defence of Mason P's dissenting view see A Burrows, 'Remedial Coherence and Punitive Damages in Equity' in S Degeling & J Edelman (eds), *Equity in Commercial Law*, Lawbook Co, Sydney, 2005, 381, esp pp 391–402. For another analysis of this case see D Morgan, '*Harris v Digital Pulse*: The Availability of Exemplary Damages in Equity' (2003) 29 *Monash Law Review* 377.

Equitable damages pursuant to *Lord Cairns' Act*

26.5   Wentworth v Woollahra Municipal Council (1982) 149 CLR 672

Court: High Court of Australia

Facts: Wentworth commenced a relator action through the New South Wales Attorney-General seeking a declaration and mandatory injunction for the demolition of her neighbour's home. She alleged that the house obstructed her views and that it had been built in breach of clause 43 of the Woollahra Planning Scheme Ordinance because the width of the land at the front alignment of the building was almost 5 feet less than the prescribed minimum width of 50 feet. Her action was dismissed on the ground that the non-compliance was minor and within the Council's discretion to both approve the building and dispense with a demolition order. The Attorney-General withdrew his fiat

---

37. See *Tringali v Stewardson Stubbs & Collett Ltd* (1966) 66 SR (NSW) 335 at 344; 83 WN (Pt 2) (NSW) 393 at 401.

38. See *Hill v Rose* [1990] VR 129 at 143–4.

39. *Re Hallett's Estate; Knatchbull v Hallett* (1880) 13 Ch D 696 at 710.

and Wentworth appealed, adding a claim for damages to her action. The Court of Appeal held she was not entitled to equitable relief because of laches on her part and hardship to her neighbours. As a result, she was not entitled to damages in equity. Wentworth appealed to the High Court.

Issue: The issue before the High Court was whether s 68 of the *Supreme Court Act 1970* (NSW), which re-enacted the provisions of *Lord Cairns' Act 1858* (UK), authorised the award of damages for breach of a public duty in cases where an injunction had been refused.

Decision: The High Court (Gibbs CJ, Mason, Murphy and Brennan JJ) unanimously dismissed Wentworth's appeal, holding that s 68 did not empower a court to award damages in lieu of an injunction to stop a breach of a statutory prohibition, unless the statute manifests an intention to create a private right of enforcement.

Extracts: The extracts from the joint judgment of the High Court provide a useful exposition of the power to award damages in equity.

Gibbs CJ, Mason, Murphy and Brennan JJ

[676] The main object of [Lord Cairns'] Act was to enable the Court of Chancery to do 'complete justice' between parties by awarding damages in those cases in which it had formerly refused equitable relief in respect of a legal right and left the plaintiff to sue for damages at common law. An incidental object of the Act was to enable the Court to award damages in lieu of an injunction or specific performance, even in the case of a purely equitable claim ...

[677] However, it has been said that neither Lord Cairns' Act nor its statutory successors gave power to award common law damages as such. The power to award common law damages was given to the Chancery Division by the *Judicature Act* 1873 and later by virtue of ss 62 and 63 of the Act. The Equity Division of the Supreme Court has power to award common law damages — it is bound to grant all such remedies as any party may appear to be entitled to in respect of any legal or equitable claim brought forward. The power to award common law damages in a case in which equitable relief is sought in respect of a legal right diminishes the importance which s 68 would otherwise have, though in some cases it may still be necessary to distinguish between the two sources of power. Here the power to award common law damages is of no avail to [Wentworth]. She does not seek common law damages, for she does not suggest that cl 43(1)(a) creates a private right.

Whether the predecessors of s 68 authorized the award of damages when equitable relief was refused has been a matter of considerable controversy. Hardie J in *Boyns v Lackey*[40] thought that damages could not be given in cases where the plaintiff has 'failed to establish a right, as at the date of the institution of the suit to equitable relief', adopting the view ... [that] is apparently supported by the comments of Starke J in *King v Poggioli*[41] and Dixon J in *J C Williamson Ltd v Lukey and Mulholland*.[42] The competing

40. (1958) 58 SR (NSW) 395 at 405.
41. (1923) 32 CLR 222 at 247.
42. (1931) 45 CLR 282 at 295.

view is that damages may be awarded if the plaintiff's case is such as to attract equitable relief but for the existence of a discretionary defence which is found to prevail.[43] The foundation for this opinion is to be found in cases in which the courts, having refused equitable relief on discretionary grounds, have awarded damages or directed an inquiry as to damages. However, in at least some of these cases it appears that the court was awarding, or entertaining a claim for, common law damages. So, in *Fullers' Theatres Ltd v Musgrove*[44] this Court refused equitable relief without prejudice to the plaintiff's [678] claim for damages at common law. In *Summers v Cocks*[45] the Court apparently relied on the *Judicature Act* power to award common law damages in addition to, if not to the exclusion of, the Lord Cairns' Act provision. And in *Dell v Beasley*,[46] McCarthy J held that the plaintiff's case for equitable relief having been refused on discretionary grounds, she was entitled to damages under Lord Cairns' Act or at common law.

Cairns LJ (later Lord Cairns LC) seems to have thought that the power to award damages conferred by the 1858 Act could be exercised if the plaintiff made out as at the commencement of the suit the ingredients of a case for equitable relief, notwithstanding that ultimately he failed to obtain that relief on discretionary grounds. In *Ferguson v Wilson*, after quoting the words of the section, he said:

> That, of course, means where there are, at least at the time of bill filed, all those ingredients which would enable the Court, *if it thought fit*, to exercise its power and decree specific performance — among other things where there is the subject matter whereon the decree of the Court can act — in a case of that kind, the Court has a discretionary power to award, under certain circumstances, damages in substitution for, or in addition to, the decree for specific performance. The object obviously was to enable the Court of Chancery to do 'complete justice', as it was called, a phrase which assumed that there was the power in the Court of Chancery to make a decree to some extent, but not to make a decree to the whole extent which the case required. (Emphasis supplied.)[47]

Subsequently in *Sayers v Collyer*[48] Bowen and Fry LJJ thought that nominal damages could be awarded under the 1858 Act even though the plaintiff's case for an injunction was defeated by acquiescence. More recently in *Landau v Curton*[49] Cross J followed this approach to the Act and awarded damages in respect of a purely equitable claim when the equitable right to an injunction was lost by acquiescence.

It is obvious that a discretionary defence to a claim for equitable relief does not, if made out, operate as a defence to a claim for common law damages for infringement of the legal right on which the case for equitable relief is based. Although damages under s 68 are not common law damages and they are expressed by the statute to be given in lieu of, or in addition to, the basic claim for equitable [679] relief, it conforms to the

---

43. See *Goldsbrough, Mort & Co Ltd v Quinn* (1910) 10 CLR 674 at 701.
44. (1923) 31 CLR 524.
45. (1927) 40 CLR 321.
46. [1959] NZLR 89 at 97.
47. *Ferguson v Wilson* (1866) LR 2 Ch 77 at 91–2.
48. (1884) 28 Ch D 103.
49. [1962] E Gaz 369.

main object of the statute if damages in such a case are awarded under the section, even though the claim for equitable relief is defeated by a discretionary defence such as laches, acquiescence or hardship. We are content to assume, without finally deciding, that this is so.

The crucial issue, then, is whether s 68 authorizes an award of damages for infringement of a statutory duty which does not create a civil cause of action …

[681] No doubt in some situations, of which *Day v Pinglen*[50] may be a good example, it would be advantageous if the court had jurisdiction or power to award damages to the plaintiff who has a [682] special interest, in lieu of protecting the public right by declaration or injunction. The award of compensation may in some situations in which the public right has already been infringed do greater justice between the plaintiff and the defendant, although it would not necessarily achieve anything for other members of the public who stand to gain from enforcement of the public duty. Indeed, there is some risk that the legitimate expectation of the general public that the law will be enforced by injunction, even a mandatory injunction, may be compromised if it be acknowledged that the court has power to award damages to an individual in lieu of granting an injunction to compel observance of the public duty.

If we are now to declare that s 68 applies to public as well as to private wrongs, we must ignore the insights which the history of Lord Cairns' Act offers. We know that it was called into existence with the principal object of enabling the Court of Chancery to do justice between the parties by awarding damages for infringement of private rights, whether legal or equitable. Equity's incapacity to award damages for infringement of private rights was the problem which the statute sought to solve. In 1858 it would not have occurred to anyone that, apart from public nuisance, damages might be awarded to an individual on violation of a public right or for non-performance of a public duty. And public nuisance, when actionable at the suit of an individual, is, despite its name, a personal cause of action for a tort. Certainly it could not have been supposed in 1858 that Lord Cairns' Act was intended to authorize an award of damages in favour of a plaintiff, who, asserting neither a personal cause of action nor violation of a private right, complained only of the violation of a public right created by statute or the non-performance of a public duty imposed by statute. And there is nothing in the later enactments, including s 68 of the Act, to suggest that they were intended to go beyond the scope of the 1858 statute.

Moreover, the very terms of the section suggest that it is exclusively preoccupied with private rights. The opening words of par (a) and the whole of par (b) deal with private rights. And, as Richmond J noted in *Birkenhead*[51] the expression the 'party injured' suggests that the statute contemplated the ordinary jurisdiction of the court in case of actual or threatened interference with private rights.

It is, to say the least of it, curious that s 68 should become the source of a power to award damages for breach of a statutory provision — in this case cl 43 — when the assumption underlying [683] the argument is that the clause does not create a civil action for damages. And it is no less curious that in such a case s 68 should become the source of power to award damages, not to every member of the public who suffers damage, but only to those who suffer special damage, when the cause of the damage is a breach of a

---

50. (1981) 148 CLR 289.
51. *Attorney-General (NZ) v Birkenhead Borough* [1968] NZLR 383 at 392–3.

public duty. We think that the history and the terms of s 68 show that it was not intended to authorize the award of damages for breach of a statutory prohibition which manifests no intention to create a private cause of action for damages.

For these reasons we consider that [Wentworth] has no case for damages under s 68.

Comment

1. See Radan & Stewart at **26.43–26.46**.

26.6   Johnson v Agnew
[1980] AC 367

Court: House of Lords

Facts: On 1 November 1973, when they were in arrears with the repayments of mortgages over a property in Buckinghamshire, the Johnsons entered into a written contract for its sale to Agnew. On the same day the Johnsons contracted to purchase another property and arranged for a loan from a bank to enable them to purchase the property. The price agreed to be paid by Agnew was in excess of the sums required by the Johnsons to discharge the mortgages over the Buckinghamshire property as well as repay the loan that they had arranged for the purchase of the other property. Agnew failed to complete. On 26 November 1974 the Johnsons obtained a summary order for specific performance of the contract. Meanwhile the mortgagees of the Buckinghamshire property exercised their rights of sale over the property. Part of the Buckinghamshire property was sold at auction on 3 April 1975, with the remaining part sold at auction on 20 June 1975. The two mortgagee sales were completed on 11 July 1975 and 18 July 1975 respectively. The mortgagee sales meant that compliance by Agnew with the order for specific performance was impossible after the first mortgagee sale on 3 April 1975. The Johnsons initiated a claim for damages against Agnew.

When the case was before the Court of Appeal, it ordered that the order for specific performance be discharged. It further held that the Johnsons were entitled to damages under *Lord Cairns' Act* and ordered an inquiry as to damages. Before that inquiry took place Agnew appealed to the House of Lords.

Issues: The issues before the House of Lords were whether the Johnsons were entitled to seek damages, given that compliance with the order for specific performance was impossible, and if so, on what basis such damages were to be assessed.

Decision: The House of Lords (Lords Wilberforce, Salmon, Fraser of Tulleybelton, Keith of Kinkel and Scarman) unanimously held in favour of the Johnsons. Lord Wilberforce, who delivered the only speech in the case, held that, provided the order for specific performance was first formally vacated by the court, the Johnsons were entitled to claim damages for breach of contract against Agnew. A court had jurisdiction to order such damages pursuant to the provisions of *Lord Cairns' Act*.

Extracts: The extracts from the speech of Lord Wilberforce set out the principles that apply to the assessment of damages pursuant to the successor provisions of *Lord Cairns' Act*.

Lord Wilberforce

[399] It is now necessary to deal with questions relating to the measure of damages. The Court of Appeal, while denying the [Johnsons'] right to [400] damages at common law, granted damages under Lord Cairns' Act. Since, on the view which I take, damages can be recovered at common law, two relevant questions now arise. (1) Whether Lord Cairns' Act provides a different measure of damages from the common law: if so, the [Johnsons] would be in a position to claim the more favourable basis to them. (2) If the measure of damages is the same, on what basis they should be calculated.

Since the decision of this House, by majority, in *Leeds Industrial Co-operative Society Ltd v Slack*[52] it is clear that the jurisdiction to award damages in accordance with s 2 of Lord Cairns' Act ... may arise in some cases in which damages could not be recovered at common law; examples of this would be damages in lieu of a quia timet injunction and damages for breach of a restrictive covenant to which the plaintiff was not a party. To this extent the Act created a power to award damages which did not exist before at common law. But apart from these, and similar cases where damages could not be claimed at all at common law, there is sound authority for the proposition that the Act does not provide for the assessment of damages on any new basis. The wording of s 2 'may be assessed in such manner as the court shall direct' does not so suggest, but clearly refers only to procedure.

In *Ferguson v Wilson*,[53] Turner LJ sitting in a court which included Sir Hugh Cairns himself expressed the clear opinion that the purpose of the Act was to enable a court of equity to grant those damages which another court might give ... In *Wroth v Tyler*,[54] however, Megarry J, relying on the words 'in lieu of specific performance' reached the view that damages under the Act should be assessed as on the date when specific performance could have been ordered, in that case as at the date of the judgment of the Court. This case was followed in *Grant v Dawkins*.[55] If this establishes a different basis from that applicable at common law, I could not agree with it, but in *Horsler v Zorro*[56] Megarry J went so far as to indicate his view that there is no inflexible rule that common law damages must be assessed as at the date of the breach. Furthermore, in *Malhotra v Choudhury*[57] the Court of Appeal expressly decided that, in a case where damages are given in substitution for an order for specific performance, both equity and the common law would award damages on the same basis — in that case as on the date of judgment. On the balance of these authorities and also on principle, I find in the Act no warrant for the court awarding damages differently from common law damages, but the question is left open on what date such damages, however awarded, ought to be assessed.

The general principle for the assessment of damages is compensatory, ie, that the innocent party is to be placed, so far as money can do so, in the same position as if the contract had been performed. Where the contract is one of sale, this principle normally leads to assessment of damages as at the date of the breach — a principle recognised and

---

52. [1924] AC 851.
53. (1866) LR 2 Ch 77 at 88.
54. [1974] Ch 30.
55. [1973] 3 All ER 897.
56. [1975] Ch 302 at 316.
57. [1980] Ch 52.

embodied **[401]** in s 51 of the Sale of Goods Act 1893. But this is not an absolute rule: if to follow it would give rise to injustice, the court has power to fix such other date as may be appropriate in the circumstances.

In cases where a breach of a contract for sale has occurred, and the innocent party reasonably continues to try to have the contract completed, it would to me appear more logical and just rather than tie him to the date of the original breach, to assess damages as at the date when (otherwise than by his default) the contract is lost. Support for this approach is to be found in the cases. In *Ogle v Earl Vane*[58] the date was fixed by reference to the time when the innocent party, acting reasonably, went into the market: in *Hickman v Haynes*[59] at a reasonable time after the last request of the defendants (buyers) to withhold delivery. In *Radford v De Froberville*,[60] where the defendant had covenanted to build a wall, damages were held measurable as at the date of the hearing rather than at the date of the defendant's breach, unless the plaintiff ought reasonably to have mitigated the breach at an earlier date.

In the present case if it is accepted, as I would accept, that the [Johnsons] acted reasonably in pursuing the remedy of specific performance, the date on which that remedy became aborted (not by the [Johnsons'] fault) should logically be fixed as the date on which damages should be assessed. Choice of this date would be in accordance both with common law principle, as indicated in the authorities I have mentioned, and with the wording of the Act 'in substitution for ... specific performance'. The date which emerges from this is April 3, 1975 — the first date on which mortgagees contracted to sell a portion of the property. I would vary the order of the Court of Appeal by substituting this date for that fixed by them — viz November 26, 1974.

Comment
1. See Radan & Stewart at **26.54**.

---

58. (1867) LR 2 QB 275; LR 3 QB 272.
59. (1875) LR 10 CP 598.
60. [1978] 1 All ER 33.

27

RESCISSION

Introduction

27.1 This chapter deals with the remedy of rescission. Such a right generally arises where a vitiating factor is established in relation to the formation of the contract which renders it voidable. The essence of rescission is a cancellation of the contract, provided that the parties can be restored to their pre-contractual positions (*restitutio in integrum*). The right to rescind can be lost in a variety of circumstances.

The cases extracted in this chapter discuss the following:

- the meaning of *restitutio in integrum*: *Alati v Kruger* (1955) 94 CLR 216;
- the availability of partial rescission: *Vadasz v Pioneer Concrete (SA) Pty Ltd* (1995) 184 CLR 102; and
- the loss of the right to rescind due to affirmation of a contract: *Coastal Estates Pty Ltd v Melevende* [1965] VR 433.

The meaning of *restitutio in integrum*

27.2   Alati v Kruger (1955) 94 CLR 216

Court: High Court of Australia

Facts: Kruger purchased a fruit shop business from Alati in Brisbane for the sum of £700. He alleged that Alati and his agents assured him in pre-contractual negotiations that the average takings of the business were £100 per week. A written contract was executed in which Alati agreed to obtain the landlord's consent to an assignment of the lease of the shop premises to Kruger. It also contained clause 21 which repeated Alati's statement as to weekly takings. After a couple of weeks, Kruger sought legal advice because the weekly takings were less than half of the amount expected. Of several courses of action open to him, Kruger sought to rescind the contract and sue to recover his purchase money with interest and damages. Alati argued that the purported rescission was invalid because a true restitution was not possible.

Issue: The issue before the High Court was whether Kruger's purported rescission of the contract was valid and whether the requirements of *restitutio in integrum* had been met in this case.

> **Decision:** The High Court (Dixon CJ, Webb, Fullagar, Kitto and Taylor JJ) unanimously held that Kruger was entitled to rescind the contract.
>
> **Extracts:** The extracts from the joint judgment of Dixon CJ, Webb, Kitto and Taylor JJ address the issues of rescission and the differences between the common law and equitable interpretations of *restitutio in integrum*.

Dixon CJ, Webb, Kitto and Taylor JJ

[222] On the footing which must be accepted, that the contract had been induced by a fraudulent representation made by [Alati] to [Kruger], the latter had a choice of courses open to him. He might sue for damages for breach of the warranty contained in cl 21 [of the purchase agreement], for the statement in that clause clearly formed one of the terms of the contract and was not only a representation; but he could not do this and rescind the contract for misrepresentation. Secondly, he might sue to recover as damages for fraud the difference between the price he had paid and the fair value of the property at the time of the contract,[1] but that again would involve affirming the purchase. Or, thirdly, provided that he was in a position to restore to [Alati] substantially that which he had received under the contract, he might avoid the purchase and sue to recover his purchase money back from [him], with interest and also with damages for any loss which he may have suffered through carrying on the business in the meantime ...

[223] The validity of his rescission depended ... only upon the question whether *restitutio in integrum* was possible in the circumstances as they existed at the commencement of the action ...

If the case had to be decided according to the principles of the common law, it might have been argued that at the date when [Kruger] issued his writ he was not entitled to rescind the purchase, because he was not then in a position to return to [Alati] *in specie* that which he had received under the contract, in the same plight as that in which he had received it.[2] But it is necessary here to apply the doctrines of equity, and equity has always regarded as valid the disaffirmance of a contract induced by fraud even though precise *restitutio in integrum* is not possible, if the situation is such that, by the exercise of its powers, including the power to take accounts of profits and to direct inquiries as to allowances proper to be made for deterioration, it can do what is practically just between the parties, and by so [224] doing restore them substantially to the *status quo*.[3] It is not that equity asserts a power by its decree to avoid a contract which the defrauded party himself has no right to disaffirm, and to revest property the title to which the party cannot affect. Rescission for misrepresentation is always the act of the party himself.[4] The function of a court in which proceedings for rescission are taken is to adjudicate upon the validity of a purported disaffirmance as an act avoiding the transaction *ab initio*, and, if it is valid, to

---

1. *Holmes v Jones* (1907) 4 CLR 1692.
2. *Clarke v Dickson* (1858) 120 ER 463.
3. *Erlanger v New Sombrero Phosphate Co.* (1878) 3 App Cas 1218 at 1278, 1279; *Brown v Smitt* (1924) 34 CLR 160 at 165, 169; *Spence v Crawford* [1939] 3 All ER 271 at 279, 280.
4. *Reese River Silver Mining Co v Smith* (1869) LR 4 HL 64 at 73.

give effect to it and make appropriate consequential orders.[5] The difference between the legal and the equitable rules on the subject simply was that equity, having means which the common law lacked to ascertain and provide for the adjustments necessary to be made between the parties in cases where a simple handing back of property or repayment of money would not put them in as good a position as before they entered into their transaction, was able to see the possibility of *restitutio in integrum*, and therefore to concede the right of a defrauded party to rescind, in a much wider variety of cases than those which the common law could recognize as admitting of rescission. Of course, a rescission which the common law courts would not accept as valid cannot of its own force revest the legal title to property which had passed, but if a court of equity would treat it as effectual the equitable title to such property revests upon the rescission.

In the present case, what changes affecting the possibility of restitution had occurred in the short period between [the time] when [Kruger] took possession of the business and … when he issued the writ? He had had possession of the premises, and although that might have sufficed at common law to preclude rescission,[6] it could hardly do so in equity, since a money payment could compensate for any difference there might be between the rental value of the premises and the rent paid by [Kruger] to the landlords. The title to the term created by the lease had been vested in [Kruger] by assignment, but that was subject to any right which he had to disaffirm the transaction. The title would revest in equity [225] when he elected to rescind, and he was in a position to make a legal re-assignment with the landlords' consent. He had taken over (as he said in evidence) about twenty pounds' worth of stock, but while of course he could not restore that to [Alati] *in specie* he could pay or allow for its value, and nothing more could in justice be required. The business itself had deteriorated but this would not matter, for, as the trial judge has found, it was not due to any fault on [Kruger's] part, and even at common law the necessity to return property in its original condition was qualified so as to allow for incidents for which the buyer was not responsible, such as those to which the property was liable either from its inherent nature[7] or in the course of the exercise by the buyer of those rights over it which the contract gave.[8] No other change had occurred. The case was therefore typical of the class of cases in which a defrauded purchaser is regarded by a court exercising equitable jurisdiction as entitled to rescind the purchase and obtain a decree, on proper terms, declaring and giving effect to the rescission as an avoidance of the transaction from the beginning.

There remains, however, the question whether [Kruger] lost his right to such a decree by his conduct in discontinuing the business and leaving the premises before judgment was given in the action. The remedy is discretionary and if [Kruger] had acted unconscientiously during the pendency of the action, as by causing the loss of a valuable leasehold and goodwill by discontinuing the business and abandoning the premises without giving [Alati] a reasonable opportunity to take them back, no doubt the court might refuse relief. But nothing of that kind happened. The term was, of course, still vested at law in [Kruger], and it is not impossible that, despite low takings and actual losses, the business had some residual

---

5. *Abram Steamship Co Ltd v Westville Shipping Co Ltd* [1923] AC 773.
6. *Blackburn v Smith* (1848) 154 ER 707 at 711.
7. *Newbigging v Adam* (1886) 34 Ch D 582 at 588; *Adam v Newbigging* (1888) 13 App Cas 308 at 330.
8. *Head v Tattersall* (1871) LR 7 Exch 7 at 12.

goodwill. But it is impossible to convict [Kruger] of any unfairness in the circumstances. The service of the writ had given [Alati] clear notice that if the case alleged against him were made out at the trial the business and the lease would be held to have been his all along. He knew from the judge's announcement of his findings that in fact the issues of fact in the case had gone against him. He could have applied for the appointment by the court of a receiver and manager to preserve the property pending the determination of the case, but he made [226] no such application. He did not even make any offer to [Kruger] to take the property back or suggest any *modus vivendi*. He took his chance, contenting himself with such maintenance of the business as [Kruger's] continuing conduct of it might afford. But [Kruger] was under no duty to go on indefinitely, working for nothing and incurring losses, especially after the judge had announced findings of fact in his favour. It does not appear from the material before us whether he gave [Alati] any specific warning of his intention to give up the business and leave the premises, but, even if he did not, [Alati] had ample opportunity to protect his interests, and his inaction is far more likely to have been due to an opinion that neither the lease nor the business was worth worrying about, particularly in view of the competition which the 'super-market' had created, than to any expectation that [Kruger] would obligingly continue to act as an unpaid manager.

For these reasons the appeal must fail. It is desirable, however, to make one or two variations in the judgment of the Supreme Court, because, as framed, it makes [Kruger's] right to be repaid his purchase money conditional upon his re-assigning the lease to [Alati] and delivering to [him] all other property the subject of the contract. The lease cannot now be re-assigned, and the other property referred to would include the stock-in-trade which obviously cannot now be returned, and the chattels referred to in the schedule to the contract which now may or may not be available for re-delivery. The judgment should therefore be varied so as to order [Kruger] to return to the defendant Alati such of the chattels mentioned in the schedule to the contract as he is able to return, and to order [Alati] to repay to [Kruger] the balance of the purchase money (£700) and interest thereon which shall remain after deducting the value as at the date of the contract of such of the scheduled chattels as [Kruger] cannot return, the value as at that date of the stock-in-trade which [Kruger] received from [Alati] under the contract, the damages awarded in the judgment of the Supreme Court, and any amount which ought to be allowed in [Alati's] favour in respect of [Kruger's] use of any of the property comprised in the contract.

Comment

1. See Radan & Stewart at **27.5–27.8, 27.21–27.22**.

Partial rescission

27.3 Vadasz v Pioneer Concrete (SA) Pty Ltd
(1995) 184 CLR 102

Court: High Court of Australia

Facts: Vadasz and his wife were the sole shareholders of Vadipile Drilling Pty Ltd, which conducted a foundation piling business. The company purchased ready-mixed concrete from Pioneer Concrete (SA) Pty Ltd, and had accrued debts of over $200,000 to Pioneer for concrete already supplied up to July 1992. At that time, Pioneer advised it would immediately stop further concrete deliveries to Vadipile unless Vadasz executed a personal guarantee. Vadasz was informed by Pioneer's employees that the guarantee would cover Vadipile's future debts, but the guarantee document provided for the payment of 'all monies which are now or may at any time' be due from Vadipile. Vadasz signed the guarantee without reading it. Vadipile continued to incur debts on the delivered concrete and, in November of the same year, was sued by Pioneer for the entire outstanding debt, amounting to over $350,000. Vadasz argued that the guarantee was unenforceable. The trial judge found that Pioneer's employees had misrepresented the effect of the guarantee, without indicating whether the misrepresentation was fraudulent, and that Vadasz had at all times understood the guarantee would cover future debts only. The court ruled he was entitled to equitable relief, but that this would mean the guarantee would be unenforceable only as far as past debts were concerned. Vadasz was ordered to pay over $170,000 for post-guarantee debts on the basis that the guarantee was rescinded only as regards past indebtedness. Vadasz's appeal to the Full Court of the Supreme Court was dismissed. He then appealed to the High Court.

Issue: The issue before the High Court was whether the trial judge was entitled to order partial rescission of the guarantee so that Vadasz remained liable to Pioneer for the debts incurred after the guarantee was signed.

Decision: The High Court (Deane, Dawson, Toohey, Gaudron and McHugh JJ) unanimously upheld the trial judge's decision to partially rescind the guarantee contract.

Extracts: The extracts from the High Court's joint judgment focus on the court's reasoning in allowing partial rescission of the contract, thereby enabling Pioneer to enforce Vadasz's obligation for future debts even though Pioneer had misrepresented the nature of the agreement.

Deane, Dawson, Toohey, Gaudron and McHugh JJ

[110] [I]t should be remembered that the trial judge held that [Vadasz] was 'entitled to equitable relief on the ground of [Pioneer's] misrepresentation'. And his Honour held that [Pioneer] was entitled in equity ... to enforce [Vadasz'] liability under the guarantee for future indebtedness. Had [Vadasz] sought to rely on the common law, he would not have been entitled to rescission because the contract did not remain completely executory and 'because he was not then in a position to return to [Pioneer] in specie that which he had received under the contract, in the same plight as that in which he had [111] received it'.[9] Complete restitution was not and is not possible in the circumstances of the present case where the consideration which moved from [Pioneer] to [Vadasz] was, in the words of the guarantee, [Pioneer's] 'having agreed or agreeing to sell goods ... or giving credit' to a company owned by [Vadasz] and his wife and where, in reliance upon the guarantee, [Pioneer] in fact supplied on credit to that company, which was or became insolvent,

---

9. *Alati v Kruger* (1955) 94 CLR 216 at 223.

large quantities of concrete which have been used and cannot be returned. That being so, the assumption of fraud does not avail [Vadasz] at common law.

Thus we are very much in the realm of equity. Indeed ... [Vadasz] did not really seek to attack the conclusion of the trial judge and the Full Court that the appropriate relief in the circumstances of the present case is equitable in its nature in the sense that its origins can be traced to the old Court of Chancery. [Vadasz'] case is that the appropriate equitable relief was the unconditional rescission or setting aside of the guarantee in its entirety. In that respect it is useful to have regard to what was said by Mason J in *Commercial Bank of Australia Ltd v Amadio*:

> Historically, courts have exercised jurisdiction to set aside contracts and other dealings on a variety of equitable grounds. They include fraud, misrepresentation, breach of fiduciary duty, undue influence and unconscionable conduct. In one sense they all constitute species of unconscionable conduct on the part of a party who stands to receive a benefit under a transaction which, in the eye of equity, cannot be enforced because to do so would be inconsistent with equity and good conscience.[10]

Where, as in this case, the court has granted equitable relief in the shape of rescission of a contract, the result is to set aside the contract ab initio. While equity followed the law in requiring restitution as a condition of rescission where the contract had been wholly or partly executed, it allowed greater flexibility in the basis upon which restitution and accounting between the parties may be ordered. Thus, equity did not require complete restitution of the position which existed before the contract but allowed its remedies, particularly an order for monetary accounts, to be utilised to achieve practical restitution and justice ...

[112] In the present case, [Vadasz] obtained the benefit which he sought as consideration for entering the contract of guarantee, namely, the subsequent supply on credit by [Pioneer] of goods to Vadipile. In those circumstances, a practical restoration of the status quo which existed before the execution of the guarantee and the subsequent supply of goods on credit by [Pioneer] would involve not only a cancellation of [Vadasz'] obligations under the guarantee but either a return of the goods subsequently supplied by [Pioneer] or the actual payment, either by Vadipile or [Vadasz], of an amount equivalent to the value of the goods which were subsequently supplied in reliance upon [Vadasz'] guarantee of payment of their price.

However, [Vadasz] does not offer to pay [Pioneer] the amount which Vadipile has failed to pay for those subsequently supplied goods. Nor does he offer to submit to terms or conditions which would ensure that the purchase price of those goods, which has not been suggested to exceed their true value, is received by [Pioneer]. As has been said, [Vadasz] seeks to be relieved completely and unconditionally from all liability under the guarantee, leaving [Pioneer] without either its subsequently supplied goods or any payment for them. If such complete and unconditional relief is to be granted, it must be on some basis other than mere entitlement to a practical restoration of the status quo upon rescission or 'disaffirmance' of a contract induced by fraud. The only such basis that comes to mind is equity's general jurisdiction, in setting aside contracts and other dealings on equitable grounds, to ensure the observance of the requirements of good

---

10. *Commercial Bank of Australia Ltd v Amadio* (1983) 151 CLR 447 at 461.

conscience and practical justice. Thus in *O'Sullivan v Management Agency & Music Ltd*[11] an exclusive management agreement made by a young composer was **[113]** set aside by reason of undue influence because of a fiduciary relationship between the parties. The Court of Appeal upheld rescission even though the parties could not be restored to their original position. In their judgments the members of the Court of Appeal pointed out that a contract may be set aside in equity so long as 'the court can achieve practical justice between the parties'[12] and that 'the court will do what is practically just in the individual case'[13] so long as 'it is possible to achieve what is practically just by granting rescission and restitution together with orders for accounts'.[14]

In the present case, the consideration provided by [Pioneer] involved the supply of goods upon credit to Vadipile. Any need for restitution arises by reason of Vadipile's insolvency. [Pioneer] points to the fact that goods were supplied on credit in pursuance of its promise given as consideration for [Vadasz's] guarantee and says in effect: 'I would not have made further deliveries of concrete to Vadipile and risked non-payment if [Vadasz] had not guaranteed payment for those deliveries'. In the way in which the action between the parties was constituted, practical justice is achieved, so [Pioneer's] argument runs, by holding [Vadasz] liable on a money claim for that proportion of Vadipile's debt incurred after [he] signed the guarantee. As Cussen J noted in *Bank of Victoria Limited v Mueller*, in the context of insisting that equity shall be done as a condition of setting aside a guarantee: 'This is, of course, something quite different from rectification, although in some cases its effect may be much the same'.[15]

The idea of a Court of Equity using its powers to do 'what is practically just' was referred to by Lord Blackburn in *Erlanger v New Sombrero Phosphate Co* well over 100 years ago. In contrasting the relief available in law and in equity on rescission of a contract, in particular the ability of equity to take account of profits and make allowance for deterioration of property, his Lordship said:

> And I think the practice has always been for a Court of Equity to give this relief whenever, by the exercise of its powers, it can do what is practically just, though it cannot restore the parties precisely to the state they were in before the contract.[16] ...

[114] In *Amadio*, Deane J referred to what was said by Cussen J in [*Bank of Victoria Ltd v Mueller*] in support of the proposition:

> Where appropriate, an order will be made which only partly nullifies a transaction liable to be set aside in equity pursuant to the principles of unconscionable dealing ... [T]he order will, in an appropriate case, be made conditional upon the party obtaining relief doing equity.[17]

Thus unconscionability works in two ways. In its strict sense, it provides the justification for setting aside a transaction. More loosely, it provides the justification for not setting

---

11. [1985] QB 428.
12. *O'Sullivan v Management Agency Ltd* [1985] QB 428 at 458.
13. *O'Sullivan v Management Agency Ltd* [1985] QB 428 at 466.
14. *O'Sullivan v Management Agency Ltd* [1985] QB 428 at 471.
15. *The Bank of Victoria Limited v Mueller* [1925] VLR 642 at 659.
16. *Erlanger v New Sombrero Phosphate Company* (1878) 3 App Cas 1218 at 1278–9.
17. *Commercial Bank of Australia Ltd v Amadio* (1983) 151 CLR 447 at 481.

aside the transaction in its entirety or in doing so subject to conditions, so as to prevent one party obtaining an unwarranted benefit at the expense of the other.

[115] In *Amadio* this Court upheld an order setting aside a mortgage in its entirety where the mortgagors believed they were committing themselves to securing their son's overdraft to a limit of $50,000 and for six months only. The reason for not setting aside the mortgage only to the extent that it involved a liability in excess of $50,000 was that the Amadios would not have entered into the transaction at all, had they known the true financial position of their son. In the present case it cannot be maintained that [Vadasz] would not have entered into the guarantee had it been confined to the future indebtedness of Vadipile. Rather, the evidence is that he would have done so, if not happily, because it was the only way to secure future supplies of concrete for Vadipile ... He stood to benefit personally from the operations of the company ...

The concern of equity, in moulding relief between the parties is to prevent, nullify, or provide compensation for, wrongful injury. If it appears that the other party would not have entered into the contract at all if the true position were known, the contract may be set aside in its entirety as in *Amadio*.

[Vadasz] is 'seeking the assistance of a court of equity and he who seeks equity must do equity'.[18] The Court must look at what is practically just for both parties, not only [for Vadasz]. To enforce the guarantee to the extent of future indebtedness is to do no more than hold [Vadasz] to what he was prepared to undertake independently of any misrepresentation.

Comments

1. See Radan & Stewart at **27.14–27.17**.
2. For a discussion of this case see A Robertson, 'Partial Rescission, Causation and Benefit' (2001) 17 *Journal of Contract Law* 163.

Loss of the right to rescind by affirmation

27.4   Coastal Estates Pty Ltd v Melevende
[1965] VR 433

Court: Full Court of the Supreme Court of Victoria

Facts: In September 1960, Melevende purchased eight blocks of land from Coastal Estates in a seaside subdivision on Westernport Bay by way of an instalment contract for the sum of £1768. He became aware by 1961 that Coastal Estates, through its agents, had misrepresented the value of the blocks and that he had contracted to pay far more than the blocks were worth. He tried to renegotiate the terms of the agreement with Coastal Estates without success and even tried to sell the blocks. By this time he had already paid the deposit and instalment payments totalling just over £1000. Although he was aware of the fraudulent misrepresentation, Melevende was not aware that he had a right to rescind the contract on that basis until he sought legal advice

---

18. *Cheese v Thomas* [1994] 1 WLR 129 at 136.

two years after the contract had been entered into. He rescinded the contract and began proceedings in the County Court to recover £1000. Coastal Estates defended on the grounds that Melevende had affirmed the contract by making regular instalment payments, trying to renegotiate the contract, seeking finance from his employer and trying to sell the land. It also counter-claimed for moneys due under the contract. The County Court found Melevende was unaware of his right to elect to affirm or rescind the contract at the relevant times, having become aware of his rights only when he sought advice. It held his conduct did not amount to affirmation and that his rescission was valid. Judgment was given in his favour in the sum of £1000 as claimed. Coastal Estates appealed to the Full Court of the Supreme Court.

Issue: The main issue before the Full Court was whether Melevende's conduct amounted to affirmation of the contract on the grounds that it was inconsistent with maintaining at the same time a right to rescind.

Decision: The Full Court (Herring CJ, Sholl and Adam JJ) unanimously held that Melevende had not affirmed the contract and upheld the validity of its rescission.

Extracts: The extracts from the judgments of Sholl J and Adam J deal not only with the general proposition that affirmation does not come into play until there is knowledge of the right to rescind, but also with the main qualification or exception to that principle.

Sholl J

[443] This case requires us to decide just what will and what will not amount to affirmation, given on the part of the defrauded party a full knowledge, or a certain and correct assumption, of the falsity of the material representations. Here, there was no evidence that [Melevende] knew at any time before he saw his solicitor in September 1962 that he had a legal right to rescind the contract *ab initio* for fraud, and I think on the whole of the evidence the proper inference is that he did not know that. In my opinion, the law is this. Assuming that rescission is still possible (if necessary, with the aid of equitable orders), and that the defrauded party fully knows, or positively and correctly assumes, the falsity of the representations which induced the contract, then:

(1) If he knows that he has a legal right to rescind or affirm the contract on that ground —
   (a) if he expressly communicates to the other party what his choice is, he makes an election, once and for all, which is binding upon him;
   (b) if he does anything which is referable only to a decision to adhere to the contract — ie, which he has a right to do, as against the opposite party, or is obliged to do, only if the contract stands — that is an election and he is bound thereafter to go on with it, unless, perhaps, what he does is a trifling and unconsidered action.

(2) If the defrauded party does not know that he has a legal right to rescind, he is not bound by acts which on the face of them are referable only to an intention to affirm the contract, unless those acts are 'adverse to' the opposite party, ie, unless they involve something to the other party's prejudice or detriment, as eg, if the defrauded party goes into possession of property sold to him by the contract, or accepts some other benefit thereunder. This is a form of estoppel, for the other party has in such a case acted to his prejudice upon a representation, made by the defrauded party's conduct,

that the latter is going on with the contract. The law does not require the representor in such a case to inquire of the representee whether he knows his legal rights.

(3) Acts of the defrauded party which are not adverse in the above sense, such as payments made by him to the other party, or to others (eg, rates), or negotiations for sale, are some but not conclusive evidence of a binding election made with knowledge of his rights. They may be enough to pass to him the shifting onus of proof so that he has to show non-knowledge of his rights at the time, but they do not of themselves involve an estoppel. They may, however, form part of the foundation for an estoppel, eg, if the opposite party, misled by such an act into supposing that the other is proceeding with the contract, refuses a more advantageous offer for the property the subject of the contract, or otherwise acts to his prejudice.

(4) Except in special classes of case, such as contracts to take shares in companies, where the representee must disaffirm with great promptness after knowledge (because the rights of creditors and other shareholders are affected), the defrauded party, subject to the above principles, need not make his election within any fixed time. He may defer a decision — 'suspend judgment', as it is put in some of the cases — and he may negotiate for a variation of the contract, or as to terms on which he may be relieved of it, but if he does these things he takes the risk of rescission becoming impossible or inequitable meanwhile, or of his inaction being treated as warranting an inference of knowledge and an intention to elect for affirmation of the contract.

Adam J

[451] It remains then to consider whether the proper inference from the evidence is, as [Coastal Estates] claims, that [Melevende] affirmed the contract during 1962 so as to have precluded himself from rescinding when he brought his action.

What is affirmation which deprives a party of a right of rescission in these circumstances? The right to rescind for misrepresentation may be lost in a variety of ways, some depending on the principle of election, others not. Once a representee has, by discovery of the truth, been put to his election, he will of course lose his right to rescind once he has elected not to rescind. Once he has made his election, he cannot resile from it. But not only will a party lose any right to elect in favour of rescission [452] by reason of his once having elected to affirm, he may apart altogether from this principle of election lose his right to rescind before he has made any election. He may lose his right of avoidance where by reason of his own conduct, or of other circumstances, it would be unjust or inequitable that he retain any right to elect. One example is where third parties have acquired rights under the contract which would be defeated by an avoidance of the contract. Another example is where rescission would be unjust to the representor because it has become impossible to restore him to the position in which he was at the making of the contract. *Restitutio in integrum* is not only a consequence of rescission, its possibility is indispensable to the right to rescind. Again delay in electing to rescind may make it unjust to others that the right to elect continue. For this reason the right of rescission for misrepresentation in general must be promptly exercised in transactions regarding company shares.

In my opinion, affirmation as a defence to a claim to rescind a contract rests on the principle that having elected to adhere to a contract after discovery of the falsity of the representations inducing it, the right to rescind is lost. In other words affirmation is the determination of an election by affirming the contract.

Affirmation may take the form of an express communication from the representee that he has elected to treat the contract as binding, or conduct of his in relation to the contract or its subject-matter from which the proper inference is that he has so elected. Where in addition to knowing all material facts, which would entitle him to avoid the contract, the representee is aware also that he has the choice open either to avoid or to affirm, it is a question of fact whether his conduct evidences a determination of his election. Before he will be held to have elected his conduct must be unequivocal. More difficult problems arise where the representee, while knowing the facts which in law give him the choice to avoid or affirm, is in fact unaware that he has any choice in the matter. In such a case it would seem on principle that no question can arise of his having made an election. In the nature of things how can one elect between alternative courses, unless one is aware that alternative courses are open? In other branches of the law, where questions of election arise — eg under the Workers Compensation Acts[19] or under the well-known equitable doctrine of election as between estates — actual knowledge of the existence of the right to elect as between alternatives has been considered essential. The relevance of such knowledge where the right of election arises in cases of contracts induced by misrepresentation is more obscure.

There are not wanting in the authorities statements to the effect that a party may effectually elect to affirm a contract, although unaware that he has any option to avoid it — and that knowledge of his right to elect upon discovery of fraud will be conclusively presumed.[20] Furthermore in many of the cases the test whether a representee has affirmed a contract after discovery of the fraud which induced him to enter into it, is stated to be whether he has so acted as to show unequivocally that he elected to treat the contract as binding without any discussion of the relevance of his knowledge or absence of knowledge of his right to elect.[21]

[453] The conclusion I have reached after considering the foregoing and other authorities which were cited to us — particularly the leading case of *Clough v London & North Western Railway Co*[22] — is that the ultimate question to be answered in cases where affirmation is relied upon as a defence to a rescission is whether the representee has after discovery of the falsity of the relevant misrepresentations, in truth elected to affirm the contract and thereby elected not to avoid it. Because the making of an election necessarily presupposes a knowledge that a choice between alternative courses is open, in general, no question of affirmation can arise in the absence of such knowledge. There appears, however, to be one important qualification upon this. If a representee, after discovery of the facts which entitle him to avoid a contract, exercises, in an unequivocal manner, rights under the contract adversely to the other party he will in general be deemed to have elected to affirm it, although not aware of his right to elect. In the case

---

19. *Dey v Victorian Railway Commissioners* (1949) 78 CLR 62.
20. *O'Connor v SP Bray Ltd* (1936) 36 SR (NSW) 248; *Evans v Benson and Co* [1961] WALR 13.
21. *Scarf v Jardine* (1882) 7 App Cas 345 at 361; *Abram Steamship Co Ltd v Westville Shipping Co Ltd* [1923] AC 773; *Brown v Smitt* [1924] VLR 333; *Watson v Burton* [1956] 3 All ER 929; *Tropical Traders v Groonan* (1964) 37 ALJR 497 at 500.
22. (1871) LR 7 Exch 26.

of a representee unaware of his right of election there is, I consider, a distinction to be drawn between acts done by him in exercise of rights under the contract adversely to the other party which, were the contract not on foot, could not be justified, and acts which do no more than show that the representee recognized the contract as still subsisting, but are not prejudicial or adverse to the other party. Such a distinction may be explained as an application of the doctrine of estoppel, or of the rule against approbating and reprobating, or perhaps more broadly on general considerations of justice. Strictly speaking I would think that the so-called affirmation without knowledge of any right to elect should be regarded as an example of the loss of a right to rescind apart from the principle of election, and that it tends only to confusion to treat it as of the same species as a true election to affirm …

[454] I do not find these conclusions inconsistent with any of the authorities binding on this Court. The foregoing observations are applicable in this case because on the evidence it seems proper to infer that [Melevende] was in fact unaware that he had any right to repudiate the contract until he consulted his solicitors in September 1962 just prior to commencement of these proceedings. Indeed if, as I think, the ultimate onus of establishing all elements of the defence of affirmation rests on the representor, it would be sufficient perhaps to say that the evidence fails to establish affirmatively that [Melevende] had sufficient knowledge of his rights at any relevant time. This being so the question is not whether [Melevende], after discovery of the facts, did any act which recognized the continued existence of the contract, but any act in exercise of his contractual rights adversely to [Coastal Estates]. The payment of instalments of purchase money merely discharged an obligation which [Melevende] supposed to be irrevocably binding on him — it certainly did not amount to the exercise of any contractual right by him adversely to [Coastal Estates]; the payment of rates stands in no different position; in any case the payment in 1962 was made after [Melevende] had elected to rescind, and the negotiations with [Coastal Estates] for release from or variations of the contract would seem to carry the matter no further.

No doubt had it been proved that [Melevende] was actually aware that he could, if he chose, have repudiated the contract for fraud, his conduct after knowledge of the fraud in paying instalments of purchase money would have provided most cogent evidence of a considered affirmation by him of the contract and precluded his later rescinding it; but any such inference of actual election is impossible to draw in the absence of any such awareness of his rights.

Comments
1. See Radan & Stewart at **27.25–27.28**.
2. The correctness of the decision in this case is not beyond dispute as is discussed in Radan & Stewart at **27.29–27.31**.

28

CONSTRUCTIVE TRUSTS

Introduction

28.1   This chapter deals with constructive trusts. These species of trust are not necessarily dependent upon an actual, inferred or presumed intention to create a trust. Constructive trusts can arise in numerous situations but the extracts in this chapter deal with the following three issues:

- the nature of constructive trusts and the use of unconscionability as a basis of their imposition: *Muschinski v Dodds* (1985) 160 CLR 583;
- constructive trusts imposed on stolen property: *Black v S Freedman & Co* (1910) 12 CLR 105; and
- constructive trusts and the doctrine of knowing receipt: *The Bell Group Ltd (in liq) v Westpac Banking Corporation (No 9)* (2009) 70 ACSR 1.

The nature of constructive trusts and the use of unconscionability as a basis for their imposition

28.2   Muschinski v Dodds (1985) 160 CLR 583

Court: High Court of Australia

Facts: Hilga Muschinski and Robert Dodds were in a long-term de facto relationship which broke down. The main asset of the relationship was land at Picton on the southwestern outskirts of Sydney. Muschinski had provided the entirety of the purchase price of $20,000 from the sale of her previous home. The property was in a bad state of repair and the parties planned on restoring it, building a new prefabricated house on the land, and using the land to run an arts and crafts business. The parties agreed that they would use the proceeds of the sale of Muschinski's house to provide the purchase moneys and that Dodds would use his earnings and whatever moneys he obtained from his divorce settlement to pay for the prefabricated house. The parties' plans never came to fruition. Some repair work was done by Dodds and the total respective financial contributions of the parties upon the breakdown of their relationship were $25,259.45 from Muschinski and $2549.77 from Dodds.

The land was registered in the names of Muschinski and Dodds as tenants in common in equal shares. Muschinski claimed that Dodds' half interest was held on trust for her. Dodds sought an order for the sale of the land and the division of the net proceeds into equal shares.

At trial, and on appeal to the Court of Appeal, the matter was treated as one of resulting trust, with a presumption of resulting trust arising in Muschinski's favour. Both the trial judge and the Court of Appeal found that the presumption of resulting trust had been rebutted by the evidence of Muschinski's intention to grant Dodds an interest in return for his promises to work on the property and in the proposed business. No constructive trust was found to have arisen. Muschinski appealed to the High Court.

Issue: The issue was whether a constructive trust could arise to protect the contributions which were made by Muschinski.

Decision: A majority of the High Court (Gibbs CJ, Mason and Deane JJ; Brennan and Dawson JJ dissenting) found that a constructive trust should be ordered to protect Muschinski's beneficial interest. Gibbs CJ believed that there should be an equitable accounting on the sale of the property, on the basis that the parties were joint and several debtors. Gibbs CJ recognised that Muschinski had a right to contribution against Dodds for the recovery of one-half of the amount paid under the contract, unless the parties had agreed (either expressly or impliedly) that no such right would arise between them. Gibbs CJ could find no evidence of such an agreement and therefore saw no impedient to an order for contribution (although it should be noted that his Honour agreed with the orders proposed by Deane J).

Deane J (with whom Mason J agreed) took a more radical approach. His Honour began by finding that the presumption of resulting trust had been rebutted, but that a constructive trust should be imposed. Deane J expressly disagreed with the approach of Gibbs CJ regarding her right to claim equitable contribution from Dodds. Instead, Deane J thought it more appropriate to consider Dodds' obligations as arising from the joint endeavour of the parties. Deane J found that Dodds' behaviour was unconscionable, in particular, his assertion of legal title in the face of the contributions made by Muschinski. It followed that equity required a constructive trust to adjust the rights and obligations of the parties to compensate for the disproportion between the parties' contributions to the purchase price. However, Deane J did not believe that it was unconscionable for Dodds to retain his half-share in the residue of the proceeds of sale of the property, once each party had been reimbursed for their contributions to purchase price and improvements. Deane J ordered that the property was to be held on constructive trust by both parties to repay to each her or his respective contribution and as to the residue for them both in equal shares, effective from the date of judgment. Any remaining proceeds were held equally as tenants in common.

Brennan J in dissent (with whom Dawson J agreed) also found the presumption of resulting trust to have been rebutted. Brennan J found that, as Dodds had received his legal interest as a result of his promise to improve the property, he was bound by a personal equitable obligation to compensate for his failure to make substantial improvements. However, as Muschinski had chosen to make a proprietary claim, and not a claim of personal equitable obligation, Brennan J believed her appeal should be dismissed.

Extracts: In this extract Deane J discusses the nature of the constructive trust as a remedial institution, and the use of unconscionability as a basis for its imposition.

Deane J

[611] ...There was no express or implied agreement, arrangement or understanding between the parties that they should hold their legal interests upon trust for themselves in shares corresponding to their respective contributions. To the contrary, the evidence leads inexorably to the conclusion — expressed in concurrent findings of fact in the courts below — that it was their shared intention that, from the time of purchase, each should have a full one-half beneficial, as well as legal, interest in the property. Mrs Muschinski's intention was that her own and Mr Dodds' interest or, to use her word, 'status' in the whole venture should be equal: it should be a 'joint venture', a 'partnership'. The explanation of that intention lay in her expectation of Mr Dodds' future financial contributions and in her desire to use the arrangements in relation to the purchase and development of the property as a means of strengthening the stability of her relationship with him. As she said (under cross-examination):

> Mr Dodds was going to provide a home for me, no matter what. He was going to build a home and pay for it for the rest of his life. ... He was willing to provide whatever he had and whatever he was going to earn after; he was going to contribute to our future home and happiness

and

> I expected the purchase of the Picton property to improve our relationship, to increase that happiness, because we had many arguments about the colour scheme of the house and it was always referred to, 'Yes, it is your house. I have nothing to say here' ... I thought this would restore our relationship to quite a happier one.

Nor, upon a proper assessment of the evidence, is there room for a finding of an express or implied contract between Mrs Muschinski and Mr Dodds to the effect that, if things fell apart in respect of both their personal relationship and their planned development of the land, they would hold the property either upon trust to repay their respective contributions and then for themselves equally or upon trust for themselves in shares according to their respective contributions. There is no suggestion at all of any express contract to that effect and no adequate foundation for the implication of one. As the learned trial judge found, it was not the intention of either of them that Mr Dodds' equal beneficial interest should be acquired by [612] stages as he contributed towards the planned joint endeavour. Their planned future association and joint activity provided the occasion for, and the explanation of, the arrangement between them. That arrangement was, however, to the effect that Mr Dodds' beneficial interest in the property should be immediate and unconditional. It was not qualified to provide for the uncontemplated double contingency that their personal relationship would fail and that the proposed venture involving the development and joint use of the land would crumble under the yoke of inauspicious stars.

In these circumstances, there is no occasion for recourse to the presumption of the law of equity that, where two or more persons advance the purchase price of property in different shares, the person or persons to whom the legal title is transferred holds or hold the property upon resulting trust in favour of those who provided the purchase price in the shares in which they provided it.[1] That presumption performs much the same function as a civil onus of proof. General statements to the effect that it is not lightly to be rebutted should not, in my respectful view, now be accepted as good law.[2] That is not, of course, to deny that the facts which call the presumption into operation may, in the circumstances of a particular case, also lead to such a strong inference of an intended trust that convincing evidence would be necessary to rebut it.[3] Even in such a case however, the presumption operates by reference to the presumed intention of the party whose contribution exceeds his or her proportionate share; it cannot prevail over the actual intention of that party as established by the overall evidence, including the evidence of the parties' respective contributions.

It follows that no relief is available to Mrs Muschinski on the grounds of breach of express or implied agreement or of express or implied trust. The question remains whether the circumstances of the case are such as to entitle her to claim relief on some other ground. In particular, the question arises whether she is entitled to claim relief by way of declaration of, or order imposing, a constructive trust. It was submitted on behalf of Mrs Muschinski that she was entitled to a declaration of constructive trust based on broad notions of fairness and unjust enrichment.

The nature and function of the constructive trust have been the subject of considerable discussion throughout the common law world for several decades.[4] [613] At times, disputing factions have tended to polarize the discussion by reference to competing rallying points of 'remedy' and 'institution'. The perceived dichotomy between those two catchwords has, however, largely been the consequence of lack of definition. In a broad sense, the constructive trust is both an institution and a remedy of the law of equity. As a remedy, it can only properly be understood in the context of the history and the persisting distinctness

---

1. *Calverley v Green* (1984) 155 CLR 242 at 268–269.
2. *Calverley v Green* (1984) 155 CLR at 265–266, 269–270.
3. *Wirth v Wirth* (1956) 98 CLR 228 at 241–242.
4. See, particularly, Pound, 'Equitable Remedies' (1919–1920) 33 *Harvard Law Review* 420–423; Scott, 'Constructive Trusts' (1955) 71 *Law Quarterly Review* 39; Maudsley, 'Proprietary Remedies for the Recovery of Money' (1959) 75 *Law Quarterly Review* 234; Waters, *The Constructive Trust*, 1964; Goff and Jones, *The Law of Restitution*, 1978, esp. Chs 1 and 2; Oakley, *Constructive Trusts*, 1978; John Wade, 'Trusts, the Matrimonial Home and De Facto Spouses' (1978–1980) 6 *University of Tasmania Law Review* 97; J D Davies, 'Informal Arrangements Affecting Land' (1976–1979) 8 *Sydney Law Review* 578; Underhill, *Law Relating to Trusts and Trustees* (1979), Ch 7; John L Dewar, 'The Development of the Remedial Constructive Trust' (1982) 60 *Canadian Bar Review* 265; Pettit, *Equity and the Law of Trusts*, 1984, v and Ch 10; Hanbury and Maudsley, *Modern Equity*, 1985, Ch 12.

of the principles of equity that enlighten and control the common law. The use or trust of equity, like equity itself, was essentially remedial in its origins. In its basic form it was imposed, as a personal obligation attaching to property, to enforce the equitable principle that a legal owner should not be permitted to use his common law rights as owner to abuse or subvert the intention which underlay his acquisition and possession of those rights. This was consistent with the traditional concern of equity with substance rather than form. In time, the relationships in which the trust was recognized and enforced to protect actual or presumed intention became standardized and were accepted into conveyancing practice (particularly in relation to settlements) and property law as the equitable institutions of the express and implied (including resulting) trust. Like express and implied trusts, the constructive trust developed as a remedial relationship superimposed upon common law rights by order of the Chancery Court. It differs from those other forms of trust, however, in that it arises regardless of intention. For that reason, it was not as well suited to development as a conveyancing device or as an instrument of property law. Indeed, whereas the rationale of the institutions of express and implied trust is now usually identified by reference to intention, the rationale of the constructive trust must still be found essentially in its remedial function which it has predominantly retained.[5]

The constructive trust shares, however, [614] some of the institutionalized features of express and implied trust. It demands the staple ingredients of those trusts: subject-matter, trustee, beneficiary (or, conceivably, purpose), and personal obligation attaching to the property.[6] When established or imposed, it is a relationship governed by a coherent body of traditional and statute law. Viewed in its modern context, the constructive trust can properly be described as a remedial institution which equity imposes regardless of actual or presumed agreement or intention (and subsequently protects) to preclude the retention or assertion of beneficial ownership of property to the extent that such retention or assertion would be contrary to equitable principle.

There is, however, a more limited sense in which there is some superficial plausibility in the notions of 'institution' and 'remedy' as competing characterizations of the constructive trust. If 'institution' is understood as connoting a relationship which arises and exists under the law independently of any order of a court and 'remedy' is defined as referring to the actual establishment of a relationship by such an order, the catchwords of 'institution' and 'remedy' do serve the function of highlighting a conceptual problem that persists about the true nature of a constructive trust. Even in this more limited sense, however, any perceived dichotomy between the two notions tends to prove ephemeral upon closer examination. Equity acts consistently and in accordance with principle. The old maxim that equity regards as done that which ought to be done is as applicable to enforce equitable obligations as it is to create them and, notwithstanding that the constructive trust is remedial in both origin and nature there does not need to have been a curial declaration or order before equity will recognize the prior existence of a constructive trust.[7] Where an equity court would retrospectively impose a constructive trust by way of equitable remedy, its availability as such a remedy provides the basis for, and governs the content of, its existence inter partes independently of any formal order

---

5. Waters, *The Constructive Trust*, 1964, pp 37–39.
6. Sir Frederick Jordan, *Chapters on Equity in New South Wales*, 1947, Stephen (ed) pp 17–18.
7. Scott, *Law of Trusts*, 1967, vol V, par 462.4.

declaring or enforcing it. In this more limited sense, the constructive trust is also properly seen as both 'remedy' and 'institution'. Indeed, for the student of equity, there can be no true dichotomy between the two notions.

The acknowledgment of the institutional character of the constructive trust does not involve a denial of its continued flexibility as a remedy.[8] The institutional character of the trust has never completely obliterated its remedial origins even in **[615]** the case of the more traditional forms of express and implied trust. This is a fortiori in the case of constructive trust where, as has been mentioned, the remedial character remains predominant in that the trust itself either represents, or reflects the availability of, equitable relief in the particular circumstances. Indeed, in this country at least, the constructive trust has not outgrown its formative stages as an equitable remedy and should still be seen as constituting an in personam remedy attaching to property which may be moulded and adjusted to give effect to the application and interplay of equitable principles in the circumstances of the particular case. In particular, where competing common law or equitable claims are or may be involved, a declaration of constructive trust by way of remedy can properly be so framed that the consequences of its imposition are operative only from the date of judgment or formal court order or from some other specified date. The fact that the constructive trust remains predominantly remedial does not, however, mean that it represents a medium for the indulgence of idiosyncratic notions of fairness and justice. As an equitable remedy, it is available only when warranted by established equitable principles or by the legitimate processes of legal reasoning, by analogy, induction and deduction, from the starting point of a proper understanding of the conceptual foundation of such principles.[9] Viewed as a remedy, the function of the constructive trust is not to render superfluous, but to reflect and enforce, the principles of the law of equity.

Thus it is that there is no place in the law of this country for the notion of 'a constructive trust of a new model' which, '[b]y whatever name it is described, ... is ... imposed by law whenever justice and good conscience' (in the sense of 'fairness' or what 'was fair') 'require it'.[10] Under the law of this country — as, I **[616]** venture to think, under the present law of England[11] — proprietary rights fall to be governed by principles of law and not by some mix of judicial discretion,[12] subjective views about which party 'ought to win'[13] and 'the formless void of individual moral opinion'.[14] Long before Lord

---

8. *Wirth v Wirth* (1956) 98 CLR at 238.
9. See generally Sir Frank Kitto's Foreword to the first edition of Meagher, Gummow and Lehane, *Equity: Doctrines and Remedies*, 1975, pp v–vii, and see also, for example, *In re Diplock* [1948] Ch 465 at 481–482; *Pettitt v Pettitt* [1970] AC 777 at 793, 801, 809, 825; *Cowcher v Cowcher* [1972] 1 WLR 425 at 430 ([1972] 1 All ER 943 at 948); R P Meagher and W M C Gummow, *Jacobs' Law of Trusts in Australia*, Butterworths, Sydney, 1977, [1301]–[1302], [1325]–[1329]; *Allen v Snyder* [1977] 2 NSWLR 685 at 689, 702ff; Oakley, *Constructive Trusts*, 1978, pp 1–10; Pettit, *Equity and the Law of Trusts*, 1984, pp 4–6.
10. *Eves v Eves* [1975] 1 WLR 1338 at 1341, 1342; [1975] 3 All ER 768 at 771, 772 per Lord Denning MR; and *Hussey v Palmer* [1972] 1 WLR 1286 at 1289–1290; [1972] 3 All ER 744 at 747.
11. *Burns v Burns* [1984] Ch 317.
12. *Wirth v Wirth* (1956) 98 CLR at 232, 247.
13. Maudsley, 'Constructive Trusts' (1977) 28 *Northern Ireland Legal Quarterly* 123, esp. at 123, 137, 139–140.
14. *Carly v Farrelly* [1975] 1 NZLR 356 at 367; *Avondale Printers & Stationers Ltd v Haggie* [1979] 2 NZLR 124 at 154.

Seldon's anachronism identifying the Chancellor's foot as the measure of Chancery relief, undefined notions of 'justice' and what was 'fair' had given way in the law of equity to the rule of ordered principle which is of the essence of any coherent system of rational law. The mere fact that it would be unjust or unfair in a situation of discord for the owner of a legal estate to assert his ownership against another provides, of itself, no mandate for a judicial declaration that the ownership in whole or in part lies, in equity, in that other.[15] Such equitable relief by way of constructive trust will only properly be available if applicable principles of the law of equity require that the person in whom the ownership of property is vested should hold it to the use or for the benefit of another. That is not to say that general notions of fairness and justice have become irrelevant to the content and application of equity. They remain relevant to the traditional equitable notion of unconscionable conduct which persists as an operative component of some fundamental rules or principles of modern equity.[16]

The principal operation of the constructive trust in the law of this country has been in the area of breach of fiduciary duty. Some textwriters have expressed the view that the constructive trust is confined to cases where some pre-existing fiduciary relationship can be identified.[17] Neither principle nor authority requires however that it be confined to that or any other category or categories of case.[18] Once its predominantly remedial character is accepted, **[617]** there is no reason to deny the availability of the constructive trust in any case where some principle of the law of equity calls for the imposition upon the legal owner of property, regardless of actual or presumed agreement or intention, of the obligation to hold or apply the property for the benefit of another.[19] In the United States of America, a general doctrine of unjust enrichment has long been recognized as providing an acceptable basis in principle for the imposition of a constructive trust.[20] It may be that the development of the law of this country on a case by case basis will eventually lead to the identification of some overall concept of unjust enrichment as an established principle constituting the basis of decision of past and future cases. Whatever may be the position in relation to the law of other common law countries[21] however, no such general principle is as yet established, as a basis of decision as distinct from an informative generic label for purposes of classification, in Australian law. The most that can be said at the present time is that 'unjust enrichment' is a term commonly used to identify the notion underlying a variety of distinct categories of case in which the law has recognized an obligation on the part of a defendant to account for a benefit derived at the expense of a plaintiff.[22] It therefore becomes necessary to consider whether there is

---

15. *Hepworth v Hepworth* (1963) 110 CLR 309 at 317–318.
16. For example, *Legione v Hateley* (1983) 152 CLR 406 at 444; *Commercial Bank of Australia Ltd v Amadio* (1983) 151 CLR 447 at 461–464, 474–475.
17. See, for example, *Lewin on Trusts*, Mowbray (ed), 1964, p 141.
18. See generally Professor Austin, 'Constructive Trusts' in Finn (ed), *Essays in Equity*, 1985, especially at pp 196–201; Waters, *The Constructive Trust*, 1964, pp 28ff.
19. Hanbury and Maudsley, *Modern Equity*, 1985, p 301; Pettit, *Equity and the Law of Trusts*, 1984, p 55.
20. See, for example, Scott, *Law of Trusts*, 1967, vol V, par 461.
21. See as to Canada, *Pettkus v Becker* (1980) 117 DLR (3d) 257 and, as to New Zealand, *Hayward v Giordani* [1983] NZLR 140 at 148.
22. Goff and Jones, *The Law of Restitution*, 1978, p 11.

any narrower and more specific basis on which, independently of the actual intention of the parties, Mrs Muschinski can claim to be entitled to relief by way of constructive trust in the particular circumstances of the present case.

As has been said, the payments made by Mrs Muschinski on account of the price and associated costs of the property were made by her pursuant to the overall arrangement between herself and Mr Dodds. It was the common intention of the parties, at the time those particular payments were made, that the burden of them should be borne by Mrs Muschinski alone. As I presently see the matter, it follows that Mrs Muschinski had no right to claim reimbursement from Mr Dodds in respect of an appropriate part of those payments under any doctrine of contribution.[23] It is, however, unnecessary that I form any concluded view in that regard since I would not, in any [618] event, consider it appropriate to act on the basis that Mrs Muschinski was entitled to relief by way of contribution in circumstances where she advanced neither claim nor argument for relief on that basis either in this Court or in the courts below and where factual material relevant to such a claim may, as a consequence, remain unexplored. Indeed, an essential basis of the argument on behalf of Mrs Muschinski before this Court was that she had assumed and discharged the burden of paying the whole of the purchase price of the Picton land under and in accordance with the overall arrangement between Mr Dodds and herself.

Nor has it been suggested that there was a true partnership or contractual joint venture between the parties. The case has been approached and argued on the basis that they were not partners and that the overall arrangement between them, while consensual, was a non-contractual one. That does not mean, however, that particular rules applicable to regulate the rights and duties of the parties to a failed partnership or contractual joint venture might not be relevant in the search for some more general or analogous principle applicable in the circumstances of the collapse of the consensual commercial venture and personal relationship in the present case.

Both common law and equity recognize that, where money or other property is paid or applied on the basis of some consensual joint relationship or endeavour which fails without attributable blame, it will often be inappropriate simply to draw a line leaving assets and liabilities to be owned and borne according to where they may prima facie lie, as a matter of law, at the time of the failure. Where there are express or implied contractual provisions specially dealing with the consequences of failure of the joint relationship or endeavour, they will ordinarily apply in law and equity to regulate the rights and duties of the parties between themselves and the prima facie legal position will accordingly prevail. Where, however, there are no applicable contractual provisions or the only applicable provisions were not framed to meet the contingency of premature failure of the enterprise or relationship, other rules or principles will commonly be called into play. If, in the last-mentioned case, the relevant relationship is merely contractual and the contract has been frustrated without fault on either side, the present tendency of the common law is that contributions made should be refunded at least if there has been a complete failure of consideration

---

23. *Coulls v Bagot's Executor and Trustee Co Ltd* (1967) 119 CLR 460 at 488; *Gadsden v Commissioner of Probate Duties* [1978] VR 653 at 660–662.

in performance.[24] **[619]** If the relevant relationship is a partnership, the prima facie rule of equity on premature dissolution is, as in the case of an ordinary dissolution, that the parties are, after the discharge of partnership debts, entitled to be repaid their respective capital contributions. More important for present purposes, if a premium has been paid by a fixed term partner who is not to be held responsible for the premature dissolution, an equity court will order a refund or partial refund of the premium to the extent that its retention by the other partner would be unconscionable.[25] If the relevant relationship is not a partnership but takes the form of a contractual joint venture for the pursuit of some commercial advantage, a similar prima facie rule of equity applies in the event of the premature collapse of the joint venture and the consequent preclusion of the attainment of the commercial advantage, namely, that, to the extent that the joint funds allow, the joint venturers are entitled to the proportionate repayment of their capital contributions to the abortive joint venture. This is so notwithstanding that it was the common understanding or agreement that the funds advanced were to be applied for the purposes of the joint venture and that the return from them would take the form, not of a repayment of capital contributed but of a share in the proceeds of the joint venture when it was carried to fruition.[26]

The prima facie rules respectively entitling a fixed term partner to a proportionate refund of his or her premium and a contractual joint venturer to a proportionate repayment of his or her capital contribution on the premature dissolution of the partnership or collapse of the joint venture are properly to be seen as instances of a more general principle of equity. That more general principle of equity can also be readily related to the general equitable notions which find expression in the common law count for money had and received[27] and to the rationale of the particular rule of contract law to which reference has been made.[28] Like most of the traditional doctrines of equity, it **[620]** operates upon legal entitlement to prevent a person from asserting or exercising a legal right in circumstances where the particular assertion or exercise of it would constitute unconscionable conduct.[29]

The circumstances giving rise to the operation of the principle were broadly identified by Lord Cairns L.C., speaking for the Court of Appeal in Chancery, in *Atwood v. Maude*[30] **[108]** where 'the case is one in which, using the words of Lord Cottenham in *Hirst v. Tolson*,[31]

---

24. *Fibrosa Spolka Akcyjna v Fairbairn Lawson Combe Barbour Ltd* [1943] AC 32; *Denny, Mort and Dickson Ltd v James B Fraser and Co Ltd* [1944] AC 265 at 275; and, generally, Treitel, *Law of Contract*, 1983, pp 695ff.

25. *Atwood v Maude* (1868) 3 Ch App 369.

26. See, for example, *Allen v Kent* (1957) 136 A (2d) 540 at 541; *Ewen v Gerofsky* (1976) 382 NYS (2d) 651 at 653; *Legum Furniture Corporation v Levine* (1977) 232 SE (2d) 782 at 785–786; and see, generally, 'Joint Ventures', 48A *Corpus Juris Secundum*, 452–453, 463.

27. *Moses v Macferlan* (1760) 2 Burr 1005 at 1012 [97 ER 676 at 680–681]; *J & S Holdings Pty Ltd v NRMA Insurance Ltd* (1982) 61 FLR 108 at 120.

28. *Fibrosa* [1943] AC at 61ff especially at 72.

29. Story, *Commentaries on Equity Jurisprudence*, Perry (ed), 1877, vol 2, par 1316; *Legione v Hateley* (1983) 152 CLR at 444.

30. (1868) LR 3 Ch App at 375.

31. (1850) 42 ER 521.

a payment has been made by anticipation of something afterwards to be enjoyed [and] where ... circumstances arise so that future enjoyment is denied'. Those circumstances can be more precisely defined by saying that the principle operates in a case where the substratum of a joint relationship or endeavour is removed without attributable blame and where the benefit of money or other property contributed by one party on the basis and for the purposes of the relationship or endeavour would otherwise be enjoyed by the other party in circumstances in which it was not specifically intended or specially provided that that other party should so enjoy it. The content of the principle is that, in such a case, equity will not permit that other party to assert or retain the benefit of the relevant property to the extent that it would be unconscionable for him so to do.[32]

The circumstances of the present case provide the necessary context for the operation of that general principle of the law of equity. Mrs Muschinski's payment of the purchase price of the Picton property, which was transferred into the joint names of Mr Dodds and herself, was made on the basis and for the purposes of their planned venture with respect to the land. The substratum of that planned joint endeavour was removed without attributable blame. Mr Dodds is left as a half-owner of the property in circumstances (i.e., the collapse of the joint endeavour) to which the parties did not advert and in which it was not specifically intended or specially provided that Mr Dodds should enjoy such a benefit at Mrs Muschinski's expense. In these circumstances, the operation of the relevant principle is to preclude Mr Dodds from asserting or retaining, against Mrs Muschinski, his one-half ownership of the property to the extent that it would be unconscionable for him so to [621] do. In assessing whether or to what extent such an assertion or retention of legal entitlement by Mr Dodds would constitute unconscionable conduct, one is not left at large to indulge random notions of what is fair and just as a matter of abstract morality. Notions of what is fair and just are relevant but only in the confined context of determining whether conduct should, by reference to legitimate processes of legal reasoning, be characterized as unconscionable for the purposes of a specific principle of equity whose rationale and operation is to prevent wrongful and undue advantage being taken by one party of a benefit derived at the expense of the other party in the special circumstances of the unforeseen and premature collapse of a joint relationship or endeavour.

If the venture between Mrs Muschinski and Mr Dodds had been merely a commercial one involving the purchase, development, partial realization and use of the Picton land, there would be little room for argument about the appropriate characterization, for the purposes of the relevant principle of equity, of Mr Dodds' conduct in seeking to assert and retain the full benefit derived by him from Mrs Muschinski's contribution without making any allowance to compensate her for the disproportion between those contributions and his own. The basis upon which Mrs Muschinski made her contributions was that Mr Dodds would, in due course, contribute, both in money and by labour, to the subsequent development. Their planned endeavour collapsed at a time when Mrs Muschinski had made all or almost all of her expected contribution to the overall venture, but Mr Dodds had made almost none of his. The parties had neither adverted to nor made special provision to deal with that situation. If no more

---

32. *Atwood v Maude* (1868) LR 3 Ch App at 374–375, and *Lyon v Tweddell* (1881) 17 Ch D 529 at 531 per Jessel MR.

than the commercial relationship had been involved, Mr Dodds' conduct in seeking to catch and retain the unfair advantage of unforeseen circumstances by asserting his legal entitlement of a one-half interest in the property without assenting to any adjustment to compensate Mrs Muschinski for the unintended gross disproportion between their respective contributions would plainly be unconscionable for the purposes of the relevant principle of equity. Indeed, if the relationship between the parties had been merely a commercial one, such conduct on the part of Mr Dodds would be of the very type which the relevant principle exists to preclude.

As has been seen however, the relationship between the parties in the present case was not merely a commercial one. It was a mixture of the commercial and the personal. The personal relationship provided the context and explains the content of the planned commercial venture. If the personal relationship had survived for years after the collapse of the commercial venture and the property [622] had been unmistakenly devoted to serve solely as a mutual home, any assessment of what would and would not constitute unconscionable conduct would obviously be greatly influenced by the special considerations applicable to a case where a husband and wife or persons living in a 'de facto' situation contribute, financially and in a variety of other ways, over a lengthy period to the establishment of a joint home. In the forefront of those special considerations there commonly lies a need to take account of a practical equation between direct contributions in money or labour and indirect contributions in other forms such as support, home-making and family care. In fact, of course, the personal relationship also failed in the present case. The Picton property was not devoted to serve as a mutual home for a lengthy period after the collapse of the planned commercial venture. There is no consideration or combination of considerations arising from the personal relationship between the parties which could properly be seen as negating or overriding the unconscionable character of Mr Dodds' conduct in seeking, in the circumstances, to assert and retain the benefit of a full one-half interest in the property without making any allowance for the fact that Mrs Muschinski has contributed approximately ten-elevenths of the cost of its purchase and actual improvement.

Nor does the fact that Mr Dodds is seeking to take advantage of the overall arrangement which the parties framed to meet the exigencies of their personal relationship deprive his conduct of its unconscionable character. In circumstances where the parties neither foresaw nor attempted to provide for the double contingency of the premature collapse of both their personal relationship and their commercial venture, it is simply not to the point to say that the parties had framed that overall arrangement without attaching any condition or providing any safeguard specifically to meet the occurrence of that double contingency. As has been seen, the relevant principle operates upon legal entitlement. It is the assertion by Mr Dodds of his legal entitlement in the unforeseen circumstances which arose on the collapse of their relationship and planned venture which lies at the heart of the characterization of his conduct as unconscionable. Indeed, it is the very absence of any provision for legal defeasance or other specific and effective legal device to meet the particular circumstances which gives rise to the need to call in aid the principle of equity applicable to preclude the unconscionable assertion of legal rights in the particular class of case.

It follows that equity requires that the rights and obligations of the parties be adjusted to compensate for the disproportion between their contributions to the purchase and improvement of the Picton property. In the absence of any suggestion of direct payment by **[623]** Mr Dodds to Mrs Muschinski to achieve a like result, that adjustment requires, at the least, that the parties be proportionately repaid their respective contributions to the extent allowed by the proceeds of any sale. It becomes necessary to consider their entitlement in equity to share in any surplus after the discharge of any debts incurred in their joint undertaking and the repayment to them of their respective contributions. As has been seen, the extent to which the relevant principle of equity operates to qualify legal entitlement is only that to which it positively appears that it would be unconscionable for one party to assert or retain the benefit of property contributed by the other party. There could well be circumstances in which equity and good conscience would require that the party who has made the major contribution to a failed joint endeavour should obtain a correspondingly greater share of any surplus remaining after repayment of the respective contributions. The conclusion which I have reached in all the circumstances of the present case is, however, that Mrs Muschinski has failed to establish that it would be unconscionable conduct on the part of Mr Dodds to assert and retain the one-half share in the residue of the proceeds of sale of the Picton property to which his legal entitlement and the consensual arrangement between them otherwise entitles him.

There remains the question whether there should be a declaration that the Picton property is held by the parties upon constructive trust. In my view, there should. That property was acquired, in pursuance of the consensual arrangement between the parties, to be held and developed in accordance with that arrangement. The contributions which each party is entitled to have repaid to her or him were made for, or in connexion with, its purchase or development. The collapse of the commercial venture and the failure of the personal relationship jointly combined to lead to a situation in which each party is entitled to insist upon realization of the asset, repayment of her or his contribution and distribution of any surplus. In these circumstances, the appropriate order to give effect to the rights and obligations of the parties is an order declaring that the Picton property is held by them upon constructive trust. Lest the legitimate claims of third parties be adversely affected, the constructive trust should be imposed only from the date of publication of reasons for judgment of this Court.

I would allow the appeal.

Comments

1. See Radan & Stewart at **28.7–28.10, 28.150–28.190**.
2. Deane J's approach was accepted by a majority of the High Court in *Baumgartner v Baumgartner* (1987) 164 CLR 137. In *West v Mead* [2003] NSWSC 161, Campbell J provided a detailed breakdown of the requirements of the *Muschinski/ Baumgartner* trust and listed three requirements:
   - There must be both a joint relationship or endeavour, where funds are spend towards a common benefit;
   - The joint relationship or endeavour must have come to an end 'without attributable blame'; and
   - There must be unconscionability/unconscientiousness — it must be unconscionable for the benefit of contributions provided by one party to be retained by the other.

Constructive trusts and stolen property

28.3   Black v S Freedman & Co (1910) 12 CLR 105

Court: High Court of Australia

Facts: John and Isabella Black were married. John began stealing large amounts from his employer. Some of the money was deposited in an account in his wife's name. When he realised that his thieving would soon be discovered he absconded, with stolen funds and some circular notes (an older form of traveller's cheque) which were in his wife's name. He was arrested with the money and notes in his possession.

Issue: The issue was whether a constructive trust could be employed to fasten onto the stolen funds and circular notes.

Decision: The High Court (Griffiths CJ, Barton and O'Connor JJ) found that a constructive trust could be placed over the bank account, stolen funds and circular notes. It made no difference as to whether the stolen property was real or personal property.

Extracts: In this extract from the decisions of Griffiths CJ and O'Connor J there is a discussion of when constructive trusts are imposed on stolen property.

Griffith CJ

[108] Taking all these transactions together, I have no doubt the whole amount claimed by his wife, consisting of the four sums I have mentioned, can be identified as part of the stolen money.

Then the question is whether it can be claimed from her. It is suggested that in following trust property there is a distinction between real and personal property which gets into the hands of a volunteer. But the rule appears to be the same with respect to all kinds of property. ... Dealing with this particular point, Sir George Jessel MR, in the case of *In re Hallett's Estate*,[33] said this, amongst other things:

> The modern doctrine of equity as regards property [109] disposed of by persons in a fiduciary position is a very clear and well established doctrine. You can, if the sale was rightful, take the proceeds of the sale, if you can identify them. If the sale was wrongful, you can still take the proceeds of the sale, in a sense adopting the sale for the purpose of taking the proceeds, if you can identify them.

He points out that you very often cannot identify the proceeds. In the present case I think they are sufficiently identified — I mean there is a sufficient prima facie case of identification in the absence of any explanation. Of course it is not sufficient if the money is taken by the other party bona fide for valuable consideration. There the money cannot be recovered back. But it has been laid down in cases decided long ago that if the

---

33.   (1880) 13 Ch D 696 at 708.

alienee is a volunteer the estate may be followed into his hands whether he had notice of the trust or not. In the present case, did the wife take the money as a volunteer? In my opinion the proper inference to be drawn from the evidence is that the husband — supposing there was no question of stealing — presented the money to his wife. He intended her, no doubt, to keep it, in one sense, and that it should go to her account at the Savings Bank, where it became under the local law her money for her separate use, but that is quite irrelevant to the question whether she took it as a volunteer or not. I think that where a man pays a large sum of money to his wife, and no more appears, the inference is that it is a present. Therefore the doctrine of equity is applicable. The money is identified; it came into her hands as a volunteer, and she is liable to repay it. It was pointed out by Sir George Jessel, in a well known case, that a man may at a certain stage be innocent, but that, if he knows that he has got the advantage of a fraud to which he was no party and says he will keep it, then he becomes himself a party to the fraud and is liable to the jurisdiction of the Court of Equity. In the present case the wife says she holds this money for her separate use and claims it for herself, knowing now, at any rate, the circumstances under which it came to be given to her. In those circumstances I am of opinion that there was a case made on the plaintiffs' evidence for the defendants to answer. They thought, not unnaturally on the whole, that it was better not to go into the witness box, and [110] they must take the consequences. In my opinion the learned Judge was quite right, and the appeal should be dismissed.

O'Connor J

[110] I agree. The only part of the case which really presented a question worthy of investigation is that which related to the right of the wife to retain these moneys. But there is no doubt about that on the facts ... Where money has been stolen, it is trust money in the hands of the thief, and he cannot divest it of that character. If he pays it over to another person, then it may be followed into that other person's hands. If, of course, that other person shows that it has come to him bona fide for valuable consideration, and without notice, it then may lose its character as trust money and cannot be recovered. But if it is handed over merely as a gift, it does not matter whether there is notice or not. The only question therefore is: what were the plaintiffs obliged to prove in this case? Were they obliged to prove affirmatively that the wife had received this money as a volunteer? I think they were. I think they were bound to give prima facie evidence of that. But the circumstances afford prima facie evidence of it. There is no evidence to rebut the prima facie case which is to be inferred from the facts, which is this: The husband was stealing money regularly; he wanted to have some place in which to put it away safely, and for that purpose he gave up the account which he had in the Savings Bank and put a small balance of about 17s into an account which a month or so before his wife had opened; then apparently regularly the proceeds of his crime were paid into this account. It is absurd to put payments made under those circumstances on the same footing as payments made by the thief to a stranger. In this case they were paid into the wife's account; the wife dealt with them and allowed her account to be used for the purpose of this [111] money being paid in, and there is no doubt that, when the catastrophe came at the end and he was obliged to go, she went with him to the bank, got the money out on her requisition as she was bound to do, and the circular notes were paid for out of that.

When the husband is afterwards charged with the ownership of those notes, he says they are his own money. The wife is asked afterwards about this claim of her husband's to the circular notes and she says nothing. Considering that these circular notes were bought out of money which purported to be her money, paid for by her and afterwards claimed by her, and that she was asked in reference to this claim, surely she was under a duty to say something. She says nothing, and that is evidence that is entitled to be considered. In all the circumstances, I am of opinion that there was a prima facie case, that she was a volunteer, and that this money retains its character as trust money and she cannot be allowed to keep it.

Comment

1. See Radan & Stewart at **28.129–28.139**.

Constructive trusts and the doctrine of knowing receipt

28.4   The Bell Group Ltd (in liq) v Westpac Banking Corporation (No 9) (2009) 70 ACSR 1

Court: Supreme Court of Western Australia

Facts: The Bell Group of companies was a large corporate conglomeration which primarily represented the interests of the late Robert Holmes A'Court. The stock market crashed in 1987 and the A'Court interests were sold to the Bond group. After discovering the poor financial state of the Bell Group a number of Australian banks requested that their securities be refinanced. The effect of the refinancing was to vastly improve the banks' security position to the detriment of other investors.

Later the Bond group failed and the Bell Group soon followed. Liquidators were appointed who claimed (amongst many things) that the directors had breached their fiduciary duties when agreeing to the financial restructure and that the banks had knowingly received property which they knew was being provided in breach of fiduciary duty. The rule against knowingly receiving trust property is known as the first limb of the rule in *Barnes v Addy* (1874) 9 Ch App 244.

Issue: The issue was whether the banks were subject to the rule in *Barnes v Addy* and whether they had breached the rule.

Decision: Owen J found that the banks were subject to the first limb of the rule in *Barnes v Addy* and had breached it. No formal orders were made but the parties were encouraged to negotiate a settlement in light of Owen J's findings.

Extracts: In this extract Owen J reviews the development of the rule in England and Australia and provides a summary of the modern elements of the rule. Owen J also decides that the rule could be applied outside of the trust context to other breaches of fiduciary duty.

Owen J

[287] I propose to start by going to *Barnes* [*v Addy*.[34]] The trustees of conventional trust funds had entered into a transaction that was in breach of trust and losses had accrued. The beneficiaries of the trust sued both the surviving trustee and the solicitors who had advised the trustees on the impugned transaction. The appeal concerned only the claim against the solicitors. The solicitors had no knowledge of, or reason to suspect, a dishonest design in the transaction and no funds had passed into their hands. The claim against them failed.

The issue in the case was, in essence, whether persons who were not themselves trustees should be made responsible as constructive trustees for the breaches of trust that were committed by trustees. Lord Selborne LC said:

> Now in this case we have to deal with certain persons who are trustees, and with certain other persons who are not trustees. That is a distinction to be borne in mind throughout the case. Those who create a trust clothe the trustee with a legal power and control over the trust property, imposing on him a corresponding responsibility. That responsibility may no doubt be extended in equity to others who are not properly trustees, if they are found either making themselves trustees *de son tort*, or actually participating in any fraudulent conduct of the trustee to the injury of the *cestui que trust*. But, on the other hand, strangers are not to be made constructive trustees merely because they act as the agents of trustees in transactions within their legal powers, transactions perhaps of which a court of Equity may disapprove, unless those agents receive and become chargeable with some part of the trust property, or unless they assist with knowledge in a dishonest and fraudulent design on the part of the trustees ... If those principles were disregarded, I know not how anyone could, in transactions admitting of doubt as to the view which a court of Equity might take of them, safely discharge the office of solicitor, of banker, or of agent of any sort to trustees. But, on the other hand, if persons dealing honestly as agents are at liberty to rely on the legal power of the trustees, and are not to have the character of trustees constructively imposed upon them, then the transactions of mankind can safely be carried through; and I apprehend those who create trusts do expressly intend in the absence of fraud and dishonesty, to exonerate such agents of all classes from the responsibilities which are expressly incumbent, by reason of the fiduciary relation, upon the trustees.[35]

[289] It is common to refer to Lord Selborne's dictum as containing two 'limbs'. First, his Lordship referred to an agent of the trustee who receives and becomes chargeable with some part of the trust property. This is concerned with the liability of a person as a recipient of trust property. Second, his Lordship referred to an agent of the trustee assisting with knowledge in a dishonest and fraudulent design on the part of the trustee. This limb is concerned with the liability of a person as an accessory to a trustee's breach of trust. It is now common to refer to the first limb by the shorthand phrase 'knowing receipt' or 'receipt liability' or 'recipient liability' and to the second limb as 'knowing participation' or 'knowing assistance'. The phrase 'accessory liability' is also used in *Barnes* cases and

---

34. (1874) LR 9 Ch App 244.
35. *Barnes v Addy* (1874) LR 9 Ch App 244 at 251–2.

commentary. It is most often applied to second limb situations but is sometimes used to describe third party liability under the rule generally.

The issue that has produced the most litigation as the *Barnes* principles have developed relates to the level and type of 'knowledge' that has to be established before a third party will be held liable. Doubts about that issue probably explain the tendency in modern cases and publications to describe the limbs by the phrases 'receipt liability' and 'accessory liability' rather than 'knowing receipt' and 'knowing participation'. That having been said, the latest pronouncement of the High Court (to which I will refer in some detail shortly) cautions against straying too far from the formulation of the second limb in *Barnes*.

Lord Selborne's formulation has come in for its share of criticism.[36] In *Royal Brunei Airlines Sdn Bhd v Tan*[37](*Royal Brunei*) Lord Nicholls referred to it as a 'straitjacket'[38] for the accessory liability principle. In delivering the opinion of the House his Lordship bemoaned the restrictions that had grown up in relation to one aspect of accessory liability. He said:

> What has gone wrong? Their Lordships venture to think that the reason is that, ever since the *Selangor* case[39] highlighted the potential uses of equitable remedies in connection with misapplied company funds, there has been a tendency to cite and interpret and apply Lord Selborne LC's formulation in *Barnes v Addy* ... as though it were a statute. This has particularly been so with the accessory limb of Lord Selborne LC's apothegm. This approach has been inimical to analysis of the underlying concept.[40]

These sentiments are consistent with the approach taken by equity over the past few decades, particularly as it has extended its reach into disputes that are essentially commercial in nature. The historical development of equity was (at least in part) a response to the perceived rigidity of common law principles. It was a means of tempering an injustice that had been brought about by strict adherence to a common law rule, whether substantive or procedural. Therein lay the seeds of a tension that was to last for centuries: how to balance the need for certainty of outcome (the perceived strength of the common law) with the need to provide a remedy where the justice of the case so dictated but where no remedy was otherwise available (the raison d'etre of equity).

[290] Equity has generally spoken in terms of remedies, maxims and principles rather than rules. It has always been concerned with substance rather than form. It is not surprising then that equity stems from underlying principles and so-called 'rules' are, in reality, no more than guidelines. In an extra-judicial publication, 'Equity's Role in the Twentieth Century',[41] Sir Anthony Mason said: 'equitable principles were shaped with a view to inhibiting unconscionable conduct and providing relief against it'. In the same

---

36. See, for example, M Bryan, 'Clearing Up After Breaches of Fiduciary Duty' (1995) 5 *Bond L Rev* 67 at 70 and 93.
37. [1995] 2 AC 378; [1995] 3 All ER 97 (*Royal Brunei*).
38. [1995] 2 AC 378 at 385; [1995] 3 All ER 97 at 102.
39. [1968] 2 All ER 1073; [1968] 1 WLR 1555.
40. [1995] 2 AC 378 at 386; [1995] 3 All ER 97 at 103.
41. Sir Anthony Mason (1997) 8 *King's College LJ* 1.

article he described the principles as incorporating 'broad standards which, in borderline cases at least, call for an exercise of value judgment'.

The so-called rules are not mandatory prescriptions to be applied rigidly. They are there to guide the proper application of accepted principles to the facts of an individual case. But the emphasis has always been on the identification and application of established principle. This approach is exemplified by the well-known dictum of Deane J in *Muschinski v Dodds*:

> [A constructive trust is not] a medium for the indulgence of idiosyncratic notions of fairness and justice. As an equitable remedy, it is available only when warranted by established equitable principles or by the legitimate processes of legal reasoning, by analogy, induction and deduction, from the starting point of a proper understanding of the conceptual foundation of such principles.[42]

Nonetheless, Lord Selborne's dichotomy is still generally accepted, certainly in Australia: see, for example, *Tableau Holdings Pty Ltd v Joyce*[43] and, more recently, *Farah Constructions [Pty Ltd v Say-Dee Pty Ltd]*.[44] It is important to see it as the starting point from which the juridical exercise proceeds.

The jurisprudence that has developed since *Barnes* was decided permits the following observations to be made concerning the liability of a third party. I do not think any of these points are contentious. First, the underlying principles apply in Australia.[45] Second, the reference to 'an agent' in Lord Selborne's apothegm (or is it apophthegm?) is not confined to agents in the strict sense. It can extend to third parties who have dealings with the trustee on their own behalf rather than as agent for the trustee.[46] The banking cases are a good example of a relationship operating in two spheres. In its dealings with a customer, a bank acts sometimes as an agent (for example, when it does no more than collect a cheque on behalf of the customer) and sometimes in its own right (for example, when it takes money from the customer to reduce an overdraft balance). Third, at least in relation to accessory liability, the principles that are applicable to trustees in the strict sense have been extended to other fiduciaries in some circumstances.[47] Fourth, the accessory liability principle can apply even though no trust property has passed to the third party.[48]

The arguments advanced in this case have raised issues as to the state of the law in a number of areas and, in the analysis that follows, I will concentrate on them. In this general discussion of the law I will revert to the word 'dishonesty' because it is shorter than the phrase 'conscious wrongdoing' and because it is the word most commonly occurring in the authorities. The contentious matters that I have identified include those that follow.

---

42. (1985) 160 CLR 583 at 615; 62 ALR 429 at 451; 11 Fam LR 930 at 950; [1985] HCA 78.
43. [1999] WASCA 49 at [31].
44. (2007) 230 CLR 89.
45. *Consul Developments Pty Ltd v DPC Estates Pty Ltd* (1974) 132 CLR 373 at 408; 5 ALR 231 at 260–1 (*Consul Developments*) per Stephen J.
46. See, for example, *Re Montagu's*.
47. *Consul Developments* (1974) 132 CLR 396–7; 5 ALR 250–1 per Gibbs J.
48. *Baden Delvaux v Societe Generale pour Favoriser le Developpement du Commerce et de l'Industrie en France SA* [1993] 1 WLR 509 at 572 (*Baden*).

[291] First, before a third party can be held liable, is it necessary to establish that the fiduciary was dishonest? Is it necessary to establish that the third party was dishonest? Second, what is entailed in the concept of 'knowledge' for 'knowing receipt' and 'knowing participation'? For example, must the knowledge be 'actual' or can it be 'constructive' and does the answer differ depending on whether the question is asked in relation to receipt liability or accessory liability? And where liability stems from involvement in a breach of trust or breach of a fiduciary duty, what must the stranger 'know'? Does there have to be knowledge of the precise breach? Third, in relation to receipt liability, must the third party have received 'trust property' (in the strict sense) before liability can be established?

There is a further question. Where a third party knowingly participates in a breach of duty by the fiduciary, can a claim be maintained against the third party where the claimant (a corporation) concedes that it also knowingly participated in the breach by the fiduciary (the directors) of duties owed to individual corporations? Because this question depends on the corporate group structure and the way the transaction documents were framed, I will deal with it in a later section in which the factual elements are discussed rather than in this section, which is devoted to an analysis of general legal principles.

Before I come to those specific questions I will examine the leading modern authorities in which the jurisprudence is outlined. In doing so I wish only to paint a broad picture of how the principles have developed. I will have to come back to a more detailed consideration of some of the authorities in relation to specific issues, particularly what is meant by a 'dishonest and fraudulent design' and what is entailed in the concept of 'knowing' about such a design.

21.2.2. *Barnes*: the modern authorities

21.2.2.1. The *Consul Developments* litigation[49]

A solicitor (Walton) owned and controlled a group of companies that was engaged in the purchase, renovation and resale of old houses. The companies, including the plaintiff company (DPC), employed a manager (Grey) whose duties included finding properties for DPC and other group companies. Walton employed a clerk (Clowes) in his legal practice. Clowes was managing director of his own property investment company (Consul) and decided that Consul should enter the same field as DPC. Grey told Clowes that certain properties were available but that neither DPC nor any other company in Walton's group of companies could afford to acquire them. Clowes had other information suggesting that Walton's companies were in financial difficulty. Clowes and Grey agreed that they would share equally in any profits and losses from the project. Consul then acquired the properties but Grey did not advise Walton.

DPC complained that Grey's conduct in arranging for the purchase by the defendant of the properties in circumstances in which he (Grey) could profit from the acquisition was a breach of the fiduciary duties Grey owed to DPC. At trial DPC sought a declaration that the properties were held on trust for it, as well as an account of profits earned by Consul as a result of the purchase and holding of those properties. As Consul (through Clowes) owed no fiduciary duties to Walton or to DPC, DPC pursued the claim under the *Barnes* principles. The claim was brought against both Grey and Consul. Grey did not defend the suit.

---

49. *Consul Developments* (1974) 132 CLR 373; 5 ALR 231.

[292] The trial judge dismissed the claims by DPC on the basis that it had no standing to prosecute because any duty of a fiduciary nature that may have been owed or breached by Grey was not owed to DPC. The appeal from that decision to the New South Wales Court of Appeal is reported as *DPC Estates Pty Ltd v Grey & Consul Developments Pty Ltd*[50] (*DPC Estates*). By a majority, the court reversed the decision of the trial judge. All members found that DPC had standing to claim breach of a fiduciary duty owed to it. Once the issue of standing had been resolved it was clear Grey had breached his fiduciary duty to the plaintiff. The remaining question was whether Consul was also accountable.

The court considered the level of knowledge required for the plaintiff to succeed against the third party. The plaintiff argued that constructive notice was sufficient, and that the circumstances put Clowes on enquiry. Although he may not have known of the breach of fiduciary duty, he ought to have known of it. Clowes' behaviour was said to show he had refrained from making appropriate enquiries. Jacobs P, who dissented, held that if Clowes had deliberately refrained from making enquiries, he would be infected with a guilty state of mind. However in Jacobs P's view, this was contrary to the finding of the trial judge: that Clowes had *not* deliberately refrained from making enquiries, and thus did not have the requisite knowledge. Hardie and Hutley JJA found that Clowes did have sufficient knowledge of Grey's fraudulent design to render Consul liable.

According to Jacobs P, the case failed to attract the doctrine of constructive notice, because there had been no receipt of trust property ... [H]is Honour observed of the *Barnes* principle:

> [A] distinction must be drawn between a person who receives trust property for his own benefit, as a volunteer or otherwise, and others who deal with a fiduciary, but do not actually receive trust property. In the latter case a person is not to be held responsible as a constructive trustee unless, even though no trust property passes into his hands, he is cognisant of a dishonest design on the part of the trustee.[51]

Jacobs P considered case authority including *Selangor United Rubber Estates Ltd v Cradock (No 2)*[52] and *Karak Rubber Co Ltd v Burden*[53] which suggested that actual *or* constructive notice could impose constructive trusteeship on a third party in a case of knowing assistance. His Honour ruled that Lord Selborne's dicta in *Barnes* could not be extended in this way. In his view, something more than constructive knowledge was required. There must be 'actual knowledge of the fraudulent or dishonest design, so that the person concerned can truly be described as a participant in that fraudulent or dishonest activity'. Actual knowledge could be acquired 'either through knowing or purposely refraining from finding out'.

Jacobs P distinguished the circumstances of the case from one where it is alleged that confidential information had come into the hands of a person and been put to use in

---

50. [1974] 1 NSWLR 443 (*DPC Estates*).
51. *Consul Developments* (1974) 132 CLR 373 at 457–458.
52. [1968] 1 All ER 567; [1968] 1 WLR 319.
53. (No 2) [1972] 1 All ER 1210; [1972] 1 WLR 602.

breach of its confidential nature. In such a case, the confidential information would itself be property. In that situation, it would be a case of knowing receipt and constructive notice would be sufficient. The plaintiffs had unsuccessfully applied to amend their pleadings to include such a claim in the appeal suit.

Hardie JA said that it was significant that Consul entered into a joint venture with the manager. This meant that Clowes and Grey were acting 'in concert to use for their respective profits the knowledge, information and [293] opportunities which [Consul] had acquired'.[54] Grey used Consul to implement his fraudulent scheme, and Consul was a participant in the scheme by reason of the knowledge and circumstances of its managing director, Clowes, who took advantage of his position as a clerk in Walton's employ to exploit opportunities which he knew belonged to the Walton's companies.

Hutley JA seemed to view the circumstances differently to Hardie JA, though he arrived at the same result; namely, that Clowes had sufficient knowledge of Grey's fraudulent and dishonest design to fall within Lord Selborne's principle.[55] His Honour's analysis of the findings of fact seemed to indicate that he thought Clowes had an idea that something was wrong with Grey's behaviour, rather than actual knowledge of the breach. However, Hutley JA concluded that Clowes, knowing that Grey had obligations to DPC, had been put on enquiry to seek out information concerning the nature of the obligations. Clowes was therefore, '[to] be regarded as a party to an arrangement which he knew was wrong and was calculated to encourage Grey to proceed with his plan to profit personally from his position of trust'.[56]

In *Consul Developments* the High Court dealt with the resulting appeal. By a majority (Barwick CJ, Gibbs and Stephen JJ, McTiernan J dissenting), Consul's appeal was allowed and the decision of the trial judge was reinstated.

Gibbs J reviewed the case law relating to the knowledge requirements. His Honour indicated that the decisions in *Selangor* and *Karak Rubber Co* could not resolve this case, because no trust property was received by Consul. The plaintiffs had argued that the information that Grey had concerning the subject properties was confidential information in which DPC had a relevant interest. That argument was rejected. Gibbs J looked at the purpose underpinning the rules about conflict of interest and knowing participation. He noted two alternative purposes, both leading him to conclude that a knowing assistant should be made to account for profits resulting from a breach in which he or she participated.

First, the conflict rule operated as a deterrent, to discourage people in a position of confidence from being swayed by interest rather than duty. Other persons should similarly be deterred from knowingly assisting in a violation of that duty. Second, it was contrary to equitable principle to allow a person to retain a benefit that he or she had gained from a breach of fiduciary duty. On the same principle it was unacceptable to allow other persons who knowingly took part in the breach to benefit from it.

In Gibbs J's view, following *Selangor*, the meaning of 'dishonest and fraudulent' was to be understood by reference to equitable principles and encompassed a breach of trust or a breach of fiduciary duty. While Gibbs J assumed that *Selangor* was correct (without finally

---

54. *DPC Estates* [1974] 1 NSWLR 443 at 462.
55. See, for example, *DPC Estates* [1974] 1 NSWLR 443 at 470.
56. *DPC Estates* [1974] 1 NSWLR 443 at 469.

deciding the point), it seems that he viewed the test as being neither wholly objective nor wholly subjective. His Honour said:

> It may be that it is going too far to say that a stranger will be liable if the circumstances would have put an honest and reasonable man on inquiry, when the stranger's failure to inquire has been innocent and he has not wilfully shut his eyes to the obvious. On the other hand, it does not seem to me to be necessary to prove that a stranger who participated in a breach of trust or fiduciary duty with knowledge of all the circumstances did so actually knowing that what he was doing was improper. It would not be just that a person who had full knowledge of all the facts could escape liability [294] because his own moral obtuseness prevented him from recognizing an impropriety that would have been apparent to an ordinary man.[57]

Had it been proved that Clowes knew, or that an honest and reasonable person with knowledge of the facts known to Clowes would have known, that Grey was breaching his duties in arranging for Consul to buy the properties, Consul would have been held accountable. However, on the findings of fact made by the trial judge, Clowes believed that Grey was not acting in breach of his fiduciary duty in participating in the purchase. Clowes did not 'actually' know, or have reason to believe, that Grey was in breach of his duty, and in the circumstances an honest and reasonable man would not have thought it necessary to enquire further. It was not shown that Clowes was attempting to persuade Grey to act contrary to his duty. The plaintiffs therefore failed to establish that Consul had knowledge in the wide sense accepted by *Selangor*.

Stephen J (with whom Barwick CJ agreed) looked at the trial judge's reasons at length. His Honour considered whether the findings supported a conclusion of actual knowledge, in particular whether Clowes' concealment of the purchase, and whether his feeling that it was 'somehow wrong' for Clowes and Grey to collude in commercial ventures similar to those undertaken by Walton, was evidence that Clowes had actual knowledge. Stephen J concluded that they did not: the requisite knowledge had to relate specifically to a breach of fiduciary duty. His Honour said:

> This further reason is, then, the only evidence from which the plaintiff could hope to show that Clowes had actual knowledge of Grey's breach of duty. To my mind it shows no such thing; the sense of wrongdoing [if] attributed to Clowes is quite unrelated to an awareness that Grey's scheme involved breach of fiduciary duty.[58]

Stephen J considered that the plaintiff had also failed to establish that Clowes had wilfully shut his eyes to the truth. Clowes' failure to make enquiries of Walton was due to reasons other than a suspicion of Grey's fraud. Clowes thought that Walton did not want to purchase the properties and he had reason to believe that Walton could not afford the properties in any event.

Having reviewed the authorities, Stephen J noted the difficulty in reconciling the English authorities. In *Carl Zeiss Stiftung v Herbert Smith & Co [No 2]*[59] it had been held that

---

57. *Consul Developments* (1974) 132 CLR 373 at 398.
58. *Consul Developments* (1974) 132 CLR 373 at 407.
59. [1969] 2 Ch 276.

constructive notice would only render the assistant a constructive trustee if trust property had been received. But this seemed contrary to the conclusions reached in *Selangor* and *Karak Rubber Co*. Stephen J was critical of the development in those cases, which he considered:

> [C]ontain[ed] statements of principle certainly not expressed as confining constructive notice to cases in which the defendant has received trust property but which instead speak of it as sufficing to establish knowledge, where knowledge is necessary 'to hold a stranger liable as constructive trustee in a dishonest and fraudulent design' (*Selangor*).[60]

His Honour noted that, in both cases, trust property had passed through the defendants' hands and where the plaintiff succeeded it was because the defendant had been shown to have actual knowledge of the relevant breach. In Stephen J's view, the line of authorities before *Selangor* did not support the notion that, in cases where there had been no receipt of trust property, constructive notice of breach could impose a constructive trust on a defendant. It seems that Stephen J was not prepared to extend the doctrine of constructive **[295]** notice any further in cases of accessory liability.[61] In the case before the High Court, Consul had not received any trust property and could not be held to account for the purchased properties. Stephen J expressed his conclusion on the knowledge question in these terms:

> In my view the state of the authorities as they existed before *Selangor* did not go so far, at least in cases where the defendant had neither received nor dealt in property impressed with any trust, as to apply to them that species of constructive notice which serves to expose a party to liability because of negligence in failing to make inquiry. If a defendant knows of facts which themselves would, to a reasonable man, tell of fraud or breach of trust the case may well be different, as it clearly will be if the defendant has consciously refrained from enquiry for fear lest he learn of fraud. But to go further is, I think, to disregard equity's concern for the state of conscience of the defendant.[62]

…

21.2.2.2. Recent developments in the English courts

Two recent decisions from the highest levels of authority in the English courts seem to reflect a shift away from the ascertainment of facts known by the third party (that is, 'knowledge') to an enquiry about whether the third party acted dishonestly.

In 1995, in *Royal Brunei*, the Privy Council dealt with a specific aspect of the accessory liability principle, namely, the requirement that there must be a 'dishonest and fraudulent design on the part of the trustees'.

In *Royal Brunei*, a company had acted as the agent of the plaintiff airline in respect of the sale of passenger and cargo transportation. The defendant was the managing director and principal shareholder of the company. The company was required to hold the proceeds of sales on trust for the airline, until the moneys were paid over. The money

---

60. *Consul Developments* (1974) 132 CLR 373 at 411.
61. *Consul Developments* (1974) 132 CLR 373 at 413.
62. *Consul Developments* (1974) 132 CLR 373 at 412.

was instead paid into a separate account and used for the company's own purposes, with the knowledge and participation of the defendant. The company became insolvent and the airline sought to recover from the defendant personally. It could not be shown that the company's breach of trust was dishonest.

The trial judge found for the airline but the Court of Appeal of Brunei Darussalam allowed the appeal on that basis that:

> As long standing and high authority shows, conduct which may amount to a breach of trust, however morally reprehensible, will not render a person who has knowingly assisted in the breach of trust liable as a constructive trustee if that conduct falls short of dishonesty.[63]

[296] The 'long standing and high authority' included, most notably, *Belmont Finance Corporation Ltd v Williams Furniture Ltd (No 1)*,[64] where Goff LJ cautioned against departing from the 'safe path of the principle as stated by Lord Selborne LC to the uncharted sea of something not innocent ... but still short of dishonesty'.[65]

The Privy Council differed from the Court of Appeal and, as the passage that I have set out earlier in this section demonstrates, approached the problem not as if Lord Selborne's had prescribed an all-encompassing rule, but by bearing in mind the principles that underpin the liability in equity of strangers to a trust. This is aptly illustrated by Lord Nicholls' example, *Royal Brunei*:

> Take a case where a dishonest solicitor persuades a trustee to apply trust property in a way the trustee honestly believes is permissible but which the solicitor knows full well is a clear breach of trust ... It cannot be right that in such a case the accessory liability principle would be inapplicable because of the innocence of the trustee ... Indeed, if anything, the case for liability of the dishonest third party seems stronger where the trustee is innocent, because in such a case the third party alone was dishonest and that was the cause of the subsequent misapplication of the trust property.[66]

Lord Nicholls went on to note that the position would be the same if, instead of procuring the breach, the third party dishonestly assisted in the breach. The example his Lordship gave is where the trustee himself proposed to deal with the trust property in good faith, but in a manner which the solicitor knew to be a breach of trust.

The Privy Council concluded that the liability of the third party should not depend on the state of mind of another, namely, the trustee. It was held that dishonesty was a necessary element of accessory liability, but it was dishonesty on the part of the accessory, not the trustee, that was essential to such a claim.

Their Lordships also remarked on the meaning of 'dishonesty' in the context of the accessory's state of mind. It was held to be an objective standard, that is, 'not acting as an honest person would in the circumstances'.[67]

---

63. [1995] 2 AC 378 at 383–4; [1995] 3 All ER 97 at 101.
64. [1979] Ch 250; [1979] 1 All ER 118.
65. [1979] Ch 250 at 274; [1979] 1 All ER 118 at 135.
66. [1995] 2 AC 378 at 384; [1995] 3 All ER 97 at 101.
67. *Royal Brunei* [1995] 2 AC 378 at 389; [1995] All ER 97 at 105.

The House of Lords had occasion to consider some aspects of the *Barnes* principles and the *Royal Brunei* case in *Twinsectra Ltd v Yardley*.[68] A solicitor (Leach) was acting for Yardley to negotiate a loan of £1m from Twinsectra Ltd Leach did not deal directly with Twinsectra. Another firm of solicitors (Sims) represented themselves to Twinsectra as acting on Yardley's behalf. Sims received the loan money having undertaken that the money would only be applied to the purchase of property by Yardley. Contrary to the undertaking and following assurances by Yardley, Sims turned the money over to Leach. Leach did not ensure that the money was used solely for the acquisition of property and £357,720 was used for other purposes.

The loan was not repaid. Twinsectra sued Yardley, Sims and Leach. The claim against Leach was for the £357,720 that was used for purposes other than buying property. Twinsectra argued that the payment by Sims to Leach was a breach of trust; Leach was therefore said to be liable for dishonestly assisting in the breach of trust in accordance with *Royal Brunei*. The case led to consideration of the standards of honesty and knowledge required to establish accessory liability under the second limb of *Barnes*.

[297] The trial judge held that there was no trust, because the terms of the undertaking were too vague, and Twinsectra did not intend to create a trust. The trial judge also held that Leach, in receiving the money and paying it to Yardley without concerning himself about its application, had been misguided but not dishonest. He had shut his eyes to some problems, but thought he held the money for Yardley without restriction. The Court of Appeal reversed this finding and held that Leach had been dishonest. The Court of Appeal justified overturning the trial judge's decision on dishonesty because the trial judge had only considered conscious dishonesty and not 'Nelsonian blindness', which they said was relevant in the circumstances of the case.

The House of Lords agreed with the Court of Appeal in the conclusion that there was a trust. Though unusual, it was not void for uncertainty. The undertaking given by Sims meant that the money was not to be at Yardley's free disposal; it was for the sole purpose of acquiring property. Sims was only to turn the money over to enable the acquisition of property. This meant that while the money was in Sims' client account, it remained Twinsectra's money until it was applied for the acquisition of property in accordance with the undertaking.

The question for the House of Lords was whether Leach, in receiving the money and paying it to Yardley without concerning himself about its application, could be said to have acted dishonestly. Leach had testified that, in paying out the money, he was simply acting in accordance with his client's instructions. This was inconsistent with the pleaded defence that was to the effect that Leach believed the money would be used for the purpose set out in the undertaking.

The House of Lords found that Leach had been aware of all of the facts and therefore could not be said to have been dishonest by deliberately failing to make enquiries for fear of finding out something he did not want to know. On that basis, the Court of Appeal should not have overturned the trial judge's finding concerning dishonesty and should not have substituted its own finding.

Lord Millett opined that accessory liability did not depend on dishonesty in the normal sense: it was sufficient that Leach knew all the facts that made it wrongful for him to participate in the way in which he did. Lord Hoffmann disagreed, seeing this view as

---

68. [2002] 2 AC 164; [2002] 2 All ER 377; [2002] UKHL 12 (*Twinsectra*).

a departure from *Royal Brunei*. On his Lordship's analysis of *Royal Brunei*, for the conduct to be wrongful, more than mere knowledge of the facts is required. There must be 'a dishonest state of mind ... consciousness that one is transgressing ordinary standards of honest behaviour'.[69] Here, there were no relevant facts of which Leach could be unaware: Leach believed that the money was at Yardley's disposal. If this was Leach's honest belief, he had not been dishonest.

Lord Hoffmann qualified the scope of his statement, noting that a person might dishonestly assist in the commission of a breach of trust without a full appreciation of the legal meaning of the arrangement. A relevantly dishonest state of mind might result if the defendant knew that he was helping to deal with money to which the recipient was not entitled. But that was not the instant case.

Lord Hutton considered the standard that should be applied to determine whether a person has acted dishonestly. In his Lordship's opinion, there were three possible standards:

- purely subjective: the person is only regarded as dishonest if he or she transgresses his or her own standard of honesty, even if that standard is contrary to that of reasonable and honest people; **[298]**
- purely objective: if the person's conduct is dishonest by the ordinary standards of reasonable and honest people, even if he or she does not realise it, he or she is judged as dishonest; or
- combined standard: to establish dishonesty, the defendant's conduct must be dishonest by the ordinary standards of reasonable and honest people, and he himself or she herself must also realise that by those standards his or her conduct was dishonest.

Having noted that the courts have rejected the 'purely subjective' standard, Lord Hutton differed from Lord Millett's interpretation of what Lord Nicholls had said in *Royal Brunei*. Lord Millett, it is to be remembered, found that liability depended on knowledge rather than dishonesty. In Lord Hutton's analysis of *Royal Brunei*,[70] it was a statement of general principle that 'dishonesty is a necessary ingredient of accessory liability and knowledge is not an appropriate test'. Lord Hutton opined that an objective standard should be added, and the 'combined' test should be characterised thus:

[36] [D]ishonesty requires knowledge by the defendant that what he was doing would be regarded as dishonest by honest people, although he should not escape a finding of dishonesty because he sets his own standards of honesty and does not regard as dishonest what he knows would offend the normally accepted standards of honest conduct.[71]

Lord Millett, in his dissent on the question of whether Leach's conduct had been dishonest, said that liability for knowing receipt is restitutionary and based on the receipt itself rather than fault. His Lordship then contrasted this position with the doctrine of knowing assistance. He advocated an approach where the condition of liability is intentional wrongdoing, and not conscious dishonesty. Thus, according to Lord Millett:[72]

---

69. *Twinsectra* [2002] 2 AC 164 at [20].
70. *Twinsectra* [2002] 2 AC 164 at [31]–[32].
71. *Twinsectra* [2002] 2 AC 164 at [36].
72. *Twinsectra* [2002] 2 AC 164 at [105], [107] and [107].

[105] There is no basis for requiring actual knowledge of the breach of trust, let alone dishonesty, as a condition of [recipient] liability. Constructive notice is sufficient and may not even be necessary. There is powerful academic support for the proposition that the liability of the recipient is the same as in other cases of restitution, that is to say strict but subject to a change of position defence.

...

[107] The accessory's liability for having assisted in a breach of trust is quite different. It is fault-based, not receipt-based. The defendant is not charged with having received trust moneys for his own benefit, but with having acted as an accessory to a breach of trust. The action is not restitutionary; the claimant seeks compensation for wrongdoing. The cause of action is concerned with attributing liability for misdirected funds. Liability is not restricted to the person whose breach of trust or fiduciary duty caused their original diversion. His liability is strict. Nor is it limited to those who assist him in the original breach. It extends to everyone who consciously assists in the continuing diversion of the money.

Lord Millett then summarised the position of knowing assistance in the English courts leading up to *Royal Brunei* and thereafter:

[110] Prior to the decision in *Royal Brunei Airlines Sdn Bhd v Tan* the equitable claim was described as 'knowing assistance'. It gave a remedy against third parties who knowingly assisted in the misdirection of funds. The accessory was liable if he knew all the relevant facts, in particular the fact that the principal was not entitled to deal with the funds entrusted to him as he had done or was proposing to do. Unfortunately, the **[299]** distinction between this form of fault-based liability and the liability to make restitution for trust money received in breach of trust was not always observed, and it was even suggested from time to time that the requirements of liability should be the same in the two cases ...

[111] Behind the confusion there lay a critical issue: whether negligence alone was sufficient to impose liability on the accessory. If so then it was unnecessary to show that he possessed actual knowledge of the relevant facts. Despite a divergence of judicial opinion, by 1995 the tide was flowing strongly in favour of rejecting negligence. It was widely thought that the accessory should be liable only if he actually knew the relevant facts. It should not be sufficient that he ought to have known them or had the means of knowledge if he did not in fact know them.

[112] There was a gloss on this. It is dishonest for a man deliberately to shut his eyes to facts which he would prefer not to know. If he does so, he is taken to have actual knowledge of the facts to which he shut his eyes.[73]

It seems that Lord Millett, also, considered the applicable standard of 'dishonesty' to contain both subjective and objective elements, but leaned towards the objective approach. He considered the question that the House had to answer was not whether Lord Nicholls in *Royal Brunei* was using the word 'dishonesty' in a subjective or objective sense,

---

73. *Twinsectra* [2002] 2 AC 164 at [110]–[112].

but rather whether the plaintiff must establish that an accessory had a dishonest state of mind. In Lord Millett's opinion, while subjective elements of tests previously applied by the courts related to the defendant's knowledge, experience and attributes, these factors could only be interpreted in light of the standard of honesty and the recognition of wrongdoing. His Lordship said:

> [122] The [question is whether an honest person would] appreciate that what he was doing was wrong or improper, not whether the defendant himself actually appreciated this ... Neither an honest motive nor an innocent state of mind will save a defendant whose conduct is objectively dishonest ... equity looks to man's conduct, not to his state of mind.[74]

As to the knowledge required to establish accessory liability, Lord Millett considered that it was sufficient that the defendant knew that the money was not at the free disposal of the principal, or that he knew that he was assisting in a dishonest scheme. He characterised the relationship between the breaching principal and the accessory in this way:

> [137] The gravamen of the charge against the principal is not that he has broken his word, but that having been entrusted with the control of a fund with limited powers of disposal he has betrayed the confidence placed in him by disposing of the money in an unauthorised manner. The gravamen of the charge against the accessory is not that he is handling stolen property, but that he is assisting a person who has been entrusted with the control of a fund to dispose of the fund in an unauthorised manner. He should be liable if he knows of the arrangements by which that person obtained control of the money and that his authority to deal with the money was limited, and participates in dealing with the money in a manner which he knows is unauthorised.[75]

In the result, Lord Millett found it unnecessary to consider whether Leach realised that honest people would regard his conduct as dishonest. His knowledge that he was assisting Sims to default in the latter's undertaking to Twinsectra was sufficient to establish accessory liability.

I have spent some time discussing Lord Millett's dissenting opinion in *Twinsectra* because some commentators have suggested it is closer to the Australian position as disclosed in *Consul Developments*.[76]

[300] The Privy Council returned to these issues in *Barlow Clowes International Ltd (in liq) v Eurotrust International Ltd*[77] (*Barlow*). In that case a submission had been made (citing what Lord Hutton had said in *Twinsectra*) that the requisite state of mind for accessory liability was conscious dishonesty; namely, that the person concerned must be aware that the conduct would, by ordinary standards, be regarded as dishonest. At trial, the judge had found that by normal standards the defendant had been dishonest but that his own standard was different and that this, it was submitted, was not enough to ground accessory liability. The Privy Council said:

---

74. *Twinsectra* [2002] 2 AC 164 at [122].
75. *Twinsectra* [2002] 2 AC 164 at [137].
76. See, for example, P M McDermott, 'The Twinsectra Case (Knowing Assistance; Quistclose)' (2003) 77 *Australian Law Journal* 290 at 291.
77. [2006] 1 All ER 333; [2006] UKPC 37 (*Barlow*).

[15] Their Lordships accept that there is an element of ambiguity in these remarks which may have encouraged a belief, expressed in some academic writing, that the *Twinsectra* case had departed from the law as previously understood and invited inquiry not merely into the defendant's mental state about the nature of the transaction in which he was participating but also into his views about generally acceptable standards of honesty. But they do not consider that this is what Lord Hutton meant. The reference to 'what he knows would offend normally accepted standards of honest conduct' meant only that his knowledge of the transaction had to be such as to render his participation contrary to normally acceptable standards of honest conduct. It did not require that he should have had reflections about what those normally acceptable standards were.

[16] Similarly in the speech of Lord Hoffmann, the statement[78] that a dishonest state of mind meant 'consciousness that one is transgressing ordinary standards of honest behaviour' was in their Lordships' view intended to require consciousness of those elements of the transaction which make participation transgress ordinary standards of honest behaviour. It did not also require him to have thought about what those standards were.[79]

At [17] their Lordships dealt with the facts of *Twinsectra*. The defendant, a solicitor, had received on behalf of his client a payment from another solicitor whom he knew had given an undertaking to pay it to the client only for a particular use. The defendant believed that the undertaking did not apply to him and that he held the money unconditionally. That being so, he was bound to pay it upon his client's instructions without restriction on its use. The defendant was acquitted of dishonesty.

Neither the trial judge nor the House had undertaken any enquiry into the views of the defendant about ordinary standards of honest behaviour. The defendant had taken a particular view of the law and had acted in accordance with that view. The majority in the House of Lords considered that a solicitor who held this view of the law, even though he knew all the facts, was not by normal standards dishonest. Having thus explained *Twinsectra*, their Lordships continued:

[18] Their Lordships therefore reject [the] submission that the judge failed to apply the principles of liability for dishonest assistance which had been laid down in the *Twinsectra* case. In their opinion they were no different from the principles stated in *Royal Brunei Airlines Sdn Bhd v Tan* ... which were correctly summarised by the judge.[80]

21.2.2.3. The Australian position following *Royal Brunei*

There are some Australian decisions in the years after 1995 in which Lord Nicholls' formulation in *Royal Brunei* has been adopted: see, for example, *News Ltd v Australian Rugby Football League Ltd*[81] (reversed on appeal but on the basis that there had been no breach of a relevant fiduciary duty); *Pascoe Ltd (in liq) v Lucas*[82] **[301]** (interestingly, a case involving some of the companies in the BCHL and JNTH groups); *Beach Petroleum*

---

78. *Twinsectra* [2002] 2 AC 164 at [20].
79. *Barlow* [2006] 1 All ER 333 at [15]–[16].
80. *Barlow* [2006] 1 All ER 333 at [18].
81. (1996) 58 FCR 447 at 546–7; 135 ALR 33 at 125–6.
82. (1999) 75 SASR 246; 33 ACSR 357; [1999] SASC 519 at [243].

NL v Abbott Tout Russell Kennedy.[83] Some judicial officers and academic commentators have expressed the view that there is little difference in the approaches contained in *Consul Developments* and *Royal Brunei.*[84] But in *Farah Constructions*[85] (which I will come to shortly), the High Court classified the suggestion discounting any difference between the traditional approach (that is, the approach in *Consul Developments*) and that adopted in *Royal Brunei* as 'not soundly based'.

In other Australian authorities, the judicial officers concerned have cautioned against moving away from what was said in *Consul Developments.*[86] In *NCR Australia Pty Ltd v Credit Connection Pty Ltd (in liq)*[87] (*NCR Australia*) Austin J, in relation to accessory liability, was referred to 'a substantial number of authorities' including *Royal Brunei.* However, his Honour said that the current Australian law was to be found in *Consul Developments* and that it he would be guided by the judgments in that case.

Austin J discussed the majority judgments in *Consul Developments* at some length. He referred to the passage in the reasons of Stephen J[88] to the effect that the plaintiff had not only failed to establish actual knowledge against the relevant defendant, but had also failed to establish that the defendant wilfully shut his eyes to the truth for fear that he should learn of the fiduciary's dishonesty. Both actual knowledge and calculated 'abstention from enquiry' were missing. As Austin J pointed out, Stephen J:

(a) rejected the view that liability for knowing assistance would arise in cases of 'that species of constructive notice which serves to expose a party to liability because of negligence in failing to make inquiry'; and

(b) said that it would be different if 'the defendant has consciously refrained from inquiry for fear lest he learn of fraud'; but

(c) cautioned that, to go further would be to disregard equity's concern for the state of conscience of the defendant.

Austin J also noted the observation of Stephen J[89] that the defendant was in a situation in which a reasonable and honest man would not have had knowledge of circumstances telling of a breach of duty. That, he said, was the furthest extent to which any possible doctrine of constructive notice may go in such a case. His Honour also referred to the passage from the reasons of Gibbs J[90] that I have set out in section 21.2.2.1. Against the background of those observations concerning *Consul Developments*, Austin J said, *NCR Australia* at [168]–[169]:

[168] What seems to emerge from these observations is that liability arises where the defendant has assisted in the trustee's dishonest and fraudulent design and:

---

83. (1999) 48 NSWLR 1; 33 ACSR 1; [1999] NSWCA 408 at [403] –[417].

84. See, for example, *Sixty-Fourth Throne Pty Ltd v Macquarie Bank Ltd* (1996) 130 FLR 411 at 477; H A J Ford & W A Lee, *Principles of the Law of Trusts*, Looseleaf edition, LawBook Company, Sydney, 1996+, [22690].

85. *Farah Constructions* (2007) 230 CLR 89 at [164].

86. See, for example, *Cadwallader v Bajco Pty Ltd* [2002] NSWCA 328 at [199] per Heydon JA.

87. [2004] NSWCA 1 (*NCR Australia*).

88. *Consul Developments* (1974) 132 CLR 373 at 407–408; 5 ALR 231 at 260–1.

89. *Consul Developments* (1974) 132 CLR 373 at 413.

90. *Consul Developments* (1974) 132 CLR 373 at 398.

(a) has actual knowledge of the dishonest and fraudulent design; or

(b) has deliberately shut his or her eyes to such a design; or

(c) has abstained in a calculated way from making such inquiries as an honest and reasonable person would make, where such inquiries would have led to discovery of the dishonest and fraudulent design; or **[302]**

(d) has actual knowledge of facts which to a reasonable person would suggest a dishonest and fraudulent design.

[169] But there is no liability if the defendant merely knows facts that would have been investigated by a reasonable person acting diligently, thereby discovering the truth, where the defendant has innocently but carelessly failed to make the appropriate investigations.[91]

Many of the cases involving recipient liability concern real property. This often brings into question the concept of indefeasibility of title under the Torrens system. In relation to issues such as dishonesty, this requires that attention be given to the fraud exception in statutory provisions such as s 68 of the *Transfer of Land Act 1893 (WA)*.[92] The indefeasibility principles were not called in aid in this case. I mention this because some of the Transactions were registered mortgages of Torrens system land.

A leading authority concerning recipient liability is *Koorootang Nominees Pty Ltd v Australia and New Zealand Banking Group Ltd*[93] *(Koorootang)*. The plaintiff was a trustee company and the second defendant, Jeffries, was its managing director. Jeffries' own businesses were in financial difficulties and owed money to ANZ. Jeffries informed ANZ that the plaintiff was the trustee of a non-active trust and consequently security was taken over the trust property. But the bank had notice that this was not correct; the plaintiff was the trustee of merged family estates and held the property on trust for the beneficiaries. Hansen J found that the banks had actual knowledge that the property was trust property and were wilfully blind to the question whether the trust property had been misapplied (which therefore also constituted actual knowledge).

But his Honour nevertheless undertook a lengthy and detailed analysis of the conflicting English and Australian case law on the question whether constructive knowledge on the part of the recipient would suffice to establish liability under the first limb of *Barnes*. His Honour's conclusions were, I think, shaped by his view that recipient liability is predicated on the notion of restitution. For this reason he concluded that there is a fundamental distinction between accessory liability and recipient liability. His Honour said:

the former being a claim that a third party acted as an accessory to a principal wrongdoer and thereby committed a wrong himself, the latter being a restitution-based claim that the defendant has been unjustly enriched at the expense of a trust beneficiary.[94]

---

91. *NCR Australia* [2004] NSWCA 1 at [168–169].
92. See, for example, *Macquarie Bank Ltd v Sixty-Fourth Throne Pty Ltd* [1998] 3 VR 133 *(Macquarie)*; *LHK Nominees Pty Ltd v Kenworthy* (2002) WAR 517; [2002] WASCA 291; *Tara Shire Council v Garner* [2003] 1 Qd R 556; [2002] QCA 232 *(Tara Shire)*.
93. [1998] 3 VR 16 *(Koorootang)*.
94. *Koorootang* [1998] 3 VR 16 at 105.

Therefore, given that the first limb is a doctrine designed to restore misapplied trust property, it was not necessary to establish dishonesty or a want of probity. It was sufficient for a plaintiff to establish that the defendant, at the time of receipt, had the requisite knowledge that the relevant property was (a) trust property and (b) that it had been misapplied. The requisite knowledge was taken to include any of the first four categories as expressed in *Baden Delvaux v Societe Generale pour Favoriser le Developpement du Commerce et de l'Industrie en France SA*[95] *(Baden)*.

Hansen J also expressed a tentative view that, on the presumption that recipient liability is restitutionary-based, liability should be strict, subject only to defences of bona fide purchase and change of position. But since the parties had not argued the case in that manner, he declined to rule on that basis. **[303]**

21.2.2.4. The *Farah Constructions* litigation

This brings me to the most recent pronouncements by the High Court about the *Barnes* principles, namely *Farah Constructions*.

Mr Farah Elias was involved in real estate developments and controlled several defendant companies, including Farah Constructions Pty Ltd. Farah Constructions and Say-Dee entered into a joint venture agreement where they were to acquire a nominated property. They planned to refurbish some units and rent them, while they sought redevelopment approval from the local council. Say-Dee was to contribute a majority of the funds; Mr Elias was (among other things) responsible for managing the progress of the development application as well as the ultimate construction and sale of the development. Upon completion of the joint venture, the profits were to be distributed equally between Say-Dee and Farah Constructions.

The council declined to approve the redevelopment on the basis that the land area was too small, but indicated that it might be inclined to support a redevelopment if neighbouring properties were amalgamated. Mr Elias used this knowledge to acquire some of the neighbouring properties through another company controlled by him, through his wife and two daughters. There was an issue about whether Mr Elias had disclosed to Say-Dee the knowledge he had received from the council, as well as whether the subsequent acquisitions of the neighbouring properties had been disclosed.

A *Barnes* claim was made against Mrs Elias and her daughters. The only knowledge imputed to them was the fact that Mr Elias acted as their agent and thus they were taken to be fixed with his knowledge. The claim against them was dependent on there being a breach of fiduciary duty by Mr Elias. It was common ground that Mr Elias owed fiduciary duties to Say-Dee, but it was disputed whether the scope of these duties covered the acts in question. Another contentious issue was whether there had been adequate disclosure by Mr Elias.

The trial judge found for the defendants on both these threshold issues, and so did not go on to consider the *Barnes* claim. In *Say-Dee Pty Ltd v Farah Constructions Pty Ltd*[96] the New South Wales Court of Appeal ruled that there had been a breach of fiduciary duty, and also found Mrs Elias and her daughters liable as recipients of trust property, using a traditional approach to the first limb of *Barnes*. It was held that the constructive

---

95. [1993] 1 WLR 509 *(Baden)*.
96. [2005] NSWCA 309.

knowledge imputed to Mrs Elias and her daughters was sufficient to satisfy the knowledge test under this limb, despite the fact that the recipients were 'innocent' or at least not dishonest.

Tobias JA, with whom Mason P and Giles JA agreed, also endorsed what he described as an 'alternate' basis for relief under a 'restitutionary approach' to the first limb of *Barnes*, following the view to which Hansen J had inclined in *Koorootang*. The court held that the respondents (Mr Elias and others) were strictly liable and the knowledge (actual or otherwise) of the recipient was irrelevant. A plaintiff need only prove that there was an enrichment of the defendant at the expense of the plaintiff such that it was unjust to retain the trust property (subject of course to the exception where there had been a bona fide purchase in good faith or where a person had changed their position as a result).

In a joint judgment the High Court allowed the appeal and restored the trial judge's original orders. The claim under the first limb of *Barnes* failed because there was no receipt of property, no agency and insufficient notice or knowledge to give rise to recipient liability.

[304] The High Court noted in *Farah Constructions*[97] that in recent times it has been assumed, 'but rarely if at all decided', that the first limb applies not only to persons dealing with trustees, but also to persons dealing with other types of fiduciaries:

> For example, in *DPC Estates Pty Ltd v Grey and Consul Development Pty Ltd*,[98] Jacobs P assumed that if property were received by a stranger from a fiduciary in breach of fiduciary duty, the first limb applied. See also *El Ajou v Dollar Land Holdings plc*[99] per Hoffmann LJ.[100]

The High Court declined to proffer any further views on this issue, since the case was conducted on a mutual assumption that the first limb applied in the circumstances.

In relation to recipient liability, the traditional formulation, as I understand it to have been expressed by Lord Selborne, is that there must be receipt of 'trust property'. In dealing with this issue the High Court asked '[d]id the Court of Appeal establish that Mrs Elias and her daughters received property to which a fiduciary obligation attached?' This is a slightly broader formulation than Lord Selborne's and could conceivably apply to company property, to which a director's fiduciary obligations would attach. But later the High Court noted that the acquisition of the land was not sufficient to satisfy the first limb because the three units were not 'trust property or the traceable proceeds of trust property'.[101] This appears to be a reversion to the more traditional formulation of what constitutes receivable property.

The other 'property' which Mrs Elias and her daughters had arguably received was the information obtained by Mr Elias that the land would be the subject of an alternate redevelopment approval. The High Court found that this was not confidential information, and even if it was, it did not have the requisite proprietary character. Nor had this information been passed to Mrs Elias and her daughters.

---

97. *Farah Constructions* (2007) 230 CLR 89 at [113].
98. [1974] 1 NSWLR 443 at 459–460.
99. [1994] 2 All ER 685 at 700.
100. *Farah Constructions* (2007) 230 CLR 89 at [113] footnote 54.
101. *Farah Constructions* (2007) 230 CLR 89 at [119].

In relation to notice, the High Court held that, because there was no agency established on the facts, there could be no notice to Mrs Elias and her daughters. Because there was therefore no question of those defendants having knowledge the High Court did not discuss the level of knowledge required under the first limb.

But their Honours said that it was a 'grave error' for the Court of Appeal to endorse the restitutionary theory for recipient liability. It was unjust because it had not been argued by the parties, and it was confusing because the Court of Appeal had in effect endorsed Hansen J's imposition of strict liability, without actually abandoning the notice test traditionally required under the first limb of *Barnes*. This, the High Court said, flew in the face of the received view of *Barnes* and of the 'seriously considered dicta' of a majority of the High Court in *Consul Developments*.

The second limb of *Barnes* was not considered by the Court of Appeal but arose in the High Court, where it was held that no accessorial liability arose on the facts. But the comments of the court *Farah Constructions* on the divergence between the traditional test in Australia and the Privy Council decision in *Royal Brunei* are worth repeating:

[160] As conventionally understood in Australia, the second limb makes a defendant liable if that defendant assists a trustee or fiduciary with knowledge of a dishonest and fraudulent design on the part of the trustee or fiduciary. **[305]**

[161] Several points of a general nature should be made here. The first concerns the scope of the second limb. This was not expressed by Lord Selborne LC as an exhaustive statement of the circumstances in which a third party who has not received trust property and who has not acted as a trustee *de son tort* nevertheless may be accountable as a constructive trustee. Before *Barnes v Addy*, there was a line of cases in which it was accepted that a third party might be treated as a participant in a breach of trust where the third party had knowingly induced or immediately procured breaches of duty by a trustee where the trustee had acted with no improper purpose; these were not cases of a third party assisting the trustee in any dishonest and fraudulent design on the part of the trustee.

[162] Secondly, the distinction has been recognised in the Australian case law but, on one reading of *Royal Brunei Airlines Sdn Bhd v Tan*, may have been displaced by the Privy Council in favour of a general principle of 'accessory liability' expressed as follows:

A liability in equity to make good resulting loss attaches to a person who dishonestly procures or assists in a breach of trust or fiduciary obligation. It is not necessary that, in addition, the trustee or fiduciary was acting dishonestly, although this will usually be so where the third party who is assisting him is acting dishonestly. 'Knowingly' is better avoided as a defining ingredient of the principle.

[163] Thirdly, whilst the different formulations of principle may lead to the same result in particular circumstances, there is a distinction between rendering liable a defendant participating with knowledge in a dishonest and fraudulent design, and rendering liable a defendant who dishonestly procures or assists in a breach of trust or fiduciary obligation where the trustee or fiduciary need not have engaged in a dishonest or fraudulent design. The decision in *Royal Brunei* has been referred to in this court several times but not in terms foreclosing further consideration of the subject in this

court, in particular, further consideration of the apparent necessity to displace the acceptance in *Consul Development Pty Ltd v DPC Estates Pty Ltd* of the formulation of the second limb of *Barnes v Addy* were *Royal Brunei* to be adopted in this country. Until such an occasion arises in this court, Australian courts should continue to observe the distinction mentioned above and, in particular, apply the formulation in the second limb of *Barnes v Addy*.

[164] On the present appeal, specific reliance was not placed by Say-Dee upon *Royal Brunei*, although there was a suggestion, not soundly based, discounting any difference between what might be called the traditional approach and that adopted in *Royal Brunei*. The changes to the law in Australia which were sought by Say-Dee did not include any adoption of a cause of action of the kind expressed in the passage in *Royal Brunei* set out above. Accordingly, it is unnecessary to decide now how far *Royal Brunei*, and subsequent decisions in the House of Lords and Privy Council, have modified the second limb of *Barnes v Addy* or, rather, restated the form of liability operating antecedently to and independently of *Barnes v Addy*, and if so, whether these changes should be adopted in Australia.[102] [Footnotes omitted]

In explaining the 'distinction' referred to in *Farah Constructions* at [162]–[163], the High Court cited an article by C Harpum, 'The Stranger as Constructive Trustee (Part 1)'.[103] In it the author describes knowing inducement (as opposed to knowing assistance) in this way:

A stranger who knowingly induces a trustee to commit a breach of trust will be liable as a constructive trustee. The motive for the inducement is irrelevant. It is also immaterial whether the trustee commits the breach of trust innocently or for some ulterior purpose.

The author went on to express the following summary of the knowing assistance principle: **[306]**

A stranger will be liable as a constructive trustee if he knowingly assists a trustee to commit a dishonest and fraudulent breach of trust. This residual category of liability covers the case of a stranger who renders significant assistance in the commission of a breach of trust short of inducing it, and who may never have received any part of the trust property. The foundation of his liability is his implication in a fraud by the trustee. If that fraudulent element is lacking, the stranger will not be accountable.[104]

Apart from its interest as a commentary on juridical method and the relationship between an intermediate and an ultimate appellate court, *Farah Constructions* is significant in at least four respects that are relevant to this litigation. First, the distinction between knowing assistance and knowing inducement is important. The two causes of action exist side by side, but they are different, having some elements that are common and others that are not.

---

102. *Farah Constructions* (2007) 230 CLR 89 at [160]–[164].
103. (1986) 102 *Law Quarterly Review* 114 at 115–116.
104. C Harpum, 'The Stranger as Constructive Trustee (Part 1)' (1986) 102 *Law Quarterly Review* 114 at 116.

Second, the comment of Lord Nicholls in *Royal Brunei*[105] that, in relation to the accessory liability principle, the *Baden* scale of knowledge is 'best forgotten' does not represent the law in Australia. On the contrary, the High Court indicated that while *Consul* provides authoritative guidance on the question of knowledge for the second limb of *Barnes*, the five categories found in *Baden* assist in an analysis of those principles.

Third, liability for knowing receipt depends on receipt of trust property and on notice of the requisite kind. Liability does not depend on the doctrine of restitution based on the unjust enrichment of the third party at the expense of the entity to whom the duties were owed. This is not to say that there could not, in some circumstances, be a restitutionary cause of action. But it would be independent of the *Barnes* principle and would have to be applied in accordance with conventional restitution law concepts.

Fourth, the High Court noted, *Farah Constructions*,[106] that recent authorities assumed (although it had rarely if at all been decided) that the first limb of *Barnes* applied not only to persons dealing with trustees, but also to persons dealing with at least some other types of fiduciary. The appellants had not contended to the contrary and, accordingly, the High Court saw no need to examine the correctness of that assumption. In this respect I note that in *Kalls Enterprises*[107] the Court of Appeal examined the authorities in which the first limb of *Barnes* has been applied to breach of fiduciary duty by a director of a company. Giles JA said that this represented a 'line of authority [which] should be followed until the High Court says otherwise'.[108] That is what I propose to do.

21.2.3. *Barnes* and the dishonest fiduciary

In relation to accessory liability, Lord Selborne spoke of assisting in a 'dishonest and fraudulent design' on the part of the trustees. The question arises whether that is to be taken literally, that is, as involving actual dishonesty or fraud (as in fraudulent design) in a pejorative sense. An alternative construction is that the phrase is broad enough to incorporate other activity involving infractions of generally accepted conduct but of a type that would attract a lesser degree of opprobrium. A third possibility is that it applies (in the case of a trustee) to any breach of a trust obligation.

In *Royal Brunei*, the Privy Council moved away from the phrase 'dishonest and fraudulent design on the part of the trustees' almost entirely. Their Lordships opined that what was relevant was the state of mind of the third party assisting in a breach of trust, not that of the trustee who perpetrated the breach. Lord Nicholls said:

> [307] [The trustee's] state of mind is essentially irrelevant to the question whether the *third party* should be made liable to the beneficiaries for the breach of trust ... In this regard dishonesty on the part of the third party would seem to be a sufficient basis for his liability, irrespective of the state of mind of the trustee who is in breach of trust. It is difficult to see why, if the third party dishonestly assisted in a breach, there should be a further prerequisite to his liability, namely that the trustee must also have been acting dishonestly. The alternative view would mean that a dishonest third party is liable if the

---

105. [1995] 2 AC 378 at 392; [1995] 3 All ER 97 at 108.
106. (2007) 230 CLR 89 at [113].
107. [2007] NSWCA 191; (2007) 25 ACLC 1094 at [152]–[158].
108. [2007] NSWCA 191; (2007) 25 ACLC 1094 at [159].

trustee is dishonest, but if the trustee did not act dishonestly that of itself would excuse a dishonest third party from liability. That would make no sense.[109]

Similar views have been expressed (both before and after *Royal Brunei*) in academic commentary on the direction of Australian law.[110]

The members of the High Court who decided *Farah Constructions* appear not to share Lord Nicholls' incredulity at such an outcome. The High Court[111] went back to Lord Selborne's formulation of the principle in *Barnes* itself and to what was said in *Consul Developments*. Their Honours said that Say-Dee's submission involved an abandonment of 'the "dishonest and fraudulent design" integer' and a reformulation of the second limb so that liability would attach to a third party who had not received a direct financial benefit but who had 'participated in a significant way in a significant breach of duty/trust with actual knowledge of the essential facts which constituted the breach'. That submission was rejected and the conclusion announced in this way:

> [179] The relevant passages in *Consul* establish for Australia that 'dishonest and fraudulent designs' can include not only breaches of trust but also breaches of fiduciary duty; but *any breach of trust or breach of fiduciary duty relied on must be dishonest and fraudulent.*[112] [Emphasis added]

Their Honours had little to say about the meaning of the phrase 'dishonest and fraudulent design', although they did comment that a person can act dishonestly, judged by the standards of ordinary, decent people, without appreciating that the act in question was dishonest by those standards.[113] Admittedly, that was in the context of a discussion concerning the requirement of 'knowledge' expressed in the second limb and was probably directed more at the state of mind of the third party than it was at the erring fiduciary. Nonetheless, as a matter of principle it is difficult to see why a similar approach should not be taken in relation to dishonesty on the part of the fiduciary. In other words, the test has objective elements so that, like the 'morally obtuse' third party, a fiduciary cannot escape liability by failing to recognise an impropriety that would have been apparent to an ordinary person applying the standards of such a person.[114]

In its common usage 'dishonest' is the antonym of 'honest'. And honesty means marked by uprightness or probity, being fundamentally sincere and truthful. As it is used in relation to accessory liability, I doubt it goes as far as dishonesty in, for example, a criminal law context or actual fraud in a common law sense. As the High Court pointed out in *Farah Constructions*[115] Gibbs J in *Consul Developments* did not categorise all breaches of fiduciary duty as 'dishonest and fraudulent' and said that this phrase is to be judged 'according to the plain principles of a court of equity'. It seems, therefore, that the impugned [308]

---

109. [1995] 2 AC 378 at 385; [1995] 3 All ER 97 at 102.

110. See, for example, Waters, *Equity, Fiduciaries and Trusts*, 1993, Ch 10, 213–14; H A J Ford & W A Lee, *Principles of the Law of Trusts*, Looseleaf edition, LawBook Company, Sydney, 1996+, [22690].

111. (2007) 230 CLR 89 at [179]–[185].

112. (2007) 230 CLR 89 at [179].

113. *Farah Constructions* (2007) 230 CLR 89 at [173].

114. *Farah Constructions* (2007) 230 CLR 89 at [177].

115. (2007) 230 CLR 89 at [183].

conduct must be attended by circumstances that would attract a degree of opprobrium raising it above the level of a simple breach of trust or breach of a fiduciary duty. This is consistent with the discussion in *Farah Constructions* on the facts of that case.[116] It is implicit in what is said[117] that a breach of fiduciary duty by a company officer that may be excused under s 1318 of the Corporations Act would not be regarded as part of a 'dishonest and fraudulent design' and thus would not ground an accessory liability claim.

In any event, if the mere fact of a breach were sufficient to ground liability, the cautionary note in *Farah Constructions* that 'any breach of trust or breach of fiduciary duty relied on must be dishonest and fraudulent' would be robbed of meaning. So too would the strongly worded rejection of what the High Court described as an attempt to abandon 'the "dishonest and fraudulent design" integer'.[118] Unless some real meaning is given to the phrase 'dishonest and fraudulent design', there would be no significant difference from the approach advocated in *Royal Brunei*. And the High Court also referred to an 'imputation of commercial dishonesty' (admittedly made against the third party rather than the errant fiduciary) which, their Honours noted, was a serious allegation that ought to have been pleaded and particularised and assessed in the way mentioned in *Briginshaw v Briginshaw*[119] (*Briginshaw*).

...

21.2.4. *Barnes* and degrees of knowledge

The question of what a stranger, implicated in a breach of trust, must 'know' before liability can attach has created significant controversy in various parts of the common law world over a long period. Particular controversy has attended the question whether (and if so to what extent) constructive knowledge would suffice. It seems to me that, in relation to the second limb, this aspect of the controversy has been authoritatively settled in Australia by *Farah Constructions* and, accordingly, I am spared the stygian task of examining the earlier decisions.

I have already mentioned the adoption in *Farah Constructions* of the five categories of knowledge enunciated by Peter Gibson J in *Baden*. This is what the High Court said on the knowledge issue: **[311]**

[171] What is required by the requirement of 'knowledge' expressed in the second limb?

[172] In the passage in which Lord Selborne formulated the second limb in terms of assisting with knowledge in a dishonest and fraudulent design on the part of the trustees, he contrasted those 'actually participating in any fraudulent conduct of the trustee' and those 'dealing honestly as agents'.

[173] As a matter of ordinary understanding, and as reflected in the criminal law in Australia, a person may have acted dishonestly, judged by the standards of ordinary, decent people, without appreciating that the act in question was dishonest by those

---

116. (2007) 230 CLR 89 especially at [181]–[186].
117. (2007) 230 CLR 89 at [184] for example.
118. (2007) 230 CLR 89 at [180].
119. (1938) 60 CLR 336 (*Briginshaw*).

standards. Further, as early as 1801, Sir William Grant MR stigmatised those who 'shut their eyes' against the receipt of unwelcome information.

[174] Against this background, it has been customary to analyse the requirement of knowledge in the second limb of *Barnes v Addy* by reference to the five categories agreed between counsel in *Baden v Société Générale pour Favoriser le Développement du Commerce et de l'Industrie en France SA*:

'(i) actual knowledge; (ii) wilfully shutting one's eyes to the obvious; (iii) wilfully and recklessly failing to make such inquiries as an honest and reasonable man would make; (iv) knowledge of circumstances which would indicate the facts to an honest and reasonable man; (v) knowledge of circumstances which would put an honest and reasonable man on inquiry.'

In *Bank of Credit and Commerce International (Overseas) Ltd v Akindele*[120]('*BCCI*'), Nourse LJ observed that the first three categories have generally been taken to involve 'actual knowledge', as understood both at common law and in equity, and the last two as instances of 'constructive knowledge' as developed in equity, particularly in disputes respecting old system conveyancing. After noting that in *Royal Brunei* the Privy Council had discounted the utility of the *Baden* categorisation, Nourse LJ in *BCCI* went on to express his own view that the categorisation was often helpful in identifying the different states of knowledge for the purposes of a knowing assistance case.

[175] Although *Baden* post-dated the decision in *Consul*, the five categories found in *Baden* assist in an analysis of that for which *Consul* provides authoritative guidance on the question of knowledge for the second limb of *Barnes v Addy*.

[176] Thus, support in *Consul* can be found for categories (i), (ii) and (iii). Further, *Consul* also indicates that category (iv) suffices. However, in *Consul*, Stephen J held that knowledge of circumstances which would put an honest and reasonable man on inquiry, later identified as the fifth category in *Baden*, would not suffice. Gibbs J left open the possibility that constructive notice of this description would suffice. Barwick CJ agreed with Stephen J.

[177] The result is that *Consul* supports the proposition that circumstances falling within any of the first four categories of *Baden* are sufficient to answer the requirement of knowledge in the second limb of *Barnes v Addy*, but does not travel fully into the field of constructive notice by accepting the fifth category. In this way, there is accommodated, through acceptance of the fourth category, the proposition that the morally obtuse cannot escape by failure to recognise an impropriety that would have been apparent to an ordinary person applying the standards of such persons.

[178] These conclusions in *Consul* as to what is involved in 'knowledge' for the second limb represent the law in Australia. They should be followed by Australian courts, unless and until departed from by decision of this court.[121] [Footnotes omitted.]

---

120. [2000] 3 WLR 1423 ('*BCCI*').
121. *Farah Constructions* (2007) 230 CLR 89 at [171]–[178].

This is the reason that in section 21.2.2.3 I discussed at some length the judgment of Austin J in *NCR Australia*.[122] His Honour has there encapsulated the practical effect of what has to be established before a third party will be held liable for knowing assistance in a breach of duty. And there is also clear recognition in that passage that the threshold for second limb liability is a 'dishonest and fraudulent design' on the part of the fiduciary.

[312] It seems to me, however, that the answer to the question is less clear in relation to recipient liability. As Giles JA pointed out in *Kalls Enterprises*,[123] Lord Selborne did not refer to knowledge in connection with the first limb. The High Court in *Farah Constructions*[124] defined the first limb in this way: 'persons who receive trust property become chargeable if it is established that they have received it with notice of the trust'. The question that arises is what (in terms of knowledge) constitutes 'notice of the trust' for these purposes.

In *Kalls Enterprises*[125] Giles JA implicitly accepted (at least in relation to recipient liability) the correctness of what was said by Anderson J in *Hancock Family Memorial Foundation Ltd v Porteous*[126] (*Hancock*) on this issue. Anderson J commenced[127] by looking at accessory liability and concluded that, in order to succeed, a plaintiff must establish that the third party's conduct was dishonest, that is, lacking in probity. Whether the third party had so acted was to be judged by objective standards, that is, that the third party had not acted as an honest person would in the circumstances. The extent to which, following *Farah Constructions* and its exhortation to adhere strictly to the dicta in *Consul Developments*, it is necessary to focus on whether the third party was 'dishonest' rather than on what the third party 'knew', is something that I do not need to examine further. I am relying on *Hancock* in so far as it relates to knowing receipt rather than knowing assistance. Turning his attention to the first limb, Anderson J said, again:[128]

> [79] As to recipient liability, there is less certainty about what must be proved to sheet home liability to the non-trustee but I adopt, with respect, the reasoning and conclusions of Hansen J in *Koorootang Nominees Pty Ltd v Australia & New Zealand Banking Group Ltd* ... on the question. In the first place, it is not necessary to establish that a recipient of trust property acted dishonestly or with want of probity. Recipient liability may be established if the defendant had actual or constructive knowledge at the time he received the relevant property that: (a) it was trust property; and (b) it was being misapplied. The defendant will be taken to have constructive knowledge if it is proved that he wilfully shut his eyes to the obvious; that he wilfully and recklessly failed to make such inquiries as an honest and reasonable man would make in the circumstances; and that he knew of circumstances which would indicate the true facts to an honest and reasonable man.

---

122. [2004] NSWCA 1 at [168].
123. [2007] NSWCA 191; (2007) 25 ACLC 1094 at [112].
124. (2007) 230 CLR 89 at [112].
125. [2007] NSWCA 191; (2007) 25 ACLC 1094 at [176].
126. (1999) 32 ACSR 124; 151 FLR 191; [1999] WASC 55 (*Hancock*).
127. (1999) 32 ACSR 124; 151 FLR 191; [1999] WASC 55 at [79].
128. (1999) 32 ACSR 124; 151 FLR 191; [1999] WASC 55 at [79].

If all that is proved is that the defendant had knowledge of circumstances which would put an honest and reasonable man on inquiry, that is not enough.[129]

This, then, seems to cover actual knowledge in one or more of the first three categories in *Baden* and constructive knowledge coming within the fourth category but it eschews the fifth category. If this is correct, then at least in this respect the test for knowledge in relation to accessory liability (as explained in *Farah Constructions*) and the test for recipient liability (as outlined in *Hancock* and *Koorootang*) seem to have come together. This is probably more by accident than design and, given the history of *Barnes* jurisprudence, the confluence of thinking is likely to be short-lived.

What is it that the third part must 'know' before liability can attach? In *Hancock*, Anderson J held that the third party must know, at the time he received the relevant property, that it was trust property and that it was being misapplied. The same basic principle has been put in various ways in other cases. For example, in *Spangaro v Corporate Investment Australia Funds Management Ltd*[130] Finkelstein J observed that a plaintiff must prove that the defendant was in receipt of trust property and had knowledge that the property received was trust property, and of circumstances [313] attendant on the transfer of that property that made the transfer a breach of trust. His Honour went on to say that 'knowledge means a third party's knowledge that the relevant property was trust property being misapplied or transferred pursuant to a breach of fiduciary duty or trust'.[131]

It is important to go back to what was said by Stephen J in *Consul Developments* ... about constructive knowledge. It is not necessary for a plaintiff to establish something along these lines: 'The recipient turned his mind to the question whether the proposed transfer of property was a breach of fiduciary duty, decided it was, but opted to go ahead anyway'. Using the language of Stephen J, it may be sufficient (all other elements being satisfied) if 'a defendant knows of facts which themselves would, to a reasonable man, tell of fraud or breach of trust'.

The resulting law, as I apprehend it, is that for a third party to be held liable for knowing receipt:

(a) there must be a 'trust';
(b) the trustee must have misapplied 'trust property';
(c) the third party must have received trust property;
(d) at the time of receiving the trust property, the third party must have known of the trust and of the misapplication of the trust property; and
(e) the third party will be taken to have 'known' in the relevant sense if the third party:
   (i) has actual knowledge of the trust and the misapplication of trust property; or
   (ii) has deliberately shut his or her eyes to those things; or
   (iii) has abstained in a calculated way from making such enquiries as an honest and reasonable person would make, about the trust and the application of the trust property; or
   (iv) knows of facts which to an honest and reasonable person would indicate the existence of the trusts and the fact of misapplication. ...

---

129. See *Koorootang* [1998] 3 VR 16 at 85 and 105.
130. (2003) 47 ACSR 285; [2003] FCA 1025 at [55].
131. (2003) 47 ACSR 285; [2003] FCA 1025 at [58].

21.2.5. Recipient liability and trust property

21.2.5.1. The concept of trust property

The next question that I wish to address is the meaning of 'trust property' in these circumstances. By 'these circumstances' I mean where a director of a company deals with assets of the company in a way that constitutes a breach of a fiduciary duty that the director owes to the company. It is in this section that the discussion of the somewhat peculiar nature of the trust property is developed. It must be remembered that one of the reasons why the claim under the first limb of *Barnes* failed in *Farah Constructions* was that the claimants did not establish that the third party had received trust property. Similarly, in *Rogers v Kabriel*,[132] Young J noted that under the first limb [314] liability is imposed 'only in respect of trust property in a strict sense'. His Honour found that the moneys paid over in that case were not 'trust property in a strict sense, or at all'.

In a detailed and considered submission the banks contend that in this respect (among myriad others) there was a fatal flaw in the plaintiffs' case. They submit that trust property is unique because it involves the recognition of two separate proprietary interests, not present in the case of property owned absolutely (as in the case of property owned by a company in its own right). In the case of trust property there is both a beneficial interest and a legal interest, ownership of the former residing in the beneficiary, ownership of the latter being vested in the trustee. Beneficial ownership is, in itself, a proprietary interest, capable of assignment.

According to this line of reasoning, a company director has no interest — legal or beneficial — in the property of the company. A company (unlike a trust) has legal personality and the company is the absolute owner of its own property. There are no separate legal and beneficial estates involved.[133] Such property is assigned, transferred and paid away on a daily basis without any issues of beneficial interests intervening. No person other than the company has any beneficial interest in that property and (unlike the case of a trust) there is no reason for a third party to consider whether or not other beneficial interests exist.

The banks also submit that the whole thesis of liability for knowing receipt is that the transferor (the trustee) is no more than the legal owner of the property. Thus, when a stranger receives trust property, prima facie he receives property that is not beneficially owned by the transferor. A recipient of trust property who knows he is dealing with a trustee is immediately on notice that the property is not owned absolutely by the trustee. A recipient of company property, on the other hand, knows that the company is the absolute owner of the property. According to this submission, the concept that the same principle governs knowing receipt of trust property and bargains negotiated at arm's length between major corporate entities is specious.

As a matter of basic principle, there is a certain attraction in that line of reasoning. But, in my view, the weight of authority suggests that the phrase 'trust property' in modern *Barnes* jurisprudence has a broader meaning than 'trust property in the strict sense'. The difficulties are well illustrated by dicta in *Farah Constructions* itself. The High

---

132. [1999] NSWSC 368 at [173].
133. See *Federal Commissioner of Taxation v Linter Textiles Australia Ltd (in liq)* (2005) 220 CLR 592; 215 ALR 1; [2005] HCA 20 at [30] (*Linter Textiles*).

Court gave clear direction that the law is to be understood in the way described in *Barnes* and *Consul Developments*. Their Honours concluded, in *Farah Constructions*,[134] that the claim under the first limb failed because (as well as the absence of a requisite level of notice), there was 'no relevant receipt of trust property'. But in the following paragraph they posed the question (and later answered it, in the negative): 'Did the Court of Appeal establish that Mrs Elias and her daughters received property *to which a fiduciary obligation attached?*' (emphasis added). This is not the first time that such language has appeared in a judgment. In *Evans v European Bank Ltd*[135] *(Evans)*, Spigelman CJ (with whom the other members of the court agreed) said: 'In my opinion, it is an essential aspect of accessorial liability for "knowing receipt" that the act of transfer of the property ... must be in breach of a fiduciary obligation'. [315]

Spigelman CJ went on[136] to extract various formulations of this proposition from the authorities. One such formulation is 'a disposal of his assets in breach of fiduciary duty'.[137]

Regard should also be had in this respect to the reasons of Gibbs J in *Consul Developments*. His Honour noted[138] that although Lord Selborne spoke of dishonesty and fraud it was clear that the principle extended to the case where a person received trust property and dealt with it in a manner inconsistent with trusts of which he was cognizant. Gibbs J posed the question whether the principle applied to impose liability on strangers who knowingly participated in a breach of fiduciary duty committed by a person who was not a trustee or was at most a constructive trustee. His Honour went on to say[139] that 'the principle under discussion extends to the case where a stranger has knowingly participated in a breach of fiduciary duty committed by a person who is not a trustee even though nothing that might properly be regarded as trust property — even property stamped with a constructive trust — has been received'.

In *Farah Constructions* the High Court assumed (leaving it open to re-visitation on a future occasion) that the first limb applies not only to persons dealing with trustees, but also to persons dealing with some other types of fiduciaries. If that is the case, then the broadening of the phrase 'trust property', as used by Lord Selborne, to property to which a fiduciary obligation attaches, is not a particularly large step. I accept that 'trust property' and 'property to which a fiduciary obligation attaches', are not the same thing. It is difficult to imagine a species of 'trust property' that is not also 'property to which a fiduciary obligation attaches' but the reverse does not necessarily apply.

Comment

1. See Radan & Stewart at **28.93–28.128**.

---

134. (2007) 230 CLR 89 at [115].
135. (2004) 61 NSWLR 75; [2004] NSWCA 82 at [160] *(Evans)*.
136. (2004) 61 NSWLR 75; [2004] NSWCA 82 at [161].
137. *El Ajou v Dollar Land Holdings plc* [1994] 2 All ER 685 at 700; [1994] 1 BCLC 464 at 478 *(El Ajou)*; *Bank of Credit & Commerce International (Overseas) Ltd v Akindele* [2001] Ch 437 at 448; [2000] 4 All ER 221 at 229.
138. (1974) 132 CLR 373 at CLR 396.
139. (1974) 132 CLR 373 at 396–7.

29

TRACING

Introduction

29.1 Tracing is a remedy that allows beneficiaries to pursue trust property when it is wrongly taken and used by trustees or bestowed on others. Tracing allows the property to be followed through the hands that receive it, as well as into the new property that may have been created from or mixed with the trust property. The extracts in this chapter deal with the following issues:

- the nature of tracing: *Foskett v McKeown* [2001] 1 AC 102; and
- tracing mixed property in the hands of trustees from more than one trust: *Re French Caledonia Travel* (2003) 59 NSWLR 361.

The nature of tracing

29.2   Foskett v McKeown [2001] 1 AC 102

Court: House of Lords

Facts: Timothy Murphy was the main person in charge of a development scheme where people could buy plots of land in Algarve in Portugal. Under the terms of the scheme people could purchase the land and the proceeds would be held on trust. If the land was not transferred to them within two years the money had to be repaid with interest.

Two hundred and twenty people purchased lots but the lots were never developed. Murphy dissipated the funds. Part of the funds (£20,440) were used to pay premiums on a life insurance policy. Premiums were paid in 1986, 1987, 1988, 1989 and 1990. The first two premiums had been paid using Murphy's own funds. There was a dispute about what money had been used to pay the third premium, but it was clear that the last two premiums had been paid out of the purchasers' trust.

The policy provided for a death benefit which was in favour of Murphy's wife (who received a 1/10th share) and his three children (who received the rest in equal amounts). The right to the death benefit arose after the second premium was paid.

Murphy killed himself in 1991. The purchasers claimed that they were entitled to trace their money through the policy into the sum paid out to the children (they did not pursue the amount paid to Mrs Murphy). They believed they were entitled to a proportionate share of the policy money which was equivalent to two-fifths. The majority of the Court of Appeal upheld the purchasers' claim but limited it to an amount in restitution which was equivalent to the amount of the two premiums together with interest. The beneficiaries were denied a proportionate share of the policy proceeds. The majority found no causal link between the misappropriation of the funds and the right to the policy proceeds, as the right to whole-of-life cover arose after the first two premiums, and was not causally related to the misappropriated funds.

The purchasers appealed to the House of Lords.

Issue: The issue was whether the purchasers could claim a two-fifths share of the payout to the children or whether their claim was limited to the amount of money taken from the trust plus interest.

Decision: A majority of the House (Lord Browne-Wilkinson, Lord Hoffman and Lord Millet; Lord Steyn and Lord Hope of Craighead dissenting) found that the purchasers' money could be traced. The purchasers' rights were proprietorial and not based on restitution.

Extracts: In this extract Lord Millet describes the nature of tracing and the fact that it is a process based on property rights.

Lord Millett

[126] My Lords, this is a textbook example of tracing through mixed substitutions. At the beginning of the story the plaintiffs were beneficially entitled under an express trust to a sum standing in the name of Mr Murphy in a bank account. From there the money moved into and out of various bank accounts where in breach of trust it was inextricably mixed by Mr Murphy with his own money. After each transaction was completed the plaintiffs' money formed an indistinguishable part of the balance standing to Mr Murphy's credit in his bank account. The amount of that balance represented a debt due from the bank to Mr Murphy, that is to say a chose in action. At the penultimate stage the plaintiffs' money was represented by an indistinguishable part of a different chose in action, viz, the debt prospectively and contingently due from an insurance company to its policyholders, being the trustees of a settlement made by Mr Murphy for the [127] benefit of his children. At the present and final stage it forms an indistinguishable part of the balance standing to the credit of the respondent trustees in their bank account.

Tracing and following

The process of ascertaining what happened to the plaintiffs' money involves both tracing and following. These are both exercises in locating assets which are or may be taken to represent an asset belonging to the plaintiffs and to which they assert ownership. The processes of following and tracing are, however, distinct. Following is the process of following the same asset as it moves from hand to hand. Tracing is the process of identifying a new asset as the substitute for the old. Where one asset is exchanged for another, a claimant can elect whether to follow the original asset into the hands of the new owner or to trace its value into the new asset in the hands of the same owner. In practice his choice is often dictated by the circumstances. In the present case the plaintiffs do not seek to follow the money any further once it reached the bank or insurance company, since its identity was lost in the hands of the recipient (which in any case obtained an unassailable title as a bona fide purchaser for value without notice of the plaintiffs' beneficial interest). Instead the plaintiffs have chosen at each stage to trace the money into its proceeds, viz, the debt presently due from the bank to the account holder or the debt prospectively and contingently due from the insurance company to the policy holders.

Having completed this exercise, the plaintiffs claim a continuing beneficial interest in the insurance money. Since this represents the product of Mr Murphy's own money as well as theirs, which Mr Murphy mingled indistinguishably in a single chose in action, they claim a beneficial interest in a proportionate part of the money only. The transmission of a claimant's property rights from one asset to its traceable proceeds is part of our law of property, not of the law of unjust enrichment. There is no 'unjust factor' to justify restitution (unless 'want of title' be one, which makes the point). The claimant succeeds if at all by virtue of his own title, not to reverse unjust enrichment. Property rights are determined by fixed rules and settled principles. They are not discretionary. They do not depend upon ideas of what is 'fair, just and reasonable'. Such concepts, which in reality mask decisions of legal policy, have no place in the law of property.

A beneficiary of a trust is entitled to a continuing beneficial interest not merely in the trust property but in its traceable proceeds also, and his interest binds every one who takes the property or its traceable proceeds except a bona fide purchaser for value without notice. In the present case the plaintiffs' beneficial interest plainly bound Mr Murphy, a trustee who wrongfully mixed the trust money with his own and whose every dealing with the money (including the payment of the premiums) was in breach of trust. It similarly binds his successors, the trustees of the children's settlement, who claim no beneficial interest of their own, and Mr Murphy's children, who are volunteers. They gave no value for what they received and derive their interest from Mr Murphy by way of gift.

Tracing

We speak of money at the bank, and of money passing into and out of a bank account. But of course the account holder has no money at the bank. [128] Money paid into a bank account belongs legally and beneficially to the bank and not to the account holder. The bank gives value for it, and it is accordingly not usually possible to make the money itself the subject of an adverse claim. Instead a claimant normally sues the account holder rather than the bank and lays claim to the proceeds of the money in his hands. These consist of the debt or part of the debt due to him from the bank. We speak of tracing money into and out of the account, but there is no money in the account. There is merely a single debt of an amount equal to the final balance standing to the credit of the account holder. No money passes from paying bank to receiving bank or through the clearing system (where the money flows may be in the opposite direction). There is simply a series of debits and credits which are causally and transactionally linked. We also speak of tracing one asset into another, but this too is inaccurate. The original asset still exists in the hands of the new owner, or it may have become untraceable. The claimant claims the new asset because it was acquired in whole or in part with the original asset. What he traces, therefore, is not the physical asset itself but the value inherent in it.

Tracing is thus neither a claim nor a remedy. It is merely the process by which a claimant demonstrates what has happened to his property, identifies its proceeds and the persons who have handled or received them, and justifies his claim that the proceeds can properly be regarded as representing his property. Tracing is also distinct from claiming. It identifies the traceable proceeds of the claimant's property. It enables the claimant to substitute the traceable proceeds for the original asset as the subject matter of his claim. But it does not affect or establish his claim. That will depend on a number of factors including the nature of his interest in the original asset. He will normally be able to maintain the same claim to the substituted asset as he could have maintained to the original asset. If he held only a security interest in the original asset, he cannot claim more than a security interest in its proceeds. But his claim may also be exposed to potential defences as a result of intervening transactions. Even if the plaintiffs could demonstrate what the bank had done with their money, for example, and could thus identify its traceable proceeds in the hands of the bank, any claim by them to assert ownership of those proceeds would be defeated by the bona fide purchaser defence. The successful completion of a tracing exercise may be preliminary to a personal claim[1] or a proprietary one, to the enforcement of a legal right[2] or an equitable one.

Given its nature, there is nothing inherently legal or equitable about the tracing exercise. There is thus no sense in maintaining different rules for tracing at law and in equity. One set of tracing rules is enough. The existence of two has never formed part of the law in the United States.[3] There is certainly no logical justification for allowing any distinction between them to produce capricious results in cases of mixed substitutions by insisting on the existence of a fiduciary relationship as a precondition for applying equity's tracing rules. The existence of such a relationship may be relevant to the nature of the claim which the plaintiff can maintain, whether personal or proprietary, but that is a different matter. I agree with the passages which my noble and learned friend, Lord Steyn, has cited from Professor Birk's **[129]** essay 'The Necessity of a Unitary Law of Tracing',[4] and with Dr Lionel Smith's exposition in his comprehensive monograph The Law of Tracing.[5]

This is not, however, the occasion to explore these matters further, for the present is a straightforward case of a trustee who wrongfully misappropriated trust money, mixed it with his own, and used it to pay for an asset for the benefit of his children. Even on the traditional approach, the equitable tracing rules are available to the plaintiffs. There are only two complicating factors. The first is that the wrongdoer used their money to pay

---

1. As in *El Ajou v Dollar Land Holdings plc* [1993] 3 All ER 717.
2. As in *Trustees of the Property of F C Jones & Sons v Jones* [1997] Ch 159.
3. See Scott, *Law of Trusts*, 1989, s 515, pp 605–609.
4. P Birk, 'The Necessity of a Unitary Law of Tracing' in *Making Commercial Law, Essays in Honour of Roy Goode*, 1997, pp 239–258.
5. Smith, *The Law of Tracing*, 1997, pp 120–130, 277–279 and 342–347.

premiums on an equity-linked policy of life assurance on his own life. The nature of the policy should make no difference in principle, though it may complicate the accounting. The second is that he had previously settled the policy for the benefit of his children. This should also make no difference. The claimant's rights cannot depend on whether the wrongdoer gave the policy to his children during his lifetime or left the proceeds to them by his will; or if during his lifetime whether he did so before or after he had recourse to the claimant's money to pay the premiums. The order of events does not affect the fact that the children are not contributors but volunteers who have received the gift of an asset paid for in part with misappropriated trust moneys.

Comments

1. See Radan & Stewart at **29.3–29.5, 29.39–29.48.**
2. What if the children in *Foskett* had taken the money and purchased property with it prior to the court decision? In *Commonwealth Bank of Australia v Saleh* [2007] NSWSC 903 Einstein J, at [39], summarised the principles of tracing as they affect third parties, like the children:

   - where trust property is transferred to a volunteer who takes without notice, and there is no question of mixing, then the volunteer will hold the property on trust for the rightful beneficiaries;
   - where the trust moneys were used to pay off a secured creditor, the trust was not entitled to be subrogated to the rights of the secured creditor who was repaid …;
   - if the volunteer purchased property with a mixed fund including trust moneys then the beneficiary would be allowed a charge over the property in order to secure repayment of the trust moneys used for the purchase …;
   - if an asset is purchased with mixed funds and it increases in value, the beneficiary will not be entitled to any proportionate share in that increase in value. In this respect, careful consideration needs to be given to renovations or improvements made upon real property.

Tracing mixed property in the hands of trustees from more than one trust

---

29.3   Re French Caledonia Travel (2003) 59 NSWLR 361

Court: Supreme Court of New South Wales

Facts: The case concerned a travel agency which was run by French Caledonia Travel Service Pty Ltd ('French Calendonia'). The company ran a trust account where it would hold moneys from clients that were then to be paid to travel providers. On occasion money was also transferred from this account into another cash deposit account. Proper accounting of these amounts had never been done so it was not clear what funds could be attributed to these transfers.

French Caledonia became insolvent and was placed under administration and then in liquidation. Claims against the company totalled $1.43 million but the trust account held only $97,000. The cash deposit account totalled $75,000. The liquidator sought directions from the court as to how to distribute the funds amongst the creditors.

Issue: The issue was whether the court should distribute the funds according to the principle of 'first in-first out' (known as the rule in *Clayton's case*) or whether it should distribute the funds based on proportionate contributions and losses (the *pari passu* approach).

Decision: Campbell J found against the application of *Clayton's case* as a matter of principle, regardless of whether there was enough information upon which to allocate withdrawals to particular deposits. Additionally, Campbell J found that the rule was not appropriate to the situation at hand where money was drawn from the account to pay the expenses of particular travellers, regardless of whether that traveller's money had been the first in, last in or somewhere in between.

Extracts: In this extract Campbell J reviews and explains a number of important tracing authorities from *Clayton's case* up to modern times.

Campbell J

Clayton's Case itself

[368] *Clayton's Case*[6] related to how the liabilities of a partnership of bankers to a customer should be borne amongst the partners. Devaynes was a member of a partnership of five bankers. Clayton was a customer of that partnership. At the time of Devaynes' death, Clayton's account with the partnership had a credit balance. The four surviving partners continued on the banking business, but became insolvent some time later.

[369] Clayton continued to make deposits to, and withdrawals from, his account with the partnership during the time that the four surviving partners operated it. At the time of the bankruptcy of the four surviving partners, the partnership owed Clayton a significant sum. The estate of Devaynes was solvent. Hence Clayton tried to throw liability onto Devaynes' estate, to the extent he could.

At the death of Devaynes, Clayton's account with the partnership had a balance of £1,713 in credit. After the death of Devaynes, and before paying any more money into the account, Clayton drew out money which reduced his cash balance to £453. Thereafter, he continued to make both payments and withdrawals of large sums. At the time of the bankruptcy of the remaining four partners, his cash balance exceeded £1,713.

Clayton alleged that the estate of Devaynes remained a debtor to him in the sum of £453 (minus the proportion attributable to £453 of dividends he had received from the bankruptcy of the surviving partners).

The problem which required solution in *Clayton's Case* was one involving identification of the debtor, in a relationship between banker and customer. It arose from the need to decide which of two potential debtors — the partnership of five, or the partnership of

---

6. *Devaynes v Noble* (1816) 35 ER 781 (*Clayton's Case*).

four — continued to owe a debt to Clayton. That problem was solved by appropriating payments out of the bank account, to work out whether the debt which was owing by the partners to Clayton at the time of Devaynes' death had been repaid or not.

Sir William Grant MR held that Clayton's claim failed. He noted[7] that the common law contained two irreconcilable strands of authority concerning the way in which an appropriation was to be made in the situation where a debtor owed several debts to a creditor, and made a payment which did not completely repay those debts. One strand of authority was derived from the civil law, the other was one which the common law had developed for itself. Sir William distinguished both those strands of authority from the case before him by saying:

> ... They were all cases of distinct insulated debts, between which a plain line of separation could be drawn. But this is a case of a banking account, where all the sums paid in form one blended fund, the parts of which have no longer any distinct existence ... In such a case, there is no room for any other appropriation than that which arises from the order in which the receipts and payments take place, and are carried into the account. Presumably, it is the sum first paid in, that is first drawn out. It is the first item on the debit side of the account, that is discharged, or reduced, by the first item on the credit side. The appropriation is made by the very act of setting the two items against each other. Upon that principle, all accounts current are settled, and particularly cash accounts. When there has been a continuation of dealings, in what way can it be ascertained whether the specific balance due on a given day has, or has not, been discharged, but by examining whether payments to the amount of that balance appear by the account to have been made? You are not to take the account backwards, and strike the balance at the head, instead of the foot, of it. A man's banker breaks, owing him, on the whole account, the balance of £1,000. It would surprise one to hear the customer say, 'I have been fortunate enough to draw out all that I paid in during the last four years; but there is £1,000, which I paid in five years ago, that I hold myself never to have drawn out; and, therefore, if I can find any body who was answerable for the debts of the banking house, such as they [370] stood five years ago, I have a right to say that it is that specific sum which is still due to me, and not the £1,000 that I paid in last week'. That is exactly the nature of the present claim. Mr Clayton travels back into the account, 'till he finds a balance, for which Mr Devaynes was responsible; and then he says, — 'That is a sum which I have never drawn for. Though standing in the centre of the account, it is to be considered as set apart, and left untouched. Sums above it, and below it, have been drawn out; but none of my drafts ever reached or affected this remnant of the balance due to me at Mr Devaynes's death.' What boundary would there be to this method of re-moulding an account?[8]

And:

> If appropriation be required, here is appropriation in the only way that the nature of the thing admits. Here are payments, so placed in opposition to debts, that, on the ordinary principles on which accounts are settled, this debt is extinguished.[9]

---

7.   (1816) 35 ER 781 at 791–792.
8.   (1816) 35 ER 781 at 793.
9.   (1816) 35 ER 781 at 793.

Sir William Grant also relied upon the fact that the customer had not informed the banker that any other method of appropriation was to be adopted, and had received statements of account drawn up as though a first-in first-out method of appropriation was being adopted. He said:

> ... He makes no objection to it, — and the report [of the Master] states that the silence of the customer after the receipt of his banking account is regarded as an admission of its being correct. Both debtor and creditor must, therefore, be considered as having concurred in the appropriation.[10]

A third reason for reaching the conclusion that Clayton's claim failed was that Clayton drew from the account immediately after the death of Devaynes:

> ... he drew, and that to a considerable extent, when there was no fund, except this balance, out of which his drafts could be answered. What was there, in the next draft he drew, which could indicate that it was not to be paid out of the residue of the same fund, but was to be considered as drawn exclusively on the credit of money more recently paid in? No such distinction was made; nor was there any thing from which it could be inferred. I should, therefore say, that on Mr Clayton's express authority the fund was applied in payment of his drafts in the order in which they were presented.[11]

...

Re Hallett's Estate — an account of the case

[375] ... *Re Hallett's Estate; Knatchbull v Hallett*[12] was an action for administration of the deceased estate of a solicitor. The plaintiff in the action was one of the solicitor's general creditors. Other claimants against the estate were the trustee of the solicitor's marriage settlement, and one of the solicitor's clients, Mrs Cotterill. There was a dispute as to their respective entitlements to money standing in the solicitor's bank account.

[376] At the start of business on 3 November 1877, the solicitor's bank account had (simplifying figures somewhat) £1,796 standing to its credit. On 3 November he paid in £341, concerning which he had a fiduciary obligation to account to Mrs Cotterill. On 14 November, he paid in two amounts. The bank account records the order in which they were paid in. First he paid in £770, a sum which he had a fiduciary obligation to hold on the trusts of the marriage settlement. Then he paid in £1804, which was another amount concerning which he had a fiduciary obligation to account to Mrs Cotterill. Each of the payments connected with Mrs Cotterill was one where Hallett had sold an asset of Mrs Cotterill, which his obligation had been to keep in specie. Hallett, then, before his death, drew out various sums for his own purposes, so that the balance to his credit at the time of his death (if nothing more had been paid in by him after 14 November) would have been £1,708. He had, however, paid in other sums, so that he had at the time of his death a balance at his bankers of £3,029. For a reason which does not appear from the report, only £2,600 of this amount was paid into court to the credit of an action for the administration of his estate.

---

10. (1816) 35 ER 781 at 793.
11. (1816) 35 ER 781 at 794.
12. (1879) 13 Ch D 696.

The reported case was a priority dispute about entitlement to that £2,600. The trustees of the marriage settlement claimed the whole amount of £770. Mrs Cotterill claimed £1,708, on the basis that that was the sum remaining in the banker's hands out of the proceeds of the sale of her assets. It is to be observed that the total amount claimed by the trustees and Mrs Cotterill together was £2,478, which was less than the £2,600 paid into court.

The trial judge, Fry J, held that the two creditors to whom Hallett owed a fiduciary obligation prevailed over the general creditors, but that the rule in *Clayton's Case* applied as between the two creditors to whom Hallett owed a fiduciary obligation. He specifically rejected[13] an argument that the amount which remained in the bank account should be divided rateably between the trustees of the marriage settlement and Mrs Cotterill. In consequence, as Mrs Cotterill's money had been paid in last, she had established her right to the £1,708 she claimed, and the trustees of the marriage settlement received nothing.

Appeals against the decision of Fry J by the general creditors were dismissed.[14] Insofar as the general creditors disputed the decision of Fry J that the trustee of the marriage settlement prevailed over the general creditors, the argument turned on a question of fact, concerning whether certain bonds from which the £770 was derived had been appropriated to become assets of the marriage settlement. Fry J's decision on that point was upheld.[15] Insofar as the general creditors disputed the decision of Fry J that Mrs Cotterill prevailed over the general creditors, it sufficed that Mrs Cotterill established that Hallett had owed her a fiduciary obligation concerning the asset which he had wrongly sold, and (because various earlier statements that 'money has no earmark' no longer applied to prevent tracing in equity into a mixed fund) that fiduciary obligation enabled Mrs Cotterill to trace into the bank account and obtain a charge over it — and that charge meant that she prevailed over the general (unsecured) creditors.[16]

As well, the trustees of the marriage settlement and Mrs Cotterill *both* appealed against the decision that the claim of the trustees was to be governed by *Clayton's Case*. Mrs Cotterill's appeal involved a repudiation of the argument which she had put to Fry J. Fry J summarised the argument which she put to him by saying:

> In this case Mrs *Cotterill* claims to have [377] such portion of the residue of the balance standing to the credit of the late Mr *Hallett's* banking account as may be attributable to her after applying the rule in *Clayton's Case* to that account.[17]

Mrs Cotterill had not, at first instance, made a claim to anything larger than £1708, and the case had been argued at first instance as though that £1,708 was part of the £1,804 paid into the account on 14 November. She did not make any claim at all to the £341 which had been paid into the account on 3 November. Presumably, this stance was taken because her counsel assumed that the application of *Clayton's Case* would result in her money being eroded, in part, by drawings which Hallet made for his own purposes after

13. (1879) 13 Ch D 696 at 703–704.
14. (1879) 13 Ch D 696 at 705–724.
15. (1879) 13 Ch D 696 at 706–707.
16. (1879) 13 Ch D 696 at 707–724.
17. (1879) 13 Ch D 696 at 701.

14 November, notwithstanding that Hallet paid money of his own into the account after 14 November.

The appeal by the trustees and Mrs Cotterill succeeded. The basis of the appeal succeeding, so far as Sir George Jessel MR was concerned, was that a trustee who created a mixed fund was presumed, consistently with honesty, to draw his own money out first. If the trustee mixed his own coins with trust coins in a bag, and drew some coins out of the bag, he would be presumed to be taking his own money out first — and the fact that the money was in a bank account, instead of a bag, made no difference. He said:

> ... It is obvious he must have taken away that which he had a right to take away, his own £100. What difference does it make if, instead of being in a bag, he deposits it with his banker, and then pays in other money of his own, and draws out some money for his own purposes? Could he say that he had actually drawn out anything but his own money? His money was there, and he had a right to draw it out, and why should the natural act of simply drawing out the money be attributed to anything except to his ownership of money which was at his bankers.[18]

Baggallay LJ gave a fuller account of the facts than had been given below, including the fact[19] that the balance to the credit of the account never fell below the aggregate of the two sums of money which had been paid in on 14 November. He says[20] that if the principle that the drawings of Mr Hallett will be appropriated to his own money standing in the account from time to time, were to be applied thoroughly, Mrs Cotterill would have been entitled to the full sum of £1,804 of her money which had been paid in on 14 November, and not merely to the £1,708 which she claimed.

Thus, there never was any competition, on the appeal, between the respective claims of the trustee of the marriage settlement, and Mrs Cotterill. Both were able to be satisfied in full, as to the claims which they had made at first instance. The judgment on the appeal showed that Mrs Cotterill could well have succeeded had she made a more ambitious claim at first instance, but on appeal she was limited by the case she had put at first instance. Thus the decision in the Court of Appeal provides no authority as to whether or not the rule in *Clayton's Case* ought apply to decide the Problem.

There are, however, some dicta in the Court of Appeal in Hallett's Case about the role which *Clayton's Case* plays in tracing. Sir George Jessel MR said that the rule in *Clayton's Case* was:

> ... a very convenient rule, and I have nothing to say against it unless there is evidence either of agreement to the contrary or of circumstances from which a contrary intention must be presumed, and then of course that which is a mere presumption of law gives way to those other considerations. Therefore, it does appear to me that there is nothing in the [378] world laid down by Sir *William Grant* in *Clayton's Case*, or in the numerous cases which follow it, which in the slightest degree affect the principle, which I consider to be clearly established.[21]

---

18. (1879) 13 Ch D 696 at 727–728.
19. (1879) 13 Ch D 696 at 731.
20. (1879) 13 Ch D 696 at 731.
21. (1879) 13 Ch D 696 at 728.

The 'principle' had been identified:

> ... Now, first upon principle, nothing can be better settled, either in our own law, or, I suppose, the law of all civilised countries, than this, that where a man does an act which may be rightfully performed, he cannot say that that act was intentionally and in fact done wrongly. A man who has a right of entry cannot say he committed a trespass in entering. A man who sells the goods of another as agent for the owner cannot prevent the owner adopting the sale, and deny that he acted as agent for the owner. It runs throughout our law, and we are familiar with numerous instances in the law of real property. A man who grants a lease believing he has sufficient estate to grant it, although it turns out that he has not, but has a power which enables him to grant it, is not allowed to say he did not grant it under the power. Wherever it can be done rightfully, he is not allowed to say, against the person entitled to the property or the right, that he has done it wrongfully. That is the universal law.[22]

It was as an example of the application of that principle to the case of a trustee who had blended trust monies with his own that Sir George gave the 'coins in a bag' example, which I have mentioned.[23] The sense of Sir George's reasons, as I follow them, is that the presumption which would ordinarily arise from *Clayton's Case* was rebutted in the case where a trustee had mixed trust money with his own money in a bank account, because a different presumption, that the trustee had acted honestly and drawn his own money out first, displaced it.

Baggallay LJ[24] noted that in *Pennell v Deffell*[25] the court had stated:

> ... that, as a general principle, the rule in *Clayton's Case* must be applied to the banking accounts of trustees for the purpose of determining the proportions in which the *cestuis que trust* and the general creditors, or the several classes of their *cestuis que trust*, are entitled to the debt due from the bankers in closing the account. ...

However, Baggallay LJ said: ... that such presumption was liable to be rebutted, or its effect modified, by any equities affecting Mr Greenwood, and those claiming through him, unless there was sufficient reason to the contrary'.[26] ('Greenwood' is presumably a misnomer for 'Green'.) Baggallay LJ held that in *Pennell v Deffell* there was such an equity, namely 'the obligation ... of attributing to the trustee, when the circumstances would admit of it, an intention to act honestly'.[27] He, like Jessel MR, regards the failure of the Court of Appeal in Chancery to apply that principle as fundamentally undermining the decision in *Pennell v Deffell*. Concerning that decision, he says:

> ... I cannot regard it as satisfactory, if it is to be considered as establishing as a general proposition that in all such cases as that then under their consideration the presumption of an honest intention on the part of the trustee is to be altogether disregarded, however

---

22. (1879) 13 Ch D 696 at 727.
23. At 377 [50] supra.
24. (1879) 13 Ch D 696 at 738.
25. (1853) 43 ER 551.
26. (1879) 13 Ch D 696 at 739.
27. (1879) 13 Ch D 696 at 739–740.

favourable to such a presumption the circumstances of any particular case may be, and that the rule of appropriating in strict order of date the drawings out to the payments in is alone to be applied. On the contrary, I entertain a very decided opinion that in cases like *Pennell v Deffell*, or in such as that which is the subject of the present appeal, full effect should be given to [379] the principle of attributing the honest intention whenever the circumstances of the case admit of such a presumption.[28]

That amounts to saying he was declining to follow *Pennell v Deffell*.

He went on to say:

> ... It may, of course, happen that, through the acts of a trustee, whether wilfully dishonest or not, the ultimate balance may not be sufficient to meet the full amounts of all the trust monies which may have been paid into a blended banking account, and the question then raised may be as to the various claims in respect of distinct trusts; in such a case the strict application of the general rule of appropriating in order of date the drawings out to the payments in may, and probably would, be correct. ...[29]

That is, of course, only obiter dicta.

Thesiger LJ dissented, on the ground that previous authority, namely *Pennell v Deffell*, required a different conclusion to that which the majority had arrived at.

...

Re Oatway — account of the case

[385] ... *Re Oatway; Hertslet v Oatway*[30] involved a trustee who paid £3,000 of trust money into his own banking account (which was then in credit), purchased shares with money withdrawn from the account, then spent the rest of the money in the account. Joyce J held that the beneficiaries of the trust were entitled to the proceeds of sale of the shares. When a trustee mixes trust money and his own money in a bank account, and there is a credit in the bank account:

> ... it is settled that he is not entitled to have the rule in *Clayton's Case* applied so as to maintain that the sums which have been drawn out and paid away so as to be incapable of being recovered represented pro tanto the trust money, and that the balance remaining is not trust money, but represents only his own monies paid into the account ... It is, in my opinion, equally clear that when any of the money drawn out has been invested, and the investment remains in the name or under the control of the trustee, the rest of the balance having been afterwards dissipated by him, he cannot maintain that the investment which remains represents his own money alone, and that what has been spent can no longer be traced and recovered was the money belonging to the trust. In other words, when the private money of the trustee and that which he held in a fiduciary capacity have been mixed in the same banking account, from which various payments have from time to time been made, then, in order to determine to whom any remaining balance or any investment that may have been paid for out of the account ought to be deemed to belong, the trustee must be debited with all the sums

---

28. (1879) 13 Ch D 696 at 743.
29. (1879) 13 Ch D 696 at 743.
30. [1903] 2 Ch 356.

that have been withdrawn and applied to his own use so as to be no longer recoverable, and the trust money in like manner be debited with any sums taken out and duly invested in the names of the proper trustees ...[31]

Note that this is the language of ex post facto accounting, not of presumption of intention.

Even though the amount standing in the account at the time the shares were purchased included money which was the trustee's, of an amount greater than the purchase price of the shares, this did not mean that the trustee was entitled to the shares:

> ... he was never entitled to withdraw the [purchase price of the shares] from the account, or at all events, that he could not be entitled to take that sum from the account and hold it or the investment made therewith, freed from the charge in favour of the trust, unless or until the trust money paid into the account had been first restored, and the trust fund reinstated by due investment of the money in the joint names of the proper trustees, which was never done.[32]

The purchase price of the shares was less than the £3,000 of trust money which had been paid into the bank account. Though the shares rose in value somewhat between the time of purchase and time of sale, the proceeds of sale [386] were less than £3,000. Because the beneficiaries had a charge over the shares for £3,000, they were entitled to the whole of the proceeds of sale.

Re Oatway — matters arising

The principle in *Re Oatway* has been applied by the High Court of Australia in *Scott v Scott*.[33] The principle in *Re Oatway* enables a beneficiary to claim an equitable interest in an asset purchased from a mixed fund. There is another principle which prohibits a trustee from making a profit from his trust. Scott combined those two principles to enable a beneficiary, who could trace his money through a mixed account into a particular asset, to claim a proportionate beneficial interest in that asset, rather than merely a charge, if the value of the asset had gone up since the date of purchase. The House of Lords reached a similar conclusion in *Foskett v McKeown*.[34]

There are two different senses in which the caselaw talks about there being a 'charge' over assets in, or acquired from, a mixed fund. One sense is that which applies when a court grants a remedy of a charge over a particular item of property, ordering that that item of property be used as a fund from which a particular monetary amount is to be raised. The other sense is the sense in which there is, even prior to the grant of a remedy by the court, a charge over all the assets which are in, or have been acquired from, the mixed fund. A charge in that sense arises from the way in which equity reasons towards the granting of a remedy. When a trustee has wrongfully taken property from a trust fund, his first obligation is, so far as the trust property can be seen as remaining in his

---

31. [1903] 2 Ch 356 at 360.
32. [1903] 2 Ch 356 at 361.
33. (1963) 109 CLR 649.
34. [2001] 1 AC 102 at 130 per Lord Millet (with whom Lord Browne-Wilkinson (at 111) and Lord Hoffman (at 115) agreed concerning this point).

hands, to make restitution — that is, to put back in specie into the trust fund whatever of the trust property he still retains. Until he has performed that obligation, equity will not permit him to assert that he has unfettered ownership of *any* of the property into which any part of the trust property has been converted or mixed. In this way, there is a potential for any of the property into which the trust property has been converted or mixed to be the subject of, eventually, an order for restitution in specie. That all the property into which the trust property has been converted or mixed is subject to this potential for being the property which might be seized upon as the subject of an order means that it is all subject to a charge, in this second sense. A charge of this second type arises as soon as the wrongful conversion or mixing occurs, because from that time the converted property or mixed fund is potentially subject to this sort of an order to restore the trust fund.

When tracing can occur into an asset purchased with money taken out of the mixed fund, and not only into what remains of the mixed fund in the bank account, this means identification of the property over which the court grants a proprietary remedy is an ex post facto exercise, and depends upon what property remains at the time of the hearing, out of all the property over which a charge (in the second sense) once existed. It also follows from this that a beneficiary, in exercising rights arising from tracing, has to some extent an election about which property he will take, over which a charge (in the second sense) continues to exist at the date of the hearing. As H A J Ford and W A Lee, *Principles of the Law of Trusts*, say: 'The beneficiary's right of property in the targeted property crystallises only when the court makes a proprietary order with respect to it'.[35]

[387] That a beneficiary has this right to elect, at the time of trial, whether he will seek a remedy against what remains of the mixed fund, or against an asset or assets purchased from the mixed fund, assists in showing that the explanation of tracing given in *Hallett's Case* based upon a presumption of honest intention in making a withdrawal from the mixed fund, is not adequate. The explanation is not adequate in two ways. First, (and this is not a consequence of the beneficiary's right of election concerning remedies) in many factual situations a presumption of honesty on the part of the trustee does not enable one to decide whether a particular withdrawal of money from a trust account has been of trust money, or the trustee's own money. If a withdrawal from a trust account is made, and invested in some investment which is of a kind which might well retain its value, or increase in value, presuming that the trustee is honest does not enable one to say whether the money withdrawn is trust money, or not. Second, remedies which follow the identification of the property which is charged with the obligation to restore the trust fund, are granted over that item or those items of property which, at the time of the trial, have values which will provide the best remedy to the beneficiary. The values of items of property into which a mixed fund has been converted might fluctuate significantly between the time of their acquisition and the time of trial. Presuming the trustee to be honest at the time of making a withdrawal is not enough to identify the property over which the remedy will, eventually, be granted.

---

35. H A Ford & W A Lee, *Principles of the Law of Trusts*, Looseleaf edition, LawBook Company, Sydney, 1996+, [17210].

The fact that a beneficiary has a right to elect, at the time of trial, which asset or assets he will claim a remedy against also creates a serious problem for the application of *Clayton's Case* to withdrawals from a mixed bank account. When *Clayton's Case* applies, it operates to effect an appropriation of the withdrawal, at either the time that the withdrawal is made, or the time that the current account is drawn up (if that is later than the withdrawal). In the situation where money of two different beneficiaries has been paid, successively, into a bank account, and a withdrawal is made of an account equal to the amount of the first beneficiary's money, the operation of *Clayton's Case* would mean that the withdrawal is treated as being, definitely, from the time the appropriation is made, a withdrawal of the money first paid in. In a situation where, from a mixed account of that kind, one withdrawal is made and dissipated, then another withdrawal is made and invested with spectacular success, it should be possible for both beneficiaries to trace into the successful investment. For a charge (in the second sense) exists over the whole mixed fund, in favour of both beneficiaries — the defaulting trustee cannot assert an unqualified title to the mixed fund until both beneficiaries have had their respective trust funds restored. Yet, if *Clayton's Case* is rigidly applied, the appropriation would be regarded as having been made, and there would be none of the money of the first beneficiary remaining in the account, which could be traced into the successful investment.

...

Re Diplock

[401] ... *Re Diplock; Diplock v Wintle*[36] involved a deceased estate which the executors, acting on a mistaken view as to the correct construction of the will, distributed to many charities. The next-of-kin, who on the true construction of the will had been entitled to the assets which were distributed, sought to recover from the charities. The judgment of the Court of Appeal (Lord Greene MR, Wrottesley LJ and Evershed LJ) dealt first with the next-of-kin's claim to have a right in personam to recover from the various wrongly paid charities. The court held that the next-of-kin had that right, subject only to an obligation to give credit for an amount (to be divided rateably between the various charities) which the next-of-kin had recovered from the executors. The court went on to express their views on whether, as well, the next-of-kin had a claim in rem against any of the assets of the charities.[37] They did this[38] in deference to the detailed argument they had received, because their views on the topic might be material to an application for leave to appeal to the House of Lords, and because those views would be relevant if the House of Lords were to uphold an appeal against the court's decision about the availability of the right of recovery in personam. As well though (and importantly for present purposes), the right of recovery in personam was one which the court allowed without interest on the amounts recovered. (The unavailability of interest in the action in personam might have been a peculiarity of that particular case, rather than a universal rule.[39]) If the next-of-kin were to succeed in their claims in rem, interest might possibly have been paid.

---

36. [1948] 1 Ch 465.
37. [1948] 1 Ch 465 at 516ff.
38. [1948] 1 Ch 465 as explained at 516–517.
39. *Westdeutsche Landesbank Girozentrale v Islington London Borough Council* [1996] AC 669 at 694, 729.

In summary, the Court of Appeal in *Re Diplock* held that there could be tracing into assets held by a volunteer, such as the charities involved in *Re Diplock*. Their Lordships held that tracing can occur into a mixed fund **[402]** (such as the bank account of a charity) even if the person who does the mixing is not a fiduciary, but rather is a volunteer.[40] *Sinclair v Brougham*[41] was not decided on a different principle to that applied in *Hallett's Case* — it was decided on the same principle: '... but in its application to new facts fresh light was thrown upon it, and it was shown to have a much wider scope than a narrow reading of *Hallett's Case* itself would suggest'.[42] The court said that, in *Sinclair v Brougham* the House of Lords had applied *Hallett's Case*, so that the class of depositors shared rateably with the class of shareholders, and said:

> ... this application of the principle is an extension of it since, although the right of individuals to trace their own money (if they could) was preserved in the order of the House, the order provided for tracing the aggregate contributions of the two classes as classes. *Hallett's Case* was, of course, based on the right of an individual to follow what he could in equity identify as his own money. The extension of the principle in *Sinclair v Brougham* was the obvious and, indeed, on the facts, the only practical method of securing a just distribution of the assets.[43]

There were three specific distributions to charities concerning which the court discussed the application of *Clayton's Case*. The fullest discussion appears concerning a distribution of estate money made to Dr Barnardo's Homes. The next-of-kin claimed a right to trace into some loan securities, of face value of £40,000, which Dr Barnardo's Homes had purchased for a little less than the face value. The purchase was made using funds drawn on the charity's current account. On 14 December 1936, that account was in credit some £46,000. Then, on 14 December, £3,000 of Diplock money was paid in. Over the next week or so around £22,000 was withdrawn. Then the £39,000-odd, used to purchase the loan securities, was withdrawn. Thus, if *Clayton's Case* applied, the loan securities would have been purchased, as to roughly three thirty-ninths, with Diplock money. The court said the following, about whether *Clayton's Case* ought be applied:

> ... It might be suggested that the corollary of treating two claimants on a mixed fund as interested rateably should be that withdrawals out of that fund ought to be attributed rateably to the interests of both claimants. But in the case of an active banking account this would lead to the greatest difficulty and complication in practice and might in many cases raise questions incapable of solution. What then is to be done? In our opinion, the same rule as that applied in *Clayton's Case* should be applied. This is really a rule of convenience based on so-called presumed intention. It has been applied in the case of two beneficiaries whose trust money has been paid into a mixed banking account from which drawings were subsequently made, and, so far as we know, its application has not been adversely criticised.[44] In such a case both claimants are innocent, neither

---

40. [1948] 1 Ch 465 at 523–526.
41. [1914] AC 398.
42. [1948] 1 Ch 465 at 526.
43. [1948] 1 Ch 465 at 526–527.
44. See *Hallett's Case* (1880) 13 Ch D 696 per Fry J and in *In Re Stenning* [1895] 2 Ch 433 per North J.

is in a fiduciary relation to the other, and if the mixed fund had not been drawn upon they would be entitled to rateable charges upon it. Exactly the same occurs where the claimants are not two beneficiaries but one beneficiary and one volunteer, and we think, accordingly, that the same principle should be adopted.[45]

Thus, the court held that the securities were subject to a charge for the £3,000 of Diplock money which had gone into them.

[403] The court also decided, without further discussion, that *Clayton's Case* might also be applied to decide whether certain investments of St George's Hospital, purchased from a banking account into which Diplock money had been paid, were ones in relation to which a tracing order could be made.[46]

This is to be contrasted with the decision reached concerning the Royal Sailors Orphan Girls School and Home. At a time when it held £9,700 of War Stock, it used £2,000 of Diplock money to buy more War Stock. The War Stock was uncertified inscribed stock, such that the newly purchased stock could not be identified from the previously held stock. Further, various sales of War Stock were made by the charity before it was given notice of the claim of the next-of-kin. The court rejected the view that *Clayton's Case* should be applied to those stockholdings, saying:

> We do not accept the view that the case ought to be treated as though it were subject to the rule in *Clayton's Case*. We see no justification for extending that rule beyond the case of a banking account. Here, before the sales took place, the mass of stock, if the question had then been raised, would have been regarded in equity as belonging rateably to the charity and to the Diplock estate. The only equitable way of treating the situation appears to us to be to regard each sum of stock withdrawn from the mass as having been made up in the same proportions. In so far as, upon this principle, withdrawals represented in part Diplock money and the sums received on the sale of the stock withdrawn were expended on general purposes and cannot now be traced into any existing asset, that amount of Diplock money must be regarded as having disappeared. But in respect of so much of the Diplock interest as is not thus accounted for, we are of opinion that the claim to a rateable proportion of the stock still held is established.[47]

In relation to those charities concerning which a tracing claim succeeded, the court held that the next-of-kin were entitled to a sum representing the interest in fact earned by the investments into which the Diplock money was traced.[48] As no interest was payable on amounts which the Diplock next-of-kin could recover from charities pursuant to the action in personam, the fact that interest was allowed on those items where a claim in rem could be made out means that the court's decisions about how *Clayton's Case* affects a tracing remedy cannot be dismissed as mere obiter dicta.

...

---

45. [1948] 1 Ch 465 at 553–554.
46. [1948] 1 Ch 465 at 550.
47. [1948] 1 Ch 465 at 555–556.
48. [1948] 1 Ch 465 at 557.

Should *Re Diplock* be followed?

[412] ... The discussion of English cases in Part C of this judgment has shown that only English case after *Hallett* which has adopted *Clayton's Case* as the means for deciding which of several beneficiaries whose assets have been mixed will be treated as being withdrawn is *Re Diplock*. A judge of the Supreme Court of New South Wales is not bound to follow decisions of the English Court of Appeal, and such decisions are followed only to the degree of the persuasiveness of their reasoning.[49] I did not regard the reasons which led the Court of Appeal in *Re Diplock* to apply the rule in *Clayton's Case* as being persuasive. In the passage which I have quoted,[50] their Lordships acknowledge that two claimants on a mixed fund should be interested in it rateably for as long as the fund is not depleted. That is uncontentious. The only conclusion which they consider, as following for that proposition, is that withdrawals from the mixed fund ought be attributed rateably to the interests of both claimants. That is not the whole picture which arises from two claimants on the mixed fund being interested rateably. The right of election of the claimants, concerning whatever property they might be able to trace into at the time of trial, the charge each has over the fund and any asset acquired from it, and the possibility of them having a proportionate beneficial interest in assets purchased from the mixed fund, mean that the possible avenues for tracing are not so limited. It is not necessary to be able to decide, at the time a withdrawal is made, whose money is being withdrawn. In other words, the task that *Clayton's Case* is designed to perform is not one which needs to be carried out, for tracing to occur.

Their Lordships say, '... in the case of an active banking account this would lead to the greatest difficulty and complication in practice and might in many cases raise questions incapable of solution'. That remark is one which arises [413] from their assumption that the only way of effecting tracing is to attribute withdrawals rateably to the interests of both claimants. Its strength is limited accordingly. As well, though, the principles of law in this area are ones which deal with claims to trace where the facts are simple, and as well as ones where the facts are complex. That the tracing of the asset of a particular beneficiary which has become mixed might in some circumstances be complex, or prove impossible, if proper principles are adopted, is not a reason for denying the application of proper principles in those circumstances where they can be applied. It is well-known that, outside this particular area of mixing of trust funds of two beneficiaries, or of a beneficiary and an innocent volunteer, tracing is a complex exercise, and sometimes plaintiffs seeking to make out a tracing claim fail to discharge their onus of proof. That is not a reason for changing the principles. As well, as *Sinclair v Brougham* makes clear, the principle which underlies tracing can sometimes result in members of a class being entitled to an equitable interest in property, even in circumstances where an individual member of that class could not discharge the onus of proof to trace into individual assets. Further, it is not as though tracing is the only remedy which a beneficiary has when there has been a breach of trust. While the first duty of a trustee who has mixed assets in breach of trust is to put back into the trust fund such of the trust assets as still remain in his hands, such a trustee also has a duty to make good the trust fund from his own assets.

---

49. *Cook v Cook* (1986) 162 CLR 376 at 390, 394; *Sharah v Healey* [1982] 2 NSWLR 223 at 227–228.
50. At 402 [131] supra.

This personal obligation of the trustee means that tracing is usually only of practical importance in circumstances where the trustee has disappeared or is insolvent.

Insofar as the Court of Appeal relied upon the previous occasions when *Clayton's Case* had been applied in a case of two beneficiaries whose trust money had been paid into a mixed banking account from which drawings were subsequently made (the decision of Fry J in *Hallett's Case*, and North J in *Re Stenning*), the weaknesses which I have previously identified concerning the application of *Clayton's Case* in those decisions makes the reliance of the Court of Appeal on them unpersuasive. The account given elsewhere in these reasons for judgment of the proper basis for tracing through mixed funds,[51] and how the interest of two beneficiaries whose funds are mixed can be traced without resort to *Clayton's Case* lead me to not follow *Re Diplock* in so far as it applied *Clayton's Case*.

Other Australian decisions

Whether *Clayton's Case* should be used to solve the Problem, has not been considered by the High Court of Australia. There is one decision of a single judge of an Australian Supreme Court which certainly applies *Clayton's Case* for the purpose of solving the Problem.[52] Two other decisions of a single judge of a State Supreme Court may also provide some authority for the use of *Clayton's Case* in this area: *Re Laughton;*[53] *Re Joscelyne; Allen's Plaster Products Pty Ltd v Prudential Assurance Co Ltd.*[54]

Various decisions of Australian superior courts have declined to apply *Clayton's Case* to decide how the loss should fall between several beneficiaries whose funds had been mixed.[55] In [414] these cases the impossibility of carrying out the tracing exercise was a factor which led to the court's conclusion to effect a pari passu distribution. In *Australian Securities and Investments Commission v Enterprise Solutions 2000 Pty Ltd*[56] orders were made under s 1114 of the *Corporations Law* (Cth) for the distribution of the assets of a managed investments scheme which had been placed into receivership. A rateable distribution was ordered amongst the investors, partly on the basis that no particular investor could identify his money in any asset. In *Australian Securities & Investments Commission v Nelson,*[57] Austin J gave directions to a liquidator for the distribution of funds held on trust for various investors which had become mixed. His Honour expressed the view[58] that Australian authority had reached the point where the rateable solution was to be preferred to the first in, first out approach when trust funds are mixed, regardless of whether it was impossible on the facts to apply the first in, first out approach. In *Re Global Finance Group Pty Ltd (In liq); Ex parte Read and Herbert,*[59] McLure J dealt with tracing claims of great complexity, arising from the

---

51. Particularly at 386 [83]–[86], 400 [127], 411 [151]–[154] supra and 418 [176]–[185] infra.
52. *Hodges & Hurley v Kovacs Estate Agency Ltd* [1961] WAR 19 at 24.
53. [1962] Tas SR 300.
54. [1963] Tas SR 4.
55. *Re Jones (decd); Ex parte Mayne* (1953) 16 ABC 169; *Windsor Mortgage Nominees Pty Ltd v Cardwell* (1979) ACLC ¶40-540 at 32,199–32,200; *Australian Securities Commission v Melbourne Asset Management Nominees Pty Ltd* (1994) 49 FCR 334 at 358–359, 365.
56. [2001] QSC 082 (Chesterman J, 27 March 2001, unreported).
57. (2003) 44 ACSR 719.
58. (2003) 44 ACSR 719 at 723 [24]–[26].
59. (2002) 26 WAR 385.

mixing of funds held on various trusts. However, the forensic frame in which her Honour was working was one where no party contended that *Clayton's Case* provided the appropriate method of allocating losses amongst the beneficiaries.[60] Thus the decision cannot assist in deciding whether *Clayton's Case* ought be used to solve the Problem.

There is no Australian authority which is binding on me and is to the contrary of the dictum of the Court of Appeal in *Keefe's Case* that the decision of Kearney J in *Hagan v Waterhouse*[61] should be approved. That dictum of the Court of Appeal is itself not binding on me.[62] However, that the Court of Appeal pronounced that dictum at all is a matter which, from my position in the judicial hierarchy, needs to be accorded considerable weight.

Australian text writers favour not using *Clayton's Case* to solve the Problem. *Jacobs' Law of Trusts in Australia*[63] continues not to favour it.

H A J Ford and W A Lee, *Principles of the Law of Trusts*[64] refers to cases where consideration has been given to whether *Clayton's Case* operates to allocate losses between several beneficiaries whose money has been mixed, and says:

> In some of these cases judges correctly reject the application of *Clayton's Case* as irrelevant. *Clayton's Case* provides a means of ascertaining each depositor's entitlement within the bank account; but it has never been applied to differentiate between depositors if a subsequent deficiency arises in the account. Then each depositor is entitled to the proportion that his or her ascertained entitlement bears to the value remaining in the account.

> Unfortunately some commentators have entertained an opinion that *Clayton's Case* applies as between existing depositors at the date when the account becomes deficient in the wake of a delinquent withdrawal, allocating the delinquent withdrawal amongst the depositors on a first in first out basis, so that the withdrawal that creates the deficiency is attributed to those clients whose deposits in the account are earlier, later deposits being paid in full ...

[415] Most commentators repudiate that opinion. Scott[65] observes:

> The rule is so clearly arbitrary and unfair that one must suspect the soundness of the reasons on which it is based; and indeed, the only basis turns out to be the application of presumptions based on fictions.

Birks[66] says that this exception should be regarded as 'open to review'. Goff & Jones[67] condemn it. Moffatt[68] doubts it as do Underhill & Hayton.[69] It has been expressly rejected

---

60. (2002) 26 WAR 385 at 430 [227].
61. (1991) 34 NSWLR 308.
62. *Hepburn v TCN Channel Nine Pty Ltd* [1984] 1 NSWLR 386.
63. R P Meagher and W M C Gummow, *Jacobs' Law of Trusts in Australia*, Butterworths, Sydney, 1977, p 749 [2711]–[2712].
64. H A Ford & W A Lee, *Principles of the Law of Trusts*, Looseleaf edition, LawBook Company, Sydney, 1996+, [17250].
65. Scott, *Law of Trusts*, 1998, para 519.
66. Birks, *Law of Restitution*, 1989, p 364.
67. Goff & Jones, *The Law of Restitution*, 1986, p 59.
68. Moffatt, *Trusts Law Text and Materials*, 1994.
69. Underhill & Hayton, *Law of Trusts & Trustees*, 1995, pp 860–861.

by the Ontario Court of Appeal in *Ontario (Securities Commission) v Greymac Credit Corp*.[70] *Jacobs'*[71] offers the same view. *Lewin on Trusts*[72] having considered it say that the application of the rule is arbitrary.

...

Conclusion — *Clayton's Case* not applicable

[416] ...The principles upon which tracing operates, and the proper scope of application of the rule in *Clayton's Case*, both favour the rule in *Clayton's Case* not being used to allocate losses suffered by beneficiaries whose funds are mixed. This conclusion is arrived at as a matter of principle, regardless of **[417]** whether or not there is sufficient information to enable an allocation of withdrawals to deposits, in accordance with *Clayton's Case*, to be made in any particular case.

Alternatively, distinguishing *Clayton's Case*

Even if I were wrong in the conclusion I have just come to, I would not, on the facts, apply *Clayton's Case* in the present case. The situation in which *Clayton's Case* came to be applied in *Re Diplock* is distinguishable from the situation of the trust accounts of French Caledonia Travel.

The situation under consideration in *Re Diplock* was that of a charity, which had been given money from the Diplock estate to which it thought it was entitled. It paid that money into its general account, and then drew against the general account. It had no consciousness that the money received from the Diplock account was, at that time, anything other than its own money. In those circumstances, the presumed intention which arises from *Clayton's Case* has some reality. It is not really comparable with the situation of the operator of a trust account containing money which it knows is money of many beneficiaries.

The fact that the trust account operated by French Caledonia was the type it was — where money was contributed by numerous intending travellers, each intending to pay for their own travel — is in itself a reason why, as between trustee and the beneficiaries, *Clayton's Case* ought not be treated as applying. If such a trust account were operated properly, the intention one would presume, when any money was drawn from the trust account, to pay the expenses of any particular traveller, was that it was the money of that traveller which was being drawn upon, regardless of whether, of the money then standing in the trust account, that traveller's money had been paid in first, last, or somewhere in between. If the operator of such a trust account misappropriated money from it, the intention one would presume is that the operator was wrongly taking money of all the people whose money was in the account.

Part E — pari passu distribution?

Having concluded that the liquidator should not apply *Clayton's Case* does not of itself lead to a conclusion about what manner of distribution the liquidator should adopt.

---

70. (1986) 30 DLR (4th) 1.
71. R P Meagher and W M C Gummow, *Jacobs' Law of Trusts in Australia*, Butterworths, Sydney, 1977, [2712].
72. Mowbray, Tucker, Le Poidevin, Simpson and Brightwell, *Lewin on Trusts*, 2000, pp 41–53, 41–47.

To say that he should adopt a 'pari passu distribution' glosses over some questions of principle, and of evidence.

Roscoe v Winder

James Roscoe (Bolton) Ltd v Winder[73] concerned a person who paid trust money into his personal bank account, spent everything in that bank account apart from £25, and then replenished the bank account. Sargant J held that the beneficiary could trace only in relation to £25. His Honour accepted[74] that if there was evidence that the intention of the trustee, in replenishing the account, was to substitute the additional monies for the original trust monies, that intention could be given effect to. But in circumstances where the account in question was a general trading account of the trustee, the mere fact of payment in of funds was not enough to result in such an intention being attributed to the trustee.

James Roscoe v Winder is authority for the 'lowest intermediate balance rule'. Under it, absent any payment in of money with the intention of making good earlier depredations, tracing cannot occur through a mixed account for **[418]** any larger sum than is the lowest balance in the account between the time the beneficiary's money goes in, and the time the remedy is sought. In a case where the type of tracing being attempted involves detailed analysis of what has become of the property of a particular beneficiary, and into what other assets it has been converted or mixed, the lowest intermediate balance rule is fundamental to a principled approach to tracing. Remembering that the aim of tracing is to identify property which is still in the hands of a defendant, and which can be seen to be in substance the property of the plaintiff, no more than the lowest intermediate balance in a mixed account can meet that test. It is only to the extent of the lowest intermediate balance that the beneficiary can say 'you cannot in conscience deny that your right to get money out of your bank account is property which you hold on trust, and which you must put back into the trust fund'.

Equality is equity?

The maxim 'equality is equity' does not require that the available funds be divided between all people who can establish that, at one time, they had a claim on a bank account in which property held on trust for several people have been mixed. It can readily enough be accepted that if several people have an equal right to be paid from a particular fund, and the fund proves insufficient, their claims will abate rateably. This happens in relation to general legacies,[75] and with the proportionate abatement of provable debts which creditors sustain in a bankruptcy or winding up. Rateable abatement does not automatically apply whenever there is a mixed fund because there is a preliminary question, the answer to which cannot be assumed, of whether all the claimants on the fund, in the form the fund takes at the time of trial, have claims which are equal.

---

73. [1915] 1 Ch 62.
74. [1915] 1 Ch 62 at 69.
75. *Re Farmer; Nightingale v Whybrow* [1939] Ch 573; *Re Wilson (decd); Hartley v Marie Curie Hospital* [1940] Ch 966.

There are two senses of 'have claims which are equal' which apply here. The first concerns whether, in relation to the amount of money of a beneficiary which has gone into a mixed fund, and for which that beneficiary has in one sense a claim, the beneficiary has a charge over whatever property remains from that fund for the whole of the amount of his money which went in. If it can be demonstrated that some beneficiaries have a charge over those assets for the whole amount of their money which went into the fund, while others have a charge over those assets for only part of their money which went into the fund, their claims are not equal. An example of how this happens is found in the extract from *Re Walter J Schmidt & Co; Ex parte Feuerbach*[76] contained in the quotation from *Re Registered Securities Ltd*.[77] Modifying the example so that it talks of charges, rather than proportions, at the beginning of February A has a charge on the fund for $3000 and B has a charge on the fund for $5000. The depletion during February means that A's charge on the fund is reduced to one for $1500, and B's charge is reduced to one for $2500. At the beginning of March A and B have those charges for $1500 and $2500 respectively, and C has a charge for his full $5000. Thus, even though A, B and C each has a claim for $5000, because the charges they can demonstrate over the fund at the beginning of March are not equal, their claims as at that date are not equal.

The other sense in which claims might be unequal arises once the amount of the various charges of beneficiaries on the fund has been established. Then a question arises of whether in accordance with the equitable principles **[419]** concerning priorities, or indeed whether by reference to any personal equities whatever which exist between the various claimants, there is any reason to treat any of the claimants as postponed to any of the others.

An example of such a personal equity is to be found in *Re Hobourn Aero Components Ltd's Air Raid Distress Fund; Ryan v Forrest*[78] at first instance (Cohen J) and in the Court of Appeal (Lord Greene MR, Morton LJ and Somervell LJ).[79] Nearly all the employees of a company agreed to deductions being made from their wages to set up a fund. The fund was administered by a committee, referred to as trustees, which had a discretion about making payments from the fund. There appeared to be a consensus that the purposes for which payments could be made were providing benefits in cash or kind to former members of the Fund who were on active service, and making grants to members in distress as a result of enemy action. The question for decision concerned how to distribute a surplus in the fund. The case proceeded on the implicit assumption that the fund was held on trust. All judges held that the fund was not held on charitable trusts, because a personal relationship to a particular entity (namely the employer company) was needed before an individual was eligible for a benefit, and distributions were made regardless of the means of recipients.

Cohen J held that the fund should be distributed on the basis that:

> … each donor retained an interest in the amount of his contributions except so far as they are applied for the purposes for which they were subscribed. Moreover, the rule in *Clayton's Case* is not applicable in such a case (see *In re British Red Cross Balkan Fund*). …[80]

---

76. 298F 314 (1923).

77. [1991] 1 NZLR 545, at 553 (quoted at 406 [142]).

78. [1946] Ch 86.

79. *Re Hobourn Aero Components Ltd's Air Raid Distress Fund; Ryan v Forrest* [1946] Ch 194.

80. [1946] Ch 86 at 97.

As to the manner of distribution, Cohen J referred to two cases in which orders had been made for distribution of a fund without requiring the bringing into hotchpot of benefits received. He said:

> ... But in both those cases the decision to this effect was based on the difficulty and the expense involved in ascertaining the amount of the respective benefits and the persons to whom they were paid. In the present case I was told by ... the company's accountant, that while considerable labour would be involved, there would be no difficulty in ascertaining the amounts of the benefits or the recipients, and I have come to the conclusion that I should not be justified in deviating from the general principle, that a person seeking to participate in the distribution of a fund must bring into hotchpot anything he has already received therefrom. ...[81]

He declared that:

> ... the fund now available for distribution ought to be distributed amongst all the persons who during their employment by Hobourn Aero Components, Ld, contributed to the fund at any time after December 12, 1940, in proportion to the total amount contributed by them respectively to the fund, each such person bringing into hotchpot any amount received by him by way of benefit out of the fund.[82]

The appeal concerned only the question of whether the fund was charitable, not the manner in which it should be distributed once it was decided it was not charitable.

The manner of distribution supports the view that all the contributors have a charge over the fund in which their contributions are mixed, to support their interest in the fund by way of a contingent resulting trust if the committee [420] were not to exercise its discretion and distribute the entire fund. As contributions are made week by a week, so the interest of each contributor increases; as the fund is expended, so the interest of each contributor is proportionately decreased. Further, the requirement to bring into hotchpot benefits received from the fund is an illustration of a personal equity which results in the charge which one contributor has being held to be of lower priority than the charge which another contributor has, though with the possibility of becoming of equal ranking if one of the chargees performed an action which he had no obligation to perform, but the performance of which was a precondition to his charge being accorded equal rank.

The appropriate way of dividing available assets between beneficiaries whose money has been mixed in an account might also depend upon what other remedies in rem the various beneficiaries have. If there is a situation where the money of A and B is mixed in an account, some of it is withdrawn and used to purchase an asset, and then the money of C is placed in the account, and both the asset, and the account, are available at the time of trial, a liquidator might be directed to administer the fund in accordance with principles of marshalling, so that A and B satisfied themselves from the asset (which only they could trace into) to the extent that they could, leaving C to claim a higher percentage of his claim from the account balance than A and B are permitted to claim

---

81. [1946] Ch 86 at 97.
82. [1946] Ch 86 at 97–98.

from the account balance. In *Re Global Finance Group Pty Ltd*,[83] McLure J held that, on the facts of the case before her, a division of available monies pari passu between all claimants was inappropriate.

These examples show how it cannot be said that, as a matter of law, a fund in which assets of several beneficiaries have become mixed should always be distributed amongst all beneficiaries, pro rata to their claims.

Tracing principles applied to classes

As *Crace-Calvert's Case*[84] and *Sinclair v Brougham* show, it is possible for there to be tracing which does not depend upon identifying the transmogrifications which the assets of a particular beneficiary have gone through. Sometimes, a liquidator seeking to administer a fund will know nothing more than that the fund is held on trust, and that there are a number of potential claimants to the fund, whose merits he cannot on any rational basis distinguish between. In such a situation, it may be appropriate for the court to direct a liquidator that he is justified in distributing the fund amongst the claimants proportionately to their claims. It is relevant to this that in *Sinclair v Brougham* the fact of monies being mixed was enough for the House to decide that there should be a pro rata distribution, and the paucity of evidence meant that there was no reason to depart from a pro rata distribution.

Sometimes, however, there might be facts which show that claimants fall into particular classes, such that the amount of the charge which one class has on the assets which remain is likely to be a smaller proportion of the amount of their money which went in than is the case with another class. If, for instance, there was a time when a trust account was completely depleted, beneficiaries whose money went into that trust account before the day of depletion could not have any equitable right at all to the sum which stands in the account at the date of trial. If the account in which the mixing occurred at any time reached a particularly low level, it may be that those people whose money was paid into the account before that low level was reached ought be **[421]** accorded a smaller dividend on the amount of their claim than people whose money was paid in after that low level was reached. In carrying out such calculations, estimation and inference can be appropriate if precise evidence is not available.

Sometimes, likewise, there might be facts which showed that claimants fall into particular classes such that one class has a higher priority for the charge it can establish than does the other class.

While a liquidator must distribute funds of the company, or under his control through the company being trustee of trusts, in accordance with legal entitlements of people to those funds, the court's findings about what legal entitlements exist depend upon the evidence which is placed before the court, and inferences properly drawn from that evidence. When distribution of a fund is made by reference to classes of claimants, the available evidence is frequently evidence about the nature of a fund and the types of contribution which have gone into it. It is because the evidence is at this level of generality that the court reaches conclusions about the beneficial ownership of the fund by saying

---

83. (2002) 26 WAR 385.
84. *Guardian Permanent Benefit Building Society, Re (Crace-Calvert's Case)* (1882) 23 Ch D 440.

that it is divided amongst claimants in some particular way. If ever the court is able to give a remedy founded on tracing some individual claimants, it is because evidence is available which enables the property of those individual claimants to be more specifically traced. It should not be a cause for surprise that evidence of these different types can lead to different types of conclusion.

It is possible to recognise that, on the basis of evidence of a liquidator's investigations taken to a certain stage, distribution among claimants proportionately to their claims is proper, while at the same time recognising the theoretical possibility that further investigation might turn up facts which showed, in some way, inequality amongst the various claims. If ever a liquidator is in significant doubt about whether he ought conduct further investigations to see whether any such facts emerge, he can always ask the Court for directions on that topic.

In *Law Society of Upper Canada v Toronto-Dominion Bank*[85] the Ontario Court of Appeal held that beneficiaries whose money had been mixed in an account, and wrongly depleted, should share whatever balance remained in the account pro rata to their contributions, without regard to the 'lowest intermediate balance rule'. One reason for this conclusion was pragmatic — that performing the calculations required to identify the proportions in which the fund was held following each deposit or withdrawal would be extremely complicated in principle, and often not achievable in fact. The second was that the fund was a blended fund, and when it was wrongly depleted it was the fund as a whole which was wrongly depleted, not any particular beneficiary's contributions.

I do not accept that either of these reasons leads to a conclusion that, always and regardless of the facts of the individual case, the lowest intermediate balance rule has no part to play in deciding how a mixed fund of several beneficiaries should be distributed in specie. As to the first reason, whether performing the calculations to carry out a full tracing exercise is complicated, or achievable, will depend upon the particular case being considered. Further, it is not as though the only available alternatives are full analysis of every transaction in the account, and dividing between all claimants equally. As to the second reason, while it is true that, when a depletion occurs from a fund, it [422] is the fund as a whole, as it exists at that time, which is depleted, accretions to the fund after that time are, self evidently, not affected by that depletion.

In the present case, the liquidator puts no facts before the Court which lead to a conclusion that the various claimants ought be divided into various classes which are given different dividends. There is no reason to believe that there are any assets purchased from the accounts, into which some beneficiaries can trace but not others. The funds available are comparatively small, and likely to be completely, or substantially, depleted by the liquidator's own costs if the liquidator tried to carry out a more extensive analysis of the accounts. In these circumstances, the liquidator is justified in distributing amongst all the claimants, proportionately to their claims as assessed by him.

Comment

1. See Radan & Stewart at **29.25–29.37**.

---

85. (1998) 169 DLR (4th) 353.

30

OTHER EQUITABLE REMEDIES

Introduction

30.1 This chapter deals with a number of equitable remedies. The extracted cases discuss the following:

- the availability of rectification of contracts entered into as the result of a common mistake: *Ryledar Pty Ltd v Euphoric Pty Ltd* (2007) 69 NSWLR 603;
- the availability of rectification of contracts entered into as the result of a unilateral mistake: *George Wimpey UK Ltd v V I Construction Ltd* [2005] EWCA 77; and
- the availability of an account of profits in equity: *Dart Industries Inc v The Decor Corporation Pty Ltd* (1993) 179 CLR 101.

Rectification for common mistake

30.2   Ryledar Pty Ltd v Euphoric Pty Ltd
(2007) 69 NSWLR 603

Court: Court of Appeal of New South Wales

Facts: Ryledar was a petrol retailer operating under the business name Volume Plus. Euphoric distributed Mobil petroleum products and entered into a supply agreement with Ryledar in May 1998, which was varied in March 1999. The original contract was expressed to have a two-year term, expiring in May 2000, which the 1999 agreement extended by six months to November 2000. However, the original contract also provided an option for three 'renewal periods' of one year each. The agreement also referred to a rebate entitlement in favour of Ryledar for gas and auto distillate. Litigation was initiated by Euphoric for recovery of moneys that required construction of the agreements in relation to the option terms and the application of the rebate to Ryledar's outlets.

Issues: The principal issues before the Court of Appeal were (i) whether Ryledar was entitled to the rebate for distillate supplied to its sites located outside its 'Sydney Metro locations' and (ii) whether Euphoric breached the agreement by denying Ryledar's entitlement to exercise the option for the first renewal period.

Decision: The Court of Appeal (Mason P, Tobias and Campbell JJA) unanimously rejected Ryledar's appeal and upheld Euphoric's interpretation of the agreement between the parties as varied.

> **Extracts:** The extracts below from the separate judgments of Tobias JA and Campbell JA outline the principles to be applied for rectification of contracts in equity.

Tobias JA

[629] The relevant legal principles

As is observed in Meagher Gummow & Lehane *Equity, Doctrines & Remedies*,[1] it is of the upmost importance for a proper appreciation of the basis of the equitable doctrine of rectification to realise that the court, by its orders, merely reforms the instrument in which the parties have mistakenly expressed their agreement. The learned authors then cite the following passage from the judgment of Denning LJ in *Frederick E Rose (London) Ltd v William H Pim Junior & Co Ltd*:

> In order to get rectification it is necessary to show that the parties were in complete agreement on the terms of their contract but by an error wrote them down wrongly.[2] ...

[632] [I]n *Club Cape Schanck Resort Co Ltd v Cape Country Club Pty Ltd* ... Tadgell JA [agreed with] the proposition that 'the court may order rectification of a document which contains words used purposely, but mistakenly as to their effect, so as to give effect to the true intention of the parties'.[3]

His Honour observed that in *Commissioner of Stamp Duties (NSW) v Carlenka* the mistake or misapprehension in that case was '... such as to produce a fundamental inconsistency between what the words used in the deed, when properly interpreted, were apt to achieve and what the maker of the deed had antecedently determined to achieve by using them'.[4]

His Honour concluded in these terms:

> ... rectification will be ordered only to give effect to the common intention [positively] shown. So, since the equitable doctrine of rectification exists for the purpose, in effect, of ordering actually or notionally the textual amendment of the document, it will not be available to achieve the amendment of a particular document just because the document is shown not to conform with a common intention of the parties to it. It must be shown further that words or expressions or other text inserted into or deleted from the document would give effect to the common intention.[5]

Phillips JA, after referring to the proposition that rectification is possible only where the written word fails to give effect to the parties' common intention,[6] summarised the relevant principles in the following passage:

> ... I venture to suggest that the principle upon which rectification depends always remains the same; it depends in every case upon a want of correspondence between the form of the

---

1. 4th ed (2002), LexisNexis Butterworths, Australia at 886 [26–010].
2. [1953] 2 QB 450 at 461.
3. *Club Cape Schanck Resort Co Ltd v Cape Country Club Pty Ltd* (2001) 3 VR 526 at 528.
4. *Club Cape Schanck Resort Co Ltd v Cape Country Club Pty Ltd* (2001) 3 VR 526 at 530.
5. *Club Cape Schanck Resort Co Ltd v Cape Country Club Pty Ltd* (2001) 3 VR 526 at 531.
6. *Club Cape Schanck Resort Co Ltd v Cape Country Club Pty Ltd* (2001) 3 VR 526 at 538.

document (that is, in the words actually used) and the common intention of the parties at the time when the document is executed. Where the disconformity is the product of a common mistake, that mistake may be as to what words have been employed in the document or the meaning or effect of such words as appear. But whatever the common mistake, the lack of correspondence must be between the form of the document and the common intention, if rectification is to be available. In *Rose v Pim* the parties were mistaken as to the effect of their words, but there was no disconformity between the words employed and what was held to be their common intention — so rectification was not available. In *Carlenka*, there was a lack of correspondence between form and intention so rectification was available. Of course, whatever the nature or source of the underlying mistake of the parties, the common intention of the parties at the time of the execution of the document remains a matter of fact, which accounts, I believe for such variations as occur in result. The result in any given case will depend upon whether in the particular circumstances of that case there is (as a matter of fact) the requisite disconformity between the document as executed and the common intention of the parties. It is not enough that the parties have made a mistake about their document (whether the mistake be about the words used, their meaning or their effect); that mistake may serve to explain such disconformity (if any) as is seen to exist, but it cannot be a substitute for it.[7] ...

[633] More recently, in *Mander Pty Ltd v Clements*,[8] McKechnie J stated the relevant legal principle in terms of what Denning LJ had said in *Frederick E Rose (London) Ltd v William H Pim Junior & Co Ltd*,[9] namely, that in order to get rectification it was necessary to show that the parties were in complete agreement on the terms of their contract, but by an error wrote them down wrongly ...

[641] According to *Carter on Contracts*,[10] it is sufficient for proving a continuing common intention to establish some manifestation or disclosure by words, conduct or outward expression of the accord which the subsequent instrument fails to express. Such an external (or objective) manifestation of intention although sufficient, is not necessary provided that the party seeking rectification has proved that both parties had the necessary common intention. However, the learned author suggests that in view of the requirement that the party seeking rectification to adduce clear and convincing evidence of the required common intention, lack of any outward manifestation of it may well signify that the party seeking rectification will not be able to discharge the relevant onus of proof.

The proposition that there is a requirement for an outward expression of intention was rejected by L Bromley QC in his article 'Rectification in Equity'.[11] Bromley's thesis was that although the presence or absence of an outward expression of accord may well go to whether the burden of proof can be discharged, it was not per se a requirement of rectification: rather, because the actual correction of instruments by rectification was only one of the ways in which the Court of Chancery acted in matters of conscience, what was required to be ascertained was the parties' subjective or real or true intention.

---

7. *Club Cape Schanck Resort Co Ltd v Cape Country Club Pty Ltd* (2001) 3 VR 526 at 539.
8. (2005) 30 WAR 46.
9. [1953] 2 QB 450 at 461.
10. Vol 1, LexisNexis Butterworths, Sydney, 2002, at 52,521 [22-460].
11. (1971) 87 *Law Quarterly Review* 532.

Thus ... David Wright[12] ... refers with approval to Bromley's suggestion that there is no need for an outward (or objective) expression of intention and that the relevant consideration is the subjective intention of the parties given that the ancient equitable remedy of rectification is an application of the maxim that 'equity looks to the intent, rather than to the form'. The lack of any need to establish some outward expression of accord was confirmed by Clarke J in the *NSW Medical Defence Union* case[13] and by Gummow J in *Elders Trustee and Executor Co Ltd v E G Reeves Pty Ltd*.[14] Therefore, it is the need to establish the subjective common intention of the parties which is critical, especially where the parties' dealings prior to the execution of the instrument sought to be rectified are inconclusive.

In any event, no basis exists in any of the authorities to which I have referred which suggests that the subjective intention of the parties is irrelevant, as Ryledar submitted. In *Commissioner of Stamp Duties (NSW) v Carlenka*,[15] **[642]** Mahoney AP stated that in the context of rectification the term 'intention' referred to that which was subjectively seen and intended to be effected by the relevant document. Such an approach is consistent ... with the following observation of Pearce LJ in *Earl v Hector Whaling Ltd*: 'It is a question of fact and degree what weight of evidence is needed to overcome [the] inherent probability, and to establish that, the parties did not mean what they wrote'.[16] ...

It follows from the foregoing that first, the common intention which must be established by clear and convincing proof to justify rectification must be the actual or true common intention of the parties. Second, evidence of that intention may be ascertained not only from the external or outward expressions of the parties manifested by their objective words or conduct but also from evidence of their subjective states of mind.

Third, where, for instance, the correspondence between and/or conduct of the parties establishes a positive lack of an 'objective' common intention, then that evidence must be taken in conjunction with the evidence (if any) of their subjective states of mind to determine whether the necessary common intention has been established. In the example posited, that would be highly unlikely.

Fourth, in *Westland Savings Bank v Hancock*[17] it was held by Tipping J that a party subsequently acting as if the instrument stood in the form into which it is sought to be rectified was strong evidence of that party's intention at the time to execute the instrument in its rectified form. Such conduct is obviously of significance but, depending on other evidence, if any, is not necessarily conclusive although in the absence of any such evidence it may be.

Fifth, it follows that where the correspondence and/or conduct positively establishes the necessary common intention, then assertions by the party opposing rectification of his or her subjective state of mind which is inconsistent with that party's outward manifestation of his or her intention, being unexpressed and uncommunicated, is

---

12. D Wright, 'Rectification' in P Parkinson (ed), *The Principles of Equity*, 2nd ed, Lawbook Co, Sydney, 2003, p 977.
13. *NSW Medical Defence Union Ltd v Transport Industries Insurance Co Ltd* (1986) 6 NSWLR 740.
14. (1987) 78 ALR 193 at 253–4.
15. *Commissioner of Stamp Duties (NSW) v Carlenka Pty Ltd* (1995) 41 NSWLR 329 at 630.
16. *Earl v Hector Whaling Ltd* [1961] 1 Lloyd's Rep 459 at 468.
17. [1987] 2 NZLR 21 at 31.

unlikely to trump his or her expressed intention. But this is because that party is unlikely to be believed.

Sixth, where as in the present case, the outward expression of the parties' common intention is at best inconclusive, then establishing that the subjective states of mind of the parties evinces the relevant common intention becomes critical if the necessary standard of proof to support an order for rectification is to be achieved.

Campbell JA

[655] Rectification and intention
The first [additional remark] is Mr Rayment's submission that it is possible, for the purpose of deciding whether to grant rectification, to determine the common intention of the parties objectively, and ignore any inconsistent evidence which established that, subjectively speaking, no such common intention was held. That submission runs counter to fundamental principle about the basis on which rectification of contracts is granted.

It is now clearly established that what is necessary for rectification of a document is a common intention of the parties that continues to the time of execution of the document in question, but that an antecedent concluded contract is not needed. It is not sufficient to show that a written instrument does not represent the common intention of the parties — as well, it must be shown what their common intention was.[18]

As well, it is commonplace that the task of the court in deciding whether a contract has been entered, and in construction of contracts, is to ascertain the common intention of the parties.

Thus, both for the purpose of deciding whether a contract has been entered and construing it, and for the purpose of deciding whether to grant rectification of a contract already entered, a court seeks to ascertain the common intention of the parties to the contract. However, the use of the single expression 'common intention' masks two quite different concepts — what counts as a 'common intention' for one of these purposes is significantly different to what counts as a 'common intention' for the other of these purposes.

The type of intention relevant to contract formation and construction
For the purpose of deciding whether a contract has been entered, or what construction it bears, the common intention that the court seeks to ascertain is what is sometimes called the 'objective intention' of the parties. That is the intention that a reasonable person, with the knowledge of the words and actions of the parties communicated to each other, and the knowledge that the parties had of the surrounding circumstances, would conclude that the parties had, concerning the subject matter of the alleged contract.

There is also authoritative recognition that a factor to be taken into account in deciding whether a contract has been entered and if so what are its terms is 'the purpose and object of the transaction'.[19] [656] In *Pacific Carriers Ltd v BNP Paribas*,[20] the joint judgment of Gleeson CJ, Gummow J, Hayne J, Callinan J and Heydon J recognised the appropriateness of taking into account the purpose and object of the transaction, and continued:

---

18. *Slee v Warke* (1949) 86 CLR 271 at 281.
19. *Pacific Carriers Ltd v BNP Paribas* (2004) 218 CLR 451 at 462; *Toll (FGCT) Pty Ltd v Alphapharm Pty Ltd* (2004) 219 CLR 165 at 179.
20. *Pacific Carriers Ltd v BNP Paribas* (2004) 218 CLR 451 at 462.

In *Codelfa Constructions Pty Ltd v State Rail Authority of NSW*,[21] Mason J set out with evident approval the statement by Lord Wilberforce in *Reardon Smith Line Ltd v Hansen-Tangen*:

> 'In a commercial contract it is certainly right that the court should know the commercial purpose of the contract and this in turn presupposes knowledge of the genesis of the transaction, the background, the context, the market in which the parties are operating'.[22]

But the purpose and object of the transaction is itself ascertained objectively — it is ascertained by considering what a reasonable observer, in the situation of the parties, would conclude was the purpose and object of the transaction. In *Prenn v Simmonds*, Lord Wilberforce noted that Lord Blackburn's judgment in *River Wear Commissioners v Adamson*[23] had said that the task involved in construction required one to: '... inquire beyond the language and see what the circumstances were with reference to which the words were used, and the object, appearing from those circumstances, which the person using them had in view'.[24] (Emphasis added).

Lord Wilberforce also said: 'the commercial, or business object, of the transaction, *objectively ascertained*, may be a surrounding fact' (emphasis added), and, '... evidence of negotiations, or of the parties' intentions ... ought not to be received, and evidence should be restricted to evidence of the factual background known to the parties at or before the date of the contract, including evidence of the "genesis" and *objectively* the "aim" of the transaction'.[25] (Emphasis added).

There are some statements to the effect that there can be some exceptional cases where the subjective intention of the parties can be taken into account in deciding whether a contract has been entered or not, in situations where the parties were playacting, or 'joking, or doing or saying anything that was intended to be taken other than at face value'.[26] These are not, it seems to me, a real exception to the objective theory of contract. Rather, a subjective intention not to enter a contract comes to be taken into account, in situations like those of playacting or joking, because there is some form of communication between the parties, or context, such that a reasonable person would realise that the words were not intended to be taken at face value. Similarly, a subjective intention to use words with some meaning other than the meaning that an ordinary hearer of the words would put on them, if the hearer were not in the specific context in which the words were spoken, comes to be taken into account, in deciding what are the terms of the contract, only because there is some form of communication between the parties, or context, such that a reasonable person would realise that the more usual meaning of the words was not intended. But a subjective intention to use words with

---

21. (1982) 149 CLR 337 at 350.
22. *Reardon Smith Line Ltd v Hansen-Tangen* [1976] 3 All ER 570 at 574.
23. (1877) 2 App Cas 743 at 763.
24. *Prenn v Simmonds* [1971] 1 WLR 1381 at 1384.
25. *Prenn v Simmonds* [1971] 1 WLR 1381 at 1385.
26. *Australian Broadcasting Corporation v XIVth Commonwealth Games Ltd* (1988) 18 NSWLR 540 at 550 per Gleeson CJ; *Air Great Lakes Pty Limited v K S Easter (Holdings) Pty Ltd* (1985) 2 NSWLR 309 at 330–1.

some meaning other than their usual meaning, not communicated in any way to the person with whom one is dealing, and not ascertainable from [657] the context within which one is speaking or acting, is not sufficient to stop a contract being entered in which the terms are accorded the meaning that a reasonable observer would take them to have. Similarly, a subjective intention not to contract, not communicated in any way to the person with whom one is dealing, and not ascertainable from the context within which one is speaking or acting, is not sufficient to stop a contract being entered. Thus, the only reason why it can be said that the subjective intention of the person who is playacting or joking is taken into account is because a reasonable person, in the context in which the words in question are communicated, would realise that they were not to be taken at face value. This is, it seems to me, an application of the objective theory of contract, not an exception to it.

The type of intention relevant to rectification

By contrast, the type of intention that is relevant to rectification of a contract is the subjective intention — sometimes called the actual intention — of the parties.

In *Codelfa Construction Pty Ltd v State Rail Authority of New South Wales*, Mason J said:

> The implication of a term is to be compared, and at the same time contrasted, with rectification of the contract. In each case the problem is caused by a deficiency in the expression of the consensual agreement. A term which should have been included has been omitted. The difference is that with rectification the term which has been omitted and should have been included *was actually agreed upon*; with implication the term is one which it is presumed that the parties would have agreed upon had they turned their minds to it — it is not a term that they have actually agreed upon. Thus, in the case of the implied term the deficiency in the expression of the consensual agreement is caused by the failure of the parties to direct their minds to a particular eventuality and to make explicit provision for it. *Rectification ensures that the contract gives effect to the parties' actual intention*; the implication of a term is designed to give effect to the parties' presumed intention.[27] (Emphasis added).

Parol evidence admissible

One way in which it can be seen that it is subjective intention that matters for rectification, concerns the evidence admissible in a rectification suit. Notwithstanding that the contract that it is sought to rectify is in writing, and notwithstanding the common law rule that parol evidence is not admissible to contradict a written agreement, parol evidence is receivable, in an action seeking rectification, to establish what was the intention of each of the parties to the contract.[28]

It is also possible to have evidence from the draftsperson of the document stating what his or her instructions were, and that particular words were included in the document by mistake.

---

27. (1982) 149 CLR 337 at 346.
28. *Ball v Storie* (1823) 57 ER 84 at 88; *NSW Medical Defence Union Ltd v Transport Industries Insurance Co Ltd* (1986) 6 NSWLR 740 at 751, 752; *Farrow Mortgage Services Pty Ltd (in liquidation) v Slade and Nelson* (1996) 38 NSWLR 636 at 642; *Commissioner of Stamp Duties (NSW) v Carlenka Pty Ltd* (1995) 41 NSWLR 329 at 332; *Brambles Holdings Ltd v Bathurst City Council* (2001) 53 NSWLR 153 at 164; *Green v AMP Life* (2005) 13 ANZ Insurance Cases 90-124 (86,632) at 86,665.

[658] Lord Hardwicke explained why parol evidence was admissible in this way in *Baker v Paine*: 'How can a mistake in an agreement, be proved but by parol evidence? It is not read to contradict the face of the agreement which the court would not allow, but to prove a mistake therein, which cannot otherwise be proved ...'[29]

Not only is parol evidence from the parties admissible to prove their intention, it is of considerable importance. In *Fowler v Fowler*,[30] Lord Chelmsford LC said:

> Upon the question of rectifying a deed, the denial of one of the parties, that it is contrary to his intention, ought to have considerable weight. Lord Thurlow, in *Irnham v Child* says, 'The difficulty of proving that there has been a mistake in a deed is so great, that there is no instance of its prevailing against a party insisting that there was no mistake'.[31] And Lord Eldon, in *Marquis of Townshend v Stangroom*, after observing that Lord Thurlow seems to say that the proof must satisfy the Court what was the concurrent intention of all the parties, adds, 'And it must never be forgotten to what extent the Defendant, one of the parties, admits or denies the intention.'[32]

Outward expression of accord

There is ongoing debate about whether it is necessary for there to be an 'outward expression of accord' before rectification can be granted. That debate is noted (but not resolved — 'it *may* not be necessary to show that the accord found outward expression ...' (Emphasis added)) in *Pukallus v Cameron*.[33]

That debate stems from the decision of the English Court of Appeal in *Joscelyne v Nissen*. Russell LJ,[34] speaking for the Court, said ... that an outward expression of accord was a requirement for rectification. In *Joscelyne v Nissen*, the parties had made their intentions clear to each other before signing the document in question, and the sole point at issue was whether it was necessary for there to be an antecedent *concluded contract* before rectification could be granted, so those remarks were obiter. The only explanation for them contained in the judgment is that closely similar language was used[35] ... to explain the decision in *Frederick E Rose (London) Ltd v William H Pim Junior & Co Ltd*.[36] [This] was a case where parties had to all outward appearances entered an oral contract for the sale and purchase of horsebeans, then had accurately recorded that oral contract in writing. Each thought that 'horsebeans' was the same as 'feveroles', because a representative of the defendant had misinformed a representative of the plaintiff that that was the case. In fact 'feveroles' were a particular type of horsebeans, more valuable than the type of horsebeans that were delivered in purported performance of the contract. It was held that no rectification was available in those circumstances. *Joscelyne v Nissen* described *Frederick E Rose (London) Ltd v William H Pim Jnr & Co Ltd* as:

---

29. *Baker v Paine* (1750) 27 ER 1140 at 1141.
30. (1859) 45 ER 97 at 106–7.
31. *Irnham v Child* (1781) 28 ER 1006.
32. *Marquis of Townshend v Stangroom* (1801) 31 ER 1076.
33. (1982) 180 CLR 447 at 452.
34. *Joscelyne v Nissen* [1970] 2 QB 86 at 99.
35. *Joscelyne v Nissen* [1970] 2 QB 86 at 97.
36. [1953] 2 QB 450.

... a case in which there was nothing that could be described as an outward expression between the parties of an accord on what was to be involved in a term of the proposed agreement ... The decision ... does not assert or reinstate the view that an antecedent complete concluded contract is required for rectification: it only shows that prior accord on a term or the meaning of a phrase to be used must have been outwardly expressed or communicated between the parties.[37]

That explanation of [the *Frederick E Rose* case] is puzzling — in [that case] **[659]** there *had* been communication between the negotiating parties of the incorrect information that feveroles were the same as horsebeans ...

[660] Caution is needed in evaluating the case law relating to whether or not an outward expression of accord is needed. That is because it is not clear how much (or how little) is involved in an assertion, or denial, of the need for an 'outward expression of accord'. It is not clear just what the phrase means. One possibility is that the parties have said 'we agree', or something similar, or performed an act like shaking hands or opening a bottle of champagne that is commonly recognised as an indication of a consensus having been reached. Another possibility is that each of the parties has in some fashion stated (though not to each other) his or her belief that an accord has been reached. Another is that the expression should be taken as performing the work that, in its context in *Joscelyne v Nissen*, it was designed to perform, namely of indicating that identical subjective intentions, of parties involved in a contractual negotiation, to use a word with a meaning different to its actual meaning is not enough to give rise to rectification unless those subjective intentions of the negotiators have not only become known to each other, but as well they have in some way stated that they propose to use the word with a meaning different to its actual meaning. There is no point in multiplying examples.

In my view, when the fundamental requirement for granting rectification is a continuing common intention of the parties, it is of more assistance to concentrate on what is needed before an intention of the parties to a negotiation counts as a *common* intention. In my view, when that intention relates to the terms upon which they will contract with each other, it is still necessary for them to know enough of each other's intentions for it to be said that there is a *common* intention. They might come to know of each other's intentions in this way through those intentions being directly stated, or they might come to know of them through the various other means by which one person's intention can become known to another person. Those means can sometimes involve a process of conscious and deliberate inference. Those means can sometimes involve simply perceiving a *gestalt* in a series of events. Those means can depend to some extent on the people involved sharing a common understanding of how particular bodies of knowledge or markets or social institutions they are operating in work — the experienced surgeon, or the experienced chess player, can sometimes see what another surgeon, or chess player, is seeking to do, in a way that an inexperienced person cannot. What matters for present purposes is that for a negotiating party to perform actions or say words from which the other party can gather his or her intention is itself a form of communication. Negotiation of any contract takes place in a context in which various facts are known or assumed by the negotiating parties. Sometimes, for example, if a contract is negotiated

---

37. *Joscelyne v Nissen* [1970] 2 QB 86 at 97.

in a context where there are well understood business practices and conventions, and nothing is said about those practices and conventions not applying, it can be legitimate to conclude that both parties to the contract intended to act in accordance with those practices and conventions, even if they did not expressly communicate to each other that they intended to act in accordance with those practices and conventions. This view of what is needed before an intention is a common intention, accords, it seems to me, with the Australian case law since *Joscelyne* ...

[665] Assistance from the rationale for rectification

That the common intention must be in some manner disclosed is also consistent with the rationale on which rectification is granted.

In *Simpson v Vaughan*, Lord Hardwicke saw the justification for granting rectification as lying in mistake. He rectified a bond binding two people, that had not been stated to bind them severally, saying:

> Now here is a reasonable presumption that this bond was either through fraud, or for want of skill, made a joint, instead of a joint and several bond; for *Baker*, one of the obligors who filled it up, is only a tradesman, and intirely unacquainted with the common form of bonds, where money is lent to two persons; but I do not think it was a fraud in *Baker*, but merely a *mistake*, and this is a head of equity on which the Court always relieves.[38]

Simonds J, in *Crane v Hegeman-Harris Co Inc* ... also identified the rationale of rectification as lying in mistake, saying:

> ... in order that this Court may exercise its jurisdiction to rectify a written instrument it is not necessary to find a concluded and binding contract between the parties antecedent to the agreement which it is sought to rectify ... it is sufficient if you find a common continuing intention in regard to a particular provision or aspect of the agreement. If you find that in regard to a particular point the parties were in agreement up to the moment when they executed their formal instrument, and the formal instrument does not conform with that common agreement, then this court has jurisdiction to rectify although it may be that there was, until the formal instrument was executed, no concluded and binding contract between the parties. ... if it were not so, it would be a strange thing, for the result would be that two parties binding themselves by a mistake to which each had equally contributed, by an instrument which did not express their real intentions, would yet be bound by it.[39]

[666] The judgment of Simonds J in that case was endorsed by the Court of Appeal in England, and part of the passage that I have just quoted (from 'if it were not so' onwards) was quoted by Rich J, Dixon J and Williams J in *Slee v Warke*.[40] While Simonds J's account is correct as far as it goes, it points to only one aspect of the problem that rectification aims to remedy. It does not go on to identify why it is that mistake ought result in a court administering equitable jurisdiction ordering rectification, and does not explain why granting rectification of the contract, rather than some other remedy such as rescission is the appropriate response to the problem.

---

38. *Simpson v Vaughan* (1739) 26 ER 415 at 416.
39. *Crane v Hegeman-Harris Co Inc* [1971] 1 WLR 1390 at 1391.
40. (1952) 86 CLR 271 at 280–1.

A fuller account of the rationale for the granting of a remedy of rectification is given in Story, *Commentaries on Equity Jurisprudence as Administered in England and America*. The author started by considering how the principles upon which equity granted rectification compared with the principle of the common law under which parol evidence was not admissible to vary or add to written contracts, and continued:

> The same principle lies at the foundation of each class of decisions, that is to say, the desire to suppress frauds and promote general good faith and confidence in the formation of contracts. The danger of setting aside the solemn engagements of parties when reduced to writing, by the introduction of parol evidence substituting other material terms and stipulations, is sufficiently obvious. But what shall be said where those terms and stipulations are suppressed or omitted by fraud or imposition? Shall the guilty party be allowed to avail himself of such a triumph over innocence and credulity to accomplish his own base designs? That would be to allow a rule introduced to suppress fraud to be the most effectual promotion and encouragement of it. And hence Courts of Equity have not hesitated to entertain jurisdiction to reform all contracts where a fraudulent suppression, omission, or insertion of a material stipulation exists, notwithstanding to some extent it breaks in upon the uniformity of the rule as to the exclusion of parol evidence to vary or control contracts; wisely deeming such cases to be a proper exception to the rule, and proving its general soundness.
>
> It is upon the same ground that equity interferes in cases of written agreements where there has been an innocent omission or insertion of a material stipulation contrary to the intention of both parties and under the mutual mistake. To allow it to prevail in such a case would be to work a surprise, or fraud, upon both parties; and it certainly upon the one who is the sufferer. As much injustice would to the full be done under such circumstances as would be done by a positive fraud or an inevitable accident. A Court of Equity would be of little value if it could suppress only positive frauds, and leave mutual mistakes, innocently made, to work intolerable mischiefs contrary to the intention of parties. It would be to allow an act originating in innocence to operate ultimately as a fraud, by enabling the party who receives the benefit of the mistake to resist the claims of justice under the shelter of a rule framed to promote it. In a practical view there would be as much mischief done by refusing relief in such cases as there would be introduced by allowing parol evidence in all cases to vary written contracts.[41]

In other words, the type of unconscientiousness that is prevented by the availability of the equity to rectify a written contract is that that would occur if a party to the contract sought the benefit of those legal rights he would have if the document contained the agreement that the parties had made, when the document does not accurately state the common intention that the parties had …

[667] It is because the avoidance of unconscientious taking advantage of the common mistake is the rationale of the remedy that it does not matter that the mistaken drafting of the agreement was carried out by the plaintiff, or that the plaintiff is a legal practitioner.[42]

---

41. *Commentaries on Equity Jurisprudence as Administered in England and America*, 13th ed, 1886, at 168–169, [154]–[155].

42. *Ball v Storie* (1823) 57 ER 84 at 88.

That the rationale for granting rectification is to avoid unconscientious departure from the common intention, assists in deciding what is required for there to be a 'common intention'. If two negotiating parties each had a particular intention about the agreement they would enter, and their intentions were identical, but that intention was disclosed by neither of them, and they later entered a document that did not accord with that intention, what would be the injustice or unconscientiousness in either of them enforcing the document according to its terms?

Conclusion

For the reasons I have given, the common intention that is required to grant rectification is subjective. Even though there is a requirement for the intention to be disclosed before it can count as a common intention, that disclosure need not be by words that say in substance 'this is my intention'. The need for disclosure fills the role of being a limitation on the types of subjective intention that can be enforced through the remedy of rectification, or a limitation on the circumstances in which a subjective intention must exist before it can be enforced through the remedy of rectification. It still remains [668] that proof of the subjective intention of the parties to the contract is fundamental to the grant of rectification. Hence it is not possible to ignore a factual finding by the trial judge, to the effect that he was not satisfied that [Euphoric] intended the rebate to apply in relation to deliveries to any location within New South Wales outside the Sydney Metro locations, and look only to the correspondence for the purpose of finding a 'common intention'.

Comment

1. See Radan & Stewart at **30.8–30.18**.

Rectification for unilateral mistake

30.3   George Wimpey UK Ltd v V I Construction Ltd
[2005] EWCA 77

Court: Court of Appeal of England and Wales

Facts: Wimpey entered into a contract with VI Construction (VIC) under which Wimpey agreed to purchase land from VIC for the purposes of residential development. The price of the land was to be determined by a complex mathematical formula. Wimpey's representative in the negotiations made the mistake of omitting an element of the formula which resulted in the deal being less advantageous to Wimpey. VIC knew of the omission of the element from the formula. Wimpey sought rectification of the contract setting out the formula for determining the price.

Issue: The issue before the Court of Appeal was whether Wimpey was entitled to rectification based upon VIC's knowledge of Wimpey's mistake.

Decision: The Court of Appeal (Peter Gibson, Sedley LJJ and Blackburne J) unanimously held that Wimpey was not entitled to the remedy of rectification. The court held that the

---

mere fact that a mistake has been made, even a serious one, is an insufficient basis for a claim for rectification. One has to establish that the other party knew of the mistake in circumstances such as to make its conduct dishonest or unconscionable. Peter Gibson LJ and Blackburne J took the view that VIC, inexperienced in property development, was entitled to assume that Wimpey, a very experienced property developer, knew what it was doing when omitting the particular element in the price formula, rendering Wimpey's mistake a product of its own carelessness. Sedley LJ took a different approach, assessing VIC's conduct from the perspectives of honourable and reasonable behaviour in the context of an arm's-length commercial negotiation and concluded that VIC had no legal or moral responsibility.

Extracts: The extracts from the judgments of Peter Gibson LJ and Sedley LJ set out the principles applicable to rectification for unilateral mistake and their different approaches in the context of the facts of this case.

Peter Gibson LJ

[36] The modern authorities on unilateral mistake commence with the decision of Pennycuick J in *A Roberts & Co Ltd v Leicestershire County Council* where he said:

> ... a party is entitled to rectification of a contract upon proof that he believed a particular term to be included in the contract, and that the other party concluded the contract with the omission or a variation of that term in the knowledge that the first party believed the term to be included.[43]

[37] In *Riverlate Properties Ltd v Paul* this court ... approved the principle stated in *Roberts* but commented:

> Whether there was in any particular case knowledge of the intention and mistake of the other party must be a question of fact to be decided upon the evidence. Basically it appears to us that it must be such as to involve the lessee in a degree of sharp practice.[44]

[38] The requirements of the jurisdiction to rectify for unilateral mistake were considered further in [*Thomas Bates Ltd v Wyndham's (Lingerie) Ltd*]. That case concerned a claim for rectification of a rent review clause in a lease. When executing the lease, the tenants' officer, Mr Avon, noticed that the rent review clause in the lease drafted by the landlords was defective in not including a provision in default of agreement. The trial judge held that the conduct of Mr Avon, who had not given evidence, amounted to sharp practice. This court did not approve that stricture but found that the tenants knew of the omission and of the landlords' mistake. Buckley LJ ... suggested that the reference in *Riverlate* to 'sharp practice' might be obiter, and continued:

> In that case the lessee against whom the lessor sought to rectify a lease was held to have had no such knowledge as would have brought the doctrine into play. The reference to

---

43. *A Roberts & Co Ltd v Leicestershire County Council* [1961] Ch 555 at 570.
44. *Riverlate Properties Ltd v Paul* [1975] Ch 133 at 140.

'sharp practice' may thus be said to have been an obiter dictum. Undoubtedly I think in any such case the conduct of the defendant must be such as to make it inequitable that he should be allowed to object to the rectification of the document. If this necessarily implies some measure of 'sharp practice', so be it; but for my part I think that the doctrine is one which depends more on the equity of the position. The graver the character of the conduct involved, no doubt the heavier the burden of proof may be; but, in my view, the conduct must be such as to affect the conscience of the party who has suppressed the fact that he has recognised the presence of a mistake. For this doctrine — that is to say the doctrine of *A Roberts v Leicestershire County Council* — to apply I think it must be shown: first, that one party A erroneously believed that the document sought to be rectified contained a particular term or provision, or possibly did not contain a particular term or provision which, mistakenly, it did contain; secondly, that the other party B was aware of the omission or the inclusion and that it was due to a mistake on the part of A; thirdly, that B has omitted to draw the mistake to the notice of A. And I think there must be a fourth element involved, namely, that the mistake must be one calculated to benefit B. If these requirements are satisfied, the court may regard it as inequitable to allow B to resist rectification to give effect to A's intention on the ground that the mistake was not, at the time of execution of the document, a mutual mistake.[45]

I accept that as the authoritative statement of the requirements for rectification for unilateral mistake.

[39] Before I leave that case, I should refer to the observations of Brightman LJ on the standard of proof, where he said:

The standard of proof required in an action of rectification to establish the common intention of the parties is, in my view, the civil standard of balance of probability. But as the alleged common intention ex hypothesi contradicts the written instrument, convincing proof is required in order to counteract the cogent evidence of the parties' intention displayed by the instrument itself. It is not, I think, the standard of proof which is high, so differing from the normal civil standard, but the evidential requirement needed to counteract the inherent probability that the written instrument truly represents the parties' intention because it is a document signed by the parties. The standard of proof is no different in a case of so-called unilateral mistake such as the present.[46]

[40] In *The Nai Genova*[47] rectification was unsuccessfully sought of an escalation clause in a charter-party which provided for a base figure in US dollars to be increased by reference to Italian inflation. The plaintiffs claimed that an accord had been reached that the base figure should be in lire rather than dollars, but that when the defendants prepared a draft charter-party, they put the base figure in dollars. Slade LJ ... noted ... that the effect of allowing rectification for unilateral mistake was to impose on the defendants a contract which, at the time of its execution, they did not intend to make. He reviewed the authorities and found it a significant feature that they all required actual knowledge by

---

45. *Thomas Bates Ltd v Wyndham's (Lingerie) Ltd* [1981] 1 WLR 505 at 515–6.
46. *Thomas Bates Ltd v Wyndham's (Lingerie) Ltd* [1981] 1 WLR 505 at 521.
47. *Agip SpA v Navigazione Alta Italia SpA* [1984] 1 Lloyd's Rep 353.

the defendant of the existence of the plaintiff's mistake. He accepted that there could be a case of an implied misrepresentation that a proffered draft gave effect to an accord and of a resultant estoppel if it was intended or reasonably foreseeable that the representation would be relied on and if the representee relied on that representation. However, Slade LJ said ... that on the facts those conditions were not satisfied, as it had not been shown that the defendants intended or could have foreseen that the plaintiff would rely on any such representation when the defendants could have reasonably assumed that the plaintiffs would have read the escalation clause for themselves and would have noted any objection when discussing the clause with the defendants. Slade LJ said that the greater the degree of the carelessness in not detecting the error, the more unrealistic it became for the plaintiffs to assert that the reliance on the representation was foreseeable. He thought it significant that the plaintiff's witnesses did not attempt to blame the defendants for their mistake. He was unpersuaded that there had been sharp practice by the defendants or that it would be inequitable to allow them to resist the claim for rectification.

[41] In *Commission*[48] the primary question determined by this court was whether the parties had entered into a binding agreement whereby the claimant had granted the defendant a put option. This court held that they had not. However, it went on to consider whether, if wrong on that, the contract should be rectified on the ground of unilateral mistake. That was on the basis that the claimant mistakenly believed that there was no agreement to grant the put option, while the defendant knew of the mistake or its conduct was such that it was unconscionable to insist on the performance of the contract. The trial judge held that the claimant was not entitled to rectification because the defendant did not have actual knowledge of the mistake and only actual knowledge would do.

[42] [In *Commission*] Stuart-Smith LJ expressed the view that actual knowledge was not always necessary and that a fraudulent misrepresentation, intended to mislead and succeeding in misleading, when coupled with suspicion of a mistake, would suffice to allow rectification to be granted.[49] That was one of the passages which the judge [in this case] quoted ... The judge also quoted the following passage[50] from Stuart-Smith LJ's judgment:

> Did [the defendant] have actual knowledge of the mistake? The judge held not; they merely suspected it. [Counsel for the claimant] submits that the judge was in error and he should have found actual knowledge. His attention was drawn to the analysis of various forms of knowledge made by Peter Gibson J in *Baden v Société Générale pour Favoriser le Développement du Commerce et de l'Industrie en France SA (Note)*[51] and cited by Millett J in *Agip (Africa) Ltd v Jackson*:[52]
>
> > Knowledge may be proved affirmatively or inferred from circumstances. The various mental states which may be involved were analysed by Peter Gibson J in *Baden's* case as comprising: (i) actual knowledge; (ii) wilfully shutting one's eyes to the obvious;

---

48. *Commission for the New Towns v Cooper (Great Britain) Ltd* [1995] Ch 259.
49. *Commission for the New Towns v Cooper (Great Britain) Ltd* [1995] Ch 259 at 280.
50. *Commission for the New Towns v Cooper (Great Britain) Ltd* [1995] Ch 259 at 280–1.
51. [1993] 1 WLR 509. (Note: This case was decided in 1984.)
52. [1990] Ch 265 at 293.

(iii) wilfully and recklessly failing to make such inquiries as an honest and reasonable man would make; (iv) knowledge of circumstances which would indicate the facts to an honest and reasonable man; (v) knowledge of circumstances which would put an honest and reasonable man on inquiry. According to Peter Gibson J, a person in categories (ii) or (iii) will be taken to have actual knowledge, while a person in categories (iv) or (v) has constructive notice only. I gratefully adopt the classification but would warn against over refinement or a too ready assumption that categories (iv) or (v) are necessarily cases of constructive notice only. The true distinction is between honesty and dishonesty. It is essentially a jury question. If a man does not draw the obvious inferences or make the obvious inquiries, the question is: why not? If it is because, however foolishly, he did not suspect wrongdoing or, having suspected it, had his suspicions allayed, however unreasonably, that is one thing. But if he did suspect wrongdoing yet failed to make inquiries because 'he did not want to know' (category (ii)) or because he regarded it as 'none of his business' (category (iii)), that is quite another. Such conduct is dishonest, and those who are guilty of it cannot complain if, for the purpose of civil liability, they are treated as if they had actual knowledge.

[43] Stuart-Smith LJ then referred to the trial judge's view that actual knowledge within category (i) was needed, but disagreed with that view, saying that categories (ii) and (iii) also constituted actual knowledge in law. He described the defendant's conduct in raising a smokescreen about one matter other than the put option as 'dishonest and intended to deceive'. He also found that there had been a fraudulent misrepresentation by the defendant. He therefore found the defendant's conduct unconscionable and the circumstances such that equity required the contract to be rectified ...

[45] Mr Fetherstonhaugh [on behalf of Wimpey] relies on *Commission* as holding that actual knowledge by the non-mistaken party of the mistaken party's mistake is not a requisite of the jurisdiction to rectify for unilateral mistake. He relies on the views expressed in that case that knowledge in categories (ii) and (iii) suffices. But he criticizes as illogical the reasoning of Millett J in *Agip (Africa) Ltd.* that knowledge in those categories involves dishonesty, at any rate to the extent that this court adopted that reasoning as applicable to what knowledge of the mistaken party's mistake is needed for rectification. Why, he asks, if rectification can be ordered if the non-mistaken party has actual knowledge of the mistaken party's mistake, but there is neither dishonesty nor sharp practice, should knowledge in categories (ii) and (iii), which is the equivalent in law of actual knowledge, involve dishonest behaviour for the purposes of rectification? I see force in that submission. However, Mr Fetherstonhaugh's difficulty, as it seems to me, lies, first, in this court's acceptance in *Commission* of the reasoning of Millett J in the context of rectification for unilateral mistake and this court's application of that reasoning to a case of dishonest conduct, and, second, in the judge's acceptance of the same approach ... in finding dishonest conduct when concluding that VIC had knowledge (in categories (ii) and (iii)) of Wimpey's mistake. I do not accept that it is open to Wimpey to rely on the judge's finding ... that VIC had such knowledge but to say that such knowledge was without dishonesty or sharp practice where it is plain that the judge's remarks ... were permeated by his finding of dishonesty, which, because of *Commission*, he thought was required.

[46] In any event, I cannot see that Wimpey has discharged the onus on it of providing convincing proof that VIC did have knowledge in either of categories (ii) and (iii) of

Wimpey's mistake. These were arm's length negotiations for the sale of property for residential development between, on the one hand, VIC, with no relevant experience and, on the other, Wimpey with its vast experience …

[47] [I]n the light of all the circumstances, in my judgment, Wimpey has failed to provide convincing evidence that VIC shut its eyes to the obvious or wilfully and recklessly failed to do what an honest and reasonable person would have done in the circumstances, and it would not be inequitable to allow VIC to resist the claim for rectification …

[51] I recognise that the mistake has had serious consequences for Wimpey and brought a benefit to VIC to an extent which it did not foresee in putting forward the formula. But that is not determinative of whether Wimpey can successfully invoke the exceptional jurisdiction to rectify for unilateral mistake. For the reasons given, I do not think it can.

Sedley LJ

[57] [The trial judge] was bound by authority to consider whether an honourable and reasonable person would have drawn Wimpey's attention to the omission of [the particular element] from the final formula …

[58] There is, as it seems to me, a paradox in the notion of what an honourable and reasonable person would do in the context of an arm's-length commercial negotiation. This is a context in which honour (or honesty) and rationality (or reasonableness) are frequently not on speaking terms. I doubt whether Mr Fetherstonhaugh's submission that the two epithets qualify each other does more than compound the paradox.

[59] Take the present case. An honourable person negotiating for VIC would probably have asked Wimpey if they realised that [the particular element] had been left out, but I very much doubt whether a reasonable negotiator would have done so. His first duty would have been to his own principal, whose interests undoubtedly lay in leaving [the particular element] out and not alerting Wimpey to the omission.

[60] The phrase 'honest and reasonable' is not a term of art. It is a judicial attempt to sketch a line beyond which conduct may be regarded as unconscionable or inequitable. Its duality, however, is a recognition that honesty alone is too pure a standard for business dealings because it omits legitimate self-interest; while reasonableness alone is capable of legitimising Machiavellian tactics.

[61] Mistake is a concept which sits awkwardly in this space. Absent a prior accord which has simply not been carried into effect, absent also a dishonest inducement to contract, one is looking for a mistake on the claimant's own part which the defendant was honour-bound, despite his own legitimate business interests, to point out to him. I am unable to accept that this was such a case on any tenable view of the evidence.

[62] There are at least two kinds of mistake. One is a literal misunderstanding of some fact material to the proposed contract. The other is an error of judgment in entering into the contract. I find it difficult to think that the second kind has any relevance to the law of unilateral mistake. Nobody is bound, even in honour, to help his opposite number to negotiate to the best advantage.

[63] What then was the material fact that Wimpey misunderstood? That [the particular element] was omitted? They had only to look at VIC's draft to see that it was. Their mistake was failing to renegotiate it, and that seems to me an error of judgment, not of fact.

[64] Mr Fetherstonhaugh's submissions in effect have recognised this. He submits that VIC must have realised that, unless Wimpey had undergone a sudden fit of altruism, they had overlooked the omission of [the particular element]. I think that this is a more convincing analysis of the evidence than [that by counsel for VIC], and more consistent with the judge's appraisal of the witnesses. But it seems to me to take Wimpey into a dead end, for I do not see how either honesty tempered with reasonableness or reasonableness tempered with honesty can have required VIC to point out to Wimpey where the latter's own best interests lay.

[65] In saying this I recognise that sharp practice has no defined boundary. An arm's-length negotiation between parties of unequal competence and resources may well place greater constraints of honest and reasonable conduct on the stronger party than on the weaker. But the present case practically reverses the paradigm: it is the weaker party which is accused by the stronger of having unconscionably misled it by failing to draw the stronger party's attention to its own oversight ...

[67] If ever a party was entitled to assume that its opponent knew what it was doing, it was VIC in its negotiations with one of the country's largest construction and development enterprises. In my judgment the mistake made by Wimpey was a result of their own corporate neglect for which VIC bore no legal or — so far as it matters — moral responsibility.

Comments

1. See Radan & Stewart at **30.19–30.23**.
2. For a discussion of this case see E Palser, 'Rectification for Unilateral Mistake: How Heavy is the Burden of Proof?' [2006] *Lloyd's Maritime and Commercial Law Quarterly* 139.
3. For a discussion of the circumstances in which rectification is available for unilateral mistake see D McLauchlan, 'The "Drastic" Remedy of Rectification for Unilateral Mistake' (2008) 124 *Law Quarterly Review* 608.

Account of profits

30.4   Dart Industries Inc v The Decor Corporation Pty Ltd (1993) 179 CLR 101

Court: High Court of Australia

Facts: Dart had a registered patent over a type of press button seal or lid used in plastic kitchen canisters. Two other companies, Rian and Decor, were involved respectively in the manufacture and sale of plastic canisters that contained seals in breach of Dart's patent. Dart succeeded in obtaining judgment against the companies for patent infringement. It elected for an account of profits and the trial judge ordered both companies to account. Issues arose concerning the deductibility from profits of overhead costs, with Dart arguing that only overhead costs attributable to the manufacture and sale of the infringing products should be deductible from profits. Dart appealed to the High Court and the two companies filed cross applications.

Issues: The two principal issues before the High Court were (i) whether any part of the infringers' general overhead costs is allowable as a deduction to determine the profits made from infringement and (ii) whether the infringers must account for profits made from the manufacture and sale of the plastic canisters as a whole, or merely from the patented press button seals that formed part of the canisters.

Decision: The High Court (Mason CJ, Deane, Dawson, Toohey and McHugh JJ) unanimously dismissed Dart's appeal and refused leave to the companies to cross-appeal. It held that the infringers were at liberty to prove the various overhead costs that were attributable to the profits made, and to show how and in what proportion the overheads should be allocated in relation to the infringing product.

Extracts: The extracts from the joint judgment of Mason CJ, Deane, Dawson and Toohey JJ outline the High Court's approach to account of profits as an equitable remedy.

Mason CJ, Deane, Dawson and Toohey JJ

[110] Damages and an account of profits are alternative remedies. An account of profits was a form of relief granted by equity whereas [111] damages were originally a purely common law remedy. As Windeyer J pointed out in *Colbeam Palmer Ltd v Stock Affiliates Pty Ltd*,[53] even now[54] an account of profits retains its equitable characteristics in that a defendant is made to account for, and is then stripped of, profits which it has dishonestly made by the infringement and which it would be unconscionable for it to retain. An account of profits is confined to profits actually made, its purpose being not to punish the defendant but to prevent its unjust enrichment.[55] The ordinary requirement of the principles of unjust enrichment that regard be paid to matters of substance rather than technical form[56] is applicable.

But it is notoriously difficult in some cases, particularly cases involving the manufacture or sale of a range of products, to isolate those costs which are attributable to the infringement from those which are not so attributable.[57] Whilst it is accepted that mathematical exactitude is generally impossible, the exercise is one that must be undertaken, and some assistance may be derived from the principles and practices of commercial accounting. Unfortunately, neither the Australian nor the English authorities contain any precise analysis of the problem.

Leplastrier & Co Ltd v Armstrong-Holland Ltd involved an account of profits arising from the manufacture and sale of concrete mixing machines in breach of a patent. Harvey CJ in Eq drew a distinction between the profits made from the manufacture and sale of the infringing machines, which were to be accounted for, and the profits of the business in

---

53. (1968) 122 CLR 25 at 34.

54. See *Patents Act 1952* (Cth) s 118(1); *Patents Act 1990* (Cth) s 122.

55. *My Kinda Town Ltd v Soll* [1983] RPC 15 at 55; *Potton Ltd v Yorkclose Ltd* (1989) 17 FSR 11 at 14, 15; *Sheldon v Metro-Goldwyn Pictures Corp* (1940) 309 US 390 at 399.

56. See *Baltic Shipping Co v Dillon* (1993) 176 CLR 344 at 376.

57. See *Siddell v Vickers* (1892) 9 RPC 152 at 162–3; *My Kinda Town Ltd v Soll* [1983] RPC 15 at 57–8.

connexion with the sale of those machines, which were not.[58] He expressed the view that the defendant bore the onus of establishing that the costs were incurred in the manufacture of the machines and observed:

> [112] Under no circumstances can he, in my opinion, deduct interest on his capital employed in the business. Under no circumstances can he claim any remuneration to himself, nor under any circumstances can he claim in my opinion any director's fees for carrying on the business. I have no desire at the present stage to say exactly what can be taken into account as the costs of manufacture. It is clear that costs of material can be taken; it is clear that costs of wages can be deducted. It is possible that other costs may be taken, but I think the test which is to be applied is that the only expenses which can be deducted are those which were solely referable to the manufacture of the machines. If, for instance, for the purpose of manufacturing these machines the defendant found it necessary to install a particular piece of machinery which was useful for making these machines and for nothing else, then it might be that depreciation of this machinery would be a proper item to allow him as part of his costs of manufacturing the machines; if his machinery is used partly for the purpose of making these machines and partly for the purpose of other machines it may be proper to allow him such depreciation for wear and tear on the value of his machinery as may be properly allocated to the work which has been done on the infringing machines as compared with the work done on other machines.[59]

In giving the first direction, [the trial judge] relied upon this passage in the judgment of Harvey CJ in Eq and adopted the language of his Honour, saying that only costs which are 'solely referable' to manufacture or sale of the infringing article may be deducted.[60]

Dart relies upon the same passage to support its submission that the correct accounting principle to employ in the taking of an account of profits is incremental costing rather than absorption costing. Incremental costing takes account only of the change in costs incurred by the manufacture or sale of a particular product and does not seek to apportion to the manufacture or sale of that product any part of general overheads, such as rent, light, heating or office expenses, which cannot be identified as a direct result of producing that product. Absorption costing on the other hand is a costing method whereby general overheads are apportioned by some appropriate means, often by sales or volume, to the manufacture or sale of each product.

Dart's argument, based on incremental costing as the proper method for taking an account of profits of infringing activities, is as follows. The profit should be calculated by taking the gross revenue received from the manufacture and sale of the infringing product and deducting from it direct costs, such as materials or labour, [113] solely due to the manufacture or sale of the infringing product, and also deducting overheads, but only to the extent that they were increased by the manufacture or sale of the infringing product. Otherwise, the defendant would be able to deduct expenditure which it would have incurred in any event. This should not be allowed because if any of the revenue from the sale or manufacture could be set off against general overheads which would

---

58. *Leplastrier & Co Ltd v Armstrong-Holland Ltd* (1926) 26 SR (NSW) 585 at 591.
59. *Leplastrier & Co Ltd v Armstrong-Holland Ltd* (1926) 26 SR (NSW) 585 at 593.
60. *Dart Industries Inc v Decor Corporation Pty Ltd* (1990) 20 IPR 144 at 151.

have been incurred without the infringing activities, the defendant would profit from the infringing activities. The defendant would gain by reducing the cost of its overheads, but would not have to account to the plaintiff for this gain.

Not only does Dart rely on the passage cited from the judgment of Harvey CJ in Eq but it maintains that the same principle is to be seen in the judgment of Windeyer J in *Colbeam Palmer Ltd v Stock Affiliates Pty Ltd*. That was a case of infringement of a trade mark in which Windeyer J ordered an account of profits. In doing so, he directed that the cost of selling and delivering the infringing articles be taken into account. But he added:

> This will include any costs directly attributable to such sales and deliveries. But it should not, I think, include any part of the general overhead costs, managerial expenses and so forth of the defendant's business, as it seems that all these would have been incurred in any event in the ordinary course of its business in which as it was put in evidence the painting sets were a 'side line'.[61]

The explanation of the direction given by Windeyer J is that mentioned by him, namely, that the infringing articles were a side line. There appears to have been unused capacity in the defendant's business in the form of overheads which would have been incurred whether or not the infringing articles had been sold and delivered. The sale and delivery of the infringing articles took up that surplus capacity or some of it, and none of the overhead costs was attributable to the infringing activities because those costs would have been incurred in any event.

But there was no evidence in this case that Decor or Rian had unused or surplus capacity. There was evidence that the infringing canisters were an integral part of one consistent product range produced, marketed and sold according to a common system. From this it might be inferred that, had those companies not been engaged in the manufacture and marketing of the infringing press button seal canisters, their capacity for those activities would have **[114]** been taken up in the manufacture and marketing of alternative products.

Thus the cost of manufacturing and marketing the press button seal canisters may have included the cost of forgoing the profit from the manufacture and marketing of alternative products. The latter cost is called an opportunity cost. 'Opportunity cost' can be defined as 'the value of the alternative foregone by adopting a particular strategy or employing resources in a specific manner ... As used in economics, the opportunity cost of any designated alternative is the greatest net benefit lost by taking an alternative'.[62] The practical reality of this concept was recognized in *Schnadig Corp v Gaines Manufacturing Co Inc*, where the Court stated: 'The alternative available uses of the facilities devoted to the infringement must be considered, and these too will vary'.[63]

In calculating an account of profits, the defendant may not deduct the opportunity cost, that is, the profit forgone on the alternative products. But there would be real inequity if a defendant were denied a deduction for the opportunity cost as well as being denied a deduction for the cost of the overheads which sustained the capacity that would

---

61. *Colbeam Palmer Ltd v Stock Affiliates Pty Ltd* (1968) 122 CLR 25 at 39.
62. *Kohler's Dictionary for Accountants*, 6th ed, 1983, pp 362–3.
63. *Schnadig Corp v Gaines Manufacturing Co Inc* (1980) 620 F 2d 1166 at 1175.

have been utilized by an alternative product and that was in fact utilized by the infringing product. If both were denied, the defendant would be in a worse position than if it had made no use of the patented invention. The purpose of an account of profits is not to punish the defendant but to prevent its unjust enrichment.

Where the defendant has forgone the opportunity to manufacture and sell alternative products it will ordinarily be appropriate to attribute to the infringing product a proportion of those general overheads which would have sustained the opportunity. On the other hand, if no opportunity was forgone, and the overheads involved were costs which would have been incurred in any event, then it would not be appropriate to attribute the overheads to the infringing product. Otherwise the defendant would be in a better position than it would have been in if it had not infringed. It is not relevant that the product could not have been manufactured and sold without these overheads. Nor is it relevant that absorption method accounting would attribute a proportion of the overheads to the infringing product. The equitable principle of an account of profits is not to compensate the plaintiff, nor to fix a fair price for the [115] infringing product, but to prevent the unjust enrichment of the defendant.

Of course, further possibilities may in some cases be open on the evidence. Overhead costs might have been increased by the manufacture and sale of the infringing product, or overhead costs might have been reduced had the infringing product not been produced. In either case it may be appropriate to attribute the difference in overhead costs to the infringing product.

It does not appear that in *Leplastrier & Co Ltd v Armstrong-Holland Ltd* the concept of opportunity cost played any part in the reasoning of Harvey CJ in Eq. In allowing the deduction only of expenses 'solely referable' to the manufacture of the infringing product, he seems to have intended to exclude overheads except to the extent that they were increased by the manufacture of the infringing product. The examples that he gave indicate such an approach. But this is hardly surprising since the English authorities, even the more recent ones, have not grappled with the concept. Whilst they recognize[64] that the purpose of ordering an account of profits is not to inflict punishment, but is limited to compelling the defendant to surrender profits improperly made, there is little examination of the principles to be employed in ascertaining which profits were derived from the infringement.[65] ...

[118] In *My Kinda Town Ltd v Soll*,[66] Slade J was inclined to think that in the taking of an account of profits the onus of proof fell upon neither party. As we have said, a different view was taken by Harvey CJ in Eq in *Leplastrier & Co Ltd v Armstrong-Holland Ltd* where he expressed the opinion that the onus is on the defendant to establish that any item of costs was incurred in relation to the manufacture of the infringing articles. The view of Harvey CJ in Eq would seem to be the preferable one, at least so far as it requires that the defendant establish that the overheads in any particular category are attributable to the manufacture or sale of the infringing product. It is a view which is supported by the

---

64. See *My Kinda Town Ltd v Soll* [1983] RPC 15 at 55.
65. See *Crosley v Derby Gas-Light Co* (1838) 40 ER 992; *Peter Pan Manufacturing Corp v Corsets Silhouette Ltd* [1963] RPC 45 at 59–60; *My Kinda Town Ltd v Soll* [1983] RPC 15; *Potton Ltd v Yorkclose Ltd* (1989) 17 FSR 11.
66. [1983] RPC 15 at 57.

United States authorities[67] and may also be justified because the relevant facts are likely to be peculiarly within the knowledge of the defendant.

In the present case, the trial judge accepted that the manufacture and sale of the infringing goods was not a side line. He found that [119] Decor's range of canisters with press button seals formed part of a much larger range of container systems, storage systems and canisters. On the evidence, the share of sales of the canisters with press button seals varied from 3.1 per cent to 1.3 per cent over a six-year period after they were added to Decor's existing range, and that percentage was similar to the percentage of sales of other types of containers in Decor's range.

Decor contends that it is possible to identify some overheads as direct costs which may be attributed to the press button seal canisters as actually incurred in respect of them, namely, the cost of product development/royalty expenses, media advertising, industrial design registration, legal fees and tooling expenses. It seeks to allocate all remaining overheads which are indirect costs by reference to the proportion which sales of canisters with press button seals bear to total sales.

Whether Decor and Rian should succeed in their contentions depends upon whether, as a matter of fact and substance, the overheads which they seek to have deducted are attributable to the manufacture and sale of the infringing product. In arriving at an answer, the Court must consider such questions as whether the overheads in any particular category were increased by the manufacture or sale of the product, whether they represent costs which would have been reduced or would have been incurred in any event, and whether they were surplus capacity or would, in the absence of the infringing product, have been used in the manufacture or sale of other products. Dealing with the last of these questions may require the use of the concept of opportunity cost. If any of the categories are to be brought into account, the proportion to be allocated to the infringing product must be determined and it is here that approximation rather than precision may be necessary. But such an approach has long been accepted. As was said in *Colburn v Simms*:

> The Court, by the account, as the nearest approximation which it can make to justice, takes from the wrongdoer all the profits he has made by his piracy, and gives them to the party who has been wronged.[68]

It follows that we consider that [the trial judge] was in error in directing that 'no part of general overhead costs is allowable as a deduction' and that the Full Court was substantially correct in directing, as it did, that '[Decor and Rian] are at liberty to show that various [120] categories of overhead contributed to the obtaining of the relevant profit, and to show how and in what proportion they should be allocated in the taking of the account of profits'. But it would be better, we think, if the word 'contributed' were replaced by the words 'are attributable'.

The application by Decor and Rian for special leave to cross-appeal may be dealt with more shortly. In considering whether the profits for which an account was ordered should include those arising from the manufacture and sale of the canisters as well as the press

---

67. See *Westinghouse Electric & Manufacturing Co v Wagner Electric & Manufacturing Co* (1912) 225 US 604 at 620–2; *Duplate Corp v Triplex Safety Glass Co* (1936) 298 US 448 at 458.

68. *Colburn v Simms* (1843) 67 ER 224 at 231.

button seals which were fitted to them, the trial judge correctly identified the problem when he said:

> The basic legal principle is that the relevant profits are those accruing to [Decor and Rian] from their use and exercise of [Dart's] patented invention. Where [Decor and Rian's] products are, as here, composites of the invention and other features the determination of such a question is one of fact.[69]

In answering the question which he posed, [the trial judge] found that 'sales of press button canisters are for present purposes attributable to use of the patented invention' and for that reason directed that the profits for which Decor and Rian had to account included the profits from the containers to which the press button seals were fitted.[70]

The Full Court identified the same question in somewhat different terms:

> [Dart] cannot gainsay that it is only entitled to the profits obtained by the infringement. If, for example, a patented brake is wrongfully used in the construction of a motor car, the patentee is not entitled to the entire profits earned by sales of the motor car. He must accept an appropriate apportionment. But the question is how that principle shall be applied to a situation where the patent relates to the essential feature of a single item ... it seems to us that it was open to the judge to find, and he correctly found, that what characterised the infringing product was the press button lid, without which this particular container would never have been produced at all.[71]

The questions posed by the trial judge and the Full Court concerning the apportionment of a total profit both accurately reflect the correct principle which was expressed in this Court by Windeyer J in *Colbeam Palmer Ltd v Stock Affiliates Pty Ltd* as follows:

> [121] The true rule, I consider, is that a person who wrongly uses another man's industrial property — patent, copyright, trade mark — is accountable for any profits which he makes which are attributable to his use of the property which was not his ...

> If one man makes profits by the use or sale of some thing, and that whole thing came into existence by reason of his wrongful use of another man's property in a patent, design or copyright, the difficulty disappears and the case is then, generally speaking, simple. In such a case the infringer must account for all the profits which he thus made.[72]

It is true that there is some divergence between [the trial judge] and the Full Court in relation to whether, in the circumstances of this case, primary emphasis should be placed on reason for sale or reason for production. Nonetheless, the overall approach of both accurately reflects the application of the correct general principle in the resolution of what is ultimately a question of fact.

Comment

1. See Radan & Stewart at **30.25–30.29**.

---

69. *Dart Industries Inc v Decor Corporation Pty Ltd* (1990) 20 IPR 144 at 152.
70. *Dart Industries Inc v Decor Corporation Pty Ltd* (1990) 20 IPR 144 at 154.
71. *Dart Industries Inc v Decor Corporation Pty Ltd* (1991) 33 FCR 397 at 407.
72. *Colbeam Palmer Ltd v Stock Affiliates Pty Ltd* (1968) 122 CLR 25 at 42–3.

31

EQUITABLE DEFENCES

Introduction

31.1 This chapter deals with a number of generally available defences to equitable remedies. The availability of these defences in any particular case is a matter for the discretion of the court.

The cases extracted in this chapter discuss the following:

- the availability of the defence of unclean hands: *Black Uhlans Inc v New South Wales Crime Commission* [2002] NSWSC 1060;
- the equitable defence of laches: *Lamshed v Lamshed* (1963) 109 CLR 440;
- the defence to an action in equity by the application of limitation legislation by analogy: *Italiano Oliveri v Invocare Pty Ltd* [2008] NSWSC 1138; and
- the defence of set-off in equity: *AWA Ltd v Exicom Australia Pty Ltd* (1990) 19 NSWLR 705.

Unclean hands

31.2 Black Uhlans Inc v New South Wales Crime Commission [2002] NSWSC 1060

Court: Supreme Court of New South Wales

Facts: Wilson, who was a member of the Black Uhlans motorcyle club, was convicted for drug trafficking. A forfeiture order was later made under proceeds of crime legislation vesting his property in the Public Trustee. The property included premises at Peakhurst that contained the Black Uhlans' clubhouse. Wilson had purchased the property in 1991 for $400,000 after obtaining a $227,500 mortgage from Citibank. But the club sought a declaration that Wilson held the real estate on trust for it, and that the beneficial ownership of the property should not be forfeited. It argued that Wilson was the only club member who owned property and had a job, and so had the best chance of obtaining a bank loan. It was proved that part of the funds Wilson had used to acquire the clubhouse was provided by the club through its members. The club contended that Wilson held a proportionate share of the property on trust for the club under resulting trust principles. However, it was argued against this by a variety of defendants (represented by the Crime Commission [CC]) that the club could not invoke the

---

principle of resulting trusts, since it did not come before the court with 'clean hands'. This was because it had knowingly participated in Wilson's false application for the bank loan that provided the balance of purchase moneys.

Issue: The issue before the Supreme Court was whether, notwithstanding the resulting trust, equitable relief to the club should be denied through the operation of the 'unclean hands' defence.

Held: Campbell J found in favour of the club and held that its fraudulent activity did not deprive it of its entitlement under the law of resulting trusts. The club's conduct related only to how Wilson obtained the loan and did not relate to its contribution to the funds for the purchase of the clubhouse.

Extracts: The extracts from the judgment of Campbell J highlight that the 'unclean hands' defence requires a court to identify the equity that the court would be prepared to uphold, and then satisfy itself that the disentitling conduct had an immediate and necessary relation to the equity sued for, that it amounted to a moral and illegal depravity, and that it was directed at the defendant.

Campbell J

[157] The [CC] submit that the [Club] ought not receive any equitable relief, by way of enforcing the existence of a resulting trust, because of unclean hands on the part of the [Club]. They say that the only way in which the Peakhurst property was able to be purchased was through obtaining a loan from Citibank. Further, that loan from Citibank was obtained only by [Wilson and the club's solicitor] telling Citibank a pack of lies, and submitting to Citibank a set of fabricated documents. The Club was party to the deception of Citibank, in that its officers agreed to the scheme that involved [Wilson] being presented to Citibank as a man of substance. The [CC] say that even though officers of the Club might not have known all the details about the way in which Citibank was deceived, there was still a joint enterprise to deceive, under circumstances such that the conduct of [Wilson and the club's solicitor], in carrying through that joint enterprise, is to be attributed to the Club.

[158] That someone who comes to equity must have clean hands is an equitable maxim. Such a maxim provides an explanation for the circumstances in which equity recognises rights, and confers remedies, across a broad range of equity's jurisdiction. The approach to the recognition of rights and conferring of remedies which the maxim articulates has resulted in various specific principles of law which are recognised as part of the substantive law of equity. The law of promissory estoppel provides one example. However, the maxim remains of ongoing importance, as a guide to how cases not governed by specific rules of substantive law ought be decided, or as a guide to how specific rules of substantive law ought be extrapolated.

[159] The unclean hands maxim requires the Court to look at the conduct of the litigant who seeks the assistance of equity, rather than the conduct of the defendant. Further, it is conduct which the litigant who seeks the assistance of equity has engaged in in the past which is required to be looked at. In this way it differs from the maxim that he who seeks equity must do equity, which looks at the conduct which a litigant who seeks the assistance of equity undertakes to engage in in the future.

[160] Some examples of the circumstances in which the maxim has been the basis on which a case has been decided illustrate the breadth of application of the maxim. Thus, specific performance of a contract will not be granted at the suit of a plaintiff who has made a relevant misrepresentation to the defendant.[1] Unclean hands can be a ground for refusing relief against forfeiture of a lease.[2] It can be a ground on which a court declines to enforce a trust.[3] It can be a basis upon which the beneficiary of a trust, who has led the trustee to commit a breach of trust, can be denied a remedy for that breach.[4] It can provide a ground for refusing an injunction to enforce a negative contractual stipulation, if that contract has been procured by a misrepresentation of the plaintiff.[5] It can provide a basis for refusing an injunction to enforce a restrictive covenant, if a person entitled to the benefit of the covenant has represented it will not be enforced, and that representation is acted upon by the person bound by the covenant.[6] Where the plaintiff and the defendant are both bound by restrictive covenants arising under a common building scheme, and the plaintiff is in serious breach of the covenant, unclean hands provides a basis on which the plaintiff cannot obtain an injunction to require the defendant to observe the restrictive covenant.[7] It can provide a basis for refusing an injunction to prevent passing off, where the reputation which the plaintiff seeks to have protected has itself been built up by deceptive means.[8] It can provide a basis for refusing equitable relief to prevent a breach of copyright where the work contained false statements calculated to deceive the public.[9] Further, some cases have held that it can provide a basis for refusing equitable relief in circumstances where a plaintiff has engaged in, or advocated, immorality of some kind.[10]

[161] However, the operation of the maxim is not triggered by *any* act of wrongful conduct by a defendant, regardless of its nature or connection to the subject matter of the suit …

[163] Brandeis J has referred to there being a limitation on the types of bad conduct which trigger the operation of the maxim by saying: *'Equity does not demand that its suitors shall have led blameless lives'.*[11] Young J has expressed the limitations on the operation of the maxim by saying, *'Unless there is established one of the equitable defences, then general naughtiness or the desire of the court to censor the plaintiff's conduct, does not enter into the equation when one is considering whether the plaintiff should get relief'.*[12]

[164] A test for the circumstances in which the maxim operates was provided in *Dering v Earl of Winchelsea*. That case arose from the appointment of a Mr Dering as a collector of

---

1. *Cadman v Horner* (1810) 34 ER 221; *Wall v Stubbs* (1815) 56 ER 31.
2. *Litvinoff v Kent* (1918) TLR 298; *Gill v Lewis* [1956] 2 QB 1.
3. *Gascoigne v Gascoigne* [1918] 1 QB 223; *In Re Emery's Investment Trusts* (1959) Ch 410; *Tinker v Tinker* [1970] P 136.
4. *Cory v Gertcken* (1816) 56 ER 250.
5. *Hewson v Sydney Stock Exchange Ltd* [1968] 2 NSWR 224.
6. *Greater Sydney Development Association Ltd v Rivett* (1929) 29 SR (NSW) 356 at 360–1.
7. *Goddard v Midland Railway Company* (1891) 8 TLR 126.
8. *Kettles and Gas Appliances Ltd v Anthony Hordern and Sons Ltd* (1934) 35 SR (NSW) 108.
9. *Slingsby v Bradford Patent Truck and Trolley Co* [1905] WN 122; [1906] WN 51.
10. *Glyn v Weston Feature Film Company* [1916] 1 Ch 261, and cases referred to in Ashburner's *Principles of Equity*, 2nd ed, p 467, cf now *Stephens v Avery* [1988] 1 Ch 449.
11. *Loughrin v Loughrin* 292 US 216 at 229 (1934).
12. *FAI Insurances Ltd v Pioneer Concrete Services Ltd* (1987) 15 NSWLR 552 at 554.

customs duties. In connection with the appointment, bonds for his proper performance were given to the Crown by his elder brother (Sir Edward Dering) and two others. When Mr Dearing fell into arrears in making payments to the Crown, the Crown sued Sir Edward Dering on his bond, and recovered the full amount of the arrears. In this action, Sir Edward Dering sought contribution from the other two sureties. Those sureties resisted the action on the ground that Sir Edward Dering had unclean hands. This argument was dealt with by Lord Chief Baron Eyre ... as follows:

> The misconduct imputed to Sir Edward is that he encourages his brother in gaming and other irregularities; that he knew his brother had no fortune of his own, and must necessarily be making use of the public money, and that Sir Edward was privy to his brother's breaking the orders of the Lords of the Treasury, to keep the money in a particular box, and in a particular manner, &c this may all be true, and such a representation of Sir Edward's conduct certainly places him in a bad point of view; ... [A] man must come into a Court of Equity with clean hands; but when this is said, it does not mean a general depravity; it must have an immediate and necessary relation to the equity sued for; it must be a depravity in a legal as well as in a moral sense. In a moral sense, the companion, and perhaps the conductor, of Mr Dering, may be said to be the author of the loss, but to legal purposes, Mr Dering himself is the author of it, and if the evil example of Sir Edward led him on, this is not what the Court can take cognisance of.[13]

[165] What is meant by the expression *'an immediate and necessary relation to the equity sued for'* is best explained by reference, first, to cases where an allegation of unclean hands was made, but did not result in the plaintiff failing to be granted relief ...

[168] *Meyers v Casey* concerned a horse-owner who had been disqualified for 12 months for *'suspicious practices'* in connection with a particular race. The disqualification had initially been effected by the stewards at Mooney Valley. He had appealed against that decision to the committee of the Victoria Racing Club, which had received fresh evidence, and upheld the decision. He also sought an injunction restraining the Victoria Racing Club from expelling him. In fact the stewards did not have power to disqualify a person (as opposed to a horse) for *'suspicious practices'*, but the committee had such power. The majority in the High Court held that the decision of the committee was valid, even though it was taken on appeal from an invalid decision. The majority in the High Court also held that the injunction restraining the Victoria Racing Club from expelling him should be granted, because there was a threat to expel him without according him natural justice. Barton ACJ said that the *'clean hands'* doctrine should have had no role to play in connection with the challenge to the validity of the decision of the committee. He said:

> His Honour who tried the case dismissed the action on the ground that the plaintiff, in seeking the assistance of equity, did not come into Court with clean hands. I do not think that his case can be met by the application of the maxim. The merits of the plaintiff's conduct were not in issue before his Honour. The case raised by the claim and met by the defence was based purely on the asserted illegality of the decision against him. It was not its correctness, but its validity, that was contested in the Supreme Court.

---

13. *Dering v Earl of Winchelsea* (1787) 29 ER 1184 at 1184–5.

Its correctness was assumed for the purpose of the argument, but was not admitted as a fact. The plaintiff could not have been heard to declare his innocence in that proceeding. Evidence as to the turpitude or integrity of his conduct was not admissible on the case made.[14]

[169] In other words, the equity which the plaintiff was suing for was an injunction to prevent him being disqualified by a decision made by a body which had no power to disqualify him. When that was the equity being sued for, the fact that (as the committee held) he had engaged in conduct which warranted his disqualification did not have a sufficient connection to the equity which was sued for ...

[171] In *Moody v Cox* the plaintiff was a purchaser of real estate who sought to rescind the contract of purchase, on grounds of misrepresentation and nondisclosure. The defendants were trustees, and were also solicitors who, it was held, were acting as solicitors for the plaintiff in that particular transaction. The court held the defendants guilty of both misrepresentation, and breach of an obligation to disclose material facts known to the defendants. The plaintiff had given one of the solicitors a bribe, at a time when the plaintiff wished the transaction to proceed. The defendants, by seeking specific performance of the contract, waived their entitlement to rescind by reason of that bribe. Even so, the defendants argued that the giving of the bribe amounted to unclean hands on the part of the plaintiff, which disentitled him to the equitable remedy of rescission.

[173] Scrutton LJ said:

> ... Equity will not apply the principle about clean hands unless the depravity, the dirt in question on the hand, has an immediate and necessary relation to the equity sued for. In this case the bribe has no immediate relation to rectification, if rectification were asked, or to rescission in connection with a matter not in any way connected with the bribe.[15] ...

[175] *Dow Securities Pty Ltd v Manufacturing Investments Ltd* was an application by a corporation to restrain presentation of a winding up petition. The plaintiff admitted that it owed the debt referred to in a statutory demand, but asserted it had a cross-claim for a greater amount. The defendant submitted that the plaintiff ought not be granted an injunction because of its unclean hands, in that the admitted debt of the plaintiff to the defendant arose from a transaction which was illegal under section 125 of the Companies Act 1961, and that to grant relief will enable the plaintiff to avoid repayment of a loan which should never have been made. Wootten J accepted that if there had been a breach of section 125, that would be conduct of a type appropriate to attract the doctrine of unclean hands, because it would be misconduct *'in a legal as well as a moral sense'*. However, that conduct did not have *'an immediate and necessary relation to the equity sued for'*. He said:

> [The plaintiff's] rights, viz, to have its counterclaim determined by due process, exists, if at all, by reason of circumstances wholly independent of the alleged misconduct; the wrong it complains of, viz, the threat to winding up when it has not in fact *'neglected'* to pay its debt, is wholly independent of the misconduct ... The right which the court

---

14. *Meyers v Casey* (1913) 17 CLR 90 at 101–2.
15. *Moody v Cox* [1917] 2 Ch 71 at 87–8.

of equity is asked to protect or assist was not itself brought into existence or induced by the conduct complained of.[16] ...

[177] With these cases are to be contrasted cases where the plaintiff's unclean hands have resulted in relief being denied ...

[178] *Gascoigne v Gascoigne* was a case where a husband put a lease of land in his wife's name and built a house upon the land with his own money. He used his wife's name in the transaction, with her knowledge and connivance, for the purpose of misleading, defeating and delaying present or future creditors. After the parties separated, the husband sought a declaration that the wife was trustee for him of the property. He succeeded at first instance, but on appeal he failed. The Divisional Court (Lawrence and Lush JJ) said:

> ... What the learned judge has done is this: he has permitted the plaintiff to rebut the presumption [of advancement] which the law raises by setting up his own illegality and fraud, and to obtain relief in equity because he has succeeded in proving it. The plaintiff cannot do this; and, whether the point was taken or not in the County Court this court cannot allow a judgment to stand which has given relief under such circumstances as that.[17]

[179] *Gascoigne* was a case where it was necessary for the plaintiff to prove his own bad conduct to rebut the presumption of advancement and thus to establish the trust he sued to enforce ... If a plaintiff needs to prove his own bad conduct to be able to prove the circumstances which he says entitles him to an equitable remedy, that bad conduct has an immediate and necessary relation to the equity sued for.

[180] By contrast, *Griffiths v Griffiths* was a case where a husband claimed an enlarged beneficial interest in the matrimonial home (which had been conveyed into the name of his wife) by reason of having effected improvements. The wife alleged that his claim must fail because of his unclean hands, in that he had represented to the Law Society for the purpose of obtaining a legal aid certificate, and to a court bailiff for the purpose of avoiding a distraint, that the house belonged exclusively to the wife. Arnold J rejected this argument:

> [I]n my judgement the point is a bad one because he is not, in preferring his claim to the improvements, relying upon his own disreputable act, as, for example, does a man who seeks to enforce a resulting or express trust of property transferred by him to his wife by saying *'oh, the transfer was only to defraud my creditors.'* Nor is he doing the other thing which is forbidden, by the doctrine of promissory estoppel, of reversing a previous contention where, but only where, the party against whom the contention is made has in the meantime altered his or her position in reliance on the previous contention. He falls between the two stalls; for it is no ingredient in the claim that he behaved wrongly, and therefore he escapes from the principle of *Gascoigne v Gascoigne* and it is not suggested that the wife relied on his disclaimer or either of his disclaimer is in such a way as to make it unfair to her that the position should now be reversed.[18] ...

---

16. *Dow Securities Pty Ltd v Manufacturing Investments Ltd* (1981) 5 ACLR 501 at 508–9.
17. *Gascoigne v Gascoigne* [1918] 1 KB 223 at 226.
18. *Griffiths v Griffiths* [1973] 1 WLR 1454 at 1456–7.

[181] The two tests ... (*'immediate and necessary relation to the equity sued for'* and *'a depravity in a legal as well as in a moral sense'*) do not provide a complete guide to the circumstances in which the *'unclean hands'* maxim will be applied to deprive the litigant with the unclean hands of a remedy. Those two tests are a necessary condition for the application of the *'unclean hands'* maxim, but not a sufficient condition. Equitable relief is always discretionary, and other factors can influence the exercise of the discretion ... In *Littlewood v Caldwell*[19] a plaintiff was refused an injunction to restrain the plaintiff's former partner from interfering in the partnership business, receiving debts or drawing bills, and for an account and dissolution of the partnership, on the ground that the plaintiff had removed the partnership books and refused the defendant access to them. The defendant said that, because the partnership books were missing, he was unable to file an answer to the plaintiff's claim. The plaintiff's application was refused because of his removal of the books — but that refusal was expressly stated to be without prejudice to any future application which might thereafter be made. Thus, the order specifically left open the possibility of the plaintiff returning the books and of a situation arising where his having once removed them no longer made it unjust to grant an injunction.

[182] Further, the weight which is accorded to bad conduct on the part of the plaintiff can differ depending upon the relief which is sought, and the alternatives for relief which the plaintiff has open to him. In *Vigers v Pike* Lord Cottenham noted that there is a,

> ... marked distinction made by the Court of Equity between what is necessary to resist a suit for the specific performance of a contract, and what is necessary to support a suit to set aside a deed executed and an arrangement completed, and consequently to resist a suit founded upon such deed and growing out of such arrangement. When the Court simply refuses to enforce the specific performance of the contract it leaves the party to his remedy at Law; but if it were to refuse to administer equities founded upon a deed executed, it would leave the party applying without remedy, and his opponent in possession of that for which what was sought to be obtained was reserved as an equivalent.[20]

[183] If refusal of relief might occasion injustice to people who are not parties, the court might decide to grant relief notwithstanding bad conduct on the part of the plaintiff, if the transaction is objectionable on the grounds of public policy, *'the relief not being given for their sake but for the sake of the public'*.[21]

[184] In applying the unclean hands principle in the present case, it is necessary first to identify what is the equity which (absent unclean hands) I would be prepared to uphold. It is the equity of resulting trust, relating to those contributions which the Club has made to the purchase price of the Peakhurst property from its own money.

[185] It is not necessary for the Club to prove anything about the circumstances in which Citibank was misled to be able to prove the facts which make good that claim to a beneficial interest. The equity which the Club asserts is one which originally arose

---

19. (1822) 147 ER.
20. *Vigers v Pike* (1842) 8 ER 220 at 251–2.
21. *Vauxhall Bridge Co v Spence (Earl)* (1821) Jac 64 at 67; *Money v Money (No2)* [1966] 1 NSWR 348 at 351–2; *New South Wales Diary Corporation v Murray Goulburn Co-Operative Company Limited* (1990) 171 CLR 363 at 409.

against [Wilson] by reason of the Club's money providing part of the purchase price, and operated to impose equitable obligations on him, concerning his legal ownership of the property — the circumstances in which [Wilson] came to have money to make his own contribution to the purchase price of the property have no immediate and necessary relation to that. Another way of putting this is that even accepting (as I do) that the Peakhurst property would probably not have been purchased at all if Citibank had not been misled, that misleading of Citibank did not make any contribution to the proportionate beneficial interest which recognition of the resulting trust would give to the Club. ... In my view the principle of unclean hands provides no reason for refusing to recognise that particular resulting trust. If the Club were to claim an entitlement to part of the beneficial interest in the property derived from [Wilson's] contributions the position might be different — but I do not need to decide that question.

Comment

1. See Radan & Stewart at **31.8–31.12**.

Laches

31.3   Lamshed v Lamshed
(1963) 109 CLR 440

Court: High Court of Australia

Facts: In 1956 Lamshed entered into a contract for sale of his grazing property in South Australia to Lamshed & Co, a company representing his brother and other members of his extended family. Some weeks later, after denying its validity in conversations with the sale agent and others, Lamshed formally repudiated the contract by a letter from his solicitors. About four months later, the company commenced proceedings seeking specific performance, to which Lamshed filed a defence. No further action was taken after the close of pleadings and the company did not set the matter down for trial until almost five years had passed. It did so shortly after Lamshed contracted to sell the property to another party, who placed a caveat on the title. The company's delay was explained by the belief of its principals that Lamshed would eventually proceed with the sale once land values declined sufficiently.

Issue: The issue before the High Court was whether the company was disentitled to the remedy of specific performance due to laches for failing to prosecute the action with reasonable diligence.

Decision: The majority of the High Court (Kitto and Windeyer JJ; McTiernan J dissenting) held that the company was guilty of laches and therefore dismissed its application for specific performance.

Extracts: The extracts from the judgment of Kitto J highlight the main features of the equitable defence of laches, holding that in this case the prejudice to Lamshed was demonstrated by his being left indefinitely in a position of not knowing whether or not the contract would be enforced against him.

Kitto J

[452] There was a time in the history of equity jurisprudence when the case of *Gibson v Patterson*[22] was regarded as a decision that in equity time was of no consequence and delay no impediment to decreeing specific performance of agreements. It seems that Lord *Loughborough* first showed that the case decided no such thing,[23] and the doctrine has ever since been maintained that the special remedy of specific performance is available to those only who are prompt to claim it. [453] The degree of promptness required depends on the nature of the case and all its circumstances. Accordingly there is little point in citing cases for the purpose of comparing the period of delay in the present case with the delay which has been considered fatal to claims for specific performance in the circumstances of other cases. The bare fact of delay is not enough. Where there is nothing at all in the circumstances to justify either a conclusion that the delay has been to the prejudice of the defendant or of any third party, or a conclusion that the plaintiff ought to be regarded as having abandoned any rights he ever had, specific performance is not ordinarily refused.[24] But a circumstance which is of importance, where it exists, is that the defendant has denied that he is bound by the contract. The case in which that has occurred has been called 'the typical case' for refusing specific performance by reason of a delay of even a few months.[25] 'In such cases (as those of purported rescission for breach of contract or under a special condition as to title) the purchaser who wishes to attack the validity of the rescission must always come very promptly to a court of equity. It is natural and reasonable that this should be required of him, for the vendor is not to be placed indefinitely in the position of not knowing whether he can safely deal with the property in question on the footing that the contract has ceased to exist'.[26] By parity of reasoning, a definite denial by one party that he has ever become bound by a contract of sale to which the other seeks to hold him places a clear obligation upon that other to sue promptly if he is to obtain from a court of equity a decree for specific performance. Equity will not allow the possibility of its making such a decree to be held unfairly long over the head of the party who denies the existence of the contract and asserts a right to deal with the property as his own. This is a particular application of the general principle of laches as expounded in *Lindsay Petroleum Co v Hurd*[27] and *Erlanger v New Sombrero Phosphate Co.* To repeat words from the latter case, 'a court of equity requires that those who come to it to ask its active interposition to give them relief, should use due diligence, after there has been such notice or knowledge as to make it inequitable to lie by'.[28]

[454] Plainly it would have been inequitable for [Lamshed & Co] in the present case, if [it] wanted specific performance, to lie by until 26th March 1962, continuing to assert the existence of a contract but taking no proceedings and leaving [Lamshed] in the position of not knowing whether any money he might spend on the property would benefit him or [Lamshed & Co], or whether he was free to sell the property to a third party, or whether

---

22. (1737) 26 ER 8.
23. See note to *Lloyd v Collett* (1793) 29 ER 992.
24. *Fitzgerald v Masters* (1956) 95 CLR 420 at 433.
25. *Fitzgerald v Masters* (1956) 95 CLR 420 at 433.
26. *Fitzgerald v Masters* (1956) 95 CLR 420 at 433.
27. (1874) LR 5 PC 221 at 239, 240.
28. *Erlanger v New Sombrero Phosphate Co* (1878) 3 App Cas 1218 at 1279.

his estate, if he should die, would include the property or the purchase money for which [Lamshed & Co] said that he had agreed to sell it ...

[455] The case is therefore not one of bare delay; it is not even one in which all that can be said against the granting of relief is that [Lamshed & Co's] delay has unfairly placed [Lamshed] in a position of uncertainty over a substantial period; it is a case in which a defendant, not precipitately but at length, in circumstances which made it not altogether unreasonable to do so, has prejudiced his position; and it is a case in which third parties, not shown to be in any way at fault and not being warned by any caveat on the title, have acquired interests which will be defeated if a decree for specific performance should now be made. It seems to me a clear case for refusing relief on the ground of delay unless the law be that delay after action brought cannot afford a defence to a suit for specific performance.

Fry LJ did not think that that was the law. In par 1100 of his book[29] he mentioned, as one form of delay that might constitute laches disentitling a plaintiff to the aid of the court, delay in not diligently prosecuting his action when instituted. He cited in this connexion *Moore v Blake*,[30] in which Lord *Manners* as Lord Chancellor of Ireland held that laches in not prosecuting a suit was as strong a reason for refusing the discretionary remedy of specific performance as laches in not commencing a suit. The actual decision in that case was reversed on appeal to the House of Lords,[31] and expressions in the speeches of Lord *Eldon* and Lord *Redesdale* may seem at first sight to suggest [456] that a defence of delay in prosecuting a suit must fail if (as is the case here) the defendant might have moved to have the suit dismissed for want of prosecution. But the real point of the case seems to have been that the suit was for specific performance of an agreement to grant a lease subject to the payment to the defendant of a debt owing to him by the plaintiff. As is said in the last two lines of the report, the defendant might refuse to execute the lease until paid his debt. He was in the position of a mortgagee of the promised lease. Delay by the plaintiff in prosecuting the suit was therefore delay in paying the mortgage debt. Their Lordships appear to have considered that the defendant's proper remedy for that delay was to move, as a means of foreclosure, that the suit be dismissed for want of prosecution. The circumstances were very special. What is important in the judgments is Lord *Eldon's* acknowledgement of 'those cases which justify a dismissal on the ground that, though begun in due time, it (the suit) has not been prosecuted with due diligence'.[32] Lord *Manners'* judgment as a statement of general principle as to delay seems to be unimpaired and indeed reinforced.

Comment

1. See Radan & Stewart at **31.13–31.19**.

---

29. Fry, 6th ed, (1921, p 514).
30. (1808) 1 Ball & B 62.
31. *Moore v Blake* (1816) 3 ER 1147.
32. *Moore v Blake* (1816) 3 ER 1147 at 1152.

Limitation legislation by analogy

31.4   Italiano Oliveri v Invocare Pty Ltd
[2008] NSWSC 1138

Court: Supreme Court of New South Wales

Facts: Oliveri initiated proceedings for specific performance of a contract alleged to have been entered into between himself and Invocare in respect of the supply to Oliveri of 'a vault suitable for the interment of nine persons, with a floor of no less than 300 millimetres above the surrounding kerb and gutter'. At an interlocutory stage of proceedings Invocare applied to have them summarily dismissed on the ground that they were statute barred by virtue of the provisions of ss 14 and 23 of the *Limitation Act 1969* (NSW). Section 14 imposed a six-year period within which to commence claims 'founded on contract'. Section 23 stipulated that s 14 did not apply to an application for equitable relief except in so far as s 14 could be applied by analogy to the equitable proceedings.

Issue: The issue before the Supreme Court was whether Oliveri's application for specific performance was statute barred by application of s 14 by analogy.

Decision: McLaughlin AsJ held that Oliveri's application for specific performance was no barred by application of s 14 by analogy.

Extracts: The extracts from the judgment of McLaughlin AsJ detail and apply the principles relating to the application of limitations legislation provisions by analogy in relation to an application for specific performance of a contract.

McLaughlin AsJ

[24] The application by analogy of the limitation provisions of section 14 to a cause of action for specific performance of a contract has been considered in a number of decided cases.

[25] Those cases have been conveniently collated in the English Court of Appeal in *P & O Nedlloyd BV v Arab Metals Co & Ors*,[33] in the judgment of Moore-Bick LJ ...

[26] Moore-Bick LJ commenced his review of the appropriateness of the relevant authorities relating to what can be described as limitation by analogy, by referring to the decision of Lord Westbury, the Lord Chancellor, in *Knox v Gye* ... [where] his Lordship said:

> For where the remedy in Equity is correspondent to the remedy at Law, and the latter is subject to a limit in point of time by the Statute of Limitations, a Court of Equity acts by analogy to the statute, and imposes on the remedy it affords the same limitation ... Where a Court of Equity frames its remedy upon the basis of the Common Law, and supplements the Common Law by extending the remedy to parties who cannot have an action at Common Law, there the Court of Equity acts in analogy to the statute; that is, it adopts the statute as rule of procedure regulating the remedy it affords.[34]

---

33. [2007] 1 WLR 2288.
34. *Knox v Gye* (1872) LR 5 HL 656 at 674–5.

[27] His Lordship Moore-Bick LJ also referred in *P & O Nedlloyd BV* to more recent English decisions, including the decision of the English Court of Appeal in *Paragon Finance plc v D B Thakerer & Co*[35] and *Nelson v Rye*.[36] His Lordship then said:

These passages support the conclusion that if a statutory limitation provision, properly interpreted, applies to the claim under consideration, equity will apply it in obedience to the statute, as indeed it must. However, even if the limitation period does not apply because the claim is for an exclusively equitable remedy, the Court will nonetheless apply it by analogy if the remedy in equity is 'correspondent to the remedy at law'. In other words, where the suit in equity corresponds with an action at law, a court of equity adopts the statutory rule as its own rule of procedure.[37]

[28] After referring to a number of other relatively recent authorities, His Lordship continued:

It is not surprising that equity should apply by analogy the limitation periods applicable to claims at law for an account and for damages for breach of duty, whether in contract or tort, to claims for an account and for equitable compensation. In each case the same facts give rise to a claim, whether at law or in equity, and the same kind of relief is obtainable. A claim for specific performance raises different considerations, however, both because relief comparable to that available from the courts of equity was not available from the common law courts and because the facts needed to support a claim for specific performance are not in all respects the same as those necessary to support a claim for breach of contract.[38] ...

[29] His Lordship then continued:

The fact that the common law courts could not grant a coercive remedy comparable to a decree of specific performance strongly suggests that there is no case in which (to use the language of Lord Westbury in *Knox v Gye*) 'the remedy in equity is correspondent to the remedy at law' or 'the suit in equity corresponds with an action at law'. At most it can be said that there are some cases in which the facts giving rise to a claim at law for damages for breach of contract will also be sufficient to justify the intervention of equity.

However, in cases where the facts capable of supporting a claim for equitable relief differ from those capable of supporting a claim at law, or where the equitable remedy differs in a material respect from that available at law, there is not the same reason to deprive the court of the power to grant equitable relief in an appropriate case by adopting the statutory limitation period by analogy.[39]

[30] After ... referring to the decision of the House of Lords in *Hasham v Zenab*,[40] His Lordship further said:

---

35. [1999] 1 All ER 400.
36. [1996] 1 WLR 1378.
37. *P & O Nedlloyd BV v Arab Metals Co & Ors* [2007] 1 WLR 2288 at 2304.
38. *P & O Nedlloyd BV v Arab Metals Co & Ors* [2007] 1 WLR 2288 at 2306.
39. *P & O Nedlloyd BV v Arab Metals Co & Ors* [2007] 1 WLR 2288 at 2306–7.
40. [1960] AC 316.

It is therefore wrong in principle to treat specific performance as merely an equitable remedy for an existing breach of contract. Moreover, since a claim for specific performance may be made as soon as the contract has been entered into, it is very arguable that, if the limitation period were to be applied by analogy, it would be necessary to regard the cause of action as accruing at that moment with the unfortunate result that the claim could become time-barred before any need for relief had arisen. This lends further support to the conclusion that the application of the limitation period by analogy is not appropriate in relation to claims for specific performance.[41]

[31] His Lordship concluded his review of various cited authorities by stating:

> In my view that question must be answered by reference to the nature of the remedy and the circumstances in which it is available. Both factors point to the conclusion that claims for specific performance fall outside the scope of the principle identified by Lord Westbury in *Knox v Gye* and applied by this court in *Companhia de Seguros Imperio v Heath*.[42] The remedy is available in circumstances where no cause of action exists at law, so the factual circumstances giving rise to a claim need not be the same as those which would support a claim for breach of contract, and no comparable remedy is available at law.[43] ...

[40] In *The Duke Group Ltd (in liq) v Alamin Investments Ltd*, Doyle CJ considered the principles developed by equity in relation to the application of limitation periods by analogy, including the circumstances in which equity will decline to apply an analogous limitation period. His Honour said:

> Before applying the statutory time limit by analogy, I must be satisfied that in all the circumstances it is just to do so. It is not just a question of finding a sufficient similarity between the equitable claim and the claim that is subject to a statutory time limit. This point has not attracted a great deal of attention in the cases referred to. Nevertheless, in accordance with basic principle it is necessary for me to consider whether it is just in all the circumstances to apply the statutory time limit.[44]

[41] A similar view was expressed in the New Zealand case *Matai Industries Ltd v Jenson*.[45] Buss JA in *Hewitt v Henderson* states:

> In my opinion, the authorities which I have reviewed support the proposition that equity will not apply a limitation period by analogy where there are circumstances which make the application of the statute unconscionable.[46]

[42] The conclusions of Buss JA concerning an application for dismissal of proceedings in circumstances such as those in the instant application, where it is submitted the claim must be defeated by the expiry of the appropriate limitation period, referred to the salutary admonition in the joint judgment of Dawson, Gaudron and McHugh JJ in *Wardley Australia Limited v Western Australia*, where their Honours emphatically said:

---

41. *P & O Nedlloyd BV v Arab Metals Co & Ors* [2007] 1 WLR 2288 at 2308.
42. [2001] 1 WLR 112.
43. *P & O Nedlloyd BV v Arab Metals Co & Ors* [2007] 1 WLR 2288 at 2309–10.
44. *The Duke Group Ltd (in liq) v Alamin Investments Ltd* [2004] SASC 415 at [135].
45. [1989] 1 NZLR 525.
46. *Hewitt v Henderson* [2006] WASCA 233 at [25].

We should, however, state in the plainest of terms that we regard it as undesirable that limitation questions of the kind under consideration should be decided in interlocutory proceedings in advance of the hearing of the action, except in the clearest of cases. Generally speaking, in such proceedings, insufficient is known of the damage sustained by the plaintiff and of the circumstances in which it was sustained to justify a confident answer to the question.[47] ...

[45] In the instant case ... the question of application by analogy of the limitation period to a cause of action for specific performance of a contract by its very nature must require full consideration of all the circumstances of the case and a consideration of the question whether [Oliveri] is ultimately entitled to specific performance.

[46] It is not possible to determine the entitlement of [Oliveri] to that remedy until all the evidence in the case is complete and at the end of a final hearing of the proceedings. The remedy by way of specific performance is a discretionary remedy, although that discretion must be exercised in accordance with established principles. It cannot be known at this stage of the proceedings whether [Oliveri] will be entitled to obtain that remedy. If he is entitled to obtain the remedy for specific performance, then on my understanding of the effect of section 23 of the *Limitation Act* the Court must look to whether or not by analogy the provisions of section 14 have application.

[47] If a plaintiff is entitled to specific performance of a contract I do not see how the provisions of section 14 can have application by analogy, since the provisions of section 14 expressly apply to a cause of action founded on contract. Such a cause of action appears to me to be a cause of action at common law, which would result only in an award of damages to a successful plaintiff.

[48] There can be no analogy between such an award of damages and the equitable remedy of specific performance. If, therefore, [Oliveri] is ultimately entitled to that remedy of specific performance, the limitation period contained in section 14 does not apply.

Comment

1. See Radan & Stewart at **31.22–31.28**.

Equitable set-off

31.5   AWA Ltd v Exicom Australia Pty Ltd
(1990) 19 NSWLR 705

Court: Supreme Court of New South Wales

Facts: AWA entered into a contract to sell its Australian telecommunications business, including a variety of assets and goodwill, to Exicom. The sale price was agreed to be subject to adjustment as specified in the contract, with the final adjusted sum amounting to $62m. Several months after completion, Exicom commenced proceedings against AWA seeking damages for breach of warranty and for breach of s 52 of the *Trade*

---

47. *Wardley Australia Limited v Western Australia* [1992] 175 CLR 514 at 533.

Practices Act 1974 (Cth) due to allegedly misleading and deceptive information in the deed of sale. AWA then took action against Exicom, claiming an amount of almost $900,000 plus interest as money payable upon the transfer of the business to AWA under certain provisions in the deed. Exicom's defence stated that it was entitled to a set-off against AWA's claim 'for such part of the amount due to it pursuant to its claim in [the breach of warranty] proceedings ... as is equal to' AWA's claim. AWA applied to have Exicom's defence struck out on the ground that it could not be pleaded as a defence. Exicom argued it was entitled to an equitable set-off, agreeing that AWA would be entitled to judgment if the defence were struck out. It then applied for a stay of execution if that were to eventuate.

Issue: The issue before the Supreme Court was whether Exicom was entitled to plead its defence by way of equitable set-off in the circumstances of the case.

Decision: Giles J dismissed AWA's application to strike out Exicom's defence. The question of stay of execution did not arise as a result.

Extracts: The extracts from the judgment of Giles J address the criteria to be met for the availability of set-off in equity.

Giles J

[707] 1. Equitable set-off

AWA accepted that the appropriate approach was that described by Woodward J in *D Galambos & Son Pty Ltd v McIntyre*:

> I believe that the relevant principles to be extracted from the authorities are as follows:-
>
> (i)   Failure in part to perform a contract, or defective performance of a contract requiring work to be done again or directly reducing the value of work done or goods supplied, may be raised as a defence to an action for money due under that contract.
>
> (ii) Claims for money due under a contract and for damages for breach of the same contract (arising, for example, from delay) may be set-off against each other where the equity of the case requires that it should be so. This will depend upon how closely the respective claims are related, particularly as to time and subject-matter. The general conduct of the respective parties will, as always, be relevant to the granting of such equitable relief.
>
> (iii) Even where one of the claims is not in terms based upon the contract, but it flows out of and is directly connected with it, a court may be prepared to recognise an equitable set-off.
>
> (iv) The above statements of principle cannot be regarded as having universal application. They do clearly apply to contracts for work and labour, but special considerations are relevant in other areas such as bills of exchange.[48]

It will be necessary to address the authorities in more detail, but this will suffice to develop the respective contentions. AWA acknowledged that Exicom's claims, or at least its claims

---

48. *D Galambos & Son Pty Ltd v McIntyre* (1974) 5 ACTR 10 at 25-266.

for breach of warranty, might found an equitable set-off as a defence to a claim by AWA for the purchase price, or part of the purchase price, payable under the deed. Its argument was that its [708] claims were of a different character, and were insufficiently closely related to Exicom's claims, and insufficiently connected with the contract recorded in the deed, for the recognition of an equitable set-off. Exicom argued that there was such a close relationship and connection between the claims that an entitlement to set-off should be recognised, and in particular said that there was a close connection between the claims because it would not have entered into the deed at all, or not on the terms contained in the deed, but for the alleged misleading and deceptive conduct, so that its (Exicom's) claims went to the root of AWA's claims. It further argued that on an application to strike out a defence it would not be right to accede to the application if it were arguable that it was entitled to an equitable set-off, so that AWA should fail where the question was arguable even if on full consideration the conclusion might be that there was no equitable set-off ...

[710] Equitable set-off has been considered in a number of cases since *D Galambos & Son Pty Ltd v McIntyre* ... These cases make it clear that the test is not as simple as whether Exicom's claim relates to the sale price as distinct from other payments for which the deed provides. While it is correct that the mere fact that Exicom has a claim against AWA is insufficient for an equitable set-off, all the circumstances must be considered in order to determine whether what Woodward J referred to as 'the equity of the case' requires that AWA be restrained from proceeding to judgment upon its claim without there being determined and set-off against it Exicom's claim.

This consideration should be undertaken bearing in mind the juristic basis of an equitable set-off. Prior to the *Judicature Act*, an equitable set-off was enforced by an injunction obtained in equity to restrain the plaintiff at law from proceedings with his action without giving credit to the defendant for the amount of his cross-demand. Hence it was not enough simply to point to a cross-demand: there had to be shown '... some equitable ground for the defendant being protected against his adversary's demand'.[49] Hence also where that equitable ground was shown the defendant had a defence to the claim, and more than just a cross-demand. The so-called equitable set-off could be better described as an equitable defence,[50] [711] and operates to reduce or extinguish the plaintiff's claim.[51]

Thus the effect of an equitable set-off is not just a restraint upon enforcement of a judgment, but a restraint which if imposed will have important consequences if (for example) the plaintiff be insolvent. Its effect is not just procedural. There must be something additional to the fact of a cross-demand to cause the court, in the exercise of its equitable jurisdiction, to require the plaintiff to set-off against his claim the claim of the defendant.

---

49. See *Rawson v Samuel* (1841) 41 ER 451 at 458 per Lord Cottenham LC.
50. *Henriksens Rederi A/S v THZ Rolimpex ('The Brede')* [1974] QB 233 at 248–9; *Sidney Raper Pty Ltd v Commonwealth Trading Bank of Australia* [1975] 2 NSWLR 227 at 236; *Altarama Ltd v Camp* (1980) 5 ACLR 513 at 519.
51. *Stewart v Latec Investments Ltd* [1968] 1 NSWR 432; *Stehar Knitting Mills Pty Ltd v Southern Textile Converters Pty Ltd* [1980] 2 NSWLR 514 at 518 per Hutley JA; *Covino v Bandag Manufacturing Pty Ltd* [1983] 1 NSWLR 237 at 238 per Hutley JA and *Tooth & Co Ltd v Rosier* (Wood J, 7 June 1985, unreported).

That requirement has often been expressed in language to the effect that the equitable set-off must go to the root of or impeach the title of the plaintiff's claim. What is meant by such phrases, particularly in the light of the more recent cases, itself needs explanation. In *D Galambos & Son Pty Ltd v McIntyre*, Woodward J extracted from the language used by Lord Cottenham LC in *Rawson v Samuel* and the cases to which his Lordship referred that the prerequisites of an equitable set-off were clear cross-claims for debts or damages which were:

> ... so closely related as to subject-matter that the claim sought to be set-off impeached the other *in the sense that it made it positively unjust that there should be recovery without deduction.*[52] (Emphasis added.)

In *British Anzani (Felixstowe) Ltd v International Marine Management (UK) Ltd*,[53] Forbes J referred to the essential attribute of a valid equitable set-off that the equity must go to the very root of the plaintiff's claim, but went on to adopt as a felicitously expressed statement of the principle the passage in the judgment of Parker J in *Compania Sud Americana de Vapores v Shipmair BV (The 'Teno')*:

> ... where the cross-claim not only arises out of the same contract as the claim but is so directly connected with it that it would be manifestly unjust to allow the claimant to recover without taking into account the cross-claim there is a right of set-off in equity of an unliquidated claim.[54]

His Lordship went on to say that it was not necessary that the cross-claim arose out of the same contract as the claim, but could be sufficient if it arose otherwise provided there was the requisite close connection, and after citing a passage from *Hanak v Green*[55] said:

> ... In other words, in considering questions of this kind it is what is obviously fair or manifestly unjust that will determine the solution. This is because today, while it is necessary to look back before the *Judicature Act* to discover the broad principles upon which equity would grant relief, it may not be helpful to seek to find out from the cases what a court of equity would have done in a similar case. The principle may be derived from the older cases. The application of that principle should be reached by a consideration of what today would be regarded as fair or just.[56]

In *Tooth & Co Ltd v Smith*,[57] Clarke J observed that a determination as to [712] whether an equitable set-off exists in any particular case requires an examination of the closeness of the respective claims, and that no general rule can be laid down except by stating that such a set-off will arise when there exist circumstances which make it unjust or inequitable that a plaintiff should be permitted to proceed with his claim. In *Tooth & Co Ltd v Rosier*,[58] while continuing to acknowledge the necessity that the set-off 'raise an

---

52. *D Galambos & Son Pty Ltd v McIntyre* (1974) 5 ACTR 10 at 18.
53. [1980] QB 137 at 145.
54. *Compania Sud Americana de Vapores v Shipmair BV (The 'Teno')* [1977] 2 Lloyd's Rep 289 at 297.
55. [1958] 2 QB 9.
56. *British Anzani (Felixstowe) Ltd v International Marine Management (UK) Ltd* [1980] QB 137 at 145 at 155.
57. (Clarke J, 5 September 1984, unreported).
58. (Wood J, 7 June 1985, unreported).

equity which impeaches, or is essentially bound up with, or goes to the root of title of the plaintiff's claims', Wood J observed that as presently advised he saw no fault in the test thus expressed by Clarke J, and in *Sydmar Pty Ltd v Statewise Developments Pty Ltd*, Smart J appeared to accept that test and referred to 'the evolution and development that has taken place in this area of the law and which is reflected in *Galambos*, the modern English cases and the cases in this court'.[59] To the modern English cases can now be added *Bank of Boston Connecticut v European Grain and Shipping Ltd*,[60] where the House of Lords appeared to distinguish between the concept of the cross-demand being such as 'impeached the title to the legal demand' found in *Rawson v Samuel* and the test of a cross-demand 'flowing out of and inseparably connected with the dealings and transactions which also give rise to the claim' found in *Newfoundland Government v Newfoundland Railway Co*,[61] and to prefer the latter.[62] (It may be that the application of the test in charterparty cases such as that before their Lordships is particularly constrained by authority.)

In the consideration of all the circumstances of the case no mechanical test can be applied. Relevantly, although it is of course a matter to be taken into account, it is not determinative that Exicom's claim relates to the sale price as distinct from the other payments for which the deed provides (although as will be seen I do not accept that such a neat distinction can be drawn). Conversely, although it is again a matter to be taken into account it is not determinative that both claims arise under the deed. The ultimate question is whether, bearing in mind that the existence of Exicom's claim is not enough and that something more is needed, sufficient to warrant the intervention of equity to protect Exicom, it would be unjust or inequitable that AWA should be permitted to proceed with its claim. Primarily that throws up the relationship and closeness of connection between the claims. That the ultimate question is one of equity's intervention is shown by the observations that the general conduct of the parties will be relevant to the granting of equitable relief.[63] Those observations were given effect in *APM Wood Products Pty Ltd v Kimberley Homes Pty Ltd*[64] where an equitable set-off was denied notwithstanding closeness of the respective claims because the cross-claimant's failure to investigate, quantify or press its cross-claim disentitled it in equity from maintaining the cross-claim as defence.

In my view the respective claims as revealed in AWA's summons and Exicom's amended summons, fleshed out by reference to the deed, are so closely related that it would be unjust and inequitable that AWA should be permitted to proceed with its claim without Exicom being able to prosecute its claim as an equitable defence. With the possible exception of AWA's first claim, both AWA and Exicom make claims under the deed. It is true that **[713]** AWA's claims rely upon cl 7 and cl 9 for payments consequential upon the transfer of the business, and that Exicom's claim under the deed is for damages for breach of warranty under cl 11, but both claims are by way of working out the bargain between the parties

59. *Sydmar Pty Ltd v Statewise Developments Pty Ltd* (1987) 73 ALR 289 at 296; 11 ACLR 616 at 623.
60. [1989] AC 1956 at 1101–3.
61. (1888) 13 App Cas 199.
62. *Bank of Boston Connecticut v European Grain and Shipping Ltd* [1989] AC 1956 at 1106.
63. *D Galambos & Son Pty Ltd v McIntyre* (1974) 5 ACTR 10 at 26 and *Sydmar Pty Ltd v Statewise Developments Pty Ltd* (1987) 73 ALR 289 at 296; 11 ACLR 616 at 623.
64. (Cole J, 17 February 1989, unreported).

in relation to the sale of the business and the assets. One element of the bargain was the disposition of expenses incurred and liabilities undertaken, and of moneys received, with respect to orders accepted and contracts undertaken but incomplete as at the date of completion; another element was recompense to Exicom should information warranted by AWA turn out to be incorrect. Neither came directly into the calculation of the sale price, but in a wider sense both affected what Exicom paid for what it obtained in the transaction. The consequential adjustments could readily have been treated in the deed as adjustments to the sale price, but in whatever formal way they were treated Exicom would presumably have paid $X more if it had not been required to reimburse $X to AWA for accrued expenses or had been entitled to retain $X received after completion in respect of sales prior to completion. In that wider sense AWA's first claim can be seen as flowing out of and connected with the transaction. ...

The relationship is in my view a close one — the respective claims both go to the fundamental issue of the sale price of the business and the assets — and the inequity if Exicom were unable to maintain an equitable set-off would be considerable. AWA would be entitled to judgment for a sum in the vicinity of $900,000 due in the working out of the bargain between the parties, and Exicom would be left with its claim also in the working out of the bargain between the parties. That Exicom additionally bases its claim upon contravention of the *Trade Practices Act* (Cth) does not detract from this, and I do not think it necessary to consider whether or not Exicom's position is improved by its argument that it would not have entered into the transaction on the terms on which it did but for the alleged misleading and deceptive conduct.

I should note that AWA placed particular reliance upon *Rawson v Samuel*, referring to the Lord Chancellor's observation:

> It was said that the subjects of the suit in this Court, and of the action at law, arise out of the same contract; but the one is for an account of transactions under the contract, and the other for damages for the breach of it. The object and subject-matters are, therefore, totally distinct; and the fact that the agreement was the origin of both does not form any bond of union for the purpose of supporting an injunction.[65]

AWA submitted that its claim founded upon cl 7 and cl 9 of the deed was in the nature of a claim for an account of transactions under the contract, while Exicom's claim was a claim for damages for breach of the contract, and said that *Rawson v Samuel* required that the respective claims be regarded as unconnected for the purposes of equitable set-off. The passage cited above, and some following paragraphs, were adopted by Griffith CJ, with whom Barton J concurred, in *Hill v Ziymack*,[66] in a case on similar facts to those in *Rawson v Samuel*.

I do not think that the Lord Chancellor should be taken to have meant that in no circumstances could an action for damages for breach of a [714] contract be set-off against a claim for an amount due under the contract. An action for an account is rather different from an action for damages, since of its nature it can produce a result in favour of either party. Later passages show that his Lordship was conscious that the plaintiff had already obtained judgment and that the claim to an account was complicated and uncertain,

---

65. *Rawson v Samuel* (1841) 41 ER 451 at 458.
66. (1908) 7 CLR 352 at 361.

observing that there were not even cross-demands as it could not be assumed that the balance of the account would be found to be in favour of the defendants.

Certainly his Lordship has not been taken as so saying. Even before *D Galambos & Son Pty Ltd v McIntyre* claims for damages under contracts were set-off against claims for money due thereunder.[67] It is not necessary to rely on the more controversial cases of *Morgan & Son Ltd v S Martin Johnson & Co Ltd*[68] and *Hanak v Green*, but in *Sun Candies Pty Ltd v Polites*,[69] Mann CJ allowed the equitable set-off of a claim for breach of warranty as to the value of a business against a claim for the unpaid balance of purchase money.

Going then to *D Galambos & Son Pty Ltd v McIntyre*, a claim for damages for substantial inconvenience and discomfort flowing from breach of a building contract was allowed as an equitable set-off against a claim for money due under the building contract. In *British Anzani (Felixstowe) Ltd v International Marine Management (UK) Ltd*, a claim for damages for breach of agreements to construct and then lease warehouses, the breach being in relation to the condition of the floor of the warehouses, was allowed as an equitable set-off against a claim to rent under the lease; in *Tooth & Co Ltd v Rosier*, it seems that an agreement between the plaintiff and the principal debtor whereby the plaintiff was to pay to the principal debtor the value of the goodwill of a hotel was seen as an equitable set-off against the principal debtor's obligations under the lease of the hotel (but I would respectfully reserve my opinion on whether it could be available to the guarantor); and in *Sydmar Pty Ltd v Statewise Developments Pty Ltd*, claims of breach of contractual obligations in relation to the supervision, management and promotion of mining operations at three particular locations were seen as potentially giving rise to an equitable set-off against a claim for a consultancy fee and royalty payable under the same agreement but with respect to mining operations at different locations.

It seems to me that these cases demonstrate that there is no such general embargo upon an equitable set-off as that which AWA sought to find in *Rawson v Samuel*, and I do not think that AWA's claim was of the nature of an action for an account if such an action is in a special position. I do not think it is, but no doubt the nature of the action is a matter to be taken into account in deciding whether the 'equity of the case' takes it to the other side of the line. By way of illustration of cases on the other side of the line, in *Tooth & Co Ltd v Smith* an equitable set-off was declined where the defendant sought to set-off a claim of fraud and breach of fiduciary duty inducing payments in 1977 and 1979 in relation to the transfer of a hotel against a sum payable under a deed made in 1983 compromising a dispute in relation to the payment for the hotel, and in *Devoe Prufcoat Pty Ltd v Altex Industrial Paints Ltd*[70] it was held that a [715] claim for damages for breach of a distribution agreement consisting of failure to grant the right to distribute a particular range of products could not constitute an equitable set-off against a claim for money payable pursuant to the distribution agreement for other goods sold and delivered.

---

67. See *Young v Kitchin* (1878) 3 Ex D 127; *Lowe v Holme* (1883) 10 QBD 286 and *Newfoundland Government v Newfoundland Railway Co* (1888) 13 App Cas 199.
68. [1949] 1 KB 107.
69. [1939] VLR 132.
70. (Cole J, 15 March 1989, unreported).

It follows that I consider that Exicom is entitled to plead the matters the subject of its claim in [the breach of warranty] proceedings ... as an equitable defence in [AWA's proceedings for moneys payable under the contract] ... and that AWA's application to strike out its defence must fail.

Comment
1. See Radan & Stewart at **31.29–31.38**.

INDEX